ROYAL BOROUGH OF GREENWICH

Follow us on twitter  @green

Blackheath Library
Tel: 020 8858 1131

D0532680

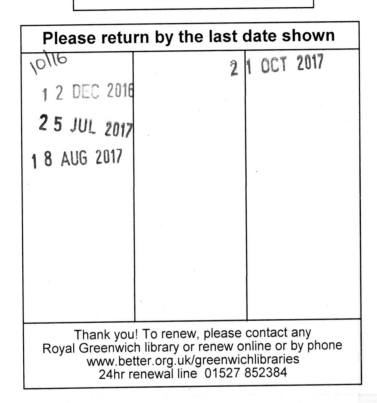

Please return by the last date shown

10/16		2 1 OCT 2017
1 2 DEC 2016		
2 5 JUL 2017		
1 8 AUG 2017		

Thank you! To renew, please contact any
Royal Greenwich library or renew online or by phone
www.better.org.uk/greenwichlibraries
24hr renewal line 01527 852384

GREENWICH LIBRARIES

3 8028 02265588 7

Published by AA Publishing, which is a trading name of AA Media Limited whose registered office is: Fanum House, Basing View, Basingstoke, Hampshire RG21 4EA. Registered number 06112600

47th edition published 2016
© AA Media Limited 2016

AA Media Limited retains the copyright in the current edition. © 2016 and in all subsequent editions, reprints and amendments to editions.

The information contained in this directory is sourced from the AA's establishment database. All rights reserved. No part of this publication may be reproduced, stored in a retrieval system, or transmitted in any form or by any means – electronic, photocopying, recording, or otherwise – unless the written permission of the publishers has been given beforehand. This book may not be sold, resold, hired out or otherwise disposed of by way of trade in any form of binding or cover other than that in which it is published, without the prior written consent of all relevant Publishers. The contents of this publication are believed correct at the time of printing. Nevertheless the Publisher cannot be held responsible for any errors or omissions or for changes in the details given in this guide or for the consequences of any reliance on the information provided in the same. This does not affect your statutory rights. Assessments of AA inspected establishments are based on the experience(s) of the hotel and restaurant inspectors on the occasion(s) of their visit(s), therefore the descriptions in this guide represent an element of subjective opinion that may not reflect a reader's own opinion on another occasion.

AA Media Limited strives to ensure accuracy of the information in this guide at the time of printing. Due to the constantly evolving nature of the subject matter the information is subject to change. AA Media Limited gratefully receive advice from readers of any necessary updates.

Every effort has been made to trace copyright holders, and we apologise in advance for any unintentional omissions or errors. We would be pleased to apply any corrections in a following edition of this publication.

Typeset by Servis Filmsetting Ltd, Stockport

Printed in Italy by Printer Trento SRL, Trento

Directory compiled by the AA Lifestyle Guides Department and managed in the Librios Information Management System and generated from the AA establishment database system.

Maps prepared by the Mapping Services Department of AA Publishing.

Maps © AA Media Limited 2016.

Contains Ordnance Survey data © Crown copyright and database right 2016.

This is based upon Crown Copyright and is reproduced with the permission of Land & Property Services under delegated authority from the Controller of Her Majesty's Stationery Office.
© Crown copyright and database rights 2016 PMLPA No. 100497

Republic of Ireland mapping based on © Ordnance Survey Ireland/Government of Ireland Copyright Permit number MP0000116

Information on National Parks in England provided by the Countryside Agency (Natural England).

Information on National Parks in Scotland provided by Scottish Natural Heritage.

Information on National Parks in Wales provided by The Countryside Council for Wales.

A CIP catalogue record for this book is available from the British Library.

ISBN: 978-0-7495-7831-2

A05406

GREENWICH LIBRARIES	
BL	
3 8028 02265588 7	
Askews & Holts	05-Oct-2016
914.106	£14.99
5173188	

Contents

Welcome to the AA B&B Guide 2017

For over 45 years, our readers have been using *The AA B&B Guide* to find many different types of accommodation, for a multitude of reasons. As the AA inspects such a wide range of establishments, we hope that this guide will prove an invaluable asset in helping you to find the right place to stay.

Who's in the guide?

From the most stylish and sophisticated urban boutique accommodation to family-run homes in the countryside; from ultra-chic luxury to charmingly rustic home-from-home comfort and many points between, *The AA B&B Guide 2017* has it all. Throughout the year, our specially trained team of expert inspectors are visiting, grading and advising the Guest Accommodation that appears in this guide. Each one is judged on its presentation, quality of accommodation, leisure facilities, breakfasts and evening meals, service, hospitality, conference facilities and cleanliness and housekeeping. They are then rated according to our classification system (pages 8 and 9).

Our inspectors also choose their Guest Accommodation of the Year for England, Scotland, Wales, and Northern Ireland, as well as the Friendliest B&B of the Year and the Funkiest B&B of the Year.

Gold Stars

All of the Guest Accommodation in this guide is of a high standard, but some are a cut above, and those with Gold Stars are in the top ten percent of their Star rating. At these establishments you can expect a little more of everything: more comfort, more extras, and more attention. From three to five Gold Stars, this is the best of British Guest Accommodation.

Silver Stars

These properties offer a superior level of quality within their Star rating, high standards of hospitality, service and cleanliness.

Premier Collection

All five-Star establishments, whether Gold, Silver or Black Stars, are part of the Premier Collection, and these entries are highlighted in the guide. This allows the reader to see at a glance those Guest Accommodations that have met all the criteria required by the Guest Accommodation Scheme and reached the highest rating possible.

Rosettes

Some of the B&Bs in this guide have their own restaurants, and many of them serve food that has been awarded AA Rosettes; including a few that have reached the four and five Rosette level, making them among the finest restaurants in the world. These are regularly visited by the AA Inspectorate who award Rosettes strictly on the basis of the inspector's experience alone.

Many establishments in the guide designated as Restaurants with Rooms have been awarded AA Rosettes for the quality of their food.

Anonymous inspection

Any Guest Accommodation applying for AA recognition receives an unannounced visit by one of the AA's professional inspectors to check standards. The inspector pays his or her own bill (rather than it being paid by the establishment).

After staying overnight at the Guest Accommodation, the inspector will make themselves known to a member of staff and ask to speak to the manager. Once a rating is awarded, regular visits are made by our inspectors to check that standards are being maintained.

If the accommodation changes hands, the new owners must reapply for classification, as AA recognition is not transferable.

Tell us what you think

We welcome your feedback about the B&Bs included in this guide, and about the guide itself. You can write to us at: The AA B&B Guide, 8th floor, Fanum House, Basing View, Basingstoke, Hampshire RG21 4EA or email us at **lifestyleguides@theAA.com**

How to use the AA B&B Guide

1.
| CAMBRIDGE | Map 12 TL45 |

Benson House

2. ★★★★ 🛏 GUEST HOUSE

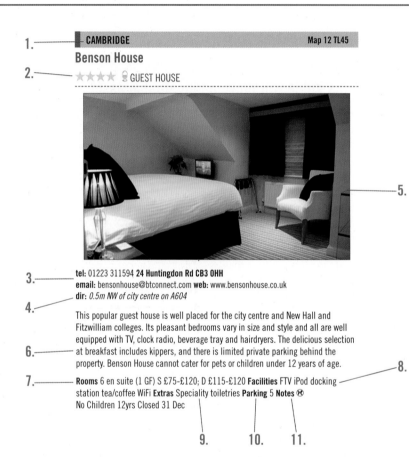

5.

3. **tel:** 01223 311594 **24 Huntingdon Rd CB3 0HH**
email: bensonhouse@btconnect.com **web:** www.bensonhouse.co.uk

4. **dir:** *0.5m NW of city centre on A604*

6. This popular guest house is well placed for the city centre and New Hall and Fitzwilliam colleges. Its pleasant bedrooms vary in size and style and all are well equipped with TV, clock radio, beverage tray and hairdryers. The delicious selection at breakfast includes kippers, and there is limited private parking behind the property. Benson House cannot cater for pets or children under 12 years of age.

8.

7. **Rooms** 6 en suite (1 GF) S £75-£120; D £115-£120 **Facilities** FTV iPod docking station tea/coffee WiFi **Extras** Speciality toiletries **Parking** 5 **Notes** ⊗ No Children 12yrs Closed 31 Dec

9.   **10.**   **11.**

1. Location, map reference & name

Each country is listed in alphabetical order by county then location. The Channel Islands and Isle of Man follow the England section and the Scottish Islands follow the Scotland section. Establishments are listed alphabetically in descending order of Stars, with Gold Stars appearing first in each rating.

The map page number refers to the atlas at the back of the guide and is followed by the National Grid Reference. To find the location, read the first figure across and the second figure vertically within the lettered square. Farmhouse entries also have a six-figure National Grid Reference, which can be used with Ordnance Survey maps or **www.ordnancesurvey.co.uk**.

You can find routes at **theAA.com** or **www.AAbookings.ie**. London has its own Plans (see end of atlas), and London establishments have a Plan number based on these.

If the establishment's name is shown in italics, then details have not been confirmed by the proprietor for this edition.

2. Classification & designator

See pages 8 and 9.

Five-Star establishments are highlighted as Premier Collection, and they are listed on page 24.

🏵 **Rosettes** The AA's food award, see page 11.

🥚 **Egg cups and** 🥧 **pies** These symbols indicate that, in the experience of the inspector, either breakfast or dinner (or both) are really special, and have an emphasis on freshly prepared local ingredients.

3. Email address & website

Email and website addresses are included where they have been specified by the establishment. Such websites are not under the control of AA Media Limited, who cannot accept any responsibility or liability in respect of any and all matters whatsoever relating to such websites.

4. Directions & distances

Distances in **directions** are given in miles (m) and yards (yds), or kilometres (km) and metres (mtrs) in the Republic of Ireland.

5. Photographs

Establishments may choose to include a photograph.

6. Description

Written by the inspector at the time of his or her visit.

7. Rooms

The number of letting bedrooms (rms), or rooms with a bath or shower en suite are shown. Bedrooms that have a private bathroom (pri facs) adjacent are indicated.

The number of bedrooms in an annexe of equivalent standard are also shown. Charges are per night:

S bed and breakfast per person

D bed and breakfast for two people sharing a room. If an asterisk (*) follows the prices this indicates 2016 prices.

The euro € is the currency of the Republic of Ireland.

Prices are indications only, so check before booking. Some places may offer free accommodation to children provided they share their parents' room.

8. Facilities

Most bedrooms will have TV. If this is important to you, please check when booking. If **TV4B** appears, this means that there are TVs in four bedrooms.

If **Dinner** is shown, you may have to order in advance. Please check when booking.

For other abbreviations and symbols, see panel on the right of this page.

9. Extras

Anything the establishment offers in rooms that are more than expected e.g. speciality toiletries, trouser press, mineral water, home-made biscuits etc.

10. Parking

Parking is usually followed by the number of spaces. Motorists should be aware that some establishments may charge for parking. Please check when booking.

11. Notes

Although many establishments allow dogs, they may be excluded from some areas of the accommodation and some breeds, particularly those requiring an exceptional license, may not be accepted at all. Under the Equality Act 2010, access should be allowed to guide dogs and assistance dogs. Please check the establishment's policy when making your booking.

No children children cannot be accommodated, or a minimum age may be specified, e.g. No Children 4yrs means no children under four years old.

Establishments with special facilities for children (**ch fac**) may include a babysitting service or baby-intercom system, playroom or playground, laundry facilities, drying and ironing facilities, cots, high chairs and special meals. If you have very young children, check facilities before booking.

No coaches is published in good faith from details supplied by the establishment. Inns have well-defined legal obligations towards travellers; in the event of a query the customer should contact the proprietor or local licensing authority.

Additional facilities such as lifts or any leisure activities available are also listed.

LB indicates that Short or Leisure Breaks are available. Contact the establishment for details.

Establishments are open all year unless **Closed** days/dates/months are shown. Some places are open all year but offer a restricted service (**RS**) in low season. If the text does not say what the restricted services are you should check before booking.

Civ Wed 50 The establishment is licensed for civil weddings and can accommodate 50 guests for the ceremony.

⊛ shows that **credit/debit cards are not accepted**, but check when booking. Where credit cards are accepted there may be an extra charge.

Smoking Since 1 July 2007 smoking has been banned by law in all public places in the United Kingdom and Ireland. However, the proprietor can designate one or more bedrooms with ventilation systems where the occupants can smoke, but communal areas must be smoke-free. Communal areas include the interior bars and restaurants in pubs and inns. We indicate number of smoking rooms (if any).

Conference facilities Conf indicates that facilities are available. The total number of delegates that can be accommodated is shown, plus maximum numbers in various settings (theatre, classroom and boardroom).

Key to symbols and abbreviations

★★★	Classification (see page 8–9)
◉	AA Rosette award (see page 11)
A	Associate entry (see page 9)
U	Unclassified rating (see page 9)
♀	A very special breakfast, with an emphasis on freshly prepared local ingredients
⊖	A very special dinner, with an emphasis on freshly prepared local ingredients
S	Single room
D	Double room (2 people sharing)
pri fac	Private facilities
fmly	Family bedroom
GF	Ground floor bedroom
LB	Short/Leisure breaks
*	2016 prices
ch fac	Special facilities for children
TVL	Lounge with television
Lounge	Lounge without television
TV4B	Television in four bedrooms
STV	Satellite television
FTV	Freeview television
WiFi	Wireless internet
⊛	Credit/debit cards not accepted
tea/coffee	Tea and coffee-making facilities
Conf	Conference facilities
rms	Bedrooms in main building
Etr	Easter
fr	From
RS	Restricted service
🔒	Secure storage
⊗	No dogs
⊡	Indoor swimming pool'
⊡	Heated indoor swimming pool
↖	Outdoor swimming pool
↖	Heated outdoor swimming pool
⚘	Croquet lawn
♔	Tennis court
⚑	Golf (followed by number of holes)

AA Inspected Guest Accommodation

The AA inspects and classifies more than 2,100 guest houses, farmhouses, inns and restaurants with rooms for its Guest Accommodation Scheme, under common quality standards agreed between the AA, VisitBritain, VisitScotland and VisitWales. AA recognised establishments pay an annual fee according to the classification and the number of bedrooms. The classification is not transferable if an establishment changes hands.

The AA presents several awards within the Guest Accommodation Scheme, including the **AA Friendliest B&B of the Year**, which showcases the very finest hospitality in the country; **AA Guest Accommodation of the Year Awards**, presented to establishments in England, Scotland, Wales, and Northern Ireland, and **AA Funkiest B&B of the Year**. See pages 12-15 for this year's winners.

Stars

AA Stars classify guest accommodation at five levels of quality, from one at the simplest, to five offering the highest quality. In order to achieve a one-Star rating an establishment must meet certain minimum entry requirements. For example:
- A cooked breakfast or substantial continental option is provided
- The proprietor and/or staff are available for your arrival, departure and at all meal times
- Once registered, guests have access to the establishment at all times unless previously notified
- All areas of operation meet minimum quality requirements for cleanliness, maintenance and hospitality as well as facilities and the delivery of services
- A dining room or similar eating area is available unless meals are served in bedrooms

To obtain a higher Star rating, an establishment must provide increased quality standards across all areas, with particular emphasis in four key areas:
- Cleanliness and housekeeping
- Hospitality and service
- Quality and condition of bedrooms, bathrooms and public rooms
- Food quality

There are also particular requirements in order for an establishment to achieve three, four or five Stars, for example:
Three Stars and above
- access to both sides of all beds for double occupancy
- bathrooms/shower rooms cannot be used by the proprietor
- there is a washbasin in every guest bedroom (either in the bedrooms or the en suite/private facility)
Four Stars
- half of bedrooms must be en suite or have private facilities
Five Stars
- all bedrooms must be en suite or have private facilities

Establishments applying for AA recognition are visited by one of the AA's qualified accommodation inspectors as a mystery guest. Inspections are a thorough test of the accommodation, food, and hospitality. The inspector completes a full report, resulting in a recommendation for the appropriate Star rating. After this first visit, the establishment will receive a regular visit to check that standards are maintained. If it changes hands, the new owners must re-apply for classification, as standards can change.

Guests can expect to find the following minimum standards at all levels:

- Pleasant and helpful welcome and service, and sound standards of housekeeping and maintenance
- Comfortable accommodation equipped to modern standards
- Bedding and towels changed for each new guest, and at least weekly if the room is taken for a long stay
- Adequate storage, heating, lighting and comfortable seating
- A sufficient hot water supply at reasonable times
- A full cooked breakfast. (If this is not provided, the fact must be advertised and a substantial continental breakfast must be offered.)

When an AA inspector has visited a property, and evaluated all the aspects of the accommodation for comfort, facilities, attention to detail and presentation, you can be confident the Star rating will help you make the right choice.

★ Gold Star Award
AA Gold Stars are awarded to the very best Guest Accommodation within the three, four, or five Star ratings.

★ Silver Star Award
Guest Accommodation with Silver Stars offer a superior level of quality within their Star rating, high standards of hospitality, service and cleanliness.

Accommodation Designators
Along with the Star ratings, six designators have been introduced. The proprietors, in discussion with our inspectors, choose which designator best describes their establishment:

Bed & Breakfast
A private house run by the owner with accommodation for no more than six paying guests.

Guest House
Run on a more commercial basis than a B&B, the accommodation provides for more than six paying guests and there are usually more services; for example staff as well as the owner may provide dinner.

Farmhouse
The B&B or guest house accommodation is part of a working farm or smallholding.

Inn
The accommodation is provided in a fully licensed establishment. The bar will be open to non-residents and can provide food in the evenings.

Restaurant with Rooms
This is a destination restaurant offering overnight accommodation, with dining being the main business, and open to non-residents. The restaurant should offer a high standard of food and restaurant service at least five nights a week. A liquor licence is necessary and there is a maximum of 12 bedrooms.

Guest Accommodation
Any establishment that meets the minimum entry requirements is eligible for this general category.

[U] Unclassified entries
A small number of establishments in this guide have this symbol because their Star classification was not confirmed at the time of going to press. This may be due to a change of ownership or because the establishment has only recently joined the AA rating scheme. For up-to-date information on these and other new establishments check **theAA.com**.

[A] Associate entries
These establishments have been inspected and rated by VisitBritain, VisitScotland or VisitWales, and have joined the AA scheme on a marketing-only basis.

AA Advertised
These establishments are not rated or inspected by the AA, but are displayed for advertising purposes only.

Useful information

What follows is a selection of things we think it is worth bearing in mind when planning a stay. We hope you'll find them useful.

Arriving at the accommodation
There may be restricted access to some establishments, particularly in the late morning and the afternoon, so do check when booking.

Booking
Book as early as possible, particularly for the peak holiday period (early June to the end of September) and for Easter and other public holidays. In some parts of Scotland the skiing season is also a peak holiday period.

Some establishments only accept weekly bookings from Saturday, and some require a deposit on booking.

Prices
Minimum and maximum prices are shown for one (S) and two people (D) per night and include a full breakfast. If dinner is also included this is indicated in brackets (incl dinner). Where prices are for the room only, this is indicated.

Prices in the guide include VAT (and service where applicable), except the Channel Islands where VAT does not apply.

Where proprietors have been unable to provide us with their 2017 charges we publish the 2016 price as a rough guide (shown by an asterisk *). Where no prices are given, please make enquiries direct.

London prices
London prices tend to be higher than outside the capital, and normally only bed and breakfast is provided, although some establishments do provide a full meal service.

Cancellation
If you have to cancel a booking, let the proprietor know at once. If the room cannot be re-let you may be held legally responsible for partial payment; you could lose your deposit or be liable for compensation, so consider taking out cancellation insurance.

Food and drink
Some guest accommodation provides evening meals, ranging from a set meal to a full menu. Some even have their own restaurant. You may have to arrange dinner in advance, at breakfast or on the previous day, so do ask when booking.

Food Allergies
From December 2014 an EU regulation came into force making it easier for those with food allergies to make safer food choices when eating out. There are 14 allergens listed in the regulation, and pubs and restaurants are required to list any of these that are used in the dishes they offer. These may highlighted on the menus or customers can ask staff for full information. Remember, if you are allergic to a food and are in any doubt speak to a member of staff. For further information see: www.food.gov.uk/science/allergy-intolerance/label/labelling-changes

If you book on bed, breakfast and evening meal terms, you may find that the tariff includes only the set menu. If there is a carte you may be able to order from this and pay a supplement.

On Sundays, many establishments serve the main meal at midday, and provide only a cold supper in the evening. In some parts of Britain, particularly in Scotland, high tea (i.e. a savoury dish followed by bread and butter, scones and cakes) is sometimes served instead of, or as an alternative to, dinner.

Farmhouses: Sometimes the land has been sold and only the house remains, but many are working farms and some farmers are happy to allow visitors to look around, or even to help feed the animals. However, you should always exercise care and never leave children unsupervised. Although the directory entry states the acreage and the type of farming, do check when booking to make sure that it matches your expectations. The farmhouses are listed under towns or villages, but do ask for directions when booking.

Inns: Traditional inns often have a cosy bar, convivial atmosphere, good beer and hearty pub food. Those listed in the guide will provide breakfast in a suitable room, and should also serve light meals during licensing hours. The character of the properties vary according to whether they are country inns or town establishments. Check before you book, including arrival times as these may be restricted to licensed opening hours.

Facilities for disabled guests

The Equality Act 2010 details the legal rights of disabled people, including access to goods, services and facilities, and means that service providers may have to consider making adjustments to their premises. For more information about the Act see www.gov.uk/definition-of-disability-under-equality-act-2010 or www.gov.uk/government/policies/creating-a-fairer-and-more-equal-society.

We recommend that you always telephone in advance to ensure that the establishment you have chosen has appropriate facilities. The establishments in this guide should be aware of their obligations under the Act.

Please note: AA inspectors are not accredited to make inspections under the National Accessibility Scheme. We indicate in entries if an establishment has ground floor rooms; and if a B&B tells us they have disabled facilities this is included in the description.

AA Rosette Awards

The AA awards Rosettes to over 2,000 restaurants that we regard as the best in the UK & Ireland

◉
Excellent local restaurants serving food prepared with care, understanding and skill, using good quality ingredients.

◉◉
The best local restaurants, which aim for and achieve higher standards and better consistency, and where a greater precision is apparent in the cooking. There will be obvious attention to the selection of quality ingredients.

◉◉◉
Outstanding restaurants that demand recognition well beyond their local area.

◉◉◉◉
Among the very best restaurants in the British Isles, where the cooking demands national recognition.

◉◉◉◉◉
The finest restaurants in the British Isles, where the cooking compares with the best in the world.

AA Bed &Breakfast Awards 2016–17

Each year the AA celebrates the best that our Guest Accommodation Scheme has to offer. Our inspectors nominate those places that they feel to be a cut above the rest, and award winners are chosen from these nominations. Held this year at The Landmark London Hotel, the AA Bed & Breakfast Awards 2016–17 recognised and rewarded almost 30 very deserving finalists, for demonstrating all-round excellence and unfailing standards and for providing outstanding service to their guests. All finalists were treated to a drinks reception, followed by a formal four-course celebratory luncheon. They also received a personalised certificate and an engraved Villeroy & Boch decanter.

FRIENDLIEST B&B OF THE YEAR

THE OLD BAKERY B&B ★★★★ ⬤ ⬤
HINDOLVESTON, NORFOLK page 225

After five years of thinking about a change of career, Mike and Alison Thomas found the perfect place for their new business. They spent six months renovating this delightful Georgian building, once the village bakery, before opening in July 2011, and they've been welcoming guests to their home ever since. As soon as they walked through the front door for the first time, they felt a peaceful sense of sanctuary, which is exactly what they offer guests. From a welcome cup of tea and home-made cake on arrival, to helping guests make the most of their stay with a wealth of local knowledge and a 'nothing is too much bother' attitude, it's no wonder The Old Bakery has many guests who frequently return for a relaxing break in the beautiful Norfolk countryside, having built a strong and enduring relationship with Mike and Alison.

See page 16 for an interview with Mike and Alison.

Below: (l to r) Giovanna Grossi, AA Group Area Manager; Thomas Messett from eviivo; Alison Thomas & Mike Thomas, The Old Bakery; Peter Jensen, Head of AA Hotel & Hospitality Services

FUNKIEST B&B OF THE YEAR

SNOOZE ★★★★
BRIGHTON, EAST SUSSEX page 296

Located in the heart of Brighton, Snooze is run by owners Tony Mead and Paul Munton, who have created a unique boutique B&B. Following a programme of refurbishment in the last couple of years, Snooze now offers individually styled rooms which glory in a really eclectic mix of both contemporary decor and vintage furnishings. Each room is themed, with all contents individually sourced to fit the chosen theme. There is a real retro style running throughout the property, and there are two 1970s-influenced suites on the top floor, spacious and oozing style. The dining room is a feature in its own right with a collection of mis-matched tables and furnishings, sometimes linked to Brighton. The ceiling has been created by a local graffiti artist as a modern take on the Michaelangelo ceiling in the Sistine Chapel.

GUEST ACCOMMODATION OF THE YEAR FOR ENGLAND

KATESHILL HOUSE ★★★★★ ♀
BEWDLEY, WORCESTERSHIRE page 331

A few minutes' walk from the heart of this riverside town and secluded from the road by mature planting, Kateshill House's manicured gardens feature a 500-year-old Sweet Chestnut. Lovingly refurbished and constantly refreshed by Judith and Graham, the house was awarded five Gold Stars and a Breakfast Award on joining the scheme. Twenty-first-century comforts blend seamlessly with Georgian splendour; high ceilings, full height sash windows and a host of period features, along with fresh flowers, fruit and a small decanter of wine. Judith's attention to detail is impressive, whether selecting a decorative upholstery trim or ensuring the highest standards of cleanliness. The house is seasonally decorated; the spectacular Christmas displays are a delight.

AA Bed &Breakfast Awards 2016–17

GUEST ACCOMMODATION OF THE YEAR FOR SCOTLAND

THE DULAIG ★★★★★

GRANTOWN-ON-SPEY, HIGHLAND page 379

Located in the heart of Speyside and the Cairngorms, built in 1910, and furnished in the Arts and Crafts style, The Dulaig is lovingly run by Carol and Gordon Bulloch. The property is set in 1.5 acres of stunning grounds, which are sometimes opened to the public and feature a menagerie of wildlife. The three rooms are beautifully appointed and feature high quality beds, furnishings and fittings. Gordon and Carol provide real Scottish hospitality and they love to interact with guests and give advice on the area. There's a large comfortable lounge and a beautiful dining room where breakfast is served; featuring several courses and leaving guests full until dinner. No stay would be complete without a visit from The Cake Fairy who leaves different cakes in guest rooms each day.

GUEST ACCOMMODATION OF THE YEAR FOR WALES

CAEMORGAN MANSION ★★★★★

CARDIGAN, CEREDIGION page 403

Located five minutes from Cardigan and ten minutes from local beaches, this beautiful property is set in its own grounds, and offers five luxurious appointed bedrooms with every home comfort. There is also a popular restaurant with dinner and breakfast awards as well as a conference and meeting room, ideal for small weddings. The property has recently been completely refurbished and during this time the owners also focused on ensuring the house was more eco-friendly. Proprietors David and Beverley Harrison-Wood do their best to see that all guests are extremely well cared for and adopt a very hands-on approach. This property is well deserving of the AA Five Star Guest House rating, and is a worthy winner of this award.

ARDTARA COUNTRY HOUSE ★★★★ ◉◉
MAGHERA, COUNTY LONDONDERRY page 433

This beautiful Victorian property set in eight wooded acres of grounds is located within easy reach of the Giant's Causeway and the North Antrim Coast. It was built as a family home in the late 19th century by linen baron Harry Jackson Clark who lived here with numerous children and grandchildren until his death in 1956. It offers nine elegant, beautifully appointed bedrooms with high ceilings and antique furnishings. There are also two comfortable lounges with original wall tapestries and antique furnishings, as well as a large dining room with beautiful fireplaces. Afternoon tea is available. Guests are made to feel extremely welcome by the friendly team and this property is a worthy winner of Northern Ireland Guest Accommodation of the Year.

Back to the Old House –
The Old Bakery B&B, Hindolveston

by Julia Hynard

A new career and a return – quite by chance – to the ancestral home

Neither Mike nor Alison Thomas had any experience of the hospitality trade before opening their B&B less than five years ago. That doesn't mean that they hadn't thought long and hard about it and thoroughly done their homework. They had been visiting B&Bs for years, in the UK, Ireland, France and as far afield as Canada, taking photos and making notes about the things they enjoyed and the aspects of a B&B stay that appealed to them. As winners of this year's AA Friendliest B&B, this diligence has certainly paid off.

A change of career

The couple were living in Sussex. Alison was working in HR at a bank when following a restructure she was moved to a job based in Cambridge. The post had such a large area of operation, including East Anglia, outside the M25 area and up as far as Grimsby and across to High Wycombe, that it didn't matter where within the area she actually lived as she would be travelling anyway. Mike had spent 34 years in supermarket management and was ready for a career change, and after four or five years thinking about it, it seemed the right time to put the B&B plan into action.

Mike and Alison really fell for the North Norfolk coast, the beaches and the countryside, and the minute they stepped into the Old Bakery at Hindolveston, they knew they'd found the right place, both for its location and ambience. Alison explains that a previous owner, a vicar, had used the house for healing retreats, and that they were immediately struck by its atmosphere of peace and calm – the perfect sanctuary.

The AA inspected the Old Bakery just six weeks after they had opened for business and they were awarded the AA Four Star Gold Award and a Breakfast Award. As novices they were surprised by this early success, but the first two sets of guests booked into the accommodation (quite independently) extended their stay, so they knew they must be getting something right! They set about renovating another room, as they only had one to offer, and creating a self-catering cottage on site.

As a career change for Mike it was a winner. Though new to the trade, his remit at Morrisons had included responsibility for cafés, so he had the food and hygiene experience, and both he and Alison had the customer service background and ethos.

◁ The Old Bakery B&B in bloom

The growing and cooking of food

A shared passion, brought into play in their new enterprise, was the growing and cooking of food. As dedicated allotmenteers, the Thomas's produce much of the fruit and veg served at the Old Bakery, including 15 varieties of fruit and 20 different types of vegetable. Local food – and not just the home-grown produce – is very much a feature of their menus, which highlights local seafood, including Cromer crab, and meat from the butcher in the neighbouring village who makes 40 different kinds of sausage. Mike takes his shopping seriously, doing the rounds of producers and suppliers in the area to choose the best local fare. Indeed the quails' eggs from the nearby village of Great Snoring inspired Mike's legendary Great Snoring Breakfast: quails' eggs on a tomato bruschetta nestling on a Portobello mushroom, sitting on top of an English muffin. Other breakfast options include kippers from the Cley smokehouse, pancakes with mixed berries from the garden, and toast with home-made preserves.

'Many of their guests return and are soon like old friends...'

On being the friendliest

Meeting new people is a pleasure for both Mike and Alison. Guests are greeted with a welcoming cuppa and home-made cake in either the dining hall or garden, depending on the season. Mike and Alison ask them about their plans for their stay and give advice on places to visit and eat in the locality. Many of their guests return and are soon like old friends, sharing their photos of children, grandchildren and travels with the Thomases. The couple feel that it is important to give time to chatting to guests, not to impose but to establish common ground, build rapport and to bond, so that guests feel comfortable and relaxed.

Unexpected events

One of the things Mike had looked forward to in his career change was a quieter run up to Christmas – this had always been an exhausting period in the supermarket trade. But he hadn't reckoned on the Thursford Christmas Spectacular, the biggest Christmas show in the country, which runs through November and December and is only six miles away! So business is always brisk at this time of year, accommodating guests who come for the show and usually stay for one night, so there are lots of quick changes, and running guests to the show and picking them up afterwards.

Another surprise was the 1940s themed events put on by the North Norfolk Railway Poppy Line, which are taken very seriously by their aficionados. One morning the Thomases found all their guests (who didn't know each other) sitting down for breakfast in vintage 1940s dress! Some of these 40s fans have become their most loyal and regularly returning guests. So much so that they have been invited to a 40s themed wedding and are now on the lookout for suitable attire for the occasion.

◁ Mike making bread

△ Mike, Alison and friends

A family business

Mike and Alison work well as a team running the family business, each with their designated tasks. Their children, Stephen and Claire, are grown up and live respectively in London and Somerset, but enjoy their visits to Norfolk. Claire had just graduated when they started the B&B and was involved as they got themselves going, particularly helping with the cooking as she is an excellent cook. She now works as a speech therapist with dyslexic children but returns in the school holidays.

For Mike the B&B is a full-time commitment, while Alison also works outside the business. She accepted redundancy from the bank in 2012 and became, for nine months, the "second chef and waitress, who never did things quite as Mike would have done", but then took up a temporary contract – staff health and wellbeing for a local NHS trust – and is still doing the job three years later. She feels that from a relationship point of view, living and working together, it's good to have some time away. Her B&B responsibilities include the accounts, admin and cooking meals at weekends.

Quilting and coaching

Alison brings added value to the business by sharing her unique skills with some of the guests who come for her quilting retreats.

The retreats, usually over a weekend, see guests working on their quilts, while Alison demonstrates what she is doing on hers. She is also a trained coach and guests can book life/career coaching as part of their stay. Sometimes she will coach a couple in separate and joint sessions. Other times one of the guests will have signed up for the coaching while the other explores the attractions of the vicinity. Coaching might take place over a few days as part of a break or can be an intensive 24 hours.

A return to the ancestral home

The Old Bakery dates back to the 1700s and was originally part of a large estate which included a windmill (now a private residence at the bottom of the garden), a granary and five cottages. The building has been in its time a village store, bakery and post office. On buying the property, Mike and Alison, who thought they had no prior connection with Norfolk were in for quite a shock. Mike's brother had been working on the family tree and had recognised the name of the village from his research. Looking back he discovered that ancestors of theirs had lived in Hindolveston during the 1800s, and by extraordinary coincidence in the very same property.

"So you see," said Alison, "It really was meant to be!"

Wales: Land of Our Fathers

by Gwyneth Rees

At around a sixth the size of England, with just three million people, Wales is the *cwtch* of Britain. This evocative Welsh word – pronounced 'cutsh' – can mean a snug, cosy place of warmth and comfort, or a hug.

It's a place where people still know each other, and the name of the local vicar and pub landlord; but don't be mistaken, this is no sleepy backwater. It is a nation of bravado and fire, a nation where – as they boast at the Principality Stadium come match day – *y ddraig goch* (the red dragon) roars. At the moment, Wales – or Cymru, rather – is definitely breathing fire.

You'll probably have heard that it rains – and yes, it does. That's what makes the grass so very green and lush and the air so fresh; but Wales, particularly the coastal regions, also has some serious micro-climates where, if you're lucky, the sun beats down on you. What is more, short of a truly tropical climate, this nation has every conceivable holiday attraction you could wish for.

Just take its history and culture, for instance. Even if you spent a year trying, you wouldn't see half of its castles or dolmens – ancient Neolithic tombs with enormous capstones. Now mostly under the care of Cadw, the Welsh government's historical environment arm, these ancient monuments are around every corner, perched on cliffs overlooking tidal estuaries or acting as lookouts on flat-topped hills. Clearly those who constructed these fortresses and sacred sites capitalised on the natural beauty of the land.

Fortunately, this beauty still exists today – from the craggy mountains of the north to the central verdant valleys and crumpled coasts. There's also no better place to try outdoor pursuits, and even if you're planning a tour of the main cities – say, Cardiff, Swansea and Aberystwyth – you'll never be more than 20 minutes from remote landscapes where you can walk, cycle or meditate to your heart's content. It's this heady mix of culture and nature that makes Wales so appealing. Take this hearty brew and add a friendly, humorous, self-deprecating psyche – prone to singing, taking the mickey, drinking beer and chattering away in its own mother tongue – and you've got a

killer destination. There are no pretensions here – a spade is a spade and a leek a leek. Rain is rain, so put your coat on.

There's more though, like the sense of space, good food and sandy beaches galore, where seagulls mug you for your fish and chips and the waves tempt you in on your bodyboard. Again, due to Wales' status as a cwtch, all these gems are often found close together. It is one of the reasons why Wales is so popular with film crews in need of an array of different backgrounds without the hassle of long-distance travel. The Welsh, of course, know this, though they're not a nation to boast. They spent 700 years fighting the English and fending off arrogant unfounded appraisals of their culture and intellect, but now they've got a Welsh Assembly, their language back and, most important, their own spirit and identity. The Welsh do still, of course, retain a good-natured antipathy to their neighbours. Some of the identities of Wales are perhaps slightly clichéd – the male voice choirs, the coal town brass bands, the sheep-shearing farmers – but there's also so much that's new and refreshing. The nation is leading the environmental and safe-cycling movements across Britain. There are plenty of stylish and boutique restaurants and B&Bs. Hillsides scarred by industry are being turned into world-class mountain-biking venues and the Eisteddfod, an ancient literary competition, is growing mightier year on year. There's plenty of adventure; be that surfing in Snowdonia, trampolining in Cardiff or zip-lining across a mining town.

A Land of Vision

The film and TV industries have done much to revive the image of the Welsh. A small sampling of the recent generation of big Welsh names on the small or silver screens would include Ruth Jones (of Bridgend) and Rob Brydon (of Swansea) – both from popular sitcom *Gavin & Stacey*; Newport's own Michael Sheen (who has played everything from a vampire lord to Brian Clough), Eve Myles from Ystradgynlais in Powys, (star of *Torchwood* and *Broadchurch*), or Erin Richards from Penarth who is now a star of Warner Brothers' *Gotham* TV series.

Importantly, Wales remains real, alive and gritty. It's not a Celtic pastiche. Here, at the height of summer, you can still find low-key campsites next to glorious blue-flag beaches (Wales has upwards of 40), usually with a relaxed seaside café just a stroll away. The westbound M4 comes to an end in Carmarthen, an hour from the coast, and much of the northern terrain is only accessible by winding country roads used regularly by tractors, and so Wales has managed to keep its original charm. Traditional communities do still exist, work and function here.

◁ View towards Cwm Bychan in the Rhinogs in Snowdonia National Park

Wales is a nation with a vision, too, and one that's embraced reinvention. It's got heaps of independent businesses, from the super-cool, eco-minded Howies alternative clothing store to dairy good producer, Rachel's Organics, which led the organic farming revolution in the UK, and still has a dairy based in Aberystwyth. It's got sporting prowess – not just rugby but also a premier league football team in Swansea, and a national side that had a very successful UEFA Euro 2016 Championship (their first). It's gaining more and more powers from Westminster, and has abundant history to fall back on. The iconic oval ball is being kicked high over the goalposts and it's going to land somewhere good.

'Wales is a nation with a vision, too, and one that's embraced reinvention.'

Food

Wales has had a food renaissance of late, with a distinct move towards organic and locally sourced produce, preferably sold at local farmers' markets. If you're into meat, then try Welsh Black beef, an ancient breed descended from pre-Roman cattle, or salt-marsh lamb, which is reared in coastal locations such as Harlech in Snowdonia. The lamb's saline-rich diet imparts a sweet, delicate – though not salty – flavour. Other delights include oysters from the Conwy Estuary and Menai Strait, crab and lobster from Pembroke or Penclawdd cockles from The Mumbles, harvested on the Gower and sold at Swansea's farmers' market. Laver bread, despite its misleading name, is also a product of the water. It's a nutritious seaweed, cooked until it becomes like jelly, and then often mixed with oats and served in a traditional Welsh breakfast. Cawl is another favourite, a hearty soup of lamb, leeks and potatoes.

Cheeses are big business, too. The best known is Caerphilly, a crumbly white variety from south Wales. Other types include Y Fenni and Tintern, Black Bomber from Snowdonia and Collier's Powerful Welsh Cheddar. Recently, artisan cheese-makers, such as Carmarthenshire's Caws Cenarth and

Pembrokeshire's Pant Mawr, have become increasingly popular. Cheese is also linked to a favourite Welsh export – rarebit, effectively a tasty mix of ale, cheese and mustard that's grilled on toast. Historians say its original name was Welsh rabbit – the idea being that the Welsh were too poor to buy meat, so referred to cheese as if it were meat as a joke – but rarebit has stuck.

For pudding, the Welsh love nothing more than a slab of Bara Brith, their old-fashioned fruited tea bread; or a Welsh cake, a type of flat scone cooked on a griddle and sprinkled liberally with caster sugar. Finally, if it's a little seasoning you're after, nothing beats the Isle of Anglesey's Halen Môn Sea Salt, now used by top chefs throughout the world.

Drink

Beer is the national drink of Wales, with SA Brain and Felinfoel breweries existing since the late 19th century. Even though pubs are closing across the nation, microbreweries are booming. There are also more than 20 vineyards in Wales, a leading one being Penarth Vineyard, which makes fruity wines. If spirits are more your thing, then try Wales' leading whisky (or wysgi, as it is in Welsh) – Penderyn – which was launched in 2004. It's not just alcohol though. The Welsh have a lot of water, and they bottle it. Leading brands include Brecon Carreg, Cerist Natural Mineral Water and Tŷ Nant.

Art

Wales has spawned a number of great artists, both ancient and modern. Names from the past include Richard Wilson, one of the founders of the Royal Academy; Augustus John and his sister, Gwen; and James Dickson Innes who painted landscapes in a primitive, post-Impressionist style. More contemporary painters include Sir Kyffin Williams, who died in 2006 and painted rural landscapes. In a similar vein, John Knapp-Fisher brought us images similar to Williams', yet a touch bleaker and more melancholy. Sadly he also died recently, in 2015. Among living artists, Helen Elliott creates the most endearing and cheerful works, while Eloise Govier is a young fine artist who paints extravagantly in neon colours, and has expanded into sculpture.

Music

Rumour has it that when Welsh babies are born, their first cry is a rendition of that old favourite hymn, 'Calon Lân'. Known to many as the 'Land of Song', no nation on earth, it seems, can rival their honey baritones and nonconformist choral harmonies. It's the might of this talent that's produced some of the nation's most famous exports. Let's run a few names by you: Tom Jones, Katherine Jenkins, Charlotte Church, Cerys Matthews,

Bryn Terfel, Shakin' Stevens, Bonnie Tyler and Shirley Bassey. It seems that all Welsh people are proud of their voices, and come match day in the Principality Stadium, you can hear the combined efforts of 70,000 fans throwing their heads back to thunder out the anthem Hen Wlad Fy Nhadau (Land of My Fathers). Even if most of them are dressed as giant leeks and daffodils, it's a formidable spectacle. New Zealand may have the Haka, but Wales has singing en masse.

As early as the first century there are references to the Welsh being a musical race, with scholars writing of bards – professional poets who wrote and sang songs of eulogy. From the early 19th century there are records of traditional Welsh songs and also a growing movement of folk music, accompanied by the national instrument, the harp. These were performed in folk dancing sessions, at festivals or traditional parties similar to Scottish ceilidhs. The Eisteddfod (festival) also grew in popularity from the mid-1850s when a brutal English attack on the Welsh education system sparked public anger, leading to a renewed national pride. Its resurgence brought together musical tradition with poetry, the influence of chapel and the joy of choral music.

During the industrial boom there was also the rise of the male voice choirs, such as the Morriston Orpheus Choir and Treorchy Male Voice Choir. Although they dwindled in prominence with the collapse of the coal-mining communities, lately they've seen something of a resurgence, helped by television shows such as the BBC's *Last Choir Standing*. These choirs have helped keep national songs alive too. Favourite hymns include the 19th-century 'Calon Lân' (A Pure Heart), sung in Welsh before almost every test match, and 'Men of Harlech', a military song and march about the seven-year siege of Harlech castle (1461–68). It gained international recognition when it featured in the 1964 film *Zulu*. 'Myfanwy', composed by Dr Joseph Parry, is another favourite of the choirs, as too is 'Cwm Rhondda', commonly known as Bread of Heaven and usually sung in English. As for the national anthem, – 'Hen Wlad Fy Nhadau' ('Land of My Fathers') – it was written and composed by son and father Evan and James James, of Pontypridd, Glamorgan, in 1856. Although first performed in the vestry of the original Capel Tabor, Maesteg, it only really became a hit when it was sung at the Llangollen Eisteddfod of 1858. As it gained popularity at patriotic gatherings, its original 6/8, quick-waltz tempo slowed to accommodate large crowds. In 1905, it became the first national anthem to be sung before a game was played – Wales were playing host to the first touring New Zealand team, and went on to win in a match that was dubbed the 'game of the century'.

Since then the Welsh music scene has continued to flourish, and change. During World War I singer-songwriter Ivor Novello became an international star – his name is still connected to one of the biggest annual British singing awards. In the 1950s Harry Secombe became a major force in Welsh music, mixing his massive operatic voice with the surreal comedy of The Goons. Come the 1960s, and musicians such as Tom Jones, Shirley Bassey took the popular music world by storm; while in a quieter way John Cale, as part of US band the Velvet Underground and later as a solo artist, had a massive influence on the music that fed into the punk movement of the 70s and 80s. Welsh pop continued to flourish in the 80s, with artists like Bonnie Tyler and Michael Barratt, aka Shakin' Stevens. Later, in the 1990s, Welsh bands such as the Manic Street Preachers, Super Furry Animals and Stereophonics didn't sing in Welsh, but helped towards creating a strong Welsh identity through their lyrics and accents.

The growth of the Welsh National Opera, established in 1946, and stars such as Bryn Terfel, helped draw global attention to the giant lungs of this small nation. Further support came from Radio 1 DJ John Peel, who championed Welsh-language punks Anhrefn and experimentalists Datblygu. Today, although not as prolific as the Cool Cymru 1990s, there's a vivid music scene. Popstar Duffy released her album *Rockferry* to global acclaim, winning a Grammy in 2009, and more recently Catfish and the Bottlemen won the 2016 Brit Award for Best British Breakthrough Act. Alternative rock band Feeder, from Newport, have carved out a name for themselves, as have Cardiff's Los Campesinos! Although punk bands Blackout and Funeral For A Friend have both decided to call it a day, there are plenty of up and comers to take their place. The popularity of music festivals – particularly The Green Man, held in August each year in the Brecon Beacons – has boosted interest in alternative Welsh music. The 160-piece Welsh choir Côr Glanaethwy even came close to winning *Britain's Got Talent* in 2015. Wales is still the land of song, and has much to sing about.

If you've enjoyed reading this feature, find out more by seeking out *The AA Guide to Wales*, packed with information on this fascinating nation.

★★★★★ The Premier Collection

ENGLAND

BERKSHIRE

HURLEY
The Olde Bell Inn

WARGRAVE
Copperfields

BUCKINGHAMSHIRE

BEACONSFIELD
Crazy Bear Beaconsfield

CAMBRIDGESHIRE

ELTON
The Crown Inn

CHESHIRE

BURWARDSLEY
The Pheasant Inn

CHESTER
Mitchell's of Chester
Stone Villa Chester

CONGLETON
Whitethorn Bed & Breakfast

WARMINGHAM
The Bear's Paw

CORNWALL & ISLES OF SCILLY

BUDE
Pot and Barrel B&B

FALMOUTH
Anacapri

LAUNCESTON
Wheatley Farm

LOOE
The Beach House

LOSTWITHIEL
The Old Chapel B&B

MEVAGISSEY
Pebble House
Portmellon Cove Guest House

PADSTOW
Padstow Townhouse
Penjoly Guest House
St Petrocs & Bistro
The Seafood Restaurant

PENZANCE
Camilla House

PERRANUTHNOE
Ednovean Farm

POLPERRO
Trenderway Farm

ST AUSTELL
Anchorage House
Lower Barn

ST MELLION
Pentillie Castle & Estate

WADEBRIDGE
Wadebridge Bed and Breakfast

CUMBRIA

AMBLESIDE
Nanny Brow

BORROWDALE
Hazel Bank Country House

BRAMPTON
Lanercost Bed and Breakfast

CARTMEL
L'Enclume

CROSTHWAITE
The Punchbowl Inn
   at Crosthwaite

GLENRIDDING
Glenridding House

GRASMERE
Moss Grove Organic

GRIZEDALE
Grizedale Lodge

KIRKBY LONSDALE
Hipping Hall
Plato's
The Sun Inn

KIRKBY STEPHEN
Cheskin House
The Inn at Brough

LUPTON
Plough Inn

NEAR SAWREY
Ees Wyke Country House

NEWBY BRIDGE
Hill Crest Country Guest House
The Knoll Country House

PENRITH
Brooklands Guest House
River Garth

TROUTBECK
Broadoaks Country House

WINDERMERE
Applegarth Villa & Restaurant
The Howbeck
Lindeth Fell Country House
Windermere Suites

DERBYSHIRE

BELPER
Bridge Hill House
Dannah Farm Country House

BRADWELL
The Samuel Fox Country Inn

DARLEY DALE
Ashford Grange

HOPE
Underleigh House

NEWHAVEN
The Smithy

DEVON

AXMINSTER
Kerrington House

BRATTON FLEMING
Bracken House

CHILLATON
Tor Cottage

CULLOMPTON
Muddifords Court Country House

DARTMOUTH
Appletree Court House
Mounthaven
Nonsuch House
Strete Barton House

ERMINGTON
Plantation House

ILFRACOMBE
The Habit Boutique Rooms

LUSTLEIGH
Eastwrey Barton

LYNMOUTH
The Heatherville

NEWTON ABBOT
Bulleigh Barton Manor

PAIGNTON
The P&M Paignton RESIDENCE

SIDMOUTH
The Salty Monk

TEDBURN ST MARY
Frogmill Bed & Breakfast

TIVERTON
Fernside Bed and Breakfast

TORQUAY
The Albaston
Carlton Court
The Cary Arms
Kingston House
Lanscombe House
Linden House
The Marstan
Meadfoot Bay Guest House
The 25 Boutique B&B
Tyndale B&B

TOTNES
Stoke Gabriel Lodgings -
  Badgers Retreat

DORSET

BRIDPORT
The Shave Cross Inn

BROADWINDSOR
The Old George

CHRISTCHURCH
Druid House
The Lord Bute & Restaurant

DORCHESTER
Little Court

SHERBORNE
The Kings Arms
Munden House
The Rose and Crown Inn, Trent

SWANAGE
Swanage Haven

WIMBORNE MINSTER
Les Bouviers Restaurant
  with Rooms

ESSEX

DEDHAM
The Sun Inn

GESTINGTHORPE
The Pheasant

GREAT YELDHAM
The White Hart

STANSTED MOUNTFITCHET
Linden House

WIX
Dairy House Farm

GLOUCESTERSHIRE

BARNSLEY
The Village Pub

BLAISDON
Blaisdon House B&B

BOURTON-ON-THE-WATER
The Dial House

CHELTENHAM
Beaumont House
The Bradley
Cleeve Hill House

CIRENCESTER
The Fleece at Cirencester

LOWER SLAUGHTER
The Slaughters Country Inn

NETHER WESTCOTE
The Feathered Nest Country Inn

STOW-ON-THE-WOLD
Old Stocks Inn
The Porch House

HAMPSHIRE

BARTON-ON-SEA
Pebble Beach

SOUTHAMPTON
Ennio's Restaurant
  & Boutique Rooms
THE PIG in the Wall
White Star Tavern,
  Dining and Rooms

WINCHESTER
Giffard House

HEREFORDSHIRE

BOLSTONE
Prickett's Place

HEREFORD
Somerville House

LEDBURY
Verzon House

LEINTWARDINE
The Lion
Upper Buckton

LEOMINSTER
Hills Farm

ROSS-ON-WYE
Wilton Court Restaurant
  with Rooms

HERTFORDSHIRE

WELWYN
The Wellington

ISLE OF WIGHT

GODSHILL
Koala Cottage

NITON
Enchanted Manor

TOTLAND BAY
Sentry Mead

VENTNOR
The Hambrough
The Leconfield

KENT

BENENDEN
Beacon Hall House B&B

DEAL
Sutherland House

DOVER
The Marquis at Alkham

EGERTON
Frasers

MAIDSTONE
Maiden's Tower at Leeds Castle

MARDEN
Merzie Meadows

ROYAL TUNBRIDGE WELLS
Danehurst House

LANCASHIRE

BLACKBURN
The Millstone at Mellor

CLITHEROE
The Assheton Arms

WHITEWELL
The Inn at Whitewell

LEICESTERSHIRE

KEGWORTH
Kegworth House

LINCOLNSHIRE

HEMSWELL
Hemswell Court

HOUGH-ON-THE-HILL
The Brownlow Arms

MARKET RASEN
The Advocate Arms

STAMFORD
Meadow View

WINTERINGHAM
Winteringham Fields

LONDON POSTAL DISTRICTS

LONDON SW3
San Domenico House
Sydney House Chelsea

LONDON SW7
The Exhibitionist

LONDON W1
The Marble Arch by Montcalm
The Piccadilly London West End

NORFOLK

BLAKENEY
Blakeney House

CLEY NEXT THE SEA
Old Town Hall House

NORWICH
Brasteds
38 St Giles

SHERINGHAM
The Eiders Bed & Breakfast

THORPE MARKET
The Green House B&B

THURSFORD
Holly Lodge

NORTHUMBERLAND

BELFORD
Market Cross Guest House

MORPETH
St Mary's Inn

STOCKSFIELD
The Duke of Wellington Inn

NOTTINGHAMSHIRE

ELTON
The Grange

HOLBECK
Browns

RETFORD
Blacksmiths

OXFORDSHIRE

ABINGDON-ON-THAMES
B&B Rafters

FARINGDON
Buscot Manor B&B

KINGHAM
The Wild Rabbit

OXFORD
The Bocardo
Burlington House

STADHAMPTON
The Crazy Bear

WITNEY
Old Swan & Minster Mill

WOODSTOCK
The Glove House

SHROPSHIRE

LUDLOW
The Charlton Arms
The Clive Bar & Restaurant
   with Rooms
Old Downton Lodge

MARKET DRAYTON
Ternhill Farm House

OSWESTRY
Greystones

SHREWSBURY
Darwin's Townhouse
Drapers Hall
Porter House SY1

WELLINGTON
The Old Orleton Inn

SOMERSET

AXBRIDGE
The Oak House

BATH
Apple Tree Guest House
Apsley House
Chestnuts House
Dorian House
One Three Nine
Paradise House
River House and Friary
   Coach House
Tasburgh House Guest House
Waterhouse
The Windsor Townhouse

CHEW MAGNA
The Bear & Swan

CORTON DENHAM
The Queens Arms

DULVERTON
Tarr Farm Inn

FIVEHEAD
Langford Fivehead

FROME
Lullington House

HOLCOMBE
The Holcombe Inn

LYMPSHAM
Batch Country House

WESTON-SUPER-MARE
Church House

WITHYPOOL
Kings Farm

YEOVIL
Little Barwick House

STAFFORDSHIRE

LICHFIELD
Netherstowe House
Pipe Hill House

RUGELEY
Colton House

TAMWORTH
Oak Tree Farm

SUFFOLK

BURY ST EDMUNDS
Clarice House

ELVEDEN
The Elveden Inn

HOLTON
Valley Farm

IXWORTH
Ixworth House

LAVENHAM
Lavenham Great House
   'Restaurant With Rooms'

LONG MELFORD
Long Melford Swan

MILDENHALL
The Bull Inn

NEWMARKET
The Packhorse Inn

SOUTHWOLD
Sutherland House

STOKE-BY-NAYLAND
The Angel Inn

THORNHAM MAGNA
Thornham Hall

YAXLEY
The Auberge

SURREY

CHIDDINGFOLD
The Crown Inn

SUSSEX, EAST

BOREHAM STREET
Boreham House

DITCHLING
The Bull

EASTBOURNE
Ocklynge Manor

HASTINGS & ST LEONARDS
The Cloudesley
Stream House

HERSTMONCEUX
Wartling Place

LEWES
Broadacres

NORTHIAM
Knelle Dower B&B

RYE
Jeake's House
Manor Farm Oast
Willow Tree House

SUSSEX, WEST

CHICHESTER
Rooks Hill
The Royal Oak Inn

CHILGROVE
The White Horse

LITTLEHAMPTON
Berry House
Glendales

LODSWORTH
The Halfway Bridge Inn

SIDLESHAM
The Crab & Lobster

WARWICKSHIRE

ILMINGTON
The Howard Arms

STRATFORD-UPON-AVON
Cherry Trees

WEST MIDLANDS

SOLIHULL
Hampton Manor

WILTSHIRE

BOX
The Northey Arms

BURTON
The Old House at Home

CORSHAM
The Methuen Arms

DEVIZES
Blounts Court Farm
The Peppermill

EDINGTON
The Three Daggers

PEWSEY
Red Lion Freehouse

WORCESTERSHIRE

ABBERLEY
The Manor Arms

BEWDLEY
Kateshill House

BROADWAY
Abbots Grange
Mill Hay House
Russell's

WICHENFORD
Laughern Hill Estate

YORKSHIRE, EAST RIDING OF

BEVERLEY
Newbegin House

BRIDLINGTON
Marton Grange

NORTH NEWBALD
Boxtree House Boutique B&B

SOUTH DALTON
The Pipe and Glass Inn

YORKSHIRE, NORTH

AMPLEFORTH
Shallowdale House

ASENBY
Crab Manor

AUSTWICK
The Traddock

BAINBRIDGE
Yorebridge House

CLAPHAM
The New Inn

CONEYSTHORPE
Lime Kiln House

CRAYKE
The Durham Ox

FILEY
All Seasons Guesthouse

GOLDSBOROUGH
Goldsborough Hall

GRASSINGTON
Ashfield House
Grassington House

HARROGATE
The Grafton Boutique B&B

HETTON
The Angel Inn

KEXBY
Kexby House

KIRKBY FLEETHAM
Black Horse Inn

KNARESBOROUGH
General Tarleton Inn

LEEMING BAR
Little Holtby

LEVISHAM
Moorlands Country House

LEYBURN
Braithwaite Hall
Capple Bank Farm
Low Mill Guest House

MIDDLETON TYAS
The Coach House

OLDSTEAD
The Black Swan at Oldstead

OSMOTHERLEY
The Cleveland Tontine

PICKERING
17 Burgate

RIPON
Mallard Grange
The Old Coach House

WEST WITTON
The Wensleydale Heifer

YORK
The Judge's Lodging

YORKSHIRE, WEST

HALIFAX
Shibden Mill Inn

HAWORTH
Ashmount Country House

HUDDERSFIELD
315 Bar and Restaurant

ISLE OF MAN

PORT ST MARY
Aaron House

CHANNEL ISLANDS

JERSEY

ST AUBIN
The Panorama

SCOTLAND

ABERDEENSHIRE

ELLON
Aikenshill House

ANGUS

INVERKEILOR
Gordon's

ARGYLL & BUTE

BARCALDINE
Ardtorna

OBAN
Blarcreen House

EDINBURGH, CITY OF

EDINBURGH
Kew House
Six Brunton Place
21212
The Witchery by the Castle

FIFE

PEAT INN
The Peat Inn

HIGHLAND

BRACHLA
Loch Ness Lodge

CROMARTY
The Factor's House

DAVIOT
Daviot Lodge

DORNOCH
Links House at Royal Dornoch
2 Quail

GRANTOWN-ON-SPEY
The Dulaig

INVERNESS
Trafford Bank

MEY
Mey House Luxury Rooms
and Breakfast

NAIRN
Boath House

POOLEWE
Pool House

LOTHIAN, WEST

LINLITHGOW
Arden Country House

PERTH & KINROSS

ALYTH
Tigh Na Leigh Guesthouse

PERTH
The Townhouse

SCOTTISH BORDERS

MELROSE
Fauhope Country House

PEEBLES
Kingsmuir House

STIRLING

STIRLING
Victoria Square Guest House

STRATHYRE
Creagan House

SCOTTISH ISLANDS

ISLE OF ISLAY

GLENEGEDALE
Glenegedale House

ISLE OF SKYE

STRUAN
Ullinish Country Lodge

WALES

ISLE OF ANGLESEY

BEAUMARIS
The Bull - Beaumaris

CARMARTHENSHIRE

LLANARTHNE
Llwyn Helyg Country House

ST CLEARS
Coedllys Country House

CEREDIGION

ABERAERON
Feathers Royal

ABERYSTWYTH
Awel-Deg

CARDIGAN
Caemorgan Mansion

CONWY

ABERGELE
The Kinmel Arms

BETWS-Y-COED
Penmachno Hall

CONWY
The Groes Inn
Sychnant Pass Country House

LLANDUDNO
Bryn Derwen

LLANDUDNO JUNCTION
Queens Head

RHOS-ON-SEA
Plas Rhos

TAL-Y-CAFN
Bodnant Welsh Food Centre

TREFRIW
Yr Hafod Country House

DENBIGHSHIRE

LLANDYRNOG
Pentre Mawr Country House

RUTHIN
Firgrove Country House B&B

ST ASAPH
Tan-Yr-Onnen Guest House

GWYNEDD

ABERDYFI
Penhelig Arms

CAERNARFON
Plas Dinas Country House

DOLGELLAU
Tyddynmawr Farmhouse

PWLLHELI
The Old Rectory

MONMOUTHSHIRE

WHITEBROOK
The Whitebrook

PEMBROKESHIRE

EGLWYSWRW
Ael y Bryn

PEMBROKESHIRE

FISHGUARD
Erw-Lon Farm

HAVERFORDWEST
The Paddock
Slebech Park Estate

NARBERTH
Canaston Oaks

SOLVA
Crug Glâs Country House

ST DAVIDS
Ramsey House

TENBY
Trefloyne Manor

POWYS

BRECON
Peterstone Court

SWANSEA

REYNOLDSTON
Fairyhill

VALE OF GLAMORGAN

HENSOL
Llanerch Vineyard

PENARTH
Restaurant James Sommerin

NORTHERN IRELAND

COUNTY ANTRIM

BUSHMILLS
Causeway Lodge
Whitepark House

REPUBLIC OF IRELAND

COUNTY CLARE

LAHINCH
Moy House

COUNTY CORK

KINSALE
Friar's Lodge

SHANAGARRY
Ballymaloe House

DUBLIN

DUBLIN
Glenogra Town House
Harrington Hall

COUNTY KERRY

DINGLE
Castlewood House
Gormans Clifftop House &
   Restaurant

KILLARNEY
Fairview Guest House
Foleys Town House

KILLORGLIN
Carrig House Country House
   & Restaurant

COUNTY MEATH

SLANE
Tankardstown

COUNTY MONAGHAN

GLASLOUGH
The Castle at Castle
   Leslie Estate

COUNTY TIPPERARY

THURLES
The Castle
Inch House Country House
   & Restaurant

COUNTY WEXFORD

CAMPILE
Kilmokea Country Manor
   & Gardens

GOREY
Clonganny House

WEXFORD
Killiane Castle Country
   House & Farm

England

BEDFORDSHIRE

BEDFORD
Map 12 TL04

The Knife and Cleaver

★★★★★ ⚙️⚙️ INN

tel: 01234 930789 & 07554 790130 **The Grove, Houghton Conquest MK45 3LA**
email: info@theknifeandcleaver.com **web:** www.theknifeandcleaver.com
dir: S of Bedford on A6, turn right to Houghton Conquest. Over rdbt, pass post office, right at next rdbt. Left to The Knife and Cleaver

This charming inn offers guests a choice of spacious, well-appointed bedrooms with sleek modern bathrooms. Set in the heart of the pretty village of Houghton Conquest it is very popular with locals and serves an extensive range of seasonal dishes for lunch and dinner. Free WiFi is available throughout and pets are accepted by prior arrangement.

Rooms 9 en suite (9 GF) S £99-£109; D £99-£109* **Facilities** FTV tea/coffee Dinner available WiFi **Conf** Max 20 Thtr 20 Class 20 Board 20 **Parking** 25 **Notes** LB

DUNSTABLE
Map 11 TL02

The Highwayman

★★★ INN

tel: 01582 601122 **London Rd LU6 3DX**
email: 6466@greeneking.co.uk **web:** www.oldenglish.co.uk
dir: N'bound: M1 junct 9, A5, 6m on right. S'bound: M1 junct 11, A505, left on A5 towards London. Property on left

The Highwayman continues to prove popular with business guests, partly due to its convenient location just south of the town, and also for the ample parking available. The accommodation is comfortable, well equipped and cheerfully decorated. The public areas include a large public bar where meals are available.

Rooms 51 en suite (6 fmly) (23 GF) **Facilities** STV FTV TVL tea/coffee Dinner available WiFi **Parking** 76 **Notes** ⊗

HENLOW
Map 12 TL13

The Crown

★★★★★ ⚙️ INN

tel: 01462 812433 **2 High St SG16 6BS**
email: rooms@crownpub.co.uk **web:** www.crownpub.co.uk
dir: On B659 (High St)

The Crown is situated on the High Street in Henlow with easy access from the A1. It's a traditional pub with a modern feel and an attractive beer garden where guests can relax in the summer. Bedrooms all have plenty of useful features such as smart TV, free WiFi, hair straighteners and Nespresso coffee machines. Guests can enjoy dinner in the restaurant which makes good use made of high quality, seasonal ingredients.

Rooms 5 annexe en suite (1 fmly) (5 GF) **Facilities** STV FTV Lounge tea/coffee Dinner available WiFi **Extras** Speciality toiletries, mineral water, fresh milk **Parking** 72 **Notes** ⊗ Closed 25-26 Dec No coaches

LEIGHTON BUZZARD
Map 11 SP92

The Heath Inn

★★★ INN

tel: 01525 237816 & 237390 **76 Woburn Rd, Heath and Reach LU7 0AR**
email: enquiries@theheathinn.com **web:** www.theheathinn.com

Situated in the quiet village of Heath and Reach, close to Leighton Buzzard, this traditional inn offers comfortable accommodation. Good quality dishes and a range of cask ales are available in both the bar and restaurant.

Rooms 16 en suite (5 fmly) (8 GF) S £55-£65; D £65-£85* **Facilities** FTV TVL tea/coffee Dinner available WiFi 🐾 **Parking** 50

BERKSHIRE

BEENHAM
Map 5 SU56

The Six Bells

★★★★ 🍺 INN

tel: 0118 971 3368 **The Green RG7 5NX**
email: info@thesixbells.co.uk **web:** www.thesixbells.co.uk
dir: Exit A4 between Reading & Newbury, follow signs for Beenham

Not far from Thatcham and Newbury, The Six Bells is a friendly, traditional pub with comfortable, well-appointed bedrooms and good service. The restaurant serves a range of excellent, well-prepared dishes, dinner is recommended.

Rooms 4 en suite **Facilities** FTV tea/coffee Dinner available **Conf** Max 40 Thtr 40 Class 40 Board 25 **Parking** 20 **Notes** ⊗ No Children 16yrs No coaches

BOXFORD
Map 5 SU47

Bell @ Boxford

★★★ 🅰 INN

tel: 01488 608721 **Lambourn Rd RG20 8DD**
email: paul@bellatboxford.com **web:** www.bellatboxford.com
dir: M4 junct 14, A338 towards Wantage. Right onto B4000 to x-rds signed Boxford

Paul and Helen Lavis have been the hosts at this traditional Berkshire inn for over twenty years. The restaurant offers a varied and comprehensive menu, seven days a week, along with relaxed service and good value prices. The bedrooms all come complete with power shower, HDTV, WiFi, trouser press and hairdryers, and the location is ideal for Newbury and Hungerford.

Rooms 9 en suite (4 GF) S £50-£80; D £56-£90* **Facilities** FTV DVD tea/coffee Dinner available Direct Dial WiFi Pool table **Conf** Max 12 Board 12 **Parking** 35

CHIEVELEY
Map 5 SU47

Crab & Boar
★★★★ ◉◉ RESTAURANT WITH ROOMS

tel: 01635 247550 **Wantage Rd RG20 8UE**
email: info@crabandboar.com **web:** www.crabandboar.com
dir: 1.5m W of Chieveley on B4494

Part of The Epicurean Collection, this recently refurbished and renovated former pub has been appointed to a very high standard and bedrooms include a full range of modern amenities. Some ground floor rooms have a small private patio area complete with a luxury private hot tub. The warm and cosy restaurant offers an extensive and award-winning range of dishes, using the best suppliers in the south.

Rooms 9 en suite 5 annexe en suite (8 GF) D £110-£220* **Facilities** FTV tea/coffee Dinner available Direct Dial WiFi Hot tub suites **Extras** Home-made biscuits **Conf** Max 14 Thtr 14 Class 14 Board 14 **Parking** 80 **Notes** LB No coaches

Ye Olde Red Lion
★★★★ ◉ INN

tel: 01635 248379 & 07764 579808 **Green Ln RG20 8XB**
email: redlion@toucansurf.com **web:** www.yeolderedlion.com
dir: M4 junct 13 N towards Oxford for 300yds, onto slip road signed Chieveley. Left at junct, 300yds on left

Situated in the quiet village of Chieveley, just five miles north of Newbury, this traditional inn offers comfortable en suite accommodation in the adjoining 15th-century house. The cosy pub offers a good range of real ales, and dinner can be enjoyed in the restaurant where good use is made of local and seasonal produce.

Rooms 5 annexe en suite (3 GF) S £80-£90; D £90-£100 **Facilities** FTV tea/coffee Dinner available WiFi **Parking** 30 **Notes** No Children 14yrs

HUNGERFORD
Map 5 SU36

The Swan Inn
★★★★ ◉ INN

tel: 01488 668326 **Craven Rd, Inkpen RG17 9DX**
email: enquiries@theswaninn-organics.co.uk **web:** www.theswaninn-organics.co.uk
dir: 3.5m SE of Hungerford. S on Hungerford High St past rail bridge, left to Hungerford Common, right signed Inkpen

This delightful village inn dates back to the 17th century, has open fires and beams in the bar, and the bonus of a smart restaurant. Bedrooms are generally spacious and well equipped. Organic produce is available from the on-site farm shop, so the bar, restaurant and breakfast menus all feature local organic produce too.

Rooms 10 en suite (2 fmly) S £70-£80; D £85-£105* **Facilities** FTV Lounge tea/coffee Dinner available Direct Dial WiFi ⓑ **Extras** Trouser press **Conf** Max 40 Thtr 40 Class 40 Board 12 **Parking** 50 **Notes** ⊗ Closed 25-26 Dec

HURLEY
Map 5 SU88

Premier Collection

The Olde Bell Inn
★★★★★ ◉◉ INN

tel: 01628 825881 **High St SL6 5LX**
email: oldebellreception@coachinginn.co.uk **web:** www.theoldebell.co.uk
dir: M4 junct 8/9 follow signs for Henley. At rdbt take A4130 to Hurley, turn right to Hurley Village, 800yds on right

Dating in part to 1135, this charming coaching inn has lots of original features, with timber framed buildings and extensive landscaped gardens. Dinner can be enjoyed in the award-winning restaurant, and the kitchen uses some of the inn's own home-grown seasonal produce. There is a range of individually-styled bedrooms, each with a modern well-equipped bathroom. Both The Tithe Barn and Malthouse cater for functions and private parties, and there is a range of business facilities.

Rooms 11 en suite 37 annexe en suite (21 GF) D £79-£279* **Facilities** FTV tea/coffee Dinner available Direct Dial WiFi ⓦⓑ 18 **Conf** Max 130 Thtr 130 Class 80 Board 52 **Parking** 80 **Notes** LB Civ Wed 160

Find out more about AA Inspected Guest Accommodation on page 8

KINTBURY — Map 5 SU36

The Dundas Arms

★★★★ ⬡ INN

tel: 01488 658263 **53 Station Rd RG17 9UT**
email: info@dundasarms.co.uk **web:** www.dundasarms.co.uk
dir: A34 onto A4, turn left, signed Kintbury, into Station Rd

Part of The Epicurean Collection, The Dundas Arms is quite a unique property; the location next to the canal is inviting, with service of food and drinks to the canal side being available. There are also extensive garden areas and ample car parking. The en suite bedrooms are comfortable and well equipped; some have their own private waterside patio areas. Food is a highlight of the stay with local produce featuring highly on the menu.

Rooms 8 en suite (2 fmly) (5 GF) D £80–£155* **Facilities** FTV Lounge tea/coffee Dinner available Direct Dial WiFi Fishing **Conf** Max 16 **Parking** 60 **Notes** LB

KNOWL HILL — Map 5 SU87

Bird in Hand Country Inn

★★★★ ⬡ INN

tel: 01628 826622 & 822781 **Bath Rd RG10 9UP**
email: info@birdinhand.co.uk **web:** www.birdinhand.co.uk
dir: M4 junct 8/9, A404 towards Henley. At junct 9b onto A4 towards Reading, 3m, Knowl Hill on right after BP garage

The Bird in Hand Country Inn is just four miles from Maidenhead, and dates back, in part, to the 14th century. Bedrooms are arranged around a brick courtyard and all are well equipped. Guests can relax in the Oak Lounge Bar, which has plenty of traditional charm and old English character, and dining is available either in the bar or the restaurant.

Rooms 10 en suite 12 annexe en suite (1 fmly) (6 GF) S £80–£89; D £90–£160* **Facilities** FTV iPod docking station tea/coffee Dinner available Direct Dial WiFi ⬡ **Extras** Robes & slippers in some rooms **Conf** Max 50 Thtr 50 Class 30 Board 40 **Parking** 80 **Notes** LB

MAIDENHEAD — Map 6 SU88

Pinkneys Court Mews

★★★★ ⬡ BED AND BREAKFAST

tel: 01628 633253 & 07989 572167 **Lee Ln SL6 6PE**
email: pinkneyscourtmews@outlook.com **web:** www.bedbreakfastmaidenhead.co.uk
dir: M4 junct 8/9 onto A404(M) to Maidenhead West. Exit after 2m & at rdbt onto A4 towards Maidenhead. Left at next rdbt, then right to Pinkneys Green. At Pinkneys Arms pub left into Lee Ln, on left

Situated within easy reach of Henley, Marlow, Maidenhead and Windsor, this attractive country house bed and breakfast offers convenient but quiet and tranquil surroundings. Attractively furnished bedrooms with designer fabrics provide a homely touch. Finish your stay with an enjoyable breakfast featuring locally sourced, fresh ingredients. A conservatory, terrace and garden are available.

Rooms 4 en suite S £70–£90; D £80–£100* **Facilities** FTV DVD Lounge tea/coffee WiFi ⬡ 18 **Extras** Speciality toiletries, snacks **Parking** 4 **Notes** ⊗ No Children 12yrs

NEWBURY — Map 5 SU46

Pilgrims Guest House

★★★★ GUEST ACCOMMODATION

tel: 01635 40694 **Oxford Rd RG14 1XB**
email: office@pilgrimsgh.co.uk **web:** www.pilgrimsnewbury.co.uk
dir: In Newbury exit A4 at Waitrose rdbt onto B4494 towards Wantage, 0.5m on left

Located close to the town centre, this smartly presented house has comfortable bedrooms with modern bathrooms; some rooms are located in an annexe. WiFi is provided throughout the property and breakfast is served in the bright dining room. Parking is available.

Rooms 13 rms (9 en suite) 4 annexe en suite (1 fmly) (3 GF) S £45–£59; D £65* **Facilities** FTV Lounge tea/coffee WiFi ⬡ **Parking** 17 **Notes** ⊗ Closed 24 Dec–2 Jan

Rookwood Farm House

★★★★ GUEST ACCOMMODATION

tel: 01488 608676 **Stockcross RG20 8JX**
email: charlotte@rookwoodfarmhouse.co.uk **web:** www.rookwoodfarmhouse.co.uk
dir: 2m W of Newbury, at junct A4 & A34 onto B4000, 0.75m to Stockcross, 1st right signed Woodspeen, bear left, 1st on right

Rookwood Farm House enjoys wonderful views and is very much a family home. Bedrooms are attractively presented and feature fine pieces of furniture. Breakfast is served at one large table in the kitchen. The coach house has a kitchen and sitting room and, during the summer, visitors can enjoy the beautiful gardens and outdoor pool.

Rooms 2 rms (1 en suite) (1 pri facs) 2 annexe en suite (1 fmly) **Facilities** TVL tea/coffee WiFi ⬡ ⬡ ⬡ 9 ⬡ **Conf** Max 16 Board 16 **Parking** 4 **Notes** ⊗ Civ Wed 200

PANGBOURNE — Map 5 SU67

Weir View House

★★★★ GUEST ACCOMMODATION

tel: 0118 984 2120 **9 Shooters Hill RG8 7DZ**
email: info@weirview.co.uk **web:** www.weirview.co.uk
dir: A329 N from Pangbourne, after mini rdbt under rail bridge, opposite The Swan pub

A warm welcome is guaranteed at this delightful house, overlooking the River Thames in the village of Pangbourne. The spacious modern bedrooms have been finished to a very high standard and the thoughtful extras include a well-stocked mini-bar. A continental breakfast is served in the bright and airy dining room, and freshly cooked meals can be delivered to your room from the pub across the road.

Rooms 9 en suite (6 fmly) (3 GF) **Facilities** FTV DVD TVL tea/coffee Direct Dial WiFi ⬡ **Extras** Mini-bar chargeable; robes/slippers in some rooms **Conf** Max 10 Board 10 **Parking** 10 **Notes** ⊗

| READING | Map 5 SU77 |

The French Horn
★★★★ ◉◉ RESTAURANT WITH ROOMS

tel: 0118 969 2204 **Sonning RG4 6TN**
email: info@thefrenchhorn.co.uk **web:** www.thefrenchhorn.co.uk
dir: From A4 into Sonning, follow B478 through village over bridge, on right, car park on left

This long-established Thames-side establishment has a lovely village setting and retains the traditions of classic hospitality. The restaurant is a particular attraction and has been awarded two AA Rosettes. Bedrooms, including four cottage suites, are spacious and comfortable; many offer stunning views over the river. A private boardroom is available for corporate guests.

Rooms 12 en suite 8 annexe en suite (4 GF) (4 smoking) **Facilities** FTV iPod docking station Lounge tea/coffee Dinner available Direct Dial WiFi ↨ 18 Fishing ♨ **Extras** Speciality toiletries, safe, mineral water **Conf** Max 14 Board 14 **Parking** 43 **Notes** ⊗ Closed 1-2 Jan RS 25 Dec eve closed for dinner No coaches

The Wee Waif
★★★ INN

tel: 0118 944 0066 **Old Bath Rd, Charvil RG10 9RJ**
web: www.oldenglish.co.uk

The Wee Waif can be found on the outskirts of Reading and has easy access to the transport network. The lodge-style accommodation is appointed with guest comfort in mind. All-day dining is available from the popular Hungry Horse restaurant and bar, where breakfast is also served. Ample parking is provided.

Rooms 42 en suite (21 GF) **Facilities** FTV tea/coffee Dinner available WiFi Pool table **Conf** Max 30 Thtr 30 Class 30 Board 30 **Parking** 50 **Notes** ⊗

| SLOUGH | Map 6 SU97 |

Furnival Lodge
★★★★ ◭ GUEST HOUSE

tel: 01753 570333 **53-55 Furnival Av SL2 1DH**
email: info@furnival-lodge.co.uk **web:** www.furnival-lodge.co.uk
dir: Just off A355 (Farnham Rd), adjacent to BP garage

In operation for more than twenty years, Furnival Lodge offers modern and spacious rooms, complete with power showers in the en suite bathrooms. Bedrooms are pleasantly decorated and guests have the use of a comfortable lounge.

Rooms 10 en suite (1 fmly) (3 GF) **Facilities** TVL WiFi **Parking** 7 **Notes** ⊗

| THATCHAM | Map 5 SU56 |

The Bunk Inn
★★★★★ ◉◉ INN

tel: 01635 200400 **Curridge RG18 9DS**
email: info@thebunkinn.co.uk **web:** www.thebunkinn.co.uk

The Bunk Inn is a quintessential English pub set in the pretty village of Curridge, close to Newbury Racecourse. The en suite bedrooms have plenty of character and offer impressive quality and comfort. Great beers and ales are served in peak condition in the characterful bar and great food is served, both at breakfast and at dinner, which has achieved two AA Rosettes. Private parties can be accommodated and there is plenty of parking.

Rooms 9 en suite **Facilities** tea/coffee Dinner available WiFi **Extras** Speciality toiletries **Parking**

| WARGRAVE | Map 5 SU77 |

Premier Collection

Copperfields
★★★★★ BED AND BREAKFAST

tel: 0118 348 4791 & 07802 483044 **15 Dark Ln RG10 8JU**
email: robertdavis48@hotmail.co.uk

An impressive house surrounded by manicured lawns, Copperfields is located in a quiet residential area and only a few miles from Henley-on-Thames. The four rooms have been very well appointed and differ in style and size; the smaller double has a private bathroom. Evening meals can be provided upon prior request. Breakfast is served at the communal table overlooking the garden. Secure parking and free WiFi available.

Rooms 4 rms (2 en suite) (2 pri facs) **Facilities** FTV TVL TV3B WiFi ↖ ♨ **Parking** 5 **Notes** ⊗ ☻

| WINDSOR | Map 6 SU97 |

Rainworth House
★★★★ GUEST ACCOMMODATION

tel: 01753 856749 **Oakley Green Rd SL4 5UL**
email: info@rainworthhouse.com **web:** www.rainworthhouse.com
dir: Off A308 Windsor to Maidenhead road. Take 1st left into Oakley Green Rd

In well-kept grounds near Windsor, this smart property has six individually-styled bedrooms. The richly decorated rooms are well equipped and are ideal for both business and leisure guests. Public areas include a comfortable lounge, and the dining area is a sociable setting for breakfast. Parking is available.

Rooms 6 rms (5 en suite) (1 pri facs) (2 fmly) **Facilities** FTV Lounge tea/coffee Direct Dial WiFi ♨ **Parking** 10

WINDSOR *continued*

Innkeeper's Lodge Old Windsor

★★★★ INN

tel: 08451 551551 *(Calls cost 2p per minute plus your phone company's access charge)*
Staright Rd, Old Winsdor SL4 2RR
email: info@innkeeperslodge.com **web:** www.innkeeperslodge.com

At Innkeeper's Lodge you'll find accommodation with comfort and character in equal measure, and everything needed for a relaxing stay, from easy check-in and free parking to complimentary breakfast and a cosy pub serving great value food and drink on the doorstep. Each Lodge has quality rooms, and there are Lodges in a variety of locations from towns and cities to countryside settings across the UK.

Rooms 15 en suite (2 fmly) (7 GF) **Facilities** FTV tea/coffee Dinner available WiFi **Parking Notes** ⊗

76 Duke Street B&B

★★★★ BED AND BREAKFAST

tel: 01753 620636 & 07884 222225 **76 Duke St SL4 1SQ**
email: bedandbreakfast@76dukestreet.co.uk **web:** www. 76dukestreet.co.uk
dir: *M4 junct 6 onto A332. Keep in left lane, take 1st slip road into Maidenhead Rd. At rdbt turn left, at 2nd set of lights turn left into Vansittart Rd. Duke St 1st turn on right, No 76 5th house on left*

A Victorian property situated in a quiet residential area of Windsor, just 200 metres from the River Thames and a 10 minute walk along the riverside into the centre. A warm welcome can be expected and lots of thoughtful accessories are available along with free WiFi. Guests can enjoy a selection of freshly cooked items at breakfast, made with fresh quality ingredients.

Rooms 1 rms (1 pri facs) D £85-£95 **Facilities** FTV Lounge TVL tea/coffee WiFi **Extras** Chocolates, home-made biscuits/cakes, fresh fruit **Notes** ⊗ ⊜

The Windsor Trooper

★★★ INN

tel: 01753 670123 **97 St Leonards Rd SL4 3BZ**
email: thewindsortrooper@live.co.uk **web:** www.thetrooperinnwindsor.com
dir: *M4 junct 6, at rdbt follow signs for Windsor, then straight over next 2 rdbts signed Staines-on-Thames, take 1st road on left*

Located close to many popular attractions and within walking distance of the town centre, this traditional inn provides comfortable annexed accommodation, including a family room. Dinner is served in the bright and airy conservatory, where a range of daily specials are often available. A freshly prepared breakfast is served and limited secure parking is available.

Rooms 4 en suite 4 annexe en suite (1 fmly) (3 GF) S £70-£90; D £70-£90 (room only) **Facilities** FTV tea/coffee Dinner available WiFi Pool table **Extras** Speciality toiletries **Parking** 5 **Notes** LB ⊗

Quarters

★★★★ GUEST ACCOMMODATION

tel: 0118 979 7071 **14 Milton Rd RG40 1DB**
email: elaineizod@hotmail.com **web:** www.quarterswokingham.com
dir: *From town centre on A321 towards Henley & Twyford. Left at 1st mini rdbt into Milton Rd*

Located just a short walk from the town centre, a warm welcome is assured at Quarters. Stylishly decorated bedrooms are well equipped and spacious. A hearty breakfast is served around the communal dining table.

Rooms 3 en suite S £50-£55; D £65-£70* **Facilities** FTV DVD iPod docking station tea/coffee WiFi **Notes** ⊗ No Children 12yrs ⊜

The Emmbrook Inn

★★★ INN

tel: 0118 978 2552 **Emmbrook Rd RG41 1HG**
email: embrookinn@btconnect.com **web:** http://emmbrookinn.com
dir: *M4 junct 10 onto A329, 2m to inn*

Situated close to the M4, with direct routes to London and the south west, this traditional English inn offers comfortable en suite accommodation, situated adjacent to the pub. Home-cooked meals can be enjoyed, along with a good range of real cask conditioned ales. An enclosed garden and front patio are available for summer drinks. Ample parking to the rear.

Rooms 12 en suite (6 GF) **Facilities** STV FTV tea/coffee Dinner available WiFi **Parking** 24 **Notes** ⊗ No Children 14yrs No coaches

Westfield House

★★★★ ⓺ ⊜ BED AND BREAKFAST

tel: 0117 962 6119 **37 Stoke Hill, Stoke Bishop BS9 1LQ**
email: admin@westfieldhouse.net **web:** www.westfieldhouse.net
dir: *1.5m NW of city centre in Stoke Bishop*

A genuine welcome is assured at this friendly, family-run B&B in a quiet location on the edge of Durdham Downs. The very well-equipped bedrooms offer high levels of quality and comfort. Home-cooked dinners are available by arrangement, and in summer these can be enjoyed on the patio overlooking the large rear garden.

Rooms 3 en suite S £98-£115; D £99-£135 **Facilities** FTV DVD TVL tea/coffee Dinner available Direct Dial WiFi ⤵ **Conf** Max 10 Board 10 **Parking** 5 **Notes** LB ⊗ No Children 11yrs

Valley Farm

★★★★ BED AND BREAKFAST

tel: 01275 332723 & 07799 768161 **Sandy Ln BS39 4EL**
email: valleyfarm2010@btinternet.com

(For full entry see Stanton Drew (Somerset))

The Washington

★★★ GUEST HOUSE

tel: 0117 973 3980 **11-15 St Pauls Rd, Clifton BS8 1LX**
email: washington@cliftonhotels.com
web: www.cliftonhotels.com/bristolhotels/washington/
dir: *A4018 into city, right at lights opposite BBC, house 200yds on left*

This large terraced house is within walking distance of the city centre and Clifton Village. The bedrooms are well equipped for business guests. Public areas include a modern reception lounge and a bright basement breakfast room. The property has secure parking and a rear patio garden.

Rooms 46 rms (40 en suite) (4 fmly) (10 GF) **Facilities** FTV tea/coffee Direct Dial Licensed WiFi Reduced rate pass local health club & Bristol Zoo **Extras** Fresh fruit - complimentary **Parking** 16 **Notes** Closed 23-31 Dec

BUCKINGHAMSHIRE

AMERSHAM	Map 6 SU99

The Crown

★★★★★ ◉ ⬡ INN

tel: 01494 721541 **16 High St HP7 0DH**
email: reception@thecrownamersham.com **web:** www.thecrownamersham.com
dir: *M40 junct 2 onto A355, continue to Amersham. Onto Gore Hill, left into The Broadway*

Originally a 16th-century coaching inn, The Crown now offers a mix of quirky, modern minimalist style blended with the character of the original building. High quality food is served daily along with a notable breakfast that will set your day off to a good start.

Rooms 29 en suite 9 annexe en suite (1 fmly) (9 GF) D £115-£300* **Facilities** STV FTV Lounge TVL tea/coffee Dinner available Direct Dial WiFi ⬤ ⬤ Spa facility access **Extras** Speciality toiletries, snacks, wine - free **Conf** Max 120 Thtr 120 Class 100 Board 18 **Parking** 38 **Notes** No coaches Civ Wed 50

The Potters Arms

★★★ ⬡ INN

tel: 01494 726222 **Fagnall Ln, Winchmore Hill HP7 0PH**
email: info@pottersarms.co.uk **web:** www.pottersarms.co.uk
dir: *From Beaconsfield on A355, left into Magpie Ln. Follow road to Winchmore Hill*

Situated in a rural location in Buckinghamshire, close to Amersham, this traditional pub offers comfortable accommodation. A warm welcome will be received, and guests can enjoy a range of classic pub favourites in the bar and restaurant. The inn has become well known for its popular Comedy Nights, attracting some top comedians.

Rooms 4 en suite S £75-£85; D £80-£95* **Facilities** FTV TVL tea/coffee Dinner available WiFi **Parking** 20

ASTON CLINTON	Map 5 SP81

Innkeeper's Lodge Aylesbury (East)

★★★★ ⬡ INN

tel: 08451 551551 *(Calls cost 2p per minute plus your phone company's access charge)*
London Rd HP22 5HP
email: info@innkeeperslodge.com **web:** www.innkeeperslodge.com

At Innkeeper's Lodge you'll find accommodation with comfort and character in equal measure, and everything needed for a relaxing stay, from easy check-in and free parking to complimentary breakfast and a cosy pub serving great value food and drink on the doorstep. Each Lodge has quality rooms, and there are Lodges in a variety of locations from towns and cities to countryside settings across the UK.

Rooms 11 en suite (4 fmly) (3 GF) **Facilities** FTV tea/coffee Dinner available Direct Dial WiFi **Parking Notes** ⊗

AYLESBURY	Map 11 SP81

Innkeeper's Lodge Aylesbury (South)

★★★★ ⬡ INN

tel: 08451 551551 *(Calls cost 2p per minute plus your phone company's access charge)*
40 Main St, Weston Turville HP22 5RW
email: info@innkeeperslodge.com **web:** www.innkeeperslodge.com

At Innkeeper's Lodge you'll find accommodation with comfort and character in equal measure, and everything needed for a relaxing stay, from easy check-in and free parking to complimentary breakfast and a cosy pub serving great value food and drink on the doorstep. Each Lodge has quality rooms, and there are Lodges in a variety of locations from towns and cities to countryside settings across the UK.

Rooms 16 en suite (5 GF) **Facilities** FTV tea/coffee Dinner available Direct Dial WiFi **Parking Notes** ⊗

BEACONSFIELD	Map 6 SU99

Premier Collection

Crazy Bear Beaconsfield

★★★★★ ◉ ⬡ GUEST ACCOMMODATION

tel: 01494 673086 **75 Wycombe End, Old Town HP9 1LX**
email: enquiries@crazybear-beaconsfield.co.uk **web:** www.crazybeargroup.co.uk
dir: *M40 junct 2, 3rd exit from rdbt, next rdbt 1st exit. Over 2 mini rdbts, on right*

Located in the heart of the old town, this former inn dating from Tudor times has been completely restored to create an exciting and vibrant environment. Award-winning cuisine in both the Thai and the English restaurants, classic cocktails and an extensive wine list can all be enjoyed. The Terrace and the Moroccan-style lounge offer a calming environment in which to relax. The bedrooms are individually appointed with unusual fabrics and dazzling colour schemes. Resident guests can also enjoy the swimming pool and Jacuzzi. The Crazy Bear Beaconsfield is well equipped to cater for private parties, weddings and business meetings. Limited secure parking available.

Rooms 6 en suite 26 annexe en suite (2 GF) **Facilities** STV Dinner available Direct Dial Licensed WiFi ⬤ Jacuzzi **Extras** Fruit, mineral water - complimentary **Conf** Max 100 Thtr 100 Class 100 Board 60 **Parking** 12 **Notes** ⊗ Civ Wed 100

BRILL
Map 11 SP61

The Pheasant
★★★★ ⬥ INN

tel: 01844 239370 **39 Windmill St HP18 9TG**
email: info@thepheasant.co.uk **web:** www.thepheasant.co.uk
dir: *M40 junct 7, take A329 Thame, A418 Aylesbury. At next rdbt take B4011, through Long Crendon, right signed Brill*

The Pheasant is a popular local pub with well-appointed rooms some of which offer views of the Grade II listed windmill. The mill is owned by the village and is open to the public at certain times of the year. At The Pheasant all the rooms have been nicely configured to offer comfort and practicality. Real ale and cocktails are served at the bar, while the restaurant offers simple yet delicious dishes using local produce. Free parking and WiFi is available.

Rooms 2 en suite 2 annexe en suite (1 GF) S £75; D £95* **Facilities** FTV Lounge tea/coffee Dinner available WiFi **Notes** RS 25-26 Dec rooms available, no bkfst No coaches

Poletrees Farm *(SP660160)*
★★★★ FARMHOUSE

tel: 01844 238276 **Ludgershall Rd HP18 9TZ**
email: poletrees.farm@btinternet.com
dir: *Exit S from A41 signed Ludgershall/Brill, after railway bridge 0.5m on left*

Located between the villages of Ludgershall and Brill, this 16th-century farmhouse retains many original features including a wealth of exposed beams. The bedrooms are in converted outbuildings, and the cosy dining room is the setting for a wholesome breakfast.

Rooms 4 annexe en suite (4 GF) S £45-£50; D £90-£100* **Facilities** FTV TVL tea/coffee **Parking** 6 **Notes** LB ⊗ No Children 12yrs 110 acres sheep

CHALFONT ST GILES
Map 6 SU99

The Ivy House
★★★ ⬥ INN

tel: 01494 872184 **London Rd HP8 4RS**
email: alfie@theivyhousechalfont.co.uk **web:** www.ivyhousechalfontstgiles.co.uk

This popular traditional English inn is more than 250 years old, and has retained some lovely period features. Situated in the heart of the Chiltern Vale surrounded by countryside it makes a popular venue for walkers or even for those heading to London, which is only 40 minutes away. Rooms are comfortably equipped and guests can enjoy dinner in the attractive restaurant, which also has a very good range of real ales and wines.

Rooms 5 en suite **Facilities** FTV tea/coffee Dinner available WiFi ⚓ 18 **Parking** 40

DENHAM
Map 6 TQ08

The Falcon Inn
★★★★ ⬥ INN

tel: 01895 832125 **Village Rd UB9 5BE**
email: mail@falcondenham.com **web:** www.falcondenham.com
dir: *M40 junct 1, follow A40 & Gerrards Cross signs. Approx 200yds, right into Old Mill Rd, pub opposite village green*

This 18th-century inn stands in the heart of the picturesque village of Denham, opposite the green. The en suite bedrooms, with smart shower rooms, are well equipped and display original features. Carefully prepared dishes, together with a good selection of wines, are served at both lunch and dinner in the cosy restaurant.

Rooms 4 en suite **Facilities** FTV DVD tea/coffee Dinner available WiFi ⚓ 18 ⚓ **Extras** Fresh fruit, bottled water, speciality toiletries **Notes** No Children 10yrs

GREAT MISSENDEN
Map 6 SP80

Nags Head Inn & Restaurant
★★★★ ⊚ INN

tel: 01494 862200 **London Rd HP16 0DG**
email: goodfood@nagsheadbucks.com **web:** www.nagsheadbucks.com
dir: *N of Amersham on A413, left at Chiltern hospital into London Rd signed Great Missenden*

This delightful 15th-century inn, located in the picturesque Chiltern Hills, has a great reputation locally thanks to its extensive menu of local produce and carefully prepared dishes. Individually-designed bedrooms are comfortable with a modern twist ensuring a home-from-home feel. Ample parking is available.

Rooms 5 en suite (1 fmly) S £75-£115; D £75-£135* **Facilities** FTV DVD tea/coffee Dinner available WiFi ⚓ **Extras** Speciality toiletries, mineral water - free **Conf** Max 50 **Parking** 40 **Notes** Closed 25 Dec

HIGH WYCOMBE
Map 5 SU89

Clifton Lodge

★★★ GUEST HOUSE

tel: 01494 440095 **210 West Wycombe Rd HP12 3AR**
email: mail@cliftonlodgehotel.com **web:** www.cliftonlodgehotel.com
dir: *A40 from town centre towards Aylesbury, on right after BP station & opposite phone box*

Located west of the town centre, this long-established, owner-managed guest house provides a range of bedrooms, popular with a regular commercial clientele. Public areas include an attractive conservatory-dining room and a cosy lounge. Ample parking behind the property.

Rooms 32 rms (20 en suite) (1 fmly) (7 GF) **Facilities** FTV Lounge tea/coffee Dinner available Licensed WiFi **Conf** Max 25 Thtr 25 Class 20 Board 15 **Parking** 28 **Notes** LB ⊗

Fox Country Inn

★★★ INN

tel: 01491 638814 **Ibstone HP14 3XT**
email: info@foxcountryinn.co.uk **web:** www.foxcountryinn.co.uk
dir: *M40 junct 5 follow signs to Ibstone, 1.5m on left*

This stylish modern inn enjoys a peaceful rural location on the outskirts of High Wycombe. The modern bedrooms are all attractively presented and have a host of thoughtful little extras. Free WiFi is available throughout. The bar and restaurant are contemporary and open-plan in style and food is served all day in the bar and on the terrace.

Rooms 18 en suite (2 fmly) (10 GF) S £60-£70; D £70-£80* **Facilities** FTV tea/coffee Dinner available Direct Dial WiFi **Parking** 23 **Notes** Civ Wed 50

MARLOW
Map 5 SU88

The Prince of Wales

★★★ INN

tel: 01628 482970 **1 Miller Rd SL7 1PX**
email: prince-of-wales@tiscali.co.uk **web:** www.the-prince-of-wales.co.uk

The Prince of Wales offers well-appointed bedrooms that meet the needs of both business and leisure travellers; some rooms are annexed and have private access. The traditional inn offers a range of ales and an appealing Thai and British menu. There is a large patio that proves ideal for relaxation in the warmer months. Ample, secure parking is available.

Rooms 3 en suite 3 annexe en suite (1 GF) **Facilities** FTV tea/coffee Dinner available WiFi **Parking** 22

NEWTON BLOSSOMVILLE
Map 11 SP95

The Old Mill

★★★ INN

tel: 01234 881273 **Clifton Rd MK43 8AN**
email: enquiries@oldmill.uk.com **web:** www.oldmill.uk.com
dir: *M1 junct 14 onto A509 towards Wellingborough. In Emberton right into Newton Rd*

In the quiet and attractive village of Newton Blossomville, in the Borough of Milton Keynes, this traditional inn offers comfortable accommodation. The inn remains a friendly locals' pub and guests can also enjoy a game of skittles. A traditional pub menu offers a good range of dishes, and a selection of real ales is on offer.

Rooms 5 en suite (2 fmly) **Facilities** FTV tea/coffee Dinner available WiFi ⓑ
Extras Bottled water, fresh milk **Notes** LB No coaches

WADDESDON
Map 11 SP71

The Five Arrows

★★★★★ ◉◉ ⓢ RESTAURANT WITH ROOMS

tel: 01296 651727 **High St HP18 0JE**
email: reservations@thefivearrows.co.uk **web:** www.waddesdon.org.uk/fivearrows
dir: *On A41 in Waddesdon. Into Baker St for car park*

This Grade II listed building with its elaborate Elizabethan-style chimney stacks stands at the gates of Waddesdon Manor and was named after the Rothschild family emblem. Individually styled en suite bedrooms are comfortable and well appointed. Friendly staff are on hand to offer a warm welcome. Alfresco dining is possible in the warmer months.

Rooms 8 en suite 8 annexe en suite (2 fmly) (3 GF) S £70-£100; D £80-£235* **Facilities** FTV tea/coffee Dinner available WiFi ⓑ **Conf** Max 20 Thtr 20 Class 20 Board 20 **Parking** 40 **Notes** ⊗ No coaches Civ Wed 60

WOOBURN GREEN
Map 6 SU98

The Old Bell

★★★★ ⌂ INN

tel: 01628 523117 **HP10 0PL**
email: oldbellwooburn@hotmail.co.uk **web:** www.oldbellwooburn.co.uk
dir: *M40 junct 2, A355 towards Beaconsfield. Take A40 through Beaconsfield. Left onto B4440 to Wooburn Green. At T-junct left into Town Ln. Old Bell on left*

Dating back to the 16th century, this former coaching inn retains many of its original features, with low beams and real fires in the cosy bar. The Old Bell has a very good range of real ales, including guest ales, while the award-winning restaurant features some excellent local produce. Bedrooms are very stylish and retain many of the period features that make this place unique. Free WiFi along with ample secure parking is available for guests.

Rooms 6 en suite 1 annexe en suite (2 fmly) (1 GF) S £90-£95; D £99-£140 **Facilities** FTV tea/coffee Dinner available WiFi ⌁ 18 **Parking** 14 **Notes** LB Closed 1 Jan RS 25-26 Dec Bar & restaurant closes at 4pm

CAMBRIDGESHIRE

BALSHAM
Map 12 TL55

The Black Bull Inn

★★★★ ◉ INN

tel: 01223 893844 **27 High St CB21 4DJ**
email: info@blackbull-balsham.co.uk **web:** www.blackbull-balsham.co.uk
dir: *From S: M11 junct 9 towards Newmarket, exit signed Balsham, in centre of village. From N: M11 junct 10, A505 signed Newmarket (A11), exit signed Balsham.*

This privately owned 16th-century, Grade II listed free house is set in the pretty village of Balsham. There are five spacious en suite bedrooms located alongside the pub which provide very high levels of quality and comfort. Excellent food is served at lunch and dinner every day.

Rooms 5 annexe en suite (1 fmly) (5 GF) S £90-£115; D £115-£145* **Facilities** FTV DVD Lounge tea/coffee Dinner available WiFi ⓑ **Conf** Max 30 Thtr 30 Class 24 Board 20 **Parking** 20 **Notes** LB

BURWELL   Map 12 TL56

Deerview

★★★★ BED AND BREAKFAST

tel: 01638 741885 & 07554 300501 **133A North St CB25 0BB**
email: bookings@deerview.biz **web:** www.deerview.biz
dir: A14 junct 35 onto A1303 then B1102. Through Burwell, take last turn on right, at end turn left, 500yds to Deerview

Deerview enjoys a prominent position in the heart of the peaceful village of Burwell. Bedrooms are all spacious, attractively presented and very well equipped. A warm welcome is guaranteed from the friendly owners, and the freshly prepared breakfasts are not to be missed. The house is ten minutes from the famous Wicken Fen and a short drive from Newmarket, Ely, and Cambridge. Secure parking is available, and there is free WiFi for guests.

Rooms 4 en suite (1 fmly) (2 GF) S fr £40; D fr £85* **Facilities** FTV DVD tea/coffee WiFi 🛁 **Extras** Bottled water, snacks - complimentary **Parking** 4 **Notes** ⊗

CAMBRIDGE   Map 12 TL45

Benson House

★★★★ 🍴 GUEST HOUSE

tel: 01223 311594 **24 Huntingdon Rd CB3 0HH**
email: bensonhouse@btconnect.com **web:** www.bensonhouse.co.uk
dir: 0.5m NW of city centre on A604

This popular guest house is well placed for the city centre and New Hall and Fitzwilliam colleges. Its pleasant bedrooms vary in size and style and all are well equipped with TV, clock radio, beverage tray and hairdryers. The delicious selection at breakfast includes kippers, and there is limited private parking behind the property. Benson House cannot cater for pets or children under 12 years of age.

Rooms 6 en suite (1 GF) S £75-£120; D £115-£120 **Facilities** FTV iPod docking station tea/coffee WiFi **Extras** Speciality toiletries **Parking** 5 **Notes** ⊗ No Children 12yrs Closed 31 Dec

Rose Corner

★★★★ BED AND BREAKFAST

tel: 01223 563136 & 07733 027581 **42 Woodcock Close, Impington CB24 9LD**
email: enquiries@rose-corner.co.uk **web:** www.rose-corner.co.uk
dir: 4m N of Cambridge. A14 junct 32, B1049 N into Impington, exit Milton Rd into Woodcock Close

Rose Corner is a detached property in a quiet cul-de-sac in the popular village of Impington, north of the city. Its spacious bedrooms are carefully furnished and thoughtfully equipped, and breakfast is served in the comfortable lounge/dining room overlooking the rear gardens.

Rooms 5 rms (3 en suite) S £38-£40; D £75-£80* **Facilities** FTV TVL tea/coffee WiFi 🛁 **Parking** 5 **Notes** ⊗ No Children 11yrs

The Old Red Lion Inn

★★★★ ⍟ 🍴 INN

tel: 01223 892909 & 894217 **Horseheath CB21 4QF**
email: info@theoldredlion.co.uk **web:** www.theoldredlion.co.uk
dir: Leave A11 at Fourwentway, take A1307 (Haverhill). Continue past Linton after dual carriageway left to Horseheath

The Old Red Lion is situated in Horseheath and is a traditional inn offering modern, comfortable accommodation. A good range of real ales are available in the bar where guests can relax by the fire, or enjoy a drink on the outdoor patio in summer. A wide range of dishes are available in the restaurant and all dishes are home-made and ingredients locally sourced.

Rooms 12 annexe en suite (1 fmly) (7 GF) S £70-£90; D £80-£105 (room only)* **Facilities** STV FTV tea/coffee Dinner available WiFi **Extras** Bottled water **Conf** Max 30 **Parking** 30 **Notes** No coaches

AA ★★★
HAMDEN
GUEST HOUSE

Comfortable en-suite bedrooms 2½ miles from Cambridge City Centre. Frequent bus service. Car park. Local shops. Pubs and restaurants within walking distance.

89 High Street, Cherry Hinton, Cambridge CB1 9LU
Tel: (01223) 413263
e-mail: info@hamdenguesthouse.co.uk
web: www.hamdenguesthouse.co.uk

Hamden Guest House

★★★ GUEST HOUSE

tel: 01223 413263 & 07543 049010 **89 High St, Cherry Hinton CB1 9LU**
email: info@hamdenguesthouse.co.uk **web:** www.hamdenguesthouse.co.uk
dir: *3m SE of city centre. From M11 exit A1134 to Cherry Hinton; from A14 exit N on A1303 signed Cambridge & Cherry Hinton*

Expect a warm welcome at this small, family-run guest house, which is just a short drive from the city centre. The pleasant bedrooms are generally quite spacious and equipped with many thoughtful extras. Public rooms include a large kitchen-dining room where breakfast is served at individual tables.

Rooms 5 en suite (2 fmly) (1 GF) S £40; D £60 **Facilities** FTV tea/coffee WiFi **Parking** 6 **Notes** LB ⊗ No Children 5yrs

See advert on opposite page

The Alpha Milton Guest House

★★★ GUEST ACCOMMODATION

tel: 01223 311625 **61-63 Milton Rd CB4 1XA**
email: info@alphamilton.com **web:** www.alphamilton.com
dir: *0.5m NE of city centre*

The Alpha Milton Guest House is in a residential area just a short walk from the city centre. The attractive lounge-dining room overlooks the rear garden, and the pleasant bedrooms all have a good range of facilities.

Rooms 8 rms (7 en suite) (1 pri facs) (2 fmly) (2 GF) **Facilities** FTV DVD tea/coffee WiFi **Parking** 8 **Notes** ⊗

The Carpenters Arms

★★★ ⊛ INN

tel: 01223 367050 **182-186 Victoria Rd CB4 3DZ**
email: hello@carpentersarmscambridge.co.uk **web:** www.carpentersarmscambridge.co.uk
dir: *Phone for directions*

The Carpenters Arms has recently re-opened as a family-friendly gastropub, and is located only ten minutes' walk from the centre of Cambridge. Accommodation is available, and guests can enjoy award-winning meals in the vibrant and friendly restaurant below, alongside a good selection of real ales and craft beers. Guests can also enjoy home-made stone-baked pizza from the wood-burning pizza oven.

Rooms 5 rms (2 en suite) (3 pri facs) (3 fmly) **Facilities** FTV tea/coffee Dinner available WiFi ⚓ **Conf** Max 30 Thtr 30 Class 15 Board 15 **Parking** 6 **Notes** LB

Southampton Guest House

★★★ GUEST HOUSE

tel: 01223 357780 **7 Elizabeth Way CB4 1DE**
email: southamptonhouse@btinternet.com **web:** www.southamptonguesthouse.com
dir: *0.5m E of city centre*

The proprietors provide a friendly service at this terraced guest house, situated on the city's inner ring road, and just a short walk from the Grafton Centre. Guests can expect well-equipped bedrooms and a comprehensive choice at breakfast.

Rooms 5 en suite (3 fmly) (1 GF) S £40-£55; D £55-£65* **Facilities** tea/coffee Direct Dial WiFi **Parking** 8 **Notes** ⊗ ⊜

CAMBRIDGE *continued*

Red Lion

Ⓤ

tel: 01223 497070 & 497085 **Station Rd, Whittlesford Bridge CB22 4NL**
email: reservations@hiexpresscambridgeduxford.co.uk

Currently the rating for this establishment is not confirmed. This may be due to a change of ownership or because it has only recently joined the AA rating scheme.

Rooms 18 en suite **Facilities** FTV iPod docking station Lounge tea/coffee Dinner available Direct Dial Licensed WiFi **Conf** Max 200 Thtr 200 Class 74 Board 40 **Parking** 80 **Notes** ⊗ Civ Wed 70

| **ELTON** | **Map 12 TL09** |

Premier Collection

The Crown Inn
★★★★★ ⌂ INN

tel: 01832 280232 **8 Duck St PE8 6RQ**
email: inncrown@googlemail.com **web:** www.thecrowninn.org
dir: *A1 junct 17, A605 W. In 3.5m right signed Elton, 0.9m, left signed Nassington. On village green*

Expect a warm welcome at this delightful village pub, situated opposite the village green. The property dates back to the 16th century. It retains many of its original features, such as a large inglenook fireplace and oak-beamed ceilings. The smartly decorated bedrooms are tastefully appointed and thoughtfully equipped. Public rooms include a large open-plan lounge bar, a small relaxed dining area to the front, and a tastefully appointed circular restaurant.

Rooms 3 en suite 5 annexe en suite (3 fmly) (5 GF) **Facilities** FTV tea/coffee Dinner available Direct Dial WiFi ⌂ **Conf** Max 40 Thtr 25 Class 40 Board 25 **Parking** 15 **Notes** ⊗ RS Sun eve & Mon (ex BH) Restaurant only closed No coaches

| **ELY** | **Map 12 TL58** |

Lazy Otter Pub Restaurant
★★★★ INN

tel: 01353 649780 **Cambridge Rd, Stretham CB6 3LU**
email: thelazyotter@btconnect.com **web:** www.lazy-otter.com

The Lazy Otter enjoys an idyllic position, nestled on the banks of the River Ouse, ideally located between Cambridge and Ely. Comfortable bedrooms are all of a high standard. The restaurant overlooks the river with its boats and barges, and enjoys some lovely Fen scenery. The bar offers a range of real ales and guests can relax by roaring log fires in the cooler months. There is a very popular restaurant and the freshly cooked breakfasts are enjoyable. This is an ideal base from which to explore the countryside and delightful historic market towns.

Lazy Otter Pub Restaurant

Rooms 3 en suite **Facilities** FTV DVD iPod docking station tea/coffee Dinner available WiFi ⌂ **Parking** 60

See advert on opposite page

The Anchor Inn
★★★★ ◉ INN

tel: 01353 778537 **Bury Ln, Sutton Gault CB6 2BD**
email: anchorinn@popmail.bta.com **web:** www.anchor-inn-restaurant.co.uk
dir: *W of Ely. Sutton Gault signed from B1381 at S end of Sutton*

The Anchor inn is a 17th-century traditional inn, situated outside the city of Ely, in a quiet riverside location. Bedrooms are modern, yet retain some period charm, and guests can enjoy award-winning food in the restaurant.

Rooms 4 en suite **Facilities** FTV tea/coffee Dinner available Direct Dial WiFi **Extras** Bottled water, fresh milk **Parking** 10 **Notes** ⊗ RS 25-26 Dec Open for lunch only

The Three Pickerels
★★★★ INN

tel: 01353 777777 **19 Bridge Rd, Mepal CB6 2AR**
email: info@thethreepickerels.co.uk **web:** www.thethreepickerels.co.uk

Situated in the tranquil village of Mepal on the outskirts of Ely, this property sits on the banks of the New Bedford River and has views of the surrounding area. Public rooms include a smart bar, a dining room and a lovely lounge overlooking the river. The smartly appointed bedrooms are comfortable and well equipped.

Rooms 4 en suite (1 fmly) **Facilities** FTV TVL tea/coffee Dinner available WiFi Fishing Pool table **Parking** 40 **Notes** ⊗

The Village Inn
★★★ INN

tel: 01353 663763 **80 Main St, Witchford CB6 2HQ**
email: tarobinson@hotmail.co.uk **web:** www.villageinnwitchford.co.uk

The Village Inn offers two comfortable, well-appointed bedrooms and is located in the peaceful village of Witchford. Dinner is available in the evenings and the bar has a good choice of ales and beers. The historic town of Ely and the city of Cambridge are a short drive away. Free WiFi is available along with secure parking.

Rooms 2 rms **Facilities** Dinner available WiFi **Parking**

FEN DRAYTON
Map 12 TL36

Thorn House Bed & Breakfast
★★★★ BED AND BREAKFAST

tel: 01954 232092 & 07773 777473 **Church St CB24 4SG**
email: thornhousebandb@yahoo.co.uk **web:** www.thornhousebandb.co.uk
dir: *From Huntingdon - take 2nd Fenstanton exit signed 'dairy site'. Right & immediately left. Before A14 turn left to Fen Drayton. At T-junct turn right, left at mini rdbt, 1st right into Church St*

Thorn House Bed & Breakfast is located on the edge of Fen Drayton Nature Reserve and only 15 minutes from both Cambridge and Papworth. It is also a good base for those wishing to do the guided St Ives to Cambridge busway. The property itself offers comfortable and quiet accommodation. There is a private lodge to the rear that comes complete with a fridge and microwave, and also two rooms available in the main part of the house, which also share a comfortable lounge. A warm welcome will be received from Nicky, and for those wanting dinner nearby, there is a pub just three minutes' walk away.

Rooms 3 rms (1 en suite) 1 annexe en suite (1 fmly) (1 GF) S £58-£89; D £68-£99*
Facilities STV FTV DVD iPod docking station TVL tea/coffee WiFi ♿ 18 **Extras** Robes
Parking 3 **Notes** LB

GREAT ABINGTON
Map 12 TL54

Three Tuns
★★★★ ⊜ INN

tel: 01223 891467 **75 High St CB21 6AB**
email: email@thethreetuns-greatabington.co.uk
web: www.thethreetuns-greatabington.co.uk

Visitors are guaranteed a warm welcome at this charming 16th-century inn set in a prominent position in the heart of the pretty village of Great Abington. The very popular restaurant has a well-deserved reputation for its Thai cuisine and the bar has a good selection of real ales. The purpose-built bedrooms are beautifully presented and offer guests stylish and comfortable accommodation along with high quality bathrooms. Free WiFi is available throughout the property and secure parking is provided.

Rooms 9 annexe en suite (1 fmly) (9 GF) S £75-£120; D £90-£150 (room only)*
Facilities STV FTV tea/coffee Dinner available WiFi **Extras** Speciality toiletries
Parking 20 **Notes** Closed 1 Jan

The Lazy Otter

Cambridge Rd, Stretham, Ely, Cambridgeshire CB6 3LU
Tel: 01353 649780 • Email: thelazyotter@btconnect.com
Website: www.lazyotter.co.uk

HINXTON
Map 12 TL44

The Red Lion Inn
★★★★ ◉ INN

tel: 01799 530601 **32 High St CB10 1QY**
email: info@redlionhinxton.co.uk **web:** www.redlionhinxton.co.uk
dir: *Nbound only: M11 junct 9, towards A11, left onto A1301. Left to Hinxton. Or M11 junct 10, A505 towards A11/Newmarket. At rdbt 3rd exit onto A1301, right to Hinxton*

The Red Lion Inn is a 16th-century free house pub and restaurant, set in the pretty conservation village of Hinxton and offering high quality purpose-built accommodation. In the winter guests can relax by the well-stoked fire, while in summer they can enjoy the attractive walled garden which overlooks the village church.

Rooms 8 annexe en suite (2 fmly) (8 GF) S £95-£120; D £120-£150* **Facilities** FTV DVD Lounge tea/coffee Dinner available Direct Dial WiFi ⚫ **Conf** Max 20 Thtr 20 Class 15 Board 15 **Parking** 43 **Notes** LB

HUNTINGDON
Map 12 TL27

The Abbot's Elm
★★★★ ◉◉ INN

tel: 01487 773773 **Abbots Ripton PE28 2PA**
email: info@theabbotselm.co.uk **web:** www.theabbotselm.co.uk
dir: *A1(M) junct 13 onto A14 towards Huntingdon. At 1st rdbt straight on (A141 Spittals Way). Left at 2nd rdbt signed Abbots Ripton. 3m in village centre*

This Grade II listed thatched country inn is situated in the quiet village of Abbots Ripton, near the ancient market town of Huntingdon. Bedrooms are modern and comfortable, and guests can enjoy a range of real ales and fine wines in the spacious and smartly appointed bar and restaurant. The food, cooked by chef-patron Julia, has been awarded two AA Rosettes.

Rooms 3 en suite (3 GF) S £65-£69.50; D £80-£90* **Facilities** STV Lounge tea/coffee Dinner available WiFi **Extras** Robes; filtered water - complimentary **Parking** 50 **Notes** No coaches

LITTLEPORT
Map 12 TL58

The Gate House
★★★★ ⚑ BED AND BREAKFAST

tel: 01353 863840 & 07940 120023 **2B Lynn Rd CB6 1QG**
email: edna@thegatehousebandb.co.uk **web:** www.thegatehousebandb.co.uk
dir: *On A10 between Ely & King's Lynn. Cross railway line in Littleport, next right into Lynn Rd, last house on left*

This new-build house has a range of beautifully presented, stylish bedrooms and is a short walk from Littleport railway station. Rear-facing rooms have lovely views of a spur on the River Great Ouse. Conveniently located close to Cambridge, Newmarket and Ely, it is an ideal base to explore this lovely region. The freshly prepared breakfasts include award-winning local produce and should not be missed. Both ample secure parking and free WiFi are available.

Rooms 3 rms (2 en suite) (1 pri facs) **Facilities** FTV DVD Lounge tea/coffee WiFi **Extras** Robes, slippers, home-made biscuits **Parking** 4 **Notes** ⊗

MELBOURN
Map 12 TL34

The Sheene Mill
★★★★ ◉◉ RESTAURANT WITH ROOMS

tel: 01763 261393 **39 Station Rd SG8 6DX**
email: reservations@sheenemill.com **web:** www.sheenemill.com
dir: *M11 junct 10 onto A505 towards Royston. Right to Melbourn, pass church on right, on left before old bridge*

This 16th-century watermill is ideally situated just off the A10, a short drive from both Cambridge and Royston. The bedrooms are individually decorated and well equipped; some rooms overlook the mill pond and terrace. Public rooms include a comfortable lounge, a bar, conservatory and a delightful restaurant overlooking the pond.

Rooms 9 en suite (3 fmly) S £90; D £105-£125* **Facilities** FTV Lounge tea/coffee Dinner available WiFi ⚡ 18 Sauna ⚫ **Extras** Speciality toiletries - complimentary **Conf** Max 180 Thtr 120 Class 120 Board 60 **Parking** 60 **Notes** ⊗ Civ Wed 120

UFFORD
Map 12 TF00

The White Hart
★★★★ ⚑ INN

tel: 01780 740250 **Main St PE9 3BH**
email: info@whitehartufford.co.uk **web:** www.whitehartufford.co.uk

Just five miles from Stamford and ten miles from Peterborough, this charming 17th-century inn is home to Ufford Ales, which are served in the bar. The property is built from local stone and retains many of its original features. The delightful bedrooms are tastefully furnished and thoughtfully equipped. Public rooms include a lounge bar, conservatory and restaurant.

Rooms 6 en suite 4 annexe en suite (6 GF) **Facilities** tea/coffee Dinner available WiFi ⚡ 18 ⚫ **Conf** Max 30 Thtr 30 Class 20 Board 20 **Parking** 30 **Notes** Civ Wed 30

WOODHURST
Map 12 TL37

Falcon's Nest
★★★ GUEST ACCOMMODATION

tel: 01487 741140 **The Raptor Foundation, The Heath, St Ives Rd PE28 3BT**
email: info@raptorfoundation.org.uk **web:** www.raptorfoundation.org.uk
dir: *On B1040 between St Ives & Somersham*

Located just a few miles from St Ives, Falcon's Nest is in the grounds of The Raptor Foundation estate. There are eight en suite rooms all with kitchenette facilities. As a resident you also get free entry into the Raptor Centre and can see many different birds of prey. Breakfasts are available at an additional cost and served in the Silent Wings Tea Room.

Rooms 8 en suite (1 fmly) (8 GF) S £47.50; D £47.50-£75 (room only)* **Facilities** FTV DVD tea/coffee WiFi ⚡ 18 Entry to The Raptor Foundation Bird of Prey Park **Conf** Class 50 **Parking** 56 **Notes** LB ⊗

CHESHIRE

ALDERLEY EDGE
Map 16 SJ87

Innkeeper's Lodge Alderley Edge

★★★★ INN

tel: 08451 551551 *(Calls cost 2p per minute plus your phone company's access charge)*
5-9 Wilmslow Rd SK9 7QN
email: info@innkeeperslodge.com **web:** www.innkeeperslodge.com

Situated between Wilmslow and picturesque Alderley Edge, and only 12 miles from Manchester. Bedrooms are modern and offer good space and comfort. The cosy pub and restaurant offer of wide range of drinks and food. Complimentary WiFi is provided and there is on-site parking.

Rooms 11 en suite (3 fmly) **Facilities** FTV tea/coffee Dinner available WiFi
Parking 50 **Notes** ⊗

BURWARDSLEY
Map 15 SJ55

Premier Collection

The Pheasant Inn

★★★★★ ◉ INN

tel: 01829 770434 **Higher Burwardsley CH3 9PF**
email: info@thepheasantinn.co.uk **web:** www.thepheasantinn.co.uk
dir: *From A41, left to Tattenhall, right at 1st junct & left at 2nd Higher Burwardsley. At post office left, signed*

This delightful 300-year-old inn sits high on the Peckforton Hills and enjoys spectacular views over the Cheshire Plain. Well-equipped, comfortable bedrooms are housed in an adjacent converted barn. Creative dishes are served either in the stylish restaurant or in the traditional, beamed bar where real fires are lit in the winter months.

Rooms 2 en suite 10 annexe en suite (2 fmly) (5 GF) S £105-£145;
D £115-£190* **Facilities** FTV tea/coffee Dinner available Direct Dial WiFi ⌁ 18
Parking 80

CHESTER
Map 15 SJ46

See also Malpas

Premier Collection

Mitchell's of Chester

★★★★★ ◉ GUEST HOUSE

tel: 01244 679004 **28 Hough Green CH4 8JQ**
email: welcome@mitchellsofchester.com **web:** www.mitchellsofchester.com
dir: *1m SW of city centre. A483 onto A5104, 300yds on right in Hough Green*

A warm welcome is assured at this delightfully restored and elegant Victorian house, located on the south side of the Dee, within a 20-minute walk of the city centre. Bedrooms are very well equipped and delightfully furnished; and enjoy stylish en suite bathrooms. Guests have use of a beautiful lounge and dining room, where sumptuous breakfasts, featuring lots of local produce, are served. Both of these rooms reflect the Victorian setting.

Rooms 3 en suite S £70-£110; D £94-£110* **Facilities** FTV DVD TVL tea/coffee
Licensed WiFi **Extras** Speciality toiletries - complimentary **Parking** 5 **Notes** LB ⊗
No Children 8yrs Closed 21 Dec-2 Jan

Premier Collection

Stone Villa Chester

★★★★★ GUEST ACCOMMODATION

tel: 01244 345014 & 07764 282015 **Stone Place, Hoole Rd CH2 3NR**
email: info@stonevillachester.co.uk **web:** www.stonevillachester.co.uk
dir: *0.5m NE of city on A56 Hoole Rd*

Stone Villa Chester is a welcoming retreat, away from the bustling city, yet within walking distance of city centre attractions. Bedrooms have comfortable beds and a wealth of accessories which creates a home-from-home experience. Hearty breakfasts feature local produce and home-made jams. Secure parking is a bonus.

Rooms 10 en suite (2 fmly) (3 GF) S £60-£100; D £90-£150 **Facilities** FTV DVD
iPod docking station Lounge tea/coffee Licensed WiFi ⌁ **Conf** Max 10 Board 10
Parking 10 **Notes** ⊗

CHESTER *continued*

Coach House Inn

★★★★ ⬤ INN

tel: 01244 351900 & 351143 **29 Northgate St CH1 2HQ**
email: info@coachhousechester.co.uk **web:** www.coachhousechester.co.uk
dir: *Phone for detailed directions*

Ideally located in the centre of the city, this inn has been appointed to provide high standards of comfort and good facilities. Its sumptuous bedrooms have a wealth of thoughtful extras; some have views over the Town Hall Square and the cathedral. Imaginative food is served in the bistro-style restaurant and in the cosy bar area. Staff offer informal service and a warm welcome.

Rooms 8 en suite (3 fmly) **Facilities** FTV tea/coffee Dinner available Direct Dial WiFi **Notes** ⊗ Closed 25 Dec

Lavender Lodge

★★★★ GUEST ACCOMMODATION

tel: 01244 323204 **46 Hoole Rd CH2 3NL**
email: bookings@lavenderlodgechester.co.uk **web:** www.lavenderlodgechester.co.uk
dir: *1m NE of city centre on A56, opposite All Saints Church*

A warm welcome is assured at this smart, late Victorian house located within easy walking distance of Chester's central attractions. The comfortable bedrooms are equipped with thoughtful little extras and have modern bathrooms. Hearty breakfasts are served in the attractive dining room.

Rooms 5 rms (4 en suite) (1 pri facs) (2 fmly) (2 GF) S £45-£90; D £75-£100 **Facilities** FTV tea/coffee WiFi 🔒 **Parking** 4 **Notes** LB ⊗ Closed 24 Dec-2 Jan

Green Gables

★★★★ GUEST HOUSE

tel: 01244 372243 **11 Eversley Park CH2 2AJ**
email: perruzza_d@hotmail.com **web:** www.greengableschester.co.uk
dir: *Off A5116 Liverpool Rd signed Countess of Chester Hospital, right at 3rd pedestrian lights to Eversley Park*

Green Gables is an attractive Victorian house with pretty gardens, set in a quiet residential area close to the city centre. The well-equipped bedrooms include a family room, and there is a large, comfortable sitting room. The bright breakfast room is strikingly decorated. Off-street parking is a bonus.

Rooms 2 en suite (1 fmly) S £50-£80; D £80-£100* **Facilities** FTV DVD TVL tea/coffee WiFi 🔒 **Parking** 8 **Notes** ⊗ ⬤

Hamilton Court

★★★★ GUEST HOUSE

tel: 01244 345387 **Hamilton St, Hoole CH2 3JG**
email: hamiltoncourth@aol.com **web:** www.hamiltoncourtchester.co.uk
dir: *M53 junct 12, over 2 rdbts. Pass All Saints church on left, Hamilton St 2nd on left*

This friendly guest house offers a peaceful street location just a few minutes' walk from Chester railway station and city centre. Bedrooms are spacious and comfortable, and equipped with a range of thoughtful extras. Hearty breakfasts are served in the traditionally decorated dining room. Off-road parking is available.

Rooms 11 en suite (4 fmly) (1 GF) **Facilities** FTV Lounge tea/coffee Licensed WiFi ⚡ 18 **Parking** 6 **Notes** Closed 22 Dec-3 Jan

The Old Farmhouse B&B

★★★★ BED AND BREAKFAST

tel: 01244 332124 & 07949 820119 **9 Eggbridge Ln, Waverton CH3 7PE**
email: jmitchellgreenwalls@hotmail.com **web:** www.chestereggbridgefarm.co.uk
dir: *From A41 at Waverton left into Moor Ln, left into Eggbridge Ln, over canal bridge, house on right before shops*

The Old Farmhouse, dating from the 18th century, is located in a village community three miles south of the city centre. The cosy bedrooms are equipped with a wealth of thoughtful extras, and the hearty breakfasts feature local and home-made produce.

Rooms 2 rms (1 en suite) (1 pri facs) D £65-£80 **Facilities** FTV TVL tea/coffee WiFi 🔒 **Parking** 6 **Notes** LB ⊗ No Children 7yrs Closed 13-28 Feb RS Xmas & New Year continental breakfast only

Innkeeper's Lodge Chester Christleton

★★★ INN

tel: 08451 551551 *(Calls cost 2p per minute plus your phone company's access charge)* **Whitchurch Rd CH3 6AE**
email: info@innkeeperslodge.com **web:** www.innkeeperslodge.com

Innkeeper's Lodge Chester Christleton (locally known as The Cheshire Cat) offers guests comfortable bedrooms with classic decor and thoughtful amenities; some in the main house, and some in converted cottages alongside the canal. A popular lunch venue with locals, the inn provides well cooked meals served in cosy rooms, each with its own style, and most with a real fire. Large attractive outside areas are available for dining in warmer weather, with access to the canalside to walk off your meal.

Rooms 14 en suite (3 fmly) (4 GF) **Facilities** FTV tea/coffee Dinner available Direct Dial WiFi **Parking Notes** ⊗

George & Dragon

★★★ INN

tel: 01244 380714 **1 Liverpool Rd CH2 1AA**
email: 7783@greeneking.co.uk **web:** www.oldenglish.co.uk

This former old coaching inn with its black and white Tudor façade, is situated just five minutes from the city centre. This is a traditional inn with sports viewing, cask ales, dining and weekly entertainment, and a late bar until midnight. Bedrooms of various sizes are available. Parking is available on site.

Rooms 14 en suite (2 fmly) S £54; D £75* **Facilities** FTV DVD tea/coffee Dinner available WiFi Pool table 🔒 **Parking** 20 **Notes** ⊗

Glen Garth

★★★ GUEST ACCOMMODATION

tel: 01244 310260 **59 Hoole Rd CH2 3NJ**
email: glengarthguesthouse@btconnect.com **web:** www.glengarthguesthouse.co.uk
dir: Exit M53 onto A56, 0.5m E of city

Situated within easy walking distance of the city, family-run Glen Garth provides well-equipped bedrooms, and hearty breakfasts served in the pleasant rear dining room. Friendly, attentive service is a strength here.

Rooms 5 rms (3 en suite) (2 pri facs) (3 fmly) S £35-£45; D £75-£100* **Facilities** FTV DVD tea/coffee WiFi ⌁ 18 **Parking** 5 **Notes** LB ⊗

The Oaklands

★★ INN

tel: 01244 345528 **93 Hoole Rd, Hoole CH2 3NB**
email: 7878@greeneking.co.uk **web:** www.oldenglish.co.uk

This busy and popular public house is conveniently located for access to both the city centre and the M56. A wide range of food is available in the stylish open-plan bar and dining area. Bedrooms come in various sizes, and service is friendly and attentive.

Rooms 14 rms (13 en suite) (1 pri facs) (2 fmly) (4 GF) **Facilities** FTV TVL tea/coffee Dinner available WiFi **Parking** 30 **Notes** ⊗

CONGLETON	Map 16 SJ86

Premier Collection

Whitethorn Bed & Breakfast (SJ842607)

★★★★★ ⌂ FARMHOUSE

tel: 07771 967352 **Whitethorn Farm, Watery Ln, Astbury CW12 4RR**
email: whitethornbandb@aol.co.uk **web:** www.astburybedbreakfast.co.uk
dir: S of Congleton on A34. Turn left after Astbury church into Watery Ln, 1st farm on right

Dating back to the 17th century, this working arable farm has been bought right up to date, offering peace and tranquillity in luxurious surroundings. Bedrooms are spacious, with a real focus on guest comfort. Large gardens overlook the surrounding fields, with a variety of walks over the 600 acre farm. Hearty breakfasts made with local produce leave a positive lasting impression. An outdoor swimming pool is heated during summer months.

Rooms 5 en suite (1 fmly) **Facilities** FTV iPod docking station tea/coffee WiFi ⌁ Fishing **Extras** Robes **Parking** 5 **Notes** 600 acres arable

CREWE	Map 15 SJ75

Corner Farm

Ⓤ

tel: 01270 841429 **2 Pit Ln, Hough CW2 5JQ**
email: leafarm@hotmail.com **web:** www.cornerfarmathough.co.uk
dir: M6 junct 16 onto A500 towards Nantwich. 1st rdbt, take 1st left, 2nd rdbt follow signs to Hough. Over railway bridge, pass White Hart pub, left into Pit Ln, Corner Farm immediately on right

Currently the rating for this establishment is not confirmed. This may be due to a change of ownership or because it has only recently joined the AA rating scheme.

Rooms 3 en suite (1 fmly) S £36-£38; D £60-£65 **Facilities** FTV DVD TVL tea/coffee WiFi 🔒 **Parking** 8 **Notes** ⊗ ⊗ ⌂

FARNDON	Map 15 SJ45

The Farndon

★★★★ ⌂ INN

tel: 01829 270570 **High St CH3 6PU**
email: enquiries@thefarndon.co.uk **web:** www.thefarndon.co.uk
dir: Just off A534 in village on main street

Located close to Chester and the north Wales coast, The Farndon is a family-run coaching inn that dates in part to the 16th century and offers traditional hospitality with a modern twist. The attractive bedrooms are well equipped, and downstairs the bar offers a selection of real ales and fine wines, together with a wide range of imaginative dishes and welcoming log fires.

Rooms 5 en suite S £70-£90; D £85-£105* **Facilities** STV FTV Lounge TVL tea/coffee Dinner available WiFi **Parking** 15 **Notes** LB No coaches

HOLMES CHAPEL	Map 15 SJ76

Holly Tree Farm (SJ802709)

★★★★ FARMHOUSE

tel: 01477 571257 & 07979 910800 **Holmes Chapel Rd SK11 9DT**
email: davidathollies@aol.com **web:** www.hollytreefarm.org
dir: On A535 Holmes Chapel Rd in front of Jodrell Bank

Situated close to Jodrell Bank, Holly Tree Farm offers a good base for both business travellers or for those visiting the local attractions. Bedrooms are located in the adjacent house and are attractive and well equipped. Hearty breakfasts, served in the farmhouse, are based on local produce from the farm's own shop.

Rooms 4 en suite (1 fmly) (1 GF) **Facilities** FTV TVL tea/coffee WiFi ch fac 🔒 **Extras** Mini-fridge **Parking** 3 **Notes** ⊗ 100 acres beef/sheep/poultry

KNUTSFORD	Map 15 SJ77

Belle Epoque

★★★★ ◉◉ RESTAURANT WITH ROOMS

tel: 01565 633060 **60 King St WA16 6DT**
web: www.thebelleepoque.com

This long established fixture on the north west dining scene has welcomed guests for over 40 years. The opulent, boutique styling lives up to its name throughout the bar and restaurant where imaginative French-leaning cuisine is the centrepiece. Accommodation is in seven rooms of varying size. All are equipped to a modern standard.

Rooms 7 en suite **Facilities** Dinner available

MALPAS   Map 15 SJ44

Hampton House Farm *(SJ505496)*

★★★★ ☕ FARMHOUSE

tel: 01948 820588 **Stevensons Ln, Hampton SY14 8JS**
email: enquiries@hamptonhousefarm.co.uk **web:** www.hamptonhousefarm.co.uk
dir: *2m NE of Malpas. Exit A41 into Cholmondeley Rd, next left*

Hampton House is located on a quiet farm and offers thoughtfully appointed
accommodation and a warm welcome. Parts of the house are reputed to date from
1600, and its stylish decor highlights the many period features, including a wealth
of exposed beams.

Rooms 2 en suite S £50-£80; D £75-£80* **Facilities** TVL tea/coffee WiFi 🔒
Parking 12 **Notes** ⊗ No Children 12yrs ⊛ 180 acres mixed

NANTWICH   Map 15 SJ65

The Cheshire Cat

★★★★ ☕ INN

tel: 01270 623020 **26 Welsh Row CW5 5ED**
email: hello@thecatatnantwich.com **web:** www.thecatat.com
dir: *M6 junct 15 follow signs to Nantwich. Left off B5341 onto Welsh Row, right into First
Wood St*

Originally built in the early 17th century as almshouses for six widows, this property
has been restored with a modern 21st-century twist. The inn offers comfortable,
attractive accommodation. Imaginative dinners are served in the restaurant with
its oak beams and glass atrium. Weekends are lively with a bustling bar.

Rooms 11 en suite 3 annexe en suite (3 fmly) (5 GF) **Facilities** FTV TVL tea/coffee
Dinner available Direct Dial WiFi **Extras** Speciality toiletries **Conf** Max 30 **Parking** 20
Notes ⊗

SANDBACH   Map 15 SJ76

Innkeeper's Lodge Sandbach, Holmes Chapel

★★★ INN

tel: 08451 551551 *(Calls cost 2p per minute plus your phone company's access charge)*
Brereton Green CW11 1RS
email: info@innkeeperslodge.com **web:** www.innkeeperslodge.com

Peacefully located in rural Cheshire, close to historic Sandbach, the lodge provides
comfortable, modern bedrooms. It is attached to the Bears Head Vintage Inn, an
attractive black-and-white building that has real fires, spacious dining areas and a
wide choice of cask ales and food. A continental buffet breakfast is complimentary
for all guests.

Rooms 25 en suite (6 fmly) (10 GF) **Facilities** FTV tea/coffee Dinner available WiFi
Parking Notes ⊗

TARPORLEY   Map 15 SJ56

Alvanley Arms Inn

★★★★ INN

tel: 01829 760200 **Cotebrook CW6 9DS**
email: info@alvanleyarms.co.uk **web:** www.alvanleyarms.co.uk
dir: *M56 junct 10, follow signs for Whitchurch then A49*

This historic inn, bedecked with flowers in summer, dates back to the 17th century
and the bar and dining areas still feature the original beams. Bedrooms are well
equipped with complimentary WiFi access. The Alvanley Arms offers a wide choice
of home-cooked meals that utilise local produce. The inn is perfectly placed for
visiting the adjoining Shire Horse Centre and Countryside Park, which is popular
with families, and also Delamere Forest Park and Oulton Park race circuit.

Rooms 7 en suite **Facilities** FTV DVD Lounge TVL tea/coffee Dinner available WiFi
⚓ 18 🔒 **Parking** 30 **Notes** ⊗

Food Allergies

A recent EU regulation makes it easier
for those with food allergies to choose
safer foods when eating out. 14 allergens
are listed in the regulation, and pubs and
restaurants must now list any of these
used in the dishes they offer.

WARMINGHAM   Map 15 SJ76

The Bear's Paw
★★★★★ ⊛ INN

tel: 01270 526317 **School Ln CW11 3QN**
email: info@thebearspaw.co.uk **web:** www.thebearspaw.co.uk
dir: M6 junct 17, A534, A533 signed Middlewich & Northwich. Continue on A533, left into Mill Ln, left into Warmingham Ln. Right into Plant Ln, left into Green Ln

Located beside a small river in a rural Cheshire village, this fully modernised 19th-century red-brick inn provides spacious boutique bedrooms that have a wealth of practical extras and feature deeply comfortable beds. The friendly team serves imaginative food, which makes use of quality seasonal produce, in an attractive open-plan dining room. Relaxed lounge areas are also available.

Rooms 17 en suite (4 fmly) S £105-£135; D £115-£175* **Facilities** STV FTV iPod docking station Lounge tea/coffee Dinner available Direct Dial WiFi **Extras** Apple TV - deposit required **Parking** 75 **Notes** LB

CORNWALL & ISLES OF SCILLY

BODINNICK   Map 2 SX15

The Old Ferry Inn
★★★ ⊜ INN

tel: 01726 870237 **PL23 1LX**
email: info@oldferryinn.co.uk **web:** www.oldferryinn.co.uk
dir: From Liskeard on A38 to Dobwalls, left onto A390. After 3m left onto B3359 signed Looe. Right at sign for Lerryn/Bodinnick/Polruan

The Old Ferry Inn has stood on the edge of the Fowey Estuary for over four hundred years, overlooking the Bodinnick to Fowey ferry service. 'Ferryside', the childhood home of Daphne du Maurier, is at the bottom of the hill. There are plenty of coastal walks, historical buildings, fishing and wildlife nearby, with the famous Eden Project just a few miles away. A range of local beers and Cornish ciders are available, and meals can be enjoyed while gazing out over the amazing river views.

Rooms 12 rms (10 en suite) (2 pri facs) (1 fmly) D £80-£150* **Facilities** FTV Lounge TVL tea/coffee Dinner available WiFi **Parking** 6 **Notes** LB No coaches

BODMIN   Map 2 SX06

Mennabroom Farm (SX161703)
★★★★ ⊜ ⌂ FARMHOUSE

tel: 01208 821272 **Warleggan PL30 4HE**
email: enquiries@mennabroom.com **web:** www.mennabroom.co.uk
dir: A30 take exit signed Colliford Lake. After 2.8m turn right signed Mennabroom Farm and Cottages, turn right into Mennabroom

In the heart of Bodmin Moor, this extremely comfortable farmhouse offers a haven of peace and tranquillity for visitors to the beautiful West Country. Rooms are well appointed with quality furnishings and very comfortable beds. Guests are welcomed with afternoon tea, dinner is available on request and breakfast uses the farm's home-produced eggs, bacon and sausages. Self-catering cottages are also available.

Rooms 2 en suite S £65; D £85* **Facilities** FTV DVD Lounge tea/coffee Dinner available WiFi ⛱ **Extras** Speciality toiletries - complimentary **Parking** 6 **Notes** LB 40 acres sheep/pigs/beef

BUDE   Map 2 SS20

Pot and Barrel B&B
★★★★★ ⊜ BED AND BREAKFAST

tel: 01288 355305 **Crooklets Beach EX23 8NE**
email: chris@potandbarrel.co.uk **web:** www.potandbarrel.com
dir: From town centre follow signs for Crooklets Beach. Crooklets Inn on right, turn left towards sea, pass unmade track. Take sharp right hairpin bend, proceed up hill

Originally an elegant Edwardian gentleman's residence, built 1910, the Pot and Barrel offers two well-appointed bedrooms both furnished and decorated to a high standard. There is a guest lounge, with a cosy fire during the winter months, and the dining room has distracting coastal views. The sun lounge also boasts excellent views. A high quality breakfast with plenty of choice, including daily changing specials, is on offer each morning.

Rooms 2 en suite (1 GF) S £77.40-£86.40; D £86-£96 **Facilities** FTV Lounge TVL tea/coffee WiFi ⛱ **Extras** Robes, fresh milk - complimentary **Parking** 3 **Notes** LB ⊗ No Children 16yrs

Bangors Organic
★★★★ ⊜ ⌂ GUEST HOUSE

tel: 01288 361297 **Poundstock EX23 0DP**
email: info@bangorsorganic.co.uk **web:** www.bangorsorganic.co.uk
dir: 4m S of Bude. On A39 in Poundstock

Situated a few miles south of Bude, this renovated Victorian establishment offers elegant accommodation with a good level of comfort. Bedrooms are furnished to a high standard with bathrooms worthy of special mention, being impressively spacious and luxurious. Breakfast and dinner, featuring organic, local and home-made produce, are served in the pleasant dining room. The establishment is certified as organic by the Soil Association.

Rooms 2 en suite **Facilities** TVL tea/coffee Dinner available Licensed WiFi ⛱ Badminton **Parking** 10 **Notes** ⊗ No Children 10yrs

BUDE *continued*

Pencarrol Guest House

★★★★ GUEST HOUSE

tel: 01288 352478 **21 Downs View EX23 8RF**
email: pencarrol21@gmail.com
dir: *0.5m N of Bude. N from Bude into Flexbury village*

This cosy guest house is only a short walk from Bude centre and Crooklets Beach, and has glorious views over the golf course. Bedrooms are attractively furnished and there is a first-floor lounge. Breakfast is served at separate tables in the dining room.

Rooms 5 rms (3 en suite) (2 pri facs) (2 fmly) S £34-£36; D £72-£76* **Facilities** FTV tea/coffee WiFi 🔒 **Notes** LB ⊗ No Children 10yrs Closed Nov-Feb 🚭

The Old Wainhouse Inn

★★★ INN

tel: 01840 230711 & 07752 190514 **Wainhouse Corner, St Gennys EX23 0BA**
email: wainhouse10@yahoo.co.uk **web:** www.oldwainhouseinn.co.uk
dir: *On A39 between Bude & Camelford*

This popular roadside pub provides an ideal base from which to explore the wonderful countryside and dramatic coastline; the South West Coast Path is close by. The convivial bar is the focus here, with plenty of friendly banter always on offer and helpful local advice readily available. Bedrooms and bathrooms provide good levels of comfort with simple styling. Food in the bar and restaurant includes a Sunday roast and vegetarian options.

Rooms 4 en suite S fr £47.50; D fr £95* **Facilities** FTV tea/coffee Dinner available WiFi Pool table 🔒 **Conf** Max 50 Class 50 **Parking** 25

Sea Jade Guest House

★★★ GUEST ACCOMMODATION

tel: 01288 353404 & 07737 541540 **15 Burn View EX23 8BZ**
email: seajadeguesthouse@yahoo.co.uk **web:** www.seajadeguesthouse.co.uk
dir: *A39 turn right follow signs for Bude & golf course*

A warm welcome awaits at this popular establishment which is within a few minutes' walk of both the town and beaches. Bedrooms are light and airy with simple, contemporary styling; some have views across the golf course. Breakfast is a generous offering and guaranteed to get the day off to a satisfying start.

Rooms 8 rms (7 en suite) (1 pri facs) (4 fmly) (2 GF) **Facilities** FTV TVL tea/coffee WiFi ⅃ 18 🔒 **Notes** LB ⊗ 🚭

CALLINGTON Map 3 SX36

Woodpeckers

★★★★ 🛎 GUEST HOUSE

tel: 01579 363717 **Rilla Mill PL17 7NT**
email: alisonmerchant@talktalk.net **web:** www.woodpeckersguesthouse.co.uk
dir: *5m NW of Callington. Exit B3254 at Upton Cross x-rds for Rilla Mill*

Set in a conservation village, in a wooded valley, by a tumbling stream, this modern, detached house offers cosy, well-equipped bedrooms with numerous thoughtful extras. Home-cooked dinners, using the best of local ingredients, are available by prior arrangement. The hot tub in the garden is an additional feature.

Rooms 3 en suite S fr £75; D £75-£80* **Facilities** STV FTV tea/coffee Dinner available Gym 🔒 Spa/Hot tub **Parking** 7 **Notes** LB ⊗ 🚭

CRACKINGTON HAVEN Map 2 SX19

Trevigue *(SX137956)*

★★★★ 🛎 🍴 FARMHOUSE

tel: 01840 230492 & 07903 110037 **Trevigue Farm EX23 0LQ**
email: trevigue@talk21.com **web:** www.trevigue.com/bed-and-breakfast

Peace and tranquillity are two of the many qualities of Trevigue, a beautiful 16th-century farmhouse set in 500 acres of stunning North Cornish cliff land. Your host will make you feel at home and cater for all your needs in order to make your stay as stress-free as possible. Rooms are beautifully appointed and equipped. Dinner and breakfast use the freshest of local produce. There is also a self-catering cottage. AA Friendliest B&B of the Year Award Finalist 2016-2017.

Rooms 4 en suite (1 fmly) **Facilities** FTV iPod docking station Lounge TVL TV3B tea/coffee Dinner available Licensed WiFi 🔒 **Conf** Max 45 Class 45 Board 20 **Parking** 8 **Notes** ⊗ No Children 8yrs Civ Wed 45 500 acres beef

CRAFTHOLE Map 3 SX35

The Liscawn

★★★★ INN

tel: 01503 230863 **PL11 3BD**
email: enquiries@liscawn.co.uk **web:** www.liscawn.co.uk

This attractive, historic 14th-century inn enjoys an imposing position in the rolling Cornish countryside. Bedrooms, many with pleasant views, have a homely feel, and all are comfortable and have impressive modern facilities. Public areas have an engaging charm and the restaurant provides a relaxing environment with an impressive menu selection. Breakfasts are tasty and freshly cooked.

Rooms 7 en suite 4 annexe en suite (5 fmly) (3 GF) S £60-£70; D £90-£110 **Facilities** FTV Lounge TVL tea/coffee Dinner available WiFi 🛎 ⅃ 18 🔒 **Conf** Max 30 Thtr 30 Class 30 Board 30 **Parking** 60 **Notes** LB Civ Wed 120

FALMOUTH Map 2 SW83

Premier Collection

Anacapri

★★★★★ GUEST ACCOMMODATION

tel: 01326 311454 **Gyllyngvase Rd TR11 4DJ**
email: anacapri@btconnect.com **web:** www.hotelanacapri.co.uk
dir: *A39 (Truro to Falmouth), straight on at lights. Over next 2 rdbts into Melvill Rd,
down hill, 2nd right into Gyllyngvase Rd, Anacapri on right*

With stunning views out across the sea and beach, this well managed property
offers friendly, attentive service from a young and upbeat team, with jolly
managers Peter and June at the helm to oversee guest care. Smart and
extremely comfortable bedrooms are spacious, and many rooms enjoying
splendid sea views. Public areas are varied and include a smart bar and lounge
where guests can enjoy drinks and snacks, and ample seating is provided on the
delightful sea facing patio. A superb establishment where guests are made to
feel welcome and at home. The hosts are ready to offer all sorts of interesting
and additional information on the location and region.

Rooms 16 en suite (3 fmly) (2 GF) S fr £37.50; D fr £75 **Facilities** FTV Lounge tea/
coffee Licensed WiFi 🏊 **Parking** 18 **Notes** LB ⊗

Bosanneth Guest House

★★★★ ⚬ 🍴 GUEST ACCOMMODATION

tel: 01326 314649 **Gyllyngvase Hill TR11 4DW**
email: stay@bosanneth.co.uk **web:** www.bosanneth.co.uk
dir: *From Truro on A39 follow signs for beaches/docks, 3rd right mini rdbt Melvil Rd, 3rd
right into Gyllyngvase Hill*

This well situated property, just a two-minute walk from the beach, offers stylish
and individually decorated bedrooms and a very warm welcome from the friendly
hosts. Some bedrooms have a sea view, and dinner is served each evening. A full
Cornish breakfast is served in the dining room.

Rooms 8 en suite **Facilities** FTV Lounge tea/coffee Dinner available Licensed WiFi
Extras Speciality toiletries, robes **Parking** 7 **Notes** ⊗ No Children Closed Nov

Who are **the AA's award-
winning B&Bs? For details
see pages 12-15**

The Rosemary

★★★★ GUEST ACCOMMODATION

tel: 01326 314669 **22 Gyllyngvase Ter TR11 4DL**
email: stay@therosemary.co.uk **web:** www.therosemary.co.uk
dir: *A39 Melvill Rd signed to beaches & seafront, right into Gyllyngvase Rd, 1st left*

Just a short walk from the beach, this welcoming establishment is conveniently
located for exploring the local area. The well-equipped bedrooms all provide
impressive levels of comfort and quality, with many having the added bonus of
wonderful views across Falmouth Bay. Breakfast is a generous and tasty start to
the day, and is served in the light and airy dining room. Other facilities include a
bar and guest lounge, while outside a decked area and rear garden are also
available for guests.

Rooms 8 en suite (2 fmly) S £50-£55; D £79-£110* **Facilities** FTV DVD Lounge tea/
coffee Licensed WiFi 🏊 **Extras** Speciality toiletries **Parking** 2 **Notes** LB Closed end
Oct-9 Feb

Melvill House

★★★★ GUEST ACCOMMODATION

tel: 01326 316645 **52 Melvill Rd TR11 4DQ**
email: melvillhouse@btconnect.com **web:** www.melvill-house-falmouth.co.uk
dir: *On A39 near town centre & docks*

Well situated for the beach, the town centre and the National Maritime Museum on
the harbour, Melvill House is a family-run establishment with a relaxed atmosphere.
Some bedrooms have four-poster beds, and breakfast is served in the smart dining
room. Ample parking.

Rooms 7 en suite (2 fmly) (1 GF) S £45-£55; D £75-£90* **Facilities** FTV TVL tea/
coffee WiFi 🏊 **Parking** 8 **Notes** LB ⊗

FALMOUTH *continued*

The Rathgowry

★★★★ GUEST HOUSE

tel: 01326 313482 **Gyllyngvase Hill TR11 4DN**
email: enquiries@rathgowry.co.uk **web:** www.rathgowry.co.uk
dir: *A39 into Falmouth, over 1st & 2nd rdbts. After 300mtrs turn right into Gyllyngvase Hill, half way down on left*

Located in a quieter residential area yet only a few minutes' stroll from the beach and 15 minutes from the town centre, this traditionally styled property offers a range of differently sized, well-equipped bedrooms and bathrooms. There are extra thoughtful touches in the rooms, and free WiFi is provided throughout the property. A varied menu is offered at breakfast including ample choice of cereals and preserves, with a bumper full English cooked option.

Rooms 9 rms (7 en suite) (2 pri facs) (1 fmly) S £41-£46; D £82-£94* **Facilities** FTV tea/coffee WiFi **Extras** Bottled water, fresh milk **Parking** 7 **Notes** ⊗ Closed Nov-Mar

Rosemullion

★★★★ GUEST ACCOMMODATION

tel: 01326 314690 **Gyllyngvase Hill TR11 4DF**
email: gail@rosemullionhotel.co.uk **web:** www.rosemullionhotel.co.uk

Recognisable by its mock-Tudor exterior, this warm and friendly establishment is well situated for both the town centre and the beach. Some of the comfortable bedrooms are on the ground floor, while a few rooms on the top floor have views to Falmouth Bay. Breakfast, served in the panelled dining room, is freshly cooked and there is a well appointed lounge.

Rooms 13 rms (11 en suite) (2 pri facs) (3 GF) **Facilities** FTV Lounge tea/coffee WiFi **Parking** 18 **Notes** ⊗ No Children Closed 23-31 Dec

The Westcott Guest House

★★★★ GUEST HOUSE

tel: 01326 311309 **Gyllyngvase Hill TR11 4DN**
email: thewestcott@outlook.com **web:** www.thewestcottfalmouth.co.uk

The Westcott is a modern guest house situated just minutes from Falmouth beach and within easy walking distance of busy Falmouth harbour with its many interesting shops, art galleries, restaurants and trendy bars, a foodies' paradise. The hosts are friendly and attentive and really know how to make their guests feel at home. The bedrooms are very well appointed; in addition there is a large guest lounge with an honesty bar and lots of extra thoughtful touches. There is some private parking.

Rooms 9 en suite **Facilities** FTV TVL tea/coffee Licensed WiFi Pool table 🛁 **Extras** Sweets **Parking** 7 **Notes** LB ⊗ No Children 12yrs Closed 14 Dec-14 Jan

Eden Lodge

★★★ GUEST HOUSE

tel: 01326 212989 & 07715 696218 **54 Melvill Rd TR11 4DQ**
email: info@edenlodgefalmouth.co.uk **web:** www.edenlodgefalmouth.co.uk
dir: *On A39, on left 200yds past Fox Rosehill Gardens*

Very well located on Melvill Road, and with off-road parking, Eden Lodge boasts comfortable rooms and a swimming pool. The friendly hosts serve dinner by arrangement and do all they can to ensure a comfortable stay for their guests.

Rooms 5 rms (4 en suite) (2 fmly) (1 GF) **Facilities** FTV TVL tea/coffee Dinner available Licensed WiFi 🏊 Gym 🛁 Massage & aromatherapy by appointment **Parking** 9 **Notes** ⊛

Trevoil Guest House

★★★ GUEST HOUSE

tel: 01326 314145 & 07966 409782 **25 Avenue Rd TR11 4AY**
email: alan.jewel@btconnect.com **web:** www.trevoil-falmouth.co.uk
dir: *Exit A39 (Melvill Rd) left into Avenue Rd, 150yds from Maritime Museum*

Located within walking distance of the town centre, the friendly Trevoil is a comfortable and relaxed place to stay. Breakfast is enjoyed in the light, pleasant dining room.

Rooms 8 rms (4 en suite) (3 fmly) (1 GF) **Facilities** FTV tea/coffee WiFi **Parking** 6

GWEEK	Map 2 SW72

Black Swan

★★★★ INN

tel: 01326 221502 **TR12 6TU**
web: www.blackswangweek.co.uk
dir: *In village centre*

The Black Swan inn is in the picturesque village of Gweek, a stone's throw from the popular Cornish Seal Sanctuary. This delightful inn has been restored to its former glory, and the stylish en suite bedrooms are comfortable and enhanced with homely touches. Food is sourced with care, ensuring local produce is used whenever possible; an extensive blackboard menu showcases pub classics and favourites. The selection of Cornish ales is not to be missed.

Rooms 4 en suite **Facilities** FTV tea/coffee Dinner available WiFi Pool table **Parking** 15

HAYLE	Map 2 SW53

The Penellen

★★★★ GUEST ACCOMMODATION

tel: 01736 753777 **64 Riviere Towans, Phillack TR27 5AF**
email: penellen@btconnect.com **web:** www.penellen.co.uk
dir: *From A30 onto B3301 through Hayle. Turn opposite petrol station, road bears to left, into private road*

Superbly situated at the water's edge, this personally run, friendly property has splendid views of the beach and coastline. Bedrooms are well equipped and comfortable, many with patio doors and stunning views to wake up to each morning. The dining room is spacious with a bright and airy feel. The cheerful hosts provide attentive service. Food is a strength, with good quality produce on offer.

Rooms 5 en suite (2 fmly) **Facilities** FTV tea/coffee WiFi **Parking** 10 **Notes** ⊗ Closed Nov-Feb

HELSTON	Map 2 SW62

See also St Keverne

Tregaddra Farmhouse B&B *(SW697216)*

★★★★ FARMHOUSE

tel: 01326 240235 & 07773 518223 **Cury Cross Lanes TR12 7BB**
email: june@tregaddra.co.uk **web:** www.tregaddra.co.uk
dir: *From Helston on B3083, at Wheel Inn turn left at x-rds. 1st farm on left after 0.5m*

This 18th-century farmhouse, on a working farm, offers the perfect base for exploring the Lizard Peninsula and south west Cornwall. All bedrooms are individually appointed and very comfortable; two have balconies overlooking the open countryside. A farmhouse Aga breakfast is served at individual tables in the attractive dining room. A swimming pool (seasonal) and tennis court are also available.

Rooms 4 en suite S £40-£60; D £75-£89 **Facilities** FTV DVD Lounge TVL tea/coffee Dinner available WiFi ⚡ ☺ ⚓ 18 **Extras** Speciality toiletries **Parking** 4 **Notes** LB ⊗ No Children 10yrs 300 acres beef/arable

LANEAST

Map 2 SX28

Stitch Park B&B

★★★★ ☕ 🍴 BED AND BREAKFAST

tel: 01566 86687 **Stitch Park PL15 8PN**
email: katehandford@btinternet.com **web:** www.stitchpark.co.uk
dir: A30 from Exeter. At Kennards House junct follow signs for North Cornwall & Wadebridge (A395). After 4m, pass through Pipers Pool then left for Laneast, village signed. Pass church on right, Church Way on left. Around corner, Stitch Park next bungalow on left

Located just a few miles from Launceston, this modern bungalow is a perfect base from which to explore the beautiful coast and countryside. The views along the Inny Valley to Dartmoor beyond are breathtaking and always changing with the seasons. There is a comfortable lounge in which to relax, while bedrooms offer high quality and a host of extras; likewise bathrooms with a range of toiletries, fluffy towels and robes. Breakfast is a real treat, with eggs from the resident hens and other tasty local produce. Dinner is also available by prior arrangement.

Rooms 3 en suite (3 GF) D £70-£75* **Facilities** FTV DVD TVL tea/coffee Dinner available WiFi 🔧 **Extras** Speciality toiletries, chocolates - complimentary **Parking** 4 **Notes** ⊗ No Children 14yrs ◉

LAUNCESTON

Map 3 SX38

Premier Collection

Wheatley Farm (SX245926)

★★★★★ ☕ FARMHOUSE

tel: 01566 781232 **Maxworthy PL15 8LY**
email: valerie@wheatley-farm.co.uk **web:** www.farmstay-cornwall.co.uk
dir: From A39 at Wainhouse Corner follow signs to Canworthy Water. At T-junct, left & after 1.5m turn left at sign to Wheatley Farm. 1st farm on left

This working dairy farm dates back to 1871 and was originally part of the estate of Lord Bedford. Surrounded by wonderful rolling countryside, the family have been farming here for five generations. A pot of tea is always on offer for arriving guests with every effort made to ensure a relaxing and rewarding stay. Bedrooms all provide high levels of comfort, likewise the modern bathrooms. Breakfast is a treat, served in the lovely dining room complete with original slate floor and imposing granite fireplace. Additional facilities include a guest lounge, heated indoor swimming pool, spa and sauna.

Rooms 4 en suite **Facilities** FTV DVD TVL tea/coffee Dinner available WiFi 🔧 Sauna Pool table 🔔 Spa bath **Parking** 4 **Notes** ⊗ No Children Closed Nov-Mar 232 acres dairy

Hurdon Farm (SX333828)

★★★★ 🍴 FARMHOUSE

tel: 01566 772955 **PL15 9LS**
email: hurdonfarm@hotmail.co.uk **web:** www.hurdonfarm.weebly.com
dir: A30 onto A388 to Launceston, at rdbt exit for hospital, 2nd right signed Trebullett, premises 1st on right

Genuine hospitality is assured at this delightful 18th-century granite farmhouse. The bedrooms are individually furnished and decorated, and equipped with numerous extras. The delicious dinners, which need to be booked in advance, use only the best local produce, and include home-made puddings and the farm's own clotted cream.

Rooms 6 en suite (1 fmly) (1 GF) S £37-£40; D £70-£76* **Facilities** FTV TVL tea/coffee Dinner available WiFi **Parking** 10 **Notes** LB ⊗ Closed Nov-Apr ◉ 400 acres mixed

Bradridge Farm (SX328938)

★★★★ FARMHOUSE

tel: 01409 271264 & 07748 253346 **PL15 9RL**
email: angela@bradridgefarm.co.uk **web:** www.bradridgefarm.co.uk
dir: 5.5m N of Launceston. Exit B3254 at Ladycross sign for Boyton, Bradridge 2nd farm on right after Boyton school

This late Victorian farmhouse stands in glorious countryside on the border of Devon and Cornwall. The well-presented bedrooms have many considerate extras, and the Aga-cooked breakfasts feature farm-fresh eggs.

Rooms 4 rms (3 en suite) (1 fmly) S £40; D fr £75* **Facilities** FTV Lounge TVL tea/coffee WiFi Fishing **Parking** 6 **Notes** LB ⊗ Closed Nov-Mar ◉ 250 acres arable/beef/sheep/hens

Middle Tremollett Farm B&B (SX297757)

★★★★ ☕ FARMHOUSE

tel: 01566 782416 & 07973 435529 **Coad's Green PL15 7NA**
email: btrewin@btinternet.com **web:** www.tremollett.co.uk
dir: A30 onto B3257, through village of Coad's Green. Turn right signed Tremollett, 1st on left at bottom of hill

Genuine hospitality is assured at this delightful granite farmhouse surrounded with breathtaking views of the countryside. The bedrooms are individually furnished and decorated, and equipped with numerous extras. The delicious breakfasts use only the best local produce, and include home-made produce and the farm's own eggs.

Rooms 2 en suite S £38-£42; D £72-£84 **Facilities** FTV TVL tea/coffee WiFi ⚓ 18 🔔 **Extras** Speciality toiletries **Parking** 3 **Notes** LB ⊗ No Children 12yrs Closed Dec-Feb 100 acres arable/beef/sheep

LAUNCESTON *continued*

Tyne Wells House

★★★★ BED AND BREAKFAST

tel: 01566 775810 **Pennygillam PL15 7EE**
email: btucker@talktalk.net **web:** www.tynewells.co.uk
dir: *0.6m SW of town centre. Exit A30 onto Pennygillam rdbt, house off rdbt*

Situated on the outskirts of town, Tyne Wells House has panoramic views over the countryside. There's a relaxed and friendly atmosphere and the bedrooms are neatly furnished. A hearty breakfast is served in the dining room, which overlooks the garden.

Rooms 3 rms (2 en suite) (1 pri facs) (1 fmly) S £35-£45; D £60-£70 **Facilities** FTV DVD tea/coffee WiFi ♨ **Extras** Shared fridge **Parking** 4 **Notes** LB ⊗ ⊜

LEEDSTOWN	Map 2 SW63

Little Pengelly Farm *(SW614327)*

★★★★ FARMHOUSE

tel: 01736 850452 **Trenwheal TR27 6BP**
email: maxine@littlepengelly.co.uk **web:** www.littlepengelly.co.uk
dir: *From Hayle on B3302 towards Helston. Through Leedstown, after 2m at top of hill turn left. 1st house on right*

Little Pengelly Farm is situated in beautiful countryside about five miles from both the north and south coasts of the Cornish peninsula. B&B and self-catering accommodation are on offer, as well as a tea room serving freshly baked scones with home-made jam. The three guest rooms are bright and comfortable and enjoy views of the garden or courtyard. A farmhouse breakfast is served in the conservatory overlooking the gardens. A laundry service and free WiFi are available, and there is ample parking on site.

Rooms 3 rms (2 en suite) (1 pri facs) (1 fmly) D £75-£105* **Facilities** FTV tea/coffee WiFi ♨ **Extras** Speciality toiletries - complimentary **Parking** 10 **Notes** LB ⊗ Closed 23 Dec-2 Jan 10 acres arable

LISKEARD	Map 2 SX26

See also Callington

Redgate Smithy

★★★★ ⬤ BED AND BREAKFAST

tel: 01579 321578 **Redgate, St Cleer PL14 6RU**
email: enquiries@redgatesmithy.co.uk **web:** www.redgatesmithy.co.uk
dir: *3m NW of Liskeard. Exit A30 at Bolventor/Jamaica Inn into St Cleer Rd for 7m, B&B just past x-rds*

This 200-year-old converted smithy is on the southern fringe of Bodmin Moor near Golitha Falls. The accommodation offers smartly furnished, cottage-style bedrooms with many extra facilities. A wide choice of freshly cooked breakfasts is served in the conservatory, and there are several eating options nearby.

Rooms 3 rms (2 en suite) (1 pri facs) S £60-£65; D £83 **Facilities** FTV DVD Lounge tea/coffee WiFi ♨ **Parking** 3 **Notes** LB No Children 12yrs Closed 22 Oct-14 Mar

Trecarne House

★★★★ GUEST ACCOMMODATION

tel: 01579 343543 & 07950 262682 **Penhale Grange, St Cleer PL14 5EB**
email: trish@trecarnehouse.co.uk **web:** www.trecarnehouse.co.uk
dir: *B3254 N from Liskeard to St Cleer. Right at Post Office, 3rd left after church, 2nd right, house on right*

A warm welcome awaits at Trecarne House, a large family home, peacefully located on the edge of the village. The stylish and spacious bedrooms enjoy magnificent country views and have many thoughtful extras. The buffet-style breakfast offers a wide choice, which can be enjoyed in the dining room or bright conservatory overlooking rolling countryside.

Rooms 3 en suite (2 fmly) S £65-£75; D £80-£90 (room only) **Facilities** FTV DVD iPod docking station TVL tea/coffee Dinner available WiFi ch fac ♨ Table tennis Trampoline **Extras** Speciality toiletries, robes, slippers **Conf** Max 25 **Parking** 6 **Notes** LB ⊗

Cheesewring

★★★ INN

tel: 01579 362321 **Minions PL14 5LE**
email: thecheesewring@gmail.com **web:** www.cheesewringhotel.co.uk
dir: *From Liskeard at rdbt into St Cleer Rd (B3254) (St Cleer). 1m, left signed St Cleer. Through St Cleer. At T-junct right (Minions), 2m to Minions*

This attractive and historic inn has an imposing position on the edge of Dartmoor, a great location for some beautiful walks and observation of the abundant wildlife. Each of the guest rooms is warm and inviting, and all have impressive modern facilities. A good choice of dishes is offered at lunch and dinner in the atmospheric restaurant-bar, and there are lovely open fires to relax in front of.

Rooms 3 en suite S £45; D £70* **Facilities** FTV tea/coffee Dinner available WiFi **Parking** 30

Elnor Guest House

★★★ GUEST HOUSE

tel: 01579 342472 **1 Russell St PL14 4BP**
email: infoelnorguesthouse50@talktalk.net **web:** www.elnorguesthouse.co.uk
dir: *Exit A38 from Plymouth into town centre, house on right opposite florist on road to railway station, pass British Legion & The Railway pub*

Elnor is a well-established, friendly guest house, close to the town centre and railway station, and just a short drive from Bodmin Moor and other places of interest. Bedrooms are neatly presented and well equipped, and some are on the ground floor. A cosy lounge is available to guests.

Rooms 6 rms (4 en suite) 3 annexe en suite (3 fmly) (4 GF) S £35-£40; D £65-£70* **Facilities** FTV TVL tea/coffee Direct Dial WiFi ♨ **Parking** 7 **Notes** ⊗ Closed end Nov-end Jan ⊜

LOOE   Map 2 SX25

Premier Collection

The Beach House
★★★★★ GUEST ACCOMMODATION

tel: 01503 262598 **Marine Dr, Hannafore PL13 2DH**
email: enquiries@thebeachhouselooe.co.uk web: www.thebeachhouselooe.co.uk
dir: *From Looe W over bridge, left to Hannafore & Marine Drive, on right after Tom Sawyers B&B*

As its name would suggest, this property has panoramic sea views and is just a short walk from the harbour, restaurants and town. Some rooms have stylish hand-made furniture, and the bedrooms are well equipped and have many extras. Hearty breakfasts are served in the first-floor dining room, providing a good start for walking the South West Coast Path which passes right by the house.

Rooms 5 en suite (4 GF) D £85-£135* **Facilities** FTV Lounge tea/coffee WiFi 🦢 Beauty treatment room **Extras** Speciality toiletries, fresh fruit - complimentary **Parking** 6 **Notes** LB ⊗ No Children 16yrs Closed Xmas

Bucklawren Farm *(SX278540)*
★★★★ FARMHOUSE

tel: 01503 240738 **St Martin-by-Looe PL13 1NZ**
email: info@bucklawren.co.uk web: www.bucklawren.co.uk
dir: *2m NE of Looe. Off B3253 to Monkey Sanctuary, 0.5m right to Bucklawren, farmhouse 0.5m on left*

This spacious 19th-century farmhouse stands in 400 acres of farmland just a mile from the beach. The attractive bedrooms, including one on the ground floor providing wheelchair access, are well equipped, and the front-facing rooms have spectacular views across fields to the sea. Breakfast is served in the dining room with stunning views of the rolling countryside.

Rooms 6 en suite (3 fmly) (1 GF) S £55-£65; D £80-£90 **Facilities** FTV Lounge TVL tea/coffee WiFi 🦢 **Extras** Speciality toiletries, fridge **Parking** 6 **Notes** LB ⊗ No Children 5yrs Closed 20-27 Dec 400 acres arable/beef

LOOE *continued*

Meneglaze Guest House

★★★★ GUEST HOUSE

tel: 01503 269227 & 07717 288497 **Shutta PL13 1LU**
email: dannycornwall@outlook.com **web:** www.meneglaze.com
dir: *A387, opposite railway station turn into Shutta, 100yds on left*

Built in 1860, this delightful guest house was formerly a sea captain's house. It has a private parking area and offers modern comfort and style just a five-minute, easy walk from the centre of Looe. Meneglaze maintains elements of its seafaring days with hints of the nautical throughout the decor. All rooms have tea and coffee making facilities, mini-bar fridges, sumptuous towelling gowns, Egyptian cotton bedding, flat-screen TV with Freeview and free WiFi. Breakfasts are hearty and proudly Cornish. Expect the best quality home-made marmalades and jams and the finest (award winning) Hog's Pudding available each morning.

Rooms 4 en suite **Facilities** FTV iPod docking station tea/coffee WiFi ⓑ **Extras** Safe, fridge, fruit, flowers **Parking** 6 **Notes** LB ⊗ No Children 14yrs

Polraen Country House

★★★★ ⚇ 🚭 GUEST ACCOMMODATION

tel: 01503 263956 **Sandplace PL13 1PJ**
email: enquiries@polraen.co.uk **web:** www.polraen.co.uk
dir: *2m N of Looe at junct A387 & B3254*

This 18th-century stone house, formerly a coaching inn, sits in the peaceful Looe Valley. The charming hosts provide friendly service in a relaxed atmosphere, and the bedrooms and public areas are stylishly co-ordinated and well equipped. The licensed bar, lounge and dining room overlook the garden, and there are facilities for children. The excellent evening meals feature local produce and are served Wednesday to Saturday from April to October.

Rooms 5 en suite (2 fmly) D £75-£112* **Facilities** FTV Lounge TVL tea/coffee Dinner available Licensed WiFi ⚲ 18 ⓑ **Conf** Max 30 Thtr 30 Class 16 Board 16 **Parking** 20 **Notes** LB ⊗ Closed 23-28 Dec RS Nov-Mar No bar or evening dinner service

Trehaven Manor

★★★★ ⚇ 🚭 GUEST ACCOMMODATION

tel: 01503 262028 **Station Rd PL13 1HN**
email: enquiries@trehavenhotel.co.uk **web:** www.trehavenhotel.co.uk
dir: *In East Looe between railway station & bridge. Trehaven's drive adjacent to The Globe public house*

Run by a charming family, this former rectory is in a stunning location with magnificent views of the estuary. Many of the attractive bedrooms have views, and all are particularly well equipped. There is also a cosy lounge bar. Dinner, by arrangement, specialises in Oriental cuisine, and breakfast features traditional fare; the meals are memorable.

Rooms 7 en suite (1 fmly) (1 GF) **Facilities** TVL tea/coffee Dinner available Licensed **Parking** 8 **Notes** ⊗

Tremaine Farm (SX194558)

★★★★ FARMHOUSE

tel: 01503 220417 **Pelynt PL13 2LT**
email: rosemary@tremainefarm.co.uk **web:** www.tremainefarm.co.uk
dir: *5m NW of Looe. B3359 N from Pelynt, left at x-rds*

Convenient for Fowey, Looe and Polperro, this pleasant working farm offers a relaxing and rewarding stay. The proprietors provide friendly hospitality and attentive service, and the spacious and stylish bedrooms are well equipped with impressive bathrooms. A hearty breakfast is served in the dining room and there is also a spacious and comfortable guest lounge.

Rooms 3 en suite (1 fmly) S £40; D £76-£80* **Facilities** FTV DVD iPod docking station TVL tea/coffee WiFi **Extras** Fridge **Parking** 6 **Notes** LB ⊗ 🚭 250 acres arable/sheep

Trenake Manor Farm (SX190555)

★★★★ FARMHOUSE

tel: 01503 220835 & 07812 982775 **Pelynt PL13 2LT**
email: lorraine@cornishfarmhouse.co.uk **web:** www.cornishfarmhouse.co.uk
dir: *A38 onto A390 then B3359. Right at small x-rds, signed Trenake Farm*

This welcoming 15th-century farmhouse is surrounded by countryside and makes a good base for touring Cornwall. Bedrooms have thoughtful finishing touches and there is a comfortable lounge. Breakfast, using local produce, is served in the cosy dining room. You may see the milking cows passing the end of the garden.

Rooms 3 en suite (1 fmly) S £30-£50; D £80* **Facilities** STV FTV Lounge TVL tea/coffee Dinner available WiFi ⓑ **Parking** 10 **Notes** LB ⊗ 🚭 1000 acres dairy/beef/arable

Dovers House

★★★★ GUEST ACCOMMODATION

tel: 01503 265468 & 07545 584150 **St Martin's Rd PL13 1PB**
email: dovershouse@btconnect.com **web:** www.dovershouse.co.uk
dir: *From Saltash on A38, at Trerulefoot rdbt turn left onto A374. After 1m right onto A387, at Widegates stay on B3253, pass Tregoad Park, on left. Continue up hill, 1st house on left*

In a rural setting on the outskirts of Looe, making it an ideal centre for exploring the stunning Cornish coastline. Dovers House is a comfortable place which provides a good base to relax. Bedrooms are light and airy and furnished to a consistently high standard. Breakfast is served in the dining room, which faces the beautiful gardens. Private parking is also provided.

Rooms 4 en suite (1 fmly) **Facilities** FTV Lounge tea/coffee WiFi **Extras** Fridge, fresh milk **Parking** 4 **Notes** ⊗ No Children 8yrs

Commonwood Manor

★★★★ ☺ GUEST ACCOMMODATION

tel: 01503 262929 & 07795 258699 **St Martins Rd PL13 1LP**
email: director@commonwoodmanor.com **web:** www.commonwoodmanor.com
dir: *From centre of Looe, on A387, right onto B3253, 200yds on right*

Commonwood Manor is a building steeped in history, with high ceilings, panoramic views of the Looe valley, and grand fireplaces. Recent refurbishments respect the tradition and history of the building, but you can still look forward to all the comforts you'd expect from a modern guest accommodation. Despite the grand surroundings, the atmosphere is relaxed, with a family-run feel. Bedrooms are situated over three floors offering great views. Breakfast is served daily in the family kitchen, a substantial offering that makes for a great start to the day.

Rooms 8 en suite (1 fmly) S £45-£60; D £55-£115* **Facilities** STV Lounge tea/coffee Licensed WiFi ⬠ ⬠⬠ 18 Pool table **Conf** Max 30 Thtr 20 Class 30 **Parking** 14 **Notes** LB Civ Wed 65

Little Harbour

★★★ GUEST HOUSE

tel: 01503 262474 & 07846 575262 **Church St PL13 2EX**
email: littleharbour@btconnect.com **web:** www.littleharbour.co.uk
dir: *From West Looe harbour, right into Princess Sq, guest house on left*

Little Harbour is situated almost on Looe's harbour in the historic old town; it is in a pleasant and convenient spot and some parking is available. The proprietors are friendly and attentive, and bedrooms are well appointed and attractively decorated. Breakfast is served, freshly cooked, in the dining room.

Rooms 5 en suite (1 fmly) **Facilities** STV FTV TVL tea/coffee WiFi ⬠ **Conf** Max 14 **Parking** 3 **Notes** LB No Children 5yrs

The Ship Inn

★★★ INN

tel: 01503 263124 **Fore St PL13 1AD**
email: reservations@smallandfriendly.co.uk **web:** www.smallandfriendly.co.uk

This lively family pub is located in the very heart of bustling East Looe and has a local following. The bedrooms are comfortable and equipped with all the expected facilities. A wide range of popular dishes is served at lunch and during the evenings, with light refreshments available throughout the day.

Rooms 8 en suite (1 fmly) **Facilities** FTV tea/coffee Dinner available WiFi Pool table ⬠ **Notes** LB

LOSTWITHIEL   Map 2 SX15

Premier Collection

The Old Chapel B&B

★★★★★ ☺ GUEST ACCOMMODATION

tel: 01579 321260 & 07979 234743 **West Taphouse PL22 0RP**
email: enquiries@theoldchapelbandb.co.uk **web:** www.theoldchapelbandb.co.uk
dir: *From Bodmin follow signs to Lostwithiel. In town, turn left onto A390. After 3m into West Taphouse, last property on left*

Friendly hosts Greg and Kimberley offer a genuine welcome at The Old Chapel. The beautifully refurbished bedrooms and bathrooms are well equipped with additional thoughtful touches, including chocolates, shortbread biscuits and fresh milk for tea and coffee. The region has much to offer, as sightseeing and activities are plentiful. The hosts have designed their own "Carless breaks" for those who wish to enjoy their trip with the option of leaving the car at home.

Rooms 4 rms (3 en suite) (1 pri facs) (1 fmly) S £60-£90; D £65-£95 **Facilities** FTV DVD tea/coffee Dinner available WiFi ⬠ **Extras** Home-made biscuits, sweets, flowers - free **Parking** 6 **Notes** LB ⊗ No Children 13yrs

Hazelmere House

★★★★ ☺ BED AND BREAKFAST

tel: 01208 873315 **58 Grenville Rd PL22 0RA**
email: hazelmerehouse@aol.com **web:** www.hazelmerehouse.co.uk

Hazelmere House is a professionally run B&B where guests are welcomed with a smile and made to feel at home. The rooms are very well appointed and equipped. All three rooms offer great views over the beautiful Fowey Valley and beyond. The award-winning breakfast is served at the communal table in the formal dining room. The garden offers peace and tranquillity.

Rooms 3 en suite **Facilities** STV FTV iPod docking station TVL tea/coffee WiFi ch fac ⬠ ⬠⬠ 18 Riding ⬠ **Extras** Speciality toiletries **Parking** 6 **Notes** ⊜

Penrose B&B

★★★★ GUEST ACCOMMODATION

tel: 01208 871417 & 07766 900179 **1 The Terrace PL22 0DT**
email: enquiries@penrosebb.co.uk **web:** www.penrosebb.co.uk
dir: *In Lostwithiel on A390 (Edgcumbe Rd) into Scrations Ln, turn 1st right for parking*

Just a short walk from the town centre, this grand Victorian house offers comfortable accommodation and a genuine homely atmosphere. Many of the bedrooms have the original fireplaces and all are equipped with thoughtful extras. Breakfast is a generous offering and is served in the elegant dining room, with views over the garden. WiFi access is also available.

Rooms 7 en suite (3 fmly) (2 GF) S £35-£80; D £45-£100* **Facilities** FTV DVD TVL tea/coffee WiFi ⬠ **Parking** 8 **Notes** LB ⊜

LUXULYAN
Map 2 SX05

Ivy Cottage

★★★★ BED AND BREAKFAST

tel: 01726 850796 & 07707 038966 **PL30 5DW**
web: www.ivycottage-luxulyan.co.uk
dir: *A30 exit at Innis Downs onto A391. Follow signs to Eden Project. At rdbt take 1st exit signed Luxulyan. Pass Kings Arms pub, over rail bridge to top of hill. Turn right & at church sharp left, 1st cottage on right*

This welcoming cottage is surrounded by countryside and is an ideal base for touring Cornwall. Bedrooms have thoughtful finishing touches and there is a picturesque garden to relax in with abundant wildlife, and you can watch the friendly cows in the farmers' fields. Breakfast, using local produce, is enjoyed in the cosy dining room. Private parking is provided.

Rooms 2 en suite S £60-£70; D £75-£85* **Facilities** FTV TVL tea/coffee Lift WiFi ⚓ 18 ⚓ **Parking** 3 **Notes** ⊗ Closed 15 Oct-Mar ⊜

MARAZION
Map 2 SW53

Blue Horizon

★★★★ BED AND BREAKFAST

tel: 01736 711199 Fore St TR17 0AW
email: stay@bluehorizon-marazion.co.uk **web:** www.bluehorizon-marazion.co.uk
dir: *E end of village centre*

Located in the heart of this market town, the rear of this establishment is almost at the water's edge and offers superb views of the sea from its garden, some of the bedrooms and the breakfast room. The atmosphere is laid back and relaxed. There are a number of additional facilities available (charged), including a laundry room, sauna cabin and barbecue facilities. Ample parking is also available.

Rooms 5 en suite D £85-£95* **Facilities** FTV tea/coffee WiFi Sauna ⚓ Hot tub in cabin **Parking** 6 **Notes** ⊗ Closed Oct-Mar RS 22-30 Jul & 24 Aug-1 Sep continental bkst only

The Marazion

★★★★ INN

tel: 01736 710334 **The Square TR17 0AP**
email: enquiries@marazionhotel.co.uk **web:** www.marazionhotel.co.uk
dir: *In village square opposite Out of Blue gallery*

Within 50 metres of one of Cornwall's safest beaches, this family-run establishment offers a relaxed atmosphere with friendly service. The individually furnished and decorated bedrooms are comfortable, and many have the benefit of stunning views across to St Michael's Mount. The Cutty Sark public bar is a great place to sit and enjoy a drink and listen to local banter, while the restaurant provides a wide range of meals to suit all tastes and budgets.

Rooms 11 en suite (2 fmly) S £81-£147; D £81-£147* **Facilities** FTV Lounge tea/coffee Dinner available WiFi ⚓ **Parking** 20 **Notes** Closed Nov No coaches

St Michaels Bed and Breakfast

★★★★ 🛡 BED AND BREAKFAST

tel: 01736 711348 & 07518 945279 **The Corner House, Fore St TR17 0AD**
email: stmichaelsbandb@hotmail.com **web:** www.stmichaels-bedandbreakfast.co.uk
dir: *From A30 at Newtown rdbt, exit signed Marazion. At T-junct turn left, into Marazion, 800mtrs on left next to methodist chapel*

A relaxed yet professional approach, comfortable accommodation and award-winning breakfasts make St Michaels the ideal place to stay when visiting the ancient market town of Marazion, the sandy beaches of Mount's Bay or St Michael's Mount. Top floor rooms enjoy sea views, and parking is available.

Rooms 6 en suite (1 GF) S £85-£95; D £100-£120* **Facilities** FTV DVD tea/coffee WiFi ⚓ **Parking** 6 **Notes** ⊗ No Children 12yrs

Glenleigh House

★★★ GUEST HOUSE

tel: 01736 710308 **Higher Fore St TR17 0BQ**
email: glenleighbandb@hotmail.co.uk **web:** www.glenleigh-marazion.co.uk
dir: *A394 to Penzance, opposite Fire Engine Inn*

Glenleigh House, overlooking St Michael's Mount and the sweeping panorama of Mount's Bay, has been owned and run by the Hales family for more than 30 years. With eight comfortable and well-appointed bedrooms (many with views to the Mount and the sea), you can be assured of a comfortable stay. Built in 1898 as the home of a prosperous farmer, the house retains its original Victorian charm while providing modern amenities such as free WiFi. Expect a filling breakfast of your choice to set you up for the day.

Rooms 8 en suite (1 GF) **Facilities** FTV TVL tea/coffee WiFi **Parking** 8 **Notes** LB ⊗ No Children 8yrs Closed Nov-Mar

Silver Stars The AA Silver Star rating denotes a B&B that we highly recommend. They have a superior level of quality within their star rating, high standards of hospitality, service and cleanliness.

MEVAGISSEY
Map 2 SX04

Premier Collection

Pebble House
★★★★★ ⌂ GUEST ACCOMMODATION

tel: 01726 844466 & 07973 714392 **Polkirt Hill PL26 6UX**
email: hello@pebblehousecornwall.co.uk **web:** www.pebblehousecornwall.co.uk
dir: B3273 to Mevagissey, into village & follow one-way system. Pass Ship Inn on right, up hill keeping sea on left to T-junct. Pebble House on right

This property is affectionately known as 'THE house with THE view' which certainly provides an accurate description. Providing boutique-style accommodation, all the rooms are en suite and individual in design – modern, contemporary, quirky, and providing excellent comfort. You can buy pretty much everything you see in the house if you wish. Light snacks, picnics, cream teas and a range of drinks are available, along with a hearty breakfast featuring daily specials. Please note that Pebble House can only accommodate children aged over 16.

Rooms 6 en suite (1 GF) S £120-£215; D £120-£215* **Facilities** STV FTV DVD iPod docking station tea/coffee Licensed WiFi 🏋 **Extras** Speciality toiletries **Parking** 6 **Notes** LB ⊗ No Children 16yrs

Premier Collection

Portmellon Cove Guest House
★★★★★ ⌂ GUEST ACCOMMODATION

tel: 01726 843410 & 07747 440002 **121 Portmellon Park, Portmellon PL26 6XD**
email: stay@portmellon-cove.com **web:** www.portmellon-cove.com
dir: A390 onto B3273 into Mevagissey. Through village, up Polkirt Hill. 1st left into Porthmellon Rd, pass pub, right into Porthmellon Park, on right

Portmellon Cove Guest House lies in a quiet, peaceful, sandy cove less than a mile from the pretty fishing village of Mevagissey. This well-run family property offers inviting sea-view rooms, free parking and WiFi. All three rooms are well equipped with a generous mini-bar and beverage tray. Award-winning breakfasts are served in the bright and airy dining room which enjoys views across the garden and out to sea. Close to The Lost Gardens of Heligan, the Eden Project, the coastal path and cycleways, most of Cornwall's many attractions can be reached within an hour.

Rooms 3 en suite **Facilities** FTV DVD iPod docking station Lounge tea/coffee Licensed WiFi 🏋 18 🏋 **Extras** Mini-bar, snacks, robes, fridge **Parking** 5 **Notes** LB ⊗ No Children 12yrs Closed Nov-Mar

Stone's Throw Cottage
★★★★ BED AND BREAKFAST

tel: 01726 844605 **5 Polkirt Hill PL26 6UR**
email: info@stones-throw-cottage-mevagissey.com **web:** www.stones-throw-cottage-mevagissey.com
dir: From St Austell take B3273 to Mevagissey

A beautifully restored fisherman's cottage set in the centre of Mevagissey, a minute's walk from the quaint historic harbour, shops, bars and restaurants. The friendly host offers cheerful hospitality, alongside bedrooms and bathrooms that have been sympathetically refurbished and well equipped. Comfort and quality is assured in the additional thoughtful touches, including chocolates, assorted teas and fresh milk for tea and coffee. Sumptuous beds ensure a good night's sleep. Perfectly located for sightseeing and activities.

Rooms 3 rms (2 en suite) (1 pri facs) S £50-£85; D £60-£95* **Facilities** FTV DVD tea/coffee WiFi **Extras** iPads **Notes** LB ⊗

Tanglewood House B&B
★★★★ ⌂ BED AND BREAKFAST

tel: 01726 843657 **Valley Rd PL26 6SB**
email: stay@tanglewoodbandb.co.uk **web:** www.tanglewoodbandb.co.uk
dir: From St Austell follow signs to Mevagissey on B3273, Tanglewood on right

Just a short stroll from Mevagissey, this is a perfect base from which to explore popular attractions such as The Eden Project and The Lost Gardens of Heligan. Set within attractive and peaceful grounds, Tanglewood offers a warm welcome, and every effort is made to ensure an enjoyable and memorable stay. Bedrooms provide impressive levels of quality with all expected modern comforts, while bathrooms come complete with robes and cosseting towels. Breakfast uses locally sourced produce, including free-range eggs, and is served downstairs in the dining room, overlooking the garden.

Rooms 3 en suite **Facilities** FTV Lounge tea/coffee WiFi 🏋 18 **Parking** 7 **Notes** ⊗ No Children 8yrs

MITCHELL
Map 2 SW85

The Plume of Feathers
★★★★ 🍺 INN

tel: 01872 510387 & 511122 **TR8 5AX**
email: theplume@hospitalitycornwall.com **web:** www.theplumemitchell.co.uk
dir: Just off A30 & A3076, follow signs

The Plume of Feathers is a very popular inn, with origins dating back to the 16th century, situated close to Newquay and the beaches. The restaurant offers a varied menu which relies heavily on local produce. The stylish bedrooms are decorated in neutral colours and have wrought-iron beds with quality linens. The garden makes an ideal place to enjoy a meal or a Cornish tea. Staff are very friendly.

Rooms 13 annexe en suite (4 fmly) (10 GF) S £80-£100; D £100-£130* **Facilities** FTV tea/coffee Dinner available WiFi **Conf** Max 65 **Parking** 40 **Notes** LB No coaches

MORWENSTOW
Map 2 SS21

West Point B&B

★★★★ BED AND BREAKFAST

tel: 01288 331594 & 07443 567963 **West Point, Crimp EX23 9PB**
email: bramhill@hotmail.co.uk **web:** www.budebedandbreakfast.co.uk
dir: A361 to Barnstaple onto A39 towards Bude. 7m after Clovelly rdbt on right

Ideally placed for exploring the beautiful countryside and coasts of north Cornwall and north Devon, this smartly appointed establishment is surrounded by colourful gardens with far-reaching views to the rear. Guests are assured of a genuine welcome plus the freedom of all-day access. Both bedrooms are comfortable, light and airy; one has a French-style king-size bed and patio doors leading to the garden. Additional facilities include a guest lounge and dining room where local farm produce is on offer whenever possible.

Rooms 2 en suite (1 fmly) (2 GF) S £45-£50; D £70-£80 **Facilities** FTV TVL tea/coffee WiFi 🔒 **Extras** Speciality toiletries, home-made biscuits **Parking** 4 **Notes** LB ⊗ Closed 22 Dec-2 Jan ⊛

MULLION
Map 2 SW61

Colvennor Farmhouse

★★★★ BED AND BREAKFAST

tel: 01326 241208 **Cury TR12 7BJ**
email: colvennor@btinternet.com **web:** www.colvennorfarmhouse.com
dir: A3083 (Helston-Lizard), over rdbt at end of airfield, next right to Cury/Poldhu Cove, farm 1.4m on right at top of hill

This peacefully located Grade II listed former farmhouse is a wonderfully relaxing base from which to explore the picturesque delights of The Lizard. Parts of the house date back to the 17th century, but modern comforts are now in place, with bedrooms and bathrooms offering high levels of quality and character. Breakfast makes good use of excellent local produce and is served in the attractive dining room. Guests also have a lovely lounge at their disposal, with a log-burner to keep the chill off in cooler months. There is also a large garden.

Rooms 3 en suite (1 GF) S £55-£60; D £70-£80* **Facilities** FTV DVD TVL tea/coffee WiFi ⌁ 18 🔒 **Parking** 3 **Notes** ⊗ No Children 10yrs ⊛

NEWQUAY
Map 2 SW86

Lewinnick Lodge

★★★★ RESTAURANT WITH ROOMS

tel: 01637 878117 **Pentire Headland TR7 1QD**
email: thelodge@hospitalitycornwall.com **web:** www.hospitalitycornwall.com/lewinnicklodge
dir: From A392, at rdbt exit into Pentire Rd then Pentire Ave. Turn right to Lewinnick Lodge

Set above the cliffs of Pentire Headland, looking out across the mighty Atlantic, guests are guaranteed amazing coastal views here at Lewinnick Lodge. The bedrooms were designed by Guy Bostock and are modern, spacious, and offer many thoughtful extras; some have open-plan bathrooms. Modern British food (with an emphasis on fresh fish) is served all day.

Rooms 11 en suite (1 fmly) **Facilities** FTV iPod docking station tea/coffee Dinner available Direct Dial Lift WiFi 🔒 Surf board store **Extras** Speciality toiletries, robes, bottled water - free **Parking** 50 **Notes** No coaches

Meadow View

★★★ GUEST ACCOMMODATION

tel: 01637 873132 **135 Mount Wise TR7 1QR**
email: meadowview135@hotmail.com **web:** www.meadowviewnewquay.co.uk
dir: A392 into Newquay to Mountwise, Meadow View on left before rdbt to Pentire

Expect a warm welcome at Meadow View, which is just a short walk from the town centre and Fistral Beach which is famous for surfing. The bedrooms are comfortable and some have countryside views. A hearty breakfast is served in the pleasant dining room and there is a cosy sun lounge to relax in. Waterworld, The Eden Project, and the Pentire peninsula with its rolling green coastline are all just a short drive away.

Rooms 7 en suite (2 fmly) **Facilities** FTV tea/coffee WiFi 🔒 **Parking** 7 **Notes** LB ⊗ No Children 5yrs Closed 7 Nov-mid Feb ⊛

The Three Tees

★★★ GUEST ACCOMMODATION

tel: 01637 872055 **21 Carminow Way TR7 3AY**
email: greg@3tees.co.uk **web:** www.3tees.co.uk
dir: A30 onto A392 signed Newquay. Right at Quintrell Downs rdbt signed Porth, over x-rds, 3rd right

Located in a quiet residential area just a short walk from the town and beach, this friendly family-run establishment is comfortable and well equipped. Guests have use of a lounge, a bar and a sun lounge, and breakfast is served in the dining room, where snacks are available throughout the day. The bar serves light snacks in the evenings. In addition to the bedrooms in the main house, a family annexe is also available, and offers flexible, level-access accommodation.

Rooms 8 rms (7 en suite) (1 pri facs) 1 annexe en suite (4 fmly) (2 GF) D £70-£80* **Facilities** FTV DVD TVL tea/coffee Licensed WiFi 🔒 **Parking** 9 **Notes** LB Closed Nov-Feb

Rolling Waves

★★★ GUEST HOUSE

tel: 01637 873236 **Alexandra Rd, Porth TR7 3NB**
email: enquiries@rollingwaves.co.uk **web:** www.rollingwaves.co.uk
dir: A30 onto A392, A3058 towards Newquay. B3276 to Porth, pass Mermaid public house

Rolling Waves is a family-owned and run guest house with great views across the bay. The bedrooms are comfortable, the hosts friendly and welcoming, and dinner is available on request.

Rooms 8 rms (7 en suite) (1 pri facs) (2 fmly) (4 GF) S £33-£43; D £60-£92* **Facilities** FTV TVL tea/coffee Dinner available Licensed WiFi **Parking** 7 **Notes** LB ⊗

Avalon

★★★ GUEST ACCOMMODATION

tel: 01637 877522 & 07870 320346 **4 Edgcumbe Gardens TR7 2QD**
email: enquiries@avalonnewquay.co.uk **web:** www.avalonnewquay.co.uk
dir: From A30 at Quintrell Downs rdbt onto A3058 signed St Columb Minor. Left in 1m opposite Rocklands

Conveniently situated within walking distance of the town centre and the beaches, in a quiet residential area, Avalon provides comfortable accommodation, and enjoys the benefit of on-site parking. Guests may enjoy the front-facing sun terrace during summer months. Golfing holiday offers are available.

Rooms 6 rms (5 en suite) (1 pri facs) (1 fmly) S £25-£35; D £55-£65* **Facilities** FTV tea/coffee WiFi 🔒 **Parking** 6 **Notes** LB

The Croft

★★★ GUEST ACCOMMODATION

tel: 01637 871520 **37 Mount Wise TR7 2BL**
email: info@the-crofthotel.co.uk **web:** www.the-crofthotel.co.uk
dir: *In town centre near Towan Beach, junct Mount Wise & Mayfield Rd*

Located just minutes away from the town centre and beach, The Croft is a comfortable place to stay, and the friendly hosts create a homely atmosphere. A full English breakfast is served in the informal bar-dining room.

Rooms 7 rms (5 en suite) (2 pri facs) (3 fmly) D £60-£75* **Facilities** FTV tea/coffee Licensed WiFi 🅿 **Parking** 7 **Notes** LB ⊗ No Children 3yrs

Porth Lodge

★★★ INN

tel: 01637 874483 **Porth Bean Rd TR7 3LT**
email: info@porthlodgehotel.co.uk **web:** www.porthlodgehotel.co.uk

Porth Lodge is a popular venue with its own bowling alley. Staff here are friendly and helpful, and the bedrooms are very comfortable and well equipped. Meals are available every day.

Rooms 16 en suite (1 fmly) **Facilities** FTV tea/coffee Dinner available WiFi ⌁ 18 Pool table 🅿 Ten pin bowling alley **Conf** Thtr 40 Class 30 Board 20 **Parking** 20

St Breca

★★★ GUEST HOUSE

tel: 01637 872745 **22 Mount Wise TR7 2BG**
email: enquiries@stbreca.co.uk **web:** www.stbreca.co.uk
dir: *A30 onto A392. Follow signs to Newquay, then to Mount Wise*

This friendly guest house is conveniently located a few minutes' walk from the town centre, beaches and other amenities. It provides soundly maintained, modern bedrooms, and separate tables are provided in the attractive breakfast room.

Rooms 10 rms (8 en suite) (2 pri facs) (3 fmly) (2 GF) **Facilities** FTV DVD tea/coffee WiFi **Parking** 3 **Notes** ⊗

PADSTOW

Map 2 SW97

Premier Collection

Padstow Townhouse

★★★★★★ ◉◉◉◉ 🍽 RESTAURANT WITH ROOMS

tel: 01841 550950 **16/18 High St PL28 8BB**
web: www.paul-ainsworth.co.uk

This cosy 18th-century townhouse offers six individually styled suites, providing all home comforts as well as some little luxuries. Each suite has its own 40" curved TV complete with Apple TV, as well as free WiFi. The suites are all named after desserts – rhubarb & custard, toffee apple, honeycomb – and are influenced by the style and feel of the 1920s or 30s. Breakfast is served in Rojano's in the Square, and guests are welcome to dine there (it has one AA Rosette) or at the four AA-Rosetted Paul Ainsworth at No.6 restaurant.

Rooms 6 en suite S £255-£355; D £280-£380* **Facilities** Dinner available WiFi **Extras** Speciality toiletries

Premier Collection

Penjoly Guest House

★★★★★ 🛏 GUEST HOUSE

tel: 01841 533535 **Padstow Rd PL28 8LB**
email: penjoly.padstow@btopenworld.com **web:** www.penjolypadstow.co.uk
dir: *1m S of Padstow. Off A389 near Padstow Holiday Park*

Penjoy is a very professionally run establishment, where attention to detail and quality are noteworthy throughout. Bedrooms are delightfully decorated and complemented by an impressive range of extras. Breakfast is served in the attractive breakfast room or in the conservatory, and a guest lounge is also available. This is a perfect base for exploring the West Country's delights, and for seeking out the great restaurants of Cornwall. Guests have the convenience of off-road parking.

Rooms 3 en suite (3 GF) S £85.50-£103.50; D £95-£115 **Facilities** STV FTV DVD iPod docking station TVL tea/coffee WiFi **Extras** Robes **Parking** 10 **Notes** ⊗ No Children 16yrs 🐾

Premier Collection

The Seafood Restaurant

★★★★★ ◉◉◉ 🍽 RESTAURANT WITH ROOMS

tel: 01841 532700 **Riverside PL28 8BY**
email: reservations@rickstein.com **web:** www.rickstein.com
dir: *Into town centre, down hill (Station Rd), follow signs to harbour car park, opposite car park*

Food lovers continue to beat a well-trodden path to this famous restaurant. Situated on the edge of the harbour, just a stone's throw from the shops, The Seafood Restaurant offers chic and comfortable bedrooms that boast numerous thoughtful extras; some have views of the estuary and a couple have private balconies with stunning sea views. Service is relaxed and friendly; booking is essential for both accommodation and a table in the restaurant.

Rooms 16 en suite 6 annexe en suite (12 fmly) (3 GF) S £154-£313.50; D £154-£313.50* **Facilities** FTV DVD tea/coffee Dinner available Direct Dial Lift WiFi 🅿 Cookery School **Extras** Speciality toiletries, robes, mini-bar **Parking** 13 **Notes** LB Closed 24-26 Dec RS 24 Dec limited restaurant service times No coaches

Premier Collection

St Petrocs & Bistro

★★★★★ ◉ RESTAURANT WITH ROOMS

tel: 01841 532700 **4 New St PL28 8EA**
email: reservations@rickstein.com **web:** www.rickstein.com
dir: *A39 onto A389, follow signs to Padstow town centre*

One of the oldest buildings in town, this charming establishment is just up the hill from the picturesque harbour. Style, comfort and individuality are all great strengths here, particularly so in the impressively equipped bedrooms. Breakfast, lunch and dinner all reflect a serious approach to cuisine, and the popular restaurant has a relaxed, bistro style. Comfortable lounges, a reading room and lovely gardens complete the picture.

Rooms 10 en suite (2 fmly) D £156-£280* **Facilities** FTV Lounge tea/coffee Dinner available Direct Dial WiFi **Parking** 4 **Notes** LB Closed 24-26 Dec No coaches

PADSTOW *continued*

The Old Mill House

★★★★ ⚇ GUEST ACCOMMODATION

tel: 01841 540388 **Little Petherick PL27 7QT**
email: enquiries@theoldmillhouse.com **web:** www.theoldmillhouse.com
dir: *2m S of Padstow. In centre of Little Petherick on A389*

The Old Mill House is situated in an Area of Outstanding Natural Beauty, a couple of miles from the busy town of Padstow with its pretty harbour with many shops, bars and restaurants. This 16th-century property, a former corn mill house, has been sympathetically converted and is beautifully decorated and well equipped. Family-run, it offers good levels of comfort and quality. Dinner is served in the restaurant with a good selection of dishes to suit all tastes. Traditional afternoon teas may be served in the garden and a good hearty 'Full Cornish' breakfast is made with locally sourced produce and ingredients.

Rooms 7 en suite (2 fmly) S £70-£110; D £85-£125* **Facilities** FTV DVD Lounge tea/coffee Dinner available Licensed WiFi ⚿ Hot tub on request **Extras** Sherry, fresh milk, snacks **Notes** LB Closed 20 Dec-1 Feb

Rick Stein's Café

★★★★ BED AND BREAKFAST

tel: 01841 532700 **10 Middle St PL28 8AP**
email: reservations@rickstein.com **web:** www.rickstein.com
dir: *A389 into town, one way past church, 3rd right*

Another Rick Stein success story, this is a lively café by day, restaurant by night, and offers good food and quality accommodation just a short walk from the harbour. Three bedrooms are available – each is quite different but all have high standards of comfort. Friendly and personable staff are always on hand.

Rooms 3 en suite (1 fmly) S £113-£176; D £113-£176* **Facilities** FTV DVD tea/coffee Dinner available Direct Dial Licensed WiFi ch fac ⚿ Cookery school **Extras** Speciality toiletries; mini-bar - chargeable **Notes** LB Closed 24-26 Dec RS 24 Dec limited service times

Wingfield House

★★ ⚇ BED AND BREAKFAST

tel: 01841 532617 **Dennis Ln PL28 8DP**
email: besidetheseaside@btinternet.com **web:** www.wingfieldhouse.co.uk
dir: *Into Padstow on A389, 1st right into Sarahs Ln. At bottom of hill, right into Dennis Ln, 3rd entrance on right*

Wingfield House is a very friendly, traditional bed and breakfast a few minutes' walk from Padstow town centre. The comfortable bedrooms are well appointed and have shared or private facilities. Hearty breakfasts are served at a large table in the dining room, and guests have the use of a TV lounge. There is off-road parking.

Rooms 3 rms (1 pri facs) (2 fmly) **Facilities** FTV TVL tea/coffee WiFi **Parking** 5 **Notes** LB ⊜

PAR Map 2 SX05

The Britannia Inn & Restaurant

★★★★ ⊜ INN

tel: 01726 812889 & 815796 **St Austell Rd PL24 2SL**
email: info@britanniainn.com **web:** www.britanniainn.com
dir: *On A390 between Par & St Austell, next to Cornish Market World*

This long established inn is situated between Par and St Austell and is just a five-minute drive from The Eden Project. There is a very genuine welcome here and a collective effort to ensure guests are well looked after and enjoy their stay. A choice of bars is available, together with attractive gardens, function room and range of dining options. The extensive menu features plenty of Cornish produce with a range of daily specials also offered. Bedrooms offer contemporary style and comfort with impressive, high quality bathrooms.

Rooms 7 en suite (4 fmly) S £70-£100; D £90-£150* **Facilities** FTV tea/coffee Dinner available Direct Dial WiFi ⚿ **Conf** Max 75 Thtr 60 Class 45 Board 50 **Parking** 105 **Notes** RS 25 Dec open 12-2 drinks only

The Royal Inn

★★★★ INN

tel: 01726 815601 **66 Eastcliffe Rd, Tywardreath PL24 2AJ**
email: info@royal-inn.co.uk **web:** www.royal-inn.co.uk
dir: *Adjacent to Par railway station*

Situated next to the railway station on the edge of Tywardreath, this free house provides high standards of comfort and quality. Only five minutes from Par Sands and four miles from The Eden Project, it is an ideal base for exploring Cornwall. The open-plan bar area has slate floors and a large open fire; the atmosphere is relaxed and diners can choose from the bar menu or dine more formally in the restaurant or conservatory. All twin rooms have sofa beds (suitable for children under 14), and the family suite is suitable for families of four or five.

Rooms 15 en suite (8 fmly) (4 GF) **Facilities** STV FTV tea/coffee Dinner available WiFi Pool table ⚿ **Conf** Max 20 Thtr 8 Class 8 Board 20 **Parking** 17 **Notes** LB Closed 23-26 Dec & 30 Dec-1 Jan

PENRYN Map 2 SW73

Prospect House

★★★★ GUEST ACCOMMODATION

tel: 01326 373198 **Commercial Rd TR10 8AH**
email: stay@prospecthouse-penryn.co.uk **web:** www.prospecthouse-penryn.co.uk
dir: *Exit A39 at Treluswell rdbt onto B3292, right at Penryn town centre sign. Left at junct to town hall, left into Saint Gluivas St, at bottom on left*

Prospect House is an attractive building close to the waterside, and was built in 1820 for a ship's captain. The original charm of the house has been carefully maintained and the attractive bedrooms are well equipped. A comfortable lounge is available, and freshly cooked breakfasts are served in the elegant dining room.

Rooms 3 en suite D £80-£85* **Facilities** FTV Lounge tea/coffee WiFi **Parking** 4 **Notes** ⊗

PENZANCE   Map 2 SW43

Premier Collection

Camilla House

★★★★★ GUEST ACCOMMODATION

tel: 01736 363771 **12 Regent Ter TR18 4DW**
email: enquiries@camillahouse.co.uk **web:** www.camillahouse.co.uk
dir: *A30 to Penzance, at rail station follow road along harbourfront into Promenade Rd. Opposite Jubilee Bathing Pool, Regent Terrace 2nd right*

A warm welcome is assured at this charming Victorian property, located in a quiet residential area facing the sea and only a short walk from Penzance's beach and town centre attractions. Bedrooms, some with views towards the coast, are spacious and attractively appointed. There's a stylish guest lounge with many homely features, and breakfast should not to be missed. Secure car parking is provided.

Rooms 8 rms (7 en suite) (1 pri facs) (1 GF) **Facilities** FTV DVD TVL tea/coffee WiFi 🔒 **Parking** 7 **Notes** ⊗ Closed Nov-Mar

Premier Collection

Ednovean Farm *(SW538295)*

★★★★★ FARMHOUSE

tel: 01736 711883 **TR20 9LZ**
email: info@ednoveanfarm.co.uk **web:** www.ednoveanfarm.co.uk

(For full entry see Perranuthnoe)

Mount Royal

★★★★ GUEST ACCOMMODATION

tel: 01736 362233 **Chyandour Cliff TR18 3LQ**
email: mountroyal@btconnect.com **web:** www.mountroyalpenzance.com
dir: *From A30 onto coast road into town*

Part Georgian and part Victorian, the spacious Mount Royal has splendid views over Mount's Bay and is convenient for the town's attractions. There's a gracious elegance throughout with the impressive dining room retaining its original fireplace and ornate sideboard. Parking available to the rear of the property.

Rooms 6 en suite (1 fmly) (1 GF) S £100-£130; D £100-£130 **Facilities** FTV Lounge tea/coffee WiFi 🔒 **Extras** Speciality toiletries **Parking** 8 **Notes** LB ⊗ Closed Oct-May

The Dunedin

★★★★ GUEST ACCOMMODATION

tel: 01736 362652 **Alexandra Rd TR18 4LZ**
email: info@dunedinhotel.co.uk **web:** www.dunedinhotel.co.uk
dir: *A30 to Penzance, at rail station along harbour front into Promenade Rd, right into Alexandra Rd, Dunedin on right*

The Dunedin is in a tree-lined avenue just a stroll from the promenade and town centre. The friendly proprietors provide a relaxed atmosphere, and bedrooms that are well equipped and smartly decorated to a high standard. Hearty breakfasts are served in the dining room.

Rooms 8 en suite (2 fmly) (2 GF) S £60-£65; D £72-£85 **Facilities** FTV DVD tea/coffee WiFi 🔒 **Notes** LB ⊗ No Children 12yrs Closed 31 Oct-3 Jan ⊛

The Old Vicarage

★★★★ BED AND BREAKFAST

tel: 01736 711508 & 07736 101230 **Churchtown, St Hilary TR20 9DQ**
email: johnbd524@aol.com **web:** www.oldvicaragepenzance.co.uk
dir: *5m E of Penzance. Off B3280 in St Hilary*

Guests will certainly feel very much at home after the friendly welcome they'll receive on arrival at The Old Vicarage. The spacious bedrooms are thoughtfully equipped, and there is a comfortable lounge and extensive gardens. Guests can also take advantage of the trekking and riding school, run by the proprietors, who own a small stud farm.

Rooms 4 en suite (2 fmly) (1 GF) S fr £45; D £70-£80* **Facilities** FTV Lounge tea/coffee WiFi ⚲ 18 Riding **Parking** 8 **Notes** LB

The Dolphin Tavern

★★★ INN

tel: 01736 364106 **Quay St TR18 4BD**
email: dolphintavern@tiscali.co.uk **web:** www.dolphintavern.co.uk
dir: *Opposite Penzance harbour*

The Dolphin Tavern is a traditional inn just a few yards away from Penzance harbour, usefully located for the Scillonian ferry. Rooms are comfortable and well presented, and the staff are friendly and attentive. Food is available in the bar and restaurant daily from a wide menu which also offers daily-changing specials.

Rooms 3 en suite D £70-£100* **Facilities** FTV tea/coffee Dinner available WiFi 🔒 Pool table in winter only **Notes** ⊗ No coaches

Find out more about the AA's awards for food excellence on page 11

PENZANCE *continued*

Fountain Tavern

★★★ INN

tel: 01736 369340 **Saint Clare St TR18 2PD**
email: contact@fountaintavernpenzance.co.uk **web:** www.fountaintavernpenzance.co.uk
dir: *A30 into Penzance. At Eastern Green rdbt take 2nd right, follow signs to West Cornwall Hospital. Pass hospital, on left*

This friendly inn at the top of Penzance's high street boasts attractively-styled, comfortable rooms with all the amenities needed for a pleasant stay. The popular inn offers a dining room (set apart from the popular central bar area) for dinner and breakfast. Local ales are a real feature in the bar along with the inviting atmosphere. The welcoming team are key to the business here, making for a memorable experience overall.

Rooms 5 rms (4 en suite) D £50-£114* **Facilities** FTV tea/coffee Dinner available WiFi **Parking** 3 **Notes** LB

The Swordfish Inn

★★★ INN

tel: 01736 362830 **The Strand, Newlyn TR18 5HN**
email: info@swordfishinn.co.uk **web:** www.swordfishinn.co.uk
dir: *1m SW of Penzance*

Situated in the very heart of the fishing village of Newlyn, The Swordfish has been totally renovated to provide modern comforts in a traditional and convivial environment. The spacious, comfortable bedrooms are well appointed, as are the en suite shower rooms. This establishment is a popular venue for locals and tourists alike.

Rooms 4 en suite **Facilities** FTV tea/coffee WiFi **Notes** ⊗ No coaches

The Summer House

Ⓤ

tel: 01736 363744 & 07768 608439 **Cornwall Ter TR18 4HL**
email: reception@summerhouse-cornwall.com **web:** www.summerhouse-cornwall.com
dir: *A30 to Penzance, at rail station follow along harbour onto Promenade, pass Jubilee Pool, right after Queens Hotel. Summer House 30yds on left*

Currently the rating for this establishment is not confirmed. This may be due to a change of ownership or because it has only recently joined the AA rating scheme.

Rooms 5 en suite **Facilities** FTV DVD TVL tea/coffee Licensed WiFi **Extras** Fresh milk, chocolates, mini-fridge **Parking** 5 **Notes** ⊗ No Children 16yrs Closed Oct-Etr

PERRANUTHNOE	Map 2 SW52

Premier Collection

Ednovean Farm *(SW538295)*

★★★★★ 🏠 FARMHOUSE

tel: 01736 711883 **TR20 9LZ**
email: info@ednoveanfarm.co.uk **web:** www.ednoveanfarm.co.uk
dir: *Off A394 towards Perranuthnoe at Dynasty Restaurant, farm drive on left on bend by post box*

Tranquillity is guaranteed at this 17th-century farmhouse, which looks towards the countryside towards Mount's Bay. The bedrooms are individually styled and are very comfortable. The impressive Mediterranean-style gardens are ideal for relaxing and taking in the superb views. In addition to the sitting room, there is also a garden room and several patios. Breakfast is served at a magnificent oak table.

Rooms 3 en suite (3 GF) D £100-£140 **Facilities** FTV DVD iPod docking station Lounge tea/coffee WiFi **Extras** Speciality toiletries, slippers, robes **Parking** 4 **Notes** LB ⊗ No Children 16yrs Closed 24-28 Dec 22 acres grassland/stud

POLPERRO	Map 2 SX25

Premier Collection

Trenderway Farm *(SX214533)*

★★★★★ 🏠 FARMHOUSE

tel: 01503 272214 **Pelynt PL13 2LY**
email: stay@trenderwayfarm.com **web:** www.trenderwayfarm.co.uk
dir: *Take A387 from Looe to Polperro, right at signpost to Pelynt. 3rd left at signed junct to farm. Continue down lane to gravel car park*

Warm hospitality awaits at this delightful 16th-century farmhouse set on a 200-acre working farm. Stylish bedrooms, both in the farmhouse and in the adjacent barns, offer high levels of comfort and include WiFi access. Hearty breakfasts are served in the conservatory overlooking the lake, and free-range eggs from the farm, as well as high quality local produce, are served.

Rooms 2 en suite 5 annexe en suite (2 GF) S £99-£189; D £99-£189 **Facilities** FTV DVD TVL tea/coffee Licensed WiFi 🎣 Lakes Falconry school **Extras** Speciality toiletries; mini-bar - chargeable **Conf** Max 100 Thtr 100 Class 50 Board 15 **Parking** 8 **Notes** LB No Children 16yrs Civ Wed 120 200 acres beef/sheep/orchards

Penryn House

★★★★ GUEST ACCOMMODATION

tel: 01503 272157 **The Coombes PL13 2RQ**
email: enquiries@penrynhouse.co.uk **web:** www.penrynhouse.co.uk
dir: *A387 to Polperro, at mini rdbt left down hill into village (ignore restricted access). 200yds on left*

Penryn House has a relaxed atmosphere and offers a warm welcome. Every effort is made to ensure a memorable stay. Bedrooms are neatly presented and reflect the character of the building. After a day exploring, enjoy a drink at the bar and relax in the comfortable lounge.

Rooms 12 en suite (3 fmly) S £45-£60; D £75-£105* **Facilities** FTV Lounge tea/coffee Licensed WiFi ⌨ **Parking** 13 **Notes** LB

PORT GAVERNE Map 2 SX08

Port Gaverne

★★★★ INN

tel: 01208 880244 **PL29 3SQ**
email: eat@portgavernehotel.co.uk **web:** www.portgavernehotel.co.uk

This traditional inn is located a tiny and peaceful cove on Cornwall's dramatic north coast, one headland away and five minutes' walk from Port Isaac. Accommodation is spread over 15 en suite bedrooms, all comfortably furnished, well-maintained, and spotlessly clean. No two are the same. You'll find antique furniture, nooks and crannies, a wonderfully comfortable bed, and good food here. All rooms come complete with full satellite TV, radio, direct-dial telephone and coffee and tea-making facilities. Also available is a relaxing sitting room, outside terrace and sunny beer garden.

Rooms 15 en suite (4 fmly) S £90-£135; D £110-£160* **Facilities** STV FTV DVD Lounge tea/coffee Dinner available Direct Dial WiFi ⌨ 18 ⚿ **Extras** Speciality toiletries, Nespresso coffee machine **Conf** Max 12 Board 12 **Parking** 17 **Notes** LB No coaches

PORTHLEVEN Map 2 SW62

Kota Restaurant with Rooms

★★★ ⦿⦿ ⊜ RESTAURANT WITH ROOMS

tel: 01326 562407 **Harbour Head TR13 9JA**
email: kota@btconnect.com **web:** www.kotarestaurant.co.uk
dir: *B3304 from Helston into Porthleven. Kota on harbour opposite slipway*

Overlooking the water, this 300-year-old building is the home of Kota Restaurant ('kota' being the Maori word for 'shellfish'). The bedrooms are approached from a granite stairway to the side of the building. The family room is spacious and has the benefit of harbour views, while the smaller, double room is at the rear of the property. The enthusiastic young owners ensure guests enjoy their stay here, and a meal in the two AA Rosette award-winning restaurant should not be missed. Food and drink is also served in the Kota Kai Bar & Kitchen. Breakfast features the best local produce.

Rooms 2 annexe en suite (1 fmly) S £60-£85; D £65-£95* **Facilities** FTV DVD tea/coffee Dinner available WiFi ⌨ 18 ⚿ **Parking** 1 **Notes** ⊗ Closed Jan-10 Feb No coaches

PORTLOE Map 2 SW93

The Lugger

★★★★★ ⦿⦿ ⊜ INN

tel: 01872 501322 **TR2 5RD**
email: reservations.lugger@bespokehotels.com **web:** www.bespokehotels.com/thelugger
dir: *A390 to Truro, B3287 to Tregony, A3078 (St Mawes Rd), left for Veryan, left for Portloe*

This delightful inn enjoys a unique setting adjacent to the slipway of the harbour, where fishing boats still come and go. Bedrooms, some in adjacent buildings and cottages, are contemporary in style and are well equipped. There is a sitting room which reflects the original character of the property, with beams and open fireplaces creating a cosy atmosphere. The modern restaurant enjoys superb views, and in warmer months, a sun terrace overlooking the harbour proves a popular place to enjoy a meal.

Rooms 5 en suite 17 annexe en suite (1 GF) **Facilities** FTV Lounge tea/coffee Dinner available Direct Dial WiFi **Parking** 26 **Notes** No coaches Civ Wed 50

Carradale

★★★★ BED AND BREAKFAST

tel: 01872 501508 **TR2 5RB**
email: barbara495@btinternet.com **web:** www.carradale-bnb.co.uk
dir: *Off A3078 into Portloe, B&B 200yds from Ship Inn*

Carradale lies on the outskirts of this picturesque fishing village, a short walk from the South West Coast Path. It provides warm hospitality, a good level of comfort and well equipped bedrooms. There is an upper-floor lounge with a TV, and breakfast is served around a communal table in the pleasant dining room.

Rooms 2 rms (1 en suite) (1 pri facs) (1 fmly) (2 GF) S £40-£45; D £70-£75 **Facilities** TVL TV1B tea/coffee WiFi ⚿ **Parking** 5 **Notes** ⊗ ⊜

REDRUTH

Map 2 SW64

Old Railway Yard

★★★★ ⬛ ⬤ BED AND BREAKFAST

tel: 01209 314514 & 07970 595598 **Lanner Hill TR16 5TZ**
email: g.s.collier@btinternet.com **web:** www.old-railway-yard.co.uk
dir: A393 Redruth/Falmouth road, at brow of hill before Lanner village, turn right into Tram Cross Ln, 125mtrs on right

Warm, genuine service and hospitality awaits you at The Old Railway Yard, where a warm and friendly welcome is assured from owners Graham and Suzanne. The Old Railway Yard is located in the heart of Cornwall, minutes away from the A30, perfect for exploring all the region offers. Beautifully equipped rooms provide everything you need, and a superb full Cornish breakfast with many extras will set you up well for the day ahead, especially the freshly prepared home-made bread. The Old Railway Yard was the AA Friendliest B&B of the Year 2015-2016.

Rooms 3 rms (2 en suite) (1 pri facs) (1 GF) S £65-£85; D £75-£85* **Facilities** FTV DVD TVL tea/coffee Dinner available Licensed WiFi ⬛ Hot tub **Parking** 8 **Notes** ⊗ No Children 6yrs

Lanner Inn

★★ INN

tel: 01209 215611 **The Square, Lanner TR16 6EH**
email: info@lannerinn.co.uk **web:** www.lannerinn.co.uk
dir: 2m SE of Redruth. In Lanner on A393

Conveniently situated for access to Redruth and the A30, this traditional inn is situated in the centre of Lanner and has a good local following. The property has a dining room and a bar in addition to the comfortable bedrooms. This inn is owner-run and managed, and the team of staff are very friendly.

Rooms 3 en suite 1 annexe en suite (2 fmly) (1 GF) **Facilities** FTV tea/coffee WiFi Pool table ⬛ **Parking** 16

RUAN HIGH LANES

Map 2 SW93

Trenona Farm Holidays *(SW915411)*

★★★ FARMHOUSE

tel: 01872 501339 & 07775 698953 **TR2 5JS**
email: info@trenonafarmholidays.co.uk **web:** www.trenonafarmholidays.co.uk
dir: A390 onto A3078, signed St Mawes. 6m on left

Trenona Farm is located on the Roseland Peninsula, surrounded by rolling countryside and close to lots of beautiful sandy beaches. The area provides many attractions, great restaurants and pubs and is very popular with walkers. A warm welcome awaits guests (and well-behaved dogs). Well-equipped rooms are warm and comfortable and a good hearty farmhouse breakfast is provided in the attractive dining room.

Rooms 4 rms (3 en suite) (1 pri facs) (3 fmly) S £40-£50; D £70* **Facilities** FTV TVL tea/coffee WiFi **Extras** Fridge, fresh milk **Parking** 8 **Notes** LB Closed Nov-mid Mar 250 acres arable/beef

ST AGNES

Map 2 SW75

Driftwood Spars

★★★★ ⬤ GUEST ACCOMMODATION

tel: 01872 552428 **Trevaunance Cove TR5 0RT**
email: info@driftwoodspars.co.uk **web:** www.driftwoodspars.co.uk
dir: A30 to Chiverton rdbt, right onto B3277, through village. Driftwood Spars 200yds before beach

Partly built from shipwreck timbers, this 18th-century building attracts locals and visitors alike. The attractive bedrooms, some in an annexe, are decorated in a bright, seaside style with many interesting features. Local produce, including delicious seafood, is served in the informal dining room and in the restaurant, together with a range of hand-pulled beers.

Rooms 9 en suite 6 annexe en suite (4 fmly) (5 GF) S £50-£100; D £86-£145* **Facilities** FTV tea/coffee Dinner available Direct Dial Licensed WiFi Pool table Table football **Conf** Max 70 Thtr 70 Class 25 Board 20 **Parking** 40 **Notes** LB RS 25 Dec no lunch/dinner, no bar in evening Civ Wed 76

Penkerris

★★ GUEST HOUSE

tel: 01872 552262 **Penwinnick Rd TR5 0PA**
email: penkerris@gmail.com **web:** www.penkerris.co.uk
dir: A30 onto B3277 to village, Penkerris on right after village sign

Set in gardens on the edge of the village, this Edwardian house has a relaxed and welcoming atmosphere. Period features abound, and the best possible use is made of space in the bedrooms. Home-cooked evening meals are served by prior arrangement. Ample parking is available.

Rooms 7 rms (4 en suite) (3 fmly) S £25-£50; D £50-£70* **Facilities** FTV TVL tea/coffee Dinner available Licensed WiFi ch fac Badminton Volleyball **Parking** 9 **Notes** LB

ST AUSTELL	Map 2 SX05

Premier Collection

Anchorage House

★★★★★ 〓 GUEST ACCOMMODATION

tel: 01726 814071 **Nettles Corner, Tregrehan Mills PL25 3RH**
email: info@anchoragehouse.co.uk **web:** www.anchoragehouse.co.uk
dir: 2 m E of town centre off A390, opposite St Austell Garden Centre

Georgian-style Anchorage House is set in an acre of carefully landscaped gardens at the end of a private lane. Guests are met upon arrival with afternoon tea, often served on the patio. The luxurious and elegant bedrooms are equipped to the highest standard with sumptuous beds, and include satellite TV, fresh fruit, magazines, bottled water and chocolates. Guests also have use of the indoor heated pool, hot tub and gym. The house is a short distance from many of Cornwall's major tourist attractions.

Rooms 4 en suite 1 annexe en suite (1 GF) S £70-£80; D £110-£145*
Facilities STV FTV DVD Lounge tea/coffee WiFi ✆ Gym ⚓ Hot tub
Extras Speciality toiletries **Parking** 6 **Notes** ✪ No Children 16yrs Closed Dec-Feb

Premier Collection

Lower Barn

★★★★★ 〓 GUEST ACCOMMODATION

tel: 01726 844881 & 07825 270962 **Bosue, St Ewe PL26 6ET**
email: janie@lowerbarns.co.uk **web:** www.lowerbarns.co.uk
dir: 3.5m SW of St Austell. Off B3273 at x-rds signed Lost Gardens of Heligan, Lower Barn signed 1m on right

Nestled in a corner of south Cornwall, close to the sea and within walking distance of the Lost Gardens of Heligan and the South West Coast Path, Lower Barn is a luxury boutique retreat, ideal for couples who crave a bit of romance. Warm colours throughout create a Mediterranean feel, and staff offer informal and genuine hospitality. Bedrooms have a host of extras. Breakfast is served around a large table or on the patio deck overlooking the garden, which has a hot tub.

Rooms 6 en suite (1 fmly) (1 GF) S £75-£85; D £100-£160* **Facilities** FTV DVD tea/coffee Dinner available WiFi Sauna ⚓ Hot tub Spa treatments Sauna in Nook suite **Parking** 7 **Notes** LB ✪ Closed Jan Civ Wed 20

The Gables

★★★★ 〓 GUEST ACCOMMODATION

tel: 01726 72638 & 07971 821854 **1 Edgcumbe Rd PL25 5DU**
email: barbara@gablesguesthousebnb.co.uk **web:** www.gablesguesthousebnb.co.uk

A warm welcome is assured at The Gables. The house offers a range of bedrooms with en suite or private facilities. A superb location for those wishing to visit The Eden Project, The Lost Gardens of Heligan and many other Cornish destinations. Memorable breakfasts are served in the conservatory or delightful gardens.

Rooms 4 rms (2 en suite) (2 pri facs) **Facilities** FTV Lounge tea/coffee WiFi **Extras** Home-made biscuits - complimentary **Parking** 4 **Notes** ✪ No Children 12yrs RS Xmas wk

Langdale House

★★★★ BED AND BREAKFAST

tel: 01726 71404 & 07764 531050 **1A Southbourne Rd PL25 4RU**
email: stay@langdalehousecornwall.co.uk **web:** www.langdalehousecornwall.co.uk
dir: On A390 St Austell bypass, 0.5m S of town centre

Handy for the town centre, this is an ideal choice for both business and leisure guests and a great place to relax, unwind and re-charge the batteries. Quality and comfort levels are high throughout, both in the elegant bedrooms and the impressive bathrooms. The welcome is warm and friendly with every effort to ensure an enjoyable and rewarding stay. Breakfast is served in the attractive dining room, with a good range of dishes offered. Super-fast WiFi is provided.

Rooms 3 en suite **Facilities** FTV tea/coffee WiFi ⚓ **Extras** Speciality toiletries **Parking** 3 **Notes** ✪ No Children 5yrs

Ancient Shipbrokers

★★★★ BED AND BREAKFAST

tel: 01726 843370 **1 Higher West End, Pentewan PL26 6BY**
email: shipbrokers1@btinternet.com **web:** www.pentewanbedandbreakfast.com
dir: From St Austell on B3273, at Mill Garage turn left signed Pentewan, over bridge bear right & pass Ocean Sports. Next left into private road, Higher West End

The Ancient Shipbrokers overlooks Pentewan harbour and one of the best sandy beaches in Cornwall. The house has bags of history and character, and has been decorated tastefully and sympathetically. A large area of the garden is given over to wild flowers and trees, and there is also a kitchen garden. The dining room enjoys a wonderful view out across the harbour and the beach, and is the ideal venue for home-cooked breakfasts. Private parking is available on-site or in the village car park. Help with luggage and free WiFi is provided. There is also space for storing bicycles, surf boards and wetsuits. Self-catering is available.

Rooms 3 en suite (1 fmly) **Facilities** FTV DVD tea/coffee WiFi ⚓ **Parking** 3 **Notes** LB ✪ Closed 20 Dec-5 Jan

Visit shop.theAA.com

for a wide variety of AA publications, including Walking books, Lifestyle Guides, Atlases, and International Travel Guides

ST AUSTELL *continued*

Polgreen Farm *(SX008503)*

★★★★ FARMHOUSE

tel: 01726 75151 **London Apprentice PL26 7AP**
email: polgreen.farm@btinternet.com **web:** www.polgreenfarm.co.uk
dir: *1.5m S of St Austell. Exit B3273, left on entering London Apprentice & signed*

Guests regularly return for the friendly welcome at this peaceful establishment located just south of St Austell. The spacious and well-equipped bedrooms are divided between the main house and an adjoining property, and each building has a comfortable lounge. Breakfast is served in a pleasant conservatory overlooking the garden.

Rooms 2 rms (1 en suite) (1 pri facs) 4 annexe en suite (1 fmly) (1 GF) S £35-£45; D £66-£74 **Facilities** FTV Lounge TVL tea/coffee WiFi **Parking** 8 **Notes** LB ⊗ ⊛ 64 acres livestock

The Bugle Inn

★★★ INN

tel: 01726 850307 **57 Fore St, Bugle PL26 8PD**
email: thebugleinn@gmail.com **web:** www.bugleinn.co.uk
dir: *A30 onto A391. In Bugle at x-rds*

The Bugle Inn is a warm and inviting establishment, with its origins dating back to the 17th century. It's situated in the heart of the Cornish countryside, between Bodmin and St Austell, handy for The Eden Project. Traditional pub food and drink are served in a characterful building with a lovely open fire. Bedrooms are attractive with a cosy feel.

Rooms 5 en suite (1 fmly) **Facilities** FTV tea/coffee Dinner available Direct Dial WiFi Pool table

---

ST BURYAN **Map 2 SW42**

Tregurnow Farm *(SW444242)*

★★★★ ⬭ FARMHOUSE

tel: 01736 810255 **TR19 6BL**
email: tregurnow@lamorna.biz **web:** www.lamorna.biz
dir: *From Newlyn take B3315, after 4m black & white sign on left just past turn for Lamorna Cove*

Tucked away near St Buryan, Tregurnow Farm offers traditional, quality farmhouse bed and breakfast and self-catering facilities. Peace and quiet, stunning views and hearty breakfasts are hallmarks of a stay here. Close to Mousehole, Minack Theatre and Penzance, this is a good base for touring the far south-west of the county.

Rooms 3 en suite S £60-£67.50; D £80-£95* **Facilities** FTV Lounge TVL WiFi Pool table ⬭ **Extras** Fridge **Parking** 10 **Notes** ⊗ No Children 5yrs Closed Xmas 100 acres mixed

---

ST IVES **Map 2 SW54**

Downsfield Bed and Breakfast

★★★★ GUEST ACCOMMODATION

tel: 01736 796659 **Longstone Hill TR26 2LJ**
email: sharonp27@hotmail.com **web:** www.downsfieldbnb.co.uk
dir: *On main road between Carbis Bay & St Ives*

A warm welcome awaits you at Downsfield from the lovely hosts Sharon and Phil. Decorated and furnished to an exceptionally high standard this accommodation will feel like a home from home. There is private parking, which is invaluable in St Ives during the summer. Rooms are spacious and well equipped with very good levels of comfort. Within walking distance of St Ives with its many unique shops and restaurants. A great location for exploring the region and stunning coastal attractions.

Rooms 5 en suite (2 fmly) (1 GF) **Facilities** FTV TVL tea/coffee WiFi ⬭ **Extras** Speciality toiletries, gowns, chocolate **Parking** 5 **Notes** ⊗ No Children 4yrs

Lamorna Lodge

★★★★ ⬭ GUEST ACCOMMODATION

tel: 01736 795967 & 07837 638620 **Boskerris Rd, Carbis Bay TR26 2NG**
email: lamorna@tr26.wanadoo.co.uk **web:** www.lamorna.co.uk
dir: *A30 onto A3074, right after playground in Carbis Bay, establishment 200yds on right*

A warm welcome is assured at Lamorna Lodge, which is just a short walk from Carbis Bay beach. Wonderful views over St Ives Bay to Godrevy Lighthouse can be enjoyed from the spacious lounge, a view also shared by some of the stylish bedrooms. Breakfast makes great use of local Cornish produce and is served in the elegant surroundings of the dining room. The stylish terrace enjoys lovely sea views.

Rooms 9 en suite (2 fmly) (2 GF) **Facilities** FTV Lounge tea/coffee WiFi ⬭ **Conf** Max 18 Thtr 18 Class 18 Board 18 **Parking** 9 **Notes** ⊗ Closed 5 Nov-10 Mar

The Nook

★★★★ GUEST ACCOMMODATION

tel: 01736 795913 **Ayr TR26 1EQ**
email: info@nookstives.co.uk **web:** www.nookstives.co.uk
dir: *A30 to St Ives left at NatWest, right at rdbt & left at top of hill*

The Nook is an ideal base for exploring Cornwall's spectacular coastline, gardens and countryside. The comfortable bedrooms are furnished in a contemporary style and are equipped with numerous facilities. There is a wide variety on offer at breakfast, from full English or continental, to scrambled eggs with smoked salmon.

Rooms 11 en suite (1 fmly) (1 GF) **Facilities** FTV DVD TVL tea/coffee WiFi **Parking** 10 **Notes** ⊗

CORNWALL & ISLES OF SCILLY 69 ENGLAND

The Rookery

★★★★ GUEST ACCOMMODATION

tel: 01736 799401 **8 The Terrace TR26 2BL**
email: therookerystives@hotmail.com **web:** www.rookerystives.com
dir: A3074 through Carbis Bay, right fork at Porthminster Hotel, The Rookery 500yds on left

Aptly named, The Rookery stands in an elevated position overlooking the town and sandy beach. The attractive bedrooms include one which is on the ground floor and a luxurious suite, all of which are well equipped and offer a good level of comfort. Breakfast is served in the first-floor dining room at separate tables.

Rooms 7 en suite (2 fmly) (1 GF) **Facilities** FTV tea/coffee WiFi ⚓ **Parking** 7 **Notes** ⊗ No Children 7yrs

Thurlestone Guest House

★★★★ GUEST ACCOMMODATION

tel: 01736 796369 **St Ives Rd, Carbis Bay TR26 2RT**
email: thurlestoneguesthouse@yahoo.co.uk **web:** www.thurlestoneguesthouse.co.uk
dir: A3074 to Carbis Bay, pass convenience store on left, 0.25m on left next to Carbis Bay Holidays Office

This granite former chapel, built in 1843, now offers stylish, comfortable accommodation. The welcoming proprietors provide a relaxed environment, and many guests return regularly. The property offers a cosy lounge bar and well-equipped bedrooms, some with sea views.

Rooms 6 en suite (1 fmly) (1 GF) D £75-£110 **Facilities** STV FTV DVD TVL tea/coffee Licensed WiFi ⚓ **Extras** Safe **Parking** 5 **Notes** LB ⊗ Closed Nov-Mar

Chy Conyn

★★★★ BED AND BREAKFAST

tel: 01736 798068 **8 Ayr Ter TR26 1ED**
email: chyconyn@hotmail.co.uk **web:** www.chyconyn.co.uk

Located in a pleasant residential area, just above the town, Chy Conyn offers accommodation in a range of sizes. All rooms come with plenty of useful extras. Breakfast is served in the relaxing and well-presented dining room. WiFi is available, and there is a car park to the rear of the property.

Rooms 4 rms (3 en suite) (1 pri facs) (1 fmly) **Facilities** FTV DVD tea/coffee WiFi **Parking** 3 **Notes** ⊗ No Children 3yrs Closed Nov-28 Dec

Coombe Farmhouse

★★★★ BED AND BREAKFAST

tel: 01736 740843 **TR27 6NW**
email: coombefarmhouse@aol.com **web:** www.coombefarmhouse.com
dir: 1.5m W of Lelant. Exit A3074 to Lelant Downs

Built of sturdy granite, this early 19th-century farmhouse is in a delightful location tucked away at the southern foot of Trencrom Hill, yet convenient for St Ives. The comfortable bedrooms are attractively decorated. There is a conservatory lounge, and substantial breakfasts, featuring farm-fresh eggs, are served in the dining room overlooking the garden.

Rooms 3 rms (2 en suite) (1 pri facs) S £50; D £80-£86* **Facilities** FTV Lounge TV2B tea/coffee WiFi **Extras** Bottled water - complimentary **Parking** 3 **Notes** ⊗ No Children 16yrs Closed Dec 📧

The Mustard Tree

★★★★ GUEST HOUSE

tel: 01736 795677 & 07840 072323 **Sea View Meadows, St Ives Rd, Carbis Bay TR26 2JX**
email: enquiries@mustard-tree.co.uk **web:** www.mustard-tree.co.uk
dir: A3074 to Carbis Bay, The Mustard Tree on right opposite Methodist church

Set in delightful gardens and with sea views, this attractive house is just a short drive from the centre of St Ives, and the coastal path that leads from Carbis Bay to St Ives. The pleasant bedrooms are very comfortable and have many extras. A splendid choice is offered at breakfast, with vegetarian and continental options.

Rooms 9 rms (8 en suite) (1 pri facs) (1 fmly) (4 GF) S £36-£46; D £72-£99* **Facilities** FTV DVD TVL tea/coffee WiFi ⚓ **Extras** Guest PC available, fridge **Conf** Max 20 **Parking** 9 **Notes** ⊗

The Old Count House

★★★★ GUEST HOUSE

tel: 01736 795369 & 07853 844777 **1 Trenwith Square TR26 1DQ**
email: counthouse@btconnect.com **web:** www.theoldcounthouse-stives.co.uk
dir: Follow signs to St Ives, house between leisure centre & school

Situated in a quiet residential area with on-site parking, The Old Count House is a granite building, where Victorian mine workers collected their wages. Guests are assured of a warm welcome and an extensive choice at breakfast. Bedrooms vary in size, with all rooms being well equipped. The town centre, with all its restaurants, is only a five-minute walk away.

Rooms 10 rms (9 en suite) (1 pri facs) (2 GF) S £52-£58; D £82-£88* **Facilities** FTV DVD Lounge TVL tea/coffee WiFi Sauna ⚓ Excercise bike Massage chair **Parking** 9 **Notes** ⊗ No Children Closed Nov & 20-29 Dec

Old Vicarage

★★★★ GUEST HOUSE

tel: 01736 796124 **Parc-an-Creet TR26 2ES**
email: stay@oldvicarage.com **web:** www.oldvicarage.com
dir: From A3074 in town centre take B3306, 0.5m right into Parc-an-Creet

This former Victorian rectory stands in secluded gardens in a quiet part of St Ives and is convenient for the seaside, town and Tate St Ives. The bedrooms are enhanced by modern facilities. A good choice of local produce is offered at breakfast, plus home-made yogurt and preserves.

Rooms 6 en suite (4 fmly) S £53-£72; D £76-£104* **Facilities** FTV TVL tea/coffee Licensed WiFi **Parking** 12 **Notes** LB ⊗ Closed Dec-Jan Civ Wed 35

The Regent

★★★★ GUEST ACCOMMODATION

tel: 01736 796195 **Fernlea Ter TR26 2BH**
email: keith@regenthotel.com **web:** www.regenthotel.com
dir: In town centre, near bus & railway station

This popular and attractive property stands on an elevated position convenient for the town centre and seafront. The Regent has well-equipped bedrooms, some with spectacular sea vistas, and the comfortable lounge also has great views. The breakfast choices, including vegetarian, are excellent.

Rooms 10 rms (8 en suite) (1 fmly) S £50-£95; D £95-£126* **Facilities** Lounge TVL tea/coffee WiFi ⚓ **Parking** 12 **Notes** LB ⊗ No Children 16yrs

ST IVES *continued*

The Sloop Inn

★★★ INN

tel: 01736 796584 **The Wharf TR26 1LP**
email: sloopinn@btinternet.com **web:** www.sloop-inn.co.uk
dir: *On St Ives harbour by middle slipway*

This attractive, historic inn has an imposing position on the harbour. Each of the guest rooms has a nautical name, many enjoy pleasant views, and all have impressive modern facilities. A good choice of dishes is offered at lunch and dinner in the atmospheric restaurant-bar.

Rooms 22 en suite (6 fmly) (5 GF) S £85.50; D £104-£119* **Facilities** FTV tea/coffee Dinner available WiFi 🔒 **Parking** 8 **Notes** LB No coaches

ST KEVERNE	Map 2 SW72

Gallen-Treath Guest House

★★★ 🍴 GUEST HOUSE

tel: 01326 280400 & 07579 967836 **Porthallow TR12 6PL**
email: gallentreath@btclick.com **web:** www.gallen-treath.com
dir: *1.5m SE of St Keverne in Porthallow*

Gallen-Treath Guest House has super views over the countryside and sea from its elevated position above Porthallow. Bedrooms are individually decorated and feature many personal touches. Guests can relax in the large, comfortable lounge complete with balcony. Hearty breakfasts and dinners (by arrangement) are served in the bright dining room.

Rooms 5 en suite (1 fmly) (1 GF) S £33-£40; D £66-£80* **Facilities** FTV TVL tea/coffee Dinner available Licensed WiFi **Parking** 6

ST KEW	Map 2 SX07

Tregellist Farm

★★★★ BED AND BREAKFAST

tel: 01208 880537 & 07970 559637 **Tregellist PL30 3HG**
email: mail@tregellistfarm.co.uk **web:** www.tregellistfarm.co.uk
dir: *On B3314 between Pendoggett & St Endellion, take turn brown signed to St Kew & Tregellist Farm*

Tregellist Farm is located in beautiful countryside close to Port Isaac, and convenient for Lanhydrock, Pencarrow, The Lost Gardens of Heligan, Padstow and The Eden Project. All bedrooms are en suite, with flat-screen TVs, hospitality trays with fresh milk daily. Served at separate tables in the dining room, breakfast is sourced locally and includes fresh eggs from the farm.

Rooms 2 en suite 2 annexe en suite (1 fmly) (2 GF) **Facilities** FTV DVD TVL tea/coffee WiFi 🔒 **Parking** 6 **Notes** ⊗ Closed Xmas & New Year

ST MARY'S (ISLES OF SCILLY)	Map 2 SV91

Crebinick House

★★★★ GUEST HOUSE

tel: 01720 422968 **Church St TR21 0JT**
email: aa@crebinick.co.uk **web:** www.crebinick.co.uk
dir: *House 500yds from quay through Hugh Town; (airport bus to house)*

Many guests return time and again to this friendly, family-run house close to the town centre and the seafront. The granite-built property dates from 1760 and has smart, well-equipped bedrooms; two are on the ground floor. There is a quiet lounge for relaxing.

Rooms 4 en suite (2 GF) **Facilities** FTV Lounge tea/coffee WiFi **Notes** LB ⊗ No Children 10yrs Closed Nov-Mar

ST MAWGAN	Map 2 SW86

The Falcon Inn

★★★★ INN

tel: 01637 860225 **TR8 4EP**
email: thefalconinnstmawgan@gmail.com **web:** www.thefalconinnstmawgan.co.uk
dir: *A30 towards Newquay airport, follow signs for St Mawgan. Turn right, signed, Falcon Inn at bottom of hill*

The Falcon is a traditional village pub offering good food and drink along with well-presented and comfortable en suite bedrooms. The owners and friendly staff create a pleasant atmosphere. Its quiet location, along with plenty of off-street parking, make this a popular venue. Please note that the pub is closed 3-6pm; access to the accommodation will be arranged for these times.

Rooms 3 en suite **Facilities** FTV tea/coffee Dinner available Direct Dial WiFi ⛹ 18 🔒 **Conf** Thtr 30 Class 20 Board 20 **Parking** 20

ST MELLION	Map 3 SX36

Premier Collection

Pentillie Castle & Estate

★★★★★ 🍴 GUEST ACCOMMODATION

tel: 01579 350044 **Paynters Cross PL12 6QD**
email: contact@pentillie.co.uk **web:** www.pentillie.co.uk
dir: *From A38 Saltash onto A388 to Callington & St Mellion. After 3.1m right to Cargreen & Landulph. 100yds on left*

Pentillie Castle and Estate has a great deal to offer. For a start, it's in a peaceful location in the heart of the Tamar Valley on the Cornwall and Devon border. It has established gardens, formal lawns and breath-taking views stretching over 2,000 acres of land. The property has been lovingly renovated to its former glory; the comfortable and well equipped rooms are warm and inviting. Supper and breakfast are served in the elegant dining room with views of the gardens. The beautifully designed lounge and drawing room are the perfect setting to read the paper or enjoy a glass of wine from the honesty bar.

Rooms 9 en suite (1 GF) D £125-£250* **Facilities** FTV DVD Lounge TVL tea/coffee Dinner available Licensed WiFi ⛹ 🎣 ⛹ 36 Pool table 🔒 **Extras** Speciality toiletries, robes, slippers, shortbread **Conf** Max 30 Thtr 30 Class 24 Board 24 **Parking** 100 **Notes** LB Civ Wed 120

SALTASH	Map 3 SX45

Smeaton Farm *(SX387634)*

★★★★ 🍴 🚜 FARMHOUSE

tel: 01579 351833 & 07813 027657 **PL12 6RZ**
email: info@smeatonfarm.co.uk **web:** www.smeatonfarm.co.uk
dir: *1m N of Hatt & 1m S of St Mellion just off A388*

This elegant Georgian farmhouse is surrounded by 450 acres of rolling Cornish farmland, providing a wonderfully peaceful place to stay. Home to the Jones family, the atmosphere is relaxed and hospitable, with every effort made to ensure that guests have a comfortable and rewarding break. Bedrooms are spacious, light and airy. Enjoyable dinners often feature home-reared meats, and the sausages at breakfast come highly recommended.

Rooms 3 en suite (1 fmly) S £55-£80; D £75-£95* **Facilities** FTV DVD Lounge TVL tea/coffee Dinner available Licensed WiFi ⛹ 18 Riding 🔒 Cornish maze Guided farm tours **Extras** Speciality toiletries, snacks, fruit **Conf** Max 10 Board 10 **Parking** 8 **Notes** LB ⊗ 450 acres arable/beef/sheep

Hay Lake Farm Bed & Breakfast

★★★★ BED AND BREAKFAST

tel: 01752 851209 & 07989 426306 **Landrake PL12 5AE**
email: ianbiffen@hotmail.co.uk **web:** www.haylakefarm.co.uk
dir: *A38 at Landrake turn into West Ln. 0.75m on left before x-rds*

This modern, comfortable bed and breakfast offers spacious and well-equipped en suite accommodation. Hay Lake Farm is ideal for those exploring both north and south coasts of Cornwall, and is within easy reach of many National Trust properties as well as The Eden Project. Stables are available.

Rooms 3 en suite (2 fmly) (1 GF) S £50; D £85 **Facilities** FTV DVD tea/coffee WiFi &
Extras Speciality toiletries - complimentary **Parking** 6

Crooked Inn

★★★★ INN

tel: 01752 848177 **Stoketon Cross, Trematon PL12 4RZ**
email: info@crooked-inn.co.uk **web:** www.crooked-inn.co.uk
dir: *1.5m NW of Saltash. A38 W from Saltash, 2nd left to Trematon, sharp right*

The friendly animals that freely roam the courtyard add to the relaxed country style of this delightful inn. The spacious bedrooms are well equipped, and freshly cooked dinners are available in the bar and conservatory. Breakfast is served in the cottage-style dining room.

Rooms 15 annexe en suite (5 fmly) (7 GF) **Facilities** FTV tea/coffee Dinner available WiFi ⚡ **Extras** Speciality toiletries, fresh milk **Conf** Max 60 **Parking** 45
Notes Closed 25 Dec

ISLES OF SCILLY
See St Mary's & Tresco

TORPOINT   Map 3 SX45

The Devon and Cornwall

★★★ INN

tel: 01752 822320 **1 West St, Millbrook PL10 1AA**
email: thedevonandcornwall@hotmail.co.uk **web:** www.thedevonandcornwall.co.uk
dir: *From Torpoint Ferry onto A374, follow signs for Antony. Turn left into village & follow road to T-junct. Turn left to Millbrook, follow road*

This cosy village inn, popular with the locals, offers a great location for those wishing to explore Devon and the south Cornwall coastline. All bedrooms are en suite, comfortable and modern. Meals are served daily.

Rooms 5 en suite (2 fmly) S £45-£55; D £70-£80* **Facilities** FTV tea/coffee Dinner available WiFi & **Notes** LB

TRESCO (ISLES OF SCILLY)   Map 2 SV81

New Inn

★★★★ ⊛ INN

tel: 01720 422849 & 423006 **TR24 0QQ**
email: contactus@tresco.co.uk **web:** www.tresco.co.uk
dir: *By New Grimsby Quay*

This friendly, popular inn is located at the island's centre point and offers bright, attractive and well-equipped bedrooms, many with splendid sea views. Guests have an extensive choice from the menu at both lunch and dinner and can also choose where they take their meals – either in the airy bistro-style Pavilion, the popular bar which serves real ales, or the elegant restaurant. A heated outdoor pool is also available.

Rooms 16 en suite (2 fmly) (2 GF) **Facilities** FTV DVD Lounge tea/coffee Dinner available Direct Dial WiFi ⚡ ⚓ Fishing Pool table Use of local leisure spa
Extras Speciality toiletries **Notes** LB No coaches

TRURO
Map 2 SW84

Bodrean Manor Farm *(SW851480)*

★★★★ FARMHOUSE

tel: 07970 955857 **Trispen TR4 9AG**
email: bodrean@hotmail.co.uk **web:** www.bodreanmanorfarm.co.uk
dir: *3m NE of Truro. A30 onto A39 towards Truro, left after Trispen signed Frogmore & Trehane, farm drive 100yds*

This friendly farmhouse is located in peaceful countryside, convenient for Truro or as a touring base. It has all the charm of an historic house but is styled and fitted with modern facilities. Bedrooms are thoughtfully and extensively equipped, and the bathrooms are well provisioned with soft towels and a host of toiletries. The home-cooked breakfast is served around a large, communal table in the smartly appointed dining room. Storage for motorbikes and cycles is available.

Rooms 3 rms (2 en suite) (1 pri facs) (1 fmly) **Facilities** FTV TVL tea/coffee WiFi **Parking** 6 **Notes** ⊗ ⊜ 220 acres mixed

Bissick Old Mill

★★★★ GUEST HOUSE

tel: 01726 882557 **Ladock TR2 4PG**
email: enquiries@bissickoldmill.plus.com **web:** www.bissickoldmill.co.uk
dir: *6m NE of Truro. Exit B3275 in Ladock centre by Falmouth Arms pub*

This charming family-run guest house in a former mill dates back some 300 years. Low ceilings, beams, stone walls and an impressive fireplace all contribute to its character. Equally inviting is the hospitality extended to guests, who are instantly made welcome. The high-spec bedrooms are all en suite and feature Egyptian cotton sheets along with many extras. The breakfast is a memorable aspect of any stay with the menu offering a range of freshly prepared hot dishes.

Rooms 3 en suite 1 annexe en suite (1 fmly) (1 GF) **Facilities** FTV DVD TVL tea/coffee Direct Dial WiFi **Parking** 6 **Notes** LB ⊗

Merchant House

★★★★ GUEST ACCOMMODATION

tel: 01872 272450 **49 Falmouth Rd TR1 2HL**
email: reception@merchant-house.co.uk **web:** www.merchant-house.co.uk
dir: *A39 Truro, on approaching centre proceed across 1st & 2nd rdbts onto bypass. At top of hill turn right at twin mini rdbt into Falmouth Rd. 100mtrs on right*

Merchant House is just a short stroll from the city centre. A range of bedrooms are offered, some of which have benefited from the ongoing refurbishment programme, all offering good levels of comfort. Public areas are smartly appointed with period features retained where possible. The bar provides an engaging venue for a refreshing glass of something, perhaps accompanied by a tasty dish from the bar menu, and the friendly team are flexible and helpful.

Rooms 27 en suite (3 fmly) (4 GF) **Facilities** FTV TVL tea/coffee Direct Dial Licensed WiFi ⚓ Drying room Launderette **Conf** Max 64 Thtr 64 Class 48 Board 36 **Parking** 30 **Notes** Closed 24-27 Dec

Oxturn House

★★★★ ⬙ BED AND BREAKFAST

tel: 01726 884348 **Ladock TR2 4NQ**
email: oxturnhouse@hotmail.com **web:** www.oxturnhouse.co.uk
dir: *6m NE of Truro. B3275 to Ladock, take lane opposite Falmouth Arms, up hill 200yds, 1st right after end 30mph sign, Oxturn on right*

A friendly welcome is assured at Oxturn House, a large family house, set slightly above the village and close to a pub and several dining venues. Bedrooms are spacious and a pleasant lounge is available. In summer you can enjoy the country views from the patio. Hearty breakfasts are served in the dining room.

Rooms 2 rms (1 en suite) (1 pri facs) **Facilities** FTV TVL tea/coffee WiFi **Parking** 4 **Notes** ⊗ No Children 12yrs Closed Nov-Feb ⊜

Donnington Guest House

★★★ GUEST ACCOMMODATION

tel: 01872 222552 & 07787 555475 **43 Treyew Rd TR1 2BY**
email: info@donnington-guesthouse.co.uk **web:** www.donnington-guesthouse.co.uk

A well located property, just 12 minutes' walk from the city centre. It is actually two houses operating as one, with breakfast being taken in the breakfast room of one of them. Well-appointed bedrooms, a friendly host and good off-road parking make this a very popular venue.

Rooms 14 rms (12 en suite) (2 pri facs) (2 fmly) (2 GF) **Facilities** FTV DVD tea/coffee ⚵ 18 ⚓ **Extras** Fridge **Parking** 11 **Notes** ⊜

The Laurels

★★★ BED AND BREAKFAST

tel: 07794 472171 **Penwethers TR3 6EA**
email: annie.toms@hotmail.com **web:** www.thelaurelsbedandbreakfast.com
dir: *From A39 onto A390 (Tregolls Rd), through 3 rdbts. Take exit towards Redruth (Treyew Rd) next left to Penwethers*

The Laurels is a traditional bed and breakfast operation offering comfortable accommodation in a home-from-home environment. It is ideally located in a quiet location, yet is just minutes from the cathedral city of Truro. Off-road parking is available.

Rooms 3 rms (1 en suite) (1 pri facs) (2 fmly) S £45-£50; D £65-£70* **Facilities** FTV Lounge TV2B tea/coffee WiFi ⚓ **Extras** Chocolates **Parking** 3 **Notes** ⊗ ⊜

Resparveth Farm *(SW914499)*

★★★ FARMHOUSE

tel: 01726 882382 & 07929 234206 **Grampound Rd TR2 4EF**
email: resparveth.farm@gmail.com **web:** www.resparvethfarmbnb.co.uk
dir: *A30 exit signed Fraddon/Grampound Road (B3275). Continue on A3058, through Grampound Road village, turn right at B&B sign*

The young owners of this traditional farmhouse bed and breakfast do all they can to make a stay as comfortable as possible. This is a handy location for St Austell, The Eden Project and Truro, offering comfortable rooms and freshly cooked breakfasts at one large table in the breakfast room featuring an original Cornish range.

Rooms 3 en suite S £50-£60; D £60-£69 **Facilities** FTV DVD tea/coffee WiFi ⚶ ⚓ Drying room Feeding of animals Farm experience **Parking** 4 **Notes** LB ⊗ 60 acres beef/sheep/bees/pigs/arable

Elerkey Guest House

★★★★ GUEST HOUSE

tel: 01872 501261 & 501160 **Elerkey House TR2 5QA**
email: anne@elerkeyguesthouse.co.uk **web:** www.elerkeyguesthouse.co.uk
dir: *In village, 1st left after church & water gardens*

This peaceful home is surrounded by attractive gardens in a tranquil village. The proprietors and their family provide exemplary hospitality and many guests return time and again. The pleasantly appointed bedrooms have many considerate extras.

Rooms 4 en suite (1 fmly) S £65-£90; D £70-£90 **Facilities** FTV DVD Lounge tea/coffee Direct Dial WiFi 🛜 Art gallery & gift shop **Extras** Mineral water **Parking** 5 **Notes** LB ⊗ Closed Xmas-New Year

Premier Collection

Wadebridge Bed and Breakfast

★★★★★ BED AND BREAKFAST

tel: 01208 816837 & 07740 255092 **Orchard House, Elmsleigh Rd PL27 7HA**
email: info@wadebridgebedandbreakfast.net
web: www.wadebridgebedandbreakfast.net
dir: *From Bodmin A389 into Wadebridge. Pass Trelawney Garden Centre on right, continue to rdbt. Exit onto A39. At next rdbt left into West Hill. After phone box on left, take next left into Elmsleigh Rd, 1st house on left*

This contemporary house is just a short walk from the town centre and provides an ideal base from which to explore the area. Bedrooms offer impressive levels of comfort and quality, and one has a balcony with lovely views over the town and countryside. Bathrooms offer all the expected mod cons with under floor heating, invigorating showers and fluffy towels. Generous and tasty breakfasts are served in the dining room with a garden patio available for alfresco dining. Secure storage is available for bikes and surf boards.

Rooms 3 en suite S £75-£95; D £80-£100 **Facilities** FTV DVD TVL tea/coffee WiFi 🛜 **Extras** Bottled water, fresh milk, speciality toiletries **Parking** 3 **Notes** LB ⊗ No Children Closed Jan-Feb

Alston House

★★★★ 🍴 RESTAURANT WITH ROOMS

tel: 01434 382200 **Townfoot CA9 3RN**
email: alstonhouse@fsmail.net **web:** www.alstonhouse.co.uk
dir: *On A686 opposite Spar garage*

Located at the foot of the town, this family-owned restaurant with rooms provides well-equipped, stylish and comfortable accommodation. The kitchen serves both modern and traditional dishes with flair and creativity. Alston House runs a café during the day, serving light meals and afternoon teas.

Rooms 7 en suite (3 fmly) **Facilities** DVD tea/coffee Dinner available WiFi 🎣 9 Fishing **Conf** Max 70 Thtr 70 Class 30 Board 30 **Parking** 20 **Notes** Civ Wed

Premier Collection

Nanny Brow

★★★★★ GUEST ACCOMMODATION

tel: 015394 33232 & 07746 103008 **Clappersgate LA22 9NF**
email: unwind@nannybrow.co.uk **web:** www.nannybrow.co.uk
dir: *M6 junct 36 onto A590 & A591 through Windermere. At lights bear left onto A593, left again at rugby pitch & left over bridge. Through Clappersgate, 0.5m on right*

Nanny Brow provides high quality throughout. Each room is thoughtfully decorated with contemporary furnishings, antique furniture, and original arts and crafts. The property is situated in Clappersgate, close to Ambleside, standing high above the road overlooking the beautiful Langdale Valley. A drink from the bar menu can be enjoyed in the quiet guest lounge where you will find plenty of information regarding local walks.

Rooms 12 en suite 2 annexe en suite (2 GF) S £115-£265; D £130-£280* **Facilities** FTV DVD Lounge tea/coffee Licensed WiFi 🛜 **Extras** Robes, champagne, chocolates, flowers - chargeable **Conf** Max 26 Thtr 26 Class 12 Board 12 **Parking** 15 **Notes** LB ⊗ No Children 12yrs Civ Wed 32

Find out more about the AA Friendliest B&B of the Year on page 17

AMBLESIDE *continued*

Riverside

★★★★ ⌚ GUEST HOUSE

tel: 015394 32395 & 32440 **Under Loughrigg LA22 9LJ**
email: info@riverside-at-ambleside.co.uk **web:** www.riverside-at-ambleside.co.uk
dir: *A593 from Ambleside to Coniston, over stone bridge, right into Under Loughrigg Ln, Riverside 150yds left*

Riverside is a Victorian house, whose owners offer a most friendly welcome. It is situated on a quiet lane by the River Rothay, below Loughrigg Fell. Bedrooms all have lovely views, are very comfortable and stylishly furnished, and feature many thoughtful extras. A log-burning stove warms the lounge in winter. Guests can use the garden which has seating for the morning and evening sun. An award-winning hearty Lakeland breakfast is a highlight of any stay and features local produce along with home baking and preserves.

Rooms 6 en suite D £114-£134 **Facilities** FTV DVD iPod docking station TVL tea/coffee Licensed WiFi ⌀ **Parking** 6 **Notes** ⊗ No Children 10yrs Closed 13 Dec-22 Jan

Innkeeper's Lodge Ambleside, Lake District

★★★★ INN

tel: 08451 551551 *(Calls cost 2p per minute plus your phone company's access charge)*
The White Lion, Market Place LA22 9DB
email: info@innkeeperslodge.com **web:** www.innkeeperslodge.com

Charming 18th-century inn situated in the heart of Ambleside close to Windermere and within easy reach of the M6. The modern, well equipped bedrooms are very well appointed with a range of modern facilities. Public areas include a large open-plan lounge bar with a roaring open fire and a selection of seating options; dinner and full English breakfast are available in the smart dining room.

Rooms 7 en suite (4 fmly) **Facilities** FTV tea/coffee Dinner available WiFi **Conf** Max 20 **Parking** 7 **Notes** ⊗

Wanslea Guest House

★★★★ GUEST HOUSE

tel: 015394 33884 **Low Fold, Lake Rd LA22 0DN**
email: information@wanslea.co.uk **web:** www.wanslea.co.uk
dir: *On S side of town, opposite garden centre*

Located between town centre and lakeside pier, this Victorian house provides a range of thoughtfully furnished bedrooms, some of which are individually themed and equipped with spa baths. Comprehensive breakfasts are served in the spacious dining room and a cosy lounge is available.

Rooms 10 en suite (1 fmly) **Facilities** FTV Lounge TV8B tea/coffee WiFi ⌀ **Notes** ⊗ No Children 12yrs Closed 23-26 Dec

The Old Vicarage

★★★★ A GUEST ACCOMMODATION

tel: 015394 33364 **Vicarage Rd LA22 9DH**
email: info@oldvicarageambleside.co.uk **web:** www.oldvicarageambleside.co.uk
dir: *In town centre. Exit Compston Rd left into Vicarage Rd*

This charming early Victorian house stands in quiet landscaped grounds with private parking, close to the town centre. Bedrooms are mostly spacious, some having four-posters and spa baths, and all have video players, fridges and CD players. There also is a splendid pool, sauna and a hot tub.

Rooms 15 en suite (4 fmly) (2 GF) **Facilities** FTV DVD Lounge tea/coffee WiFi ⌀ ⌀ Riding Sauna Pool table ⌀ Hot tub **Extras** Mini-fridge **Parking** 17 **Notes** Closed 23-28 Dec

■ BOOT   **Map 18 NY10**

Brook House Inn

★★★★ ⌀ INN

tel: 01946 723288 **CA19 1TG**
email: stay@brookhouseinn.co.uk **web:** www.brookhouseinn.co.uk
dir: *In village centre. 0.5m NE of Dalegarth station*

Located in the heart of Eskdale, this impressive inn dates from the early 18th century and has been renovated to offer comfortable accommodation with smart, modern bathrooms for weary walkers and travellers. Wholesome meals using local produce are served in the traditionally furnished dining room or attractive bar – the latter features real ales and country memorabilia.

Rooms 8 en suite (2 fmly) **Facilities** FTV tea/coffee Dinner available WiFi **Conf** Max 35 **Parking** 24 **Notes** LB Closed 25 Dec

BORROWDALE

Map 18 NY21

Premier Collection

Hazel Bank Country House

★★★★★ ◉ ⌂ GUEST ACCOMMODATION

tel: 017687 77248 & 07775 701069 **Rosthwaite CA12 5XB**
email: info@hazelbankhotel.co.uk **web:** www.hazelbankhotel.co.uk
dir: B5289 from Keswick towards Borrowdale, left after sign for Rosthwaite

Set on an elevated position surrounded by four acres of gardens and woodland, Hazel Bank Country House enjoys wonderful views of Borrowdale. The approach to this grand Victorian house is impressive, reached via a picturesque hump back bridge and a winding drive. Bedrooms are sumptuous and all are en suite. Carefully cooked dishes are served in the elegant dining room; the daily changing four-course menu features fresh local ingredients. There is a friendly atmosphere here and the proprietors are very welcoming.

Rooms 7 en suite (1 GF) **Facilities** FTV iPod docking station Lounge tea/coffee Dinner available Licensed WiFi ⌂ **Extras** Speciality toiletries, chocolates, bottled water **Parking** 9 **Notes** LB ⊗ No Children 12yrs Closed 30 Nov-30 Jan

BOWNESS-ON-WINDERMERE

See Windermere

BRAITHWAITE

Map 18 NY22

The Cottage in the Wood

★★★★ ◉◉◉ ⌂ RESTAURANT WITH ROOMS

tel: 017687 78409 & 07730 312193 **Whinlatter Pass CA12 5TW**
email: relax@thecottageinthewood.co.uk **web:** www.thecottageinthewood.co.uk
dir: M6 junct 40, A66 W. After Keswick exit for Braithwaite via Whinlatter Pass (B5292), establishment at top of pass

This charming property sits on wooded hills with striking views of Skiddaw, and is conveniently placed for Keswick. The owners provide excellent hospitality in a relaxed manner. The award-winning food, freshly prepared and locally sourced, is served in the bright and welcoming conservatory restaurant with its stunning views. The comfortable bedrooms are well appointed and have many useful extras.

Rooms 9 en suite **Facilities** FTV Lounge tea/coffee Dinner available Direct Dial WiFi ⌂ **Parking** 15 **Notes** ⊗ No Children 10yrs Closed Jan RS Mon closed No coaches

The Royal Oak

★★★★ INN

tel: 017687 78533 **CA12 5SY**
email: info@royaloak-braithwaite.co.uk **web:** www.royaloak-braithwaite.co.uk
dir: In village centre

The Royal Oak, in the pretty village of Braithwaite, has delightful views of Skiddaw and Barrow, and is a good base for tourists and walkers. Some of the well-equipped bedrooms are furnished with four-poster beds. Hearty meals and traditional Cumbrian breakfasts are served in the restaurant, and there is an atmospheric, well-stocked bar.

Rooms 10 en suite (1 fmly) **Facilities** STV FTV tea/coffee Dinner available WiFi ⌂ **Parking** 20 **Notes** LB

BRAMPTON

Map 21 NY56

Premier Collection

Lanercost Bed and Breakfast

★★★★★ ◷ ⌂ GUEST ACCOMMODATION

tel: 016977 42589 & 07976 977204 **Lanercost CA8 2HQ**
email: info@lanercostbedandbreakfast.co.uk
web: www.lanercostbedandbreakfast.co.uk
dir: Follow signs to Lanercost Priory, then signs to B&B

Built in 1840 in the grounds of Lanercost Priory, close to Hadrian's Wall, this property offers individually designed bedrooms of a good size with quality fixtures and fittings. Public areas are welcoming and enhanced with artwork and *objets d'art*. The hearty, award-winning breakfasts use local produce and make a wonderful start to the day, and dinners are equally good.

Rooms 4 en suite S £83-£88* **Facilities** FTV iPod docking station Lounge tea/coffee Dinner available Licensed WiFi ⌂ 18 Fishing Riding ⌂ **Extras** Speciality toiletries, home-made biscuits - free **Conf** Max 10 Thtr 10 Class 10 Board 10 **Parking** 10 **Notes** LB ⊛

Abbey Bridge

★★★★ ⌂ GUEST ACCOMMODATION

tel: 016977 3841 **Lanercost CA8 2HG**
email: tim@abbeybridge.co.uk **web:** www.abbeybridge.co.uk
dir: M6 junct 43. A69 to Brampton, follow signs for Lanercost Priory. Through town, 2m on left, next to Lanercost Bridge

The Abbey Bridge has a long history and is a beautifully presented property offering wonderful hospitality and high standards of comfort. Previously an inn and pub but also a Temperance Inn until regaining its license in the 1970s, the property is currently fully licensed, and comprises two buildings, The Blacksmiths and the main house. Walkers are well catered for, with a boot and wet kit room which even boasts boot drying equipment. Located close to Hadrian's Wall and even closer to Lanercost Priory, it's an ideal base to tour the surrounding area with Edinburgh, Newcastle, the North Pennines and the Lakes all within easy reach, as the A69 is just minutes away. Dinner is available by prior arrangement.

Rooms 4 en suite 3 annexe en suite (1 GF) S £65-£70; D £85-£90* **Facilities** FTV TVL tea/coffee Dinner available Licensed WiFi ⌂ **Parking** 7 **Notes** ⊗ Closed Nov-Mar

BRAMPTON *continued*

The Blacksmiths Arms

★★★★ INN

tel: 016977 3452 & 42111 **Talkin Village CA8 1LE**
email: blacksmithsarmstalkin@yahoo.co.uk web: www.blacksmithstalkin.co.uk
dir: *B6413 from Brampton to Castle Carrock, after level crossing 2nd left signed Talkin*

Dating from the early 19th century and used as a smithy until the 1950s, this friendly village inn offers good home-cooked fare and real ales, with two Cumbrian cask beers always available. Bedrooms are well equipped, and three are particularly smart. An extensive menu and daily specials are offered in the cosy bar lounges or the smart, panelled Old Forge Restaurant.

Rooms 5 en suite 3 annexe en suite (2 fmly) (3 GF) S £60-£65; D £80-£90
Facilities FTV tea/coffee Dinner available Direct Dial WiFi ⚓ 18 🔒 **Parking** 20
Notes ⊗ No coaches

| CARLISLE | Map 18 NY35 |

See also Brampton

The Angus

★★★★ GUEST ACCOMMODATION

tel: 01228 523546 **14-16 Scotland Rd CA3 9DG**
email: hotel@angus-hotel.co.uk web: www.angus-hotel.co.uk
dir: *0.5m N of city centre on A7*

Situated just north of the city and built on the actual foundations of Hadrian's Wall, this family-run establishment is ideal for business and leisure. A warm welcome is assured and the accommodation is well equipped. Dinner is available by prior arrangement, providing enjoyable food and home baking. There is also a comfortable lounge available for the guests.

Rooms 10 en suite (2 fmly) S £55-£68; D £69-£89 **Facilities** FTV Lounge tea/coffee Dinner available Direct Dial Licensed WiFi 🔒 **Notes** LB

No1 Guest House

★★★★ BED AND BREAKFAST

tel: 01228 547285 & 07899 948711 **1 Etterby St CA3 9JB**
email: sheila@carlislebandb.co.uk web: www.carlislebandb.co.uk
dir: *M6 junct 44 onto A7, right at 7th lights into Etterby St, house 1st on left*

This small friendly house is on the north side of the city within walking distance of the centre. The attractive, well-equipped en suite bedrooms consist of a double, a twin and a single room. Hearty traditional breakfasts featuring the best of local produce, are served in the ground-floor dining room.

Rooms 3 en suite **Facilities** FTV tea/coffee Dinner available WiFi **Parking** 1
Notes LB ⊗

| CARTMEL | Map 18 SD37 |

Premier Collection

L'Enclume

★★★★★ ◉◉◉◉◉ RESTAURANT WITH ROOMS

tel: 015395 36362 **Cavendish St LA11 6PZ**
email: info@lenclume.co.uk web: www.lenclume.co.uk
dir: *From A590 turn left for Cartmel before Newby Bridge*

L'Enclume is a delightful 13th-century property in the heart of a lovely village, and offers incredible 21st-century cooking that draws foodies from far and wide.

Once the village forge (l'enclume is French for 'the anvil') it's now the location for some of Britain's best food, and Simon Rogan's imaginative and adventurous cooking may be sampled in the stylish restaurant. Individually designed, modern, en suite rooms, of varying sizes and styles, and are either in the main property or dotted about the village only a few moments' walk from the restaurant.

Rooms 5 en suite 11 annexe en suite (3 fmly) (3 GF) S £90-£150; D £129-£219*
Facilities STV DVD iPod docking station tea/coffee Dinner available Direct Dial WiFi **Parking** 4 **Notes** ⊗ No coaches

| CONISTON | Map 18 SD39 |

Wheelgate Country Guest House

★★★★ GUEST HOUSE

tel: 015394 41418 **Little Arrow LA21 8AU**
email: enquiry@wheelgate.co.uk web: www.wheelgate.co.uk
dir: *1.5m S of Coniston, on W side of road*

A charming Lakeland cottage nestled at the base of Coniston Old Man and close to the lake and village itself. Think oak beams, low ceilings and snug nooks to relax. Popular with walkers and those who like a peaceful Lakes stay, a warm and personal welcome can be expected along with hearty breakfast and comfortable bedrooms. A cosy bar also available.

Rooms 4 en suite 3 annexe en suite (3 GF) S £35-£39; D £64-£78* **Facilities** FTV Lounge tea/coffee Licensed WiFi 🔒 **Parking** 5 **Notes** LB ⊗ No Children 8yrs

| CROSTHWAITE | Map 18 SD49 |

Premier Collection

The Punchbowl Inn at Crosthwaite

★★★★★ ◉◉ 🍷 INN

tel: 015395 68237 **Lyth Valley LA8 8HR**
email: info@the-punchbowl.co.uk web: www.the-punchbowl.co.uk
dir: *M6 junct 36 signed Barrow, on A5074 towards Windermere, turn right for Crosthwaite. At E end of village beside church*

Located in the stunning Lyth Valley alongside the village church, this historic inn has been renovated to provide excellent standards of comfort and facilities. Its sumptuous bedrooms have a wealth of thoughtful extras, and imaginative food is available in the elegant restaurant or in the rustic-style bar with open fires. A warm welcome and professional service is assured.

Rooms 9 en suite **Facilities** FTV Dinner available Direct Dial WiFi 🔒
Extras Speciality toiletries, home-made scones & jam **Parking** 25
Notes No coaches Civ Wed 50

GLENRIDDING
Map 18 NY31

Premier Collection

Glenridding House
★★★★★ 🍴 GUEST ACCOMMODATION

tel: 017684 82874 & 07966 486701 **CA11 0PH**
email: stay@glenriddinghouse.com **web:** www.glenriddinghouse.com
dir: M6 junct 40 onto A66, then A592 to Glenridding. Turn sharp second left

Glenridding House is a wonderful Georgian Lakeside villa which sits right on the shores of Ullswater. Used as a holiday home by Charles Darwin, this once derelict building has been lovingly restored. Bedrooms differ in size, and a number boast stunning views of the lake and surrounding fells. An excellent location for those touring this unspoilt area of the Lake District.

Rooms 6 rms (6 pri facs) (1 GF) **Facilities** FTV Lounge tea/coffee Dinner available Licensed WiFi Fishing 🛁 Packed lunches available **Conf** Max 30 Thtr 30 Class 30 Board 30 **Parking** 30 **Notes** ⊗ No Children 18yrs Civ Wed 50

GRANGE-OVER-SANDS
Map 18 SD47

Birchleigh Guest House
★★★★ GUEST HOUSE

tel: 015395 32592 & 07527 844403 **Kents Bank Rd LA11 7EY**
email: birchleigh@btinternet.com **web:** www.birchleighguesthouse.com
dir: M6 junct 36, A590 signed Windermere, then Barrow. At Meathop Rdbt left onto B5277 to Grange-Over-Sands. At 1st rdbt left, at 2nd rdbt right. At T-junct left into Kents Bank Rd. 3rd house on left after car park

This homely and welcoming guest house is situated in the heart of town providing four comfortable and tastefully-decorated modern bedrooms. Expect a hearty breakfast served in the well appointed dining room with a separate lounge area available for guests.

Rooms 4 en suite (1 fmly) **Facilities** FTV Lounge tea/coffee WiFi 🛁 **Extras** Fresh milk **Parking** 2 **Notes** ⊗

GRASMERE
Map 18 NY30

Premier Collection

Moss Grove Organic
★★★★★ 🍴 GUEST ACCOMMODATION

tel: 015394 35251 **LA22 9SW**
email: enquiries@mossgrove.com **web:** www.mossgrove.com
dir: From S: M6 junct 36 onto A591 signed Keswick. From N: M6 junct 40 onto A591 signed Windermere

Located in the centre of Grasmere, this impressive Victorian house has been appointed using as many natural products as possible, as part of an ongoing dedication to cause minimal environmental impact. The stylish bedrooms are decorated with beautiful wallpaper and natural clay paints, featuring hand-made beds and furnishings. Bose home entertainment systems, flat-screen TVs and luxury bathrooms add further comfort, one room even has a hot tub. Extensive continental breakfasts are served in the spacious kitchen, where guests can help themselves and dine at the large wooden dining table.

Rooms 11 en suite (2 GF) **Facilities** STV DVD iPod docking station Lounge tea/coffee Licensed WiFi 🛁 **Extras** Speciality toiletries - complimentary **Parking** 11 **Notes** LB No Children 14yrs Closed 24-25 Dec

GRIZEDALE
Map 18 SD39

Premier Collection

Grizedale Lodge
★★★★★ 🍴 GUEST HOUSE

tel: 015394 36532 **LA22 0QL**
email: enquiries@grizedale-lodge.com **web:** www.grizedale-lodge.com
dir: From Hawkshead follow signs S to Grizedale. Lodge 2m on right

Set in the heart of Grizedale Forest Park, close to the Go Ape centre and two miles from Hawkshead, this lovely property offers quiet and tranquil surroundings. Hospitality is warm here, and Richard and Debs will be keen to welcome you into their home. The comfortable lounge with open log fire and views of the forest, makes this an ideal place to relax. All the rooms are well decorated and some offer four-poster beds. Expect superb home-cooked dinners and appetising breakfasts. Mountain bike storage also available.

Rooms 8 en suite (1 fmly) (2 GF) D £95-£160* **Facilities** FTV DVD Lounge tea/coffee Dinner available Licensed WiFi 🛁 **Extras** Speciality toiletries **Parking** 12

HAWKSHEAD
Map 18 SD39

See also Near Sawrey

Premier Collection

Ees Wyke Country House
★★★★★ ◉ 🍴 GUEST HOUSE

tel: 015394 36393 **LA22 0JZ**
email: mail@eeswyke.co.uk **web:** www.eeswyke.co.uk

(For full entry see Near Sawrey)

The Queen's Head Inn & Restaurant
★★★★ ◉ INN

tel: 015394 36271 **Main St LA22 0NS**
email: info@queensheadhawkshead.co.uk **web:** www.queensheadhawkshead.co.uk
dir: M6 junct 36, then A590 to Newby Bridge. Over rdbt, 1st right into Hawkshead

This 16th-century inn features a wood-panelled bar with low, oak-beamed ceilings and an open log fire. An excellent selection of quality dishes and local ales are served throughout the day. Accommodation has benefited from a complete refurbishment and bedrooms are comfortable and stylishly decorated with modern amenities.

Rooms 10 en suite 3 annexe en suite (1 fmly) (2 GF) **Facilities** FTV DVD iPod docking station tea/coffee Dinner available WiFi 🛁 **Extras** Speciality toiletries, robes

HAWKSHEAD *continued*

Sun Inn

★★★★ ⬤ INN

tel: 015394 36236 **Main St LA22 0NT**
email: rooms@suninn.co.uk **web:** www.suninn.co.uk
dir: *M6 junct 36 onto A591 (Ambleside). Follow signs to Hawkshead, in centre of village*

The Sun Inn is a charming 17th-century building located in the heart of the peaceful village of Hawkshead on the quieter side of Windermere. It has retained a great deal of original character, with wooden panelling, oak beams, and stone floors, and exposed brickwork. Bedrooms differ in size but are all well appointed and presented, with local hand-made furniture making the best of the available space. Food is very good, and the bar boasts a number of local real ales, with an open fire adding to the charm in the colder months.

Rooms 8 en suite (1 fmly) **Facilities** FTV tea/coffee Dinner available WiFi Pool table ⬤ **Extras** Wine/champagne, flowers, chocolates - chargeable

Kings Arms

★★★ INN

tel: 015394 36372 **LA22 0NZ**
email: info@kingsarmshawkshead.co.uk **web:** www.kingsarmshawkshead.co.uk
dir: *M6 junct 36, A591, left onto A593 at Waterhead. 1m, onto B5286 to Hawkshead, Kings Arms in main square*

The Kings Arms is a traditional Lakeland inn in the heart of a conservation area. The cosy, thoughtfully equipped bedrooms retain much character and are traditionally furnished. A good choice of freshly prepared food is available in the lounge bar and the neatly presented dining room.

Rooms 8 en suite (3 fmly) S £59-£69; D £88-£102 **Facilities** FTV DVD tea/coffee Dinner available Direct Dial WiFi ⬤ Fishing Riding ⬤ Bowling green **Notes** LB Closed 25 Dec

HOLMROOK

Map 18 SD09

The Lutwidge Arms

★★★★ INN

tel: 019467 24230 **CA19 1UH**
email: mail@lutwidgearms.co.uk **web:** www.lutwidgearms.co.uk
dir: *M6 junct 36, A590 towards Barrow. Follow A595 towards Whitehaven & Workington, property in village centre*

This Victorian roadside inn is family run and offers a welcoming atmosphere. Its name comes from the Lutwidge family of Holmrook Hall, whose lineage included Charles Lutwidge Dodgson, better known as Lewis Carroll. The bar and restaurant offer a wide range of meals during the evening. Bedrooms are smart and comfortable, and the new Orangery has transformed the garden and dining areas.

Rooms 11 en suite 5 annexe en suite (5 fmly) (5 GF) **Facilities** FTV TVL tea/coffee Dinner available WiFi Pool table ⬤ **Conf** Max 20 Thtr 20 Class 20 Board 20 **Parking** 30 **Notes** LB ⊗ No Children 5yrs

IREBY

Map 18 NY23

Woodlands Country House

★★★★ ⬤ ⬤ GUEST HOUSE

tel: 016973 71791 **CA7 1EX**
email: stay@woodlandsatireby.co.uk **web:** www.woodlandsatireby.co.uk
dir: *M6 junct 40, A66, pass Keswick, at rdbt right onto A591. At Castle Inn right signed Ireby, 2nd left signed Ireby. Pass church on left, last house in village*

Previously a vicarage, this lovely Victorian home is set in well-tended gardens that attract lots of wildlife. Guests are given a warm welcome by the friendly owner and delicious home-cooked evening meals are available by prior arrangement. A peaceful lounge and cosy bar with snug are also available. Bedrooms are attractively furnished and thoughtfully equipped.

Rooms 4 en suite 3 annexe en suite (3 fmly) (3 GF) S £55-£75; D £85-£98* **Facilities** FTV Lounge TVL tea/coffee Dinner available Licensed WiFi **Extras** Home-made shortbread, sweets, mineral water - free **Parking** 11 **Notes** LB

IRTHINGTON

Map 21 NY46

The Golden Fleece

★★★★ ⬤ INN

tel: 01228 573686 & 07766 736924 **Rule Holme CA6 4NF**
email: info@thegoldenfleececumbria.co.uk **web:** www.thegoldenfleececumbria.co.uk
dir: *M6 junct 44 onto A689 signed Brampton. 1m past Carlisle Airport, on left*

The Golden Fleece is a rural inn set beside the A689, close to Carlisle and Hadrian's Wall. Public areas include a feature bar with local real ales on draught, and a cosy lounge area with a fire. The dining room is split between several areas helping to create a sense of intimacy. Bedrooms and bathrooms are all modern in appearance. The full Cumbrian breakfasts are not to be missed, and friendly staff provide a true Cumbrian welcome. There is ample parking.

Rooms 8 en suite (4 fmly) D £85-£95* **Facilities** FTV DVD iPod docking station Lounge tea/coffee Dinner available WiFi ⬤ 18 Fishing ⬤ **Extras** Speciality toiletries, home-made cakes **Conf** Max 150 Thtr 120 Class 70 Board 70 **Parking** 100 **Notes** Closed 1-8 Jan Civ Wed 100

KENDAL
Map 18 SD59

The Punch Bowl

★★★★ ⭐ INN

tel: 015395 60267 **Barrows Green LA8 0AA**
email: punch_bowl@hotmail.co.uk **web:** www.thepunchbowla65.com
dir: *M6 junct 36 onto A65 signed Kendal. After 4m, on left*

Expect a warm welcome at this friendly pub within easy reach of local transport links and perfectly situated at the gateway to the Lake District. Two tasteful letting rooms are comfortable and well equipped for the modern traveller. Dinner is traditional and wholesome 'pub grub', and breakfasts are a hearty affair.

Rooms 2 en suite **Facilities** FTV Lounge TVL tea/coffee Dinner available WiFi Pool table 🛇 **Extras** Bottled water, Kendal mintcake **Parking** 40

KESWICK
Map 18 NY22

Amble House

★★★★ ⭐ GUEST HOUSE

tel: 017687 73288 **23 Eskin St CA12 4DQ**
email: info@amblehouse.co.uk **web:** www.amblehouse.co.uk
dir: *400yds SE of town centre. Exit A5271 (Penrith Rd) into Greta St & Eskin St*

An enthusiastic welcome awaits you at this Victorian mid-terrace house, close to the town centre and in an ideal location for exploring the Lakes. The thoughtfully equipped bedrooms have co-ordinated decor and are furnished in pine. Healthy breakfasts are served in the attractive dining room.

Rooms 5 en suite S £50-£65; D £64-£88* **Facilities** tea/coffee WiFi 🛇 **Extras** Speciality toiletries **Notes** LB 🛇 No Children 16yrs Closed 24-26 Dec

Badgers Wood

★★★★ ⭐ GUEST HOUSE

tel: 017687 72621 **30 Stanger St CA12 5JU**
email: enquiries@badgers-wood.co.uk **web:** www.badgers-wood.co.uk
dir: *In town centre off A5271 (main street)*

Anne and Andrew at Badgers Wood welcome guests to this delightful Victorian terrace house, located in a quiet area close to the town centre. The smart bedrooms are furnished to a high standard and are well equipped and have lovely views; the attractive breakfast room at the front of the house overlooks the fells. Off-road parking is an added benefit. Special diets gladly catered for.

Rooms 6 en suite S £43-£45; D £78-£80* **Facilities** FTV DVD tea/coffee WiFi 🛇 **Parking** 6 **Notes** 🛇 No Children 12yrs Closed Nov-Jan

Brocklehurst B&B

★★★★ ⭐ BED AND BREAKFAST

tel: 017687 74897 **Brocklehurst, Sunset Hill CA12 4RN**
email: brocklehurst.keswick@gmail.com **web:** www.brocklehurstkeswick.co.uk
dir: *From A66 E of Keswick, exit signed Burns. 300mtrs on right*

Ideally located on the edge of Keswick town centre, this ground floor accommodation was converted from what was the old Storms Farm Dairy, known locally as the 'lemonade factory'. En suite bedrooms are well appointed with a

separate guest lounge available. Breakfast is a highlight and makes great use of local quality produce to ensure guests are well fed prior to the day's events. A quiet peaceful location with off-road parking.

Rooms 2 en suite (2 GF) **Facilities** FTV DVD TVL tea/coffee **Parking** 2 **Notes** 🛇 No Children 12yrs Closed Xmas-New Year 🛇

Dalegarth House

★★★★ ⭐ ⭐ GUEST ACCOMMODATION

tel: 017687 72817 **Portinscale CA12 5RQ**
email: allerdalechef@aol.com **web:** www.dalegarth-house.co.uk
dir: *Off A66 to Portinscale, pass Farmers Arms, 500yds on left*

This friendly, family-run establishment stands on an elevated position in the village of Portinscale, and has fine views from the well-tended garden. The attractive bedrooms are well equipped, and there is a peaceful lounge, a well-stocked bar, and a spacious dining room where the resident owner-chef produces hearty breakfasts and delicious evening meals.

Rooms 8 en suite 2 annexe en suite (1 fmly) (2 GF) S £46; D £92-£114* **Facilities** FTV Lounge tea/coffee Dinner available Licensed WiFi 🛇 **Extras** Home-made cakes - complimentary **Parking** 10 **Notes** LB 🛇 No Children 12yrs Closed 24 Nov-1 Mar

The Edwardene

★★★★ ⭐ GUEST ACCOMMODATION

tel: 017687 73586 **26 Southey St CA12 4EF**
email: info@edwardenehotel.com **web:** www.edwardenehotel.com
dir: *M6 junct 40, A66 follow 1st sign to Keswick, right into Penrith Rd. Sharp left by war memorial into Southey St, 150mtrs on right*

Located close to the heart of the town centre, this Victorian Lakeland stone building retains many of its original features. Bedrooms are well equipped with many thoughtful extras provided throughout. A comfortable lounge is available, and the generous Cumbrian breakfast is served in the stylish dining room.

Rooms 11 en suite (1 fmly) S £51-£56; D £92-£122* **Facilities** FTV Lounge TVL tea/coffee Licensed WiFi 🛇 **Extras** Speciality toiletries **Parking** 1 **Notes** LB 🛇 No Children 2yrs

Rooms 36

★★★★ GUEST ACCOMMODATION

tel: 017687 72764 & 74416 **36 Lake Rd CA12 5DQ**
email: andy@rooms36.co.uk **web:** www.rooms36.co.uk
dir: *M6 junct 40, A66 to Keswick. From Main St in Keswick follow Borrowdale (B5289) signs. Right at next mini rdbt into Heads Rd (B5289), 4th right into The Heads, left at end into Lake Rd*

Refurbished to a high standard, Rooms 36 overlooks Hope Park at the end of Lake Road. Modern bedrooms feature iPod docking stations, Tassimo coffee machines, comfortable beds and Herdwick wool carpets as standard. En suites are well appointed and public area decor is enhanced with wonderful artwork by local artist Tessa Kennedy.

Rooms 6 en suite (4 fmly) **Facilities** STV FTV iPod docking station Lounge TVL tea/coffee WiFi 🛇 **Parking** 2

KESWICK *continued*

Brundholme

★★★★ ⚲ GUEST ACCOMMODATION

tel: 017687 73305 & 07739 435401 **The Heads CA12 5ER**
email: bazaly@hotmail.co.uk **web:** www.brundholme.co.uk

Centrally located, overlooking Hope Park with some bedrooms boasting wonderful views of surrounding fells, this Victorian property is just minutes' walk from the town centre in one direction and the theatre in the other. Limited off-road parking is available. Bedrooms are comfortable and well appointed, and the well cooked traditional Lakeland breakfast will set you up for the day. Service is relaxed and friendly.

Rooms 4 en suite (1 GF) D £80-£85* **Facilities** FTV tea/coffee WiFi **Extras** Fridges **Parking** 6 **Notes** ⊗

Eden Green Guest House

★★★★ GUEST HOUSE

tel: 017687 72077 **20 Blencathra St CA12 4HP**
email: enquiries@edengreenguesthouse.com **web:** www.edengreenguesthouse.com
dir: A591 Penrith Rd into Keswick, under railway bridge, 2nd left, house 500yds on left

This mid-terrace house, faced with local stone, offers well-decorated and furnished bedrooms, some with fine views of Skiddaw. Traditional English and vegetarian breakfasts are served in the neat breakfast room, and packed lunches can be provided on request.

Rooms 5 en suite (1 fmly) (1 GF) S £40-£50; D £70-£85* **Facilities** FTV DVD iPod docking station tea/coffee WiFi 🔒 **Notes** LB ⊗ No Children 8yrs

Claremont House

★★★★ GUEST ACCOMMODATION

tel: 017687 72089 **Chestnut Hill CA12 4LT**
email: info@claremonthousekeswick.co.uk **web:** www.claremonthousekeswick.co.uk
dir: A591 N into Chestnut Hill. Pass Manor Brow on left, Claremont House 100yds on right

This impressive 19th-century house has commanding views over Keswick and beyond, and is set in mature grounds where red squirrels regularly visit. It is within walking distance of the town and is ideal for walkers. Guests can expect comfortable bedrooms, a hearty breakfast and friendly service. The resident owners also offer a hot drink and cake on your arrival. Free WiFi is also available.

Rooms 6 en suite (1 fmly) (1 GF) S £45-£50; D £70-£86* **Facilities** FTV tea/coffee WiFi 🔒 **Extras** Flowers, wine, chocolate - chargeable **Parking** 8 **Notes** LB ⊗ No Children 8yrs Closed 24-26 Dec

Craglands Guest House

★★★★ GUEST ACCOMMODATION

tel: 017687 74406 **Penrith Rd CA12 4LJ**
email: craglands@msn.com **web:** www.craglands-keswick.co.uk
dir: 0.5m E of Keswick centre on A5271 (Penrith Rd) at junct A591

This Victorian house occupies an elevated position within walking distance of the town centre. The good value accommodation provides attractive, well equipped bedrooms. Pauline and Mark offer a warm welcome and serve delicious breakfasts with local produce and home-made breads.

Rooms 7 rms (5 en suite) **Facilities** FTV tea/coffee WiFi 🔒 **Parking** 6 **Notes** ⊗ No Children 8yrs

Cragside

★★★★ GUEST ACCOMMODATION

tel: 017687 73344 **39 Blencathra St CA12 4HX**
email: cragside-keswick@hotmail.com **web:** www.cragside-keswick.co.uk
dir: A591 Penrith Rd into Keswick, under rail bridge, 2nd left

Expect warm hospitality at Cragside, located within easy walking distance of the town centre. The attractive bedrooms are well equipped, and many have fine views of the fells. Hearty Cumbrian breakfasts are served in the breakfast room, which overlooks the small front garden. Visually or hearing impaired guests are catered for, with Braille information, televisions with teletext, and a loop system installed in the dining room.

Rooms 4 en suite (1 fmly) S £50-£70; D £70-£85 **Facilities** FTV DVD tea/coffee WiFi **Notes** No Children 5yrs

Dorchester House

★★★★ GUEST ACCOMMODATION

tel: 017687 73256 **17 Southey St CA12 4EG**
email: dennis@dorchesterhouse-keswick.co.uk **web:** www.dorchesterhouse-keswick.co.uk
dir: 200yds E of town centre. Exit A5271 (Penrith Rd) into Southey St, 150yds on left

A warm welcome awaits at Dorchester House, just a stroll from the town centre and its amenities. The comfortably proportioned, well-maintained bedrooms offer pleasing co-ordinated decor. Hearty breakfasts are served in the attractive ground-floor dining room.

Rooms 8 rms (7 en suite) (1 pri facs) (2 fmly) **Facilities** FTV tea/coffee WiFi **Notes** ⊗ No Children 6yrs

Elm Tree Lodge

★★★★ GUEST ACCOMMODATION

tel: 017687 71050 & 07980 521079 **16 Leonard St CA12 4EL**
email: info@elmtreelodge-keswick.co.uk **web:** www.elmtreelodge-keswick.co.uk
dir: Exit A66, pass ambulance depot, left before pedestrian crossing, left into Southey St. 3rd left into Helvellyn St, 1st right into Leonard St, property 3rd on right

Close to the town centre, Elm Tree Lodge is a tastefully decorated Victorian house that offers a variety of rooms. Bedrooms feature stripped pine, period furniture, crisp white linen and modern en suites or private shower room. Hearty breakfasts are served in the charming dining room and feature local produce. A friendly welcome is guaranteed.

Rooms 4 rms (3 en suite) (1 pri facs) S £45-£50; D £62-£85* **Facilities** FTV tea/coffee WiFi 🔒 **Parking** 2 **Notes** LB ⊗ No Children 8yrs

The George

★★★★ 🍴 INN

tel: 017687 72076 **Saint Johns St CA12 5AZ**
email: rooms@thegeorgekeswick.co.uk **web:** www.thegeorgekeswick.co.uk
dir: M6 junct 40, A66, take left filter road signed Keswick, pass pub on left. At x-rds left into Station St, 150yds on left

Located in the centre of town, this property is Keswick's oldest coaching inn. There is an abundance of character with wooden beamed bar, cosy seating areas and an atmospheric, candle-lit dining room. Food is a highlight with a wide choice of freshly prepared dishes. Bedrooms are simply presented and comfortable. Parking permits and storage for cycles are available.

Rooms 12 en suite (2 fmly) **Facilities** FTV tea/coffee Dinner available 🔒 **Parking** 4 **Notes** No coaches

Hedgehog Hill Guest House

★★★★ GUEST HOUSE

tel: 017687 80654 **18 Blencathra St CA12 4HP**
email: keith@hedgehoghill.co.uk **web:** www.hedgehoghill.co.uk
dir: *M6 junct 40, A66 to Keswick. Left into Blencathra St*

Expect warm hospitality at this Victorian terrace house. Hedgehog Hill Guest House is convenient for the town centre, local attractions and many walks. Bedrooms are comfortably equipped and offer thoughtful extras. Hearty breakfasts are served in the light and airy dining room with vegetarians well catered for.

Rooms 6 rms (4 en suite) S £31–£32; D £74–£80* **Facilities** FTV tea/coffee WiFi ❦ **Extras** Fair Trade snacks **Notes** ⊗ No Children 12yrs Closed 23-26 Dec

Rickerby Grange

★★★★ GUEST ACCOMMODATION

tel: 017687 72344 **Portinscale CA12 5RH**
email: stay@rickerbygrange.co.uk **web:** www.rickerbygrange.co.uk
dir: *W of Keswick on A66, turn left at Portinscale junct. Pass The Farmers public house, then 2nd right into Rickerby Ln. 50yds on right*

Rickerby Grange is ideally positioned in a private lane in the pretty village of Portinscale one mile from Keswick. This family-run property offers a genuine warm welcome to all, including walkers and cyclists (by prior arrangement). Even the family dog is welcome. Bedrooms are pleasantly furnished and most are en suite. A small but well-stocked bar is available, and drinks can be enjoyed in the lounge area or in the garden.

Rooms 9 rms (8 en suite) (1 pri facs) 1 annexe en suite (3 fmly) (1 GF) **Facilities** FTV tea/coffee Licensed WiFi ❦ **Parking** 14

The Royal Oak at Keswick

★★★★ INN

tel: 017687 74584 **Main St CA12 5HZ**
email: relax@royaloakkeswick.co.uk **web:** www.royaloakkeswick.co.uk
dir: *M6 junct 40, A66 to Keswick town centre to war memorial x-rds. Left into Station St. Inn 100yds*

Located on the corner of the vibrant market square this large, friendly 18th-century coaching inn offers a wide range of meals throughout the day and evening. There is a fully stocked bar complete with well-kept cask ales. Bedrooms vary in size but all are contemporary, smartly presented and feature quality accessories such as LCD TVs. There is also a drying room.

Rooms 19 en suite (2 fmly) S £80–£160; D £80–£160* **Facilities** FTV tea/coffee Dinner available **Notes** LB

Skiddaw Croft B&B

★★★★ GUEST ACCOMMODATION

tel: 017687 72321 **Portinscale CA12 5RD**
email: info@skiddawcroft.co.uk **web:** www.skiddawcroft.co.uk
dir: *A66 past Keswick, turn left signed Portinscale. Pass Farmers Arms pub, over brow of hill, 3rd property on left*

Located in the peaceful village of Portinscale, just a few hundred metres away from the majestic Derwentwater, Skiddaw Croft was built in 1913 and has recently enjoyed extensive investment, with numerous projects taking place inside and out.

A warm, genuine welcome awaits all guests on arrival, with the offer of refreshments and home baking. Well appointed, modern bedrooms enjoy a variety of views; the lake from the front, and sometimes Cat Bells (depending on the time of year), while from the rear you can see Skiddaw. Off road car parking is a bonus, and Portinscale is handy for the A66, Keswick and further afield.

Rooms 6 rms (4 en suite) (2 fmly) S £40; D £75–£80* **Facilities** FTV Lounge tea/coffee WiFi ❦ **Extras** Speciality toiletries - complimentary **Parking** 5 **Notes** No Children 8yrs Closed Dec-Feb

Avondale Guest House

★★★★ Ⓐ GUEST ACCOMMODATION

tel: 017687 72735 & 07917 855474 **20 Southey St CA12 4EF**
email: enquiries@avondaleguesthouse.com **web:** www.avondaleguesthouse.com
dir: *A66 to Keswick. A591 towards town centre, left at war memorial into Station St. Sharp left into Southey St, 100yds on right*

Just a short walk from Keswick town centre, Avondale is a great base for cyclists and walkers. The pleasantly decorated bedrooms each have flat-screen digital TV, radio alarm clock, hairdryer and fan. Complimentary tea- and coffee-making facilities are provided along with a selection of biscuits. Breakfast is mainly made from excellent local produce, with the exception of the award-winning black pudding, from the Outer Hebrides. Visitors can take a boat trip on Derwentwater, or visit the world renowned 'Theatre by the Lake', just a short stroll away.

Rooms 6 en suite S £46–£48; D £92–£96* **Facilities** FTV Lounge tea/coffee WiFi ❦ **Extras** Fresh milk **Notes** LB ⊗ No Children

Sandon Guesthouse

★★★★ Ⓐ GUEST HOUSE

tel: 017687 73648 **13 Southey St CA12 4EG**
email: sandonguesthouse@gmail.com **web:** www.sandonguesthouse.co.uk
dir: *200yds E of town centre. Exit A5271 (Penrith Rd) into Southey St*

This spacious Victorian residence close to the market square offers en suite bedrooms (except the single room) thoughtfully equipped with many extras. Expect warm hospitality from the friendly resident owners.

Rooms 6 rms (5 en suite) (1 pri facs) S £40–£46; D £80–£92* **Facilities** FTV DVD tea/coffee WiFi ❦ **Notes** ⊗ No Children 8yrs Closed 24 Dec (day), 25-26 Dec

Springs Farm B&B *(NY274227)*

★★★ FARMHOUSE

tel: 017687 72144 & 07816 824253 **Springs Farm, Springs Rd CA12 4AN**
email: springsfarmkeswick@gmail.com **web:** www.springsfarmcumbria.co.uk
dir: *A66 into Keswick, left at T-junct onto Chestnut Hill. After 200yds right on Manor Brow, then left into Springs Road. 0.5m at end of road*

(Please note: Springs Farm is currently closed due to flooding. Telephone Springs Farm for current information.) Part of a working beef farm, the farmhouse was built around 150 years ago. Guests can expect comfortable accommodation and a well-cooked breakfast with eggs from the farm's own hens. Springs Farm B&B is ideally located in the heart of the countryside but surprising close to the town centre, which is an easy 10-minute walk away.

Rooms 3 en suite **Facilities** STV FTV DVD iPod docking station TVL tea/coffee WiFi ❦ Farm shop Tea room **Parking** 6 **Notes** Closed 19-29 Dec ⊜ 180 acres beef

KIRKBY IN FURNESS
Map 18 SD28

Low Hall Farm (SD232812)
★★★★ FARMHOUSE

tel: 01229 889220 **LA17 7TR**
email: tracey.edmondson@btinternet.com **web:** www.low-hall.co.uk
dir: M6 junct 36 onto A590. At rdbt signed Workington follow A595, through Askam in Furness. After 2.5m turn right, signed Low Hall Farm then 1st left

Low Hall is a lovely Victorian farmhouse owned by Holker Hall Estates and run by Peter and Tracey Edmondson. The farm is a working beef and sheep farm set in peaceful countryside, offering spectacular views of the Duddon Estuary and Lakeland fells. Low Hall is a very spacious farmhouse, with all rooms offering high quality furnishings. A traditional farmhouse English breakfast is served in the bright and airy dining room, and there is a comfortable living room with wood-burning stove. Ironing facilities are available.

Rooms 3 en suite S £40-£45; D £65-£70 **Facilities** FTV TVL tea/coffee WiFi **Extras** Speciality toiletries - complimentary **Parking** 4 **Notes** ⊗ No Children 14yrs 366 acres beef/sheep

KIRKBY LONSDALE
Map 18 SD67

Premier Collection

Hipping Hall
★★★★★ ⊛⊛⊛ ⓠ RESTAURANT WITH ROOMS

tel: 015242 71187 **Cowan Bridge LA6 2JJ**
email: info@hippinghall.com **web:** www.hippinghall.com
dir: M6 junct 36, A65 through Kirkby Lonsdale towards Skipton. On right after Cowan Bridge

Close to the market town of Kirkby Lonsdale, Hipping Hall offers spacious bedrooms, designed using soft shades with sumptuous textures and fabrics; the bathrooms use natural stone, slate and limestone to great effect. There are also three spacious cottage suites that create a real hideaway experience. The sitting room, with large, comfortable sofas has a traditional feel. The 3 AA Rosette-worthy restaurant is a 15th-century hall with tapestries and a minstrels' gallery that is as impressive as it is intimate.

Rooms 7 en suite 8 annexe en suite (5 GF) **Facilities** FTV Lounge Dinner available Direct Dial WiFi ⏎ **Extras** Speciality toiletries, fruit **Parking** 30 **Notes** No Children 12yrs No coaches Civ Wed 42

Premier Collection

The Sun Inn
★★★★★ ⊛⊛ ⓠ RESTAURANT WITH ROOMS

tel: 015242 71965 **6 Market St LA6 2AU**
email: email@sun-inn.info **web:** www.sun-inn.info
dir: From A65 follow signs to town centre. Inn on main street

The Sun is a 17th-century inn situated in a historic market town, overlooking St Mary's Church. The atmospheric bar features stone walls, wooden beams and log fires with real ales available. Delicious meals are served in the bar or the more formal, modern restaurant. Traditional and modern styles are blended together in the beautifully appointed rooms with excellent en suites.

Rooms 11 en suite (1 fmly) (8 GF) S £80-£179; D £110-£189* **Facilities** FTV tea/coffee Dinner available WiFi ⏎⏎ 18 🔒 **Extras** Bath robes, speciality toiletries **Notes** LB Closed 25 Dec No coaches

Premier Collection

Plato's
★★★★★ ⓠ ⟵ RESTAURANT WITH ROOMS

tel: 015242 74180 **2 Mill Brow LA6 2AT**
email: hello@platoskirkby.co.uk **web:** www.platoskirkbylonsdale.co.uk
dir: M6 junct 36, A65 Kirkby Lonsdale, after 5m at rdbt take 1st exit, onto one-way system

Tucked away in the heart of the popular market town, Plato's is steeped in history. Sumptuous bedrooms have a wealth of thoughtful extras, and imaginative food is available in the elegant restaurant with its open-plan kitchen. The lounge bar is more rustic in style with fires to relax by. A warm welcome and professional service is assured. The Pop Shop offers Plato's cuisine to take away.

Rooms 8 en suite **Facilities** FTV DVD iPod docking station TVL tea/coffee Dinner available WiFi ⏎ 18 **Notes** No coaches

Pheasant Inn
★★★★ ⊛ INN

tel: 015242 71230 **Casterton LA6 2RX**
email: info@pheasantinn.co.uk **web:** www.pheasantinn.co.uk
dir: M6 junct 36, A65 for 7m, left onto A683 at Devils Bridge, 1m to Casterton centre

This friendly family-run inn is perfectly situated in a quiet village near the picturesque market town of Kirkby Lonsdale. Real ales are a speciality, along with hearty but refined cooking served in the oak-panelled dining room. Spacious and comfortable accommodation is provided.

Rooms 10 en suite (1 GF) **Facilities** FTV Lounge tea/coffee Dinner available Direct Dial **Parking** 20 **Notes** No coaches

The Copper Kettle
★★★ ▲ GUEST ACCOMMODATION

tel: 015242 71714 **3-5 Market St LA6 2AU**
email: gamble_p@btconnect.com **web:** www.copperkettlekirkbylonsdale.co.uk
dir: In town centre, down lane by Post Office

Built between 1610 and 1640 The Copper Kettle is situated in the heart of this small quaint market town, which nestles on the banks of the River Lune. The bedrooms, all of which retain their old world 17th-century charm, are comfortable and atmospheric. Home-cooked meals and hearty breakfasts are served in the cosy restaurant.

Rooms 5 en suite (2 fmly) **Facilities** FTV tea/coffee Dinner available Licensed WiFi 🔒 **Parking** 3

KIRKBY STEPHEN
Map 18 NY70

Premier Collection

Cheskin House

★★★★★ 🏠 ⬤ GUEST ACCOMMODATION

tel: 01539 587667 **CA17 4NY**
email: info@cheskinhouse.com **web:** www.cheskinhouse.com

This 270-year-old farmhouse has recently been lovingly restored and refurbished to an impressive standard. Situated in the stunning Eden Valley and only a short drive from the Lake District and the M6, this property is the place to go for food lovers. Local Cumbrian produce features at both breakfast and dinner, with afternoon tea also provided for arriving guests. The luxurious bedrooms have Egyptian linens and a host of thoughtful touches. The property also features a wine studio, conservatory and orangery.

Rooms 2 en suite D £115-£140* **Facilities** STV iPod docking station Lounge tea/coffee Dinner available Licensed WiFi **Extras** Sherry, chocolates, fruit - complimentary **Parking Notes** ⊗ No Children 16yrs

Premier Collection

The Inn at Brough

★★★★★ ◉ INN

tel: 01768 341252 **Main St, Brough CA17 4AY**
email: enquiries@theinnatbrough.co.uk **web:** www.theinnatbrough.co.uk
dir: M6 junct 38, A685 to Kirkby Stephen, then Brough. A66 exit to Brough & Kirkby Stephen

This former 18th-century coaching inn is located in the picturesque Eden Valley and enjoys easy access to the A66 for those travelling north or south. Deeply comfortable bathrooms feature a host of luxury touches while bathrooms feature Villeroy & Boch fittings and local toiletries. A stay here would not be complete without sampling the wonderful food on offer; both at dinner and at breakfast.

Rooms 14 en suite 2 annexe en suite (2 fmly) (2 GF) S £65-£85; D £100-£200* **Facilities** FTV DVD tea/coffee Dinner available WiFi ⬇ 18 🔒 **Extras** Robes, slippers, soft drinks **Conf** Max 100 Thtr 60 Class 60 Board 30 **Parking** 25 **Notes** LB

Tranna Hill

★★★★ 🏠 GUEST ACCOMMODATION

tel: 015396 23227 & 07989 892368 **Newbiggin-on-Lune CA17 4NY**
email: trannahill@hotmail.com **web:** www.trannahill.co.uk
dir: M6 junct 38 onto A685 towards Brough. After 5m turn left towards Great Asby then immediately left to Kelleth. 100mtrs on right

Tranna Hill is set in its own grounds on the edge of the village of Newbiggin-on-Lune, a short distance from the M6 and A66. This period building offers fantastic views of the surrounding fells. Bedrooms are comfortable, well appointed and equipped with lots of books, maps and guides. The sitting/dining room has a log-burning stove and the gardens have seating on the patio.

Rooms 3 en suite (1 fmly) S £48-£53; D £68-£74 **Facilities** FTV DVD TVL tea/coffee WiFi ⬇ 9 🔒 **Extras** Speciality toiletries, chocolates **Parking** 8 **Notes** LB ⊗

LITTLE LANGDALE
Map 18 NY30

Three Shires Inn

★★★★ ⬤ INN

tel: 015394 37215 **LA22 9NZ**
email: enquiry@threeshiresinn.co.uk **web:** www.threeshiresinn.co.uk
dir: Exit A593, 3m from Ambleside at 2nd junct signed Langdales. 1st left after 0.5m, 1m along lane

Enjoying an outstanding rural location, this family-run inn was built in 1872. The brightly decorated bedrooms are individual in style and many offer panoramic views. The attractive lounge features a roaring fire in the cooler months and there is a traditional bar with a great selection of local ales. Meals can be taken in either the bar or cosy restaurant.

Rooms 10 en suite (1 fmly) **Facilities** FTV Lounge TVL tea/coffee Dinner available WiFi 🔒 Use of local country club **Parking** 15 **Notes** Closed 25 Dec RS Dec & Jan wknds & New Year only No coaches

LONGTOWN
Map 21 NY36

The Sycamore Tree

★★★★ GUEST ACCOMMODATION

tel: 01228 791919 **40/42 Bridge St CA6 5UD**
email: jfothergill2008@googlemail.com **web:** www.sycamoretreelongtown.co.uk
dir: On A7

The Sycamore Tree is located on the high street of Longtown just four miles from Gretna and the Scottish border. Choose from a four-poster or a king-size family room. If you are staying on one of the 'steak nights' be sure to reserve a table for dinner.

Rooms 2 en suite (2 fmly) S £45; D £70* **Facilities** FTV tea/coffee Dinner available Licensed WiFi **Extras** Robes, slippers, bottled water - free **Notes** ⊗ Closed 1st 2wks Sep & 26 Dec

LOWESWATER
Map 18 NY12

Kirkstile Inn

★★★★ ⬤ INN

tel: 01900 85219 **CA13 0RU**
email: info@kirkstile.com **web:** www.kirkstile.com
dir: A66 onto B5292 into Lorton, left signed Buttermere. Follow signs to Loweswater, left signed Kirkstile Inn

This historic 16th-century inn lies in a valley surrounded by mountains. Serving great food and ale, its rustic bar and adjoining rooms are a mecca for walkers. There is also a cosy restaurant offering a quieter ambiance. Bedrooms retain their original character. There is a spacious family suite in an annexe, with two bedrooms, a lounge and a bathroom.

Rooms 7 en suite 3 annexe en suite (1 fmly) (2 GF) S £63.50-£90; D £105-£117* **Facilities** TVL TV3B tea/coffee Dinner available WiFi **Parking** 30 **Notes** LB Closed 25 Dec No coaches

LOWESWATER *continued*

Grange Country House

★★★★ ◕ GUEST ACCOMMODATION

tel: 01946 861211 & 861570 **CA13 0SU**
email: info@thegrange-loweswater.co.uk **web:** www.thegrange-loweswater.co.uk
dir: *Exit A5086 for Mockerkin, through village. After 2m left signed Loweswater Lake. Grange Country House at bottom of hill on left*

The delightful Grange Country House is set in extensive grounds in a quiet valley at the north western end of Loweswater and proves popular with guests seeking peace and quiet. It has a friendly relaxed atmosphere and cosy public areas which include a small bar serving a great range of local beers; a residents' lounge and an attractive dining room with dinner served by prior arrangement. The bedrooms are well equipped and comfortable, some with four-poster beds.

Rooms 8 en suite (2 fmly) (1 GF) **Facilities** FTV Lounge TVL tea/coffee Dinner available Licensed WiFi ⬤ **Extras** Speciality toiletries **Conf** Max 25 Thtr 25 Class 25 Board 25 **Parking** 20

| **LUPTON** | **Map 18 SD58** |

Premier Collection

Plough Inn

★★★★★ ◕ INN

tel: 015395 67700 **Cow Brow LA6 1PJ**
email: info@theploughatlupton.co.uk **web:** www.theploughatlupton.co.uk
dir: *M6 junct 36 onto A65 towards Kirkby Lonsdale. Through Nook, up hill, inn on right*

This delightful inn's interior is open plan and a real delight; modern but with a rustic farmhouse appearance. There are large beams, and a log-burning stove in the lounge surrounded by comfortable sofas where you can relax and read the papers. The bedrooms are well proportioned and reflect the inn's high standards; all have feature bathrooms with roll-top baths and walk-in showers. The staff are excellent and guests are made to feel like part of the family. The inn is open all year and serves food every day.

Rooms 6 en suite (1 fmly) **Facilities** FTV Lounge tea/coffee Dinner available Direct Dial WiFi ♨ 18 ⬤ **Extras** Speciality toiletries **Parking** 50
Notes No coaches

| **MILNTHORPE** | **Map 18 SD48** |

The Cross Keys

★★★★ INN

tel: 015395 62115 **1 Park Rd LA7 7AB**
email: stay@thecrosskeyshotel.co.uk **web:** www.thecrosskeyshotel.co.uk

This early 19th-century coaching inn has a wealth of history and is located in the heart of the town. In its modern incarnation it offers well-equipped and comfortable accommodation and a pub serving good food and a range of cask ales. Ample parking is provided and there is a large function space and separate snooker and pool games rooms.

Rooms 8 en suite (2 fmly) **Facilities** STV FTV tea/coffee Dinner available Direct Dial WiFi ♨ 18 Fishing Snooker Pool table ⬤ **Conf** Max 60 Thtr 60 Class 30 Board 40 **Parking** 40 **Notes** LB

| **NEAR SAWREY** | **Map 18 SD39** |

Premier Collection

Ees Wyke Country House

★★★★★ ◉ ⬤ GUEST HOUSE

tel: 015394 36393 **LA22 0JZ**
email: mail@eeswyke.co.uk **web:** www.eeswyke.co.uk
dir: *On B5285 on W side of village*

A warm welcome awaits at this elegant Georgian country house with views over Esthwaite Water and the surrounding countryside. The thoughtfully equipped bedrooms have been decorated and furnished with care. There is a charming lounge with an open fire, and a splendid dining room where a carefully prepared five-course dinner is served. Breakfasts have a fine reputation due to the skilful use of local produce.

Rooms 8 en suite (1 GF) **Facilities** FTV Lounge tea/coffee Dinner available Licensed WiFi ⬤ **Extras** Sherry, peanuts **Parking** 12 **Notes** ⊗
No Children 12yrs

| **NEWBY BRIDGE** | **Map 18 SD38** |

Premier Collection

The Knoll Country House

★★★★★ ⬤ ◕ GUEST ACCOMMODATION

tel: 015395 31347 **Lakeside LA12 8AU**
email: info@theknoll-lakeside.co.uk **web:** www.theknoll-lakeside.co.uk
dir: *A590 W to Newby Bridge, over rdbt, signed right for Lake Steamers, house 0.5m on left*

This delightful Edwardian villa stands in a leafy dell on the western side of Windermere. Public areas have many original features, including open fires in the cosy lounge and dining room. The attractive bedrooms vary in outlook, and are all very stylish. Proprietor and chef Jenny Mead and her enthusiastic team extend a very caring and natural welcome. Jenny also prepares a good range of excellent dishes at breakfast and dinner.

Rooms 8 en suite 1 annexe rm (1 pri facs) **Facilities** STV FTV DVD iPod docking station Lounge TVL tea/coffee Dinner available Direct Dial Licensed WiFi ⬤ **Extras** Fruit & wine in 1 room **Conf** Max 30 Thtr 30 Class 18 Board 12 **Parking** 9 **Notes** ⊗ No Children 16yrs Closed 24-26 Dec Civ Wed 40

Follow us on Facebook
www.facebook.com/TheAAUK
Find us on Facebook

Premier Collection

Hill Crest Country Guest House

★★★★★ 🛏 GUEST HOUSE

tel: 015395 31766 **Brow Edge LA12 8QP**
email: enquiries@hotelnewbybridge.co.uk **web:** www.hillcrestnewbybridge.co.uk
dir: M6 junct 36 follow signs for Barrow (A590). 1m after Newby Bridge, turn left into Brow Edge Rd, continue on up incline. 4th house on right

Hill Crest Country Guest House is set in picturesque surroundings with stunning views, and offers a high standard of en suite accommodation. All rooms are individual and well maintained. A cosy guest lounge leads into the conservatory breakfast room, where breakfast is served, making good use of fresh local produce. Warm and genuine hospitality is guaranteed. AA Friendliest B&B of the Year Award Finalist 2016-2017.

Rooms 3 en suite (1 fmly) (1 GF) S £60-£80; D £88-£110* **Facilities** iPod docking station TVL tea/coffee WiFi 🔒 Discounted rates at nearby health & fitness club **Extras** Speciality toiletries **Parking** 3 **Notes** LB ⊗ Closed 23-26 Dec

Lyndhurst Country House

★★★★ 🛏 GUEST HOUSE

tel: 015395 31245 **LA12 8ND**
email: chris@lyndhurstcountryhouse.co.uk **web:** www.lyndhurstcountryhouse.co.uk
dir: On junct of A590 & A592 at Newby Bridge rdbt

This 1920s house is situated close to the southern tip of Lake Windermere. Accommodation consists of three comfortable, tastefully decorated bedrooms, each with en suite shower room. Hearty breakfasts feature local produce and are served in the pleasant dining room, which also has a lounge area opening onto the garden.

Rooms 3 en suite D £85-£90* **Facilities** FTV Lounge tea/coffee WiFi 🔒 **Parking** 3 **Notes** LB ⊗ No Children 8yrs Closed 23-28 Dec

PENRITH   Map 18 NY53

Premier Collection

Brooklands Guest House

★★★★★ 🛏 GUEST HOUSE

tel: 01768 863395 **2 Portland Place CA11 7QN**
email: enquiries@brooklandsguesthouse.com **web:** www.brooklandsguesthouse.com
dir: M6 junct 40, follow sign for TIC, left at town hall, 50yds on left

In the bustling market town of Penrith, this beautifully appointed house offers individually furnished bedrooms with high quality accessories and some luxury touches. Nothing seems to be too much trouble for the friendly owners and, from romantic breaks to excellent storage for cyclists, all guests are very well looked after. Delicious breakfasts featuring Cumbrian produce are served in the attractive dining room.

Rooms 6 en suite (1 fmly) S £40-£70; D £85-£95 **Facilities** FTV iPod docking station tea/coffee WiFi 🔒 **Extras** Speciality toiletries, fresh fruit - complimentary **Parking** 2 **Notes** LB ⊗ No Children 3yrs Closed 24 Dec-4 Jan

Premier Collection

River Garth

★★★★★ 🛏 GUEST HOUSE

tel: 01768 863938 & 07718 763273 **Eamont Bridge CA10 2BH**
email: rivergarth@hotmail.co.uk **web:** www.rivergarth.co.uk
dir: M6 junct 40, A66 E towards Scotch Corner. At rdbt 4th exit to Shap, 150yds over bridge & continue for 200yds, turn right at "Keep Clear" road marking. Last bungalow facing river with balconies

The River Garth is in an elevated position overlooking the River Eamont. Spacious and well-presented bedrooms cater well for the needs of the guest, and two of them have balconies looking out on the river. The lounge dining room is comfortable and breakfast uses the finest local produce.

Rooms 3 en suite (1 fmly) S £50-£70; D £70-£90* **Facilities** STV FTV TVL tea/coffee WiFi 🔒 **Extras** Speciality toiletries, bottled water, sweets - free **Parking** 6 **Notes** LB ⊗ 🚭

Albany House

★★★★ 🛏 🍽 GUEST HOUSE

tel: 01768 863072 **5 Portland Place CA11 7QN**
email: info@albany-house.org.uk **web:** www.albany-house.org.uk
dir: Left at town hall into Portland Place. 30yds on left

A well-maintained Victorian house close to Penrith town centre. Bedrooms are comfortable and thoughtfully equipped. Wholesome breakfasts using local ingredients are served in the attractive breakfast room. Good quality dinners are served at the weekend – advance bookings are required.

Rooms 5 rms (3 en suite) (2 pri facs) (1 fmly) S £40-£75; D £70-£80 **Facilities** FTV tea/coffee Dinner available WiFi 🔒 **Extras** Speciality toiletries, bottled water, chocolates **Notes** LB ⊗

Brandelhow Guest House

★★★★ 🛏 GUEST HOUSE

tel: 01768 864470 **1 Portland Place CA11 7QN**
email: enquiries@brandelhowguesthouse.co.uk **web:** www.brandelhowguesthouse.co.uk
dir: In town centre on one-way system, left at town hall

Situated within easy walking distance of central amenities, this friendly guest house is also convenient for the Lakes and M6. The bedrooms are thoughtfully furnished and some are suitable for families. Breakfasts, make great use of quality local produce, are served in a Cumbria-themed dining room overlooking the pretty courtyard garden. Afternoon and high teas are available by arrangement.

Rooms 5 rms (4 en suite) (1 pri facs) (2 fmly) **Facilities** FTV tea/coffee WiFi **Notes** ⊗ Closed 31 Dec & 1 Jan

PENRITH *continued*

Glendale Guest House

★★★★ GUEST HOUSE

tel: 01768 210061 **4 Portland Place CA11 7QN**
email: glendaleguesthouse@yahoo.co.uk **web:** www.glendaleguesthouse.com
dir: *M6 junct 40, follow town centre signs. Pass castle, turn left before town hall*

This friendly, family-run guest house is part of a Victorian terrace just a short stroll from the town centre and convenient for the Lakes and Eden Valley. Drying facilities are available. Bedrooms vary in size, but all are attractive, well equipped and well presented. Hearty breakfasts are served at individual tables in the charming ground-floor dining room.

Rooms 7 en suite (3 fmly) **Facilities** FTV tea/coffee WiFi **Notes** ⊗

Stoneybeck Inn

★★★★ ⊛ INN

tel: 01768 862369 **Bowscar CA11 8RP**
email: reception@stoneybeckinn.co.uk **web:** www.stoneybeckinn.co.uk

This inn enjoys panoramic views over the Cumbrian Fells, and is ideally located for easy access to the M6, and as a base for touring the Lakes and beyond. Recently added bedrooms are finished to an impressive standard with a number of luxurious touches. The inn has built up a strong following locally for both its food and drink. Monthly pudding nights and the Sunday carvery are not to be missed. Extensive conference and banqueting facilities are also on site, as well as complimentary parking.

Rooms 7 en suite (2 GF) S £79-£95; D £89-£105* **Facilities** FTV Lounge tea/coffee Dinner available WiFi ⌗ **Conf** Max 200 Thtr 200 Class 130 Board 60 **Parking** 50 **Notes** ⊗ Civ Wed 200

Acorn Guest House

★★★★ GUEST HOUSE

tel: 01768 868696 & 07814 719894 **Scotland Rd CA11 9HL**
email: info@acorn-guesthouse.co.uk **web:** www.acorn-guesthouse.co.uk

Located within easy walking distance of the town centre, Acorn Guest House is ideal for walkers and cyclists as well as guests using Penrith as their base to tour the area. Bedrooms are en suite and are all well presented and spacious. Breakfast makes good use of quality local produce. A small bar, along with drying facilities, is also available.

Rooms 7 en suite (2 fmly) S £50-£57; D £78-£95 **Facilities** FTV Lounge TVL tea/coffee Dinner available Licensed WiFi ⌗ **Conf** Max 20 Thtr 12 Class 18 Board 20 **Parking** 13 **Notes** LB ⊗

RAVENSTONEDALE **Map 18 NY70**

The Black Swan

★★★★ ⌕ ⊖ INN

tel: 015396 23204 **CA17 4NG**
email: enquiries@blackswanhotel.com **web:** www.blackswanhotel.com
dir: *M6 junct 38. Black Swan on A685, W of Kirkby Stephen*

Set in the heart of this quiet village, the inn is popular with visitors and locals and offers a very friendly welcome. Bedrooms are individually styled and comfortably equipped. There is an informal atmosphere in the bar areas and home-made meals can be taken in the bar or the stylish dining room. Relax by the fire in the cooler months and enjoy the riverside garden in the summer.

Rooms 10 en suite 6 annexe en suite (3 fmly) (3 GF) S £75-£150; D £85-£150 **Facilities** FTV iPod docking station Lounge tea/coffee Dinner available WiFi ⌔ ⌗ 9 Fishing Riding Snooker ⌕ **Extras** Speciality toiletries, snacks, water, robes **Conf** Max 14 Thtr 14 Class 14 Board 14 **Parking** 20 **Notes** LB

The Fat Lamb

★★★★ ⊖ INN

tel: 015396 23242 **Crossbank CA17 4LL**
email: enquiries@fatlamb.co.uk **web:** www.fatlamb.co.uk
dir: *On A683, between Kirkby Stephen & Sedbergh*

Solid stone walls and open fires feature at this 17th-century inn. The bedrooms are comfortable and all are en suite. An accessible ground-floor room with en suite wet room is available. Guests can enjoy a choice of dining options: well-cooked dishes using local produce are served in either the traditional bar or the more formal dining room. There is also a beer garden.

Rooms 12 en suite (4 fmly) (5 GF) S £64; D £108 **Facilities** Lounge tea/coffee Dinner available WiFi ⌗ 18 ⌕ Private 5-acre nature reserve **Conf** Thtr 60 Class 30 Board 30 **Parking** 60 **Notes** LB

RYDAL
See Ambleside

SHAP **Map 18 NY51**

Brookfield Guest House

★★★★ GUEST HOUSE

tel: 01931 716397 **CA10 3PZ**
email: info@brookfieldshap.co.uk **web:** www.brookfieldshap.co.uk
dir: *M6 junct 39, A6 towards Shap, 1st accommodation off motorway, on right*

In a quiet rural location within easy reach of the M6, inviting Brookfield Guest House stands in well-tended, attractive gardens. Bedrooms are thoughtfully appointed and well maintained. There is a comfortable lounge, and a small bar area next to the traditional dining room where substantial, home-cooked breakfasts are served at individual tables.

Rooms 4 rms (3 en suite) (1 pri facs) **Facilities** FTV TVL tea/coffee Licensed WiFi ⌗ **Parking** 20 **Notes** ⊗ No Children 12yrs Closed Nov-1 Mar ⊜

TEMPLE SOWERBY   Map 18 NY62

The Kings Arms
★★★★ ⇔ INN

tel: 017683 62944 **CA10 1SB**
email: enquiries@kingsarmstemplesowerby.co.uk
web: www.kingsarmstemplesowerby.co.uk
dir: *M6 junct 40, E on A66 to Temple Sowerby, Kings Arms in village*

The Kings Arms is located in the peaceful village of Temple Sowerby, just a couple of minutes from the A66 bypass and a short drive from Center Parcs. The property dates back over 400 years and offers a good deal of charm and character. Quality food is served in the small restaurant or in the bar itself which has an open fire. Comfortable, well-appointed accommodation makes this an ideal base for touring this delightful area.

Rooms 8 en suite (5 fmly) S £65-£70; D £85-£120* **Facilities** FTV Lounge tea/coffee Dinner available WiFi Fishing 🅿 **Parking** 20 **Notes** LB

Skygarth Farm *(NY612261)*
★★★ FARMHOUSE

tel: 017683 61300 **CA10 1SS**
email: skygarth@outlook.com **web:** www.skygarth.co.uk
dir: *Off A66 at Temple Sowerby for Morland, Skygarth 500yds on right, follow signs*

Skygarth is just south of the village, half a mile from the busy main road. The house stands in a cobbled courtyard surrounded by cowsheds, with gardens to the rear, where red squirrels feed. There are two well-proportioned bedrooms and an attractive lounge where tasty breakfasts are served.

Rooms 2 rms (2 fmly) S £40; D £60-£66* **Facilities** FTV TVL tea/coffee WiFi 🅿 **Extras** Bottled water, biscuits - complimentary; robes **Parking** 4 **Notes** ⊗ Closed Dec-Jan ⊛ 200 acres mixed

---

TROUTBECK (NEAR WINDERMERE)   Map 18 NY40

Premier Collection

Broadoaks Country House
★★★★★ ⇔ GUEST ACCOMMODATION

tel: 015394 45566 **Bridge Ln LA23 1LA**
email: enquiries@broadoakscountryhouse.co.uk
web: www.broadoakscountryhouse.co.uk
dir: *Exit A591 junct 36 pass Windermere. Filing station on left, 1st right 0.5m*

This impressive Lakeland stone house has been restored to its original Victorian grandeur and is set in seven acres of landscaped grounds with stunning views of the Troutbeck Valley. Individually furnished bedrooms are well appointed and en suite bathrooms feature either whirlpool or Victorian roll top baths. Spacious day rooms include the music room, featuring a Bechstein piano. Meals are served by friendly and attentive staff in the elegant dining room.

Rooms 11 en suite 8 annexe en suite (8 fmly) (7 GF) **Facilities** STV FTV DVD iPod docking station tea/coffee Dinner available Direct Dial Licensed WiFi 🛥 Fishing Arrangement with local leisure facility **Extras** Speciality toiletries **Conf** Max 62 Thtr 40 Class 45 Board 45 **Parking** 40 **Notes** Civ Wed 100

WASDALE HEAD   Map 18 NY10

Wasdale Head Inn
★★★★ INN

tel: 019467 26229 & 26333 **CA20 1EX**
email: reception@wasdale.com **web:** www.wasdale.com
dir: *Leave A595 at Santon Bridge or Gosforth if travelling S. Follow signs for Wasdale*

Wasdale Head is known as the birthplace of British climbing for good reason. The setting of this popular inn is breathtaking, surrounded by the fells with the brooding Wast Water close by. Inside, the decor is enhanced with *objets d'art* and photos of climbers and mountains. Bedrooms and public areas are comfortable, and the service is relaxed and informal. Real ales and good food are served in the rustic bar while a separate restaurant is available for residents.

Rooms 11 en suite 9 annexe en suite (2 fmly) (5 GF) **Facilities** FTV Lounge tea/coffee Dinner available Direct Dial WiFi 🅿 **Extras** Bath salts, robes - complimentary **Conf** Max 20 Thtr 20 Class 20 Board 20 **Parking** 30 **Notes** LB No coaches Civ Wed 50

WINDERMERE   Map 18 SD49

Premier Collection

Applegarth Villa & Restaurant
★★★★★ ⓠ ⇔ GUEST ACCOMMODATION

tel: 015394 43206 **College Rd LA23 1BU**
email: info@lakesapplegarth.co.uk **web:** www.lakesapplegarth.co.uk
dir: *M6 junct 36, A591 towards Windermere. On entering town left after NatWest Bank into Elleray Rd. 1st right into College Rd, Applegarth on right*

This period building in the heart of Windermere offers elegantly furnished accommodation with luxurious bathrooms. The attractive conservatory dining room offers stunning views of the mountains and serves locally sourced produce. The oak-panelled bar has an open fire and is a perfect retreat on a winter evening. Private off-road parking is a bonus.

Rooms 15 en suite 7 annexe en suite (2 GF) S £90-£150; D £140-£475* **Facilities** FTV iPod docking station tea/coffee Dinner available Direct Dial Licensed WiFi 🅿 7 suites with outdoor hot tubs **Extras** Speciality toiletries, bottled water, fruit - free **Parking** 27 **Notes** LB No Children 18yrs

Over 2,100 places, from country inns and historic taverns to town hostelries and gastro-pubs. Now in its 20th year.

AA

THE **PUB** GUIDE 2017

BRITAIN'S BEST PUBS FOR BEER AND FOOD

shop.theAA.com

WINDERMERE *continued*

Premier Collection

Lindeth Fell Country House

★★★★★ ☺ GUEST ACCOMMODATION

tel: 015394 43286 & 44287 **Lyth Valley Rd, Bowness-on-Windermere LA23 3JP**
email: kennedy@lindethfell.co.uk **web:** www.lindethfell.co.uk
dir: *1m S of Bowness on A5074*

Lindeth Fell offers luxury bed and breakfast accommodation, perfectly located overlooking Lake Windermere in the heart of the Lake District. A few minutes' drive from Bowness with its boutique shops, cinema, lively restaurants and cafés, this elegant Edwardian country house has high ceilings and beautiful architecture, sympathetically and stylishly restored with both period and contemporary features. The 14 individually-designed bedrooms have crisp Egyptian cotton bed linen, deluxe fluffy towels, White Company toiletries, sherry decanters, DAB radio/Bluetooth, and flat-screen TV. Many have superb lake views. All have tea/coffee trays, and the Master rooms have Nespresso coffee machines.

Rooms 14 en suite (2 fmly) (1 GF) S £68-£95; D £136-£240* **Facilities** FTV iPod docking station Lounge tea/coffee Direct Dial Licensed WiFi ⚓ Fishing ⚓ Use of leisure facilities at nearby hotel **Extras** Speciality toiletries, sherry - complimentary **Conf** Max 12 Class 12 Board 12 **Parking** 20 **Notes** LB ⊗ Closed Jan

Premier Collection

Windermere Suites

★★★★★ ☺ BED AND BREAKFAST

tel: 015394 47672 **New Rd LA23 2LA**
email: reservations@windermeresuites.co.uk **web:** www.windermeresuites.co.uk
dir: *Through village on one-way system towards Bowness-on-Windermere. 50mtrs past The Ellerthwaite*

Close to Windermere and Bowness, Windermere Suites is a very special boutique town house which offers eight individual suites, all combining contemporary designer furniture with cutting edge entertainment technology and sheer elegance. Each suite has its own lounge area, and the bathrooms have large spa baths complete with TV, mood lighting and power showers. Rooms also have mini-bars, and room service is available up to 10pm. An unusual feature is the "living showroom" element, if you like an item of furniture or decoration you can order it to buy at a discount.

Rooms 8 en suite (3 GF) S £150-£220; D £180-£270* **Facilities** STV FTV DVD iPod docking station TVL tea/coffee Licensed WiFi Free use of nearby spa & leisure club **Extras** Mini-bar, safe **Parking** 9 **Notes** LB ⊗

Premier Collection

The Howbeck

★★★★★ GUEST HOUSE

tel: 015394 44739 **New Rd LA23 2LA**
email: relax@howbeck.co.uk **web:** www.howbeck.co.uk
dir: *A591 through Windermere town centre, left towards Bowness*

The Howbeck is a delightful Victorian villa, convenient for the village and the lake. Bedrooms are well appointed and feature lovely soft furnishings, along with luxurious spa baths in some cases. There is a bright lounge with internet access and an attractive dining room where home-prepared hearty Cumbrian breakfasts are served at individual tables.

Rooms 10 en suite 1 annexe en suite (3 GF) **Facilities** STV FTV TVL tea/coffee Dinner available Licensed WiFi Free membership to nearby spa & leisure club **Parking** 12 **Notes** ⊗ Closed 24-25 Dec

Follow us on twitter
@TheAA_Lifestyle

The Cottage

★★★★ ≊ GUEST ACCOMMODATION

tel: 015394 44796 **Elleray Rd LA23 1AG**
email: enquiries@thecottageguesthouse.com **web:** www.thecottageguesthouse.com
dir: A591, past Windermere Hotel, in 150yds left into Elleray Rd. The Cottage 150yds on left

Built in 1847, this attractive house is one of the oldest in Windermere and offers a blend of modern and traditional styles. The tastefully furnished bedrooms are well equipped and comfortable. A wide choice of freshly cooked breakfasts is served in the spacious dining room at individual tables.

Rooms 8 en suite (2 GF) S £40-£49; D £75-£100* **Facilities** FTV DVD tea/coffee **Parking** 8 **Notes** ⊗ No Children 11yrs Closed Nov-Jan

Dene House

★★★★ GUEST ACCOMMODATION

tel: 015394 48236 **Kendal Rd LA23 3EW**
email: denehouse@ignetics.co.uk **web:** www.denehouse-guesthouse.co.uk
dir: From Lake Rd, turn opposite St Martins Church into Kendal Rd. 400yds on right

Detached property situated on the edge of the village a short walk from pubs, restaurants and Lake Windermere. Bedrooms are individually furnished and tastefully decorated, one room is situated on the ground floor offering ease of access; facilities include wine chillers, iPod docking stations and WiFi. Breakfast is served at individual tables in the smart dining room and the property has a beautiful terrace garden.

Rooms 7 rms (6 en suite) (1 pri facs) (1 GF) **Facilities** FTV iPod docking station tea/coffee WiFi Gym Use of pool at nearby hotel - charged **Parking** 7 **Notes** LB ⊗ No Children 12yrs

Fairfield House and Gardens

★★★★ ≊ GUEST HOUSE

tel: 015394 46565 **Brantfell Rd, Bowness-on-Windermere LA23 3AE**
email: tonyandliz@the-fairfield.co.uk **web:** www.the-fairfield.co.uk
dir: Into Bowness town centre, turn opposite St Martin's Church & sharp left by Spinnery restaurant, house 200mtrs on right

Situated just above Bowness and Lake Windermere, this Lakeland country house is tucked away in a half acre of secluded, peaceful gardens. The house has been beautifully appointed to combine Georgian and Victorian features with stylish, contemporary design. Guests are shown warm hospitality and can relax in the delightful lounge. Bedrooms are well furnished, varying in size and style with some featuring luxurious bathrooms. Delicious breakfasts are served in the attractive dining room or on the terrace in warmer weather.

Fairfield House and Gardens

Rooms 8 en suite (3 GF) S £59-£94; D £79-£94 **Facilities** FTV DVD Lounge tea/coffee Licensed WiFi ⌣ ⚲ 18 ⚿ **Conf** Max 20 Thtr 20 Class 10 Board 12 **Parking** 10 **Notes** LB No Children 10yrs Closed Xmas

Glenville House

★★★★ ≊ GUEST HOUSE

tel: 015394 43371 **Lake Rd LA23 2EQ**
email: mail@glenvillehouse.co.uk **web:** www.glenvillehouse.co.uk
dir: At Windermere station/tourist info centre, turn left into village. Straight through, on right opposite vets

Glenville House is very conveniently located in a pleasant area, and good parking is a bonus. The house is well appointed and the bedrooms have comfortable beds and many accessories to make your stay relaxing and enjoyable. The friendly proprietors make guests welcome, and breakfast is taken in a pleasant room at individual tables. AA Friendliest B&B of the Year Award Finalist 2016-2017.

Rooms 7 en suite (1 GF) S £65-£80; D £70-£110* **Facilities** FTV iPod docking station tea/coffee WiFi **Parking** 7 **Notes** LB ⊗ No Children 18yrs Closed 6-30 Jan

The Hideaway at Windermere

★★★★ ≊ GUEST ACCOMMODATION

tel: 015394 43070 **Phoenix Way LA23 1DB**
email: eatandstay@thehideawayatwindermere.co.uk
web: www.thehideawayatwindermere.co.uk
dir: Exit A591 at Ravensworth B&B, into Phoenix Way, The Hideaway 100mtrs on right

Quietly tucked away, this beautiful Victorian Lakeland house is personally run by owners Richard and Lisa. Delicious food, individually designed bedrooms and warm hospitality ensure an enjoyable stay. There is a beautifully appointed lounge looking out to the garden, and the dining area is split between two light and airy rooms. Breakfast is freshly prepared using the best local ingredients and service is attentive and friendly. Bedrooms vary in size and style; the larger rooms feature luxury bathrooms. Tea and home-made cake is included and served each day.

Rooms 10 en suite 1 annexe en suite D £85-£165* **Facilities** FTV Lounge tea/coffee Direct Dial Licensed WiFi ⚿ Off-site spa facilities available **Parking** 15 **Notes** LB ⊗ No Children 16yrs Closed Jan-mid Feb

WINDERMERE *continued*

Holly-Wood Guest House

★★★★ 🛏 GUEST HOUSE

tel: 015394 42219 **Holly Rd LA23 2AF**
email: info@hollywoodguesthouse.co.uk **web:** www.hollywoodguesthouse.co.uk
dir: *M6 junct 36 left onto A590 signed Kendal then A591 towards Windermere, left into town, left again into Ellerthwaite Rd, next left into Holly Rd*

This attractive Victorian end terrace is located in a quiet residential area just a few minutes' walk from Windermere town centre. Guests are offered a friendly welcome, comfortable, well equipped bedrooms and a freshly prepared breakfast. Limited off-street parking is also available.

Rooms 6 en suite S £45; D £75-£100 **Facilities** FTV iPod docking station tea/coffee WiFi 🛜 **Extras** Speciality toiletries, home-made snacks - free **Parking** 3 **Notes** ⊗ No Children 18yrs Closed 23-27 Dec

Rockside Guest House

★★★★ 🛏 GUEST HOUSE

tel: 015394 45343 **25 Church St LA23 1AQ**
email: enquiries@rockside-guesthouse.co.uk **web:** www.rockside-guesthouse.co.uk

Rockside Guest House was built in 1847 from Lakeland stone, and is owner-managed by Martin and Caroline. They have modernised the building to provide all mod cons, yet retained many of the original features. Situated at the head of the village, Rockside is a two minute walk from local transport links, restaurants, pubs and shops, and only 20 minutes' walk from Lake Windermere. Breakfast offers a range of options for all tastes, from a substantial full breakfast to lighter bites and vegetarian alternatives, all prepared with quality local produce and served with home-made marmalade and jams.

Rooms 9 en suite D £75-£95* **Facilities** FTV tea/coffee WiFi **Parking** 9 **Notes** ⊗ No Children 14yrs Closed Nov-Feb

The Wild Boar Inn, Grill & Smokehouse

★★★★ 🏵 INN

tel: 015394 45225 **Crook LA23 3NF**
email: thewildboar@englishlakes.co.uk **web:** www.thewildboarinn.co.uk
dir: *2.5m S of Windermere on B5284. From Crook 3.5m, on right*

Steeped in history, this former coaching inn enjoys a peaceful rural location close to Windermere. Public areas include a welcoming lounge and a cosy bar where an extensive choice of wines, ales and whiskies are served. The Grill & Smokehouse features quality local and seasonal ingredients. Bedrooms, some with four-poster beds, vary in style and size. Leisure facilities are available close by.

Rooms 34 en suite (2 fmly) (9 GF) **Facilities** FTV TV33B tea/coffee Dinner available Direct Dial WiFi Use of leisure facilities at sister hotel **Conf** Thtr 40 Class 10 Board 20 **Parking** 60 **Notes** LB Civ Wed 100

Blenheim Lodge

★★★★ GUEST ACCOMMODATION

tel: 015394 43440 **Brantfell Rd, Bowness-on-Windermere LA23 3AE**
email: enquiries@blenheim-lodge.com **web:** www.blenheim-lodge.com
dir: *From Windermere to Bowness village, left at mini rdbt, next 2 lefts, then up to top of Brantfell Rd & turn right*

From a peaceful position above Bowness, Blenheim Lodge has stunning panoramic views of Lake Windermere. Bedrooms are well equipped featuring antique furnishings and pocket-sprung mattresses. Most beds are antiques themselves and include two William IV four-posters and three Louis XV examples. There is a comfortable lounge and a beautifully decorated dining room.

Rooms 11 rms (10 en suite) (1 pri facs) (2 fmly) (2 GF) S £60-£65.50; D £90-£155 **Facilities** FTV TVL tea/coffee Licensed WiFi 🛜 Free fishing permits **Parking** 11 **Notes** LB ⊗ No Children 8yrs Closed 25 Dec RS 24-27 Dec may open, phone for details

The Haven

★★★★ 🛏 BED AND BREAKFAST

tel: 015394 88583 **10 Birch St LA23 1EG**
email: info@thehavenwindermere.co.uk **web:** www.thehavenwindermere.co.uk
dir: *On A5074 enter one-way system, 3rd left into Birch St*

Built from Lakeland slate and stone, The Haven is just a 50 metres from the town centre and shops. The bright, spacious bedrooms offer en suite facilities and one has a Victorian brass bed. A hearty Cumbrian breakfast is served in the well-appointed dining room that doubles as a lounge. The Haven benefits from limited off-road parking, available on a first come first served basis. The well-presented hanging baskets and planters outside are lovely. A warm and genuine welcome from the owners adds to the friendly first impression created.

Rooms 3 en suite (1 fmly) **Facilities** FTV DVD Lounge tea/coffee WiFi 🛜 **Parking** 3 **Notes** LB ⊗ No Children 7yrs

The Old Court House

★★★★ GUEST HOUSE

tel: 015394 45096 **Lake Rd LA23 3AP**
email: alitheoch@gmail.com **web:** www.theoch.co.uk
dir: *On Windermere-Bowness road at junct Longlands Rd*

Guests are given a warm welcome at this attractive former Victorian police station and courthouse, located in the centre of Bowness. Comfortable, pine-furnished bedrooms offer a good range of extra facilities. Freshly prepared breakfasts are served in the bright ground-floor dining room.

Rooms 6 en suite (2 GF) **Facilities** tea/coffee WiFi **Parking** 6 **Notes** ⊗ No Children 10yrs

Bonny Brae Guest House

★★★ GUEST HOUSE

tel: 015394 22699 & 07765 778046 **West Beck, 11 Oak St LA23 1EN**
email: stay@bonnybraewindermere.com **web:** www.bonnybraewindermere.com

A warm and genuine welcome awaits you at Bonny Brae, situated in the heart of Windermere village, just a short walk from cafés, shops and travel links. Accommodation is comfortable, and breakfast makes good use of local produce.

Rooms 5 en suite (1 fmly) S £65; D £75-£85 **Facilities** FTV DVD iPod docking station tea/coffee WiFi 🔒 **Notes** ⊗ No Children 7yrs

Brook House

★★★ GUEST HOUSE

tel: 015394 44932 **30 Ellerthwaite Rd LA23 2AH**
email: stay@brookhouselakes.co.uk **web:** www.brookhouselakes.co.uk
dir: *M6 junct 36, A591, through one-way system. Ellerthwaite Rd 2nd left, 200yds on right*

Brook House is a Lakeland stone Victorian guest house set in a quiet part of Windermere and offers a very relaxed friendly atmosphere. Accessible with or without a car and close to all amenities, it is a perfect base for exploring the Lake District. Bedrooms include a family room and a single. Private parking and a guest lounge are also available. 'Whisky Warmer' weekends are run throughout the winter.

Rooms 5 en suite (1 fmly) **Facilities** FTV Lounge tea/coffee WiFi **Extras** Speciality toiletries - complimentary **Parking** 5 **Notes** ⊗ No Children 8yrs

Ellerdene Guesthouse

★★★ GUEST HOUSE

tel: 015394 43610 **12 Ellerthwaite Rd LA23 2AH**
email: info@ellerdene.co.uk **web:** www.ellerdene.co.uk
dir: *M6 junct 36 follow signs for Kendal then Windermere (A591). Follow one-way system, take 2nd left after pedestrian crossing into Ellerthwaite Rd. On right opposite Holly Rd*

Ellerdene is a welcoming guest house situated in the heart of Windermere village, perfectly situated for all local amenities. Accommodation features modern, stylishly designed rooms which are comfortable and thoughtfully equipped. Expect a generous, freshly-cooked breakfast served in the bright and spacious dining room.

Rooms 6 rms (5 en suite) (1 pri facs) (1 fmly) (1 GF) S £30-£40; D £64-£75* **Facilities** FTV DVD tea/coffee WiFi 🔒 **Extras** Fridge **Notes** LB No Children 6yrs Closed 7 Nov-16 Jan

Adam Place Guest House

★★★ GUEST HOUSE

tel: 015394 44600 & 07484 826762 **1 Park Av LA23 2AR**
email: adamplacewindermere@yahoo.co.uk **web:** www.adamplacelakedistrict.co.uk
dir: *Exit A591 into Windermere, through town centre, left into Ellerthwaite Rd & Park Av*

Located in a mainly residential area within easy walking distance of lake and town centre, this stone-built Victorian house has been renovated to provide comfortable and homely bedrooms. Comprehensive breakfasts are served in the cosy dining room and there is a pretty patio garden.

Rooms 5 en suite (2 fmly) **Facilities** FTV DVD tea/coffee WiFi 🔒 **Notes** LB ⊗ No Children 6yrs

Green Gables Guest House

★★★ GUEST HOUSE

tel: 015394 43886 **37 Broad St LA23 2AB**
email: info@greengablesguesthouse.co.uk **web:** www.greengablesguesthouse.co.uk
dir: *A591 into Windermere, 1st left after pelican crossing, opposite car park*

Aptly named, Green Gables is a friendly guest house looking onto Elleray Gardens. Just a short walk from the centre, the house is attractively furnished and offers bright, fresh and well appointed bedrooms. There is a comfortable bar-lounge, and substantial breakfasts are served in the spacious dining room.

Rooms 7 rms (4 en suite) (3 pri facs) (3 fmly) (1 GF) **Facilities** TVL tea/coffee Licensed **Notes** ⊗ Closed 23-27 Dec

| WORKINGTON | Map 18 NY02 |

The Sleepwell Inn

★★★★ GUEST ACCOMMODATION

tel: 01900 65772 **Washington St CA14 3AX**
email: info@washingtoncentralhotel.co.uk
web: www.washingtoncentralhotelworkington.com
dir: *M6 junct 40, W on A66. At bottom of Ramsay Brow left into Washington St, 300yds on left opposite church*

The Sleepwell Inn offers comfortable and well-appointed accommodation and is situated just 100 metres from its sister property, the Washington Central Hotel. Guests have full use of the Washington's facilities and that is where breakfast is served. Off-road parking is available to the rear. Rooms differ in size and style at The Sleepwell, with some inter-connecting rooms available. A calming, natural colour scheme has been used in the bedrooms to create a chic, contemporary feel.

Rooms 24 en suite (4 fmly) (12 GF) S £55-£65; D £80 (room only)* **Facilities** FTV Lounge TVL tea/coffee Dinner available Direct Dial Licensed WiFi ⬇ 18 🔒 Facilities available at Washington Central Hotel **Parking** 32 **Notes** LB ⊗ Civ Wed 300

DERBYSHIRE

ASHBOURNE   Map 10 SK14

Compton House

★★★★ GUEST ACCOMMODATION

tel: 01335 343100 **27-31 Compton DE6 1BX**
email: jane@comptonhouse.co.uk **web:** www.comptonhouse.co.uk
dir: *A52 from Derby into Ashbourne, over lights at bottom of hill, house 100yds on left opposite garage*

Within easy walking distance of the central attractions, this conversion of three cottages has resulted in a house with good standards of comfort and facilities. Bedrooms are filled with homely extras and comprehensive breakfasts are served in the cottage-style dining room. Parking available.

Rooms 5 en suite (1 fmly) (1 GF) S £50-£55; D £70-£80 **Facilities** FTV TVL tea/coffee WiFi 🛁 **Parking** 5 **Notes** ⊗

Mercaston Hall *(SK279419)*

★★★★ FARMHOUSE

tel: 01335 360263 & 07836 648102 **Mercaston DE6 3BL**
email: mercastonhall@btinternet.com **web:** www.mercastonhall.com
dir: *Exit A52 in Brailsford into Luke Ln, 1m, right at 1st x-rds, house 1m on right*

Located in a pretty hamlet, this medieval building retains many original features. Bedrooms are homely, and additional facilities include an all-weather tennis court and a livery service. WiFi access is also available. This is a good base for visiting local stately homes, the Derwent Valley mills and Dovedale.

Rooms 3 en suite S £65-£75; D £75-£95* **Facilities** FTV DVD Lounge tea/coffee WiFi 🎣 Fishing 🛁 **Extras** Fridge **Parking** 3 **Notes** Closed Xmas ⊛ 60 acres mixed

The Wheel House

★★★★ 🥂 BED AND BREAKFAST

tel: 01335 372837 **Belper Rd, Hulland Ward DE6 3EE**
email: thewheelhouse@btinternet.com **web:** www.thewheelhouse.co.uk
dir: *Between Ashbourne & Belper on A517*

This comfortably furnished house is set in open countryside on the main road between Ashbourne and Belper. The bedrooms are furnished in a country style and are named after authors. A cosy lounge is available. Breakfasts are hearty, and guests can expect friendly and attentive service.

Rooms 3 en suite **Facilities** FTV TVL tea/coffee WiFi 🛁 **Extras** Bottled water, jar of sweets - complimentary **Parking** 5 **Notes** ⊗

BAKEWELL   Map 16 SK26

Wyedale Bed & Breakfast

★★★★ BED AND BREAKFAST

tel: 01629 812845 **Wyedale House, 25 Holywell DE45 1BA**
web: www.wyedale.co.uk
dir: *500yds SE of town centre, off A6 (Haddon Rd)*

Wyedale is close to the town centre and is ideally based for a relaxing stay or touring. Bedrooms, one of which is on the ground floor, are spacious and pleasantly decorated. Breakfast is served in the attractive dining room, which overlooks the rear patio.

Rooms 4 en suite (1 fmly) (1 GF) **Facilities** tea/coffee WiFi 🎣 Fishing 🛁 **Parking** 4 **Notes** ⊗ Closed 31 Dec RS 24 Dec ⊛

Wyeclose

★★★ BED AND BREAKFAST

tel: 01629 813702 **5 Granby Croft DE45 1ET**
email: wyeclosebnb@gmail.com **web:** www.wyeclosebnb.co.uk
dir: *From centre of Bakewell onto A6 (Matlock St) left into Granby Rd & 2nd right into Granby Croft*

Located in a quiet cul-de-sac in the town centre, this Edwardian house provides thoughtfully furnished bedroom accommodation with smart modern bathrooms, and an attractive dining room, which is the setting for comprehensive breakfasts. Original family art is a feature in the ground-floor areas.

Rooms 2 rms (1 en suite) (1 pri facs) D £70 **Facilities** FTV DVD tea/coffee WiFi 🛁 **Parking** 3 **Notes** ⊗ No Children 8yrs Closed Xmas & New Year

BEELEY   Map 16 SK26

The Devonshire Arms at Beeley

★★★★ ⊛ INN

tel: 01629 733259 & 01756 718111 **Devonshire Square DE4 2NR**
email: enquiries@devonshirebeeley.co.uk **web:** www.devonshirebeeley.co.uk
dir: *B6012 towards Matlock, pass Chatsworth House. After 1.5m turn left, 2nd entrance to Beeley*

The Devonshire Arms at Beeley is a charming 18th-century village inn, located on the Chatsworth Estate, with Chatsworth House itself only a short drive away. With fourteen stylish and well-appointed rooms and suites, this is the ideal place to stay for exploring one of Britain's best-loved stately homes, the pretty villages on the estate, and the wild and natural beauty of the Peak District National Park. Local produce is fully evident on the menu, and the inn serves an array of dishes. Eat in the cosy bar area, The 'Malt Vault' - a private seating area suited to groups of up to twelve; or the contemporary, colourful Brasserie. In the summer months there is an 'alfresco' terrace too, with parasols beside the brook.

Rooms 4 en suite 10 annexe en suite (2 fmly) (2 GF) **Facilities** FTV DVD tea/coffee Dinner available Direct Dial WiFi **Parking** 30 **Notes** No coaches

BELPER   Map 11 SK34

Premier Collection

Dannah Farm Country House

★★★★★ 🥂 GUEST ACCOMMODATION

tel: 01773 550213 & 550630 **Bowmans Ln, Shottle DE56 2DR**
email: slack@dannah.co.uk **web:** www.dannah.co.uk
dir: *A517 from Belper towards Ashbourne, 1.5m right into Shottle after Hanging Gate pub on right, over x-rds & right*

Part of the Chatsworth Estates at Shottle, in an elevated position with stunning views, this impressive Georgian house and its outbuildings have been renovated to provide luxurious, individually styled bedrooms. Two have private hot tubs, one has a sauna, and there is a Spa Cabin and 'Secret Garden' hot tub that can be booked separately. The elegant dining room is the setting for memorable breakfasts, which make use of the finest local produce. Excellent supper platters are also available by prior arrangement.

Rooms 8 en suite (1 fmly) (2 GF) S £95-£110; D £185-£295* **Facilities** FTV DVD iPod docking station Lounge tea/coffee Licensed WiFi Sauna 🛁 Leisure cabin hot tub **Extras** Bath robes, speciality toiletries, honesty bar **Parking** 20 **Notes** LB ⊗ Closed 24-26 Dec

Premier Collection

Bridge Hill House

★★★★★ ☺ GUEST ACCOMMODATION

tel: 07931 931011 & 01773 599859 **34a Lodge Dr DE56 2TP**
email: info@bridgehillhouse.co.uk **web:** www.bridgehillhouse.co.uk
dir: In town centre turn onto A517 signed Ashbourne. After 350mtrs right into Belper Ln, then left into Lodge Drive. Continue up hill, right into drive alongside Number 34

Bridge Hill House is a modern property designed by its owners and built using local stone on what used to be part of the extensive Strutt family estate. Some evidence of its former life remains, including the ice house and underground arched tunnels which are now listed. A warm welcome is assured, and home-made afternoon bakes and cakes are not to be missed. Award-winning breakfasts are served in the open-plan family room which has far-reaching views across Belper and beyond. Attractively presented en suite accommodation is all located on the ground floor, and rooms are decorated in soft tones with a host of thoughtful extras provided. Local guided tours by prior arrangement.

Rooms 4 en suite (4 GF) S £75–£129; D £85–£149* **Facilities** FTV iPod docking station Lounge tea/coffee WiFi 🔒 **Parking** 6 **Notes** LB ⊗ No Children 16yrs

Ladygate Farm Bed and Breakfast

★★★★ ☺ BED AND BREAKFAST

tel: 01663 745562 & 07885 593123 **Briargrove Rd SK22 1AY**
email: liz@ladygatefarm.co.uk **web:** www.ladygatefarm.co.uk
dir: From Marple Bridge follow signs to Mellor/New Mills. After 3m left into Briargrove Rd, 0.5m on left at bottom of hill

Beautifully restored, this former farm house is both peaceful and homely, and is surrounded by picturesque Derbyshire countryside. Known as the location for the BBC drama The Village, Heyfield is just two miles away. Lyme House, Kinder Scout and the start of the Pennine Way are also within easy reach. Stylish bedrooms are well equipped with comfortable beds, a wealth of thoughtful extras and smart modern bathrooms. Served at the large dining table, Aga-cooked breakfasts include sausage and bacon from a local award-winning butcher. Hosts Liz and Dave will be happy to recommend a number of local dining options.

Rooms 3 rms (2 en suite) (1 pri facs) S £65; D £85–£90 **Facilities** FTV DVD TVL tea/coffee WiFi 🔒 **Extras** Robes, fruit, fresh flowers, speciality toiletries **Parking** 3 **Notes** LB ⊗ No Children 12yrs

Premier Collection

The Samuel Fox Country Inn

★★★★★ ⊛⊛ INN

tel: 01433 621562 **Stretfield Rd S33 9JT**
email: enquiries@samuelfox.co.uk **web:** www.samuelfox.co.uk
dir: M1 junct 29, A617 towards Chesterfield, A619 signed Baslow & Buxton, 2nd rdbt A623 for 7m, take B6049 to Bradwell, through village on left

Named after Bradwell's most famous son, industrial magnate Samuel Fox, who built the steelworks at Stocksbridge, The Samuel Fox Country Inn is modern and stylish yet retains its rustic charm. Bedrooms are both immaculately presented

and extensively equipped, and service is highly attentive. The restaurant has breathtaking views and serves modern British cuisine, awarded two AA Rosettes.

Rooms 4 en suite S £95; D £130* **Facilities** FTV tea/coffee Dinner available WiFi ⛷ 18 🔒 **Extras** Home-made chocolates, hand-made cookies, sherry **Conf** Max 20 Thtr 12 Class 12 Board 10 **Parking** 15 **Notes** LB ⊗ Closed 2-17 Jan

Alpine Lodge Guest House

★★★★ GUEST HOUSE

tel: 01298 26155 & 07808 283408 **1 Thornsett, Hardwick Mount SK17 6PS**
email: sales@alpinelodgebuxton.co.uk **web:** http://alpinelodgebuxton.co.uk
dir: A515 onto Hardwick St. Take right hand fork into Hardwick Mount, just past church on left

Alpine Lodge is particularly welcoming to walkers and cyclists. It offers elegant, stylishly furnished accommodation on a tree-lined residential road, close to the town centre. All rooms have en suite shower facilities or private bathrooms with large baths, separate showers and luxurious toiletries. A hospitality tray with fresh milk is provided in each room. Non-allergenic duvets and pillows are available on request, and all beds have fresh crisp cotton sheets and duvet covers. Buxton Opera House and the tranquil Pavilion Gardens are 10 minutes' stroll away. The Peak District National Park and Derbyshire Dales are on the doorstep.

Rooms 5 rms (4 en suite) (1 pri facs) (1 fmly) S £65–£70; D £85–£95 **Facilities** FTV tea/coffee WiFi 🔒 **Extras** Speciality toiletries, bottled water - free **Parking** 4 **Notes** ⊗ No Children 1yr

Oldfield Guest House

★★★★ ☺ GUEST HOUSE

tel: 01298 78264 **8 Macclesfield Rd SK17 9AH**
email: avril@oldfieldhousebuxton.co.uk **web:** www.oldfieldhousebuxton.co.uk
dir: On B5059 0.5m SW of town centre

Located within easy walking distance of the centre, Oldfield Guest House is an impressive Victorian house with some original stained-glass windows, providing spacious bedrooms with modern en suites. Comprehensive breakfasts are served in the bright dining room, and a cosy lounge is available, making this a home-from-home experience.

Rooms 4 en suite (1 GF) D £85–£90* **Facilities** FTV DVD TVL tea/coffee WiFi ⛷ 18 🔒 **Extras** Speciality toiletries, bottled water - free **Parking** 7 **Notes** LB ⊗ No Children 8yrs Closed Xmas

BUXTON *continued*

Roseleigh

★★★★ GUEST ACCOMMODATION

tel: 01298 24904 **19 Broad Walk SK17 6JR**
email: enquiries@roseleighhotel.co.uk **web:** www.roseleighhotel.co.uk
dir: *A6 to Morrisons rdbt, into Dale Rd, right at lights, 100yds left by Swan pub, down hill, right into Hartington Rd*

This elegant property has a prime location overlooking Pavilion Gardens, and the quality furnishings and decor highlight the many original features. The thoughtfully furnished bedrooms have smart modern shower rooms, and a comfortable lounge is also available.

Rooms 14 rms (12 en suite) (2 pri facs) (1 GF) S £44-£98; D £70-£98* **Facilities** FTV Lounge tea/coffee WiFi **Parking** 9 **Notes** ⊗ No Children 6yrs Closed 6 Dec-20 Jan

---

CASTLETON   Map 16 SK18

Innkeeper's Lodge Castleton, Peak District

★★★ INN

tel: 08451 551551 *(Calls cost 2p per minute plus your phone company's access charge)*
Castle St S33 8WG
email: info@innkeeperslodge.com **web:** www.innkeeperslodge.com

This property enjoys an excellent location, nestled amongst the hills of Hope Valley and surrounded by the wild moors and sheer rock edges. Dating back to the 1800s this coaching inn provides modern spacious accommodation. The welcoming lounge bar is a popular place to eat with food served all day. Free WiFi available along with on-site car parking.

Rooms 15 en suite (4 fmly) (3 GF) **Facilities** FTV tea/coffee Dinner available Direct Dial WiFi **Parking Notes** ⊗

CHESTERFIELD   Map 16 SK37

Church Villa B&B

★★★ BED AND BREAKFAST

tel: 01246 850254 **29 Church Ln, Temple Normanton S42 5DB**
email: churchvilla@btinternet.com **web:** www.churchvilla29.co.uk
dir: *M1 junct 29 onto A617. After 2m turn to Temple Normanton. Take 3rd right signed Holmewood, right again into Birkin Ln. Next right into Church Ln, opposite church notice board*

Church Villa B&B is a charming cottage situated on the outskirts of Chesterfield, ideally placed for visiting the Peak District. It has comfortable, well-equipped bedrooms which come complete with many thoughtful extras. Breakfast and home-cooked dinners are served in the dining room, which has a 100-year old vine, and overlooks the country garden. A guest lounge is also available.

Rooms 3 en suite S £50-£55; D £60-£75* **Facilities** FTV DVD TVL tea/coffee Dinner available WiFi 🛞 **Extras** Robes **Parking** 3 **Notes** LB ⊗

CHINLEY   Map 16 SK08

The Old Hall Inn

★★★★ ⚑ INN

tel: 01663 750529 **Whitehough SK23 6EJ**
email: info@old-hall-inn.co.uk **web:** www.old-hall-inn.co.uk

This 16th-century, family-run inn is located in some prime walking country. The rooms are all en suite and one has a balcony overlooking the garden. All rooms have flat-screen TVs and WiFi. Breakfast comes as full English or continental style, while other meals can be eaten in the Old Hall's Minstrel Gallery restaurant. The bar features many ales from local breweries as well as an extensive wine list.

Rooms 7 en suite 4 annexe en suite S £65-£90; D £79-£140* **Facilities** FTV DVD tea/coffee Dinner available WiFi 🛞 **Conf** Max 16 Board 16 **Parking** 20 **Notes** LB

CROMFORD   Map 16 SK25

Alison House

★★★★ GUEST ACCOMMODATION

tel: 01629 822211 **Intake Ln DE4 3RH**
email: info@alison-house-hotel.co.uk **web:** www.alison-house-hotel.co.uk
dir: *From A6, SE of Cromford, right into Intake Ln*

This well furnished and spacious 18th-century house stands in seven acres of well-tended grounds just a short walk from the village. Public rooms are comfortable and charming, and bedrooms come in a variety of sizes. All are furnished to a high standard, and The Arkwright Suite is a favourite with honeymooners.

Rooms 15 en suite (2 fmly) (4 GF) **Facilities** TVL tea/coffee Dinner available Direct Dial Licensed WiFi 🛝 🛞 **Conf** Max 40 Thtr 40 Class 40 Board 40 **Parking** 30 **Notes** Civ Wed 80

DALBURY
Map 10 SK23

The Black Cow
★★★★ ⊛ INN

tel: 01332 824297 **The Green, Dalbury Lees DE6 5BE**
email: enquiries@theblackcow.co.uk **web:** www.theblackcow.co.uk
dir: From Derby A52 signed Ashbourne, Kirk Langley; turn into Church Lane, then Long Lane, follow signs to Dalbury Lees

The Black Cow is set in the centre of the village overlooking the green. It is a traditional pub with friendly staff and hand-pulled ales. There is a beer garden and children's play area. Comfortable bedrooms come with flat-screen TVs and complimentary WiFi. The en suite bathrooms are well equipped with high standards of decor. Bar and dining room areas are very comfortable.

Rooms 7 en suite (2 fmly) **Facilities** FTV Lounge TVL tea/coffee Dinner available WiFi ⚓ 18 ⚿ **Extras** Speciality toiletries, bottled water **Parking** 22

DARLEY DALE
Map 16 SK26

Premier Collection

Ashford Grange
★★★★★ BED AND BREAKFAST

tel: 01629 734575 **Oakwood Dr DE4 2BT**
email: info@ashfordgrange.co.uk **web:** www.ashfordgrange.co.uk
dir: N of Matlock on A6, pass Old Hackney Ln on right, next right into Darley Lodge Drive & Oakwood Drive

Located in the Derwent Valley and built in the grounds of the former manor house using local stone, Ashford Grange is a modern house full of creature comforts, and a warm welcome is assured. Rooms are spacious and attractively decorated in co-ordinating colours, and all offer high quality en suite facilities. The Hayloft located in the adjacent building has its own private entrance. Home baked afternoon treats and breakfasts are served in the dining room overlooking the garden and hills beyond, or weather permitting on one of the garden terraces.

Rooms 2 en suite 1 annexe en suite S £100-£140; D £115-£155 **Facilities** FTV tea/coffee WiFi ⚓ 18 Fly fishing available **Extras** Speciality toiletries, flowers, robes, slippers **Parking** 3 **Notes** LB ⊗ No Children Closed Xmas-New Year

DERBY
Map 11 SK33

See also Belper & Melbourne

The Derby Conference Centre
★★★★ GUEST ACCOMMODATION

tel: 01332 861842 & 861831 **London Rd DE24 8UX**
email: enquiries@thederbyconferencecentre.com
web: www.thederbyconferencecentre.com
dir: M1 junct 25, A52 towards Derby. Filter left onto A5111 signed Ring Road. At Raynesway Park rdbt 3rd exit signed Ring Road/Alvaston. At next rdbt A6 towards Derby centre. Pass Wickes, left into entrance

Formerly a railway training centre, this Grade II listed art deco building has modern public areas, meeting rooms and accommodation, yet original features such as the wall paintings by Norman Wilkinson still remain. Extensive conference facilities include a lecture theatre. Complimentary WiFi and on-site parking available.

Rooms 50 en suite (10 GF) S £40-£65; D £46-£75* **Facilities** FTV Lounge TVL tea/coffee Dinner available Licensed WiFi ⚓ 18 ⚿ **Conf** Max 1000 Thtr 350 Class 60 Board 40 **Parking** 200 **Notes** ⊗ Closed 24 Dec-4 Jan

A38 Woodlands B&B
★★ BED AND BREAKFAST

tel: 01332 293658 & 07792 547964 **300 Burton Rd DE23 6AD**
email: info@a38woodlands.com **web:** www.a38woodlands.com
dir: From city centre on A5250 to Littleover, opposite Stone Hill Rd, above the International Hotel

Run by a friendly husband and wife team, the A38 Woodlands B&B is situated within easy walking distance of Derby city centre. This Victorian town house provides a choice of en suite room configurations; singles to large family accommodation. All offer microwaves and refrigeration; however some have additional kitchen facilities on prior request. A hearty home-cooked breakfast is provided in the small conservatory. WiFi available. Limited on-site parking.

Rooms 10 en suite (3 fmly) (4 GF) S £25-£35; D £35-£45 (room only) **Facilities** FTV tea/coffee WiFi ⚿ **Extras** Fridge, microwave **Parking** 6 **Notes** LB ⊗

EDALE
Map 16 SK18

Stonecroft Country Guesthouse
★★★★ ⚘ GUEST HOUSE

tel: 01433 670262 **Stonecroft S33 7ZA**
email: enquiries@stonecroftguesthouse.co.uk **web:** www.stonecroftguesthouse.co.uk
dir: From A6187 in Hope follow signs for Edale. After 4.5m, pass large car park on right, turn right (marked No Through Road). 3rd house after church

A warm welcome awaits you at this beautifully located guest house in the quiet village of Edale. Bedrooms are comfortable and feature luxurious extras such as fluffy bathrobes and well equipped beverage trays. Award-winning breakfasts are served round a communal breakfast table, and dietary requirements are especially well catered for. A large lounge area is provided with a roaring log fire, perfect for those winter evenings. A limited amount of on-site parking is available.

Rooms 3 rms (2 en suite) (1 pri facs) S £50-£60; D £99-£110* **Facilities** FTV iPod docking station TVL tea/coffee WiFi ⚿ **Extras** Robes, speciality toiletries, fruit, chocolates **Parking** 3 **Notes** LB ⊗ No Children 10yrs Closed Xmas

EYAM
Map 16 SK27

Barrel Inn

★★★ ⊜ INN

tel: 01433 630856 **Bretton S32 5QD**
email: barrelinn@btconnect.com **web:** www.thebarrelinn.co.uk
dir: *From Baslow on A623, turn right signed Foolow. At next T junct, turn left & immediately right opposite pond. 1m on left*

Laying claim to be the highest pub in Derbyshire, the Barrel Inn dates back to 1597 and provides the visitor with a warm and homely base from which to explore the area. Oak-beamed ceiling and flagstones are a feature in the bar area, while the restaurant offers a wide selection of meals. On a clear day it is possible to see five counties.

Rooms 4 annexe en suite (1 fmly) (3 GF) **Facilities** DVD tea/coffee Dinner available WiFi **Parking** 20 **Notes** ⊗

FOOLOW
Map 16 SK17

The Bulls Head Inn

★★★★ INN

tel: 01433 630873 **S32 5QR**
email: wilbnd@aol.com **web:** www.thebullatfoolow.co.uk
dir: *Off A623 into Foolow*

Located in the village centre, this popular inn retains many original features and offers comfortable, well-equipped bedrooms. Extensive and imaginative bar meals are served in the traditionally furnished dining room or in the cosy bar areas. The inn welcomes well-behaved dogs in the bar (and even muddy boots on the flagstone areas).

Rooms 3 en suite (1 fmly) **Facilities** tea/coffee Dinner available ⌁ 18 **Parking** 20

FROGGATT
Map 16 SK27

The Chequers Inn

★★★★ ⊛⊛ ⊜ INN

tel: 01433 630231 **S32 3ZJ**
email: info@chequers-froggatt.com **web:** www.chequers-froggatt.com
dir: *On A625 between Sheffield & Bakewell, 0.75m from Calver*

The Chequers Inn is a very popular 16th-century inn offering an extensive range of interesting two AA Rosette-worthy dishes, with a clear focus on local produce. The bedrooms are comprehensively equipped with all modern comforts and the hospitality is warm and sincere. This is a good location for touring Derbyshire and the Peak District National Park, and visiting Chatsworth.

Rooms 7 en suite S £109-£119; D £109-£119* **Facilities** FTV tea/coffee Dinner available WiFi **Parking** 45 **Notes** LB ⊗ Closed 25 Dec No coaches

GREAT HUCKLOW
Map 16 SK17

The Queen Anne

★★★ ⊜ INN

tel: 01298 871246 **SK17 8RF**
email: angelaryan100@aol.com **web:** www.queenanneinn.co.uk
dir: *Exit A623 onto B6049 to Great Hucklow*

Set in the heart of this pretty village, The Queen Anne has been a licensed inn for over 300 years and to this day acts a hub for the local community. Meals are served in the cosy bar and dining room which benefits from a wealth of original features. During summer months meals can be taken in the pretty garden with far reaching views across Derbyshire countryside. Bedrooms are tucked away to the rear of the property in a separate building with direct access. Both rooms are comfortable and have modern shower rooms en suite. Ample parking and free WiFi are available.

Rooms 2 annexe en suite (2 GF) S £53-£59; D £72-£75* **Facilities** FTV DVD TVL tea/coffee Dinner available WiFi **Parking** 20 **Notes** LB ⊗ No Children 10yrs Closed Xmas & New Year

HARDSTOFT
Map 16 SK46

COCO at the Shoulder

★★★★ ⊜ INN

tel: 01246 850276 **Deep Ln S45 8AF**
email: book@cocoattheshoulder.co.uk **web:** www.cocoattheshoulder.co.uk
dir: *B6039 follow signs for Hardwick Hall, 1st right after turning off B6039*

This 300-year-old country pub offers a friendly atmosphere along with real ales and log fires. Home-cooked meals are skilfully prepared and served throughout the informal bar and the stylish restaurant; breakfasts include home-made sausages and black pudding. Bedrooms vary in size but all are well furnished and complimentary WiFi is provided. There is also a function room available.

Rooms 4 en suite (1 fmly) **Facilities** FTV tea/coffee Dinner available WiFi **Extras** Bottled water, home-made biscuits **Conf** Max 80 Thtr 80 Class 40 Board 40 **Parking** 50

HARTINGTON
Map 16 SK16

Bank House Guest House

★★★★ GUEST ACCOMMODATION

tel: 01298 84465 **Market Place SK17 0AL**
web: www.visitbankhouse.co.uk
dir: *B5054 into village centre*

Bank House is a very well-maintained Grade II listed Georgian building that stands in the main square of this delightful village. Bedrooms are neat and fresh in appearance, and there is a comfortable television lounge. A hearty breakfast is served in the ground-floor cottage-style dining room.

Rooms 5 rms (3 en suite) (3 fmly) S £40-£45; D £62-£70 **Facilities** FTV TVL tea/coffee WiFi ⚓ **Parking** 2 **Notes** LB ⊗ Closed Xmas RS 22-28 Dec ⊛

The Jug and Glass Inn

★★★ INN

tel: 01298 84848 **Ashbourne Rd SK17 0BA**
email: enquiries@jugandglass.biz **web:** www.jugandglass.biz
dir: *On A515 between Buxton & Ashbourne at Hartington junct*

Set in the High Peak National Park, The Jug and Glass Inn is a family-run establishment where the husband and wife team ensure their guests are warmly welcomed and made to feel at home. There is a choice of well-presented rooms with flat-screen TV provided. The inn is the perfect base for exploring the Derbyshire countryside with Matlock, Ashbourne and Buxton all within a 10-minute drive.

Rooms 9 en suite (1 fmly) (4 GF) **Facilities** FTV DVD tea/coffee Dinner available ⚓ **Parking** 20 **Notes** RS Nov-Apr Closed Mon-Tue No coaches

HARTSHORNE
Map 10 SK32

Bulls Head
★★★ INN

tel: 01283 215299 **1 Woodville Rd DE11 7ET**
email: dougbec1955@netscape.net **web:** www.bullsheadhartshorne.co.uk

This family-run inn offers friendly hospitality; a good base from which to explore the surrounding National Forest, with convenient links to the motorway network. Rooms are comfortable and well appointed. Hearty meals are served daily in the cosy bar area. Parking and free WiFi are available.

Rooms 5 rms (3 en suite) **Facilities** FTV DVD tea/coffee Dinner available WiFi ⅃ 18 🅿 **Parking** 40 **Notes** ⊗ No coaches

HATHERSAGE
Map 16 SK28

The Plough Inn
★★★★★ ⊚ INN

tel: 01433 650319 **Leadmill Bridge S32 1BA**
email: sales@theploughinn-hathersage.co.uk **web:** www.theploughinn-hathersage.co.uk
dir: 1m SE of Hathersage on B6001. Over bridge, 150yds beyond at Leadmill

This delightful 16th-century inn with beer garden has an idyllic location by the River Derwent. A selection of real ales and imaginative food is served in the spacious public areas, and original fireplaces and exposed beams have been preserved. The attractive, well-equipped bedrooms include several luxury rooms, and WiFi access is available throughout.

Rooms 3 en suite 3 annexe en suite (3 fmly) (2 GF) S £80-£105; D £105-£140* **Facilities** FTV DVD iPod docking station tea/coffee Dinner available Direct Dial WiFi ⅃ 18 🅿 **Extras** Fruit, water - complimentary **Parking** 50 **Notes** LB Closed 25 Dec No coaches

HAYFIELD
Map 16 SK08

Fuchsia Bank Cottage
★★★★ BED AND BREAKFAST

tel: 07852 964773 **Bank Vale Rd SK22 2EZ**
email: markfuchs@me.com **web:** www.fuchsiabankcottage.co.uk

This family-run property benefits from a secluded location at the foot of Lantern Pike in Hayfield, which came to fame recently as the setting for BBC drama *The Village*. Kinder Scout and Lyme Park are both within easy reach, with Manchester a little over half an hour away. Annexed from the main house there is just one attractively presented en suite room, filled with thoughtful accessories and creature comforts. Double doors lead on to the patio and the main garden. Breakfast is served in the comfort of your room. Ample parking and free WiFi are also available.

Rooms 1 en suite **Facilities** tea/coffee WiFi **Notes** ⊛

HOPE
Map 16 SK18

Premier Collection

Underleigh House
★★★★★ ⊜ GUEST ACCOMMODATION

tel: 01433 621372 **Lose Hill Ln S33 6AF**
email: info@underleighhouse.co.uk **web:** www.underleighhouse.co.uk
dir: From village church on A6187 into Edale Rd, 1m left into Lose Hill Ln

Situated at the end of a private lane, surrounded by glorious scenery, Underleigh House was converted from a barn and cottage that dates from 1873, and now offers carefully furnished and attractively decorated bedrooms with modern facilities. One room has a private lounge and others have access to the gardens. There is a very spacious lounge with comfortable chairs and a welcoming log fire. Memorable breakfasts are served at one large table in the dining room.

Rooms 4 en suite (1 GF) S £75-£105; D £95-£125* **Facilities** FTV DVD TVL tea/coffee Direct Dial Licensed WiFi 🔒 **Extras** Speciality toiletries, fruit, sweets - free **Parking** 6 **Notes** LB ⊗ No Children 12yrs Closed Xmas, New Year & Jan

Stoney Ridge
★★★★ ⊜ GUEST ACCOMMODATION

tel: 01433 620538 **Granby Rd, Bradwell S33 9HU**
email: info@stoneyridge.org.uk **web:** www.stoneyridge.org.uk
dir: From N end of Bradwell on B6049 into Gore Ln, uphill, pass Ye Olde Bowling Green Inn, left into Granby Rd

This large, split-level bungalow stands in attractive mature gardens at the highest part of the village and has extensive views. Hens roam freely in the landscaped garden, and their fresh eggs add to the hearty breakfasts. Bedrooms are attractively furnished and thoughtfully equipped, and there is a spacious comfortable lounge to relax in.

Rooms 4 rms (3 en suite) (1 pri facs) S £60-£70; D £60-£82* **Facilities** STV FTV TVL tea/coffee WiFi 🔒 **Extras** Sweets **Parking** 6 **Notes** LB ⊗ No Children 14yrs RS Nov proprietors holiday

Round Meadow Barn
★★★ BED AND BREAKFAST

tel: 01433 621347 & 07836 689422 **Parsons Ln S33 6RB**
email: geof@harrisrmb.freeserve.co.uk **web:** www.mysite.freeserve.com/rmbarn
dir: Exit A625 (Hope Rd) N onto Parsons Ln, over rail bridge, in 200yds right into hay barnyard, through gates, across 3 fields, house on left

This converted barn, with original stone walls and exposed timbers, stands in open fields in the picturesque Hope Valley. The bedrooms are large enough for families and there are two modern bathrooms. Breakfast is served at one large table adjoining the family kitchen.

Rooms 3 rms (1 en suite) (2 pri facs) (1 fmly) **Facilities** FTV tea/coffee Direct Dial WiFi 🔒 **Parking** 8 **Notes** ⊛

MARSH LANE — Map 16 SK47

Ravencar Farm Bed and Breakfast (SK406791)

★★★★ FARMHOUSE

tel: 01246 433717 & 07786 911950 **Main Rd S21 5RH**
email: helenmrshcfish@aol.com **web:** www.ravencarbandb.co.uk

A warm welcome awaits you at this friendly family run farmhouse which is conveniently located on the border between South Yorkshire and Derbyshire and close to the M1. Bedrooms are well appointed and provide a number of modern accessories such as in-room fridges, well-stocked hospitality trays and flat-screen televisions. Breakfasts are served in the dining room which overlooks the gardens. Full cooked breakfasts are available as well as a wide range of lighter options.

Rooms 3 en suite (1 fmly) (1 GF) **Facilities** FTV DVD tea/coffee WiFi Riding 🛁
Extras Fruit juice, mineral water - free **Parking** 12 **Notes** 6 acres non-working/horses

MATLOCK — Map 16 SK35

Castle Green B&B

★★★★ BED AND BREAKFAST

tel: 01629 581349 & 07584 162988 **Butts Dr DE4 3DJ**
email: john@castlegreenbandb.co.uk **web:** www.castlegreenbandb.co.uk
dir: *A615 into Matlock, pass British Red Cross on left, opposite Castle Green & Butts Drive*

Located in the peaceful grounds of the former Ernest Bailey mansion, the property is nestled in a wooded valley with views of Riber Castle; the house is within walking distance of Matlock. A warm welcome awaits and the accommodation is well equipped and very comfortable. Breakfast is served in the dining room on the ground floor. Other facilities include WiFi and on site parking.

Rooms 6 en suite (1 fmly) (1 GF) S £55; D £78-£85* **Facilities** FTV tea/coffee WiFi
🛁 **Extras** Speciality toiletries **Parking** 8 **Notes** LB ⊗

The Pines

★★★★ 🍽 BED AND BREAKFAST

tel: 01629 732646 & 07796 437333 **12 Eversleigh Rd, Darley Bridge DE4 2JW**
email: info@thepinesbandb.co.uk **web:** www.thepinesbandb.co.uk
dir: *From Bakewell or Matlock take A6 to Darley Dale. Turn at Whitworth Hotel onto B5057, pass Square & Compass pub & The 3 Stags Heads, The Pines on right*

Dating from the 1820s, this home as been authentically restored and stands in a secluded and pretty garden. Three spacious en suite bedrooms are stylishly furnished using rich fabrics. Comprehensive breakfasts, making use of quality local produce, offer a hearty start to the day. The Pines makes an ideal location for visiting the Peak District.

Rooms 3 en suite S £50-£60; D £80-£90* **Facilities** FTV tea/coffee Dinner available
WiFi 🛁 **Parking** 5 **Notes** LB

The Red Lion

★★★ INN

tel: 01629 584888 **Matlock Green DE4 3BT**
dir: *500yds SE of town centre on A632*

This comfortable free house is a good base for exploring Matlock and the surrounding Derbyshire countryside. Each bedroom is comfortably furnished, and

one comes complete with a four-poster. Public areas include a games area with open fires, and a restaurant where a wide selection of meals is on offer. Private parking is a bonus.

Rooms 6 en suite **Facilities** tea/coffee Dinner available WiFi Pool table **Parking** 20
Notes ⊗

MELBOURNE — Map 11 SK32

The Coach House

★★★★ BED AND BREAKFAST

tel: 01332 862338 **69 Derby Rd DE73 8FE**
email: enquiries@coachhouse-hotel.co.uk **web:** www.coachhouse-hotel.co.uk
dir: *Off B587 in village centre*

The Coach House sits in the heart of a conservation area, close to Donington Park and East Midlands Airport. This traditional cottage has been restored to provide good standards of comfort and facilities. Bedrooms are thoughtfully furnished, and a lounge and secure parking are available.

Rooms 6 en suite (1 fmly) (3 GF) S £48-£55; D £70-£80* **Facilities** FTV TVL tea/coffee WiFi 🛁 **Parking** 5 **Notes** LB ⊗

Harpur's of Melbourne

★★★★ 🏵 INN

tel: 01332 862134 **2 Derby Rd DE73 8FE**
email: info@harpursofmelbourne.co.uk **web:** www.harpursofmelbourne.co.uk
dir: *From A50 exit signed Melbourne/Swadlincote. Continue for 5m, in centre of Melbourne on left*

Starting life back in the late 18th century as two houses, before becoming the Melbourne Hotel in the mid-19th century, Harpur's continues to welcome guests from far and wide. After extensive refurbishment this is now a modern inn and restaurant, with an increasingly strong following not only for its ales but also for its food; dishes use some of the finest local ingredients. Situated in the attractive Georgian town of Melbourne and steeped in history, Harpur's offers comfortably appointed en suite accommodation within easy reach of the National Forest.

Rooms 4 en suite D £49.95-£150 (room only)* **Facilities** FTV tea/coffee Dinner available WiFi 🛁 **Conf** Max 50 Thtr 50 Class 30 Board 30 **Parking** 20 **Notes** LB No coaches

MICKLEOVER — Map 10 SK33

The Great Northern

★★★★ INN

tel: 01332 514288 **Station Rd DE3 9FB**
email: greatnorthernderby@yahoo.co.uk **web:** www.thegreatnorthern.co.uk
dir: *From N - A38 to Markeaton Island, take 3rd exit. Then 2nd left into Radbourne Ln, 3rd left into Station Rd*

Bedrooms at The Great Northern are in a converted barn; the three boutique-style rooms are well appointed and thoughtfully equipped. This modern inn with friendly staff provides imaginative food, and a selection of local cask ales. Free WiFi and ample parking are provided. A meeting room is available for small parties or private dining.

Rooms 3 en suite (1 fmly) (1 GF) S £80; D £90-£100* **Facilities** FTV DVD tea/coffee Dinner available WiFi **Conf** Max 80 Thtr 80 Class 50 Board 25 **Parking** 80 **Notes** ⊗

NEWHAVEN
Map 16 SK16

Premier Collection

The Smithy

★★★★★ 🍴 GUEST ACCOMMODATION

tel: 01298 84548 **SK17 0DT**
email: lynnandgary@thesmithybedandbreakfast.co.uk
web: www.thesmithybedandbreakfast.co.uk
dir: *0.5m S of Newhaven on A515. Adjacent to Biggin Ln, private driveway opposite Ivy House*

Set in a peaceful location close to the Tissington and High Peak trails, this 17th-century drovers' inn and blacksmith's workshop has been carefully renovated. Bedrooms, which are in a former barn, are well equipped. Enjoyable breakfasts, which include free-range eggs and home-made preserves, are served in the forge, which features the original bellows on the vast open hearth.

Rooms 4 en suite (2 GF) S £45-£50; D £75-£95* **Facilities** FTV DVD Lounge tea/coffee WiFi 🏌 **Conf** Max 20 Thtr 15 Board 10 **Parking** 8 **Notes** LB ⊗ No Children 🐾

NEW MILLS
Map 16 SK08

Pack Horse Inn

★★★★ 🅰 INN

tel: 01663 742365 **Mellor Rd SK22 4QQ**
email: info@packhorseinn.co.uk **web:** www.packhorseinn.co.uk

The Pack Horse Inn sits on the edge of the Peak District, ideally located within easy reach of Stockport, Manchester and Sheffield. Some bedrooms are in a converted barn and still have original oak beams. The other rooms are in the main building. The friendly bar has at least three hand-pulled, regularly changing guest ales together with Tetley bitter. Traditional bar meals and snacks are available, or a more formal meal is served in the dining room which overlooks the patio area, where guests can eat and drink in the warmer weather.

Rooms 12 en suite **Facilities** Dinner available

PILSLEY
Map 16 SK27

Holly Cottage

★★★★ 🍴 BED AND BREAKFAST

tel: 01246 582245 **DE45 1UH**
email: hollycottagebandb@btinternet.com **web:** www.hollycottagebandb.co.uk
dir: *Follow brown tourist signs for Chatsworth & Pilsley. Holly Cottage next to post office in Pilsley*

A warm welcome is assured at this mellow stone cottage, part of a combined Post Office and shop in the conservation area of Pilsley, which is owned by the adjacent Chatsworth Estate. The cosy bedrooms feature a wealth of thoughtful extras, and comprehensive breakfasts, utilising quality local produce, are taken in an attractive pine-furnished dining room.

Rooms 3 en suite **Facilities** FTV iPod docking station tea/coffee WiFi **Notes** LB ⊗ No Children 10yrs

The Devonshire Arms at Pilsley

★★★ INN

tel: 01246 583258 **The High St DE45 1UL**
email: res@devonshirehotels.co.uk **web:** www.devonshirepilsley.co.uk
dir: *From A619, in Baslow, at rdbt take 1st exit onto B6012. Follow signs to Chatsworth, 2nd right to Pilsley*

The newest addition to the Devonshire Hotels and Restaurants group, The Devonshire Arms at Pilsley is just two miles from Chatsworth House, and also a minute's walk from the Chatsworth farm shop which provides much of the food served. It is an intimate yet traditional 18th-century village inn with a selection of cosy bedrooms, some in the inn and some in the farmhouse next door. The inn has a bartering system in place, allowing locals to exchange home-grown fruit and veg for a pint or two of local ale at the bar.

Rooms 7 en suite 6 annexe en suite (2 fmly) (3 GF) **Facilities** FTV Lounge tea/coffee Dinner available WiFi 🏌 **Parking** 16 **Notes** RS 24-26 Dec & 31 Dec-1 Jan Xmas & New Year packages No coaches

REPTON
Map 10 SK32

The Boot Inn

★★★★★ 🍴 INN

tel: 01283 346047 **12 Boot Hill DE65 6FT**
email: info@thebootatrepton.co.uk **web:** www.thebootatrepton.co.uk
dir: *From Repton Cross into Brook End, The Boot on right*

The Boot can trace its history back to the 17th century when it was a coaching inn, and was also used for legal sessions and proceedings prior to the completion of the Court House opposite, which now forms part of Repton School. It is a delightful village inn, and has recently undergone a complete refurbishment to provide a contemporary dining area and bar, made homely with attractive artwork, exposed original features and wood-burning stoves. The Boot also has its own micro-brewery, producing brews like Boot Beer, Tuffer's Old and Clod Hopper. En suite bedrooms are individually decorated, each tastefully furnished with an emphasis on comfort. Carefully prepared dishes make great use of quality, local produce at breakfast and dinner. Free WiFi and on-site parking are available. The Boot Inn is the AA Pub of the Year for England 2016-2017.

Rooms 9 en suite (4 fmly) S £79-£120; D £79-£120 (room only) **Facilities** FTV DVD tea/coffee Dinner available WiFi **Parking** 8 **Notes** LB No coaches

ROWSLEY
Map 16 SK26

Grouse and Claret

★★★★ INN

tel: 01629 733233 **Station Rd DE4 2EB**
email: grouseandclaret.matlock@marstons.co.uk **web:** www.grouseclaretpub.co.uk

The Grouse and Claret is an 18th-century inn ideally located on the A6 between Matlock and Bakewell, within easy striking distance of the Peak District National Park. Public rooms feature a large open-plan area with a range of seating styles to suite all needs; a range of food is available from the all-day menu which features freshly spit roast chickens. The bedrooms are modern and well equipped.

Rooms 8 en suite (2 fmly) **Facilities** FTV tea/coffee Dinner available WiFi **Parking** 75 **Notes** ⊗

WILLINGTON
Map 10 SK22

The Dragon

★★★★ ⛲ INN

tel: 01283 704795 **11 The Green DE65 6BP**
email: info@thedragonatwillington.co.uk **web:** www.thedragonatwillington.co.uk
dir: Junct of A50/A38 follow signs for Willington. At mini rdbt turn left, The Dragon on left

Situated on the bank of the Trent and Mersey canal, this village inn has been welcoming guests by land and water for over 150 years. It's ideally situated for those wishing to explore south Derbyshire's attractions and unspoilt countryside. The beautifully appointed en suite rooms are located in the neighbouring cottage and benefit from private parking and complimentary WiFi. A cooked breakfast includes award-winning local sausages which are a must!

Rooms 7 annexe en suite (2 GF) S £49.95-£69; D £49.95-£79 (room only) **Facilities** FTV tea/coffee Dinner available WiFi ⛲ **Conf** Max 50 Thtr 50 Class 45 Board 45 **Parking** 20 **Notes** LB No coaches

WINSTER
Map 16 SK26

Brae Cottage

★★★★ 🅰 GUEST ACCOMMODATION

tel: 01629 650375 **East Bank DE4 2DT**
web: www.braecottagewinster.co.uk
dir: A6 onto B5057, driveway on right past pub

Brae Cottage lies in the heart of this Peak District village, a stone's throw from the Old Bowling Green Inn. The bedrooms are in converted outbuildings and have a wealth of thoughtful extras. Comprehensive breakfasts, featuring home-made or local produce, are served at an antique table in the carefully furnished cottage.

Rooms 2 annexe en suite (1 fmly) (2 GF) S £55-£65; D £65-£80* **Facilities** tea/coffee ⛲ **Extras** Mineral water - complimentary **Parking** 2 **Notes** ⊗ No Children 11yrs Closed Nov-Feb ⊛

YOULGREAVE
Map 16 SK26

The George

★★★ INN

tel: 01629 636292 **Church St DE45 1UW**
dir: 3m S of Bakewell in Youlgreave, opposite church

The public bars of the 17th-century George are popular with locals and tourists. Bedroom styles vary, and all have shower rooms en suite. Breakfast is served in the lounge bar, and a range of bar meals and snacks is available.

Rooms 3 en suite (1 fmly) **Facilities** FTV DVD tea/coffee Dinner available WiFi Fishing ⛲ **Parking** 12

DEVON

ASHBURTON
Map 3 SX77

Greencott

★★★★ GUEST HOUSE

tel: 01803 762649 **Landscove TQ13 7LZ**
web: www.stayawhile.co.uk/southwest/Greencott/Greencott.html
dir: 3m SE of Ashburton. Exit A38 at Peartree junct, Landscove signed on slip road, village green 2m on right, opposite village hall

Greencott has a peaceful village location and superb country views. Your hosts extend a very warm welcome and there is a relaxed home-from-home atmosphere. Service is attentive and caring and many guests return time and again. Bedrooms are attractive, comfortable and very well equipped. Delicious breakfasts are served around an oak dining table.

Rooms 2 en suite S £27.50-£30; D £55-£60* **Facilities** FTV TVL tea/coffee ⛲ **Parking** 3 **Notes** LB ⊗ Closed 25-26 Dec ⊛

Gages Mill Country Guest House

★★★★ GUEST ACCOMMODATION

tel: 01364 652391 **Buckfastleigh Rd TQ13 7JW**
email: katestone@gagesmill.co.uk **web:** www.gagesmill.co.uk
dir: Off A38 at Peartree junct, turn right then left at fuel station, Gages Mill 500yds on left

Conveniently situated within easy access of the A38, this Grade II listed building was formerly a woollen mill. Very much a family home, there is a relaxed and welcoming feel here with every effort made to ensure a rewarding and memorable stay. The bedrooms provide good standards of comfort and many have lovely views across the surrounding fields. Breakfast provides a substantial and enjoyable start to the day with plenty of choice for all appetites.

Rooms 7 en suite (1 fmly) (1 GF) S £65; D £80-£85* **Facilities** iPod docking station TVL tea/coffee Licensed WiFi ⛲ **Parking** 7 **Notes** ⊗ Closed Nov-Feb ⊛

The Rising Sun

★★★ INN

tel: 01364 652544 **Woodland TQ13 7JT**
email: enquiries@therisingsunwoodland.co.uk **web:** www.therisingsunwoodland.co.uk
dir: From A38 take exit signed Woodland & Denbury, 1.5m on left

Conveniently situated for access to Dartmoor and the stunning countryside, The Rising Sun is situated in woodland, perfect for the keen walker. The property has a dining room and a bar in addition to its comfortable bedrooms. The inn is owner-run and managed, with friendly staff. There's an ample range offered on the menu, along with a good selection of wines and beers. Lovely open fires on the winter evenings create a cosy relaxed atmosphere.

Rooms 4 en suite (1 fmly) (2 GF) **Facilities** FTV tea/coffee Dinner available WiFi ⚓ **Parking** 20

ATHERINGTON
Map 3 SS52

West Down *(SS582228)*

★★★★ 🚜 FARMHOUSE

tel: 01769 560551 **Little Eastacombe EX37 9HP**
email: info@westdown.co.uk **web:** www.westdown.co.uk
dir: *0.5m from Atherington on B3227 to Torrington, turn right, 100yds on left*

Set within 25 acres of lush Devon countryside, this farmhouse makes a good base for exploring the area. A peaceful atmosphere and caring hospitality are assured. Bedrooms are equipped with a host of thoughtful extras, and every effort is made to ensure an enjoyable stay. One bedroom has wheelchair access and a large wet room. A choice of homely lounges is available; breakfast and very good dinners are served in the sun lounge.

Rooms 1 en suite 2 annexe en suite (2 GF) S £53-£55; D £84-£88* **Facilities** Lounge TVL tea/coffee Dinner available WiFi ⚓ **Parking** 8 **Notes** LB ⊗ ☺ 25 acres sheep/ chickens

AXMINSTER
Map 4 SY29

Premier Collection

Kerrington House

★★★★★ ⚑ 🚜 GUEST ACCOMMODATION

tel: 01297 35333 **Musbury Rd EX13 5JR**
email: info@kerringtonhouse.com **web:** www.kerringtonhouse.com
dir: *0.5m from Axminster on A358 towards Seaton, house on left*

This former Victorian gentleman's residence has been decorated and furnished to very high standards to make guests as comfortable as possible. Bedrooms and bathrooms include a range of welcome extras. Afternoon tea may be enjoyed in the comfortably furnished lounge or, in the warmer months, outside overlooking the landscaped gardens. Locally sourced produce is used both at breakfast and at dinner, which is available by prior arrangement.

Rooms 5 en suite (2 fmly) (2 GF) S £80-£90; D £125-£130* **Facilities** FTV DVD iPod docking station Lounge tea/coffee Dinner available Licensed WiFi ⚓ **Extras** Speciality toiletries, sherry, chocolates - free **Conf** Max 12 Board 12 **Parking** 6 **Notes** LB ⊗

BAMPTON
Map 3 SS92

Newhouse Farm *(SS892228)*

★★★★ ⚑ 🚜 FARMHOUSE

tel: 01398 351347 **EX16 9JE**
email: anne.boldry@btconnect.com **web:** www.newhouse-farm-holidays.co.uk
dir: *5m W of Bampton on B3227*

Set in 42 acres of rolling farmland, this delightful farmhouse provides a friendly and informal atmosphere. The smart, rustic-style bedrooms are well equipped with modern facilities, and imaginative and delicious home-cooked dinners, using the best local produce, are available by arrangement. Home-made bread and preserves feature at breakfast which can be enjoyed outside on the patio in the summer.

Rooms 3 en suite (1 GF) D £70-£85* **Facilities** FTV tea/coffee Dinner available WiFi Fishing **Parking** 3 **Notes** LB ⊗ No Children 10yrs Closed Nov-Feb ☺ 42 acres beef/sheep

The Swan

★★★★ ⑧⑧ INN

tel: 01398 332248 **Station Rd EX16 9NG**
email: info@theswan.co **web:** www.theswan.co

The Swan is a traditional hostelry offering good food, good beer and a wide selection of wines coupled with comfortable, well-equipped bedrooms and en suite bathrooms. Each bedroom has a flat-screen TV, and other modern media staples. Staff are very friendly and do all they can to make a stay comfortable. Breakfast is a hearty affair using good local ingredients, and the menu in the evening, which has been awarded two AA Rosettes, offers a great choice for all.

Rooms 3 en suite S £70-£95* **Facilities** FTV iPod docking station tea/coffee Dinner available WiFi Fishing Riding Gym ⚓ **Extras** Speciality toiletries, espresso machine, snacks **Notes** LB Closed 25-26 Dec

Weston House

★★★★ BED AND BREAKFAST

tel: 01398 332094 & 07958 176799 **6 Luke St EX16 9NF**
email: peter@westonhousedevon.co.uk **web:** www.westonhousedevon.co.uk
dir: *On B3227, in village, opposite church*

Located in the heart of Bampton within easy reach of many local attractions and gardens, Weston House offers comfortable, well-equipped bedrooms and hearty breakfasts using quality local ingredients. Owner Catherine Stott is an artist who teaches, and many of her pieces are tastefully displayed throughout the house. Public parking is available within a few minutes' walk.

Rooms 3 rms (2 en suite) (1 pri facs) S £55-£75; D £70-£80* **Facilities** FTV DVD tea/coffee WiFi ⚓ Drying facilities **Extras** Speciality toiletries, home-made biscuits - free **Notes** LB ⊗ Closed 20-28 Dec

BARNSTAPLE
Map 3 SS53

The Spinney

★★★★ GUEST ACCOMMODATION

tel: 01271 850282 & 07775 335654 **Shirwell EX31 4JR**
email: stay@thespinneyshirwell.co.uk **web:** www.thespinneyshirwell.co.uk
dir: *From Barnstaple on A39, past hospital towards Lynton*

This elegant, 18th-century former rectory is located in the heart of north Devon, three miles from the historic market town of Barnstaple. The Spinney offers stylishly decorated, en suite accommodation in muted colours with thoughtful extras. Local farm sausages feature at breakfast which is served in the conservatory. Ample private parking is available.

Rooms 5 rms (4 en suite) (1 pri facs) (1 fmly) **Facilities** FTV DVD Lounge tea/coffee WiFi ⚓ **Extras** Chocolates, water - complimentary **Parking** 7 **Notes** LB ⊗ No Children 10yrs

BARNSTAPLE *continued*

Cresta Guest House

★★★ GUEST HOUSE

tel: 01271 374022 **26 Sticklepath Hill EX31 2BU**
email: contact@crestaguesthouse.co.uk **web:** www.crestaguesthouse.co.uk
dir: *On A3215, 0.6m W of town centre, top of hill on right*

A warm welcome is assured at this family-run establishment, situated on the western outskirts of Barnstaple. The well-equipped, individually styled bedrooms are smartly appointed and include ground-floor rooms. A hearty breakfast is served in the modern and comfortable dining room.

Rooms 6 en suite 2 annexe en suite (2 fmly) (2 GF) **Facilities** FTV tea/coffee WiFi 🌣
Parking 6 **Notes** ⊗ Closed 2wks Xmas

| BEESANDS | Map 3 SX84 |

The Cricket Inn

★★★★★ 🌣 🍷 INN

tel: 01548 580215 **TQ7 2EN**
email: enquiries@thecricketinn.com **web:** www.thecricketinn.com
dir: *From Kingsbridge follow A379 towards Dartmouth, at Stokenham mini rdbt turn right for Beesands*

Dating back to 1867 this charming seaside inn is situated almost on the beach at Start Bay. The well-appointed bedrooms have fantastic views, comfortable beds and flat-screen TVs. The daily-changing fish menu includes locally-caught crabs, lobster and perhaps hand-dived scallops.

Rooms 7 en suite (1 fmly) **Facilities** FTV tea/coffee Dinner available WiFi **Parking** 30
Notes No coaches

| BIDEFORD | Map 3 SS42 |

The Pines at Eastleigh

★★★★ GUEST ACCOMMODATION

tel: 01271 860561 **The Pines, Eastleigh EX39 4PA**
email: info@thepinesateastleigh.co.uk **web:** www.thepinesateastleigh.co.uk
dir: *A39 onto A386 signed East-the-Water. 1st left signed Eastleigh, 500yds next left, 1.5m to village, house on right*

This charming Grade II listed house is set in seven-acre grounds with lovely views across rolling farmland towards Lundy Island and Hartland Point. This makes a wonderful location from which to explore this beautiful area, and your welcoming hosts will help with any local information required. The bedrooms are located both in the main house and adjacent courtyard – all provide impressive levels of quality and comfort and have stylish bathrooms. Tasty breakfasts are served in the elegant dining room; a guest lounge, with an honesty bar, is also available.

Rooms 10 en suite (1 fmly) (5 GF) S £75-£85; D £90-£105* **Facilities** FTV DVD TVL TV8B tea/coffee Licensed WiFi 🌣 **Conf** Max 25 Thtr 20 Board 20 **Parking** 10
Notes LB No Children 9yrs

| BISHOPSTEIGNTON | Map 3 SX97 |

Cockhaven Arms

★★★ INN

tel: 01626 775252 **Cockhaven Rd TQ14 9RF**
email: contact@cockhavenarms.co.uk **web:** www.cockhavenarms.co.uk
dir: *From A381 follow brown tourist signs*

Cockhaven Arms is a friendly, family-run inn that dates back to the 16th century. Bedrooms are well equipped and many enjoy views across the beautiful Teign estuary. A choice of dining options is offered, and traditional and interesting dishes, along with locally caught fish, prove popular.

Rooms 10 en suite (2 fmly) **Facilities** FTV tea/coffee Dinner available WiFi 🌣 18
Conf Max 144 Thtr 100 Class 100 Board 24 **Parking** 30 **Notes** LB Closed 26 Dec
Civ Wed 80

| BLACKAWTON | Map 3 SX85 |

The George Inn

★★★ INN

tel: 01803 712342 **Main St TQ9 7BG**
email: tgiblackawton@yahoo.co.uk **web:** www.blackawton.com
dir: *From Totnes on A381 through Halwell. Left onto A3122 towards Dartmouth, turn right to Blackawton*

Situated in the heart of Blackawton, this village local offers a warm welcome to all. A proper, unspoilt pub, it enjoys an engaging traditional atmosphere and a real sense of community. Bedrooms offer good levels of comfort and quality, likewise the modern bathrooms; while public areas have an inviting, rustic charm. A wide range of food options are offered, with local produce used as much as possible. Lovely views across the rolling countryside can be enjoyed from the terrace and garden.

Rooms 4 en suite (1 fmly) **Facilities** FTV DVD tea/coffee Dinner available WiFi 🌣
Parking 12 **Notes** No coaches

BOVEY TRACEY
Map 3 SX87

Courtenay House
★★★ BED AND BREAKFAST

tel: 01626 835363 & 07774 260446 **76 Fore St TQ13 9AE**
email: info@courtenayhouse.co.uk **web:** www.courtenayhouse.co.uk
dir: *A38 from Exeter towards Plymouth. Follow B3344 Chudleigh Knighton signs. At T-junct in Bovey Tracey, right, follow Town Centre signs into Fore St. House on left after Orchard Terrace*

Courtenay House is located in the heart of the historic town of Bovey Tracey and is the perfect base to explore the area. The bedrooms are well furnished and equipped with a range of useful amenities. A freshly cooked breakfast is served in the Tea Room just off the Antique Shop.

Rooms 3 rms (2 en suite) (1 pri facs) (1 GF) S £45; D £75-£80* **Facilities** FTV tea/coffee WiFi **Notes** LB No Children 16yrs Closed 24 Dec-6 Jan

BRATTON FLEMING
Map 3 SS63

Premier Collection

Bracken House
★★★★★ BED AND BREAKFAST

tel: 01598 711810 & 07970 275881 **EX31 4TG**
email: info@brackenhouse.co.uk **web:** www.brackenhouse.co.uk
dir: *From M5 (junct 27) A361 to South Molton, right on A399 for 7m, left to Bratton Fleming for 2m. Sign end of drive opposite Baptist Chapel.*

Bracken House, a former Victorian rectory, has four en suite bedrooms and is situated on the edge of the popular north Devon village of Bratton Fleming. It is within easy driving distance of the spectacular coast, Exmoor and many other local attractions, including National Trust properties, the gardens at RHS Rosemoor, Castle Hill, Marwood and Tapeley Park. The drawing room, with its cosy open fire, has lovely views over the garden and towards Hartland through the large bay window. The dining room where a full English breakfast is served each morning has a wood-burner which is lit during those cooler mornings.

Rooms 4 en suite (1 fmly) (1 GF) S £65-£75; D £90-£120* **Facilities** FTV DVD Lounge tea/coffee WiFi 🏌 🔥 **Extras** Speciality toiletries **Parking** 6 **Notes** ⊗ Closed 23-26 Dec Civ Wed 20

BRIXHAM
Map 3 SX95

Anchorage Guest House
★★★★ ⓢ GUEST HOUSE

tel: 01803 852960 & 07950 536362 **170 New Rd TQ5 8DA**
email: enquiries@brixham-anchorage.co.uk **web:** www.brixham-anchorage.co.uk
dir: *A3022, enter Brixham, left at lights at junct with Monksbridge Rd. Pass Toll House immediately on right*

Conveniently located within walking distance of the town centre and harbour, this is an excellent choice for anyone looking to explore the many attractions of this popular holiday area. The dining room and the bedrooms have a light, bright contemporary style, with many extra facilities provided to ensure a comfortable stay. Guests are welcome to use the delightful garden, and on-site parking is a bonus.

Rooms 7 rms (6 en suite) (1 pri facs) (4 GF) **Facilities** FTV tea/coffee WiFi 🔥 **Parking** 6 **Notes** ⊗ No Children

The Melville
★★★★ GUEST HOUSE

tel: 01803 852033 **45 New Rd TQ5 8NL**

Situated in Brixham, The Melville is close to the harbour, as well as having easy access to Dartmoor and other local attractions. The comfortable en suite rooms have digital televisions and tea/coffee making facilities, making The Melville a relaxing base for your holiday or short break.

Rooms 7 en suite (1 fmly) S £40-£46; D £60-£90* **Facilities** STV FTV Lounge tea/coffee Licensed WiFi **Extras** Filtered water **Parking** 4 **Notes** LB ⊗ No Children 6yrs Closed Nov

BUCKFAST
Map 3 SX76

Furzeleigh Mill
★★★ GUEST ACCOMMODATION

tel: 01364 643476 **Old Ashburton Rd TQ11 0JP**
email: enquiries@furzeleigh.co.uk **web:** www.furzeleigh.co.uk
dir: *Exit A38 at Dartbridge junct, right at end slip road, right signed Ashburton/Prince Town (NB do not cross River Dart bridge), 200yds right*

This Grade II listed, 16th-century converted corn mill stands in its own grounds and is a good base for touring Dartmoor. Spacious family rooms are available as well as a lounge and a bar. All meals are served in the dining room and use local produce.

Rooms 14 en suite (2 fmly) S £35-£59; D £55-£85* **Facilities** FTV TVL tea/coffee Dinner available Licensed WiFi 🔥 **Conf** Max 20 Thtr 20 **Parking** 32 **Notes** LB No Children 6yrs Closed 23 Dec-2 Jan

BUCKFASTLEIGH
Map 3 SX76

Kilbury Manor
★★★★ ⓢ GUEST ACCOMMODATION

tel: 01364 644079 **Colston Rd TQ11 0LN**
email: info@kilburymanor.co.uk **web:** www.kilburymanor.co.uk
dir: *Off A38 onto B3380 to Buckfastleigh, left into Old Totnes Rd, at bottom turn right, Kilbury Manor on left*

Dating back to the 17th century, this charming Devon longhouse is situated in the tranquil surroundings of the Dart Valley with access to the river across the meadow. Bedrooms have an abundance of character and are located in the main house and in adjacent converted barns; all provide high levels of comfort. The stylish bathrooms are also appointed to impressive standards. Breakfast is served in the elegant dining room with local produce very much in evidence.

Rooms 4 rms (3 en suite) (1 pri facs) (1 GF) S £60-£80; D £70-£90* **Facilities** FTV DVD tea/coffee WiFi **Parking** 5 **Notes** No Children 7yrs 🐾

CHILLATON
Map 3 SX48

Premier Collection

Tor Cottage

★★★★★ 🛏 GUEST ACCOMMODATION

tel: 01822 860248 **PL16 OJE**
email: info@torcottage.co.uk **web:** www.torcottage.co.uk
dir: A30 Lewdown exit through Chillaton towards Tavistock, 300yds after Post Office right signed 'Bridlepath No Public Vehicular Access' to end

Tor Cottage, located in its own valley with 18 acres of grounds, is a welcome antidote to the fast pace of everyday life. Rooms are spacious and elegant; the cottage-wing bedroom has a separate sitting room, and the garden rooms have their own wood-burners. The gardens are delightful, with a stream and heated outdoor pool. An exceptional range of dishes is offered at breakfast, which can be enjoyed either in the conservatory dining room or on the terrace.

Rooms 1 en suite 3 annexe en suite (3 GF) S £98; D £150-£155* **Facilities** FTV DVD TVL tea/coffee WiFi ⚡ 🛁 **Parking** 8 **Notes** LB ⊗ No Children 14yrs Closed mid Dec-beg Feb

CHRISTOW
Map 3 SX88

Hyner Farm (SX835820)

★★★★ FARMHOUSE

tel: 01647 252923 & 07781 186133 **EX6 7NT**
email: preston916@btinternet.com **web:** www.hynerfarm-bandb-devon.co.uk
dir: A38 take exit signed Teign Valley. Follow brown tourist signs for Canonteign Falls. Turn sharp left signed No Through Road at Canonteign Falls exit

This beautiful rural farmhouse, located in the middle of the Teign Valley has three highly individual bedrooms. All are richly decorated and well equipped; ideal for business or leisure use. Public areas include a comfortable lounge and a dining area with inglenook fire place; a sociable setting for breakfast. There is also parking, all in characterful grounds.

Rooms 3 en suite (3 smoking) S £40-£100; D £70-£100* **Facilities** FTV DVD TVL tea/coffee WiFi ⚡ 18 🛁 **Parking** 3 **Notes** LB 120 acres beef/grass

CHULMLEIGH
Map 3 SS61

The Old Bakehouse

★★★★ 🛏 GUEST HOUSE

tel: 01769 580074 & 580137 **South Molton St EX18 7BW**
email: holly@oldbakehousedevon.co.uk **web:** www.oldbakehousedevon.co.uk
dir: A377 onto B3096 into village centre, left into South Molton St, 100yds on left

This 16th-century thatched house is situated in the centre of Chulmleigh, a hilltop town which stands above a beautiful river valley. The charming bedrooms are equipped with many extras such as DVD players (library available) and are located across a pretty, secluded courtyard garden in the former village bakery. A wealth of beams, thick cob walls and wood-burning stove all contribute to the character and comfort. A generous choice is offered at breakfast with an emphasis on excellent local produce.

Rooms 3 en suite (1 GF) S £60; D £90 **Facilities** FTV DVD Lounge tea/coffee ⚡ 18 🛁 **Extras** Home-made biscuits, flowers **Notes** LB ⊗ No Children 11yrs

CLOVELLY
Map 3 SS32

East Dyke Farmhouse (SS312235)

★★★★ 🛏 FARMHOUSE

tel: 01237 431216 **East Dyke Farm, Higher Clovelly EX39 5RU**
email: helen.goaman@btinternet.com **web:** www.bedbreakfastclovelly.co.uk
dir: A39 onto B3237 at Clovelly Cross rdbt, farm 500yds on left

Adjoining an Iron Age hill fort, this working farm has glorious views of Bideford Bay in the distance. The farmhouse has a friendly atmosphere and the open fires, beams and stone floors add to its charm and character. The three bedrooms are spacious and furnished in co-ordinated fabrics with thoughtful little extras. A key feature here is the breakfast – local produce and delicious home-made preserves are served around one large table.

Rooms 3 rms (2 en suite) (1 pri facs) (1 fmly) S £45-£55; D £65-£75* **Facilities** FTV TVL tea/coffee WiFi 🛁 **Extras** Fridge **Parking** 6 **Notes** Closed 24-26 Dec RS Dec-Feb Advance bookings only ⊜ 350 acres beef/arable

COLEFORD
Map 3 SS70

The New Inn

★★★★ INN

tel: 01363 84242 **EX17 5BZ**
email: enquiries@thenewinncoleford.co.uk **web:** www.thenewinncoleford.co.uk
dir: Exit A377 into Coleford, 1.5m to inn (signed)

Originally dating back to the 13th century, The New Inn is a charming thatched village inn with much to offer, and is a relaxing base from which to explore this beautiful corner of Devon. Bedrooms are spacious, comfortable and well appointed with lovely beds and lots of period features. Roaring fires, flagged floors, and Captain the resident parrot, all combine to create an engaging atmosphere. A choice of carefully prepared dishes is on offer in the restaurant and bar lounges, with local produce strongly featured.

Rooms 6 en suite (4 fmly) (1 GF) S £60-£69; D £85-£95* **Facilities** FTV DVD tea/coffee Dinner available Direct Dial WiFi ⚡ 18 🛁 **Extras** Bottled water - complimentary **Parking** 50 **Notes** LB Closed 25-26 Dec No coaches

CREDITON
Map 3 SS80

The Lamb Inn

★★★★ 🍺 INN

tel: 01363 773676 **The Square, Sandford EX17 4LW**
email: thelamb@gmail.com **web:** www.lambinnsandford.co.uk

The Lamb Inn is the sort of quintessential local which any village would be proud to have. This is a proper unpretentious pub with a very welcoming and engaging atmosphere, where good-natured banter is on offer to accompany a refreshing pint. Food is not to be missed; accomplished cooking makes good use of quality, local produce, and breakfasts are generous. Bedrooms and bathrooms offer impressive levels of quality with contemporary styling.

Rooms 7 en suite S £69; D £89-£130* **Facilities** Dinner available

CROYDE
Map 3 SS43

The Whiteleaf

★★★★ ♀ ➣ GUEST HOUSE

tel: 01271 890266 **Croyde Rd EX33 1PN**
web: www.thewhiteleaf.co.uk
dir: On B3231 entering Croyde, on left at 'Road Narrows' sign

A warm family welcome awaits guests at this attractive house within easy walking distance of the pretty village and the sandy beach. Each of the well-equipped bedrooms has its own charm, and three rooms have decked balconies. Ambitious and imaginative dinners, using fresh seasonal produce, are served in the elegant restaurant.

Rooms 5 en suite (2 fmly) S £68-£72; D £82-£140* **Facilities** FTV Lounge tea/coffee Dinner available Direct Dial Licensed WiFi ⚓ **Extras** Mini-bar **Parking** 10 **Notes** LB ⊗ Closed 24-27 Dec

CULLOMPTON
Map 3 ST00

Premier Collection

Muddifords Court Country House

★★★★★ ♀ GUEST ACCOMMODATION

tel: 01884 820023 & 07890 273730 **Willand EX15 2QG**
email: info@muddifords.co.uk **web:** www.muddifordscourt.co.uk
dir: M5 junct 27 onto A38 (Wellington). After 1m at rdbt right onto B3181, at rdbt (4m) right signed Halberton/Willand. Over mini rdbt, 500mtrs turn right (Sampford Peverell). 200mtrs on right

Muddifords Court has been developed into a high quality establishment, with the added benefit of a range of flexible meeting space to accommodate weddings, conferences and special events. The rooms have been finished to a high standard and are sumptuously appointed; some offer attractive views over the Culm Valley and beyond. A choice of freshly prepared breakfasts is served in the main dining room. Self-catering huts are available in the private copse.

Rooms 5 en suite 2 annexe en suite (1 GF) D £90-£145 (room only)* **Facilities** FTV DVD TVL tea/coffee Licensed WiFi ⚓ **Extras** Sherry **Conf** Max 100 Thtr 100 Class 80 Board 60 **Parking** 70 **Notes** ⊗ Closed 24 Dec-2 Jan Civ Wed 120

Lower Ford Farm (SS978095)

★★★★ ➣ FARMHOUSE

tel: 01884 252354 **EX15 1LX**
email: lowerfordfarm@hotmail.com **web:** www.lowerfordfarm-accommodation.co.uk
dir: M5 junct 28 Cullompton, take road by Manor House Hotel. At Whitedown x-rds turn left then 1st left

A peacefully located 15th-century farmhouse, Lower Ford Farm offers naturally welcoming hospitality with a real home-from-home atmosphere. Surrounded by delightful countryside, this working farm provides a peaceful retreat. Bedrooms are comfortably furnished and equipped with some welcome extras to add to guest comfort. A spacious lounge is also available. In addition to the large farmhouse breakfast, the home-cooked dinners (available by prior arrangement) should not be missed.

Rooms 3 en suite (1 fmly) S £34; D £68* **Facilities** FTV DVD TVL tea/coffee Dinner available WiFi ⛳ ⚓ **Parking** 6 **Notes** ⊗ Closed Nov-Jan ➣ 450 acres beef/sheep/arable

Weir Mill Farm (ST040108)

★★★★ FARMHOUSE

tel: 01884 820803 **Jaycroft, Willand EX15 2RE**
email: rita@weirmill-devon.co.uk **web:** www.weirmill-devon.co.uk
dir: 2m N of Cullompton. M5 junct 27, B3181 to Willand, left at rdbt onto B3340 signed Uffculme, 50yds right into Willand Moor Rd, after Lupin Way left into lane

Set in extensive farmland, this charming 19th-century farmhouse offers comfortable accommodation with a relaxed and homely atmosphere. The spacious bedrooms are attractively decorated and equipped with an impressive range of thoughtful extras. A good choice is offered at breakfast in the well-appointed dining room.

Rooms 3 en suite (1 fmly) S £45; D £75 **Facilities** FTV tea/coffee WiFi ⚓ **Parking** 5 **Notes** ⊗ ➣ 100 acres arable/beef

DARTMEET
Map 3 SX67

Brimpts Farm

★★★ GUEST ACCOMMODATION

tel: 01364 631450 **PL20 6SG**
email: info@brimptsfarm.co.uk **web:** www.brimptsfarm.co.uk
dir: Dartmeet at E end of B3357, establishment signed on right at top of hill

A popular venue for walkers and lovers of the great outdoors, Brimpts Farm is peacefully situated in the heart of Dartmoor and has been a Duchy of Cornwall farm since 1307. Bedrooms are simply furnished and many have wonderful views across the moor. Additional facilities include a sauna and spa, and a children's play area.

Rooms 10 en suite 3 annexe rms (3 pri facs) (2 fmly) (7 GF) S £40; D £70-£80 **Facilities** Lounge TVL TV1B tea/coffee Licensed WiFi Sauna Pool table ⚓ Farm walks & trails Hot tub **Conf** Max 60 Thtr 60 Class 40 Board 25 **Parking** 50 **Notes** LB

DARTMOUTH
Map 3 SX85

Premier Collection

Nonsuch House
★★★★★ GUEST ACCOMMODATION

tel: 01803 752829 **Church Hill, Kingswear TQ6 OBX**
email: enquiries@nonsuch-house.co.uk **web:** www.nonsuch-house.co.uk
dir: *A3022 onto A379 2m before Brixham. Fork left onto B3205. Left up Higher Contour Rd, down Ridley Hill, house on bend on left at top of Church Hill*

Nonsuch House is a delightful Edwardian property with fabulous views across the Dart estuary. The marvellous hosts combine friendliness with unobtrusive service. Bedrooms are spacious and superbly appointed, each with a spectacular panorama of the harbour. Fresh, local ingredients are served at dinner, including top-quality meat, fish, and farmhouse cheeses. Breakfast, served on the patio in good weather, features freshly squeezed juice, local sausages and home-baked bread.

Rooms 4 en suite (2 fmly) (2 GF) S £95-£145; D £135-£185* **Facilities** FTV DVD iPod docking station Lounge tea/coffee Dinner available WiFi ⚓
Extras Speciality toiletries, home-made biscuits - free **Parking** 4 **Notes** LB ⊗ No Children 10yrs RS Sat & Tue-Wed no dinner available

Premier Collection

Strete Barton House
★★★★★ GUEST HOUSE

tel: 01803 770364 **Totnes Rd TQ6 ORU**
email: info@stretebarton.co.uk **web:** www.stretebarton.co.uk

(For full entry see Strete)

Premier Collection

Appletree Court House
★★★★★ BED AND BREAKFAST

tel: 01803 835630 & 07944 407969 **4c Church Rd TQ6 9HQ**
email: enquiries@appletreecourthouse.co.uk **web:** www.appletreecourthouse.co.uk
dir: *Follow signs for town centre, down hill, turn right into Townstal Rd. 1st right into Church Rd, signed*

Appletree Court House is a very high quality bed and breakfast tucked away in a quiet location, yet just a few minutes' walk from the centre of Dartmouth. Hosts John and Christine are very experienced and make every effort to make their guests feel relaxed and at home. Service is very attentive and breakfast is a real treat - a great start to the day.

Rooms 2 rms (1 en suite) (1 pri facs) (1 fmly) D £100-£130* **Facilities** FTV DVD Lounge tea/coffee WiFi ⚓ 27 ⚓ Leisure facilities at golf & country club
Extras Speciality toiletries, robes **Parking** 2 **Notes** ⊗

Premier Collection

Mounthaven
★★★★★ BED AND BREAKFAST

tel: 01803 839061 & 07919 274751 **Mount Boone TQ6 9PB**
email: enquiries@mounthavendartmouth.co.uk
web: www.mounthavendartmouth.co.uk
dir: *A379, right into Townstal Rd, opposite Royal Naval College gates. 1st left into Mount Boone, halfway down on right*

Set on the hillside of Mount Boone, Mounthaven has a superb view of the town and the estuary yet is only a few minutes' walk from the town centre. The hosts are experienced and professional and a very warm welcome is assured. Bedrooms are individually decorated and each enjoys a view of historic Dartmouth or the sea.

Rooms 3 en suite **Facilities** STV FTV DVD TVL tea/coffee WiFi ⚓ 18 ⚓ **Parking** 5 **Notes** ⊗ No Children 16yrs ⊕

Hill View House
★★★★ GUEST ACCOMMODATION

tel: 01803 839372 **76 Victoria Rd TQ6 9DZ**
email: enquiries@hillviewdartmouth.co.uk **web:** www.hillviewdartmouth.co.uk
dir: *Phone for detailed directions*

Centrally located, Hill View House is a fully refurbished five-storey late Victorian town house. A warm welcome is guaranteed and the house is located only minutes from the heart of Dartmouth. Bedrooms are comfortably furnished, serviced to a high standard, and come equipped with a range of accessories. Breakfast is served in the light and airy dining room. Free WiFi is accessible throughout.

Rooms 4 en suite 1 annexe en suite S £42-£47; D £60-£70* **Facilities** TVL tea/coffee WiFi ⚓ 18 **Extras** Speciality toiletries **Parking** 3 **Notes** ⊗ No Children 14yrs

Bayards Cove Inn

★★★★ ⌂ GUEST ACCOMMODATION

tel: 01803 839278 **27 Lower St TQ6 9AN**
email: bayardscove@gmail.com **web:** www.bayardscoveinn.co.uk

There is a real sense of history at this charming waterside establishment, once a Tudor merchant's house, located a few steps from where the Pilgrims set sail on the Mayflower in 1621. Every effort is made to ensure guests have a relaxed and rewarding stay. A café and wine bar by day; evening opening times vary, with a tapas menu available on selected nights. Bedrooms are comfortable, and individually styled. Bathrooms provide all the expected modern necessities with cosseting towels and quality toiletries. Breakfast is a generous affair, with a range of continental and cooked options, all showcasing the best of local produce.

Rooms 7 en suite (2 fmly) **Facilities** FTV DVD Lounge tea/coffee Dinner available Licensed WiFi ♿ 18 🔒 **Extras** Magazines - complimentary

Cherub's Nest

★★★★ GUEST ACCOMMODATION

tel: 01803 832482 **15 Higher St TQ6 9RB**
email: cherubsnest4bb@aol.com **web:** www.cherubsnest.co.uk
dir: From Lower Dartmouth ferry along Lower St, left into Smith St, left into Higher St, Cherub's Nest 50yds on left

Dating from 1710, this former merchant's house, bedecked with flowers during the summer, is located in the very heart of historic Dartmouth. Full of character, the individually decorated bedrooms vary in size, but all are attractive and well equipped. A choice of breakfasts is served in the cosy dining room.

Rooms 3 en suite **Facilities** FTV tea/coffee WiFi **Notes** ⊗ No Children 10yrs

DODDISCOMBSLEIGH — Map 3 SX88

The Nobody Inn

★★★★ ◎ INN

tel: 01647 252394 **EX6 7PS**
email: info@nobodyinn.co.uk **web:** www.nobodyinn.co.uk
dir: From A38 turn off at top of Haldon Hill, follow signs to Doddiscombsleigh

Dating back to the 16th century, this fascinating inn is something of a mecca for lovers of wine, whisky and local ale — the choices are extensive. Let's not forget the impressive food, much of which is sourced locally including an extensive cheese selection. Bedrooms and bathrooms have been appointed to provide high levels of quality, comfort and individuality. Reassuringly, the bars and lounges remain unchanged with charmingly mis-matched furniture, age-darkened beams and an inglenook fireplace.

Rooms 5 rms (4 en suite) (1 pri facs) S £50-£75; D £99-£105* **Facilities** FTV DVD tea/coffee Dinner available Direct Dial WiFi 🔒 **Conf** Max 24 **Parking** 25 **Notes** No Children 5yrs Closed 25 Dec No coaches

DUNKESWELL — Map 3 ST10

The Old Kennels

★★★★ BED AND BREAKFAST

tel: 01823 681138 **Stentwood EX14 4RW**
email: info@theoldkennels.co.uk **web:** www.theoldkennels.co.uk

Located in the heart of the beautiful Blackdown Hills, on the Devon-Somerset border, The Old Kennels is in a quiet rural location and makes an ideal base for exploring this vibrant area. Accommodation includes a cosy two bedroom loft apartment, furnished with antique furniture and vintage details. It has a compact lounge area with TV, microwave, fridge, kettle and sink. The roof terrace and garden area have far-reaching views across the fields and valley. A continental breakfast is served in the main house, from which the resident alpacas can be seen grazing in the fields.

Rooms 2 annexe rms 1 annexe en suite (1 pri facs) (1 fmly) S £50-£60; D £100* **Facilities** FTV TVL tea/coffee WiFi ♿ 18 🔒 25 acres of woodland Arts & crafts courses **Extras** Fresh milk **Conf** Max 12 Board 12 **Parking** 10 **Notes** LB ⊗

ERMINGTON — Map 3 SX65

Premier Collection

Plantation House

★★★★★ ◎◎ ⌂ RESTAURANT WITH ROOMS

tel: 01548 831100 & 830741 **Totnes Rd PL21 9NS**
email: info@plantationhousehotel.co.uk **web:** www.plantationhousehotel.co.uk

Peacefully situated in the picturesque South Hams, this former rectory provides an intimate and relaxing base from which to explore the area. Quality, comfort and individuality are hallmarks throughout, with bedrooms offering impressive standards and a host of thoughtful extras. The stylish bathrooms come equipped with fluffy towels, robes and under-floor heating. A drink beside the crackling log fire is the ideal prelude to dinner, where skill and passion underpin menus focusing upon wonderful local produce. Breakfast is equally enjoyable, with superb eggs provided by the resident hens.

Rooms 8 en suite S £55-£85; D £95-£230* **Facilities** DVD iPod docking station Lounge tea/coffee Dinner available Direct Dial WiFi ♿ 18 Fishing Riding Massage & Therapies **Extras** Speciality toiletries, fruit, robes, mineral water **Conf** Max 16 **Parking** 30 **Notes** LB No coaches

EXETER — Map 3 SX99

Chi Restaurant & Bar with Accommodation

★★★★ ◎ RESTAURANT WITH ROOMS

tel: 01626 890213 **Fore St, Kenton EX6 8LD**
email: enquiries@chi-restaurant.co.uk **web:** www.chi-restaurant.co.uk
dir: 5m S of Exeter. M5 junct 30, A379 towards Dawlish, in village centre

This former pub has been spectacularly transformed into a chic and contemporary bar, allied with a stylish Chinese restaurant. Dishes are beautifully presented with an emphasis on quality produce and authenticity, resulting in a memorable dining experience. Bedrooms are well equipped and all provide good levels of space and comfort, along with modern bathrooms.

Rooms 5 en suite (1 fmly) S £45-£50; D £62.10-£69 (room only)* **Facilities** FTV DVD TVL tea/coffee Dinner available Direct Dial WiFi 🔒 **Parking** 26 **Notes** ⊗ No coaches

EXETER *continued*

Innkeeper's Lodge Exeter, Clyst St George

★★★ INN

tel: 08451 551551 *(Calls cost 2p per minute plus your phone company's access charge)*
Clyst St George EX3 0QJ
email: info@innkeeperslodge.com **web:** www.innkeeperslodge.com

This welcoming inn is just a short drive from the centre of Exeter and very convenient for access to the M5. Surrounded by rolling fields, this is an excellent base for exploring the East Devon coast, with Exmouth close by and Topsham also worth a visit. Bedrooms all provide impressive levels of comfort and quality with all the requirements for the business and leisure guest. The pub has a warm and inviting atmosphere with crackling log fires and cosy hideaways, so sit back and enjoy a drink and a satisfying meal.

Rooms 21 en suite (6 fmly) (8 GF) **Facilities** FTV tea/coffee Dinner available Direct Dial WiFi **Parking Notes** ⊗

Innkeeper's Lodge Exeter, Middlemoor Lodge

★★★ INN

tel: 08451 551551 *(Calls cost 2p per minute plus your phone company's access charge)*
Rydon Ln, Middlemoor EX2 7HL
email: info@innkeeperslodge.com **web:** www.innkeeperslodge.com
dir: *M5 junct 29 onto A30 towards Honiton/Exeter Airport. Right into Honiton Rd, take 1st exit at next 2 rdbts, then 2nd exit at next rdbt, property on left*

Having recently undergone a total refurbishment, this conveniently located establishment is ideally suited for both business and leisure guests. It's just a short drive from the city centre, and is also close to the airport and Digby and Sowton station. Contemporary styled bedrooms offer good levels of comfort and quality. A Toby Carvery is adjacent.

Rooms 1 en suite 37 annexe en suite (1 fmly) (28 GF) D £49-£129* **Facilities** FTV tea/coffee Dinner available WiFi **Conf** Max 40 **Parking** 200 **Notes** ⊗

EXMOUTH — Map 3 SY08

The Devoncourt

★★★ GUEST ACCOMMODATION

tel: 01395 272277 **16 Douglas Av EX8 2EX**
email: enquiries@devoncourt.com **web:** www.devoncourthotel.com
dir: *M5/A376 to Exmouth, follow seafront to Maer Rd, right at T-junct*

The Devoncourt stands in four acres of mature, subtropical gardens, sloping gently towards the sea and overlooking two miles of sandy beaches. It offers extensive leisure facilities, and the smartly furnished bedrooms are exceptionally well equipped. The spacious public areas are available to timeshare owners as well as guests. For meals there is a choice between the informal bar and the restaurant.

The Devoncourt

Rooms 52 en suite 2 annexe en suite (35 fmly) (8 GF) **Facilities** FTV DVD TVL tea/coffee Dinner available Direct Dial Lift Licensed WiFi ⊗ ⬥ ⬥ ⬥ ⬥ 18 Snooker Sauna Gym Sun shower Jacuzzi **Parking** 50 **Notes** ⊗ Civ Wed 100

HALWELL — Map 3 SX75

Stanborough Farm *(SX767527)*

★★★★ FARMHOUSE

tel: 01548 821306 & 07807 787327 **Halwell TQ9 7JQ**
email: stanboroughfarm@hotmail.com **web:** www.stanboroughfarm.co.uk
dir: *From Halwell turn right signed Moreleigh, farm on left*

A warm welcome is received on arrival at this working dairy farm. After a comfortable night's sleep, a freshly cooked farmhouse breakfast, using produce from the farm whenever possible, is served in the attractive breakfast room overlooking the garden. Both en suite bedrooms have been appointed to a high standard and offer all the comforts required by the modern traveller. An ideal location for exploring the South Hams. There are two country pubs within walking distance.

Rooms 3 en suite **Facilities** FTV Lounge TV2B tea/coffee WiFi **Parking** 4 **Notes** ⊗ ⊛ 130 acres dairy/poultry

HAYTOR VALE
Map 3 SX77

Rock Inn
★★★★★ ⊛⊛ INN

tel: 01364 661305 & 661465 **TQ13 9XP**
email: inn@rock-inn.co.uk **web:** www.rock-inn.co.uk
dir: A38 onto 382 to Bovey Tracey, in 0.5m left onto B3387 to Haytor

Dating back to the 1750s, this former coaching inn is in a pretty hamlet on the edge of Dartmoor. Each named after a Grand National winner, the individually decorated bedrooms have some nice extra touches. Bars are full of character, with flagstone floors and old beams, and offer a wide range of dishes, cooked with imagination. The food has been awarded two AA Rosettes.

Rooms 9 en suite S £80-£100; D £100-£160* **Facilities** FTV DVD Lounge tea/coffee Dinner available Direct Dial WiFi 🔒 **Parking** 10 **Notes** LB Closed 25-26 Dec No coaches

HOLSWORTHY
Map 3 SS30

The Hollies Farm Guest House *(SS371001)*
★★★★ FARMHOUSE

tel: 01409 253770 & 07972 510014 **Clawton EX22 6PN**
email: theholliesfarm@hotmail.com **web:** www.theholliesfarm.co.uk
dir: Exit A388 at Clawton signed vineyard, left in 1.5m. The Hollies in lane on left, by farm buildings, after T-junct, signed. At end of farm lane, fork right

This sheep and beef farm offers comfortable, modern accommodation with a family atmosphere. There are pleasant views across the countryside from some bedrooms, and all are well appointed. Breakfast is served in the conservatory. There is also a barbecue area with a gazebo.

Rooms 3 en suite (2 fmly) **Facilities** FTV DVD TVL tea/coffee WiFi ⚓ 18 🔒 **Parking** 6 **Notes** LB ⊗ Closed 24-25 Dec ⊜ 25 acres beef/sheep

Barton Gate Farm Guesthouse
★★★ BED AND BREAKFAST

tel: 07768 402640 & 07831 739206 **Pancrasweek EX22 7JT**
email: paularaefrancis@me.com **web:** www.bartongatedevon.co.uk
dir: From Holsworthy take A3072 to Bude, 3.1m on right

This relaxed and welcoming establishment is ideally located for exploring and is within easy access of the coast. Every effort is made to ensure guests enjoy a rewarding stay with plenty of local information always on offer. Hospitality is also extended to animals, with anything from a hamster to a horse more than welcome. Bedrooms are located in a newly converted stable block, all offering good levels of comfort, and the advantage of inter-connecting doors for families. A choice of continental or traditional English breakfast is served in the light and airy dining room. Additional facilities include a games room, lounge, nail bar and a large exercise field for dogs.

Rooms 3 en suite (3 fmly) (3 GF) D £75-£140* **Facilities** FTV DVD Lounge TVL tea/coffee ch fac Pool table 🔒 Table tennis, 4G WiFi **Parking** 30 **Notes** LB

HONITON
Map 4 ST10

Threshays
★★★ BED AND BREAKFAST

tel: 01404 43551 & 07811 675800 **Awliscombe EX14 3QB**
email: threshays@btinternet.com **web:** www.stayat.co.uk/threshays
dir: 2.5m NW of Honiton on A373

A converted threshing barn, situated on a non-working farm, Threshays has wonderful views over open countryside. With tea and cake offered on arrival, this family-run establishment provides comfortable accommodation in a friendly atmosphere. The lounge-dining room is a light and airy setting for enjoying breakfasts. Ample parking is a bonus.

Rooms 2 rms (1 fmly) S £37; D £64* **Facilities** TVL tea/coffee WiFi **Parking** 4 **Notes** ⊗ ⊜

HOPE COVE
Map 3 SX64

Cottage
★★★★ ⊜ GUEST ACCOMMODATION

tel: 01548 561555 **TQ7 3HJ**
email: info@hopecove.com **web:** www.hopecove.com
dir: From Kingsbridge on A381 to Salcombe. 2nd right at Marlborough, left for Inner Hope

Glorious sunsets can be seen over the attractive bay from this popular accommodation. Friendly and attentive service from the staff and management mean many guests return here. Bedrooms, many with sea views and some with balconies, are well equipped. The restaurant offers an enjoyable dining experience.

Rooms 32 rms (31 en suite) (1 pri facs) (5 fmly) (5 GF) S £52-£125; D £104-£210* (incl.dinner) **Facilities** FTV DVD Lounge TVL tea/coffee Dinner available Direct Dial Licensed WiFi ch fac ⚓ 18 🔒 Table tennis **Conf** Max 70 Thtr 60 Class 60 Board 30 **Parking** 50 **Notes** LB Closed early Jan-early Feb

ILFRACOMBE
Map 3 SS54

Premier Collection

The Habit Boutique Rooms
★★★★★ ⊛⊛ 🍷 RESTAURANT WITH ROOMS

tel: 01271 863272 & 07931 551487 **46-48 Fore St EX34 9DN**
email: info@thehabitboutiquerooms.com **web:** www.thehabitboutiquerooms.com
dir: Into Ilfracombe on A361, continue to High St until road splits. Take slight left, 100yds on left

The Habit Boutique Rooms occupy a fully refurbished grand old Victorian building close to Ilfracombe seafront. The rooms, many offering stunning views over the Bristol Channel, are of high quality throughout. There is also an elegant yet relaxed, fine dining restaurant which has been awarded two AA Rosettes; a large bar and a lounge area with soaring ceilings extending out on to a large deck; and a fully equipped Pilates studio and beauty treatment rooms. AA Funkiest B&B of the Year Award Runner-Up 2016-2017.

Rooms 11 en suite (4 fmly) **Facilities** FTV Lounge tea/coffee Dinner available WiFi 🔒 Well-being studio **Extras** Speciality toiletries, robes, slippers, mini-bar **Conf** Max 28 Thtr 28 Class 16 Board 12 **Notes** LB ⊗ No coaches

ILFRACOMBE *continued*

Marine Court

★★★★ ⚑ GUEST HOUSE

tel: 01271 862920 & 07791 051778 **Hillsborough Rd EX34 9QQ**
email: info@marinecourthoteldevon.co.uk **web:** www.marinecourthoteldevon.co.uk
dir: *M5 junct 27, A361 to Barnstaple, continue to Ilfracombe*

Marine Court is a well-established guest house offering comfortable, well appointed rooms in a handy location. Guests are assured a very warm welcome from the hosts who do all they can to ensure a comfortable stay. Guests have use of a small bar lounge where drinks can be served, and off-road parking is a bonus.

Rooms 8 en suite **Facilities** FTV DVD iPod docking station Lounge tea/coffee Licensed WiFi **Extras** Mini-bar **Parking** 8 **Notes** ⊗ No Children 16yrs Closed Nov-Mar

The Olive Branch

★★★★★ ◉◉ ⚑ GUEST ACCOMMODATION

tel: 01271 879005 & 07860 418343 **56 Fore St EX34 9DJ**
email: enquiries@olivebranchguesthouse.co.uk **web:** www.olivebranchguesthouse.co.uk
dir: *A361 into Ilfracombe, through lights into High St. At end, fork left into Fore St, continue straight down, pass no entry signs, on left hand side*

A Georgian Grade II listed building situated in the heart of Ilfracombe with easy access to the seafront and only minutes away from all local amenities. Bedrooms are all en suite and decorated to high standards, all offering very good comfort. The restaurant has been awarded two AA Rosettes, and the excellent breakfast is a great way to start the day.

Rooms 5 en suite **Facilities** FTV DVD tea/coffee Dinner available WiFi ⚲ **Extras** Speciality toiletries, bottled water, magazines **Notes** LB ⊗ No Children 15yrs Closed Nov-Feb

Collingdale Guest House

★★★★ ⚑ GUEST HOUSE

tel: 01271 863770 **13 Larkstone Ter EX34 9NU**
email: thecollingdale@gmail.com **web:** www.thecollingdale.co.uk
dir: *Take A399 E through Ilfracombe, on left past B3230 turning*

Overlooking the harbour, this Victorian guest house is within easy walking distance of the town centre and seafront. The well-presented bedrooms, many with sweeping sea views, are furnished to a high standard with many thoughtful extras. One room has its own balcony. The comfortable lounge and elegant dining room share the magnificent views. A cosy bar is also available for a tipple before bedtime.

Rooms 9 rms (8 en suite) (1 pri facs) (3 fmly) S £55-£65; D £75-£95* **Facilities** FTV TVL tea/coffee Licensed WiFi ⚓ 18 **Extras** Mineral water - complimentary **Notes** LB ⊗ No Children 8yrs Closed Nov-Feb

Norbury House

★★★★ GUEST HOUSE

tel: 01271 863888 **Torrs Park EX34 8AZ**
email: info@norburyhouse.co.uk **web:** www.norburyhouse.co.uk
dir: *From A399 to end of High St/Church St. At mini rdbt after lights take 1st exit into Church Rd. Bear left into Osbourne Rd. At T-junct left into Torrs Park. House at top of hill on right*

This detached Victorian residence has a refreshingly different, contemporary style, and the genuinely warm welcome is allied with a helpful and attentive approach. A variety of bedroom styles is offered but all provide impressive levels of comfort and quality. An elegant lounge leads through to a conservatory which has an honesty bar. Outside, the peaceful terraced gardens have lovely views. Breakfast features quality, local produce.

Rooms 6 en suite (2 fmly) **Facilities** FTV tea/coffee Licensed WiFi **Conf** Max 18 Thtr 14 Class 14 Board 12 **Parking** 6 **Notes** ⊗

| KENTISBURY | Map 3 SS64 |

Nightingails

★★★★ ⚑ GUEST ACCOMMODATION

tel: 01271 883545 **Kentisbury Mill EX31 4NF**
email: info@nightingails.co.uk **web:** www.nightingails.co.uk
dir: *M5 junct 27, A361 towards Barnstaple, then A399 to Blackmoor Gate. Left at Blackmoor Gate onto A39, right onto B3229 at Kentisbury Ford, 1m on right*

Originally consisting of an 18th-century cottage and mill, this relaxing hideaway has been sympathetically renovated to provide impressive levels of comfort, allied with caring hospitality. Bedrooms offer an appealing blend of old and new, with views over the extensive gardens. A guest lounge is also provided with plenty of local information for those wanting to explore the dramatic coast and countryside.

Breakfast is Aga-cooked and includes eggs laid by the resident hens, together with other wonderful local produce.

Rooms 5 en suite S £40; D £80-£84* **Facilities** FTV DVD Lounge tea/coffee Dinner available WiFi **Parking** 6 **Notes** LB Closed Xmas

LEWDOWN Map 3 SX48

Lobhill Farmhouse

★★★★ BED AND BREAKFAST

tel: 01566 783542 & 07817 244687 **EX20 4DT**
email: jane.colwill@btopenworld.com **web:** www.lobhillbedandbreakfast.co.uk
dir: *Exit A30 at Sourton Cross, follow signs for Lewdown onto old A30. Lobhill 1m before Lewdown*

Ideally situated for easy access to moorland and the Devon and Cornwall coasts, this stone farmhouse dates back some 130 years. Peacefully located, its renovation has resulted in impressive levels of quality, yet it still retains a reassuringly traditional and homely feel. Bedrooms (including one on the ground floor with separate access) have free WiFi and views of the countryside. Tasty and satisfying breakfasts are cooked on the Aga and served either in the dining room or at the kitchen table. Guests are welcome to make use of the lovely gardens and summerhouse, or explore the woodland walks.

Rooms 4 en suite (1 fmly) (1 GF) S £55; D £75-£95* **Facilities** FTV DVD iPod docking station Lounge tea/coffee WiFi Fishing Riding Vineyard tours **Extras** Home-made biscuits, local fudge **Parking** 8 **Notes** LB

LUSTLEIGH Map 3 SX78

Premier Collection

Eastwrey Barton

★★★★★ GUEST ACCOMMODATION

tel: 01647 277338 **Moretonhampstead Rd TQ13 9SN**
email: info@eastwreybarton.co.uk **web:** www.eastwreybarton.co.uk
dir: *On A382 between Bovey Tracey & Moretonhampstead, 6m from A38 (Drumbridges junct)*

Warm hospitality and a genuine welcome are hallmarks at this family-run establishment, situated inside the Dartmoor National Park. Built in the 18th century, the house retains many original features and has views across the Wray Valley. Bedrooms are spacious and well equipped, while public areas include a cosy lounge warmed by a crackling log fire. Breakfast and dinner showcase local produce with an impressive wine list to accompany the latter.

Rooms 5 en suite (1 fmly) S £115; D £125-£140* **Facilities** FTV Lounge tea/coffee Dinner available Licensed WiFi **Parking** 18 **Notes** No Children 10yrs

LYNMOUTH Map 3 SS74

Premier Collection

The Heatherville

★★★★★ GUEST ACCOMMODATION

tel: 01598 752327 & 753893 **Tors Park EX35 6NB**
email: theheatherville@aol.com **web:** www.heatherville.co.uk
dir: *Exit A39 into Tors Rd, 1st left fork into Tors Park*

This wonderful Victorian establishment stands high above Lynmouth, and the views across the wooded valley are quite superb. There is an abundance of charm and quality here at The Heatherville, and bedrooms are individually styled with comfort and character. Public rooms are also inviting with an elegant lounge and snug bar, while the dining room is the attractive venue for skilfully prepared dinners and substantial breakfasts.

Rooms 6 en suite D £105-£130* **Facilities** FTV DVD Lounge tea/coffee Dinner available Licensed WiFi **Parking** 6 **Notes** LB No Children 16yrs Closed Nov-Mar

East Lyn House

★★★★ GUEST HOUSE

tel: 01598 752540 **17 Watersmeet Rd EX35 6EP**
email: eastlynhousehotel@gmail.com **web:** www.eastlynhouse.co.uk

Just a short stroll from the centre of the village and the harbour, this is a perfect place to stay to enjoy this picturesque location. Bedrooms provide all the expected comforts with comfy beds ensuring a good rest before the day's activities. Public areas include a bar and lounge, while outside a wonderful terrace looks out over the River Lyn, with stunning views up the densely wooded valley. Breakfast is a tasty start to the day, and can be served on the terrace in summer months. Parking is also available.

Rooms 8 en suite (1 fmly) **Facilities** FTV DVD Lounge TVL tea/coffee Licensed WiFi **Parking** 8 **Notes** No Children 8yrs

LYNTON Map 3 SS74

Gable Lodge Guest House

★★★★ GUEST ACCOMMODATION

tel: 01598 752367 **35 Lee Rd EX35 6BS**
email: gablelodge@btconnect.com **web:** www.gablelodgelynton.co.uk
dir: *M5 junct 23 onto A39 to Lynmouth. Right up hill to Lynton, right at top of hill signed Lynton. Continue through town, Gable Lodge on right*

Gable Lodge is a Grade II listed, family-run Victorian establishment just a short stroll from the centre of this small town. The welcome is warm and genuine with plenty of local information, help and advice always available to help ensure a memorable stay. Bedrooms all provide good levels of comfort and quality with lovely views an added bonus. Generous breakfasts are served in the dining room, and evening meals also available on request. Additional facilities include a guest lounge and parking.

Rooms 6 en suite (2 fmly) S £42-£46; D £61-£72* **Facilities** FTV DVD iPod docking station TVL tea/coffee Dinner available Licensed WiFi **Extras** Mini-fridge, fresh milk **Parking** 5 **Notes** LB Closed Xmas

LYNTON *continued*

Sinai House

★★★★ GUEST HOUSE

tel: 01598 753227 **Lynway EX35 6AY**
email: enquiries@sinaihouse.co.uk **web:** www.sinaihouse.co.uk
dir: *A39 onto B3234 through town, pass church, house on right overlooking main car park*

Originally built in 1850, this grand house stands in half an acre of terraced gardens, just a short stroll from the centre of town. Spectacular views can be enjoyed from many of the comfy, well-appointed bedrooms, likewise from the elegant guest lounge. The welcome is warm and genuine with every effort made to ensure a relaxed and rewarding stay. In addition to the satisfying breakfasts, bar snacks are also available, served either in the spacious dining room or snug bar.

Rooms 8 rms (6 en suite) (2 pri facs) S £40; D £152-£156 **Facilities** FTV DVD Lounge tea/coffee Licensed WiFi 🔒 **Parking** 8 **Notes** ⊗ No Children 12yrs Closed Xmas

South View Guest House

★★★★ GUEST HOUSE

tel: 01598 753728 **23 Lee Rd EX35 6BP**
email: titfords@hotmail.co.uk **web:** www.southviewguesthouselynton.co.uk

South View was built in 1905, when Lynton was expanding to provide additional accommodation for the burgeoning tourist trade. Now newly refurbished, South View offers comfortable accommodation in a central location within Lynton. Breakfast is served in the contemporary dining room, with a good selection on offer. Hosts Martin and Catherine are on hand to welcome and help throughout your stay.

Rooms 5 en suite **Facilities** WiFi

Rockvale

★★★★ ⒶGUEST ACCOMMODATION

tel: 01598 752279 **Hollerday Dr, Lee Rd EX35 6HQ**
email: enquiries@rockvalelynton.com **web:** www.rockvalelynton.com
dir: *From A39 follow signs to Lynton, then town hall. In Lee Rd, turn opposite Costcutter supermarket into Hollerday Drive*

Rockvale was once the residence of a Victorian merchant, and now offers all the comforts of home, with accommodation to suit families, couples and single travellers. Rockvale has a warm, friendly atmosphere, great views, and good food, with a licensed bar. Guests have use of a lounge with log fire, and evening meals are served at 7pm, though an earlier sitting may sometimes be arranged if necessary. This is an ideal base for exploring, close to the North Devon coast and with easy access to the stunning countryside of the Exmoor National Park.

Rooms 7 rms (6 en suite) (1 pri facs) (3 fmly) S £35-£45; D £65-£85* **Facilities** STV Lounge TVL tea/coffee Dinner available Licensed WiFi 🔒 **Parking** 7 **Notes** ⊗ Closed 31 Oct-13 Mar

The Fernery

★★★ BED AND BREAKFAST

tel: 01598 753265 & 07970 857459 **Lydiate Ln EX35 6AJ**
email: info@thefernerylynton.com **web:** www.thefernerylynton.com
dir: *B3234 to Lynton into Castle Hill. Then Lee Rd, turn left into Cross St. Left into Lydiate Ln, 300mtrs on right*

Nestled in a quiet street within a few minutes' walk of the town centre, The Fernery provides a comfortable, convenient base for exploring the North Devon coast and Exmoor. Rooms are bright and have very comfortable beds, and breakfast features local quality produce. There is on-street parking nearby and two public car parks not far away.

Rooms 3 en suite **Facilities** FTV DVD Lounge tea/coffee WiFi 🔒 **Notes** ⊗

MEDDON
Map 2 SS21

The West Country Inn

★★★ INN

tel: 01237 441724 & 07977 496535 **Bursdon Moor EX39 6HB**
email: thewestcinn@aol.com **web:** www.westcountryinn.co.uk
dir: *On A39 S of Clovelly*

Originally a coaching inn, dating back to the 16th century, this traditional and welcoming establishment is ideally placed for exploring this picturesque area. The bedrooms provide good levels of comfort and have all that's needed to ensure a relaxing stay. The well-stocked bar has a range of local ales and provides a convivial focal point with plenty of good-natured banter always on offer. A range of good, honest dishes are served either in the bar or adjacent dining room. Additional facilities include a spa and gym.

Rooms 9 en suite (1 fmly) **Facilities** FTV Lounge TVL tea/coffee Dinner available WiFi Gym Pool table 🔒 Hot tub **Conf** Max 100 Thtr 100 Class 70 Board 70 **Parking** 100

NEWTON ABBOT
Map 3 SX87

Premier Collection

Bulleigh Barton Manor

★★★★★ 🍽 BED AND BREAKFAST

tel: 01803 873411 & 07973 422678 **Ipplepen TQ12 5UA**
email: liz@escapetosouthdevon.co.uk **web:** www.escapetosouthdevon.co.uk
dir: *From A381 follow signs to Bulleigh and Compton Castle. Bear left along narrow lane, after 1.5m Bickley Mill signed on left, drive directly opposite turning*

Warm hospitality and a genuine welcome are hallmarks at this family-run establishment. This wonderful house dates back to the 1400s and is steeped in history. Today it offers en suite bedrooms providing comfortable accommodation in a peaceful countryside location. Breakfast is a hearty affair featuring locally sourced produce.

Rooms 3 en suite S £80-£115; D £90-£125* **Facilities** FTV DVD Lounge tea/coffee WiFi ⚡ 🔒 **Extras** Home-made fudge & cakes, fresh milk - free **Parking** 4 **Notes** LB No Children 16yrs

Bulleigh Park Farm *(SX860660)*

★★★★ FARMHOUSE

tel: 01803 872254 **Ipplepen TQ12 5UA**
email: southdevonaccommodation@gmail.com
web: www.southdevonaccommodation.co.uk
dir: *3.5m S of Newton Abbot. Exit A381 at Parkhill Cross, by petrol station, for Compton, 1m, signed*

Bulleigh Park is a working farm; stock includes a rare breed of sheep, the Devon Closewool. Expect a warm friendly welcome at this family home set in glorious tranquil countryside, but centrally located for the coast and Dartmoor. The breakfasts are notable for their wealth of fresh, local and home-made produce, and the porridge is cooked using a secret recipe. Home-made tea and cakes greet guests on arrival. The local inn is just a short stroll away.

Rooms 2 en suite (1 fmly) S £50-£55; D £80-£85 **Facilities** FTV iPod docking station Lounge TVL tea/coffee WiFi 🛁 **Extras** Mini-fridge **Parking** 6 **Notes** LB No Children 5yrs Closed Dec-1 Mar 60 acres beef/sheep/hens

---

NOSS MAYO   Map 3 SX54

Worswell Barton Farmhouse B&B *(SX549464)*

★★★★ FARMHOUSE

tel: 01752 872977 **Worswell Barton PL8 1HB**
email: info@worswellbarton.co.uk **web:** www.worswellbarton.co.uk
dir: *M5 onto A38, exit at Smithaleigh & follow signs to Yealmpton (B3186). Continue to Newton Ferrers then Noss Mayo. At Bridgend, up hill to church then Stoke Rd/Cross Rd continue to end*

Worswell Barton is very much a working farm, owned by the National Trust and home to the same family for over 65 years. The farmhouse can trace its roots back to the Domesday Book with period features adding to the charm and character. Bedrooms and bathrooms are up-to-date and provide all the necessary contemporary comforts. Breakfast is served around the dining table with wonderful eggs from the farm and locally produced bacon and sausages. The setting is quite spectacular, a haven for those wishing to relax and unwind, surrounded by stunning coastal scenery. There are many local walks, with the South West Coast Path just a short walk from the farm.

Rooms 4 rms (2 en suite) (2 pri facs) **Facilities** FTV TVL tea/coffee WiFi 🛁 **Extras** Robes, slippers - complimentary **Parking** 4 **Notes** ⊗ Closed Nov-Jan 🐾 1000 acres mixed

---

OKEHAMPTON   Map 3 SX59

See also Holsworthy

Meadowlea Guest House

★★★★ GUEST HOUSE

tel: 01837 53200 **65 Station Rd EX20 1EA**
email: meadowlea65@btinternet.com **web:** www.meadowleaguesthouse.co.uk
dir: *From A30 onto B3260, after 2m left at lights, then 3rd right into Station Rd. 200yds on left*

A well-presented period house, Meadowlea has been modernised over the years but still retains its Victorian essence. A range of comfortably appointed rooms for all budgets, some with shared facilities, is offered. There is a well appointed sitting room in which to relax and local produce is used on the breakfast menu. Should you wish to eat in, after a long day exploring the local area, guests are welcome to use the breakfast room, which is suitably equipped. Secure storage for bicycles is available.

Rooms 7 rms (4 en suite) (1 fmly) S £35-£50; D £60-£75 **Facilities** FTV Lounge tea/coffee WiFi 🛁 Drying room for boots & coats **Extras** Bottled water - complimentary **Parking** 2 **Notes** ⊗

OTTERY ST MARY   Map 3 SY19

Fluxton Farm

★★ BED AND BREAKFAST

tel: 01404 812818 **Fluxton EX11 1RJ**
email: ann@fluxtonfarm.co.uk **web:** www.fluxtonfarm.co.uk
dir: *2m SW of Ottery St Mary. B3174, W from Ottery over river, left, next left to Fluxton*

A haven for cat lovers, Fluxton Farm offers comfortable accommodation with a choice of lounges and a large garden, complete with pond and ducks. Set in peaceful farmland four miles from the coast, this 16th-century longhouse has a wealth of beams and open fireplaces.

Rooms 7 en suite S £27.50-£35* **Facilities** FTV Lounge tea/coffee WiFi 🛁 **Parking** 15 **Notes** LB No Children 8yrs RS Nov-Apr pre-booked & wknds only 🐾

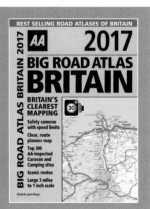

To help you navigate safely and easily, use the AA Big Road Atlas Britain 2017. Available from: shop.theAA.com

BEST SELLING ROAD ATLASES OF BRITAIN

AA 2017 BIG ROAD ATLAS BRITAIN

BRITAIN'S CLEAREST MAPPING
Safety cameras with speed limits
Clear, route planner map
Top 300 AA-inspected Caravan and Camping sites
Scenic routes
Large 3 miles to 1 inch scale

theAA.com/shop

PAIGNTON

Map 3 SX86

Premier Collection

The P&M Paignton RESIDENCE

★★★★★ BED AND BREAKFAST

tel: 01803 523118 & 07803 290568 **2 Kernou Rd TQ4 6BA**
email: mail@paignton-residence.com **web:** www.paignton-residence.com
dir: *Follow signs to seafront, into Kernou Rd, close to cinema*

A warm welcome is guaranteed in this smart B&B, very conveniently located within walking distance of Paignton seafront. All eight bedrooms are comfortably furnished, serviced to a high standard, and come equipped with a range of accessories. Breakfast is served in the light and airy dining room. Free WiFi is available throughout.

Rooms 8 en suite (1 GF) D £80-£125* **Facilities** FTV DVD iPod docking station tea/coffee WiFi ♨ Sauna in 1 room **Conf** Max 10 Thtr 10 Class 10 Board 10 **Parking** 2 **Notes** ⊗ No Children 16yrs

Devon House Guest House

★★★★ GUEST HOUSE

tel: 01803 528080 & 07777 642340 **20 Garfield Rd TQ4 6AX**
email: dhgh@btconnect.com **web:** www.devonhouseguesthouse.co.uk
dir: *In Paignton follow signs to seafront & Esplanade Rd. Into Torbay Rd, then Garfield Rd*

Devon House has been lovingly restored and is conveniently located to explore Paignton and its surrounding areas. All rooms offer comfortable beds and a range of facilities to meet the needs of a varied clientele, including families. A freshly cooked breakfast is served in the attractive dining room on the ground floor.

Rooms 8 en suite (2 fmly) **Facilities** FTV tea/coffee WiFi **Notes** ⊗

Beaches

★★★★ BED AND BREAKFAST

tel: 01803 665448 & 07854 940747 **9 Manor Rd TQ3 2HT**
email: mikemitchell21@hotmail.com **web:** www.beachesbandb.co.uk
dir: *From A38 follow signs to Torquay, then Paignton, then Preston. Take one way system at sea front, right into Manor Rd*

Situated just a few hundred metres from Paignton seafront, this guest accommodation offers bright, spacious, well-equipped rooms with comfortable beds. Breakfast is served in the light, airy breakfast room and guests have use of complimentary WiFi, a well-appointed guest lounge, and free off-road parking.

Rooms 6 en suite (2 fmly) **Facilities** FTV TVL tea/coffee WiFi ♨ **Extras** Speciality toiletries **Parking** 4 **Notes** LB ⊗ RS Oct-Jan wknds only

The Clydesdale

★★★★ GUEST HOUSE

tel: 01803 558402 & 07872 342486 **5 Polsham Park TQ3 2AD**
email: theclydesdale@hotmail.co.uk **web:** www.theclydesdale.co.uk
dir: *Exit A3022 (Torquay Rd) into Lower Polsham Rd, 2nd right into Polsham Park*

Tucked away in a quiet residential area, this is an ideal location from which to explore the varied attractions of Paignton and the wider Torbay area. The welcome is warm and genuine, with every effort made to ensure a relaxed and rewarding stay. The bedrooms are well appointed and provide all the expected modern comforts. Breakfast is served in the dining room; a separate guest lounge is also available.

Rooms 7 en suite (1 fmly) (2 GF) S £27-£30; D £54-£60 **Facilities** FTV TVL tea/coffee WiFi ♨ **Parking** 6 **Notes** LB ⊗ Closed Xmas & New Year RS Nov-Feb open by prior arrangement

Collerton Lodge Bed and Breakfast

★★★★ BED AND BREAKFAST

tel: 01803 554018 & 669045 **332 Totnes Rd TQ4 7HD**
email: sandra.singleton@sky.com **web:** www.collertonlodge.co.uk
dir: *A3022 to Paignton then left onto A385 towards Totnes. 100yds on right*

Ideally situated for access to the Torbay area, this warm and welcoming establishment offers high standards of accommodation, with every effort made to ensure an enjoyable stay. Bedrooms all provide impressive levels of comfort and quality with all the expected necessities, likewise the modern bathrooms with robes also provided. Breakfast is a generous and tasty offering, served in the conservatory with lovely views over the surrounding houses and fields. Ample parking is also provided, along with a guest lounge.

Rooms 5 en suite (1 fmly) **Facilities** FTV DVD Lounge TVL tea/coffee WiFi ⌛ 18 ♨ **Parking** 5 **Notes** ⊗ No Children 5yrs

Merritt House Bed & Breakfast

★★★★ GUEST ACCOMMODATION

tel: 01803 528959 **7 Queens Rd TQ4 6AT**
email: bookings@merritthouse.co.uk **web:** www.merritthouse.co.uk
dir: *From Paignton seafront, right into Torbay Rd, 1st left into Queens Rd, house on right*

Handily located for the town centre and the lovely beach, this is an ideal choice from which to explore this popular holiday area. A warm welcome is assured along with a slice of cake, the perfect way to start a relaxing break. Bedrooms provide good levels of comfort with ground floor rooms available. Breakfast is a treat with a range of tantalising options on offer. Off-road parking available.

Rooms 7 en suite (3 GF) **Facilities** FTV DVD tea/coffee WiFi ♨ **Parking** 4 **Notes** LB ⊗ No Children 12yrs

The Wentworth Guest House

★★★★ GUEST HOUSE

tel: 01803 557843 **18 Youngs Park Rd, Goodrington TQ4 6BU**
email: enquiries@wentworthguesthouse.co.uk **web:** www.wentworthguesthouse.co.uk
dir: *Through Paignton on A378, 1m left at rdbt, sharp right into Roundham Rd, right & right again into Youngs Park Rd*

Quietly located opposite a pretty park, this is an ideal location for exploring the many and varied attractions of the English Riviera. Goodrington's lovely beaches are just a short stroll, and the town centre is a 10-15 minute walk away. The caring owners are always on hand to assist with local information. Bedrooms offer good levels of comfort and include both a dog-friendly room and family rooms. Breakfast is served in the informal dining room with a cosy guest lounge also provided.

Rooms 10 en suite (2 fmly) S £32-£49; D £57-£74* **Facilities** FTV TVL tea/coffee Licensed WiFi **Parking** 5 **Notes** LB Closed 19 Dec-4 Jan

Merriedale Guest House

★★★ GUEST HOUSE

tel: 01803 553013 & 07950 819716 **21 Garfield Rd TQ4 6AX**
email: merriedale@gmx.co.uk **web:** www.merriedale.com
dir: *A380 to Torquay, 2nd exit at rdbt (Kerswell Gdns). 1st exit at next rdbt Churscombe Cross into Marldon Rd (B3060). Right into Torquay Rd (A3022), bear left into Hyde Rd, left into Torbay Rd & left into Garfield Rd*

Overlooking Victoria Park, this friendly and welcoming establishment is perfectly situated to explore the local area, as it's just a short walk from the town centre and the wonderful sandy beach. Every effort is made to help guests enjoy a relaxing stay, with local information and advice readily offered. Bedrooms and bathrooms all offer good levels of quality and all the expected comforts. Breakfast is a satisfying start to the day and is served in the well-appointed dining room.

Rooms 6 rms (5 en suite) (1 pri facs) S £28-£34; D £56-£64* **Facilities** FTV tea/coffee WiFi **Extras** Bottled water - complimentary **Parking** 6 **Notes** LB ⊗ No Children 7yrs

The Park

★★★ GUEST ACCOMMODATION

tel: 01803 557856 **Esplanade Rd TQ4 6BQ**
email: stay@theparkhotel.net **web:** www.theparkhotel.net
dir: *On Paignton seafront, nearly opposite pier*

This large establishment has a prominent position on the seafront with excellent views of Torbay. The pleasant bedrooms are spacious, and available in a number of options; several have sea views. Entertainment is provided in the lounge on some evenings. Dinner and breakfast are served in the spacious dining room, which overlooks the attractive front garden.

The Park

Rooms 47 en suite (5 fmly) (3 GF) **Facilities** tea/coffee Dinner available Lift Licensed WiFi 🛇 Games room with 3/4 snooker table & table tennis **Conf** Max 120 Thtr 80 Class 120 Board 40 **Parking** 38

Lazy Days

Ⓤ

tel: 01803 520854 **10 Queens Rd TQ4 6AT**
email: peteandirenelazydays2@gmail.com **web:** www.lazydaysguesthousepaignton.co.uk

Currently the rating for this establishment is not confirmed. This may be due to a change of ownership or because it has only recently joined the AA rating scheme.

Rooms 6 en suite S £41.25-£60; D £55-£80*

PLYMOUTH   Map 3 SX45

Jewell's

★★★★ GUEST ACCOMMODATION

tel: 01752 254760 **220 Citadel Rd, The Hoe PL1 3BB**
email: jewellsguest@btconnect.com **web:** www.jewellsguesthouse.com
dir: *A38 towards city centre, follow sign for The Barbican, then The Hoe. Left at lights, right at top of road into Citadel Rd. Jewell's 0.25m*

This smart, comfortable, family-run establishment is only a short walk from The Hoe and is convenient for the city centre, the Citadel and the Barbican. Bedrooms come with a wide range of extra facilities, and breakfast is served in the pleasant dining room. Some secure parking is available.

Rooms 10 rms (7 en suite) (5 fmly) **Facilities** FTV tea/coffee WiFi **Parking** 3 **Notes** LB ⊗

PLYMOUTH *continued*

Rainbow Lodge Guest House

★★★★ GUEST HOUSE

tel: 01752 229699 & 07584 472723 **29 Athenaeum St, The Hoe PL1 2RQ**
email: info@rainbowlodgeplymouth.co.uk **web:** www.rainbowlodgeplymouth.co.uk
dir: *A38 onto A374. Follow City Centre signs for 3m, into Exeter St. Bear left into Breton Side at lights, follow road, left into Athenaeum St at Walrus pub*

Located in a peaceful area of Plymouth, Rainbow Lodge Guest House is within easy walking distance of the town centre, the Barbican and harbour. Service is the highlight of the stay, ensuring that all needs and wants are catered for. The ten guest bedrooms provide a comfortable night's sleep. Free WiFi is available and a full English breakfast is offered daily in the delightful breakfast room.

Rooms 10 rms (6 en suite) (1 pri facs) (2 fmly) (1 GF) S £36-£42; D £49-£69*
Facilities FTV tea/coffee WiFi **Notes** ⊗ No Children 5yrs Closed 21 Dec-1 Jan

The Firs Guest Accommodation

★★★ GUEST ACCOMMODATION

tel: 01752 262870 & 300010 **13 Pier St, West Hoe PL1 3BS**
email: thefirsguesthouseinplymouthdevon@hotmail.com
web: www.thefirsinplymouth.co.uk
dir: *A374 into city centre, follow signs to The Hoe. Continue on Hoe Rd, with sea on left, 1st right at mini rdbt into Pier St*

A well located and well established house on the West Hoe with convenient on-street parking. Friendly owners and comfortable rooms make it a popular destination.

Rooms 7 rms (3 en suite) (2 fmly) **Facilities** FTV tea/coffee Dinner available WiFi 🛆 Fishing trips can be arranged

The Lamplighter

★★★ GUEST ACCOMMODATION

tel: 01752 663855 **103 Citadel Rd, The Hoe PL1 2RN**
email: stay@lamplighterplymouth.co.uk **web:** www.lamplighterplymouth.co.uk
dir: *Near war memorial*

With easy access to The Hoe, The Barbican and the city centre, this comfortable house provides a good base for leisure or business. Bedrooms, including family rooms, are light and airy and furnished to a consistent standard. Breakfast is served in the dining room, which has an adjoining lounge area.

Rooms 9 rms (7 en suite) (2 pri facs) (2 fmly) S £40; D £60* **Facilities** FTV TVL tea/coffee WiFi 🛆 **Parking** 4

SEATON	Map 4 SY29

Mariners

★★★★ ⌂ GUEST ACCOMMODATION

tel: 01297 20560 **East Walk Esplanade EX12 2NP**
web: www.marinershotelseaton.co.uk
dir: *Off A3052 signed Seaton, Mariners on seafront*

Located just yards from the beach and cliff paths, this comfortable establishment has a friendly and relaxed atmosphere. Bedrooms, some with sea views, are well equipped, and public rooms are light and airy. The dining room is the venue for enjoyable breakfasts that utilise quality local produce; afternoon teas are also available on the seafront terrace.

Rooms 8 en suite (1 fmly) (1 GF) D £80-£110* **Facilities** FTV tea/coffee WiFi 🛆 **Parking** 8 **Notes** LB ⊗ No Children 5yrs Closed Nov-Jan

Beaumont Guest House

★★★★ GUEST HOUSE

tel: 01297 20832 & 07775 713667 **Castle Hill EX12 2QW**
email: beaumont.seaton@talktalk.net **web:** www.beaumont-seaton.co.uk
dir: *In Seaton, from Harbour Rd head W to Marine Place on seafront. Beaumont Guest House at beginning of Castle Hill*

Dating back to the days of Victorian splendour, this elegant establishment is just a few steps away from the wonderful beach at Seaton. A warm and genuine welcome awaits, with plenty of helpful local advice always on offer. Bedrooms have great sea views and provide all the expected modern comforts, with a ground floor room also being available. Breakfast provides a tasty start to the day, served in the attractive dining room.

Rooms 5 en suite (1 fmly) (1 GF) S £55-£60; D £73-£85* **Facilities** FTV tea/coffee WiFi **Parking** 6 **Notes** LB ⊗ Closed Xmas & New Year

SHALDON	

See Teignmouth

SIDMOUTH	Map 3 SY18

See also Ottery St Mary

Premier Collection

The Salty Monk

★★★★★ ⊚⊚ ⌂ RESTAURANT WITH ROOMS

tel: 01395 513174 **Church St, Sidford EX10 9QP**
email: saltymonk@btconnect.com **web:** www.saltymonk.co.uk
dir: *On A3052 opposite church in Sidford*

Set in the village of Sidford, this attractive property dates from the 16th century. There's plenty of style and appeal here and each bedroom has a unique identity. Bathrooms are equally special with multi-jet showers, spa baths and cosseting robes and towels. The output from the kitchen is impressive with excellent local produce very much in evidence, served in the elegant surroundings of the restaurant. A mini-spa facility is available.

Rooms 5 en suite 1 annexe en suite (3 GF) S £85-£140; D £130-£190*
Facilities FTV Lounge tea/coffee Dinner available WiFi ⌁ 18 Sauna Gym 🛆 Outdoor hot tub Massage therapists **Extras** Speciality toiletries, bottled water - free **Parking** 20 **Notes** LB Closed 1wk Nov & Jan No coaches

Cheriton Guest House

★★★★ ⌂ GUEST ACCOMMODATION

tel: 01395 513810 & 07899 793314 **Vicarage Rd EX10 8UQ**
email: info@cheriton-guesthouse.co.uk **web:** www.cheriton-guesthouse.co.uk

Located just a 10-minute stroll from the seafront, Cheriton Guest House is a convenient base for exploring Sidmouth. A flexible approach to guest requirements is adopted here, and every effort is made to ensure a comfortable stay. Bedrooms provide good levels of comfort with all the expected extras; public rooms include a stylish lounge and airy breakfast room.

Rooms 8 en suite **Facilities** FTV Lounge tea/coffee WiFi **Parking** 7 **Notes** ⊗

The Groveside

★★★★ GUEST HOUSE

tel: 01395 513406 **Vicarage Rd EX10 8UQ**
email: info@thegroveside.co.uk **web:** www.thegroveside.co.uk
dir: *0.5m N of seafront on A375*

Conveniently situated a short, level walking distance from the town centre, The Groveside offers boutique-style accommodation. A number of influences, such as art deco, have been used to impressive effect in the bedrooms, while bathrooms also show individuality and flair. Guests are assured of attentive service and a relaxed and friendly atmosphere. On-site parking is a bonus.

Rooms 9 en suite **Facilities** FTV Lounge tea/coffee WiFi **Conf** Max 14 Class 14 Board 14 **Parking** 9 **Notes** LB ⊗ No Children 12yrs ⌨

Mincombe Barn Bed & Breakfast

★★★★ ⌂ BED AND BREAKFAST

tel: 01395 597858 & 07753 747941 **Roncombe Ln, Sidbury EX10 0QN**
email: mincombebarn@outlook.com **web:** www.mincombebarn.com
dir: *N of Sidmouth on A375, through Sidbury, right to Roncombe (1.5m)*

Set in 20 acres of peaceful pasture and woodland, Mincombe Barn is midway between Honiton and Sidmouth, within the East Devon Area of Outstanding Natural Beauty, a UNESCO World Heritage Site, with the Blackdown Hills just to the north. Each room is individually designed to be elegant, comfortable and practical. All rooms can be made as either a twin or double. Breakfast is served daily with ingredients sourced locally along with fresh eggs daily on site.

Rooms 3 en suite (3 GF) **Facilities** FTV Lounge tea/coffee WiFi ch fac ⌄ 18 ⌨ **Extras** Home-made biscuits **Parking** 8 **Notes** LB ⌨

The Old Farmhouse

★★★★ GUEST ACCOMMODATION

tel: 01395 512284 **Hillside Rd EX10 8JG**
dir: *A3052 from Exeter to Sidmouth, right at Bowd x-rds, 2m left at rdbt, left at mini rdbt, next right, over hump-back bridge, bear right on the corner*

This beautiful 16th-century thatched farmhouse, in a quiet residential area just a stroll from the Esplanade and shops, has been lovingly restored. Bedrooms are attractively decorated, and the charming public rooms feature beams and an inglenook fireplace. The welcoming proprietors provide memorable dinners, (by prior arrangement) using traditional recipes and fresh local ingredients.

Rooms 3 en suite 3 annexe en suite (1 fmly) (1 GF) S £50-£65; D £70-£82* **Facilities** FTV Lounge TVL tea/coffee Dinner available WiFi ⌄ 18 **Extras** Speciality toiletries **Parking** 4 **Notes** LB ⊗ No Children 12yrs Closed Nov-Feb ⌨

Glendevon

★★★★ GUEST ACCOMMODATION

tel: 01395 514028 & 07960 052475 **Cotmaton Rd EX10 8QX**
email: enquiries@glendevonsidmouth.co.uk **web:** www.glendevonsidmouth.co.uk
dir: *A3052 onto B3176 to mini rdbt. Right, house 100yds on right*

Located in a quiet residential area just a short walk from the town centre and beaches, this stylish Victorian house offers neat, comfortable bedrooms. Guests are assured of a warm welcome from the resident owners.

Rooms 8 en suite S £42-£47; D £84-£94* **Facilities** FTV DVD TVL tea/coffee WiFi ⌨ **Notes** ⊗ No Children 10yrs ⌨

Rose Cottage Guest House

★★★★ GUEST HOUSE

tel: 01395 597357 **Greenhead, Sidbury EX10 0RH**
web: www.rosecottagesidbury.co.uk
dir: *At junct of A375 & Greenhead*

Rose Cottage is a very well appointed, comfortable property in the quiet village of Sidbury, with the resort of Sidmouth close by. Roz, and son Luke, do all they can to make you feel very welcome and at home. Rooms are well appointed, there is a guest lounge to enjoy, and there is off-road parking. Very good quality, locally sourced produce is used for breakfast, which is served in the well appointed dining room.

Rooms 6 en suite **Facilities** FTV Lounge tea/coffee WiFi ⌨ **Parking** 6

<table>
<tr><td>**SOURTON**</td><td style="text-align:right">Map 3 SX59</td></tr>
</table>

Bearslake Inn

★★★★ ⌂ INN

tel: 01837 861334 **Lake EX20 4HQ**
email: enquiries@bearslakeinn.com **web:** www.bearslakeinn.com
dir: *A30 from Exeter onto A386 signed Sourton & Tavistock, 2m on left from junct*

Situated on the edge of the Dartmoor National Park, this thatched inn is believed to date back to the 13th century and was originally part of a working farm. There is character in abundance here with beams, flagstone floors and low ceilings, all of which contribute to an engaging atmosphere. Bedrooms have great individuality and provide period features combined with contemporary comforts. Local produce is very much in evidence on the menu, with dinner served in the attractive Stable Restaurant. The beer garden is bordered by a moorland stream with wonderful views across open countryside.

Rooms 6 en suite (3 fmly) (1 GF) S £68.50-£100; D £110-£135* **Facilities** FTV DVD tea/coffee Dinner available Direct Dial WiFi ⌨ **Parking** 35 **Notes** LB

Collaven Manor

★★★★ ⌂ ⌂ GUEST ACCOMMODATION

tel: 01837 861522 **EX20 4HH**
email: collavenmanor@gmail.com **web:** www.collavenmanor.co.uk
dir: *A30 onto A386 to Tavistock, 2m on right*

This delightful 15th-century manor house is quietly located in five acres of well-tended grounds. The friendly proprietors provide attentive service and ensure a relaxing environment. Charming public rooms have old oak beams and granite fireplaces, provide a range of comfortable lounges, and include a well stocked bar. In the restaurant, a daily-changing menu offers interesting dishes.

Rooms 8 en suite (1 fmly) **Facilities** FTV Lounge Dinner available Direct Dial Licensed WiFi ch fac ⌄ Bowls **Conf** Max 14 Thtr 14 Class 14 Board 14 **Parking** 50 **Notes** LB Closed Dec-Jan Civ Wed 50

SOUTH MOLTON · Map 3 SS72

Sampson Barton Guest House

★★★★ ⌂ GUEST HOUSE

tel: 01769 572466 **Kings Nympton EX37 9TG**
email: mail@sampsonbarton.co.uk **web:** www.sampsonbarton.co.uk
dir: *From South Molton follow signs for George Nympton & Kings Nympton. Through George Nympton, down hill, over bridge, 1st right into lane signed Sampson & Sletchcott. Up hill, 0.75m on left*

Dating back some 400 years, this charming former farmhouse is the perfect place to relax. A reviving cup of tea on arrival in front of the warming wood-burner sets the scene, with helpful local information always on hand. Bedrooms offer good levels of comfort, likewise the contemporary bathrooms. Dinner is a treat, with wonderful local produce on offer. Breakfast is also impressive with eggs supplied by the resident hens. A stroll around the wonderful gardens is a must; find a peaceful vantage point and gaze over the rolling Devon countryside.

Rooms 6 rms (5 en suite) (1 pri facs) (1 fmly) S £65; D £82-£92* **Facilities** FTV TVL tea/coffee Dinner available Licensed WiFi ⌂ **Extras** Speciality toiletries - complimentary **Parking** 6 **Notes** LB ⊗

The Coaching Inn

★★★ INN

tel: 01769 572526 **Queen St EX36 3BJ**
web: www.thecoaching-inn.co.uk
dir: *In town centre*

This long-established former coaching inn has been providing a warm welcome to weary travellers for many years. Situated in the heart of this bustling town, guests are assured of a relaxing stay in a genuine, family-friendly atmosphere. Bedrooms provide good levels of comfort. An extensive menu is provided with an emphasis on quality and value for money.

Rooms 10 en suite (2 fmly) S £35; D £70* **Facilities** FTV tea/coffee Dinner available WiFi Pool table ⌂ **Conf** Max 100 Thtr 80 Class 50 Board 60 **Parking** 40

SOUTH ZEAL · Map 3 SX69

The Oxenham Arms and Restaurant

★★★★ ⌂ INN

tel: 01837 840244 **EX20 2JT**
email: info@theoxenhamarms.co.uk **web:** www.theoxenhamarms.com
dir: *From A30, follow signs for A382 Moreton Hampstead/Winkleigh/Torrington. Over mini rdbt towards South Zeal, after 2m, right into village*

Dating back to the 12th century, there is a tangible sense of the past at this fascinating inn. Still very much the village local, it was first licensed in 1477, and boasts a standing stone dating back some 5000 years. Extensive refurbishment has blended contemporary styling with the historic features. Bedrooms have plenty of character and no two are alike, with a number of four-posters available. The stylish restaurant offers accomplished cuisine with a range of dishes, all making good use of quality, local produce. In summer, meals can be taken in the extensive garden with stunning views of Dartmoor.

Rooms 7 en suite (3 fmly) S £115-£145; D £118-£150* **Facilities** FTV DVD Lounge TVL tea/coffee Dinner available WiFi ♨ ⚲ 18 Fishing Riding ⌂ Free loan of bicycles **Extras** Bottled water **Conf** Max 30 Thtr 30 Class 25 Board 30 **Parking** 7 **Notes** LB

STRETE · Map 3 SX84

Premier Collection

Strete Barton House

★★★★★ ⌂ GUEST HOUSE

tel: 01803 770364 **Totnes Rd TQ6 ORU**
email: info@stretebarton.co.uk **web:** www.stretebarton.co.uk
dir: *Off A379 coastal road into village, just below church*

This delightful 16th-century former farmhouse blends stylish accommodation with original character. The bedrooms are very comfortably furnished and well equipped with useful extras. Breakfast makes good use of quality local produce and is served in the spacious dining room. Guests are also welcome to use the comfortable lounge, complete with log-burning stove. The village lies between Dartmouth and Kingsbridge and has easy access to the beautiful South Hams as well as many local pubs and restaurants.

Rooms 5 rms (4 en suite) (1 pri facs) 1 annexe en suite S £105-£165; D £105-£165* **Facilities** FTV DVD iPod docking station Lounge tea/coffee WiFi ⚲ 18 ⌂ **Extras** Speciality toiletries, guest fridge **Parking** 3 **Notes** LB No Children 8yrs

TAVISTOCK · Map 3 SX47

Premier Collection

Tor Cottage

★★★★★ ⌂ GUEST ACCOMMODATION

tel: 01822 860248 **PL16 OJE**
email: info@torcottage.co.uk **web:** www.torcottage.co.uk

(For full entry see Chillaton)

TEDBURN ST MARY — Map 3 SX89

Premier Collection

Frogmill Bed & Breakfast

★★★★★ 🍴 BED AND BREAKFAST

tel: 01647 272727 & 24088 **EX6 6ES**
email: frogmillbandb@btinternet.com **web:** www.frogmillbandb.co.uk
dir: *From A30 take exit signed Cheriton Bishop. Take Tedburn road, then left towards Crediton. After 1m left to Froggy Mill, 1m on left*

Situated in the heart of Devon, this former mill house is as picturesque as can be, complete with thatch and a babbling brook. The grounds are spectacular, with around 10 acres of woodland and pasture. The welcome is just as impressive; a cream tea in the garden is offered on arrival. The comfortable bedrooms offer quality and individuality and include a separate, self-contained suite away from the main building; the bathrooms have soft towels and invigorating showers. Food is a real treat here – the eggs for breakfast provided by the resident hens. In addition to the elegant dining room, a lounge, with deep leather sofas and a wood-burner, is provided.

Rooms 2 en suite 1 annexe en suite (1 fmly) (1 GF) S £65-£70; D £80-£100 **Facilities** FTV iPod docking station Lounge tea/coffee WiFi 🔒 **Extras** Fruit, chocolates - free; robes **Parking** 6 **Notes** LB ⊗

TEIGNMOUTH — Map 3 SX97

Potters Mooring

★★★★ GUEST ACCOMMODATION

tel: 01626 873225 **30 The Green, Shaldon TQ14 0DN**
email: info@pottersmooring.co.uk **web:** www.pottersmooring.co.uk
dir: *A38 onto A380 signed Torquay, B3192 to Teignmouth & Shaldon, over river, follow signs to Potters Mooring*

A former sea captain's residence dating from 1625, Potters Mooring has been appointed to provide charming accommodation of a very high standard, including a four-poster room. The friendly proprietors make every effort to ensure an enjoyable stay, and the Captain Potter's breakfast features tasty local produce.

Rooms 9 en suite

TIVERTON — Map 3 SS91

Premier Collection

Fernside Bed and Breakfast

★★★★★ 🍴 BED AND BREAKFAST

tel: 01884 860025 & 07885 192331 **Fernside Cottage, Templeton EX16 8BP**
email: enquiries@fernsidecottage-bed-and-breakfast.co.uk
web: www.fernsidecottage-bed-and-breakfast.co.uk
dir: *M25 junct 27, A361 signed Barnstaple. In approx 4m at Stonelands Cross left signed Rackenford & Templeton. Left at T-junct signed Templeton. 2nd right signed Templeton. In Templeton Bridge at T-junct right signed Witheridge. B&B up hill on right*

This charming thatched cottage is within easy reach of Tiverton and the M5, and sits in rolling countryside, a haven of peace and tranquillity. Expect high quality bedrooms with wonderful beds, smart bathrooms, Aga-cooked breakfasts and a really warm welcome from two very caring hosts.

Rooms 2 en suite **Facilities** FTV iPod docking station Lounge tea/coffee WiFi Riding 🔒 **Extras** Speciality toiletries, robes, home-made biscuits **Parking** 3 **Notes** ⊗ No Children 18yrs Closed 12 Dec-6 Jan ⊗

Stoodleigh B&B

★★★★ BED AND BREAKFAST

tel: 01398 351163 & 07789 982305 **Barton House, Stoodleigh EX16 9PP**
email: bookings@stoodleighbandb.co.uk **web:** www.stoodleighbandb.co.uk
dir: *A361 from Tiverton towards Barnstaple. At Stoodleigh Cross turn right, follow signs to Stoodleigh, left bend into Long Ln, then West End Ln. Behind hall in village*

Within easy reach of Exmoor National Park, this is a perfect choice for anyone looking for a peaceful base from which to explore some beautiful countryside. Rest and relaxation are assured, with a warm welcome always on offer. Bedrooms provide all the expected contemporary comforts, likewise the well-appointed bathrooms. Breakfast makes use of wonderful local produce, served in the attractive dining room.

Rooms 3 en suite (1 fmly) S £65-£75; D £75-£85* **Facilities** FTV TVL tea/coffee WiFi 🔒 **Parking** 4 **Notes** LB Closed 24-25 Dec ⊗

Quoit-At-Cross *(ST923188)*

★★★ FARMHOUSE

tel: 01398 351280 **Stoodleigh EX16 9PJ**
email: quoit-at-cross@hotmail.co.uk **web:** www.quoit-at-cross.co.uk
dir: *M5 junct 27 for Tiverton. A396 N for Bampton, after 3.5m turn left over bridge for Stoodleigh, farmhouse on 1st junct in village centre*

This delightful stone-built farmhouse commands lovely views over rolling Devonshire countryside and is a great place from which to explore this picturesque area. A warm and genuine welcome is assured, along with a homely and relaxed atmosphere. The comfortable, attractive bedrooms are well furnished and have many extra facilities. A crackling fire keeps the lounge snug and warm during colder nights, while in the summer the pretty garden is available to guests. The property has alpacas and ponies, and supervised access can be arranged.

Rooms 4 en suite (2 fmly) S £40-£45; D £70-£80* **Facilities** FTV DVD TVL tea/coffee Dinner available WiFi Fishing Riding Pool table 🔒 Wildlife garden & farm wildlife trail **Extras** Speciality toiletries, snacks, fridge available **Conf** Max 15 **Parking** 4 **Notes** LB Closed Xmas ⊗ 160 acres mixed

TORBAY

See Brixham, Paignton and Torquay

TORQUAY — Map 3 SX96

Premier Collection

Carlton Court

★★★★★ BED AND BREAKFAST

tel: 01803 297318 & 07794 613051 **18 Cleveland Rd TQ2 5BE**
email: stay@carlton-court.co.uk **web:** www.carlton-court.co.uk
dir: *A380 onto A3022, straight ahead at 3 sets of lights. Stay in left lane, straight ahead at 2 sets of lights. Into right lane at Torre station, down hill. After 100yds left into Cleveland Rd, straight over at x-rds, 700yds on right*

This elegant detached Victorian villa has been sensitively refurbished to provide impressive levels of quality and comfort, while retaining many original period features. Service and hospitality are hallmarks here, and every effort is made to ensure guests feel both welcomed and relaxed, with helpful local information always on offer. Bedrooms provide high standards with a range of types available, including suites and ground-floor rooms. Quality is equally high in bathrooms, with lovely warm towels and robes. All rooms also feature chiller fridges. Breakfast is served in the well-appointed dining room, overlooking the garden, and provides a wonderful start to the day.

Rooms 6 en suite (2 GF) **Facilities** FTV DVD tea/coffee WiFi **Extras** Fresh milk, bottled water, speciality toiletries **Parking** 7 **Notes** ⊗ No Children 16yrs

TORQUAY *continued*

Premier Collection

Kingston House

★★★★★ ⌂ GUEST ACCOMMODATION

tel: 01803 212760 **75 Avenue Rd TQ2 5LL**
email: stay@kingstonhousetorquay.co.uk **web:** www.kingstonhousetorquay.co.uk
dir: *From A3022 to Torquay, turn right at Torre Station down Avenue Rd, Kingston House approx 0.4m on left*

Dating from around 1870, this elegant Victorian house, just a short stroll from the seafront, is well positioned for those visiting the area on business or for pleasure. There is always plenty of helpful advice and information readily available. Tea and cakes are served on arrival in the inviting guest lounge; an ideal way to start a relaxing break. Bedrooms offer impressive quality with wonderfully comfortable beds; likewise bathrooms come equipped with cosseting towels and robes. Breakfast offers a number of tasty options, served in the well-appointed dining room.

Rooms 5 en suite (1 GF) S £85-£105; D £90-£120 **Facilities** FTV iPod docking station TVL tea/coffee WiFi **Extras** Speciality toiletries, chocolates, bottled water **Parking** 5 **Notes** ⊗ No Children 16yrs Closed Dec-Feb

Premier Collection

The Marstan

★★★★★ ⌂ GUEST HOUSE

tel: 01803 292837 **Meadfoot Sea Rd TQ1 2LQ**
email: enquiries@marstanhotel.co.uk **web:** www.marstanhotel.co.uk
dir: *A3022 to seafront, left onto A379 Torbay Rd & Babbacombe Rd, right into Meadfoot Rd, Marstan on right*

This elegant, mid-19th-century villa provides high levels of comfort and quality throughout. The hospitality and service are excellent, and every effort is made to create a relaxed atmosphere. Public areas include an impressive dining room, a bar and a comfortable lounge. Outdoors, guests can enjoy a heated swimming pool and hot tub in the secluded garden.

Rooms 9 en suite (1 fmly) (2 GF) **Facilities** FTV iPod docking station Lounge tea/coffee Direct Dial Licensed WiFi ⌇ Hot tub **Parking** 8 **Notes** LB ⊗

Premier Collection

Meadfoot Bay Guest House

★★★★★ ⌂ GUEST ACCOMMODATION

tel: 01803 294722 **Meadfoot Sea Rd TQ1 2LQ**
email: stay@meadfoot.com **web:** www.meadfoot.com
dir: *A3022 to seafront, onto A379, right into Meadfoot Rd, 0.5m on right*

The Meadfoot Bay Guest House is a family-run guest house situated in the Meadfoot conservation area, just north of Torquay harbour, and only 200 metres from a delightful Blue Flag beach. Rooms vary in size and facilities, and include standard, superior, superior deluxe and The St Andrews Suite. Free parking is available in the private car park, and free WiFi is a bonus. Meadfoot Bay is completely non-smoking.

Rooms 15 en suite (2 GF) S £60-£148; D £94-£159* **Facilities** FTV Lounge TVL tea/coffee Licensed WiFi ⌇ 18 Access to nearby health club **Parking** 15 **Notes** LB ⊗ No Children 14yrs Closed Nov-Mar

Premier Collection

The 25 Boutique B&B

★★★★★ ⌂ BED AND BREAKFAST

tel: 01803 297517 **25 Avenue Rd TQ2 5LB**
email: stay@the25.uk **web:** www.the25.uk
dir: *A3022 into Torquay, pass railway station, into Avenue Rd. Just past lights*

The 25 Boutique B&B is located within easy walking distance of Torquay's Abbey Sands beach, town centre and harbour. A warm and friendly atmosphere, attention to detail and attentive yet unobtrusive service is on offer from the proprietors. The six rooms and suites are named after local beaches, and all benefit from individual design, modern en suites and amenities, free WiFi, and fridges with fresh milk and bottled water. Each room is individually designed combining the latest trends with a classic twist to highlight the period features. A full English breakfast is served in the light and contemporary breakfast room. Off-street parking is available.

Rooms 6 en suite S £84-£144; D £99-£159 **Facilities** FTV DVD iPod docking station Lounge tea/coffee Licensed WiFi ⌇ **Extras** Speciality toiletries, home-made biscuits, robes **Parking** 10 **Notes** LB ⊗ No Children 18yrs Closed Xmas & New Year

Find out more about the **AA Funkiest B&B of the Year** on page 13

Premier Collection

The Albaston

★★★★★ GUEST ACCOMMODATION

tel: 01803 212100 **27 St Marychurch Rd TQ1 3JF**
email: contact@albastonhotel.co.uk **web:** www.albastonhotel.co.uk
dir: *A380 to centre (Riviera Way), left onto B3119. Over 1st rdbt & 2nd double rdbt, straight ahead at lights. Turn right into St Marychurch Rd, 0.5m on left*

The Albaston is a detached Victorian residence offering quality guest accommodation, suitable for either business or pleasure. Located in the heart of Torquay, it's an ideal base for exploring the English Riviera. The town centre, harbour and beach are within walking distance, as is Babbacombe Bay, and The Albaston is one of the closest properties to the International Language Schools. On offer are the guest lounge, private south facing Japanese-style decking area and Oscars bar, local beers, lager and wine all on offer. Breakfast is served in the newly refurbished dining room, all freshly cooked with locally sourced or produced ingredients. CCTV-monitored parking and unrestricted on-street parking available.

Rooms 9 en suite D £85-£125* **Facilities** FTV DVD Lounge TVL tea/coffee Licensed WiFi **Parking** 6 **Notes** ⊗ No Children 14yrs

Premier Collection

The Cary Arms

★★★★★ INN

tel: 01803 327110 **Babbacombe Beach TQ1 3LX**
email: enquiries@caryarms.co.uk **web:** www.caryarms.co.uk
dir: *A380 at Ashcombe Cross onto B3192 to Teignmouth. Right at lights to Torquay on A379, left at lights to Babbacombe. Left into Babbacombe Downs Rd, left into Beach Rd*

Located on the water's edge at Babbacombe, this seaside retreat is very well appointed; the rooms have sea views and nearly all have terraces or balconies. Bedrooms and bathrooms are fitted to a high standard with many thoughtful extras and unique touches to make a stay memorable. This is a popular dining venue whether eating inside, or on the terraces that lead down to the water's edge; in summer there's a barbecue and wood-fired oven. The dedicated staff will assist in planning your day, or simply share local knowledge.

Rooms 12 en suite (4 fmly) (3 GF) **Facilities** FTV Lounge tea/coffee Dinner available WiFi ⅃ 18 Fishing Pool table Spa treatment room Sea fishing **Extras** Speciality toiletries, sloe gin, confectionery **Conf** Max 24 Thtr 24 Class 24 Board 24 **Parking** 15 **Notes** No coaches Civ Wed 42

Premier Collection

Lanscombe House

★★★★★ GUEST ACCOMMODATION

tel: 01803 606938 & 07928 928570 **Cockington Village TQ2 6XA**
email: stay@lanscombehouse.co.uk **web:** www.lanscombehouse.co.uk
dir: *From Torquay seafront, head towards Paignton. At Livermead turn right signed Cockington Village & Country Park. 0.5m along valley, at entrance to village*

Located in the peaceful village of Cockington, in the heart of Cockington Country Park, and close to the attractions of Torquay, Lanscombe House offers sumptuous en suite accommodation. The building is surrounded by lovely secluded gardens that are perfect on a summer's day, or guests may choose to relax in the elegant lounge. Ample private parking is available. Lanscombe House does not accept dogs, or children under 16 years of age.

Rooms 5 en suite S £100-£120; D £105-£125 **Facilities** FTV Lounge tea/coffee Licensed WiFi ⅃ ⚓ **Extras** Speciality toiletries, local confectionery - free **Parking** 10 **Notes** LB ⊗ No Children 16yrs Closed mid Oct-Etr

Premier Collection

Linden House

★★★★★ GUEST ACCOMMODATION

tel: 01803 212281 & 07786 075359 **31 Bampfylde Rd TQ2 5AY**
email: susanelliott488@btinternet.com **web:** www.lindenhousetorquay.co.uk
dir: *Phone for directions*

This grand Victorian house has timeless elegance and charm, and offers impressive levels of contemporary comfort combined with stylish period features. Tea and cake is always available on arrival, along with a friendly welcome and the offer of help with local information and advice. Bedrooms and bathrooms offer high levels of quality with individual styling, and everything necessary to ensure a relaxing and rewarding stay. Spacious public areas include a lovely lounge with views over the garden; and the airy dining room is the venue for the wonderful breakfasts that are guaranteed to get the day off to a tasty and satisfying start.

Rooms 6 en suite 1 annexe en suite (1 GF) **Facilities** FTV TVL tea/coffee WiFi **Extras** Home-made chocolates **Parking** 6 **Notes** No Children 16yrs Closed 21 Dec-6 Jan

The AA on Social Media - follow us:

twitter: @TheAA_Lifestyle
facebook: www.facebook.com/TheAAUK

 Find us on Facebook

TORQUAY *continued*

Premier Collection

Tyndale B&B

★★★★★ BED AND BREAKFAST

tel: 01803 380888 **68 Avenue Rd TQ2 5LF**
email: info@tyndaletorquay.co.uk **web:** www.tyndaletorquay.co.uk
dir: *A380 onto A3022, follow sea front signs into Avenue Rd, on right hand side of 1st lights*

A warm and genuine welcome is extended to all guests arriving at Tyndale. The location is very convenient, being within walking distance of the town and beach, with good off-road parking. Bedrooms have been recently refurbished to create impressive levels of comfort and quality, likewise the stylish bathrooms, complete with cosseting towels and snuggly robes. Breakfast is a real treat with a number of options to tantalise the taste buds, a tasty and fulfilling start to the day.

Rooms 4 en suite (1 GF) D £75-£115* **Facilities** FTV tea/coffee WiFi
Extras Speciality toiletries, fridge, bottled water **Parking** 7 **Notes** LB ⊗
No Children 15yrs

The Cleveland

★★★★ GUEST ACCOMMODATION

tel: 01803 297522 **7 Cleveland Rd TQ2 5BD**
email: info@clevelandbandbtorquay.co.uk **web:** http://clevelandbandbtorquay.co.uk
dir: *A3022 into Torquay, at lights by Torre Station take right hand fork. 1st left into Cleveland Rd, at far end on left*

Located in a peaceful area of Torquay, this family-run guest accommodation is within easy walking distance of Abbey Sands beach, town centre and harbour. Service is the highlight of any stay, ensuring that all needs and wants are catered for. The seven guest bedrooms are all en suite, and are ideal for a comfortable night's sleep. A south-facing sun terrace and garden are also on offer for guest use. There is also a fully licensed bar and lounge. Free WiFi and off-street parking are available, with a full English breakfast offered daily within a delightful breakfast room.

Rooms 7 en suite (2 fmly) (1 GF) S £39-£50; D £59-£110* **Facilities** FTV Lounge tea/coffee Licensed WiFi **Extras** Bottled water, robes in suites **Parking** 7 **Notes** ⊗

The Downs, Babbacombe

★★★★ GUEST ACCOMMODATION

tel: 01803 328543 **41-43 Babbacombe Downs Rd, Babbacombe TQ1 3LN**
email: manager@downshotel.co.uk **web:** www.downshotel.co.uk
dir: *From Torquay, A329 to Babbacombe. Off Babbacombe road turn left into Princes St. Left into Babbacombe Downs Rd, 20mtrs on left*

Built in the 1850s, this elegant building forms part of a seafront terrace with direct access to the promenade and Babbacombe Downs. The warmth of welcome is matched by attentive service, with every effort made to ensure a rewarding and relaxing stay. Bedrooms offer impressive levels of comfort and most have spectacular views across Lyme Bay with balconies being an added bonus. For guests with limited mobility, assisted access is available to the first floor. Additional facilities include the convivial lounge/bar and spacious restaurant where enjoyable dinners and breakfasts are offered.

Rooms 12 en suite (4 fmly) **Facilities** FTV TVL tea/coffee Dinner available Direct Dial Licensed WiFi **Parking** 8

See advert on opposite page

The Downs
Babbacombe

Room with a View...........?

**Winners of South Devon's
Bed & Breakfast, Guest House & Inn of the Year 2013**

Situated directly above Babbacombe & Oddicombe beaches, we are fully licensed, family run guest accommodation with 12 en-suite bedrooms. 8 have private balconies which enjoy fabulous unobstructed views across Babbacombe Downs and Lyme Bay. All rooms have flat screen Freeview digital TV's and hot drinks tray. There is stairlift access to first floor accommodation & we are child and dog friendly. Our spacious Restaurant and Lounge Bar ensure you have plenty of room to enjoy your surroundings. Free WiFi access. Optional evening meal available. Open all year.

41-43 Babbacombe Downs Road, Babbacombe, TQ1 3LN t. 01803 328543

www.downshotel.co.uk

TORQUAY *continued*

Headland View

★★★★ ⌂ GUEST HOUSE

tel: 01803 312612 **37 Babbacombe Downs Rd, Babbacombe TQ1 3LN**
email: reception@headlandview.com **web:** www.headlandview.com
dir: *Follow signs for Babbacombe Theatre & Model Village*

Positioned on Babbacombe Downs, this elegant Victorian house boasts superb views of the coast of Lyme Bay, a World Heritage Site. Bedrooms are individually styled, with most having French doors leading onto balconies overlooking the spectacular bay. The many period features enhance the character and appeal of the building. A spacious guest lounge is available, while the excellent breakfasts are served in the pretty dining room.

Rooms 6 rms (4 en suite) (2 pri facs) S £60-£70; D £75-£85* **Facilities** FTV DVD iPod docking station Lounge TVL tea/coffee WiFi 🛁 **Extras** Speciality toiletries, bottled water - free **Parking** 6 **Notes** LB ⊗ No Children 10yrs Closed Dec-Jan

Orestone Manor

★★★★★ ◉◉ ⌂ RESTAURANT WITH ROOMS

tel: 01803 328098 **Rockhouse Ln, Maidencombe TQ1 4SX**
email: info@orestonemanor.com **web:** www.orestonemanor.com
dir: *N of Torquay on A379, on sharp bend in village of Maidencombe*

Set in an fabulous location overlooking the bay, Orestone Manor has a long history of providing fine food and very comfortable accommodation, coupled with friendly, attentive service. Log fires burn in cooler months, and there is a conservatory, a bar and a sitting room for guests to enjoy. AA Rosettes have been awarded for the uncomplicated modern cuisine which is based on quality local produce.

Rooms 11 en suite 3 annexe en suite (6 fmly) (3 GF) S £95-£315; D £110-£325* **Facilities** STV FTV iPod docking station Lounge tea/coffee Dinner available Direct Dial WiFi ch fac 🛁 **Extras** Speciality toiletries **Conf** Max 90 Thtr 90 Class 60 Board 30 **Parking** 38 **Notes** LB Closed Jan No coaches Civ Wed 90

Garway Lodge Guest House

★★★★ ⌂ GUEST HOUSE

tel: 01803 293126 & 07483 315176 **79 Avenue Rd TQ2 5LL**
email: info@garwaylodge.co.uk **web:** www.garwaylodge.co.uk
dir: *On A3022, 100mtrs past Torre Station on left*

Garway Lodge is in the heart of Torquay and offers accommodation exclusively for adults. The bedrooms are spacious and stylish, and include a ground floor room. Business guests are particularly welcomed and there is free on-site parking and free WiFi. Residents have use of a small honesty bar, and an extensive breakfast menu is offered. The seafront and harbourside restaurants are a level walk away.

Rooms 6 en suite (1 GF) S £33-£45; D £58-£75 **Facilities** FTV DVD iPod docking station tea/coffee Licensed WiFi 🛁 **Extras** Speciality toiletries, honesty bar **Parking** 6 **Notes** LB No Children

The Iona

★★★★ ⌂ GUEST ACCOMMODATION

tel: 01803 294918 **5 Cleveland Rd TQ2 5BD**
email: stay@hoteliona.co.uk **web:** www.hoteliona.co.uk
dir: *A380 to Riviera rdbt, 1st exit onto A3022 towards seafront. Take left into Vine Rd, right into Cleveland Rd*

Dating back to the 1860s, this grand Victorian villa is situated in a quiet location just a short stroll from the town centre, harbour and many attractions. A variety of bedroom sizes is offered; all provide good levels of comfort and the expected necessities. Public areas are elegant with a number of period features retained. Dinner and breakfast are served in the light and airy conservatory.

Rooms 8 en suite **Facilities** FTV DVD iPod docking station Lounge TVL tea/coffee Dinner available WiFi 🛁 **Parking** 8 **Notes** No Children 5yrs Closed 31 Dec-1 Mar

Kelvin House

★★★★ GUEST ACCOMMODATION

tel: 01803 209093 **46 Bampfylde Rd TQ2 5AY**
email: kelvinhousehotel@hotmail.com **web:** www.kelvinhousehotel.co.uk
dir: *M5 junct 31, A380, A3032 (Newton Rd) into Torquay. At lights at Torre Station right into Avenue Rd. Bampfylde Rd on left*

This attractive Victorian house was built in the 1880s and sits on a lovely tree-lined road. It is a family-run property with a relaxed, friendly home-from-home atmosphere. All bedrooms are en suite and have been appointed to a high standard with many extras. A large elegant sitting room is available for guests, and hearty breakfasts are served in the dining room, or on the patio in good weather. Close to good transport links, it makes an ideal base for touring the Torquay Riviera.

Rooms 8 en suite (1 fmly) (2 GF) **Facilities** FTV TVL tea/coffee Licensed WiFi **Parking** 6 **Notes** ⊗

Kingsholm

★★★★ GUEST ACCOMMODATION

tel: 01803 297794 **539 Babbacombe Rd TQ1 1HQ**
email: thekingsholm@virginmedia.com **web:** www.kingsholmhotel.co.uk
dir: *From A3022 left onto Torquay seafront, left at clock tower rdbt, Kingsholm 400mtrs on left*

An elegant, personally-run establishment situated in a conservation area, only 350 metres from the bustling harbour, this fine Edwardian house offers excellent accommodation that is appointed to a high standard; many rooms overlook Torwood Gardens. All bedrooms have Freeview TV, free WiFi, hairdryers and hospitality trays. There is also a guest lounge, a spacious dining room with separate tables and a licensed bar. Parking is free. Owners June and Carl offer a friendly welcome.

Rooms 9 en suite S £36-£42; D £55-£75* **Facilities** FTV TVL tea/coffee Licensed WiFi **Parking** 9 **Notes** ⊗ No Children 10yrs Closed 17 Nov-1 Mar

The Robin Hill

★★★★ GUEST ACCOMMODATION

tel: 01803 214518 & 07940 559925 **74 Braddons Hill Road East TQ1 1HF**
email: reservations@therobinhill.co.uk **web:** www.robinhillhotel.co.uk
dir: *From A38 to seafront then left to Babbacombe. Pass theatre to Clock Tower rdbt, take 1st exit & through 2 sets of lights, Braddons Hill Road East on left after museum*

Dating back to 1896, this fascinating building has character in abundance and is located a short stroll from the harbour and shops. Every effort is made to ensure a stay is enjoyable; assistance is readily available at all times. Bedrooms, in varying styles, provide all the expected necessities. Public areas include the inviting lounge, plus a light and airy dining room where breakfast is served.

Rooms 10 en suite (3 fmly) (1 GF) D £60-£120* **Facilities** FTV iPod docking station Lounge TVL tea/coffee Licensed WiFi 🛢 **Parking** 10 **Notes** LB Closed 20 Dec-4 Jan

Aveland House

★★★★ 🍵 GUEST ACCOMMODATION

tel: 01803 326622 **Aveland Rd, Babbacombe TQ1 3PT**
email: avelandhouse@aol.com **web:** www.avelandhouse.co.uk
dir: *A3022 to Torquay, left onto B3199 (Hele Rd) into Westhill Rd. Then Warbro Rd, 2nd left into Aveland Rd*

Set in well-tended gardens in a peaceful area of Babbacombe, close to the South West Coast Path, beaches, shops and attractions, Aveland House is within easy walking distance of Torquay harbour and town. This family-run house offers warm and attentive service. The attractive bedrooms are well equipped, with free WiFi throughout. A pleasant bar and two comfortable TV lounges are available. Hearing-impaired visitors are especially welcome, as both the proprietors are OCSL signers. Evening meals and bar snacks are available by arrangement. Coeliacs and special diets can be catered for.

Rooms 10 en suite S £45-£55; D £78-£98 **Facilities** Lounge TVL tea/coffee Dinner available Licensed WiFi 🛢 **Parking** 10 **Notes** LB ⊗ No Children 12yrs RS Sun no evening meals

Babbacombe Palms Guest House

★★★★ GUEST HOUSE

tel: 01803 327087 **2 York Rd, Babbacombe TQ1 3SG**
email: reception@babbacombepalms.com **web:** www.babbacombepalms.com
dir: *A379 to Torquay, pass golf club on left. Follow signs to St Marychurch, straight over at lights. 3rd turning on left into York Rd*

Babbacombe Palms has a convenient location, in a pleasant residential area within strolling distance of the town's many attractions. There is a very friendly atmosphere here and guests are made to feel welcome. Bedrooms are comfortably appointed; there is a cosy bar where guests can relax, and a spacious dining room where freshly-cooked breakfasts are served.

Rooms 8 rms (7 en suite) (1 pri facs) (2 fmly) (1 GF) S fr £45; D £55-£70* **Facilities** FTV TVL tea/coffee Licensed WiFi **Notes** LB ⊗

Barclay Court

★★★★ GUEST ACCOMMODATION

tel: 01803 292791 **29 Castle Rd TQ1 3BB**
email: enquiries@barclaycourt.co.uk **web:** www.barclaycourt.co.uk
dir: *M5 onto A38 then A380 to Torquay. A3022 Newton Rd left onto Upton Rd, right towards Lymington Rd. Right to Castle Circus, Castle Rd on left*

The delightful, personally-run Barclay Court is within easy walking distance of Torquay's attractions and offers a friendly, relaxed atmosphere. Individually decorated rooms vary in size, but all are en suite and well equipped. There is a games room on the lower-ground floor and the garden is a quiet retreat, especially in the summer months.

Rooms 4 en suite 6 annexe en suite (1 fmly) (1 GF) S £30-£35; D £60-£90 **Facilities** FTV TVL tea/coffee WiFi 🛢 Games room **Parking** 7 **Notes** ⊗ Closed 25 Dec & New Year RS Nov-Mar Limited rooms available

Brooklands

★★★★ GUEST HOUSE

tel: 01803 296696 & 07900 417855 **5 Scarborough Rd TQ2 5UJ**
email: enquiries@brooklandsguesthousetorquay.com
web: www.brooklandsguesthousetorquay.com
dir: *From seafront into Belgrave Rd. Scarborough Rd 300mtrs on right*

This personally-run, Victorian, terraced property is convenient for the seafront, town centre and Princess Theatre, making it an ideal base for exploring the English Riviera. The en suite bedrooms have good facilities with a thoughtful range of extras, including a fridge in each room and a selection of toiletries. Generous breakfasts are served at individual tables in the attractive breakfast room. On-street parking is available at the rear on request. Guests are welcome to drink in the neighbouring RAF Association Social Club (by prior arrangement).

Rooms 5 en suite (1 fmly) S £35-£45; D £55-£65 **Facilities** FTV tea/coffee WiFi 🛢 **Extras** Snacks, beverages - complimentary **Parking** 1 **Notes** LB ⊗ No Children 5yrs

The Coppice

★★★★ GUEST ACCOMMODATION

tel: 01803 297786 & 211085 **Barrington Rd TQ1 2QJ**
email: reservations@coppicehotel.co.uk **web:** www.coppicehotel.co.uk
dir: *1m from harbour on Babbacombe Rd, opposite St Matthias Church*

Friendly and comfortable, The Coppice is a popular choice and occupies a convenient location within walking distance of the beaches and shops. In addition to the indoor and outdoor swimming pools, evening entertainment is often provided in the spacious bar. Bedrooms are bright and airy with modern amenities.

Rooms 39 en suite (10 fmly) (28 GF) S £30-£65; D £60-£130* (incl.dinner) **Facilities** FTV Lounge tea/coffee Dinner available Licensed WiFi 🕙 ⤳ 🎣 9 Sauna Gym Pool table **Conf** Max 60 Thtr 60 Class 60 Board 60 **Parking** 20 **Notes** LB ⊗

TORQUAY *continued*

The Elmington

★★★★ GUEST ACCOMMODATION

tel: 01803 605192 **St Agnes Ln, Chelston TQ2 6QE**
email: mail@elmington.co.uk **web:** www.elmington.co.uk
dir: *At rear of rail station*

Set in sub-tropical gardens with views over the bay, this splendid Victorian villa has been lovingly restored. The comfortable bedrooms are brightly decorated and vary in size and style. There is a spacious lounge, bar and dining room. Additional facilities include an outdoor pool and terrace.

Rooms 19 en suite **Facilities** FTV Lounge TVL tea/coffee Licensed WiFi ⚓ ♨ ↕ Pool table ♿ **Parking** 24 **Notes** LB ⊗ Closed Nov-Mar

Harmony Bed & Breakfast

★★★★ GUEST ACCOMMODATION

tel: 01803 293918 **67 Avenue Rd TQ2 5LG**
email: enquiries@harmonyhotel.co.uk **web:** www.harmonyhotel.co.uk
dir: *A380 onto A3022 (Riviera Way). At Torre Station, right onto A3022 (Avenue Rd). On left at junct with Vine Rd*

Harmony is a family run establishment within walking distance of the town and a level walk from the seafront. A warm welcome is extended to all guests and every effort made to ensure a relaxing and rewarding stay. Bedrooms all provide impressive levels of quality with all the necessities required and wonderful comfy beds. Breakfast is a tempting and tasty offering with use of local produce where possible, a great start to the day! Ample parking is also an asset here.

Rooms 8 en suite (2 fmly) (2 GF) S £50-£60; D £65-£80* **Facilities** FTV DVD Lounge tea/coffee WiFi **Extras** Mineral water, sweets - complimentary **Parking** 10 **Notes** LB ⊗

Newton House

★★★★ GUEST ACCOMMODATION

tel: 01803 297520 **31 Newton Rd TQ2 5DB**
email: newtonhouse_torquay@yahoo.com **web:** www.newtonhouse-tq.co.uk
dir: *From Torre station bear left at lights, Newton House 40yds on left*

You are assured of a warm welcome at Newton House, which is close to the town centre and attractions. The comfortable bedrooms, some on the ground floor, have thoughtful extras, and a lounge is available. Breakfast is enjoyed in the pleasant dining room.

Rooms 9 en suite (3 fmly) (5 GF) **Facilities** FTV Lounge tea/coffee WiFi ♿ Drying room for hikers **Extras** Snacks, chocolate, sweets - complimentary **Parking** 15 **Notes** ⊗

Peppers

★★★★ GUEST ACCOMMODATION

tel: 01803 293856 **551 Babbacombe Rd TQ1 1HQ**
email: enquiries@hotel-peppers.co.uk **web:** www.hotel-peppers.co.uk
dir: *A3022 to seafront, left on to B3199 towards harbour. At clock tower rdbt, turn left, 250mtrs on left*

Dating back to the Edwardian era, Peppers has much to offer and is conveniently located just a short walk from the harbour. Hospitality is assured, with every effort made to ensure a relaxing and rewarding stay. Bedrooms are elegantly appointed and all provide impressive levels of quality and comfort. Additional facilities include a spacious guest lounge and an intimate bar. The contemporary dining room is the venue for tasty breakfasts with a generous choice on offer. At the rear of the property, a sun terrace leads to the car park.

Rooms 10 rms (9 en suite) (1 pri facs) **Facilities** FTV TVL tea/coffee Licensed WiFi **Extras** Bottled water - complimentary **Parking** 9 **Notes** ⊗ No Children 10yrs Closed 18 Dec-18 Jan

The Norwood

★★★★ ◪ GUEST ACCOMMODATION

tel: 01803 294236 & 07741 662861 **60 Belgrave Rd TQ2 5HY**
email: enquiries@norwoodhoteltorquay.co.uk **web:** www.norwoodhoteltorquay.co.uk
dir: *From Princess Theatre towards Paignton, at 1st lights right into Belgrave Rd, over x-rds, 3rd building on left*

The Norwood is just a short walk from the seafront, town centre and Conference Centre. All the individually decorated bedrooms are en suite and four-poster rooms are available. There are excellent choices at breakfast, from traditional full English to lighter options; dinner is available by prior arrangement, and the hosts are happy to cater for special dietary requests. Packed lunches and takeaway breakfasts are also available.

Rooms 9 en suite (5 fmly) (1 GF) S £38-£44; D £58-£68* **Facilities** FTV tea/coffee Dinner available Licensed WiFi **Extras** Speciality toiletries - complimentary **Parking** 3 **Notes** LB

TOTNES	Map 3 SX86

Premier Collection

Stoke Gabriel Lodgings - Badgers Retreat

★★★★★ ♿ BED AND BREAKFAST

tel: 01803 782003 & 07785 710225 **2 Orchard Close, Stoke Gabriel TQ9 6SX**
email: info@stokegabriellodgings.com **web:** www.stokegabriellodgings.com
dir: *In Stoke Gabriel, pass Baptist church, take left fork into Paignton Rd. 100mtrs to entrance on left by public bench*

Stoke Gabriel Lodgings is an attractive example of contemporary architecture, positioned high above the River Dart just outside Stoke Gabriel, near Totnes. It was only completed in 2010 and has been designed to take full advantage of its location. David and Helen offer a warm welcome as well as a delicious Devon cream tea on arrival. Bedrooms are spacious and lavishly furnished with comfortable seating, and en suites that come complete with wet shower areas and heated towel rails. Patio doors open to a private balcony overlooking the garden and countryside. Outside, the newly planted garden landscape can be enjoyed from the large terrace or conservatory. Breakfast is a delight, while dinner can be taken at one of many local pubs and restaurants.

Rooms 3 en suite (1 fmly) S £75-£80; D £100-£110 **Facilities** STV FTV DVD iPod docking station Lounge TVL tea/coffee WiFi ch fac ♨ ♿ **Extras** Speciality toiletries, fruit/snacks, mineral water **Parking** 6 **Notes** ⊗ ⊜

Dartington Hall

★★★★ ◉◉ GUEST ACCOMMODATION

tel: 01803 847135 & 84170 **The Darington Hall Trust TQ9 6EL**
email: reservations@dartingtonhall.com **web:** www.dartingtonhall.com

Dartington Hall is a Grade I listed property set within a 1200-acre estate in the South Hams. It is the HQ of the Dartington Hall Trust, a charity specialising in the arts, social justice and sustainability. Surrounding a distinctive 14th-century courtyard, accommodation offers a mix of heritage and modern day comforts. A full range of facilities are available, along with guest parking. The award-winning White Hart Restaurant serves breakfast, lunch and dinner.

Rooms 50 rms (39 en suite) (11 pri facs) (10 fmly) (10 GF) S £60-£104; D £89-£139* **Facilities** STV FTV DVD TVL tea/coffee Dinner available Direct Dial Licensed WiFi ↖ ☺⛵ Fishing **Extras** Speciality toiletries, fruit **Conf** Max 500 Thtr 300 Class 200 Board 60 **Parking** 200 **Notes** LB ⊗ Civ Wed 169

YARCOMBE Map 4 ST20

The Belfry at Yarcombe

★★★★ ⬙ ⬗ RESTAURANT WITH ROOMS

tel: 01404 861234 **EX14 9BD**
email: stay@thebelfryatyarcombe.co.uk **web:** www.thebelfrycountryhotel.com
dir: On A30, in village of Yarcombe opposite church

Built in the late 1860s and originally the village school, The Belfry at Yarcombe now offers bright and clean accommodation. Six comfortable en suite rooms are on offer along with a pleasant guest lounge and south-facing terrace, views across the village and valley are a highlight. Breakfast is served in the restaurant, where dinner is also available Thursday through Saturday. WiFi and off-street parking available.

Rooms 6 en suite (2 GF) S £60-£70; D £92-£99 **Facilities** FTV TVL tea/coffee Dinner available Direct Dial WiFi ⬙ **Extras** Speciality toiletries, fresh milk & juice **Conf** Max 12 Board 12 **Parking** 7 **Notes** LB ⊗ No Children 10yrs RS Sun-Wed restaurant closed No coaches

YELVERTON Map 3 SX56

Tor Royal

★★★★ BED AND BREAKFAST

tel: 01822 890189 & 07892 910666 **Princetown PL20 6SL**
email: stay@torroyal.co.uk **web:** www.torroyal.co.uk
dir: A38 exit at Ashburton, follow signs to Princetown/Two Bridges. Turn right to Princetown & left opposite Country Charm shop, Tor Royal on right

This peacefully located Grade II listed former country house is a wonderfully relaxing base from which to explore the picturesque delights of Dartmoor. Parts of the house date back to the 17th century, but modern comforts are now in place, with bedrooms and bathrooms offering high levels of quality and character. Breakfast makes use of excellent local produce, served in the attractive dining room. Guests also have a lovely lounge at their disposal, with an open fire to keep the chill off in cooler months. There is also a large garden.

Rooms 5 en suite (1 GF) **Facilities** FTV DVD TVL TV4B tea/coffee WiFi ⬙ **Conf** Max 30 Class 25 Board 20 **Parking** 10 **Notes** LB ⊗ RS Xmas & New Year Civ Wed 50

Burrator Inn

★★★★ ⬙ ⬗ INN

tel: 01822 853121 **Dousland PL20 6NP**
email: reservations@theburratorinn.co.uk **web:** www.theburratorinn.com
dir: From Yelverton on B3212 to Dousland

This lively pub is located in the very heart of Dousland, near Yelverton, and has a good local following. The bedrooms are comfortable and equipped with all the expected facilities. A wide range of popular dishes served all day, and the very cheerful and upbeat staff are ready and willing to meet the needs of their guests. Good selection of wines and local beers. Great for all ages and families.

Rooms 7 en suite (3 fmly) S £55-£75; D £55-£85* **Facilities** FTV DVD tea/coffee Dinner available WiFi Pool table **Parking** 40 **Notes** Closed 25 Dec

Overcombe House

★★★★ ⬙ GUEST HOUSE

tel: 01822 853501 **Old Station Rd, Horrabridge PL20 7RA**
email: enquiries@overcombehotel.co.uk **web:** www.overcombehotel.co.uk
dir: Signed 100yds off A386 at Horrabridge

Many guests return on a regular basis to enjoy this delightful, family-run establishment. Genuine hospitality is a great strength, and every effort is taken to ensure an enjoyable and memorable stay. Given its location, this is a perfect base for exploring the rugged beauty of the Dartmoor National Park, just on the doorstep. Bedrooms are all neatly presented; many have lovely views across the countryside.

Rooms 8 en suite (2 GF) S £65-£87.50; D £80-£100* **Facilities** FTV DVD tea/coffee Licensed WiFi ⬙ **Parking** 7 **Notes** ⊗ No Children 12yrs Closed 24 Dec-2 Jan

DORSET

ASKERSWELL
Map 4 SY59

The Spyway Inn

★★★★ 🍽 🛏 INN

tel: 01308 485250 **DT2 9EP**
email: spywaytim@hotmail.com **web:** www.spyway-inn.co.uk
dir: *From A35 follow Askerswell sign, then follow Spyway Inn sign*

Peacefully located in the rolling Dorset countryside, this family-run inn offers a warm and genuine welcome. Bedrooms are spacious and well appointed with a number of extras provided, including bath robes. Real ales are on tap in the bar. Menus feature home-cooked food, with many dishes making use of local produce both at dinner and breakfast. The extensive beer garden, with wonderful views, is popular in summer. AA Friendliest B&B of the Year Award Runner-Up 2016-2017.

Rooms 3 en suite (1 fmly) S £50; D £49.50-£80* **Facilities** FTV tea/coffee Dinner available WiFi **Extras** Robes **Parking** 40 **Notes** LB ⊗

BEAMINSTER
Map 4 ST40

Hill Farm B&B

★★ BED AND BREAKFAST

tel: 01308 861037 **DT8 3SQ**
email: rkpjones1955@yahoo.co.uk **web:** www.hillfarmbandbdorset.com
dir: *Off A356 between Crewkerne & Maiden Newton*

Hill Farm offers a peaceful rural setting, and cosy and comfortable accommodation. There is a relaxed atmosphere, and a good hearty breakfast is served in the traditional dining room adorned with historical artefacts and family pictures. This is a perfect spot from which to explore the stunning south coast and surrounding areas.

Rooms 2 rms (1 en suite) (1 pri facs) D £85* **Facilities** TVL tea/coffee WiFi 🛁 **Parking** 4 **Notes** ⊗ ⊠

Portman Lodge

Built in 1873, *Portman Lodge* is the main wing and entrance into a large Victorian property, originally part of Lord Portman's estate. It is thought to have been a residence for choristers for St Martin's Church. Many of the original fixtures and fittings remain, in particular the attractive Victorian tiled floor in the entrance hall and corridor.

The individually decorated bedrooms, with twin, double or kingsize beds, are supremely comfortable, with ensuite rooms, plentiful hot water, powerful showers and white fluffy towels.

Substantial cooked tasty breakfasts, including a varied range of locally sourced produce, are served around a large table in our lovely dining room.

There is a good choice of pubs and restaurants for lunch and dinner in the beautiful Georgian market town of Blandford, just five minutes walk away, so no need to get into your car.

Recommended in the area: Kingston Lacy, Lulworth Cove, Jurassic Coast, Corfe Castle, Abbotsbury Swannery and Gardens

Whitecliff Mill Street, Blandford Forum, Dorset DT11 7BP
Tel: 01258 453727
Mobile: 07860 424235 (Gerry) • 07785 971743 (Pat)
Website: www.portmanlodge.co.uk
Email: enquiries@portmanlodge.co.uk

BLANDFORD FORUM

BLANDFORD FORUM

Map 4 ST80

Portman Lodge

★★★★ BED AND BREAKFAST

tel: 01258 453727 **Whitecliff Mill St DT11 7BP**
email: enquiries@portmanlodge.co.uk **web:** www.portmanlodge.co.uk
dir: *One-way system, follow signs from town centre to Shaftesbury & hospital. On right past Our Lady of Lourdes church (on left)*

Victorian building once used as a music school, this substantial detached house now provides elegant accommodation and a warm welcome. All bedrooms and bathrooms are well decorated and comfortably furnished. Breakfast utilises good quality ingredients and is served at a communal table.

Rooms 3 en suite 2 annexe en suite (1 fmly) S fr £65; D £80-£85* **Facilities** STV tea/coffee WiFi 🛎 **Parking** 8 **Notes** No Children 10yrs 🚭

see advert on opposite page

BOURNEMOUTH

Map 5 SZ09

Washington House

★★★★ GUEST ACCOMMODATION

tel: 01202 556111 **3 Durley Rd BH2 5JQ**
email: info@washingtonhousehotel.com **web:** www.washingtonhousehotel.com

This Grade II listed Victorian villa has much to offer, not least of which a great location, just a short walk from the seafront and the Bournemouth International Centre. Recently refurbished throughout, the bedrooms provide individuality, style and comfort, likewise the modern bathrooms. Public areas are equally impressive; the elegant dining room is the venue for breakfast, an extensive continental offering. A guest lounge is also provided, and there is parking available.

Rooms 13 en suite (2 fmly) (4 GF) S £49.50-£120 (room only)* **Facilities** FTV Lounge tea/coffee Licensed WiFi **Parking** 12 **Notes** 🚭

Pinedale

★★★ GUEST ACCOMMODATION

tel: 01202 553733 & 292702 **40 Tregonwell Rd, West Cliff BH2 5NT**
email: thepinedalehotel@btconnect.com **web:** www.thepinedalehotel.co.uk
dir: *A338 at Bournemouth West rdbt, signs to West Cliff, Tregonwell Rd 3rd left after passing Wessex Hotel*

This friendly guest accommodation is enthusiastically run by two generations of the same family, and offers comfortable accommodation within a short walk of the seafront and local attractions. The fresh-looking bedrooms are equipped with useful extras. There is also an attractive licensed bar and an airy dining room where you can enjoy wholesome home-cooked breakfasts.

Rooms 15 rms (10 en suite) (1 fmly) S £23-£37; D £52-£84* **Facilities** FTV TVL tea/coffee Direct Dial Licensed WiFi 🛎 **Parking** 15 **Notes** 🚭 Closed 24 Dec-2 Jan

Trouville Lodge

★★★ GUEST ACCOMMODATION

tel: 01202 552262 **9 Priory Rd BH2 5DF**
email: reception@trouvillehotel.com **web:** www.trouvillehotel.com

Professionally run, this well-managed establishment offers an impressive standard of accommodation and facilities. Bedrooms are situated in an annexe to the Trouville Hotel next door. All rooms are stylishly appointed and comfortably furnished. Facilities are in the hotel. The Deauville restaurant offers a very good menu choice, and the well-stocked Le Café Bar provides an informal and pleasant environment. There is also a large pool and sauna as well as a resident beautician.

Rooms 19 en suite (4 fmly) (4 GF) **Facilities** FTV tea/coffee Dinner available Licensed WiFi 🏊 Sauna Gym Leisure facilities available at Trouville Hotel **Parking** 14 **Notes** LB

BRIDPORT

Map 4 SY49

Premier Collection

The Shave Cross Inn

★★★★★ 🍴 INN

tel: 01308 868358 **Marshwood Vale DT6 6HW**
email: roy.warburton@virgin.net **web:** www.theshavecrossinn.co.uk
dir: *From B3165 turn at Birdsmoorgate & follow brown signs*

This historic inn has been providing refreshment to weary travellers for centuries and continues to offer a warm and genuine welcome. The snug bar is dominated by a wonderful fireplace with crackling logs creating just the right atmosphere. Bedrooms are located in a separate Dorset flint and stone building. Quality is impressive throughout with wonderful stone floors and oak beams, combined with feature beds and luxurious bathrooms. Food, using excellent local produce, has a distinct Caribbean and international slant, including a number of authentic dishes.

Rooms 7 en suite (1 fmly) (3 GF) **Facilities** STV FTV tea/coffee Dinner available Direct Dial WiFi Pool table **Parking** 29 **Notes** No Children RS Mon (ex BH) closed for lunch & dinner No coaches

BRIDPORT *continued*

Oxbridge Farm (SY475977)

★★★★ FARMHOUSE

tel: 01308 488368 & 07766 086543 **DT6 3UA**
email: jojokillin@hotmail.com **web:** www.oxbridgefarm.co.uk
dir: *From A3066 Bridport to Beaminster. Take 1st right signed Oxbridge 1m*

Oxbridge Farm sits in the rolling hills of west Dorset in an Area of Outstanding Natural Beauty. The bedrooms are well equipped and offer a very good level of comfort. A hearty breakfast is served in the attractive dining room which benefits from wonderful countryside views.

Rooms 4 rms (3 en suite) (1 pri facs) (2 fmly) (1 GF) **Facilities** FTV Lounge TV3B tea/coffee Dinner available WiFi ⚓ 18 **Parking** 6 **Notes** LB ⊛ Civ Wed 200 40 acres sheep

BROADWINDSOR
Map 4 ST40

Premier Collection

The Old George

★★★★★ ⊜ GUEST ACCOMMODATION

tel: 01308 868434 **The Square DT8 3QD**
email: theoldgeorge@gmail.com **web:** www.theoldgeorge-broadwindsor.co.uk

Located in the peaceful and quintessentially English village of Broadwindsor, this comfortable listed Georgian house was converted sympathetically from a pub to a family home fifty years ago, and is an ideal retreat for those seeking peaceful surroundings. King Charles II slept in the adjacent property in 1651. Each of the bedrooms has its own character, and a range of thoughtful extras such as fresh flowers, bottled water and magazines. A pub offering a selection of evening meals is just a stone's throw away. Home-cooked breakfasts are also served in the comfortable dining room.

Rooms 3 en suite **Facilities** FTV DVD TVL tea/coffee WiFi 🐾 🔒 **Extras** Speciality toiletries **Parking** 2 **Notes** ⊗ ⊛

CHIDEOCK
Map 4 SY49

The Anchor Inn

★★★★ ⊜ 🍺 INN

tel: 01297 489215 **Seatown DT6 6JU**
email: contact@theanchorinnseatown.co.uk **web:** www.theanchorinnseatown.co.uk
dir: *Turn off A35 in Chideock into Duck Street, 0.75m down lane to sea*

This long established inn has much to offer, not least of which is its superb position, just a few steps away from the sea. There is a simple and rustic nautical style throughout the bars, combined with an engaging and good humoured atmosphere. Bedrooms are spacious with wonderful bathrooms and the added luxury of quality toiletries and cosseting robes. Food is not to be missed, a varied menu with excellent quality local seafood is always on offer. Breakfast also makes use of impressive local produce.

Rooms 3 en suite (2 fmly) S £105-£135; D £120-£150* **Facilities** FTV tea/coffee Dinner available Direct Dial WiFi **Extras** Speciality toiletries, slippers, gowns **Parking** 8 **Notes** Closed 24 Dec-1 Jan No coaches

CHRISTCHURCH
Map 5 SZ19

Premier Collection

Druid House

★★★★★ ⊜ GUEST ACCOMMODATION

tel: 01202 485615 **26 Sopers Ln BH23 1JE**
email: reservations@druid-house.co.uk **web:** www.druid-house.co.uk
dir: *From A35 exit at Christchurch main rdbt into Sopers Ln, establishment on left*

Overlooking the park, this delightful family-run establishment is just a stroll from the high street, the priory and the quay. Bedrooms, some with balconies, are very comfortably furnished, and have many welcome extras including CD players. There is a pleasant rear garden, a patio and a relaxing lounge and bar areas.

Rooms 8 en suite (3 fmly) (4 GF) **Facilities** FTV DVD iPod docking station tea/coffee Direct Dial Licensed WiFi **Parking** 8 **Notes** ⊗

Premier Collection

The Lord Bute & Restaurant

★★★★★ ◉◉ GUEST ACCOMMODATION

tel: 01425 278884 **179-181 Lymington Rd, Highcliffe on Sea BH23 4JS**
email: mail@lordbute.co.uk **web:** www.lordbute.co.uk
dir: *A337 towards Highcliffe*

The elegant Lord Bute stands directly behind the original entrance lodges of Highcliffe Castle, close to the beach and historic town of Christchurch. Bedrooms have been finished to a very high standard with many thoughtful extras including spa baths. The excellent food served in the restaurant has been awarded two AA Rosettes. Conferences and weddings are catered for.

Rooms 9 en suite 4 annexe en suite (1 fmly) (6 GF) S £125-£245; D £125-£245* **Facilities** FTV Lounge tea/coffee Dinner available Direct Dial Licensed WiFi **Conf** Max 25 Thtr 25 Class 15 Board 18 **Parking** 40 **Notes** LB RS Mon Restaurant closed (open bkfst) Civ Wed 120

Grosvenor Lodge

★★★★ GUEST HOUSE

tel: 01202 499008 **53 Stour Rd BH23 1LN**
email: bookings@grosvenorlodge.co.uk **web:** www.grosvenorlodge.co.uk
dir: *A35 from Christchurch to Bournemouth, at 1st lights left into Stour Rd. Lodge on right*

Grosvenor House is a friendly and popular guest house near the centre of this historic town. The bedrooms are brightly and individually decorated and have lots of useful extras. Hearty breakfasts are served in the cheerful dining room, and there are many local restaurants for lunch and dinner.

Rooms 7 en suite (4 fmly) (1 GF) **Facilities** FTV DVD iPod docking station tea/coffee WiFi ☕ **Parking** 10 **Notes** ⊗

Avon Breeze

★★★★ ☕ BED AND BREAKFAST

tel: 01425 279102 & 07896 128026 **21 Fulmar Rd BH23 4BJ**
email: info@avonbreeze.co.uk **web:** http://avonbreeze.co.uk
dir: *A35 follow signs for Christchurch. At Sainsburys, signs for Mudeford. At Mudeford quay, turn into Falcon Dr, left & left again*

Avon Breeze is situated on the edge of the New Forest, a few minutes' level walk from the harbour, beach and local pubs. This contemporary home offers two comfortable en suite rooms as well as the use of a conservatory. Breakfast consists of locally-sourced, organic ingredients. Ample off-street parking is available.

Rooms 2 en suite (2 GF) **Facilities** FTV DVD iPod docking station tea/coffee WiFi ☕ **Extras** Bottled water, chocolate - complimentary **Parking** 3 **Notes** ⊗ No Children Closed Oct-Mar RS Apr one room only open ◉

The Rothesay

★★★★ GUEST ACCOMMODATION

tel: 01425 274172 **175, Lymington Rd, Highcliffe on Sea BH23 4JS**
email: reservations@therothesayhotel.com **web:** www.therothesayhotel.com
dir: *A337 to Highcliffe towards The Castle, 1m on left*

Set on the edge of Highcliffe, The Rothesay is a great base for exploring the Dorset and Hampshire coast. Highcliffe Castle is just a five-minute walk away, and there are cliff-top walks and views to the Isle of Wight. The indoor pool is a real bonus, as are the pretty gardens and large car park.

Rooms 12 en suite 3 annexe en suite (1 fmly) (7 GF) **Facilities** FTV TVL tea/coffee Licensed WiFi ☘ Sauna Pool table **Conf** Max 30 Thtr 30 Class 30 Board 30 **Parking** 21 **Notes** ⊗ No Children 8yrs

Riversmead

★★★★ GUEST ACCOMMODATION

tel: 01202 487195 **61 Stour Rd BH23 1LN**
email: riversmead.dorset@googlemail.com **web:** www.riversmeadbb.co.uk
dir: *A338 to Christchurch. Left turn to town centre, turn right over railway bridge*

Ideally located close to the town centre, beaches and the New Forest, with excellent access to local transport links, Riversmead is the perfect base for a short break or longer stay. This comfortable house offers a range of facilities including enclosed off-road parking, fridges in rooms, and an excellent breakfast.

Rooms 3 en suite (1 fmly) S £50-£60; D £65-£75* **Facilities** FTV DVD tea/coffee WiFi **Parking** 9 **Notes** LB No Children 10yrs

The White House

★★★★ GUEST ACCOMMODATION

tel: 01425 271279 **428 Lymington Rd, Highcliffe on Sea BH23 5HF**
email: enquiries@thewhitehouse-christchurch.co.uk
web: www.thewhitehouse-christchurch.co.uk
dir: *Off A35, signs to Highcliffe. After rdbt The White House 200yds on right*

This charming Victorian house is just a short drive from Highcliffe beach, the New Forest, and the historic town of Christchurch. Comfortable, well-appointed accommodation is provided, and a generous, freshly-cooked breakfast is served in the cosy dining room.

Rooms 6 en suite **Facilities** FTV tea/coffee WiFi **Parking** 6 **Notes** LB ⊗

CHRISTCHURCH *continued*

Brantwood Guest House

★★★ GUEST ACCOMMODATION

tel: 01202 473446 **55 Stour Rd BH23 1LN**
email: brantwoodbookings@gmail.com **web:** www.brantwoodguesthouse.com
dir: *A338 Bournemouth, 1st exit to Christchurch, right after railway bridge, cross lights, 200yds on right*

Brantwood Guest House offers relaxed and friendly guest accommodation where the proprietors create a home-from-home atmosphere. Bedrooms and bathrooms are all well decorated and comfortably furnished. The town centre is just a stroll away and off-road parking is available.

Rooms 5 en suite (2 fmly) (1 GF) **Facilities** FTV tea/coffee WiFi **Parking** 5 **Notes** ⊗

Southern Comfort Guest House

★★★ BED AND BREAKFAST

tel: 01202 471373 **51 Stour Rd BH23 1LN**
email: southerncomfortgh@gmail.com **web:** www.christchurchguesthouse.co.uk
dir: *A338 onto B3073 towards Christchurch, 2m onto B3059 (Stour Rd). 100yds on right*

This family-run establishment is well located for exploring the charms of Christchurch. Bedrooms all provide good levels of comfort with a variety of different configurations; a ground floor room is available. Breakfast is served in the attractive dining room with a generous cooked offering. Car parking is also provided.

Rooms 6 en suite (5 fmly) (1 GF) S £30-£35; D £60-£75* **Facilities** FTV tea/coffee WiFi **Parking** 6 **Notes** LB ⊗ Closed 24-27 Dec & Jan

| CORFE MULLEN | Map 4 SY99 |

Kenways

★★★ BED AND BREAKFAST

tel: 01202 280620 **90a Wareham Rd BH21 3LQ**
email: eileen@kenways.com **web:** www.kenways.co.uk
dir: *2m SW of Wimborne. Off A31 to Corfe Mullen. Over B3074 rdbt, B&B 0.3m on right*

Expect to be welcomed as one of the family at this homely bed and breakfast situated between Wimborne Minster and Poole. The spacious bedrooms are well provisioned with thoughtful extras, and breakfast is served in the pleasant conservatory overlooking attractive gardens.

Rooms 3 rms (3 pri facs) (1 fmly) (2 GF) **Facilities** FTV DVD TVL tea/coffee WiFi Table tennis Snooker table **Parking** 4

| CRANBORNE | Map 5 SU01 |

The Inn at Cranborne

★★★★ ⊜ INN

tel: 01725 551249 **5 Wimborne St BH21 5PP**
email: info@theinnatcranborne.co.uk **web:** www.theinnatcranborne.co.uk
dir: *On B3078 in centre of village*

A delightful 17th-century inn, lovingly restored and full of special touches, The Inn at Cranborne is located in a peaceful village just a short drive from the New Forest and the Jurassic Coast. Nine comfortable and beautifully appointed en suite rooms are available. Breakfast (a real treat here), lunch and dinner are served in the bar and dining room areas. Off-street parking is available.

Rooms 9 en suite (2 fmly) S £75-£130; D £85-£150* **Facilities** FTV DVD iPod docking station Lounge TVL tea/coffee Dinner available WiFi ⌀ 18 ⌀ **Extras** Speciality toiletries, ground coffee, fresh milk **Conf** Max 10 Thtr 10 Board 10 **Parking** 25 **Notes** LB

| DORCHESTER | Map 4 SY69 |

Premier Collection

Little Court

★★★★★ ⊜ GUEST ACCOMMODATION

tel: 01305 261576 **5 Westleaze, Charminster DT2 9PZ**
email: info@littlecourt.net **web:** www.littlecourt.net
dir: *A37 from Dorchester, 0.25m right at Loders Garage, Little Court 0.5m on right*

Built in 1909 in the style of Lutyens, Little Court sits in over four acres of attractive grounds and gardens, complete with tennis courts and swimming pool. The property has been appointed to a very high standard and the friendly proprietors are on hand to ensure a pleasant stay. A delicious breakfast, including home-grown produce, can be enjoyed in the stylish dining room.

Rooms 8 en suite (1 fmly) **Facilities** FTV Lounge tea/coffee Licensed WiFi ⌀ ⌀ ⌀ 18 Gym **Parking** 10 **Notes** LB ⊗ Closed Xmas & New Year

Westwood House

★★★★ GUEST ACCOMMODATION

tel: 01305 268018 **29 High West St DT1 1UP**
email: reservations@westwoodhouse.co.uk **web:** www.westwoodhouse.co.uk
dir: *On B2150 in town centre*

Originally built in 1815, Westwood House is centrally located in this historic town and is ideal for leisure visitors as well as business travellers. Run by a husband and wife team, this attractive property offers well-appointed rooms with modern facilities presented in an informal, stylish environment.

Rooms 7 rms (5 en suite) (2 pri facs) (2 fmly) **Facilities** FTV DVD tea/coffee WiFi ⌀ **Extras** Speciality toiletries, fresh milk **Notes** ⊗

Baytree House Dorchester

★★★★ BED AND BREAKFAST

tel: 01305 263696 **4 Athelstan Rd DT1 1NR**
email: info@baytreedorchester.com **web:** www.bandbdorchester.co.uk
dir: 0.5m SE of town centre

Baytree House Dorchester is a friendly, family-run bed and breakfast situated in the heart of the town, not far from the village of Higher Bockham, birthplace of Thomas Hardy. The bedrooms are furnished in an appealing contemporary style and provide high levels of comfort. Breakfast is served farmhouse style in the open-plan kitchen/dining area. Parking is available.

Rooms 6 en suite **Facilities** FTV iPod docking station tea/coffee **Parking** 3 **Notes** ⊗

The Brewers Arms

★★★ INN

tel: 01305 889361 **Martinstown DT2 9LB**
email: contact@thebrewersarms.com **web:** www.thebrewersarms.com
dir: W of Dorchester on A35, after 2m turn left signed Martinstown. Right into village, 0.5m on right

The Brewers Arms is very much a traditional country local, situated in the heart of a picturesque village. A warm welcome is assured and the atmosphere at the bar is good-natured and friendly. Bedrooms are located in an adjacent building and are entirely self-contained. Each one is spacious and well appointed with all the necessities to ensure a comfortable and relaxing stay. The menu offers a range of popular favourites, served either in the restaurant or the bar area. An extensive garden is also available.

Rooms 2 annexe en suite (2 GF) S £80-£90; D fr £90* **Facilities** FTV tea/coffee Dinner available WiFi **Extras** Speciality toiletries, bottled water **Parking** 20 **Notes** LB

EVERSHOT — Map 4 ST50

The Acorn Inn

★★★★ ◉ INN

tel: 01935 83228 **28 Fore St DT2 0JW**
email: stay@acorn-inn.co.uk **web:** www.acorn-inn.co.uk
dir: From A37 between Yeovil & Dorchester, follow Evershot & Holywell signs, 0.5m to inn

This delightful 16th-century coaching inn is located in the heart of the village. Many of the bedrooms feature interesting four-poster beds, and all the rooms have been individually decorated and furnished. The public areas retain many original features including oak panelling, open fires and stone-flagged floors. Fresh local produce is included on the varied menu.

Rooms 10 en suite (2 fmly) S £89-£210; D fr £99* **Facilities** STV FTV TVL tea/coffee Dinner available Direct Dial WiFi 🔒 Use of spa opposite - charged **Extras** Speciality toiletries, robes, home-made biscuits **Conf** Max 30 Thtr 30 Board 30 **Parking** 40 **Notes** LB

FARNHAM — Map 4 ST91

Museum Inn

★★★★ ◉◉ 🍷 INN

tel: 01725 812702 **DT11 8DE**
email: enquiries@museuminn.co.uk **web:** www.museuminn.co.uk
dir: Off A354 between Salisbury & Blandford Forum

Part of The Epicurean Collection and located in a peaceful Dorset village, this traditional inn offers cosy log fires, flagstone floors and a welcoming bar combined with efficient service and a friendly welcome. Bedrooms include larger, stylish rooms in the main building or a selection of cosy rooms in an adjacent building. Food here, whether dinner or breakfast, uses the finest quality produce and really should not be missed.

Rooms 4 en suite 4 annexe en suite (2 fmly) (4 GF) S £90-£160; D £90-£160* **Facilities** FTV Lounge tea/coffee Dinner available Direct Dial WiFi 🌊 18 Fishing Riding **Extras** Speciality toiletries **Conf** Max 30 Thtr 30 Class 24 Board 20 **Parking** 24 **Notes** LB

HIGHCLIFFE

For accommodation details see Christchurch

LYME REGIS — Map 4 SY39

See also Axminster (Devon)

St Cuthberts

★★★★ BED AND BREAKFAST

tel: 01297 445901 **Charmouth Rd DT7 3HG**
email: info@stcuthbertsoflyme.co.uk **web:** www.stcuthbertsoflyme.co.uk
dir: A35 from Dorchester, at Charmouth rdbt onto B3052 for 2m. Establishment on opposite side of road to "Welcome to Lyme Regis" sign

Located just a ten minute walk above the main town and harbour, this detached home is set within mature gardens and has its own parking. Bedrooms and bathrooms offer plenty of quality and comfort, as well as many thoughtful extras. A lounge with a log-burning stove and a decked terrace are available for guests. Breakfast, served around one large table, offers a varied choice including delicious pancakes with bacon and maple syrup.

Rooms 3 en suite (1 GF) S fr £65; D fr £85* **Facilities** FTV DVD TVL tea/coffee 🌊 18 🔒 **Parking** 3 **Notes** ⊗ No Children 7yrs ⊗

Kersbrook

★★★★ 🍷 GUEST ACCOMMODATION

tel: 01297 442596 **Pound Round DT7 3HX**
email: alex@kersbrook.co.uk **web:** www.kersbrook.co.uk

Just a stroll from the town centre and the famous Cobb, this thatched property provides an excellent base for exploring the fascinating delights of Lyme Regis. Dating back to 1790, there is character and charm in abundance, with facilities including a bar and lounge. Breakfast is a treat, the ideal start to a day of exploration. Bedrooms are traditionally styled, allied with modern bathrooms; an appealing combination.

Rooms 14 rms (13 en suite) (1 pri facs) (1 fmly) (4 GF) S £55-£65; D £95-£135* **Facilities** FTV Lounge tea/coffee Licensed WiFi 🌊 18 Fishing 🔒 **Parking** 13 **Notes** LB ⊗

LYME REGIS *continued*

The Mariners

★★★★ INN

tel: 01297 442753 **Silver St DT7 3HS**
email: enquiry@hotellymeregis.co.uk **web:** www.hotellymeregis.co.uk
dir: *A35 onto B3165 (Lyme Rd). Mariners is pink building opposite road to The Cobb (Pound Rd)*

This delightful building combines traditional character and ambience with a modern and stylish look. Bedrooms and bathrooms vary in size, but include a range of welcome extras; many have views over the bay. Public areas include a relaxing lounge, comfortable bar and modern restaurant. Guests can choose a full dinner, which makes great use of local fish and seafood, or a varied range of lighter options from the bar menu. Outdoor seating is available.

Rooms 14 en suite (2 fmly) **Facilities** FTV Lounge tea/coffee Dinner available Direct Dial WiFi ⅃ 18 Fishing **Conf** Max 30 Thtr 24 Class 16 Board 30 **Parking** 20

MILTON ABBAS · Map 4 ST80

Hambro Arms

★★★★ INN

tel: 01258 880233 **DT11 0BP**
email: info@hambroarms.com **web:** www.hambroarms.com
dir: *From A354 follow signs for Milton Abbas, in village*

The village of Milton Abbas is something very special. Much admired and featured on many a postcard, it is situated in the heart of Dorset. Identical thatched cottages that once housed the local estate workers line either side of the gently winding road. The Hambro Arms occupies one such thatched building, and is a charming and quintessential village hostelry. Step inside for a genuine welcome and enjoy the refurbished bars, restaurant and lounge, all retaining their original character. Food demonstrates a genuine commitment to quality, local produce; likewise the tasty and substantial breakfast. Impressive bedrooms provide all the expected comforts combined with historic charm.

Rooms 4 en suite (1 fmly) S £76-£104; D £86-£114* **Facilities** FTV Lounge tea/coffee Dinner available WiFi ⚓ **Parking** 15

MOTCOMBE · Map 4 ST82

The Coppleridge Inn

★★★ INN

tel: 01747 851980 **SP7 9HW**
email: thecoppleridgeinn@btinternet.com **web:** www.coppleridge.com
dir: *Exit A350 to Motcombe, under railway bridge, 400yds, right to Mere, inn 300yds on left*

This village inn set in 15 acres offers ten en suite bedrooms located in a pretty courtyard. All bedrooms have been appointed to a high standard and provide a very comfortable stay. Staff offer a warm welcome, and the inn serves good food with many daily specials. There are tennis courts and boules, plus a children's play area. Clay pigeon shooting can also be arranged.

Rooms 10 en suite (2 fmly) (10 GF) S £65; D £100* **Facilities** FTV DVD TVL tea/coffee Dinner available Direct Dial WiFi ch fac ☕ ⚓ Boules pitch **Extras** Mini-bar **Conf** Max 60 Thtr 60 Class 60 Board 30 **Parking** 100 **Notes** LB Civ Wed 120

PIDDLEHINTON · Map 4 SY79

Longpuddle

★★★★ BED AND BREAKFAST

tel: 01300 348532 & 07711 965109 **4 High St DT2 7TD**
email: ann@longpuddle.co.uk **web:** www.longpuddle.co.uk
dir: *From Dorchester (A35) take B3143, after entering village 1st thatched house on left after village cross*

This purpose-built annexe accommodation is perfectly located for exploring the delightful Dorset countryside and coast. Bedrooms are spacious, very well furnished and equipped with thoughtful extras such as mini-fridges. Breakfast is served in the dining room of the main house, where the guest lounge overlooks the lovely gardens.

Rooms 2 annexe en suite (2 fmly) D £80-£90* **Facilities** FTV TVL tea/coffee WiFi **Parking** 3 **Notes** RS Dec-Jan Prior bookings only

---

PLUSH · Map 4 ST70

The Brace of Pheasants

★★★★ INN

tel: 01300 348357 **DT2 7RQ**
email: info@braceofpheasants.co.uk **web:** www.braceofpheasants.co.uk
dir: *A35 onto B3142, right to Plush 1.5m*

Situated in the heart of Dorset, The Brace of Pheasants is a picturesque thatched pub that offers a warm and genuine welcome to both visitors and locals alike. Very much a traditional inn, its atmosphere is convivial, with plenty of good-natured conversation. Bedrooms are split between the main building and the former skittle alley – all offer exceptional standards of comfort and individual style, with wonderful bathrooms. The food here should not be missed, with excellent local produce used to create an appealing menu.

Rooms 4 en suite 4 annexe en suite (4 GF) **Facilities** FTV tea/coffee Dinner available Direct Dial WiFi **Parking** 15 **Notes** Closed 25 Dec

---

POOLE · Map 4 SZ09

Acorns Guest House

★★★★ GUEST ACCOMMODATION

tel: 01202 672901 **264 Wimborne Rd, Oakdale BH15 3EF**
email: enquiries@acornsguesthouse.co.uk **web:** www.acornsguesthouse.co.uk
dir: *On A35, approx 1m from town centre, opposite Esso station*

A warm welcome is assured at Acorns Guest House, located with easy access to the town, ferry terminal, business parks and attractions. The bedrooms are furnished to a high standard, and an English breakfast is served in the charming dining room. There is also a quiet cosy lounge.

Rooms 4 en suite (1 GF) D £70-£80 **Facilities** FTV DVD Lounge tea/coffee WiFi ⚓ **Parking** 6 **Notes** LB ⊗ No Children 14yrs Closed 23 Dec-1 Jan ⊜

Milsoms Poole

★★★★ RESTAURANT WITH ROOMS

tel: 01202 609000 **47 Haven Rd, Canford Cliffs BH13 7LH**
email: poole@milsomshotel.co.uk **web:** www.milsomshotel.co.uk

Milsoms Poole is located in the Canford Cliffs area, moments from some of the country's best beaches and the picturesque Purbeck Hills. Comfortable and stylish en suite accommodation is situated above the popular seafood Loch Fyne

Restaurant. The friendly and helpful team provide a warm welcome. Limited on-site parking is available.

Rooms 8 en suite (1 GF) **Facilities** FTV tea/coffee Dinner available WiFi **Parking** 12 **Notes** ⊗ No coaches

Towngate Guest House

★★★ GUEST HOUSE

tel: 01202 668552 **58 Wimborne Rd BH15 2BY**
email: ayoun19@ntlworld.com **web:** www.towngateguesthouse.net
dir: B3093 from town centre, guest house on right

Guests are assured of a warm welcome at this centrally located house, within walking distance of the town centre and harbour, and just a short drive from the ferry terminal. The well-equipped bedrooms are comfortable and nicely furnished.

Rooms 3 en suite S £45-£50; D £65-£70 **Facilities** FTV tea/coffee WiFi ⊕ **Parking** 4 **Notes** ⊗ No Children 10yrs Closed mid Dec-mid Jan ⊛

Seacourt

★★★ GUEST ACCOMMODATION

tel: 01202 674995 **249 Blandford Rd, Hamworthy BH15 4AZ**
email: seacourtguesthouse@hotmail.co.uk
dir: Off A3049/A35 signed to Hamworthy

Within a short distance of the ferry port and town centre, this friendly establishment is well maintained and efficiently run. The comfortable bedrooms, some located on the ground floor, are all nicely decorated and equipped with useful extra facilities. Breakfast is served in the pleasant dining room at separate tables.

Rooms 5 en suite (1 fmly) (3 GF) (5 smoking) S £47; D £64 **Facilities** FTV DVD tea/coffee WiFi **Extras** Use of microwave & fridge **Parking** 5 **Notes** ⊗ No Children 5yrs ⊛

PORTESHAM
Map 4 SY68

Kings Arms

★★★★ INN

tel: 01305 871342 **2 Front St DT3 4ET**
web: www.kingsarmsportesham.co.uk
dir: On B3157 coastal road

Situated on the coast road, approximately half way between Weymouth and Dorchester, this long-established and popular village local is a great base from which to explore the area. The atmosphere is warm and welcoming with good-natured banter at the bar. Local produce features on the menu with a range of dishes for all tastes. Bedrooms are located to the side of the pub, all with level access and a private entrance.

Rooms 3 en suite (1 fmly) (3 GF) S £75-£95; D £95-£140* **Facilities** tea/coffee Dinner available WiFi **Extras** Speciality toiletries **Parking** 20

PORTLAND
Map 4 SY67

Queen Anne House

★★★★ GUEST ACCOMMODATION

tel: 01305 820028 **2/4 Fortuneswell DT5 1LP**
email: margaretdunlop@tiscali.co.uk **web:** www.queenannehouse.com
dir: A354 to Portland then Fortuneswell. House on left 200mtrs past Royal Portland Arms

This delightful, Grade II listed building is a charming and comfortable place to stay; particularly delightful are the Italianate gardens to the rear. Ideal for business

and leisure travellers, Queen Anne House is close to Portland Bill, Weymouth and Chesil Beach. The bedrooms are particularly attractive and pleasantly furnished. Breakfast, taken at one large table, offers a wide range of options.

Rooms 3 en suite S £55-£65; D £80-£90* **Facilities** FTV TVL tea/coffee WiFi ⊕ **Parking** 4 **Notes** ⊗ ⊛

Portland Lodge

★★★ GUEST ACCOMMODATION

tel: 01305 820265 **Easton Ln DT5 1BW**
email: info@portlandlodge.com **web:** www.portlandlodge.com
dir: Signs to Easton/Portland Bill, rdbt at Portland Heights Hotel 1st right. Portland Lodge 200yds

Situated on the fascinating island of Portland, this modern, lodge-style establishment provides comfortable accommodation including a number of ground-floor bedrooms. Breakfast is served in the spacious dining room with a friendly team of staff on hand. This is an ideal location for those wishing to explore the World Heritage coastline.

Rooms 30 annexe en suite (15 fmly) (7 GF) S £35-£60; D £45-£80 (room only)* **Facilities** FTV tea/coffee WiFi **Parking** 30 **Notes** LB ⊗

PUNCKNOWLE
Map 4 SY58

Offley Bed & Breakfast

★★★★ GUEST ACCOMMODATION

tel: 01308 897044 & 07792 624977 **Looke Ln DT2 9BD**
web: www.offleybedandbreakfast.info
dir: Off B3157 into village centre, left after Crown Inn into Looke Ln, 2nd house on right

With magnificent views over the Bride Valley, this village house provides comfortable, quality accommodation. Guests are assured of a warm, friendly welcome, and this is an ideal base from which to enjoy the numerous local attractions. There are several local inns, one in the village which is just a gentle stroll away.

Rooms 3 rms (2 en suite) (1 pri facs) S £45; D £70* **Facilities** FTV TVL tea/coffee ⚲ ⚲ **Extras** Fruit, flowers - complimentary **Parking** 4 **Notes** LB ⊛

SHAFTESBURY
Map 4 ST82

La Fleur de Lys Restaurant with Rooms

★★★★★ ⚙⚙ RESTAURANT WITH ROOMS

tel: 01747 853717 **Bleke St SP7 8AW**
email: info@lafleurdelys.co.uk **web:** www.lafleurdelys.co.uk
dir: From junct of A30 & A350, 0.25m towards town centre

Located just a few minutes' walk from the famous Gold Hill, this light and airy restaurant with rooms combines efficient service with a relaxed and friendly atmosphere. Bedrooms, which are suitable for both business and leisure guests, vary in size but all are well equipped, comfortable and tastefully furnished. A relaxing guest lounge and courtyard are available for afternoon tea or pre-dinner drinks. The excellent food has been awarded two AA Rosettes.

Rooms 8 en suite (2 fmly) (1 GF) S £80-£130; D £100-£170 **Facilities** FTV Lounge tea/coffee Dinner available Direct Dial WiFi ⚲ **Extras** Home-made biscuits, fresh milk - complimentary **Conf** Max 12 Board 10 **Parking** 10 **Notes** LB ⊗ Closed 1-21 Jan No coaches

SHAFTESBURY *continued*

The Fontmell

★★★★ ⬚ INN

tel: 01747 811441 **Crown Hill, Fontmell Magna SP7 0PA**
email: info@thefontmell.com **web:** www.thefontmell.com

This warm and welcoming pub was formerly known as The Crown, but was re-named following extensive refurbishment in 2010. The result is a stylish and comfortable environment, complete with a stream flowing between the bar and the dining room. Relaxation is guaranteed; a great place to linger over a pint at the bar, or curl up on the sofa and peruse the newspapers. Bedrooms offer impressive quality and comfort, and each has its own unique identity. The kitchen presents a range of flavour-packed dishes, based on the best of local, seasonal produce.

Rooms 6 rms (6 pri facs) **Facilities** FTV DVD TVL tea/coffee Dinner available Direct Dial WiFi ⬚ ⅃ 18 Fishing Riding ⬚ **Parking** 30 **Notes** No coaches

SHERBORNE	Map 4 ST61

See also Corton Denham (Somerset)

Premier Collection

Munden House

★★★★★ ⬚ GUEST ACCOMMODATION

tel: 01963 23150 **Munden Ln, Alweston DT9 5HU**
email: stay@mundenhouse.co.uk **web:** www.mundenhouse.co.uk
dir: *A352 from Sherborne, left onto A3030 to Alweston, at Oxfords Bakery sign, turn left into Mundens Ln. Munden House 100yds on right*

Munden House is a delightful property set in a quiet lane away from the main road, with pleasant views over the surrounding countryside. Bedrooms and bathrooms come in a variety of shapes and styles but all are very well decorated and furnished; the beds are especially comfortable. Guests are welcome to use the lounge and garden. Breakfast includes a selection of high quality hot and cold dishes, all carefully prepared to order.

Rooms 5 en suite 3 annexe en suite (2 fmly) (4 GF) D £85–£140* **Facilities** FTV Lounge tea/coffee Licensed WiFi ⬚ ⬚ **Extras** Speciality toiletries, mineral water - free **Parking** 11 **Notes** LB

Premier Collection

The Kings Arms

★★★★★ ⬚ INN

tel: 01963 220281 **Charlton Horethorne DT9 4NL**
email: admin@thekingsarms.co.uk **web:** www.thekingsarms.co.uk
dir: *From A303 follow signs for Templecombe & Sherborne onto B3145 to Charlton Horethorne*

Situated in the heart of this engaging village, The Kings Arms offers impressive standards throughout. The experienced owners have created something for everyone with a convivial bar, snug and choice of dining environments, including the garden terrace with lovely countryside views. Bedrooms have individuality, quality and style with marble bathrooms, robes and wonderful showers. Food is taken seriously here, with an assured team producing a menu showcasing the best of local produce.

Rooms 10 en suite (1 fmly) D fr £135* **Facilities** FTV DVD Lounge tea/coffee Dinner available Direct Dial Lift WiFi ⬚ ⅃ 18 **Conf** Thtr 70 Class 45 Board 50 **Parking** 30 **Notes** Closed 25 Dec RS 26 Dec no dinner served No coaches

The Rose and Crown Inn, Trent

★★★★★ ⊜ INN

tel: 01935 850776 **Trent DT9 4SL**
email: info@theroseandcrowntrent.co.uk **web:** www.theroseandcrowntrent.co.uk
dir: *Just off A30 between Sherborne & Yeovil*

The Rose and Crown dates from the 14th century and is a quintessential country inn with a long and interesting history. Packed full of character, this is a place where relaxation comes easily, with crackling fires adding to the atmosphere and charm. Bedrooms are accessed externally, and each has high levels of comfort and quality, with stylish bathrooms and cosseting extras. They also have patio areas with lovely views across the rolling countryside. Food is taken seriously here and creative and flavoursome dishes are offered.

Rooms 3 annexe en suite (3 GF) S £65-£100; D £75-£125 **Facilities** FTV DVD iPod docking station Lounge tea/coffee Dinner available WiFi ⚓ **Extras** Speciality toiletries, home-made cookies **Parking** 30 **Notes** No coaches

The Alders

★★★★ BED AND BREAKFAST

tel: 01963 220666 **Sandford Orcas DT9 4SB**
email: info@thealdersbb.com **web:** www.thealdersbb.com
dir: *3m N of Sherborne. Off B3148 signed Sandford Orcas, near Manor House in village*

Located in the charming conservation area of Sandford Orcas and set in a lovely walled garden, this delightful property offers attractive, well-equipped bedrooms. Guests have their own entrance leading from the garden. A large inglenook fireplace with a wood-burning stove can be found in the comfortable sitting room, which also features the owner's watercolours. Massage therapies are available.

Rooms 3 en suite (1 fmly) S £60-£75; D £70-£85 **Facilities** FTV TVL tea/coffee WiFi ⚓ **Parking** 4 **Notes** ⊗ ⊜

STURMINSTER NEWTON Map 4 ST71

The Old Post Office

★★★ BED AND BREAKFAST

tel: 01258 475590 **Marnhull Rd, Hinton St Mary DT10 1NG**
email: info@northdorsetbandb.co.uk **web:** www.northdorsetbandb.co.uk
dir: *A30 onto B3092 signed Sturminster Newton, on right after 5m*

Built in the 1830s, The Old Post Office provides pleasant and relaxing accommodation with charming features such as low doorways and unusual angles in the floors and walls. Comfortable beds are provided in the two rooms; one is en suite and the other has private facilities. Guests are welcome to use the pleasant rear garden and relaxing guest lounge where a TV is provided (rather than in the bedrooms). Off-street parking is available.

Rooms 2 rms (1 en suite) (1 pri facs) S £55-£60; D £70-£75* **Facilities** TVL tea/coffee WiFi ⚓ **Parking** 2 **Notes** ⊗ No Children 16yrs ⊜

SWANAGE Map 5 SZ07

Swanage Haven

★★★★★ ⌕ ⊜ GUEST HOUSE

tel: 01929 423088 **3 Victoria Rd BH19 1LY**
email: info@swanagehaven.com **web:** www.swanagehaven.com

Swanage Haven is a boutique-style guest house close to Swanage beach and the coastal path. Exclusively for adults, the accommodation is contemporary, with many extras such as fluffy robes, slippers, hot tub and WiFi. The hands-on owners provide excellent hospitality with a relaxed and friendly service. The breakfasts are superb – top quality organic and local produce are featured on the extensive menu.

Rooms 7 en suite **Facilities** FTV TVL tea/coffee Dinner available Licensed WiFi ↝ ⚓ 18 Hot tub Holistic treatment room **Parking** 7 **Notes** ⊗ No Children 16yrs

The Castleton

★★★★ GUEST ACCOMMODATION

tel: 01929 423972 **1 Highcliffe Rd BH19 1LW**
email: stay@thecastleton.co.uk **web:** www.thecastleton.co.uk
dir: *From town centre follow seafront towards Studland Rd, 110yds after leaving Promenade on right*

A charming and luxurious Victorian house, full of character and located just 100 metres from Swanage's glorious beach. The Castleton provides elegant, well-equipped bedrooms and bathrooms, and is just a short stroll along the seafront from the town centre and its many attractions. Breakfast is served at separate tables in the light-filled dining area.

Rooms 10 en suite (2 fmly) (1 GF) S £60-£80; D £100-£238* **Facilities** FTV DVD TVL tea/coffee WiFi ⚓ 18 ⚓ **Parking** 4 **Notes** ⊗ Closed Dec-2 Jan

SWANAGE *continued*

Rivendell

★★★★ ⚜ GUEST HOUSE

tel: 01929 421383 **58 Kings Rd BH19 1HR**
email: kevin@rivendell-guesthouse.co.uk **web:** www.rivendell-guesthouse.co.uk

This beautiful period house, located within easy reach of the beach and town centre, has been lovingly restored to retain many of the original features. The bedrooms have been upgraded to a very good standard and can accommodate a diverse clientele. An award-winning breakfast is served in the cosy dining room.

Rooms 9 en suite (1 fmly) **Facilities** FTV DVD TVL tea/coffee WiFi **Notes** ⊗

Corner Meadow

★★★★ BED AND BREAKFAST

tel: 01929 423493 & 07930 486347 **24 Victoria Av BH19 1AP**
email: geogios@hotmail.co.uk **web:** www.cornermeadow.co.uk
dir: *In Victoria Av, opposite main beach car park*

Diane and Roy make guests feel very welcome at their comfortable and well appointed bed and breakfast, just five minutes' level walk from the beach, steam railway and town centre. All bedrooms are en suite, and private parking is available at the rear of the premises.

Rooms 4 en suite (1 fmly) (1 GF) S £72-£76; D £86-£94 **Facilities** FTV DVD WiFi ⚄
Extras Fridge **Parking** 4 **Notes** ⊗ Closed 6 Oct-1 May ⚐

The Limes

★★★★ GUEST HOUSE

tel: 01929 422664 **48 Park Rd BH19 2AE**
email: info@limeshotel.net **web:** www.limeshotel.net
dir: *Follow one-way system, signed to Durlston Country Park. Pass Trattoria restaurant on left, right into Park Rd, 200mtrs on right*

Ideally located for both the town centre and the seafront, this comfortable establishment offers a variety of different bedroom shapes and sizes. In addition to the pleasant dining room, guests are free to use the small bar area and the popular games room.

Rooms 12 rms (10 en suite) (7 fmly) S £46-£58; D £97-£98 **Facilities** FTV DVD Lounge tea/coffee Licensed WiFi Pool table ⚄ **Conf** Max 25 Thtr 25 Class 20 Board 16 **Parking** 8 **Notes** LB

Caythorpe House

★★★ GUEST ACCOMMODATION

tel: 01929 422892 **7 Rempstone Rd BH19 1DN**
email: enquiries@caythorpehouse.co.uk **web:** www.caythorpehouse.co.uk
dir: *A351 to Swanage. Right at lights opposite church, Caythorpe House at junct*

Conveniently located just a short stroll from the seafront and town centre, this elegant Edwardian villa is a perfect place from which to enjoy the many delights Swanage has to offer. A warm and genuine welcome is assured, with every effort made to ensure a relaxing and rewarding break whether for business or pleasure. Bedrooms are light and airy with all the expected comforts, and a variety of configurations to suit all needs. Breakfast is a satisfying start, and helpful advice for the day ahead is always on offer. A guest lounge is also provided and there is ample off-road parking.

Rooms 7 rms (4 en suite) (3 fmly) (2 GF) S £42-£45; D £84-£90* **Facilities** FTV DVD iPod docking station TVL tea/coffee WiFi ⚄ **Parking** 6 **Notes** ⊗ No Children 10yrs Closed 17 Oct-1 Apr

Oxford House

★★★ GUEST ACCOMMODATION

tel: 01929 422247 **5 Park Rd BH19 2AA**
email: enquiries@theoxfordswanage.com **web:** www.theoxfordswanage.co.uk
dir: *Follow signs for town centre, pass Mowlem Theatre on left. Turn left opposite White Swan, 2nd right into Park Rd*

Located just a three-minute walk from Swanage pier, Oxford House offers relaxed and informal accommodation. The property also benefits from being close to the town centre and beach. Cooked breakfasts are served in the front dining room.

Rooms 6 rms (5 en suite) (1 pri facs) (2 fmly) S £40; D £70-£80 **Facilities** FTV DVD tea/coffee WiFi **Notes** ⊗ No Children 5yrs Closed Oct-Mar

TARRANT MONKTON	**Map 4 ST90**

The Langton Arms

★★★★ ⚐ INN

tel: 01258 830225 **DT11 8RX**
email: info@thelangtonarms.co.uk **web:** www.thelangtonarms.co.uk
dir: *Exit A354 in Tarrant Hinton to Tarrant Monkton, through ford, Langton Arms opposite*

Tucked away in a sleepy Dorset village, The Langton Arms offers stylish, light and airy accommodation and is a good base for touring this attractive area. Bedrooms, all at ground-floor level in the modern annexe, are very well equipped and comfortable. Diners can choose between the relaxed bar-restaurant and the more formal Stables Restaurant, which offers innovative and appetising dishes. Breakfast is served in the conservatory dining room just a few steps across the pretty courtyard.

Rooms 6 annexe en suite (6 fmly) (6 GF) S £80; D £100* **Facilities** FTV tea/coffee Dinner available Direct Dial WiFi **Conf** Max 70 Thtr 70 Class 70 Board 70 **Parking** 100 **Notes** Closed 25-26 Dec Civ Wed 60

WAREHAM	**Map 4 SY98**

Kingston Country Courtyard

★★★★ GUEST ACCOMMODATION

tel: 01929 481066 **Kingston, Nr Corfe Castle BH20 5LR**
email: relax@kingstoncountrycourtyard.com **web:** www.kingstoncountrycourtyard.com
dir: *Through Corfe Castle towards Swanage (A351), turn right onto B3069. Through village, up steep hill, sharp left hand bend, Kingston Country Courtyard 0.25m on left*

Situated amid the beautiful Purbeck Hills, the views from this house include historic Corfe Castle and the distant shores of the Isle of Wight. A variety of comfortable guest bedrooms is on offer and breakfast is served in the spacious dining hall.

Rooms 25 en suite (3 fmly) (21 GF) S £40-£85; D £100-£170* **Facilities** FTV Lounge tea/coffee Licensed WiFi ⚄ **Conf** Max 100 Thtr 100 Class 100 Board 50 **Parking** 100 **Notes** LB Closed 24 Dec-3 Jan RS wknds may be closed due to weddings Civ Wed 130

Worgret Manor

★★★ GUEST ACCOMMODATION

tel: 01929 552957 **Worgret Rd BH20 6AB**
email: admin@worgretmanor.co.uk **web:** www.worgretmanor.co.uk
dir: *A351 to Wareham. Take A352 signed Dorchester. 0.5m to manor on left*

Worgret Manor is a grand Georgian manor house perfectly situated for exploration of this beautiful area with the Saxon market town of Wareham just a mile away. Comfortable bedrooms provide good levels of space with period features adding to the character and charm. Breakfast provides a satisfying start to the day and friendly and helpful service is always on offer.

Rooms 3 en suite (1 GF) **Facilities** FTV tea/coffee Licensed WiFi ⌛ **Parking** 8 **Notes** ⊗ No Children 16yrs

WEST LULWORTH   Map 4 SY88

Bishops
★★★★ 🍴 GUEST ACCOMMODATION

tel: 01929 400552 & 07956 102371 **Lulworth Cove BH20 5RQ**
email: bishopscottagelulworth@gmail.com **web:** www.bishopscottage.co.uk

Bishops is located 100 metres from beautiful Lulworth Cove, and offers high quality en suite bedrooms, a bar that opens daily, and a restaurant offering fish and vegetarian dishes. During spring and summer guests can enjoy afternoon tea outside. Breakfast is served in the contemporary dining room, with dishes based on locally sourced ingredients. Additional facilities include an outdoor pool with seating area offering stunning views of the cove.

Rooms 6 en suite 2 annexe en suite (2 fmly) **Facilities** STV FTV TVL tea/coffee Dinner available Licensed WiFi ⌇ Riding ⌛ **Extras** Robes, snacks **Notes** Civ Wed 150

WEYMOUTH   Map 4 SY67
See also Portland

Swallows Rest
★★★★ 🍴 BED AND BREAKFAST

tel: 01305 785244 & 07747 753656 **Martleaves Farm, South Rd, Wyke Regis DT4 9NR**
email: jane.furlong@btinternet.com **web:** www.swallowsrestselfcatering.co.uk
dir: *From Weymouth on Portland road, follow brown tourism signs*

This beautiful rural B&B with coastal views has highly individual bedrooms. Each is richly decorated and well equipped; ideal for any type of break. Public areas include a comfortable lounge and the dining area, which is a sociable setting for breakfast. Parking is available, and there is also a campsite, and some self-catering apartments. The owners have their own pigs, chickens, ducks and alpacas, and the grounds are full of character.

Rooms 5 en suite (1 fmly) S £50-£80; D £75-£115* **Facilities** FTV TVL tea/coffee WiFi ⌛ **Extras** Speciality toiletries, home-made cakes, chocolates **Parking** 16 **Notes** LB ⊗ No Children 5yrs Closed 24-26 Dec Civ Wed 30

The Esplanade
★★★★ 🍴 GUEST ACCOMMODATION

tel: 01305 783129 & 07515 657116 **141 The Esplanade DT4 7NJ**
email: stay@theesplanadehotel.co.uk **web:** www.theesplanadehotel.co.uk
dir: *On seafront, between Jubilee Clock & pier bandstand*

Dating from 1835, this attractive property is located on the seafront and offers wonderful views from the elegant dining room and stylish first-floor lounge. There's a genuine enthusiasm here, with a warm welcome assured. The comfortable bedrooms are thoughtfully equipped, including Egyptian cotton sheets and towels, and many rooms have sea views. Breakfast is a showcase of local produce with an extensive menu.

Rooms 11 en suite (3 fmly) (2 GF) **Facilities** FTV TVL tea/coffee Licensed WiFi **Parking** 9 **Notes** ⊗ Closed Nov-Feb

Florian Guest House
★★★★ GUEST HOUSE

tel: 01305 773836 & 07460 442166 **59 Abbotsbury Rd DT4 0AQ**
email: enquiryflorian@aol.com **web:** www.florianguesthouse.co.uk
dir: *At junct of A354 & A353 into Abbotsbury Rd. 500yds on left after St Pauls Church*

Situated about ten minutes' walk from the town centre, beach and local attractions, this welcoming property offers bedrooms in a range of shapes and sizes, and is ideally situated for a family seaside holiday or a short break. Breakfast is taken in the comfortably furnished downstairs dining area.

Rooms 6 rms (5 en suite) (1 pri facs) (1 fmly) (1 GF) S £40-£68; D £45-£75 (room only)* **Facilities** FTV DVD tea/coffee WiFi ⌛ **Extras** Fridge **Parking** 5 **Notes** LB ⊗

Kingswood
★★★★ GUEST ACCOMMODATION

tel: 01305 784926 & 07899 770920 **55 Rodwell Rd DT4 8QY**
email: kingwood55@sky.com **web:** www.kingswoodhotel.com
dir: *On A354 up hill towards Portland from inner harbour, on left after lights*

Handily located for both Weymouth and Portland, this welcoming establishment provides spacious guest accommodation, including larger suites with jacuzzi baths. The building has a long and interesting history, including a period when it was commandeered for American officers during World War II. The bedrooms are well appointed and comfortable, as are the public areas. Breakfast is served in the attractive dining room. Just a stroll away is Brewers Quay, a lovely area in which to while away an hour or two.

Rooms 10 rms (9 en suite) (1 pri facs) (2 GF) **Facilities** FTV Lounge tea/coffee WiFi **Extras** Fridges in most rooms **Parking** 20 **Notes** LB ⊗ Closed Nov-Feb

WEYMOUTH *continued*

St John's Guest House

★★★★ GUEST ACCOMMODATION

tel: 01305 775523 **7 Dorchester Rd DT4 7JR**
email: stjohnsguesthouse@googlemail.com **web:** www.stjohnsguesthouse.co.uk
dir: *Opposite St John's Church*

Located just 70 yards from the beach, St John's is an elegant building from around 1880. Hospitality here is warm and genuine, and the property has an appealing, uncluttered style. Standards are high throughout. Bedrooms have comfy beds and are all well equipped with such extras as DVD players and WiFi access. Breakfast is served in the light and airy dining room, a satisfying and tasty start to the day.

Rooms 7 en suite (2 fmly) (2 GF) **Facilities** FTV DVD tea/coffee WiFi **Parking** 10 **Notes** ⊗ No Children 4yrs

Barnes's Rest Weymouth

★★★ BED AND BREAKFAST

tel: 01305 779354 & 07582 707749 **165 Dorchester Rd DT4 7LE**
email: barnessrest@hotmail.co.uk **web:** www.bandbbarnessrestweymouth.co.uk
dir: *A354 into Weymouth. At Manor rdbt 1st exit onto B3159 (Dorchester Rd), on right just past doctors surgery*

This Victorian family home is ideally located for those visiting Weymouth for either business or pleasure. The welcome is warm and inviting, with every effort made to ensure a relaxing and rewarding stay. The handy location is just a ten minute stroll from the seafront. Bedrooms and bathrooms are light and airy with modern facilities and all the required necessities. Breakfast is served around the dining table with an ample choice for all appetites. Safe storage facilities are available for bikes and outdoor gear.

Rooms 3 en suite D £60-£87* **Facilities** FTV tea/coffee WiFi 🔒 **Parking** 2 **Notes** LB ⊗

Wadham Guesthouse

★★★ GUEST HOUSE

tel: 01305 779640 & 07717 899213 **22 East St DT4 8BN**
email: shirleystephenson@btconnect.com **web:** www.wadhamhouse.co.uk
dir: *Off S end of A353 The Esplanade*

This pleasant town centre property offers a range of rooms, and is a good base for touring or for a short stay. The comfortable bedrooms are attractively decorated, and home-cooked breakfasts are served in the ground-floor dining room. Parking permits are available.

Rooms 9 en suite (1 GF) S £38-£43; D £76-£86* **Facilities** FTV tea/coffee WiFi **Notes** LB ⊗ No Children 5yrs Closed Xmas & New Year RS Jan-Feb Limited rooms available

Beaufort Guesthouse

★★★ GUEST HOUSE

tel: 01305 782088 **24 The Esplanade DT4 8DN**
web: www.beaufortguesthouse.co.uk

Just a few steps from the sandy beach, this friendly, family-run establishment is ideally located for a seaside break. Bedrooms are soundly appointed with all the necessary essentials, likewise the modern showers. Some of the rooms have the added bonus of sea views. Breakfast is served in the lounge diner, which also has a bar to refresh and revive after a hard day enjoying the many and varied local attractions.

Rooms 6 rms (5 en suite) (1 pri facs) (1 fmly) S £30-£35; D £60-£70 **Facilities** FTV TVL tea/coffee Licensed WiFi **Notes** LB ⊗ Closed 23 Dec-1 Jan

The Cavendale

★★★ BED AND BREAKFAST

tel: 01305 786960 **10 The Esplanade DT4 8EB**
email: thecavendale@gmail.com **web:** http://weymouth.co.uk
dir: *Phone for directions*

Conveniently located right on the seafront with splendid views from some of the rooms, this cosy bed and breakfast offers a range of bedroom sizes, some with private bathrooms. Guests are welcome to use the lounge, where in addition to a large range of videos, they can join in with the current on-the-go jigsaw. Helpfully, parking permits for nearby car parks are available.

Rooms 9 rms (6 en suite) (3 pri facs) (5 fmly) S £32-£36; D £68-£75* **Facilities** FTV DVD TVL tea/coffee WiFi **Extras** Fridges in en suite rooms **Notes** LB ⊗ Closed 24 Dec-2 Jan

The Edenhurst

★★★ GUEST HOUSE

tel: 01305 771255 **122 The Esplanade DT4 7ER**
email: enquiries@edenhurstweymouth.com **web:** www.edenhurstweymouth.com
dir: *Phone for directions*

Just a step across the road from the beach and within walking distance of the railway and bus stations, this smartly presented establishment is a perfect base from which to explore the local area. A number of bedroom styles are offered, some having balconies and wonderful sea views; all have modern bathrooms. Breakfast is served in the elegant, sea-facing dining room, and a guest lounge is also provided.

Rooms 12 rms (11 en suite) (1 pri facs) (4 fmly) S £39-£51; D £78-£115*
Facilities FTV TVL tea/coffee WiFi **Extras** Bottled water - complimentary **Notes** LB ⊗

The Lugger Inn

★★★ INN

tel: 01305 766611 & 07787 872737 **30 West St, Chickerell DT3 4DY**
email: info@theluggerinn.co.uk **web:** www.theluggerinn.co.uk
dir: *Follow B3157 coastal road to Bridport. 3m from centre of Weymouth turn right at Chickerell Hill into West St*

The Lugger is a charming inn, within easy reach of Weymouth. It offers comfortable accommodation in a peaceful setting. Carefully prepared dinners are enjoyed in the warm atmosphere of the bar-restaurant. The inn benefits from outside seating and ample parking space.

Rooms 14 en suite (6 fmly) (3 GF) S £72-£82; D £82-£95* **Facilities** STV FTV TVL tea/coffee Dinner available WiFi ⌂ 18 ☕ **Conf** Max 50 Class 50 Board 30 **Parking** 30

WIMBORNE MINSTER   Map 5 SZ09

Premier Collection

Les Bouviers Restaurant with Rooms

★★★★★ ◉◉ ☕ RESTAURANT WITH ROOMS

tel: 01202 889555 **Arrowsmith Rd, Canford Magna BH21 3BD**
email: info@lesbouviers.co.uk **web:** www.lesbouviers.co.uk
dir: *A31 onto A349. Left in 0.6m. In approx 1m right into Arrowsmith Rd. Establishment approx 100yds on right*

Les Bouviers is an excellent restaurant with rooms in a great location, set in five and a half acres of grounds. Food is obviously a highlight of any stay here, as is the friendly, attentive service. Chef patron Leonard James Coward's team turn out impressive cooking, which has been recognised with two AA Rosettes. The bedrooms are extremely well equipped and the beds are supremely comfortable. Cream teas can be taken on the terrace.

Rooms 6 en suite (4 fmly) **Facilities** FTV DVD Lounge tea/coffee Dinner available Direct Dial WiFi ch fac All bathrooms have steam showers or air baths **Extras** Robes, slippers, mineral water **Conf** Max 120 Thtr 100 Class 100 Board 100 **Parking** 50 **Notes** LB RS Sun eve restricted opening & restaurant closed Civ Wed 120

COUNTY DURHAM

BARNARD CASTLE   Map 19 NZ01

Homelands Guest House

★★★★★ ☕ GUEST HOUSE

tel: 01833 638757 & 07725 363330 **85 Galgate DL12 8ES**
email: enquiries@homelandsguesthouse.co.uk **web:** www.homelandsguesthouse.co.uk
dir: *From A1(M) onto A67 to Barnard Castle. Guest house on left on A67(Galgate)*

This beautiful Victorian town house is conveniently located for the Yorkshire Dales and is only 20 minutes from the A1(M). Guests are welcome to use the attractive lounge, where there is an honesty bar and complimentary WiFi is also provided. The attractively presented bedrooms are thoughtfully equipped and include a garden room. Breakfast features a wide choice of hot and cold items and high quality, locally sourced ingredients. The friendly proprietors also welcome families.

Rooms 4 rms (3 en suite) (1 pri facs) 1 annexe en suite (1 fmly) (1 GF) S £50-£55; D £85-£90 **Facilities** FTV Lounge tea/coffee Dinner available Licensed WiFi ☕

Three Horseshoes

★★★★ INN

tel: 01833 631777 **5-7 Galgate DL12 8EQ**
email: info@three-horse-shoes.co.uk **web:** www.three-horse-shoes.co.uk

The Three Horseshoes is a family-owned and run inn. It is modern with very good design throughout the refurbished bedrooms, en suite bathrooms, and public areas. Real ales and home-cooked food are a feature, with an ever-changing menu and competitively priced wine list. Private parking and sun terrace add to the features of this beautifully restored inn.

Rooms 7 en suite 4 annexe en suite (1 fmly) (2 GF) S £70-£115; D £80-£125*
Facilities FTV DVD tea/coffee Dinner available Direct Dial WiFi ☕ **Parking** 12 **Notes** ⊗

Strathmore Lawn East

★★★★ ☕ GUEST ACCOMMODATION

tel: 01833 637061 & 07790 006920 **81 Galgate DL12 8ES**
email: strathmorelawn@gmail.com **web:** www.strathmorelawneast.co.uk
dir: *From A66 to Barnard Castle, through town centre into Galgate. On right opposite chemist*

Located just five minutes' walk from the main high street, pubs and restaurants, Strathmore Lawn East is a great base for visiting the Yorkshire Dales. Expect a warm and friendly welcome at this Victorian town house, where bedrooms are comfortable, pleasantly furnished and well equipped. Memorable breakfasts with local produce, home-made bread and preserves are served in the pleasant dining room with guests seated at one table. Special dietary requirements and individual preferences are catered for.

Rooms 3 rms (2 en suite) (1 pri facs) 1 annexe en suite D £80 **Facilities** FTV Lounge tea/coffee Dinner available WiFi ⌂ 18 ☕ **Extras** Bottled water, speciality toiletries - free **Notes** LB No Children 2yrs Closed 22 Dec-4 Jan

CHESTER-LE-STREET — Map 19 NZ25

The Lambton Worm

★★★★ ⊜ INN

tel: 0191 387 1162 **North Rd DH3 4AJ**
email: info@thelambton.com web: www.thelambton.com
dir: *A1(M) junct 63 onto A167, 0.7m on left*

Named after a local legend that inspired Bram Stoker's 1911 novel, *The Lair of the White Worm*, this boutique inn offers comfortable and well-appointed bedrooms. Real ales come from the local parent company, Sonnet 43 Brew House, while the award-winning food is locally sourced and of a very good standard. The team are friendly and helpful making this property a real little gem.

Rooms 14 en suite (2 fmly) **Facilities** FTV iPod docking station Lounge tea/coffee Dinner available WiFi ⅃ 18 🔒 **Parking** 24 **Notes** ⊗

CROOK — Map 19 NZ13

The Quarry Burn Guest House and Restaurant

★★★★ ⟟ ⊜ GUEST HOUSE

tel: 01388 608336 & 07967 826413 **1 Helmington Square, Hunwick DL15 0LH**
email: jbell27@sky.com web: www.thequarryburn.co.uk

The Quarry Burn Guest House and Restaurant is ideally located in the quiet village of Hunwick, within easy striking distance of Durham city centre and the A1. A family run business, it's a well-established restaurant which added four contemporary bedrooms in 2015. Quality decor, flooring and comfortable beds, with smart TVs and WiFi throughout. The lively restaurant serves popular, freshly prepared dishes, and service is warm and genuine. The secluded beer garden is a real sun trap and a perfect place to sit and have a drink in fine weather.

Rooms 4 en suite (2 fmly) S £65; D £85* **Facilities** FTV TVL tea/coffee Dinner available Licensed WiFi **Notes** ⊗ RS Mon Pub closed, accommodation available

DURHAM — Map 19 NZ24

The Old Mill

★★★★ ⊜ INN

tel: 01740 652928 **Thinford Rd, Metal Bridge DH6 5NX**
email: office@oldmilldurham.co.uk web: www.oldmilldurham.co.uk
dir: *5m S of Durham. A1(M) junct 61, A688 S for 1.5m, left at rdbt, sharp right*

This traditional, family-owned inn is in a countryside setting yet is only a mile from the A1. There is a friendly atmosphere and the bar and dining areas are full of character. Food is served throughout the day and evening, with the vast menu displayed on blackboards. Bedrooms are spacious and well equipped. Complimentary WiFi is provided.

Rooms 12 en suite S £60-£65; D £70-£75* **Facilities** STV FTV DVD tea/coffee Dinner available Direct Dial WiFi 🔒 **Conf** Max 40 Thtr 40 Class 40 Board 25 **Parking** 40 **Notes** ⊗ Closed 26 Dec RS 25 Dec bookings only

The Kingslodge Inn

★★★ ⊜ INN

tel: 0191 370 9977 **Waddington St, Flass Vale DH1 4BG**
email: enquiries@kingslodgeinn.co.uk web: www.kingslodgeinn.co.uk

In a wonderful location, just minutes away from the city centre but surrounded by woodland, The Kingslodge Inn has undergone a massive refurbishment programme with very good results. Modern bedrooms are well appointed offering quality and comfort. The inn offers a wide array of beverages with real ales always on tap. Food, as with the other properties in The Inn Collection, is very good, with a wide choice on offer. Service and hospitality are both warm and genuine. Outdoor seating in the gardens is an added benefit as is the off-road car parking.

Rooms 23 en suite (3 fmly) (2 GF) S £79-£125; D £95-£125* **Facilities** FTV tea/coffee Dinner available WiFi **Parking** 25

The Garden House Inn

AA Advertised

tel: 0191 386 3395 **Framwellgate Peth DH1 4NQ**
email: gardenhouseinn@hotmail.co.uk web: www.gardenhouseinn.com

Close to the centre of Durham and the River Wear, The Garden House Inn is a classic British pub with a welcoming bar complete with exposed beams and dark wood furniture. Bedrooms are comfortable and stylishly decorated.

Rooms 6 en suite

HESLEDEN — Map 19 NZ43

The Ship Inn

★★★★ ⊜ INN

tel: 01429 836453 & 07760 767448 **High Hesleden TS27 4QD**
email: sheila@theshipinn.net web: www.theshipinn.net
dir: *A19 onto B1281 signed Blackhall. Follow Hesleden signs to High Hesleden*

The Ship Inn has some wonderful sea views from its well-appointed and comfortable bedrooms. The bar is cosy and welcoming and has an impressive selection of well-kept real ales. Dinner is served in the spacious, comfortable restaurant and log fires burn brightly on cooler evenings. Sympathetically restored over a number of years, many of the original features of this fine old property are still in place. Free WiFi and secure parking is provided.

Rooms 6 en suite 3 annexe en suite (3 fmly) (6 GF) S £70-£75; D fr £85* **Facilities** STV FTV DVD TV7B tea/coffee Dinner available WiFi 🔒 **Extras** Fruit - complimentary **Conf** Max 45 Thtr 45 Class 25 Board 25 **Parking** 25 **Notes** ⊗ RS Mon

LANCHESTER
Map 19 NZ14

The Old Post Office
★★★★ GUEST HOUSE

tel: 01207 528420 & 07917 108481 **27 Front St DH7 0LA**
email: keithgill51@talktalk.net **web:** www.theoldpostofficelanchester.com
dir: *From Durham on A691, follow signs to Consett. Turn left signed Lanchester village centre, then immediately right into Front St. On right hand side by post box*

Located in the historic town of Lanchester, this Grade II listed building dates back to 1788 and has been lovingly restored by the current owners. Bedrooms are spacious and very comfortable, with thoughtful extras provided as standard. Great care has gone into choosing suppliers for breakfast items, and the delightful gardens to the rear add to the quality of this wonderful property.

Rooms 3 en suite (1 fmly) **Facilities** FTV Lounge tea/coffee WiFi 🔒 **Extras** Fruit - complimentary **Parking** 3

PETERLEE
Map 19 NZ44

The Bell Guest House
★★★★ GUEST HOUSE

tel: 0191 586 3863 **Sunderland Rd SR8 4PF**
email: info@thebellguesthouse.com **web:** www.thebellguesthouse.com
dir: *From A19 onto A1086 (Sunderland road)*

The Bell Guest House is located in Horden, just a few minutes from the sea. The house gets its name from the previous owner Henry Bell who purchased the property back in 1925. It has recently been refurbished but kept plenty of its charm and character. Bedrooms are well appointed and comfortable, while the coach bar and lounge are warm and welcoming. The Bell Guest House is ideally located for Hartlepool, Sunderland, Newcastle and Durham.

Rooms 9 en suite (2 fmly) S £39-£50; D £75* **Facilities** FTV TVL tea/coffee Licensed WiFi 🔒 **Notes** Closed 24-26 Dec

SEAHAM
Map 19 NZ44

The Seaton Lane Inn
★★★★ INN

tel: 0191 581 2038 **Seaton Ln, Seaton Village SR7 0LP**
email: info@seatonlaneinn.com **web:** www.seatonlaneinn.com
dir: *A19 S of Sunderland on B1404 between Seaham & Houghton*

Set on the edge of the quiet village of Seaton, close to Seaham and the A19, the inn is popular with visitors and locals alike and is a blend of modern and traditional. The emphasis is on food here with interesting home-made dishes offered in the restaurant and bar. The bedrooms, located in the adjoining building, are modern, spacious and smartly furnished.

Rooms 18 en suite (1 GF) **Facilities** FTV TVL tea/coffee Dinner available Direct Dial WiFi ⚓ 18 Fishing **Extras** Speciality toiletries **Parking** 36 **Notes** ⊗

ESSEX

CHELMSFORD
Map 6 TL70

The Lion Inn
★★★★ INN

tel: 01245 394900 **Main Rd, Boreham CM3 3JA**
email: info@lioninnhotel.co.uk **web:** www.lioninnhotel.co.uk
dir: *A12 junct 19 onto B1137 to Maldon. 0.75m on right*

The Lion Inn offers stylish and comfortably appointed accommodation; well-equipped with flat-screen TVs, free WiFi, and full air-conditioning it appeals to leisure and business guests alike. Many rooms benefit from balconies or direct access to the private garden. The spacious bar and restaurant is open-plan style with additional seating in the Victorian conservatory. Guests can enjoy a wide selection of good classic pub dishes with a continental twist; a cooked and continental breakfast is served daily.

Rooms 15 en suite 8 annexe en suite (1 fmly) (9 GF) D £110-£250* **Facilities** tea/coffee Dinner available Direct Dial WiFi **Conf** Max 150 Thtr 150 Class 50 Board 20 **Parking** 150 **Notes** ⊗ Closed 24-26 Dec RS All BHs No coaches Civ Wed

CLACTON-ON-SEA | Map 7 TM11

The Chudleigh

★★★★ GUEST ACCOMMODATION

tel: 01255 425407 **13 Agate Rd, Marine Parade West CO15 1RA**
email: chudleighhotel@btconnect.com **web:** www.chudleighhotel.com
dir: With sea on left, cross lights at pier, turn into Agate Rd at mini rdbt

Conveniently situated for the seafront and shops, this immaculate property has been run by the friendly owners Peter and Carol Oleggini for more than 50 years. Bedrooms are most attractive with co-ordinating decor and well chosen fabrics. Breakfast is served in the smart dining room and there is a cosy lounge with plush sofas.

Rooms 10 en suite (2 fmly) (2 GF) S £55; D £85 **Facilities** FTV TVL tea/coffee Direct Dial Licensed WiFi 🔒 **Extras** Speciality toiletries, chocolates - free **Parking** 7 **Notes** No Children 18 months Closed Oct RS 1wk Mar/Apr

Pond House B&B (TM143164)

★★★★ 🍴 FARMHOUSE

tel: 01255 820458 & 07855 914064 **Earls Hall Farm, Earls Hall Dr CO16 8BP**
email: brenda_lord@farming.co.uk **web:** www.earlshallfarm.info
dir: A133 onto B1027 signed St Osyth, after 2m turn right into Earls Hall Drive. Follow to end & signs for Pond House

This charming Victorian farmhouse is surrounded by mature gardens and enjoys lovely countryside views. Bedrooms are all attractively presented, very comfortable and equipped with a host of thoughtful little extras. Guests can enjoy woodland walks on this working farm, or watch the birds while enjoying a hearty breakfast from the extensive menu (sourced locally wherever possible). Home-made cake and refreshments are offered in the sitting room on arrival, and on return from days out.

Rooms 2 en suite S £55-£60; D £75-£80* **Facilities** FTV DVD Lounge tea/coffee WiFi 🚣 18 Fishing 🔒 **Extras** Juice, snacks, magazines **Parking** 3 **Notes** LB ⊗ No Children 12yrs 300 acres arable/beef

COLCHESTER | Map 13 TL92

Black Bond Hall Bed and Breakfast

★★★★ BED AND BREAKFAST

tel: 01206 735776 & 07909 516013 **Lodge Ln, Langenhoe CO5 7LX**
email: gill@blackbondhall.co.uk **web:** www.blackbondhall.co.uk
dir: A12 junct 26 signed to Mersea (B1025). Through Abberton & Langenhoe pass x-rds & garage, 1st left into School Rd & Fingringhoe Range. 1st right into Lodge Ln, on right

Black Bond Hall is ideally situated for Colchester and attractions such as The Beth Chatto Gardens, Dedham, Rowhedge, Abberton Reservoir, Mersea Island and Fingringhoe Nature Reserves. The two comfortable double rooms provide tea- and coffee-making facilities, TV, WiFi and hairdryer. Guests can expect a warm welcome, with home-made cake on arrival, as well as tea and coffee. Breakfast is sourced from local produce and is served in either the modern breakfast room overlooking the garden, or the traditional dining room. There are local pubs for evening meals.

Rooms 2 en suite D £90* **Facilities** FTV tea/coffee WiFi 🛏 🔒 **Extras** Snacks **Parking** 8 **Notes** LB ⊗ No Children 12yrs 🚭

DEDHAM | Map 13 TM03

Premier Collection

The Sun Inn

★★★★★ 🌸🌸 🍴 INN

tel: 01206 323351 **High St CO7 6DF**
email: office@thesuninndedham.com **web:** www.thesuninndedham.com
dir: In village centre opposite church

The Sun Inn is a charming 15th-century coaching inn situated in the centre of Dedham, opposite the church. The carefully decorated bedrooms include four-poster and half-tester beds, along with many thoughtful touches. The open-plan public rooms have a wealth of character with inglenook fires, oak beams and fine oak panelling, and the food in the restaurant has been awarded two AA Rosettes.

Rooms 7 en suite S £90-£130; D £145 **Facilities** FTV DVD iPod docking station Lounge tea/coffee Dinner available WiFi 🔒 **Extras** Speciality toiletries, mineral water **Parking** 15 **Notes** LB Closed 25-28 Dec

GESTINGTHORPE | Map 13 TL83

Premier Collection

The Pheasant

★★★★★ 🌸 🍴 INN

tel: 01787 465010 & 461196 **Audley End CO9 3AU**
email: thepheasantpb@aol.com **web:** www.thepheasant.net
dir: Phone for directions

Close to the Suffolk/Essex border, The Pheasant enjoys stunning countryside views and a lovely location in the heart of the village of Gestingthorpe. The bar is charming and features wood-burning stoves, low ceilings and a good choice of local real ales. Dinner is not to be missed and much of the produce is grown on the pub's own plot of land. The five spacious bedrooms in the coach house are beautifully presented and are all individually designed. An ideal base from which to explore the surrounding countryside and pretty Suffolk villages.

Rooms 5 en suite (2 fmly) (2 GF) **Facilities** FTV tea/coffee Dinner available Direct Dial WiFi 🚣 18 🔒 **Extras** Speciality toiletries, home-made cookies **Parking** 25 **Notes** LB Closed 1st 2wks Jan No coaches

GREAT DUNMOW — Map 6 TL62

Dunmow Guest House
★★★★ BED AND BREAKFAST

tel: 01371 859138 & 07740 724626 **46 Stortford Rd CM6 1DL**
email: enquiries@dunmowguesthouse.co.uk web: www.dunmowguesthouse.co.uk
dir: *On Stortford Rd, 100yds from Queen Victoria pub, on opposite side of road*

Dunmow Guest House is conveniently located, close to Stansted Airport and a short walk into the pretty market town of Great Dunmow. The historic villages of Thaxted and Saffron Walden are nearby, as are many historic houses and the Freeport designer village. Spacious modern bedrooms are beautifully presented and feature super king-size beds. The indoor pool is very popular with guests as are the games room and fantastic home cinema.

Rooms 3 rms (2 en suite) (1 pri facs) S £89-£125; D £89-£125* **Facilities** FTV DVD TVL tea/coffee WiFi 🦢 Private cinema Games room **Extras** Speciality toiletries, soft drinks - complimentary **Parking** 3 **Notes** ⊗ No Children 18yrs

Harwood House
★★★★ GUEST ACCOMMODATION

tel: 01371 874627 **52 Stortford Rd CM6 1DN**
email: info@harwoodhousestansted.com web: www.harwoodhousestansted.com
dir: *M11 junct 8 onto A120 signed Stansted/Colchester. Exit onto B1256 signed Great Dunmow, over 3 rdbts & take 1st exit at 4th. Harwood House on left*

A charming period house located in the quaint market town of Great Dunmow. Harwood House offers guests large comfortable bedrooms and a warm welcome is guaranteed from the friendly proprietors. Ample secure parking is provided and the house is conveniently located close to the main road network and a short drive from Stansted Airport. Free WiFi is available throughout the house and freshly cooked breakfasts are served in conservatory breakfast room.

Rooms 8 en suite (1 fmly) (3 GF) S £55-£65; D £60-£85 (room only)* **Facilities** FTV iPod docking station Lounge TVL tea/coffee Licensed WiFi 🔓 **Parking** 20 **Notes** ⊗

GREAT TOTHAM — Map 7 TL81

The Bull & Willow Room at Great Totham
★★★★ ◉◉ RESTAURANT WITH ROOMS

tel: 01621 893385 & 894020 **2 Maldon Rd CM9 8NH**
email: reservations@thebullatgreattotham.co.uk web: www.thebullatgreattotham.co.uk
dir: *Exit A12 at Witham junct to Great Totham*

A 16th-century coaching inn located in the village of Great Totham, The Bull is now a very stylish restaurant with rooms that offers en suite bedrooms with satellite TVs with Freeview; WiFi is available throughout. Guests can enjoy dinner in the gastro-pub or in the two AA Rosette award-winning fine dining restaurant, The Willow Room.

Rooms 4 annexe en suite (2 GF) S fr £80; D fr £90* **Facilities** STV FTV Lounge tea/coffee Dinner available WiFi 🔓 18 **Conf** Max 60 Thtr 40 Class 40 Board 16 **Parking** 80 **Notes** LB Closed 25 Dec

GREAT YELDHAM — Map 13 TL73

Premier Collection

The White Hart
★★★★★ ◉◉ INN

tel: 01787 237250 **Poole St CO9 4HJ**
email: restaurant@whitehartyeldham.com web: www.whitehartyeldham.com
dir: *On A1017 in village*

The White Hart is a large timber-framed character building that includes the main restaurant and bar areas while the bedrooms are located in the converted coach house; all are smartly appointed and well equipped with many thoughtful extras. The comfortable lounge and bar and the beautifully landscaped gardens provide areas for relaxation. Locally sourced produce is used on menus in the main house restaurant which is popular with local residents and guests alike.

Rooms 13 en suite (2 fmly) (6 GF) **Facilities** FTV TVL tea/coffee Dinner available Direct Dial WiFi **Conf** Max 200 Thtr 200 Class 200 Board 50 **Parking** 80 **Notes** LB Closed 1-18 Jan Civ Wed 130

HARWICH — Map 13 TM23

The Goodlife Guesthouse
★★★ GUEST ACCOMMODATION

tel: 01255 556565 & 242440 **162 High St, Dovercourt CO12 3AT**
email: mike@clickyourfingers.com web: www.goodlifehotel.co.uk
dir: *On Dovercourt High Street, opposite park*

This recently renovated establishment is located in the centre of Harwich. The accommodation is modern in style and very spacious, both in the bedrooms and the main dining and lounge areas. There is a private car park located on site, and a park directly opposite with good views of the sea which is only 150 metres from the house. A cooked breakfast is served daily in the dining area.

Rooms 10 en suite (2 fmly) S £42-£44; D £47-£53 (room only)* **Facilities** STV FTV TVL tea/coffee Lift Licensed WiFi 🔓 9 Snooker Pool table 🔓 **Parking** 24

HATFIELD HEATH — Map 6 TL51

Lancasters Farm (TL544149)
★★★★ FARMHOUSE

tel: 01279 730220 **Chelmsford Rd CM22 7BB**
dir: *A1060 from Hatfield Heath for Chelmsford, 1m left on sharp right bend, through white gates*

Guests are made to feel at home at this delightfully spacious house, which is at the heart of this large working arable farm close to Stansted Airport. Bedrooms vary in size and style, but all are smartly decorated and thoughtfully equipped. Garaging can be arranged, as can transport to and from the airport.

Rooms 4 rms (3 en suite) (1 pri facs) S £48; D £96* **Facilities** FTV Lounge tea/coffee WiFi **Parking** 6 **Notes** ⊗ No Children 12yrs Closed 14 Dec-4 Jan ⊜ 260 acres arable

MALDON
Map 7 TL80

The Bell

★★★ GUEST HOUSE

tel: 01621 843208 **2 Silver St CM9 4QE**
email: info@thebellmaldon.co.uk **web:** www.thebellmaldon.co.uk
dir: *Phone for directions*

Centrally located to explore the historic town of Maldon and surrounding areas, this attractive guest house used to be a pub in a previous life and many original features can still be found around the property. The bedrooms offer good accommodation, while breakfast is served in the former cellar. Limited parking is available.

Rooms 4 rms (2 en suite) (2 pri facs) S £50-£90; D £60-£100* **Facilities** FTV DVD TVL tea/coffee Direct Dial WiFi 🏃 18 🔒 **Parking** 2 **Notes** LB ⊗ No Children 6yrs ⌨

MANNINGTREE
Map 13 TM13

Premier Collection

Dairy House Farm *(TM148293)*

★★★★★ FARMHOUSE

tel: 01255 870322 & 07749 073974 **Bradfield Rd CO11 2SR**
email: bridgetwhitworth353@gmail.com **web:** www.dairyhousefarm.info

(For full entry see Wix)

SAFFRON WALDEN
Map 12 TL53

Bendysh Hall Bed & Breakfast *(TL606389)*

★★★★ FARMHOUSE

tel: 01799 599220 & 07950 750684 **Ashdon Rd, Radwinter CB10 2UA**
email: info@bendyshhallbedandbreakfast.co.uk
web: www.bendyshhallbedandbreakfast.co.uk
dir: *From Saffron Walden on B1053 towards Radwinter, through village, turn left signed Ashdon. Bendysh Hall 1m on right*

Bendysh Hall Bed & Breakfast is located in a quiet spot close to Saffron Walden and offers a comfortable night's sleep. A beautiful Grade II listed building that has been thoughtfully renovated over the years keeping some of the period features of the house. The farm consists of 300 acres of land and guests are welcome to take a walk/cycle through the woods. A hearty breakfast makes good use made of high quality ingredients and eggs from the farm.

Rooms 3 rms (2 en suite) (1 pri facs) D £70-£90* **Facilities** FTV DVD Lounge TVL tea/coffee WiFi Fishing 🔒 **Extras** Snacks - complimentary; robes **Parking** 10 **Notes** LB No Children 5yrs 300 acres arable/poultry

The Cross Keys

★★★★ ⌨ INN

tel: 01799 522207 **32 High St CB10 1AX**
email: info@theoldcrosskeys.co.uk **web:** www.theoldcrosskeys.co.uk

Enjoying a prominent position in the busy market town of Saffron Walden, The Cross Keys is an authentic coaching inn dating back some 850 years. It offers guests a range of beautifully presented, individually styled bedrooms. The stylish restaurant is very popular and there is a real buzz in the small bar area in the evenings. Free WiFi is available, along with some secure parking.

Rooms 9 en suite S £90-£110; D £100-£120* **Facilities** FTV iPod docking station tea/coffee Dinner available WiFi 🏃 18 **Parking** 6 **Notes** ⊗ No coaches

The Crown Inn

★★★ ⌨ INN

tel: 01799 522475 **Little Walden CB10 1XA**
email: pippathecrown@aol.com **web:** www.thecrownlittlewalden.co.uk
dir: *M11 junct 9 follow signs for Saffron Walden. In Saffron Walden, left at lights signed Thaxted. At mini rdbt left towards Little Walden (B1052)*

This charming country inn enjoys a prominent position in the pretty village of Little Walden and has a choice of three cosy, comfortable bedrooms. All are individually styled and well equipped. Free WiFi is available throughout the property and there is secure parking for guests. There's a great atmosphere in the authentic bar, and an extensive choice of home-cooked meals on the evening menu.

Rooms 3 en suite S fr £75* **Facilities** FTV DVD tea/coffee Dinner available WiFi **Conf** Max 40 Thtr 40 Class 30 Board 30 **Parking** 30

SOUTHEND-ON-SEA
Map 7 TQ88

The Ilfracombe House

★★★★ GUEST ACCOMMODATION

tel: 01702 351000 **9-13 Wilson Rd SS1 1HG**
email: info@ilfracombe-hotel.co.uk **web:** www.ilfracombe-hotel.co.uk
dir: *500yds W of town centre. Exit A13 at Cricketers pub into Milton Rd, 3rd left into Cambridge Rd, 4th right, car park in Alexandra Rd*

The Ilfracombe House lies in Southend's conservation area, just a short walk from the cliffs, gardens and the beach. The public rooms include a dining room, lounge and a cosy bar, and the well-equipped bedrooms include deluxe options and two four-poster rooms.

Rooms 20 en suite (4 fmly) (2 GF) **Facilities** STV FTV DVD TVL tea/coffee Dinner available Direct Dial Licensed WiFi **Extras** Mini-fridge **Conf** Max 15 **Parking** 9 **Notes** ⊗

STANSTED AIRPORT

Map 6 TL52

See also Bishop's Stortford (Hertfordshire)

The White House

★★★★ GUEST ACCOMMODATION

tel: 01279 870257 **Smiths Green CM22 6NR**
email: enquiries@whitehousestansted.co.uk **web:** www.whitehousestansted.co.uk
dir: *M11 junct 8, B1256 towards Takeley. Through lights at Four Ashes x-rds. 400yds, corner of B1256 & Smiths Green*

The White House is a delightful 16th-century property situated close to Stansted Airport (but not on the flight path). The stylish bedrooms feature superb beds, luxurious bathrooms and many thoughtful touches. Traditional breakfasts, served in the farmhouse-style kitchen, are made from local ingredients; evening meals are available at the Lion and Lamb, a nearby pub/restaurant owned by the proprietors, who can usually provide transport to and from The White House.

Rooms 3 rms (2 en suite) (1 pri facs) (3 fmly) S £50-£70; D £70-£80* **Facilities** FTV DVD tea/coffee Dinner available WiFi 🔒 **Extras** Robes, speciality toiletries, bottled water **Conf** Max 25 **Parking** 6 **Notes** ⊗ Closed 24-25, 31 Dec & 1 Jan

STANSTED MOUNTFITCHET

Map 12 TL52

Premier Collection

Linden House

★★★★★ 🏠 GUEST HOUSE

tel: 01279 813003 **1-3 Silver St CM24 8HA**
email: stay@lindenhousestansted.co.uk **web:** www.lindenhousestansted.co.uk
dir: *M11 junct 8 towards Newport on A120, on right after windmill*

Linden House enjoys a prominent position in the heart of Stansted Mountfitchet and is a short drive from the airport. This fine property has individually designed bedrooms, all beautifully presented and very luxurious. The cosy bar has a good choice of local ales and an extensive wine list. Freshly-cooked breakfasts are not to be missed. Free WiFi is available throughout the property and there is parking nearby.

Rooms 9 en suite (1 fmly) (2 GF) **Facilities** DVD iPod docking station tea/coffee Dinner available Licensed WiFi **Extras** Speciality toiletries, home-made cookies **Notes** LB ⊗

THAXTED

Map 12 TL63

Steepleview Bed & Breakfast

★★★★ BED AND BREAKFAST

tel: 01371 831263 & 07949 589325 **Steepleview, 61 Newbiggen St CM6 2QS**
email: info@steepleviewthaxted.co.uk **web:** www.steepleviewthaxted.co.uk

Steepleview is a charming family run B&B in the pretty village of Thaxted and offers guests a choice of beautifully presented, well equipped and comfortable bedrooms. Breakfast is served in the well-appointed breakfast room and the conservatory lounge is available for guests. Free WiFi is available along with secure parking and Steepleview is ideally located for Stansted Airport.

Rooms 2 en suite **Facilities** FTV iPod docking station Lounge tea/coffee WiFi 🔒 **Parking** 2 **Notes** ⊗ Closed Xmas

The Farmhouse Inn

★★★ INN

tel: 01371 830864 **Monk Street CM6 2NR**
email: info@farmhouseinn.org **web:** www.farmhouseinn.org
dir: *M11 to A120 to B184, 1m from Thaxted, between Thaxted & Great Dunmow*

This 16th-century inn overlooks the Chelmer Valley, and is surrounded by open countryside. The property is ideally situated in the quiet hamlet of Monk Street about two miles from the historic town of Thaxted. Bedrooms are pleasantly decorated and equipped with modern facilities. Public rooms include a cosy lounge bar and a large, smartly appointed restaurant.

Rooms 11 annexe en suite **Facilities** FTV tea/coffee Dinner available WiFi **Conf** Max 80 Thtr 80 Class 60 Board 50 **Parking** 35

THORPE BAY

See Southend-on-Sea

TOPPESFIELD

Map 12 TL73

Ollivers Farm

★★★ BED AND BREAKFAST

tel: 01787 237642 **CO9 4LS**
web: www.essex-bed-breakfast.co.uk
dir: *500yds SE of village centre. Off A1017 in Great Yeldham to Toppesfield, farm 1m on left before T-junct to village*

Full of charm and character, this impressive 16th-century farmhouse is set amid pretty landscaped gardens in a peaceful rural location. Bedrooms are pleasantly decorated and thoughtfully equipped. Public rooms have a wealth of original features including exposed beams and there is a huge open fireplace in the reception hall.

Rooms 3 rms (1 en suite) (1 pri facs) S £50; D £75-£90* **Facilities** FTV Lounge tea/coffee WiFi 🔒 Shed for bikes **Parking** 4 **Notes** ⊗ No Children 10yrs Closed 23 Dec-1 Jan ⊛

WIX
Map 13 TM12

Premier Collection

Dairy House Farm (TM148293)
★★★★★ FARMHOUSE

tel: 01255 870322 & 07749 073974 **Bradfield Rd CO11 2SR**
email: bridgetwhitworth353@gmail.com **web:** www.dairyhousefarm.info
dir: Exit A120 into Wix, turn at x-rds to Bradfield, farm 1m on left

This Georgian house stands amid 550 acres of arable land, and is blessed with stunning views of the surrounding countryside. Extensively renovated in the Victorian style, it has original decorative tiled floors, moulded cornices and marble fireplaces. The spacious bedrooms are carefully furnished and equipped with many thoughtful touches. Breakfast is served in the elegant antique-furnished dining room and there is a cosy lounge.

Rooms 3 en suite S £55-£60; D £76-£86* **Facilities** FTV DVD TVL tea/coffee WiFi 🔒 Farm reservoir fishing **Extras** Home-made cake - complimentary **Parking** 8 **Notes** ⊗ No Children 12yrs ☙ 550 acres arable

GLOUCESTERSHIRE

ALDERTON
Map 10 SP03

Corner Cottage Bed and Breakfast
★★★★ 🛏 BED AND BREAKFAST

tel: 01242 620630 **Stow Rd GL20 8NH**
email: info@stayatcornercottage.co.uk **web:** www.stayatcornercottage.co.uk
dir: M5 junct 9 E onto A46 to rdbt then B4077 (Stow). Turn left opposite Alderton garage into Willowbank Rd, left again into drive & follow signs to car park

There is a warm and genuine welcome for all guests arriving at Corner Cottage, with helpful local advice always on offer if required. The location is an ideal base from which to explore this picturesque area, with Tewkesbury only a short drive away. Bedrooms offer good levels of comfort, with modern, well-appointed bathrooms. Breakfast is a generous and tasty offering, served around the table in the lounge-diner.

Rooms 4 en suite S £55-£80; D £70-£80* **Facilities** FTV TVL tea/coffee WiFi **Parking** 8 **Notes** ⊗ No Children 18yrs Closed Xmas/New Year & Jan

Tally Ho Bed & Breakfast
★★★★ BED AND BREAKFAST

tel: 01242 621482 & 07966 593169 **20 Beckford Rd GL20 8NL**
email: tallyhobb@aol.com **web:** www.cotswolds-bedandbreakfast.co.uk
dir: M5 junct 9, A46 signed Evesham, through Ashchurch. Take B4077 signed Stow-on-the-Wold & Alderton. Left in 1.5m opposite garage signed Alderton. Into village, pass Gardeners pub on right, Tally Ho on left

Convenient for the M5, this friendly establishment stands in a delightful quiet village. Bedrooms, including two on the ground floor, offer modern comforts and attractive co-ordinated furnishings. Breakfast is served in the stylish dining room, and for dinner, the village pub is just a stroll away.

Rooms 3 en suite (1 fmly) (2 GF) S £50-£55; D £70-£75 **Facilities** FTV DVD tea/coffee WiFi **Parking** 3 **Notes** LB

AMBERLEY
Map 4 SO80

The Amberley Inn
★★★★ 🛏 INN

tel: 01453 872565 **Culver Hill GL5 5AF**
email: enquiries@theamberleyinn.co.uk **web:** www.theamberleyinn.co.uk
dir: From A46 follow signs for Amberley, up Culver Hill, in village centre on left

This delightful inn is just outside Stroud, with walks from the door in all directions across the Woodchester Valley and commons. Pets are especially welcome here. Bedrooms offer a range of sizes with some located above the main inn and others in the separate Garden House. A range of real ales and wines are available in the traditional, welcoming bar and a selection of delicious bar and restaurant meals are offered, making good use of fine quality local produce.

Rooms 8 en suite 5 annexe en suite (2 fmly) (1 GF) S £65-£85; D £85-£105* **Facilities** FTV Lounge tea/coffee Dinner available Direct Dial WiFi ⚓ 18 🔒 **Extras** Speciality toiletries, robes **Conf** Max 30 **Parking** 7 **Notes** LB Civ Wed 35

ARLINGHAM
Map 4 SO71

The Old Passage Inn
★★★★ ◉◉ 🛏 RESTAURANT WITH ROOMS

tel: 01452 740547 **Passage Rd GL2 7JR**
email: oldpassage@btconnect.com **web:** www.theoldpassage.com
dir: A38 onto B4071 through Frampton on Severn. 4m to Arlingham, through village to river

Delightfully located on the very edge of the River Severn, this relaxing restaurant with rooms combines high quality food with an air of tranquillity. Bedrooms and bathrooms are decorated in a modern style, and have a collection of welcome extras including a well-stocked mini-bar. The menu offers a wide range of seafood and shellfish dishes including crab, oysters and lobsters from Cornwall, kept alive in seawater tanks. An outdoor terrace is available in warmer months.

Rooms 2 en suite **Facilities** FTV DVD Lounge tea/coffee Dinner available WiFi 🔒 **Extras** Mini-bar - chargeable **Parking** 30 **Notes** Closed 25 & 26 Dec RS Jan-Feb closed for dinner Tue & Wed No coaches

BARNSLEY
Map 5 SP00

Premier Collection

The Village Pub
★★★★★ 🛏 INN

tel: 01285 740000 & 740241 **GL7 5EF**
email: reservations@barnsleyhouse.com **web:** www.thevillagepub.co.uk
dir: On B4425 in centre of village

With a village location as its name suggests, this delightful establishment provides high quality accommodation and an efficient but relaxed style of hospitality and service. Owned by the same company as Barnsley House Hotel (across the road), guests here can enjoy an informal stay with high standards. The bar-dining room serves an excellent choice of top quality, seasonal produce and a varied choice of wines and ales. The bedrooms and bathrooms come in a range of sizes and all are comfortably furnished and equipped.

Rooms 6 rms (6 pri facs) (1 fmly) S £119-£139; D £129-£149* **Facilities** STV FTV DVD iPod docking station tea/coffee Dinner available Direct Dial WiFi 🐾⚓ 18 Riding **Parking** 20 **Notes** LB

BERKELEY
Map 4 ST69

The Malt House
★★★ INN

tel: 01453 511177 **22 Marybrook St GL13 9BA**
email: the-malthouse@btconnect.com **web:** www.themalthouse.uk.com
dir: *A38 into Berkeley, at town hall follow road to right, premises on right past hospital & opposite school*

Conveniently located for business and leisure travellers, this family-run inn has a convivial atmosphere. Bedrooms are soundly appointed while public areas include a choice of bars, a skittle alley and an attractive restaurant area. Local attractions include Berkeley Castle, and the Wildfowl & Wetlands Trust at Slimbridge.

Rooms 9 en suite (2 fmly) **Facilities** FTV tea/coffee Dinner available WiFi Pool table Skittle Alley **Parking** 30 **Notes** ⊗

BIBURY
Map 5 SP10

The Catherine Wheel
★★★★ ⌨ INN

tel: 01285 740250 **Arlington GL7 5ND**
email: rooms@catherinewheel-bibury.co.uk **web:** www.catherinewheel-bibury.co.uk
dir: *On B4425 between Burford & Cirencester*

This family-run inn provides a pleasant welcome and traditional country pub ambience. A range of seating is available in the cosy bar, or in the more formal dining room where a selection of carefully prepared dishes is offered throughout the day and evening. Bedrooms are in an adjacent building and include smaller standard rooms or larger superior rooms – all comfortably furnished and with some welcome extras.

Rooms 4 annexe en suite (4 GF) **Facilities** FTV DVD TVL tea/coffee Dinner available WiFi ⚓ **Parking** 23

BLAISDON
Map 10 SO71

Premier Collection

Blaisdon House B&B
★★★★★ ⌂ BED AND BREAKFAST

tel: 01452 830437 **GL17 0AH**
email: stay@blaisdonhouse.com **web:** www.blaisdonhouse.com
dir: *From A4136 follow signs for Blaisdon, opposite pub in village*

This delightful house was previously a vicarage with parts dating back to the 12th century. The new owners have spent many months completely renovating and updating the property to provide three high quality bedrooms and bathrooms, with a feel of luxury throughout. Tea is offered in the relaxing lounge on arrival. A carefully prepared delicious breakfast makes good use of local produce, served around a large table in the spacious dining room. There are many local walks from the house and the helpful proprietors are always glad to assist. The village inn is ideal for dinner, and is just opposite. AA Friendliest B&B of the Year Award Finalist 2016-2017.

Rooms 3 en suite S £60-£99; D £70-£125* **Facilities** STV FTV DVD Lounge tea/coffee WiFi ⚓ **Extras** Speciality toiletries **Parking** 3 **Notes** ⊗ No Children 13yrs

BOURTON-ON-THE-WATER
Map 10 SP12

Premier Collection

The Dial House
★★★★★ ⊛⊛⊛ ⌂ RESTAURANT WITH ROOMS

tel: 01451 822244 **High St GL54 2AN**
email: info@dialhousehotel.com **web:** www.dialhousehotel.com

With an idyllic location in the middle of the delightful village of Bourton-on-the-Water, this high quality accommodation offers a well judged mix of professional and efficient service with a relaxed and friendly ambience. Bedrooms and bathrooms offer a range of shapes and sizes and all are decorated and maintained to high standards. Off-street car parking and a pleasant garden are provided to the rear of the property. Dinner is a highlight, offering a range of carefully prepared dishes that combine fine English produce with French culinary techniques.

Rooms 9 en suite 5 annexe en suite (7 GF) **Facilities** FTV DVD Lounge tea/coffee Dinner available Direct Dial WiFi ⚓ Hot tub **Extras** Speciality toiletries **Conf** Max 20 Thtr 14 Class 14 Board 16 **Parking** 15 **Notes** No Children 10yrs Closed 1-8 Jan No coaches

The Mousetrap Inn
★★★ INN

tel: 01451 820579 **Lansdowne GL54 2AR**
email: thebatesies@gmail.com **web:** www.mousetrap-inn.co.uk

The Mousetrap Inn is a traditional and informal Cotswold hostelry located on the edge of this idyllic village just a few minutes' stroll from the centre. A selection of real ales and also home-cooked dinners (except Sundays and Mondays) are offered in the relaxed bar. Bedrooms and bathrooms vary in size and include three at ground floor level. Breakfast includes home-made sausages and free-range eggs.

Rooms 10 en suite (3 GF) **Facilities** tea/coffee Dinner available WiFi **Parking** 10 **Notes** ⊗ No Children 10yrs

CHELTENHAM   Map 10 SO92

Premier Collection

Beaumont House

★★★★★ GUEST ACCOMMODATION

tel: 01242 223311 **56 Shurdington Rd GL53 OJE**
email: reservations@bhhotel.co.uk **web:** www.bhhotel.co.uk
dir: S side of town on A46 to Stroud

Built as a private residence, popular Beaumont House exudes genteel charm.
Public areas include a large lounge and an elegant dining room which overlooks
the garden. The accommodation includes studio bedrooms on the top floor. These
complement the 'Out of Asia' and 'Out of Africa' bedrooms, which are luxuriously
furnished and very well equipped. Bedrooms situated to the rear of the building
have views over Leckhampton Hill, and there are also bedrooms on the lower
ground floor.

Rooms 16 en suite (3 fmly) S £75-£85; D £90-£284* **Facilities** STV FTV Lounge
tea/coffee Direct Dial Licensed WiFi 🏊 **Extras** Fruit, mineral water - free; mini-
bar - chargeable **Parking** 16 **Notes** ⊗ RS 25-26 Dec
No housekeeping services

Premier Collection

The Bradley

★★★★★ 🍴 GUEST ACCOMMODATION

tel: 01242 519077 & 07502 225031 **19 Royal Pde, Bayshill Rd GL50 3AY**
email: enquiries@thebradleyhotel.co.uk **web:** www.thebradleyhotel.co.uk

The Bradley is a boutique townhouse in the centre of Regency Cheltenham, just
a few minutes' stroll from the local shops and the town centre. Bedrooms and
bathrooms offer plenty of quality and comfort, and come in a range of shapes
and sizes. Breakfast utilises the best quality produce, and is served in the
elegant dining room. Parking permits can generally be arranged if booked in
advance.

Rooms 8 en suite (1 GF) S £90-£190; D £95-£195* **Facilities** FTV iPod docking
station Lounge tea/coffee Dinner available Licensed WiFi **Parking** 3
Notes No Children 9yrs

Premier Collection

Cleeve Hill House

★★★★★ 🍴 GUEST ACCOMMODATION

tel: 01242 672052 **Cleeve Hill GL52 3PR**
email: info@cleevehill-hotel.co.uk **web:** www.cleevehill-hotel.co.uk
dir: 3m N of Cheltenham on B4632

Many of the bedrooms and the lounge at this Edwardian property have
spectacular views across to the Malvern Hills. Room shapes and sizes vary but
all are comfortably furnished with many welcome extras; some have four-poster
beds. There is a relaxing guest lounge, and an honesty bar is in place.
Breakfast, served in the pleasant conservatory, offers a good selection of
carefully presented hot and cold items.

Rooms 10 en suite (1 GF) S £58-£68; D £98-£105* **Facilities** STV FTV DVD
Lounge tea/coffee Direct Dial Licensed WiFi **Parking** 11 **Notes** ⊗
No Children 8yrs

The Battledown Bed and Breakfast

★★★★ 🍴 BED AND BREAKFAST

tel: 01242 233881 & 07807 142069 **125 Hales Rd GL52 6ST**
email: info@thebattledown.co.uk **web:** www.thebattledown.co.uk
dir: 0.5m E of town centre. A40 onto B4075, 0.5m on right

Simon, Sarah and their daughter Isabella welcome you to their home, The
Battledown, a French colonial-style villa that was built in 1855. It is conveniently
located for the town centre, all of the events in Cheltenham and the surrounding
Cotswold countryside.

Rooms 7 en suite (2 fmly) S fr £65; D fr £85* **Facilities** FTV DVD Lounge tea/coffee
WiFi 🏊 **Parking** 7 **Notes** LB ⊗

Clarence Court

★★★★ 🍴 GUEST ACCOMMODATION

tel: 01242 580411 **Clarence Square GL50 4JR**
email: enquiries@clarencecourthotel.com **web:** www.clarencecourthotel.com

Situated in an attractive, tree-lined Georgian square, this property was once owned
by the Duke of Wellington. The building is charming and its elegant public rooms
reflect the grace of a bygone age. Spacious bedrooms offer ample comfort and
quality, and have many original features. The convenience of the peaceful location
is a great asset, only a five-minute stroll from the town centre. A varied range of
carefully prepared dishes is offered in the café-restaurant from noon to 9pm.

Rooms 20 en suite (3 fmly) (7 GF) S £65-£85; D £85-£150* **Facilities** FTV DVD TVL
tea/coffee Dinner available Direct Dial Licensed WiFi Free use of Fitness First
Leisure Club (Adults) **Parking** 21

Hope Orchard

★★★★ GUEST ACCOMMODATION

tel: 01452 855556 **Gloucester Rd, Staverton GL51 0TF**
email: info@hopeorchard.com **web:** www.hopeorchard.com
dir: A40 onto B4063 at Arlecourt rdbt. Hope Orchard 1.25m on right

Situated midway between Gloucester and Cheltenham, Hope Orchard is a good base
for exploring the area. The comfortable bedrooms are next to the main house, all are
on the ground floor, and each has its own separate entrance. There is a large
garden, and ample off-road parking is available.

Rooms 8 en suite (8 GF) **Facilities** FTV DVD tea/coffee Direct Dial WiFi 🏊
Extras Fridge, microwave **Parking** 10 **Notes** Closed 23 Dec-2 Jan

Malvern View

★★★★ GUEST ACCOMMODATION

tel: 01242 672017 & 07917 714929 **Cleeve Hill GL52 3PR**
web: www.malvernview.com
dir: B4632 from Cheltenham towards Winchcombe & Stratford-upon-Avon. Through
Southam & Cleeve Hill, Malvern View on right

Located just outside Cheltenham, most rooms in this comfortable accommodation
have delightful views over the countryside towards the Malverns and beyond.
Bedrooms and bathrooms here are all comfortably furnished and include some
welcome extras. Breakfast is made to order and offers a range of well-presented
options. Off-street car parking is another welcome feature.

Rooms 7 rms (6 en suite) (1 pri facs) (2 fmly) S £80; D £90-£120* **Facilities** FTV
iPod docking station Lounge tea/coffee Licensed WiFi ⚓ 18 🏊 **Conf** Max 30 Thtr 18
Class 30 Board 18 **Parking** 12 **Notes** LB Closed 4-29 Jan RS wknds min 2 night stay

Map 10 SP13

The Kings

★★★★ ◉◉ ⚲ RESTAURANT WITH ROOMS

tel: 01386 840256 & 841056 **The Square, High St GL55 6AW**
email: info@kingscampden.co.uk **web:** www.kingscampden.co.uk
dir: *In centre of town square*

Located in the centre of this delightful Cotswold town, The Kings effortlessly blends a relaxed and friendly welcome with efficient service. Bedrooms and bathrooms come in a range of shapes and sizes and all are appointed to a high level of quality and comfort. Dining options, whether in the main restaurant or the comfortable bar area, serve a tempting menu to suit all tastes, from light salads and pasta, to meat and fish dishes.

Rooms 14 en suite 5 annexe en suite (3 fmly) (3 GF) S £130-£305; D £130-£305*
Facilities FTV tea/coffee Dinner available Direct Dial WiFi **Conf** Thtr 30 Class 20
Board 20 **Parking** 14 **Notes** LB ⊗ Civ Wed 60

Lygon Arms

★★★★ ⚲ INN

tel: 01386 840318 & 840089 **High St GL55 6HB**
email: sandra@lygonarms.co.uk **web:** www.lygonarms.co.uk
dir: *In town centre near church*

This charming and welcoming inn sits on Chipping Campden's high street – a tranquil location with lots of tempting antique shops. Well managed by a friendly team, the inn has a cosy bar with open log fires and oak beams. Spacious and very well-appointed accommodation is provided in the main building and in mews houses. Both breakfast and dinner are hearty and should not be missed.

Rooms 10 en suite (3 fmly) (1 GF) **Facilities** FTV tea/coffee Dinner available Direct
Dial WiFi **Parking** 12 **Notes** No coaches

The Seagrave Arms

★★★★ ◉◉ RESTAURANT WITH ROOMS

tel: 01386 840192 **Friday St, Weston-sub-Edge GL55 6QH**
email: enquiries@seagravearms.com **web:** www.seagravearms.com
dir: *From Moreton-in-Marsh take A44 towards Evesham. Approx 7m right onto B4081 signed Chipping Campden. Becomes Sheep St. At junct with High Street, left into Dyers Ln. 0.5m over Dovers Hill, into Weston-sub-Edge, becomes Church St. Inn on left*

Part of The Epicurean Collection, this Grade II listed, 400-year-old house is set in the heart of the Cotswolds. It offers modern accommodation in the main house and also rooms around the courtyard. The inn is full of character, serving award-winning seasonal food every day of the week, with occasional specialist nights. Staff are warm and friendly, and the bar offers local ales and good wines. There is ample parking and attractive gardens.

Rooms 5 en suite 3 annexe en suite (3 GF) **Facilities** FTV tea/coffee Dinner available
WiFi **Parking Notes** No coaches

Holly House

★★★★ BED AND BREAKFAST

tel: 01386 593213 **Ebrington GL55 6NL**
email: jeffreyhutsby@yahoo.co.uk **web:** www.hollyhousebandb.co.uk
dir: *B4035 from Chipping Campden towards Shipston on Stour, 0.5m left to Ebrington & signed*

Set in the heart of the pretty Cotswold village of Ebrington, this late Victorian house offers thoughtfully equipped accommodation. Bedrooms are housed in buildings that were formerly used by the local wheelwright, and offer level access, seclusion and privacy. Quality English breakfasts are served in the light and airy dining room. For other meals, the village pub is just a short walk away.

Rooms 2 en suite 1 annexe en suite (2 fmly) (3 GF) S £55-£80; D £75-£85*
Facilities FTV Lounge tea/coffee WiFi **Parking** 5 **Notes** ⊗ ⊜

Map 4 ST78

The Moda House

★★★★ GUEST ACCOMMODATION

tel: 01454 312135 **1 High St BS37 6BA**
email: enquiries@modahouse.co.uk **web:** www.modahouse.co.uk
dir: *In town centre*

This popular, Grade II listed Georgian house has an imposing position at the top of the High Street. It has been appointed to provide modern bedrooms of varying shapes and sizes, and has comfortable public areas that have retained many original features. Room facilities include satellite TV and phones.

Rooms 8 en suite 3 annexe en suite (3 GF) S £62-£67; D £87-£105* **Facilities** STV
FTV Lounge TVL tea/coffee Direct Dial Licensed WiFi **Conf** Max 20 Thtr 10 Board 10
Notes No Children 16yrs

CIRENCESTER | Map 5 SP00

Premier Collection

The Fleece at Cirencester

★★★★★ 🍽 ☕ INN

tel: 01285 658507 **Market Place GL7 2NZ**
email: relax@thefleececirencester.co.uk **web:** www.thefleececirencester.co.uk

Located in the heart of the market town of Cirencester, this country inn has been finished to a high standard with guests and comfort in mind. Bedrooms are sumptuous, and many thoughtful touches add to the stay. Public areas include a traditional bar featuring Thwaites cask ales, a cosy lounge and a popular restaurant.

Rooms 28 en suite (1 fmly) **Facilities** FTV Lounge tea/coffee Dinner available WiFi **Parking** 8

Greensleeves

★★★★ BED AND BREAKFAST

tel: 01285 642516 & 07971 929259 **Baunton Ln, Stratton GL7 2LN**
email: johnps1@tesco.net **web:** www.greensleeves4u.co.uk
dir: From Cirencester, follow signs for Stratton. Right into Baunton Ln

Guests are ensured of a warm and friendly welcome from proprietor John, at this delightful property, just a short drive from Cirencester. Smart en suite accommodation, with off-street parking, is well equipped with a host of facilities to ensure both leisure and corporate guests feel at home. Delicious breakfasts feature home-baked bread.

Rooms 3 en suite **Facilities** FTV DVD tea/coffee WiFi ⚽ 🐾 **Parking** 5

The Old Brewhouse

★★★★ BED AND BREAKFAST

tel: 01285 656099 **7 London Rd GL7 2PU**
email: info@theoldbrewhouse.com **web:** www.theoldbrewhouse.com

The Old Brewhouse dates back to the 17th century and is situated in the centre of Cirencester, a short walking distance from a range of shops and restaurants. This butter-coloured town house has been fully refurbished to a high standard. Bedrooms are comfortable, many with original features, and all have good quality en suite bathrooms. The conservatory provides a comfortable seating area and leads onto a pretty courtyard garden, an unusual feature. A small car park is located to the rear of the property.

Rooms 10 en suite

COLEFORD | Map 4 SO51

The Rock B&B

★★★★ GUEST ACCOMMODATION

tel: 01594 837893 **Hillersland GL16 7NY**
email: chris@stayattherock.com **web:** www.stayattherock.com
dir: A40 at Monmouth onto A4136. 5m, left at Five Acres into Park Rd. At Christchurch right, immediately left towards Symonds Yat Rock, 0.75m S of Symonds Yat Rock

The Rock B&B offers stylish modern accommodation and is located on the outskirts of Coleford, near the famous Symonds Yat Rock. Bedrooms are attractively presented and very comfortable, with new garden rooms making the most of the spectacular views over the Wye Valley. Very popular with walkers, The Rock also caters well for business guests. Breakfasts are served in the spacious dining room overlooking the garden.

Rooms 7 annexe en suite (5 GF) S £40-£45; D £60-£90* **Facilities** FTV Lounge tea/coffee WiFi 🛁 Hot tub **Parking** 20 **Notes** LB No Children 12yrs

The Miners Country Inn

★★★ 🍽 INN

tel: 01594 836632 **Chepstow Rd, Sling GL16 8LH**
web: www.theminerssling.co.uk
dir: 1m from Coleford town centre

The Miners is a real family affair, set in the heart of the Forest of Dean. First impressions are of a quintessential pub with beamed ceilings, stone floors and a bar offering an array of local ales. A strong local trade makes for a bustling atmosphere, but really it's the food that's the focus. The chef-patron uses locally sourced ingredients, and suppliers are championed on blackboards and menus, with most supplying the inn exclusively. Dishes are well conceived and offer classic hearty fare with a modern twist. Bedrooms are light and airy, with modern en suite bathrooms.

Rooms 4 en suite **Facilities** FTV tea/coffee Dinner available

COWLEY | Map 10 SO91

The Green Dragon Inn

★★★★ ☕ INN

tel: 01242 870271 **Cockleford GL53 9NW**
email: green-dragon@buccaneer.co.uk **web:** www.green-dragon-inn.co.uk

The Green Dragon offers all the charm and character of an English country pub combined with a relaxed atmosphere and carefully prepared food made with local produce; dinner is particularly recommended. Bedrooms, some at ground floor level, are individually furnished and vary in size. There is a terrace at the front where guests may enjoy a drink on warmer days.

Rooms 9 annexe en suite (3 fmly) (4 GF) S £70-£105; D £95-£175* **Facilities** tea/coffee Dinner available Direct Dial WiFi **Extras** Fresh milk, fruit **Conf** Max 100 Thtr 100 Class 65 Board 65 **Parking** 40 **Notes** LB Closed 25 Dec eve-26 Dec eve & 1 Jan eve

DIDMARTON | Map 4 ST88

The Kings Arms

★★★★ ☕ INN

tel: 01454 238245 **The Street GL9 1DT**
email: enquiries@kingsarmsdidmarton.co.uk **web:** www.kingsarmsdidmarton.co.uk
dir: M4 junct 18, A46 towards Stroud. 6m, right onto A433. 3m to Didmarton. Kings Arms on left

Part of The Epicurean Collection, The Kings Arms is a real gem. Bedrooms, converted from the old stables, are extremely comfortable, and are named after hounds who ran with the local hunt. Locally sourced produce is cooked with passion and presented with flair. The inn has been fully restored but retains its stone-flagged floors, heavy wooden tables, rustic walls and simple decoration. Real ales are also a feature. Outside, the garden provides a great space in the summer.

Rooms 6 en suite **Facilities** FTV tea/coffee Dinner available WiFi **Conf** Max 30 Thtr 30 Board 18 **Parking Notes** No coaches

THE WHARF HOUSE

AWARD-WINNING WATERSIDE RESTAURANT WITH ROOMS

MODERN BRITISH AND EUROPEAN CUISINE WITH A TWIST

Tasting Menu at The Wharf House Six Courses only £39.99 per person.

Lighter lunches including paninis from £4.50 and deli boards from £13 now available.

Luxury accommodation with stunning riverside views.

01452 332 900
www.thewharfhouse.co.uk

Over, Gloucester, GL2 8DB
enquiries@thewharfhouse.co.uk

Directions: Turn off the A40 at traffic lights
250 yds west of Over Roundabout
(junction A40/A417). GR SO 816197

All profits from The Wharf House will be used for the promotion and restoration of the Hereford & Gloucester Canal.

EBRINGTON
Map 10 SP14

The Ebrington Arms
★★★★★ ◉◉ 🍸 INN

tel: 01386 593223 **GL55 6NH**
email: info@theebringtonarms.co.uk **web:** www.theebringtonarms.co.uk
dir: *From Chipping Campden take B4035 towards Shipston on Stour, left to Ebrington*

Nestled in the quiet, unspoilt village of Ebrington, just a couple of miles from Chipping Campden, this 17th-century inn offers an excellent selection of real ales, fine wines and really enjoyable award-winning cuisine utilising the finest of produce. Food is served in the friendly bar or in the cosy dining room where the open fire roars on chilly days. Bedrooms are full of character and include some welcome extras. A large beer garden and car park are also available.

Rooms 5 en suite **Facilities** FTV tea/coffee Dinner available WiFi **Extras** Home-made cookies, sherry - complimentary **Conf** Max 32 Thtr 32 Class 32 Board 25 **Parking** 10 **Notes** ⊗

FALFIELD
Map 4 ST69

The Park
★★★★ ⬤ GUEST ACCOMMODATION

tel: 01454 260550 **Gloucester Rd GL12 8DR**
email: info@theparkfalfield.co.uk **web:** www.theparkfalfield.co.uk
dir: *M5 junct 14 follow signs for A38 & Falfield (B4509). 1m on left*

With easy access to the M5 this stylish accommodation has recently been completely refurbished throughout to provide high levels of quality and comfort. Bedrooms offer a range of shapes and sizes and an impressive black and white decor theme runs throughout the building. Guests can enjoy breakfast and dinner in the comfortable dining room or a light snack in the bar area. Welcome extras include a full license and ample car parking. The pleasant surrounding gardens with outdoor seating also make this a popular wedding venue.

Rooms 10 en suite (1 fmly) **Facilities** FTV DVD TVL tea/coffee Dinner available Direct Dial Licensed WiFi **Conf** Thtr 70 Class 24 Board 30 **Parking** 50 **Notes** ⊗ Civ Wed 100

FRAMPTON MANSELL
Map 4 SO90

The Crown Inn
★★★★ ⬤ INN

tel: 01285 760601 **GL6 8JG**
email: enquiries@thecrowninn-cotswolds.co.uk **web:** www.thecrowninn-cotswolds.co.uk
dir: *Off A419 signed Frampton Mansell, 0.75m at village centre*

This establishment was a cider house in the 17th century, and guests today will find that roaring log fires, locally brewed ales and traditional, home-cooked food are all on offer. The comfortable, well-equipped bedrooms are in an annexe, and ample parking is available.

Rooms 12 annexe en suite (1 fmly) (4 GF) S £69.50-£89.50; D £89.50-£105* **Facilities** tea/coffee Dinner available WiFi **Conf** Max 40 **Parking** 35 **Notes** LB

GLOUCESTER
Map 10 SO81

The Wharf House Restaurant with Rooms
★★★★ ◉ RESTAURANT WITH ROOMS

tel: 01452 332900 **Over GL2 8DB**
email: enquiries@thewharfhouse.co.uk **web:** www.thewharfhouse.co.uk
dir: *From A40 between Gloucester & Highnam exit at lights for Over. Establishment signed*

The Wharf House was built to replace the old lock cottage and, as the name suggests, it is located at the very edge of the river; it has pleasant views and an outdoor terrace. The bedrooms and bathrooms have been finished to a high standard, and there are plenty of guest extras. Seasonal, local produce can be enjoyed both at breakfast and dinner in the delightful AA Rosetted restaurant.

Rooms 7 en suite (1 fmly) (1 GF) D fr £95* **Facilities** STV FTV DVD Lounge tea/coffee Dinner available WiFi Fishing 🛁 **Extras** Speciality toiletries - free; Mini-bar - chargeable **Parking** 37 **Notes** Closed 22 Dec-8 Jan RS Sun & Mon Check in before 6pm/rest closed evening No coaches

See advert on page 153

GUITING POWER
Map 10 SP02

Guiting Guest House

★★★★ BED AND BREAKFAST

tel: 01451 850470 **Post Office Ln GL54 5TZ**
email: info@guitingguesthouse.com web: www.guitingguesthouse.com

Guiting Power is a quintessential, beautiful and peaceful Cotswold village, surrounded by stunning countryside, and well placed for exploring the entire region. Guiting Guest House is very close to the village shop, post office, the church and two excellent pubs. A 16th-century Cotswold-stone farmhouse with warming log fires in the winter, and a delightful garden, it offers comfortable rooms, breakfasts with local produce and home-made bread, and a friendly, peaceful atmosphere; all of which have made it a favourite with guests from all over the world. There are lots of walks right from the garden gate. Some bedrooms have four-poster beds, and baskets of fresh fruit and flowers provide a personal touch. Hairdryer, bathrobes and toiletries are provided for extra comfort.

Rooms 5 rms (4 en suite) (1 pri facs) (2 GF) **Facilities** FTV Lounge tea/coffee WiFi ♨ ♨ **Extras** Fresh fruit, flowers, robes - complimentary **Notes** ⊗ Closed 25-26 Dec

HYDE
Map 4 SO80

The Ragged Cot

★★★★ ⊜ INN

tel: 01453 884643 & 07976 011198 **Cirencester Rd GL6 8PE**
email: info@theraggedcot.co.uk web: www.theraggedcot.co.uk
dir: *M5 junct 13 onto A419 signed Stroud/Cirencester. At Ashton Down Airfield rdbt, right signed Minchinhampton. 2m on left*

Originally a 17th-century coaching inn, the property has been extended and offers a modern, large, airy bar and restaurant with a selection of good quality bedrooms equipped for the modern day traveller. An extensive collection of ever-changing artwork is an interesting feature. This friendly inn serves a wide selection of real ales and a menu focusing on locally sourced ingredients.

Rooms 9 en suite (4 GF) **Facilities** FTV DVD tea/coffee Dinner available WiFi ♨ 36
Extras Speciality toiletries **Parking** 30 **Notes** No coaches

LECHLADE ON THAMES
Map 5 SU29

The Riverside

★★★ INN

tel: 01367 252534 **Park End Wharf GL7 3AQ**

Located on the banks of the Thames, with an unrivalled position in Lechlade, this traditional inn is within easy reach of Swindon, Cirencester and the Cotswolds. Comfortable accommodation is located adjacent to the inn with its own entrance, all rooms are en suite with some suitable for families. Great British fare is served either in the main bar and dining rooms or, weather permitting, outside. Owned by the Arkell's family brewers, a great range of traditionally brewed beers is available.

Rooms 6 en suite

LOWER SLAUGHTER
Map 10 SP12

Premier Collection

The Slaughters Country Inn

★★★★★ ⍟⍟ INN

tel: 01451 822143 **GL54 2HS**
email: info@theslaughtersinn.co.uk web: www.theslaughtersinn.co.uk
dir: *Exit A429 at 'The Slaughters' sign, between Stow-on-the-Wold & Bourton-on-the-Water. In village centre*

This attractive 17th-century inn is set in beautiful grounds beside the River Eye. Inside, contemporary high quality bedrooms, all with modern bathrooms, blend well with the more traditional bar area with its beamed ceilings, open fires, and flagstone floors. The Eton Restaurant is an attractive setting where modern British cooking sits next to more classical dishes and there's a comfortable lounge in which to relax. Parking is a bonus.

Rooms 19 en suite 12 annexe en suite (3 fmly) (6 GF) **Facilities** FTV DVD tea/coffee Dinner available Direct Dial WiFi ♨ **Conf** Thtr 80 Class 50 Board 36 **Parking** 45 **Notes** Civ Wed 80

MARSHFIELD
Map 4 ST77

Snow at the Barn

★★★★ ⍟ BED AND BREAKFAST

tel: 01225 892339 & 07973 382028 **The Barn, Chippenham Rd SN14 8NY**
email: snowatthebarn@icloud.com web: www.snowatthebarn.co.uk
dir: *M4 junct 18, A46 towards Bath. After 3m left at Cold Ashton rdbt onto A420 towards Chippenham. 3m turn right into Tormarton Rd then left into Chippenham Rd, barn on right*

Located in the pleasant village of Marshfield, this friendly accommodation offers a relaxed ambience just a short drive from Bath. Guests are welcomed with tea and cake and are assured of attentive hospitality throughout their stay. Breakfast includes a good selection of carefully-prepared hot and cold dishes, all served around one large table in the comfortable dining room. Off-street car parking is also provided.

Rooms 3 en suite D £85-£90* **Facilities** FTV iPod docking station tea/coffee WiFi ♨ 18 Riding ♨ **Parking** 6 **Notes** ⊗ ⍟

NAILSWORTH · Map 4 ST89

Wild Garlic Restaurant and Rooms

★★★★ ◉◉ ⬢ RESTAURANT WITH ROOMS

tel: 01453 832615 **3 Cossack Square GL6 0DB**
email: info@wild-garlic.co.uk **web:** www.wild-garlic.co.uk
dir: M4 junct 18, A46 towards Stroud. Enter Nailsworth, left at rdbt, immediately left. Establishment opposite Britannia pub

Situated in a quiet corner of charming Nailsworth, this restaurant with rooms offers a delightful combination of welcoming, relaxed hospitality and serious cuisine. The spacious and well-equipped bedrooms are situated above the award-winning restaurant. The small and friendly team of staff ensure guests are very well looked after throughout their stay.

Rooms 3 en suite (2 fmly) **Facilities** STV FTV DVD tea/coffee Dinner available WiFi ⌁ 18 Fishing Riding Shooting **Extras** Speciality toiletries, spring water - free **Notes** ⊗ No coaches

NAUNTON · Map 10 SP12

Mill View Guest House

★★★★ GUEST HOUSE

tel: 01451 850586 & 07887 553571 **2 Mill View GL54 3AF**
email: patricia@millview.myzen.co.uk **web:** www.millviewguesthousecotswolds.com
dir: Exit B4068 to E end of village

Mill View Guest House takes its name from the historic watermill opposite, and the owners of this former family home aim to provide every comfort. A warm welcome and attentive care is assured in this non-smoking house, which has one ground floor bedroom, equipped for easier access. The accommodation provides a good base for walkers or for touring Gloucestershire.

Rooms 3 en suite (1 GF) S £50-£65; D £70-£85* **Facilities** FTV DVD iPod docking station TVL tea/coffee Dinner available WiFi ☕ **Extras** Snacks, sherry - complimentary **Parking** 4 **Notes** LB ⊗ ⊛

NETHER WESTCOTE · Map 10 SP22

Premier Collection

The Feathered Nest Country Inn

★★★★★ ◉◉◉ ⬢ INN

tel: 01993 833030 **OX7 6SD**
email: info@thefeatherednestinn.co.uk **web:** www.thefeatherednest.co.uk
dir: A424 between Burford & Stow-on-the-Wold, follow signs

Located in the picturesque Cotswold village of Nether Westcote, with rolling views over the Evenlode Valley, this charming village inn offers a cosy base from which to explore the pretty countryside. There are four luxurious en suite bedrooms, all individually designed combining quality antiques and modern extras. Service is attentive and helpful while and food is a delight, offering a selection of carefully crafted dishes using the best of quality, seasonal produce. Fish is delivered fresh from the coast, and meals can be enjoyed on the charming outdoor terrace in warmer weather.

Rooms 4 en suite **Facilities** STV FTV DVD TVL tea/coffee Dinner available Direct Dial WiFi **Extras** Home-made biscuits, fruit - complimentary; robes **Parking** 45 **Notes** ⊗ Closed 25 Dec RS Mon (ex BHs) No coaches Civ Wed 200

NEWENT · Map 10 SO72

Three Choirs Vineyards

★★★★ ◉ RESTAURANT WITH ROOMS

tel: 01531 890223 **GL18 1LS**
email: info@threechoirs.com **web:** www.three-choirs-vineyards.co.uk
dir: On B4215 N of Newent, follow brown tourist signs

This thriving vineyard continues to go from strength to strength and provides a wonderfully different place to stay. The restaurant, which overlooks the 100-acre estate, enjoys a popular following thanks to well-executed dishes that make good use of local produce. Spacious, high quality bedrooms are equipped with many extras, and each opens onto a private patio area which has lovely views.

Rooms 11 annexe en suite (1 fmly) (11 GF) S £130-£195; D £140-£195* **Facilities** FTV DVD Lounge tea/coffee Dinner available Direct Dial WiFi Wine tasting Vineyard Tours **Conf** Max 20 Thtr 20 Class 15 Board 20 **Parking** 11 **Notes** LB Closed 24-26 Dec & 31 Dec-6 Jan No coaches

Kilcot Inn

★★★★ ⬢ INN

tel: 01989 720707 **Ross Rd GL18 1NA**
email: info@kilcotinn.com **web:** www.kilcotinn.com

The inviting Kilcot Inn deals in the best traditions of hospitality, food and drink. From the selection of real ales and local ciders on tap, to the high quality produce used in the delicious dishes in the bar/restaurant there is something for everyone. The bedrooms and bathrooms above the inn provide high levels of quality and comfort. Outdoor seating is also available, including a pleasant garden area to the rear of the property.

Rooms 4 en suite S £75-£85; D £75-£85* **Facilities** FTV Lounge tea/coffee Dinner available WiFi ☕ **Parking** 40

OLD SODBURY · Map 4 ST78

The Sodbury House

★★★★ GUEST HOUSE

tel: 01454 312847 **Badminton Rd BS37 6LU**
email: info@sodburyhouse.co.uk **web:** www.sodburyhouse.co.uk
dir: M4 junct 18, A46 N, 2m left onto A432 to Chipping Sodbury, house 1m on left

This comfortably furnished, 19th-century farmhouse stands in six acres of grounds. The bedrooms, some located on the ground floor and some in buildings adjacent to the main house, have many extra facilities. Breakfast offers a varied choice and is served in the spacious breakfast room.

Rooms 6 en suite 3 annexe en suite (1 fmly) (2 GF) **Facilities** FTV Lounge TVL tea/coffee WiFi ⌣ ♨ **Conf** Thtr 40 Class 25 Board 20 **Parking** 30 **Notes** ⊗ Closed 24 Dec-3 Jan

PAINSWICK
Map 4 SO80

The Falcon

★★★★ ♨ ⌣ INN

tel: 01452 814222 **New St GL6 6UN**
email: info@falconpainswick.co.uk **web:** www.falconpainswick.co.uk
dir: On A46 in centre of Painswick

The Falcon is an imposing Cotswold stone building that dates back to 1554, and sits on the main street of this attractive Cotswold village. Overlooking St Mary's church with its famous clipped yews, it's also within easy driving distance of Cheltenham Racecourse. Bedrooms are all individually designed and well equipped with comfortable beds, crisp white linen and very good quality toiletries. With an eclectic mix of furnishings, and chalky white and muted duck egg blue walls, this popular place has a charming atmosphere with a good mix of locals and tourists. The kitchen serves an accomplished bistro-style menu awash with locally-sourced, seasonal ingredients.

Rooms 8 en suite 3 annexe en suite (1 fmly) (1 GF) **Facilities** FTV tea/coffee Dinner available WiFi ⌣ 18 ♨ **Extras** Speciality toiletries **Conf** Max 30 Thtr 30 Class 20 Board 20 **Parking** 20

PUCKLECHURCH
Map 4 ST77

Orchard Cottage Bed & Breakfast

AA Advertised

tel: 0117 937 3284 **18 Homefield Rd BS16 9QD**
email: davidmstacey@gmail.com **web:** www.orchardcottagebandb.co.uk

Orchard Cottage is adjacent to Pucklechurch conservation area, and is a completely private duplex apartment with its own entrance and free parking, available for B&B or self-catering. The apartment includes a lounge with designer furniture, LCD TV, WiFi, iPod dock, fridge and tea/coffee making facilities. The bedroom has a round window with a lovely view of the conservation area barn. The apartment is suitable for adults only.

Rooms 1 en suite **Facilities** STV FTV DVD iPod docking station TVL tea/coffee WiFi ♨ **Parking** 4 **Notes** ⊗ No Children 18yrs

ST BRIAVELS
Map 4 SO50

The Florence

★★★★ GUEST ACCOMMODATION

tel: 01594 530830 **Bigsweir GL15 6QQ**
email: enquiries@florencehotel.co.uk **web:** www.florencehotel.co.uk
dir: On A466 between Monmouth & Chepstow

Located on the very edge of the river with delightful views over the surrounding countryside, this large detached house offers guests comfortable accommodation in a relaxing setting. Off-street car parking is provided and dinner is available by prior arrangement. A small bar and guest lounge is also provided.

Rooms 3 en suite 3 annexe en suite (1 fmly) (1 GF) **Facilities** Lounge tea/coffee Dinner available Licensed WiFi Fishing ♨ **Parking** 30 **Notes** LB ⊗ No Children 10yrs Closed Nov-Feb

STOW-ON-THE-WOLD
Map 10 SP12

Premier Collection

Old Stocks Inn

★★★★★ ⦿ ⌣ RESTAURANT WITH ROOMS

tel: 01451 830666 **The Square GL54 1AP**
email: info@oldstocksinn.com **web:** www.oldstocksinn.com
dir: From A429 turn into Market Sq, located opposite Town Hall

The Old Stocks has been lovingly restored, and offers a mix of modern facilities and 17th-century charm. Bedrooms are well designed and make good use of space; there are some unique features in the 'great' rooms. Cuisine is at the heart of the operation, with a café, restaurant and bar making up the impressive ground floor. Award-winning breakfasts are served in the restaurant, whilst lunch and dinner also offer award-winning dining.

Rooms 13 en suite 3 annexe en suite (4 fmly) (3 GF) S £129-£249; D £129-£275* **Facilities** FTV iPod docking station Lounge tea/coffee Dinner available Direct Dial WiFi ♨ **Extras** Mini-bar, Nespresso machine **Conf** Max 16 Thtr 10 Board 16 **Parking** 10 **Notes** No coaches

Premier Collection

The Porch House

★★★★★ ⦿⦿ ⌣ INN

tel: 01451 870048 **Digbeth St GL54 1BN**
web: www.porch-house.co.uk/home
dir: Short walk from main square, on left

Originally built in 975 AD, the Porch House is reputed to be England's oldest inn, and many of the original features can be seen today in the beautifully presented public areas. The inn has thirteen individually styled bedrooms, all equipped to a high standard, with WiFi available throughout. Guests have a choice of cosy authentic bars – with exposed stone walls and log fires – for casual dining. The award-winning restaurant is very well appointed and the unmissable breakfast features lots of local produce.

Rooms 13 en suite (2 fmly) (2 GF) S £89-£219; D £89-£219* **Facilities** STV FTV Lounge TVL tea/coffee Dinner available WiFi ♨ **Conf** Max 12 **Parking** 4

STOW-ON-THE-WOLD *continued*

Woodlands Guest House

★★★★ ⚲ GUEST ACCOMMODATION

tel: 01451 832346 **Upper Swell GL54 1EW**
email: amandak247@talktalk.net **web:** www.woodlands-guest-house.co.uk
dir: *Upper Swell 1m from Stow-on-the-Wold, take B4077 (Tewkesbury Road)*

Situated in the small hamlet of Upper Swell, Woodlands provides an ideal base for exploring the many charming nearby villages. This establishment enjoys delightful rural views and has comfortably appointed bedrooms with a good range of extra accessories. Breakfast is served in the welcoming dining room around the communal dining table. Off-road parking is available.

Rooms 5 en suite (2 GF) **Facilities** FTV tea/coffee WiFi **Parking** 8 **Notes** LB ⊗

Aston House

★★★★ BED AND BREAKFAST

tel: 01451 830475 **Broadwell GL56 0TJ**
email: fja@astonhouse.net **web:** www.astonhouse.net
dir: *A429 from Stow-on-the-Wold towards Moreton-in-Marsh, 1m right at x-rds to Broadwell, Aston House 0.5m on left*

Peacefully located on the edge of the village of Broadwell, this is an ideal base from which to explore the Cotswolds. A warm and genuine welcome is guaranteed and every effort is made to ensure a relaxed and enjoyable stay. Great care and attention are hallmarks here, and bedrooms come equipped with many thoughtful extras such as electric blankets.

Rooms 2 en suite D £90-£95 **Facilities** FTV tea/coffee WiFi ♿ Stairlift **Extras** Chocolates **Parking** 2 **Notes** ⊗ No Children 10yrs Closed Nov-Feb ✉

Corsham Field Farmhouse *(SP217249)*

★★★★ FARMHOUSE

tel: 01451 831750 **Bledington Rd GL54 1JH**
email: farmhouse@corshamfield.co.uk **web:** www.corshamfield.co.uk
dir: *A436 from Stow towards Chipping Norton. After 1m bear right onto B4450 (Bledington Rd), 1st farm on right in 0.5m, opposite Oddington turn*

This charming farmhouse offers superb views over the peaceful Cotswold countryside and has comfortable, well furnished bedrooms located in the main house or an adjoining cottage. The garden with relaxing chairs and tables provides a lovely spot for picnics and observing the wildlife. Freshly prepared breakfast is served in the spacious dining room/lounge, and the local pub is only five minutes' walk away for dinner.

Rooms 7 rms (5 en suite) (2 pri facs) (3 fmly) (2 GF) S £50-£65; D £60-£85* **Facilities** FTV Lounge tea/coffee WiFi **Extras** Speciality toiletries, sweets **Parking** 10 **Notes** LB ⊗ ✉ 100 acres arable

The Kings Head Inn

★★★★ ⬤ INN

tel: 01608 658365 **The Green, Bledington OX7 6XQ**
email: info@kingsheadinn.net **web:** www.kingsheadinn.net
dir: *4m SE off B4450*

In prime position on the delightful village green near the river, this 16th-century inn has spacious public areas with open fires, uneven floors, beams and wood furnishings. The comfortable restaurant offers an excellent dining experience and

the bedrooms have been creatively decorated and well furnished; some rooms are in a converted annexe.

Rooms 6 en suite 6 annexe en suite (3 GF) **Facilities** FTV TVL tea/coffee Dinner available Direct Dial WiFi **Parking** 24 **Notes** ⊗ Closed 25-26 Dec RS wkdays Closed every afternoon 3-6 low season No coaches

---

THORNBURY   Map 4 ST69

Thornbury Lodge

★★★★ GUEST ACCOMMODATION

tel: 01454 281144 **Bristol Rd BS35 3XL**
email: info@thornburygc.co.uk **web:** www.thornburygc.co.uk
dir: *M5 junct 16, A38 towards Thornbury. At lights (Berkeley Vale Motors) turn left, 1m on left*

With good access to both the M4 and M5, this lodge offers a popular retreat for both business and leisure guests, and is surrounded by pleasant scenery including a golf course. Dinner and breakfast can be enjoyed in the clubhouse-style dining area where an abundant choice is offered. Spacious and comfortable bedrooms are located in a lodge adjacent to the main clubhouse. An excellent golf driving range is also available.

Rooms 7 en suite 4 annexe en suite (11 fmly) (7 GF) S £70-£90; D £75-£95 (room only)* **Facilities** FTV TVL tea/coffee Dinner available Direct Dial Licensed WiFi ⅃ 36 Driving range Practice putting green **Conf** Max 165 Thtr 165 Class 60 Board 40 **Parking** 200 **Notes** LB ⊗ Closed 25 Dec Civ Wed 120

WICK   Map 4 ST77

Blue Lodge Farm *(ST692740)*

★★★★ FARMHOUSE

tel: 0117 937 2254 & 07748 733740 **Lodge Rd, Abson BS30 5TX**
email: info@bluelodgefarm.co.uk **web:** www.bluelodgefarm.co.uk
dir: *Phone for directions*

Peacefully located and surrounded by countryside, this pleasant farm offers a relaxed environment and yet is only a short drive from Bath or Bristol. Bedrooms and bathrooms are spacious and comfortable and all have their own front door, being located in a modern, purpose-built annexe. A garden and car park are both available for guest use. Breakfast make use of good quality produce and is served in the main building.

Rooms 3 annexe en suite (1 fmly) (3 GF) **Facilities** FTV Lounge WiFi ♿ **Extras** Speciality toiletries, fruit - complimentary **Parking** 6 **Notes** ⊗ ✉ 52 acres beef

WINCHCOMBE

Map 10 SP02

The Lion Inn

★★★★ ◉ INN

tel: 01242 603300 **37 North St GL54 5PS**
email: reception@thelionwinchcombe.co.uk **web:** www.thelionwinchcombe.co.uk
dir: *In town centre (parking in Chandos St)*

This 15th-century inn is situated in the centre of historic Winchcombe, a pretty Cotswold village. The accommodation has been recently updated to offer comfortable bedrooms that make the most of the historic elements of the property. Close by is Sudeley Castle, where Queen Katherine Parr, sixth wife of Henry VIII, is buried, while Cheltenham Racecourse is not far away. A seasonal menu is offered in the award-winning restaurant enhanced by daily-changing dishes. Parking is available in the pay and display car park to the rear of the property.

Rooms 7 en suite (1 fmly) D £110-£190* **Facilities** Dinner available Direct Dial WiFi **Extras** Speciality toiletries - complimentary **Conf** Max 20 Thtr 20 Class 12 Board 20

Sudeley Hill Farm *(SP038276)*

★★★★ ◉ FARMHOUSE

tel: 01242 602344 **GL54 5JB**
email: scudamore4@aol.com
dir: *Exit B4632 in Winchcombe into Castle St. White Hart Inn on corner, farm 0.75m on left*

Located on an 800-acre mixed arable and sheep farm, this 15th-century stone farmhouse is full of original features including fireplaces and exposed beams. Genuine hospitality is always on offer here together with a relaxed and welcoming atmosphere. The comfortable bedrooms are filled with thoughtful extras, and memorable breakfasts are served in the elegant dining room that overlooks the immaculate gardens.

Rooms 3 en suite (1 fmly) S £50-£60; D £75-£85* **Facilities** FTV DVD TVL tea/coffee WiFi ◉ **Parking** 10 **Notes** ◉ Closed Xmas ◉ 800 acres sheep/arable/pigs

Wesley House

★★★★ ◉◉ ◉ RESTAURANT WITH ROOMS

tel: 01242 602366 **High St GL54 5LJ**
email: enquiries@wesleyhouse.co.uk **web:** www.wesleyhouse.co.uk
dir: *In town centre*

This 15th-century, half-timbered property is named after John Wesley, founder of the Methodist Church, who stayed here while preaching in the town. Bedrooms are small and full of character. In the rear dining room, where the food has been awarded two AA Rosettes, a unique lighting system changes colour to suit the mood required, and also highlights the various floral displays created by a world-renowned flower arranger. A glass atrium covers the outside terrace.

Rooms 5 en suite **Facilities** FTV Lounge tea/coffee Dinner available WiFi ◉ **Conf** Thtr 30 Class 40 **Notes** ◉ RS Sun eve & Mon Restaurant closed Civ Wed 60

GREATER MANCHESTER

ALTRINCHAM

Map 15 SJ78

Ash Farm Country House

★★★★ GUEST ACCOMMODATION

tel: 0161 929 9290 **Park Ln, Little Bollington WA14 4TJ**
email: ashfarm@gmail.com **web:** www.ashfarm.co.uk
dir: *M56 junct 7 onto A56 at Lymm Rd 1st right into Park Ln, house at bottom of lane on right, just before The Swan with Two Nicks pub*

A warm welcome is guaranteed at this charming 18th-century National Trust farmhouse, which enjoys a peaceful location along a quiet country lane. The bedrooms are attractively presented and public areas include a book-filled lounge with its crackling log fire and cosy sofas. Free WiFi is available and the house is equally popular with business and leisure guests. Dunham Massey Hall and Deerpark is a short stroll from the house while Manchester Airport is just a 15-minute drive away.

Rooms 3 rms (2 en suite) (1 pri facs) 1 annexe en suite (1 GF) S £51-£71; D £86-£101* **Facilities** FTV Lounge tea/coffee Licensed WiFi ◉ **Extras** Robes, mineral water, chocolates **Conf** Max 10 Class 10 **Parking** 12 **Notes** ◉ No Children 12yrs Closed 22 Dec-2 Jan

ASHTON-UNDER-LYNE

Map 16 SJ99

Broadoak

★★★★ ◉ INN

tel: 0161 330 2764 **69 Broadoak Rd OL6 8QD**
email: broadoakhotel@googlemail.com **web:** www.broadoakhotel.co.uk
dir: *M60 junct 23 follow signs to Oldham (A627). Right at lights into Wilshaw Ln. Right at rdbt, Broadoak on right*

This inn is popular with locals, and ideally situated for Manchester, with excellent transport links to the ring road and the city. Hearty meals are served in the pub restaurant by friendly staff, often accompanied by live jazz. Accommodation is stylish with a range of modern amenities including complimentary WiFi and flat-screen TVs. Family suite available. Functions are also catered for.

Rooms 7 en suite (1 fmly) S £85-£120; D £90-£120* **Facilities** FTV Lounge TVL tea/coffee Dinner available Direct Dial WiFi ◉ **Conf** Max 100 Thtr 100 Class 50 Board 50 **Parking** 25 **Notes** LB ◉ No coaches

CHEADLE
Map 16 SJ88

The Governors House
★★★ INN

tel: 0161 488 4222 **43 Ravenoak Rd, Cheadle Hulme SK8 7EQ**
email: **4718@greeneking.co.uk** web: **www.oldenglish.co.uk**

Located close to Manchester and Stockport, this establishment is an ideal base for exploring the Cheshire countryside. Bedrooms are tastefully decorated and furnished, with a good range of accessories. The bar and restaurant are popular with residents and locals, and alfresco dining can be enjoyed in the summer months. Children are welcome. Park and Fly Manchester service is available.

Rooms 9 en suite (1 fmly) **Facilities** FTV tea/coffee Dinner available Direct Dial WiFi **Conf** Thtr 20 Class 14 Board 14 **Parking** 87 **Notes** ⊗ No coaches

DELPH
Map 16 SD90

The Old Bell Inn
★★★★★ ◉ INN

tel: 01457 870130 **5 Huddersfield Rd OL3 5EG**
email: **info@theoldbellinn.co.uk** web: **www.theoldbellinn.co.uk**
dir: *M62 junct 22 onto A672. In Denshaw onto A6052, through Delph to x-rds with A62. Turn left, 100yds on left*

Formerly a coaching inn, dating back to 1835, and situated in a rural village yet close to motorway links, The Old Bell has a quiet ambience allied with refined service. Hospitality is a real strength of the young and enthusiastic team. Bedrooms offer space, quality and comfort. The conservatory lounge is the perfect place to finish the evening after dinner in the modern restaurant.

Rooms 18 en suite (1 fmly) S £59.50-£69.50; D £95-£125* **Facilities** FTV TVL tea/coffee Dinner available Direct Dial WiFi **Parking** 20 **Notes** ⊗

MANCHESTER
Map 15 SJ89

The Ascott
★★★★ GUEST ACCOMMODATION

tel: 0161 950 2453 **6 Half Edge Ln, Ellesmere Park, Eccles M30 9GJ**
email: **ascotthotelmanchester@yahoo.co.uk** web: **www.ascotthotelmanchester.co.uk**
dir: *M602 junct 2, left into Wellington Rd, 0.25m, right into Abbey Grove & left into Half Edge Ln*

Set in a mainly residential area close to major routes, this early Victorian house, once the home of the Mayor of Eccles, provides thoughtfully furnished bedrooms with smart modern bathrooms. A choice of breakfast rooms is available and there is an elegant lounge.

Rooms 14 en suite (1 fmly) (4 GF) **Facilities** FTV Lounge TVL tea/coffee Direct Dial WiFi **Parking** 12 **Notes** ⊗ Closed 22 Dec-2 Jan RS Sun & Fri Closed 1-5pm

OLDHAM
Map 16 SD90

The White Hart Inn
★★★★★ ◉◉ INN

tel: 01457 872566 **51 Stockport Rd, Lydgate OL4 4JJ**
email: **bookings@thewhitehart.co.uk** web: **www.thewhitehart.co.uk**

Located on the edge of the Pennines in the small village of Lydgate, this inn is the perfect combination of modern style and old-world tradition. A choice of dining options is provided; the Brasserie serving good quality home cooking, and the restaurant, which has been awarded two AA Rosettes and provides a more formal approach. Bedrooms are comfortable and well-appointed with amenities such as flat-screen TV, complimentary WiFi and well-stocked hospitality trays. Weddings and events are catered for in a purpose-built suite.

Rooms 12 en suite **Facilities** Dinner available WiFi **Notes** Closed 24-26 Dec & 1 Jan

STOCKPORT
Map 16 SJ89

Innkeeper's Lodge Stockport
★★★ INN

tel: 08451 551551 *(Calls cost 2p per minute plus your phone company's access charge)* **271 Wellington Rd, North Heaton Chapel SK4 5BP**
email: **info@innkeeperslodge.com** web: **www.innkeeperslodge.com**

At Innkeeper's Lodge you'll find accommodation with comfort and character in equal measure, and everything needed for a relaxing stay, from easy check-in and free parking to complimentary breakfast and a cosy pub serving great value food and drink on the doorstep. Each Lodge has quality rooms, and there are Lodges in a variety of locations from towns and cities to countryside settings across the UK.

Rooms 22 en suite (1 fmly) (1 GF) **Facilities** FTV tea/coffee Dinner available WiFi **Parking Notes** ⊗

HAMPSHIRE

ALTON
Map 5 SU73

The Anchor Inn
★★★★ ◉◉ INN

tel: 01420 23261 **Lower Froyle GU34 4NA**
email: **info@anchorinnatlowerfroyle.co.uk** web: **www.anchorinnatlowerfroyle.co.uk**
dir: *From A3 follow Bentley signs & inn signs*

The Anchor Inn is located in the tranquil village of Lower Froyle. Luxury rooms are designed to reflect the traditional English inn style with charming decor, pictures, and a selection of books. The restaurant welcomes both residents and non-residents with classic pub cooking, which has been awarded two AA Rosettes, served in impressive surroundings, with feature wooden floors and period furnishings.

Rooms 5 en suite **Facilities** STV FTV DVD tea/coffee Dinner available Direct Dial WiFi **Extras** Mini-fridge **Conf** Board 30 **Parking** 30 **Notes** Civ Wed 45

The Angel
★★★★ GUEST ACCOMMODATION

tel: 01730 828111 **Gosport Rd GU34 3NN**
email: **info@angelcitylodge.com** web: **www.angelcitylodge.com**
dir: *On A32 between Alton & West Meon*

The Angel offers a choice of accommodation to meet the needs of a varied clientele; the annexe rooms are particularly suited to business travellers. All rooms offer free WiFi and powerful showers. The bar is well stocked, while the restaurant is very popular, especially the daily carvery. The Angel also offers meeting space for business meetings, ceremonies or family gatherings. Plenty of parking space provided.

Rooms 21 en suite 19 annexe en suite (6 fmly) **Facilities** FTV TVL tea/coffee Dinner available Licensed WiFi **Conf** Max 60 Thtr 40 Class 40 Board 40 **Parking** 150 **Notes** LB ⊗

ANDOVER
Map 5 SU34

The George and Dragon
★★★★ ⊛ INN

tel: 01264 736277 **The Square, Hurstbourne Tarrant SP11 0AA**
email: info@georgeanddragon.com **web:** www.georgeanddragon.com
dir: *N of Andover on A343, in middle of village*

With a history dating back to the 16th century, this former coaching inn has been given a new lease of life with a complete renovation. The results are impressive, with wonderfully comfortable beds, stylish decor and contemporary bathrooms. The bar is the focus downstairs, where a pre-dinner drink can be enjoyed before sampling the very enjoyable output from the kitchen. Crackling fires and low beams add to the charm of this revitalised village local.

Rooms 8 en suite (1 fmly) S £70-£75; D £75-£125* **Facilities** FTV tea/coffee Dinner available WiFi 🐾 **Conf** Max 22 Board 22 **Parking** 17

The White Horse
★★★ 🍺 INN

tel: 01264 772401 & 07823 320043 **Thruxton SP11 8EE**
email: enquiries@whitehorsethruxton.co.uk **web:** www.whitehorsethruxton.co.uk
dir: *Off A303, 4m from Andover town centre*

Situated in the heart of the Test Valley, this 15th-century Grade II listed inn is ideally situated for both business and leisure guests. Beneath the thatch, a warm welcome is assured, with every effort made to ensure a relaxing and rewarding stay. Bedrooms are well appointed and comfortable, while public areas include a spacious bar, a choice of dining areas and some lovely gardens. Food is a delight, with quality local produce utilised in flavoursome and creative dishes.

Rooms 4 en suite (2 fmly) **Facilities** FTV DVD iPod docking station TVL tea/coffee Dinner available WiFi 🐾 **Extras** Mineral water **Parking** 50 **Notes** No coaches

The Hatchet Inn
★★★ INN

tel: 01264 730229 **Lower Chute SP11 9DX**
email: info@thehatchetinn.co.uk **web:** www.thehatchetinn.co.uk
dir: *A303 exit signed Weyhill/Monxton onto A343. Follow signs for The Chutes*

Dating back to the 13th century, this picturesque thatched inn is very much the traditional village local, providing a warm welcome to all. Bedrooms offer good levels of comfort with all the necessities required to ensure a relaxing and rewarding stay. A good choice is offered at dinner, while breakfast provides a tasty start to the day. Many original features remain in the bar and public areas, all adding to the unique charms of this popular hostelry. Additional facilities include gun cabinets for those shooting in the area.

Rooms 7 annexe en suite (2 fmly) (3 GF) **Facilities** FTV TVL tea/coffee Dinner available WiFi 🐾 **Conf** Max 20 Board 20 **Parking** 50 **Notes** LB

ASHURST
Map 5 SU31

Kingswood Cottage
★★★★ 🍴 BED AND BREAKFAST

tel: 023 8029 2582 & 07866 455322 **10 Woodlands Rd SO40 7AD**
email: kingswoodcottage@yahoo.co.uk **web:** www.kingswoodcottage.co.uk
dir: *Off A35 Lyndhurst to Ashurst, in village turn right over bridge signed Woodlands. Gates on right after 1st turning*

Kingswood Cottage is located in Ashurst village, a quiet area just three miles from Lyndhurst yet with easy access to Southampton, which is only six miles away. Bedrooms are comfortably appointed with traditionally-styled decor and furnishings. Bedrooms have views of the spacious well-tended gardens which guests can enjoy year round. A hearty cooked or continental breakfast is served in the dining room and conservatory area. Guests can enjoy home-made refreshments on arrival.

Rooms 3 en suite S £40-£75; D £70-£85* **Facilities** FTV TVL tea/coffee WiFi 🐾 **Extras** Bottled water, speciality toiletries - free; robes **Parking** 3 **Notes** LB ⊗ No Children 5yrs Closed 12 Dec-2 Jan ⊜

Forest Gate Lodge
★★★★ BED AND BREAKFAST

tel: 023 8029 3026 **161 Lyndhurst Rd SO40 7AW**
email: forestgatelodge161@hotmail.co.uk **web:** www.forestgatelodge.co.uk

Forest Gate Lodge is located in Ashurst, just a short drive from all that the New Forest has to offer. Bedrooms have modern decor and furnishings, and come equipped with digital TV, DVD and free WiFi access. There is a guest lounge on the ground floor and guests can enjoy a cooked or continental breakfast in the dining room. Off-road parking is available, and there are restaurants and pubs within a short walking distance of the property.

Rooms 5 en suite D £75-£80* **Facilities** FTV DVD iPod docking station TVL tea/coffee WiFi Riding 🐾 **Parking** 6 **Notes** LB ⊗ No Children 5-12yrs ⊜

ASHURST *continued*

The Willows

★★★ BED AND BREAKFAST

tel: 023 8029 2745 & 07980 937862 **72 Lyndhurst Rd SO40 7BE**
email: thewillowsashurst@hotmail.co.uk **web:** www.thewillowsbandb.co.uk
dir: *M27 junct 3 onto M271. 1.5m, at rdbt take A35 signed Lyndhurst. In Ashurst, The Willows on right before bus stop*

This property is on the edge of the New Forest, and is convenient for Ashurst railway station and the M27. The bedrooms are traditional in style but with modern fixtures and furnishings including free WiFi; the bathrooms have high-quality fixtures. Guests can enjoy a cooked or continental breakfast in the dining room.

Rooms 3 en suite (1 fmly) **Facilities** FTV tea/coffee WiFi **Parking** 4 **Notes** No Children 5yrs Closed 2wks Xmas & New Year

BARTON-ON-SEA
Map 5 SZ29

Premier Collection

Pebble Beach

★★★★★ ◉ ♨ RESTAURANT WITH ROOMS

tel: 01425 627777 **Marine Dr BH25 7DZ**
email: mail@pebblebeach-uk.com **web:** www.pebblebeach-uk.com
dir: *A35 from Southampton onto A337 to New Milton, left into Barton Court Av to clifftop*

Situated on the clifftop, the restaurant at Pebble Beach boasts stunning views towards The Needles. Bedrooms and bathrooms (situated above the restaurant) are well equipped and provide a range of accessories. A freshly cooked breakfast is served in the main restaurant, or outside on the wonderful terrace. Next door, Petit Pebbles delicatessen is a recent addition and well worth a visit.

Rooms 4 rms (3 en suite) (1 pri facs) D £69.95-£349.95* **Facilities** FTV tea/coffee Dinner available WiFi **Extras** Speciality toiletries **Conf** Max 8 Thtr 8 Class 8 Board 8 **Parking** 20 **Notes** ⊗ RS 25 Dec & 1 Jan dinner not available No coaches

BASINGSTOKE
Map 5 SU65

Innkeeper's Lodge Basingstoke

★★★ INN

tel: 08451 551551 *(Calls cost 2p per minute plus your phone company's access charge)*
Andover Rd, Clerken Green, Oakley RG23 7EP
email: info@innkeeperslodge.com **web:** www.innkeeperslodge.com

Located on the quiet outskirts of the town, Innkeeper's Lodge Basingstoke provides a good level of comfort and quality through the accommodation and public areas. Bedrooms are well appointed and fitted with extras tailored to the modern traveller. Meals and drinks are served in The Beach Arms, adjacent to the Lodge; a wide choice on the menu is sure to suit any appetite and all tastes.

Rooms 22 en suite (4 fmly) (22 GF) **Facilities** FTV tea/coffee Dinner available Direct Dial WiFi **Parking** 45 **Notes** ⊗

BRANSGORE
Map 5 SZ19

Tothill House

★★★★ BED AND BREAKFAST

tel: 01425 674414 **Black Ln, off Forest Rd BH23 8EA**
email: enquiries@tothillhouse.com **web:** www.tothillhouse.com
dir: *M27 onto A31 or A35, between Burley & Bransgore*

Built for an admiral in 1908, Tothill House is located in the southern part of the New Forest. The garden backs on to the forest, and is frequently visited by deer, ponies and other wildlife. The spacious bedrooms are furnished to a high standard, reflecting the character of the house. There is an elegant library, and a generous breakfast is served in the dining room.

Rooms 3 rms (2 en suite) (1 pri facs) **Facilities** Lounge tea/coffee WiFi ♨ **Parking** 6 **Notes** ⊗ No Children 16yrs Closed Nov-Feb ⊛

BROCKENHURST
Map 5 SU30

The Filly Inn

★★★★ INN

tel: 01590 623449 **Lymington Rd SO42 7UF**

Conveniently located in the New Forest, this traditional inn offers a characterful restaurant and bar, and has retained many original features. All the bedrooms are en suite with stylish decor and very comfortable furnishings. There is plenty of parking on site and a large garden for guests to enjoy. Both cooked and continental breakfasts are served in the main restaurant.

Rooms 5 en suite **Facilities** FTV Dinner available **Parking**

BROOK
Map 5 SU21

The Bell Inn
★★★★ ⊛ INN

tel: 023 8081 2214 **SO43 7HE**
email: bell@bramshaw.co.uk web: www.bellinnbramshaw.co.uk
dir: *M27 junct 1 onto B3079, 1.5m on right*

This delightful inn is part of the Bramshaw Golf Club and is an ideal base for visiting the New Forest. Bedrooms are spacious and have been refurbished to a high standard. Public areas are full of character, and there is a welcoming bar, a popular restaurant and a comfortable lounge.

Rooms 25 en suite 2 annexe en suite (1 fmly) (8 GF) S £69-£79; D £89-£179* **Facilities** TVL tea/coffee Dinner available Direct Dial WiFi ⅃ 36 ⊕ Boules Garden chess **Conf** Max 40 Thtr 40 Class 16 Board 24 **Parking** 150 **Notes** LB ⊛ Civ Wed 50

BURGHCLERE
Map 5 SU46

Carpenters Arms
★★★ INN

tel: 01635 278251 **Harts Ln RG20 9JY**
email: thecarpenters.burghclere@arkells.com
web: www.carpentersarms-burghclere.co.uk
dir: *A34 Newbury Tothill Services, at rdbt take 2nd exit signed Burghclere. At end of road, turn left, 200m on right.*

Located in a tranquil setting just a couple of miles outside Newbury, this traditional inn offers comfortably appointed bedrooms boasting some traditional features and modern furnishings. All rooms are annexed, plenty of on-site parking available and guests can enjoy breakfast, lunch or dinner with a range of traditional pub dishes in the conservatory restaurant or bar.

Rooms 4 annexe en suite (1 fmly) S £40-£69; D £45-£79 (room only)* **Facilities** FTV tea/coffee Dinner available **Parking** 18 **Notes** No coaches

CLANFIELD
Map 5 SU71

The Rising Sun Inn
★★★ INN

tel: 023 9259 6975 & 07702 262339 **North Ln PO8 0RN**
email: enquiries@therisingsunclanfield.co.uk web: www.therisingsunclanfield.co.uk
dir: *A3 between Petersfield & Horndean, exit signed Clanfield/Chalton. Follow brown signs*

The family-run Rising Sun Inn is in the quiet village of Clanfield yet just off the A3 and so within a short drive of both Portsmouth and Chichester. The three bedrooms are fresh and modern with comfortable accommodation, well equipped with both digital TVs and WiFi. Food is served daily and guests can enjoy a selection of traditional pub classics. A cooked and continental breakfast is served each morning in the restaurant.

Rooms 3 en suite S £55-£85; D £65-£95* **Facilities** FTV iPod docking station tea/coffee Dinner available WiFi ⊕ **Extras** Fresh milk **Parking** 24 **Notes** No coaches

DUMMER
Map 5 SU54

Tower Hill House
★★★ BED AND BREAKFAST

tel: 01256 398340 **Tower Hill, Winchester Rd RG25 2AL**
email: martin.hyndman@virgin.net web: www.accommodationinbasingstoke.co.uk
dir: *In village. M3 junct 7, A30 towards Winchester, 2nd left, opposite sign for North Waltham*

Ideally situated for access to the M3 and A30, while overlooking fields and countryside, this family-run bed and breakfast is in the pretty village of Dummer, just 10 minutes away from the centre of Basingstoke. Bedrooms are simply, but comfortably furnished and a well-prepared breakfast is served in the cheerful dining room.

Rooms 4 en suite **Facilities** tea/coffee WiFi **Parking** 6

EMSWORTH
Map 5 SU70

36 on the Quay
★★★★★ ⊛⊛⊛ RESTAURANT WITH ROOMS

tel: 01243 375592 & 372257 **47 South St PO10 7EG**
web: www.36onthequay.co.uk
dir: *Last building on right in South St, which runs from square in centre of Emsworth*

Occupying a prime position with far-reaching views over the estuary, this 16th-century house is the scene for some accomplished and exciting cuisine. The elegant restaurant occupies centre stage with peaceful pastel shades, local art and crisp napery together with glimpses of the bustling harbour outside. The contemporary bedrooms offer style, comfort and thoughtful extras.

Rooms 5 en suite 2 annexe en suite **Facilities** FTV iPod docking station tea/coffee Dinner available WiFi **Parking** 6 **Notes** Closed 3wks Jan, 1wk late May

Hollybank House
★★★★ BED AND BREAKFAST

tel: 01243 375502 **Hollybank Ln PO10 7UN**
email: anna@hollybankhouse.com web: www.hollybankhouse.com
dir: *1m N of town centre. A259 onto B2148, 1m right into Southleigh Rd, 3rd left into Hollybank Ln, house at top*

This Georgian country house stands in a 10-acre woodland garden complete with tennis court on the outskirts of Emsworth, and looks out to Chichester Harbour. The attractive entrance hall leads into spacious lounge and dining rooms where light streams through the deep Georgian windows. Bedrooms are comfortable and home-made goods feature on the breakfast menu. Emsworth has a variety of restaurants, pubs and harbour walks.

Rooms 4 en suite (1 fmly) S £60-£70; D £85-£95* **Facilities** FTV DVD Lounge tea/coffee WiFi ⊴⊰ ⊕ **Parking** 85

EMSWORTH *continued*

The Jingles

★★★★ ⊜ GUEST ACCOMMODATION

tel: 01243 373755 **77 Horndean Rd PO10 7PU**
email: info@thejingles.co.uk **web:** www.thejingles.co.uk
dir: *A3 (M) junct 2, follow signs for Emsworth, 4m, 1st building in Emsworth on right*

The Jingles is a family-run business, located in the charming maritime village of Emsworth. Situated adjacent to open farmland, it's a great location for exploring both Portsmouth and Chichester. All bedrooms are en suite and decorated to a high standard. The dining room is the setting for a cooked English breakfast, and a drawing room is available for relaxing in. WiFi is available if required.

Rooms 28 en suite (2 fmly) (7 GF) **Facilities** FTV Lounge tea/coffee Licensed WiFi ◒ **Extras** Bottled water - complimentary **Parking** 35 **Notes** ⊗ Closed 24 Dec-2 Jan

The Crown

★★★ INN

tel: 01243 372806 **High St PO10 7AW**
email: thecrownemsworth@aol.com **web:** www.thecrownemsworth.com

A historic property conveniently located in the centre of town with ample parking at the back. Long winding stairs and uneven corridors lead to well-appointed bedrooms which offer a range of amenities such as flat-screen TVs and WiFi. Freshly prepared food is served in the well-stocked bar and the restaurant.

Rooms 9 rms (7 en suite) (2 pri facs) (2 fmly) **Facilities** FTV tea/coffee Dinner available WiFi ⚓ 18 **Conf** Max 48 Thtr 48 Class 36 Board 24 **Parking** 16

FAREHAM   Map 5 SU50

Wisteria House

★★★★ BED AND BREAKFAST

tel: 01329 511940 & 07742 400242 **14 Mays Ln, Stubbington PO14 2EP**
email: info@wisteria-house.co.uk **web:** www.wisteria-house.co.uk
dir: *M27 junct 9, A27 to Fareham. Right onto B3334, at rdbt left into Mays Ln*

Wisteria House is located on the edge of the village of Stubbington, just a short walk from local amenities, and only one mile from the beach at Lee-on-the-Solent. Attention to detail is key at this B&B, guaranteeing a return visit by those who stay here. The charming and comfortable bedrooms have en suite bathrooms, are located on the ground floor, and also have WiFi. Off-road parking is available.

Rooms 2 en suite (2 GF) **Facilities** FTV tea/coffee WiFi **Parking** 2 **Notes** ⊗ No Children 8yrs

FARNBOROUGH   Map 5 SU85

The Alexandra Pub

★★★ INN

tel: 01252 519964 **74 Victoria Rd GU14 7PH**
email: thealex@alexandrapub.co.uk **web:** www.alexandrapub.co.uk
dir: *M3 junct 4 onto A331 (Farnborough), at 1st rdbt take 2nd exit. Follow signs for A331 Hawley/Farnborough, at next rdbt 3rd exit. At next rdbt 1st exit onto Farnborough Rd (A325). 3rd exit at next rdbt into Victoria Rd*

Named after a young Danish princess who became a much loved queen, The Alexandra pub remains at the heart of the local community. The inn has been refurbished to a good standard and retains its warm and welcoming feel. There are three well equipped en suite rooms offering comfortable accommodation. The bar is well stocked and the restaurant offers freshly cooked and popular dishes. Secure parking is provided at the rear of the inn, as well as a dedicated smoking area.

Rooms 3 en suite S £45-£65; D £55-£70 (room only)* **Facilities** STV FTV DVD Lounge TVL tea/coffee Dinner available WiFi Pool table **Parking** 16 **Notes** LB Closed 24-25 Dec No coaches

HAWKLEY   Map 5 SU72

The Hawkley Inn

★★★★ ⊜ INN

tel: 01730 827205 **Pococks Ln GU33 6NE**
email: info@hawkleyinn.co.uk **web:** www.hawkleyinn.co.uk
dir: *A3 Liss rdbt towards Liss B3006. Right at Spread Eagle, follow brown tourist signs. After 3m, left to village centre*

The Hawkley Inn captures all that is required of a traditional inn and more. There are five beautifully appointed double rooms, which offer all the comforts required by discerning travellers. The bar is well stocked including a range of real ales while the chef-proprietor is passionate about local produce and prepares award-winning dishes. The rear garden is a haven of tranquillity.

Rooms 5 en suite (1 fmly) **Facilities** STV FTV tea/coffee Dinner available WiFi ⚓ 18 **Parking** 4

HAYLING ISLAND
Map 5 SU70

Ravensdale

★★★★ BED AND BREAKFAST

tel: 023 9246 3203 & 07802 188259 **19 St Catherines Rd PO11 0HF**
email: phil.taylor@tayloredprint.co.uk **web:** www.ravensdale-hayling.co.uk
dir: A27 onto A3023 at Langstone, cross Hayling Bridge, 3m to mini rdbt, right into Manor Rd, 1m. Right by Barley Mow into Station Rd, 3rd left into St Catherines Rd

A warm welcome awaits you at this comfortable home, quietly situated near the beach and golf course. Bedrooms are attractive, very comfortable and enhanced with numerous thoughtful extras. One room is a triple and has its own separate facilities. Home cooking can be enjoyed at breakfast in the dining room, and there is also a lounge area.

Rooms 3 rms (2 en suite) (1 pri facs) (1 fmly) D £78–£80 **Facilities** FTV DVD TVL tea/coffee WiFi **Extras** Flowers, chocolates - complimentary **Parking** 4 **Notes** ⊗ No Children 8yrs Closed last 2wks Dec & 1st 2wks Jan ⚭

HIGHCLERE
Map 5 SU45

The Yew Tree

★★★★★ ⚜⚜ RESTAURANT WITH ROOMS

tel: 01635 253360 **Hollington Cross RG20 9SE**
email: info@theyewtree.co.uk **web:** www.theyewtree.co.uk
dir: 1m S of Highclere village

Part of The Epicurean Collection, this attractive 17th-century country inn has comfortable bedrooms, decorated with William Morris print wallpaper and retaining traditional features, giving it an overall cosy feel. Great British cooking can be enjoyed in the attractively-decorated restaurant, where good use is made of high-quality produce and fresh ingredients. The garden, with its own bar and dining areas, is a real bonus.

Rooms 8 rms **Facilities** FTV Lounge tea/coffee Dinner available WiFi ⚓ **Parking** 22 **Notes** No coaches

HURSLEY
Map 5 SU42

The Kings Head

★★★★ ⚜ INN

tel: 01962 775208 **Main Rd SO21 2JW**
email: enquiries@kingsheadhursley.co.uk **web:** www.kingsheadhursley.co.uk
dir: M3 junct 11, follow signs for A3090 & Hursley

Part of The Epicurean Collection, The Kings Head is a traditional inn a short drive from Winchester in an idyllic quiet village. Bar and restaurant areas are smart yet cosy, and quality food is available. Rooms are exceptionally well presented with comfortable beds and a host of extras to make your stay even more enjoyable. Full English breakfast can be enjoyed each morning in the Snug.

Rooms 7 en suite 1 annexe en suite S £75–£85; D £90–£115* **Facilities** FTV Lounge tea/coffee Dinner available WiFi Skittle alley **Conf** Max 50 **Parking** 30 **Notes** No coaches

ISLE OF WIGHT
See Isle of Wight

LEE-ON-THE-SOLENT
Map 5 SU50

West Wind Guest House

★★★★ GUEST ACCOMMODATION

tel: 023 9255 2550 & 07748 010102 **197 Portsmouth Rd PO13 9AA**
email: info@west-wind.co.uk **web:** www.west-wind.co.uk
dir: M27 junct 11 follow Gosport & Fareham signs, B3385 for Lee-on-the-Solent. At seafront left along Marine Pde, 600mtrs left into Portsmouth Rd. West Wind on right

This family-run guest accommodation is found in a quiet, residential area within walking distance of the beach and town centre. The bedrooms are comfortable and nicely appointed, some with flat-screen TV and all with free WiFi. There is an attractive breakfast room and off-street parking.

Rooms 6 en suite (1 GF) S £50–£55; D £65–£70* **Facilities** FTV DVD iPod docking station tea/coffee WiFi **Parking** 6 **Notes** ⊗ No Children 8yrs

LISS
Map 5 SU72

The Jolly Drover

★★★★ ⚬ INN

tel: 01730 893137 **London Rd, Hillbrow GU33 7QL**
email: thejollydrover@googlemail.com **web:** www.thejollydrover.co.uk
dir: From Liss on B3006, at junct with B2070

Situated on the West Sussex/Hampshire border this traditional inn prides itself on local ales, good home-cooked food and a warm welcome. It is popular with both business and leisure guests due to its close proximity to Petersfield and transport links. Rooms are situated in the traditional outbuildings, and have been fitted in a comfortable modern style with all expected guest amenities. Free WiFi is available. A large beer garden to the rear of the inn is the perfect place to enjoy a summer's day, and ample parking is available.

Rooms 6 annexe rms (6 pri facs) (1 fmly) (6 GF) **Facilities** FTV tea/coffee Dinner available WiFi **Extras** Bottled water **Parking** 48 **Notes** LB ⊗ Closed 25-26 Dec & 1 Jan

LYMINGTON
Map 5 SZ39

Britannia House

★★★★ BED AND BREAKFAST

tel: 01590 672091 & 07808 792639 **Station St SO41 3BA**
email: enquiries@britannia-house.com **web:** www.britannia-house.com
dir: Follow signs to railway station, at corner of Station St & Mill Ln

Built in 1865 as the Britannia Commercial Hotel, Britannia House occupies a quiet location only two minutes' walk from the quay, waterfront and the High Street with its many shops, pubs and restaurants. Rooms are elegant with a refined air, there is a charming lounge and breakfast is taken in the homely kitchen.

Rooms 3 en suite 2 annexe en suite (2 GF) S £65–£129; D £75–£129 **Facilities** FTV Lounge tea/coffee WiFi ⚓ **Parking** 4 **Notes** LB ⊗ No Children 8yrs

LYNDHURST
Map 5 SU30

The Rufus House

★★★★ 🛎 GUEST ACCOMMODATION

tel: 023 8028 2930 **Southampton Rd SO43 7BQ**
email: stay@rufushouse.co.uk **web:** www.rufushouse.co.uk
dir: *From Lyndhurst centre onto A35 (Southampton Rd), 300yds on left*

Located on the edge of town, this delightful family-run Victorian property is well situated for exploring the New Forest. The brightly decorated bedrooms are appointed to a high standard, while the turret lounge and the garden terrace are great spots for relaxing.

Rooms 10 en suite (1 fmly) (2 GF) **Facilities** tea/coffee WiFi ⌁ 18 **Parking** 12 **Notes** ⊗ No Children 5yrs

Temple Lodge

★★★★ 🛎 GUEST ACCOMMODATION

tel: 023 8028 2392 **2 Queens Rd SO43 7BR**
email: templelodge@btinternet.com **web:** www.templelodge-guesthouse.com
dir: *M27 junct 2/3 onto A35 to Ashurst & Lyndhurst. Temple Lodge on 2nd corner on right, opposite forest*

Temple Lodge is a well appointed Victorian house with very friendly hosts, who welcome back returning guests year after year. Guests will enjoy easy access to the New Forest and Lyndhurst town centre, with good off-road parking. The bedrooms are furnished with comfort in mind and feature lots of thoughtful extras including mini-bars, some bedrooms have sofas too. The breakfasts should not be missed.

Rooms 6 en suite (1 fmly) D £70-£120* **Facilities** FTV DVD TVL tea/coffee WiFi ⌁ **Extras** Mini-fridge with snacks/soft drinks - chargeable **Parking** 6 **Notes** LB ⊗ No Children 12yrs

Whitemoor House

★★★★ 🛎 GUEST ACCOMMODATION

tel: 023 8028 3043 **Southampton Rd SO43 7BU**
email: whitemoorhouse@talktalk.net **web:** www.whitemoorhouse.co.uk
dir: *0.5m NE of town centre on A35 towards Southampton*

Situated just on the edge of Lyndhurst, this very well run establishment offers comfortable, smartly-decorated bedrooms, well equipped and all en suite. Breakfast is impressive, with home-made preserves and an extensive selection of cold items; there are plenty of hot options too, most sourced from local suppliers. Guests can relax in the cosy lounge, which opens on to the patio overlooking the well-kept grounds. There is also an honesty bar, free WiFi and parking on site.

Rooms 7 en suite S £57; D £74-£94* **Facilities** FTV DVD TVL tea/coffee Licensed WiFi ⌁ 18 🛆 **Extras** Mini-bar - chargeable; home-made cake on arrival **Parking** 7 **Notes** ⊗ No Children 12yrs Closed Nov-Jan ⊛

Clayhill House

★★★★ BED AND BREAKFAST

tel: 023 8028 2304 **SO43 7DE**
email: clayhillhouse@tinyworld.co.uk **web:** www.clayhillhouse.co.uk
dir: *Exit M27 junct 2. A35 to Lyndhurst then A337 signed Brockenhurst, 0.75m*

Set at the edge of this attractive town, and convenient for visiting the New Forest and coastal attractions nearby, Clayhill House is a well-appointed property, which offers friendly service and comfortable accommodation. The bedrooms are particularly well equipped with thoughtful extras. Freshly cooked breakfasts are served in the dining room.

Rooms 3 en suite (1 fmly) S £55-£90; D £75-£90* **Facilities** FTV tea/coffee WiFi 🛆 **Parking** 6 **Notes** LB ⊗ No Children 14yrs Closed 22 Dec-4 Jan

NORTHINGTON
Map 5 SU53

The Woolpack Inn

★★★★ ⓢ 🛎 INN

tel: 01962 734184 **Totford SO24 9TJ**
email: info@thewoolpackinn.co.uk **web:** www.thewoolpackinn.co.uk
dir: *On B3046 S of Basingstoke*

Part of The Epicurean Collection, this attractive country inn, tucked away in Hampshire's Candover Valley, offers a traditional feel with lots of character. The flint and brick building dates back to 1880 and many original features can be seen throughout. The inviting bar has flagstone floors, leather armchairs and open fires, while the dining room features smart fabrics, candle-lit tables and the same relaxed, friendly atmosphere. There is also a wood-fired outdoor kitchen and a small private dining room. Bedrooms, each named after a game bird, are richly furnished and very well equipped. All of them have a contemporary en suite bath or shower room.

Rooms 7 en suite (1 fmly) (4 GF) **Facilities** FTV tea/coffee Dinner available Direct Dial WiFi ⌁ 18 Fishing Riding Pool table **Conf** Max 15 Thtr 15 Class 12 Board 12 **Parking** 50

PETERSFIELD
Map 5 SU72

The Old Drum

★★★★ INN

tel: 01730 300208 **16 Chapel St GU32 3DP**
email: info@theolddrum.com **web:** www.theolddrum.com

Located in the very centre of Petersfield, this inn has been recently refurbished to offer stylish and contemporary accommodation. The bar is open daily and has an inviting ambience, busy with residents and locals alike. Breakfast, lunch and dinner are available daily in the restaurant. There is an outside courtyard with seating, perfect for the summer months. There's no parking on site; however a large carpark to the rear of the inn is less than a minute's walk away.

Rooms 5 en suite (1 fmly) S £90-£110; D £110-£130* **Facilities** STV FTV Lounge TVL tea/coffee Dinner available WiFi 🛆 **Extras** Speciality toiletries, fruit **Conf** Max 15 Class 15 **Notes** LB ⊗ Closed 25 Dec & 1-3 Jan No coaches

| **RAKE** | **Map 5 SU82** |

The Flying Bull Inn

★★★★ INN

tel: 01730 892285 **London Rd GU33 7JB**
email: info@theflyingbull.com **web:** www.theflyingbull.com
dir: *From A3 Sbound, take exit for Liphook & follow signs for B2070. In Rake on right hand side*

This traditional inn is set in the village of Rake, near Liss and close to both Petersfield and Haslemere. Bedrooms and bathrooms are well appointed offering guests comfortable accommodation. There is plenty of parking available, and a well-tended outside seating area in addition to the bar and restaurant. A cooked or continental breakfast is served in the restaurant; lunch and dinner are available daily.

Rooms 7 en suite (1 fmly) (5 GF) **Facilities** FTV Lounge tea/coffee Dinner available WiFi ⌣ ⚡ 18 🔒 **Parking** 35 **Notes** LB

| **RINGWOOD** | **Map 5 SU10** |

Moortown Lodge

★★★★ GUEST ACCOMMODATION

tel: 01425 471404 **244 Christchurch Rd BH24 3AS**
email: enquiries@moortownlodge.co.uk **web:** www.moortownlodge.co.uk
dir: *1m S of Ringwood. Exit A31 at Ringwood onto B3347, follow signs to Sopley. Lodge adjacent to David Lloyd Leisure Club*

Moortown Lodge was originally a Georgian hunting lodge and is conveniently located ten miles from the Dorset coast, not far from Christchurch, and just five minutes south of Ringwood. A warm welcome is assured, with every effort made to ensure a relaxed and rewarding stay. Bedrooms offer impressive levels of comfort combined with individual styling and a host of additional facilities. The elegant dining room is the venue for satisfying breakfasts which make use of local New Forest produce. Moortown Lodge is a very convenient base for exploring this delightful area.

Rooms 7 en suite (1 fmly) (2 GF) S £75-£96; D £75-£119* **Facilities** FTV DVD Lounge tea/coffee Direct Dial WiFi Reduced rates at local David Lloyds Leisure Club **Extras** Speciality toiletries, robes, bottled water **Parking** 8 **Notes** ⊗ No Children 3yrs

Little Forest Lodge

★★★★ GUEST HOUSE

tel: 01425 478848 **Poulner Hill BH24 3HS**
email: enquiries@littleforestlodge.co.uk **web:** www.littleforestlodge.co.uk
dir: *1.5m NE of Ringwood on A31*

A warm welcome is extended to guests, and their pets, at this charming Edwardian house where the manicured lawns run into two acres of woodland. Bedrooms are pleasantly decorated, and equipped with thoughtful extras. The attractive wood-panelled dining room and the delightful lounge, with bar and wood-burning fire, overlook the gardens. A very convenient base from which to explore this picturesque area.

Rooms 5 en suite 1 annexe en suite (2 fmly) (1 GF) **Facilities** FTV Lounge tea/coffee Licensed WiFi 🔒 **Parking** 7

Amberwood

★★★★ GUEST ACCOMMODATION

tel: 01425 476615 **3/5 Top Ln BH24 1LF**
email: maynsing1@sky.com **web:** www.amberwoodbandb.co.uk
dir: *A31 onto B3347, over rdbt, left into School Ln, left into Top Ln*

This delightful Victorian home is situated in a quiet residential area within easy walking distance of the town centre. Bedrooms are attractively furnished and decorated, with many thoughtful extras. A substantial breakfast is served around one large table in the conservatory, which overlooks the well-tended garden. A lounge is also available.

Rooms 2 en suite (1 fmly) **Facilities** FTV TVL tea/coffee Direct Dial WiFi **Parking** 2 **Notes** ⊗ No Children 12yrs Closed Xmas & New Year ◉

Lamb Inn

★★★ INN

tel: 01425 473721 **2 Hightown Rd BH24 1NW**
email: anitaandbrum@gmail.com **web:** www.lambinnringwood.co.uk

This traditional inn is situated in the market town of Ringwood and provides a convenient location for exploring the beautiful New Forest. A very warm and genuine welcome is always on offer, with a helpful team to ensure your stay is relaxed and rewarding. Bedrooms provide good levels of comfort, and two rooms are located externally with separate entrance. The bar is the hub of activity with friendly banter to accompany the good choice of food and drink on offer.

Rooms 3 rms (2 en suite) (1 pri facs) 2 annexe en suite (2 GF) S £45-£80; D £50-£90 **Facilities** FTV tea/coffee Dinner available WiFi Pool table **Parking** 6 **Notes** LB No Children No coaches

| **ROMSEY** | **Map 5 SU32** |

The Mill Arms

★★★★ INN

tel: 01794 340401 **Barley Hill, Dunbridge SO51 0LF**
email: mill.arms@btconnect.com **web:** www.themillarms.co.uk
dir: *M27 junct 2 onto A3090 then left onto A27 (Salisbury road). Turn right into Danes Rd, straight over into Saunders Ln. At T-junct left into Barley Hill*

The Mill Arms is a traditional inn set in a quiet village with easy access to the New Forest and surrounding towns, cities and the South Coast. Guests are assured of a warm welcome, friendly service and great food. Bedrooms are comfortable, well equipped and furnished, and there is free WiFi. Good on-site parking is a bonus.

Rooms 6 annexe en suite (1 fmly) S £75-£90; D £75-£90 (room only)* **Facilities** FTV tea/coffee Dinner available WiFi 🔒 **Extras** Bottled water - complimentary **Conf** Max 100 Thtr 70 Class 30 Board 30 **Parking** 40 **Notes** Closed 25 Dec No coaches

ST MARY BOURNE
Map 5 SU45

Bourne Valley Inn
★★★★ ⊛ INN

tel: 01264 738361 **SP11 6BT**
email: enquiries@bournevalleyinn.com **web:** www.bournevalleyinn.com
dir: S of St Mary Bourne on B3048

Part of The Epicurean Collection, the Bourne Valley Inn is located in the rural village of St Mary Bourne. Ample customer car parking and large riverside beer gardens are real features. The inn is both children and dog friendly, and accommodation is all en suite and in keeping with the style of this rustic building. Food is a highlight with mostly local produce being used. Sunday lunch is a real treat. Hospitality from the young and enthusiastic management and team is excellent.

Rooms 9 en suite (3 GF) **Facilities** FTV Lounge tea/coffee Dinner available WiFi Fishing **Conf** Max 80 **Parking**

SOUTHAMPTON
Map 5 SU41

Premier Collection

Ennio's Restaurant & Boutique Rooms
★★★★★ ⬗ ☕ RESTAURANT WITH ROOMS

tel: 023 8022 1159 & 07748 966113 **Town Quay Rd SO14 3AS**
email: info@ennios.co.uk **web:** www.ennios.co.uk
dir: Opposite Red Funnel Ferry terminal

This fine property, lovingly converted from a former Victorian warehouse, offers luxurious accommodation on Southampton's waterfront. All rooms are en suite and are furnished to a very high standard, including mini-bars and over-sized showers. Downstairs, the popular Ennio's Restaurant and bar is the ideal setting in which to dine, offering an authentic Italian atmosphere and a wonderful selection of dishes. There is limited parking available to the rear of the building.

Rooms 10 en suite D £96.75-£125* **Facilities** FTV iPod docking station tea/coffee Dinner available WiFi **Extras** Speciality toiletries, mini-bar **Parking** 6 **Notes** LB ⊗ Closed 24-26 Dec No coaches

Premier Collection

THE PIG in the Wall
★★★★★ ☕ INN

tel: 023 8063 6900 **8 Western Esplanade SO14 2AZ**
email: info@thepiginthewall.com **web:** www.thepighotel.com

Located close to the city centre, this beautifully restored property has high quality bedrooms in all shapes and sizes, all with air-conditioning, some with roll-top baths, all with their own larder of goodies and Nespresso machine. There is secure parking and the deli-bar showcases local produce. Its homely, relaxed, 'shabby-chic' in style and there is an extensive continental breakfast available to guests each morning.

Rooms 12 en suite (2 GF) **Facilities** FTV DVD Lounge tea/coffee Dinner available Direct Dial WiFi **Extras** Nespresso - free; stocked larder - chargeable **Parking** 12 **Notes** ⊗ No coaches

Premier Collection

White Star Tavern, Dining and Rooms
★★★★★★ ⊛⊛ INN

tel: 023 8082 1990 **28 Oxford St SO14 3DJ**
email: reservations@whitestartavern.co.uk **web:** www.whitestartavern.co.uk
dir: M3 junct 14, A33 towards Ocean Village

This stylish tavern is conveniently located in the popular Oxford Street area, a moment's walk from the city centre. Bedrooms take their name from the ships of the White Star Line and are smartly appointed and well equipped with many thoughtful extras. The main bar and restaurant areas provide comfortable seating in stylish surroundings. Two AA Rosette award-winning cuisine is served in the White Star restaurant while in the morning an à la carte breakfast is served in the bar area. Private meeting space is also available.

Rooms 13 en suite **Facilities** FTV DVD iPod docking station TVL tea/coffee Dinner available Direct Dial WiFi **Extras** Mini-bar, fresh milk & bottled water **Conf** Max 12 Thtr 12 Board 12 **Notes** ⊗ Closed 25-26 Dec

Alcantara Guest House
★★★★ ⬗ GUEST ACCOMMODATION

tel: 023 8033 2966 **20 Howard Rd, Shirley SO15 5BN**
email: alcantaraguesthouse@sky.com **web:** www.alcantaraguesthouse.co.uk
dir: 0.5m NW of city centre. Exit A3057 into Howard Rd

A warm welcome is assured at this Victorian property, named after an ocean liner to reflect the establishment's shipping connections. Bedrooms are comfortable and well decorated and have many thoughtful extras. An appetising breakfast can be served in the bright and airy dining room. Secure off-road parking is available.

Rooms 9 rms (6 en suite) (1 fmly) (2 GF) S £40-£52; D £78* **Facilities** FTV tea/coffee WiFi ⬗ **Parking** 7 **Notes** ⊗ No Children 12yrs RS 2wks Xmas

Landguard Lodge
★★★★ GUEST HOUSE

tel: 023 8063 6904 **21 Landguard Rd SO15 5DL**
email: info@landguardlodge.co.uk **web:** www.landguardlodge.co.uk
dir: 500yds NW of Southampton Central station. Off A3057 Shirley Rd into Landguard Rd, between Hill Ln & Shirley Rd

This smart and well cared for Victorian house is in a quiet residential area, just a 10-15 minute walk from the railway station, or there is off-street parking available. The bedrooms are bright, comfortable and well equipped with many thoughtful extras. Breakfast is served in the sunny breakfast room.

Rooms 11 en suite (1 fmly) (2 GF) S fr £48; D fr £80* **Facilities** FTV tea/coffee WiFi ⬗ **Parking** 3 **Notes** ⊗ No Children 5yrs

City Park Guest House
★★★ GUEST ACCOMMODATION

tel: 023 8022 5391 **4-6 The Polygon SO15 2BN**
email: info@cityparkguesthouse.com **web:** www.cityparkguesthouse.com

City Park Guest House is a family run business with a friendly atmosphere. Located in Southampton city centre close to the train and coach stations. Also an ideal location for the Mayflower Theatre which is only a three minute walk away. Comfortable accommodation is on offer with limited parking available.

Rooms 12 rms (9 en suite) (1 fmly) (2 GF) **Facilities** FTV DVD tea/coffee WiFi ⬗ **Parking** 2 **Notes** ⊗

Prince Consort

★★★ INN

tel: 023 8045 2676 **Victoria Rd, Netley SO31 5DQ**
email: info@theprinceconsortpub.co.uk **web:** www.theprinceconsortpub.co.uk
dir: *Premises situated next to main entrance of Royal Victoria Country Park*

The Prince Consort is situated just five minutes' walk from the seafront, and enjoys a friendly atmosphere. Food is available every evening in the spacious bar and restaurant. Bedrooms are contemporary and well presented, with smart, fully tiled en suites. Outdoor seating is a real bonus, as is the on-site parking.

Rooms 7 annexe en suite (1 fmly) (5 GF) **Facilities** STV FTV tea/coffee Dinner available WiFi **Conf** Max 40 Class 40 Board 20 **Parking** 25

The Brimar Guest House

★★ GUEST ACCOMMODATION

tel: 023 8086 2950 **10-14 High St, Totton SO40 9HN**
email: info@brimar-guesthouse.co.uk **web:** www.brimar-guesthouse.co.uk
dir: *3m W of city centre, exit A35 (Totton bypass) into Totton High St*

This property offers practical, comfortable accommodation at reasonable prices. Not all rooms are en suite but bathrooms are well situated. Breakfast is served in the dining room or as a take-away option. The Brimar is well placed for the M27 and Southampton docks, and off-road parking is available.

Rooms 21 rms (8 en suite) (7 pri facs) (2 fmly) (8 GF) S £45-£50; D £90-£100* **Facilities** FTV WiFi **Parking** 20 **Notes** ⊗

STOCKBRIDGE Map 5 SU33

The Greyhound on the Test

★★★★★ ◉◉ ⸮RESTAURANT WITH ROOMS

tel: 01264 810833 **31 High St SO20 6EY**
email: info@thegreyhoundonthetest.co.uk **web:** www.thegreyhoundonthetest.co.uk
dir: *9m NW of Winchester, 8m S of Andover. Off A303*

This charming restaurant with rooms has the River Test at its rear and the two AA Rosette award-winning food is a real draw. In addition, the luxury bedrooms are generally spacious, beautifully styled and come with a host of extras. Bathrooms are modern and have high quality towels and toiletries. There is also ample parking and well-kept grounds.

Rooms 10 en suite (1 GF) **Facilities** FTV DVD Lounge tea/coffee Dinner available WiFi ⚓ 18 Fishing Riding **Extras** Speciality toiletries - free; honesty bar **Conf** Max 12 Board 12 **Parking** 28 **Notes** Closed 24-25 Dec No coaches

The Three Cups Inn

★★★★ ◉ ⸮INN

tel: 01264 810527 **High St SO20 6HB**
email: manager@the3cups.co.uk **web:** www.the3cups.co.uk

Standing on Stockbridge high street, The Three Cups Inn dates from the 15th century. A former coaching inn, it has bags of charm and character and there are many cask ales to try in the cosy bar. The bedrooms are individually furnished, comfortable and equipped to a high standard. Excellent food is available every evening, served in both the cosy, snug-like dining room and the Orangery overlooking the garden.

Rooms 8 en suite (3 fmly) **Facilities** FTV tea/coffee Dinner available WiFi Fishing **Extras** Speciality toiletries, fresh milk **Parking** 15 **Notes** No coaches

The Peat Spade Inn

★★★★ ◉ INN

tel: 01264 810612 **Village St, Longstock SO20 6DR**
email: info@peatspadeinn.co.uk **web:** www.peatspadeinn.co.uk
dir: *M3 junct 8, A303 W approx 15m, then take A3057 Stockbridge/Andover*

In a delightfully tranquil setting between the historic cities of Winchester and Salisbury, Longstock is just north of Stockbridge, in the heart of the Test Valley, known for its fly fishing and picture-postcard villages. The inn has lots of character, with bedrooms located in the main building and the adjacent former peat house; all are comfortable and furnished in a modern style yet in keeping with the date of the original building. The inn is popular for both dining and drinking; the modern British menus are well balanced and use seasonal ingredients sourced from the local area.

Rooms 3 rms (3 pri facs) 5 annexe rms (5 pri facs) (3 GF) D £110-£160* **Facilities** FTV tea/coffee Dinner available Direct Dial WiFi ⚓ 18 Fishing Riding ⚫ Shooting **Extras** Bottled water, mini-fridge, speciality toiletries **Conf** Max 16 Board 16 **Parking** 19

WARNFORD Map 5 SU62

George & Falcon

★★★★ ⚋ INN

tel: 01730 829623 **Warnford Rd SO32 3LB**
email: reservations@georgeandfalcon.com **web:** www.georgeandfalcon.com
dir: *Adjacent to A32 in village*

Set in the picturesque village of Warnford, close to major transport links to Winchester, Portsmouth and Southampton, the George & Falcon offers tastefully appointed bedroom that retain the charm and character of a coaching inn yet provide modern facilities. Traditional fare is served in the popular restaurant and bar, and there is a large decking area which proves a useful addition in summer months.

Rooms 6 en suite (1 fmly) S £60-£90; D £65-£129 (room only)* **Facilities** FTV Lounge tea/coffee Dinner available WiFi ⚓ 18 Fishing Riding ⚫ **Extras** Speciality toiletries, mineral water **Conf** Max 30 Thtr 30 Class 15 Board 15 **Parking** 47 **Notes** LB Civ Wed 135

WHITCHURCH Map 5 SU44

White Hart Whitchurch

★★★ INN

tel: 01256 892900 **The Square RG28 7DN**
email: thewhitehart.whitchurch@arkells.com

Located in the centre of Whitchurch the White Hart is steeped in history and has served the local community for over 500 years. En suite rooms are well equipped some of which are located in an adjacent building. The inn is very popular with locals and diners alike. A very warm welcome from the friendly team is assured. Owned by Arkell's family brewers, a great range of traditionally brewed beers are available.

Rooms 10 en suite (3 fmly) **Facilities** FTV tea/coffee Dinner available WiFi **Parking** 12 **Notes** No coaches

WINCHESTER
Map 5 SU42

Premier Collection

Giffard House

★★★★★ GUEST HOUSE

tel: 01962 852628 **50 Christchurch Rd SO23 9SU**
email: giffardhotel@aol.com **web:** www.giffardhotel.co.uk
dir: *M3 junct 11, at rdbt 3rd exit onto A333 (St Cross road) for 1m. Pass BP garage on right, next left, 2nd right. 150mtrs on left*

Expect a warm welcome at Giffard House, a stunning Victorian property, close to the university. The accommodation is luxurious, comfortable and well equipped for both the business and leisure traveller. Beds are made up with crisp linen, and breakfast is served in the dining room. There is also a fully licensed bar in the elegant conservatory. Parking is a real bonus.

Rooms 13 en suite (1 fmly) (4 GF) **Facilities** STV FTV Lounge tea/coffee Direct Dial Licensed WiFi 🔒 **Extras** Speciality toiletries **Conf** Max 15 Thtr 15 Class 15 Board 13 **Parking** 13 **Notes** ⊗ Closed 24 Dec-2 Jan

The Old Vine

★★★★ INN

tel: 01962 854616 **8 Great Minster St SO23 9HA**
email: reservations@oldvinewinchester.com **web:** www.oldvinewinchester.com
dir: *M3 junct 11 towards St Cross, right at Green Man Pub, left into Symonds St, left into Little Minster St*

Overlooking the cathedral, this Grade II listed 18th-century inn mixes the elegance of days gone by with chic, modern comfort. The beautifully appointed bedrooms are named after designers and blend antique with contemporary, and the attractive dining room serves quality fare using local produce. There is permit parking.

Rooms 5 en suite 1 annexe en suite (2 fmly) S £120-£160; D £130-£200* **Facilities** FTV tea/coffee Dinner available WiFi 🔒 **Extras** Speciality toiletries, water, fruit juices - free **Notes** No coaches

The Wykeham Arms

★★★★★ ◉◉ 🍷 INN

tel: 01962 853834 **75 Kingsgate St SO23 9PE**
web: www.wykehamarmswinchester.co.uk
dir: *Immediately S of Cathedral, by Kingsgate and opposite Winchester College*

This is one of the oldest and best-loved public houses in Hampshire and is situated just south of the ancient cathedral. Bedrooms are sited in both the main house and annexe. All areas are furnished to a high standard with excellent facilities. Dining in the restaurant or bar is recommended - walls are adorned from top to bottom with every kind of bijouterie imaginable and the regularly changing menu uses fresh ingredients.

Rooms 14 en suite **Facilities** FTV Lounge tea/coffee Dinner available Direct Dial WiFi 🏌 18 🔒 **Extras** Mineral water - complimentary; robes in some rooms **Conf** Max 20 Thtr 20 Class 20 Board 20 **Parking** 10 **Notes** No Children 14yrs

Running Horse Inn

★★★★ ◉◉ INN

tel: 01962 880218 **88 Main Rd, Littleton SO22 6QS**
email: info@runninghorseinn.co.uk **web:** www.runninghorseinn.co.uk
dir: *B3049 from Winchester 1.5m, turn right into Littleton after 1m, Running Horse on right*

Situated in a pretty rural location, yet with easy access to the M3, this is a great location for business and leisure travellers visiting Hampshire. Offering quality accommodation, the Running Horse Inn is minimalist in its design, and provides comfortable beds and a small workstation area. Highlights of a stay here are a meal in the smart restaurant or a drink in the bar.

Rooms 15 annexe en suite (1 fmly) (9 GF) **Facilities** FTV tea/coffee Dinner available WiFi **Parking** 40 **Notes** No coaches

24 Clifton Road

★★★ BED AND BREAKFAST

tel: 01962 851620 **SO22 5BU**
email: a.williams1997@btinternet.com
dir: *500yds NW of city centre. B3090 Romsey Rd W from city centre, Clifton Rd 2nd right*

This delightful house is in a quiet residential area close to the railway station and High Street. It combines town-house elegance with a homely cottage charm, and is handy for local walks. The bedroom is comfortably furnished and the bathroom has a deep claw-foot bath. There is a lounge and a dining room.

Rooms 1 rm (1 pri facs) S £40; D £70 **Facilities** TVL tea/coffee WiFi 🔒 **Parking** 2 **Notes** ⊗ No Children 6yrs ⊛

HEREFORDSHIRE

ADFORTON
Map 9 SO47

Brick House Farm

★★★★ 🍽 BED AND BREAKFAST

tel: 01568 770870 **SY7 0NF**
email: info@adforton.com **web:** www.adforton.com
dir: *On A4110 in Adforton opposite St Andrew's Church*

Very much at the heart of the village community, this 16th-century longhouse provides high standards of comfort and good facilities. Superb beds and smart, modern private bathrooms can be found in the thoughtfully furnished accommodation. Comprehensive breakfasts featuring locally-sourced produce are served in the cosy, combined sitting and dining room. A warm welcome is assured.

Rooms 2 rms (2 pri facs) **Facilities** STV FTV Lounge tea/coffee WiFi **Parking** 2 **Notes** No Children 12yrs

---

ASTON INGHAM Map 10 SO62

New House Farm B&B (SO685229)

★★★★ ⌒ FARMHOUSE

---

tel: 01452 830484 & 07811 707487 **Barrel Ln GL17 0LS**
email: scaldbrain@btinternet.com **web:** www.newhousefarm-accommodation.co.uk
dir: A40 onto B4222, Barrel Ln on right before Aston Ingham; or M50 junct 3 towards Newent, right at Kilcot to Aston Ingham (B4222)

Located in tranquil wooded countryside, this working farm is a good spot for a touring base on the Gloucestershire-Herefordshire border. Set in 80 acres, the welcoming farmhouse will certainly appeal to nature lovers, and there is a comfortable lounge. Breakfast consists of a good selection of carefully prepared local produce.

Rooms 3 en suite (1 fmly) S £60-£90; D £80-£110* **Facilities** FTV DVD Lounge TVL tea/coffee WiFi 🕸 🌢 Clay pigeon shooting **Conf** Max 15 **Parking** 10 **Notes** LB ⊗ Closed Xmas & New Year 80 acres sheep/cattle/woodland

---

AYMESTREY Map 9 SO46

Mount Pleasant Lodge

★★★★ BED AND BREAKFAST

---

tel: 01568 708031 **HR6 9SU**
email: mountpleasantlodge@gmail.com **web:** www.mplaymestrey.co.uk
dir: Head from Leominster towards Kingsland, signed Amestrey approx 2.5m

A detached family home offering plenty of quality and comfort throughout, ideally located for guests visiting nearby attractions including a number of National Trust properties. Bedrooms and bathrooms provide good space and comfort along with some welcome extras. The freshly cooked breakfast offers a range of good quality local produce. Off-street parking, a comfortable conservatory and a pleasant garden are all available for guests to enjoy.

Rooms 3 en suite S £55-£75; D £75-£90* **Facilities** FTV DVD Lounge tea/coffee WiFi 🌢 **Extras** Snacks, filtered water - complimentary **Parking** 5 **Notes** LB ⊗ Closed Xmas & New Year ⊛

Farm Breakfasts B&B

★★★ BED AND BREAKFAST

---

tel: 01568 709055 **HR6 9ST**
web: www.farmbreakfasts.co.uk

Farm Breakfasts B&B is reputed to be the oldest house in Aymestrey and dates back to the 1500s. Ideally located for Leominster and Ludlow, the property is located midway on the Moritmer Trail and is great for walkers and cyclists. The property is full of original features like sloping ceilings and exposed wood; and there's a comfortable lounge with a log-burner. Bedrooms are well equipped for modern travellers. The whole property can be reserved on a self-catering basis or for small groups. Dinners are available on request using very good quality, locally sourced produce.

Rooms 3 en suite (1 fmly) **Facilities** TVL tea/coffee Dinner available WiFi

---

BODENHAM Map 10 SO55

The Coach House at England Gate's Inn

★★★★ ⌒ INN

---

tel: 01568 797286 **HR1 3HU**
email: englandsgate@btconnect.com **web:** www.englandsgate.co.uk
dir: Just off A417

This fine black and white 16th-century inn is run by the McNeil family, who pride themselves on quality service. It is set in attractive gardens which are ideal for alfresco dining on warmer days. The detached coach house has comfortable bedrooms with modern en suite facilities; the views are spectacular from the upstairs rooms. Continental breakfast is served in the coach house dining area on weekdays, and a full cooked breakfast is available at weekends.

Rooms 7 en suite (2 fmly) (4 GF) **Facilities** FTV DVD tea/coffee Dinner available Direct Dial WiFi 🌢 **Extras** Bottled water **Conf** Max 12 Board 12 **Parking** 30

BOLSTONE Map 10 SO53

Premier Collection

Prickett's Place

★★★★★ ⌒ BED AND BREAKFAST

---

tel: 01432 870221 **HR2 6LZ**
email: prickettsplace@btinternet.com **web:** www.prickettsplace.com
dir: M50 junct 4 onto A49, right towards Hoarwithy. Follow signs for Cottage of Content public house, turn left then turn right, Prickett's Place on left

Surrounded by magnificent countryside in the beautiful Wye Valley, Prickett's Place is peacefully located just seven miles from Hereford and nine miles from Ross-on-Wye. Bedrooms are very well furnished and equipped with welcome extras. Guests can enjoy tea in the garden upon arrival and also have use of a comfortable lounge. An excellent selection of high-quality ingredients is offered at breakfast.

Rooms 1 en suite 1 annexe en suite (1 fmly) S £55; D £74-£78 **Facilities** FTV DVD TVL tea/coffee WiFi 🌢 Canoeing **Extras** Speciality toiletries, fruit, fridge in annexe **Parking** 6 **Notes** LB ⊗ No Children 7yrs Closed Xmas & New Year

---

BREDWARDINE Map 9 SO34

Red Lion

★★★ INN

---

tel: 01981 500303 **HR3 6BU**
email: info@redlion-hotel.com **web:** www.redlion-hotel.com
dir: Off A438, Hereford to Brecon road

This traditionally styled inn is set in a pleasant village and provides an ideal base for exploring the local countryside and river walks. Popular with anglers, the inn has a fishing theme running throughout the public areas. Bedrooms offer a range of shapes and sizes, and are located either above the inn or in an adjacent annexe. Home cooked meals are served at both lunch and dinner.

Rooms 7 en suite 3 annexe en suite (1 fmly) (2 GF) **Facilities** FTV TVL tea/coffee Dinner available WiFi Fishing 🌢 **Parking** 20 **Notes** LB Closed Dec-1 Mar RS Mar-May closed Sun eve to Wed am

EWYAS HAROLD   Map 9 SO32

The Temple Bar Inn

★★★★ ◉◉ INN

tel: 01981 240423 **HR2 0EU**
email: phillytemplebar@btinternet.com **web:** www.thetemplebarinn.co.uk
dir: From Pontrilas (A465) onto B4347 signed Ewyas Harold. After 1m left into village. On right in 0.1m

Standing in the centre of the village, The Temple Bar Inn has been lovingly refurbished and brought back to life by the owners, with the help of local craftsmen, and is now the hub of the community. Smart bedrooms are well equipped for the modern traveller and complemented by modern en suite bathrooms. There is a bustling bar area with a separate games room and a small dining room serving high quality, locally sourced seasonal dishes.

Rooms 3 en suite (1 fmly) S £60; D £85* **Facilities** FTV tea/coffee Dinner available WiFi Pool table **Extras** Speciality toiletries, fresh milk - complimentary **Conf** Max 45 Thtr 45 Class 24 Board 16 **Parking** 10 **Notes** Closed 25 Dec RS 1wk Nov & 1wk Jan/Feb no L or D avail No eve meals all year Sun-Tue

GARWAY   Map 9 SO42

Garway Moon Inn

★★★★ ◻ INN

tel: 01600 750270 **HR2 8RQ**
email: info@garwaymooninn.co.uk **web:** www.garwaymooninn.co.uk
dir: From Hereford, S on A49. Right onto A466, right again onto B4521. At Broad Oak turn right to Garway

This traditional old hostelry is situated in peaceful and picturesque surroundings. Bedrooms are located above the inn and provide good quality and comfort. This 'proper' pub offers a selection of real ales and ciders, with a relaxed and welcoming ambience in the bar. Dinner should not be missed with high quality produce from local suppliers — many of whom might be found sitting in the bar. The home-made burgers are especially recommended.

Rooms 3 en suite (2 fmly) **Facilities** STV FTV DVD Lounge tea/coffee Dinner available WiFi **Extras** Bottled water - complimentary **Conf** Max 12 Board 12 **Parking** 20

HEREFORD   Map 10 SO53

Premier Collection

Somerville House

★★★★★ GUEST ACCOMMODATION

tel: 01432 273991 **12 Bodenham Rd HR1 2TS**
email: enquiries@somervillehouse.net **web:** www.somervillehousehereford.co.uk
dir: A465, at Aylestone Hill rdbt towards city centre, left at Southbank Rd, leading to Bodenham Rd

Situated in a quiet, tree-lined residential road, Somerville House is a detached late-Victorian villa that provides a boutique-style experience. Expect a warm and friendly welcome from Rosie and Bill who offer quality accommodation with high standards of luxury and comfort. All bedrooms are spacious, with a good range of quality extras. Breakfast is served at individual tables in the light and contemporary dining room. There is a terraced garden to the rear where guests can sit and relax, or indoors, they can make use of the comfortable lounge. There is ample parking.

Rooms 12 en suite (2 fmly) (1 GF) S £65-£95; D £85-£125* **Facilities** FTV DVD Lounge tea/coffee Licensed WiFi ◻ Arrangement with health spa **Extras** Speciality toiletries, chocolate, bottled water **Conf** Max 10 Thtr 10 Class 10 Board 10 **Parking** 10 **Notes** LB ◉

The Steppes

★★★★ ◻ BED AND BREAKFAST

tel: 01432 851536 & 07974 960956 **Hemhill, Lumber Ln HR1 4AL**
email: info@thesteppeshereford.co.uk **web:** www.thesteppeshereford.co.uk
dir: E of Hereford on A438, left in Lugwardine into Lumber Lane

Peacefully located in a quiet village this delightful property offers a tranquil and relaxing environment. Bedrooms and bathrooms are very well equipped and are located adjacent to the 16th-century cottage where breakfast is taken. The proprietors take great pride in their breakfast offering delicious daily special dishes in addition to home-made bread, jams and even honey from bees in the garden. For dinner, a pleasant pub is just a short stroll away.

Rooms 4 annexe en suite (3 GF) S £70-£90; D £80-£90 **Facilities** FTV DVD tea/coffee WiFi ◻ **Parking** 4 **Notes** ◉ No Children 15yrs

The Bay Horse Inn

★★★★ INN

tel: 01432 273351 **236 Kings Acre Rd HR4 0SD**
email: info@bayhorseinnhereford.co.uk **web:** www.bayhorseinnhereford.co.uk
dir: On A438, pass Wyevale garden centre, 100yds on left

Located just outside the city centre, The Bay Horse Inn combines comfortable bedrooms and bathrooms with an excellent range of food available during the day and evening. There is a relaxed ambience and welcoming service throughout. Guests also benefit from the use of a car park and a range of outdoor seating in warmer weather. A good selection of real ales, wine and bottled ciders are available.

Rooms 8 annexe en suite (3 fmly) (4 GF) S fr £59; D fr £69* **Facilities** FTV TVL tea/coffee Dinner available WiFi **Conf** Max 60 Thtr 35 Class 60 Board 20 **Parking** 56 **Notes** ◉ Closed 26 Dec

No 21

★★★★ GUEST ACCOMMODATION

tel: 01432 279897 & 07967 525403 **21 Aylestone Hill HR1 1HR**
email: jane@21aylestonehill.co.uk **web:** www.21aylestonehill.co.uk
dir: On A4103 from Worcester to rdbt at approach to Hereford. Take 1st exit to town centre (A465)

A warm welcome awaits visitors to this peaceful detached property, not far from the train station and the centre of Hereford. All the bedrooms and smart modern bathrooms are appointed to a high standard. The bedrooms are spacious with many extras; one ground-floor room, with a wet room, is ideal for guests that have difficulty with stairs. Breakfast is served in the spacious dining room at the front of the property, and there is ample secure parking.

Rooms 4 en suite (1 fmly) (1 GF) S £45-£50; D £70-£80* **Facilities** FTV TVL tea/coffee WiFi ◻ **Extras** Orange juice, bottled water, fresh milk - free **Parking** 8

Sink Green Farm (SO542377)

★★★★ FARMHOUSE

tel: 01432 870223 Rotherwas HR2 6LE
email: enquiries@sinkgreenfarm.co.uk web: www.sinkgreenfarm.co.uk
dir: 3m SE of city centre. Exit A49 onto B4399 for 2m

This charming 16th-century farmhouse stands in attractive countryside and has many original features, including flagstone floors, exposed beams and open fireplaces. Bedrooms are traditionally furnished and one has a four-poster bed. The pleasant garden has a comfortable summer house, hot tub and barbecue.

Rooms 3 en suite S £40-£50; D £80-£100 Facilities FTV iPod docking station Lounge TVL tea/coffee WiFi 🔒 Hot tub Extras Home-made biscuits Parking 10 Notes LB ⊛ 180 acres beef

Heron House

★★★ 🅰 BED AND BREAKFAST

tel: 01432 761111 Canon Pyon Rd, Portway HR4 8NG
email: info@theheronhouse.com web: www.theheronhouse.com
dir: A4103 onto A4110 to Portway x-rds, Heron House 200yds on left

Originally an 18th-century cottage, Heron House was considerably extended about 30 years ago. It is quietly located at Burghill, some four miles north of Hereford. The accommodation consists of one twin and one double room, both with modern furnishings and equipment. Separate tables are provided in the breakfast room.

Rooms 2 rms (1 en suite) Facilities DVD tea/coffee Parking 5 Notes ⊛ No Children 10yrs ⊛

KIMBOLTON — Map 10 SO56

Grove Farm B&B (SO518611)

★★★ FARMHOUSE

tel: 01568 613425 & 07890 471314 Grove Farm HR6 0HE
email: fiona@grovefarmdirect.co.uk web: www.grovefarmdirect.co.uk
dir: A49 N of Leominster onto A4112, signed Leysters. Into Kimbolton, turn left at pub, 500mtrs on left

Located in the Herefordshire countryside, this working farm offers a proper farmhouse feel with plenty of animals around and a friendly welcome with tea and cake on arrival. Bedrooms offer a range of shapes and sizes including one on the ground floor. Breakfast includes home-produced sausages and bacon in addition to apple juice from a nearby farm. For dinner, the local pub is just a few minutes stroll along the lane, or you could prepare something yourself in the guest kitchen which has a microwave and a fridge/freezer among other useful things. Dogs are welcome.

Rooms 3 en suite (1 fmly) (1 GF) Facilities FTV Lounge tea/coffee Dinner available WiFi ch fac ⅃ 18 🔒 Table tennis Extras Fresh milk, home-made cake Conf Max 20 Thtr 20 Class 20 Board 20 Parking 6 Notes 40 acres pigs/sheep/orchard

LEDBURY — Map 10 SO73

Premier Collection

Verzon House

★★★★★ ⊛⊛ 🍴 RESTAURANT WITH ROOMS

tel: 01531 670381 Trumpet HR8 2PZ
email: info@verzonhouse.com web: www.verzonhouse.com
dir: M50 junct 2 follow signs to Ledbury. Left at rdbt for Hereford. Follow A438 3m then Verzon is on right

Located on the main road, just a short distance from Ledbury, this delightful restaurant with rooms offers contemporary styling that mixes well with a more traditional country house feel, creating a relaxing ambience. Bedrooms offer a range of shapes and sizes, most with glorious views over the countryside towards the Malvern Hills. Dinner and breakfast provide a range of tempting, high-quality dishes all prepared with care and attention.

Rooms 8 en suite (1 fmly) Facilities FTV tea/coffee Dinner available Direct Dial WiFi ⅃ 18 Sauna Gym Extras Speciality toiletries, fruit, water - free Conf Max 20 Board 20 Parking 35 Notes Civ Wed 60

LEINTWARDINE — Map 9 SO47

Premier Collection

The Lion

★★★★★ ⊛ 🍴 RESTAURANT WITH ROOMS

tel: 01547 540203 & 540747 High St SY7 0JZ
email: enquiries@thelionleintwardine.co.uk web: www.thelionleintwardine.co.uk
dir: Beside bridge on A4113 (Ludlow to Knighton road) in Leintwardine

This quiet country restaurant with rooms in the picturesque village of Leintwardine, set beside the River Teme, is just a short distance from Ludlow and Craven Arms. The interior is stylish and the contemporary bedrooms are all en suite. Dining is taken seriously here and the modern, imaginative food uses the freshest local ingredients. The well-stocked bar offers a selection of real ales and lagers and there is a separate drinkers' bar too. The Lion is particularly popular with families as the garden has a secure children's play area, and in warmer months guests can eat alfresco. The friendly staff help to make any visit memorable.

Rooms 8 en suite (1 fmly) Facilities FTV Lounge tea/coffee Dinner available Direct Dial WiFi Fishing 🔒 Extras Home-made shortbread - complimentary Conf Max 25 Class 25 Board 25 Parking 25 Notes ⊛ Closed 25 Dec

LEINTWARDINE *continued*

Premier Collection

Upper Buckton *(SO384733)*

★★★★★ 🚜 FARMHOUSE

tel: 01547 540634 **Buckton SY7 0JU**
email: ghlloydco@btconnect.com **web:** www.upperbuckton.co.uk
dir: *From Leintwardine on A4113 to Walford. Right into narrow road signed Buckton. 2nd farm on left*

Upper Buckton is a Georgian house surrounded by beautiful grounds that slope gently down to the mill stream and out to the motte. Beyond this lies the ha-ha, old fashioned meadowland, the River Teme and the forested Wigmore Rolls. The house is comfortably furnished with interesting paintings and antique furniture. Of the three bedrooms, two have an en suite bathroom and one has private facilities and beds are fitted with electric blankets. An enjoyable home-cooked dinner is available by prior arrangement. In the cooler months the sitting room is a pleasant place to take afternoon tea and enjoy an after-dinner coffee around the log fire.

Rooms 3 rms (2 en suite) (1 pri facs) D fr £100 **Facilities** FTV Lounge tea/coffee Dinner available Licensed WiFi Table tennis **Extras** Speciality toiletries **Parking** 3 **Notes** LB ⊗ ⊜ 360 acres arable/potatoes/sheep

| LEOMINSTER | Map 10 SO45 |

Premier Collection

Hills Farm *(SO564638)*

★★★★★ ⌂ FARMHOUSE

tel: 01568 750205 **Leysters HR6 0HP**
email: stay@thehillsfarm.co.uk **web:** www.thehillsfarm.co.uk
dir: *Off A4112 (Leominster to Tenbury Wells), on outskirts of Leysters*

Set in a peaceful location with views over the countryside, this property dates in part from the 16th century. The friendly, attentive proprietors provide a relaxing and homely atmosphere. The attractive bedrooms, in the converted barns, are spacious and comfortable. Breakfasts, served in the dining room and conservatory, feature fresh local produce.

Rooms 3 annexe en suite (1 GF) D £88-£90 **Facilities** FTV iPod docking station Lounge tea/coffee WiFi 🔒 **Extras** Fridge, microwave, crockery, cutlery **Parking** 8 **Notes** ⊗ No Children 12yrs Closed Nov-Mar 120 acres arable

| MATHON | Map 10 SO74 |

Weobley Cross Cottage Bed & Breakfast

★★★★ BED AND BREAKFAST

tel: 01684 541488 & 07891 696795 **South End Ln WR13 5PB**
email: apwcross@gmail.com **web:** www.bedandbreakfastmalvernhills.co.uk
dir: *From Great Malvern on A449 towards Ledbury, fork right for Colwall & through Wyche Cutting. Right onto B4232 (West Malvern Rd), after 1m sharp left into Harcourt Rd. Travel 2m towards Mathon at the sign for South End pull onto the driveway.*

Expect a warm welcome from Anne, Peter and Hetty the dog at this peaceful cottage in the countryside, situated in the small village of Mathon, west of the Malvern Hills which border Herefordshire and Worcestershire. Surrounded by beautifully tended gardens the house offers two comfortable ground-floor en suite rooms, which are tastefully decorated in an eclectic cottage style. The conservatory makes an ideal venue for breakfast on cooler mornings.

Rooms 2 en suite (2 GF) D £80-£95 **Facilities** FTV Lounge tea/coffee WiFi 🔒 **Extras** Speciality toiletries, bottled water - free **Parking** 2 **Notes** LB ⊗ Closed Dec-Jan

| ROSS-ON-WYE | Map 10 SO52 |

Premier Collection

Wilton Court Restaurant with Rooms

★★★★★ ◉◉ ⌂ RESTAURANT WITH ROOMS

tel: 01989 562569 **Wilton Ln HR9 6AQ**
email: info@wiltoncourthotel.com **web:** www.wiltoncourthotel.com
dir: *M50 junct 4, A40 towards Monmouth at 3rd rdbt left signed Ross-on-Wye, 1st right, on right*

Dating back to the 16th century, Wilton Court has great charm and a wealth of character. Standing on the banks of the River Wye, just a short walk from the town centre, there is a genuinely relaxed, friendly and unhurried atmosphere created by hosts Roger and Helen Wynn and their reliable team. Bedrooms are tastefully furnished and well equipped, while public areas include a comfortable lounge, traditional bar and pleasant restaurant with a conservatory extension overlooking the garden. High standards of food, using fresh, locally sourced ingredients, are offered.

Rooms 11 en suite (1 fmly) (1 GF) S £100-£150; D £125-£185* **Facilities** FTV DVD Lounge tea/coffee Dinner available Direct Dial WiFi 🐾 🔒 18 Fishing 🔒 **Extras** Kimonos, bottled water **Conf** Thtr 50 Class 20 Board 20 **Parking** 20 **Notes** LB Closed 3-15 Jan

Benhall Farm

★★★★ ⌂ BED AND BREAKFAST

tel: 01989 563900 & 07900 264612 **Wilton HR9 6AG**
email: info@benhallfarm.co.uk **web:** www.benhallfarm.co.uk
dir: *From Wilton rdbt (A40 & A49 junct), take exit towards M50. On dual-carriageway immediately left at No Through Road sign. Benhall Farm at end of lane*

A warm welcome can be expected at Benhall Farm, a modern working dairy and arable farm of 335 acres which forms part of the Duchy of Cornwall Estate. The farm is on the outskirts of Ross-on-Wye on the banks of the river and has easy access to the M50, Hereford, Abergavenny, Monmouth, and the Forest of Dean. The bedrooms are comfortable, spacious and many guest extras are provided, including

WiFi. A lounge is available for guests' use and the dining room is the venue for hearty breakfasts served at the communal table. Parking is available to the front of the property.

Rooms 3 en suite D £80-£84* **Facilities** FTV DVD TVL tea/coffee WiFi Fishing ⚓ **Extras** Fridge, home-made biscuits, fresh milk **Parking** 6 **Notes** LB ⊗ Closed 20 Dec-10 Jan

Forest View Guest House

★★★★ GUEST ACCOMMODATION

tel: 01600 890210 & 07881 247068 **Symonds Yat East HR9 6JL**
web: www.forestviewguesthouse.co.uk
dir: A40 onto B4229 signed Goodrich, then B4432 for Symonds Yat East

Delightfully located on the banks of the river, guests can take part in a range of activities such as walking and canoeing, literally on the doorstep. Bedrooms and bathrooms are comfortably furnished and most have views over the river and the forest beyond. In addition to carefully prepared breakfast, guests also have the option of a range of home-cooked dinners served in the pleasant dining room. A small bar and lounge is provided.

Rooms 10 en suite (2 GF) **Facilities** FTV DVD Lounge TVL tea/coffee Dinner available Licensed WiFi ⌥ 18 Fishing ⚓ **Extras** Speciality toiletries, snacks **Conf** Max 20 Thtr 20 Class 20 Board 20 **Parking** 15 **Notes** ⊗ No Children 12yrs

Lea House

★★★★ ☕ GUEST ACCOMMODATION

tel: 01989 750652 & 07495 713603 **Lea HR9 7JZ**
email: enquiries@leahouse.co.uk **web:** www.leahouse.co.uk
dir: 4m SE of Ross on A40 towards Gloucester, in Lea

This former coaching inn, near Ross-on-Wye, has a relaxed atmosphere and makes a good base for exploring the Forest of Dean and the Wye Valley. The individually furnished bedrooms are thoughtfully equipped and very homely. Breakfast in the oak-beamed dining room offers home-made breads, freshly squeezed juice, fresh fruit platters, local sausages and fish choices.

Rooms 3 rms (2 en suite) (1 pri facs) (1 fmly) S £58-£70; D £82-£92* **Facilities** FTV TVL tea/coffee WiFi ⚓ **Parking** 4 **Notes** LB

Thatch Close

★★★★ GUEST ACCOMMODATION

tel: 01989 770300 **Llangrove HR9 6EL**
email: info@thatchclose.co.uk **web:** www.thatchclose.co.uk
dir: Off A40 at Symonds Yat West/Whitchurch junct to Llangrove, right at x-rds after Post Office & before school. Thatch Close 0.6m on left

Standing in 13 acres, this sturdy 18th-century farmhouse is full of character. Expect a wonderfully warm atmosphere with a genuine welcome from your hosts. The homely bedrooms are equipped for comfort with many thoughtful extras. Breakfast is served in the elegant dining room, and a lounge is available. The extensive patios and gardens are popular in summer, providing plenty of space to find a quiet corner and relax with a good book.

Rooms 3 en suite S £55; D £80* **Facilities** TVL tea/coffee WiFi ⚓ **Parking** 8 **Notes** LB

SYMONDS YAT (EAST)   Map 10 SO51

See also Coleford (Gloucestershire)

The Royal Lodge

★★★★ ☕ ⚑ GUEST ACCOMMODATION

tel: 01600 890238 **HR9 6JL**
email: info@rhhotels.co.uk **web:** www.rhhotels.co.uk
dir: Midway between Ross and Monmouth exit A40 at signs for Goodrich & B4229 to Symonds Yat East

The Royal Lodge stands at the top end of the village overlooking the River Wye. Bedrooms are spacious and comfortable, and come complete with flat-screen TVs and many guest extras; the bathrooms offer modern facilities. There is a cosy lounge with an open fireplace and two bars are available. Meals are offered in the welcoming restaurant, which provides carefully prepared meals using fresh and local ingredients. Staff are pleasant and friendly.

Rooms 24 en suite (5 fmly) S £40-£65; D £69-£139 **Facilities** FTV DVD TVL tea/coffee Dinner available Direct Dial Licensed WiFi Fishing ⚓ **Extras** Mineral water **Conf** Max 120 Thtr 120 Class 80 Board 80 **Parking** 150 **Notes** LB Civ Wed 150

The Saracens Head Inn

For centuries the *Saracens Head Inn* has occupied its spectacular position on the east bank of the River Wye, where the river flows into a steep wooded gorge. The Inn's own ferry across the river still operates by hand, just as it has for the past 200 years.

There's a relaxed atmosphere throughout the Inn, from the flagstoned bar to the cosy lounge and dining room. The riverside terraces are a great place to watch the world go by.

The Inn has a reputation for high quality food, using fresh local ingredients where possible, with a regularly changing menu and daily specials – not to mention a tempting choice of 6 real ales (featuring local breweries), and freshly-ground coffee.

Symonds Yat East is situated in an Area of Outstanding Natural Beauty on the edge of the Forest of Dean, so a stay in one of the ten guest bedrooms is a must for exploring the unspoilt local countryside.

The Wye Valley Walk passes the Inn, as does the Peregrine cycle trail. Walking, cycling, mountain biking, river cruises, canoeing, kayaking, climbing and fishing are all available nearby.

Symonds Yat East
Ross on Wye
Herefordshire
HR9 6JL

Tel: 01600 890435
E: contact@saracensheadinn.co.uk
Web: www.saracensheadinn.co.uk

SYMONDS YAT (EAST) *continued*

Saracens Head Inn

★★★★ ⚓ INN

tel: 01600 890435 **HR9 6JL**
email: contact@saracensheadinn.co.uk web: www.saracensheadinn.co.uk
dir: *Exit A40 at South Herefordshire Motorcaravan Centre, signed Symonds Yat East, 2m*

Dating from the 16th century, the friendly, family-run Saracens Head faces the River Wye and has wonderful views. The well-equipped bedrooms are decorated in a cottage style, and there are a cosy lounge, an attractive dining room, and a popular public bar that leads onto a riverside patio. All meals are offered from a regularly changing and comprehensive menu that includes locally-sourced produce.

Rooms 8 en suite 2 annexe en suite (1 GF) S £59-£75; D £89-£138* **Facilities** FTV TVL tea/coffee Dinner available Direct Dial WiFi Fishing ⚓ **Conf** Max 25 Thtr 25 Class 25 Board 25 **Parking** 35 **Notes** No Children 12yrs No coaches

See advert on page 175

See advert on page 175

WHITCHURCH   Map 10 SO51

Norton House

★★★★ ⚓ BED AND BREAKFAST

tel: 01600 890046 & 07948 079660 **Old Monmouth Rd HR9 6DJ**
email: lynda.mwhittle@gmail.com web: www.norton-house.com

Built as a farmhouse, Norton House dates back some 300 years and has retained a lot of character, with flagstone floors and beamed ceilings. A warm and friendly welcome awaits all guests from hosts Lynda and David. The bedrooms, including a four-poster room, are individually styled and furnished for maximum comfort. Charming public areas include a snug with a wood-burning stove and comfortable lounge, a perfect location to enjoy the home-baked cakes on arrival. Excellent local produce is used to create an imaginative range of breakfast dishes. Parking is off-road, and self-catering cottages are also available.

Rooms 3 en suite S fr £60; D fr £80* **Facilities** FTV iPod docking station Lounge TVL tea/coffee WiFi ⚓ **Extras** Fruit **Parking** 5 **Notes** LB No Children 13yrs

---

WHITNEY-ON-WYE   Map 9 SO24

Rhydspence Inn

★★★★ ⚓ INN

tel: 01497 831262 **HR3 6EU**
email: info@rhydspence.com web: www.rhydspence.com
dir: *On A438 between Hereford & Brecon, on right at England/Wales border*

The Rhydspence Inn is full of character and history. Spanning the Wales-England border this popular property is ideally located for Hay-on-Wye and Hereford. Parts of the building date from 1380, and extensions were added in the 17th to 20th centuries. A friendly welcome and relaxing ambience are provided in both the bar and the dining room where locals and guests mingle. Bedrooms offer a variety of shapes and sizes and are all located above the inn. Both dinner and breakfast offer a good selection of home-made, carefully prepared dishes.

Rooms 8 en suite S £60-£120; D £70-£150* **Facilities** FTV Lounge TVL tea/coffee Dinner available WiFi Fishing **Extras** Speciality toiletries **Conf** Max 30 Thtr 30 Class 30 Board 30 **Parking** 30 **Notes** LB

YARKHILL   Map 10 SO64

Garford Farm *(SO600435)*

★★★★ FARMHOUSE

tel: 01432 890226 **HR1 3ST**
email: garfordfarm@btconnect.com
dir: *Exit A417 at Newtown x-rds onto A4103 for Hereford, farm 1.5m on left*

This black and white, timber-framed farmhouse, set on a large arable holding, dates from the 17th century. Its character is enhanced by period furnishings, and fires burn in the comfortable lounge during colder weather. The traditionally furnished bedrooms, including a family room, have modern facilities.

Rooms 2 en suite (1 fmly) S fr £45; D fr £65* **Facilities** Lounge tea/coffee WiFi ⚓ ⚓ **Parking** 6 **Notes** No Children 2yrs Closed 25-26 Dec ⊛ 200 acres arable

HERTFORDSHIRE

ASHWELL
Map 12 TL23

The Three Tuns
★★★★ ⊛ INN

tel: 01462 743343 **6 High St SG7 5NL**
email: info@thethreetunsashwell.co.uk **web:** www.thethreetunsashwell.co.uk
dir: A1(M) junct 10 follow signs for Baldock (A507), turn left signed Ashwell.
At T junct right. In Ashwell, on left of High Street

The Three Tuns is located in the picturesque village of Ashwell. This is a friendly village pub that offers comfortable accommodation and rooms have been stylishly designed. Guests can enjoy dinner in either the friendly bar or the restaurant. A patio garden is available for summer months.

Rooms 3 en suite (1 fmly) D £90-£110* **Facilities** FTV tea/coffee Dinner available WiFi **Conf** Max 20 Thtr 20 Class 12 Board 12 **Parking** 16 **Notes** No coaches

BISHOP'S STORTFORD
Map 6 TL42

The PitStop
★★★★ GUEST ACCOMMODATION

tel: 01279 725725 & 725007 **The Morgan Garage, Little Hallingbury CM22 7RA**
email: mr@melvyn-rutter.net **web:** www.the-pitstop.net
dir: 3m S of Bishop's Stortford, signed Melvyn Rutter Ltd - Morgan Garage

The PitStop offers four individually styled en suite rooms. Located above The Morgan Garage, guests can enjoy a good night's sleep, and hire a modern classic Morgan car for the day. All rooms are very well equipped and meet the needs of a varied clientele. Self-service continental breakfast can be taken in the American-style diner.

The PitStop

Rooms 4 en suite (1 fmly) D fr £89* **Facilities** FTV iPod docking station TVL Lift WiFi Hire of Morgan & MGB sports cars **Extras** Fruit, snacks - complimentary **Parking** 30 **Notes** ⊛

See advert below

Bonningtons Guest House
★★★ GUEST HOUSE

tel: 01279 507472 & 07815 704830 **George Green, Little Hallingbury CM22 7SP**
email: info@bonningtons.net **web:** www.bonningtons.net
dir: M11 junct 8 onto A120 towards Bishop's Stortford. Left at next rdbt, at lights left onto A1060 towards Hatfield Heath. In centre of Little Hallingbury, turn right opposite The George pub

Set in its own grounds, Bonningtons is a stylish guest house with a range of individually designed modern bedrooms. All bedrooms are well equipped, and free WiFi is available along with secure parking. Stansted Airport is a short drive away and daily rates for parking are available. Continental-style breakfasts are provided and there is a very good choice on offer. An ideal base from which to explore the Cambridgeshire and Essex countryside.

Rooms 6 annexe en suite (1 fmly) (4 GF) S £42.50-£49.99; D £49.99-£69.99* **Facilities** FTV Lounge tea/coffee WiFi 🛁 **Extras** Chocolates **Parking** 20

The PitStop

Superior accommodation, for ladies and gentlemen, with a motoring flavour

THE FAMILY - *(Edwardian style)*
THE DROP HEAD COUPE - *(Eastern & exotic)*
THE AERO - *(Modern contemporary)*
THE SUPER SPORTS - *(Art Deco)*
All rooms have beautiful en-suite bathrooms, internet access and TV
THE KITCHEN *(American diner style)*
help yourself to breakfast

Rooms from £89 per night, including Continental style breakfast

AA
★★★★
Guest Accommodation

FOR HIRE
2 litre Plus 4 at £220 per day

The Morgan Garage, Little Hallingbury, Nr Bishop's Stortford. CM22 7RA
T: 01279 725725 / 07803 290000 (M)   E: mr@melvyn-rutter.net   W: www.the-pitstop.net

BUNTINGFORD
Map 12 TL32

Sword Inn Hand
★★★★ INN

tel: 01763 271356 **Westmill SG9 9LQ**
email: theswordinnhandrestaurant@gmail.com web: www.theswordinnhand.co.uk
dir: *In Westmill, off A10 S of Buntingford*

Set within the peaceful village of Westmill amid rolling countryside, this charming 14th-century inn offers excellent accommodation in a friendly and relaxed atmosphere. The purpose-built, ground-floor bedrooms are located just off the rear gardens; all are very well-equipped and carefully appointed and have their own access. Character public rooms offer a choice of restaurant and bar dining options, along with a choice of draught ales.

Rooms 4 en suite (4 GF) **Facilities** STV FTV TVL tea/coffee Dinner available ⚓
Parking 25 **Notes** ⊗

MUCH HADHAM
Map 6 TL41

High Hedges Bed & Breakfast
★★★★ BED AND BREAKFAST

tel: 01279 842505 **High Hedges, Green Tye SG10 6JP**
email: info@high-hedges.co.uk web: www.high-hedges.co.uk
dir: *From B1004 turn off to Green Tye at Prince of Wales pub, turn into private road, 1st on right*

Expect a warm welcome at High Hedges, a family-run B&B conveniently located for Stansted Airport, and convenient for visiting London and Cambridge. Bedrooms are well presented and comfortable, and come with many thoughtful extra touches. A substantial breakfast is served in the pleasant dining room.

Rooms 3 rms (2 en suite) (1 pri facs) (1 fmly) (1 GF) **Facilities** FTV tea/coffee WiFi
Parking 3 **Notes** ⊗ Closed 25-26 Dec & 31 Dec-1 Jan ⊛

NUTHAMPSTEAD
Map 12 TL43

The Woodman Inn
★★★ INN

tel: 01763 848328 **SG8 8NB**
email: enquiries@thewoodman-inn.co.uk web: www.thewoodman-inn.co.uk
dir: *M11 junct 20, A505 towards Royston, left onto B1368 to Barkway, 1st left past Tally Ho, right in 2m. Inn on left. Or from Royston take A505 signed motorway (M11) & Newmarket. Right onto B1368 & then as above*

This 17th-century inn has many fine features, and is close to the Duxford Imperial War Museum. The practical bedrooms are decorated in a traditional style. The kitchen offers a good range of British meals, plus a generous breakfast.

Rooms 2 annexe en suite (2 GF) **Facilities** FTV tea/coffee Dinner available WiFi ⚲ 18
Pool table Shooting range by arrangement **Parking** 30 **Notes** RS Sun eve-Mon bar & restaurant closed

ST ALBANS
Map 6 TL10

Innkeeper's Lodge St Albans, London Colney
★★★★ INN

tel: 08451 551551 *(Calls cost 2p per minute plus your phone company's access charge)*
Barnet Rd, London Colney AL2 1BL
email: info@innkeeperslodge.com web: www.innkeeperslodge.com

Conveniently located close to the historic town of St Albans, the Colney Fox is a favourite with leisure and business guests. The charming original bar is warm and welcoming, and the log fires burn brightly on cooler evenings. The Fox is a very popular dining venue, and the extensive dinner menu caters for most tastes. The stylish bedrooms are all attractively presented while still retaining many of the inn's original features. Free WiFi is provided, ample secure parking is available and the M25 is close by.

Rooms 13 en suite **Facilities** FTV tea/coffee Dinner available WiFi **Parking** **Notes** ⊗

WELWYN
Map 6 TL21

Premier Collection

The Wellington
★★★★★ ⊚ INN

tel: 01438 714036 **High St AL6 9LZ**
email: info@wellingtonatwelwyn.co.uk web: www.wellingtonatwelwyn.co.uk
dir: *A1(M) junct 6 follow signs to Welwyn. In the High St opposite St Mary Church*

Enjoying a prominent position in the heart of the pretty village of Welwyn, The Wellington offers a range of beautifully presented, individually styled bedrooms. The most is made of the eye-catching original features in the charming restaurant, and log fires on colder evenings add to the ambience. There is a cosy bar area along with a sheltered terrace at the rear of the property. Ample secure parking is available along with free WiFi for guests.

Rooms 6 en suite **Facilities** FTV DVD iPod docking station tea/coffee Dinner available WiFi **Extras** Bottled water **Parking** 34 **Notes** ⊗ No coaches

ISLE OF WIGHT

ARRETON
Map 5 SZ58

Blandings
★★★★ BED AND BREAKFAST

tel: 01983 865720 & 865331 **Horringford PO30 3AP**
email: robin.oulton@horringford.com web: www.horringford.com/bedandbreakfast.htm
dir: *S through Arreton (B3056), pass Stickworth Hall on right, 300yds on left farm entrance signed Horringford Gdns. U-turn to left, at end of poplar trees turn right. Blandings on left*

Blandings is a detached home in the grounds of Horringford Gardens. Set in a small group of farm buildings, it was formerly the piggery and wainhouse, where the farm carts were kept. The guest bedroom has private access and a decking area for warm summer evenings. Breakfast is a highlight with local island produce gracing the table.

Rooms 1 en suite (1 GF) **Facilities** FTV tea/coffee WiFi **Parking** 3 **Notes** ⊛

BEMBRIDGE
Map 5 SZ68

The Spinnaker
★★★★ INN

tel: 01983 873572 & 872840 **1 Steyne Rd PO35 5UH**
email: info@thespinnakeriow.co.uk web: www.thespinnakeriow.co.uk
dir: *From A3055 take B3395 (Sandown Rd) towards Bembridge. After rdbt becomes Steyne Rd*

A beautifully restored Edwardian inn, set in the heart of Bembridge, open from 9am daily for breakfast, lunch and dinner. The 14 en suite rooms are appointed with modern amenities, while the decor retains the character and charm of this grand building. The bar has a fabulous snug area, chart room and many other cosy corners. The menu uses local produce and island suppliers where possible. There are two intimate function rooms available to hire. Flexible, tailor-made packages are available and advance booking is recommended.

Rooms 14 en suite (2 fmly) S £45-£90; D £60-£120* **Facilities** FTV DVD iPod docking station tea/coffee Dinner available WiFi ⬥ 9 🐾 **Conf** Max 100 Thtr 100 Class 60 Board 50 **Parking** 30 **Notes** LB No coaches Civ Wed 50

The Crab & Lobster Inn

★★★★ INN

tel: 01983 872244 **32 Forelands Field Rd PO35 5TR**
email: info@crabandlobsterinn.co.uk **web:** www.crabandlobsterinn.co.uk
dir: *From High St in Bembridge, 1st left after Boots into Forelands Rd. At right bend, left into Lane End Rd, 2nd right into Egerton Rd. At T-junct left into Howgate Rd. Road bears right & becomes Forelands Field Rd, follow brown inn signs*

The Crab & Lobster is a traditional beamed inn enjoying a coastal location overlooking Bembridge Ledge and has panoramic sea views. Bedrooms and bathrooms are traditionally fitted, comfortable and spacious, offering a good range of accessories. Locally-caught crab and lobster are a speciality.

Rooms 5 en suite (1 fmly) S £40-£80; D £65-£100* **Facilities** FTV DVD tea/coffee Dinner available WiFi **Parking** 20 **Notes** RS 24-26 Dec B&B only No coaches

---

CHALE   Map 5 SZ47

The Old House

★★★★ 🏠 BED AND BREAKFAST

tel: 01983 551368 & 07746 453398 **Gotten Manor, Gotten Ln PO38 2HQ**
email: aa@gottenmanor.co.uk **web:** www.gottenmanor.co.uk
dir: *1m N of Chale. Turn right from B3399 into Gotten Ln (opposite chapel), house at end*

Located in countryside close to the coast, this 17th-century house has 18th- and 19th-century additions. The charming rustic bedrooms have antique bathtubs. Comprehensive breakfasts using the finest ingredients are served in the cosy dining room, and there is a spacious lounge with an open fire.

Rooms 2 en suite S £70-£90; D £90-£110 **Facilities** STV FTV iPod docking station Lounge tea/coffee WiFi 🐾 🐾 **Parking** 3 **Notes** LB ⊗ No Children 12yrs ⌨

COWES   Map 5 SZ49

Mimosa Lodge

★★★★ BED AND BREAKFAST

tel: 01983 241490 & 07775 742361 **59 Baring Rd PO31 8DW**
email: info@mimosa-lodge.co.uk **web:** www.mimosa-lodge.co.uk
dir: *From East Cowes on chain ferry to West Cowes, into Mill Hill Rd. Right into Victoria Rd, at end right into Park Rd then immediately left into Ward Ave. At bottom of road, left into Baring Rd*

Located just a short distance from Cowes, this Regency-style house offers spacious and comfortable en suite bedrooms boasting many original features, alongside modern decor and fixtures that include WiFi and digital TVs. Just a short distance from the Isle of Wight Coast Path, this B&B is also ideal for walkers. Guests can expect a friendly arrival where refreshments can be enjoyed in the conservatory. A cooked and continental breakfast is served daily in the dining room.

Rooms 3 en suite (1 GF) **Facilities** FTV DVD tea/coffee WiFi **Parking** 3 **Notes** ⊗ No Children 12yrs Closed 22 Dec-2 Jan

Duke of York Inn

★★★ INN

tel: 01983 295171 **Mill Hill Rd PO31 7BT**
email: bookings@dukeofyorkcowes.co.uk **web:** www.dukeofyorkcowes.co.uk

This family-run inn is situated very close to the centre of Cowes. Comfortable bedrooms are divided between the main building and a separate annexe only seconds away. Home-cooked meals, with a number of fish and seafood dishes, feature on the menu every evening and are served in the bar and dining area; outdoor covered dining is also an option. Parking is a bonus.

Rooms 8 en suite 5 annexe en suite (1 fmly) (1 GF) S £59-£70; D £79-£100* **Facilities** FTV tea/coffee Dinner available WiFi **Parking** 10

FISHBOURNE
Map 5 SZ59

The Fishbourne

★★★★ ⇔ INN

tel: 01983 873572 & 882823 **111 Fishbourne Ln PO33 4EU**
email: info@thefishbourne.co.uk web: www.thefishbourne.co.uk
dir: *Off A3054 Newport to Ryde road, next to Wightlink Ferry Terminal*

The Fishbourne is conveniently located just along from the Wightlink Fishbourne terminal. The inn offers five stylishly decorated bedrooms with light and airy decor and modern fixtures, including LCD TV and free WiFi. Guests can enjoy breakfast, lunch or dinner served in the open-plan bar and restaurant area. On offer are a wide range of traditional pub dishes, with all produce locally sourced.

Rooms 5 en suite (2 fmly) S £45-£75; D £80-£120* **Facilities** FTV DVD iPod docking station tea/coffee Dinner available WiFi ⅃ ⑨ **Parking** 40 **Notes** LB No coaches

GODSHILL
Map 5 SZ58

Premier Collection

Koala Cottage

★★★★★ ⇔ BED AND BREAKFAST

tel: 01983 842031 **Church Hollow PO38 3DR**
email: info@koalacottage.co.uk web: www.koalacottage.co.uk
dir: *From Ryde on A3055, after 7m onto A3056 then A3020, left into Church Hollow*

Located in the heart of the picturesque village of Godshill, Koala Cottage offers three spacious and comfortably appointed bedrooms, all with external access and on-site parking. Bedrooms and bathrooms are of a high quality and guests can expect a number of thoughtful extras on arrival, including locally-made chocolates plus wine and flowers. There is a patio area and jacuzzi for guests to enjoy. Both cooked and continental breakfasts are served in the conservatory. There are a number of good pubs within a couple of minutes' walk for evening meals.

Rooms 3 en suite (3 GF) **Facilities** FTV DVD tea/coffee Direct Dial Licensed WiFi Sauna ⑧ Jacuzzi **Extras** Bottled water - complimentary **Parking** 3 **Notes** ⊗ No Children 18yrs

NEWPORT
Map 5 SZ58

Bank Cottage B&B

★★★★ BED AND BREAKFAST

tel: 01983 822255 & 07796 945019 **Dodnor Ln PO30 5TD**
email: bankcottagebnb@gmail.com web: www.bankcottagebandb.co.uk

Bank Cottage offers a one bedroom suite with private facilities and a private terrace on which to relax in warmer months. This is an ideal place for those searching for a quiet location to unwind and recharge their batteries. The suite has been well designed and can be configured to accommodate families or friends travelling together. In-room breakfast is served at the dining table, and guests can choose from a well-written breakfast menu the night before for a prompt delivery in the morning. The suite also offers all mod cons including free WiFi. Secure parking is available.

Rooms 1 rm (1 pri facs) (1 fmly) S £60-£85; D £75-£100* **Facilities** FTV TVL tea/coffee WiFi ⑧ **Extras** Slippers **Parking** 3 **Notes** ⊗

Castle Lodge

★★★ GUEST ACCOMMODATION

tel: 01983 527862 & 07789 228203 **54 Castle Rd PO30 1DP**
email: castlelodge@hotmail.co.uk web: www.castlelodgeiow.co.uk
dir: *0.5m SW of town centre. On B3323 towards Carisbrooke Castle*

Well-presented Castle Lodge is located in a quiet residential area within close walking distance of the famous Carisbrooke Castle. A comfortable stay is assured in attractive and restful bedrooms, together with a bright and airy dining room where a substantial breakfast can be enjoyed.

Rooms 2 en suite 5 annexe en suite (1 fmly) (5 GF) S £40-£60; D £50-£90* **Facilities** FTV DVD tea/coffee WiFi ⑧ **Parking** 5 **Notes** ⊗

NITON
Map 5 SZ57

Premier Collection

Enchanted Manor

★★★★★ GUEST ACCOMMODATION

tel: 01983 730215 **Sandrock Rd PO38 2NG**
email: info@enchantedmanor.co.uk web: www.enchantedmanor.co.uk

Enchanted Manor is a delightful property, set in charming grounds, and enjoys an enviable location within walking distance of the sea. The unusual theme of magic and enchantment prevails throughout the beautifully appointed suites and spacious public areas, all of which are furnished and decorated to a very high standard. A host of extra touches are provided such as DVD players, well-stocked mini-fridges and welcome baskets. Friendly, attentive service is assured.

Rooms 7 en suite (2 GF) **Facilities** STV FTV DVD Lounge tea/coffee Licensed WiFi Snooker Pool table ⑧ Spa/hot tub Massage beauty treatment room **Conf** Max 30 Board 30 **Parking** 15 **Notes** LB ⊗ No Children Civ Wed 50

RYDE
Map 5 SZ59

Lisle Court

★★★★ BED AND BREAKFAST

tel: 01983 882860 & 07773 870376 **Woodside, Wootton PO33 4JR**
email: welcome@lislecourt.org.uk web: www.lislecourt.org.uk
dir: *A3054 to Wootton Bridge. In High St into New Rd, 1m to Lisle Court*

In a prime location with views of Wootton Creek, this Victorian property offers comfortably appointed bedrooms and bathrooms. The house stands in approximately two acres of garden, with mature trees, shrubs and lawns with a small pond and swimming pool. For anyone with a boat the property has its own jetty and pontoons which dry out at low tide. A small boat/summer house on the foreshore provides a tranquil spot to sit and watch boats and wildlife on the creek.

Rooms 3 en suite S £45-£60; D £90-£100 **Facilities** FTV Lounge TVL tea/coffee WiFi ⚲ Fishing ⑧ Private jetty & pontoons **Parking** 12 **Notes** LB No Children 16yrs Closed 24 Dec-4 Jan ⊜

SANDOWN
Map 5 SZ58

The Wight

★★★★ GUEST ACCOMMODATION

tel: 01983 403722 **11 Avenue Rd PO36 8BN**
email: enquiries@wighthotel.co.uk **web:** www.wighthotel.co.uk
dir: 100yds after mini rdbt between High St & Avenue Rd

A family establishment, set in secluded grounds, only a short walk from Sandown's beach and high street shops. Bedrooms are very welcoming and are either on the ground or first floor. There's a heated swimming pool and a spa facility; there's also evening entertainment in the bar. A plentiful breakfast is served in the colourful dining room.

Rooms 41 en suite (17 fmly) (18 GF) S £40-£56; D £80-£112* **Facilities** FTV Lounge TVL tea/coffee Licensed WiFi ⊗ Snooker Sauna Gym Pool table ⬤ Steam room Jacuzzi **Parking** 36 **Notes** LB Civ Wed 80

SEAVIEW
Map 5 SZ69

The Boathouse

★★★★ ⬤ INN

tel: 01983 873572 & 810616 **Springvale Rd PO34 5AW**
email: info@theboathouseiow.co.uk **web:** www.theboathouseiow.co.uk
dir: From Seaview follow sea road, The Boathouse on corner of Springvale Rd & Puckpool Hill

This very pleasant inn has a shore-side location and is a relaxing, friendly and comfortable place to stay. Food is a focus here with fresh, local produce and speciality lobster and crab dishes. The inn provides a contemporary style throughout; bedrooms are pleasantly spacious and most have beach views. There is ample parking and a garden, where in warmer times food and drink are served.

Rooms 4 en suite (1 fmly) S £45-£75; D £80-£130* **Facilities** FTV DVD iPod docking station tea/coffee Dinner available WiFi **Parking** 20 **Notes** LB No coaches

SHANKLIN
Map 5 SZ58

Fernbank

★★★★ ⬤ GUEST ACCOMMODATION

tel: 01983 862790 **6 Highfield Rd PO37 6PP**
email: fernbank2010@btconnect.com **web:** www.fernbank-iow.co.uk
dir: Approaching Shanklin on A3020, right into Highfield Rd. 300yds on left

Located in Shanklin Old Village, Fernbank offers modern, comfortable and spacious accommodation. Home-made refreshments are available throughout the afternoon and guests can enjoy a wide range of both cooked and continental breakfasts in the airy dining room. There is an indoor swimming pool and plenty of outside space within the landscaped gardens in which to relax. Free WiFi is available throughout.

Rooms 17 en suite (1 fmly) (2 GF) S £52-£54; D £88-£102* **Facilities** FTV DVD tea/coffee Licensed WiFi ⊗ Petanque **Parking** 13 **Notes** LB ⊗ No Children 12yrs Closed Nov-Feb

The Belmont

★★★★ ⬤ GUEST ACCOMMODATION

tel: 01983 862864 & 867875 **8 Queens Rd PO37 6AN**
email: enquiries@belmont-iow.co.uk **web:** www.belmont-iow.co.uk
dir: From Sandown (on A3055), half turn left at Fiveways lights signed Ventnor. Belmont 400mtrs on right, opposite St Saviour's Church

Situated less than ten minutes' walk from Shanklin beach and only five minutes from Shanklin Old Village, The Belmont offers comfortable accommodation and several rooms with stunning sea views. The Belmont is licensed, and drinks and sandwiches are available during the day and evening. Off-road parking is a benefit, and during summer months guests can enjoy the outdoor swimming pool.

Rooms 12 en suite (2 GF) **Facilities** FTV TVL tea/coffee Dinner available Licensed WiFi ⬟ Sauna ⬤ **Parking** 9 **Notes** LB ⊗ No Children 16yrs

The Birkdale

★★★★ GUEST ACCOMMODATION

tel: 01983 862949 & 07508 591889 **5 Grange Rd PO37 6NN**
email: birkdale-iow@hotmail.co.uk **web:** www.birkdalehotel.com
dir: Follow signs for Shanklin Old Village, Grange Rd opposite car park. The Birkdale on right opposite dance school

Located right in the heart of Shanklin Old Village, The Birkdale offers spacious and stylishly decorated accommodation, well equipped and with well-stocked beverage trays, digital TV and free WiFi access. There is a traditional guest lounge and extensive range of both cooked and continental dishes for breakfast. Ample off-road parking is available, and a number of shops, cafés, pubs and restaurants are right on the doorstep of this establishment.

Rooms 7 en suite (3 GF) **Facilities** STV DVD TVL tea/coffee WiFi ⬤ **Parking** 7 **Notes** LB ⊗ No Children 16yrs

The Grange

★★★★ GUEST ACCOMMODATION

tel: 01983 867644 **9 Eastcliff Rd PO37 6AA**
email: info@thegrangebythesea.com **web:** www.thegrangebythesea.com
dir: Off A3055, High St

This delightful house specialises in holistic breaks and enjoys a tranquil yet convenient setting among manicured grounds, close to the seafront and village centre. Care has been taken over the beautifully presented bedrooms and spacious public areas. Breakfast is taken en famille (outside in fine weather).

Rooms 16 en suite (2 fmly) (6 GF) S £69-£83; D £88-£116* **Facilities** Lounge TVL tea/coffee Licensed WiFi Sauna Beauty treatments & massage **Extras** Speciality toiletries **Parking** 10 **Notes** LB ⊗ Civ Wed 100

SHANKLIN *continued*

Hayes Barton

★★★★ ⬤ GUEST ACCOMMODATION

tel: 01983 867747 **7 Highfield Rd PO37 6PP**
email: enquiries@hayesbarton.co.uk **web:** www.hayesbarton.co.uk
dir: *A3055 onto A3020 Victoria Ave, 3rd left*

Hayes Barton has the relaxed atmosphere of a family home and provides well-equipped bedrooms and a range of comfortable public areas. Dinner is available from a short selection of home-cooked dishes, and there is a cosy bar-lounge. Shanklin Old Village, beach and promenade are all within walking distance.

Rooms 9 en suite (3 fmly) (2 GF) S £64-£69; D fr £78* **Facilities** FTV DVD TVL tea/coffee Dinner available Licensed WiFi **Parking** 9 **Notes** LB No Children 3yrs Closed Oct-Apr

The Rowborough

★★★★ GUEST ACCOMMODATION

tel: 01983 866072 **32 Arthurs Hill PO37 6EX**
email: info@rowboroughhotel.com **web:** www.rowboroughhotel.com
dir: *Off A3055 Sandown Rd, on corner of Arthurs Hill & Wilton Park Rd*

A warm welcome is guaranteed at this family-run Victorian house, set in beautifully tended gardens within walking distance of Shanklin Village, Chine and beaches. All nine bedrooms are comfortably furnished, serviced to a high standard, and come equipped with Freeview TV and DVD player. Breakfast and dinner are served in the light and airy dining room, which has doors leading out to the patio and gardens. Guests can enjoy a drink at the well-stocked bar or simply relax in either the guest lounge or modern conservatory. Free WiFi is accessible throughout. Children over the age of 3 and small dogs are welcome.

Rooms 9 en suite (2 fmly) (1 GF) S £34-£42; D £68-£84* **Facilities** FTV DVD Lounge TVL tea/coffee Dinner available Licensed WiFi **Parking** 5 **Notes** LB No Children 3yrs Closed Nov-Feb

The St Leonards

★★★★ GUEST ACCOMMODATION

tel: 01983 862121 **22 Queens Rd PO37 6AW**
email: info@thestleonards.co.uk **web:** www.thestleonards.co.uk
dir: *Off A3055 into Queens Rd*

The St Leonards is located in the heart of Shanklin just a short walk away from Shankin Old Village and nearby beach. This traditional guest accommodation offers spacious and comfortably appointed rooms, all well equipped with well-stocked beverage trays, free WiFi access and digital TV. There is a comfortable guest lounge and bar on the ground floor where guests can enjoy refreshments on arrival. Breakfast is served daily and offers a good selection of both cooked and continental dishes. Off-road parking is also available.

Rooms 7 en suite (2 fmly) **Facilities** FTV Lounge TVL tea/coffee Licensed WiFi ⬤ **Parking** 6 **Notes** ⊗

TOTLAND BAY	Map 5 SZ38

Premier Collection

Sentry Mead

★★★★★ ⬤ ⬤ GUEST ACCOMMODATION

tel: 01983 753212 **Madeira Rd PO39 0BJ**
email: info@sentrymead.co.uk **web:** www.sentrymead.co.uk
dir: *From Yarmouth onto A3054 to Freshwater, 2m, straight over at rdbt, right at next rdbt into Madeira Rd, 300yds on right*

This country house is located in Totland Bay, in the west of the island. Bedrooms have been tastefully decorated to offer guests traditional yet stylish accommodation, all well equipped with WiFi and digital TV. Public areas are spacious; guests can relax in the main lounge or conservatory area, both with views of the large, well-tended garden. A selection of cooked breakfasts and continental dishes is available each morning in the dining room.

Rooms 10 en suite S £65-£105; D £75-£120* **Facilities** FTV DVD iPod docking station Lounge TVL tea/coffee Dinner available Licensed WiFi ⤓ 18 ⬤ Day membership to West Bay Country Club **Extras** Speciality toiletries, robes **Parking** 9 **Notes** LB

The Hoo

★★★★ BED AND BREAKFAST

tel: 01983 753592 **Colwell Rd PO39 0AB**
email: the.hoo@btinternet.com **web:** www.thehoo.co.uk
dir: *From Yarmouth ferry right onto A3054, 2.25m enter Colwell Common. The Hoo on corner of Colwell Rd & Warden Rd*

Located close to the port and beaches, this friendly, family home provides a peaceful setting. The house has many Japanese features and guests are asked to wear slippers. The spacious bedrooms are well equipped and comfortably furnished. English breakfast is most enjoyable and is served overlooking the attractive gardens.

Rooms 3 rms (1 en suite) (2 fmly) **Facilities** FTV tea/coffee WiFi **Parking** 1 **Notes** No Children 5yrs

The Hermitage

★★★ GUEST ACCOMMODATION

tel: 01983 752518 **Cliff Rd PO39 0EW**
email: blake_david@btconnect.com **web:** www.thehermitagebnb.co.uk
dir: *From Church Hill (B3322), right into Eden Rd, left into Cliff Rd, 0.5m on right*

The Hermitage is an extremely pet- and people-friendly establishment which occupies a stunning and unspoilt location near to the cliff top in Totland Bay. Extensive gardens are well maintained and off-road parking is a bonus. Accommodation is comfortable and guests are assured of a genuinely warm welcome here. A range of delicious items at breakfast provide a substantial start to the day.

Rooms 6 rms (5 en suite) (1 pri facs) (1 fmly) **Facilities** FTV Lounge TVL tea/coffee Dinner available WiFi 🔒 **Parking** 6 **Notes** LB

The Highdown Inn

★★★ INN

tel: 01983 752450 & 07964 322044 **Highdown Ln PO39 0HY**
email: susan@highdowninn.co.uk **web:** www.highdowninn.com

This traditional country pub and restaurant is located on a quiet crossroads, only a few minutes from nearby beaches, stunning bay views and the iconic Needles. Walkers and cyclists are welcome, as are dogs (in the bar). The bar offers real ales, an open fire and a wide range of dishes including local seafood. There is also a smartly presented dining room. There is a sunny garden with decking, vegetable plot and a children's play area.

Rooms 3 en suite **Facilities** FTV DVD tea/coffee Dinner available WiFi ⬇ 18 Riding 🔒 **Extras** Robes **Parking** 30 **Notes** No coaches

▌ VENTNOR   Map 5 SZ57

Premier Collection

The Hambrough

★★★★★ ⚲ GUEST ACCOMMODATION

tel: 01983 856333 **Hambrough Rd PO38 1SQ**
email: info@thehambrough.com **web:** www.thehambrough.com
dir: *Phone for directions*

A former Victorian villa set on the hillside above Ventnor and with memorable views out to sea, The Hambrough has a modern, stylish interior with well-equipped and boutique-style accommodation. Afternoon tea is available in the bar from Tuesday to Saturday.

Rooms 7 en suite (3 fmly) D £130-£230* **Facilities** STV DVD Lounge tea/coffee Direct Dial Licensed WiFi 🔒 **Extras** Speciality toiletries - free; mini-bar - charged **Conf** Max 40 Thtr 40 Class 20 Board 24 **Notes** LB ⊗ Civ Wed 40

The Leconfield

★★★★★★ ⊚ ⚲ GUEST ACCOMMODATION

tel: 01983 852196 **85 Leeson Rd, Upper Bonchurch PO38 1PU**
email: enquiries@leconfieldhotel.com **web:** www.leconfieldhotel.com
dir: *On A3055, 3m from Shanklin Old Village*

This country house is situated on an elevated position with panoramic sea views over the historic village of Bonchurch. Luxury bedrooms and suites are spacious and individually styled. Public rooms include two lounges and a conservatory, in addition to the Sea Scape restaurant, where freshly prepared breakfast and imaginative dinner menus are served. Additional facilities include the outdoor pool, terrace area and ample off-road parking.

Rooms 6 en suite 5 annexe en suite (3 GF) S £60-£160; D £70-£200 **Facilities** FTV DVD iPod docking station Lounge tea/coffee Dinner available Licensed WiFi 🔭 🔒 **Extras** Bath robes - complimentary **Parking** 14 **Notes** LB ⊗ No Children 16yrs Closed 24-26 Dec & 3-27 Jan

Little Rannoch

★★★★ ⚲ BED AND BREAKFAST

tel: 01983 852263 **1 Steephill Court Rd PO38 1UH**
email: littlerannoch@btinternet.com **web:** www.littlerannoch.co.uk
dir: *From Ventnor town centre onto A3055 to St Lawrence. After 1.3m turn right after botanic gardens into Steephill Court Rd, on left*

Little Rannoch is a south-facing bungalow less than a mile from Ventnor, close to Ventnor Botanic Gardens, Cricket Ground and Steephill Cove. The accommodation comprises one self-contained suite comprising of double bedroom, diningroom/kitchenette, shower room and patio with garden and sea views. The resorts of Shanklin and Sandown are within eight miles of Little Rannoch. Breakfast features local and home-made items. Off street parking available.

Rooms 1 en suite (1 GF) S £60; D £110* **Facilities** STV FTV iPod docking station tea/coffee 🔒 **Extras** Snacks, home-made biscuits **Parking** 1 **Notes** ⊗ No Children Closed Nov-1 Mar

St Maur

★★★★ GUEST ACCOMMODATION

tel: 01983 852570 & 853645 **Castle Rd PO38 1LG**
email: info@stmaur.co.uk **web:** www.stmaur.co.uk
dir: *Exit A3055 at end of Park Av into Castle Rd, premises 150yds on left*

A warm welcome awaits at this Victorian villa, which is pleasantly and quietly located in an elevated position overlooking the bay. The well-equipped bedrooms are traditionally decorated, while public areas include a spacious lounge and cosy residents' bar. The gardens here are a delight.

Rooms 8 en suite (2 fmly) S £65-£130; D £140-£160* **Facilities** STV FTV Lounge tea/coffee Dinner available Licensed WiFi 🔒 **Extras** Speciality toiletries **Parking** 8 **Notes** LB ⊗ No Children 4yrs Closed Dec

KENT

BENENDEN
Map 7 TQ83

Premier Collection

Beacon Hall House B&B

★★★★★ 🍽 BED AND BREAKFAST

tel: 01580 240434 & 07747 095749 **Rolvenden Rd TN17 4BU**
email: julie.jex@btconnect.com **web:** www.beaconhallhouse.co.uk
dir: From Benenden take B2086 towards Rolvenden for approx 1m

Beacon Hall House offers three well-appointed and well configured bedrooms, all with deeply comfortable beds, powerful showers and a host of amenities. All rooms offer relaxing views of the garden and the surrounding area. There is a tennis court and a swimming pool for guest use. Guests can also wander around the vegetable garden, as well as admiring the chicken house. The award-winning breakfast offers local produce and home-made jams, marmalade and baked goods, amongst other things.

Rooms 3 en suite (1 fmly) **Facilities** FTV DVD TVL tea/coffee Dinner available WiFi ⌁ ⌁ **Extras** Robes, slippers, speciality toiletries **Parking** 6 **Notes** ⊗ ⊛

Apple Trees B&B

★★★★ BED AND BREAKFAST

tel: 01580 240622 **Goddards Green TN17 4AR**
email: garryblanch@aol.com **web:** www.appletreesbandb.co.uk
dir: 3m E of Cranbrook. Exit A262 at Sissinghurst S into Chaple Ln, over x-rds, 2m left to Goddards Green, 1m on right

This spacious cottage is situated in the heart of the Kentish countryside, and is convenient for those visiting Sissinghurst Castle and Great Dixter. Bedrooms are attractively presented and include plenty of thoughtful extras such as flat-screen TVs and internet connection. Breakfast is served in the rustic dining room overlooking the garden.

Rooms 3 rms (1 en suite) (2 pri facs) (3 GF) S £50-£65; D £60-£75* **Facilities** TVL TV1B tea/coffee WiFi ⌁ 18 ⌁ **Parking** 6 **Notes** ⊗ ⊛

BOUGHTON STREET
Map 7 TR05

The White Horse Inn

★★★★ ⌁ INN

tel: 01227 751343 **246 The Street, Boughton-under-Blean ME13 9AL**
email: whitehorseinn@live.co.uk **web:** www.whitehorsecanterbury.co.uk
dir: M2 junct 7, slip road left towards Channel Tunnel/Canterbury/Dover. At rdbt 4th exit onto A2 then slip road left to Boughton. On left on entering village

This traditional inn is located in the picturesque village of Boughton-under-Blean, yet just a short drive from Canterbury city centre. The White Horse Inn has a spacious pub and restaurant area where lunch, dinner and breakfast are served daily. Bedrooms are all modern in style and comfortably appointed, and come well equipped with digital TV and free WiFi.

Rooms 13 en suite (3 fmly) (2 GF) S £60-£90; D £80-£120 **Facilities** FTV Lounge TVL tea/coffee Dinner available Direct Dial WiFi ⌁ 18 ⌁ **Extras** Speciality toiletries, water - free; slippers **Parking** 31 **Notes** LB

BROADSTAIRS
Map 7 TR36

The Victoria Bed and Breakfast

★★★★ BED AND BREAKFAST

tel: 01843 871010 **23 Victoria Pde CT10 1QL**
email: helen.kemp2@virgin.net **web:** www.thevictoriabroadstairs.co.uk
dir: A299 into Broadstairs, pass train station & continue on High St. Turn right into Charlotte St, 1st left then right into Victoria Parade

The Victoria Bed and Breakfast offers very comfortable seaside accommodation in an excellent location. The breakfast room/lounge and top floor bedroom have stunning sea views and the house is just thirty metres from the beach. All bedrooms are well furnished with en suite bathrooms, Freeview TV and tea/coffee making facilities. Breakfast is cooked to order, and a range of breakfast options is available with most items locally sourced. Private parking or nearby permit parking available at no charge.

Rooms 3 en suite (1 fmly) S £70-£75; D £90-£140* **Facilities** FTV DVD Lounge tea/coffee WiFi ⌁ **Extras** Fridge, fresh milk & mineral water - free **Parking** 1 **Notes** LB ⊗ RS Xmas

CANTERBURY
Map 7 TR15

House of Agnes

★★★★ GUEST ACCOMMODATION

tel: 01227 472185 **71 Saint Dunstans St CT2 8BN**
email: info@houseofagnes.co.uk **web:** www.houseofagnes.co.uk
dir: On A290 between London Rd & Orchard St, 300mtrs from Westgate

This historic 14th-century property has been appointed to provide luxury guest accommodation and offers individually themed rooms, ranging from the traditional to the more exotic. All bedrooms have a good range of amenities such as flat-screen TVs and WiFi.

Rooms 8 en suite 8 annexe en suite (2 fmly) (8 GF) S £75-£95; D £79-£135* **Facilities** FTV DVD Lounge TVL tea/coffee Licensed WiFi ⌁ ⌁ 18 ⌁ Boules Badminton **Extras** Champagne, chocolates, fruit - charges vary **Conf** Thtr 30 Class 12 Board 20 **Parking** 13 **Notes** LB ⊗ No Children 6yrs Closed 24-26 Dec

The White House

★★★★ GUEST ACCOMMODATION

tel: 01227 761836 **6 St Peters Ln CT1 2BP**
email: info@whitehousecanterbury.co.uk **web:** www.whitehousecanterbury.co.uk
dir: A2 into Canterbury. At London Rd rdbt take 2nd exit (A2050), at next rdbt 1st exit into St Peters Pl. Right at Westgate Tower rdbt, right before next rdbt. Left at end, St Peters Ln on right

The White House is an ideally located Regency property in the heart of Canterbury, within a two-minute walk of the famous cathedral. All bedrooms are modern with bright, airy decor and have LCD TVs and WiFi. Breakfast can be enjoyed in the ground-floor dining room and there's additional space for guests to relax during their stay.

Rooms 7 en suite S £69-£79; D £90-£140* **Facilities** FTV DVD tea/coffee WiFi **Notes** ⊗ No Children 16yrs Closed Jan

Yorke Lodge

★★★★ GUEST ACCOMMODATION

tel: 01227 451243 **50 London Rd CT2 8LF**
email: info@yorkelodge.com **web:** www.yorkelodge.com
dir: *M2 junct 7, A2, exit left signed Canterbury. At 1st rdbt turn left into London Rd*

Yorke Lodge stands in a tree-lined road just a ten-minute walk from the town centre and railway station. The spacious bedrooms are thoughtfully equipped and carefully decorated using a calming palette of neutral and pastel shades. Some rooms have four-poster beds. The stylish dining room leads to a conservatory which opens onto a superb terrace.

Rooms 8 en suite (1 fmly) S £65-£72; D £90-£120 **Facilities** FTV tea/coffee WiFi **Parking** 5 **Notes** LB No Children 5yrs

The Duke William

★★★★ 🍺 INN

tel: 01227 721308 **Ickham CT3 1QP**
email: info@thedukewilliamickham.com **web:** www.thedukewilliamickham.com
dir: *A257 (Canterbury to Sandwich) into Littlebourne, left opposite The Anchor into Nargate St. 0.5m, right into Drill Ln, right into The Street*

Located in the quiet village of Ickham, this village pub has been completely revamped; the public areas still offer a traditional style with exposed beams and roaring wood fires, though decor and furnishings have been modernised offering a comfortable bar and restaurant area. Bedrooms have all been refurbished; stylish decor and contemporary furnishings offer guests high quality and comfort, and are ideal for both leisure and corporate guests alike. The location here is quiet, yet is just a short drive from Canterbury.

Rooms 4 en suite S £100; D £100* **Facilities** FTV tea/coffee Dinner available WiFi **Extras** Speciality toiletries - complimentary

Canterbury Lodge

★★★★ GUEST ACCOMMODATION

tel: 01227 768767 **63 London Rd CT2 8JZ**
email: info@canterburylodge.uk **web:** www.canterburylodge.uk
dir: *M2 onto A2, 1st exit signed Canterbury. At 1st rdbt, left into London Rd*

Conveniently located on the London Road in the centre of Canterbury, this spacious property offers comfortably appointed accommodation all with en suite facilities. Rooms are well equipped and modern in style yet still showing many of the buildings original features. Free WiFi and off road parking available. Guests can enjoy a hearty cooked and continental breakfast served daily in the dining room on the ground floor.

Rooms 10 en suite (2 fmly) S £50-£65; D £70-£85* **Facilities** FTV Lounge TVL tea/coffee WiFi 🔒 **Parking** 9 **Notes** LB No Children 5yrs

The City of Canterbury Guest House

★★★★ GUEST ACCOMMODATION

tel: 01227 457455 **27 St Thomas Hill CT2 8HW**
email: n.gunn@thecityofcanterbury.co.uk **web:** www.thecityofcanterbury.co.uk
dir: *From city centre, past Westgate Towers. Straight over level crossing and up hill. Opposite University entrance*

This charming guest house is located less than one mile outside the historic city of Canterbury, directly opposite the university. The large open-plan lounge and dining room offers space for guests to relax during their stay and where a cooked and continental breakfast is served daily. Bedrooms are spacious, many with views of the city, and all offer comfortably equipped accommodation with digital TV and free WiFi throughout. There is limited parking available, which is a real benefit.

Rooms 8 en suite (2 GF) **Facilities** STV FTV TVL tea/coffee WiFi 🔒 **Parking** 4 **Notes** ⊗

Peregrine House

★★★★ GUEST ACCOMMODATION

tel: 01227 761897 **18 Hawks Ln CT1 2NU**
email: enquiries@castlehousehotel.co.uk **web:** www.theperegrinehouse.co.uk

Peregrine House is centrally located right in the heart of Canterbury. This is a sister property to Castle House. Guests register at Castle House and then take a short walk to Peregrine House, alternatively a courtesy car is available to help transport guests and their luggage. Bedrooms and bathrooms offer clean, modern comfortable accommodation. Close to the main high street, cathedral, shops and restaurants.

Rooms 13 rms (11 en suite) (2 pri facs) (5 fmly) (3 GF) **Facilities** TVL tea/coffee Dinner available Licensed WiFi **Parking** 14 **Notes** ⊗

CANTERBURY *continued*

Cathedral Gate

★★★ GUEST ACCOMMODATION

tel: 01227 464381 **36 Burgate CT1 2HA**
email: cgate@cgate.demon.co.uk **web:** www.cathgate.co.uk
dir: *In city centre. Next to main gateway into cathedral precincts*

Dating from 1438, this house has an enviable central location next to the cathedral. Old beams and winding corridors are part of the character of the property. Bedrooms are traditionally furnished, equipped to modern standards and many have cathedral views. Luggage can be unloaded at reception before parking in a nearby car park.

Rooms 12 rms (2 en suite) 12 annexe rms 10 annexe en suite (1 fmly) S £50; D £65-£120* **Facilities** FTV Lounge tea/coffee Licensed WiFi **Notes** ⊗ Closed 23-29 Dec

St Stephens Guest House

★★★ GUEST ACCOMMODATION

tel: 01227 767644 **100 St Stephens Rd CT2 7JL**
email: info@ststephensguesthouse.co.uk **web:** www.ststephensguesthouse.co.uk
dir: *A290 from city, Westgate & sharp right into North Ln, 2nd rdbt left into St Stephens Rd, right into Market Way, car park on right*

St Stephens Guest House offers well-appointed accommodation. Rooms are well equipped. It is located just ten minutes' walk from Canterbury town centre and conveniently located near the University of Kent and Christchurch College. The dining room is traditionally decorated and has views of the garden; guests can enjoy a cooked or continental breakfast.

Rooms 1 en suite 8 annexe en suite (2 fmly) (3 GF) S fr £52; D fr £73* **Facilities** FTV tea/coffee WiFi **Parking** 8 **Notes** ⊗ Closed mid Dec-mid Jan

Duke Of Cumberland

★★★ 🍺 INN

tel: 01227 831396 & 01303 844663 **The Street, Barham CT4 6NY**
email: info@dukeofcumberland.co.uk **web:** www.dukeofcumberland.co.uk
dir: *S of Canterbury on A2. Exit signed Barham, 100yds on The Street, off Valley Rd*

This traditional English pub is located in the village of Barham just a few miles outside historic Canterbury. There are three comfortably appointed en suite bedrooms, traditional in style with all modern amenities including WiFi and digital TVs. A hearty cooked breakfast is served daily and guests can enjoy lunch or dinner in the main bar and restaurant area.

Rooms 3 en suite (1 fmly) S £50-£60; D £70-£100 **Facilities** FTV DVD iPod docking station tea/coffee Dinner available WiFi ⚓ **Parking** 30

Innkeeper's Lodge Canterbury

★★★ INN

tel: 08451 551551 *(Calls cost 2p per minute plus your phone company's access charge)* **162 New Dover Rd CT1 3EL**
email: info@innkeeperslodge.com **web:** www.innkeeperslodge.com

At Innkeeper's Lodge you'll find accommodation with comfort and character in equal measure, and everything needed for a relaxing stay, from easy check-in and free parking to complimentary breakfast and a cosy pub serving great value food and drink on the doorstep. Each Lodge has quality rooms, and there are Lodges in a variety of locations from towns and cities to countryside settings across the UK.

Rooms 9 en suite (1 fmly) **Facilities** FTV tea/coffee Dinner available WiFi **Parking** **Notes** ⊗

The Corner House

Ⓤ

tel: 01227 780793 & 823000 **1 Dover St CT1 3HD**
email: matt@cornerhouserestaurants.co.uk **web:** www.cornerhouserestaurants.co.uk

Currently the rating for this establishment is not confirmed. This may be due to a change of ownership or because it has only recently joined the AA rating scheme.

Rooms 3 en suite S £75-£120; D £75-£120 (room only)* **Facilities** FTV DVD tea/coffee Dinner available Licensed WiFi ⚓ **Conf** Max 20 Class 20 Board 10 **Notes** ⊗

DARTFORD   Map 6 TQ57

The Rising Sun Inn

★★★ INN

tel: 01474 872291 **Fawkham Green DA3 8NL**
email: admin@risingsun-fawkham.com **web:** www.risingsun-fawkham.com
dir: *M25 junct 3, A20 Brands Hatch. Turn into Scratchers Ln until sign for Fawkham. Left into Brandshatch Rd, inn on left*

This popular inn overlooks the village green and is just a short drive from Brands Hatch. All the en suite bedrooms are spacious, pleasantly decorated and comfortable. There is a busy character bar, restaurant, and a patio for alfresco dining in warmer weather.

Rooms 5 en suite (1 fmly) (2 GF) **Facilities** FTV tea/coffee Dinner available WiFi **Extras** Bottled water - complimentary **Parking** 20 **Notes** ⊗ No coaches

DEAL
Map 7 TR35

Premier Collection

Sutherland House
★★★★★ GUEST ACCOMMODATION

tel: 01304 362853 **186 London Rd CT14 9PT**
email: info@sutherlandhouse.fsnet.co.uk **web:** www.sutherlandhousehotel.co.uk
dir: 0.5m W of town centre/seafront on A258

This stylish accommodation demonstrates impeccable taste with its charming, well-equipped bedrooms and a comfortable lounge. A fully stocked bar, books, free WiFi, Freeview TV and radio are some of the many amenities offered. The elegant dining room is the venue for a hearty breakfast and dinner is available by prior arrangement.

Rooms 4 en suite (1 GF) S £70-£80; D £85-£95* **Facilities** FTV DVD iPod docking station Lounge tea/coffee Dinner available Direct Dial Licensed WiFi 🛁
Extras Speciality toiletries, honesty bar **Conf** Max 12 Thtr 12 Class 12 Board 12
Parking 7 **Notes** LB No Children 5yrs

Sondes Lodge
★★★ GUEST ACCOMMODATION

tel: 01304 368741 & 07817 178186 **14 Sondes Rd CT14 7BW**
email: info@sondeslodge.co.uk **web:** www.sondeslodge.co.uk
dir: From Dover take A258 to Deal, pass Deal Castle, towards town centre. 4th right into Sondes Rd. Lodge on right

Expect a warm welcome at this smart guest accommodation situated in a side road just off the seafront and a short walk from the town centre. The pleasant bedrooms have co-ordinated fabrics and many thoughtful touches. Breakfast is served at individual tables in the lower ground-floor dining room.

Rooms 3 en suite (1 fmly) (1 GF) S £40-£50; D £60-£90* **Facilities** FTV DVD TVL tea/coffee WiFi **Extras** Bath robes, bottled water, fruit/snacks - free **Notes** ⊗

DOVER
Map 7 TR34

Premier Collection

The Marquis at Alkham
★★★★★ ◉◉ 🍴 RESTAURANT WITH ROOMS

tel: 01304 873410 & 822945 **Alkham Valley Rd, Alkham CT15 7DF**
email: info@themarquisatalkham.co.uk **web:** www.themarquisatalkham.co.uk
dir: A256 from Dover, at rdbt 1st exit into London Rd, left into Alkham Rd, Alkham Valley Rd. Establishment 1.5m after sharp bend

Located between Dover and Folkestone, this contemporary restaurant with rooms offers luxury accommodation with modern features; flat-screen TVs, WiFi, power showers and bathrobes to mention but a few. All the stylish bedrooms are individually designed and have fantastic views of the Kent Downs. The award-winning restaurant, open for lunch and dinner, specialises in modern British cuisine guided by chef Andrew King. Both continental and a choice of cooked breakfasts are offered.

Rooms 10 en suite (3 fmly) (1 GF) S £69-£129; D £79-£159 **Facilities** FTV DVD Lounge TVL Dinner available Direct Dial WiFi **Conf** Max 20 Thtr 20 Class 20 Board 16 **Parking** 22 **Notes** LB ⊗ Civ Wed 55

Hubert House Guesthouse
★★★★ GUEST HOUSE

tel: 01304 202253 **9 Castle Hill Rd CT16 1QW**
email: stay@huberthouse.co.uk **web:** www.huberthouse.co.uk
dir: On A258 by Dover Castle, down hill, 1st left. Next to White Horse pub

This charming Georgian house is within walking distance of the ferry port and the town centre. Bedrooms are sumptuously decorated and furnished with an abundance of practical extras. Breakfast, including full English and healthy options, is served in the smart bistro. Families are especially welcome.

Rooms 6 en suite (4 fmly) **Facilities** FTV tea/coffee Licensed WiFi 🛁 **Extras** Robes, fridges **Parking** 6 **Notes** Closed 24-27 Dec & 31 Dec-2 Jan

DOVER continued

Castle Guest House

★★★★ GUEST HOUSE

tel: 01304 201656 **10 Castle Hill CT16 1QW**
email: info@castle-guesthouse.com **web:** www.castle-guesthouse.co.uk
dir: *A20 Dover, follow signs for Dover Castle. At foot of hill, on right*

Castle Guest House is located in the centre of Dover just minutes from the town centre, Dover ferry port and Channel Tunnel terminal. Bedrooms are modern and comfortably appointed and include digital TV and free WiFi access. A cooked and continental breakfast is served daily in the dining room. Free off-road parking available and secure parking is available for motorbikes or bicycles (on request).

Rooms 6 en suite (2 fmly) **Facilities** FTV DVD tea/coffee WiFi 🔒 **Parking** 5 **Notes** Closed Xmas

Maison Dieu Guest House

★★★★ GUEST ACCOMMODATION

tel: 01304 204033 **89 Maison Dieu Rd CT16 1RU**
email: info@maisondieu.co.uk **web:** www.maisondieu.co.uk
dir: *M20/A20 to Dover. Left into York St, at rdbt 2nd exit. Right at lights into Ladywell, right at next lights, 100yds on left*

Maison Dieu is ideally located to offer the perfect stopover en route to and from Dover and mainland Europe. Dover ferry and cruise terminals and The White Cliffs of Dover are just five minutes away and the Channel Tunnel is ten minutes by car. Bedrooms are comfortably decorated and come well equipped with WiFi and digital TV. Guests can enjoy a cooked or continental breakfast daily in the dining room.

Rooms 7 rms (4 en suite) (1 pri facs) (4 fmly) S £34-£44; D £60-£72 (room only)* **Facilities** FTV tea/coffee WiFi 🔒 **Parking** 6 **Notes** LB ⊗ No Children 4yrs

Bleriot's

★★★ GUEST ACCOMMODATION

tel: 01304 211394 **Belper House, 47 Park Av CT16 1HE**
email: info@bleriotsguesthouse.co.uk **web:** www.bleriotsguesthouse.co.uk
dir: *A20 to Dover, left into York St, right at lights into Ladywell. Left at next lights into Park Av*

This large, family-run Victorian property is convenient for the ferry port and town centre. Guests receive a warm welcome and can enjoy a range of comfortable, spacious en suite bedrooms. The attractive dining room is the venue for a wholesome breakfast to set you up for the day.

Rooms 8 en suite (2 fmly) S £36-£37; D £54-£64 (room only)* **Facilities** FTV Lounge tea/coffee WiFi 🔒 **Parking** 8 **Notes** LB ⊗

Ardmore Guest House

★★★ GUEST ACCOMMODATION

tel: 01304 205895 **18 Castle Hill Rd CT16 1QW**
email: res@ardmoreph.co.uk **web:** www.ardmoreph.co.uk
dir: *On A258 by Dover Castle*

Dating from 1796, this delightful house is adjacent to Dover Castle. Convenient for the town centre and ferry port, the Ardmore offers comfortable accommodation and friendly hospitality. The non-smoking bedrooms are spacious and airy. Public rooms include a comfortable lounge and a well-appointed breakfast room.

Rooms 4 en suite (1 fmly) **Facilities** FTV Lounge tea/coffee WiFi **Notes** ⊗ Closed Xmas

St Martins Guest House

★★★ GUEST ACCOMMODATION

tel: 01304 205938 **17 Castle Hill Rd CT16 1QW**
email: res@stmartinsgh.co.uk **web:** www.stmartinsgh.co.uk
dir: *On A258 by Dover Castle*

Located close to the castle, ferry port and town centre, this smart guest accommodation offers a friendly welcome. The thoughtfully equipped en suite bedrooms are attractively decorated, and most rooms enjoy a sunny aspect. Breakfast is served in the pine-furnished dining room, and there is also a comfortable lounge.

Rooms 6 en suite (3 fmly) **Facilities** FTV Lounge tea/coffee WiFi **Notes** ⊗ Closed Xmas

---

EGERTON   Map 7 TQ94

Premier Collection

Frasers

★★★★★ ◉◉ ♀ GUEST ACCOMMODATION

tel: 01233 756122 **Coldharbour Farm TN27 9DD**
email: lisa@frasers-events.co.uk **web:** www.frasers-events.co.uk
dir: *Please contact Frasers for detailed directions*

Frasers is nestled at the end of a private drive on a working farm set deep in beautiful Kent countryside, halfway between Maidstone and Ashford. Bedrooms are spacious and individual in style with excellent quality furnishings ensuring a comfortable stay. Guests can enjoy an extensive cooked or continental breakfast in the main restaurant; this is also where the AA Rosette-worthy dinner is served.

Rooms 8 en suite **Facilities** FTV DVD iPod docking station tea/coffee Dinner available Licensed ⅃ 18 Fishing **Extras** Speciality toiletries, robes, slippers **Conf** Max 150 Thtr 150 Class 50 Board 50 **Parking** 50 **Notes** ⊗ Civ Wed 100

ELHAM
Map 7 TR14

Rose & Crown
★★★★ INN

tel: 01303 840890 **CT4 6TD**
web: www.theroseandcrownelham.co.uk

This Grade II listed building is located in the village of Elham just a short drive from Canterbury. This traditional inn on the high street has lots of original character. Traditional pub dishes are served daily for both lunch and dinner. Bedrooms are all annexed and very spacious. A cooked breakfast served in the main bar every morning.

Rooms 6 en suite **Facilities** FTV tea/coffee Dinner available WiFi **Parking**

FAVERSHAM
Map 7 TR06

Faversham Creek & Red Sails Restaurant
★★★★ ⚫ RESTAURANT WITH ROOMS

tel: 01795 533535 & 534689 **Conduit St ME13 7BH**
email: office@favershamcreekhotel.co.uk web: www.favershamcreekhotel.co.uk
dir: *M2 junct 6 onto A251. At T-junct left then right into The Mall. Pass railway station, continue on B2041. Left into Quay Ln*

Located in the heart of Faversham and adjacent to the Creek, this restaurant with rooms offers modern accommodation with its own individual style, and rooms named after characters from the Faversham area. Bedrooms are well equipped and ideal for both business and leisure guests alike. There is a courtyard terrace where guests can enjoy lunch or pre-dinner drinks before dining in the award-winning Red Sails Restaurant. Parking is available on site.

Rooms 6 en suite (4 fmly) **Facilities** STV FTV Lounge tea/coffee Dinner available Direct Dial WiFi **Parking** 4 **Notes** ⊗ No coaches

Garden Cottage
★★★★ GUEST ACCOMMODATION

tel: 01795 531167 **Stonebridge Lodge, West St ME13 7RU**
email: lizandtonysharp@mac.com web: www.stonebridgelodgefaversham.com
dir: *M2 junct 6 onto A251, left onto A2. Right into Ospringe Rd, left into Napleton Rd, right into Tanners St, left into West St. 1st house on right*

Located in the centre of Faversham within easy walking distance of the town and restaurants, Garden Cottage is in the garden of Stonebridge Lodge. Accommodation is spacious and comfortably appointed with modern decor and furnishings. A substantial continental breakfast can be provided in the room and there is a dining area in the room where guests can eat. The spacious gardens surrounding the cottage are dotted with ponds and waterways.

Rooms 1 annexe en suite (1 fmly) (1 GF) S fr £100; D £100-£115 **Facilities** STV FTV tea/coffee WiFi 🔒 **Extras** Fruit, snacks, fridge **Parking** 3 **Notes** ⊗ Closed 15 Dec-15 Jan 🌐

FOLKESTONE
Map 7 TR23

Rocksalt Rooms
★★★★ ⚫⚫ RESTAURANT WITH ROOMS

tel: 01303 212070 **2 Back St CT19 6NN**
email: info@rocksaltfolkestone.co.uk web: www.rocksaltfolkestone.co.uk
dir: *M20 junct 13 follow signs to harbour (A259). At harbour left onto Fish Market*

Overlooking the busy harbour, often crowded with small leisure boats, and with wonderful sea views, Rocksalt enjoys a great location in Folkestone. Bedrooms are stylish, well-appointed with original antique beds and equipped with a host of thoughtful little extras. Continental breakfasts are delivered promptly to the guests' rooms each morning, and dinner is served in the award-winning restaurant, also blessed with panoramic views.

Rooms 4 en suite (1 fmly) S £85-£115; D £85-£115* **Facilities** FTV iPod docking station tea/coffee Dinner available WiFi **Extras** Nespresso machine, fruit, speciality toiletries **Notes** ⊗ No coaches

The Relish
★★★★ GUEST ACCOMMODATION

tel: 01303 850952 **4 Augusta Gardens CT20 2RR**
email: reservations@hotelrelish.co.uk web: www.hotelrelish.co.uk
dir: *M20 junct 13 onto A2034 (0.6m), then B2064 (0.6m). Right into Earls Avenue, then left into Bouverie Rd West, right into Trinity Gardens*

Expect a warm welcome at this impressive Victorian terrace property, which overlooks Augusta Gardens in the fashionable West End of town. The bedrooms feature beautiful, contemporary natural-wood furniture, lovely co-ordinated fabrics and many thoughtful extras such as DVD players and free WiFi. Public rooms include a modern lounge-dining room, and a sun terrace where breakfast is served in the summer.

Rooms 10 en suite **Facilities** FTV DVD Lounge tea/coffee Direct Dial WiFi **Extras** Home-made cake, bottled water - complimentary **Conf** Max 12 Thtr 9 Class 9 Board 12 **Notes** ⊗ Closed 23-31 Dec

The Wycliffe
★★★ GUEST HOUSE

tel: 01303 252186 **63 Bouverie Rd West CT20 2RN**
email: wycliffeguesthouse@gmail.com web: www.wycliffehotel.com
dir: *M20 junct 13 onto A20. 2nd set of lights take middle lane & proceed straight over. After 1km turn right signed A259 Sandgate/Hastings into Earls Av. Then 2nd left into Bouverie Road West, 200mtrs on right*

The Wycliffe is located in the heart of Folkestone, just a short walk into the town centre and main promenade. Bedrooms are spacious and traditional in style with modern amenities including digital TV and free WiFi access. There is a bar and a large dining room where guests can enjoy breakfast and evening meals.

Rooms 13 rms (9 en suite) (3 fmly) S £28-£50; D £45-£80 (room only)* **Facilities** FTV TVL tea/coffee Dinner available Licensed WiFi 🔒 **Parking** 10 **Notes** LB

FOLKESTONE *continued*

Rob Roy Guest House

★★★ GUEST HOUSE

tel: 01303 253341 & 07957 412486 **227 Dover Rd CT19 6NH**
email: robroy.folkestone@gmail.com **web:** www.robroyfolkestone.co.uk

This traditional guest house is conveniently located just a couple of minutes from the harbour and town centre, and is just a short drive from the Dover Ferries and the Channel Tunnel. Bedrooms are all comfortably appointed and benefit from free WiFi, home-made biscuits and digital TVs. A cooked or continental breakfast is served in the dining room, with a choice of some daily specials. There is off-road parking, which in this area is a real benefit.

Rooms 5 rms (4 en suite) (1 pri facs) (1 fmly) (1 GF) **Facilities** STV FTV TVL tea/coffee WiFi 🛁 **Parking** 3 **Notes** Closed 24-26 Dec

---

GOUDHURST   Map 6 TQ73

The Star & Eagle

★★★★ 🛏 INN

tel: 01580 211512 **High St TN17 1AL**
email: starandeagle@btconnect.com **web:** www.starandeagle.co.uk
dir: *Off A21 to Hastings rd, take A262, inn at top of village next to church*

A warm welcome is assured at the 15th-century Star & Eagle, located in the heart of this delightful village. Within easy reach of Royal Tunbridge Wells and the Weald, this is a great base for walkers. Both bedrooms and public areas boast original features and much character. A wide range of delicious home-made dishes is available in the restaurant and bar.

Rooms 10 rms (8 en suite) (2 pri facs) S £80-£120; D £105-£160 **Facilities** FTV tea/coffee Dinner available Direct Dial WiFi 🛁 **Extras** Speciality toiletries, home-made shortbread **Conf** Max 30 Thtr 30 Class 15 Board 12 **Parking** 20 **Notes** ⊗ RS 25-26 Dec eve closed Civ Wed 50

GRAFTY GREEN   Map 7 TQ84

Who'd A Thought It

★★★★ ◉◉ GUEST ACCOMMODATION

tel: 01622 858951 **Headcorn Rd ME17 2AR**
email: joe@whodathoughtit.com **web:** www.whodathoughtit.com
dir: *M20 junct 8 onto A20 towards Lenham. After 1m take turn signed Grafty Green, follow brown tourism signs for 4-5m*

The unusually named Who'd A Thought It is located in the quiet village of Grafty Green, yet convenient for both Maidstone and Ashford. Bedrooms and bathrooms are spacious and individually designed, using eclectic furnishings and stylish decor. Bathrooms feature hot tubs or jacuzzi baths, along with speciality toiletries. The restaurant has been awarded two AA Rosettes and offers an intimate and comfortable ambience. Meals are served daily in the restaurant meals and there is also a bar menu available.

Rooms 19 annexe en suite (19 GF) S £50-£80; D £70-£475* **Facilities** STV FTV DVD iPod docking station Lounge tea/coffee Dinner available Licensed WiFi 🎣 18 Fishing **Extras** Chocolates, champagne, bottled water, robes **Conf** Max 30 Thtr 30 Class 30 Board 20 **Parking** 40 **Notes** ⊗

HALSTEAD   Map 6 TQ46

7 Motel Diner

★★★★ GUEST ACCOMMODATION

tel: 01959 535890 **London Rd, Polhill TN14 7AA**
email: reservations@7hoteldiner.co.uk **web:** www.7hoteldiner.co.uk
dir: *M25 junct 4, 2m towards Sevenoaks*

This guest accommodation is conveniently located off the M25 and is just a short drive from Sevenoaks. The well-equipped bedrooms have been stylishly decorated to offer modern, comfortable accommodation; all have custom-made furniture, flat-screen TVs and free WiFi. The lounge has a huge 50" TV with BT Sport coverage. There is an American-themed diner complete with authentic jukebox and leather booths, and all-day dining is available from 7am to 9.30pm.

Rooms 26 en suite (2 fmly) (6 GF) S £49.95-£69; D £59.95-£99 (room only)* **Facilities** FTV TVL tea/coffee Dinner available Direct Dial Licensed WiFi ♿ **Parking** 50 **Notes** ⊗

HAWKHURST   Map 7 TQ73

The Queen's Inn

★★★★ INN

tel: 01580 754233 **Rye Rd TN18 4EY**
email: info@queensinn.co.uk **web:** www.thequeensinnhawkhurst.co.uk
dir: *From M25 junct 5 take A21 to Flimwell. Turn left at lights to Hawkhurst*

The Queen's Inn has been carefully and sympathetically refurbished by the current owners after years of decline. The rooms have been individually styled in a traditional yet contemporary style, all offer en suite facilities, deep and comfortable beds and home-made goodies. The restaurant uses local seasonal produce with many items such as breads, jams and marmalade made on-site by the talented co-owner and Head Chef. Free WiFi is offered in the public areas. Parking provided.

Rooms 7 en suite (2 fmly) S £90-£100; D £100-£185 **Facilities** FTV iPod docking station Lounge tea/coffee Dinner available Direct Dial WiFi **Extras** Home-made brownies, fresh milk, robes - free **Conf** Max 100 Thtr 100 Class 50 Board 50 **Parking** 30

Tudor Rose Bed and Breakfast

★★★★ BED AND BREAKFAST

tel: 01580 754830 & 07831 620172 **1 Tudor Hall TN18 5DB**
email: rosemarie_imago@hotmail.com **web:** www.tudor-rose-bnb.com

Tudor Rose is a family-run B&B, located on the outskirts of Hawkhurst. It has four rooms, two en suite and two with private bathrooms; the family room is en suite, and has a double bed and single bed. All rooms have tea and coffee making facilities, Freeview TV, CD/DVD and WiFi. Thoughtful touches include dressing gowns, slippers, and toiletries. Full English or continental breakfast is served in the dining room.

Rooms 4 rms (2 en suite) (2 pri facs) (1 fmly) S £55-£70; D £70-£90* **Facilities** FTV DVD Lounge tea/coffee WiFi 🔒 **Extras** Robes, slippers, chocolates **Parking** 4 **Notes** LB ⊗

Applebloom Bed and Breakfast

★★★★ BED AND BREAKFAST

tel: 01580 753347 **White Rose Cottage TN18 5DZ**
email: enquiries@applebloom.co.uk **web:** www.applebloom.co.uk
dir: A21 onto A268 at Flimwell. Through Hawkhurst, after 1.1m turn right at x-rds into Conghurst Ln. 400mtrs on right

Applebloom Bed and Breakfast is set in its own attractive garden and surrounded by the beautiful Kent countryside. The two bedrooms are individually appointed and offer style, quality and comfort. Guests can relax either in the lounge, or in the garden during the warm months of the year. Breakfast is served at a communal table overlooking the garden; expect home-made and locally sourced items of the highest quality.

Rooms 2 rms (1 en suite) (1 pri facs) **Facilities** FTV Lounge tea/coffee WiFi **Parking** 2 **Notes** ⊗ No Children 12yrs 🐾

HERNE COMMON
Map 7 TR16

Westgrange House B&B

★★★ GUEST ACCOMMODATION

tel: 01227 740663 **42 Bushyfields Rd CT6 7LJ**
email: westgrangebandb@ymail.com **web:** www.westgrangehouse.co.uk

Located in a quiet and tranquil area, this family-run bed and breakfast offers comfortable rooms, all equipped with WiFi and flat-screen TVs. Off-road parking is available for all guests and a cooked and continental breakfast is served daily in the dining room. Herne Bay with its shops, bars and restaurants, is only a ten-minute drive away.

Rooms 4 rms

Visit shop.theAA.com
for the latest Hotel, Pub and Restaurant Guides

LEYSDOWN-ON-SEA
Map 7 TR07

The Ferry House Inn

★★★★ ◉ INN

tel: 01795 510214 **Harty Ferry Rd ME12 4BQ**
email: info@theferryhouseinn.co.uk **web:** www.theferryhouseinn.co.uk
dir: A249 over Sheppey Bridge, follow signs for Leysdown. Past Eastchurch, turn right before Leysdown

The Ferry House Inn is on the Isle of Sheppey, and offers spacious and comfortable accommodation as well as some fantastic views. All rooms have modern fixtures, fittings and decor. Guests can enjoy dinner in the main restaurant or in the bar area with lots of local produce sourced from surrounding farms. A cooked or continental breakfast is served daily.

Rooms 5 en suite S £50-£100; D £80-£180* **Facilities** FTV DVD iPod docking station Lounge tea/coffee Dinner available WiFi **Conf** Max 80 Thtr 80 Class 40 Board 40 **Parking** 50 **Notes** LB ⊗ No Children 12yrs Closed 24-30 Dec Civ Wed 150

MAIDSTONE
Map 7 TQ75

See also Marden

Premier Collection

Maiden's Tower at Leeds Castle

★★★★★ GUEST ACCOMMODATION

tel: 01622 767823 & 765400 **Leeds Castle Estate ME17 1PL**
email: accommodation@leeds-castle.co.uk **web:** www.leeds-castle.com
dir: M20 junct 8, follow brown tourist signs. After 3rd sign, continue over rdbt on A20. Pass Park Gate Inn on right, turn next right signed Broomfield

The Maiden's Tower was built as an annexe to the castle and used for house-parties when the castle was still a private residence. Today, it offers five beautifully appointed bedrooms – all with stunning views. All rooms are en suite and equipped with modern amenities. The venue can be hired for exclusive use for family parties or intimate ceremonies. Breakfast and dinner are served in the 17th-century, oak-beamed Fairfax Restaurant. Guests are free to explore the castle, grounds and gardens while in residence. Free parking offered.

Rooms 5 en suite D £220-£240* **Facilities** FTV DVD tea/coffee Dinner available Direct Dial Licensed WiFi 🏊 9 🔒 Facilities available within Leeds Castle grounds **Extras** Speciality toiletries, robes, coffee machine **Conf** Max 100 Thtr 100 Class 40 Board 30 **Parking** 15 **Notes** ⊗ Closed 25-26 Dec Civ Wed 100

The Black Horse Inn

★★★★ 🛏 INN

tel: 01622 737185 **Pilgrims Way, Thurnham ME14 3LD**
email: info@wellieboot.net **web:** www.wellieboot.net
dir: M20 junct 7, N A249. Right into Detling, opposite pub into Pilgrims Way for 1m

This charming inn dates from the 17th century, and the public areas showcase a wealth of oak beams, exposed brickwork and open fireplaces. The stylish bedrooms are in a series of cosy cabins behind the premises; each one is attractively furnished and thoughtfully equipped, and the bathrooms are of an equally high standard.

Rooms 27 annexe en suite (8 fmly) (27 GF) S £70-£82; D £85-£100 **Facilities** FTV tea/coffee Dinner available WiFi 🔒 **Conf** Max 80 Thtr 80 Class 40 Board 28 **Parking** 40 **Notes** LB Closed 24-27 Dec No coaches Civ Wed 100

MAIDSTONE *continued*

Stable Courtyard at Leeds Castle

★★★★ GUEST ACCOMMODATION

tel: 01622 767823 & 767786 **Leeds Castle Estate ME17 1PL**
email: accommodation@leeds-castle.co.uk **web:** www.leeds-castle.com
dir: *M20 junct 8, follow brown tourist signs. After 3rd sign, continue over rdbt on A20. Pass Park Gate Inn on right, turn next right signed Broomfield*

Stable Courtyard is located right in the heart of the grounds at Leeds Castle. The stylishly appointed bedrooms are spacious, and many benefit from excellent views of the formal gardens and lake. Guests are welcome to explore the grounds and castle as part of their stay. Dinner and breakfast are served just opposite in The Great British Kitchen Restaurant.

Rooms 22 annexe en suite (1 fmly) (5 GF) S £85-£95; D £110-£140* **Facilities** FTV DVD tea/coffee Dinner available Direct Dial Licensed WiFi ⅃ 9 **Conf** Max 90 Thtr 90 Class 40 Board 30 **Parking** 30 **Notes** ⊗ Closed 25-26 Dec Civ Wed 100

Innkeeper's Lodge Maidstone

★★★ INN

tel: 08451 551551 *(Calls cost 2p per minute plus your phone company's access charge)* **Sandling Rd ME14 2RF**
email: info@innkeeperslodge.com **web:** www.innkeeperslodge.com

Known as The White Rabbit Sandling, this Innkeeper's Lodge is situated close to the centre of town, and dates back to 1797 when it was built to house the officers' quarters of the Invicta Barracks. Lodge bedrooms are modern, spacious and well appointed with a good range of facilities. Public rooms feature plush seating and dining areas where a good choice of food is available.

Rooms 12 en suite (1 fmly) **Facilities** FTV tea/coffee Dinner available WiFi **Parking Notes** ⊗

MARDEN Map 6 TQ74

Premier Collection

Merzie Meadows

★★★★★ BED AND BREAKFAST

tel: 01622 820500 & 07762 713077 **Hunton Rd TN12 9SL**
email: pamela@merziemeadows.co.uk **web:** www.merziemeadows.co.uk
dir: *A229 onto B2079 for Marden, 1st right into Underlyn Ln, 2.5m at large Chainhurst sign, right onto drive*

Merzie Meadows is a detached property set in 20 acres of mature gardens in the Kent countryside. The generously proportioned bedrooms are housed in two wings, which overlook a terrace; each room is carefully decorated, thoughtfully equipped and furnished with well-chosen pieces. The attractive breakfast room has an Italian tiled floor and superb views of the garden.

Rooms 2 en suite (1 fmly) (2 GF) S £100; D £115-£120* **Facilities** STV FTV TVL tea/coffee WiFi **Extras** Speciality toiletries, chocolates, magazines - free **Parking** 4 **Notes** ⊗ No Children 15yrs Closed mid Dec-mid Feb ⊛

NEW ROMNEY Map 7 TR02

The Ship

★★★ INN

tel: 01797 362776 **83 High St TN28 8AZ**
email: theshiphotelandrestaurant@gmail.com **web:** www.the-ship-hotel.co.uk
dir: *M20 junct 10 onto A2070 to Brenzett. At rdbt 1st exit onto A259 to New Romney. Next to petrol station on right*

This traditional inn is located in the very centre of Romney Marsh, bedrooms are traditional in style and are all located above the main pub area. The restaurant is spacious, seating up to 70 people, and is ideal for events and functions. Main bar area, conservatory and fully heated patio offer a good array of seating areas for guests to enjoy. Breakfast, lunch and dinner are served here daily.

Rooms 10 en suite (1 fmly) **Facilities** FTV DVD tea/coffee Dinner available WiFi ⅃ 18 Pool table 🔒 **Conf** Max 130 Thtr 130 Class 80 Board 40 **Parking** 20 **Notes** LB

PEMBURY Map 6 TQ64

Camden Arms

★★★★ INN

tel: 01892 822012 **1 High St TN2 4PH**
email: food@camdenarms.co.uk **web:** www.camdenarms.co.uk
dir: *Off A21, opposite village green*

Located in a central position and just a couple of minutes' drive from Tunbridge Wells, this inn offers comfortable, well-equipped accommodation with LCD TVs, free WiFi throughout, and spacious en suite bathrooms. The large garden has outdoor seating, and the restaurant and bar area serve a large variety of local beers which change on a regular basis and pub meals are available seven days a week. Guests can enjoy a continental breakfast in the morning, or, for an extra charge, a hearty traditional English breakfast.

Rooms 15 annexe en suite (1 fmly) (8 GF) **Facilities** FTV tea/coffee Dinner available WiFi 🔒 **Extras** Trouser press **Conf** Max 50 Thtr 50 Class 24 Board 16 **Parking** 68

PLUCKLEY Map 7 TQ94

Elvey Farm

★★★★ GUEST ACCOMMODATION

tel: 01233 840442 **Elvey Ln TN27 0SU**
email: bookings@elveyfarm.co.uk **web:** www.elveyfarm.co.uk
dir: *M20 junct 8 onto A20 to Charing. Right into Station Rd signed Pluckley. At bottom of Forge Hill turn right. 1st right into Mundy Bois Rd, then 1st right into Elvey Ln*

Located in a very quiet and picturesque part of the Kentish countryside, a number of period outbuildings have been converted to offer stylish and comfortable accommodation. There is a restaurant on site, with an outside seating area, open for afternoon tea and dinner every night. Meeting rooms make this ideal for small functions, weddings or business meetings. A hearty cooked or continental breakfast is served daily in the main restaurant.

Rooms 11 en suite (6 GF) S £55-£120; D £90-£275* **Facilities** FTV DVD Lounge tea/coffee Dinner available Licensed WiFi 🔒 **Conf** Max 20 Thtr 20 Class 15 Board 12 **Parking** 30 **Notes** Civ Wed 60

QUEENBOROUGH
Map 7 TQ97

Queen Phillippa B&B
★★★★ GUEST ACCOMMODATION

tel: 01795 228756 **High St ME11 5AQ**
email: queenphillippabedandbreakfast@gmail.com **web:** www.queenphillippa.com
dir: *A249 onto the Isle of Sheppey, follow signs for Queenborough. Located opposite entrance to railway station*

This former pub has been completely renovated to provide ten en suite bedrooms, all have been completely refurbished throughout with modern decor and stylish furnishings. Rooms are well equipped with free WiFi, digital TV and beverage making facilities. Breakfast is served daily in the dining area on the ground floor where guests can enjoy a cooked or continental breakfast.

Rooms 10 en suite (10 fmly) S £45-£59.50; D £45-£85* **Facilities** FTV TVL tea/coffee WiFi ⚓ 18 **Parking** 9 **Notes** LB ⊗

SANDWICH
Map 7 TR35

The New Inn
★★★ INN

tel: 01304 612335 **2 Harnet St CT13 9ES**
email: new.inn@thorleytaverns.com **web:** www.thenewinnsandwich.com
dir: *Off A256, one-way system into town centre, inn on right*

The New Inn is situated in the heart of busy Sandwich. The large open-plan lounge bar offers an extensive range of beers and an interesting choice of home-made dishes. Bedrooms are furnished in pine and have many useful extras.

Rooms 5 en suite (3 fmly) (2 smoking) **Facilities** STV tea/coffee Dinner available Direct Dial WiFi ⚓ **Parking** 17 **Notes** No coaches

SITTINGBOURNE
Map 7 TQ96

Sandhurst Farm Forge
★★★★ BED AND BREAKFAST

tel: 01795 886854 **Seed Rd, Newnham ME9 0NE**
email: rooms.forge@btinternet.com **web:** www.sandhurstfarmforge.co.uk
dir: *Exit A2 into Newnham, into Seed Rd by church, establishment 1m on right*

A warm welcome is assured at this peaceful location, which also features a working forge. The spacious bedrooms are in a converted stable block and provide smartly furnished accommodation. Breakfast is served in the dining room adjoining the bedrooms. The owner has won an award for green tourism by reducing the impact of the business on the environment.

Rooms 2 annexe en suite (2 GF) S £50; D £80* **Facilities** STV DVD tea/coffee WiFi ⚓ **Extras** Fruit, snacks, bottled water **Parking** 6 **Notes** LB No Children 12yrs Closed 23 Dec-2 Jan

TENTERDEN
Map 7 TQ83

Little Dane Court
★★★★ BED AND BREAKFAST

tel: 01580 763389 & 07776 193399 **1 Ashford Rd TN30 6AB**
email: littledanecourt@gmail.com **web:** www.littledanecourt.co.uk
dir: *A28 to Tenterden, after 1m pass 2 red telephone boxes. Little Dane 4th house on right*

Little Dane Court has a long and fascinating history, and offers a range of well-appointed bedrooms that meet the needs of discerning travellers. All rooms are well equipped. For something a bit more individual, the Japanese-style cottage offers extra privacy and space. Breakfast is served at the communal table in the dining room or in the courtyard during the warm months of the year. The Japanese-style garden is a pocket of tranquillity.

Rooms 3 rms (2 en suite) (1 pri facs) 1 annexe en suite S £80-£110; D £100-£135* **Facilities** FTV DVD TVL tea/coffee Dinner available WiFi ⚓ **Conf** Max 10 Thtr 10 Board 10 **Parking** 6 **Notes** LB ⊗

TUNBRIDGE WELLS (ROYAL)
Map 6 TQ53

Premier Collection

Danehurst House
★★★★★ BED AND BREAKFAST

tel: 01892 527739 **41 Lower Green Rd, Rusthall TN4 8TW**
email: info@danehurst.net **web:** www.danehurst.net
dir: *1.5m W of Tunbridge Wells in Rusthall. Exit A264 into Coach Rd & Lower Green Rd*

Situated in pretty gardens in a quiet residential area, this gabled Victorian house is located to the west of the historic spa town. The house retains many original features and is attractively decorated throughout. Public areas include a comfortable lounge with a small bar. The homely bedrooms come with a wealth of thoughtful extras, and excellent breakfasts are served in the conservatory. AA Friendliest B&B of the Year Award Finalist 2016-2017.

Rooms 4 en suite D £119-£175* **Facilities** FTV DVD iPod docking station TVL tea/coffee Licensed WiFi **Extras** Speciality toiletries, Nespresso coffee machine **Parking** 6 **Notes** ⊗ No Children 12yrs Closed Xmas

Salomons
★★★★ GUEST ACCOMMODATION

tel: 01892 515152 **Salomons Estate, Broomhill Rd, Southborough TN3 0TG**
email: reception@salomons-estate.com **web:** www.salomons-estate.com
dir: *M25 junct 5, A21 signed Hastings. Then A26 (Southborough & Tunbridge Wells). In Southborough right at 2nd lights into Speldhurst Rd. 2nd left into Broomhill Rd, entrance on right*

Salomons is located on a private, 36-acre estate just a short distance from Royal Tunbridge Wells. The bedrooms are all contemporary in style with modern decor and are well equipped ideal for both business and leisure guests. Guests can enjoy breakfast, lunch and dinner in the main Manor House daily. This is also a very popular wedding venue and a great range of conference rooms are available.

Rooms 47 annexe en suite (23 GF) S £60-£75; D £90-£105* **Facilities** STV FTV tea/coffee Dinner available Direct Dial Licensed WiFi Gym **Extras** Speciality toiletries **Conf** Max 230 Thtr 230 Class 77 Board 68 **Parking** 200 **Notes** Civ Wed 200

TUNBRIDGE WELLS (ROYAL) *continued*

Innkeeper's Lodge Tunbridge Wells

★★★ INN

tel: 08451 551551 *(Calls cost 2p per minute plus your phone company's access charge)*
London Rd, Southborough TN4 0QB
email: info@innkeeperslodge.com **web:** www.innkeeperslodge.com

At Innkeeper's Lodge you'll find accommodation with comfort and character in equal measure, and everything needed for a relaxing stay, from easy check-in and free parking to complimentary breakfast and a cosy pub serving great value food and drink on the doorstep. Each Lodge has quality rooms, and there are Lodges in a variety of locations from towns and cities to countryside settings across the UK.

Rooms 14 en suite (2 fmly) **Facilities** FTV tea/coffee Dinner available WiFi **Parking**
Notes ⊗

WROTHAM	Map 6 TQ65

The Bull

★★★★ ⊛⊛ INN

tel: 01732 789800 **Bull Ln TN15 7RF**
email: info@thebullhotel.com **web:** www.thebullhotel.com
dir: *M20 junct 2, A20 (signed Paddock Wood, Gravesend & Tonbridge). At rdbt 3rd exit onto A20 (signed Wrotham, Tonbridge, Borough Green, M20 & M25). At rdbt take 4th exit into Bull Ln (signed Wrotham)*

Dating back to 1385 and first licensed in 1495, The Bull offers modern facilities yet retains many traditional features, including original exposed beams. High quality meals can be enjoyed at breakfast, lunch and dinner; the inn sources local produce from nearby farms, south coast landed fish, and real ales from the Dark Star microbrewery. Dinner can be taken in the AA two Rosette award-winning à la carte restaurant, while more relaxed fare is offered in the smokehouse bar. The bedrooms, including one four-poster room, are decorated with modern furnishings. The Buttery function room was originally the village bakery.

Rooms 11 en suite (1 fmly) S £69-£139; D £79-£159 (room only)* **Facilities** FTV tea/coffee Dinner available WiFi ↧ 18 **Extras** Speciality toiletries - complimentary **Conf** Max 100 Thtr 60 Class 60 Board 40 **Parking** 30 **Notes** Civ Wed 60

LANCASHIRE

ACCRINGTON	Map 18 SD72

The Maple Lodge

★★★★ GUEST ACCOMMODATION

tel: 01254 301284 **70 Blackburn Rd, Clayton-le-Moors BB5 5JH**
email: info@stayatmaplelodge.co.uk **web:** www.stayatmaplelodge.co.uk
dir: *M65 junct 7, follow signs for Clitheroe, right at T-junct into Blackburn Rd*

This welcoming house is convenient for the M65 and local business areas and provides modern bedrooms generously equipped with home comforts as well as an inviting lounge with well-stocked bar. Freshly cooked dinners (by arrangement) and hearty breakfasts are served in the bright dining room.

Rooms 4 en suite 4 annexe en suite (1 fmly) (4 GF) **Facilities** FTV DVD TVL tea/coffee Dinner available Direct Dial Licensed WiFi ⊜ **Parking** 6

Pilkington's Guest House

★★★ GUEST HOUSE

tel: 01254 237032 **135 Blackburn Rd BB5 0AA**
email: pilkybuses@hotmail.com **web:** www.pilkingtonsbedandbreakfast.webs.com
dir: *M65 junct 7 follow signs to Accrington town centre, establishment opposite railway station. M66 onto A56 to Accrington town centre*

Positioned close to the railway station, this family-run property has two comfortable bedrooms in the main house and four further bedrooms in the terrace which is just a short way along the street. Home-cooked breakfasts are served in the main house.

Rooms 6 rms (6 pri facs) (2 fmly) (2 GF) S fr £30; D fr £60 (room only)*
Facilities FTV DVD Lounge TVL tea/coffee WiFi ⊜ **Extras** Slippers, robes **Parking** 2 **Notes** ⊗

BARLEY	Map 18 SD84

Barley Mow

★★★★ ⊜ INN

tel: 01282 690868 **BB12 9JX**
email: info@barleymowpendle.co.uk **web:** www.seafoodpubcompany.com
dir: *M65 junct 13, at rdbt exit onto A682. Left into Pasture Ln, right into Ridge Ln, continue on Barley New Rd. Turn right*

This relaxed dining pub is full of stripped back rustic charm. Although managed by the Seafood Pub Company, there is plenty for meat lovers as there is an international flavour, with an American twist on traditional pub fare. Six bedrooms upstairs are spacious and equipped with smart-TVs, free WiFi and deeply comfortable beds. A rural location offers a peaceful setting but quick motorway links are also available.

Rooms 6 en suite (2 fmly) **Facilities** FTV tea/coffee Dinner available WiFi **Extras** Mineral water, fresh milk **Parking** 10

BLACKBURN	Map 18 SD62

Premier Collection

The Millstone at Mellor

★★★★★ ⊛⊛ INN

tel: 01254 813333 **Church Ln, Mellor BB2 7JR**
email: relax@millstonehotel.co.uk **web:** www.millstonehotel.co.uk
dir: *A677 from Blackburn (or from A59) follow signs to Mellor*

Once a coaching inn, The Millstone is situated in a village just outside the town. It provides a very high standard of accommodation and professional and friendly service. Bedrooms, some in an adjacent house, are comfortable and generally spacious, and all are very well equipped. A room for less mobile guests is also available. Meals in the AA Rosetted restaurant make excellent use of the highest quality Ribble Valley produce.

Rooms 17 en suite 6 annexe en suite (5 fmly) (8 GF) S £80-£160; D £80-£160*
Facilities STV Lounge tea/coffee Dinner available Direct Dial WiFi **Conf** Max 10 Board 10 **Parking** 40 **Notes** ⊗ No coaches

BLACKPOOL
Map 18 SD33

The Fylde International
★★★★ GUEST HOUSE

tel: 01253 623735 **93 Palatine Rd FY1 4BX**
email: fyldeinternationalblackpool@gmail.com
web: www.familyaccommodationblackpool.com
dir: *A5099 (Central Dr) into town centre, right into Palatine Rd. Property on right before lights*

This family-run guest house has a prime central location close to all of Blackpool's attractions. Accommodation is comfortable and all rooms are equipped with modern facilities. Families are well catered for with a choice of family rooms and suites available. A spacious lounge and a separate dedicated children's area ensure all guests can enjoy the relaxed and welcoming environment. A substantial buffet breakfast is served. Parking is available.

Rooms 7 en suite (4 fmly) (1 GF) **Facilities** FTV TVL tea/coffee Licensed WiFi 🛇
Parking 6 **Notes** ⊗

The Berwick
★★★★ GUEST ACCOMMODATION

tel: 01253 351496 **North Shore, 23 King Edward Av FY2 9TA**
email: enquiries@theberwickhotel.co.uk **web:** www.theberwickhotel.co.uk

Thiis establishment has a quiet North Shore setting, only a few minutes' walk from the prom, and an interesting history, as the birthplace of what would become Jaguar Motors. The bodyshop even supplied the first AA Patrol motorcycle sidecars! With private parking available, the welcome and hosting from Yvonne and Eddie is matched only by homely cooking and a hearty breakfast. Bedrooms are comfortably appointed.

Rooms 8 en suite **Facilities** FTV TVL tea/coffee Dinner available Licensed WiFi ⅃ 18 **Parking** 4 **Notes** LB ⊗ No Children 3yrs Closed mid Nov-Feb

Bona Vista
★★★★ GUEST ACCOMMODATION

tel: 01253 351396 **104-106 Queens Promenade FY2 9NX**
email: enquires@bonavistahotel.com **web:** www.bonavistahotel.com
dir: *0.25m N of Uncle Toms Cabin & Casino*

The Bona Vista has a prime seafront position on North Shore within easy reach of Blackpool's amenities. Its bright and fresh bedrooms are well equipped, some with sea views. There is a spacious dining room and a comfortable bar and sun lounge. Some 16 parking spaces are available, an absolute bonus in this busy town. Dinner by arrangement and a robust breakfast are highlights.

Rooms 16 en suite (4 fmly) **Facilities** FTV Lounge TVL tea/coffee Dinner available Licensed WiFi Pool table 🛇 **Conf** Max 50 Thtr 50 Class 50 Board 50 **Parking** 16

The Bromley
★★★★ BED AND BREAKFAST

tel: 01253 624171 & 07702 239890 **306 Promenade FY1 2EY**
email: bromleyblackpool@gmail.com **web:** www.bromleyhotelblackpool.co.uk
dir: *0.1m N past Blackpool Tower, on right*

Located on the North Shore promenade, just a short walk from many of the main attractions, The Bromley offers comfortable en suite accommodation. There is a licensed bar and lounge on the ground floor. Free WiFi is available in public areas, and off-road parking, provided at the front of the property, is a real bonus.

Rooms 13 en suite (3 fmly) (1 GF) S £45; D £65-£80 **Facilities** FTV DVD iPod docking station TVL tea/coffee Licensed WiFi 🛇 **Parking** 9 **Notes** ⊗ Closed 21-27 Dec

BLACKPOOL *continued*

The Craigmore

★★★★ GUEST HOUSE

tel: 01253 355098 **8 Willshaw Rd, Gynn Square FY2 9SH**
email: enquiries@thecraigmore.com web: www.thecraigmore.com
dir: *1m N of Tower. A584 N over Gynn rdbt, 1st right into Willshaw Rd. The Craigmore 3rd on left*

This friendly and welcoming guest house is in an attractive location overlooking Gynn Square gardens, with the Promenade and tram stops just metres away. Three of the smart and modern bedrooms are suitable for families. There is a comfortable lounge, a separate sun lounge and patio to the front, and the dining room has a small bar.

Rooms 7 en suite (3 fmly) D £50-£65* **Facilities** FTV Lounge TVL tea/coffee Licensed WiFi **Notes** LB ⊗ No Children 5yrs Closed Nov-Mar

Lynbar Guesthouse

★★★★ GUEST HOUSE

tel: 01253 294504 **32 Vance Rd FY1 4QD**
email: enquiries@lynbarhotel.co.uk web: www.lynbarhotel.co.uk
dir: *M55 until end, follow Yeadon Way/Seasiders Way to central car park. Exit car park into Central Dr, turn left then 2nd on right*

Lynbar is a welcoming, personally-run guest house with a prime central location just 300 metres from the promenade; an ideal position for the Tower, Winter Gardens and Grand Theatre. There are very comfortable beds in a choice of room sizes and very good in-room amenities. Dinner is served with advance notice and a hearty home-made breakfast with a wide choice awaits guests in the morning.

Rooms 8 rms (6 en suite) (2 pri facs) (3 fmly) S £27.50-£40; D £50-£80 **Facilities** FTV Lounge tea/coffee Dinner available Licensed WiFi **Notes** LB ⊗ No Children 2yrs Closed 22 Dec-4 Jan

Pelham Lodge

★★★★ GUEST ACCOMMODATION

tel: 01253 625127 & 07717 342897 **7-9 General St FY1 1RW**
email: info@pelhamlodge.co.uk web: www.pelhamlodge.co.uk

Situated towards the North End of Blackpool, and close to attractions such as the Winter Gardens and Blackpool Tower, Pelham Lodge is only a five minute walk from the train station. Good quality and comfortable accommodation is promised and a friendly welcome on arrival guaranteed. Limited parking available to the rear.

Rooms 15 en suite (2 fmly) (2 GF) S £35-£45; D £55-£65* **Facilities** FTV TVL tea/coffee WiFi **Extras** Bottled water - complimentary **Parking** 4 **Notes** ⊗ Closed 24-25 Dec

The Baron

★★★★ Ⓐ GUEST ACCOMMODATION

tel: 01253 622729 **296 North Promenade FY1 2EY**
email: baronhotel@f2s.com

The Baron offers comfortable surroundings only a short walk from the North Pier, Tower and centre. All rooms come complete with thoughtful extras, including free WiFi. Guests can dine at individual tables, and vegetarians and other special diets can be catered for. A passenger lift is on hand for the dining room and first and second floor bedrooms. Free parking is a plus.

Rooms 21 en suite (1 fmly) (3 GF) **Facilities** FTV DVD Lounge tea/coffee Lift Licensed WiFi **Conf** Max 20 Thtr 20 Class 20 Board 20 **Parking** 16 **Notes** ⊗ No Children 12yrs

Eden House

★★★ BED AND BREAKFAST

tel: 01253 297669 **91 Palatine Rd FY1 4BX**
email: info@edenhouseblackpool.com web: www.edenhouseblackpool.com
dir: *M55 junct 4 onto A583 pass windmill on left. Through 10 sets of lights, turn left into Palatine Rd*

A warm welcome is assured at Eden House, just off the beaten track in the centre of Blackpool, and within easy walking distance of attractions. Bedrooms are very comfortable, and are equipped with a wealth of extras for the modern traveller. Well-cooked, hearty breakfasts are served in the bright dining room.

Rooms 6 en suite (2 fmly) (1 GF) S £35; D £55-£60* **Facilities** FTV tea/coffee WiFi 🔒 **Parking** 5 **Notes** LB ⊗

Hartshead

★★★ GUEST ACCOMMODATION

tel: 01253 353133 & 357111 **17 King Edward Av, North Shore FY2 9TA**
email: info@hartshead-hotel.co.uk web: www.hartshead-hotel.co.uk
dir: *M55 junct 4, A583, A584 to North Shore, exit Queens Promenade into King Edward Av*

Popular for its location near the seafront on the quieter North Shore, the enthusiastically-run Hartshead has modern bedrooms of various sizes, all equipped with a good range of practical extras. A comfortable sun lounge is available to the front, in addition to a lounge bar. Breakfast and pre-theatre dinners are served in the bright dining room. Guaranteed off-street parking is a bonus.

Rooms 9 en suite (3 fmly) S £25-£50; D £48-£65* **Facilities** FTV DVD Lounge tea/coffee Dinner available Licensed WiFi **Parking** 7 **Notes** LB ⊗

The Abbotsford

★★★ GUEST HOUSE

tel: 01253 346417 **18 Woodfield Rd FY1 6AX**
email: abbotsford-blackpool@outlook.com web: www.abbotsford-blackpool.co.uk
dir: *M55 to end of motorway. Over rdbt into Yeadon Way, continue for 1.5m, over 2 rdbts. Turn left at football ground*

This friendly, personally-run guest house has a great location close to the promenade and handy for the Pleasure Beach and all of Blackpool's central attractions. Rooms are neat and well equipped and there is a small bar and sun lounge to relax in. Dinner is available on request and a generous breakfast is served in the bright dining room.

Rooms 9 rms (8 en suite) (1 pri facs) (2 fmly) **Facilities** FTV DVD TVL tea/coffee Dinner available Licensed WiFi Pool table **Notes** LB ⊗ Closed 15-28 Dec

Bianca Guesthouse

★★★ GUEST HOUSE

tel: 01253 752824 **25 Palatine Rd FY1 4BX**
web: www.hotelbianca.co.uk

A warm Blackpool welcome awaits at Bianca Guesthouse, situated centrally, and within easy walking distance of all the town's attractions and amenities. Homely accommodation is decorated with modern floral prints. Family rooms are available, as well as a range of cosy doubles fitted with impressively comfortable beds. There is a licensed bar for residents.

Rooms 10 en suite (2 fmly) **Facilities** FTV tea/coffee Licensed WiFi **Notes** ⊗ Closed 20-27 Dec

Braemar

★★★ GUEST ACCOMMODATION

tel: 01253 346024 & 07786 391990 **30 Lonsdale Rd FY1 6EE**
email: enquiries@braemarhotel.com **web:** www.braemarhotel.com

This friendly, family-run accommodation is positioned a short walk from both the seafront and Blackpool FC making it an ideal location to explore the bustling centre of Blackpool. Modern bedrooms are spacious and well equipped, and many have en suite bathrooms. There is a cosy bar area and small dining room, a range of lighter bar snacks or more substantial three-course, home-made dinners are available for guests.

Rooms 7 rms (4 en suite) (1 pri facs) (2 fmly) **Facilities** FTV DVD TVL tea/coffee Dinner available Licensed WiFi 🔒 **Parking** 2 **Notes** LB ⊗ Closed 25-26 Dec

Casablanca

★★★ GUEST ACCOMMODATION

tel: 01253 622574 **84 Hornby Rd FY1 4QS**
email: jdixon8969@aol.com

This personally-run and homely guest accommodation is perfectly situated within easy reach of all of Blackpool's central attractions. Accommodation is fully en suite and features modern accessories and a choice of room types. There is a comfortable lounge, breakfasts are generous and limited parking is available.

Rooms 9 en suite (2 fmly) S £30; D £50-£60* **Facilities** FTV TVL tea/coffee 🔒 **Parking** 2 **Notes** LB ⊗ Closed 20 Dec-4 Jan

The Derby

★★★ GUEST ACCOMMODATION

tel: 01253 623708 & 07809 143248 **2 Derby Rd FY1 2JF**
email: tj52way@yahoo.com **web:** www.thederbyhotel.co.uk
dir: From promenade, pass North Pier, heading N. Turn right next to Hilton Hotel into Derby Road, The Derby on right

The Derby is a family-friendly establishment offering good value, modern accommodation in a variety of sizes. Dinner is available and guests have the use of a comfortable lounge and a separate bar. Breakfast is the highlight of any stay with quality cooking and hearty portions to be expected.

Rooms 9 rms (5 en suite) (4 pri facs) (3 fmly) S £25-£35; D £50-£60 **Facilities** FTV TVL tea/coffee Dinner available Licensed WiFi 🔒 **Parking** 5 **Notes** LB

The Fairway

★★★ ⒶGUEST ACCOMMODATION

tel: 01253 623777 **34-36 Hull Rd FY1 4QB**
email: impulsedh@aol.com **web:** www.fairwayhotelblackpool.co.uk

Close to Blackpool's seafront and Tower, The Fairway is run by friendly owners and is a traditional seaside property. It is ideal for families, or those attending dance festivals, conferences or other Blackpool entertainments. There is a licensed bar, and a games area with a pool table. A full English breakfast is served and free WiFi is a bonus.

Rooms 19 en suite **Facilities** FTV DVD TVL TV18B Licensed WiFi Pool table **Notes** ⊗

BOLTON-BY-BOWLAND   Map 18 SD74

Middle Flass Lodge

★★★★ 🍽 GUEST HOUSE

tel: 01200 447259 **Settle Rd BB7 4NY**
email: middleflasslodge@btconnect.com **web:** www.middleflasslodge.co.uk
dir: 2m N of Bolton-by-Bowland. Off A59 for Sawley, N to Forest Becks, over bridge, 1m on right

Set in peaceful countryside in the Forest of Bowland, this smart house provides a warm welcome. Stylishly converted from farm outbuildings, exposed timbers feature throughout, as well as in the attractive restaurant and cosy lounge. The modern bedrooms include a family room, with stairlift access to the first floor. Thanks to the accomplished chef, the restaurant is very popular.

Rooms 5 en suite 2 annexe en suite (1 fmly) S £55-£60; D £76-£82 **Facilities** FTV TVL tea/coffee Dinner available Licensed WiFi 🔒 **Extras** Speciality toiletries - complimentary **Parking** 14 **Notes** LB ⊗

CHORLEY

See Eccleston

CLITHEROE   Map 18 SD74

Premier Collection

The Assheton Arms

★★★★★ ⓰ RESTAURANT WITH ROOMS

tel: 01200 441227 **Downham BB7 4BJ**
email: info@asshetonarms.com **web:** www.seafoodpubcompany.com
dir: A59 to Chatburn, then follow Downham signs

This historic Grade II-listed building is located in the conservation village of Downham, with stunning views of the Pendle Hills. The inn is owned by the Seafood Pub Company which means you can expect outstanding seafood. The rooms are spacious with traditional fittings yet maintain a modern feel. The team are young, friendly and guarantee a warm welcome.

Rooms 1 en suite 11 annexe en suite (4 fmly) (6 GF) **Facilities** FTV Lounge tea/coffee Dinner available WiFi ⅃ 18 🔒 **Extras** Mineral water, fresh milk **Conf** Max 20 **Parking** 18

ECCLESTON
Map 15 SD51

Parr Hall Farm

★★★★ GUEST ACCOMMODATION

tel: 01257 451917 **8 Parr Ln PR7 5SL**
email: enquiries@parrhallfarm.com **web:** www.parrhallfarm.com
dir: M6 junct 27, B5250 N for 5m to Parr Ln on right. 1st property on left

This attractive, well-maintained farmhouse, located in a quiet corner of the village yet close to the M6, dates back to the 18th century. The majority of bedrooms are located in a sympathetic barn conversion and include luxury en suite bathrooms and lots of thoughtful extras. A comprehensive continental breakfast is included in the room price.

Rooms 10 annexe en suite (1 fmly) (5 GF) S £49-£55; D £78-£85* **Facilities** FTV tea/coffee WiFi ⌘ 9 ⚓ Guided Walks **Conf** Max 15 Class 15 Board 15 **Parking** 20 **Notes** ⊗

LANCASTER
Map 18 SD46

The Fenwick Steak & Seafood Pub

★★★★ ⌖ INN

tel: 015242 21157 **Lancaster Rd, Claughton LA2 9LA**
email: info@fenwickarms.co.uk **web:** www.fenwickarms.co.uk

This charming roadside dining pub has been stylishly restored in recent years by the growing Seafood Pub Company. Comfortable and characterful public bar and restaurant areas are the setting for the fish and grill-led menu and a great choice of real ales and wines. Accommodation, even more recently opened is modern and comfortable with suites available.

Rooms 9 en suite S £70-£105; D £80-£170 (room only)* **Facilities** Dinner available WiFi **Parking**

Toll House Inn

★★★★ ⌖ INN

tel: 01524 599900 **Penny St LA1 1XT**
email: relax@tollhouseinnlancaster.co.uk **web:** http://tollhouseinnlancaster.co.uk

Ideally situated in the heart of the city, Toll House Inn has been transformed from a typical Victorian property to one that is fresh and contemporary, yet retains all the elegance of its original era. Bedrooms are modern and very well equipped. The stylish bar and brasserie are popular with both guests and local residents, serving meals and light bites throughout the day.

Rooms 28 en suite (2 fmly) (2 GF) **Facilities** FTV tea/coffee Dinner available Lift WiFi ⚓ **Conf** Max 20 Thtr 20 Board 20 **Parking** 3 **Notes** ⊗ No coaches

LANESHAW BRIDGE
Map 18 SD94

The Alma Inn

★★★★★ ⌖ INN

tel: 01282 857830 **Emmott Ln BB8 7EG**
email: reception@thealmainn.com **web:** www.thealmainn.com
dir: At end of M65 onto A6068 (Vivary Way) towards Skipton. At 3rd rdbt, 1st exit into Skipton Old Rd, after 0.5m right into Hill Ln. 0.5m on right

The Alma Inn nestles in the magnificent Pendle countryside, and dates back to 1725. It is a rural coaching inn that features open fires, stone floors and original beams. Guests can dine well in the lounge-style bars or the more lavishly appointed restaurant. The stylish rooms come in a variety of sizes, and all are thoroughly equipped with coffee machines, DAB radio and safes. Function facilities are available along with ample parking and even a helicopter landing pad.

Rooms 9 en suite (8 fmly) S £65.95; D £79.95* **Facilities** FTV iPod docking station Lounge tea/coffee Dinner available Direct Dial WiFi ⌘ 9 ⚓ **Extras** Speciality toiletries, espresso coffee machine **Conf** Max 150 Thtr 100 Class 50 Board 40 **Parking** 45 **Notes** LB Civ Wed 200

Rye Flatt Bed & Breakfast

★★★★ BED AND BREAKFAST

tel: 01282 871565 **20 School Ln BB8 7JB**
email: info@rye-flatt.co.uk **web:** www.rye-flatt.co.uk
dir: M65 onto A6068 towards Keighley. Turn right at Emmott Arms, park on left, immediately after bridge

Situated on the Lancashire and Yorkshire border with great transport links, this B&B operates from a 17th-century farmhouse which has some fantastic original features. Ideally located for business or leisure, the house features cosy bedrooms and well-equipped bathrooms. Warm hospitality and a memorable breakfast are features of any stay here. There is also a garden for sunnier days.

Rooms 2 en suite **Facilities** FTV Lounge tea/coffee WiFi ⚓ **Parking** 2 **Notes** ⊗ ⊜

LONGRIDGE
Map 18 SD63

Derby Arms

★★★★ ⌖ INN

tel: 01772 782370 **Chipping Rd PR3 2NB**
email: info@derbyarmslongridge.co.uk **web:** www.derbyarmslongridge.co.uk
dir: Phone for directions

This recently refreshed, relaxed dining pub is managed by the Seafood Pub Company so although classic British pub fare is to be expected, the emphasis is on locally landed fish. Accommodation upstairs is spacious and equipped with smart-TVs. Little luxury extras in the form of toiletries are noteworthy and a deeply comfortable bed is guaranteed. A rural location offers a peaceful setting but quick motorway links are also a boon.

Rooms 6 en suite (1 fmly) **Facilities** FTV tea/coffee Dinner available ⌘ 18 ⚓ **Conf** Max 15 Thtr 15 Class 15 Board 15 **Parking** 50

LYTHAM ST ANNES
Map 18 SD32

Strathmore

★★★ GUEST ACCOMMODATION

tel: 01253 725478 **305 Clifton Drive South FY8 1HN**
dir: In centre of St Annes opposite Post Office

The long-established, family-run Strathmore has a central location close to the promenade, and offers smartly furnished and well-equipped bedrooms. There is an elegant lounge and a smart dining room.

Rooms 5 en suite S £30-£32; D £60-£64 **Facilities** Lounge tea/coffee WiFi 🔋
Parking 5 **Notes** LB ⊗ No Children 9yrs ⊛

MORECAMBE
Map 18 SD46

Broadwater Guest House

★★★★ ⬛ GUEST HOUSE

tel: 01524 411333 **356 Marine Road East LA4 5AQ**
email: enquiries@thebroadwaterhotel.co.uk **web:** www.thebroadwaterhotel.co.uk
dir: M6 junct 34 follow signs for Morecambe, then signs for E Promenade

Located on Morecambe's seafront, Broadwater Guest House offers a refreshingly friendly welcome. Bedrooms vary in size, but all are en suite, and well equipped with thoughtful extras including free WiFi. Substantial breakfasts are served in the pleasant dining room which has sea views.

Rooms 8 en suite S £38; D £70-£75* **Facilities** FTV DVD Lounge tea/coffee WiFi
Notes ⊗ Closed Xmas-New Year

Yacht Bay View

★★★★ GUEST HOUSE

tel: 01524 414481 **359 Marine Road East LA4 5AQ**
email: yachtbayview@hotmail.com **web:** www.yachtbay.co.uk
dir: 0.5m NE of town centre on seafront promenade

This comfortable seafront guest house is situated pride of place on Morecambe's promenade. Seven guest rooms are available in a range of sizes and all smartly appointed and well equipped. The welcome is warm and generous and breakfast is a highlight of any stay.

Rooms 7 en suite (1 fmly) S £40-£45; D £65-£80* **Facilities** FTV DVD TVL tea/coffee
WiFi 🔋 **Extras** Bottled water, fresh milk **Parking Notes** ⊗

Beach Mount

★★★ GUEST ACCOMMODATION

tel: 01524 420753 **395 Marine Road East LA4 5AN**
email: beachmounthotel@aol.com **web:** www.beachmounthotelmorecambe.co.uk
dir: M6 junct 34/35, follow signs to Morecambe. Beach Mount 0.5m from town centre on
E Promenade

This spacious property overlooks the bay and features a range of room styles that includes a junior suite. Guests have use of a comfortable lounge with fully licensed bar, and breakfasts are served in a pleasant separate dining room.

Rooms 10 en suite (1 GF) S £28.25-£31.50; D £56.50-£63* **Facilities** FTV DVD
Lounge tea/coffee Licensed WiFi **Notes** LB Closed Nov-Mar

Silverwell

20 West End Road, Morecambe, Lancashire LA4 4DL
Tel: 01524 410532
Website: www.silverwellhotel.co.uk
Email: silverwell.hotel@btconnect.com

Every guest at the *Silverwell* is important, we aim to make you feel comfortable and relaxed, happy in the knowledge that whatever your needs it will be catered for.

Our food is cooked from as far as possible locally grown and organic produce, and are always happy to cater for dietary needs and vegetarians and any particular preferences.

Our proximity to the stunning Lake District and Yorkshire Dales make Morecambe the place to stay. The views over Morecambe Bay are legendary and many guests come here to enjoy the local pleasures such as walking, fishing, golf and the many festivals.

Morecambe and this guesthouse are certainly the place to come to just enjoy.

MORECAMBE *continued*

Silverwell

★★★ GUEST HOUSE

tel: 01524 410532 **20 West End Rd LA4 4DL**
email: silverwell.hotel@btconnect.com **web:** www.silverwellhotel.co.uk
dir: *Follow signs to West End, turn right at promenade, take 3rd on right, Silverwell on left*

Silverwell offers comfortable accommodation in a quiet residential street, with rooms in a range of sizes with singles and families catered for. There is a licensed bar and lounge for guests use. Evening meals are available by prior arrangement.

Rooms 14 rms (8 en suite) (6 pri facs) (3 fmly) (4 GF) (5 smoking) S £26-£35; D £52-£70 **Facilities** FTV Lounge tea/coffee Dinner available Licensed WiFi 🔒 **Conf** Max 20 Class 20 Board 12 **Notes** ⊗

See advert on page 199

ORMSKIRK   Map 15 SD40

Innkeeper's Lodge Ormskirk

★★★★ INN

tel: 08451 551551 *(Calls cost 2p per minute plus your phone company's access charge)*
Springfield Rd, Aughton L39 6ST
email: info@innkeeperslodge.com **web:** www.innkeeperslodge.com

On the edge of the pretty village of Aughton, this luxurious lodge provides smart yet affordable accommodation ideally located for a country escape or as a quiet base away from the hustle and bustle of Liverpool or Southport, and in easy reach of attractions such as Knowsley Safari Park, Chester Zoo, Formby Golf Club and Aintree racecourse. The elegant en suite rooms offer many extras and there's a Miller & Carter steakhouse.

Rooms 12 en suite (1 fmly) **Facilities** FTV tea/coffee Dinner available Lift WiFi **Notes** ⊗

PRESTON   Map 18 SD52

Birch Croft Bed & Breakfast

★★★ BED AND BREAKFAST

tel: 01772 613174 & 07761 817187 **Gill Ln, Longton PR4 4SS**
email: johnsuts@btinternet.com **web:** www.birchcroftbandb.co.uk
dir: *From A59 right at rdbt to Midge Hall. Premises 4th on left*

Situated only ten minutes away from major motorway links (M6, M65, M61) Birch Croft is on the doorstep of many attractions and close to Southport, Preston and Blackpool. This is a friendly, family-run business which offers comfortable accommodation in a very peaceful location.

Rooms 3 en suite (1 fmly) **Facilities** FTV DVD Lounge TVL tea/coffee WiFi 🔒 **Parking** 11 **Notes** LB ⊗ ⊚

SAMLESBURY   Map 18 SD53

Samlesbury Hall Lodge

★★★★ GUEST ACCOMMODATION

tel: 01254 812010 **Preston New Rd PR5 0UP**
email: info@samlesburyhall.co.uk **web:** www.samlesburyhall.co.uk
dir: *M6 junct 31 onto A59 then A677 signed Blackburn*

The gate lodge of Samlesbury Hall provides a cosy getaway for small groups, or couples looking for a romantic retreat. Accommodation comprises a large suite with two sitting rooms on one level, making it accessible for guests with mobility issues. The sitting rooms can be converted, allowing up to six guests. Breakfasts are served in the Hall or in the suite by prior arrangement. The Hall serves hearty lunches and has an antiques saleroom and an art gallery, as well as the Hall and gardens themselves to explore.

Rooms 3 en suite (3 fmly) (3 GF) S £60; D £100 (room only)* **Facilities** FTV DVD Lounge TVL TV1B tea/coffee Licensed WiFi ⬇ 9 🔒 Golf driving range Play trail Historic house **Conf** Max 150 Thtr 150 Class 150 Board 150 **Parking** 4 **Notes** ⊗ Civ Wed 120

WARTON
Map 18 SD42

The Birley Arms
★★★★ INN

tel: 01772 679988 **Bryning Ln PR4 1TN**
email: birley@thebirleyarmshotel.co.uk **web:** www.thebirleyarmshotel.co.uk
dir: *M55 junct 3 (Kirkham), 1st left, then over 3 rdbts. Straight on at mini rdbt, at next rdbt left signed Warton. 2m on left*

The Birley Arms is a smartly appointed inn situated in the charming village of Warton, between Lytham St Annes and Preston. The bedrooms are smartly decorated and equipped with modern facilities. Open-plan public areas are light and airy, and feature a conservatory, lounge bar and a restaurant.

Rooms 16 en suite (1 fmly) (8 GF) S £70-£85; D £80-£95* **Facilities** FTV DVD tea/coffee Dinner available WiFi 🛡 **Extras** Speciality toiletries - complimentary **Parking** 60 **Notes** ⊗

WHITEWELL
Map 18 SD64

Premier Collection

The Inn at Whitewell
★★★★★ 🏵 👤 INN

tel: 01200 448222 **Forest of Bowland, Clitheroe BB7 3AT**
email: reception@innatwhitewell.com **web:** www.innatwhitewell.com
dir: *M6 junct 31a, B6243 to Longridge. Left at mini rdbt. After 3 rdbts (approx 3m) sharp left (with white railings), then right. Approx 1m, left, right at T-junct. Next left, 3m to Whitewell*

This long-established culinary destination is hidden away in quintessential Lancashire countryside, just 20 minutes from the M6. The fine dining restaurant is complemented by a warren of cosy bar rooms with roaring fires, real ales and polished service. Bedrooms are richly furnished with antiques and eye-catching bijouterie, while many of the bathrooms have Victorian brass showers.

Rooms 19 en suite 4 annexe en suite (1 fmly) (2 GF) **Facilities** STV FTV DVD iPod docking station tea/coffee Dinner available Direct Dial WiFi ⌕ 18 Fishing Riding 🛡 Horse stabling can be arranged **Extras** Speciality toiletries - complimentary **Conf** Max 45 Thtr 45 Board 35 **Parking** 60 **Notes** Civ Wed 80

LEICESTERSHIRE

CROFT
Map 11 SP59

Fossebrook B&B
★★★★ GUEST ACCOMMODATION

tel: 01455 283517 & 07860 762214 **Coventry Rd LE9 3GP**
web: www.fossebrook.co.uk
dir: *From M1 exit junct 21 or M69 exit junct 1 on to A5. 6m SE of village centre on B4114*

Offering friendly guest accommodation, Fossebrook B&B stands in a quiet rural location with good access to major roads. Bedrooms are spacious, very comfortable and offer an excellent range of facilities including a range of videos in all rooms. Breakfast is served in the bright dining room overlooking pleasant gardens and grounds.

Rooms 4 en suite (4 GF) **Facilities** tea/coffee WiFi 🛡 **Extras** Snacks - complimentary **Parking** 16 **Notes** ⊗ Closed 24 Dec-2 Jan

EAST MIDLANDS AIRPORT
Map 11 SK42

Premier Collection

Kegworth House
★★★★★ 🏵 GUEST HOUSE

tel: 01509 672575 **42 High St DE74 2DA**
email: info@kegworthhouse.co.uk **web:** www.kegworthhouse.co.uk
dir: *M1 junct 24, A6 to Loughborough. 0.5m 1st right onto Packington Hill. Left at junct, Kegworth House 50yds on left*

Convenient for major roads and East Midlands Airport, this impressive Georgian house with an immaculate walled garden is lovingly maintained. The individually styled bedrooms are luxuriously appointed and equipped with a wealth of thoughtful extras. The elegant dining room is the setting for memorable dinners (by arrangement for six or more), and wholesome breakfasts featuring local produce are served in the kitchen.

Rooms 11 en suite (1 fmly) (2 GF) **Facilities** FTV DVD Lounge tea/coffee Direct Dial Licensed WiFi Free access to health club & swimming pool **Conf** Max 12 Board 12 **Parking** 25 **Notes** LB ⊗ No Children 8yrs

HUSBANDS BOSWORTH
Map 11 SP68

Croft Farm B&B *(SP634860)*
★★★★ FARMHOUSE

tel: 01858 880679 **Leicester Rd LE17 6NW**
email: janesmith06@aol.com **web:** www.croftfarm.org.uk
dir: *A5199 from Husbands Bosworth towards Leicester. Croft Farm 0.25m on left*

This very spacious and delightfully furnished house stands on the edge of the village in well-tended grounds. Bedrooms are thoughtfully equipped and there is a comfortable guests' lounge. Expect a substantial breakfast together with friendly and attentive service.

Rooms 4 en suite S £40-£45; D £75* **Facilities** DVD TVL tea/coffee WiFi **Parking** 15 **Notes** ⊗ No Children 10yrs 🐾 350 acres sheep/arable/beef/mixed

KEGWORTH
See East Midlands Airport

KNIPTON
Map 11 SK83

The Manners Arms
★★★★ 🍴 RESTAURANT WITH ROOMS

tel: 01476 879222 **Croxton Rd NG32 1RH**
email: info@mannersarms.com **web:** www.mannersarms.com
dir: *From A607 follow signs to Knipton; from A52 follow signs to Belvoir Castle*

Part of the Rutland Estate and built as a hunting lodge for the 6th Duke, The Manners Arms offers thoughtfully furnished bedrooms designed by the present Duchess. Public areas include the intimate Beater's Bar and attractive Red Coats Restaurant, popular for its imaginative menus.

Rooms 10 en suite (1 fmly) **Facilities** FTV TVL tea/coffee Dinner available Direct Dial WiFi ⌕ 18 🛡 **Conf** Max 50 Thtr 50 Class 25 Board 20 **Parking** 60 **Notes** Civ Wed 50

LONG WHATTON
Map 11 SK42

The Royal Oak

★★★★★ ◉ ⌘ INN

tel: 01509 843694 **26 The Green LE12 5DB**
email: enquiries@theroyaloaklongwhatton.co.uk **web:** www.theroyaloaklongwhatton.co.uk

The Royal Oak is a popular gastropub with rooms, located in a small village just four miles from East Midlands Airport. Members of the young team offer a warm welcome and service is attentive. The seven spacious en suite bedrooms are to the rear of the property and have been designed with comfort and style in mind. There is plenty of parking available and a small garden for the warmer months.

Rooms 7 en suite (7 GF) S £79-£99; D £79-£99* **Facilities** FTV tea/coffee Dinner available WiFi **Extras** Speciality toiletries, mineral water **Parking** 28 **Notes** ⊗

LOUGHBOROUGH
Map 11 SK51

Charnwood Lodge

★★★★ GUEST HOUSE

tel: 01509 211120 **136 Leicester Rd LE11 2AQ**
email: reservations@charnwoodlodge.com **web:** www.charnwoodlodge.com

Located within easy walking distance of the city's shopping areas and university campus, Charnwood Lodge offers a choice of well-equipped rooms, with some situated on the ground floor having private access. A spacious dining room provides comfortable surroundings for evening meals and home-cooked breakfasts. A large TV lounge and bar with period features are also available. Complimentary WiFi and ample onsite parking is provided.

Rooms 12 rms (10 en suite) (2 pri facs) 2 annexe en suite (2 fmly) (6 GF) **Facilities** FTV TVL tea/coffee Dinner available Licensed WiFi **Parking** 30 **Notes** Closed 21 Dec-5 Jan

MARKET BOSWORTH
Map 11 SK40

Softleys

★★★ ⌂ GUEST ACCOMMODATION

tel: 01455 290464 **2 Market Place CV13 0LE**
email: softleysrestaurant@gmail.com **web:** www.softleys.com
dir: On B585 in Market Place

Softleys is a Grade II listed building dating back to 1794. The bedrooms are en suite and set on the third floor offering picturesque views over Market Bosworth. Quality food is served using locally sourced ingredients.

Rooms 3 en suite (1 fmly) **Facilities** FTV tea/coffee Dinner available Direct Dial Licensed WiFi **Conf** Max 26 Thtr 26 Class 26 Board 26 **Notes** RS Sun eve & Mon no food available

QUORN
Map 11 SK51

Lavender House

★★★★ BED AND BREAKFAST

tel: 01509 412166 **118 Chaveney Rd LE12 8AD**
email: bookings@lavenderhousequorn.co.uk **web:** www.lavenderhousequorn.co.uk
dir: From High St, at mini rdbt into Meeting St, then Chaveney Rd

The owners of Lavender House extend a friendly welcome at their home, located in the idyllic village of Quorn. Built in 1927 the house has been tastefully and sympathetically renovated to retain much of its original character and charm. The downstairs room offers very easy access as well as a large walk-in shower, while upstairs a spacious three-room suite is suitable for family use. All rooms are extremely comfortable, and offer a high level of quality in both furnishings and design. The house has a large private drive with secure well-lit parking. Breakfast is served in a bright breakfast area, and evening meals can be had at the nearby pub, or in the village. The area has plenty to recommend it, with some delightful walking country very close by.

Rooms 2 en suite (1 fmly) (1 GF) **Facilities** FTV tea/coffee WiFi 🛁 **Extras** Chocolates, home-made biscuits **Parking** 3 **Notes** ⊗ No Children 6yrs ⊜

SUTTON IN THE ELMS
Map 11 SP59

The Mill on the Soar

★★★ INN

tel: 01455 282419 **Coventry Rd LE9 6QA**
email: 1968@greeneking.co.uk **web:** www.oldenglish.co.uk
dir: M1 junct 21, follow signs for Narborough, 3m, inn on left

This is a popular inn that caters especially well for family dining, and is set in grounds with two rivers and a lake. The open-plan bar offers meals and snacks throughout the day, and is divided into family and adults-only areas; for the summer months, there is also an attractive patio. Practical bedrooms are housed in a lodge-style annexe in the grounds.

Rooms 20 en suite 5 annexe en suite (19 fmly) (13 GF) **Facilities** FTV tea/coffee Direct Dial Children's outdoor play area Pool room **Parking** 80 **Notes** ⊗

LINCOLNSHIRE

ADDLETHORPE
Map 17 TF56

The Kings Head

★★★ INN

tel: 01754 871671 **Orby Rd PE24 4TR**
email: addlethorpeleisure@yahoo.co.uk **web:** www.kingsheadaddlethorpe.com

The Kings Head Pub & Campsite is a family run business, situated just off the A52 west of Skegness, near the village of Addlethorpe. A quiet location surrounded by countryside that offers a great venue for families. The accommodation at the inn has recently benefited from refurbishment. Guests can also enjoy a wide range of meals, beers and wines in the bar and restaurant.

Rooms 10 en suite (2 fmly) S £45-£55; D £65-£80* **Facilities** FTV Dinner available WiFi ⌔ 9 Pool table 🛁 **Conf** Max 40 **Parking** 40 **Notes** LB ⊗

CLEETHORPES Map 17 TA30

The Comat

★★★★ GUEST ACCOMMODATION

tel: 01472 694791 & 591861 **26 Yarra Rd DN35 8LS**
email: comat-hotel@ntlworld.com web: www.comat-hotel.co.uk
dir: *Exit A1098 (Alexandra Rd), left of library*

A short walk from the shops and seafront, the welcoming Comat offers cosy, well-equipped bedrooms. There are a range of rooms, including ground floor bedrooms and a family suite with all bedrooms featuring smart, modern en suite bath or shower rooms. Tasty English breakfasts are served in the bright dining room, and an attractive lounge is also available.

Rooms 5 en suite (2 fmly) (1 GF) S £60-£65; D £80-£90* **Facilities** FTV DVD TVL tea/coffee WiFi **Notes** LB ⊗ RS Xmas

Brier Parks Guest House

★★★★ GUEST HOUSE

tel: 01472 605591 & 07849 639923 **27 Clee Rd DN35 8AD**
email: graham.sherwood2@ntlworld.com web: www.brierparks-guesthouse.co.uk
dir: *Left at bottom of Isaac's Hill, 150yds on left*

A warm welcome awaits you at this friendly owner-run guest house. All bedrooms are en suite and offer complimentary WiFi, fridges and flat-screen TVs. Breakfast is freshly cooked to order, and there is limited parking in front of the building. The house is just a short stroll from the seafront and town centre.

Rooms 5 en suite (2 GF) D £65-£70* **Facilities** FTV TVL tea/coffee WiFi **Parking** 2 **Notes** LB ⊗ No Children 5yrs

The Nottingham House

★★★★ INN

tel: 01472 505150 & 505152 **5-7 Sea View St DN35 8EU**
email: nottinghamhousehotel@gmail.com web: www.nottinghamhousehotel.com

Located just a few minutes' walk from the seafront, a friendly welcome awaits in the two character bars and snug. The spacious bedrooms, decorated to a high standard, are well equipped with thoughtful extras including mini-fridges. Home-made meals using fresh local produce are available Wednesday to Sunday, both in the bar and in the attractive first floor restaurant which has amazing sea views. Nearby parking is available.

Rooms 3 en suite (1 fmly) S £50; D £75* **Facilities** FTV tea/coffee Dinner available WiFi ⅃ 18 Sauna Gym Pool table **Notes** Closed 25-26 Dec No coaches

Ginnie's Guest House

★★★ ⚑ GUEST HOUSE

tel: 01472 694997 **27 Queens Pde DN35 0DF**
email: enquiries@ginnies.co.uk web: www.ginnies.co.uk
dir: *From Kingsway (seafront) into Queens Parade (A1098)*

Ginnie's Guest House is a Victorian terraced house situated in a quiet location close to the Winter Gardens, Playtower, and many other amenities. Well maintained by the resident proprietor who takes pride in the many guests who return for further visits.

Rooms 7 rms (5 en suite) (2 pri facs) (3 fmly) (1 GF) S £30-£65; D £50-£70* **Facilities** FTV DVD iPod docking station TVL tea/coffee WiFi 🔒 **Extras** Speciality toiletries - complimentary **Parking** 4 **Notes** LB ⊗ RS 24-25 & 31 Dec room only

---

GRANTHAM Map 11 SK93

Beaver House

★★★ BED AND BREAKFAST

tel: 01476 565011 & 07779 002206 **School Ln, Old Somerby NG33 4AH**
email: cuttlers@btinternet.com web: www.beaverhouse.co.uk
dir: *From Grantham A52 E for 2m. At rdbt take exit signed Old Somerby, then 1st left, 1st house on right*

Beaver House is located on a mainly residential avenue in the quiet village of Old Somerby, just five minutes' drive from Grantham. The accommodation has been thoughtfully designed, and is well equipped and very comfortable. Breakfasts are served in the dining room overlooking the manicured garden, and there is a restaurant within walking distance. A highchair and travel cot can be provided.

Rooms 3 rms (1 en suite) (1 pri facs) S £40-£50; D £50-£60* **Facilities** FTV DVD TVL tea/coffee WiFi **Parking** 3 **Notes** ⊗ Closed Owner's holiday - dates vary ⊜

GREAT LIMBER Map 17 TA10

The New Inn

★★★★ ⚜⚜ INN

tel: 01469 569998 **2 High St DN37 8JL**
email: enquiries@thenewinngreatlimber.co.uk web: www.thenewinngreatlimber.co.uk
dir: *2m from Humberside Airport on A18*

The New Inn is a Grade II listed building that has been refurbished to a modern standard. It is nestled in the Brocklesby estate, with close links to nearby areas of Grimsby and Hull. Bedrooms are comfortably appointed with modern decor and amenities such as flat-screen TVs and good WiFi connectivity. Dinners served in the restaurant are the highlight of any stay, with an interesting choice of dishes available. Meals can also be enjoyed in the more relaxed bar area. Car parking is available on-site.

Rooms 10 en suite (1 fmly) (3 GF) D £80-£135 (room only)* **Facilities** FTV Lounge Dinner available WiFi 🔒 **Extras** Speciality toiletries - complimentary **Conf** Max 18 Thtr 18 Class 18 Board 18 **Parking** 15

HEMSWELL Map 17 SK99

Premier Collection

Hemswell Court

★★★★★ ≌ ⚒ GUEST ACCOMMODATION

tel: 01427 668508 **Lancaster Green, Hemswell Cliff DN21 5TQ**
email: function@hemswellcourt.com web: www.hemswellcourt.com
dir: *1.5m SE of Hemswell on A631 in Hemswell Cliff*

Originally an officers' mess, Hemswell Court is a popular venue for conferences, weddings or private gatherings. The modern bedrooms and many suites are ideal for families or groups of friends, and all rooms are well equipped. The lounges and dining rooms are enhanced by many antique pieces.

Rooms 25 en suite (3 fmly) (6 GF) S £85-£95; D £115-£145* **Facilities** Lounge TVL tea/coffee Dinner available Licensed WiFi ⅃ ⅃ **Extras** Slippers **Conf** Max 200 Thtr 200 Class 150 Board 150 **Parking** 150 **Notes** ⊗ Closed Xmas & New Year Civ Wed 200

HORNCASTLE — Map 17 TF26

Magpies Restaurant with Rooms

★★★★ ◉◉ RESTAURANT WITH ROOMS

tel: 01507 527004 **71-73 East St LN9 6AA**
email: info@magpiesrestaurant.co.uk **web:** www.magpiesrestaurant.co.uk
dir: *A158 into Horncastle, continue at lights. On left opposite Trinity Centre*

This quaint and charming property is nestled in the popular market town of Horncastle. The spacious en suite accommodation features three individually appointed rooms. All provide flat-screen TVs, complimentary WiFi, home-made biscuits, mini-bar and luxurious bathrooms. There is a cosy lounge area with wood-burning stove which is perfect for those winter evenings. The two AA Rosette award-winning restaurant provides a good choice of imaginative dishes at both lunch and dinner, and afternoon tea is also served. On-street parking is available nearby.

Rooms 3 en suite S £70-£80; D £110-£130* **Facilities** FTV iPod docking station Lounge tea/coffee Dinner available WiFi **Extras** Bottled water, home-made biscuits & jam, mini-bar **Notes** Closed 26-30 Dec & 1-7 Jan RS Mon-Tue closed No coaches

HOUGH-ON-THE-HILL — Map 11 SK94

Premier Collection

The Brownlow Arms

★★★★★ ◉ ⌂ INN

tel: 01400 250234 **High Rd NG32 2AZ**
email: armsinn@yahoo.co.uk **web:** www.thebrownlowarms.com
dir: *Take A607 (Grantham to Sleaford road). Hough-on-the-Hill signed from Barkston*

The Brownlow Arms is a beautiful 16th-century property that enjoys a peaceful location in this picturesque village, located between Newark and Grantham. Tastefully appointed and spacious public areas have many original features, and include a choice of luxurious lounges and an elegant restaurant offering imaginative cuisine. The bedrooms are stylish, comfortable and particularly well equipped.

Rooms 4 en suite 1 annexe en suite (1 GF) S £70; D £110-£120* **Facilities** FTV DVD tea/coffee Dinner available Direct Dial WiFi ⌂ **Parking** 20 **Notes** ⊗ No Children 8yrs Closed 25-27 Dec & 31 Dec-1 Jan No coaches

LINCOLN — Map 17 SK97

See also Horncastle & Marton (Village)

St Clements Lodge

★★★★ GUEST ACCOMMODATION

tel: 01522 521532 & 07906 184266 **21 Langworth Gate LN2 4AD**
email: enquiries@stclementslodge.co.uk **web:** www.stclementslodge.co.uk
dir: *350yds E of cathedral, down Eastgate into Langworth Gate*

A warm welcome awaits at St Clements Lodge, which is just a short walk from Lincoln Cathedral and castle. This constantly improving accommodation offers three very comfortable bedrooms, two of which are en suite. There is also a family room, ideal for up to four people. A full English breakfast is served, along with home-made preserves, in the elegant breakfast room. Off-road parking is available.

Rooms 3 rms (2 en suite) (1 pri facs) (1 fmly) S £70; D £85-£90 **Facilities** FTV tea/coffee WiFi ⌂ **Parking** 3 **Notes** ⊗ ⊜

Eagles Guest House

★★★★ GUEST ACCOMMODATION

tel: 01522 686346 **552A Newark Rd, North Hykeham LN6 9NG**
email: eaglesguesthouse@yahoo.co.uk **web:** www.eaglesguesthouse.co.uk
dir: *A46 onto A1434, signed Lincoln South, North Hykeham & South Hykeham. 0.5m on right opposite Cornflower Way*

This large, modern detached house is situated within easy access of the A46 and the historic city of Lincoln. The smartly appointed, thoughtfully equipped bedrooms are bright and fresh in appearance. A substantial breakfast is served in the pleasant dining room and free WiFi is available throughout the property.

Rooms 5 en suite (1 fmly) (1 GF) S £40-£50; D £50-£60* **Facilities** FTV tea/coffee WiFi **Parking** 6 **Notes** ⊗ No Children 9yrs

The Loudor

★★★★ GUEST ACCOMMODATION

tel: 01522 680333 **37 Newark Rd, North Hykeham LN6 8RB**
email: info@loudorhotel.co.uk **web:** www.loudorhotel.co.uk
dir: *3m from city centre. A46 onto A1434 for 2m, on left opposite shopping centre*

The Loudor can be found opposite the Forum shopping centre and a short walk from the sports centre. This friendly place offers well-equipped bedrooms, and breakfast is served at individual tables in the spacious dining room. There is some on-site parking.

Rooms 9 en suite 2 annexe rms (1 fmly) (2 GF) S £40-£44; D £60-£65* **Facilities** FTV Lounge tea/coffee WiFi ⌂ **Extras** Home-made biscuits **Conf** Max 30 **Parking** 8 **Notes** ⊗

The Old Bakery

★★★★ ◎◎ RESTAURANT WITH ROOMS

tel: 01522 576057 & 07949 035554 **26-28 Burton Rd LN1 3LB**
email: enquiries@theold-bakery.co.uk **web:** www.theold-bakery.co.uk
dir: Exit A46 at Lincoln North follow signs for cathedral. 3rd exit at 1st rdbt, 1st exit at next rdbt

Situated close to the castle at the top of the town, this converted bakery offers well-equipped bedrooms and a delightful dining operation. The cooking has gained two AA Rosettes, and uses much local produce. Expect good friendly service from the dedicated staff.

Rooms 3 rms (2 en suite) (1 pri facs) (1 fmly) **Facilities** FTV tea/coffee Dinner available WiFi 🕭 **Notes** ⊗ Closed 25-26 Dec, 1-16 Jan RS Mon closed No coaches

South Park Guest House

★★★★ GUEST HOUSE

tel: 01522 887136 **11 South Park LN5 8EN**
email: enquiry@southparkguesthouse.co.uk **web:** www.southparkguesthouse.co.uk
dir: 1m S of city centre on A15

A Victorian house situated on the inner ring road facing South Park. The staff are friendly and attentive, and bedrooms, though compact, are well equipped. Breakfast is served in a modern dining room overlooking the park.

Rooms 6 en suite 1 annexe en suite (2 fmly) (1 GF) **Facilities** FTV tea/coffee Dinner available WiFi **Parking** 7 **Notes** ⊗

LOUTH　　　Map 17 TF38

The Manse B&B

★★★ BED AND BREAKFAST

tel: 01507 327495 **Middlesykes Ln, Grimoldby LN11 8TE**
email: knowles578@btinternet.com **web:** www.themansebb.co.uk
dir: Grimoldby 4m from Louth on B1200. Into Tinkle St, right into Middlesykes Ln

Located on a quiet country lane, this pleasantly appointed house offers comfortable accommodation and a warm welcome. Proprietors are enthusiastic and helpful, ensuring guests enjoy their stay. Bedrooms offer a range of homely extras, and freshly cooked evening meals are available by prior arrangement. The Manse is an ideal location for exploring the delights of the Wolds.

Rooms 4 rms (3 en suite) (1 pri facs) (1 fmly) (1 GF) S £50; D £75-£80 **Facilities** FTV TVL tea/coffee Dinner available WiFi **Parking** 5 **Notes** LB ⊗ No Children 5yrs Closed 25 Dec 🍽

MARKET RASEN　　　Map 17 TF18

Premier Collection

The Advocate Arms

★★★★★ ◎◎ RESTAURANT WITH ROOMS

tel: 01673 842364 **2 Queen St LN8 3EH**
email: info@advocatearms.co.uk **web:** www.advocatearms.co.uk
dir: In town centre

Appointed to a high standard, this 18th-century property is located in the heart of Market Rasen and combines historic character with contemporary design. The operation centres around the stylish restaurant where service is friendly yet professional and the food is a highlight. The attractive bedrooms are very well equipped and feature luxury bathrooms.

Rooms 10 en suite (2 fmly) S fr £60; D £65-£110 (room only)* **Facilities** FTV tea/coffee Dinner available WiFi ⚡ 18 🕭 **Conf** Max 22 Thtr 18 Class 22 Board 18 **Parking** 6 **Notes** ⊗

Wold View House B&B

★★★ 🛏 BED AND BREAKFAST

tel: 01673 838226 & 07976 563473 **Bully Hill Top, Tealby LN8 6JA**
email: enquiries@woldviewhouse.co.uk **web:** www.woldviewhouse.co.uk
dir: A46 onto B1225 towards Horncastle, after 7m Wold View House at x-rds

Situated at the top of Bully Hill with expansive views across The Wold, this smart bed and breakfast offers modern bedrooms and warm hospitality. Ideal for walking, riding, or touring the charming nearby villages and coastline, Wold View House is just a short drive from Lincoln.

Rooms 3 rms (2 en suite) (1 pri facs) (1 fmly) S fr £50; D fr £75* **Facilities** FTV TVL tea/coffee Dinner available Licensed WiFi 🕭 **Parking** 15 **Notes** LB

MARTON (VILLAGE)　　　Map 17 SK88

Black Swan Guest House

★★★★ GUEST ACCOMMODATION

tel: 01427 718878 **21 High St DN21 5AH**
email: info@blackswanguesthouse.co.uk **web:** www.blackswanguesthouse.co.uk
dir: On A156 in village centre at junct A1500

Centrally located in the village, this 18th-century former coaching inn retains many original features, and offers good hospitality and homely bedrooms with modern facilities. Tasty breakfasts are served in the cosy dining room and a comfortable lounge with WiFi access is available. Transport to nearby pubs and restaurants can be provided.

Rooms 6 en suite 4 annexe en suite (3 fmly) (4 GF) **Facilities** FTV TVL tea/coffee Licensed WiFi 🕭 **Parking** 10

METHERINGHAM
Map 17 TF06

The Lincolnshire Poacher Inn

★★★ INN

tel: 01526 320556 & 07818 296315 **53 High St LN4 3DZ**
email: info@thelincolnshirepoacherinn.co.uk **web:** www.thelincolnshirepoacherinn.co.uk

This traditional, family-run inn is set in the small village of Metheringham. The bed and breakfast accommodation consists of uniquely appointed cottages which provide kitchen and lounge facilities. Evening meals offer a wide range of home-cooked classics and breakfast is delivered to the private dining area in your cottage.

Rooms 3 rms S £50; D £70 **Facilities** FTV DVD TVL tea/coffee Dinner available WiFi **Parking** 9 **Notes** ⊗ No coaches

NORTON DISNEY
Map 17 SK85

Norton Lodge and Conference Centre

★★★ BED AND BREAKFAST

tel: 01522 789111 **Old Harbour Farm LN6 9JR**
email: norton.lodge@virgin.net **web:** www.nortonlodge.co.uk

This rural property is set in 14 acres of countryside although still close to main road links such as the A1 and A46. Bedrooms are spacious and boast many modern accessories such as flat-screen TV and complimentary WiFi. Perfect for leisure and business guests alike the property features four conference rooms catering up to 150 guests, as well as being closely situated to the popular market town of Newark-on-Trent. Ample on-site parking is available.

Rooms 8 en suite 14 annexe en suite (2 fmly) (6 GF) **Facilities** FTV TVL tea/coffee Direct Dial Licensed WiFi 🐾 **Conf** Max 150 Thtr 150 Class 100 Board 40 **Parking** 100 **Notes** ⊗ Civ Wed 150

SCOTTER
Map 17 SE80

The White Swan

★★★★★ ◉ INN

tel: 01724 763061 **9 The Green DN21 3UD**
email: info@whiteswanscotter.com **web:** www.whiteswanscotter.com

This smartly presented property provides stylish contemporary accommodation in a peaceful village location. The restaurant is modern with vaulted ceilings and is split over three levels, while there is also a traditional pub called The Mucky Duck. A lounge bar and impressive garden add to the range of areas for guests to relax. Weddings and other special events are also well catered for. Accommodation rates include a continental breakfast or a choice of other breakfast options is also available.

Rooms 11 en suite 14 annexe en suite (2 fmly) **Facilities** FTV tea/coffee Dinner available WiFi **Conf** Max 50 Thtr 50 Class 35 Board 35 **Parking** 35 **Notes** Civ Wed 110

SCUNTHORPE
Map 17 SE81

San Pietro Restaurant Rooms

★★★★★ ◉◉ RESTAURANT WITH ROOMS

tel: 01724 277774 **11 High Street East DN15 6UH**
email: info@sanpietro.uk.com **web:** www.sanpietro.uk.com
dir: *3m from M180, follow signs for Scunthorpe town centre & railway station, left into Brigg Rd/Station Rd. Near windmill*

This family-run restaurant with rooms was purpose-built, and offers comfortable modern accommodation. Bedrooms and bathrooms provide a range of additional extras such as mini-bars, home-made cakes, complimentary WiFi and smart TVs. Dinner and breakfast are served in the annexe Ristorante. Dinner menus have an Italian influence and provide a range of choice including a chef's tasting menu as well as a full à la carte offering. Continental breakfasts are included, with a choice to upgrade to a hearty cooked breakfast. San Pietro was the AA Funkiest Bed and Breakfast of the Year 2015-2016.

Rooms 14 en suite (5 GF) S £105-£195; D £105-£195* **Facilities** STV FTV iPod docking station tea/coffee Dinner available Direct Dial Lift WiFi 🐾 18 **Extras** Speciality toiletries, home-made cake, mini-bar **Conf** Max 80 Thtr 80 Class 40 Board 30 **Parking** 25 **Notes** ⊗ Closed 25-26 Dec & Sun No coaches Civ Wed 120

SKILLINGTON
Map 11 SK82

The Cross Swords Inn

★★★ ⊟ INN

tel: 01476 861132 **The Square NG33 5HB**
email: harold@thecross-swordsinn.co.uk **web:** www.thecross-swordsinn.co.uk
dir: *Exit A1 at Colsterworth junct between Grantham & Stamford*

Very popular with the local community, this traditional inn offers three modern, well-equipped bedrooms, housed in an attractive cottage at the top of the courtyard, and named in keeping with the history of the village. All are very comfortable and coupled with smart modern bathrooms. The inn provides imaginative food and a range of real ales in a rustic period atmosphere.

Rooms 3 annexe en suite (3 GF) S £65–£70; D £80–£85 **Facilities** FTV tea/coffee Dinner available WiFi Gliding club nearby **Parking** 12 **Notes** ⊗ No Children 10yrs RS Sun eve & Mon lunch bar & restaurant closed

STAMFORD
Map 11 TF00

Premier Collection

Meadow View
★★★★★ ⚇ BED AND BREAKFAST

tel: 01780 762133 & 07833 972577 **Wothorpe Rd PE9 2JR**
web: www.bedandbreakfast-stamford.co.uk
dir: Off A1 signed Stamford, follow road past entrance to Burley House, bottom of hill, left at lights. Follow road round, 1st house on left

Meadow View is a stylish property situated just a short walk from the town centre and Burghley House. The tastefully appointed bedrooms are contemporary in style with lovely co-ordinated soft furnishings and many thoughtful touches. Breakfast is served at a large communal table in the open-plan kitchen/dining room, and guests have the use of a smartly appointed lounge with plush sofas.

Rooms 3 en suite S £65–£95; D £75–£120* **Facilities** FTV iPod docking station TVL tea/coffee WiFi ⌂ **Extras** Chocolates, sherry, still/sparkling water **Notes** LB ⊗ ⊜

The Bull & Swan at Burghley
★★★★ ⚇ ⚇ INN

tel: 01780 766412 **High St, St Martins PE9 2LJ**
email: enquiries@thebullandswan.co.uk **web:** www.thebullandswan.co.uk
dir: A1 onto Old Great North Rd, left onto B1081, follow Stamford signs

This delightful inn dates back to the 16th century when it is said to have been a gentlemen's drinking club. The public rooms include a large bar with a range of ales. There is also a separate restaurant serving AA Rosette award-winning food. The stylish bedrooms are extremely well appointed with lovely soft furnishings and a range of thoughtful touches.

Rooms 9 en suite (2 fmly) S £85–£135; D £95–£160* **Facilities** FTV iPod docking station tea/coffee Dinner available WiFi ⌂ 18 **Extras** Organic vodka **Parking** 7 **Notes** LB No coaches

Candlesticks
★★★ RESTAURANT WITH ROOMS

tel: 01780 764033 **1 Church Ln PE9 2JU**
email: info@candlestickshotel.co.uk **web:** www.candlestickshotel.co.uk
dir: B1081 into Stamford. Left onto A43. Right into Worthorpe Rd, right into Church Ln

Candlesticks is a 17th-century property situated in a quiet lane in the oldest part of Stamford, just a short walk from the centre of town. The bedrooms are pleasantly decorated and equipped with a good range of useful extras. Public rooms include Candlesticks restaurant and a cosy bar.

Rooms 8 en suite **Facilities** STV FTV Lounge tea/coffee Dinner available Direct Dial WiFi ⌂ **Parking** 8 **Notes** ⊗ RS Mon No restaurant or bar service

SWINESHEAD BRIDGE
Map 12 TF24

Boston Lodge
★★★ GUEST ACCOMMODATION

tel: 01205 820983 & 07436 269596 **Browns Drove PE20 3PX**
email: info@bostonlodge.co.uk **web:** www.bostonlodge.co.uk
dir: From A17 onto A1121 to Boston, take 1st left into Browns Drove then immediate right

A personal welcome is guaranteed at Boston Lodge. Located in a quiet village on the outskirts of Boston within easy reach of Sleaford and Lincoln, it is an ideal base for both the tourist and business traveller. Rooms are all en suite and individual in design. Ample off-road parking is a plus.

Rooms 8 en suite 1 annexe en suite (2 fmly) (3 GF) **Facilities** FTV TVL tea/coffee WiFi ⌂ **Parking** 30

WINTERINGHAM
Map 17 SE92

Premier Collection

Winteringham Fields
★★★★★ ⍟ ⍟ ⍟ ⍟ RESTAURANT WITH ROOMS

tel: 01724 733096 **1 Silver St DN15 9ND**
email: reception@winteringhamfields.co.uk **web:** www.winteringhamfields.co.uk
dir: In village centre at x-rds

This highly regarded restaurant with rooms, located deep in the countryside at Winteringham village, is six miles west of the Humber Bridge. Public rooms and bedrooms, some of which are housed in renovated barns and cottages, are delightfully luxurious. There is an abundance of charm, and period features are combined with rich furnishings and fabrics. The award-winning food is a highlight of any stay and guests can expect highly skilled dishes, excellent quality and stunning presentation.

Rooms 4 en suite 11 annexe en suite (6 fmly) (3 GF) **Facilities** iPod docking station TV11B tea/coffee Dinner available Direct Dial WiFi ⌂ **Conf** Max 50 Thtr 50 Class 50 Board 50 **Parking** 14 **Notes** LB Closed 25 Dec for 2wks, last wk Oct, 2wks Aug No coaches Civ Wed 60

WOODHALL SPA
Map 17 TF16

Oglee Guest House
★★★★ ⬤ GUEST HOUSE

tel: 01526 353512 **16 Stanhope Av LN10 6SP**
email: ogleeguesthouse@gmail.com **web:** www.oglee.co.uk
dir: *Close to junct of B1191 & B1192*

This Edwardian family home is ideally situated for exploring Lincolnshire. It is also within easy reach of several RAF bases and the well-regarded Hotchkin Golf Course. Spacious bedrooms offer a high level of comfort with modern amenities. Hearty breakfasts use local produce, feature hand-made jams and additional special dishes. Evening meals by prior arrangement.

Rooms 3 en suite (1 fmly) S £52-£55; D £74-£80* **Facilities** FTV DVD TVL tea/coffee Dinner available WiFi 🛁 **Extras** Fruit, bottled water - complimentary **Parking** 4 **Notes** LB

WOOLSTHORPE
Map 11 SK83

Chequers Inn
★★★★ ⬤ INN

tel: 01476 870701 **Main St NG32 1LU**
email: justinnabar@yahoo.co.uk **web:** www.chequersinn.net
dir: *From Melton Mowbray on A607 towards Grantham, follow brown heritage signs to Belvoir Castle. Turn left at x-rds & follow signs*

Situated in the picturesque village of Woolsthorpe in the unspoilt Vale of Belvoir, the Chequers Inn is a quintessentially English inn dating from the 17th century. It has roaring fires in the winter and a well-maintained garden for alfresco dining in the summer. The snug and bar was once the original village bakery. Bedrooms are situated in the adjacent stables and are tastefully decorated. Good food is served in the bar and in the restaurant.

Rooms 4 annexe en suite (1 fmly) (3 GF) **Facilities** FTV DVD tea/coffee Dinner available ♨ 18 🛁 **Conf** Max 80 Thtr 80 Class 80 Board 30 **Parking** 40 **Notes** Closed 25 Dec eve, 26 Dec eve & 1 Jan eve Civ Wed 80

LONDON

N4

Best Western London Highbury
PLAN 2 F5
★★★ GUEST ACCOMMODATION

tel: 020 8802 6551 **372-374 Seven Sisters Rd N4 2PG**
email: reservations@highbury.com **web:** www.bwhighbury.com
dir: *0.5m from Finsbury Park Station*

Opposite Finsbury Park and only a short tube ride from the centre of London, this establishment offers a range of well-appointed and well-equipped accommodation. There is ample and secure parking and a well-stocked bar. Hot and cold breakfasts are served in the lower-ground floor breakfast room.

Rooms 45 en suite (6 fmly) (7 GF) **Facilities** STV FTV TVL tea/coffee Direct Dial Lift Licensed WiFi 🛁 **Extras** Chocolates **Parking** 20 **Notes** ⊗

NW1

TheWesley
PLAN 1 C5
★★★★ ⬤ GUEST ACCOMMODATION

tel: 020 7380 0001 **81-103 Euston St NW1 2EZ**
email: reservations@thewesley.co.uk **web:** www.thewesley.co.uk
dir: *Euston Rd left at lights into Melton St, 1st left into Euston St, 100yds on left*

Located within walking distance of Euston station, this smart property is convenient for central London. Stylish air-conditioned bedrooms are thoughtfully equipped for business and leisure. The airy Atrium Bar and Restaurant offers drinks, light snacks and an evening menu. Extensive conference and meeting facilities are available.

Rooms 100 en suite (2 fmly) **Facilities** STV FTV iPod docking station TVL tea/coffee Dinner available Direct Dial Lift Licensed WiFi **Extras** Speciality toiletries, safe **Conf** Max 150 Thtr 150 Class 50 Board 45 **Notes** ⊗ Civ Wed

NW3

The Langorf
PLAN 2 E4
★★★★ GUEST ACCOMMODATION

tel: 020 7794 4483 **20 Frognal, Hampstead NW3 6AG**
email: info@langorfhotel.com **web:** www.langorfhotel.com
dir: *Off A41 (Finchley Rd), near Finchley Road tube station*

Located on a leafy and mainly residential avenue within easy walking distance of shops and restaurants, this elegant Edwardian property has been appointed to provide high standards of comfort and facilities. Bedrooms are furnished with flair and a warm welcome is assured.

Rooms 31 en suite (4 fmly) (3 GF) S £69-£120; D £75-£140* **Facilities** STV Lounge TVL tea/coffee Direct Dial Lift Licensed WiFi **Conf** Max 30 Thtr 30 Class 20 Board 15 **Notes** LB ⊗

La Gaffe

PLAN 2 E5

★★★ 🛌 GUEST ACCOMMODATION

tel: 020 7435 8965 & 7435 4941 **107-111 Heath St NW3 6SS**
email: info@lagaffe.co.uk **web:** www.lagaffe.co.uk
dir: On A502, 250yds N of Hampstead tube station

This family-owned and run guest accommodation, just north of Hampstead High Street, offers charm and warm hospitality. The Italian restaurant, which is open most lunchtimes and for dinner, is popular with locals. Bedrooms are compact, but all are en suite.

Rooms 11 en suite 7 annexe en suite (2 fmly) (2 GF) S £80-£110; D £105-£130
Facilities FTV tea/coffee Dinner available Direct Dial Licensed WiFi **Conf** Max 10 Board 10 **Notes** ⊗ RS 25-26 Dec Restaurant closed 25 Dec eve & 26 Dec

NW11

Martel Guest House

PLAN 2 D5

★★★ GUEST HOUSE

tel: 020 8455 1802 & 07587 655181 **27 The Ridgeway NW11 8QP**
email: reservations@bedbreakfastlondon.co.uk **web:** www.bedbreakfastlondon.co.uk

Martel Guest House is in a quiet residential area of north London, just a 15 minute underground journey from central London, and only five minutes from the M1. Restaurants and convenience stores are just a short walk away. The accommodation is nicely appointed and offers all modern comforts including air-conditioning and free WiFi. A self-service continental breakfast or a freshly cooked English breakfast are served in the family-style breakfast room overlooking the rear garden. Secure parking offered.

Rooms 9 en suite (2 fmly) (3 GF) S £60-£65; D £80-£85* **Facilities** FTV tea/coffee Direct Dial WiFi **Extras** Fridge, bottled water **Parking** 7 **Notes** ⊗

SE10

Innkeeper's Lodge London, Greenwich

PLAN 2 G3

★★★★ INN

tel: 08451 551551 (Calls cost 2p per minute plus your phone company's access charge)
291 Greenwich High Rd, Greenwich SE10 8NA
email: info@innkeeperslodge.com **web:** www.innkeeperslodge.com

At Innkeeper's Lodge you'll find accommodation with comfort and character in equal measure, and everything needed for a relaxing stay, from easy check-in and free parking to complimentary breakfast and a cosy pub serving great value food and drink on the doorstep. Each Lodge has quality rooms, and there are Lodges in a variety of locations from towns and cities to countryside settings across the UK.

Rooms 24 en suite (3 fmly) **Facilities** FTV tea/coffee Dinner available Lift WiFi **Notes** ⊗

SW1

The Windermere

PLAN 1 C1

★★★★ 🍽 🛌 GUEST ACCOMMODATION

tel: 020 7834 5163 **142/144 Warwick Way, Victoria SW1V 4JE**
email: reservations@windermere-hotel.co.uk **web:** www.windermere-hotel.co.uk
dir: B324 off Buckingham Palace Rd, on Warwick Way, at junct with Alderney St

The Windermere is a relaxed, informal and family-run establishment within easy reach of Victoria station and many of the capital's attractions. Bedrooms, although varying in size, are stylish, comfortable and well equipped. The Pimlico restaurant serves good quality evening meals and hearty cooked breakfasts.

Rooms 19 en suite (3 fmly) (3 GF) S £120-£155; D £145-£225* **Facilities** FTV iPod docking station Lounge TVL tea/coffee Dinner available Direct Dial Lift Licensed WiFi **Extras** Speciality toiletries **Notes** ⊗ No Children 3yrs

Best Western Corona

PLAN 1 C1

★★★ GUEST ACCOMMODATION

tel: 020 7828 9279 & 7487 0673 **87-89 Belgrave Rd SW1V 2BQ**
email: info@coronahotel.co.uk **web:** www.coronahotel.co.uk
dir: From Pimlico Station into Tachbrook St. 1st left into Moreton St, 1st right into Belgrave Rd

Centrally located, this elegant Victorian property is appointed to a high standard. The smart, well-equipped bedrooms offer comfortable, modern accommodation. A continental breakfast is served in the basement dining room, and room service is also available.

Rooms 51 en suite (13 fmly) (7 GF) **Facilities** FTV Lounge tea/coffee Direct Dial Lift WiFi **Notes** ⊗

SW1 *continued*

The Lidos
PLAN 1 C1

★★★ GUEST ACCOMMODATION

tel: 020 7828 1164 **43-45 Belgrave Rd, Victoria SW1V 2BB**
email: reservations@lidoshotel.com **web:** www.lidoshotel.com
dir: *From Victoria railway station exit to Wilton Rd. After 2nd set of lights into Denbigh St. Left at next lights into Belgrave Rd. On left*

The Lidos offers affordable accommodation within walking distance of Victoria Station and the tube. In addition, there's a bus stop right in front of the main entrance making access easy to all major sites. All rooms have en suite facilities and have been equipped with modern amenities. An inclusive continental breakfast is offered to all guests, and a range of restaurants and pubs can be found nearby.

Rooms 39 en suite (2 fmly) (4 GF) S £49-£149; D £59-£299 **Facilities** FTV tea/coffee Lift WiFi **Notes** ⊗

Sidney London-Victoria
PLAN 1 C1

★★★ GUEST ACCOMMODATION

tel: 020 7834 2738 **68-76 Belgrave Rd SW1V 2BP**
email: reservations@sidneyhotel.com **web:** www.sidneyhotel.com
dir: *A202 (Vauxhall Bridge Rd) into Charlwood St & junct with Belgrave Rd*

This smart Grade II listed property near Pimlico is formed from five six-storey town houses, and offers brightly decorated bedrooms that are well equipped for business use. Several rooms are suitable for families. Public areas include a bar lounge and an airy breakfast room.

Rooms 80 en suite (13 fmly) (9 GF) **Facilities** STV Lounge TVL tea/coffee Direct Dial Lift Licensed WiFi **Conf** Max 30 Thtr 30 Class 15 Board 14 **Notes** ⊗

Best Western Victoria Palace
PLAN 1 C1

★★★ GUEST ACCOMMODATION

tel: 020 7821 7113 **60-64 Warwick Way SW1V 1SA**
email: info@bestwesternvictoriapalace.co.uk **web:** www.bestwesternvictoriapalace.co.uk

An elegant, 19th-century building located in the heart of London, near to Belgravia and a five minute walk from Victoria rail, underground and coach stations. The bedrooms have en suite shower rooms. A buffet-style breakfast is served in the basement dining room.

Rooms 43 en suite 44 annexe en suite (4 fmly) (4 GF) **Facilities** FTV Lounge tea/coffee Direct Dial Lift WiFi **Notes** ⊗

Comfort Inn
PLAN 1 C1

★★★ GUEST ACCOMMODATION

tel: 020 7834 2988 **8-12 St George's Dr SW1V 4BJ**
email: info@comfortinnbuckinghampalacerd.co.uk
web: www.comfortinnbuckinghampalacerd.co.uk
dir: *From Buckingham Palace Rd into St George's Dr. Comfort Inn on left*

Located just a short walk south from Victoria station, this establishment is a good base for visiting the capital's attractions. All bedrooms and public areas are smartly appointed and offer very good levels of comfort. An extensive continental breakfast is served.

Rooms 81 en suite (13 fmly) (15 GF) **Facilities** STV TVL tea/coffee Direct Dial Lift WiFi **Conf** Max 20 Thtr 20 Class 20 Board 20 **Notes** ⊗

Comfort Inn London Westminster
PLAN 1 C1

★★★ GUEST ACCOMMODATION

tel: 020 7834 8036 **39 Belgrave Rd SW1V 2BB**
email: stay@comfortinnwestminster.co.uk **web:** www.comfortinnwestminster.co.uk
dir: *Near Victoria station*

Located a short walk from Victoria station, the Comfort Inn London Westminster offers affordable accommodation. Bedroom sizes vary, and each room is suitably appointed, with en suite compact shower rooms. A contemporary lobby is equipped with a large TV and computer desk. A self-service continental breakfast is offered in the dining room on the lower ground floor.

Rooms 54 en suite (4 fmly) **Facilities** FTV TVL tea/coffee Direct Dial Lift WiFi **Notes** LB ⊗

Comfort Inn Victoria
PLAN 1 C1

★★★ GUEST ACCOMMODATION

tel: 020 7233 6636 **18-24 Belgrave Rd, Victoria SW1V 1QF**
email: stay@comfortinnvictoria.co.uk **web:** www.comfortinnvictoria.co.uk

With a prime location close to Victoria station, this property offers brightly appointed en suite accommodation that is thoughtfully equipped for business and leisure guests. A continental breakfast is offered in the basement dining room.

Rooms 50 rms (48 en suite) (16 fmly) (9 GF) **Facilities** STV FTV TVL tea/coffee Direct Dial Lift WiFi **Notes** ⊗

The Victoria Inn
PLAN 1 C1

★★★ GUEST HOUSE

tel: 020 7834 6721 **65-67 Belgrave Rd, Victoria SW1V 2BG**
email: welcome@victoriainn.co.uk **web:** www.victoriainn.co.uk
dir: *On A3213, 0.4m SE of Victoria station, near Pimlico tube station*

A short walk from Victoria station, this Victorian property offers modern, well-equipped accommodation for business and leisure guests. There is a comfortable reception lounge, and a limited self-service buffet breakfast is available in the basement breakfast room.

Rooms 43 en suite (7 fmly) **Facilities** FTV TVL tea/coffee Direct Dial Lift WiFi **Notes** LB ⊗

Stanley House
PLAN 1 C1

★★ Ⓐ BED AND BREAKFAST

tel: 020 7834 5042 & 7834 7292 **19-21 Belgrave Rd, Victoria SW1V 1RB**
email: cmahotel@aol.com **web:** www.londonbudgethotels.co.uk
dir: *Near Victoria station*

Stanley House is conveniently situated close to Victoria station and with easy access to the West End. Plain, soundly appointed bedrooms of varying sizes are offered, with breakfasts served in the lower ground-floor dining room; guests also have use of a ground-floor television lounge area.

Rooms 44 rms (41 en suite) (7 fmly) (8 GF) **Facilities** FTV TVL Direct Dial WiFi **Notes** LB ⊗ No Children 5yrs

SW3

Premier Collection

San Domenico House
PLAN 1 B1

★★★★★ ⛬ GUEST ACCOMMODATION

tel: 020 7581 5757 **29-31 Draycott Place SW3 2SH**
email: info@sandomenicohouse.com **web:** www.sandomenicohouse.com

This stunning property in the heart of Chelsea offers beautiful, individually styled bedrooms, all with antique and period pieces, and well appointed en suites complete with Italian Spa toiletries. A sumptuous drawing room with wonderful works of art is available for guests to relax in or maybe to enjoy afternoon tea. Breakfast is served either in guests' bedrooms or in the elegant lower ground-floor dining room. Staff are friendly and attentive.

Rooms 17 en suite (4 fmly) (1 GF) (4 smoking) **Facilities** STV Lounge Dinner available Direct Dial Lift Licensed **Notes** ⊗

Premier Collection

Sydney House Chelsea
PLAN 1 A1

★★★★★ ⛬ GUEST ACCOMMODATION

tel: 020 7376 7711 & 7376 6900 **Sydney St, Chelsea SW3 6PU**
email: info@sydneyhousechelsea.co.uk **web:** www.sydneyhousechelsea.co.uk
dir: *A4 Cromwell Rd, pass Natural History Museum on left, turn next right. Sydney St on left*

Located in the heart of Chelsea, this smart Grade II listed Georgian town house offers stylish and very comfortable accommodation, well equipped for both corporate and leisure guests. There is a small bar and drawing room and room service is also available. Staff are attentive and are always on hand to ensure guests feel at home. Breakfast is a particular highlight.

Rooms 21 en suite **Facilities** STV FTV DVD Lounge tea/coffee Dinner available Direct Dial Lift Licensed WiFi **Extras** Still mineral water **Notes** ⊗ Closed 24-30 Dec

SW5

Best Western The Boltons
PLAN 2 E3

★★★★ GUEST ACCOMMODATION

tel: 020 7373 8900 **19-21 Penywern Rd, Earl's Court SW5 9TT**
email: london@theboltonshotel.co.uk **web:** www.bw-theboltonshotel.co.uk
dir: *A3220 from Cromwell Rd, follow road past Earl's Court station, 1st right into Penywern Rd. Located on left*

Located right in the heart of Earl's Court, and just around the corner from Earl's Court underground station, The Boltons offers modern and comfortably appointed rooms, all with en suite facilities, digital TVs, beverage-making facilities, and free WiFi throughout. There is a cosy dining room on the ground floor where breakfast is served, and a wide range of restaurants, cafés and bars within a short walking distance.

Rooms 56 en suite (4 fmly) (4 GF) **Facilities** FTV iPod docking station Lounge tea/coffee Direct Dial WiFi **Notes** ⊗ No Children 18yrs

SW5 *continued*

The Park Grand London Kensington

PLAN 2 E3

★★★★ GUEST ACCOMMODATION

tel: 020 7370 6831 **33-37 Hogarth Rd, Kensington SW5 0QQ**
email: info@parkgrandlondon.com **web:** www.parkgrandkensington.co.uk

Well appointed to a high standard, this property has a smart modern feel and is conveniently located for the exhibition centre, the West End and local transport links. Bedrooms are furnished and decorated to a very high standard, offering guests a comprehensive range of modern facilities and amenities.

Rooms 132 en suite (7 GF) **Facilities** STV FTV iPod docking station tea/coffee Dinner available Direct Dial Lift Licensed WiFi Gym Fitness centre **Conf** Max 15 Board 15 **Notes** ⊗

SW7

Premier Collection

The Exhibitionist

PLAN 1 A2

★★★★★ GUEST ACCOMMODATION

tel: 020 7915 0000 **8-10 Queensberry Place, South Kensington SW7 2EA**
email: info@theexhibitionisthotel.com **web:** www.theexhibitionisthotel.com
dir: Exit A4 (Cromwell Rd) opposite Natural History Museum, near South Kensington tube station

The Exhibitionist can be found close to Kensington and Knightsbridge and offers friendly hospitality, attentive service and sumptuously furnished bedrooms; some have a private terrace. Public areas include a choice of lounges (one with internet access) and an elegant bar. There is an option of English or continental breakfast, and 24-hour room service is available.

Rooms 37 en suite **Facilities** STV FTV iPod docking station Lounge tea/coffee Dinner available Direct Dial Lift Licensed WiFi **Extras** Speciality toiletries, mineral water **Conf** Max 40 Thtr 40 Class 35 Board 30 **Notes** ⊗

Best Western The Cromwell

PLAN 1 A2

★★★★ GUEST ACCOMMODATION

tel: 020 7244 1720 **110-112 Cromwell Rd, Kensington SW7 4ES**
email: reception@thecromwell.co.uk **web:** www.thecromwell.co.uk
dir: M4/A4 towards London, pass Cromwell Hospital, 0.5m

Just minutes away from Gloucester Road tube station and with easy access to all main tourist attractions, this property offers comfortable, modern accommodation. Fully air-conditioned and with free WiFi, this is an ideal location for both leisure and business guests. Amenities include an on-site meeting room, and secure parking is available nearby.

Rooms 85 en suite (11 GF) **Facilities** STV TVL tea/coffee Direct Dial Lift Licensed WiFi Gym Fitness room **Conf** Max 8 Board 8 **Notes** ⊗

The Gainsborough

PLAN 1 A2

★★★★ GUEST ACCOMMODATION

tel: 020 7957 0000 **7-11 Queensberry Place, South Kensington SW7 2DL**
email: reservations@eeh.co.uk **web:** www.eeh.co.uk
dir: Off A4 (Cromwell Rd) opposite Natural History Museum, near South Kensington tube station

This smart Georgian house is in a quiet street near South Kensington's museums. Bedrooms are individually designed with fine fabrics and quality furnishings in co-ordinated colours. A choice of breakfasts is offered in the attractive dining room. There is also a delightful lobby lounge, and 24-hour room service is available.

Rooms 48 en suite (5 fmly) (4 GF) **Facilities** STV Lounge tea/coffee Dinner available Direct Dial Lift Licensed WiFi **Conf** Max 40 Class 40 Board 30 **Notes** ⊗

SW14

The Victoria

PLAN 2 C2

★★★★ ⊛⊛ RESTAURANT WITH ROOMS

tel: 020 8876 4238 **10 West Temple Sheen SW14 7RT**
email: bookings@thevictoria.net **web:** www.thevictoria.net
dir: Off Upper Richmond Rd West into Derby Rd, then into West Temple Sheen

The Victoria is in a quiet residential area close to Richmond Park. The bedrooms are refreshingly stylish and thoughtfully equipped. The public areas consist of a small contemporary seating area, a modern bar, and an award-winning restaurant that serves imaginative and well sourced dishes. Alfresco dining is also an option.

Rooms 7 en suite (2 fmly) (3 GF) **Facilities** FTV iPod docking station tea/coffee Dinner available Direct Dial WiFi 🐾 **Parking** 10 **Notes** No coaches

W1

Premier Collection

The Marble Arch by Montcalm

PLAN 1 B4

★★★★★ GUEST ACCOMMODATION

tel: 020 7258 0777 **31 Great Cumberland Place W1H 7TA**
web: www.themarblearchlondon.co.uk

Located just a short walk from Marble Arch, this luxury boutique townhouse property offers elegant, stylish and comfortable accommodation. Bedrooms are well equipped for the modern traveller with all rooms offering media hub, WiFi and mini-bar.

Rooms 43 en suite (1 fmly) **Facilities** STV FTV TVL tea/coffee Lift Licensed WiFi **Notes** ⊗

Premier Collection

The Piccadilly London West End
PLAN 1 D3

★★★★★ GUEST ACCOMMODATION

tel: 020 7871 6000 **65-73 Shaftesbury Av W1D 6EX**
email: reservations@thepiccadillywestend.co.uk
web: www.thepiccadillywestend.co.uk
dir: *From Piccadilly Circus 300yds up Shaftesbury Av, at junct with Dean St*

In the centre of the West End, this boutique property offers plenty of warm, traditional hospitality. It's located close to two major underground stations and has a comfortable club lounge, a popular Japanese bar/restaurant, a fitness room and a small spa. High quality, recently refurbished bedrooms and bathrooms come in a variety of sizes, all well-equipped and smartly presented.

Rooms 67 en suite (6 fmly) **Facilities** FTV iPod docking station TVL tea/coffee Dinner available Direct Dial Lift Licensed WiFi Sauna Gym Steam room Treatment rooms **Extras** Fruit - complimentary; Mini-bar - chargeable **Conf** Max 12 Board 12 **Notes** LB ⊗

The Sumner
PLAN 1 B4

★★★★ GUEST ACCOMMODATION

tel: 020 7723 2244 **54 Upper Berkeley St, Marble Arch W1H 7QR**
email: hotel@thesumner.com **web:** www.thesumner.com

Centrally located and just five minutes' walk from Marble Arch, The Sumner is part of a Georgian terrace. Appointed throughout to a very high standard, this delightful property combines much of the original character of the building with modern comfort. The air-conditioned bedrooms have all been designer decorated and feature widescreen LCD TVs as well as a range of traditional amenities. The breakfast buffet is included in the rate.

Rooms 20 en suite **Facilities** FTV Lounge Direct Dial Lift Licensed WiFi **Notes** ⊗ No Children 5yrs

W2

Park Grand Paddington
PLAN 1 A4

★★★★ GUEST ACCOMMODATION

tel: 020 7298 9800 **1-2 Queens Gardens, Paddington W2 3BA**
email: info@parkgrandlondon.co.uk **web:** www.parkgrandlondon.co.uk
dir: *Exit Paddington station via Praed St, turn right. After 3 sets of lights right into Devonshire Terrace. 100mtrs to Park Grand Paddington*

Park Grand Paddington enjoys a central location moments' walk from Paddington station and Hyde Park, not to mention the city's main shopping districts and attractions. Rooms vary in size and are appointed to a very high standard. A number of stylish suites are also available. The Atlantic bar serves a range of light snacks throughout the day and evening. Additional facilities include state-of-the-art technology with free internet access, TV and fridges.

Rooms 157 en suite (11 fmly) (23 GF) **Facilities** FTV TVL tea/coffee Dinner available Direct Dial Lift Licensed WiFi Fitness room **Notes** ⊗

Best Western Mornington
PLAN 1 A3

★★★★ GUEST ACCOMMODATION

tel: 020 7262 7361 **12 Lancaster Gate W2 3LG**
email: london@mornington.co.uk **web:** www.morningtonhotel.co.uk
dir: *N of Hyde Park, off A402 Bayswater Rd*

This fine Victorian building is located in a quiet road and close to Lancaster Gate station for easy access to the West End. The bedrooms have been appointed to provide comfortable, stylish accommodation. There is a lounge bar and an attractive dining room where an extensive Scandinavian-style breakfast is served.

Rooms 70 en suite (10 fmly) (4 GF) **Facilities** STV FTV tea/coffee Direct Dial Lift Licensed WiFi **Extras** Mini-bar **Conf** Max 14 Thtr 14 Class 14 Board 14 **Notes** ⊗

Grand Royale London Hyde Park
PLAN 2 E3

★★★★ GUEST ACCOMMODATION

tel: 020 7313 7900 **1 Inverness Ter W2 3JP**
email: info@shaftesburyhotels.com **web:** www.shaftesburyhotels.com
dir: *On A40 Bayswater Rd*

Located adjacent to Hyde Park, fashionable Notting Hill and within easy reach of the West End, the Grand Royale combines its rich heritage with the needs of the modern traveller. The accommodation is contemporary in style and very well equipped. Breakfast is served in the staterooms.

Rooms 188 en suite (2 GF) **Facilities** tea/coffee Direct Dial Lift Licensed WiFi **Conf** Max 20 Thtr 20 Class 20 Board 20 **Notes** ⊗

Hyde Park Radnor
PLAN 1 A4

★★★★ GUEST ACCOMMODATION

tel: 020 7723 5969 **7-9 Sussex Place, Hyde Park W2 2SX**
email: hydeparkradnor@btconnect.com **web:** www.hydeparkradnor.com
dir: *A402 (Bayswater Rd) into Lancaster Ter & Sussex Gardens, right into Sussex Place*

This family-run property is within walking distance of Paddington station, the Underground and all London's central attractions. There is a choice of well-appointed bedrooms with modern en suites to meet the needs of a varied clientele. All rooms are well equipped with a range of useful amenities including free WiFi. The dining room is located on the lower-ground floor, where a continental buffet and a freshly-cooked breakfast are served daily.

Rooms 36 en suite (10 fmly) (5 GF) **Facilities** STV FTV TVL tea/coffee Direct Dial Lift WiFi **Notes** ⊗

Mercure London Paddington
PLAN 1 A4

★★★★ GUEST ACCOMMODATION

tel: 020 7835 2000 **144 Praed St, Paddington W2 1HU**
email: stay@mercurepaddington.com **web:** www.mercurepaddington.com

Contemporary and stylish, Mercure London Paddington enjoys a central location, adjacent to Paddington Station. Bedrooms and en suites vary in size but all are smartly appointed and boast a host of extra facilities including CD players, flat-screen TVs, room safes and internet access. A small gym, stylish lounge and meeting rooms are also available.

Rooms 83 en suite **Facilities** STV TVL tea/coffee Dinner available Direct Dial Lift Licensed WiFi Gym **Conf** Max 22 Board 22 **Notes** ⊗

W2 continued

Park Grand London Hyde Park

PLAN 1 A4

★★★★ GUEST ACCOMMODATION

tel: 020 7262 4521 **78-82 Westbourne Ter, Paddington W2 6QA**
email: reservations@londonpremierhotels.co.uk **web:** www.parkgrandhydepark.co.uk
dir: *A40 into Lancaster Terrace, at crossing left onto slip road*

This attractive property enjoys a central location within easy reach of central London shops and attractions. The en suite bedrooms and public areas have a smart contemporary feel. Although rooms vary in size, all boast many useful facilities such as free internet access, mini-fridges and irons.

Rooms 119 en suite (10 fmly) (19 GF) **Facilities** FTV Lounge tea/coffee Direct Dial Lift Licensed WiFi **Parking** 11 **Notes** ⊗

Princes Square

PLAN 2 E3

★★★★ GUEST ACCOMMODATION

tel: 020 7229 9876 **23-25 Princes Square, off Ilchester Gardens, Bayswater W2 4NJ**
email: info@princessquarehotel.co.uk **web:** www.princessquarehotel.co.uk
dir: *From Bayswater 1st left into Moscow Rd, 3rd right into Ilchester Gardens*

This fine building is in a quiet road close to a number of tube stations, with easy access to the West End. The comfortable bedrooms provide stylish accommodation, and are equipped with a range of useful amenities. A continental breakfast is served in the attractive dining room.

Rooms 50 en suite (3 fmly) (6 GF) **Facilities** STV FTV tea/coffee Direct Dial Lift WiFi **Notes** ⊗

Shaftesbury Hyde Park International

PLAN 2 E3

★★★★ GUEST ACCOMMODATION

tel: 020 7985 8300 **52-55 Inverness Ter W2 3LB**
email: info@shaftesburyhotels.com **web:** www.shaftesburyhotels.com
dir: *Off A402 (Bayswater Rd)*

A smart, modern establishment near to Bayswater, Queensway and Paddington underground stations, the Shaftesbury Hyde Park International is also within walking distance of a myriad of dining options. Bedrooms and bathrooms are decorated to a very high standard with a good range of in-room facilities including flat-screen TV, iron and ironing board and complimentary internet or WiFi access. Continental and cooked buffet breakfasts are served daily. There is a limited number of off-road parking spaces.

Rooms 70 en suite (2 GF) **Facilities** STV TVL tea/coffee Direct Dial Lift Licensed WiFi **Extras** Mini-bar, fruit, snacks **Conf** Max 12 Thtr 12 Class 8 Board 8 **Parking** 3 **Notes** ⊗

Shaftesbury Metropolis London Hyde Park

PLAN 1 A4

★★★★ GUEST ACCOMMODATION

tel: 020 7723 7723 **78-84 Sussex Gardens, Hyde Park W2 1UH**
email: gurpreet@shaftesburymetropolitan.com **web:** www.shaftesburyhotels.com

This establishment is in an ideal location close to Paddington station with express links to Heathrow Airport. Smartly decorated bedrooms with highly comfortable beds are available in a range of sizes, all with stylish en suite provision. On-site facilities include complimentary internet or WiFi, and continental and full English breakfasts are served every day. Reception is staffed 24 hours.

Rooms 90 en suite (14 GF) **Facilities** STV FTV TVL tea/coffee Direct Dial Lift Licensed WiFi Small fitness centre **Notes** ⊗

Shaftesbury Paddington Court London

PLAN 1 A4

★★★★ GUEST ACCOMMODATION

tel: 020 7745 1200 **27 Devonshire Ter W2 3DP**
email: info@paddingtoncourt.com **web:** www.paddingtoncourt.com
dir: *From A40 take exit before Paddington flyover, follow Paddington Station signs. Devonshire Ter is off Craven Rd*

This establishment benefits from its convenient location, close to Paddington station, which has links to the tube and the Heathrow Express terminal. Situated next to Hyde Park and Kensington Palace Gardens, the guest accommodation comprises smart and comfortable rooms, and a substantial breakfast is offered. Club Rooms are also available with additional extras including the exclusive use of the Club Lounge. A room is available for small meetings by prior arrangement.

Rooms 175 en suite 35 annexe en suite (43 fmly) (45 GF) S fr £47; D fr £76* **Facilities** STV FTV TVL tea/coffee Dinner available Direct Dial Lift Licensed **Notes** ⊗

Shaftesbury Premier London Notting Hill

PLAN 2 E3

★★★★ GUEST ACCOMMODATION

tel: 020 7792 1414 **5-7 Princes Square, Bayswater W2 4NP**
web: www.shaftesburyhotels.com

Situated conveniently for many attractions yet peacefully located in a quiet, leafy square, this smart establishment offers friendly, professional service and comfortable rooms. The property has stylish public rooms and offers free WiFi as well as hard-wire connectivity in the extremely well-equipped bedrooms. Breakfast is served in the dining room and offers a good choice of freshly cooked traditional breakfast and continental items.

Rooms 68 en suite (2 GF) **Facilities** STV TVL tea/coffee Direct Dial Lift WiFi Gym **Notes** ⊗

Shaftesbury Premier London Paddington
PLAN 1 A4

★★★★ GUEST ACCOMMODATION

tel: 020 7723 3434 **55-61 Westbourne Ter W2 6QA**
web: www.theshaftesbury.co.uk
dir: *Exit A40 into Lancaster Terrace*

This smart property enjoys a convenient location within walking distance of Hyde Park and of many of London's major shops and attractions. Bedrooms are smartly appointed and boast modern technology. A hearty breakfast is served in the airy dining room. Limited off-street parking (chargeable) is a bonus. The staff are friendly and attentive.

Rooms 118 en suite (7 fmly) (20 GF) S £330; D £390* **Facilities** STV TVL tea/coffee Dinner available Direct Dial Lift Licensed WiFi **Parking** 12 **Notes** ⊗

Number 63
PLAN 1 A3

★★★ GUEST ACCOMMODATION

tel: 020 7723 8575 **63 Baywater Rd W2 3PH**
email: info@number63.co.uk **web:** www.number63.co.uk

Number 63 offers a surprisingly tranquil environment just a minute's walk from Lancaster Gate tube and directly opposite Hyde Park. All bedrooms are comfortable with en suite facilities and consist of a range of singles and twins; there is also a triple room. Hot snacks are available throughout the afternoon and evening (by prior arrangement) and a good continental or cooked breakfast is served in the mornings. A meeting/function room is available. Parking can be arranged. AA Friendliest B&B of the Year Award Finalist 2016-2017.

Rooms 16 en suite (1 fmly) S £77.50; D £130-£135* **Facilities** FTV Lounge TVL tea/coffee Dinner available Direct Dial Lift Licensed WiFi **Conf** Max 32 Thtr 32 Board 24 **Notes** ⊗ No Children 5yrs Closed 22-27 Dec

Comfort Inn Hyde Park
PLAN 1 A3

★★★ GUEST ACCOMMODATION

tel: 020 7229 6424 **73 Queensborough Ter, Bayswater W2 3SU**
email: info@comforthydepark.com **web:** www.choicehotels.co.uk
dir: *Off Bayswater Rd near Queensway tube station*

A short walk from Kensington Gardens, fashionable Queensway and the underground network this property is ideally located to explore London and all that it has to offer. There is a range of practical bedrooms from double to family rooms, with bright and well-appointed bathrooms. Air conditioning, free WiFi, flat-screen LCD televisions and tea and coffee making facilities feature in all rooms. Free continental breakfast is served daily in the dining room located in the lower ground floor. Limited street parking available (chargeable).

Rooms 29 en suite (1 fmly) (3 GF) **Facilities** STV FTV tea/coffee Direct Dial Lift WiFi **Notes** ⊗

Griffin House
PLAN 1 B4

★★★ GUEST ACCOMMODATION

tel: 020 7723 6532 & 7491 0683 **10 Connaught St, Marble Arch W2 2AH**
email: info@griffinhousehotel.co.uk **web:** www.griffinhousehotel.co.uk

A compact establishment, strategically located in the heart of central London, very well connected to the public transport network and with many landmarks just a stone's throw away. Bedrooms are comfortable and have practical amenities. A substantial continental breakfast is served in the lower-ground floor breakfast room, overseen by attentive staff.

Rooms 15 rms **Facilities** STV Direct Dial WiFi 🔒 **Extras** Mini-bar **Notes** ⊗

Kingsway Park Guest Accommodation
PLAN 1 A4

★★★ GUEST ACCOMMODATION

tel: 020 7723 5677 & 7724 9346 **139 Sussex Gardens W2 2RX**
email: info@kingswaypark-hotel.com **web:** www.kingswaypark-hotel.com
dir: *A40 Ebound junct for Paddington, through to Sussex Gdns*

This Victorian property has a central location within walking distance of Marble Arch, Hyde Park and Paddington. Bedrooms offer well-equipped, good value accommodation. Public areas include a reception lounge and a basement breakfast room adorned with interesting artwork. A limited number of parking spaces is available.

Rooms 22 en suite (5 fmly) (2 GF) S £50-£180; D £70-£240* **Facilities** STV FTV Lounge TVL tea/coffee Direct Dial Licensed **Conf** Max 30 **Parking** 3 **Notes** LB ⊗

W6

Best Western Plus Seraphine
PLAN 2 D3

★★★★ GUEST ACCOMMODATION

tel: 020 8600 0555 & 8741 6464 **84 King St W6 0QW**
email: hammersmith@seraphinehotel.co.uk **web:** www.seraphinehotel.co.uk
dir: *A4 exit into Hammersmith Bridge Rd before Hammersmith flyover. Left into King St*

Located just a short walk from Hammersmith tube station, this establishment is a good base for visiting the capital's attractions. All bedrooms and public areas are smartly appointed and offer very good levels of comfort. Continental and cooked breakfast are served in the open plan Breakfast Room. The bar offers a suitable range of drinks and snacks.

Rooms 62 en suite (14 fmly) S £90-£150; D £100-£299 **Facilities** STV FTV iPod docking station Lounge TVL tea/coffee Direct Dial Lift Licensed WiFi **Extras** Bottled water **Conf** Thtr 24 Class 16 Board 16 **Notes** LB ⊗

W8

Best Western Seraphine, Kensington Gardens
PLAN 2 E3

★★★★ GUEST ACCOMMODATION

tel: 020 7368 2222 & 7938 5911 **7-11 Kensington High St W8 5NP**
email: info@seraphinehotel.co.uk **web:** www.seraphinehotel.co.uk
dir: B325 Gloucester Road, continue for 0.5m, left at A315 Kensington Road

This smart property enjoys a prime location opposite Kensington Palace and is ideally positioned for Hyde Park, The Royal Albert Hall, shops and museums. Bedrooms vary in size but all are well equipped with interactive flat-screen TV, iPod docking stations, laptop safes and free WiFi; the en suites are modern with power showers. An extensive continental breakfast is included.

Rooms 22 en suite **Facilities** STV FTV iPod docking station TVL tea/coffee Direct Dial Lift Licensed WiFi 🛁 **Extras** Bottled water - complimentary **Notes** ⊗

Best Western Seraphine Kensington Olympia
PLAN 2 E3

★★★★ GUEST ACCOMMODATION

tel: 020 7938 5911 **225 Kensington High St W8 6SA**
email: olympia@seraphinehotel.co.uk **web:** www.seraphinehotel.co.uk
dir: A4 left onto A330, then right onto A315. On corner of Kensington High St & Abingdon Rd

This chic and intimate property enjoys a prime location in the heart of High Street Kensington, and is ideally positioned for Holland Park, local attractions, shops and museums. Bedrooms vary in size but all are well equipped with interactive flat-screen TV, iPod docking stations, laptop safes and free WiFi. En suites are modern with powerful showers. An extensive continental breakfast is included and full cooked breakfasts upon request.

Rooms 35 en suite (35 fmly) **Facilities** FTV iPod docking station TVL tea/coffee Direct Dial Lift Licensed WiFi **Extras** Bottled water **Conf** Thtr 20 Board 10 **Notes** ⊗

Mercure London Kensington
PLAN 2 E3

★★★★ GUEST ACCOMMODATION

tel: 020 7244 2400 **1a Lexham Gardens, Kensington W8 5JJ**
email: stay@mercurekensington.com **web:** www.mercurekensington.com

Mercure London Kensington enjoys a prime location adjacent to the famous Cromwell Road Hospital, and is within easy reach of the V&A and the chic shops of Knightsbridge and South Kensington. Bedrooms are extremely well equipped and, along with the comfortable public areas, have a stylish, contemporary feel. The smart and popular bar is a feature.

Rooms 82 en suite **Facilities** STV TVL tea/coffee Dinner available Direct Dial Lift Licensed **Parking** 8 **Notes** ⊗

W9

The Warrington
PLAN 1 A5

★★★★ INN

tel: 020 7286 8282 **93 Warrington Crescent W9 1EH**
email: warrington@faucetinn.com **web:** www.faucetinn.com/warrington

The Warrington is a Grade II listed building that has been serving the Maida Vale community since its opening in 1857. It has a rich and intriguing history, which continues to fascinate the locals and might shock new patrons. The interiors are richly furnished with many original features still in place such as the staircase, the bar and the fireplace. There is a large events room on the first floor, while the top floor now houses five beautifully appointed en suite bedrooms; all different in size but equipped with deeply comfortable beds and all modern facilities. The bar is well stocked and the menu offers a choice of old favourites. BBQs are regularly held during the warm months of the year.

Rooms 5 en suite **Facilities** tea/coffee

W12

W12 Rooms
PLAN 2 D3

★★★★ GUEST ACCOMMODATION

tel: 020 3658 551 **54 Uxbridge Rd, Shepherd's Bush W12 8LP**
email: info@w12rooms.co.uk **web:** www.w12rooms.co.uk

Nineteen vintage-inspired bedrooms with a modern twist make a good base for a trip to London. Westfield Shopping Centre is just minutes away, with Portobello Market, Holland Park, Earls Court and famous music and sports venues close by. Most of London's major tourist attractions, including the London Eye, Buckingham Palace and the Shard are also easily accessible. W12 offers comfortable contemporary rooms on a room only basis, there are various cafés and eateries a short walk away.

Rooms 19 en suite (1 fmly) **Facilities** FTV TVL tea/coffee WiFi **Notes** ⊗ No Children 2yrs

W13

Best Western Maitrise Suites
PLAN 2 C3

★★★★ GUEST ACCOMMODATION

tel: 020 8799 3850 **50-54 The Broadway, West Ealing W13 0SU**
email: info@maitrisesuites.com **web:** www.maitrisesuites.com

This establishment offers fully serviced accommodation. The rooms are made up of studio, one and two bedroom apartments, all with kitchens and lounge areas. Bedrooms are stylish and come fully equipped with all modern amenities including digital TV and free WiFi throughout. A continental room service breakfast can be enjoyed daily. This property has parking available and is just 10 minutes from Ealing Broadway tube station.

Rooms 17 en suite (17 fmly) S £109-£350; D £109-£350 (room only) **Facilities** FTV iPod docking station Lounge tea/coffee Direct Dial Lift WiFi **Parking** 8 **Notes** ⊗

WC1

The George
PLAN 1 D5

★★★ GUEST ACCOMMODATION

tel: 020 7387 8777 **58-60 Cartwright Gardens WC1H 9EL**
email: ghotel@aol.com **web:** www.georgehotel.com
dir: From St Pancras 2nd left into Marchmont St & 1st left into Cartwright Gardens

The George is within walking distance of Russell Square and the tube, and convenient for London's central attractions. The brightly appointed bedrooms vary in size, and some have en suites. A substantial breakfast is served in the attractive ground-floor dining room.

Rooms 41 rms (31 en suite) (10 pri facs) (5 GF) S £62-£100; D £84-£138.50*
Facilities FTV Lounge TVL tea/coffee Direct Dial WiFi **Notes** ⊗

GREATER LONDON

BARNET
Map 6 TQ29

Savoro Restaurant with Rooms

★★★★ ❀ RESTAURANT WITH ROOMS

tel: 020 8449 9888 **206 High St EN5 5SZ**
email: savoro@savoro.co.uk **web:** www.savoro.co.uk
dir: *M25 junct 23, A1000. Establishment in crescent behind Hadley Green Jaguar Garage*

Set back from the main high street, the traditional frontage of this establishment belies the stylishly contemporary bedrooms within. Several have modern four-poster beds and all have well designed bathrooms. The award-winning restaurant is an additional bonus, serving food which is all freshly prepared in-house, from bread to ice cream.

Rooms 11 rms (9 en suite) (2 pri facs) (2 fmly) (3 GF) **Facilities** FTV tea/coffee Dinner available WiFi **Extras** Bottled water - complimentary **Conf** Max 20 Class 20 Board 20 **Parking** 9 **Notes** LB ⊗ No coaches

BECKENHAM
See London Plan 2 G1

Innkeeper's Lodge Beckenham

★★★ INN

tel: 08451 551551 *(Calls cost 2p per minute plus your phone company's access charge)*
422 Upper Elmers End Rd BR3 3HQ
email: info@innkeeperslodge.com **web:** www.innkeeperslodge.com

At Innkeeper's Lodge you'll find accommodation with comfort and character in equal measure, and everything needed for a relaxing stay, from easy check-in and free parking to complimentary breakfast and a cosy pub serving great value food and drink on the doorstep. Each Lodge has quality rooms, and there are Lodges in a variety of locations from towns and cities to countryside settings across the UK.

Rooms 24 en suite (1 fmly) (8 GF) **Facilities** FTV tea/coffee Dinner available Direct Dial WiFi **Parking** 40 **Notes** ⊗

CRANFORD
See London Plan 2 A3 For accommodation details see Heathrow Airport (London)

CROYDON
Map 6 TQ36

Kirkdale

★★★ GUEST ACCOMMODATION

tel: 020 8688 5898 **22 St Peters Rd CR0 1HD**
email: reservations@kirkdalehotel.co.uk **web:** www.kirkdalehotel.co.uk
dir: *A23 onto A232 W & A212 (Lower Coombe St), 500yds right*

Close to the town centre, this Victorian property retains many original features. Public areas include a small lounge bar and an attractive breakfast room, and the bedrooms have good facilities. There is a sheltered patio for use in the summer.

Rooms 16 en suite (5 GF) **Facilities** FTV TVL tea/coffee Direct Dial Licensed WiFi **Parking** 12 **Notes** ⊗

ERITH
Map 6 TQ57

Julius Lodge - Thamesmead

★★ GUEST ACCOMMODATION

tel: 020 8312 9304 & 07582 141055 **27 Holstein Way DA18 4DQ**
web: www.juliuslodge.co.uk

Julius Lodge offers good-value rooms with shared facilities, as well as a self-contained studio. All rooms are equipped with flat-screen TVs with Freeview and free WiFi is available throughout the house. Guests can relax in the comfortable seating room and enjoy free parking after 5pm.

Rooms 9 rms (1 pri facs) (1 fmly) (2 GF) **Facilities** STV FTV DVD TVL WiFi **Notes** ⊗

HARROW ON THE HILL

See London Plan 2 B5

Old Etonian

★★★ 🍽 GUEST ACCOMMODATION

tel: 020 8423 3854 & 8422 8482 **36-38 High St HA1 3LL**
email: info@oldetonian.com **web:** www.oldetonian.com
dir: *In town centre. On B458 opposite Harrow School*

In the heart of this historic part of London and opposite the prestigious school, this friendly guest accommodation is a delight. Bedrooms are attractive, well appointed and comfortable. A continental breakfast is served in the dining room, which in the evening is home to a lively restaurant. On-road parking is available.

Rooms 9 en suite (1 GF) S £69.50; D £77.50* **Facilities** FTV tea/coffee Dinner available Direct Dial Licensed WiFi 🛁 **Extras** Snacks - complimentary **Conf** Max 30 Thtr 20 Class 20 Board 20 **Parking** 3 **Notes** ⊗

HEATHROW AIRPORT (LONDON)

The Cottage   PLAN 2 B3

★★★★ GUEST ACCOMMODATION

tel: 020 8897 1815 **150-152 High St, Cranford TW5 9WB**
email: info@the-cottage.eu **web:** www.the-cottage.eu
dir: *M4 junct 3, A312 towards Feltham, left at lights, left after 1st pub on left*

This beautiful property is a peacefully situated, family-run oasis, within five minutes of Heathrow Airport. It offers comfortable and spacious accommodation, in the tastefully decorated main house and six bedrooms located at the rear of the garden, connected to the main building by a covered walkway overlooking the stunning courtyard.

Rooms 14 en suite 6 annexe en suite (4 fmly) (12 GF) **Facilities** FTV tea/coffee WiFi **Parking** 16 **Notes** ⊗ Closed 24-26 Dec & 31 Dec-1 Jan

Crompton Guest House   PLAN 2 B2

★★★★ GUEST HOUSE

tel: 020 8570 7090 **49 Lampton Rd, Hounslow TW3 1JG**
email: cromptonguesthouse@btconnect.com **web:** www.cromptonguesthouse.co.uk
dir: *M4 junct 3, follow signs for Hounslow. Into Bath Rd (A3005), left at Yates pub. 200yds on right just before bridge*

Located just a moment's walk away from Hounslow underground station this accommodation is popular with both business and leisure travellers. Bedrooms and bathrooms are comfortable and well equipped with good facilities including air

conditioning. Breakfast is served in the intimate dining room where a freshly prepared breakfast is served. Parking is a bonus and is free for up to 15 days.

Crompton Guest House

Rooms 11 en suite (7 fmly) (2 GF) S £90-£200; D £100-£250 **Facilities** STV FTV DVD iPod docking station tea/coffee Dinner available Direct Dial WiFi 🛁 **Extras** Speciality toiletries, safe, mini-bar **Parking** 12 **Notes** LB ⊗

HORNCHURCH   Map 6 TQ58

Innkeeper's Lodge Hornchurch

★★★ INN

tel: 08451 551551 *(Calls cost 2p per minute plus your phone company's access charge)* **Station Ln RM12 6SB**
email: info@innkeeperslodge.com **web:** www.innkeeperslodge.com

At Innkeeper's Lodge you'll find accommodation with comfort and character in equal measure, and everything needed for a relaxing stay, from easy check-in and free parking to complimentary breakfast and a cosy pub serving great value food and drink on the doorstep. Each Lodge has quality rooms, and there are Lodges in a variety of locations from towns and cities to countryside settings across the UK.

Rooms 12 en suite (1 fmly) **Facilities** FTV tea/coffee Dinner available WiFi **Conf** Max 60 **Parking** 40 **Notes** ⊗

HOUNSLOW

See London Plan 2 B2 For accommodation details see under Heathrow Airport (London)

ILFORD

See London Plan 2 H5

Best Western Greater London

★★★★ GUEST ACCOMMODATION

tel: 020 8514 0444 **60 Cranbrook Rd IG1 4NH**
email: info@bestwesterngreaterlondon.com **web:** www.bestwesterngreaterlondon.com

Recently refurbished, the Best Western Greater London is an ideal base from which to explore the capital. This stylish modern property enjoys a prominent position on the high street in Ilford, and secure parking can be arranged in advance at reception. The popular café serves food throughout the day and there is an extensive choice on offer at breakfast. Comfortable, modern bedrooms are all finished to a high standard and free WiFi is available for guests.

Rooms 22 en suite **Facilities** tea/coffee WiFi

Best Western Ilford

★★★★ GUEST ACCOMMODATION

tel: 020 8911 6083 **3-5 Argyle Rd IG1 3BH**
email: manager@expresslodging.co.uk **web:** www.expresslodging.co.uk
dir: *From A406 E towards Ilford, then A118 & 1st left after Ilford Station*

This establishment is conveniently located for easy access to the Queen Elizabeth II Olympic Park and central London. The accommodation is very comfortable and offers a range of amenities such as free internet and a state-of-the-art media hub. 24-hour room service and parking is also provided.

Rooms 34 en suite 26 annexe en suite (9 fmly) (15 GF) **Facilities** FTV Lounge TVL tea/coffee Dinner available Direct Dial WiFi 🔒 **Conf** Max 30 Thtr 30 Class 30 Board 30 **Parking** 12 **Notes** ⊗

MERSEYSIDE

BIRKENHEAD
Map 15 SJ38

Shrewsbury Lodge

★★★ GUEST HOUSE

tel: 0151 652 4029 & 07912 846197 **31 Shrewsbury Rd, Oxton CH43 2JB**
email: info@shrewsbury-hotel.com **web:** www.shrewsbury-hotel.com

Modern accommodation situated in a quiet residential area but within easy walking distance of local amenities and close to travel links. Family-run, it provides well-equipped bedrooms and good breakfasts are served in the pleasant dining room. Friendly, attentive service is a strength here.

Rooms 15 rms (12 en suite) (3 pri facs) (3 fmly) (4 GF) S £35-£55; D £55-£72 (room only)* **Facilities** FTV Lounge TVL tea/coffee Licensed WiFi 🐾🦮 18 Fishing Riding **Conf** Max 20 Thtr 20 Class 20 Board 20 **Parking** 12 **Notes** LB ⊗

BOOTLE
Map 15 SJ39

Breeze Guest House

★★★ GUEST HOUSE

tel: 0151 933 2576 **237 Hawthorne Rd L20 3AW**
email: breezegh@googlemail.com **web:** www.breezeguesthouse.co.uk

This pleasant family-run guest house provides a friendly place to stay. With secure parking and great transport links, it is ideally located for Anfield and Goodison Park as well as being convenient for Aintree. Dinner is available and there is a pleasant bar too. Bedrooms are spacious and comfortable.

Rooms 10 en suite (1 fmly) (1 GF) S £40-£75; D £80-£200* **Facilities** FTV DVD TVL tea/coffee Dinner available Licensed WiFi **Extras** Bottled water **Parking** 8 **Notes** LB Closed 20 Dec-5 Jan

BROMBOROUGH
Map 15 SJ38

Pesto at the Dibbinsdale Inn

★★★★ 🍽 INN

tel: 0151 334 9818 **Dibbinsdale Rd CH63 0HJ**
email: pestodibbinsdale@hotmail.com **web:** www.pestorestaurants.co.uk
dir: *M53 junct 5 onto A41 towards Birkenhead. After 2m left towards railway station, through 2 sets of lights, 2nd right into Dibbinsdale Rd. 600yds on right*

Pesto at the Dibbinsdale Inn offers plenty of those little luxuries you'd expect from a larger establishment, combined with the relaxed comfort of an independently-run inn, all in a peaceful setting. With high standards of comfort and facilities, the stylish en suite bedrooms are equipped for both leisure and business guests. With real ales on tap and open fires, the restaurant also offers Pesto's informal Italian dining experience with its piattini menu of small plates. A special party menu is available for group bookings.

Rooms 12 en suite (1 fmly) S £50-£90; D £65-£110* **Facilities** FTV Lounge tea/coffee Dinner available WiFi 🦮 18 **Parking** 25 **Notes** LB ⊗ RS 25 Dec restaurant closed

IRBY
Map 15 SJ28

Manor Garden Lodge

★★★★ BED AND BREAKFAST

tel: 0151 648 7212 & 07855 512008 **5 Manor Rd CH61 4UA**
email: markwhite7212@gmail.com **web:** www.manorgardenlodge.co.uk
dir: *M53 junct 3 onto A552 towards Heswall. Left into Arrowe Park Rd, then right into Thingwall Rd E. After 1m at T-junct turn right, then 1st right*

Located in the heart of the Wirral and handy for transport into both Liverpool and Chester, this is a B&B with a difference. The two wooden lodges at the secluded end of a neat garden are spacious and well equipped, with modern facilities and thoughtful extras. Breakfast is taken in the main house. A warm and personal welcome and service is guaranteed.

Rooms 2 annexe en suite (2 GF) S £70-£75; D £70-£75* **Facilities** FTV iPod docking station tea/coffee WiFi 🦮 18 **Parking** 2 **Notes** LB ⊗ 🍽

LIVERPOOL
Map 15 SJ39

Liverpool Gateway B&B

★★★ GUEST ACCOMMODATION

tel: 0151 298 2288 & 07714 090842 **95 Saint Oswald's St L13 5SB**
web: www.liverpoolgateway.co.uk
dir: *End of M62 through 2 pedestrian lights, through next lights, on right opposite subway*

Ideally situated for the M62 and with easy access to the city centre and its attractions, Liverpool Gateway provides comfortable accommodation, facilities and thoughtful extras for the modern traveller. Continental breakfasts are taken in a communal kitchen; secure off-road parking is provided.

Rooms 10 rms (2 GF) S £30-£40; D £45-£60* **Facilities** FTV WiFi 🔒 **Parking** 15 **Notes** ⊗ No Children 10yrs

SOUTHPORT
Map 15 SD31

Bay Tree House B&B

★★★★ ⌂ GUEST ACCOMMODATION

tel: 01704 510555 **No1 Irving St, Marine Gate PR9 0HD**
email: info@baytreehousesouthport.co.uk **web:** www.baytreehousesouthport.co.uk
dir: *3rd road right off Leicester St, approaching from rdbt off Lord St*

A warm welcome is assured at this immaculately maintained house, located a short walk from the promenade and central attractions. Bedrooms are equipped with a wealth of thoughtful extras, and delicious imaginative breakfasts are served in an attractive dining room overlooking the pretty front patio garden.

Rooms 6 en suite **Facilities** FTV DVD iPod docking station Lounge tea/coffee Direct Dial Licensed WiFi ⅃ 18 Discounts available for local swimming baths & gym **Extras** Speciality toiletries, mini-bar, snacks, robes **Parking** 2 **Notes** Closed 24 Dec-Jan

The Baytrees

★★★★ GUEST ACCOMMODATION

tel: 01704 536513 **4 Queens Rd PR9 9HN**
email: baytreeshotel@gmail.com **web:** www.baytreeshotel.co.uk
dir: *From B565 (Lord St) towards fire station, right at rdbt into Manchester Rd, left at lights, 200yds on right*

Located a short walk from Lord Street, this elegant late Victorian house has been well appointed to provide thoughtfully furnished bedrooms with smart modern en suite bathrooms. Breakfast is served in the attractive dining room overlooking the pretty rear garden, and a lounge is also available.

Rooms 12 en suite (5 fmly) (2 GF) **Facilities** FTV DVD TVL tea/coffee WiFi ⌂ **Parking** 11 **Notes** ⊗ Closed Xmas

NORFOLK

BACTON
Map 13 TG33

The Keswick

★★★★ GUEST ACCOMMODATION

tel: 01692 650468 **Walcott Rd NR12 0LS**
email: margaret@keswickhotelbacton.co.uk **web:** www.keswickhotelbacton.co.uk
dir: *On B1159 (coast road)*

This family-run property enjoys lovely sea views and is within easy driving distance of the Broads and the stunning north Norfolk coastline. The individually decorated bedrooms are all well-appointed, have modern facilities and many rooms have sea views. Public areas include a cosy lounge bar with plush, comfortable seating along with stylish conservatory restaurant.

Rooms 12 rms (10 en suite) (2 pri facs) **Facilities** FTV DVD Lounge TVL Licensed WiFi **Conf** Board 20 **Parking** 100

BAWBURGH
Map 13 TG10

The Kings Head Bawburgh

★★★★ ◉◉ INN

tel: 01603 744977 **Harts Ln NR9 3LS**
email: anton@kingsheadbawburgh.co.uk **web:** www.kingshead-bawburgh.co.uk
dir: *Exit A47 signed university & hospital onto B1108 (Whatton). 500yds right into Stocks Hill. Into centre of Bawburgh, opposite river*

The Kings Head Bawburgh is Grade II listed, was built in 1602 and is situated in the picturesque village of Bawburgh, opposite the river, only a ten-minute drive from the centre of Norwich. The pub boasts six brand new boutique-style bedrooms with modern bathrooms, and high quality fixtures and fittings throughout. The gastropub below offers award-winning food in a traditional dining area complete with oak beams, inglenook fireplace, and wood-burners. There is also a lovely outside patio where guests can eat or enjoy a drink in the summer, with a good range of real ales available. Nothing is too much trouble for the owners who will ensure all guests feel welcomed.

Rooms 6 en suite (1 fmly) **Facilities** FTV iPod docking station tea/coffee Dinner available WiFi ⅃ 27 **Extras** Speciality toiletries, home-made biscuits **Conf** Max 20 Thtr 20 Class 20 Board 12 **Parking** 51 **Notes** No coaches

BLAKENEY
Map 13 TG04

Premier Collection

Blakeney House

★★★★★ GUEST HOUSE

tel: 01263 740561 **High St NR25 7NX**
email: admin@blakeneyhouse.com **web:** www.blakeneyhouse.com
dir: *In village centre*

Blakeney House is a stunning Victorian manor house set amid two acres of attractive landscaped grounds, just a short walk from the quay and town centre. The stylish, individually decorated bedrooms have co-ordinated fabrics and many thoughtful touches. Breakfast is served at individual tables in the smart dining room, which overlooks the well-stocked front garden.

Rooms 8 rms (7 en suite) (1 pri facs) (1 fmly) **Facilities** DVD tea/coffee WiFi ⅃ 18 ⌂ **Parking** 8 **Notes** ⊗ No Children 12yrs

BROOKE
Map 13 TM29

The Old Vicarage

★★★★ BED AND BREAKFAST

tel: 01508 558329 **48 The Street NR15 1JU**
dir: *From Norwich on B1332, turn left after Kings Head pub. 1st left at fork in road to village. Immediately before church on right*

Set in mature gardens in a peaceful village, this charming house is within easy driving distance of Norwich. The individually decorated bedrooms are thoughtfully furnished and equipped, and one room has a lovely four-poster bed. There is an elegant dining room and a cosy lounge, and dinner is available by arrangement. Service is genuinely helpful, provided in a relaxed and friendly manner.

Rooms 2 en suite S £40; D £70* **Facilities** TVL tea/coffee Dinner available **Parking** 4 **Notes** LB ⊗ No Children 15yrs ◉

BURNHAM MARKET
Map 13 TF84

The Nelson Country Inn
★★★★ INN

tel: 01328 738321 **4 Creake Rd PE31 8EN**
email: stay@the-nelson.com **web:** www.the-nelson.com
dir: *From Market Pl onto Front St (at lower end). 200yds, on Creake Rd*

This country inn is set in the pretty north Norfolk village of Burnham Market, within easy reach of King's Lynn, Norwich, Hunstanton and Cromer. Bedrooms are individually styled and comfortable. Hearty meals are served daily, making good use of local and seasonal produce where possible.

Rooms 5 en suite 2 annexe en suite (2 GF) **Facilities** FTV tea/coffee Dinner available WiFi ≡ **Extras** Sweets **Conf** Max 18 Thtr 12 Class 18 Board 14 **Parking** 20

CASTLE ACRE
Map 13 TF81

Ostrich Inn
★★★★ INN

tel: 01760 755398 **Stocks Green PE32 2AE**
email: info@ostrichcastleacre.com **web:** www.ostrichcastleacre.com
dir: *0.3m on right of Castle Acre Priory*

The 15th-century Ostrich Inn is situated adjacent to the village green in the centre of Castle Acre. The warm and inviting public areas have a wealth of original features such as exposed brickwork, oak beams and open fires. The spacious bedrooms are in an adjacent building; each room is equipped with modern facilities.

Rooms 6 en suite (1 fmly) (1 GF) **Facilities** FTV Lounge tea/coffee Dinner available Direct Dial WiFi ≡ **Conf** Max 25 Thtr 25 Class 25 Board 25 **Parking** 30 **Notes** LB

CLEY NEXT THE SEA
Map 13 TG04

Premier Collection

Old Town Hall House
★★★★★ GUEST HOUSE

tel: 01263 741439 & 07813 335236 **High St NR25 7RB**
email: bookings@oldtownhallhouse.com **web:** www.oldtownhallhouse.com
dir: *On A149 in centre of Cley. On High St, opposite old red phone box*

Old Town Hall House is located in the popular little village of Cley next the Sea, which has been designated as an Area of Outstanding Natural Beauty and has a superb bird-watching reserve on its outskirts. The tastefully appointed bedrooms offer luxurious fabrics and retro accessories with a modern touch. Dinner is available on certain nights and guests can enjoy a pre-dinner drink in the lounge beforehand. James has worked in some of the finest restaurants in Europe and only high quality ingredients will be on the menu. Breakfast is equally enjoyable.

Rooms 4 en suite (1 fmly) D £95-£130* **Facilities** Lounge tea/coffee Dinner available Licensed WiFi ≡ 18 ≡ **Extras** Speciality toiletries, fresh milk - complimentary **Notes** LB ⊗

The George
★★★★ ≡ INN

tel: 01263 740652 **The High St NR25 7RN**
email: info@thegeorgehotelatcley.co.uk **web:** www.thegeorgehotelatcley.co.uk
dir: *On A149 coast road*

The George is located in Cley next the Sea, within easy reach of Blakeney and Holt. This is a great spot for bird watchers, and The George overlooks the Cley marshes and bird reserve, looking out towards Blakeney Harbour. This is a quiet little village without any street lights and retains its original charm complete with red village phone box. The rooms all provide modern amenities and have each been attractively decorated; most overlooking the marshes. Guests can enjoy a range of freshly prepared dishes in the restaurant (where food is served all day in the summer), including a fantastic lounge.

Rooms 10 en suite (1 fmly) S £120-£345; D £120-£345* **Facilities** FTV DVD tea/coffee Dinner available WiFi **Parking** 10

CROMER
Map 13 TG24

See also Sheringham

The Grove Cromer
★★★★★ ◉◉ GUEST ACCOMMODATION

tel: 01263 512412 **95 Overstrand Rd NR27 0DJ**
email: enquiries@thegrovecromer.co.uk **web:** www.thegrovecromer.co.uk
dir: *Into Cromer on A149, right at 1st mini rdbt into Cromwell Rd. At double mini rdbt straight over into Overstrand Rd, 200mtrs on left*

A charming Georgian house, The Grove Cromer sits in several acres of landscaped gardens and is a short walk from Cromer town centre, cliff walks and the beach. There are several bedroom styles to choose from; the well-appointed comfortable bedrooms in the main house and stylish garden rooms. There is an indoor heated swimming pool available for guests along with a children's play area in the woodland walk. Delicious dinners are served in the restaurant and guests are guaranteed a warm welcome at this fine property.

Rooms 10 en suite 5 annexe en suite (4 fmly) (5 GF) S £45-£65; D £100-£140* **Facilities** FTV DVD TVL tea/coffee Dinner available Direct Dial Licensed WiFi ⊗ ≡ 18 ≡ **Conf** Max 24 Thtr 24 Class 24 Board 18 **Parking** 25 **Notes** LB ⊗ Closed 2-23 Jan Civ Wed 25

The Red Lion Food and Rooms
★★★★ ≡ INN

tel: 01263 514964 **Brook St NR27 9HD**
email: info@redlion-cromer.co.uk **web:** www.redlion-cromer.co.uk
dir: *Follow one-way system, pass church on left & take next left into Brook St*

The Red Lion is a charming Victorian inn in an elevated position at the heart of the town centre, overlooking the beach and the sea. The open-plan public areas include a lounge bar, a popular restaurant and sunny conservatory. The spacious bedrooms are tastefully decorated with co-ordinated soft furnishings and include many thoughtful touches.

Rooms 15 en suite (1 fmly) S £62.50-£95; D £115-£180* **Facilities** FTV DVD iPod docking station tea/coffee Dinner available WiFi ≡ **Extras** Honesty box - chocolate, wine, snacks **Parking** 20 **Notes** LB

CROMER *continued*

Shrublands Farm *(TG246393)*

★★★★ 🎗 FARMHOUSE

tel: 01263 579297 **Church St, Northrepps NR27 0AA**
email: youngman@farming.co.uk **web:** www.shrublandsfarm.com
dir: *Exit A149 to Northrepps, through village, past Foundry Arms, cream house 50yds on left*

Expect a warm welcome from the caring host at this delightful 18th-century farmhouse, set in landscaped grounds and surrounded by 300 acres of arable farmland. Public areas include a cosy lounge with a wood-burning stove, and breakfast is served at a communal table in the elegant dining room.

Rooms 2 rms (1 en suite) (1 pri facs) S £60; D £80* **Facilities** FTV DVD TVL tea/coffee WiFi 🔒 **Extras** Speciality toiletries, snacks, confectionery - free **Parking** 5 **Notes** LB ⊗ No Children 12yrs Closed 25-26 Dec 300 acres arable

The White Horse Overstrand

★★★★★ ⬤⬤ INN

tel: 01263 579237 **34 High St, Overstrand NR27 0AB**
email: reservations@whitehorseoverstrand.co.uk **web:** www.whitehorseoverstrand.co.uk
dir: *From A140, before Cromer, turn right into Mill Rd. At bottom right into Station Rd. After 2m, bear left into High St, White Horse on left*

The White Horse Overstrand is a smartly appointed inn ideally situated in the heart of this popular village on the north Norfolk coast. The modern bedrooms are tastefully appointed and equipped with a good range of useful extras. Public rooms include a large open-plan lounge bar with comfortable seating and a relaxed dining area. Cooking is taken seriously here as is reflected in its award of two AA Rosettes.

Rooms 8 en suite (2 fmly) **Facilities** STV TVL tea/coffee Dinner available WiFi Pool table **Parking** 6 **Notes** LB

Homefield Guest House

★★★★ GUEST HOUSE

tel: 01263 837337 **48 Cromer Rd, West Runton NR27 9AD**
email: homefield@hotmail.co.uk **web:** www.homefieldguesthouse.co.uk
dir: *On A149 (coast road) between Sheringham & Cromer*

This large Victorian house was previously owned by the Canon of Cromer and is situated in the peaceful village of West Runton between Cromer and Sheringham. The pleasantly co-ordinated bedrooms have many useful extras. Breakfast, which includes locally sourced produce, is served at individual tables in the smart dining room.

Rooms 6 en suite **Facilities** STV tea/coffee WiFi 🔒 **Parking** 8 **Notes** ⊗ No Children 14yrs

The Sandcliff Guest House

★★★ GUEST HOUSE

tel: 01263 512888 **Runton Rd NR27 9AS**
email: bookings@sandcliffcromer.co.uk **web:** www.sandcliffcromer.co.uk
dir: *500yds W of town centre on A149*

Ideally situated on the seafront just a short walk from the town centre, this guest house offers a large lounge with comfortable seating and a spacious dining room where breakfast is served. The bedrooms are pleasantly decorated, thoughtfully equipped and some have superb sea views.

Rooms 23 rms (17 en suite) (6 pri facs) (10 fmly) (3 GF) S £39-£99; D £39-£99 (room only) **Facilities** FTV TVL tea/coffee WiFi ⬇ 18 🔒 **Parking** 10

Glendale Guest House

★★★ GUEST HOUSE

tel: 01263 513278 **33 Macdonald Rd NR27 9AP**
email: glendalecromer@btconnect.com **web:** www.glendalecromer.co.uk
dir: *A149 (coast road) from Cromer centre, 4th left*

Glendale Guest House is a Victorian property situated in a peaceful side road adjacent to the seafront, just a short walk from the town centre. Bedrooms are pleasantly decorated, well maintained and equipped with a good range of useful extras. Breakfast is served at individual tables in the smart dining room.

Rooms 5 rms (1 en suite) (2 pri facs) S £35-£45; D £70-£90 **Facilities** FTV tea/coffee **Parking** 2 **Notes** LB Closed 17 Oct-14 Apr

| DEREHAM | Map 13 TF91 |

Orchard Cottage

★★★★ BED AND BREAKFAST

tel: 01362 860265 **The Drift, Gressenhall NR20 4EH**
email: walkers.norfolk@btinternet.com **web:** www.walkers-norfolk.co.uk
dir: *2m NE of Dereham. Exit B1146 in Beetley to Gressenhall, right at x-rds into Bittering St, right at x-rds, 2nd right*

Orchard Cottage is an attractive Norfolk flint building situated in the historic village of Gressenhall near Dereham. The comfortable, country style bedrooms are smartly decorated and situated on the ground floor; one of the rooms has a superb wet room. Public rooms include a lounge, a dining room and a study. Dinner is available by arrangement.

Rooms 2 en suite (2 GF) S £51-£57; D £74-£80* **Facilities** FTV Lounge TVL tea/coffee Dinner available WiFi 🔒 **Parking** 2 **Notes** LB ⊗ ⬤

| DOWNHAM MARKET | Map 12 TF60 |

Crosskeys Riverside House

★★★★ BED AND BREAKFAST

tel: 01366 387777 **Bridge St, Hilgay PE38 0LD**
email: crosskeyshouse@aol.com **web:** www.crosskeys.info
dir: *2m S of Downham Market. Off A10 into Hilgay, Crosskeys on bridge*

Situated in the small village of Hilgay, in its own grounds on the banks of the River Wissey, this former coaching inn offers comfortable accommodation that includes a number of four-poster bedrooms; all rooms have river views, as well as CD players and free WiFi. Public rooms include a dining room with oak beams and an inglenook fireplace.

Rooms 4 en suite (1 fmly) (2 GF) S £45-£60; D £70-£75* **Facilities** FTV DVD Lounge tea/coffee WiFi Fishing 🔒 Rowing boat for guests use **Extras** Flowers, champagne - chargeable **Parking** 10

EDGEFIELD
Map 13 TG03

Mount Farm Barn Bed & Breakfast

★★★★ GUEST ACCOMMODATION

tel: 01263 585069 **NR24 2AE**
email: david@mountfarmbarn.co.uk **web:** www.mountfarmbarn.co.uk

Just on the outskirts of the pretty village of Holt this sympathetically converted 15th-century barn offers guests high quality accommodation in a peaceful rural setting. The bedrooms overlook the lovely Norfolk countryside; they are beautifully presented and most comfortable. The award-winning breakfast is not to be missed, and all guests are made to feel welcome, often with tea and home-made cake on arrival. This is an ideal location from which to explore north Norfolk and its coastline. Ample secure parking is available, along with WiFi.

Rooms 2 en suite (2 fmly) S £80-£110; D £95-£125* **Facilities** FTV DVD TVL tea/coffee WiFi **Extras** Fridge, fresh milk **Parking** 4 **Notes** ⊗

GORLESTON ON SEA
Map 13 TG50

Avalon

★★★★ GUEST ACCOMMODATION

tel: 01493 662114 **54 Clarence Rd NR31 6DR**
email: avalon.hotel@btinternet.com **web:** www.avalon-gorleston.co.uk
dir: *A12 past James Paget Hospital. Take 2nd exit at rdbt towards Gorleston. Next rdbt 2nd exit, 1st right*

This Edwardian terraced house is just a short walk from the promenade and beach. Breakfast is served in the smart dining. Service is both helpful and friendly. Bedrooms are pleasantly appointed, thoughtfully equipped and well furnished.

Rooms 10 en suite (6 fmly) (1 GF) **Facilities** FTV tea/coffee Dinner available WiFi **Notes** ⊗

GREAT ELLINGHAM
Map 13 TM09

Aldercarr Hall

★★★★ GUEST ACCOMMODATION

tel: 01953 455766 & 07710 752213 **Attleborough Rd NR17 1LQ**
email: bedandbreakfast@aldercarr-limited.com **web:** www.aldercarrhall.co.uk
dir: *On B1077 500yds SE of village*

Aldercarr Hall is set in extensive grounds and surrounded by open countryside on the edge of Great Ellingham. Public rooms include a comfortably appointed conservatory and a delightful dining room where breakfast is served around a large table. The excellent facilities include a health, beauty and hairdressing studio, an indoor swimming pool, a jacuzzi and a large function suite.

Rooms 3 annexe en suite (1 fmly) (3 GF) **Facilities** FTV TVL tea/coffee WiFi ⊗ ⅄ 18 Fishing Riding Sauna Pool table ⌗ **Parking** 200 **Notes** LB

GREAT MOULTON
Map 13 TM19

South Norfolk Guest House

★★★★ GUEST HOUSE

tel: 01379 677359 & 07885 351212 **Frith Way NR15 2HE**
email: info@sngh.co.uk **web:** www.southnorfolkguesthouse.co.uk
dir: *From A140 (N), in Long Stratton turn left at 1st set of lights. Through Wacton, pass sign to Coronation Hall on right. 1st property on right in Great Moulton, past house, turn right & right again*

This former village school enjoys a peaceful rural location yet is only a short drive from Norwich. A warm welcome is guaranteed from the friendly proprietors and bedrooms are all most comfortable. Ample secure parking is available for guests along with free WiFi. Delicious hot breakfasts are served in the conservatory breakfast room.

Rooms 9 en suite S £38-£66; D £57-£76* **Facilities** FTV DVD Lounge tea/coffee Dinner available WiFi ⌗ **Parking** 14 **Notes** LB

GREAT RYBURGH
Map 13 TF92

The Blue Boar Inn

★★★ ⊜ INN

tel: 01328 829212 **5 Station Rd NR21 0DX**
email: blueboarinnryburgh@gmail.com **web:** www.blueboar-norfolk.co.uk

Built in 1635, The Blue Boar has been in the heart of village life in Great Ryburgh for over three centuries. The cosy wood-beamed bar has an original inglenook fireplace and guests are guaranteed a warm welcome. Bedrooms are all comfortable, attractively presented and well equipped. The Blue Boar has been sympathetically restored in recent years and the restaurant serves an extensive choice of imaginative dishes using the best in local produce. Hearty breakfasts are cooked to order. Secure parking and free WiFi are available for guests.

Rooms 6 rms **Facilities** FTV tea/coffee Dinner available WiFi **Parking** 40

GREAT YARMOUTH
Map 13 TG50

The Classic Lodge

★★★★ BED AND BREAKFAST

tel: 01493 852851 **13 Euston Rd NR30 1DY**
email: classiclodge@uwclub.net **web:** www.classiclodge.com
dir: *A12 to A47, follow signs for seafront. Turn left at Sainsbury's, ahead at lights 200mtrs on right, 100mtrs from seafront*

The Classic Lodge is an impressive Victorian villa situated just a short stroll from the seafront and town centre. Breakfast is served at individual tables in the large lounge-dining room, and the spacious bedrooms are carefully furnished and equipped with a good range of facilities. Secure parking is provided at the rear of the property.

Rooms 3 en suite S £30-£50; D £55-£60* **Facilities** FTV TVL tea/coffee WiFi **Parking** 5 **Notes** LB ⊗ No Children 18yrs Closed Nov-Mar ⊜

GREAT YARMOUTH *continued*

Marine Lodge

★★★★ 🛏 GUEST ACCOMMODATION

tel: 01493 331120 **19-20 Euston Rd NR30 1DY**
email: res@marinelodge.co.uk **web:** www.marinelodge.co.uk
dir: *Follow signs for seafront, 300mtrs N of Britannia Pier*

This establishment's enviable seafront position has panoramic views of the bowling greens and beach, and is within easy walking distance of Britannia Pier. Bright, modern bedrooms are complemented by smart public areas that include a bar area where light snacks are available during the evening. Guests also have complimentary use of the indoor swimming pool at the sister Palm Court Hotel.

Rooms 40 en suite (5 fmly) (5 GF) **Facilities** FTV TVL tea/coffee Dinner available Lift Licensed WiFi **Conf** Thtr 50 Class 35 Board 25 **Parking** 38 **Notes** ⊗

Swiss Cottage Bed and Breakfast

★★★★ GUEST ACCOMMODATION

tel: 01493 855742 & 07986 399857 **31 North Dr NR30 4EW**
email: info@swiss-cottage.info **web:** www.swisscottagebedandbreakfast.co.uk
dir: *0.5m N of town centre. Exit A47 or A12 to seafront, 750yds N of pier. Left at Britannia Pier. Swiss Cottage on left opposite Water Gardens*

Swiss Cottage Bed and Breakfast is a charming detached property situated in a peaceful part of town overlooking the Venetian waterways and the sea beyond. The comfortable bedrooms are pleasantly decorated with co-ordinated fabrics and have many useful extras. Breakfast is served in the smart dining room and guests have use of an open-plan lounge area.

Rooms 8 en suite 1 annexe en suite (2 GF) S £45-£55; D £74-£95* **Facilities** FTV Lounge tea/coffee WiFi 🍴 **Extras** Speciality toiletries **Parking** 9 **Notes** LB No Children 16yrs Closed Nov-Feb

All Seasons Guest House

★★★★ GUEST HOUSE

tel: 01493 852713 & 07543 036475 **10 Nelson Road South NR30 3JL**
email: mpilgrimmcd@hotmail.co.uk **web:** www.allseasons-guesthouse.co.uk
dir: *Enter Great Yarmouth on A47, at rdbt 2nd exit onto A149 for 0.3m. Next rdbt 3rd exit onto B1141 for 0.4m. Left into Queens Rd, after 0.2m left into Nelson Rd*

All Seasons Guest House is smartly presented and family-run enjoying an ideal location close to the seafront and the historic South Quay area. A warm welcome is guaranteed and the freshly cooked breakfasts are not to be missed. There is a good range of comfortable well-appointed bedrooms available. Free WiFi is available and there is ample on-street parking.

Rooms 8 en suite (1 GF) **Facilities** FTV DVD TVL tea/coffee WiFi 🍴 **Extras** Snacks - complimentary **Notes** LB ⊗

The Chequers

★★★★ GUEST HOUSE

tel: 01493 853091 **27 Nelson Road South NR30 3JA**
email: mitchellsatchequers@hotmail.co.uk **web:** www.thechequersguesthouse.co.uk
dir: *Exit A47 signed seafront, right into Marine Parade & Kings Rd, 1st right*

Guests will receive a warm welcome from the caring hosts at this privately-run establishment, situated just a short walk from Wellington Pier and the beach. Public rooms include a cosy bar, residents' lounge and a smart dining room. Bedrooms are cheerfully decorated and have many thoughtful touches.

Rooms 8 rms (7 en suite) (1 pri facs) (2 fmly) **Facilities** FTV TVL tea/coffee Dinner available Licensed WiFi **Notes** ⊗

The Hamilton

★★★★ GUEST HOUSE

tel: 01493 844662 **23-24 North Dr NR30 4EW**
email: enquiries@hamilton-hotel.co.uk **web:** www.hamilton-hotel.co.uk

Overlooking the beach with fantastic views of the sea, this property is ideally situated for the theatre, tourist attractions, town centre and Yarmouth Racecourse. Public rooms include a smart lounge bar with plush leather seating, a breakfast room and a residents' lounge with comfy sofas. Bedrooms are bright and airy with many thoughtful touches; most rooms have lovely sea views.

Rooms 21 en suite (4 fmly) (2 GF) **Facilities** FTV TVL tea/coffee Dinner available Licensed WiFi ⛳ 18 **Conf** Max 40 Thtr 40 Class 26 Board 26 **Parking** 20 **Notes** LB ⊗

The Winchester

★★★★ 🛏 GUEST ACCOMMODATION

tel: 01493 843950 & 07807 733161 **12 Euston Rd NR30 1DY**
email: enquiries@winchesterprivatehotel.com **web:** www.winchesterprivatehotel.com
dir: *A12 onto A47, signs for seafront, left at Sainsbury's over lights, premises 400yds on right*

A warm welcome is assured from the friendly hosts at The Winchester, just off the seafront. The pleasant bedrooms vary in size and style and are thoughtfully equipped. Public rooms include a large lower ground-floor dining room, a small conservatory and a foyer with comfortable sofas.

Rooms 14 en suite (2 fmly) (5 GF) S £30-£40; D £60-£80* **Facilities** FTV TVL tea/coffee Dinner available WiFi 🍴 **Parking** 10 **Notes** LB ⊗ No Children 12yrs Closed Dec-Jan RS Oct-Etr No evening meals 🛏

Senglea Lodge

★★★ GUEST ACCOMMODATION

tel: 01493 859632 & 07775 698819 **7 Euston Rd NR30 1DX**
email: senglealodge@fsmail.net **web:** www.senglealodge.com
dir: *From A4 straight over 1st 2 rdbts. At lights left towards seafront. Through next lights, Lodge on right*

Senglea Lodge is a delightful terrace property situated just off the seafront and very close to the town centre. Bedrooms are pleasantly decorated, have co-ordinated soft furnishings and a good range of useful extras. Breakfast is served at individual tables in the smart open-plan lounge/dining room.

Rooms 6 rms (4 en suite) (2 fmly) (2 smoking) S £25; D £50* **Facilities** FTV TVL tea/coffee WiFi ⌚ **Notes** LB ⊗ Closed 23 Dec-2 Jan

Haydee

★★★ GUEST HOUSE

tel: 01493 844580 **27 Princes Rd NR30 2DG**
email: info@haydee.co.uk **web:** www.haydee.co.uk
dir: *Exit A47 to seafront, Princes Rd opposite Britannia Pier*

The Haydee is in a side road just a stroll from the seafront, pier and town centre. The pleasant bedrooms vary in size and style, and all are well equipped. Breakfast is served in the smart dining room and there is a cosy lounge bar.

Rooms 8 en suite (2 fmly) (2 smoking) S £25-£28; D £50-£56* **Facilities** FTV DVD TVL tea/coffee Licensed WiFi ⌚ **Notes** LB ⊗

Silverstone House

★★★ GUEST ACCOMMODATION

tel: 01493 844862 **29 Wellesley Rd NR30 1EY**
email: silverstonehouse@yahoo.co.uk **web:** www.silverstone-house.co.uk
dir: *A47 into Great Yarmouth. Over 2 rdbts, left at lights signed seafront. Over next lights, turn left*

A warm welcome is guaranteed at this family-run property. Silverstone House is conveniently located close to the seafront and a short walk to the main shopping district. This four-storey Victorian terraced house has nine well-appointed, comfortable bedrooms. Freshly prepared hot breakfasts are served to individual tables in the charming breakfast room.

Rooms 9 en suite (4 fmly) (1 GF) (4 smoking) S £25-£30; D £45-£55 **Facilities** FTV tea/coffee WiFi **Extras** Mini-fridge - complimentary **Notes** LB ⊗

Victoria

★★★ GUEST ACCOMMODATION

tel: 01493 843872 & 842132 **2 Kings Rd NR30 3JW**
email: booking@hotelvictoria.org.uk **web:** www.hotelvictoria.org.uk
dir: *Off seafront, opposite model village*

The Victoria is a large detached property situated just off the seafront close to Wellington Pier and the town centre. Bedrooms come in a variety of sizes and styles; each one is pleasantly decorated and thoughtfully equipped. Dinner and breakfast are served in the open-plan lounge/dining room. There is also a smart outdoor swimming pool.

Rooms 35 en suite 10 annexe en suite (13 fmly) (2 GF) **Facilities** FTV DVD TVL tea/coffee Dinner available Lift Licensed WiFi ⌇ Pool table ⌚ **Conf** Max 50 Thtr 50 Class 50 Board 30 **Parking** 20 **Notes** LB ⊗

Heath Farmhouse

★★★★ BED AND BREAKFAST

tel: 01986 788417 **Homersfield IP20 0EX**
email: julia.john.hunt@googlemail.com
dir: *A143 onto B1062 towards Flixton, over bridge past Suffolk sign, 2nd farm entrance on left at AA sign*

This charming 16th-century farmhouse is set amid attractive landscaped grounds that include a croquet lawn. The property retains much of its original character with exposed beams, open fireplaces and wood-burning stoves. The pleasant bedrooms are carefully furnished and have many thoughtful touches. Breakfast is served in the smart dining room overlooking the garden.

Rooms 2 rms (1 fmly) S £40; D £70* **Facilities** Lounge TVL tea/coffee WiFi ⌣ ⌚ Table tennis **Extras** Mineral water **Parking** 8 **Notes** ⊗ ⌘

**AA FRIENDLIEST B&B
OF THE YEAR 2016-2017**

The Old Bakery B&B

★★★★ ⌃ ⌂ BED AND BREAKFAST

tel: 01263 862802 & 07771 391967 **34 The Street NR20 5DF**
email: mike@theoldbakerynorfolk.co.uk **web:** www.theoldbakerynorfolk.co.uk
dir: *From A148 exit at Little Snoring signed Fulmodeston, follow signs to Hindolveston. At next junct continue for 1.3m, house on corner of turn to Foulsham*

The Old Bakery B&B is a delightful detached property which was originally the village bakery and dates back to the 17th century. The spacious, well-equipped bedrooms have pine furniture and many thoughtful touches. Breakfast, which includes fresh local ingredients, is served at a large communal table in the smart dining room. Guests have the use of a comfortable lounge with leather sofas and a log fire.

Rooms 2 en suite S £55-£65; D £70-£85* **Facilities** FTV DVD iPod docking station tea/coffee Dinner available WiFi ⌣ ⌚ **Extras** Cakes on arrival - complimentary; fridge **Parking** 4 **Notes** LB ⊗ No Children ⌘

HOLT
Map 13 TG03

The Lawns
★★★★★ ⚙ RESTAURANT WITH ROOMS

tel: 01263 713390 **26 Station Rd NR25 6BS**
email: info@lawnshotelholt.co.uk **web:** www.lawnshotelholt.co.uk
dir: A148 (Cromer road). 0.25m from Holt rdbt, turn left, 400yds along Station Rd

The Lawns is a superb Georgian house situated in the centre of this delightful north Norfolk market town. The open-plan public areas include a large wine bar, a conservatory and a smart restaurant. The spacious bedrooms are tastefully appointed with co-ordinated soft furnishings and have many thoughtful touches.

Rooms 8 en suite 2 annexe en suite (2 GF) S £85-£145; D £85-£145* **Facilities** FTV DVD TVL tea/coffee Dinner available WiFi **Extras** Speciality toiletries **Conf** Max 20 Thtr 20 Class 12 **Parking** 18

The Feathers
★★★★ INN

tel: 01263 712318 **6 Market Place NR25 6BW**
email: enquiries@thefeathershotel.com **web:** www.thefeathershotel.com

This former coaching inn enjoys a prominent position in the heart of this pretty village. Bedrooms vary in size but all are well equipped and comfortable. The bar, with its real fire, is extremely popular with locals and the dinner menu offers an extensive choice.

Rooms 13 en suite (2 fmly) **Facilities** FTV Lounge Dinner available Direct Dial WiFi ⚲ 18 ♨ **Conf** Max 100 Thtr 100 Class 80 Board 80 **Parking** 15

Holm Oaks
★★★★ GUEST HOUSE

tel: 01263 711061 & 07778 600600 **83a Cromer Rd NR25 6DY**
email: holmoaks@btinternet.com **web:** www.holmoaksatholt.co.uk

Holm Oaks enjoys a very convenient location on the outskirts of the Georgian village of Holt. The four bedrooms are all attractively presented and free WiFi is available throughout the house. Breakfast is served at individual tables in the conservatory, which overlooks the landscaped gardens. Secure parking is available. This makes an ideal base from which to explore beautiful north Norfolk.

Rooms 4 en suite (4 GF) **Facilities** FTV DVD Lounge tea/coffee WiFi **Parking** 5 **Notes** LB No Children

HORNING
Map 13 TG31

Innkeeper's Lodge Norfolk Broads, Horning
★★★ INN

tel: 08451 551551 (Calls cost 2p per minute plus your phone company's access charge) **10 Lower St NR12 8AA**
email: info@innkeeperslodge.com **web:** www.innkeeperslodge.com

At Innkeeper's Lodge you'll find accommodation with comfort and character in equal measure, and everything needed for a relaxing stay, from easy check-in and free parking to complimentary breakfast and a cosy pub serving great value food and drink on the doorstep. Each Lodge has quality rooms, and there are Lodges in a variety of locations from towns and cities to countryside settings across the UK.

Rooms 8 en suite (3 fmly) **Facilities** FTV tea/coffee Dinner available WiFi **Parking** **Notes** ⊗

HUNSTANTON
Map 12 TF64

The Neptune Restaurant with Rooms
★★★★ ⚙⚙⚙ RESTAURANT WITH ROOMS

tel: 01485 532122 **85 Old Hunstanton Rd, Old Hunstanton PE36 6HZ**
email: reservations@theneptune.co.uk **web:** www.theneptune.co.uk
dir: On A149, past Hunstanton, 200mtrs on left after post office

This charming 18th-century coaching inn, now a restaurant with rooms, is ideally situated for touring the Norfolk coastline. The smartly appointed bedrooms are brightly finished with co-ordinated fabrics and hand-made New England furniture. Public rooms feature white clapboard walls, polished dark wood floors, fresh flowers and Lloyd Loom furniture. Obviously, the food is very much a draw here with the carefully prepared, award-winning cuisine using excellent local produce; from oysters and mussels from Thornham to quinces grown on a neighbouring farm.

Rooms 5 en suite S £150-£185; D £220-£275* (incl.dinner) **Facilities** FTV tea/coffee Dinner available Direct Dial WiFi ♨ **Parking** 6 **Notes** ⊗ No Children 10yrs Closed 2wks Nov & 3wks Jan RS Oct-Apr closed Mon No coaches

Gemini Lodge Guest House
★★★★ GUEST ACCOMMODATION

tel: 01485 533902 **5 Alexandra Rd PE36 5BT**
web: www.geminilodgehunstanton.co.uk

Gemini Lodge Guest House is in an elevated position close to the centre of town and seafront. The bedrooms are smartly decorated in neutral colours with lovely co-ordinated soft furnishings and fabrics; some rooms have lovely views of the sea. Public rooms include a smart lounge with plush sofas, and breakfast is served at a large communal table in the contemporary dining room.

Rooms 3 en suite **Facilities** FTV TVL tea/coffee **Parking** 3 **Notes** No Children ⚙

The King William IV Country Inn & Restaurant
★★★★ ⚘ INN

tel: 01485 571765 **Heacham Rd, Sedgeford PE36 5LU**
email: info@thekingwilliamsedgeford.co.uk **web:** www.thekingwilliamsedgeford.co.uk
dir: A149 to Hunstanton, right at Norfolk Lavender in Heacham onto B1454, signed Docking. 2m to Sedgeford

Tucked away in the village of Sedgeford, close to Norfolk's beautiful coast line, The King William IV Country Inn & Restaurant is a family-run inn that has been welcoming travellers and locals since 1836. The menu offers classic dishes, complemented by daily specials and seasonal offerings, and guests can enjoy a drink outside in summer months. Bedrooms are full of character and offer a comfortable stay.

Rooms 9 en suite (4 fmly) S £70-£80; D £100-£125* **Facilities** Lounge tea/coffee Dinner available WiFi ⚲ 18 ♨ **Extras** Speciality toiletries **Parking** 60 **Notes** LB No coaches

The White Cottage
★★★ GUEST ACCOMMODATION

tel: 01485 532380 **19 Wodehouse Rd PE36 6JW**

A charming cottage situated in a quiet side road in Old Hunstanton, The White Cottage has been owned and run by Mrs Burton for 30 years. The spacious bedrooms are attractively decorated, and some have lovely sea views. Dinner is served in the smart dining room and there is a cosy sitting room with a television.

Rooms 3 rms (1 en suite) (1 pri facs) S £30-£40* **Facilities** TVL tea/coffee Dinner available WiFi ♨ **Parking** 4 **Notes** LB No Children 10yrs ⚙

Old Marine Inn

★★★ INN

tel: 01485 533310 **10 St Edmunds Ter PE36 5EH**
email: administrator@marinebar.demon.co.uk **web:** www.marinehotelhunstanton.com

Situated in the centre of Hunstanton, some rooms benefit from sea views, and all generally provide good levels of comfort. A range of dining options are available with either a bar meal in the Marine bar below or for something more special in the Steak and Stilton Restaurant, which offers a good range of à la carte dishes.

Rooms 10 rms D £60-£70 (room only)* **Facilities** FTV TV9B tea/coffee Dinner available WiFi ⅃ **Parking** 10

KING'S LYNN Map 12 TF62

Linden Bed & Breakfast

★★★★ ⏚ BED AND BREAKFAST

tel: 01485 609198 & 07867 686216 **Station Rd PE31 6DE**
email: info@lindenbedandbreakfast.co.uk **web:** www.lindenbedandbreakfast.co.uk
dir: From A148 onto B1153 signed Congham, 200mtrs on left before St Mary's church

In a modern house, Linden Bed & Breakfast offers three individual, well-appointed en suite bedrooms along with a spacious guest lounge, a pretty garden overlooking the Norfolk countryside and a family-style breakfast/dining room. In the warmer months, cream teas are available and light suppers can also be arranged with prior notice.

Rooms 3 en suite S £55-£63; D £70-£85* **Facilities** FTV iPod docking station TVL tea/coffee WiFi ⏚ **Extras** Speciality toiletries - complimentary **Parking** 5 **Notes** ⊗ No Children 12yrs

---

LITCHAM Map 13 TF81

Bramley

★★★★ BED AND BREAKFAST

tel: 01328 701592 & 07778 783412 **Weasenham Rd PE32 2QT**
email: bramleybandb@hotmail.co.uk **web:** www.bramley-litcham.co.uk
dir: A1065 onto B1145. Left at x-rds, left at school, 4th house on left

A warm welcome awaits at Bramley, a delightful detached house, set in a peaceful location on the fringe of the village, with ample safe parking in generous grounds. The mostly spacious bedrooms are thoughtfully furnished to ensure guest comfort and have smartly appointed en suite shower rooms. A hearty, freshly-cooked breakfast is served at individual tables in the separate, elegant dining room.

Rooms 4 en suite (1 fmly) S £35-£45; D £65-£80* **Facilities** FTV tea/coffee WiFi ⏚ **Parking** 4 **Notes** LB ⊗ ⊜

LITTLE PLUMSTEAD Map 13 TG31

Wayside B&B

★★★★ BED AND BREAKFAST

tel: 01603 721827 & 07769 655682 **Honeycombe Rd NR13 5HY**
email: info@littleplumsteadbedandbreakfast.com
web: www.littleplumsteadbedandbreakfast.com
dir: From A47 follow signs for Little Plumstead & Witton. At x-rds in Little Plumstead into Honeycombe Rd, immediately on left

Wayside B&B is a charming house conveniently located close to Norwich and the Norfolk Broads and is set in the pretty village of Little Plumstead. Bedrooms are comfortable and very well equipped. Guests can relax on the terrace, and the

continental breakfast offer a very good choice. Free WiFi is available along with secure parking.

Rooms 3 en suite 3 annexe en suite (2 fmly) (4 GF) S £44-£49; D £59-£69 **Facilities** FTV TVL tea/coffee WiFi ⏚ **Conf** Max 8 Board 8 **Parking** 6

LODDON Map 13 TM39

The Loddon Swan

★★★★ ⊛ INN

tel: 01508 528039 **23 Church Plain NR14 6LX**
email: info@theloddonswan.co.uk **web:** www.theloddonswan.co.uk
dir: A146 exit signed High Bungay Rd. Follow road into Loddon High St

The Loddon Swan is situated in the centre of Loddon, just a minute's walk from the River Chet. This popular 18th-century inn offers modern accommodation. Dinner is available in the attractive restaurant overlooking a patio garden, and guests can enjoy viewing the gallery of original artwork. Good use is made of seasonal and local produce in some innovative and enjoyable dishes.

Rooms 4 annexe en suite (2 GF) D £90-£125* **Facilities** FTV tea/coffee Dinner available WiFi Pool table **Conf** Max 30 Thtr 30 Class 20 Board 20 **Parking** 20 **Notes** No coaches

NORTH WALSHAM — Map 13 TG23

Scarborough Hill Country Inn

★★★★ ⊜ INN

tel: 01692 402151 **Old Yarmouth Rd NR28 9NA**
email: reservations@scarboroughhillcountryinn.co.uk
web: www.scarboroughhillcountryinn.co.uk

Set in five acres of landscaped gardens, Scarborough Hill Country Inn enjoys a quiet rural setting a short drive from the historic village of North Walsham. The inn offers a range of individually styled well-appointed bedrooms. The charming bar has several local ales, a good wine list and guests can relax by the log fire on colder evenings. Dinner is served in the conservatory restaurant and there is an extensive menu with a strong emphasis on local produce. WiFi is available and there is ample secure parking.

Rooms 8 en suite 1 annexe en suite (1 fmly) (1 GF) **Facilities** FTV DVD TVL tea/coffee Dinner available Direct Dial WiFi 🐾 ⬧ **Extras** Speciality toiletries, hand-made fudge **Conf** Max 80 Thtr 60 Class 50 Board 22 **Parking** 50 **Notes** No coaches Civ Wed 70

NORWICH — Map 13 TG20

Premier Collection

Brasteds

★★★★★ ⑩⑩ ⬛ RESTAURANT WITH ROOMS

tel: 01508 491112 **Manor Farm Barns, Fox Rd, Framingham Pigot NR14 7PZ**
email: enquiries@brasteds.co.uk **web:** www.brasteds.co.uk
dir: A11 onto A47 towards Great Yarmouth, then A146. 0.5m, right into Fox Rd, 0.5m on left

Brasteds is a lovely detached property set in 20 acres of mature, landscaped parkland on the outskirts of Norwich. The tastefully appointed bedrooms have beautiful soft furnishings and fabrics along with comfortable seating and many thoughtful touches. Public rooms include a cosy snug with plush sofas, and a smart dining room where breakfast is served. Dinner is available in Brasteds Restaurant, which can be found in an adjacent building.

Rooms 6 en suite (1 fmly) (3 GF) **Facilities** FTV DVD iPod docking station TVL tea/coffee Dinner available Direct Dial WiFi ⬧ **Extras** Mini-bar **Conf** Max 120 Thtr 120 Class 100 Board 40 **Parking** 50 **Notes** LB No coaches Civ Wed 160

Premier Collection

38 St Giles

★★★★★ ⬛ GUEST ACCOMMODATION

tel: 01603 662944 & 07492 050098 **38 Saint Giles St NR2 1LL**
web: www.38stgiles.co.uk

38 St Giles is a stunning Georgian, Grade II listed building that is situated in the centre of Norwich and offers boutique accommodation. All rooms are en suite and have benefited from recent refurbishment. Each contains high quality furnishings, including Bang and Olufsen televisions, and free WiFi. Guests are welcomed with home-made cake on arrival, and breakfast offers a wide selection of locally sourced and organic products.

Rooms 8 en suite (1 fmly) (1 GF) S £95–£110; D £140–£240 **Facilities** FTV Lounge tea/coffee WiFi **Extras** Speciality toiletries, home-made cakes, flowers **Parking** 3 **Notes** ⊗

Gothic House Bed & Breakfast

★★★★ ⬛ BED AND BREAKFAST

tel: 01603 631879 **King's Head Yard, Magdalen St NR3 1JE**
email: charvey649@aol.com **web:** www.gothic-house-norwich.com
dir: Follow signs for A147, exit at rdbt past flyover into Whitefriars. Right into Fishergate, at end, right into Magdalen St

Gothic House Bed & Breakfast is an elegant Grade II listed Regency town house set in a quiet courtyard in the heart of Norwich. The property retains much of its original character and the spacious bedrooms are individually decorated and have many thoughtful touches. Breakfast, which includes locally sourced produce, is served in the elegant dining room.

Rooms 2 rms (2 pri facs) S £65; D £95 **Facilities** STV FTV tea/coffee WiFi ⬧ **Extras** Speciality toiletries **Parking** 2 **Notes** ⊗ No Children 18yrs Closed Feb ⊛

The Old Rectory

★★★★ ⑩⑩ RESTAURANT WITH ROOMS

tel: 01603 700772 **103 Yarmouth Rd, Thorpe St Andrew NR7 0HF**
email: enquiries@oldrectorynorwich.com **web:** www.oldrectorynorwich.com
dir: From A47 southern bypass onto A1042 towards Norwich N & E. Left at slip road onto A1042. Follow signs to "All routes" & Thorpe St Andrew, at mini rdbt left onto A1242. Straight on at lights, entrance on right

This delightful Grade II listed Georgian property is ideally located in a peaceful area overlooking the River Yare, just a few minutes' drive from the city centre. Spacious bedrooms are individually designed with carefully chosen soft fabrics, plush furniture and many thoughtful touches; many of the rooms overlook the swimming pool and landscaped gardens. Accomplished cooking is offered via an interesting daily-changing menu, which features skilfully prepared local produce.

Rooms 5 en suite 3 annexe en suite S £85–£150; D £125–£180* **Facilities** FTV iPod docking station Lounge tea/coffee Dinner available Direct Dial WiFi 🐾 ⬧ **Extras** Robes, speciality toiletries **Conf** Max 14 Thtr 14 Class 10 Board 14 **Parking** 12 **Notes** LB ⊗ Closed 22 Dec-3 Jan RS Sun-Mon No dinner served No coaches

Old Thorn Barn

★★★★ GUEST ACCOMMODATION

tel: 01953 607785 & 07894 203208 **Corporation Farm, Wymondham Rd, Hethel NR14 8EU**
email: enquiries@oldthornbarn.co.uk **web:** www.oldthornbarn.co.uk
dir: 6m SW of Norwich. Follow signs for Lotus Cars from A11 or B1113, on Wymondham Rd

Old Thorn Barn is a delightful Grade II listed barn situated in a peaceful rural location just a short drive from the city centre. The property has stylish, thoughtfully equipped bedrooms with polished wood floors and antique pine furniture. Breakfast is served in the open-plan barn, which also has a wood-burning stove and a cosy lounge area.

Rooms 5 en suite 2 annexe en suite (7 GF) S £38-£42; D £68-£72 **Facilities** FTV TVL tea/coffee WiFi 🔒 **Parking** 14 **Notes** ⊗

Cringleford Guest House

★★★★ GUEST HOUSE

tel: 01603 451349 & 07775 725933 **1 Gurney Ln, Cringleford NR4 7SB**
email: robandkate@cringlefordguesthouse.co.uk **web:** www.cringlefordguesthouse.co.uk
dir: From A11 & A47 Thickthorn rdbt follow signs to Norwich, 0.25m slip road to Cringleford, left at junct into Colney Ln. Gurney Ln 5th on right

Cringleford Guest House is a delightful property, situated just a short drive from the hospital, University of East Anglia and major roads. The pleasant, well-equipped bedrooms have co-ordinated fabrics and pine furniture. Breakfast is served at individual tables in the smart dining room.

Rooms 5 en suite 1 annexe en suite (3 fmly) (1 GF) S £70-£85; D £110-£130* **Facilities** FTV DVD TVL tea/coffee WiFi 🔒 **Conf** Max 10 Thtr 10 Class 10 Board 10 **Parking** 6 **Notes** LB ⊗

Church Farm

★★★★ GUEST ACCOMMODATION

tel: 01603 898020 & 898582 **Church St, Horsford NR10 3DB**
email: churchfarmgh@aol.com **web:** www.churchfarmgh.co.uk
dir: 5m NW of city centre. A140 onto B1149, right at x-rds

Church Farm is set in a peaceful rural location just a short drive from Norwich airport and the city centre. The spacious bedrooms are smartly decorated, pleasantly furnished and have many considerate extras. Breakfast is served at individual tables in the conservatory-style lounge-dining room, which overlooks the garden and sun terrace.

Rooms 10 en suite (1 fmly) (3 GF) **Facilities** FTV TVL tea/coffee WiFi **Parking** 20 **Notes** ⊗

Salhouse Lodge Inn

★★★★ INN

tel: 01603 782828 **Vicarage Rd, Salhouse NR13 6HD**
web: www.salhouselodge.co.uk
dir: From A1042 (ring road), NE of Norwich centre, exit at lights into Salhouse Rd signed New Rackheath. Through New Rackheath to Salhouse. Left onto B1140 signed Wroxham. Right in Vicarage Rd at sign for inn

Situated on the outskirts of Norwich, this former rectory has extensive gardens and enjoys a peaceful rural location close to the Norfolk Broads. All the bedrooms are of a high standard and are very well equipped. Evening meals are served available and the log fire really comes into its own on cooler evenings.

Rooms 7 en suite (2 fmly) **Facilities** FTV tea/coffee Dinner available WiFi ⛳ 18 Pool table 🔒 **Parking** 50 **Notes** LB

Innkeeper's Lodge Norwich

★★★ INN

tel: 08451 551551 *(Calls cost 2p per minute plus your phone company's access charge)*
18-22 Yarmouth Rd NR7 0EF
email: info@innkeeperslodge.com **web:** www.innkeeperslodge.com

Ideally located close to the beautiful city of Norwich, with its medieval architecture, and the Norfolk Broads, this Innkeeper's Lodge has 14 well appointed bedrooms. All are attractively presented and well-equipped, and free WiFi is available. Set beside the banks of the River Yare the large garden is a pleasant place in the warmer months. There is a very popular restaurant and the lounge is spacious and comfortable.

Rooms 14 en suite (5 fmly) **Facilities** FTV tea/coffee Dinner available WiFi **Parking** 16 **Notes** ⊗

SHERINGHAM	Map 13 TG14

See also Cromer

Premier Collection

The Eiders Bed & Breakfast

★★★★★ BED AND BREAKFAST

tel: 01263 837280 **Holt Rd, Aylmerton NR11 8QA**
email: enquiries@eiders.co.uk **web:** www.eiders.co.uk
dir: From Cromer on A148, enter Aylmerton, pass garage on left. After x-rds, 2nd entrance on right

The Eiders Bed & Breakfast is just a short drive from the centre of Sheringham and is ideally placed for touring the north Norfolk coast. The tastefully appointed bedrooms have lovely co-ordinated fabrics and many extras. Breakfast is served at individual tables in the conservatory which overlooks the gardens and a duck pond. Guests have the use of a heated swimming pool which is open from May to September.

Rooms 6 en suite (2 fmly) (6 GF) S £60-£95; D £100-£140* **Facilities** FTV DVD iPod docking station TVL tea/coffee WiFi ⛳ 🔒 **Extras** Bottled water - complimentary **Parking** 7 **Notes** LB ⊗

Roman Camp Inn

★★★★ INN

tel: 01263 838291 **Holt Rd, Aylmerton NR11 8QD**
email: enquiries@romancampinn.co.uk **web:** www.romancampinn.co.uk
dir: On A148 between Sheringham & Cromer, approx 1.5m from Cromer

Roman Camp Inn provides spacious, tastefully appointed bedrooms with a good range of useful facilities including hairdryers. Five rooms are presented as deluxe, and two are suitable for disabled guests. Public rooms include a smart conservatory-style restaurant, a comfortable open-plan lounge/bar and a dining area. Room service is available, guests have complimentary use of local leisure facilities, and there is ample free parking.

Rooms 15 en suite (1 fmly) (10 GF) S fr £75; D £110-£140* **Facilities** FTV Lounge tea/coffee Dinner available Direct Dial WiFi Free use of nearby leisure complex & pool **Conf** Max 20 Thtr 20 Class 20 Board 20 **Parking** 50 **Notes** LB ⊗ Closed 25-26 Dec

The Old Barn

★★★★ 🅰 BED AND BREAKFAST

tel: 01263 838285 **Cromer Rd, West Runton NR27 9QT**
email: mkelliott2@aol.com **web:** www.theoldbarnnorfolk.co.uk
dir: A149 from Cromer to West Runton, 2m opposite church

The Old Barn is a charming property situated in the picturesque village of West Runton, just a short drive from Sheringham. There is a smart dining room and a superb beamed drawing room. The attractive bedrooms are carefully furnished and thoughtfully equipped.

Rooms 3 rms (2 en suite) (1 pri facs) (1 GF) **Facilities** FTV DVD iPod docking station TVL tea/coffee WiFi **Parking** 6 **Notes** ⊗ No Children 18yrs

SHERINGHAM *continued*

Bay Leaf Guest House

★★★ GUEST HOUSE

tel: 01263 823779 **10 St Peters Rd NR26 8QY**
email: bayleafgh@aol.com **web:** www.bayleafbandb.co.uk
dir: *A149 Cromer road into Station Rd. 1st left into Station Approach, 2nd right into St Peters Rd*

This lovely Victorian property is ideally situated just a short walk from the golf course, steam railway and town centre. There is a smart lounge bar, and breakfast is served in the conservatory-dining room which overlooks the patio. Bedrooms vary in size and style, all are comfortable.

Rooms 7 en suite (2 fmly) (2 GF) S £50-£55; D £64-£76 **Facilities** FTV tea/coffee Licensed **Parking** 5 **Notes** LB ⊗ No Children 8yrs ⊛

SNETTISHAM   Map 12 TF63

The Rose & Crown

★★★★ ⊛ INN

tel: 01485 541382 **Old Church Rd PE31 7LX**
email: info@roseandcrownsnettisham.co.uk **web:** www.roseandcrownsnettisham.co.uk
dir: *A149 towards Hunstanton. In village centre into Old Church Rd, 100yds on left*

This lovely village inn provides comfortable, well-equipped bedrooms. A range of quality meals is served in the many dining areas, complemented by a good variety of real ales and wines. Service is friendly and a delightful atmosphere prevails. A walled garden is available on sunny days, as is a children's play area.

Rooms 16 en suite (4 fmly) (2 GF) S £100-£120; D £120-£140* **Facilities** FTV Lounge tea/coffee Dinner available WiFi ⊛ **Extras** Speciality toiletries, milk, home-made biscuits **Conf** Max 80 **Parking** 60 **Notes** LB No coaches

Queen Victoria

★★★ INN

tel: 01485 541344 **19 Lynn Rd PE31 7LW**
email: info@orchardaccountancy.co.uk **web:** www.queenvictoriasnettisham.com

The Queen Victoria is located in the coastal village of Snettisham, close to the beach, not far from Sandringham. Comfortable accommodation is provided to the rear of the property, and guests can enjoy an evening meal with a good range of cask ales in this traditional inn. In warmer months guests can relax with a drink on the outside on the terrace, while the children play in the playground with a pirate ship and magic tree.

Rooms 5 rms **Facilities** Dinner available

STALHAM   Map 13 TG32

The Ingham Swan

★★★★★ ⊛⊛ RESTAURANT WITH ROOMS

tel: 01692 581099 **Sea Palling Rd, Ingham NR12 9AB**
email: info@theinghamswan.co.uk **web:** www.theinghamswan.co.uk
dir: *From A149 Stalham, into Old Market Rd towards Upper Staithe Rd/Lower Staithe Rd. At rdbt 1st exit, 2nd exit at next rdbt into Ingham Rd. Continue to Town Rd*

The Swan is a charming 14th-century former coaching inn that has been sympathetically restored and enjoys a peaceful rural location in the heart of Norfolk. Stylish, very well equipped bedrooms are most comfortable and the eye-catching original features really add to the presentation. The award-winning restaurant serves the best of Norfolk produce and there is a small bar area for pre-dinner drinks. Secure parking is available along with free WiFi for guests.

Rooms 4 annexe en suite (2 fmly) (2 GF) **Facilities** FTV tea/coffee Dinner available WiFi **Parking** 12 **Notes** ⊗ Closed 25-26 Dec

THORPE MARKET   Map 13 TG23

Premier Collection

The Green House B&B

★★★★★ ⊛ ⊜ GUEST ACCOMMODATION

tel: 01263 834701 & 07786 195213 **Cromer Rd NR11 8TH**
email: greenhouse.norfolk@btinternet.com **web:** www.greenhousenorfolk.co.uk
dir: *A140 in village of Roughton, right at mini rdbt into Thorpe Market Rd. After 1.5m turn right at x-rds, 200yds on left*

Situated only four miles away from both Cromer and the beach, a very warm welcome is offered by Rosanna and Simon who have both worked at various top hotels in London. This 16th-century property has been carefully modernised throughout, offering high quality and comfort. Plenty of care has been taken to retain period pieces of the property. Dinner can be pre-arranged and a comfortable lounge and bar area is also available for guests to relax. An attractive garden is also available for guests to use during summer months.

Rooms 5 en suite S £80-£99; D £80-£99* **Facilities** FTV DVD iPod docking station Lounge tea/coffee Dinner available Licensed WiFi ⅃ 18 ⊛ **Extras** Speciality toiletries, sweets - free **Parking** 6 **Notes** No Children 14yrs

The Barns at Thorpe Market

★★★★ ⊜ GUEST ACCOMMODATION

tel: 01263 833033 **Common Ln NR11 8TP**
email: info@bedbreakfastnorfolk.com **web:** www.bedbreakfastnorfolk.com
dir: *A140 at Roughton onto B1436. At end turn right onto A149, onto slip road just past bus stop*

This charming 18th-century converted barn offers a range of beautifully presented bedrooms overlooking a central courtyard. The bedrooms are spacious and very comfortable, and original flint walls are a real feature of the property. Thorpe Market is a short drive from Norwich and is close to the Norfolk Broads as well as a number of National Trust properties. Breakfast is served in the vaulted breakfast room, and features the best in local produce. WiFi is available for guests along with secure bike storage.

Rooms 3 en suite (3 GF) S £75-£85; D £80-£90* **Facilities** FTV tea/coffee WiFi ⊛ **Parking** 3 **Notes** ⊗ No Children 14yrs

THURSFORD
Map 13 TF93

Premier Collection

Holly Lodge

★★★★★ ⚬ ⚬ BED AND BREAKFAST

tel: 01328 878465 **The Street NR21 0AS**
email: info@hollylodgeguesthouse.co.uk **web:** www.hollylodgeguesthouse.co.uk
dir: Exit A148 into Thursford (village green on left) 2nd driveway on left past green

Holly Lodge is an award-winning 18th-century property situated in a picturesque location surrounded by open farmland. The stylish cottage bedrooms are in a converted stable block, each room individually decorated, beautifully furnished and equipped with many useful extras. The attractive public rooms have a wealth of character, with flagstone floors, oak beams and open fireplaces. There are superb landscaped grounds to enjoy.

Rooms 3 en suite (3 GF) S £80-£110; D £100-£130 **Facilities** FTV DVD Lounge TVL tea/coffee Dinner available WiFi ⚬ **Extras** Speciality toiletries, wine, home-made cakes - free **Parking** 5 **Notes** LB ⊗ No Children 14yrs

The Old Forge Seafood Restaurant

★★★ ⚬ RESTAURANT WITH ROOMS

tel: 01328 878345 **Fakenham Rd NR21 0BD**
email: sarah.goldspink@btconnect.com **web:** www.seafoodnorthnorfolk.co.uk
dir: On A148 (Fakenham to Holt road)

Expect a warm welcome at this delightfully relaxed restaurant with rooms. The open-plan public areas include a lounge bar with comfy sofas, and an intimate restaurant with pine tables. Bedrooms are pleasantly decorated and equipped with a good range of useful facilities.

Rooms 3 en suite S £35-£65; D £65-£80* **Facilities** STV FTV Lounge tea/coffee Dinner available WiFi Riding ⚬ **Parking** 14 **Notes** No Children 10yrs No coaches

TIVETSHALL ST MARGARET
Map 13 TM18

Red House Farm Bed & Breakfast

★★★★ BED AND BREAKFAST

tel: 01379 676566 & 07719 437007 **Station Rd NR15 2DJ**
email: office@redhousefarm.info **web:** www.redhousefarm.info
dir: 500mtrs from Pulham rdbt A140

A warm welcome is assured at this delightful 17th-century barn conversion, situated on a small working farm in a peaceful rural location. The tastefully appointed bedrooms have modern furniture and lovely countryside views. Breakfast, which includes home-grown produce, is served at a large communal table in the smart kitchen.

Rooms 2 en suite 2 annexe en suite (4 GF) S £40-£50; D £70-£80* **Facilities** FTV tea/coffee WiFi **Parking** 4 **Notes** ⊗

WELLS-NEXT-THE-SEA
Map 13 TF94

Kilcoroon

★★★★ BED AND BREAKFAST

tel: 01328 710270 & 07733 112108 **Chancery Ln NR23 1ER**
email: terry@kilcoroon.co.uk **web:** www.kilcoroon.co.uk
dir: Exit B1105 into Mill Rd. 3rd right into Buttlands. Property on left of Crown Hotel

Kilcoroon is a delightful, detached period property situated by the green, just off the Buttlands and a short walk from the town centre. The spacious bedrooms are pleasantly decorated with co-ordinated fabrics and equipped with modern facilities. Breakfast is served at a communal table in the elegant dining room.

Rooms 2 en suite S £70-£75; D £90 **Facilities** FTV DVD tea/coffee WiFi ⚬ **Notes** ⊗ No Children 10yrs Closed 23-31 Dec ⊛

WESTON LONGVILLE
Map 13 TG11

The Parson Woodforde

★★★★ ⚬ INN

tel: 01603 881675 **Church St NR9 5JU**
email: info@theparsonwoodforde.com **web:** www.theparsonwoodforde.com

This is a delightful inn ideally situated just a couple of miles from the A47 in the centre of a historic village; the property has a wealth of features including oak beams and open fireplaces which create a welcoming atmosphere. The smartly appointed bedrooms are modern and well equipped with a good range of facilities; public rooms include a large open plan bar, a restaurant and outside terraces.

Rooms 5 en suite (1 fmly) S £75-£85; D £85-£145* **Facilities** FTV DVD iPod docking station tea/coffee Dinner available WiFi ⚬ 27 **Extras** Bottled water - complimentary **Conf** Max 50 **Parking** 40 **Notes** Closed 2-15 Jan

WIVETON
Map 13 TG04

Wiveton Bell

★★★★ ⚬ INN

tel: 01263 740101 **The Green, Blakeney Rd NR25 7TL**
email: wivetonbell@me.com **web:** www.wivetonbell.com
dir: 1m from Blakeney

Wiveton Bell is situated in a quiet and scenic part of Norfolk. The luxurious bedrooms come complete with a whole host of accessories including flat-screen TVs, Blu-ray/DVD players, complimentary Prosecco, REN toiletries, and Egyptian cotton linens with duck and goose down bedding. Hampers containing continental breakfasts are delivered to the rooms, including fresh pastries from the local baker, and every room has outside seating. Dinner can be taken in the AA Rosette award-winning restaurant and good use is made of fresh and local ingredients.

Rooms 6 en suite (2 GF) D £90-£160* **Facilities** FTV DVD tea/coffee Dinner available WiFi ⚬ 18 **Extras** Prosecco, speciality toiletries - free **Parking** 60 **Notes** No Children Closed 25 Dec No coaches

---

WRENINGHAM   Map 13 TM19

The Bird In Hand

★★★★ ▲ INN

---

tel: 01508 489438 **Church Rd NR16 1BJ**
email: mail@davidbrake.co.uk **web:** www.birdinhandwreningham.com
dir: *S of Norwich on B1113*

The Bird In Hand is a family run free house and restaurant combining all the atmosphere of a traditional British pub with quality food and drink and comfortable surroundings. You are guaranteed a friendly welcome from the whole team who always work hard to ensure your experience is an enjoyable one. There is a large parking area, indoor and outdoor seating areas, restaurant, bar area and above all a friendly atmosphere.

Rooms 8 annexe en suite (8 GF) S £80; D £80 (room only)* **Facilities** FTV tea/coffee Dinner available WiFi **Extras** Speciality toiletries, mineral water **Conf** Max 60 Thtr 60 Class 60 Board 30 **Parking** 90 **Notes** ⊗

WROXHAM   Map 13 TG31

Delaware

★★★★ BED AND BREAKFAST

---

tel: 01603 781947 & 07805 023249 **Tunstead Rd, Hoveton NR12 8QN**
email: eilidh_villa@hotmail.co.uk **web:** www.delawarewroxham.co.uk
dir: *Into Wroxham on A1151, turn left into Horning Rd, then right into Tunstead Rd*

A charming, family-run B&B that is conveniently located close to the centre of Wroxham and the splendid Norfolk Broads. Norwich is a short drive away and Delaware makes an ideal base from which to explore the lovely county of Norfolk. Bedrooms are all comfortable, and freshly cooked breakfasts are served at individual tables. Parking is available, along with free WiFi for guests.

Rooms 3 rms (2 en suite) (1 pri facs) (1 GF) **Facilities** FTV tea/coffee WiFi ॐ **Extras** Sweets **Parking** 4 **Notes** LB ⊗ No Children 14yrs Closed Dec-Mar ☻

NORTHAMPTONSHIRE

ASHBY ST LEDGERS   Map 11 SP56

Olde Coach House

★★★★ ⊜ INN

tel: 01788 890349 **Main St CV23 8UN**
email: info@oldecoachhouse.co.uk **web:** www.oldecoachhouse.co.uk
dir: *M1 junct 18 onto A428. Follow signs for Daventry (A361), Ashby St Ledgers signed on left*

The Olde Coach House is a delightful old building, offering public areas in keeping with period, but with all the modern amenities expected by today's guests. There is

a large bar and a spacious raised dining area, with open fires and exposed beams. The accommodation is smartly presented; rooms vary in size but all are equipped to the same high standard with flat-screen TVs, iPod docking stations and wonderfully comfortable beds. The property benefits from excellent parking and outside areas for dining and drinking.

Olde Coach House

Rooms 4 en suite 11 annexe en suite (6 GF) S £75-£85; D £75-£95* **Facilities** FTV iPod docking station Lounge tea/coffee Dinner available Direct Dial WiFi ॐ 18 **Extras** Robes, speciality toiletries, snacks **Parking** 30

DESBOROUGH   Map 11 SP88

The R Inn

★★★ INN

---

tel: 01536 648050 & 763510 **11-15 Station Rd NN14 2RL**
email: enquiries@ketteringvenues.co.uk **web:** www.desboroughhotel.co.uk

The R Inn enjoys a prominent position in the peaceful village of Desborough which is located in the heart of the lovely Ise Valley. There is a popular tapas bar along with well-equipped conference facilities, and a selection of stylish bedrooms that have been refurbished to a high standard. Secure parking is available along with free WiFi for guests.

Rooms 13 en suite (2 fmly) **Facilities** FTV tea/coffee Dinner available WiFi ॐ **Conf** Max 600 Thtr 400 Class 300 Board 50 **Parking** 40 **Notes** ⊗ Civ Wed 600

EASTON-ON-THE-HILL   Map 11 TF00

The Exeter Arms

★★★★ ⊜ INN

---

tel: 01780 756321 **21 Stamford Rd PE9 3NS**
email: reservations@theexeterarms.net **web:** www.theexeterarms.net
dir: *A1 Nbound take exit signed Easton-on-the-Hill; A1 Sbound take exit signed A47/A43 Corby/Kettering, on left entering village*

This lovely village inn is situated in north-eastern Northamptonshire just a short drive from Stamford. The public rooms have many original features such as stone walls and open fireplaces; they include a lounge bar and the Orangery Restaurant which opens out onto the terrace for alfresco dining. The modern, well-equipped bedrooms are very stylish.

Rooms 5 en suite 1 annexe en suite (2 fmly) **Facilities** FTV tea/coffee Dinner available Direct Dial WiFi ॐ 18 **Parking** 40

ISLIP
Map 11 SP97

The Woolpack Inn Islip
★★★ ⊜ INN

tel: 01832 732578 6 Kettering Rd NN14 3JU
email: darren-harding@sky.com web: www.thewoolpackinnislip.co.uk
dir: A14 junct 12, right at rdbt, down hill, on left

The Woolpack Inn enjoys a prominent position close to the River Nene on the edge of the pretty village of Islip. This popular inn has been refurbished to a very high standard and has a charming bar that serves a good choice of local ales and craft beers, along with an extensive wine list. The restaurant has a real sense of style, as well as an extensive menu and a dinner that is not to be missed. Bedrooms are all comfortable and very well equipped. Free WiFi is available, along with secure parking.

Rooms 10 en suite (10 GF) Facilities FTV TVL tea/coffee Dinner available WiFi Pool table Parking 20

NASSINGTON
Map 12 TL09

The Queens Head Inn
★★★★ ⊛ INN

tel: 01780 784006 54 Station Rd PE8 6QB
email: info@queensheadnassington.co.uk web: www.queensheadnassington.co.uk
dir: A1 Nbound exit junct 17, follow signs for Yarwell, then Nassington. Queens Head on left on entering the village

The Queens Head Inn offers a friendly atmosphere and a warm welcome, situated on the banks of the River Nene in the picturesque village of Nassington. The adjacent bedrooms are constructed from local stone; each one is smartly appointed and well equipped. Public rooms include a smart lounge bar, a restaurant and a light-filled conservatory dining room.

Rooms 10 en suite (2 fmly) (10 GF) S £65-£145; D £75-£155 Facilities FTV tea/coffee Dinner available Direct Dial WiFi Fishing ⚓ Extras Home-made biscuits Conf Max 50 Thtr 50 Class 20 Board 20 Parking 45 Notes LB Civ Wed 70

NORTHAMPTON
Map 11 SP76

The Hopping Hare
★★★★ ⊛ INN

tel: 01604 580090 18 Hopping Hill Gardens, Duston NN5 6PF
email: info@hoppinghare.com web: www.hoppinghare.com
dir: Off A428, 2m from centre of Northampton

Situated in a quiet location just two miles away from Northampton city centre, this inn provides luxury accommodation meeting the needs of holidaymakers and business travellers. Rooms have been attractively decorated with high quality soft furnishings, flat-screen TVs and free WiFi. Dinner can be enjoyed in the restaurant where the food has been awarded an AA Rosette. A very good selection of dishes is available, with good use made of fresh quality ingredients sourced by local suppliers.

Rooms 20 en suite (8 fmly) (1 GF) Facilities FTV tea/coffee Dinner available Direct Dial WiFi Parking 40 Notes No coaches

WEEDON
Map 11 SP65

Narrow Boat at Weedon
★★★★ ⊛⊛ INN

tel: 01327 340333 Stowe Hill, A5 Watling St NN7 4RZ
email: info@narrowboatatweedon.co.uk web: www.narrowboatatweedon.co.uk
dir: M1 junct 16 follow signs to Flore & Weedon. In Weedon at x-rds turn left up hill, on left

The Narrow Boat at Weedon has a superb location beside the Grand Union Canal, just off the A5. Close to both Milton Keynes and Northampton, it makes an ideal location for those wishing to visit Silverstone and the Althorp Estate. There are seven very comfortable en suite bedrooms at the rear of the property, each with external access. Modern British cuisine and traditional pub classics can be enjoyed in both the bar and the restaurant, which has been awarded two AA Rosettes, or out on the heated decking area in the garden by the canal, weather permitting of course.

Rooms 7 annexe en suite (7 GF) Facilities FTV DVD tea/coffee Dinner available WiFi Conf Max 30 Class 30 Board 30 Parking 40

NORTHUMBERLAND

ALNWICK
Map 21 NU11

The Hogs Head Inn
★★★ ⊜ INN

tel: 01665 606576 Hawfinch Dr, Cawledge NE66 2BF
email: info@hogsheadinnalnwick.co.uk web: www.hogsheadinnalnwick.co.uk
dir: A1 to Alnwick, follow signs for Cawledge Park

Named after the inn featured in the Harry Potter books, the Hogs Head opened in July 2012. It is ideally located just off the A1, on the edge of Alnwick close to the castle and gardens. It offers comfortable, spacious and well-equipped bedrooms, and WiFi throughout the whole property. The bar and restaurant serve tasty dishes in comfortable, informal surroundings. This purpose-built inn also offers external seating and dining.

Rooms 53 en suite (9 fmly) (25 GF) Facilities FTV Lounge TVL tea/coffee Dinner available Lift WiFi ⅃ 18 Parking 125

BEADNELL
Map 21 NU23

The Craster Arms
★★★★ INN

tel: 01665 720272 & 07958 678280 The Wynding NE67 5AX
email: michael@crasterarms.co.uk web: www.crasterarms.co.uk
dir: From A1 junct at Brownieside Head East, through Preston and Chathill to Beadnell

Parts of The Craster Arms date back to the 15th century. The property has it all – open fire, beer garden and spacious well-appointed, comfortable bedrooms. The bar serves real ales along with good quality food using local produce and offers generous portion sizes. Well located in the peaceful village of Beadnell and just a short drive to the beach, Seahouses and Bamburgh with world famous Craster kippers available for breakfast.

Rooms 3 en suite (2 fmly) (1 GF) Facilities FTV TVL tea/coffee Dinner available WiFi ⅃ 18 Riding Pool table Parking 20

BELFORD
Map 21 NU13

Premier Collection

Market Cross Guest House

★★★★★ 🛎 🖤 GUEST HOUSE

tel: 01668 213013 & 07595 453208 **1 Church St NE70 7LS**
email: info@marketcrossbelford.co.uk **web:** www.marketcrossbelford.co.uk
dir: *Exit A1 into village, opposite church*

Market Cross Guest House goes from strength to strength; the owners have added their own personal slant to the property. Comfortable bedrooms have a whole array of personal touches including Nespresso machines, home baking and mini-fridges. Dinner by prior arrangement is wonderful and comes highly recommended, but ensure space is left for the great breakfast in the morning.

Rooms 4 en suite S £60-£100; D £80-£110 **Facilities** FTV DVD iPod docking station tea/coffee Dinner available WiFi 🔒 **Extras** Home-made snacks, mini-fridge, robes **Parking** 4 **Notes** ⊗ No Children 10yrs Closed 23-28 Dec

Purdy Lodge

★★★★ GUEST ACCOMMODATION

tel: 01668 213000 **Adderstone Services NE70 7JU**
email: reception@purdylodge.co.uk **web:** www.purdylodge.co.uk
dir: *A1 onto B1341 then immediately left*

Purdy Lodge is located just off the A1 with Alnwick, Seahouses and Bamburgh all within easy striking distance. This comfortable accommodation has a bar and restaurant along with a 24 hour café for those late arrivals. This family-run business offers warm Northumbrian hospitality and good customer care.

Rooms 20 en suite (7 fmly) (10 GF) S £63.95-£93.95; D £71.95-£101.95 **Facilities** FTV tea/coffee Dinner available Direct Dial Licensed WiFi 🔒 **Parking** 60 **Notes** Closed 25 Dec

BERWICK-UPON-TWEED
Map 21 NT95

The Rob Roy Inn

★★★★ INN

tel: 01289 306428 **Dock Rd, Tweedmouth TD15 2BE**
email: therobroy@hotmail.co.uk **web:** www.robroyberwick.co.uk

The Rob Roy Inn enjoys views over the Tweed estuary and across to the historical border town of Berwick-upon-Tweed, this family-run inn offers high standards of accommodation. The small bar is warm and welcoming and well used by guests and locals alike. Dinner (residents only) is served in the Harbour Lights Restaurant, and offers good quality food and great value for money. The town centre is only a five minute walk whilst Spittle beach and promenade is just ten minutes in the opposite direction.

Rooms 5 en suite

Lindisfarne Inn

★★★ INN

tel: 01289 381223 **Beal TD15 2PD**
email: enquiries@lindisfarneinn.co.uk **web:** www.lindisfarneinn.co.uk
dir: *Exit A1 for Holy Island*

The Lindisfarne Inn stands on the site of the old Plough Hotel at Beal, on the road leading to Holy Island. The inn has a traditional bar, rustic-style restaurant and comfortably equipped, courtyard bedrooms in the adjacent wing. Food is available all day.

Rooms 23 annexe en suite (20 fmly) (11 GF) **Facilities** FTV TVL tea/coffee Dinner available WiFi 🔒 **Parking** 25

BLYTH
Map 21 NZ38

The Commissioners Quay Inn

[U]

tel: 07929 509899 **Quay Rd NE24 3AF**
email: sean@inncollectiongroup.com **web:** www.commissionersquayinn.com

Currently the rating for this establishment is not confirmed. This may be due to a change of ownership or because it has only recently joined the AA rating scheme.

Rooms 40 en suite (10 fmly) (10 GF) S £60-£150; D £85-£250* **Facilities** FTV tea/coffee Dinner available Lift Licensed WiFi 🔒 **Parking** 90

CHATTON
Map 21 NU02

Percy Arms

★★★★ 🛎 🖤 INN

tel: 01668 215244 **Main St NE66 5PS**
email: percyarmschatton@gmail.com **web:** www.percyarmschatton.co.uk
dir: *From A1 onto B6348 signed Chatton, on Main Rd*

The Percy Arms is ideally located in the tranquil village of Chatton just a short drive from the A1. Alnwick, Seahouses, Bamburgh and Holy Island are all easily accessible, as are some wonderful beaches on the Northumbrian coastline. Refurbished to a very high standard, bedrooms and their en suites are luxurious and comfortable. The pub boasts a number of local real ales and offers a warm welcome. The decor is sympathetic to the age and style of the building, and there is a good mix of locals and residents. The food is good, with the relaxed menu making the best of what local suppliers have to offer.

Rooms 5 en suite (3 fmly) S £75-£180; D £75-£180* **Facilities** FTV TVL tea/coffee Dinner available Direct Dial WiFi ⅃ 18 🔒 **Extras** Robes **Conf** Max 40 Thtr 40 Class 40 Board 40 **Parking** 30 **Notes** LB Civ Wed 60

CRAMLINGTON
Map 21 NZ27

Innkeeper's Lodge Cramlington

★★★ INN

tel: 08451 551551 *(Calls cost 2p per minute plus your phone company's access charge)*
Blagdon Ln NE23 8AU
email: info@innkeeperslodge.com **web:** www.innkeeperslodge.com

At Innkeeper's Lodge you'll find accommodation with comfort and character in equal measure, and everything needed for a relaxing stay, from easy check-in and free parking to complimentary breakfast and a cosy pub serving great value food and drink on the doorstep. Each Lodge has quality rooms, and there are Lodges in a variety of locations from towns and cities to countryside settings across the UK.

Rooms 18 en suite (4 fmly) (10 GF) **Facilities** FTV tea/coffee Dinner available Direct Dial WiFi **Parking** 50 **Notes** ⊗

FALSTONE
Map 21 NY78

Pheasant Inn

★★★★ ⚱ 🍽 INN

tel: 01434 240382 **Stannersburn NE48 1DD**
email: stay@thepheasantinn.com **web:** www.thepheasantinn.com
dir: *From A69 (N of Hexham) take A6079 signed Otterburn & Bellingham. Left onto B6320 signed Bellingham. Before Bellingham follow Hesleyside sign, then signs for Kielder & Stannersburn*

The Pheasant Inn epitomises the traditional, charming country inn; it has character, good food and warm hospitality. Bright modern bedrooms, some with their own entrances, can all be found in stone buildings adjoining the inn. Delicious home-cooked meals are served in the bar with its low-beamed ceilings and exposed stone walls, or in the attractive dining room.

Rooms 8 annexe en suite (1 fmly) (5 GF) S fr £70; D fr £99* **Facilities** tea/coffee Dinner available WiFi ch fac ⚗ 18 🔒 **Extras** Speciality toiletries **Parking** 40 **Notes** LB Closed 4 days Xmas RS Nov-Mar closed Mon & Tue No coaches

The Blackcock Country Inn and Restaurant

★★★★ INN

tel: 01434 240200 **NE48 1AA**
email: thebcinn@yahoo.co.uk **web:** www.blackcockinn.co.uk
dir: *From Hexham take A6079 to Bellingham, then left at church. In village centre, towards Kielder Water*

This traditional, family-run village inn lies close to Kielder Water. A cosy pub, it has a homely atmosphere, with welcoming fires burning in the colder weather. The bedrooms are very comfortable and well equipped; evening meals are served here or in the restaurant. The inn is closed during the day on Wednesdays in winter.

Rooms 6 rms (4 en suite) (2 pri facs) (1 fmly) **Facilities** STV TVL tea/coffee Dinner available WiFi Fishing Riding Pool table 🔒 Children's play area Clay pigeon shooting **Extras** Robes, chocolates; pet menus - charged **Parking** 15 **Notes** LB RS Tue-Wed closed during low season

FELTON
Map 21 NU10

Birchwood House

★★★★ ⚱ GUEST ACCOMMODATION

tel: 01670 787828 **Kitswell Dene NE65 9NZ**
email: gbblewitt@btinternet.com **web:** www.birchwood-house.co.uk
dir: *Just off A1. Take 2nd Swarland exit, bear left, left again*

Ideally located for the A1, this spacious house combines very high standards of accommodation with warmth and great hospitality. Modern bedrooms and en suites cater well for the needs of the guest, and a fantastic large lounge is also made available. A well-cooked breakfast will set you up for your day regardless of your planned activities.

Rooms 3 en suite (3 GF) S £50-£55; D £70-£75* **Facilities** FTV iPod docking station TVL tea/coffee WiFi **Parking** 20 **Notes** ⊗ No Children 14yrs

FORD
Map 21 NT93

The Estate House

★★★★ GUEST HOUSE

tel: 01890 820668 & 07436 266951 **TD15 2PX**
email: admin@theestatehouse.info **web:** www.theestatehouse.info
dir: *1m from A697, follow signs to Ford on B6354*

Located in the heart of peaceful Ford village, this Edwardian house is set in its own mature gardens. A pet-friendly house that offers spacious, well-appointed accommodation with well-dressed and comfortable beds. A guests' lounge is available and during the day, the property runs a popular tea room. A wonderful base from which to tour this area of Northumberland.

Rooms 4 rms (3 en suite) (1 pri facs) (1 fmly) S £55-£75; D £60-£85* **Facilities** FTV DVD iPod docking station TVL tea/coffee Dinner available Licensed WiFi ch fac ⚗ Fishing 🔒 **Extras** Bottled water - complimentary

HAYDON BRIDGE
Map 21 NY86

Old Repeater Station

★★★★ BED AND BREAKFAST

tel: 01434 688668 & 07941 238641 **Military Rd, Grindon NE47 6NQ**
email: les.gibson@tiscali.co.uk **web:** www.hadrians-wall-bedandbreakfast.co.uk
dir: *See website for directions*

The Old Repeater Station started life out as one of a number of buildings used as Repeater Stations for British Telecom on their Newcastle to Carlisle line. Now converted into a bed and breakfast it enjoys an enviable location roughly half way along the world famous Hadrian's Wall. The Old Repeater Station offers simple practical accommodation, an ideal stop off point for people walking the wall or for guests looking to explore this historic area. Dinner by arrangement for walkers and cyclists with drying room facilities available. Family-style breakfast uses quality locally sourced produce. A comfortable lounge is available, as well as seating in the garden overlooking Sewingshield Crags.

Rooms 4 en suite (1 fmly) (2 GF) S £55-£57.50; D £65-£69* **Facilities** FTV TVL tea/coffee Dinner available Licensed WiFi 🔒 **Parking** 4 **Notes** Closed Nov-Feb

LONGFRAMLINGTON
Map 21 NU10

The Granby Inn
★★★ ⇔ INN

tel: 01665 570228 & 570362 **NE65 8DP**
email: info@thegranbyinn.co.uk **web:** www.thegranbyinn.co.uk
dir: Off A1 onto A697 signed Coldstream. On right in Longframlington

The Granby Inn is a traditional, family-run coaching inn dating back over 250 years, situated in the heart of the village. Bedrooms are comfortable and some have wonderful views right to the coast. Food is a real strength here and the team take great pride in their locally sourced produce. The bar is welcoming and reservations to eat are always recommended.

Rooms 5 en suite **Facilities** FTV DVD tea/coffee Dinner available Direct Dial WiFi ⊘
🔒 **Parking** 24 **Notes** LB ⊗ Closed 25-26 Dec, 1 Jan

MORPETH
Map 21 NZ28

Premier Collection

St Mary's Inn
★★★★★ 🍷 ⇔ INN

tel: 01670 293293 **St Mary's Ln, St Mary's Park NE61 6BL**
email: hello@stmarysinn.co.uk **web:** www.stmarysinn.co.uk
dir: In Stannington, into Church Rd, continue for 2.25m

St Mary's Inn is built on the site of St Mary's Hospital which was the county's asylum until 1996, located close to the village of Stannington just off the A1. The oak bar boasts an array of beers including a custom-made St Mary's Ale from the local Wylam Brewery. Bedrooms are bright and spacious with wonderfully comfortable beds, while the en suites are spacious with quality fixtures and fittings. Food is a highlight of the stay, with produce locally sourced and passionately prepared. Log-burning fires add to the character and charm of this location.

Rooms 11 en suite (1 fmly) **Facilities** FTV tea/coffee Dinner available Direct Dial Lift WiFi ♿ 18 🔒 **Conf** Max 18 Board 18 **Parking** 60 **Notes** No coaches

NEWTON-ON-THE-MOOR
Map 21 NU10

The Cook and Barker Inn
★★★★ ⇔ INN

tel: 01665 575234 **NE65 9JY**
email: info@cookandbarkerinn.co.uk **web:** www.cookandbarkerinn.co.uk
dir: North on A1, pass Morpeth. A1 becomes single carriageway for 8m, then dual carriageway. Up slight incline 3m, follow signs on left to Newton-on-the-Moor

Set in the heart of a quiet village, this inn is popular with visitors and locals. The emphasis is on food here with interesting home-made dishes offered in the restaurant and bar areas. Bedrooms are smartly furnished and well equipped, and are split between the main house and the adjacent annexe.

Rooms 4 en suite 14 annexe en suite (2 fmly) (7 GF) **Facilities** FTV tea/coffee Dinner available Direct Dial WiFi **Conf** Max 50 Thtr 50 Class 50 Board 25 **Parking** 64 **Notes** ⊗

SEAHOUSES
Map 21 NU23

The Olde Ship Inn
★★★★ ⇔ INN

tel: 01665 720200 **NE68 7RD**
email: theoldeship@seahouses.co.uk **web:** www.seahouses.co.uk
dir: Lower end of main street above harbour

Under the same ownership since 1910, this friendly inn overlooks the harbour and is full of character. Lovingly maintained, its sense of history is evident by the amount of nautical memorabilia on display. Public areas include a character bar, cosy snug, restaurant and guests' lounge. The individual bedrooms are smartly presented. Two separate buildings contain executive apartments, all with sea views.

Rooms 12 en suite 6 annexe en suite (4 GF) S £47; D £94-£130* **Facilities** FTV Lounge TVL tea/coffee Dinner available Direct Dial WiFi Pool table 🔒 **Parking** 18 **Notes** LB ⊗ No Children 10yrs Closed Dec-Jan No coaches

Bamburgh Castle Inn
★★★ INN

tel: 01665 720283 **NE68 7SQ**
email: enquiries@bamburghcastleinn.co.uk **web:** www.bamburghcastleinn.co.uk
dir: A1 onto B1341 to Bamburgh, B1340 to Seahouses, follow signs to harbour

Situated in a prime location on the quayside, this establishment has arguably the best view along the coast. Dating back to the 18th century, the inn has superb dining and bar areas, with outside seating available in warmer weather. There are smart, comfortable bedrooms, many with views of the Farne Islands and the inn's famous namesake, Bamburgh Castle.

Rooms 33 en suite (6 fmly) (8 GF) **Facilities** FTV TVL tea/coffee Dinner available WiFi ♿ 18 🔒 **Parking** 35 **Notes** LB

STOCKSFIELD
Map 21 NZ06

Premier Collection

The Duke of Wellington Inn

★★★★★ ⚬ ⚬ INN

tel: 01661 844446 **Newton NE43 7UL**
email: info@thedukeofwellingtoninn.co.uk **web:** www.thedukeofwellingtoninn.co.uk
dir: Off A69, follow signs to Newton, 3m from Corbridge

Set in the peaceful village of Newton in the Tyne Valley, the Duke of Wellington Inn is reputedly one of Northumberland's oldest pubs. Located close to Corbridge, in Hadrian's Wall country, not far from Newcastle and just minutes from the A69, the inn offers high standards of accommodation, food and hospitality. Generous sized bedrooms have quality beds, bedding and branded toiletries, with every small detail taken care of. The busy bar and restaurant make great used of the best local produce. Terraces outside allow the guest to make the best of the fine weather.

Rooms 7 en suite S £85-£100; D £95-£140* **Facilities** FTV DVD iPod docking station tea/coffee Dinner available Direct Dial WiFi ⚓ 36 Sauna ⚓ **Extras** Speciality toiletries **Parking** 30 **Notes** No coaches

THROPTON
Map 21 NU00

The Three Wheat Heads

★★★★ ⚬ INN

tel: 01669 620262 **NE65 7LR**
email: info@threewheatheads.co.uk **web:** www.threewheatheads.co.uk

The Three Wheat Heads is located on the edge of the Northumberland National Park just a few miles from Rothbury. All bedrooms are decorated to a high standard, and most offer picture-postcard views of the local countryside. Good food is served in a choice of areas with a beer garden to the rear also available.

Rooms 5 en suite (1 fmly) **Facilities** FTV tea/coffee Dinner available WiFi ⚓ 18 Fishing ⚓ **Parking** 14

NOTTINGHAMSHIRE

COTGRAVE
Map 11 SK63

Jerico Farm (SK654307)

★★★★ ⚬ FARMHOUSE

tel: 01949 81733 **Fosse Way NG12 3HG**
email: info@jericofarm.co.uk **web:** www.jericofarm.co.uk
dir: Off A46, signed Kinoulton. N of junct with A606

A friendly relaxed atmosphere is offered at Jerico Farm, an attractive building, which stands in the beautiful Nottinghamshire countryside just off the A46, close to Nottingham, Trent Bridge and the National Water Sports Centre. Day rooms include a comfortable lounge, and a separate dining room in which substantial, tasty breakfasts are served overlooking the gardens. Spacious bedrooms are individually appointed and thoughtfully equipped.

Rooms 3 en suite (1 fmly) **Facilities** FTV TVL tea/coffee WiFi Fishing **Extras** Speciality toiletries **Parking** 4 **Notes** ⊗ No Children 10yrs Closed 24 Dec-2 Jan 150 acres mixed

EASTWOOD
Map 11 SK44

The Sun Inn

★★★ INN

tel: 01773 712940 **6 Derby Rd NG16 3NT**
web: www.oldenglish.co.uk

Built in 1705, this Grade II listed building is located right in the centre of Eastwood, with easy access to the Derbyshire Dales for walkers, and Nottingham for shoppers. The well-equipped bedrooms are all en suite and offer modern facilities.

Rooms 15 en suite (1 fmly) **Facilities** FTV tea/coffee Dinner available WiFi Pool table **Conf** Max 15 Thtr 15 Class 8 Board 15 **Parking** 8 **Notes** ⊗

EDWINSTOWE
Map 16 SK66

The Forest Lodge

★★★★ INN

tel: 01623 824443 **Church St NG21 9QA**
email: reception@forestlodgehotel.co.uk **web:** www.forestlodgehotel.co.uk
dir: A614 into Edwinstowe. On B6034, opposite St Mary's church

Situated in the heart of Sherwood Forest, The Forest Lodge is a 17th-century coaching inn that provides the visitor with a warm and homely base from which to explore this fascinating and historic area. The bedrooms have been tastefully finished and the bar provides home comforts and good company. Food is served in the bar and in the restaurant.

Rooms 8 en suite 5 annexe en suite (2 fmly) (5 GF) **Facilities** FTV tea/coffee Dinner available WiFi ⚓ 36 ⚓ **Extras** Speciality toiletries - complimentary **Conf** Max 75 Thtr 75 Class 45 Board 50 **Parking** 35

ELTON
Map 11 SK73

Premier Collection

The Grange

★★★★★ BED AND BREAKFAST

tel: 07887 952181 **Sutton Ln NG13 9LA**
web: www.thegrangebedandbreakfastnotts.co.uk
dir: From Grantham A1 onto A52 to Elton x-rds, left 200yds, B&B on right

Parts of this lovely house date back to the early 17th century and the rooms command fine views across the gardens and rolling open countryside. Bedrooms contain many thoughtful extras and fine hospitality is assured from the proprietors. There is also a lounge as well as a reading room for residents' use, both furnished in warm tones with welcoming soft sofas and wood-burning stoves.

Rooms 3 en suite S £55-£60; D £80-£89 **Facilities** FTV DVD Lounge TVL tea/coffee WiFi ⚓ **Extras** Chocolate, snacks, orange juice, water - free **Parking** 8 **Notes** ⊗ ⊜

HOLBECK
Map 16 SK57

Premier Collection

Browns
★★★★★ ⚏ BED AND BREAKFAST

tel: 01909 720659 **The Old Orchard Cottage, Holbeck Ln S80 3NF**
email: browns.holbeck@btconnect.com **web:** www.brownsholbeck.co.uk
dir: 0.5m off A616 Sheffield-Newark road, turn for Holbeck at x-rds

Set amid beautifully tended gardens with lily-ponds and extensive lawns, this mid 18th-century cottage is a tranquil rural hideaway. Breakfasts are served in the Regency-style dining room, and the elegant bedrooms have four-poster beds and many extras. The friendly owners provide attentive service, including courtesy transport to nearby restaurants if required.

Rooms 3 annexe en suite (3 GF) S £59-£69; D £87* **Facilities** FTV DVD tea/coffee WiFi Riding ⚓ **Extras** Robes, slippers, speciality toiletries, chocolates **Parking** 3 **Notes** ⊗ No Children 17yrs Closed Xmas wk ⊕

HOLME PIERREPONT
Map 11 SK63

Holme Grange Cottage
★★★ GUEST ACCOMMODATION

tel: 0115 981 0413 **Adbolton Ln NG12 2LU**
email: jean.colinwightman@talk21.com **web:** www.holmegrangecottage.co.uk
dir: Exit A52 SE of Nottingham onto A6011. After 500yds turn right into Regatta Way, 1.25m on right

Holme Grange Cottage is ideally located in a quiet location opposite the National Water Sports Centre, and only three miles away from Nottingham city centre. The cottage has its own all-weather tennis court – ideal for the active guest. Indeed, when not providing warm hospitality and freshly cooked breakfasts, the proprietor is often on the golf course, and can advise on the best places locally to play.

Rooms 3 rms (1 en suite) (1 fmly) S £35-£41; D £60-£66* **Facilities** FTV TVL tea/coffee WiFi ⚐ ⚓ **Parking** 6 **Notes** Closed Xmas ⊕

MANSFIELD
Map 16 SK56

Bridleways Holiday Homes & Guest House
★★★★ GUEST HOUSE

tel: 01623 635725 **Newlands Rd, Forest Town NG19 0HU**
email: bridleways@outlook.com **web:** www.stayatbridleways.co.uk
dir: From Mansfield take B6030 towards New Clipstone. Right at rdbt, follow Crown Farm Industrial Park sign. 1st left into Newlands Rd. Guest house on left

Beside a quiet bridleway that leads to Vicar Water Country Park and Sherwood Pines Forest Park, this friendly guest house is a good touring base for walking, cycling or sightseeing. The double, twin and family bedrooms are particularly spacious and all are en suite. Lovely breakfasts are served in a cottage-style dining room.

Rooms 9 en suite (1 fmly) (2 GF) S £40; D £75* **Facilities** FTV tea/coffee WiFi ⚓ **Parking** 14 **Notes** ⊗

NEWARK-ON-TRENT
Map 17 SK75

Compton House
★★★★ ⚏ ⌂ GUEST HOUSE

tel: 01636 708670 **117 Baldertongate NG24 1RY**
email: info@comptonhousenewark.com **web:** www.comptonhousenewark.com
dir: 500yds SE of town centre. B6326 into Sherwood Av, 1st right into Baldertongate

Located a short walk from Newark's central attractions, this elegant period house provides high standards of comfort. Individually themed bedrooms come with a wealth of thoughtful extras and smart modern bathrooms. Comprehensive breakfasts, and wholesome dinners (by arrangement), are served in the attractive dining room and a lounge is available.

Rooms 7 rms (6 en suite) (1 pri facs) (1 fmly) (1 GF) S £55-£85* **Facilities** FTV Lounge tea/coffee Dinner available WiFi ⚓ **Extras** Magazines, mineral water - complimentary **Conf** Max 10 Thtr 10 Class 10 Board 10 **Parking** 2 **Notes** ⊗ Closed Xmas

The Hollies
★★★★ BED AND BREAKFAST

tel: 01636 707486 & 07880 722323 **41 Victoria St NG24 4UU**
email: caroline@theholliesnewark.co.uk **web:** www.theholliesnewark.co.uk

The Hollies is located in the historical town of Newark. This beautiful Georgian townhouse has recently benefited from refurbishment and offers three attractive boutique style bedrooms each with their own private bathroom or en suite. A wonderful breakfast is offer every morning. The attractive drawing room is an ideal venue for weddings and Caroline offers a Bespoke Bridal package.

Rooms 3 rms (2 en suite) (1 pri facs) S £65-£80; D £85-£100* **Facilities** FTV Lounge tea/coffee WiFi **Notes** ⊗

NOTTINGHAM
Map 11 SK53

See also Cotgrave

Beech Lodge
★★★★ GUEST ACCOMMODATION

tel: 0115 952 3314 & 07961 075939 **222 Porchester Rd NG3 6HG**
email: paulinegoodwin222@hotmail.co.uk **web:** www.beechlodgeguesthouse.com
dir: From A684 into Porchester Rd, 8th left, (Punchbowl pub on right corner), Beech Lodge on left corner

A friendly welcome is assured at Beech Lodge and the modern accommodation is well presented and suitably equipped. The ground-floor lounge is particularly comfortable, and there is a small conservatory. Breakfast is a good choice of freshly cooked and carefully presented fare served in the dining area next to the lounge.

Rooms 4 en suite (1 fmly) **Facilities** FTV TVL tea/coffee WiFi **Parking** 4 **Notes** ⊗

The Yellow House

★★★★ BED AND BREAKFAST

tel: 0115 926 2280 **7 Littlegreen Rd, Woodthorpe NG5 4LE**
email: suzanne.prewsmith1@gmail.com **web:** www.bandb-nottingham.co.uk
dir: *Exit A60 (Mansfield Rd) N from city centre into Thackeray's Ln, over rdbt, right into Whernside Rd to x-rds, left into Littlegreen Rd, house on left*

This semi-detached private house is in an easily-accessible and quiet residential suburb to the north-east of the city. The one purpose-built bedroom contains many thoughtful extras. A warm welcome is assured here and the proprietors' pet dog is also very friendly.

Rooms 1 en suite S £50-£55; D £70-£75* **Facilities** FTV tea/coffee WiFi 🔒 **Parking** 1 **Notes** ⊗ No Children Closed 24-26 & 31 Dec, 1 Jan ⊛

RETFORD	Map 17 SK78

Premier Collection

Blacksmiths

★★★★★ ◎◎ RESTAURANT WITH ROOMS

tel: 01777 818171 **Town St, Clayworth DN22 9AD**
email: will@blacksmithsclayworth.com **web:** www.blacksmithsclayworth.com
dir: *From A631, 2.4m to Clayworth*

Blacksmiths is a modern restaurant with annexed accommodation, situated in the quiet village of Clayworth, and a short drive from Retford. Meals in the restaurant are one of the many highlights of the stay, as are the hearty breakfasts which can be delivered as room-service. Bedrooms are a new addition for 2016 and have been finished to an excellent standard. Modern gadgets and accessories are provided such as climate control, large widescreen TVs, and WiFi. Thoughtful extras such as fluffy bathrobes and luxurious toiletries add to the experience. A warm welcome is guaranteed at this owner-run establishment.

Rooms 3 en suite (1 fmly) (2 GF) D £100-£150* **Facilities** FTV iPod docking station tea/coffee Dinner available WiFi 🔒 **Conf** Max 30 Thtr 28 Class 16 Board 18 **Parking** 31 **Notes** ⊗ No coaches

WORKSOP	Map 16 SK57

Acorn Lodge

★★★★ GUEST ACCOMMODATION

tel: 01909 478383 **85 Potter St S80 2HL**
email: info@acornlodgeworksop.co.uk **web:** www.acornlodgeworksop.co.uk
dir: *A1 onto A57. Take B6040 (town centre) through Manton. Lodge on right, 100mtrs past Priory*

Originally part of the community house of the Priory Church, this property has been modernised to offer comfortable, well-appointed accommodation. Good breakfasts are served in the pleasant breakfast room and ample private parking is available at the rear.

Rooms 7 en suite (2 fmly) S fr £45; D fr £60* **Facilities** FTV tea/coffee WiFi 🔒 **Parking** 15 **Notes** ⊗

OXFORDSHIRE	

ABINGDON-ON-THAMES	Map 5 SU49

Premier Collection

B&B Rafters

★★★★★ 🛎 BED AND BREAKFAST

tel: 01865 391298 & 07824 378720 **Abingdon Rd, Marcham OX13 6NU**
email: enquiries@bnb-rafters.co.uk **web:** www.bnb-rafters.co.uk
dir: *A34 onto A415 towards Witney. Rafters on A415 in Marcham adjacent to pedestrian crossing, on right*

Set amid immaculate gardens, this modern house is built in a half-timbered style and offers spacious accommodation together with a warm welcome. Bedrooms are stylishly furnished and equipped in a boutique style, and come with a range of homely extras. Comprehensive breakfasts feature local and organic produce when possible.

Rooms 4 en suite S £63-£75; D £119-£149 **Facilities** FTV DVD iPod docking station Lounge tea/coffee WiFi **Extras** Speciality toiletries, bottled water - free **Parking** 4 **Notes** ⊗ No Children 12yrs

Abbey Guest House

★★★★ BED AND BREAKFAST

tel: 01235 537020 & 07976 627252 **136 Oxford Rd OX14 2AG**
email: info@abbeyguest.uk **web:** www.abbeyguest.uk
dir: *1m from A34 Sbound, exit at North Abingdon*

A warm welcome is assured at Abbey Guest House. This well maintained property offers very comfortable, modern bedrooms with many useful extras and a relaxed atmosphere. Terry's business ethos is firmly focused on accessibility, and the guest house's website offers comprehensive information on the facilities available for disabled guests. There are a couple of local pubs nearby as well as very good bus links to Oxford from just outside the property. Freshly prepared breakfasts are served in the airy dining room overlooking the garden. Free WiFi is available throughout the house and off-road parking is provided.

Rooms 7 en suite (2 fmly) (1 GF) S £60-£85; D £100-£110* **Facilities** FTV DVD Lounge tea/coffee Lift WiFi 🔒 **Extras** Use of fridge & microwave **Parking** 7 **Notes** ⊗

ASHBURY
Map 5 SU28

The Rose and Crown

★★★ INN

tel: 01793 710222 & 07908 666196 **3 High St SN6 8NA**
email: bookings@roseandcrowninn.co.uk **web:** www.roseandcrowninn.co.uk
dir: *3m from Shrivenham or 6m from Lambourn on B4000 in Ashbury*

A traditional inn located in the village of Ashbury, at the foot of the White Horse Downs. This location is popular with leisure guests and business travellers alike, providing a peaceful retreat in a truly scenic area, yet well connected to Bath, Oxford, and Cheltenham. Rooms are well-furnished, most benefitting from an en suite bathroom. There's a popular outside terrace for the summer months, a cosy restaurant and a bar providing a good range of à la carte dishes and Arkells real ales. A continental breakfast is served.

Rooms 8 rms (7 en suite) (1 pri facs) (2 fmly) S £40-£60; D £50-£70 (room only)*
Facilities FTV Lounge TVL tea/coffee Dinner available WiFi ⚓ 18 Pool table ⚓ Games room **Conf** Max 20 Thtr 20 Class 20 Board 18 **Parking** 30 **Notes** LB

BANBURY
Map 11 SP44

The Three Pigeons Inn

★★★★★ ◉ INN

tel: 01295 275220 **3 Southam Rd OX16 2ED**
email: manager@thethreepigeons.com **web:** www.thethreepigeons.com
dir: *M40 junct 11 onto A422 signed Banbury. Left at Southam Road rdbt onto A361. Inn on left at lights*

Located in the centre of Banbury this 17th century coaching inn offers high levels of quality and comfort. Individually styled bedrooms with well-equipped bathrooms overlook the attractive courtyard garden. Low beams and uneven floors add to the inn's charm. Guests can enjoy a drink in the comfortable bar, and should not miss the carefully prepared dishes at dinner. Free WiFi and on-site parking available.

Rooms 3 en suite (1 fmly) S £110; D £130* **Facilities** STV FTV tea/coffee Dinner available Direct Dial WiFi **Conf** Max 20 Thtr 20 Class 20 Board 20 **Parking** 11 **Notes** No coaches

Ashlea Guest House

★★★★ GUEST HOUSE

tel: 01295 250539 & 07818 431429 **58 Oxford Rd OX16 9AN**
email: info@ashleaguesthouse.co.uk **web:** www.ashleaguesthouse.co.uk
dir: *M40 junct 11, follow signs to Banbury. At 2nd rdbt take 1st exit (Concord Avenue), next rdbt 1st exit. Through 3 sets of lights, then into right hand lane at 4th set of lights, opposite junction*

Ashlea Guest House is a family-run establishment where the husband and wife team ensure their guests are warmly welcomed and made to feel at home. There is a choice of well-presented rooms to suit all budgets. The guest house is the perfect base to explore the historic town of Banbury or the beautiful Cotswold countryside.

Rooms 6 rms (5 en suite) (1 pri facs) 6 annexe en suite (1 fmly) (5 GF) **Facilities** FTV DVD tea/coffee WiFi ⚓ **Parking** 13 **Notes** LB ⊗

Horse & Groom Inn

★★★★ ◡ INN

tel: 01295 722142 & 07774 210943 **Milcombe OX15 4RS**
email: horseandgroominn@gmail.com **web:** www.thehorseandgroominn.co.uk
dir: *M40 junct 11, A422 towards Banbury. Onto A361 signed Chipping Norton, past Bloxham turn right signed Milcombe. At end of village*

This 17th-century coaching house is a traditional village pub with a good atmosphere, friendly service and comfortable, well-appointed bedrooms. The restaurant offers a good choice of well-prepared and tasty dishes. The establishment is convenient for Banbury, Stratford-upon-Avon and the Cotswolds.

Rooms 4 en suite (1 fmly) **Facilities** FTV DVD iPod docking station tea/coffee Dinner available WiFi ⚓ 18 Fishing ⚓ **Conf** Max 40 Thtr 40 Class 30 Board 20 **Parking** 20

BURFORD
Map 5 SP21

The Angel at Burford

★★★★★ ◉ INN

tel: 01993 822714 **14 Witney St OX18 4SN**
email: enquiries@theangelatburford.co.uk **web:** www.theangelatburford.co.uk

Just off the high street in the picturesque market town of Burford, this 16th-century coaching inn features beamed ceilings and open fires. Guests can dine well in the restaurant, and the character bedrooms are thoughtfully equipped. Service is friendly here and families, children and dogs are all welcome.

Rooms 3 en suite D £110-£160* (incl.dinner) **Facilities** FTV DVD iPod docking station Lounge tea/coffee Dinner available WiFi ⚓ **Extras** Refreshments - complimentary **Notes** LB

The Maytime Inn

★★★★ ⌂ ◡ INN

tel: 01993 822068 **Asthall OX18 4HW**
email: info@themaytime.com **web:** www.themaytime.com

This country inn has retained its country charm albeit with some modern enhancement, and is located just a few miles outside Burford, known as 'The gateway to the Cotswolds'. The six en suite bedrooms are all individual in design, and offer a very comfortable stay. Food is available every day.

Rooms 2 en suite 4 annexe en suite (6 GF) S £95-£160; D £95-£160* **Facilities** FTV iPod docking station tea/coffee Dinner available Direct Dial WiFi ⚓ Petanque pitch **Extras** Speciality toiletries **Conf** Max 22 Thtr 15 Class 15 Board 22 **Parking** 30 **Notes** LB

The Bull at Burford

★★★★ ◎◎ 🛏 INN

tel: 01993 822220 **105 High St OX18 4RG**
email: info@bullatburford.co.uk **web:** www.bullatburford.co.uk
dir: *In town centre*

Situated in the heart of a pretty Cotswold town, The Bull was originally built in 1475 as a rest house for the local priory. It now has stylish, attractively presented bedrooms that reflect plenty of charm and character. Dinner is a must and the award-winning restaurant has an imaginative menu along with an excellent choice of wines. Lunch is served daily and afternoon tea is popular. There is a residents' lounge, and free WiFi is available.

Rooms 13 en suite 3 annexe en suite (1 fmly) (3 GF) **Facilities** STV FTV Lounge tea/coffee Dinner available WiFi **Parking** 6 **Notes** LB

The Golden Pheasant Inn

★★★★ INN

tel: 01993 823223 **91 High St OX18 4QA**
email: bournehospitality@hotmail.co.uk **web:** www.goldenpheasantburford.com

This attractive inn is set on Burford's main street and dates, in part, back to the 16th century. Bedrooms vary in size but are well furnished with attractive fabrics and some period furniture. The bar and open-plan restaurant is full of character, and lunch and dinner are served here daily.

Rooms 12 rms (11 en suite) (1 pri facs) 6 annexe en suite (5 GF) S £55-£175; D £55-£175* **Facilities** FTV TVL tea/coffee Dinner available WiFi **Parking** 8 **Notes** ⊗ Closed 24 Dec RS 25 Dec No accommodation, bar open

Potters Hill Farm (SP300148)

★★★★ FARMHOUSE

tel: 01993 878018 & 07711 045207 **Leafield OX29 9QB**
web: www.pottershillfarm.co.uk
dir: *4.5m NE of Burford. A361 onto B4437, 1st right, 1st left, 1.5m past entrance to farm buildings, on left*

Located on a working farm in peaceful parkland that's teaming with diverse wildlife, this converted coach house stands next to the farmhouse. It has been appointed to offer comfortable bedrooms with many individual features. Breakfast is served in the main farmhouse and features fresh, local produce.

Rooms 3 annexe en suite (1 fmly) (2 GF) **Facilities** FTV Lounge tea/coffee Dinner available WiFi 🐾 **Extras** Snacks, speciality toiletries **Parking** 5 **Notes** ⊗ 770 acres mixed/sheep/arable

The Inn for All Seasons

★★★ 🛏 INN

tel: 01451 844324 **The Barringtons OX18 4TN**
email: sharp@innforallseasons.com **web:** www.innforallseasons.com
dir: *3m W of Burford on A40 towards Cheltenham*

This charming 16th-century coaching inn is close to the pretty village of Burford. The individually styled bedrooms are comfortable, and include a four-poster room, as well as a family room that sleeps four. The public areas include a cosy bar with oak beams and real fires. There is a good choice on the bar menu, and evening meals feature the best of local Cotswold produce. The inn is a dog-friendly establishment and there is a ground-floor bedroom with direct access to the garden and an exercise area.

Rooms 9 en suite 1 annexe en suite (2 fmly) (1 GF) **Facilities** FTV DVD Lounge TVL tea/coffee Dinner available WiFi ⚲ 18 Fishing 🐾 **Conf** Max 40 Thtr 40 Class 20 Board 25 **Parking** 60

CHIPPING NORTON   Map 10 SP32

Premier Collection

The Feathered Nest Country Inn

★★★★★ ◎◎◎ 🛏 INN

tel: 01993 833030 **OX7 6SD**
email: info@thefeatherednestinn.co.uk **web:** www.thefeatherednestinn.co.uk

(For full entry see Nether Westcote (Gloucestershire))

Wild Thyme Restaurant with Rooms

★★★★ ◎◎ RESTAURANT WITH ROOMS

tel: 01608 645060 **10 New St OX7 5LJ**
email: enquiries@wildthymerestaurant.co.uk **web:** www.wildthymerestaurant.co.uk
dir: *On A44 in town centre off market square*

Set in the bustling Cotswold market town of Chipping Norton, this restaurant with rooms offers three en suite bedrooms that are individually designed, well equipped, and have many thoughtful extras. The restaurant serves exciting Modern British food that is presented with relaxed and friendly service.

Rooms 3 en suite S £65-£85; D £75-£95* **Facilities** FTV DVD tea/coffee Dinner available WiFi **Extras** Mineral water, home-made biscuits **Notes** ⊗ No coaches

---

CULHAM   Map 5 SU59

The Railway Inn

★★★ INN

tel: 01235 528046 **Station Rd OX14 3BT**
email: info@railwayinnculham.co.uk **web:** www.railwayinnculham.co.uk
dir: *2.5m SE of Abingdon-on-Thames on A415. Turn left signed Culham railway station*

The Railway Inn is located beside Culham railway station and is the perfect base to explore Abingdon-on-Thames, Didcot and Oxford. The inn offers a choice of comfortable and affordable rooms, a selection of real ales and home cooked food. In addition, there is a permanent marquee in the garden, which is suitable for all occasions.

Rooms 6 rms (5 en suite) (1 pri facs) 4 annexe en suite (2 fmly) S £60; D £79* **Facilities** FTV Lounge TVL tea/coffee Dinner available WiFi 🐾 **Parking** 30 **Notes** ⊗

DEDDINGTON   Map 11 SP43

The Unicorn Inn

★★★ ◎ INN

tel: 01869 338838 **Market Place OX15 0SE**
email: info@unicorndeddington.co.uk **web:** www.unicorndeddington.co.uk
dir: *M40 junct 11, A422 signed Bembury. Take A4260 to Deddington. At x-rds in Deddington turn left to Market Place*

This 17th-century inn enjoys a prominent position in the heart of the pretty village of Deddington. Bedrooms are all attractively presented and very comfortable. The charming bar is a favourite with locals, and there is an extensive choice of real ales and craft beers, as well as a large wine list. Many original features have been retained, and the low oak-beamed ceilings and real fires help create a great atmosphere. The restaurant has been awarded an AA Rosette for owner Johnny Parke's exciting menu of great local produce.

Rooms 6 en suite (1 fmly) **Facilities** FTV Lounge TVL tea/coffee Dinner available WiFi Pool table 🐾 **Conf** Max 30 Thtr 30 Class 20 Board 20

FARINGDON   Map 5 SU29

Premier Collection

Buscot Manor B&B

★★★★★ BED AND BREAKFAST

tel: 01367 252225 & 07973 831690 **SN7 8DA**
email: romneypargeter@hotmail.co.uk web: www.buscotmanor.co.uk

Delightfully located in a peaceful village, Buscot Manor dates from 1692 and is full of character and quality. Guests are welcome to use the two comfortable lounges in addition to the pleasant gardens, where tea may be enjoyed in the summer months. The two upper-floor bedrooms have traditional four-poster beds. A more contemporary room is located on the ground floor. Breakfast is taken around one large table in the elegant dining room.

Rooms 2 en suite 1 annexe en suite (3 fmly) (1 GF) **Facilities** FTV DVD Lounge TVL tea/coffee WiFi ch fac ⚓ Fishing Riding Sauna Gym ⚓ Watersports weekends available **Extras** Speciality toiletries, fruit, snacks **Conf** Max 12 Board 12 **Parking** 30

The Trout Inn

★★★★ ◉ ⛲ INN

tel: 01367 870382 **Buckland Marsh SN7 8RF**
email: info@troutinn.co.uk web: www.troutinn.co.uk
dir: *A420 Swindon to Oxford road, turn signed Bampton. Inn 2m on right*

Located in a tranquil location just a couple of miles from the village of Bampton and within a short distance to the Cotswolds, this recently refurbished inn offers stylish and comfortably appointed accommodation. The inn boasts many original features including original flagstone flooring and exposed beams yet tastefully revamped with modern furnishings and roaring log-burners. Located right on the River Thames with a large beer garden. A hearty breakfast is served daily in the restaurant and lunch and dinner is available throughout the week.

Rooms 6 en suite (1 fmly) (4 GF) D £85-£160* **Facilities** STV tea/coffee Dinner available Direct Dial WiFi **Extras** Speciality toiletries **Conf** Max 20 Thtr 20 Class 20 Board 20 **Parking** 25 **Notes** Civ Wed

The Eagle

★★★★ ◉◉ INN

tel: 01367 241879 **Little Coxwell SN7 7LW**
email: eaglelittlecoxwell@gmail.com web: www.eagletavern.co.uk
dir: *M4 junct 15, A419, A420 signed Oxford, right into village*

Located in the peaceful village of Little Coxwell, in the beautiful Vale of the White Horse, The Eagle is a traditional inn with a welcoming atmosphere and a selection of real ales. The upstairs bedrooms, in a range of shapes and sizes, are very stylish and offer good comfort and ease of use. At both breakfast and dinner there's a variety of carefully prepared, quality dishes to choose from.

Rooms 6 en suite **Facilities** FTV Lounge tea/coffee Dinner available WiFi ⚓ **Notes** No coaches

The Bell

★★★ INN

tel: 01367 358050 **13 Market Place SN7 7HP**
email: bellhotelfar@aol.com web: www.thebellhotelonline.co.uk

With a history dating back to the 14th century, this family-run inn is located in the engaging town of Faringdon, a handy base from which to explore the local area. There is character at every turn, with low beams, uneven floors and period features, all contributing to the building's individuality. Bedrooms offer a number of configurations, while public rooms include a choice of dining areas and an atmospheric bar. An extensive menu is offered with popular favourites and daily specials.

Rooms 8 en suite **Facilities** tea/coffee Dinner available WiFi

GORING   Map 5 SU68

The Miller of Mansfield

★★★★ ◉◉ RESTAURANT WITH ROOMS

tel: 01491 872829 & 07702 853413 **High St RG8 9AW**
email: reservations@millerofmansfield.com web: www.millerofmansfield.com
dir: *M4 junct 12, S on A4 towards Newbury. 3rd rdbt onto A340 to Pangbourne. A329 to Streatley, right at lights onto B4009 into Goring*

The frontage of this former coaching inn hides sumptuous rooms furnished in a distinctive and individual style. The two AA Rosette award-winning restaurant serves appealing dishes using locally sourced ingredients, and there is a comfortable bar, which serves real ales, fine wines and afternoon tea; a bar menu provides quick bites to eat.

Rooms 13 en suite (2 fmly) S £80-£140; D £100-£195* **Facilities** FTV Lounge tea/coffee Dinner available Direct Dial WiFi Boat hire & beauty therapies can be arranged **Extras** Speciality toiletries **Conf** Max 12 Board 12 **Parking** 2 **Notes** LB

HENLEY-ON-THAMES   Map 5 SU78

Phyllis Court Club

★★★★ ⛲ GUEST ACCOMMODATION

tel: 01491 570500 **Marlow Rd RG9 2HT**
email: enquiries@phylliscourt.co.uk web: www.phylliscourt.co.uk
dir: *A404 onto A4130 into town centre. Follow A4155, 150mtrs on right*

Phyllis Court was founded in 1906 as a private members' club and has welcomed many distinguished visitors over the years. Set in 18 acres, with lawns sweeping down to the Thames, it offers a unique blend of traditional elegance and modern comforts. The club takes centre stage during Henley Royal Regatta week, being positioned opposite the finishing line. The individually styled bedrooms are well appointed and very comfortable. There is restricted meal service two days before and after the regattas in June and July. An excellent range of function venues is available, and the Grade II listed Grandstand Pavilion is perfect for weddings.

Rooms 17 en suite D £165-£345* **Facilities** FTV Lounge TVL tea/coffee Dinner available Direct Dial Lift Licensed WiFi ⚓ **Extras** Speciality toiletries, trouser press, magazines **Conf** Max 250 Thtr 250 Class 100 Board 30 **Parking** 200 **Notes** RS 26-28 Dec, 2-3 Jan, regattas Jun-Jul Civ Wed 250

Badgemore Park Golf Club

★★★★ GUEST ACCOMMODATION

tel: 01491 637300 **Badgemore Park, Badgemore RG9 4NR**
email: info@badgemorepark.com **web:** www.badgemorepark.com

Located close to Henley-on-Thames, this property offers comfortable guest accommodation in quiet surroundings within the secluded and private walled gardens, situated just 100 metres away from the main clubhouse. In summer months, dinner and a bar are available until 6pm. The venue also caters well for business meetings complete with own lounge and kitchen. Free WiFi available.

Rooms 8 annexe rms 7 annexe en suite (1 pri facs) (3 fmly) (3 GF) S £80-£95; D £80-£105* **Facilities** FTV TVL tea/coffee Licensed WiFi ⅃ 18 **Extras** Bottled water **Conf** Max 120 Thtr 120 Class 60 Board 45 **Parking** 120 **Notes** Closed 25 Dec Civ Wed 120

The Baskerville

★★★★ ⊛ INN

tel: 0118 940 3332 **Station Rd, Lower Shiplake RG9 3NY**
email: enquiries@thebaskerville.com **web:** www.thebaskerville.com
dir: *2m S of Henley in Lower Shiplake. Exit A4155 into Station Rd, inn signed*

Located close to Shiplake station and just a short drive from Henley, this smart pub is perfect for a business or leisure break. The accommodation is well equipped and it is a good base for exploring the Oxfordshire countryside and surrounding areas. The award winning dinner menu, coupled with daily specials, makes good use of local produce.

Rooms 4 en suite (1 fmly) S £100-£200; D £110-£200* **Facilities** FTV tea/coffee Dinner available WiFi ⌂ **Extras** Bottled water, sweets - complimentary **Conf** Max 15 Thtr 15 Class 15 Board 15 **Parking** 15 **Notes** Closed 1 Jan No coaches

The Cherry Tree Inn

★★★★ ⊛ INN

tel: 01491 680430 **Main St, Stoke Row RG9 5QA**
email: enquiries@thecherrytreeinn.co.uk **web:** www.thecherrytreeinn.co.uk
dir: *On A4155 from Henley-on-Thames exit B481 to Sonning Common. Follow Stoke Row signs, turn right for inn*

This 400 year-old building is located in a pretty village on the outskirts of Henley-on-Thames. There are four en suite bedrooms which offer modern comforts and are set adjacent to the public house. A range of high quality wines complement the menus which often feature local produce.

Rooms 4 annexe en suite (4 GF) S £65-£100; D £75-£200 **Facilities** FTV Lounge TVL tea/coffee Dinner available WiFi ⅃ 18 **Extras** Bottled water **Parking** 30 **Notes** LB

Leander Club

★★★★ ⌂ GUEST ACCOMMODATION

tel: 01491 575782 **Leander Way RG9 2LP**
email: events@leander.co.uk **web:** www.leander.co.uk
dir: *M4 junct 8/9 follow signs for Henley (A404M & A4130). Turn right immediately before Henley Bridge to Club & car park*

This historic rowing club has opened its doors and made its delightful facilities available to guests. The location is breathtaking, particularly in the morning, when the rowers can be seen setting out on the river. The rooms are each named after various colleges and universities, and each is packed with interesting photos and memorabilia linking them with the Leander Club. Public areas also feature lots of trophies, pictures and artefacts, and it all makes for a most interesting place to stay.

Rooms 11 en suite (1 fmly) S fr £137; D fr £162* **Facilities** STV FTV Lounge TVL tea/coffee Dinner available Direct Dial Lift Licensed WiFi **Extras** Snacks - complimentary **Conf** Max 120 Thtr 120 Class 40 Board 20 **Parking** 60 **Notes** ⊗ No Children 10yrs Closed Xmas-New Year RS 1st wk Jul Henley Royal Regatta Civ Wed 120

Follow us on Facebook
www.facebook.com/TheAAUK

Find us on Facebook

HENLEY-ON-THAMES *continued*

Milsoms Henley-on-Thames

★★★★ RESTAURANT WITH ROOMS

tel: 01491 845780 & 845789 **20 Market Place RG9 2AH**
email: henley@milsomshotel.co.uk **web:** www.milsomshotel.co.uk
dir: *In centre of town, close to town hall*

Seven en suite bedrooms are located in a listed building above the Loch Fyne Restaurant in Henley's Market Place. Each bedroom is individually appointed and equipped to meet the needs of the modern traveller; particular care has been taken to incorporate original features into the contemporary design. The restaurant has a commitment to offer ethically sourced seafood.

Rooms 7 en suite (2 fmly) (1 GF) **Facilities** FTV tea/coffee Dinner available WiFi **Extras** Still & sparkling water - complimentary **Parking** 7 **Notes** ⊗ No coaches

HORNTON	Map 11 SP34

Hornton Grounds Country House *(SP384443)*

★★★★ FARMHOUSE

tel: 01295 678318 **OX15 6HH**
email: catherine@horntongrounds.com **web:** www.horntongrounds.co.uk
dir: *From Banbury onto A422 signed Stratford. Through Wroxton, pass Indian Queen pub, next right & follow long drive*

A very warm welcome waits at Hornton Grounds Country House, an impressive retreat set on a busy working farm. It's an ideal setting for those wishing to explore the north Cotswold countryside. Guests are encouraged to enjoy the extensive grounds on foot, or you can even bring your own horse (stabling available). Evening meals are available by prior arrangement.

Rooms 4 rms (2 en suite) (2 pri facs) **Facilities** TVL tea/coffee Dinner available WiFi ⌂⌣⌃ Riding ⌂ Stabling for guests horses **Parking** 8 **Notes** 200 acres pigs/beef/sheep

KINGHAM	Map 10 SP22

Premier Collection

The Wild Rabbit

★★★★★ ⍟⍟⍟ ⌁ RESTAURANT WITH ROOMS

tel: 01608 658389 **Church St OX7 6YA**
email: theteam@thewildrabbit.co.uk **web:** www.thewildrabbit.co.uk

Situated in the idyllic Cotswold village of Kingham, this Grade II listed Georgian building has been lovingly restored and now totally refurbished. The rooms are modern and offer up-to-date technology. The public areas are a real feature with a large bar and open-plan restaurant kitchen. An outside dining area has also been added. The food is exceptional, with many French influences evident in the cooking. Service is informal yet professional and very friendly. Ample car parking is available.

Rooms 11 en suite 1 annexe en suite (1 fmly) (4 GF) **Facilities** FTV DVD iPod docking station Lounge tea/coffee Dinner available WiFi ⌂ **Extras** Mini-bar - chargeable **Parking** 19 **Notes** No coaches

The Kingham Plough

★★★★ ⍟⍟⍟ ⌁ INN

tel: 01608 658327 **The Green OX7 6YD**
email: book@thekinghamplough.co.uk **web:** www.thekinghamplough.co.uk
dir: *From Chipping Norton, take B4450 to Churchill. Take 2nd right to Kingham, left at T-junct in Kingham. Pub on right.*

The Kingham Plough is a quintessential Cotswold inn set in the pretty village of Kingham, just minutes away from the well-known Daylesford Organic Estate. The en suite bedrooms have Cotswold character and offer impressive quality and comfort. The food here is a real draw, and has been recognised by achieving three AA Rosettes; the team deliver excellent results using locally sourced produce.

Rooms 4 en suite 2 annexe en suite (2 fmly) S £110-£150; D £145-£195* **Facilities** FTV DVD iPod docking station Lounge tea/coffee Dinner available WiFi ⌣ 18 ⌂ Discounted rates at local spa **Extras** Speciality toiletries, home-made biscuits - free **Parking** 25 **Notes** Closed 25 Dec No coaches

MARSTON	Map 5 SP50

Hill Farm

★★★ BED AND BREAKFAST

tel: 07976 288329 **Mill Ln OX3 0QF**
email: laura@cherbridgecottages.co.uk **web:** www.cherbridgecottages.co.uk

Hill Farm is set in its own extensive grounds yet is conveniently close to Oxford city centre. This 18th-century cottage has many original features and is most comfortable. Bedrooms are very well appointed and there is a four-poster bed in the larger bedroom. Surrounded by open countryside, there is a pretty walk to the rear of the property along with a show jumping ground and working stables. Freshly cooked breakfasts feature the best in local produce and free WiFi is available throughout the house.

Rooms 2 rms (1 en suite) (1 pri facs) **Facilities** FTV Lounge TVL tea/coffee WiFi ⌂ **Conf** Max 80 Thtr 70 Class 60 Board 50 **Parking** **Notes** ⊗ Closed 19 Dec-4 Jan

OXFORD	Map 5 SP50

Premier Collection

Burlington House

★★★★★ ⌁ GUEST ACCOMMODATION

tel: 01865 513513 **374 Banbury Rd, Summertown OX2 7PP**
email: stay@burlington-house.co.uk **web:** www.burlington-house.co.uk
dir: *Opposite Oxford Conference Centre on A4165 on corner of Hernes Rd & Banbury Rd*

Guests are assured of a warm welcome and attentive service at this smart, beautifully maintained Victorian house, within walking distance of Summertown's fashionable restaurants. Elegant, contemporary bedrooms are filled with a wealth of thoughtful extras, and some open onto a pretty patio garden. Memorable breakfasts, served in the delightful dining room, include home-made preserves, fruit breads, granola and excellent coffee.

Rooms 13 en suite 3 annexe en suite (4 GF) S £70-£99; D £94-£149* **Facilities** FTV tea/coffee Direct Dial WiFi ⌂ **Parking** 5 **Notes** ⊗ No Children 12yrs Closed 24 Dec-2 Jan

Premier Collection

The Bocardo

★★★★★ GUEST ACCOMMODATION

tel: 01865 591234 **24-26 George St OX1 2AE**
email: reservations@thebocardo.co.uk **web:** www.thebocardo.co.uk

The Bocardo is right in the heart of the city centre on George Street and located directly above Jamie's Italian Restaurant. The bedrooms here have stylish decor; all have flat-screen TVs, free WiFi and high quality bathrooms with power showers. This is a room-only establishment so breakfast is not available, however there are numerous bars, restaurants and cafés right on the doorstep.

Rooms 10 en suite **Facilities** STV WiFi **Extras** Speciality toiletries **Notes** ⊗

Galaxie

★★★★ GUEST ACCOMMODATION

tel: 01865 515688 **180 Banbury Rd OX2 7BT**
email: info@galaxie.co.uk **web:** www.galaxie.co.uk
dir: 1m N of Oxford centre, on right before shops in Summertown

In the popular Summertown area of the city, the Galaxie has a welcoming atmosphere and good-quality accommodation. The well-equipped bedrooms are all very comfortable and come with a range of extra facilities. The attractive conservatory dining room looks over the Oriental garden.

Rooms 32 rms (28 en suite) (3 fmly) **Facilities** TVL TV31B tea/coffee Direct Dial Lift WiFi **Parking** 30 **Notes** ⊗

The Oxford Townhouse

★★★★ GUEST ACCOMMODATION

tel: 01865 511122 & 722500 **88-90 Abingdon Rd OX1 4PX**
email: stay@theoxfordtownhouse.co.uk **web:** www.theoxfordtownhouse.co.uk

The Oxford Townhouse overlooks The Queen's College playing fields, and is an ideal base to explore the city. Spread over two Victorian town houses, it offers a range of modern styled spacious bedrooms that have recently benefited from full refurbishment. Freshly prepared breakfasts are served at individual tables and service is friendly and attentive. WiFi is available throughout the house and there is secure parking.

Rooms 15 en suite S £95-£130; D £130-£190* **Facilities** FTV Lounge tea/coffee WiFi **Extras** Bottled water, soft drinks - complimentary **Parking** 9 **Notes** ⊗ No Children 10yrs Closed 24-26 Dec

Parklands

★★★★ GUEST ACCOMMODATION

tel: 01865 554374 **100 Banbury Rd OX2 6JU**
email: stay@parklandsoxford.co.uk **web:** www.parklandsoxford.co.uk

Parklands enjoys a prominent position along the tree-lined Banbury road and is only a short walk from the city centre. This beautiful Victorian building was once the home of an Oxford Don and has a range of individually designed, spacious bedrooms. Secure parking is available and free WiFi is provided. The walled garden is a peaceful retreat and the residents' lounge is very well appointed.

Rooms 14 rms (13 en suite) (1 pri facs) **Facilities** FTV Lounge tea/coffee Direct Dial Licensed WiFi **Extras** Bottled water - complimentary **Parking** 14 **Notes** ⊗ No Children 18yrs

Red Mullions Guest House

★★★★ ☺ GUEST HOUSE

tel: 01865 742741 **23 London Rd, Headington OX3 7RE**
email: stay@redmullions.co.uk **web:** www.redmullions.co.uk
dir: M40 junct 8, A40. At Headington rdbt, 2nd exit signed Headington into London Rd

Red Mullions Guest House takes its name from the brick columns between the windows of the building. Modern bedrooms provide comfortable accommodation set within easy reach of motorway networks and Oxford city centre. Hearty breakfasts provide a good start to any day.

Rooms 16 rms (15 en suite) (1 pri facs) (3 fmly) (7 GF) S £90-£100; D £100-£125* **Facilities** STV FTV DVD tea/coffee WiFi **Extras** Bottled water - complimentary **Parking** 11 **Notes** ⊗

Remont Oxford

★★★★ GUEST ACCOMMODATION

tel: 01865 311020 **367 Banbury Rd OX2 7PL**
email: info@remont-oxford.co.uk **web:** www.remont-oxford.co.uk

Remont Oxford is in the popular Summertown area, some two miles from the city centre. The well-equipped bedrooms and bathrooms are modern and stylish and come with flat-screen TVs, complimentary WiFi and well-stocked beverage trays; rooms all offer high quality and comfort. Parking is available and there is a delightful garden for guests to enjoy. Cooked and continental buffet breakfasts are served in the light and airy dining room.

Rooms 18 en suite 7 annexe en suite (2 fmly) (8 GF) S £87-£140; D £97-£150* **Facilities** FTV Lounge tea/coffee Lift WiFi **Parking** 18 **Notes** ⊗

Conifers Guest House

★★★★ GUEST ACCOMMODATION

tel: 01865 763055 **116 The Slade, Headington OX3 7DX**
email: stay@conifersguesthouse.co.uk **web:** www.conifersguesthouse.co.uk
dir: Exit ring road onto A420 towards city centre. Left onto B4495 (Windmill Rd), straight over at lights, house on left past Nuffield Orthopaedic Centre

Situated in the Headington area, Conifers is within walking distance of the Headington Hospitals, the BMW plant, Cowley Business Park, and Oxford Brookes, as well as Shotover Country Park. It is an impressive Edwardian house that provides comfortable accommodation in pine-furnished bedrooms. Breakfast is served in a smart, front-facing dining room. A private car park and a large rear garden are bonuses.

Rooms 12 en suite (4 fmly) **Facilities** FTV tea/coffee WiFi **Parking** 8 **Notes** ⊗

Cotswold House

★★★★ GUEST ACCOMMODATION

tel: 01865 310558 **363 Banbury Rd OX2 7PL**
email: d.r.walker@talk21.com **web:** www.cotswoldhouse.co.uk
dir: A40 onto A423 into city centre, follow signs to Summertown, house 0.5m on right

Situated in a leafy avenue close to the northern ring road and Summertown, this well-maintained house offers comfortable, well-equipped bedrooms and a relaxed atmosphere. Enjoy a traditional, hearty breakfast with vegetarian choices, including home-made muesli and fresh fruit, served in the bright attractive dining room.

Rooms 8 en suite (2 fmly) (2 GF) S £85-£95; D £125-£150 **Facilities** FTV Lounge tea/coffee WiFi ♨ **Parking** 6 **Notes** ⊗ Closed 28 Dec-10 Jan

OXFORD *continued*

Marlborough House

★★★★ GUEST ACCOMMODATION

tel: 01865 311321 **321 Woodstock Rd OX2 7NY**
email: enquiries@marlbhouse.co.uk **web:** www.marlbhouse.co.uk
dir: *1.5m N of city centre. Exit at A34 & A44 junct for city centre, onto A4144 (Woodstock Rd), premises on right by lights*

Marlborough House is just 1.5 miles north of Oxford's historic city centre, and is within easy reach of the M40 and the A34 ring road. Custom built in 1990 to a traditional design, the house sits comfortably alongside its Victorian neighbours in a predominantly residential area. All 17 bedrooms have en suite facilities, kitchenettes and mini-bars. WiFi covers the lounge and many of the rooms.

Rooms 13 en suite 4 annexe en suite (3 fmly) (4 GF) **Facilities** FTV Lounge tea/coffee Direct Dial Licensed WiFi **Extras** Mini-bar - chargeable **Parking** 6 **Notes** ⊗

Green Gables

★★★ GUEST ACCOMMODATION

tel: 01865 725870 **326 Abingdon Rd OX1 4TE**
email: green.gables@virgin.net **web:** www.greengables.uk.com
dir: *Exit ring road onto A4144 towards city centre, Green Gables 0.5m on left*

A warm welcome is assured at Green Gables, located within easy walking distance of the city centre. Bedrooms are equipped with a range of practical and homely extras, and a comprehensive breakfast is served in the cosy dining room. Guests have free access to the internet in the smart conservatory-lounge, and some private parking is available.

Rooms 11 en suite (2 fmly) (4 GF) **Facilities** FTV Lounge tea/coffee WiFi **Parking** 9 **Notes** ⊗ No Children 5yrs Closed 23-31 Dec

Oxford Guest House

★★★ GUEST HOUSE

tel: 01865 308833 & 07855 737373 **228 London Rd, Headington OX3 9EG**
email: oxfordguesthouse@gmail.com **web:** www.theoxfordguesthouse.co.uk
dir: *M40 junct 8 onto A40 towards Oxford. At Headington rdbt take 2nd exit signed Headington into London Rd (A420). On left after 2nd set of lights*

The newly-built Oxford Guest House is located in a quiet residential area, and offers well configured rooms finished to a very good standard. All rooms have been equipped with flat-screen TVs and free WiFi. A choice of breakfasts is served daily in the well-appointed breakfast room. Off-street parking is available.

Rooms 6 en suite (1 fmly) (2 GF) S £65-£75; D £85-£115* **Facilities** STV FTV tea/coffee WiFi ⚓ **Parking** 6 **Notes** LB ⊗

All Seasons Guest House

★★★ GUEST ACCOMMODATION

tel: 01865 742215 **63 Windmill Rd, Headington OX3 7BP**
email: info@allseasonshouse.com **web:** www.allseasonshouse.com
dir: *Exit ring road onto A420 towards city centre. 1m, left at lights into Windmill Rd, house 300yds on left*

Within easy walking distance of the suburb of Headington, this double-fronted Victorian house provides comfortable, homely bedrooms equipped with practical and thoughtful extras. The inviting dining room features an original fireplace, and parking is available to the rear of the property.

Rooms 7 rms (5 en suite) (2 pri facs) (1 fmly) (1 GF) **Facilities** FTV TVL tea/coffee WiFi **Parking** 6 **Notes** ⊗

Sports View Guest House

★★★ GUEST ACCOMMODATION

tel: 01865 244268 **106-110 Abingdon Rd OX1 4PX**
email: stay@sportsviewguesthouse.co.uk **web:** www.sportsviewguesthouse.co.uk
dir: *Exit Oxford S at Kennington rdbt towards city centre, 1.25m on left*

This family-run Victorian property overlooks The Queen's College sports ground. Situated south of the city, it is within walking distance of the centre. Rooms are comfortable, and the property benefits from off-road parking.

Rooms 20 rms (19 en suite) (1 pri facs) (4 fmly) (5 GF) S £40-£65; D £70-£110* **Facilities** FTV Lounge tea/coffee WiFi ⚓ **Parking** 7 **Notes** ⊗ No Children 3yrs Closed 25-26 Dec & 1 Jan

SHRIVENHAM Map 5 SU28

The White Horse View

★★★★ BED AND BREAKFAST

tel: 01793 780301 & 07967 497926 **Cherry Bungalow, Station Rd SN6 8JL**
email: colin@thewhitehorseview.com **web:** www.thewhitehorseview.com

Located in the pretty village of Shrivenham, this bed and breakfast offers three modern en suite bedrooms set away from the main house, each with their own external seating and spectacular countryside views. Breakfasts are served in the conservatory and feature local produce. This is a good location for those wanting to walk the Ridgeway or take in the sights of historic Marlborough.

Rooms 3 en suite (1 fmly) (3 GF) S £64-£75; D £64-£75 (room only) **Facilities** FTV TVL tea/coffee WiFi Pool table **Parking** 3 **Notes** ⊗

STADHAMPTON — Map 5 SU69

Premier Collection

The Crazy Bear

★★★★★ ◉◉ 🍴 GUEST ACCOMMODATION

tel: 01865 890714 **Bear Ln OX44 7UR**
email: enquiries@crazybear-stadhampton.co.uk **web:** www.crazybeargroup.co.uk
dir: M40 junct 7, A329. In 4m left after petrol station, left into Bear Ln

This popular and attractive guest accommodation successfully combines modern chic with old world character. Cuisine is extensive and varied, with award-winning Thai and English restaurants under the same roof (both with AA Rosettes). Those choosing to make a night of it can enjoy staying in one of the concept bedrooms, all presented to a very high standard and styled with exciting themes; the 'infinity suites' have state-of-the-art facilities.

Rooms 4 en suite 12 annexe en suite (3 fmly) (4 GF) **Facilities** STV FTV Dinner available Direct Dial Licensed WiFi 🏊 **Conf** Max 40 Thtr 30 Class 30 Board 30 **Parking** 100 **Notes** ⊗ Civ Wed 200

SWINBROOK — Map 5 SP21

The Swan Inn

★★★★★ ◉◉ INN

tel: 01993 823339 **OX18 4DY**
email: swaninnswinbrook@btconnect.com **web:** www.theswanswinbrook.co.uk
dir: 1m from A40, 2m E of Burford

The idyllic location and award-winning food are only two of the reasons why this is the perfect place for a comfortable business visit or a relaxed weekend. The bar offers real ales, local lagers and an appealing wine list. The accommodation is sumptuous and combines modern facilities with traditional comfort.

Rooms 6 en suite (1 fmly) (4 GF) **Facilities** FTV tea/coffee Dinner available WiFi ⚓ 18 Riding **Parking** 20 **Notes** Closed 25 Dec No coaches

UFFINGTON — Map 5 SU38

The Fox and Hounds

★★★★ INN

tel: 01367 820680 **High St SN7 7RP**
email: enquiries@uffingtonpub.co.uk **web:** www.uffingtonpub.co.uk
dir: From A420 (S of Faringdon) follow Fernham or Uffington signs. From M4 junct 14 via Lambourn & Kingston Lisle

The Fox and Hounds is a traditional pub located in the charming village of Uffington, and an ideal base to explore the surrounding area. The two cottage-style bedrooms are well appointed and offer a range of amenities. The beamed bar is well stocked and includes a selection of real ales, while the restaurant offers a daily menu with an oriental twist.

Rooms 2 annexe en suite (2 fmly) (2 GF) S £69-£79; D £69-£79 (room only)* **Facilities** FTV DVD tea/coffee Dinner available WiFi 🍴 **Parking** 14

WALLINGFORD — Map 5 SU68

The Coachmakers Arms

★★★ INN

tel: 01491 838229 & 07855 837020 **37 Saint Mary's St OX10 0EU**
email: coachmakers37@gmail.com **web:** www.coachmakersarmswallingford.co.uk

The Coachmakers Arms enjoys a prominent position in the heart of the historic town of Wallingford. Bedrooms are all attractively presented and most comfortable. This authentic inn has bags of character, many original features and there is a good choice of real ales on offer along with an extensive wine list. The freshly cooked breakfast is not to be missed and WiFi is available for guests.

Rooms 3 en suite (1 fmly) D fr £90* **Facilities** FTV tea/coffee WiFi **Notes** No coaches

The Partridge Inn Wallingford

★★ INN

tel: 01491 839305 & 07539 261782 **32 Saint Mary's St OX10 0ET**
email: sleep@partridgeinnwallingford.co.uk **web:** www.partridgeinnwallingford.co.uk

Located in the historic market town of Wallingford, The Partridge Inn is a good base to explore the Thames Path and neighbouring village of Dorchester – famous as the location for *Midsomer Murders*. Four comfortable rooms are provided. Dinner menus are created from as much seasonal local produce as possible. Chef/owner Matt and his small team offer relaxed and friendly hospitality; in addition continental breakfast is available.

Rooms 4 rms (1 en suite) D £55-£110 (room only)* **Facilities** FTV DVD tea/coffee Dinner available WiFi **Conf** Max 20 Thtr 20 Class 20 Board 20 **Notes** ⊗ No Children 16yrs

WANTAGE — Map 5 SU38

The Star Inn

★★★★ ◉◉ INN

tel: 01235 751873 **Watery Ln, Sparsholt OX12 9PL**
email: info@thestarsparsholt.co.uk **web:** www.thestarsparsholt.co.uk
dir: From B4507, 4m W of Wantage turn right to Sparsholt. The Star Inn is signposted

Located in the picturesque village of Sparsholt, at the foot of the famous Ridgeway. At the heart of the community for over 300 years, The Star Inn offers bedrooms that are peacefully situated in a converted barn at the rear of the property, each providing a very good level of comfort. The two AA Rosette-worthy food is a highlight of any stay; excellent quality ingredients are skilfully prepared and carefully presented.

Rooms 8 en suite (1 fmly) (5 GF) S £85-£115; D £95-£135* **Facilities** FTV DVD tea/coffee Dinner available WiFi 🍴 **Extras** Speciality toiletries **Parking** 15

La Fontana Restaurant with Accommodation

★★★★ RESTAURANT WITH ROOMS

tel: 01235 868227 & 07836 730048 **Oxford Rd, East Hanney OX12 0HP**
email: anna@la-fontana.co.uk **web:** www.la-fontana.co.uk
dir: A338 from Wantage towards Oxford. Restaurant on right in East Hanney

Guests are guaranteed a warm welcome at this family-run Italian restaurant located on the outskirts of the busy town of Wantage. The stylish bedrooms are individually designed, well equipped and very comfortable. Dinner should not be missed – the menu features a wide range of regional Italian specialities.

Rooms 12 en suite 3 annexe en suite (1 fmly) (4 GF) S £67.50-£72.50; D £87.50-£125* **Facilities** FTV Lounge tea/coffee Dinner available Direct Dial WiFi **Parking** 30 **Notes** ⊗ No coaches Civ Wed 120

WANTAGE continued

Hill Barn (SU337852)

★★★ FARMHOUSE

tel: 01235 751236 & 07885 368918 **Sparholt Firs OX12 9XB**
email: jmw@hillbarn.plus.com **web:** www.hillbarnbedandbreakfast.co.uk
dir: W of B4001 on The Ridgeway, 4m N of Wantage

This working farm offers en suite bedrooms with beautiful far-reaching views over the countryside. The atmosphere is friendly, and guests are able to relax either in the sitting room or in the garden. Breakfast is a highlight with home-made jams and other produce from the farm (when available).

Rooms 3 rms (2 en suite) (1 pri facs) **Facilities** Lounge TVL TV2B tea/coffee Dinner available WiFi ⚓ **Parking** 3 **Notes** LB ⊛ 100 acres horses

WATLINGTON   Map 5 SU69

The Fat Fox Inn

★★★ ⊛ INN

tel: 01491 613040 **13 Shirburn St OX49 5BU**
email: info@thefatfoxinn.co.uk **web:** www.thefatfoxinn.co.uk
dir: M40 junct 6 onto B4009 S for 2.5m. On right in village

Just 20 minutes out of Oxford city, this inn is conveniently located for both the leisure guest, especially walkers of the nearby Ridgeway and the business traveller looking for a quiet location. Guests can enjoy lunch and dinner in the relaxed bar or in the restaurant, where the kitchen team offers well-sourced, seasonal food.

Rooms 9 en suite (1 fmly) (5 GF) **Facilities** FTV tea/coffee Dinner available WiFi ⚓ **Parking** 20

WHEATLEY   Map 5 SP50

Gidleigh House

★★★★ BED AND BREAKFAST

tel: 01865 875150 & 07733 026882 **27 Old London Rd OX33 1YW**
web: www.gidleighousebb.co.uk
dir: M40 junct 8 follow signs to Wheatley. Pass Asda on left & right turn to Hotton/Waterperry. Next right, marked private road

You are assured of a warm, personal welcome at this modern home which is located on a private road in a quiet village just ten minutes from Oxford city centre and has easy access to the M40. The two en suite rooms are spacious, very comfortable and equipped with thoughtful extras. Relax over a newspaper in the conservatory at the family-style table while your breakfast is freshly prepared.

Rooms 2 en suite (2 fmly) S fr £55; D £80-£82* **Facilities** TVL tea/coffee **Extras** Fruit, chocolates **Parking** 4 **Notes** ⊗ No Children 10yrs Closed 18 Dec-5 Jan ⊛

WITNEY   Map 5 SP31

Premier Collection

Old Swan & Minster Mill

★★★★★ ⊛ ⌂ INN

tel: 01993 774441 **Old Minster OX29 0RN**
email: enquiries@oldswanandminstermill.com
web: www.oldswanandminstermill.com
dir: Exit A40 signed Minster Lovell, through village right T-junct, 2nd left

Located within its own stunning grounds and gardens including a private stretch of the River Windrush, the Old Swan & Minster Mill are two distinct accommodation areas, both with quality and individuality. Check-in is at the Minster Mill, where guests are welcomed and escorted to their room or suite. Old Swan rooms are traditional, with old oak beams and fireplaces in some rooms, while Mill rooms are more contemporary in style, many of which feature great views of the river and grounds. Award-winning cuisine is served in the dining room. There is a two-night minimum stay at weekends.

Rooms 60 en suite (4 fmly) (19 GF) D £175-£395* **Facilities** FTV Lounge tea/coffee Dinner available Direct Dial WiFi ⌚ ⚒ ⚕ 18 Fishing Riding Gym Pool table ⚓ Petanque **Extras** Speciality toiletries, decanter of sloe gin **Conf** Max 55 Thtr 55 Class 22 Board 24 **Parking** 70 **Notes** LB No coaches Civ Wed 50

Corncroft Guest House

★★★★ GUEST ACCOMMODATION

tel: 01993 773298 **69-71 Corn St OX28 6AS**
web: www.corncroftguesthouse.com
dir: A40 to town centre, from Market Square into Corn Street, 400mtrs on left

Located in the quieter end of town, yet close to the centre, Corncroft Guest House offers comfortable well-equipped accommodation in a friendly atmosphere. Substantial breakfasts featuring local produce are served in the attractive dining room.

Rooms 11 en suite (1 fmly) (2 GF) **Facilities** FTV DVD TVL tea/coffee WiFi **Extras** Sweets - complimentary **Notes** Closed 24-26 Dec

Crofters Guest House

★★★★ GUEST ACCOMMODATION

tel: 01993 778165 & 07930 539021 **29 Oxford Hill OX28 3JU**
email: countycolours@hotmail.co.uk **web:** www.bedandbreakfastwitney.co.uk
dir: Off A40 onto B4022 (Witney East). On right just after 1st set of lights

Crofters Guest House is located on the west side of Witney, just a ten minute walk from the centre of town. There are two ground floor double en suite rooms and two twin rooms with shared facilities upstairs. A family style breakfast table arrangement is provided in the conservatory. WiFi is available throughout and off-road parking is a bonus.

Rooms 4 rms (2 en suite) (1 fmly) (2 GF) S £55-£60; D £75-£85* **Facilities** FTV TVL tea/coffee WiFi ⚓ **Parking** 5 **Notes** ⊗

WOODSTOCK
Map 11 SP41

Premier Collection

The Glove House

☆☆☆☆☆ BED AND BREAKFAST

tel: 01993 813475 & 07447 012832 **24 Oxford St OX20 1TS**
email: info@theglovehouse.co.uk **web:** www.theglovehouse.co.uk
dir: M40 junct 8 onto A40, then A44 signed to Evesham/Woodstock. Glove House on right

The Glove House is a 17th-century Grade II listed property, which has been sympathetically renovated and enjoys a prime location; Blenheim Palace is within walking distance. The three en suite bedrooms are very well appointed and ooze style, quality and comfort. Breakfast can be served in the walled garden during the summer. The Glove House was the AA Guest Accommodation of the Year for England 2015-2016.

Rooms 3 en suite (2 fmly) S £155-£205; D £170-£220* **Facilities** FTV DVD iPod docking station Lounge tea/coffee WiFi **Extras** Speciality toiletries, mini-bar **Notes** ⊗ No Children 10yrs

Duke of Marlborough Country Inn

★★★★ INN

tel: 01993 811460 **Woodleys OX20 1HT**
email: sales@dukeofmarlborough.co.uk **web:** www.dukeofmarlborough.co.uk
dir: 1m N of Woodstock on A44 x-rds

The Duke of Marlborough is just outside the popular town of Woodstock, convenient for local attractions including Blenheim Palace. Bedrooms and bathrooms are in an adjacent lodge-style building and offer high standards of quality and comfort. Dinner includes many tempting home-cooked dishes, complemented by a good selection of ales and wines.

Rooms 13 annexe en suite (2 fmly) (7 GF) S £65-£100; D £85-£140* **Facilities** FTV tea/coffee Dinner available Direct Dial WiFi ♨ **Extras** Snacks **Conf** Max 20 Thtr 20 Class 16 Board 12 **Parking** 42 **Notes** LB ⊗

The Woodstock Arms

★★★★ ⌂ INN

tel: 01993 811251 **Market St OX20 1SX**
email: book@woodstockarms.co.uk **web:** www.woodstockarms.co.uk

The Woodstock Arms enjoys a prominent position in the centre of Woodstock, and sympathetic refurbishment has retained many of the original period features. The stylish modern bedrooms are beautifully presented; beds are comfortable, and are draped with colourful wool throws. Espresso coffee machines, lots of books and luxurious bathrobes are further features. The cosy bar with its log fire is full of character, and there is a good choice of real ales along with local craft beers, and an extensive wine list. The menu includes delicious home-made pies and stone-baked pizzas. There is small sheltered courtyard at the rear of the inn which is very popular with guests. Just a short walk from Blenheim Palace, this is an ideal base from which to explore the Oxfordshire countryside.

Rooms 5 en suite **Facilities** FTV tea/coffee Dinner available WiFi **Extras** Robes

The Townhouse

★★★ GUEST ACCOMMODATION

tel: 01993 810843 **15 High St OX20 1TE**
email: townhousewoodstock@hotmail.co.uk **web:** www.woodstock-townhouse.com
dir: Off A44 into High St

This early 18th-century stone town house is full of character and offers five individually styled, cosy en suite bedrooms. Situated in the heart of the town just a short walk from Blenheim Palace, it is an ideal base for exploring many famous Cotswold locations. Breakfasts are cooked to order and served in the small conservatory room overlooking the walled garden.

Rooms 5 en suite (1 fmly) S £60-£65; D £80-£83* **Facilities** FTV TVL tea/coffee WiFi **Notes** ⊗

WOOTTON
Map 11 SP41

The Killingworth Castle

★★★★ ⊛ INN

tel: 01993 811401 & 832849 **Glympton Rd OX20 1EJ**
email: reservations@thekillingworthcastle.com **web:** www.thekillingworthcastle.com

This 17th-century roadside country inn, located just a few miles from Woodstock and Blenheim Palace, has recently undergone a full refurbishment. It has retained its country charm with many modern creature comforts added. There are eight comfortable en suite bedrooms all within a converted Cotswold stone barn less than a stone's throw from the inn, and offer a very comfortable stay in a peaceful setting. A warm welcome is assured and dinner is not to be missed.

Rooms 8 annexe en suite (4 GF) **Facilities** FTV tea/coffee Dinner available WiFi **Extras** Sherry **Parking** 40 **Notes** No Children 16yrs

RUTLAND

CLIPSHAM
Map 11 SK91

Beech House

☆☆☆☆ ⊛ 🍴 INN

tel: 01780 410355 **Main St LE15 7SH**
email: info@theolivebranchpub.com **web:** www.theolivebranchpub.com
dir: From A1 take B668 signed Stretton & Clipsham

Beech House stands over the road from the Olive Branch restaurant. Its bedrooms are furnished with style and finesse, combining crisp linens, natural wood and retro-style accessories with traditional and modern furniture. Breakfasts are served in the Olive Branch and should not be missed. Excellent lunches and dinners are also available.

Rooms 5 en suite 1 annexe en suite (2 fmly) (3 GF) S £97.50-£165; D £115-£195* **Facilities** FTV DVD tea/coffee Dinner available Direct Dial WiFi ♨ 18 ♨ **Extras** Speciality toiletries - free; fruit - charged **Conf** Max 20 Thtr 20 Class 12 Board 16 **Parking** 10 **Notes** LB No coaches

The Marquess of Exeter

★★★★ ◉ INN

tel: 01572 822477 **52 Main St LE15 9LT**
email: info@marquessexeter.co.uk **web:** www.marquessexeter.co.uk
dir: M1 junct 19, A14 to Kettering, then A6003 to Caldecott. Right into Lyddington Rd, 2m to village

Situated in the picturesque Rutland countryside, the inn is appointed with contemporary touches while retaining many original features such as timber beam ceilings, log fires and flagstone floors. The stylish bedrooms, situated across a courtyard, are individually decorated and comfortable. The food is imaginative with the chef's 'sharing dishes' being particularly noteworthy.

Rooms 17 rms (16 en suite) (1 pri facs) (3 fmly) (10 GF) S £79.50-£104.50; D £99.50-£134.50* **Facilities** FTV tea/coffee Dinner available Direct Dial WiFi **Conf** Max 50 Thtr 50 Class 40 Board 40 **Parking** 60

Fox & Hounds

★★★★★ ◉◉ INN

tel: 01572 812403 **19 The Green, Exton LE15 8AP**
email: info@afoxinexton.co.uk **web:** www.afoxinexton.co.uk

This 17th-century coaching inn overlooks the Green in the picturesque Rutland village of Exton; the property has been recently refurbished and has three individually designed bedrooms. Public areas include a lounge bar, restaurant and library; the building also has a wealth of original features and landscaped gardens.

Rooms 3 en suite S £140-£160; D £140-£160* **Facilities** STV FTV DVD Lounge tea/coffee Dinner available WiFi ⅃ 18 Fishing Riding ⚓ **Extras** Speciality toiletries **Parking** 20

Kirkee House

★★★★ BED AND BREAKFAST

tel: 01572 757401 **35 Welland Way LE15 6SL**
email: carolbeech@kirkeehouse.demon.co.uk **web:** www.kirkeehouse.co.uk
dir: S of town centre. Exit A606 (High St) into Mill St, over level crossing, 400yds on left

Located on a leafy avenue a short walk from the town centre, this immaculately maintained modern house provides comfortable bedrooms filled with homely extras. Comprehensive breakfasts, including local sausages and home-made jams, are served in the elegant conservatory-dining room which overlooks the pretty garden.

Rooms 2 en suite D £72-£75* **Facilities** FTV tea/coffee WiFi ⚓ **Parking** 2 **Notes** ⊗ No Children 7yrs ⊛

The Lake Isle

★★★★ ◉◉ ≜ RESTAURANT WITH ROOMS

tel: 01572 822951 **16 High Street East LE15 9PZ**
email: info@lakeisle.co.uk **web:** www.lakeisle.co.uk
dir: From A47, turn left at 2nd lights, 100yds on right

This attractive town house centres around a delightful restaurant and small elegant bar. There is also an inviting first-floor guest lounge, and the bedrooms are extremely well appointed and thoughtfully equipped; spacious split-level cottage suites situated in a quiet courtyard are also available. The imaginative cooking and an extremely impressive wine list are highlights here.

Rooms 9 en·suite 3 annexe rms (3 pri facs) (1 fmly) (1 GF) **Facilities** FTV Lounge tea/coffee Dinner available Direct Dial WiFi ⚓ **Extras** Home-made biscuits - complimentary **Conf** Max 16 Board 16 **Parking** 7 **Notes** Closed 1 Jan & BHs RS Sun eve & Mon lunch closed No coaches

The Crown

★★★ INN

tel: 01572 822302 **19 High St, East Uppingham LE15 9PY**
email: info@thecrownrutland.co.uk **web:** www.thecrownrutland.co.uk

Located on the high street in the centre of Uppingham, this traditional inn dates back to 1739, and with some modernisation to the bedrooms, now offers comfortable accommodation. Guests can enjoy a range of real ales, and a selection of bar meals. There is parking to the rear, and free WiFi is available.

Rooms 7 en suite (1 fmly) **Facilities** FTV TVL tea/coffee Dinner available WiFi ⚓ **Conf** Max 25 Thtr 25 Class 25 Board 25 **Parking** 10 **Notes** No coaches

Kings Arms Inn & Restaurant

★★★★ ◉◉ ≜ INN

tel: 01572 737634 **13 Top St LE15 8SE**
email: info@thekingsarms-wing.co.uk **web:** www.thekingsarms-wing.co.uk
dir: 1.5m off A6003 in village centre

This traditional village inn, with its open fires, flagstone floors and low beams, dates from the 17th century. The restaurant is more contemporary and offers a wide range of interesting, freshly produced dishes. Service is attentive and friendly. The spacious, well-equipped bedrooms are in The Old Bake House and Granny's Cottage, in the nearby courtyard.

Rooms 8 en suite (4 GF) S £65-£75; D £80-£100 (room only)* **Facilities** FTV tea/coffee Dinner available WiFi **Parking** 30

SHROPSHIRE

BISHOP'S CASTLE
Map 15 S038

The Castle

★★★★ ⬤ INN

tel: 01588 638403 **Market Square SY9 5BN**
email: stay@thecastlehotelbishopscastle.co.uk
web: www.thecastlehotelbishopscastle.co.uk
dir: *Turn off A488 into Bishop's Castle, at top of High St on left*

This medieval town on the England-Wales border is famed for its ale, and is home to the oldest working brewery in the country. Overlooking the historic town with its mixed architecture and unusually painted houses (spotty, jigsaw etc.) sits the remains of a castle. In 1719 much of the stone from this castle was used to create The Castle Hotel, built on the old Baille (or enclosed courtyard) on the instruction of a wealthy landowner. Nearly 300 years on The Castle continues to welcome guests from far and wide. Many of the comfortably furnished rooms have stunning views across the Marches. Hearty meals are served in the bar, dining room and on sunny days on the garden terrace. Offa's Dyke, The Shropshire Way and Kerry Ridgeway are all within easy striking distance.

Rooms 12 en suite S £75-£100; D £95-£150* **Facilities** FTV TVL tea/coffee Dinner available WiFi ⬤ **Conf** Max 24 **Parking** 25 **Notes** LB Closed 25 Dec No coaches

Boars Head

★★★★ INN

tel: 01588 638521 **Church St SY9 5AE**
email: info@boarsheadhotel.co.uk **web:** www.boarsheadhotel.co.uk

The Boars Head is situated in the centre of Bishop's Castle, and is a traditional inn with comfortable and spacious bedrooms in a separate annexe. The inn incorporates a post office with a cash machine and phone top-up facilities. Food is on offer all day. Parking is available to the rear of the inn.

Rooms 4 annexe en suite (1 fmly) (3 GF) **Facilities** FTV DVD iPod docking station Lounge TV3B tea/coffee Dinner available WiFi **Extras** Fridge, digital safe, mineral water **Parking** 60 **Notes** ⊗

BRIDGNORTH
Map 10 S079

The Halfway House Inn

★★★ INN

tel: 01746 762670 **Cleobury Mortimer Rd WV16 5LS**
email: info@halfwayhouseinn.co.uk **web:** www.halfwayhouseinn.co.uk
dir: *1.5m from town centre on B4363 to Cleobury Mortimer*

Located in a rural area, this 16th-century inn has been renovated to provide good standards of comfort, while retaining its original character. The bedrooms, some in converted stables and cottages, are especially suitable for families and groups.

Rooms 10 en suite (10 fmly) (6 GF) S £50-£75; D £65-£95 **Facilities** FTV TVL tea/coffee Dinner available WiFi ⬥ 18 Fishing Pool table ⬤ **Conf** Max 30 Thtr 30 Class 24 Board 20 **Parking** 30 **Notes** LB Closed 25-26 Dec RS Winter Sun eve (ex BHs) from 5pm

CHURCH STRETTON
Map 15 S049

Court Farm (S0514951)

★★★★ 🏠 FARMHOUSE

tel: 01694 771219 **Gretton SY6 7HU**
email: alison@courtfarm.eu **web:** www.courtfarm.eu
dir: *Turn off B4371 at Longville, left at x-rds, 1st on left*

Located in the village of Gretton, this Grade II listed stone-built Georgian house is on a 330-acre working farm, and its bedrooms overlook the pretty gardens. Home to the Norris family since 1898, over the years they have sympathetically restored and modernised the building. Comprehensive breakfasts are served in an elegant dining room, and a comfortable guest lounge is also available. Court Farm is an ideal base for exploring Shropshire and surrounding areas.

Rooms 2 en suite S £55-£60; D £75-£80* **Facilities** FTV TVL tea/coffee WiFi ⬤ **Parking** 4 **Notes** ⊗ No Children 12yrs ⬤ 330 acres mixed

Belvedere Guest House

★★★★ GUEST HOUSE

tel: 01694 722232 **Burway Rd SY6 6DP**
email: info@belvedereguesthouse.co.uk **web:** www.belvedereguesthouse.co.uk
dir: *Exit A49 into town centre, over x-rds into Burway Rd*

Popular with walkers and cyclists and peacefully located on the lower slopes of the Long Mynd, this impressive, well-proportioned Edwardian house has a range of homely bedrooms, equipped with practical extras and complemented by modern bathrooms. Ground-floor areas include a cottage-style dining room overlooking the pretty garden and large lounge complete with TV, a large selection of reading material and board games.

Rooms 7 rms (6 en suite) (2 fmly) S £40; D £60-£70 **Facilities** TVL tea/coffee WiFi ⬤ **Extras** Mini-fridge, snacks, bottled water - chargeable **Parking** 9 **Notes** LB Closed Xmas & Jan

The Bucks Head

★★★★ INN

tel: 01694 722898 & 07811 364416 **42 High St SY6 6BX**
email: lloyd.nutting@btconnect.com **web:** www.the-bucks-head.co.uk
dir: *A49 N or S, turn into Church Stretton. At top of town turn left, Bucks Head on right*

The Bucks Head enjoys a central location in the heart of historic Church Stretton, and is a vibrant modern inn. There are high levels of comfort and up-to-date facilities together with original charm and character. The comfortable bedrooms are complemented by smart en suite bathrooms, and the attractive open-plan public areas are the perfect setting for enjoying food and drinks. The hospitality is warm and genuine.

Rooms 4 en suite **Facilities** FTV tea/coffee Dinner available WiFi **Notes** ⊗ No Children 5yrs No coaches

DORRINGTON
Map 15 SJ40

Upper Shadymoor Farm (SJ454021)
★★★★ FARMHOUSE

tel: 01743 718670 **Stapleton SY5 7AL**
email: kevan@shadymoor.co.uk **web:** www.shadymoor.co.uk

Upper Shadymoor Farm has it all, the shabby-chic rooms, the formal dining room, the family atmosphere, the tranquil location, the farm animals, the deer park and much more. Expect a warm welcome from the Fox family and a truly enjoyable experience. Produce from the farm is used at dinner and breakfast.

Rooms 3 en suite (1 fmly) S £60-£65; D £80-£85* **Facilities** Lounge tea/coffee Dinner available WiFi Fishing ⚓ **Parking** 20 **Notes** ⊛ 200 acres beef/mixed/sheep

GRINSHILL
Map 15 SJ52

The Inn at Grinshill
★★★★★ ⊛⊛ INN

tel: 01939 220410 **The High St SY4 3BL**
email: sales@theinnatgrinshill.co.uk **web:** www.theinnatgrinshill.co.uk
dir: N of Shrewsbury on A49, after 7m turn left, inn 500yds on left

This inn is part Grade II listed and many areas have been uncovered to highlight the original features. It is located under the lee of Grinshill in a delightful village with beautiful countryside close by; the Welsh border is within easy driving distance as are Shrewsbury, Telford and Welshpool. The accommodation is comfortable, and real ales and award-winning food are available in the spacious restaurant. Guests are very welcome to make use of the grounds.

Rooms 6 en suite S £69.50-£89.50; D £89.50-£119.50 **Facilities** FTV TVL tea/coffee Dinner available WiFi ⅄ 36 ⚓ **Parking** 30 **Notes** LB Closed 1st wk Jan RS Sun, Mon & Tue no accommodation

IRONBRIDGE
Map 10 SJ60

Broseley House
★★★★ GUEST HOUSE

tel: 01952 882043 & 07790 732723 **1 The Square, Broseley TF12 5EW**
email: info@broseleyhouse.co.uk **web:** www.broseleyhouse.co.uk
dir: 1m S of Ironbridge in Broseley town centre

A warm welcome is assured at this impressive Georgian house in the centre of Broseley. Quality, individual decor and soft furnishings highlight the many original features, and the thoughtfully furnished bedrooms are equipped with a wealth of homely extras. Comprehensive breakfasts are taken in an elegant dining room; a stylish apartment is also available.

Rooms 6 en suite (2 fmly) (1 GF) **Facilities** FTV DVD iPod docking station tea/coffee WiFi ⚓ **Extras** Fridge, robes, slippers **Notes** LB No Children 5yrs

LUDLOW
Map 10 SO57

Premier Collection

Old Downton Lodge
★★★★★ ⊛⊛⊛ ⬤ RESTAURANT WITH ROOMS

tel: 01568 771826 & 07977 475881 **Downton on the Rock SY8 2HU**
email: bookings@olddowntonlodge.com **web:** www.olddowntonlodge.com
dir: From Ludlow onto A49 towards Shrewsbury, 1st left onto A4113. After 1.9m turn left signed Downton, 3m on single track road. Turn right, signed

Originally a farm, this high-end establishment has bags of character, and is a stylish, comfortable and tranquil place to stay. Bedrooms are spacious and very well appointed, with comfortable beds and luxurious bathrooms. Old Downton Lodge is within easy reach of Ludlow's many attractions, and is in a peaceful location with good parking, pleasant grounds, ideal for walks and country pursuits. There is an honesty bar and excellent wine list. Breakfast should not be missed, and the three AA Rosette-worthy dinner is a highlight, with an imaginative five- or seven-course tasting menu using local, seasonal and foraged produce, served every Tuesday to Saturday evening.

Rooms 9 en suite (5 GF) S £125-£175; D £125-£250* **Facilities** FTV DVD Lounge tea/coffee Dinner available Direct Dial WiFi **Extras** Speciality toiletries, home-made biscuits **Conf** Max 40 Thtr 40 Class 40 Board 40 **Parking** 20 **Notes** LB No Children 13yrs Closed 24-26 Dec Civ Wed 40

Premier Collection

The Clive Bar & Restaurant with Rooms
★★★★★ ⊛ ⬤ RESTAURANT WITH ROOMS

tel: 01584 856565 & 856665 **Bromfield SY8 2JR**
email: info@theclive.co.uk **web:** www.theclive.co.uk
dir: 2m N of Ludlow on A49 in Bromfield

The Clive is just two miles from the busy town of Ludlow and is a convenient base for visiting the local attractions or for business. Based at the Ludlow Food Centre, good use is made of food made on site or from the company farms, ensuring local seasonal produce at every meal. The bedrooms, located in an annexe, are spacious and very well equipped; one is suitable for families and many are on the ground-floor level. Meals are available in the well-known Clive Restaurant or in the bar areas. The property also has a small meeting room.

Rooms 14 annexe en suite (1 fmly) (10 GF) S £65-£157.50; D £70-£170* **Facilities** FTV tea/coffee Dinner available Direct Dial WiFi ⅄ 18 **Extras** Mini-bar with local produce **Conf** Max 40 Thtr 40 Class 40 Board 24 **Parking** 80 **Notes** LB ⊛ Closed 25-26 Dec

Premier Collection

The Charlton Arms

★★★★★ ◉ INN

tel: 01584 872813 **Ludford Bridge SY8 1PJ**
email: reservations@thecharltonarms.co.uk **web:** www.thecharltonarms.co.uk

The accommodation at this riverside inn reflects the character of the historic building while offering all the comforts of modern living. Diners can enjoy fresh locally-sourced ingredients and a panoramic view across the River Teme. As a free house it also offers a fine selection of local beers. There is one bedroom which has a private terrace and a hot tub, and there are decking areas to enjoy drinks or a meal on warmer days.

Rooms 9 en suite (2 fmly) **Facilities** FTV tea/coffee Dinner available WiFi 🔒
Conf Max 100 Thtr 100 Class 80 Board 70 **Parking** 30 **Notes** Civ Wed 70

37 Gravel Hill

★★★★ BED AND BREAKFAST

tel: 01584 877524 **SY8 1QR**
email: angelastraker@btinternet.com
dir: Close to town centre

This charming old house is within walking distance of the town centre. It provides good quality, thoughtfully equipped accommodation, and there is also a comfortable sitting room. Guests share one large table in the elegant breakfast room.

Rooms 2 rms (1 en suite) (1 pri facs) S £50-£80; D £80-£90* **Facilities** TVL tea/coffee WiFi 🔒 **Notes** ⊛

Angel House Bed and Breakfast

★★★★ BED AND BREAKFAST

tel: 01584 891377 & 07568 142626 **Angel Bank, Bitterley SY8 3HT**
email: angelhouse48@gmail.com **web:** www.angelhousecleehill.co.uk
dir: On A4117 towards Kidderminster

Angel House has a super location, set just outside the busy hustle and bustle of Ludlow; the house has plentiful parking and super views. The friendly proprietors are very attentive and provide a comfortable place to stay. Bedrooms are very well appointed with lots of thoughtful extras. The gardens are spacious and home to the chickens that provide breakfast eggs.

Rooms 2 en suite (1 fmly) S £75; D £85-£90 **Facilities** FTV DVD Lounge tea/coffee Dinner available WiFi 🔒 **Extras** Speciality toiletries **Parking** 3 **Notes** No Children 7yrs

★ **Symbols and abbreviations are explained on page 7**

The Cliffe at Dinham

★★★★ RESTAURANT WITH ROOMS

tel: 01584 872063 & 876975 **Halton Ln, Dinham SY8 2JE**
email: info@thecliffeatdinham.co.uk **web:** www.thecliffeatdinham.co.uk

This former gentleman's residence is a short stroll from the River Teme, with magnificent views of Ludlow Castle, just a short walk from the vibrant centre of Ludlow. The Cliffe is a successful blend of the existing Victorian features and a more contemporary style. The rooms are comfortable and well equipped. Relaxed dining from locally sourced ingredients is offered in the attractive dining room, and there is a pleasant terraced area overlooking the gardens.

Rooms 11 en suite 2 annexe en suite (3 fmly) (1 GF) **Facilities** FTV tea/coffee Dinner available Direct Dial WiFi ⚡ 18 🔒 **Extras** Bottled water **Parking** 30 **Notes** Closed 25-26 Dec

130 Corve Street B&B

★★★★ BED AND BREAKFAST

tel: 01584 875548 **130 Corve St SY8 2PG**
email: info@130corvestreet.co.uk **web:** www.130corvestreet.co.uk
dir: N side of town on B4361, adjacent to Tesco supermarket

Expect a warm welcome at this Grade II listed building, situated within easy access of the town's many amenities and restaurants. The attractive bedrooms, situated on the ground floor at the rear, are comfortable and have independent entrances. Hearty breakfasts are served in the first-floor dining room. There is secure off-road parking next to the property.

Rooms 3 en suite (3 GF) **Facilities** FTV DVD tea/coffee WiFi **Parking** 3 **Notes** ⊛ No Children 12yrs

MARKET DRAYTON	Map 15 SJ63

Premier Collection

Ternhill Farm House

★★★★★ 🍷 🍴 GUEST ACCOMMODATION

tel: 01630 638984 **Ternhill TF9 3PX**
email: info@ternhillfarm.co.uk **web:** www.ternhillfarm.co.uk
dir: On junct A53 & A41, archway off A53 to back of property

This elegant Grade II listed Georgian property, once a farmhouse, has been lovingly converted into friendly, family-run guest accommodation. Bedrooms are individually designed and offer high levels of comfort. A choice of cosy lounges is available, and the large garden is a pleasant feature. The Cottage Restaurant is cosy (for parties of up to 22 people) but contemporary. Dinner must be reserved when the room reservation is made, and menu choices are required a minimum of 24 working hours prior to arrival. In addition, The Cottage Restaurant and/or Dining Room may be reserved for pre-booked non-resident parties of between 10 and 24 people.

Rooms 7 en suite **Facilities** FTV DVD Lounge tea/coffee Dinner available Licensed WiFi **Extras** Speciality toiletries **Parking** 21 **Notes** ⊛ No Children 14yrs RS Sun & Mon restaurant closed

MARKET DRAYTON *continued*

The Four Alls Inn

★★★ ⬠ INN

tel: 01630 652995 **Woodseaves TF9 2AG**
email: inn@thefouralls.com **web:** www.thefouralls.com
dir: *On A529 1m S of Market Drayton*

This country inn provides spacious open-plan public areas and has a strong local following for its food and real ales. Bedrooms, which are in a purpose-built chalet block, offer a good balance between practicality and homeliness. The superb beer gardens are adorned with attractive floral displays in summer.

Rooms 9 annexe en suite (4 fmly) (9 GF) S fr £47; D fr £67* **Facilities** FTV tea/coffee Dinner available Direct Dial WiFi ⬠ **Conf** Max 100 Thtr 100 Class 100 Board 30 **Parking** 60 **Notes** LB ⊗ Closed 24-26 Dec

MUNSLOW Map 10 SO58

Crown Country Inn

★★★★ ◉◉ ⬠ INN

tel: 01584 841205 **SY7 9ET**
email: info@crowncountryinn.co.uk **web:** www.crowncountryinn.co.uk
dir: *Off B4368 into village*

Located between Much Wenlock and Craven Arms, this impressive pastel-coloured and half-timbered Tudor inn is full of character and charm with stone floors, exposed beams and blazing log fires during winter. The smart pine-furnished bedrooms are in a converted stable block, and the spacious public areas include two dining rooms.

Rooms 3 en suite (1 GF) S £65-£125; D £99-£125* **Facilities** FTV DVD tea/coffee Dinner available WiFi ⬠ 19 ⬠ **Conf** Max 30 Thtr 30 Class 30 Board 20 **Parking** 20 **Notes** LB No Children 12yrs Closed 25 Dec RS Closed Sun eve & Mon for food & drink No coaches

NORTON Map 10 SJ70

The Hundred House

★★★★ ◉◉ INN

tel: 01952 580240 & 0845 644 6100 *(Calls cost 7p per minute plus your phone company's access charge)* **Bridgnorth Rd TF11 9EE**
email: reservations@hundredhouse.co.uk **web:** www.hundredhouse.co.uk
dir: *M54 junct 5, follow signs for Bridgnorth (A442), midway between Bridgnorth & Telford*

This interesting property has a genuine atmosphere of rural charm, setting it apart from the modern style of country 'food destination' pubs. A rabbit warren of public bars and restaurants, it provides respite for weary travellers and locals alike, many of whom come for the excellent meals. Bedrooms are individually designed, with

quirky furnishings and decor, and are well equipped. A large beer garden provides for good weather, with well-stocked herb and flower gardens to encourage a wander.

Rooms 9 en suite (4 fmly) S £70-£115; D £75-£140* **Facilities** FTV tea/coffee Dinner available Direct Dial WiFi ⬠ 18 ⬠ **Extras** Bottled water, sweets **Conf** Max 100 Thtr 80 Class 30 Board 35 **Parking** 50 **Notes** LB RS 25 Dec Restaurant closed pm Civ Wed 120

OSWESTRY Map 15 SJ22

Premier Collection

Greystones

★★★★★ ⬠ ⬠ GUEST HOUSE

tel: 07976 740141 **Crickheath SY10 8BW**
email: enquiry@stayatgreystones.co.uk **web:** www.stayatgreystones.co.uk
dir: *From A483 follow B4396, turn right through village take No Through Road, Greystones on right*

A warm welcome is assured at this impressive detached house, set in pretty, mature gardens in the hamlet of Crickheath. The bedrooms are equipped with a wealth of thoughtful extras and smart modern bathrooms. Comprehensive breakfasts and imaginative dinners, featuring the best seasonal produce, are available in the elegant dining room. A comfortable guest lounge is also provided. Dogs are allowed by prior arrangement only.

Rooms 4 en suite (1 fmly) (1 GF) **Facilities** FTV DVD TVL tea/coffee Dinner available Licensed WiFi ⬠⬠ 18 Fishing ⬠ **Extras** Espresso machine, robes, fridge, fruit **Conf** Board 10 **Parking** 20 **Notes** No Children 14yrs

The Pentre

★★★★ ⬠ ⬠ GUEST HOUSE

tel: 01691 653952 **Trefonen SY10 9EE**
email: helen@thepentre.com **web:** www.thepentre.com
dir: *4m SW of Oswestry. Exit Oswestry-Treflach road into New Well Ln, The Pentre signed*

A 500-year-old stone farmhouse, The Pentre retains many original features, including a wealth of exposed beams and a superb inglenook fireplace where the wood-burner blazes during colder months. Bedrooms are equipped with a range of thoughtful extras, and breakfast and dinner are memorable, with quality produce cooked with flair on the Aga.

Rooms 3 en suite (1 fmly) (1 GF) S £40-£50; D £72-£80* **Facilities** FTV TVL tea/coffee Dinner available WiFi ⬠ **Extras** Speciality toiletries, snacks - free **Parking** 10 **Notes** LB ⊗ ⬠

Sebastians

★★★★★ ◉◉ ⬠ RESTAURANT WITH ROOMS

tel: 01691 655444 **45 Willow St SY11 1AQ**
email: sebastians.rest@virgin.net **web:** www.sebastians-hotel.co.uk
dir: *From town centre, take turn signed Selattyn into Willow St. 400yds from junct on left opposite Willow Street Gallery*

Sebastians is an intrinsic part of the leisure scene in Oswestry and has built up a loyal local following. Meals feature French influences, with a multi-choice set menu as well as a simpler market menu. Rooms are set around the pretty terrace courtyard, and provide very comfortable accommodation with all the comforts of home.

Rooms 2 en suite 4 annexe en suite (2 fmly) (2 GF) S £75; D £85 (room only) **Facilities** iPod docking station Lounge tea/coffee Dinner available WiFi **Extras** Speciality toiletries, fruit, sweets - free **Parking** 6 **Notes** ⊗ Closed Xmas/New Year & BHs No coaches

SHIFNAL — Map 10 SJ70

The Anvil Lodge

★★★★ GUEST ACCOMMODATION

tel: 01952 460125 & 07918 163289 **22 Aston Rd TF11 8DU**
email: michaeldavies234@btinternet.com **web:** www.anvillodge.co.uk

A friendly welcome is assured at The Anvil Lodge, just a short stroll from the market town of Shifnal. Delicious, freshly cooked breakfasts are served around the dining room table. Bedrooms are spacious, fresh in appearance and very comfortable with modern bathrooms complete with bath and separate shower. Off-road secure parking is available.

Rooms 4 annexe en suite (2 fmly) (2 GF) **Facilities** FTV **Parking** 8 **Notes** ⊗

SHREWSBURY — Map 15 SJ41

See also Criggion (Powys), Wem & Westbury

Premier Collection

Drapers Hall

★★★★★ ⊚⊚ ≗ RESTAURANT WITH ROOMS

tel: 01743 344679 **10 Saint Mary's Place SY1 1DZ**
email: goodfood@drapershallrestaurant.co.uk
web: www.drapershallrestaurant.co.uk
dir: *From A5191 (Saint Mary's St) on one-way system into St Mary's Place*

Drapers Hall is a 16th-century, timber-framed property situated in the heart of the market town of Shrewsbury. Rooms differ in size, and all offer high levels of comfort and style, including two spacious suites. Bathrooms have a high quality finish and are well equipped for the modern traveller. The original beams and wood panels are complemented by striking art work and large gilt mirrors. A smart modern bar area successfully blends with the original architectural features, and has a great vibe. Accomplished cooking from Nigel Huxley can be enjoyed in a relaxing dining environment. Parking is available on request.

Rooms 6 en suite (2 fmly) **Facilities** FTV TVL tea/coffee Dinner available WiFi **Conf** Max 20 Thtr 20 Class 20 Board 20 **Notes** ⊗

Premier Collection

Darwin's Townhouse

★★★★★ ≗ BED AND BREAKFAST

tel: 01743 343829 & 07576 076376 **37 St Julians Friars SY1 1XL**
email: info@darwinstownhouse.com **web:** www.darwinstownhouse.com
dir: *Cross English Bridge, bear left (over pedestrian crossing) into Beeches Ln. 1st left into Williams Way, turn 1st left after car park, on left*

Darwins Townhouse is a beautifully restored Georgian property. Although situated in the centre of Shrewsbury, within walking distance of the many shops and restaurants, it sits on a peaceful street near the river. Bedrooms of various sizes are stylish and comfortable, and are located either in the main house or in the garden rooms to the rear of the property. Breakfast is served in the conservatory by the friendly team, using the finest local seasonal produce. There is an honesty bar.

Rooms 12 en suite 8 annexe en suite (1 fmly) (4 GF) S £75-£95; D £95-£150 **Facilities** FTV iPod docking station Lounge TVL tea/coffee Licensed WiFi 🔔 **Extras** Speciality toiletries, robes, slippers **Conf** Max 50 Thtr 50 Class 40 Board 30

Premier Collection

Porter House SY1

★★★★★ ⊚ RESTAURANT WITH ROOMS

tel: 01743 358870 & 761220 **15 Saint Mary's St SY1 1EQ**
email: hello@porterhousesy1.co.uk **web:** www.porterhousesy1.co.uk
dir: *Follow one-way system around town, opposite St Mary's church*

This fine property is located in the heart of the town. The name comes from a cut of steak, which is relevant to the style of cuisine here, with a real emphasis on locally sourced, good quality steaks and grills, served in the award-winning vibrant restaurant or bar. The four individually designed bedrooms, including a suite, are very comfortable and have spacious and contemporary bathrooms. Breakfast offers a quality range of dishes. Secure parking is available in a nearby public car park.

Rooms 4 en suite (1 fmly) **Facilities** tea/coffee Dinner available WiFi **Notes** ⊗ No coaches

SHREWSBURY continued

The Loopy Shrew

★★★★ INN

tel: 01743 366505 15-17 Bellstone SY1 1HU
email: hello@loopyshrew.com web: www.loopyshrew.com
dir: In centre of town, follow one-way system

Sister property to Porter House SY1, The Loopy Shrew offers 12 comfortably furnished en suite rooms in the heart of historic Shrewsbury. The open plan ground floor includes a well-stocked bar, coffee lounge and split level restaurant, all of which have been recently refurbished. Long stay parking is available within a few minutes' walk.

Rooms 12 en suite S £65-£95; D £85-£200* Facilities FTV tea/coffee Dinner available WiFi Extras Speciality toiletries Conf Board 20 Notes LB ⊗ Closed 25-26 Dec

The Old Station

★★★★ BED AND BREAKFAST

tel: 01939 290905 & 07714 068305 Leaton, Bomere Heath SY4 3AP
web: www.theoldstationshropshire.co.uk
dir: M54 junct 7 onto A5 then A49 N. At Battlefield (A5124) over rdbt into Huffley Ln, left by cricket field, 100mtrs on right

This former railway station, built in 1847, is set in the heart of the Shropshire countryside yet just four miles from Shrewsbury. The railway theme continues throughout the rooms, which offer a range of shapes and sizes. Stained-glass windows are a feature throughout the house. Breakfast is served in the well furnished dining room, with some tables located on what was previously the station platform. A garden and a small lounge are provided and there is ample parking.

Rooms 6 en suite (4 fmly) (1 GF) Facilities FTV TVL tea/coffee Dinner available WiFi 🔒 Extras Fridge in 2 bedrooms Parking 11 Notes LB Closed Dec-Feb ⊜

The Haughmond

★★★★★ ◉◉ INN

tel: 01743 709918 Pelham Rd SY4 4TZ
email: contact@thehaughmond.co.uk web: www.thehaughmond.co.uk

This delightful village inn has recently undergone a complete refurbishment to provide a contemporary dining area and bar with a range of comfortable bedrooms above. All rooms offer welcome extras and WiFi, with large rain showers in the bathrooms. Carefully prepared dishes, making good use of quality, local produce, are served for breakfast and dinner. Car parking, a garden with seating and even the village shop/café are on site. A new addition is Basil's restaurant, located in the former hayloft of a large barn conversion. If you were wondering, Basil's is named after the family dog. Basil's is only open Thursday to Saturday evenings.

Rooms 5 en suite (1 fmly) S £72-£90; D £90-£120* Facilities STV FTV iPod docking station Lounge tea/coffee Dinner available WiFi 🔒 🔒 Extras Smart TVs with Netflix Conf Max 60 Thtr 40 Class 60 Board 30 Parking 30 Notes No coaches

The Old Orleton Inn

★★★★★ ⚑ INN

tel: 01952 255011 & 07515 352538 Holyhead Rd TF1 2HA
email: info@theoldorleton.com web: www.theoldorleton.com
dir: M54 junct 7, towards Wellington then 400yds on left on corner of Haygate Rd & Holyhead Rd

Facing the Wrekin, this impressive 17th-century coaching inn has been appointed in a charming contemporary style. Each of the boutique-style bedrooms is unique in design and character, yet all retain original antique features. The kitchen has a good local reputation and fresh, quality produce, sourced locally whenever possible, is used in everything from snacks to three-course dinners, which are served in the three dining rooms.

Rooms 10 en suite S £79-£99; D £99-£119* Facilities FTV iPod docking station tea/coffee Dinner available Direct Dial WiFi 🔒 18 Discounted access to local gym/spa Conf Max 15 Thtr 15 Class 15 Board 15 Parking 25 Notes LB ⊗ No Children 5yrs Closed 1st 2wks Jan No coaches

The Lord Nelson

★★ GUEST ACCOMMODATION

tel: 01952 240055 11-13 Park St TF1 3AE
web: www.hotelintelford.com
dir: Contact The Lord Nelson for detailed directions

This Grade II listed property is pleasantly located close to town and has lots of charm and character. Pleasant meals are served in the bar dining area, and service is friendly and relaxed. Bedrooms are available in a range of room sizes and are comfortably appointed.

Rooms 12 en suite Facilities FTV tea/coffee Licensed WiFi Parking 12 Notes ⊗ Closed 16 Dec-6 Jan

Aston Lodge Guest House

★★★★ BED AND BREAKFAST

tel: 01939 232577 Soulton Rd SY4 5BG
email: astonlodge@btconnect.com web: www.aston-lodge.co.uk
dir: On B5065, close to Wem railway station

Aston Lodge is an elegant Georgian house situated in a quiet, convenient position close to the train station in the heart of Wem. Some bedrooms are in the main house while the others are found in the adjoining coach house. Of the latter, two are on the ground floor and the other has its own lounge. All rooms are of a high standard and have free WiFi and high quality bathrooms. Breakfast is served in the spacious dining room using fine quality and, where possible, locally-sourced produce. A comfortable lounge is available for guest use. There is ample off-road parking and a pleasant good-sized garden.

Rooms 3 rms (2 en suite) (1 pri facs) 3 annexe en suite (1 fmly) (2 GF) Facilities FTV DVD TVL tea/coffee WiFi Parking 6 Notes ⊗ No Children 10yrs RS 25-26 Dec room only

WESTBURY — Map 15 SJ30

Barley Mow House

★★★★ BED AND BREAKFAST

tel: 01743 891234 & 07890 215412 **Aston Rogers SY5 9HQ**
email: colinrigby@astonrogers.fsnet.co.uk **web:** www.barleymowhouse.co.uk
dir: 2m S of Westbury. Exit B4386 into Aston Rogers, house 400yds opposite Aston Hall

Dating in part from the 17th century and extended in the 18th, this charming property has been restored to provide comfortable accommodation with modern facilities. The house stands in a peaceful village and is surrounded by beautifully maintained gardens.

Rooms 3 en suite (1 fmly) (1 GF) **Facilities** FTV TVL tea/coffee WiFi 🔒 **Parking** 4 **Notes** Closed Dec-1 Mar ⊛

WHITCHURCH — Map 15 SJ54

Sedgeford House

★★★★ GUEST ACCOMMODATION

tel: 01948 665598 & 07962 111679 **Sedgeford SY13 1EX**
email: enquiries@sedgefordhouse.com **web:** www.sedgefordhouse.com
dir: From N - follow A41 to Tilstock Rd (B5476) turn left & left again. From S - into Whitchurch on B5395, straight ahead

Conveniently located just a five minute walk from the centre of the market town of Whitchurch, this modern property offers spacious, well-equipped bedrooms with the addition of very good quality bathrooms. There is a genuine warm welcome from the friendly owners and they are always on hand to advise on local attractions and restaurants.

Rooms 3 en suite **Facilities** FTV TVL tea/coffee WiFi 🔒 **Parking** 3 **Notes** ⊗ Closed 23 Dec-4 Jan

SOMERSET

AXBRIDGE — Map 4 ST45

Premier Collection

The Oak House

★★★★★ ⚙⚙ 🍴 RESTAURANT WITH ROOMS

tel: 01934 732444 **The Square BS26 2AP**
email: info@theoakhousesomerset.com **web:** www.theoakhousesomerset.com
dir: M5 junct 22, A38 N, turn right towards Axbridge & Cheddar

This impressive restaurant with rooms is located in the middle of the village and provides a relaxed, high quality experience, whether guests are coming to enjoy the restaurant or to stay in one of the nine bedrooms above. Hospitality and service are delivered in an efficient and helpful manner by a young and enthusiastic team. The kitchen has a serious approach and delivers delightful dishes full of flavour, utilising the best quality produce.

Rooms 9 en suite (2 fmly) **Facilities** FTV DVD Lounge tea/coffee Dinner available WiFi **Notes** ⊗ Closed 2-5 Jan RS Sun eve & Mon eve Restaurant closed

BABCARY — Map 4 ST52

The Red Lion Inn

★★★★ 🍺 INN

tel: 01458 223230 **Main St TA11 7ED**
email: info@redlionbabcary.com **web:** www.redlionbabcary.co.uk
dir: Off A303 & A37

Tucked away in a sleepy village, this engaging country pub has so much to offer and provides an appealing blend of traditional and contemporary styles. The thatched roof, flagstone floors and crackling log fires all set the tone alongside a committed team dedicated to ensuring guests are properly looked after. Bedrooms are located in the adjacent barn and provide impressive levels of comfort and quality, with all the necessities for a thoroughly relaxing stay. Food is not to be missed, as a skilled kitchen team make excellent use of the best the area has to offer. An alternative option in spring and summer is The Den, a stylish function room in the gardens which houses a wood-fired pizza oven.

Rooms 6 annexe en suite (2 fmly) (4 GF) S £90-£110; D £110-£130* **Facilities** DVD tea/coffee Dinner available Direct Dial WiFi **Extras** Speciality toiletries, snacks **Conf** Thtr 100 Board 20 **Parking** 35

BALTONSBOROUGH — Map 4 ST53

Lower Farm (ST572346)

★★★★ FARMHOUSE

tel: 01458 850206 & 07773 497188 **Lottisham BA6 8PF**
email: dboard51@btinternet.com **web:** www.lowerfarmbandb.co.uk
dir: From Shepton Mallet take A37 over Wraxall Hill past Queens Arms. Follow road 3rd turning on right to Lottisham, 1st on right

A working farm peacefully located and surrounded by pleasant countryside, where the proprietors offer a genuine welcome and traditional farmhouse hospitality. The one en suite bedroom is spacious and well equipped, and is located on the ground floor at one end of the main building. Breakfast is taken in the comfortable dining room where a wood-burning fire adds to the ambience during the winter.

Rooms 1 en suite (1 GF) **Facilities** FTV TVL tea/coffee ⚒ **Notes** ⊗ beef/sheep

BATH — Map 4 ST76

For other locations surrounding Bath see also Box (Wiltshire), Bradford on Avon (Wiltshire), Farmborough & Frome

Premier Collection

Apple Tree Guest House

★★★★★ 🍴 GUEST HOUSE

tel: 01225 337642 **7 Pulteney Gardens BA2 4HG**
email: enquiries@appletreebath.com **web:** www.appletreeguesthouse.com
dir: A4 onto A36 into Pulteney Rd. Under railway bridge, take 2nd left into Pulteney Gdns

This charming house is quietly located, and offers a tranquil setting. Some parking is available, and the location is within walking distance of Bath's many attractions. Excellent breakfasts are served in the cosy breakfast lounge. Bedrooms are thoughtfully appointed, and beds are particularly comfortable.

Rooms 4 en suite **Facilities** FTV tea/coffee WiFi Massage & beauty treatments **Extras** Speciality toiletries - complimentary **Parking** 2 **Notes** ⊗ No Children 11yrs Closed 14 Dec-9 Jan

BATH *continued*

Premier Collection

Apsley House

★★★★★ ⊜ BED AND BREAKFAST

tel: 01225 336966 **Newbridge Hill BA1 3PT**
email: info@apsley-house.co.uk **web:** www.apsley-house.co.uk
dir: *1.3m W of city centre on A431*

Built in 1830 by the Duke of Wellington, Apsley House is within walking distance (allow around half an hour) of the city centre. The house is extremely elegant, and the spacious bedrooms have pleasant views. Some rooms have four-poster beds, and there are two family rooms. A smart breakfast room and a delightful lounge are available.

Rooms 11 en suite (2 fmly) (1 GF) S £85-£200; D £99-£240* **Facilities** STV FTV DVD iPod docking station Lounge tea/coffee Direct Dial Licensed WiFi **Extras** Speciality toiletries, bottled water, mini-bar **Parking** 12 **Notes** LB ⊗ Closed 3 days Xmas

Premier Collection

One Three Nine

★★★★★ ⊜ GUEST ACCOMMODATION

tel: 01225 314769 **139 Wells Rd BA2 3AL**
email: info@139bath.co.uk **web:** www.139bath.co.uk
dir: *M4 junct 19, A46. A4 towards Bath, A367 towards Wells & Shepton Mallet. Establishment on left 500mtrs up hill*

Overlooking the historic city of Bath, this quality establishment pairs spacious accommodation with thoughtful design. The bedrooms are comfortably equipped with a very good range of accessories, and a number of feature bathrooms add a dash of luxury. Breakfast is served in the bright and airy dining room, where an excellent choice of continental and hot items is available. Off-street parking is an advantage.

Rooms 10 en suite (1 fmly) (2 GF) **Facilities** FTV DVD tea/coffee Direct Dial WiFi **Parking** 10 **Notes** ⊗ Closed 24-25 Dec

Premier Collection

Paradise House

★★★★★ ⊜ GUEST ACCOMMODATION

tel: 01225 317723 **Holloway BA2 4PX**
email: info@paradise-house.co.uk **web:** www.paradise-house.co.uk
dir: *A36 onto A367 (Wells Rd), 3rd left, down hill into cul-de-sac, house 200yds on left*

Set in half an acre of lovely walled gardens, this Georgian house built of mellow Bath stone, is within walking distance of the city centre. Many bedrooms have fine views over the city, and all are decorated in opulent style. Furnishings are elegant, and facilities modern. The lounge is comfortable and relaxing, and breakfast is served in the smart dining room. Hospitality and service are friendly and professional.

Rooms 12 en suite (5 GF) D £130-£220 **Facilities** FTV DVD Lounge tea/coffee Direct Dial Licensed WiFi **Parking** 10 **Notes** LB ⊗ Closed 24-25 Dec

Premier Collection

Tasburgh House Guest House

★★★★★ ⊜ GUEST ACCOMMODATION

tel: 01225 425096 **Warminster Rd BA2 6SH**
email: stay@tasburghhouse.co.uk **web:** www.tasburghhouse.co.uk
dir: *On N side of A36, next to Bathampton Ln junct*

Located on the main road just outside Bath, this elegant, detached property has undergone a complete refurbishment and provides high levels of quality and comfort throughout. Relaxing public areas include a guest lounge and the delightful conservatory-style breakfast room. Bedrooms vary in size but each includes a host of extras and very comfortable beds. Guests also have use of outdoor seating on the terrace, the large garden, and off-street parking.

Rooms 14 en suite (3 fmly) (2 GF) S £95-£120; D £140-£210* **Facilities** FTV DVD Lounge tea/coffee Direct Dial Licensed WiFi ⏬ ⛳ 18 Fishing ⚓ **Extras** Speciality toiletries, fresh milk - complimentary **Conf** Max 15 Thtr 10 Class 10 Board 15 **Parking** 16 **Notes** ⊗ No Children 6yrs Closed 21-31 Dec

Premier Collection

River House and Friary Coach House

★★★★★ GUEST ACCOMMODATION

tel: 01225 722252 & 07712 437478 **Friary, Freshford BA2 7UE**
email: info@riverhousebath.com **web:** www.riverhousebath.com
dir: *A36 S of Bath, pass signs for Freshford on left, take left turn at x-rds sign down narrow lane, "No through road"*

Set in eleven acres of delightfully peaceful former monastery grounds, River House offers views over the delightful gardens, and is just five miles from Bath. Accommodation consists of four comfortable bedrooms in the main house with lounges and relaxing areas for guests to enjoy, and the separate Friary Coach House: a luxurious, self-contained building adjacent to the main house. Guests in the Coach House have the option of breakfast being delivered to their own dining room. Attentive service and a genuine welcome are assured.

Rooms 5 en suite (1 fmly) (1 GF) S fr £60; D fr £120* **Facilities** STV FTV DVD iPod docking station Lounge TVL TV4B tea/coffee Dinner available Direct Dial Licensed WiFi ch fac ⏬ ⛳ Fishing Riding Pool table ⚓ Hot tub Badminton Art Nature Trail Clock golf **Extras** Chocolates, fridge, speciality toiletries - free **Parking** 10 **Notes** LB ⊗ ☺

Silver Stars

The AA Silver Star rating denotes a B&B that we highly recommend. They have a superior level of quality within their star rating, high standards of hospitality, service and cleanliness.

Premier Collection

Chestnuts House

★★★★ GUEST ACCOMMODATION

tel: 01225 334279 **16 Henrietta Rd BA2 6LY**
email: reservations@chestnutshouse.co.uk **web:** www.chestnutshouse.co.uk
dir: *Enter Bath on A46, under flyover, right at rdbt. Follow signs for A36 Warminster, over Cleveland Bridge & turn right. 50mtrs on left*

Located just a few minutes' walk from the city centre and appointed using light shades and oak, Chestnuts' accommodation is fresh and airy. Bedrooms are attractively co-ordinated, well equipped and comfortable. Added enhancements such as WiFi make the rooms suitable for both business and leisure guests. Breakfast, which features quite an extensive buffet and daily specials, is served in the dining room that opens onto the pretty rear garden. There is a cosy lounge, and the small car park is a bonus.

Rooms 5 en suite (1 fmly) (2 GF) **Facilities** STV FTV DVD TVL tea/coffee WiFi Riding **Extras** Speciality toiletries **Parking** 5 **Notes** ⊗

Premier Collection

Dorian House

★★★★★ GUEST ACCOMMODATION

tel: 01225 426336 **1 Upper Oldfield Park BA2 3JX**
email: info@dorianhouse.co.uk **web:** www.dorianhouse.co.uk
dir: *A36 onto A367 (Wells Rd), right into Upper Oldfield Park, 3rd building on left*

This elegant Victorian property has stunning views over the city. The atmosphere is welcoming, and the accommodation high quality. Several of the rooms have fine period four-poster beds and all offer a range of extra facilities. The attractive lounge has an honesty bar and views of the terraced gardens.

Rooms 13 en suite (4 fmly) (2 GF) **Facilities** FTV iPod docking station Lounge tea/coffee Direct Dial Licensed WiFi 🔒 **Parking** 9 **Notes** LB ⊗ Closed 24-26 Dec

Premier Collection

Waterhouse

★★★★★ GUEST ACCOMMODATION

tel: 01225 721999 **Waterhouse Ln, Monkton Combe BA2 7JB**
email: waterhouse@wilsher-group.com **web:** www.waterhousebath.co.uk
dir: *From Bath on A36 to Monkton Combe, over viaduct, turn right into Waterhouse Ln. From S on A36 turn left into Waterhouse Ln, at bottom of the hill*

This 18th-century manor house is in a peaceful location just a couple of miles outside of Bath. It offers modern bedrooms and bathrooms with plenty of welcome guest extras, and a range of relaxing lounges. Guests can enjoy the garden, and country walks start straight from the front door. Breakfast is served in the contemporary dining room, and meeting rooms are also available.

Rooms 13 en suite (4 fmly) **Facilities** FTV Lounge TVL tea/coffee Lift Licensed WiFi ⚓ 18 Fishing 🔒 **Extras** Fresh milk, bottled water - free; mini-bar **Conf** Max 40 Thtr 40 Class 20 Board 16 **Parking** 45 **Notes** LB ⊗

Premier Collection

The Windsor Townhouse

★★★★★ GUEST HOUSE

tel: 01225 422100 **69 Great Pulteney St BA2 4DL**
email: sales@bathwindsorguesthouse.com **web:** www.bathwindsorguesthouse.com

An easy two-minute walk from the city centre, shops, restaurants and attractions, The Windsor is set in a Grade I listed Georgian townhouse on Great Pulteney Street, one of the finest boulevards in Europe. Inside are fifteen individually-styled, en suite bedrooms. Period features, free WiFi, air-conditioning, flat-screen TVs, tea- and coffee-making facilities, hairdryer, mini-safe and ironing board come as standard. The addition of thick soft fluffy towels, cosy Dorma duvets, pillows and luxury Gilchrist and Soames toiletries complete the package. Breakfast offers a good selection of well-prepared, hot and cold dishes, and staff are very friendly and willing to help. Parking permits are available to purchase for the street outside.

Rooms 15 en suite (1 fmly) **Facilities** STV FTV DVD iPod docking station tea/coffee Direct Dial Licensed WiFi **Extras** Speciality toiletries, mini-bar **Parking** 4 **Notes** ⊗

Astor House

★★★★ BED AND BREAKFAST

tel: 01225 429134 & 07921 139558 **14 Oldfield Rd BA2 3ND**
email: astorhouse.visitus@virgin.net **web:** www.astorhouse-bath.co.uk
dir: *A4 into Bath to lights, then follow A36 (avoiding city centre). Onto A367, then 2nd right*

Astor House offers very comfortable accommodation and personal, friendly service. Rooms are understatedly elegant, and equipped with a wealth of extras for the modern traveller. Hearty breakfasts are served in the light dining room. The location, in a quiet street, is within easy distance of all central attractions, making it an ideal base from which to explore the city.

Rooms 7 en suite (3 fmly) **Facilities** FTV Lounge TVL tea/coffee Direct Dial WiFi ⚓ 🔒 **Parking** 5 **Notes** ⊗

BATH *continued*

The Bailbrook Lodge

★★★★ ≋ GUEST HOUSE

tel: 01225 859090 **35-37 London Road West BA1 7HZ**
email: hotel@bailbrooklodge.co.uk **web:** www.bailbrooklodge.co.uk
dir: *M4 junct 18, A46 S to A4 junct, left signed Batheaston. Lodge 1st on left*

Set in extensive gardens on the eastern edge of the city, this imposing Georgian building provides smart accommodation. The well-equipped bedrooms include some with four-poster beds and period furniture, and service is professional and efficient. The inviting lounge has a small bar, and light snacks are available from noon until evening. Breakfast is served in the elegant dining room.

Rooms 15 rms (14 en suite) (1 pri facs) (5 fmly) (1 GF) S £69-£89; D £89-£129*
Facilities FTV DVD iPod docking station Lounge tea/coffee Licensed WiFi ⬤
Extras Mineral water, bath robes in some rooms **Conf** Max 20 Thtr 20 Class 10 Board 12 **Parking** 15 **Notes** LB ⊗

Beckford House B&B

★★★★ BED AND BREAKFAST

tel: 01225 310005 **59 Upper Oldfield Park BA2 3LB**
email: info@beckford-house.com **web:** www.beckford-house.com
dir: *Turn off A36 (Warminster-Bristol road) opposite Skoda showroom, Upper Oldfield Park 3rd on left*

Close to the city's attractions, this charming Victorian house provides a relaxed and friendly welcome in a quiet location. The spacious bedrooms are elegantly furnished and beautifully decorated. The house is wonderfully proportioned and there are touches of grandeur throughout. A varied choice is offered at breakfast including local and organic produce.

Rooms 2 en suite (1 fmly) **Facilities** FTV DVD iPod docking station tea/coffee WiFi ⬤
Parking 2 **Notes** ⊗ No Children 11yrs Closed 25-31 Dec ⊜

Corston Fields Farm *(ST674648)*

★★★★ FARMHOUSE

tel: 01225 873305 & 07900 056568 **Corston BA2 9EZ**
email: corston.fields@btinternet.com **web:** www.corstonfields.com
dir: *300mtrs off A39 between Corston & Marksbury on lane running adjacent to Wheatsheaf pub*

Located in peaceful countryside and surrounded by a variety of crops, this traditional farmhouse offers a relaxing stay. Spacious and well-furnished bedrooms are located in the main property, with an additional room in a separate building that has its own entrance and patio. Guests are welcome to use the comfortable lounge. The delicious breakfasts use high-quality ingredients including free-range eggs from the farm.

Rooms 1 en suite 2 annexe en suite (2 GF) **Facilities** STV FTV Lounge tea/coffee WiFi Walk around farm **Extras** Speciality toiletries, fridge **Parking** 4 **Notes** ⊗ No Children 13yrs Closed 23 Dec-2 Jan 312 acres arable

Marlborough House

★★★★ GUEST ACCOMMODATION

tel: 01225 318175 & 07960 907541 **1 Marlborough Ln BA1 2NQ**
email: mars@manque.dircon.co.uk **web:** www.marlborough-house.net
dir: *450yds W of city centre, at A4 junct with Marlborough Ln*

Marlborough House is situated opposite Royal Victoria Park and close to the Royal Crescent. Some original features remain and the rooms are decorated with period furniture and pictures. The atmosphere is relaxed, and service is attentive and friendly. The breakfast, served from an open-plan kitchen, is vegetarian and organic.

Rooms 6 en suite (3 fmly) (1 GF) S £95-£145; D £105-£165 **Facilities** FTV Lounge tea/coffee Direct Dial Licensed WiFi ⬤ **Extras** Organic toiletries, water; mini-bar - chargeable **Parking** 3 **Notes** LB Closed 24-26 Dec

School Cottages Bed & Breakfast

★★★★ ≋ BED AND BREAKFAST

tel: 01761 471167 & 07989 349428 **The Street, Near Bath BA2 0AR**
email: tim@schoolcottages.co.uk **web:** www.schoolcottages.co.uk

(For full entry see Farmborough)

Villa Claudia

★★★★ BED AND BREAKFAST

tel: 01225 329670 **19 Forester Rd, Bathwick BA2 6QE**
email: claudiaamato77@aol.com **web:** www.villaclaudia.co.uk
dir: *From A4 into Cleveland Place East (A36), at next rdbt 1st exit into Beckford Rd, left into Forester Rd*

Villa Claudia is a beautiful Victorian property located on a quiet, tree-lined residential street within easy walking distance of the city centre's attractions and restaurants. The Italian owners provide attentive and personal service. Bedrooms and bathrooms are beautifully decorated and very comfortable; a four-poster room is available. Delicious breakfasts are served in the charming dining room at a communal table.

Rooms 3 rms (1 en suite) (2 pri facs) (1 fmly) S £95-£105; D £115-£135*
Facilities FTV DVD tea/coffee WiFi **Extras** Mineral water - complimentary **Parking** 4 **Notes** ⊗ Closed 21 Dec-1 Jan

The Bath House

★★★★ GUEST ACCOMMODATION

tel: 07711 119847 & 0117 937 4495 **40 Crescent Gardens BA1 2NB**
email: info@thebathhouse.org **web:** www.thebathhouse.org
dir: *100yds from Queen Sq on A431*

Appointed to high specifications, this accommodation is stylish and just a few minutes' level walk from the city. Bedrooms are attractive, spacious, light and airy, and equipped with modern accessories, including flat-screen TVs. WiFi is also available. Breakfast is room-service only, and a full-height dining table provided in the bedroom ensures guests enjoy their meal properly. Limited parking space is available.

Rooms 4 en suite (1 GF) **Facilities** FTV iPod docking station tea/coffee WiFi ⬤
Extras Mini-fridge, air conditioning **Parking** 5 **Notes** LB ⊗ No Children 8yrs

The Hollies

★★★★ GUEST ACCOMMODATION

tel: 01225 313366 **Hatfield Rd BA2 2BD**
email: davcartwright@lineone.net **web:** www.theholliesbath.co.uk
dir: A36 onto A367 Wells Rd & Wellsway, 0.7m right opposite Devonshire Arms

This delightful house stands in impressive gardens overlooking a magnificent church, and is within easy reach of the city centre. The individually decorated, themed bedrooms are appointed to provide excellent levels of comfort and have good facilities. Breakfast in the elegant dining room is an enjoyable start to the day.

Rooms 3 rms (2 en suite) (1 pri facs) **Facilities** FTV Lounge tea/coffee WiFi 🔒
Extras Sweets **Parking** 3 **Notes** ⊗ No Children 16yrs Closed 15 Dec-15 Jan

Poplar House

★★★★ BED AND BREAKFAST

tel: 01225 852629 **9 The Batch BA1 7DR**
email: poplarhousebath@gmail.com **web:** www.poplarhousebath.co.uk
dir: M4 junct 18 onto A46 (London Rd). Left at rdbt, located on left

Located a short drive from the centre of Bath, Poplar House is a very well-maintained property that offers comfortable accommodation in a peaceful setting. Bedrooms offer a range of shapes and sizes, and guests are also welcome to use the comfortable lounge and outdoor seating terrace. Breakfast utilises good quality produce and is served around one large table in the very pleasant dining room.

Rooms 3 en suite **Facilities** FTV TVL tea/coffee WiFi ⅃ 18 🔒 **Extras** Robes, sweets - complimentary **Parking** 6 **Notes** ⊗

Brocks Guest House

★★★★ GUEST ACCOMMODATION

tel: 01225 338374 **32 Brock St BA1 2LN**
email: brocks@brocksguesthouse.co.uk **web:** www.brocksguesthouse.co.uk
dir: Just off A4 between Circus & Royal Crescent

A warm welcome is extended at this delightful Georgian property, located in the heart of the city just a few hundred yards from Royal Crescent. All rooms reflect the comfortable elegance of the Georgian era. A traditional breakfast is served in the charming dining room, which also offers a lounge area with comfortable seating.

Rooms 6 en suite (2 fmly) **Facilities** FTV Lounge tea/coffee WiFi 🔒 **Notes** ⊗ Closed 24 Dec-1 Jan

Highways House

★★★★ GUEST ACCOMMODATION

tel: 01225 421238 **143 Wells Rd BA2 3AL**
email: highwayshouse@btconnect.com **web:** www.highwayshouse.co.uk
dir: A36 onto A367 (Wells Rd), 300yds on left

Victorian Highways House is just a ten-minute walk from the city centre; alternatively, there is a frequent bus service. The bedrooms are individually styled, well equipped and homely. A spacious, attractive lounge is available, and breakfast is served in the dining room at separate tables. Parking is a bonus.

Rooms 5 en suite 2 annexe en suite (2 fmly) (3 GF) **Facilities** FTV Lounge tea/coffee WiFi **Parking** 7 **Notes** ⊗ No Children 8yrs

Pulteney House
14 Pulteney Road
Bath Somerset BA2 4HA

PH
PULTENEY HOUSE

Telephone: 01225 460991
e-mail: pulteneyhouse@gmail.com
www.pulteneyhotel.co.uk/

Pulteney House is a large, elegant Victorian house set in its own picturesque south facing gardens, with fine views of Bath Abbey. All seventeen rooms are en suite except one. All have flat screen Free View / Free Sat colour television, hospitality trays, hairdryer and all are centrally heated and tastefully decorated to a very high standard.

The Lloyd family, who provide a warm and homely welcome to all guests, have privately owned Pulteney House for the past 37 years. The large, mature gardens are always kept in beautiful condition and guests are encouraged to utilise them to the full where children can play in absolute safety.

A comfortable family television lounge is available for all guests to use as well as large secure car parking facilities. Pulteney House is ideally located with all entertainments close at hand. The city centre is just a short, enjoyable stroll away (5 – 10 minutes level walk).

BATH *continued*

Milsoms Bath

★★★★ 🍴 RESTAURANT WITH ROOMS

tel: 01225 750128 **24 Milsom St BA1 1DG**
email: bath@milsomshotel.co.uk **web:** www.milsomshotel.co.uk
dir: *M4 junct 18, A46 (Bath), 3m, through Pennsylvania. 3rd exit at rdbt onto A420 (Bristol). 1st left signed Hamswell/Park & Ride, left at junct towards Lansdown. Right at next T-junct. 5th right into George St. 1st left into Milsom St*

Located at the end of the main street in busy, central Bath, this stylish restaurant with rooms offers a range of comfortable, well-equipped accommodation. The ground-floor Loch Fyne Restaurant serves an excellent selection of dishes at both lunch and dinner, with an emphasis on the freshest quality fish and shellfish. A good selection of hot and cold items is also available in the same restaurant at breakfast.

Rooms 9 en suite D £110-£220* **Facilities** FTV Lounge tea/coffee Dinner available Direct Dial WiFi **Notes** LB ⊗ Closed 24-25 Dec No coaches

Milton House Bed & Breakfast

★★★★ BED AND BREAKFAST

tel: 01225 335632 & 07875 319567 **75 Wellsway BA2 4RU**
email: info@milton-house.co.uk **web:** www.milton-house.co.uk
dir: *A36 inner ring road onto A367 (Wells Road). After 0.5m, sharp right turn, Milton House 150yds on left*

Located in a residential area just 15 minutes' walk from the centre of Bath, this comfortable establishment is run by Gibson and Blessing Mutandwa, who offer a very warm welcome to all guests. Bedrooms come in a range of shapes and sizes and are all well furnished and equipped. A carefully prepared breakfast is provided in the comfortable dining room. Parking is available on the side streets nearby, or on the main road outside.

Rooms 4 en suite (1 fmly) **Facilities** FTV tea/coffee WiFi 🎱 **Notes** ⊗ No Children 8yrs

More than 2,000 professionally inspected restaurants, from village inns to smart city eateries. Authoritative and reliable - Over 50 years of experience.

AA

THE **RESTAURANT** GUIDE 2017

INSPECTING RESTAURANTS FOR OVER 50 YEARS

shop.theAA.com

Pulteney House

★★★★ GUEST ACCOMMODATION

tel: 01225 460991 **14 Pulteney Rd BA2 4HA**
email: pulteney@tinyworld.co.uk **web:** www.pulteneyhotel.co.uk
dir: *On A36*

This large detached property situated in a well-tended garden, is within walking distance of the city centre. Bedrooms vary in size including some annexe rooms, and are well equipped with useful facilities. Full English breakfasts are served in the dining room at individual tables. A guest lounge and car park are both welcome features.

Rooms 12 rms (11 en suite) (1 pri facs) 5 annexe en suite (3 fmly) (2 GF) S £60-£70; D £95-£160* **Facilities** STV FTV TVL tea/coffee WiFi 🎱 **Parking** 18 **Notes** LB ⊗ Closed 24-26 Dec

See advert on page 261

Wentworth House

★★★★ GUEST ACCOMMODATION

tel: 01225 339193 **106 Bloomfield Rd BA2 2AP**
email: stay@wentworthhouse.co.uk **web:** www.wentworthhouse.co.uk
dir: *From city centre on A367 (signed Shepton Mallet), right into Bloomfield Rd*

Set in an elevated position above Bath with views over the city, Wentworth House is a comfortable establishment that includes a relaxing guest lounge, bar and garden with pool and hot tub in the summer. Bedrooms offer a range of shapes and sizes – some with four posters. Breakfast is served in the spacious dining room overlooking the garden.

Rooms 19 rms (18 en suite) (1 pri facs) 1 annexe en suite (3 fmly) (9 GF) **Facilities** FTV TVL tea/coffee Direct Dial Licensed WiFi ⚡ Hot tub **Conf** Max 15 Class 15 Board 15 **Parking** 15 **Notes** LB ⊗

The Rising Sun Inn

★★★ INN

tel: 01225 425918 & 07970 773169 **3-4 Grove St BA2 6PJ**
email: therisingsunbath@gmail.com web: www.therisingsunbath.co.uk
dir: *From A46 into Bath. Left at lights, over Cleveland Bridge, 1st right into St John's Rd, leads into Grove St*

This inn has an excellent location, just a few minutes' stroll from central Bath and all its attractions. Bedrooms are comfortably furnished and come in a range of shapes and sizes. A good selection of real ales is offered at the bar along with traditional dishes and home-cooked specials.

Rooms 5 en suite (1 fmly) S £70-£115; D £80-£125* **Facilities** STV FTV tea/coffee Dinner available WiFi **Notes** No coaches

Roman City Guest House

★★★ GUEST HOUSE

tel: 01225 463668 & 07899 777953 **18 Raby Place, Bathwick Hill BA2 4EH**
email: enquire@romancityguesthouse.fsnet.co.uk web: http://romancityguesthouse.co.uk
dir: *A4 onto A36 Bathwick St, turn right at lights, straight on at rdbt. Turn left at St Mary's church into Bathwick Hill, on left*

A warm welcome is assured at this 18th-century end-of-terrace house, located just a stroll from the heart of the historic city. The spacious bedrooms, some with four-poster beds, are comfortable and well equipped with many extra facilities.

Rooms 4 rms (3 en suite) (1 pri facs) (2 fmly) **Facilities** FTV DVD tea/coffee WiFi **Conf** Board 12 **Notes** ⊛

Find out more about AA Inspected Guest Accommodation on page 8

Waltons Guest House

★★★ GUEST HOUSE

tel: 01225 426528 **17-19 Crescent Gardens, Upper Bristol Rd BA1 2NA**
email: rose@waltonsguesthouse.co.uk web: www. bathguesthouse.com
dir: *On A4 350yds W of city centre*

There is a warm welcome at Waltons Guest House, situated within strolling distance of the centre of Bath. The cosy bedrooms come with useful extra facilities, and a traditional English breakfast is served at individual tables in the dining room.

Rooms 7 en suite **Facilities** FTV tea/coffee WiFi **Notes** ⊛

See advert below

Waltons Guest House
Bath (England)

Waltons Guest House, 17 Crescent Gardens, Upper Bristol Road, Bath, BA1 2NA

Tel: +44 (0)1225 426 528

Waltons Guest House an oasis in the centre of Bath catering for Business and Tourism and just a short walk to the Royal Crescent, City Centre and Heritage attractions.
All rooms are luxury en-suite and all rates include a hearty full English breakfast cooked to order.

AA
★★★
Guest House

BRIDGWATER
Map 4 ST23

Blackmore Farm (ST247385)

★★★★ FARMHOUSE

tel: 01278 653442 **Blackmore Ln, Cannington TA5 2NE**
email: dyerfarm@aol.com **web:** www.blackmorefarm.co.uk
dir: *3m W of Bridgwater. Follow brown tourist signs on A39, before Cannington*

Dating back to the 15th century, this Grade I listed manor house is truly unique; it has a wealth of original features such as oak beams, huge open fireplaces, stone archways and even a chapel. Bedrooms located in the main house are individual in style and one has a wonderful four-poster and a lofty, oak-beamed ceiling. Additionally, some bedrooms are located in a separate area, offering flexible accommodation with wonderful views across the rolling countryside. Breakfast is taken in the grandeur of the dining room around one incredibly long table – a truly memorable experience.

Rooms 3 en suite 6 annexe en suite (1 fmly) (6 GF) S £60-£65; D £110-£120*
Facilities FTV TVL tea/coffee Licensed WiFi ⬇️⛳ 18 Fishing 🔒 Farm shop café
Extras Fruit, bath robes in some rooms - complimentary **Conf** Max 30 Board 30
Parking 10 **Notes** LB ⊗ 900 acres dairy/arable

Ash-Wembdon Farm (ST281382)

★★★★ FARMHOUSE

tel: 01278 453097 **Hollow Ln, Wembdon TA5 2BD**
email: mary.rowe@btinternet.com **web:** www.farmaccommodation.co.uk
dir: *M5, A38, A39 to Minehead, at rdbt 3rd exit into Homeburg Way, at lights take B3339, right into Hollow Ln*

Near the Quantock Hills, Ash-Wembdon Farm is a 17th-century farmhouse on a working beef and arable farm, offering homely and comfortable accommodation. All rooms have en suite showers or private bathrooms, and English or continental breakfasts are served in the guest dining room. Guests also have use of a lounge and landscaped garden.

Rooms 3 rms (2 en suite) (1 pri facs) S £40-£45; D £60-£65 **Facilities** FTV Lounge tea/coffee WiFi 🔒 **Parking** 3 **Notes** LB ⊗ No Children 12yrs Closed 22 Dec-3 Jan 340 acres arable/beef

To help you navigate safely and easily, use the AA Road Atlas Britain 2017. Available from: shop.theAA.com

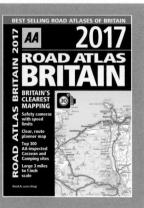

BEST SELLING ROAD ATLASES OF BRITAIN
AA
2017
ROAD ATLAS
BRITAIN
BRITAIN'S CLEAREST MAPPING
Safety cameras with speed limits
Clear, route planner map
Top 300 AA-inspected Caravan and Camping sites
Large 3 miles to 1 inch scale
theAA.com/shop

BROMPTON REGIS
Map 3 SS93

Holworthy Farm (SS978308)

★★★★ 🏡 FARMHOUSE

tel: 01398 371244 **TA22 9NY**
email: holworthyfarm@aol.com **web:** www.holworthyfarm.co.uk
dir: *2m E of Brompton Regis. Exit A396 on E side of Wimbleball Lake*

Set in the south-east corner of Exmoor, this working livestock farm has spectacular views over Wimbleball Lake. Bedrooms are traditionally furnished and well equipped. The dining room overlooking the garden is an attractive setting for breakfast. Dinner is available by arrangement.

Rooms 5 rms (3 en suite) (2 pri facs) (2 fmly) (1 GF) **Facilities** FTV DVD Lounge TVL tea/coffee Dinner available WiFi 🔒 **Extras** Bottled water - complimentary **Conf** Max 20 Class 20 Board 20 **Parking** 8 **Notes** LB ⊗ 200 acres beef/sheep

BURNHAM-ON-SEA
Map 4 ST34

Magnolia House

★★★★ GUEST HOUSE

tel: 01278 792460 **26 Manor Rd TA8 2AS**
email: enquiries@magnoliahouse.gb.com **web:** www.magnoliahouse.gb.com
dir: *M5 junct 22, follow signs to Burnham-on-Sea, at 2nd rdbt, Magnolia House on right*

Within walking distance of the town centre and beach, this elegant Edwardian house has been appointed to an impressive standard. Contemporary bedrooms offer comfort and quality with many extras such as WiFi, and a large DVD film library. Bathrooms are also modern and stylish with invigorating showers. A family suite is offered with separate, interconnecting bedrooms. Traditional full English breakfasts are served in the attractive, air-conditioned breakfast room, with vegetarian and continental options also available.

Rooms 4 en suite (2 fmly) **Facilities** FTV tea/coffee WiFi ⬇️ 18 **Parking** 7 **Notes** ⊗ No Children 5yrs

The Victoria

★★★ INN

tel: 01278 783085 **25 Victoria St TA8 1EQ**
web: www.the-victoria-hotel.co.uk

Just a short walk from the seafront at Burnham-on-Sea, The Victoria is a well established hostelry providing comfortable rooms and serving pub meals in the bar and restaurant. Some off-road parking is available on a first-come, first-served basis.

Rooms 6 rms (4 en suite) **Facilities** FTV tea/coffee Dinner available WiFi Pool table 🔒 **Parking** 6 **Notes** No Children 15yrs

CASTLE CARY
Map 4 ST63

The Pilgrims

★★★★ ◉◉ ⚲ RESTAURANT WITH ROOMS

tel: 01963 240600 **Lovington BA7 7PT**
email: jools@thepilgrimsatlovington.co.uk **web:** www.thepilgrimsatlovington.co.uk
dir: On B3153, 1.5m E of lights on A37 at Lydford

The Pilgrims describes itself as 'the pub that thinks it's a restaurant', which is pretty accurate. With a real emphasis on fresh, local and carefully prepared produce, both dinner and breakfast are the focus of any stay here. In addition, the resident family proprietors provide a friendly and relaxed atmosphere. Comfortable and well-equipped bedrooms are available in the adjacent converted cider barn.

Rooms 5 annexe en suite (5 GF) S £80-£130; D £90-£130* **Facilities** FTV Lounge tea/coffee Dinner available WiFi **Extras** Speciality toiletries **Parking** 5 **Notes** LB No Children 14yrs RS Sun lunch-Tue lunch Restaurant & bar closed to non-residents No coaches

CHARD
Map 4 ST30

Hornsbury Mill

★★★★ ⚲ GUEST ACCOMMODATION

tel: 01460 63317 **Eleighwater TA20 3AQ**
email: info@hornsburymill.co.uk **web:** www.hornsburymill.co.uk
dir: Off A358

Hornsbury Mill is a charming example of an early 19th-century corn mill, built of local flint with hamstone mullion windows. The waterwheel has been lovingly restored and turns during daylight hours; and there are four acres of beautiful gardens, making this a popular wedding venue. Bedrooms include a ground-floor room with good disabled access and facilities, and the delightful Crown Wheel Suite with four-poster bed and separate sitting room.

Rooms 10 en suite (2 fmly) (1 GF) S £70-£85; D £95-£110* **Facilities** FTV DVD Lounge tea/coffee Dinner available Direct Dial Licensed WiFi ⅃ 18 ⚱ **Conf** Max 150 Thtr 150 Class 50 Board 50 **Parking** 80 **Notes** ⊗ Closed 24 Dec-10 Jan Civ Wed 130

CHEW MAGNA
Map 4 ST56

Premier Collection

The Bear & Swan

★★★★★ ⚲ INN

tel: 01275 331100 **13 South Pde BS40 8PR**
email: thebearandswan@ohhcompany.co.uk **web:** www.ohhpubs.co.uk
dir: Chew Magna signed from A37 & A38, in centre of village

Part of a small and impressive collection of fine quality inns, this delightful village pub offers the best of traditional hospitality with an impressive range of dishes served throughout the day and evening. Recently refurbished bedrooms and bathrooms provide plenty of quality and comfort with sumptuous beds and bedding and modern, spacious showers. A well chosen selection of ales and wines completes everything required for the most relaxing of stays.

Rooms 4 en suite (1 fmly) S £85-£130; D £95-£150* **Facilities** FTV tea/coffee Dinner available Direct Dial WiFi ⚱ **Extras** Slippers **Parking** 6 **Notes** LB

CLUTTON
Map 4 ST65

The Hunters Rest

★★★★ ⚲ INN

tel: 01761 452303 **King Ln, Clutton Hill BS39 5QL**
email: paul@huntersrest.co.uk **web:** www.huntersrest.co.uk
dir: Off A37 onto A368 towards Bath, 100yds right into lane, left at T-junct, inn 0.25m on left

The Hunters Rest was originally built around 1750 as a hunting lodge for the Earl of Warwick. Set in delightful countryside, it is ideally located for Bath, Bristol and Wells. Bedrooms and bathrooms are furnished and equipped to excellent standards, and the ground floor combines the character of a real country inn with an excellent range of home-cooked meals.

Rooms 5 en suite (2 fmly) S £69.50-£85; D £105-£150 **Facilities** FTV iPod docking station tea/coffee Dinner available Direct Dial WiFi ⅃ 18 Fishing Riding ⚱ **Conf** Max 40 Thtr 40 Class 25 Board 25 **Parking** 90 **Notes** LB

Mezzé at the Warwick Arms

★★★★ ⚲ INN

tel: 01761 451200 **Upper Bristol Rd BS39 5TA**
email: clutton@mezzerestaurants.com **web:** www.mezzerestaurants.com/clutton
dir: S of Bristol on A37

Part of the Mezzé chain of inns, this delightful property provides high levels of quality and comfort. Conveniently located for Bristol Airport, the inn offers an excellent selection of dishes at dinner including a mezzé selection to tempt all tastes. Both dinner and breakfast are taken in the very comfortable dining room. Outdoor seating in the garden is also provided.

Rooms 8 en suite (1 fmly) S £60-£70; D £65-£80* **Facilities** STV FTV TVL tea/coffee Dinner available WiFi **Conf** Max 20 **Parking** 45 **Notes** ⊗

COMPTON MARTIN
Map 4 ST55

Ring O Bells

★★★★ ⚲ INN

tel: 01761 221284 **BS40 6JE**
email: ring_o_bells@btconnect.com **web:** www.ringobellscomptonmartin.co.uk
dir: On A368 between Blagdon & Chew Valley

The Ring O Bells is a delightful village inn that offers a rare combination of traditional character and hospitality with some more modern, quirky additions. The bar and dining areas are full of interest, and along with a good selection of real ales, a range of excellent dishes is offered. Bedrooms include very comfortable king-sized beds and quality showers in the bathrooms. Outdoor seating in the rear garden and car parking are both welcome features.

Rooms 1 en suite 1 annexe en suite (2 GF) S £60; D £90* **Facilities** FTV iPod docking station Lounge tea/coffee Dinner available WiFi ⅃ 18 ⚱ **Parking** 60 **Notes** LB RS Mon-Wed closed 3-6pm

CONGRESBURY
Map 4 ST46

Mezzé at the Ship and Castle
★★★★ ⏺ INN

tel: 01934 833535 **High St BS49 5BN**
email: congresbury@mezzerestaurants.com **web:** www.mezzerestaurants.com

Part of the Mezzé chain, this pleasant inn offers good quality bedrooms and bathrooms in a range of shapes and sizes. The restaurant is very well decorated and furnished in a contemporary style, providing comfortable all-day dining. The extensive menu offers the popular range of tapas dishes in addition to a more traditional menu. The pleasant rear garden is especially popular for outdoor dining.

Rooms 6 en suite (2 fmly) **Facilities** FTV DVD iPod docking station tea/coffee Dinner available WiFi **Parking** 60 **Notes** ⊗ No coaches

CORTON DENHAM
Map 4 ST62

Premier Collection

The Queens Arms
★★★★★ ◉◉ ⏺ INN

tel: 01963 220317 **DT9 4LR**
email: relax@thequeensarms.com **web:** www.thequeensarms.com
dir: A303 exit Chapel Cross signed South Cadbury & Corton Denham. Follow signs to South Cadbury. Through village, after 0.25m turn left up hill signed Sherborne & Corton Denham. Left at top of hill, pub at end of village on right

This is a proper inn located in peaceful countryside. Staff are friendly and welcoming, and the pub dog can usually be found in front of the roaring log fire in the bar. Bedrooms and bathrooms offer impressive levels of comfort, style and quality. In addition to a very good selection of real ales, this is a paradise for bottled beer lovers with a great choice from around the world. Excellent quality local produce can be found in the choice of delicious dinners which may be enjoyed in the traditional bar or character restaurant.

The Queens Arms

Rooms 5 en suite 3 annexe en suite (1 GF) S £90-£120; D £115-£135
Facilities FTV DVD iPod docking station Lounge tea/coffee Dinner available Direct Dial WiFi ⮧ 18 Riding ⬮ **Extras** Speciality toiletries, robes/slippers, sweets **Conf** Max 35 Thtr 35 Class 25 Board 30 **Parking** 20 **Notes** LB

See advert on opposite page

CREWKERNE
Map 4 ST40

Manor Farm
★★★★ GUEST ACCOMMODATION

tel: 01460 78865 & 07900 692070 **Wayford TA18 8QL**
email: theresaemery@hotmail.com **web:** www.manorfarm.biz
dir: B3165 from Crewkerne to Lyme Regis. 3m, in Clapton right into Dunsham Ln, Manor Farm 0.5m up hill on right

Just off the beaten track and well worth seeking out, this fine Victorian country house has extensive views over Clapton towards the Axe Valley. The comfortably furnished bedrooms are well equipped, and front-facing rooms enjoy splendid views. Breakfast is served at separate tables in the dining room, and a spacious lounge is also provided.

Rooms 4 en suite 1 annexe en suite (2 fmly) S £40-£60; D £80-£85* **Facilities** STV FTV TVL TV4B tea/coffee WiFi Fishing Riding ⬮ **Parking** 14 **Notes** ⊗ ⊠

The George
★★★ INN

tel: 01460 73650 **Market Square TA18 7LP**
email: georgecrewkerne@btconnect.com **web:** www.thegeorgehotelcrewkerne.co.uk
dir: In town centre on A30

Situated in the heart of town, this welcoming inn has been providing rest and sustenance for over 400 years. The atmosphere is warm and inviting, and the bar is the ideal place for a natter and a refreshing pint. Comfortable bedrooms are traditionally styled and include four-poster rooms. A choice of menus is available, served either in the bar or the attractive restaurant.

Rooms 13 rms (8 en suite) (2 pri facs) (2 fmly) S £40-£100; D £70-£150*
Facilities FTV DVD TVL tea/coffee Dinner available Direct Dial WiFi ⬮ George Suite has a hydro-therapy spa bath **Conf** Max 100 Thtr 100 Class 100 Board 50 **Notes** LB

DULVERTON

Map 3 SS92

Premier Collection

Tarr Farm Inn
★★★★★ ⊛ INN

tel: 01643 851507 **Tarr Steps, Liscombe TA22 9PY**
email: enquiries@tarrfarm.co.uk **web:** www.tarrfarm.co.uk
dir: 4m NW of Dulverton. Off B3223 signed Tarr Steps, signs to Tarr Farm Inn

Tarr Farm, dating from the 16th century, nestles on the lower slopes of Exmoor overlooking the famous old clapper bridge, Tarr Steps. The majority of rooms are in the bedroom block that provides very stylish and comfortable accommodation with an impressive selection of thoughtful touches. Tarr Farm Inn, with its character and traditional charm, draws the crowds for cream teas and delicious dinners which are prepared from good local produce.

Rooms 9 en suite (4 GF) S £75-£90; D £100-£150* **Facilities** STV DVD iPod docking station TVL tea/coffee Dinner available Direct Dial WiFi Fishing Riding ♨ **Extras** Bottled water **Conf** Max 30 Thtr 30 Class 18 Board 18 **Parking** 10 **Notes** LB No Children 10yrs No coaches

EAST LYDFORD

Map 4 ST53

Cross Keys Inn
★★★ INN

tel: 01963 240473 **TA11 7HA**
email: enquiries@crosskeysinn.info **web:** www.crosskeysinn.info
dir: From A303 take A37 at Podimore Rdbt. Approx 5m to x-rds turn right, pub immediately on right. From Shepton Mallet take A37 to Lydford On Fosse. Left at x-rds pub on right

Cross Keys Inn is a warm and welcoming establishment with a very relaxed and engaging atmosphere. There is plenty to admire with stone-flagged floors, original beams and a genuine sense of hospitality. Bedrooms offer contemporary comforts, and quality bathrooms. Food is honest and tasty and real ale lovers are very well looked after. There is also a lovely garden in which to sit, unwind, and enjoy the delights of this popular inn.

Rooms 6 en suite (1 fmly) **Facilities** FTV tea/coffee Dinner available WiFi ♨ 18 Camping site, skittle alley, function room **Extras** Speciality toiletries, bottled water - free **Conf** Max 100 Thtr 100 Class 75 Board 50 **Parking** 50

The Queens Arms

Corton Denham, Sherborne, Somerset DT9 4LR · Tel: 01963 220317
Website: www.thequeensarms.com · **Email:** relax@thequeensarms.com
Facebook: www.facebook.com/thequeensarms · **Twitter:** @queensarmspub

Double Silver Winners, Best Tourism Pub and Best B&B Accommodation – South West Tourism Excellence Awards 2014–15. Taste of Somerset Best Pub 2013, Best National Freehouse 2012 and former AA Pub of the Year 2008–9. Quintessentially English Georgian Inn, in a gloriously rural setting, with the gently rolling landscape on the Dorset/Somerset Hills. A pilgrimage for Foodies – note their own smallholding (Pigs, Cows and Hens). Snuggle up in front of the roaring open fire with newspapers, pint and a homemade pork pie – oodles of rustic charm. Their eight en-suite rooms live up to the surroundings and wonderful views, and are all decorated with understated opulence. Relax in one of the rooms and read the magazines provided with a hot mug of hot chocolate, coffee or a range of teas and teapigs.

EXFORD
Map 3 SS83

Stockleigh Lodge

★★★★ BED AND BREAKFAST

tel: 01643 831500 **TA24 7PZ**
email: stay@stockleighexford.co.uk **web:** www.stockleighexford.co.uk
dir: On B3224 through Wheddon Cross to Exford. Over river bridge into Simonsbath Rd, up hill on right

Situated at the very heart of Exmoor, Stockleigh Lodge dates from around 1900 and provides a perfect base from which to explore this spectacular area. Whether exploration is by car, foot, cycle or horseback, your hosts will be only too pleased to help with local information. Bedrooms are very comfortable and enjoy some lovely views, while public areas include a spacious guest lounge warmed by a crackling fire in cooler months. Aga-cooked breakfasts will get the day off to a satisfying start. Stabling is also available for those wishing to bring their horses on holiday.

Rooms 9 en suite (2 fmly) S £40-£45; D fr £80* **Facilities** TVL tea/coffee WiFi Riding
🐾 Stabling available for guests horses **Parking** 10

FARMBOROUGH
Map 4 ST66

School Cottages Bed & Breakfast

★★★★ 🍽 BED AND BREAKFAST

tel: 01761 471167 & 07989 349428 **The Street, Near Bath BA2 0AR**
email: tim@schoolcottages.co.uk **web:** www.schoolcottages.co.uk
dir: Exit A39 in Farmborough into The Street, 1st left opposite village school

This lovingly-restored country house is conveniently located to the south-west of Bath, in the pretty Somerset village of Farmborough. The contemporary, stylish bedrooms are equipped with WiFi, while the excellent bathrooms may include a power shower or a spa bath. Home-made jams and freshly-laid eggs contribute to the delicious breakfasts served in a charming conservatory overlooking the garden.

Rooms 3 en suite S £70-£90; D £80-£120 **Facilities** FTV TVL tea/coffee WiFi ⌁ 18 🐾
Extras Speciality toiletries, bottled water **Parking** 3 **Notes** LB ⊗ No Children 13yrs

FIVEHEAD
Map 4 ST32

Premier Collection

Langford Fivehead

★★★★★ 🏵🏵 🍽 RESTAURANT WITH ROOMS

tel: 01460 282020 **Lower Swell TA3 6PH**
email: rebecca@thelangford.co **web:** www.langfordfivehead.co.uk

Documents indicate that there has been a house on this site since 1255 and the current property retains a significant proportion of a 15th-century hall house. In keeping with the grand character found throughout the building, guests can be assured of the most pleasant of welcomes and helpful, relaxing hospitality and service. Bedrooms offer a range of shapes and styles and are decorated and equipped to very high standards (although deliberately, no TVs in bedrooms). The restaurant is a delight of home-grown and local produce, providing delicious dining at both dinner and breakfast.

Rooms 6 en suite D £150-£290* **Facilities** Dinner available **Parking**
Notes Closed 25 Jul-7 Aug & 2-15 Jan

FROME
Map 4 ST74

Premier Collection

Lullington House

★★★★★ BED AND BREAKFAST

tel: 01373 831406 & 07979 290146 **Lullington BA11 2PG**
email: info@lullingtonhouse.co.uk **web:** www.lullingtonhouse.co.uk
dir: 2.5m N of Frome. Off A36 into Lullington

Built in 1866 as a rectory, this quintessentially English, stone-built country house stands in extensive grounds and gardens, which convey an air of peace, quiet and tranquillity. The luxurious large bedrooms, some with four-poster beds, are decorated to high standards using beautiful fabrics, fine antique furniture and many extras such as WiFi, decanters of sherry, fresh flowers and well-stocked beverage trays. Breakfast is served in the impressive dining room with an excellent selection of dishes available.

Rooms 3 en suite **Facilities** FTV tea/coffee WiFi ⌁ 18 🐾 **Parking** 4 **Notes** ⊗
Closed Xmas & New Year ⊜

Archangel

★★★★ INN

tel: 01373 456111 **1 King St BA11 1BH**
email: hello@archangelfrome.com **web:** www.archangelfrome.com
dir: B3090 into Frome, into King St, just off market place

With a history dating back many centuries, this fascinating and vibrant establishment is located in the heart of the bustling town of Frome. The style here is an engaging blend of old and new, a fusion which has broad appeal for those visiting for business or leisure. Stylish bedrooms are located within the main building and also within the courtyard, the former boasting such features like roll-top zinc baths and wall murals. The bar offers a range of cocktails in addition to real ales and an extensive wine list. Food is not to be missed, the menu featuring flavoursome, well-crafted dishes.

Rooms 6 en suite 4 annexe en suite (1 fmly) (2 GF) S £70-£90; D £80-£160*
Facilities FTV DVD Lounge tea/coffee Dinner available Direct Dial WiFi **Extras** Bottled water **Conf** Max 25 Thtr 25 Class 25 Board 16 **Parking Notes** LB

Follow us on twitter
@TheAA_Lifestyle

Orchardleigh House

★★★★ GUEST ACCOMMODATION

tel: 01373 472550 & 07887 512450 **Orchardleigh BA11 2PH**
email: info@orchardleigh.net **web:** www.orchardleigh.net

Popular as a wedding venue, Orchardleigh House is a large imposing manor with a wealth of history and character. Guests can choose from a wide range of bedrooms and bathrooms, ranging from very large suites to more compact rooms, some including a bath or shower in the bedroom. Public areas are grand and include a formal dining room, billiard room and well furnished breakfast room. Delightful grounds surround the building including a full 18-hole golf course. The property can be hired for exclusive use, although regular bed and breakfast guests are also welcome.

Rooms 44 rms (40 en suite) (3 fmly) (1 GF) **Facilities** FTV iPod docking station Lounge TVL tea/coffee Licensed WiFi 🏊 ⚓ 18 Fishing Riding Snooker 🔒 **Conf** Max 165 **Parking** 85 **Notes** ⊗ Civ Wed 144

GLASTONBURY   Map 4 ST53

See also Somerton

The Glastonbury Town House

★★★★ BED AND BREAKFAST

tel: 01458 831040 & 07557 340247 **Hillclose, Street Rd BA6 9EG**
email: stay@glastonburytownhouse.co.uk **web:** www.glastonburytownhouse.co.uk
dir: *M5 junct 23 towards Glastonbury. Continue on A39, at B&Q rdbt 3rd exit, 200yds on right*

A very warm welcome is guaranteed at The Glastonbury Town House where guests can expect to have a comfortable night's rest followed by a hearty breakfast. Recently refurbished throughout by the helpful new owners, bedrooms and bathrooms here are comfortable and well equipped. Centrally located with off-street parking, the house is well placed for exploring Glastonbury Tor and the Chalice Well.

Rooms 3 en suite S £72-£75; D £72-£130 **Facilities** FTV Lounge tea/coffee Dinner available WiFi 🔒 **Extras** Speciality toiletries, bottled water, fresh milk **Parking** 3 **Notes** ⊗ No Children 5yrs

HIGHBRIDGE   Map 4 ST34

Woodlands Country House

★★★★ GUEST ACCOMMODATION

tel: 01278 760232 & 769071 **Hill Ln, Brent Knoll TA9 4DF**
email: info@woodlands-hotel.co.uk **web:** www.woodlands-hotel.co.uk
dir: *M5 junct 22 onto A38 towards Bristol. Turn left opposite Fox & Goose pub, through Brent Knoll. Right into Church Ln, then left into Hill Ln*

This charming, elegant and traditional country house is an ideal place to relax and enjoy the lovely setting and genuine hospitality. Bedrooms offer plenty of comfort and ensure a satisfying and rewarding stay. Public areas include a drawing room and snug bar with crackling fires on cooler nights. The elegant dining room is the venue for accomplished cuisine with a range of skilfully prepared dishes on offer. In the summer, the terrace is a popular option to sit, enjoy a drink and appreciate the views.

Rooms 10 en suite (1 fmly) (2 GF) **Facilities** FTV DVD Lounge tea/coffee Dinner available Direct Dial Licensed WiFi ⚓ 18 🔒 **Conf** Max 50 Thtr 50 Class 30 Board 36 **Parking** 40 **Notes** Closed 24-30 Dec Civ Wed 50

HOLCOMBE   Map 4 ST64

Premier Collection

The Holcombe Inn

★★★★★ ◉ ⚲ INN

tel: 01761 232478 **Stratton Rd BA3 5EB**
email: bookings@holcombeinn.co.uk **web:** www.holcombeinn.co.uk
dir: *From Bath or Shepton Mallet take A367 (Fosse Way) to Stratton. Follow inn signs*

Dating back to the 16th century, this inn has views towards Downside Abbey in the distance. The attentive and pleasant staff create a friendly and relaxed atmosphere. Bedrooms are individually furnished and very comfortable. Real ales are served in the open-plan bar which has an attractive split-level restaurant.

Rooms 8 en suite 2 annexe en suite (5 fmly) (2 GF) S £75-£120; D £100-£145* **Facilities** FTV DVD Lounge tea/coffee Dinner available Direct Dial WiFi **Extras** Speciality toiletries - complimentary **Conf** Thtr 40 Class 40 **Parking** 40 **Notes** LB

ILCHESTER   Map 4 ST52

Liongate House

★★★★ ⚲ BED AND BREAKFAST

tel: 01935 841741 & 07951 538692 **Northover BA22 8NG**
email: info@liongatehouse.com **web:** www.liongatehouse.com

Located in the centre of this pleasant village and a short stroll from a selection of inns and restaurants, this very comfortable accommodation demonstrates high quality throughout its bedrooms and bathrooms. The proprietors offer a genuine welcome and are very focused on customer care. Breakfast offers a range of top local produce and includes home-made bread, alongside jams made with fruit from the garden.

Rooms 3 en suite (1 fmly) (1 GF) S £65-£75; D £80-£100 **Facilities** FTV DVD tea/coffee WiFi ⚓ 18 🔒 **Extras** Fridge stocked with refreshments - free **Parking** 4 **Notes** LB ⊗

ILMINSTER
Map 4 ST31

The New Inn
★★★★ ⊜ INN

tel: 01460 52413 **Dowlish Wake TA19 0NZ**
email: newinn-ilminster@btconnect.com web: www.newinn-ilminster.co.uk
dir: *A358 or A303, follow signs for Perry's Cider, well-signed in village*

Situated in the tranquil and unspoilt village of Dowlish Wake, The New Inn is a proper local pub with a friendly welcome. All the bedrooms are on the ground floor; they are contemporary in style and located to the rear overlooking the garden. The menu offers a range of enduring favourites and daily specials, with good local produce used whenever possible. Breakfast is a substantial offering, just right for healthy appetites.

Rooms 4 annexe en suite (4 GF) **Facilities** FTV tea/coffee Dinner available **Parking** 20

Square & Compass
★★★★ INN

tel: 01823 480467 **Windmill Hill, Ashill TA19 9NX**
email: squareandcompass@tiscali.co.uk web: www.squareandcompasspub.com
dir: *M5 junct 25 onto A358. After 5m, turn right into Wood Rd, signed Windmill Hill; From Ilminster, 2m N on A358*

This peacefully located inn provides a genuinely warm welcome and traditional hospitality. The bedrooms and modern bathrooms provide high standards of quality and comfort, and are situated in converted stables adjacent to the main building. In addition to a range of excellent home-cooked meals, a selection of real ales is also available. Outdoor seating is provided in the warmer months.

Rooms 8 en suite (8 fmly) (8 GF) S £65-£75; D £85-£95* **Facilities** FTV Lounge tea/coffee Dinner available WiFi **Conf** Max 100 Class 100 Board 50 **Parking** 50 **Notes** Closed 24-26 Dec No coaches Civ Wed 120

KEYNSHAM
Map 4 ST66

Grasmere Court
★★★★ GUEST ACCOMMODATION

tel: 0117 986 2662 **22-24 Bath Rd BS31 1SN**
email: reception@grasmerecourt.co.uk web: www.grasmerecourthotel.com
dir: *On B3116 just off A4 between Bath & Bristol*

This very friendly establishment is located between Bath and Bristol. Bedrooms vary in size, with one room boasting a four-poster bed. A comfortable lounge and a well stocked bar are available, and good value, freshly prepared food is served in the attractive dining room overlooking the garden. Functions also catered for.

Rooms 16 en suite (1 fmly) (4 GF) **Facilities** FTV DVD TVL tea/coffee Dinner available Direct Dial Licensed WiFi **Extras** Bottled water **Conf** Max 30 **Parking** 13 **Notes** ⊗

LOWER LANGFORD
Map 4 ST46

The Langford Inn
★★★★ ⊜ INN

tel: 01934 863059 **BS40 5BL**
email: langfordinn@aol.com web: www.langfordinn.com
dir: *M5 junct 21, A370 towards Bristol. At lights right onto B3133 to Langford, at mini rdbt left signed Lower Langford*

Located in a peaceful village on the edge of the Mendips, this traditional country pub offers a varied selection of real ales, well-chosen wines and carefully prepared, home-made dishes. Bedrooms and bathrooms, appointed to a high standard, are housed in two converted 17th-century barns adjacent to the inn. They feature exposed beams, original brickwork and oak floors combined with modern luxuries.

Rooms 7 annexe en suite (3 fmly) (6 GF) **Facilities** FTV DVD TVL Dinner available WiFi **Conf** Max 30 Thtr 30 Class 20 Board 20 **Parking** 20

LOWER VOBSTER
Map 4 ST74

The Vobster Inn
★★★★★ ⦿⦿ ⌕ INN

tel: 01373 812920 **BA3 5RJ**
email: rdavila@btinternet.com web: www.vobsterinn.co.uk
dir: *From A361 follow signs for Whatley & Mells, then Vobster*

Peacefully located in four acres, this is a village inn where the resident proprietors offer a genuine welcome and personal attention. Bedrooms and bathrooms provide high levels of quality and comfort. Dinner menus place an emphasis on good quality, simply prepared dishes with regular seasonal changes; several dishes demonstrate the Spanish heritage of the chef proprietor.

Rooms 4 annexe en suite (2 fmly) (4 GF) **Facilities** FTV tea/coffee Dinner available WiFi Petanque **Extras** Home-made cookies - complimentary **Conf** Max 40 Thtr 25 Class 32 Board 32 **Parking** 60 **Notes** LB RS Sun eve & Mon (ex BH lunch) No food or drinks available

LYMPSHAM
Map 4 ST35

Premier Collection

Batch Country House
★★★★★ ⊜ GUEST ACCOMMODATION

tel: 01934 750371 **Batch Ln BS24 0EX**
web: www.batchcountryhouse.co.uk
dir: *M5 junct 22, take last exit on rdbt signed A370 to Weston-Super-Mare. After 3.5m, left into Lympsham, 1m, sign at end of road*

In a rural location between Weston-Super-Mare and Burnham-on-Sea, Batch Country House is a former farmhouse that offers a relaxed, friendly and peaceful environment. Bedrooms have been refurbished to provide high levels of quality and comfort, while spacious lounges overlook the extensive, well-tended gardens. The function room makes this a popular venue for wedding ceremonies. Guests can relax with a drink in the bar, where orders are taken for delicious home-cooked dinners.

Rooms 19 en suite (3 fmly) (9 GF) D £90-£100 **Facilities** Lounge TVL tea/coffee Dinner available Direct Dial Licensed WiFi **Conf** Max 250 Thtr 250 Class 200 Board 200 **Parking** 140 **Notes** LB ⊗ RS 25-26 Dec bookings only Civ Wed 260

MILVERTON
Map 3 ST12

The Globe
★★★ 🎖 INN

tel: 01823 400534 Fore St TA4 1JX
email: adele@theglobemilverton.co.uk web: www.theglobemilverton.co.uk
dir: M5 junct 27 follow B3277 to Milverton. In village centre

This popular village local was once a coaching inn, and even though it has been given contemporary styling it still retains much traditional charm. The welcome is warm and genuine with a convivial atmosphere always guaranteed. Bedrooms are appointed in a similar modern style and have comfy beds. The hard-working kitchen is committed to quality, with excellent locally-sourced produce used in impressive dishes. Continental breakfast is served.

Rooms 3 en suite (1 fmly) Facilities tea/coffee Dinner available WiFi Parking 4 Notes ⊗ Closed 20 Dec-2 Jan No coaches

MINEHEAD
Map 3 SS94

Alcombe House
★★★★ GUEST ACCOMMODATION

tel: 01643 705130 & 07549 887456 Bircham Rd, Alcombe TA24 6BG
email: info@alcombehouse.co.uk web: www.alcombehouse.co.uk
dir: A39, pass junct for Dunster, straight over at floral rdbt. Alcombe House on left

This elegant period house is a perfect base from which to explore the many and varied delights of the area. The welcome is warm and genuine with plenty of attentive service. Bedrooms provide impressive levels of quality and comfort with ample space to relax and unwind. Public areas combine contemporary and traditional styling, and include a wonderful lounge where indulgent afternoon teas can be sampled. The attractive dining room is the venue for breakfast, and dinner (by prior arrangement).

Rooms 7 en suite S £58-£65; D £79.50-£120 Facilities FTV DVD Lounge TVL tea/coffee Dinner available Licensed WiFi ⚓ 🛁 Parking 8 Notes LB No Children

Kenella House
★★★★ GUEST ACCOMMODATION

tel: 01643 703128 & 07710 889079 7 Tregonwell Rd TA24 5DT
email: kenellahouse@fsmail.net web: www.kenellahouse.co.uk
dir: Off A39 into Townsend Rd & right into Ponsford Rd & Tregonwell Rd

A warm welcome and a relaxed atmosphere are found at Kenella House, located close to the town centre, and also convenient for a visit to the steam railway. Walkers are welcomed and a heated boot cupboard is available for drying purposes. The well-maintained bedrooms are very comfortable and have many extras. Hearty breakfasts are served in the smart dining room.

Rooms 6 en suite (1 GF) S £45-£65; D £58.50-£70* Facilities FTV tea/coffee WiFi 🛁 Parking 8 Notes LB ⊗ No Children 14yrs Closed Nov-Feb 📧

MONKSILVER
Map 3 ST03

The Notley Arms Inn
★★★★★ 🎖 🍷 INN

tel: 01984 656095 Front St TA4 4JB
email: uksi@hotmail.com web: www.notleyarmsinn.co.uk
dir: From A358 at Bishop's Lydeard, onto B3224. After 5m right onto B3188 to Monksilver

The Notley Arms was re-built around 1870 and is a warm, friendly and inviting village inn. Crackling log fires, comfy sofas and attentive service all contribute to a relaxing atmosphere. Bedrooms are located in the adjacent coach house and all provide impressive levels of quality, comfort and sophistication. The bar comes well stocked with local ales; likewise the menu focuses on sourcing the best the region has to offer, with a range of flavoursome and thoroughly enjoyable dishes. A garden is also available.

Rooms 6 en suite (2 fmly) (3 GF) Facilities FTV Lounge tea/coffee Dinner available WiFi 🛁 Petanque court Extras Speciality toiletries, home-made biscuits - free Parking 20 Notes LB

NORTH WOOTTON
Map 4 ST54

Crossways
★★★★ 🎖 INN

tel: 01749 899000 Stocks Ln BA4 4EU
email: enquiries@thecrossways.co.uk web: www.thecrossways.co.uk
dir: Exit M5 junct 22 towards Shepton Mallet, 0.2m from Pilton

This family-run establishment is tucked away down a quiet lane, within easy reach of Wells and Glastonbury. The bedrooms and bathrooms are spacious, and provide high levels of quality and comfort. There is a large bar-restaurant and a smaller dining room where breakfast is served. The extensive menu (served Wednesday to Sunday) features high quality produce with a choice of traditional pub classics or an à la carte option.

Rooms 16 en suite (4 fmly) S £39-£99; D £49-£119* Facilities FTV TV15B tea/coffee Dinner available WiFi Pool table 🛁 Conf Max 150 Thtr 120 Class 60 Board 25 Parking 100 Notes Civ Wed 150

OAKHILL
Map 4 ST64

The Oakhill Inn
★★★★ 🎖 INN

tel: 01749 840442 Fosse Rd BA3 5HU
email: info@theoakhillinn.com web: www.theoakhillinn.com
dir: On A367 between Stratton-on-the-Fosse & Shepton Mallet

A welcoming country inn, offering warm hospitality, locally sourced food and a wide selection of fine ales from local microbreweries. The comfortable bedrooms include luxuries such as Egyptian cotton sheets and DVD players. In addition to lighter bar snacks, a full range of high-quality AA Rosette award-winning dishes, made with fresh local produce, is also available.

Rooms 5 en suite (1 fmly) S £65-£90; D £90-£120* Facilities FTV DVD Lounge tea/coffee Dinner available WiFi ⚓ 18 🛁 Extras Mineral water - complimentary Conf Max 30 Thtr 30 Class 30 Board 30 Parking 12 Notes LB RS 25-26 Dec 25 Dec no food, 26 Dec no dinner service

PORLOCK
Map 3 SS84

Glen Lodge Country House

★★★★ ☕ ⬤ BED AND BREAKFAST

tel: 01643 863371 & 07786 118933 **Hawkcombe TA24 8LN**
email: glenlodge@gmail.com **web:** www.glenlodge.net
dir: A39 in Porlock, turn into Parsons St at church. After 0.5m turn left over small bridge, property drive opposite

The approach to this grand country house whets the appetite for some stunning views back down the densely wooded valley to the sea beyond. This is a perfect place to relax and unwind; a cup of tea and home-made cake on the deck sets the scene with helpful advice always readily offered. Bedrooms offer impressive levels of comfort and quality, with a number of thoughtful extras. Bathrooms come complete with robes and cosseting fluffy towels. Wonderful local and home-made produce features at breakfast, likewise at dinner, which is available by prior arrangement. Additional facilities include a hot tub which enjoys wonderful views.

Rooms 5 rms (3 en suite) (2 pri facs) **Facilities** FTV DVD Lounge TVL tea/coffee Dinner available WiFi 🏊 🚶 ⛳ 18 Fishing Riding 🎱 Outdoor hot tub/jacuzzi **Extras** Speciality toiletries, robes **Parking** 6 **Notes** Closed 23 Dec-5 Jan

Tudor Cottage

★★★★ GUEST ACCOMMODATION

tel: 01643 862255 & 07855 531593 **TA24 8HQ**
email: tudorcottagebossington@btconnect.com **web:** www.tudorcottage.net
dir: M5 junct 25, A358, A39 through Minehead. 5m, follow signs for Allerford & Bossington. 1m, 1st house on left

Parts of this engaging cottage date back to the 15th century, and many period features have been retained. The welcome couldn't be warmer, with tea and cakes in the lovely garden to get your stay off to a relaxing start. The setting is a haven of peace and tranquillity with a wonderful wooded hillside as a backdrop. Bedrooms are reassuringly cosy with all the expected modern comforts. Breakfast features a host of locally-sourced produce, and light snacks are offered in the evenings.

Rooms 3 rms (1 en suite) (2 pri facs) S £60; D £80-£90* **Facilities** FTV DVD TVL tea/coffee Dinner available Licensed WiFi 🎱 **Extras** Books; mini-bar - chargeable **Parking** 3 **Notes** LB ⊗ No Children 10yrs

RADSTOCK
Map 4 ST65

The Redan Inn

U

tel: 01761 258560 **Fry's Well, Chilcompton BA3 4HA**
email: info@theredaninn.co.uk **web:** www.theredaninn.co.uk

Currently the rating for this establishment is not confirmed. This may be due to a change of ownership or because it has only recently joined the AA rating scheme.

Rooms 7 en suite S £70-£150; D £80-£180* **Facilities** tea/coffee WiFi **Extras** Speciality toiletries **Parking**

SHEPTON MALLET
Map 4 ST64

Cannards Grave Farmhouse

★★★★ GUEST ACCOMMODATION

tel: 01749 347091 **Cannards Grave BA4 4LY**
email: sue@cannardsgravefarmhouse.co.uk **web:** www.cannardsgravefarmhouse.co.uk
dir: On A37 between Shepton Mallet & The Bath and West Showground, 100yds from Highwayman pub towards showground on left

Conveniently located for the Royal Bath & West Showground, Longleat, Glastonbury and Wells, this 17th-century house provides thoughtfully equipped en suite bedrooms. There is also a well-furnished lounge, and breakfast is served in the conservatory dining room. The proprietors are very warm and hospitable.

Rooms 4 en suite 1 annexe en suite (2 fmly) (1 GF) **Facilities** FTV DVD iPod docking station TVL tea/coffee WiFi **Extras** Mineral water **Parking** 6 **Notes** ⊗

Longbridge House Bed & Breakfast

★★★★ BED AND BREAKFAST

tel: 01749 572311 & 07809 437325 **78 Cowl St BA4 5EP**
email: longbridgehouse@gmail.com **web:** www.longbridgehouse.co.uk

Guests who enjoy staying in a place with plenty of history will love this building, where the Duke of Monmouth is reputed to have stayed in 1685. The three individually designed bedrooms offer king-size beds with either en suite shower rooms, or a bathroom en suite with a roll-top bath. Thoughtful extras include fluffy robes, safes in each room, and ironing boards. Breakfast is a leisurely affair, as you watch your host prepare your food on a gorgeous red Aga, and is served either at one large table in the comfortable kitchen, or in the courtyard, weather permitting.

Rooms 3 en suite S £70-£85; D £80-£95* **Facilities** FTV DVD iPod docking station tea/coffee WiFi 🎱 **Extras** Bottled water, fluffy robes, ironing boards **Notes** ⊗ No Children

The Natterjack Inn

★★★★ ⬤ INN

tel: 01749 860253 **Evercreech Junction BA4 6NA**
email: natterjack@btconnect.com **web:** www.thenatterjackinn.co.uk
dir: On A371 between Bath & Castle Cary, 2m past Bath & West Showground heading towards Castle Cary

The Natterjack Inn offers plenty of traditional character and hospitality with a log fire, cosy seating and an excellent range of real ales and ciders. Dinner is another highlight with a varied menu to suit all tastes. Bedrooms are located in the adjacent converted cider barn, in a range of shapes and sizes that all come with very good quality bathrooms and showers. Breakfast is served in the pleasant dining room overlooking the large garden.

Rooms 5 en suite (3 GF) **Facilities** FTV tea/coffee Dinner available WiFi ⛳ 18 **Extras** Speciality toiletries, home-made biscuits - free **Parking** 20 **Notes** ⊗ No coaches

SOMERTON
Map 4 ST42

The Devonshire Arms
★★★★ ⊛ INN

tel: 01458 241271 **Long Sutton TA10 9LP**
email: mail@thedevonshirearms.com **web:** www.thedevonshirearms.com
dir: *A303 onto A372 at Podimore rdbt. After 4m left onto B3165, signed Martock & Long Sutton*

This popular village inn offers an appealing blend of traditional and contemporary styling throughout its spacious public areas and accommodation. Bedrooms are individually designed, and provide impressive levels of comfort and quality. Public areas include a convivial bar and an elegant restaurant where excellent use is made of local produce in skilfully executed dishes.

Rooms 7 en suite 2 annexe en suite (1 fmly) (2 GF) **Facilities** FTV tea/coffee Dinner available WiFi ⛄ ⛏ 18 ⚓ **Conf** Max 14 Board 14 **Parking** 6 **Notes** Closed 25-26 Dec

Somerton Court Country House
★★★★ GUEST ACCOMMODATION

tel: 01458 274694 **TA11 7AH**
email: enquiries@somertoncourt.com **web:** www.somertoncourt.com
dir: *From A303 onto A372 at Podimore rdbt. In 3m right onto B3151 to Somerton & follow signs*

Dating back to the 17th century and set in extensive gardens and grounds, this house provides a tranquil haven away from the pressures of modern life. The comfortable bedrooms have lovely views, and breakfast is served in a delightful dining room that overlooks the gardens.

Rooms 4 en suite 2 annexe en suite (1 fmly) (2 GF) S fr £65; D fr £95* **Facilities** Lounge tea/coffee WiFi Riding **Parking** 30 **Notes** LB Closed Xmas & New Year

SOUTH PETHERTON
Map 4 ST41

New Farm Restaurant
★★★★ ⛝ GUEST ACCOMMODATION

tel: 01460 240584 & 07808 563885 **Over Stratton TA13 5LQ**
email: dine@newfarmrestaurant.co.uk **web:** www.newfarmrestaurant.co.uk
dir: *From A303, at South Petherton rdbt 4th exit (travelling E) or 2nd exit (travelling W), pass Esso garage on left. Turn next left, 500mtrs on right*

Situated in the picturesque village of Over Stratton, New Farm provides an ideal base from which to explore the many surrounding attractions of Somerset and Dorset, including several nearby National Trust properties. Bedrooms vary in size and all are comfortably furnished and decorated. Dinner (available Tuesday-Saturday and other times by prior arrangement) is a highlight, as is the range of well-cooked and presented dishes served at breakfast.

Rooms 3 en suite S £55-£75; D £80-£110 **Facilities** FTV Lounge tea/coffee Dinner available Licensed WiFi **Extras** Mineral water - complimentary **Parking** 11 **Notes** LB

STANTON DREW
Map 4 ST56

Valley Farm
★★★★ BED AND BREAKFAST

tel: 01275 332723 & 07799 768161 **Sandy Ln BS39 4EL**
email: valleyfarm2010@btinternet.com
dir: *Exit B3130 into Stanton Drew, right into Sandy Ln*

Located on a quiet country lane, Valley Farm offers relaxing and friendly accommodation. All bedrooms are comfortable and well equipped, and each has pleasant views over the countryside. Breakfast is served around a communal table in the dining room and, although dinner is not available here, a number of village pubs are just a stroll away. Also conveniently located for Bath and Bristol.

Rooms 3 en suite (1 fmly) S £40-£45; D £75-£80* **Facilities** FTV TVL tea/coffee WiFi **Parking** 6 **Notes** ⊗ No Children 12yrs ⊛

STOGUMBER
Map 3 ST03

Wick House

★★★★ GUEST ACCOMMODATION

tel: 01984 656422 **Brook St TA4 3SZ**
email: sheila@wickhouse.co.uk **web:** www.wickhouse.co.uk
dir: *Off A358 into village, left at x-rds, Wick House 3rd on left*

Wick House offers homely accommodation in a pretty village on the edge of Exmoor National Park. There is a cosy lounge with a wood-burning stove, a television room, and a pleasant dining room overlooking the garden. One bedroom is designed for easier access.

Rooms 9 en suite (1 GF) S £40-£50; D £70-£90 **Facilities** FTV Lounge TVL tea/coffee Licensed WiFi 🔒 **Extras** Sweets - complimentary **Parking** 6 **Notes** LB ⊗

STREET
Map 4 ST43

The Two Brewers

★★★★ INN

tel: 01458 442421 **38 Leigh Rd BA16 0HB**
email: thetwobrewers@yahoo.com **web:** www.thetwobrewers.co.uk

The Two Brewers is a traditional inn that is very popular with locals and tourists alike and offers a genuine welcome, excellent home-cooked food and a selection of fine, real ales. The bedrooms are located in an annexe to the rear of the inn and are well equipped and comfortable. The absence of music and machines in the bar adds to the relaxing atmosphere, and the menu choices include regularly-changing blackboard specials and guest real ales.

Rooms 3 annexe en suite (1 GF) **Facilities** FTV tea/coffee Dinner available WiFi 🔒 Skittle alley **Parking** 20 **Notes** LB ⊗ Closed 25-26 Dec No coaches

TAUNTON
Map 4 ST22

Meryan House

★★★★ 🛏 GUEST ACCOMMODATION

tel: 01823 337445 **Bishop's Hull TA1 5EG**
email: meryanhousehotel@yahoo.co.uk **web:** www.meryanhouse.co.uk
dir: *1.5m W of town centre. Off Silk Mills Rd (A358)*

Set in its own grounds, just over a mile from the town centre, this 17th-century property has delightful, individually furnished rooms featuring antiques and modern facilities. Interesting dishes are available at dinner, and there is also a cosy bar and a spacious lounge.

Rooms 12 en suite (2 fmly) (2 GF) **Facilities** STV FTV DVD iPod docking station TVL tea/coffee Dinner available Licensed WiFi 🔒 **Conf** Max 25 Thtr 25 Class 25 Board 18 **Parking** 17 **Notes** RS Sun No evening meal

Brookfield House

★★★★ GUEST HOUSE

tel: 01823 272786 **16 Wellington Rd TA1 4EQ**
email: info@brookfieldguesthouse.uk.com **web:** www.brookfieldguesthouse.uk.com
dir: *From town centre follow signs to Musgrove Hospital, onto A38 (Wellington Rd), on right opposite turn to hospital*

This charming Grade II listed Georgian house is just a five-minute level walk from the town centre. The family take great pride in caring for guests, and the brightly decorated bedrooms are well equipped. Breakfast, featuring local produce, is served in the attractive dining room. The property is entirely non-smoking.

Rooms 7 en suite (1 fmly) S £72-£79; D £83-£120* **Facilities** FTV Lounge tea/coffee Dinner available WiFi 🔒 **Extras** Speciality toiletries **Parking** 8 **Notes** ⊗ No Children 7yrs

Lower Marsh Farm (ST224279)

★★★★ FARMHOUSE

tel: 01823 451331 **Kingston St Mary TA2 8AB**
email: info@lowermarshfarm.co.uk **web:** www.lowermarshfarm.co.uk
dir: *M5 junct 25. B&B between Taunton & Kingston St Mary just past King's Hall School on right*

Located at the foot of the Quantock Hills, this delightful family-run farm provides a warm welcome with a pot of tea and a slice of cake ready and waiting. Bedrooms are individually styled and reflect the traditional charm of the house; an impressive level of quality is complemented by numerous thoughtful extras. The Aga-cooked breakfast is a real treat, served in the dining room around one grand table. There is a spacious lounge warmed by a crackling log fire in winter.

Rooms 3 en suite (2 fmly) S fr £50; D fr £88 **Facilities** TVL tea/coffee WiFi 🔒 **Parking** 6 **Notes** ⊗ 300 acres arable/sheep

Creechbarn Bed & Breakfast

★★★ BED AND BREAKFAST

tel: 01823 443955 **Vicarage Ln, Creech St Michael TA3 5PP**
email: mick@somersite.co.uk **web:** www.somersite.co.uk
dir: *M5 junct 25, A358 to Creech St Michael, follow canal boat signs to end Vicarage Ln. Through brick gateposts, turn right*

Located next to the canal and on a Sustrans cycle route, this traditional Somerset barn is lovingly cared for by its owners. Bedrooms are comfortable and there is a spacious sitting room with books and TV. Breakfast is well prepared using free-range eggs and home-made bread.

Rooms 2 rms (1 en suite) (1 pri facs) S £50; D £65-£70* **Facilities** TVL TV1B tea/coffee Direct Dial WiFi 🛜 **Parking** 6 **Notes** LB Closed 20 Dec-6 Jan 🍴

TINTINHULL
Map 4 ST41

Crown & Victoria

★★★★ 🍴 INN

tel: 01935 823341 **Farm St BA22 8PZ**
email: info@thecrownandvictoria.co.uk **web:** www.thecrownandvictoria.co.uk
dir: *Off A303, signs for Tintinhull Gardens*

Appointed to a high standard, this light and airy property has very well-equipped bedrooms. The staff ensure guests are well cared for, and the contemporary bar and restaurant provide a good selection of carefully prepared dishes. The food here has been awarded an AA Rosette.

Rooms 5 en suite **Facilities** FTV DVD tea/coffee Dinner available WiFi 🛜
Extras Bottled water **Parking** 60

WATCHET
Map 3 ST04

The Georgian House

★★★★ GUEST HOUSE

tel: 01984 639279 **28 Swain St TA23 0AD**
email: georgianhouse_watchet@virgin.net **web:** www.georgian-house.info
dir: *From A39 over railway bridge into main street*

This elegant Georgian property is situated in the heart of the increasingly popular coastal resort, and is within a short walk of the impressive marina. The comfortable bedrooms combine quality and individuality. Breakfast (and dinner by arrangement) is served in the well-appointed dining room. Additional facilities for guests include a lounge and the use of the garden.

Rooms 3 en suite **Facilities** Dinner available **Parking** 2 **Notes** ⊗

Langtry Country House

★★★★ 🏆 🍴 BED AND BREAKFAST

tel: 01984 641200 & 07500 366184 **Washford TA23 0NT**
email: langtrycountryhouse@icloud.com **web:** www.langtrycountryhouse.co.uk
dir: *From A39 in Williton onto Minehead road. 2m on right just before Washford*

Dating from the early 1900s and originally a farmhouse, Langtry Country House is a convenient base from which to explore this picturesque area. A pot of tea and home-made cake is offered on arrival, and is typical of the whole-hearted commitment of the hosts to ensure guests are comfortable, relaxed and genuinely welcome. Bedrooms provide very good levels of comfort, likewise bathrooms, complete with fluffy towels and robes. The elegant dining room is the venue for superb dinners and wonderful breakfasts, with high quality produce cooked with care and skill. A guest lounge is also provided, and there are extensive gardens.

Rooms 3 en suite **Facilities** FTV DVD Lounge tea/coffee Dinner available WiFi 🛜
Extras Speciality toiletries; snacks - chargeable **Parking** 8 **Notes** ⊗
No Children 16yrs

WEDMORE
Map 4 ST44

The George

★★★★ 🍴 INN

tel: 01934 712124 **Church St BS28 4AB**
email: info@thegeorgewedmore.co.uk **web:** www.thegeorgewedmore.co.uk
dir: *M5 junct 22, follow Bristol/Cheddar signs (A38). From dual carriageway right, follow signs for Mark, then Wedmore. In village centre*

The George is a traditional inn offering plenty of character, log fires and a fine selection of ales. Bedrooms come in a variety of shapes and sizes and are located on the first floor above the inn. A range of dishes is offered at lunch and dinner to suit all tastes, and may be taken in the cosy bar or more formal dining areas. Outdoor seating and car parking are also available.

Rooms 4 en suite **Facilities** FTV DVD iPod docking station Lounge tea/coffee Dinner available WiFi ⚓ 18 🛜 **Extras** Speciality toiletries **Conf** Max 60 Thtr 30 Class 30 Board 30 **Parking** 30 **Notes** Civ Wed 100

WELLINGTON
Map 3 ST12

The Cleve Spa
★★★★ GUEST ACCOMMODATION

tel: 01823 662033 **Mantle St TA21 8SN**
email: reception@clevehotel.com **web:** www.clevehotel.com
dir: *M5 junct 26 follow signs to Wellington town centre. Continue for 600mtrs, entrance on left*

This elegant Victorian country house is situated in an elevated position with commanding views. Bedrooms provide high levels of comfort and quality, with well appointed and stylish bathrooms. Dinner and breakfast are served in the attractive restaurant, after which a stroll around the extensive grounds may be appropriate. An impressive array of leisure facilities is also offered, including indoor pool, spa bath, steam room and fully-equipped fitness studio.

Rooms 21 en suite (5 fmly) (3 GF) S £85-£115; D £100-£135* **Facilities** FTV Lounge tea/coffee Dinner available Direct Dial Licensed WiFi ⓣ Sauna Gym Spa beauty treatments **Conf** Max 250 Thtr 250 Class 100 Board 60 **Parking** 100 **Notes** LB ⊗ Closed 25 Dec-2 Jan Civ Wed 200

WELLS
Map 4 ST54

Double-Gate Farm *(ST484424)*
★★★★ FARMHOUSE

tel: 01458 832217 & 07843 924079 **Godney BA5 1RZ**
email: doublegatefarm@aol.com **web:** www.doublegatefarm.com
dir: *A39 from Wells towards Glastonbury, at Polsham right signed Godney/Polsham. 2m to x-rds, continue to farmhouse on left after inn*

Expect a warm welcome not only from the owners, but also their friendly Labradors. Set on the banks of the River Sheppey in the Somerset Levels, this comfortable farmhouse is well known for its attractive summer flower garden. Guests have use of a games room and free internet access in the lounge.

Double-Gate Farm

Rooms 1 en suite 7 annexe en suite (4 fmly) (5 GF) S £60-£80; D £80-£120* **Facilities** FTV DVD TVL tea/coffee Direct Dial WiFi Fishing Snooker ◉ Table tennis **Extras** Mini-fridges in some rooms, speciality toiletries **Parking** 9 **Notes** LB ⊗ Closed 22 Dec-5 Jan 100 acres mixed

See advert on opposite page

Crapnell Farm *(ST594456)*
★★★★ FARMHOUSE

tel: 01749 342683 **Dinder BA5 3HG**
email: pamkeen@yahoo.com **web:** www.crapnellfarm.co.uk
dir: *M5 junct 23 signed Glastonbury/Wells. Onto A371 signed Shepton Mallet. Follow signs for Dinder*

Crapnell Farm is a spacious 16th-century farmhouse located on the south side of the Mendip Hills just three miles from the city of Wells; a peaceful and relaxing location surrounded by rolling countryside. Traditionally furnished bedrooms and bathrooms are spacious, and guests are also welcome to use the comfortable lounge. Breakfast includes freshly-laid eggs from the farm's own hens.

Rooms 3 en suite (2 fmly) **Facilities** FTV TVL tea/coffee WiFi ⤵ ⤴ 18 Riding ◉ **Parking** 8 **Notes** ⊗ Closed 20 Dec-5 Jan ⊠

Visit shop.theAA.com
for a wide variety of AA publications, including Walking books, Lifestyle Guides, Atlases, and International Travel Guides

The Crown at Wells

★★★★ ☕ INN

tel: 01749 673457 **Market Place BA5 2RP**
email: stay@crownatwells.co.uk **web:** www.crownatwells.co.uk
dir: *On entering Wells follow signs for Hotels & Deliveries, in Market Place, car park at rear*

Retaining its original features and period charm, this historic inn is situated in the heart of the city, just a short stroll from the cathedral. The building's frontage has been used in many films, most famously perhaps in 2007's *Hot Fuzz*. Bedrooms, all with modern facilities, vary in size and style. Public areas focus around Anton's, the popular bistro, which has a light, airy environment and relaxed atmosphere. The Penn Bar offers an alternative eating option and real ales.

Rooms 15 en suite (2 fmly) S £65-£95; D £95-£115* **Facilities** FTV Lounge tea/coffee Dinner available WiFi ⅃ 18 🔒 **Extras** Speciality toiletries, filtered water - free **Parking** 10 **Notes** LB RS 25 Dec Bar closed

Highfield

★★★★ BED AND BREAKFAST

tel: 01749 675340 **93 Portway BA5 2BR**
web: www.wellsbandb.com
dir: *Enter Wells & signs for A371 Cheddar, Highfield on Portway after last lights at top of hill*

Within walking distance of the city and cathedral, this delightful home maintains Edwardian style and provides comfortable accommodation. There are pleasant views of the countryside and some bedrooms have balconies. A carefully prepared breakfast is served around one large table in the well furnished breakfast room. Welcome extra features include the well-tended garden and off-street parking.

Rooms 3 en suite (1 fmly) **Facilities** FTV tea/coffee WiFi ⅃ 18 **Parking** 7 **Notes** LB ⊗ No Children 2yrs Closed 23 Dec-1 Jan ⊛

Beryl

★★★★ Ⓐ BED AND BREAKFAST

tel: 01749 678738 **Hawkers Ln BA5 3JP**
email: stay@beryl-wells.co.uk **web:** www.beryl-wells.co.uk
dir: *Exit B3139 (Radstock Rd), signed The Horringtons, into Hawkers Ln opposite BP garage, to end*

Beryl is a small country mansion built in the Gothic Revival style, quietly located just one mile from the cathedral city of Wells. Bedrooms include welcome extras and enjoy splendid views of the surrounding countryside. The fine lounge (including honesty bar) and separate dining room are both suitably in keeping with the country mansion feel.

Rooms 13 rms (12 en suite) (1 pri facs) (4 fmly) S £75-£95; D £100-£160* **Facilities** FTV DVD Lounge TVL tea/coffee Direct Dial Lift Licensed WiFi ⚹ 🐾 🔒 Childrens play area **Parking** 20 **Notes** LB ⊗ Closed 24-27 Dec

19 St Cuthbert Street

★★ BED AND BREAKFAST

tel: 01749 673166 **BA5 2AW**
dir: *At bottom of High St opposite St Cuthbert's Church*

Guests are assured of a friendly welcome at this charming terraced house, which is within walking distance of the cathedral and the bus station. The accommodation is fresh, light and comfortable and the atmosphere homely. Bedrooms are well appointed and there is a relaxing lounge. Breakfast, featuring home-made marmalade, is served in the dining room around a family table.

Rooms 2 rms S £40-£45; D £70-£80* **Facilities** FTV TVL tea/coffee **Notes** ⊗ No Children 5yrs ⊛

Double-Gate Farm

Double-Gate Farm, Godney, Nr. Wells Somerset, BA5 1RZ
Tel: 01458 832217 • Fax: 01458 835612
Website: www.doublegatefarm.com
Email: doublegatefarm@aol.com

Debbie and her family warmly welcome you to Double-Gate Farm, situated on the banks of the River Sheppey in the rural heart of Somerset.
Spoilt for choice, you can choose to stay in our beautiful Georgian Farmhouse, in cosy Swallow Barn or in our spacious (fully adaptable) Riverside Suites.
All rooms are en-suite and maintained to a high standard. Breakfast is served in our Garden Dining Room – local produce used when possible.
Games Room, Tuck Shop and our own highly recommended Tea Rooms – lots of tasty food to be sampled with a good cuppa or posh coffee!
Everyone welcome.

WEST HUNTSPILL
Map 4 ST34

Crossways Inn
★★★★ INN

tel: 01278 782500 **Withy Rd TA9 3RA**
email: info@crosswaysinn.com **web:** www.crosswaysinn.com
dir: *On main A38 between M5 junct 22 & 23*

Crossways is a traditional inn serving good food and offering a very high standard of accommodation accompanied by warm friendly service. Bedrooms are very comfortable, and offer a host of extras such as iPod docks and WiFi.

Rooms 8 en suite (1 fmly) (2 GF) **Facilities** FTV iPod docking station tea/coffee Dinner available Lift WiFi Pool table 🐾 **Parking** 72

WESTON-SUPER-MARE
Map 4 ST36

Premier Collection

Church House
★★★★★ BED AND BREAKFAST

tel: 01934 633185 **27 Kewstoke Rd, Kewstoke BS22 9YD**
email: info@churchhousekewstoke.co.uk **web:** www.churchhousekewstoke.co.uk
dir: *From M5 junct 21 follow signs for Kewstoke 2.5m, next to Kewstoke Church*

In a peaceful location at the foot of Monk's Hill, Church House is a delightful property that enjoys wonderful views of the Bristol Channel and as far as Wales on clear days. The bedrooms are stylish and spacious, with lots of thoughtful extras and well-appointed en suites. Public areas include a pleasant conservatory and an elegant dining room where impressive breakfasts are served.

Rooms 5 en suite S £79-£95; D £89-£110* **Facilities** DVD iPod docking station Lounge tea/coffee WiFi ♨ 18 🐾 **Extras** Home-made cake, sweets **Parking** 6

Oakover Guest House
★★★★ GUEST HOUSE

tel: 01934 620125 & 07557 417208 **25 Clevedon Rd BS23 1DA**
email: info@oakover.co.uk **web:** www.oakover.co.uk
dir: *M25 junct 21 onto A370 (Beach Rd), at 6th rdbt left onto A3033. 2nd right into Brighton Rd. Over T-lights into Clevedon Rd*

Located just a short walk from the seafront, this well-established quality accommodation has recently been taken over by enthusiastic and welcoming new proprietors. Bedrooms and bathrooms are decorated and maintained to high standards, and provide guests with plenty of quality and comfort throughout. A good range of breakfast dishes is offered and served in the stylish breakfast room. Parking is available to the rear via a fairly narrow entrance.

Rooms 6 en suite (2 GF) S £60-£100; D £60-£100 **Facilities** FTV DVD tea/coffee WiFi **Parking** 6 **Notes** ⊗ No Children 10yrs

Camellia Lodge
★★★★ BED AND BREAKFAST

tel: 01934 613534 **76 Walliscote Rd BS23 1ED**
email: dachefs@aol.com **web:** www.camellialodge.net
dir: *200yds from seafront*

Guests return regularly for the warm welcome at Camellia Lodge, an immaculate Victorian family home, which is just off the seafront and within walking distance of the town centre. Bedrooms have a range of thoughtful touches, and carefully prepared breakfasts are served in the relaxing dining room.

Rooms 5 en suite (1 fmly) S £35-£45; D £70-£80* **Facilities** FTV DVD tea/coffee WiFi

Jamesfield Guest House
★★★★ GUEST HOUSE

tel: 01934 642898 **1A Ellenborough Park North BS23 1XH**
email: jamesfield1@aol.com **web:** www.jamesfieldguesthouse.co.uk

A well-maintained property in an ideal location, Jamesfield Guest House is a short walk from the seafront and only a few minutes' stroll from town. The bedrooms are comfortably furnished and well decorated, and include rooms on the ground floor. Guests are welcome to use the relaxing lounge, and the property also benefits from its own car park.

Rooms 7 rms (6 en suite) (1 pri facs) (1 fmly) (2 GF) S £45; D £70 **Facilities** FTV TVL tea/coffee WiFi **Parking** 9 **Notes** ⊗

Linden Lodge Guest House
★★★★ ⬤ GUEST ACCOMMODATION

tel: 01934 645797 **27 Clevedon Rd BS23 1DA**
email: info@lindenlodge.com **web:** www.lindenlodge.com
dir: *Follow signs to seafront. 0.5m S of grand pier turn into Clevedon Rd*

Just a short walk from the town centre and the seafront, Linden Lodge offers welcoming hospitality and guest care in a traditional style. Bedrooms come in a range of shapes and sizes, and all are well decorated and equipped. A good selection is offered at breakfast including home-made bread and yogurts, all served in the pleasant conservatory.

Rooms 5 en suite **Facilities** FTV tea/coffee WiFi **Parking** 3 **Notes** ⊗ No Children 18yrs

Goodrington Guest House

★★★ GUEST HOUSE

tel: 01934 623229 **23 Charlton Rd BS23 4HB**
email: vera.bishop@talk21.com **web:** www.goodrington.info
dir: *A370 Beach Rd S onto Uphill Rd, left into Charlton Rd*

The owners of Goodrington Guest House make every effort to ensure guests enjoy their stay at this charming Victorian house, tucked away in a quiet residential area. The bedrooms are comfortably furnished, and there is an attractive lounge. Families are especially welcome and this makes a good holiday base.

Rooms 3 rms (2 en suite) (1 pri facs) (1 fmly) (1 GF) S £40-£50; D £60-£65
Facilities FTV DVD TVL tea/coffee WiFi **Notes** LB ⊗ Closed Oct-Etr ⊛

Corbiere Guest House

★★★ GUEST HOUSE

tel: 01934 629607 **24 Upper Church Rd BS23 2DX**
email: corbierehotel@btinternet.com **web:** www.corbiereguesthouse.com
dir: *M5 junct 21, take 2nd exit to seafront*

Located on a residential street just a few minutes' walk from the seafront, this relaxed and welcoming accommodation offers rooms in a range of shapes and sizes. All are well furnished and have comfortable beds and bedding. Breakfast is served in the lower ground floor dining room and offers a good selection of hot and cold dishes.

Rooms 10 en suite (4 fmly) (2 GF) **Facilities** FTV DVD Lounge TVL tea/coffee Dinner available **Notes** ⊗

The Rest and Be Thankful Inn

★★★★ INN

tel: 01643 841222 **TA24 7DR**
email: stay@restandbethankful.co.uk **web:** www.restandbethankful.co.uk
dir: *M5 junct 25, A358 to Minehead, left onto B3224 at Wheddon Cross sign*

The Rest and Be Thankful Inn is situated in the highest village on Exmoor, overlooking Dunkery Beacon. The comfortable bedrooms are extremely well equipped, with extras such as mini-bars and trouser presses. The convivial bar, complete with crackling log fires, is a popular meeting point for locals and visitors alike. A range of wholesome dishes is offered in the bar, the restaurant or outside on the patio, which enjoys some lovely countryside views.

The Rest and Be Thankful Inn

Rooms 8 en suite (1 fmly) **Facilities** FTV tea/coffee Dinner available Direct Dial WiFi Pool table Skittle alley Table Tennis **Extras** Mini-bar - chargeable **Conf** Max 50 Class 50 Board 50 **Parking** 10 **Notes** Closed 25 Dec

Arden Cottage B&B

★★★★ BED AND BREAKFAST

tel: 01984 634090 & 07794 656484 **33 Long St TA4 4QU**
email: enquiries@ardencottagewilliton.co.uk
web: www.ardencottagebedandbreakfast.co.uk
dir: *M5 junct 23 to Bridgwater, then A39 signed Minehead. In Williton, over railway line, 0.5m on right*

Located in the pleasant village of Williton, Arden Cottage is full of character and history. A friendly welcome is assured, and if the timing is right may include tea and home-made cakes served in the large rear garden or the conservatory. Bedrooms offer a range of shapes and sizes, all with very comfortable beds. Breakfast utilises a good range of quality local ingredients, and a number of pubs are within easy walking distance for evening meals.

Rooms 3 en suite (1 fmly) S £37.50-£40; D £75-£80* **Facilities** iPod docking station TVL tea/coffee WiFi ⌚ Holistic massage Shibashi Tai Chi **Extras** Home-made cake on arrival, speciality toiletries **Parking** 3 **Notes** LB ⊛

The White House

★★★★ GUEST ACCOMMODATION

tel: 01984 632306 **11 Long St TA4 4QW**
email: whitehouselive@btconnect.com **web:** www.whitehousewilliton.co.uk
dir: *A39 Bridgwater to Minehead, in Williton on right prior to Watchet turning*

This Grade II listed Georgian house is in the perfect location for guests wishing to explore the beautiful Somerset countryside and coast. Many original features have been retained and add to the character of the house. Rooms are well equipped, and guests can choose whether to stay in the main house or in a room off the courtyard. Additional facilities include a bar and lounge.

Rooms 8 rms (7 en suite) (1 pri facs) 6 annexe en suite (2 fmly) (6 GF) **Facilities** FTV TVL TV13B Licensed WiFi ⌚ **Parking** 12

WINSFORD
Map 3 SS93

The Royal Oak Exmoor
★★★★ ⌂ INN

tel: 01643 851455 **Halse Ln TA24 7JE**
email: enquiries@royaloakexmoor.co.uk **web:** www.royaloakexmoor.co.uk

Originally a farm, and dating back to the 12th century, this thatched pub is very much at the heart of this picturesque Exmoor village. Character abounds throughout public areas with lots of cosy areas to sit and sup a pint and enjoy the warm and convivial atmosphere. A range of skilfully-prepared dishes make use of local, seasonal produce. Bedrooms provide impressive levels of comfort, with quality linen and wonderful beds. Breakfast is the perfect start to a day exploring this stunning area.

Rooms 10 en suite 4 annexe en suite (2 GF) **Facilities** STV Lounge tea/coffee Dinner available Direct Dial WiFi **Conf** Max 40 Thtr 40 Class 24 Board 12 **Parking** 14 **Notes** No coaches

WITHYPOOL
Map 3 SS83

Premier Collection

Kings Farm
★★★★★ ⌂ BED AND BREAKFAST

tel: 01643 831381 **TA24 7RE**
email: info@kingsfarmexmoor.co.uk **web:** www.kingsfarmexmoor.co.uk
dir: Off B3223 to Withypool, over bridge & sharp left to farm

This delightful farmhouse is set in over two acres of landscaped gardens in an idyllic valley beside the River Barle. It combines the character and charm of its 19th-century origins with modern comforts. From the carefully planned bedrooms to the sumptuously furnished sitting room, delicious home-cooked breakfasts and the warmest of welcomes, top quality is most definitely the hallmark of Kings Farm. Both stabling and fishing are available.

Rooms 2 rms (1 en suite) (1 pri facs) S fr £75; D £89-£109* **Facilities** STV FTV Lounge tea/coffee WiFi Fishing ⬤ **Extras** Speciality toiletries, fruit, chocolates - free **Parking** 3 **Notes** No Children 14yrs

WRAXALL
Map 4 ST47

The Battleaxes
★★★★ ⌂ INN

tel: 01275 857473 **Bristol Rd BS48 1LQ**
email: thebattleaxes@flatcappers.co.uk **web:** www.flatcappers.co.uk
dir: From Bristol, A370 to Weston-Super-Mare, take Clevedon exit then follow signs for Nailsea. From M5, junct 19 to Portbury, then follow signs for Nailsea

Part of the small local Flatcappers Group, this delightful inn offers a pleasing mix of traditional comfort and hospitality with some more contemporary features. Bedrooms are spacious and well equipped and free WiFi is included. Carefully prepared dishes are available throughout the day whether at breakfast, lunch or dinner. A good selection of real ales and wines by the glass adds to the relaxing ambience created throughout the bar and dining areas. A large car park is also available.

Rooms 6 en suite **Facilities** FTV iPod docking station Lounge tea/coffee Dinner available WiFi **Conf** Max 30 Thtr 30 Class 30 Board 30 **Parking** 50 **Notes** Civ Wed 90

YEOVIL
Map 4 ST51

See also Crewkerne

Premier Collection

Little Barwick House
★★★★★ ⊛⊛⊛ ⌂ RESTAURANT WITH ROOMS

tel: 01935 423902 **Barwick Village BA22 9TD**
email: littlebarwick@hotmail.com **web:** www.littlebarwickhouse.co.uk
dir: From Yeovil A37 towards Dorchester, left at 1st rdbt, 1st left, 0.25m on left

Situated in a quiet hamlet in three and half acres of gardens and grounds, this listed Georgian dower house is an ideal retreat for those seeking peaceful surroundings and good food. Just one of the highlights of a stay here is a meal in the restaurant, where good use is made of local ingredients. Each of the bedrooms has its own character, and a range of thoughtful extras such as fresh flowers, bottled water and magazines is provided.

Rooms 6 en suite **Facilities** FTV iPod docking station tea/coffee Dinner available Direct Dial WiFi ⬤ **Parking** 30 **Notes** No Children 5yrs RS Sun eve & Mon closed No coaches

Find out more about the AA B&B of the Year for England on page 13

The Masons Arms

★★★★ ☕ ⌂ INN

tel: 01935 862591 **41 Lower Odcombe BA22 8TX**
email: paula@masonsarmsodcombe.co.uk **web:** www.masonsarmsodcombe.co.uk
dir: *From A303 take A3088 to Yeovil, follow signs to Montacute after village, 3rd turning on right*

Dating back to the 16th century, The Masons Arms claims to be the oldest building in this small village on the outskirts of Yeovil. The spacious bedrooms are contemporary in style, with clean lines, a high level of comfort and a wide range of considerate extras. The friendly hosts run their own microbrewery, and their ales are available at the bar along with other brews. Public areas include a bar-restaurant, which offers a full menu of freshly prepared dishes, along with a choice of lighter snacks.

Rooms 6 en suite (1 fmly) (6 GF) **Facilities** FTV tea/coffee Dinner available Direct Dial WiFi 🛎 **Extras** Mineral water/beer in room fridge **Conf** Max 15 Class 15 Board 15 **Parking** 35 **Notes** No coaches

The Halfway House Inn Country Lodge

★★★ INN

tel: 01935 840350 & 849005 **Ilchester Rd BA22 8RE**
email: paul@halfwayhouseinn.com **web:** www.halfwayhotelyeovil.com
dir: *A303 onto A37 (Yeovil road) at Ilchester, inn 2m on left*

This roadside inn offers comfortable accommodation, which consists of bedrooms in the main house, in addition to contemporary annexe rooms, each with its own front door; all bedrooms are bright and well equipped. Meals are available in the cosy restaurant and bar, where friendly staff ensure a warm welcome.

Rooms 10 en suite 9 annexe en suite (7 fmly) (8 GF) **Facilities** STV FTV Lounge tea/coffee Dinner available WiFi Fishing **Conf** Max 90 Thtr 90 Class 60 Board 60 **Parking** 49

At Your Service B&B

★★★ BED AND BREAKFAST

tel: 01935 706932 & 07590 960339 **102 West Coker Rd BA20 2JG**
email: randall9ee@btinternet.com **web:** http://atyourserviceuk.wordpress.com

Conveniently located on the main through road, this relaxed bed and breakfast makes an ideal base from which to explore the various nearby attractions. Bedrooms come in a range of shapes and all are on the ground floor. There is a car park to the rear of the property.

Rooms 4 en suite (4 GF) S £40-£45; D £55-£70* **Facilities** FTV tea/coffee WiFi **Extras** Bottled water - complimentary **Parking** 4 **Notes** Closed 24-26 Dec

The Half Moon Inn

★★★ INN

tel: 01935 850289 **Main St, Mudford BA21 5TF**
email: enquiries@thehalfmooninn.co.uk **web:** www.thehalfmooninn.co.uk
dir: *A303 at Sparkford onto A359 to Yeovil, 3.5m on left*

Situated north of Yeovil, this delightful village inn dates from the 17th century. It has a wealth of character including exposed beams and flagstone floors. The inn proves very popular for its extensive range of wholesome food, and there is a choice of bar and dining areas. Most of the spacious, well-equipped bedrooms are on the ground floor and are situated in an adjacent building.

Rooms 14 en suite (4 fmly) (9 GF) **Facilities** STV FTV tea/coffee Dinner available WiFi 🛎 **Parking** 36 **Notes** ⊗ Closed 25-26 Dec

ABBOTS BROMLEY | Map 10 SK02

Marsh Farm (SK069261)

★★★★ FARMHOUSE

tel: 01283 840323 **WS15 3EJ**
email: marshfarmstaffs@gmail.com **web:** www.marshfarmstaffs.co.uk
dir: *1m N of Abbots Bromley on B5013*

Guests are welcome to walk around the fields at this working farm and watch the activities. The farmhouse has been modernised, and bedrooms are carefully furnished and equipped; three rooms are located in a sympathetic barn conversion. Comprehensive breakfasts are served in the spacious cottage-style dining room, which operates as a popular tea room during the summer.

Rooms 1 en suite 3 annexe en suite (1 fmly) (1 GF) S £40-£45; D £60-£65 **Facilities** FTV TVL tea/coffee WiFi 🛎 **Extras** Fresh milk, fruit **Parking** 6 **Notes** 20 acres mixed

ADBASTON | Map 15 SJ72

Offley Grove Farm (SJ761270)

★★★ FARMHOUSE

tel: 01785 280205 & 07792 641984 **Eccleshall ST20 0QB**
email: enquiries@offleygrovefarm.co.uk **web:** www.offleygrovefarm.co.uk
dir: *3m from A519 between Shebdon & Adbaston*

This attractive farm dates back to the 1800s, and is quietly located between Eccleshall and Newport making it convenient for visiting attractions such as Alton Towers, Ironbridge and the Potteries. Bedrooms are traditional, comfortable and well equipped. The lounge and gardens also provide additional space for guests to relax in. A small conference room is available along with outdoor activities.

Rooms 2 en suite (1 fmly) S £40; D £65 **Facilities** FTV DVD TVL tea/coffee WiFi Fishing 🛎 4x4 Land Rover courses Air rifle shooting **Conf** Max 20 Thtr 20 Class 12 Board 12 **Parking** 20 **Notes** ⊗ 45 acres sheep

BARTON-UNDER-NEEDWOOD
Map 10 SK11

The Three Horseshoes
★★★★ 🍺 INN

tel: 01283 716268 **2 Station Rd DE13 8DR**
email: enquiries@3horseshoesbarton.co.uk **web:** www.3horseshoesbarton.co.uk

This popular inn has been lovingly transformed with a contemporary twist. Bedrooms are individually styled. Bit 'n' Cherry restaurant, located in a converted cobbler's workshop, offers a wide selection of imaginative meals.

Rooms 3 en suite S £60-£65; D £70-£80 **Facilities** FTV tea/coffee Dinner available WiFi **Parking** 14

ECCLESHALL
Map 15 SJ82

Slindon House Farm (SJ826324)
★★★★ 🌾 FARMHOUSE

tel: 01782 791237 **Slindon ST21 6LX**
email: bonsall@btconnect.com **web:** www.slindonhousefarm.co.uk
dir: 2m N of Eccleshall on A519

This large, charming, Victorian farmhouse is fronted by a lovely garden and situated on a dairy, arable and livestock farm in the village of Slindon, some two miles from Eccleshall. It has one twin and one double-bedded room, both of which are thoughtfully equipped. Breakfast is served at individual tables in the traditionally furnished combined breakfast room and lounge.

Rooms 2 rms (1 en suite) (1 pri facs) S £50; D £70-£80* **Facilities** FTV DVD TVL tea/coffee WiFi **Parking** 4 **Notes** ⊗ Closed 23 Dec-3 Jan 🐄 175 acres arable/dairy/sheep/beef

FROGHALL
Map 10 SK04

Hermitage Working Farm (SK024476)
★★★ FARMHOUSE

tel: 01538 266515 **ST10 2HQ**
email: gapfarm69@gmail.com **web:** www.hermitagefarm.co.uk

This family run farm, peacefully located overlooking the picturesque Churnet Valley offers a warm welcome. Traditionally furnished; accommodation is split between the main house and converted farm buildings all are well equipped with stone barn conversions offering greater privacy and cooking facilities for the more independent guest. Full English breakfasts are served in the family dining room.

Rooms 3 en suite 6 annexe en suite **Facilities** FTV tea/coffee WiFi 🐾 **Parking** 10 **Notes** 105 acres beef/poultry

HALMER END
Map 15 SJ74

The Lodge B&B
★★★★ GUEST ACCOMMODATION

tel: 01782 729047 & 07973 776797 **Red Hall Ln ST7 8AX**
email: freelancedobies@aol.com **web:** www.thelodge-halmerend.co.uk
dir: M6 junct 16 onto A500, exit signed Audley, turn right into Alsager Rd. 2nd exit at rdbt, then left into Limbrick Rd (B5367). Turn right into Red Hall Ln

Set in a peaceful location, this converted barn offers warm traditional hospitality. The lodge is adjacent to Bateswood Nature reserve. The accommodation is well equipped and very comfortable. Breakfast is served in the dining room on the ground floor. WiFi is available.

Rooms 2 en suite (1 fmly) S fr £39; D fr £70* **Facilities** FTV TVL tea/coffee WiFi Fishing **Parking** 2

KINGSLEY
Map 10 SK04

The Church Farm (SK013466)
★★★★ FARMHOUSE

tel: 01538 754759 **Holt Ln ST10 2BA**
email: thechurchfarm@yahoo.co.uk **web:** www.bandbatthechurchfarm.co.uk
dir: From A52 in Kingsley into Holt Ln, 150mtrs on right opposite school drive

A warm welcome is assured at this charming farmhouse situated in the village of Kingsley. Thoughtfully equipped bedrooms with stylish furnishings are available in the main house. A hearty breakfast is served at individual tables overlooking the cottage gardens.

Rooms 3 en suite S £50; D £70* **Facilities** FTV DVD TVL TV2B tea/coffee WiFi **Extras** Speciality toiletries, fruit tea - complimentary **Parking** 6 **Notes** LB ⊗ Closed 23 Dec-2 Jan 🐄 100 acres beef/mixed

LEEK
Map 16 SJ95

Three Horseshoes Country Inn & Spa
★★★★ ⊛⊛ INN

tel: 01538 300296 **Buxton Rd, Blackshaw Moor ST13 8TW**
email: enquires@threeshoesinn.co.uk **web:** www.threeshoesinn.co.uk
dir: 2m N of Leek on A53

This traditional, family-owned hostelry provides stylish, individually designed, modern bedrooms, including several 'Garden rooms' with hot tubs. The smart brasserie, with an open kitchen and countryside views, offers modern English dishes using the best of seasonal ingredients. There is also a busy carvery, and the award-winning gardens and grounds are ideal for alfresco dining. The team are attentive and friendly. Recently opened spa facilities are available by prior arrangement.

Rooms 26 en suite (2 fmly) (10 GF) **Facilities** FTV tea/coffee Dinner available Lift WiFi **Parking** 80 **Notes** Closed 24 Dec-1 Jan

LICHFIELD
Map 10 SK10

Premier Collection

Pipe Hill House

★★★★★ BED AND BREAKFAST

tel: 01543 255751 & 07779 291219 **Walsall Rd, Pipehill WS13 8JU**
email: nick@pipehillhouse.co.uk **web:** www.pipehillhouse.co.uk
dir: From A5 rdbt at junct with A461 towards Lichfield. 1m on right

Located two miles from the centre of the cathedral city of Lichfield, this beautiful 300-year-old Georgian house is personally run by owners Nick and Annmarie. Individually designed bedrooms offer high levels of comfort and warm hospitality ensures an enjoyable stay. The comprehensive breakfast features free-range eggs and locally sourced produce, while gluten free, dairy free, low sodium and diabetic diets are catered for. Full business services are available in an adjoining barn conversion.

Rooms 3 en suite D £95-£130* **Facilities** FTV DVD iPod docking station Lounge tea/coffee Licensed WiFi ⚡ **Extras** Speciality toiletries - free; robes, slippers **Parking** 6 **Notes** ⊗ No Children 16yrs

Premier Collection

Netherstowe House

★★★★★ ⊛ GUEST HOUSE

tel: 01543 254270 **Netherstowe Ln WS13 6AY**
email: hospitality@netherstowehouse.com **web:** www.netherstowehouse.com
dir: A38 onto A5192, 0.3m on right into Netherstowe Ln. 1st left, 1st right down private drive

Netherstowe House is located in a residential area a few minutes' drive from the city centre, and provides a range of bedrooms, some of which are quite spacious. Comprehensive breakfasts are taken in a cosy dining room and a comfortable guest lounge is also available, along with a well-equipped gym.

Rooms 9 en suite 15 annexe en suite (8 fmly) (9 GF) D £89-£195 **Facilities** STV FTV DVD Lounge tea/coffee Dinner available Licensed WiFi ⬇ 18 Gym ⚡ **Extras** Robes, fruit, flowers - chargeable **Conf** Max 14 Thtr 14 Class 14 Board 14 **Parking** 45 **Notes** LB ⊗ No Children 12yrs

Innkeeper's Lodge Lichfield

★★★ INN

tel: 08451 551551 (Calls cost 2p per minute plus your phone company's access charge) **Stafford Rd WS13 8JB**
email: info@innkeeperslodge.com **web:** www.innkeeperslodge.com

Conveniently located close to the M6 Toll, M42 and Birmingham, and ideal for both the business and leisure traveller, this 18th-century property has been beautifully restored. Bedrooms are all attractively presented and are well-equipped – free WiFi is available. There is a very popular restaurant, with large gardens suitable for alfresco dining.

Rooms 9 en suite (1 fmly) **Facilities** FTV tea/coffee Dinner available WiFi **Parking** **Notes** ⊗

OAKAMOOR
Map 10 SK04

Crowtrees Farm (SK049459)

★★★★ FARMHOUSE

tel: 01538 702260 **Eaves Ln ST10 3DY**
email: dianne@crowtreesfarm.co.uk **web:** www.crowtreesfarm.co.uk
dir: Exit B5417 in village N into Eaves Ln, farm 1m on left

This impeccably maintained 200-year-old farmhouse is convenient for the Potteries, the Peak District and Alton Towers. Bedrooms are comfortable and well equipped. It is still a working farm and has splendid views. The friendly owners, along with their collection of pets, create a relaxing atmosphere.

Rooms 5 annexe en suite (3 fmly) (5 GF) **Facilities** FTV tea/coffee WiFi **Parking** 8 **Notes** LB ⊗ Closed 25-26 Dec 70 acres sheep

RUGELEY
Map 10 SK01

Premier Collection

Colton House

★★★★★ ⊜ ⊜ GUEST HOUSE

tel: 01889 578580 **Colton WS15 3LL**
email: mail@coltonhouse.com **web:** www.coltonhouse.com
dir: 1.5m N of Rugeley. Exit B5013 into Colton, 0.25m on right

Set in the pretty village of Colton, this elegant early 18th-century house has bags of original character and provides high standards of comfort and facilities. Bedrooms have a wealth of thoughtful extras. Public areas include a cosy bar, a comfortable lounge and a large garden. Dinner is by arrangement and hearty breakfasts are served in the elegant dining room.

Rooms 11 en suite **Facilities** FTV TVL tea/coffee Dinner available Licensed WiFi ⚡ **Extras** Mini-bar, robes, slippers **Conf** Max 25 Thtr 25 Class 25 Board 25 **Parking** 15 **Notes** ⊗ No Children 13yrs

STAFFORD
Map 10 SJ92

Rooks Nest (SJ960268)

★★★★ FARMHOUSE

tel: 01889 270624 & 07966 732953 **Rooks Nest Farm, Weston ST18 0BA**
email: info@rooksnest.co.uk **web:** www.rooksnest.co.uk
dir: From Stafford on A518 towards Weston. Left to Rooks Nest Farm, 1st property

Rooks Nest is in a peaceful location with panoramic views over the Trent Valley and countryside. This modern farmhouse has comfortable bedrooms with homely extras. The establishment is handy for visiting the County Showground and Stafford University, with easy access to all Staffordshire's attractions.

Rooms 2 en suite (1 fmly) **Facilities** FTV DVD tea/coffee WiFi **Parking** 4 **Notes** ⊗ ⊜ 220 acres arable/beef

STAFFORD *continued*

Leonards Croft

★★★ BED AND BREAKFAST

tel: 01785 223676 **80 Lichfield Rd ST17 4LP**
email: leonardscroft@hotmail.com **web:** www.leonardscroft.co.uk
dir: *A34 from town centre signed Cannock, 0.5m on left*

Located south of the town centre, this well-proportioned late Victorian house is conveniently positioned to appeal to both business and leisure guests. Bedrooms are practically furnished, and two are on the ground floor. A spacious lounge and complimentary WiFi are also provided. The gardens are extensive.

Rooms 9 en suite (3 fmly) (2 GF) S £45-£50; D £65-£75* **Facilities** FTV TVL tea/coffee Dinner available Licensed WiFi **Parking** 12

| STONE | Map 10 SJ93 |

Field House

★★★ BED AND BREAKFAST

tel: 01785 605712 **59 Stafford Rd ST15 0HE**
email: fieldhouse@ntlworld.com **web:** www.fieldhousehotel.co.uk
dir: *From A34, NW into town centre, right into Stafford Rd, opposite Walton Grange*

This family home stands in secluded, pretty gardens close to the town centre. The Georgian house has traditionally furnished bedrooms, some with family pieces. Guests breakfast together in the lounge-dining room, and hospitality is very welcoming.

Rooms 2 rms (1 en suite) (1 pri facs) **Facilities** STV FTV TVL tea/coffee Art tuition on request **Parking** 4 **Notes** ⊗ 📷

| TAMWORTH | Map 10 SK20 |

Premier Collection

Oak Tree Farm

★★★★★ GUEST ACCOMMODATION

tel: 01827 56807 **Hints Rd, Hopwas B78 3AA**
email: oaktreefarm1@aol.com **web:** www.oaktreefarmhotel.co.uk
dir: *2m NW of Tamworth. Off A51 in Hopwas*

A warm welcome is assured at this well-loved farmhouse, located in peaceful rural surroundings yet only a short drive from the NEC. Spacious bedrooms are filled with homely extras. The elegant dining room, adorned with Oriental artefacts, is the setting for memorable breakfasts.

Rooms 4 en suite 10 annexe en suite (4 fmly) (7 GF) S £55-£69; D £65-£85 (room only)* **Facilities** FTV TVL tea/coffee WiFi ⊗ **Parking** 20 **Notes** No Children 16yrs

The Gungate

★★★ 🍽 GUEST ACCOMMODATION

tel: 01827 63120 & 07802 987283 **62 Upper Gungate B79 8AA**
web: www.thegungate.co.uk

The Gungate is just a moment's walk from the town centre and has on-site parking. Bedrooms and bathrooms have benefited from recent investment, showcasing the Victorian splendour of the main house, while the coach house rooms are more contemporary in their appeal. Families, leisure and business guests are well catered for. A number of popular visitor attractions are located nearby.

Rooms 10 en suite (2 fmly) (1 GF) **Facilities** FTV DVD TVL tea/coffee Direct Dial Licensed WiFi 🅿 **Conf** Max 30 Thtr 30 Class 20 Board 20 **Parking** 10

Globe Inn

★★★ INN

tel: 01827 60455 **Lower Gungate B79 7AW**
email: info@theglobetamworth.com **web:** www.theglobetamworth.com

Located in the centre of Tamworth, this popular inn provides well-equipped and pleasantly decorated accommodation. The public areas include a spacious lounge bar and a relaxed dining area where a varied selection of dishes is available. There is also a function room and adjacent parking.

Rooms 18 en suite (2 fmly) (18 smoking) **Facilities** STV FTV tea/coffee Dinner available WiFi 🦮 **Conf** Thtr 90 Class 90 Board 90 **Parking** 30 **Notes** ⊗ Closed 25 Dec, 1 Jan

SUFFOLK

ALDEBURGH
Map 13 TM45

The Toll House

★★★★ GUEST HOUSE

tel: 01728 453239 **50 Victoria Rd IP15 5EJ**
email: mail@tollhousealdeburgh.com **web:** www.tollhousealdeburgh.com
dir: B1094 into town until rdbt, on right

Expect a warm welcome at this delightful red-brick property situated just a short walk from the seafront and town centre. Bedrooms are tastefully furnished, have co-ordinated fabrics and many thoughtful touches. Breakfast is served at individual tables in the smart dining room, which overlooks the garden.

Rooms 7 en suite (3 GF) S £65-£75; D £80-£90* **Facilities** FTV DVD tea/coffee WiFi **Parking** 6 **Notes** ⊗

BURY ST EDMUNDS
Map 13 TL86

Premier Collection

Clarice House

★★★★★ ֎ GUEST ACCOMMODATION

tel: 01284 705550 **Horringer Court, Horringer Rd IP29 5PH**
email: enquiries.claricebury@bannatyne.co.uk **web:** www.claricehouse.co.uk
dir: 1m SW from town centre on A143 towards Horringer

Clarice House is a large country property set amid pretty landscaped grounds a short drive from the historic town centre. The spacious, well-equipped bedrooms have co-ordinated fabrics and many thoughtful touches. Public rooms have a wealth of charm and include a smart lounge bar, an intimate restaurant, a further lounge and a conservatory. The property also has superb leisure facilities.

Rooms 13 en suite **Facilities** FTV Lounge tea/coffee Dinner available Direct Dial Lift Licensed WiFi ⓢ Sauna Gym Spa & Beauty facilities **Conf** Max 50 Thtr 50 Class 50 Board 50 **Parking** 85 **Notes** LB ⊗ No Children 5yrs Closed 24-26 Dec & 31 Dec-1 Jan Civ Wed 70

The Chantry

★★★★ GUEST ACCOMMODATION

tel: 01284 767427 **8 Sparhawk St IP33 1RY**
email: chantryhotel1@aol.com **web:** www.chantryhotel.com
dir: From cathedral S into Crown St, left into Honey Hill then right into Sparhawk St

The Chantry is an attractive Georgian property, just a short walk from the town centre. The individually decorated bedrooms are furnished with well-chosen pieces and have many extra thoughtful touches. Breakfast is served in the smart restaurant, and there is a cosy lounge-bar.

Rooms 11 en suite 3 annexe en suite (1 fmly) (1 GF) **Facilities** FTV Lounge tea/coffee Direct Dial Licensed WiFi **Parking** 14

The Abbey

★★★★ GUEST ACCOMMODATION

tel: 01284 762020 **35 Southgate St IP33 2AZ**
email: reception@abbeyhotel.co.uk **web:** www.abbeyhotel.co.uk
dir: A14 junct 44, A1302 to town centre, into Southgate St, premises 400yds

The Abbey is well placed for visiting the historic town centre. The property is split between several old buildings, the main core dating from the 15th century. The public rooms in the Tudor inn section feature a comfortable lounge and an informal dining area. Bedrooms vary in size and style, but all are comfortably furnished and well equipped.

Rooms 12 en suite (2 GF) **Facilities** FTV Lounge tea/coffee WiFi **Parking** 12 **Notes** ⊗

Dog & Partridge, The Old Brewers House

★★★★ ➡ INN

tel: 01284 764792 **29 Crown St IP33 1QU**
email: 1065@greeneking.co.uk **web:** www.oldenglish.co.uk
dir: In town centre. Exit A134 (Parkway) into Westgate St & left into Crown St. Parking located off Bridewell Ln

This charming inn is situated just a short walk from the town centre. Public rooms include a smart conservatory, a lounge bar and a a small dining area. The smartly decked terrace to the rear of the property is useful for alfresco dining. Bedrooms are pleasantly decorated, have co-ordinated fabrics, natural wood furniture and many thoughtful touches.

Rooms 9 en suite (2 fmly) (3 GF) D £89.95-£105* **Facilities** STV tea/coffee Dinner available Direct Dial WiFi **Parking** 11 **Notes** LB

The Six Bells at Bardwell

★★★★ ➡ INN

tel: 01359 250820 **The Green, Bardwell IP31 1AW**
email: sixbellsbardwell@aol.com **web:** www.sixbellsbardwell.co.uk
dir: 8m NE, off A143 on edge of village. Follow brown signs from A143

This 16th-century inn lies in the peaceful village of Bardwell. The bedrooms, in a converted stable block next to the main building, are furnished in a country style and thoughtfully equipped. Public rooms have original character and provide a choice of areas in which to relax.

Rooms 10 annexe en suite (1 fmly) (10 GF) S £62.50-£80; D £75-£95* **Facilities** FTV Lounge tea/coffee Dinner available WiFi **Parking** 50 **Notes** LB Closed 25 Dec-3 Jan

Hamilton House

★★★ BED AND BREAKFAST

tel: 01284 703022 & 07787 146553 **4 Nelson Rd IP33 3AG**
email: hamiltonhouse@hotmail.co.uk **web:** www.hamiltonhousebse.co.uk
dir: A14 junct 42, follow A1302 across rdbt, then 1st right

A warm welcome awaits at Hamilton House, a relaxing Edwardian villa, situated in a quiet side road just a short walk from the town centre. The bedrooms are brightly decorated with co-ordinated fabrics and have a good range of facilities. Breakfast is served at a large communal table in the dining room.

Rooms 4 rms (2 en suite) (1 fmly) S £30-£40; D £55-£65* **Facilities** FTV DVD tea/coffee WiFi **Notes** ⊗ ➡

BURY ST EDMUNDS *continued*

The Old Cannon Brewery

★★★ ⊜ INN

tel: 01284 768769 **86 Cannon St IP33 1JR**
email: info@oldcannonbrewery.co.uk **web:** www.oldcannonbrewery.co.uk
dir: *A14 junct 43, A134 towards town centre. At rdbt after Tesco left then sharp right into Cadney Ln, left into Cannon St, on left*

Originally a beer house and brewery, this delightful Victorian property is sure to please. The brewery's finished products can be sampled in the bar. The open-plan bar and dining area features the polished stainless steel mash tun and kettle. The well-equipped bedrooms are located in an adjacent building, and every visitor will find a bottle of beer waiting for them after they check in.

Rooms 7 annexe en suite (3 GF) S £100-£110; D £100-£140* **Facilities** STV tea/coffee Dinner available WiFi ⬤ **Parking** 7 **Notes** ⊗ No Children 10yrs No coaches

6 Orchard Street

★★★ BED AND BREAKFAST

tel: 07946 590265 **IP33 1EH**
email: mariellascarlett@me.com **web:** www.number6orchardstreet.co.uk
dir: *In town centre near St John's Church on one-way system; Northgate St turn right into Looms Ln, 2nd right into Well St, straight on into Orchard St*

Expect a warm welcome from the caring hosts at this terrace property, situated just a short walk from the town centre. The pleasant bedrooms are comfortably appointed and have a good range of useful extras. Breakfast is served at a large communal table in the cosy dining room.

Rooms 3 rms (2 en suite) (1 pri facs) **Facilities** FTV tea/coffee WiFi ⬤ **Notes** No Children 6yrs ⊜

The Black Boy

★★★ INN

tel: 01284 752723 **69 Guildhall St IP33 1QD**
web: www.theblackboypublichouse.co.uk
dir: *Exit A14 to town centre*

The Black Boy is a popular inn situated in the centre of this historic town. The spacious bedrooms have co-ordinated fabrics, pine furniture and many thoughtful touches. Public areas feature a large open-plan bar with a good selection of ales. Dinner is not served at the inn, but there is a wide variety of pubs and restaurants within a short walk. Breakfast is served daily in the bar.

Rooms 5 en suite S £35-£40; D £60-£70* **Facilities** FTV tea/coffee Dinner available WiFi Pool table **Parking** 6 **Notes** ⊗ No coaches

CAVENDISH	Map 13 TL84

The George

★★★★★ ⊛⊛ ⊜ RESTAURANT WITH ROOMS

tel: 01787 280248 **The Green CO10 8BA**
email: thegeorgecavendish@gmail.com **web:** www.thecavendishgeorge.co.uk
dir: *A1092 into Cavendish, The George next to village green*

The George is situated in the heart of the pretty village of Cavendish and has five stylish bedrooms which have retained many of their original features, as well as being comfortable and spacious. The front-facing rooms overlook the village. The award-winning restaurant is very well appointed and dinner should not be missed. Guests are guaranteed to receive a warm welcome, attentive friendly service and great food.

Rooms 5 en suite (1 fmly) **Facilities** FTV DVD tea/coffee Dinner available WiFi ⬤ **Extras** Speciality toiletries, mineral water, sweets **Notes** Closed 25 Dec & 1 Jan

DARSHAM	Map 13 TM46

Trustans Barn B&B

★★★★ GUEST ACCOMMODATION

tel: 01728 668684 & 668444 **Trustans Farm IP17 3BP**
email: sallyandrosie@trustansbarn.co.uk **web:** www.trustansbarn.co.uk
dir: *0.25m N of Yoxford on A12, turn right signed Westleton. 0.5m on right*

Trustans Barn B&B enjoys a peaceful rural location in the heart of the beautiful Suffolk countryside and is a short drive from the popular towns of Aldeburgh and Southwold. The barn has been totally refurbished and offers guests high quality, beautifully presented bedrooms and sleek modern bathrooms. There is a walled garden and ample secure parking, along with WiFi. Hearty breakfasts are served in the light-filled garden room.

Rooms 6 en suite (3 GF) D £95-£125* **Facilities** FTV tea/coffee WiFi ⬤ **Extras** Speciality toiletries **Parking** 6 **Notes** LB ⊗ No Children

ELMSWELL	Map 13 TL96

Kiln Farm Guest House

★★★★ ⊜ GUEST HOUSE

tel: 01359 240442 **Kiln Ln IP30 9QR**
email: davejankilnfarm@btinternet.com **web:** www.kilnfarmguesthouse.com
dir: *A14 junct 47 onto A1088. Entrance to Kiln Ln off E'bound slip road*

Kiln Farm Guest House is a delightful Victorian farmhouse situated in a peaceful rural location amid three acres of landscaped grounds. The bedrooms are housed in converted farm buildings, and each one is smartly decorated and furnished in country style. Breakfast is served in the smart conservatory and there is also a cosy lounge and bar area.

Rooms 2 en suite 6 annexe en suite (2 fmly) (6 GF) S £35-£40; D £70-£80* **Facilities** FTV DVD Lounge TVL tea/coffee Dinner available Licensed WiFi ⬤ **Extras** Fruit, snacks, chocolates **Parking** 20

ELVEDEN
Map 13 TL88

Premier Collection

The Elveden Inn

★★★★★ ⊜ INN

tel: 01842 890876 **Brandon Rd IP24 3TP**
email: enquiries@elvedeninn.com **web:** www.elvedeninn.com
dir: Off A11 (dual carriageway) onto B1106 (Brandon Road) towards Bury St Edmunds

This charming country inn offers a range of beautifully presented bedrooms and sleek modern bathrooms. Enjoying a peaceful location in the heart of East Anglia, the inn is part of the Guinness family-owned Elveden Estate. The bar is full of character and the terrace is a popular dining venue on warmer days. The Elveden courtyard shops are nearby and the café is very popular.

Rooms 6 en suite (2 fmly) **Facilities** FTV TV4B tea/coffee Dinner available Direct Dial WiFi **Extras** Speciality toiletries, fruit, bottled water - free **Parking** 100 **Notes** LB

EYE
Map 13 TM17

The White Horse Inn

★★★★ INN

tel: 01379 678222 **Stoke Ash IP23 7ET**
email: mail@whitehorse-suffolk.co.uk **web:** www.whitehorse-suffolk.co.uk
dir: On A140 halfway between Ipswich & Norwich

The White Horse Inn is a 17th-century coaching inn on the main A140 midway between Norwich and Ipswich. It has been run by the same family for over a decade, offering home-made, good quality food in a friendly and comfortable environment. This is complemented by well-kept local ales and cider. Comfortable bedrooms are found in the modern, purpose-built motel-style annexe. Some have air-conditioning; all are well equipped. Complimentary WiFi is available in the public areas and bedrooms.

Rooms 11 annexe en suite (1 fmly) (9 GF) **Facilities** FTV tea/coffee Dinner available Direct Dial WiFi **Conf** Max 50 Thtr 50 Class 50 Board 20 **Parking** 60 **Notes** LB ⊗

FRAMLINGHAM
Map 13 TM26

Boundary Farm

★★★★ BED AND BREAKFAST

tel: 01728 723401 & 07818 667752 **Saxmundham Rd IP13 9NU**
email: info@boundaryfarm.biz **web:** www.boundaryfarm.biz
dir: From Framlingham on B1119 towards Saxmundham. After 1.5m left at 1st x-rds signed Cransford & Badingham

Expect peace and tranquillity at this traditional 17th-century Suffolk farmhouse. All rooms are individually decorated and reflect the style of the building; in addition, all rooms offer a range of amenities to enhance comfort. Original paintings by a resident artist adorn the house. Guests can relax in the guest lounge, or by the pond during the warmer months.

Rooms 4 rms (3 en suite) (1 pri facs) S £50-£70; D £80-£95* **Facilities** FTV TVL TV3B tea/coffee WiFi ⌷ **Extras** Snacks, chocolates - free; robes, slippers **Parking** 6 **Notes** ⊗ ⊜

Colston Hall (TM316672)

★★★★ ⊜ FARMHOUSE

tel: 01728 638375 **Badingham IP13 8LB**
email: liz@colstonhall.com **web:** www.colstonhall.com
dir: On A1120 between Badingham & Peasenhall

Set in a peaceful rural location, Colston Hall offers a range of individually designed spacious bedrooms. This Elizabethan farmhouse has many original features including brick floors and oak beams. Bedrooms have lovely countryside views, overlooking the lakes and the pretty kitchen garden. The hearty breakfasts are not to be missed and the home-made marmalade is rather special.

Rooms 3 en suite 3 annexe rms 2 annexe en suite (1 pri facs) (3 GF) **Facilities** FTV DVD Lounge TVL tea/coffee WiFi Fishing Snooker Pool table ⌷ **Conf** Max 50 Thtr 50 Class 50 Board 50 **Parking** 22 **Notes** ⊗ 27 acres sheep

Church Farm (TM605267)

★★★★ FARMHOUSE

tel: 01728 723532 **Church Rd, Kettleburgh IP13 7LF**
email: abater@suffolkonline.net **web:** www.churchfarmkettleburgh.co.uk
dir: Off A12 to Wickham Market, signs to Easton Farm Park & Kettleburgh 1.25m, house behind church. Off A14, A1120 Earl Soham to Kettleburgh

This is a charming 300-year-old farmhouse situated close to the village church surrounded by superb grounds that include a duck pond, mature shrubs and sweeping lawns. The property retains exposed beams and open fireplaces. Bedrooms are pleasantly decorated and equipped with useful extras, and ground-floor rooms are available.

Rooms 2 rms (1 en suite) (1 pri facs) 2 annexe rms 1 annexe en suite (1 pri facs) (3 GF) S £45-£50; D £80-£90 **Facilities** TVL tea/coffee Dinner available WiFi Fishing ⌷ **Extras** Home-made biscuits, chocolates - complimentary **Parking** 10 **Notes** ⊜ 70 acres mixed

HOLTON
Map 13 TM47

Premier Collection

Valley Farm

★★★★★ ⊜ BED AND BREAKFAST

tel: 01986 874521 & 07971 669270 **Bungay Rd IP19 8LY**
email: mail@valleyfarmholton.co.uk **web:** www.valleyfarmholton.co.uk
dir: A144 onto B1123 to Holton, left at fork in village, left at school, 500yds on left

Expect a warm welcome from the caring hosts at this charming red-brick farmhouse situated in a peaceful rural location just a short drive from Halesworth. The individually decorated bedrooms are tastefully appointed with co-ordinated soft furnishings and many thoughtful touches. Breakfast, which features locally sourced and home-grown produce, is served at a large communal table in the smartly appointed dining room. The property has lovely landscaped grounds, a summer house, and an indoor heated swimming pool.

Rooms 2 en suite (1 fmly) S £95; D £95* **Facilities** FTV DVD iPod docking station Lounge tea/coffee WiFi ⌷ ⌷ ⌷ Boules piste **Extras** Speciality toiletries, sweets **Parking** 15 **Notes** LB ⊗

INGHAM
Map 13 TL87

The Cadogan Arms
★★★★ ◉ INN

tel: 01284 728443 **The Street IP31 1NG**
email: info@thecadogan.co.uk **web:** www.thecadogan.co.uk
dir: *4m from Bury St Edmunds, follow A134 towards Thetford*

The Cadogan Arms is a popular inn situated four miles from the centre of Bury St Edmunds. The smartly appointed bedrooms have been thoughtfully designed and have many useful extras. The open-plan public rooms are contemporary in style and they include a range of seating areas with plush leather sofas and a smart restaurant.

Rooms 7 en suite (7 fmly) S £65.50-£80; D £75.50-£100* **Facilities** FTV tea/coffee Dinner available WiFi **Extras** Bottled water **Parking** 30 **Notes** LB

IXWORTH
Map 13 TL97

Premier Collection

Ixworth House
★★★★★ ⬨ BED AND BREAKFAST

tel: 01359 230639 & 07887 903047 **St Edmund Close IP31 2HP**
email: sharyn@ixworthhouse.co.uk **web:** www.ixworthhouse.co.uk
dir: *A143 to Ixworth, opposite Fordhams Garage turn into St Edmund Close*

Built in 1908, this fine Edwardian house has been sympathetically restored and has retained many of its original features. Ixworth House enjoys a prominent position on a quiet cul de sac and is a short walk from the pretty village of Ixworth. The three spacious bedrooms are beautifully presented and there is a real sense of luxury. Hospitality is first class and freshly cooked breakfasts, served in the very well-appointed dining room, are not to be missed.

Rooms 3 en suite (1 fmly) S £70-£80; D £90-£100 **Facilities** FTV TVL tea/coffee WiFi ⬡ **Parking** 3 **Notes** ⊗

LAVENHAM
Map 13 TL94

Premier Collection

Lavenham Great House 'Restaurant With Rooms'
★★★★★ ◉◉◉ ⬨ RESTAURANT WITH ROOMS

tel: 01787 247431 **Market Place CO10 9QZ**
email: info@greathouse.co.uk **web:** www.greathouse.co.uk
dir: *Exit A1141 into Market Ln, behind cross on Market Place*

The 18th-century frontage on Market Place conceals a 15th-century timber-framed building that is now a restaurant with rooms. Lavenham Great House is a little slice of France, offering high-quality rural cuisine served by French staff. The spacious bedrooms are individually decorated and thoughtfully equipped with many useful extras; some rooms have a separate lounge area.

Rooms 5 en suite (1 fmly) S £99-£215; D £99-£235 (room only)* **Facilities** FTV DVD tea/coffee Dinner available Direct Dial WiFi ⬡ Free bicycle use for guests **Extras** Mini-bar, fruit, sherry - complimentary **Notes** LB ⊗ Closed Jan RS Sun eve & Mon Restaurant closed No coaches

LEISTON
Map 13 TM46

Field End
★★★★ GUEST HOUSE

tel: 01728 833527 & 07946 287451 **1 Kings Rd IP16 4DA**
email: herbert@herbertwood.wanadoo.co.uk **web:** www.fieldendguesthouse.co.uk
dir: *In town centre off B1122*

This Edwardian house has been appointed to a high standard and is impeccably maintained by the present owners. Bedrooms have co-ordinated soft furnishings and many thoughtful touches. Breakfast is served in an attractive dining room, which has a large sofa and a range of puzzles and games.

Rooms 5 rms (2 en suite) (1 pri facs) (1 fmly) (1 GF) S £35; D £65-£70* **Facilities** FTV DVD TVL tea/coffee WiFi **Extras** Fridges **Parking** 5 **Notes** ⊗ No Children 6mths ▣

JUST 10 MINUTES FROM NEWMARKET AND 20 MINUTES FROM BURY ST EDMUNDS, CAMBRIDGE & ELY.
AWARD WINNING AA DINING ROOMS
GREAT BRITISH BREAKFASTS & ROASTS
PUB WITH REAL ALES & LOG FIRE
PRIVATE DINING
15 BOUTIQUE & FUNKY BEDROOMS
MURDER MYSTERY & LOTS MORE...

THE BULL INN
BARTON MILLS

VOTED BEST SMALL HOTEL IN SUFFOLK

AA
★★★★ Inn

T: **01638 711001** E: reception@bullinn-bartonmills.com **www.bullinn-bartonmills.com** The Street, Barton Mills, Nr Mildenhall, Suffolk IP28 6AA

LONG MELFORD
Map 13 TL84

Premier Collection

Long Melford Swan
★★★★★ ◉◉ RESTAURANT WITH ROOMS

tel: 01787 464545 **Hall St CO10 9JQ**
email: info@longmelfordswan.co.uk **web:** www.longmelfordswan.co.uk
dir: *From A134 into Long Melford, on main road through village*

Located in the very heart of Long Melford, bedrooms have all been completely refurbished with stylish decor and modern fixtures, home-made refreshments on arrival, turn-down service and feature bathrooms. All the rooms are located just next door in Melford House, adjacent to the main bar and restaurant. This family-run business offers an excellent restaurant with attentive service and a large alfresco dining area in the walled garden. Lunch and dinner are served daily, and a range of cooked and continental dishes are offered for breakfast in the restaurant.

Rooms 2 en suite 4 annexe en suite (2 GF) **Facilities** FTV DVD iPod docking station tea/coffee Dinner available Direct Dial WiFi ⌖ 18 Spa treatments by arrangement **Extras** Speciality toiletries, fruit **Notes** LB No coaches

MILDENHALL
Map 12 TL77

Premier Collection

The Bull Inn
★★★★★ ◉ INN

tel: 01638 711001 **The Street, Barton Mills IP28 6AA**
email: reception@bullinn-bartonmills.com **web:** www.bullinn-bartonmills.com
dir: *A11 between Newmarket & Mildenhall, signed Barton Mills. Inn by Five Ways rdbt*

This delightful 16th-century coaching inn is lovingly cared for by the owners. Public rooms offer a choice of bars, a brasserie-style restaurant and a further lounge area. The contemporary bedrooms are tastefully appointed with co-ordinated soft furnishings and many thoughtful touches. All are individually designed with designer wallpaper, bespoke glass walls and many other unique elements.

The Bull Inn

Rooms 13 en suite 2 annexe en suite (1 fmly) (2 GF) S £90-£140; D £100-£175*
Facilities FTV Lounge tea/coffee Dinner available Direct Dial WiFi ⌖
Extras Speciality toiletries **Conf** Max 30 Thtr 30 Class 20 Board 20 **Parking** 50
Notes ⊗ Closed 24-26 Dec

See advert on opposite page

NEWMARKET
Map 12 TL66

Premier Collection

The Packhorse Inn
★★★★★ INN

tel: 01638 751818 **Bridge St, Moulton CB8 8SP**
email: info@thepackhorseinn.com **web:** www.thepackhorseinn.com
dir: *A14 junct 39 onto B1506. After 1.5m turn left at x-rds onto B1085 (Moulton Rd). In Moulton, left into Bridge St*

The Packhorse Inn is situated just a short drive from Newmarket in the heart of a village close to the River Kennet. The property has eight individually designed bedrooms, all tastefully appointed, with many thoughtful touches and views of the surrounding hills, after which the rooms are named. The open-plan public rooms include a choice of seating and dining areas with an eclectic collection of furniture.

Rooms 4 en suite 4 annexe en suite (2 fmly) (4 GF) S £85-£100; D £100-£175
Facilities FTV Lounge TVL tea/coffee Dinner available WiFi ⌖ 18 ⌖
Extras Speciality toiletries, mineral water, biscuits **Conf** Max 30 Thtr 30 Class 20 Board 30 **Parking** 30

NEWMARKET *continued*

Bloodstock Barn

★★★★ 🏠 BED AND BREAKFAST

tel: 01638 730263 & 07867 813628 **Mill Rd, Ashley CB8 9EE**
email: bookings@bloodstockbarn.com **web:** www.bloodstockbarn.com
dir: *A14 junct 37 onto A142 signed Newmarket. At clock tower, cross rdbt onto B1063 to Ashley/Clare. 3m, turn left at Crown pub, then 1st left into Mill Rd. 100yds on right*

This charming house enjoys a prominent position in the pretty village of Ashley and is a short drive from Newmarket. Each of the beautifully appointed bedrooms is most comfortable and has been refurbished to a high standard. The breakfasts are cooked to order and only the best in local produce is used. Bloodstock Barn is very popular with race-goers and those exploring the lovely Suffolk and Cambridge countryside. Secure parking is provided, along with WiFi.

Rooms 3 en suite (3 GF) **Facilities** FTV TVL tea/coffee WiFi 🔒 **Parking** 4 **Notes** ⊗

SIBTON
Map 13 TM36

Sibton White Horse Inn

★★★★ ⊛ 🏠 INN

tel: 01728 660337 **Halesworth Rd IP17 2JJ**
email: info@sibtonwhitehorseinn.co.uk **web:** www.sibtonwhitehorseinn.co.uk
dir: *From A12 in Yoxford take A1120 signed Sibton & Peasenhall. 3m, in Peasenhall right opposite butcher's shop. White Horse 600mtrs*

The Sibton White Horse Inn is a delightful Grade II listed 16th-century Tudor property set in open countryside, a few miles from the Suffolk coast. Public rooms include a traditional beamed bar with exposed brick fireplaces and a choice of dining areas. The attractive bedrooms are situated in a converted building adjacent to the inn.

Rooms 6 annexe en suite (3 GF) D £80-£95* **Facilities** FTV DVD tea/coffee Dinner available WiFi 🔒 **Extras** Bottled water, speciality toiletries, cafetières **Parking** 50 **Notes** LB No Children 12yrs Closed 26-27 Dec No coaches

SOUTHWOLD
Map 13 TM57

Premier Collection

Sutherland House

★★★★★ ⊛⊛ RESTAURANT WITH ROOMS

tel: 01502 724544 **56 High St IP18 6DN**
email: enquiries@sutherlandhouse.co.uk **web:** www.sutherlandhouse.co.uk
dir: *A1095 into Southwold, on High St on left after Victoria St*

Situated in the heart of the bustling town centre, this delightful 16th-century house has a wealth of character – oak beams, exposed brickwork, open fireplaces and two superb ornate plasterwork ceilings. The stylish bedrooms are tastefully decorated using co-ordinated fabrics and include many thoughtful touches. Public rooms feature a large open-plan contemporary restaurant, which has been awarded two AA Rosettes. There's a modern British menu created with care, and the food miles are listed alongside each dish.

Rooms 4 en suite (1 fmly) S £90-£100; D £125-£200 **Facilities** FTV DVD tea/coffee Dinner available Direct Dial WiFi **Conf** Max 80 Thtr 80 Class 30 Board 30 **Parking** 1 **Notes** ⊗ RS Mon Restaurant closed in winter Oct-Mar No coaches

STOKE-BY-NAYLAND
Map 13 TL93

Premier Collection

The Angel Inn

★★★★★ ⊛ 🏠 INN

tel: 01206 263245 & 07748 484619 **Polstead St CO6 4SA**
email: info@angelinnsuffolk.co.uk **web:** www.angelinnsuffolk.co.uk
dir: *From A134 onto Bear St (B1087), 2m on right in Stoke-by-Nayland*

This charming inn has welcomed guests since the 16th century. Still popular with the locals, it's well known for its food and ambience. Public areas have a wealth of character and offer a choice of dining rooms that include a smart restaurant with an original well. Bedrooms are pleasantly decorated and thoughtfully equipped.

Rooms 6 en suite **Facilities** FTV Lounge tea/coffee Dinner available WiFi 🔒 **Conf** Max 25 Thtr 15 Class 18 Board 18 **Parking** 12 **Notes** LB

SUDBURY

Map 13 TL84

The Case Restaurant with Rooms

★★★★ @ RESTAURANT WITH ROOMS

tel: 01787 210483 **Further St, Assington CO10 5LD**
email: restaurant@thecaserestaurantwithrooms.co.uk
web: www.thecaserestaurantwithrooms.co.uk
dir: Exit A12 at Colchester onto A134 to Sudbury. 7m, establishment on left

The Case Restaurant with Rooms offers dining in comfortable surroundings, along with luxurious accommodation in bedrooms that all enjoy independent access. Some bathrooms come complete with corner jacuzzi, while internet access comes as standard. In the restaurant, local produce is used in all dishes, and bread and delicious desserts are made fresh every day.

Rooms 7 en suite (2 fmly) (7 GF) S £59-£89; D £75-£99* **Facilities** FTV Lounge tea/coffee Dinner available WiFi **Extras** Speciality toiletries - free; snacks - charged **Parking** 25 **Notes** LB ⊗

THORNHAM MAGNA

Map 13 TM17

Premier Collection

Thornham Hall

★★★★★ GUEST ACCOMMODATION

tel: 01379 783314 **IP23 8HA**
email: info@thornhamhall.com **web:** www.thornhamhall.com
dir: Turn off A140 at Stoke Ash White Horse pub. After 350mtrs right before Four Horseshoes pub. Through village, pass church & into drive signed Thornham Hall

Set in a formal park, Thornham Hall enjoys a picturesque setting and the comfortable, individually styled bedrooms overlook the extensive gardens. There is a choice of reception rooms in which to relax and the Thornham estate offers guests over ten miles of walks through ancient woodland and farmland. The walled garden contains many rare apple trees. The charming town of Eye is nearby and Framlingham is a short drive away.

Rooms 3 en suite D £100-£130* **Facilities** Lounge TVL tea/coffee Licensed WiFi ⊰ ⊱ Fishing ⋒ **Parking** 10 **Notes** ⊗

WINGFIELD

Map 13 TM27

Holly Tree House

★★★★ ⬟ BED AND BREAKFAST

tel: 01379 384854 **Bleach Green IP21 5RG**
email: sharon@hollytreehousebandb.co.uk **web:** www.hollytreehousebandb.co.uk

This beautiful 16th-century timber-framed house enjoys a peaceful rural location on the Suffolk/Norfolk border. Guests are served refreshment on arrival in the garden or in the cosy lounge, depending on the weather. Bedrooms are beautifully presented and are very well equipped. The house has been sympathetically restored in recent years, and boasts many eye-catching original features as well as lovely gardens.

Rooms 2 en suite S £70; D £90-£100* **Facilities** FTV DVD iPod docking station Lounge tea/coffee WiFi ⋒ **Extras** Speciality toiletries, snacks **Parking** 4 **Notes** ⊛

WOODBRIDGE

Map 13 TM24

Cherry Tree Inn

★★★★ ⬡ INN

tel: 01394 384627 & 385213 **73 Cumberland St IP12 4AG**
email: info@thecherrytreepub.co.uk **web:** www.thecherrytreepub.co.uk

Cherry Tree Inn is a charming 17th-century inn located close to the town of Woodbridge. This authentic inn has many original features including oak beams, low ceilings and log fires. There is a great atmosphere in the bar and evening meals feature an extensive choice of freshly prepared traditional dishes. There is a good choice of cask ales available and the bedrooms are all spacious and very comfortable.

Rooms 3 annexe en suite (1 fmly) (2 GF) S £90-£120; D £100-£130* **Facilities** STV FTV DVD tea/coffee Dinner available Direct Dial WiFi ⋒ **Extras** Home-made biscuits, still/sparkling water **Parking** 30

Grove House

★★★★ ⬡ GUEST ACCOMMODATION

tel: 01394 382202 & 386236 **39 Grove Rd IP12 4LG**
email: reception@grovehousehotel.ltd.uk **web:** www.grovehousehotel.ltd.uk
dir: W of town centre on A12

Grove House is conveniently located on the outskirts of the pretty town of Woodbridge and is the perfect base from which to explore the beautiful Suffolk coastline. There is an extensive choice of rooms including a family room, as well as five that are on the ground floor with easy access. The refurbished bedrooms are all attractively presented and individually styled. There is a comprehensive choice on the dinner menu, and the comfortable lounge is ideal for pre-dinner drinks.

Rooms 11 en suite (1 fmly) (5 GF) D £55-£85* **Facilities** FTV DVD TVL tea/coffee Dinner available Licensed WiFi ⋒ **Parking** 12 **Notes** LB ⊗

YAXLEY — Map 13 TM17

Premier Collection

The Auberge

★★★★★ ◉◉ ♒ RESTAURANT WITH ROOMS

tel: 01379 783604 **Ipswich Rd IP23 8BZ**
email: aubmail@the-auberge.co.uk **web:** www.the-auberge.co.uk
dir: *On A140 between Norwich & Ipswich at x-rds with B1117*

A warm welcome awaits at The Auberge, a charming 15th-century property, which was once a rural pub but is now a smart restaurant with rooms. The restaurant has gained two AA Rosettes for the good use of fresh, quality produce in well-crafted dishes. The public areas have a wealth of character, such as exposed brickwork and beams, and the grounds are particularly well kept and attractive. The spacious bedrooms are tastefully appointed and have many thoughtful touches; one bedroom has a four-poster.

Rooms 11 annexe en suite (2 fmly) (6 GF) S £75-£90; D £95-£140* **Facilities** FTV tea/coffee Dinner available Direct Dial WiFi 🔒 **Conf** Max 30 Thtr 30 Class 20 Board 12 **Parking** 40 **Notes** LB No coaches

SURREY

ALBURY — Map 6 TQ04

The Drummond at Albury

★★★ ⊜ INN

tel: 01483 202039 **High St GU5 9AG**
web: www.thedrummondarms.co.uk

The Drummond is centrally located in this picturesque village, with attractive gardens running down to a small river at the rear of the property. The bedrooms are individually appointed and offer all the modern comforts. Breakfast is served in the light and airy conservatory while the restaurant offers mouth-watering dishes.

Rooms 9 en suite **Facilities** Dinner available **Conf** Max 40 Thtr 40 Class 40

CAMBERLEY — Map 6 SU86

Hatsue Guest House

★★★★ GUEST ACCOMMODATION

tel: 01276 22160 & 07791 267620 **17 Southwell Park Rd GU15 3PU**
email: welcome@hatsueguesthouse.com **web:** www.hatsueguesthouse.com
dir: *M3 junct 4, A331 N, A30 E, at Arena sports centre turn right. At T-junct, turn right, 2nd house on left before church*

Hatsue Guest House offers comfortable, well-appointed accommodation in a period house, which has been sympathetically updated to meet the needs of the modern guest. Flat-screen TV and free WiFi are examples of the amenities provided. The breakfast room overlooks the quiet rear garden. Ample parking is available.

Rooms 5 en suite **Facilities** FTV tea/coffee WiFi **Parking** 5 **Notes** ⊗

CHARLWOOD

For accommodation details see under Gatwick Airport (London), (Sussex, West)

CHIDDINGFOLD — Map 6 SU93

Premier Collection

The Crown Inn

★★★★★ INN

tel: 01428 682255 **The Green, Petworth Rd GU8 4TX**
email: enquiries@thecrownchiddingfold.com **web:** www.thecrownchiddingfold.com

Set in a tranquil location in a picturesque village, the inn dates back to the early 13th century. This charming property offers stylish, modern accommodation that has been tastefully finished without losing any period features. Breakfast and dinner can be enjoyed in the oak-panelled dining room, and there is a spacious bar, outside seating and small courtyard.

Rooms 8 en suite (4 fmly) **Facilities** FTV DVD iPod docking station Lounge tea/coffee Dinner available Direct Dial WiFi **Conf** Max 40 Thtr 40 Class 25 Board 28 **Parking** 15 **Notes** ⊗

CRANLEIGH — Map 6 TQ03

The Cranley

★★★ INN

tel: 01483 272827 **The Common GU6 8SQ**
email: thecranleyhotel@gmail.com **web:** www.thecranleyhotel.co.uk
dir: *From Guildford on A281 left to Cranleigh*

This traditional pub, located in the picturesque village of Cranleigh, offers freshly prepared food, at both lunch and dinner, using local produce. Regular entertainment is provided, and the rear garden is popular with families. The comfortable bedrooms have TVs and tea- and coffee-making facilities.

Rooms 7 en suite **Facilities** TVL tea/coffee Dinner available WiFi Pool table **Parking** 50 **Notes** ⊗

DORKING — Map 6 TQ14

Denbies Farmhouse B&B (TQ168510)

★★★★ FARMHOUSE

tel: 01306 876777 **London Rd RH5 6AA**
email: bandb@denbiesvineyard.co.uk **web:** www.denbies.co.uk
dir: *Off A24*

Denbies Farmhouse enjoys a wonderful location in the heart of England's largest vineyard and is a short walk to the historic market town of Dorking. Very popular with ramblers, there are many beautiful walks nearby. Bedrooms are comfortable and breakfasts are served in the conservatory with its wonderful views of the vineyard.

Rooms 7 en suite (2 fmly) (2 GF) **Facilities** STV FTV tea/coffee Licensed WiFi 🔒 **Extras** Speciality toiletries - complimentary **Parking** 14 **Notes** ⊗ 650 acres wine

EFFINGHAM — Map 6 TQ15

Sir Douglas Haig

★★★ INN

tel: 01372 456886 **The Street KT24 5LU**
email: sirdouglashaig@hotmail.com **web:** www.sirdouglashaig.co.uk
dir: *M25 junct 9, A243 then A24, at rdbt take 2nd exit onto A246. Through Bookham, at lights with golf club on left, turn right. Pub on right*

A traditional public house located in the village centre, the Sir Douglas Haig has retained a country atmosphere and offers comfortable accommodation for the modern traveller. The bar is well stocked and provides regular entertainment while the restaurant serves a choice of traditional dishes. Ample parking is available.

Rooms 7 en suite (1 fmly) **Facilities** FTV DVD tea/coffee Dinner available WiFi 🔒 **Parking** 15

GODALMING — Map 6 SU94

Innkeeper's Lodge Godalming

★★★★ 🍺 INN

tel: 08451 551551 *(Calls cost 2p per minute plus your phone company's access charge)* **Ockford Rd GU7 1RH**
email: info@innkeeperslodge.com **web:** www.innkeeperslodge.com

At Innkeeper's Lodge you'll find accommodation with comfort and character in equal measure, and everything needed for a relaxing stay, from easy check-in and free parking to complimentary breakfast and a cosy pub serving great value food and drink on the doorstep. Each Lodge has quality rooms, and there are Lodges in a variety of locations from towns and cities to countryside settings across the UK.

Rooms 14 en suite (4 fmly) **Facilities** FTV tea/coffee Dinner available Direct Dial WiFi **Conf** Max 28 **Parking Notes** ⊗

GUILDFORD — Map 6 SU94

The Angel

★★★★ GUEST ACCOMMODATION

tel: 01483 564555 **81 High St GU1 3DP**
email: reservations@angelpostinghouse.com **web:** www.angelpostinghouse.com
dir: *From A281 (Horsham Rd), turn left into High St. 200yds on left*

On the high street, in the heart of Guildford and within the popular Angel Gate area with its shops and restaurants, this historic property features a range of rooms including spacious suites and traditional doubles. All have flat-screen TVs, free WiFi, and high-quality bathrooms with power showers, some with separate baths. Rates are room-only; breakfast is available in the adjacent 'Bills' restaurant, which is also open for lunch and dinner.

Rooms 24 en suite S £115-£250; D £135-£275 (room only)* **Facilities** STV FTV Lounge tea/coffee Dinner available Licensed WiFi ⌕ 18 🔒 **Conf** Max 60 Thtr 60 Class 30 Board 30 **Notes** ⊗ Civ Wed 50

Asperion

★★★★ 🍺 GUEST ACCOMMODATION

tel: 01483 579299 **73 Farnham Rd GU2 7PF**
email: enquiries@asperion.co.uk **web:** www.asperion.co.uk
dir: *Exit A3 at Surrey University only, 2nd exit from rdbt into Chase Rd. Right into Agraria Rd to Farnham Rd junct. Turn right into Farnham Rd (A31), 3rd on right*

The stylish Asperion provides comfortable, modern and contemporary bedrooms in a convenient location close to the city centre. The owners are committed to a 'more than for profit' business ethos, part of which involves a healthy organic breakfast.

Rooms 15 rms (14 en suite) (1 pri facs) (1 fmly) (9 GF) **Facilities** FTV TVL tea/coffee Dinner available Direct Dial Licensed WiFi **Extras** Bottled water - complimentary **Parking** 11 **Notes** ⊗ No Children 12yrs Closed 21 Dec-2 Jan

HASLEMERE — Map 6 SU93

The Wheatsheaf Inn

★★★ 🍺 INN

tel: 01428 644440 **Grayswood Rd, Grayswood GU27 2DE**
email: ken@thewheatsheafgrayswood.co.uk **web:** www.thewheatsheafgrayswood.co.uk
dir: *1m N of Haslemere on A286 in Grayswood*

Situated in a small village just outside Haslemere, this well-presented inn has a friendly atmosphere. The smart conservatory restaurant, complements the attractive dining area and popular bar. Bedrooms are furnished to a good standard; all but one on the ground floor.

Rooms 7 en suite (6 GF) **Facilities** FTV tea/coffee Dinner available Direct Dial WiFi **Parking** 21 **Notes** No coaches

HORLEY

For accommodation details see under Gatwick Airport (London), (Sussex, West)

SUNBURY

See London Plan 2 A1

The Flower Pot

★★★★ 🍺 INN

tel: 01932 780741 **Thames St TW16 6AA**
email: info@theflowerpotsunbury.co.uk **web:** www.theflowerpotsunbury.co.uk
dir: *M3 junct 1, at Sunbury Cross rdbt take 6th exit (Green St). Bear left into Church Rd, right at mini rdbt into Thames St*

This upmarket coaching inn has benefited from complete refurbishment throughout, and now provides high-quality boutique en suite accommodation; each room is equipped with a wide-screen TV, an espresso machine and free WiFi. A range of tasty dishes is available in the dining area.

Rooms 8 en suite (1 fmly) D £59-£175* **Facilities** FTV Lounge TVL tea/coffee Dinner available WiFi ⌕ 18 🔒 **Extras** Speciality toiletries, coffee machines **Parking** 4 **Notes** LB

WEST END   Map 6 SU96

The Inn West End

★★★★ 🍺 INN

tel: 01276 858652 & 485842 **GU24 9PW**
email: rooms@the-inn.co.uk **web:** www.the-inn.co.uk
dir: *M3 junct 3, 3m on A322*

A convenient location, attentive service, a traditional pub, a wine shop, a restaurant and 12 individually appointed and comfortable bedrooms are available at The Inn

West End. The cottage-style bedrooms offer sumptuous beds, powerful showers and all the amenities expected by the modern traveller. The menu offers a range of dishes to meet the needs of a varied clientele with the focus on fresh and seasonal produce, locally sourced where possible. There is also a relaxing garden, ideal for barbecues during the summer months, and secure parking.

The Inn West End

Rooms 12 annexe en suite (12 GF) **Facilities** FTV tea/coffee Dinner available WiFi ⌁ 18 **Parking** 35 **Notes** No Children 10yrs No coaches

See advert below

THE INN
WEST END

STYLISH PUB & AWARD WINNING RESTAURANT
12 BEAUTIFUL BOUTIQUE EN SUITE BEDROOMS LUXURIOUS BEDS
ECLECTIC WINE LIST AND WINE SHOP ON SITE
EASY TO FIND JUST 3 MILES FROM J3 ON THE A322
ADULT FRIENDLY. NOT SUITABLE FOR INFANTS OR YOUNG CHILDREN

The Inn West End, 42 Guildford Road, West End, Surrey, GU24 9PW

Pub & Restaurant: 01276 858652
greatfood@the-inn.co.uk

Accommodation: 01276 485842
rooms@the-inn.co.uk

www.the-inn.co.uk

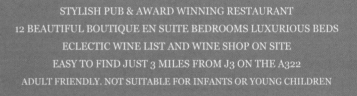

WEYBRIDGE
Map 6 TQ06

Innkeeper's Lodge Weybridge

★★★ INN

tel: 08451 551551 *(Calls cost 2p per minute plus your phone company's access charge)* **25 Oatlands Chase KT13 9RW**
email: info@innkeeperslodge.com **web:** www.innkeeperslodge.com

At Innkeeper's Lodge you'll find accommodation with comfort and character in equal measure, and everything needed for a relaxing stay, from easy check-in and free parking to complimentary breakfast and a cosy pub serving great value food and drink on the doorstep. Each Lodge has quality rooms, and there are Lodges in a variety of locations from towns and cities to countryside settings across the UK.

Rooms 19 en suite (5 fmly) (2 GF) **Facilities** FTV tea/coffee Dinner available WiFi **Parking Notes** ⊗

WOKING
Map 6 TQ05

Innkeeper's Lodge Woking

★★★ INN

tel: 08451 551551 *(Calls cost 2p per minute plus your phone company's access charge)* **Chobham Rd, Horsell GU21 4AL**
email: info@innkeeperslodge.com **web:** www.innkeeperslodge.com

Just a short walk from Woking station, a 25-minute commute from central London, this establishment is ideal for both the business or leisure traveller. It offers comfortable en suite bedrooms and attractive public areas with cosy open fires and friendly, welcoming staff. Food is served daily in The Wheatsheaf. The free on-site parking is a plus.

Rooms 33 en suite (3 fmly) (13 GF) **Facilities** FTV tea/coffee Dinner available WiFi **Parking** 28 **Notes** ⊗

Made In Sud

★★★ GUEST ACCOMMODATION

tel: 01483 723080 **14 The Broadway GU21 5AP**
email: dminardi@btinternet.com **web:** www.madeinsudwoking.co.uk

A warm welcome is guaranteed, set within walking distance of Woking train station. All bedrooms are comfortably furnished, serviced to a high standard, and come equipped with a range of accessories. Breakfast is served in the light and airy café below. Free WiFi is accessible throughout.

Rooms 8 en suite **Facilities** WiFi

EAST SUSSEX

ALFRISTON
Map 6 TQ50

The Star Inn

★★★★ INN

tel: 01323 870495 **High St BN26 5TA**
email: julie.garvin@thestaralfriston.co.uk **web:** www.thestaralfriston.co.uk
dir: *At Beddingham rdbt stay on A27 towards Eastbourne, at next rdbt 3rd exit onto Alfriston Rd. Continue to High St, Star Inn on left*

Located in the very heart of Alfriston and conveniently located close to Glyndebourne, Eastbourne and Brighton, The Star Inn is a traditional inn with cosy public areas, serving lunch and dinner daily. All of the bedrooms have benefited from a complete refurbishment offering stylish and very comfortable

accommodation. Breakfast (both cooked and continental) is served daily in the restaurant. There is also on-site parking and WiFi.

Rooms 13 en suite 24 annexe en suite (1 fmly) (12 GF) **Facilities** FTV Lounge tea/coffee Dinner available Direct Dial WiFi ⛴ **Conf** Max 110 Thtr 110 Board 28 **Parking** 30 **Notes** Civ Wed 110

BEXHILL
Map 6 TQ70

Dunselma

★★★★ Ⓐ GUEST ACCOMMODATION

tel: 01424 734144 **25 Marina TN40 1BP**
email: stay@dunselma.com **web:** www.dunselma.com

Dunselma, a seafront Edwardian town house offers guest accommodation, with all modern comforts plus the elegance and charm of yesteryear. The location is ideal for a visit to the De La Warr pavilion in Bexhill, with ample parking, beach, shops, bars, restaurants and the railway station all within walking distance. Rooms are all en suite and comfortably furnished, and many enjoy sea views. All have tea and coffee-making facilities, colour TV with digital channels, complimentary mineral water and bowls of fresh fruit. There are a limited number of free off-street parking bays, subject to availability.

Rooms 7 en suite (3 fmly) S £45-£60; D £70-£80* **Facilities** FTV Lounge tea/coffee Licensed WiFi ⛴ **Extras** Bottled water, fruit - complimentary **Notes** ⊗

BOREHAM STREET
Map 6 TQ61

Premier Collection

Boreham House

★★★★★ Ⓖ BED AND BREAKFAST

tel: 01323 833719 **Boreham Hill BN27 4SF**
email: enquiries@borehamhouse.com **web:** www.borehamhouse.com
dir: *On A271 between Herstmonceux & Battle, 100mtrs from Bull's Head pub*

This delightful Georgian manor is in a quiet location just a short drive from Bodiam Castle, Hastings and Pevensey Bay. Both sides of the property enjoy excellent views of the High Wield or across the Pevensey Marshes to the sea. Bedrooms and bathrooms are contemporary in style, yet retain many original features. There is a guest lounge, and an excellent pub just 100 metres away. Guests can enjoy a hearty cooked or continental breakfast served in the dining room, all items locally sourced.

Rooms 3 en suite (1 fmly) **Facilities** FTV Lounge tea/coffee WiFi ⛴ **Parking** 3 **Notes** ⊗

BRIGHTON & HOVE Map 6 TQ30

New Steine

★★★★ ⚨ 🍴 GUEST ACCOMMODATION

tel: 01273 695415 & 681546 **10-11 New Steine BN2 1PB**
email: reservation@newsteinehotel.com **web:** www.newsteinehotel.com
dir: A23 to Brighton Pier, left into Marine Parade, New Steine on left after Wentworth St

Close to the seafront, off the Esplanade, the New Steine provides spacious and well-appointed accommodation. The Bistro offers simple yet appealing dishes with a French and British influence; produce from farms in Sussex is used for the breakfasts. There are two meeting rooms suitable for a variety of occasions. Street parking can be arranged.

Rooms 20 rms (16 en suite) (4 pri facs) (4 fmly) (2 GF) **Facilities** FTV Lounge tea/coffee Dinner available Direct Dial Licensed WiFi 🛎 **Extras** Speciality toiletries **Conf** Max 50 Thtr 50 Class 20 Board 26 **Notes** LB No Children 4yrs

---

AA FUNKIEST B&B OF THE YEAR 2016-2017

Snooze

★★★★ GUEST ACCOMMODATION

tel: 01273 605797 **25 St George's Ter BN2 1JJ**
email: info@snoozebrighton.com **web:** www.snoozebrighton.com
dir: Follow A23 to seafront/pier. Turn left at mini rdbt opposite pier, then left into Bedford St, 2nd right into St George's Terrace

This splendid Victorian terraced property is close to the beach and the popular Kemp Town bars and restaurants. Bedrooms have a distinctly 'retro' feel and all are comfortably presented. The spacious dining room with its large bay windows is the setting for a choice of hearty breakfasts.

Rooms 8 en suite (2 GF) D £75-£150* **Facilities** FTV DVD iPod docking station tea/coffee WiFi **Extras** Speciality toiletries **Notes** ⊗

The Twenty One

★★★★ GUEST ACCOMMODATION

tel: 01273 686450 **21 Charlotte St, Marine Pde BN2 1AG**
email: enquiries@thetwentyone.co.uk **web:** www.thetwentyone.co.uk
dir: From Brighton Pier turn left into Marine Parade, 16th left turn

This stylishly-appointed town house property is situated in Kemp Town, within easy reach of clubs, bars and restaurants, and just a short walk from the beach.

Bedrooms are elegantly furnished and comfortable, with an abundance of thoughtful extras provided. The smart dining room is the setting for a delicious, freshly-cooked breakfast.

Rooms 7 en suite S £69-£79; D £119-£169 **Facilities** FTV iPod docking station Lounge tea/coffee WiFi 🛎 **Extras** iPads **Notes** LB ⊗ No Children 10yrs

---

The White House

★★★★ ⚨ GUEST ACCOMMODATION

tel: 01273 626266 **6 Bedford St BN2 1AN**
email: info@whitehousebrighton.com **web:** www.whitehousebrighton.com
dir: A23 to Brighton, follow signs to town centre. At rdbt opposite pier 1st exit, through 2 sets of lights, left into Bedford St

The White House is a small Regency residence only 100 metres from the seafront, and a short walk from Brighton's centre. There are sea views from the south-facing rooms and a courtyard garden where guests may sit and relax. All rooms are smartly and stylishly decorated and there is a relaxed atmosphere. Breakfast is served in the dining room, or alfresco. The extensive breakfast menu uses only the best quality ingredients.

Rooms 10 rms (8 en suite) (2 GF) **Facilities** FTV DVD iPod docking station tea/coffee WiFi **Notes** ⊗

No. 27 Brighton

★★★★ BED AND BREAKFAST

tel: 01273 694951 & 07921 860527 **27 Upper Rock Gardens BN2 1QE**
email: 27brightonbb@gmail.com **web:** www.27bb.co.uk
dir: A23 to Palace Pier, left onto A256 (signed Rottingdean & Newhaven). Left at 1st lights into Lower Rock Gardens, through next set of lights. On left near junct with Edward St

No. 27 Brighton has new proprietors who have refurbished the property to create an oasis of style, calm and elegance. The rooms vary in size, and have been named after places and people connected with the Prince Regent. The five rooms have been individually appointed with impeccable attention to detail. All rooms offer a range of useful amenities. Some rooms have limited en suite facilities. A choice of breakfasts is served in the well-appointed dining room.

Rooms 5 rms (3 en suite) (2 pri facs) (1 GF) S £69-£80; D £125-£160* **Facilities** FTV iPod docking station tea/coffee WiFi **Extras** Mineral water, sherry, cakes - complimentary **Notes** ⊗ No Children 16yrs

---

Brighton House

★★★★ ⚨ GUEST ACCOMMODATION

tel: 01273 323282 **52 Regency Square BN1 2FF**
email: info@brighton-house.co.uk **web:** www.brighton-house.co.uk
dir: Opposite West Pier

Situated close to the seafront is the elegant and environmentally-friendly Brighton House. Comfortably appointed bedrooms and bathrooms come in a variety of sizes and are located on four floors. An impressively abundant, organic continental breakfast is served in the spacious and elegant dining room. Parking is in the nearby underground car park.

Rooms 16 en suite (2 fmly) **Facilities** FTV tea/coffee Licensed WiFi **Notes** ⊗ No Children 12yrs

THE BULL DITCHLING

Tel 01273 843147 Email info@thebullditchling.com

The Bull, High Street, Ditchling, East Sussex BN6 8TA   Twitter @ditchlingbull

Located within the South Downs National Park, we're in a perfect location for accessing the various trails that spread out over 100 miles. Alternatively you can be on the beach or walking through the famous "Lanes" of Brighton in only 10 minutes.

We pride ourselves on producing modern british food, using ingredients from our own kitchen garden and the best local farms and estates we can source. Our true 'pub' atmosphere is supported by a vast selection of hand crafted beers, including 'Bedlam' from our own brewery and over 20 wines by the glass

Our bespoke bedrooms are designed for a comfy getaway with huge beds, crisp Egyptian cotton, beautifully appointed bathrooms and our own range of natural hand made bathroom products.

AA Rosette Award for Culinary Excellence

AA
★★★★★
Inn

www.thebullditchling.com

BRIGHTON & HOVE *continued*

Four Seasons Guest House

★★★★ GUEST ACCOMMODATION

tel: 01273 673574 **3 Upper Rock Gardens BN2 1QE**
email: info@4seasonsbrighton.co.uk **web:** www.4seasonsbrighton.co.uk
dir: *A23 signed town centre & seafront to Brighton Pier. At rdbt 1st exit, left into Marine Parade. At next lights left into Lower Rock Gardens*

Caring hosts William and Thommy provide smart accommodation with a variety of stylish contemporary bedrooms, each with ample facilities including WiFi and hairdryers. A healthy breakfast is served in the sunny dining room. Beaches, restaurants and shops are all within easy walking distance.

Rooms 7 rms (6 pri facs) (1 GF) S £55-£65; D £75-£135* **Facilities** FTV tea/coffee WiFi **Notes** LB ⊗ No Children 10yrs

Gullivers

★★★★ GUEST ACCOMMODATION

tel: 01273 681546 & 695415 **12a New Steine BN2 1PB**
email: reservation@gullivershotel.com **web:** www.gullivershotel.com
dir: *A23 to Brighton Pier, left into Marine Parade, premises 300yds on left*

Situated in an impressive Regency square close to the town and seafront, Gullivers has much to offer. Compact rooms use clever design and contemporary colours to ensure comfort, and some have quality shower rooms en suite. The lounge and brasserie, decorated with fine art, are super areas in which to relax and dine.

Rooms 12 rms (9 en suite) (3 pri facs) (2 GF) (4 smoking) **Facilities** FTV Lounge tea/coffee Dinner available Direct Dial Licensed WiFi 🐾 **Extras** Speciality toiletries - complimentary **Conf** Max 30 Thtr 30 Class 10 Board 20 **Notes** LB ⊗ No Children 4yrs

Marine View

★★★★ GUEST ACCOMMODATION

tel: 01273 603870 **24 New Steine BN2 1PD**
email: info@mvbrighton.co.uk **web:** www.mvbrighton.co.uk
dir: *From A23, left into Marine Pde, left into New Steine, 300mtrs*

Overlooking the elegant Steine Square with the sea just a glance away, this 18th-century property offers comfortable, well-designed accommodation. Plenty of accessories are provided, including free WiFi. A hearty breakfast is available in the bright lounge-dining room.

Rooms 11 rms (8 en suite) (1 pri facs) (2 fmly) (2 GF) S £35-£75; D £59-£130 **Facilities** Lounge tea/coffee WiFi **Notes** LB ⊗

Regency Lansdowne Guest House

★★★ GUEST ACCOMMODATION

tel: 01273 321830 **45 Landsdowne Place BN3 1HF**
email: rlgh@btconnect.com **web:** www.regencylansdowne.co.uk
dir: *A23 to Brighton Pier, right onto A259, 1m right into Lansdowne Place, house on left before Western Rd*

A warm welcome is guaranteed at this Regency house, located only minutes from the seafront. Comfortable bedrooms are functionally equipped with a good range of facilities, and an extensive continental breakfast is served each day at a communal table overlooking attractive gardens. On-road parking is a short walk away.

Rooms 7 rms (5 en suite) (2 pri facs) **Facilities** FTV tea/coffee Lift WiFi **Notes** ⊗ Closed 20-27 Dec

Avalon

★★★ GUEST ACCOMMODATION

tel: 01273 692344 **7 Upper Rock Gardens BN2 1QE**
email: info@avalonbrighton.co.uk **web:** www.avalonbrighton.com
dir: *A23 to Brighton Pier, left into Marine Parade, 300yds at lights left into Lower Rock Gdns, over lights, Avalon on left*

The Avalon is situated a short walk from the seafront and The Lanes. The en suite bedrooms vary in size and style but all are attractively presented with plenty of useful accessories. Parking vouchers are available for purchase from the proprietor.

Rooms 7 en suite (3 fmly) (1 GF) **Facilities** FTV DVD tea/coffee WiFi

Innkeeper's Lodge Brighton, Patcham

★★★ INN

tel: 08451 551551 *(Calls cost 2p per minute plus your phone company's access charge)* **Black Lion Harvester, London Rd, Patcham BN1 8YQ**
email: info@innkeeperslodge.com **web:** www. innkeeperslodge.com

At Innkeeper's Lodge you'll find accommodation with comfort and character in equal measure, and everything needed for a relaxing stay, from easy check-in and free parking to complimentary breakfast and a cosy pub serving great value food and drink on the doorstep. Each Lodge has quality rooms, and there are Lodges in a variety of locations from towns and cities to countryside settings across the UK.

Rooms 17 en suite (6 fmly) (1 GF) **Facilities** FTV tea/coffee Dinner available Direct Dial WiFi **Parking Notes** ⊗

| BURWASH | Map 6 TQ62 |

The Bear Inn & Burwash Motel

★★★ INN

tel: 01435 882540 **High St TN19 7ET**
email: enquiries@bear-inn-hotel-burwash.co.uk **web:** www.bear-inn-hotel-burwash.co.uk

Located in the village of Burwash, this country inn offers en suite bedrooms with external access. The inn is traditional in style and benefits from uninterrupted views of the Sussex countryside. Traditional bar meals are available daily and guests can enjoy a cooked or continental breakfast in the restaurant.

Rooms 8 en suite (8 GF) S £55; D £80* **Facilities** FTV DVD TVL tea/coffee Dinner available WiFi ⌣ ⚘ 36 Fishing Pool table ⚓ **Conf** Max 50 Thtr 50 Class 35 Board 35 **Parking** 8

| CAMBER | Map 7 TQ91 |

The Gallivant

★★★★★ ❀❀ RESTAURANT WITH ROOMS

tel: 01797 225057 **New Lydd Rd TN31 7RB**
email: beachbistro@thegallivanthotel.com **web:** www.thegallivanthotel.com

The Gallivant is located right on the edge of Camber Sands and just a short drive from the historic town of Rye. The inn offers modern, coastal-styled accommodation with light airy decor and reconditioned driftwood furniture. Rooms are well equipped and ideal for both business and leisure guests. There's a bar and the award-winning Beach Bistro serves food daily. The large function suite is open year round and is perfect for parties or weddings. The sand dunes and beach are just across the road in front of the inn.

Rooms 16 en suite 4 annexe en suite (4 fmly) (20 GF) **Facilities** FTV DVD Lounge tea/coffee Dinner available Direct Dial WiFi ⚘ 18 ⚓ **Extras** Speciality toiletries **Conf** Max 120 Thtr 120 Class 60 Board 40 **Parking** 25 **Notes** Civ Wed 150

DITCHLING Map 6 TQ31

Premier Collection

The Bull
★★★★★ @ INN

tel: 01273 843147 **2 High St BN6 8TA**
email: info@thebullditchling.com **web:** www.thebullditchling.com
dir: Exit A23 signed Pyecombe, left onto A273 signed Hassocks. Up hill, pass Pyecombe Golf Club on right, 2nd right into New Rd (B2112) to Ditchling. Right at mini rdbt, next left into car park

Dating back to 1563, The Bull is one of the oldest buildings in this famously pretty Sussex village. First used as an overnight resting place for travelling monks, the inn has also served as a courthouse and a staging post for the London-Brighton coach. Accomplished dishes, using local produce together with local ales are available in the award-winning restaurant. There is a landscaped garden with seating that enjoys stunning views over the South Downs. Bedrooms are very comfortable, offering many stylish features and a range of amenities. An extensive cooked and continental breakfast is served daily in the restaurant.

Rooms 4 en suite D £100-£180* **Facilities** FTV DVD iPod docking station tea/coffee Dinner available WiFi ⌁ 18 🔒 **Extras** Speciality toiletries, mineral water, mini-bar **Parking** 30 **Notes** LB No coaches

See advert on page 297

EASTBOURNE Map 6 TV69

Premier Collection

Ocklynge Manor
★★★★★ BED AND BREAKFAST

tel: 01323 734121 & 07979 627172 **Mill Rd BN21 2PG**
email: ocklyngemanor@hotmail.com **web:** www.ocklyngemanor.co.uk
dir: From Eastbourne Hospital follow town centre/seafront sign, 1st right into Kings Av, Ocklynge Manor at top of road

This charming home has seen a variety of uses since serving as a commanderie for the Knights of St John in the 12th century. An air of peace and relaxation is evident in the delightful public rooms, well-tended gardens and the spacious, comfortable bedrooms that come filled with thoughtful extras, including free WiFi. The hospitality is noteworthy, and home-baked bread is just one of the delights at breakfast.

Rooms 3 rms (2 en suite) (1 pri facs) S £60-£110; D £100-£130* **Facilities** FTV DVD Lounge tea/coffee WiFi 🔒 **Extras** Snacks - complimentary **Parking** 3 **Notes** ⊗ No Children 18yrs 🐾

Gyves House Guesthouse
★★★★ GUEST ACCOMMODATION

tel: 01323 721709 **20 St Aubyns Rd BN22 7AS**
email: book@gyveshouse.com **web:** www.gyvesguesthouse.co.uk
dir: On seafront between Redoubt Fortress & pier, into St Aubyns Rd, 1st house

This property is located just 30 metres from the seafront and within a short walking distance of the both the town centre and pier. Bedrooms are comfortably appointed throughout and are modern in style with high quality soft furnishings. Complimentary WiFi and digital TVs are provided in addition to well stocked beverage trays. A range of cooked and continental dishes are served daily in the main dining room.

Rooms 6 en suite S £40-£42; D £70-£75* **Facilities** FTV tea/coffee WiFi ⌁ 18 🔒 **Extras** Bottled water - complimentary **Notes** ⊗

EASTBOURNE *continued*

The Mowbray

★★★★ ☖ GUEST ACCOMMODATION

tel: 01323 720012 **2 Lascelles Ter BN21 4BJ**
email: info@themowbray.com **web:** www.themowbray.com
dir: *Opposite Devonshire Park Theatre*

The Mowbray is an elegant town house located opposite The Devonshire Park Theatre and a few minutes' walk from the seafront. Bedrooms are accessible by a lift to all floors, and vary in size, but all are attractively furnished and comfortable. Public areas include a spacious well presented lounge, small modern bar and a stylish dining room. Breakfast is home-cooked, as are evening meals, available by prior arrangement.

Rooms 12 en suite (3 fmly) (1 GF) S £35-£49; D £45-£150* **Facilities** FTV DVD iPod docking station Lounge TVL tea/coffee Dinner available Lift Licensed WiFi 🔒 **Extras** Superior rooms - fruit, bottled water, slippers **Conf** Max 20 Thtr 20 Class 10 Board 10 **Notes** LB

The Bay Lodge

★★★★ ☖ GUEST ACCOMMODATION

tel: 01323 732515 **61-62 Royal Pde BN22 7AQ**
email: baylodge@hotmail.com **web:** www.baylodge.org.uk
dir: *From A22 follow signs to seafront. Bay Lodge on right opposite Pavilion Tea Gardens*

A family-run guest accommodation, The Bay Lodge offers a warm welcome in comfortable surroundings opposite the Redoubt and Pavilion Gardens. Bedrooms are bright and spacious, some with balconies. There is a sun lounge, and a cosy bar that enjoy superb sea views.

Rooms 10 en suite (2 fmly) (2 GF) S £40-£42; D £65-£87* **Facilities** FTV Lounge tea/coffee Licensed WiFi 🔒 **Parking** 6 **Notes** LB ⊗ No Children 5yrs Closed 23 Dec-3 Jan

Arden House

★★★★ GUEST ACCOMMODATION

tel: 01323 639639 **17 Burlington Place BN21 4AR**
email: info@theardenhotel.co.uk **web:** www.theardenhotel.co.uk
dir: *On seafront, towards W, 5th turn after pier*

This attractive Regency property sits just minutes away from the seafront and town centre. Bedrooms are comfortable and bright, most with en suite bathrooms. Guests can enjoy a hearty breakfast at the beginning of the day then relax in the cosy lounge in the evening.

Rooms 11 rms (9 en suite) (2 pri facs) (1 fmly) **Facilities** STV FTV DVD TVL tea/coffee WiFi 🔒 **Parking** 3

Bella Vista

★★★★ GUEST ACCOMMODATION

tel: 01323 724222 **30 Redoubt Rd BN22 7DH**
email: stay@thebellavista.com **web:** www.thebellavista.com
dir: *500yds NE of town centre. Off A259 (Seaside Rd)*

Situated on the east side of town, just off the seafront, this is an attractive flint house with the bonus of a car park. Bedrooms are generally spacious, comfortable and neatly appointed with modern facilities including free WiFi. There is a large lounge and a dining room where dinner and breakfast is served.

Rooms 9 en suite (3 GF) **Facilities** FTV TVL tea/coffee Dinner available WiFi **Parking** 10 **Notes** ⊗

Far End Guest House

★★★★ GUEST ACCOMMODATION

tel: 01323 725666 **139 Royal Pde BN22 7LH**
web: www.farendhotel.co.uk

Located right on the seafront with excellent uninterrupted views, just one mile from the town centre, Far End is in the quieter area of Eastbourne. There's plenty of parking and a private, off-road car park for guests. Bedrooms and bathrooms are very traditional in style, many with excellent views. There is a guest lounge where guests can relax during their stay, and a dining room on the ground floor serving a cooked and continental breakfast.

Rooms 10 rms (6 en suite) (1 pri facs) **Facilities** Lounge tea/coffee **Parking**

Ivydene

★★★★ GUEST HOUSE

tel: 01323 720547 **5-6 Hampden Ter, Latimer Rd BN22 7BL**
email: ivydenehotel@hotmail.co.uk **web:** www.ivydenehotel-eastbourne.co.uk
dir: *From town centre/pier NE along seafront, towards Redoubt Fortress, into St Aubyns Rd, 1st right into Hampden Terrace*

Ivydene is made up of two Victorian houses, 5 and 6 Hampden Terrace. With adjoining doors and the two staircases still in place, this traditional building is full of character. Darren and Martin are friendly and welcoming hosts.

Rooms 14 en suite (1 GF) S £40; D £75-£85* **Facilities** FTV TVL tea/coffee Licensed WiFi **Notes** LB ⊗ No Children 16yrs Closed Dec-Mar

The Royal

★★★★ GUEST ACCOMMODATION

tel: 01323 649222 **8-9 Marine Pde BN21 3DX**
email: info@royaleastbourne.org.uk **web:** www.royaleastbourne.org.uk
dir: *On seafront 100mtrs E of pier*

The Royal enjoys a central seafront location close to the pier and within easy walking distance of the town centre. Spectacular uninterrupted sea views are guaranteed. This eco-friendly property has comfortable modern bedrooms with flat-screen TVs and free WiFi. One of the ten rooms has private facilities, while the others are en suite. A substantial continental breakfast is served. The Royal offers a full pet-sitting service and dogs stay free of charge.

Rooms 10 rms (9 en suite) (1 pri facs) (1 fmly) (1 GF) **Facilities** STV FTV DVD tea/coffee WiFi ♿ 18 🔒 Free Wi-fi **Extras** Speciality toiletries - complimentary **Notes** No Children 12yrs

The Sheldon

★★★★ GUEST ACCOMMODATION

tel: 01323 724120 **9-11 Burlington Place BN21 4AS**
email: info@thesheldonhotel.co.uk **web:** www.thesheldonhotel.co.uk
dir: *Just off The Grand Parade near bandstand*

Set in a quiet side street, this family-owned and run establishment is nestled in the heart of Eastbourne just a stone's throw from the beach, shops, theatres, restaurants and other attractions. There are rooms of many types to suit every budget, and although the premises are not licensed guests are welcome to bring their own drinks with them. All rooms have flat-screen satellite TV. Guests can get discounts at local restaurants as The Sheldon doesn't serve dinner. Free private parking and WiFi in every room.

Rooms 20 en suite (7 fmly) (2 GF) S £35-£68; D £59-£155* **Facilities** STV FTV Lounge tea/coffee Lift WiFi ⚓ 18 **Extras** Speciality toiletries **Parking** 20 **Notes** ⊗ Closed 1-20 Jan

The Sherwood

★★★★ GUEST HOUSE

tel: 01323 724002 & 07851 716706 **7 Lascelles Ter BN21 4BJ**
email: info@thesherwood.net **web:** www.thesherwood.net
dir: *Follow signs to seafront. At pier turn into Grand Parade (towards Beachy Head). Right into Lascelles Terrace*

The Sherwood is an attractive Victorian property just a minute's walk from the seafront, offering well-appointed bedrooms with comfortable, co-ordinated furnishings. The cosy lounge is great to relax in, and the attractive dining room serves a robust breakfast.

Rooms 11 en suite (2 fmly) (1 GF) **Facilities** FTV DVD TVL tea/coffee Licensed WiFi ⚓ **Extras** Bottled water **Notes** ⊗

Beachy Rise Guest House

★★★ GUEST HOUSE

tel: 01323 639171 **5 Beachy Head Rd BN20 7QN**
email: susanne234@hotmail.co.uk **web:** www.beachyrise.com
dir: *1m SW of town centre. Off B2103 Upper Dukes Rd*

This friendly, family-run guest house has a quiet residential location close to Meads. Bedrooms are individually styled with co-ordinated soft furnishings and feature some useful extras. Breakfast is served in the light and airy dining room overlooking the garden, where guests are free to wander.

Rooms 4 en suite (2 fmly) S £40-£50; D £65-£70 **Facilities** FTV tea/coffee WiFi **Notes** ⊗

HALLAND Map 6 TQ41

The Black Lion Inn

★★★ INN

tel: 01825 840304 **Lewes Rd BN8 6PN**
email: nigel.fright@btconnect.com **web:** www.theblacklioninn-halland.co.uk

This traditional inn is located on the A22 between Eastbourne and Uckfield. There is a cosy restaurant and bar area with many original features and an open fireplace; traditional pub food is served daily. Bedrooms are modern and very comfortable with digital TV and free WiFi throughout. A cooked and continental breakfast is served in the bar area.

Rooms 7 rms **Facilities** Dinner available

HASTINGS & ST LEONARDS Map 7 TQ80

Premier Collection

Stream House

★★★★★ BED AND BREAKFAST

tel: 01424 814916 & 07941 911378 **Pett Level Rd, Fairlight TN35 4ED**
email: info@stream-house.co.uk **web:** www.stream-house.co.uk
dir: *4m NE of Hastings. Exit A259 onto unclassified road between Fairlight & Cliff End*

Lovingly converted from three cottages, the Stream House stands in three acres of tranquil grounds, just one mile from Winchelsea beach. If you arrive before 6pm, you will be greeted with a complimentary cup of tea and slice of Sandra's home-made cake. The well-appointed bedrooms are beautifully decorated, and among the delightful extras provided are sherry and chocolates, along with speciality toiletries in the bathrooms. Delicious breakfasts are served in the lounge-dining room which has an original inglenook fireplace, and during warmer months you can enjoy the extensive garden with its rippling stream and Koi pond.

Rooms 3 en suite S £65-£70; D £90-£115* **Facilities** STV Lounge tea/coffee WiFi ⚓ **Extras** Speciality toiletries, Baileys, chocolates **Parking** 4 **Notes** LB ⊗ No Children 8yrs Closed Dec-Feb ▣

Premier Collection

The Cloudesley

★★★★★ GUEST ACCOMMODATION

tel: 01424 722759 & 07507 000148 **7 Cloudesley Rd TN37 6JN**
email: info@thecloudesley.co.uk **web:** www.thecloudesley.co.uk
dir: *A21 (London Rd) onto A2102, left into Tower Rd. Right into Cloudesley Rd, house on left*

The Cloudesley is located just minutes from Hastings in the quiet residential area of St Leonards, and offers high standards of quality and comfort. The bedrooms have been environmentally designed – the walls have been eco-limewashed, the hand-made beds have Siberian goosedown pillows, and the shampoos are free of parabens and sodium lauryl sulphate. There is a treatment room for holistic therapies. The two guest lounges are stylish and decorated with photographs taken by the proprietor. An extensive selection of cooked and continental dishes is available for breakfast, which includes locally sourced, organic ingredients.

Rooms 5 en suite **Facilities** iPod docking station Lounge tea/coffee Dinner available Licensed WiFi Holistic therapies & massage **Extras** Speciality toiletries, mini-fridge **Notes** ⊗ No Children 6yrs ▣

Eagle House

★★★ GUEST ACCOMMODATION

tel: 01424 430535 **Pevensey Rd TN38 0JZ**
email: info@eaglehousehotel.co.uk **web:** www.eaglehousehotel.co.uk
dir: *Exit seafront into London Rd, 5th turn on left into Pevensey Rd. 150mtrs on right*

Eagle House is a Victorian property situated in a peaceful residential area within easy walking distance of the shops, college and seafront. Public areas are sumptuously decorated in a traditional style and the spacious 'retro' bedrooms are simply furnished. A hearty breakfast can be enjoyed in the dining room, which overlooks the gardens.

Rooms 21 rms (19 en suite) (3 fmly) (3 GF) S £45-£55; D £65-£85* **Facilities** FTV TVL tea/coffee Dinner available Licensed WiFi **Parking** 9 **Notes** ⊗

Premier Collection

Wartling Place

★★★★★ ⬠ GUEST ACCOMMODATION

tel: 01323 832590 **Wartling Place, Wartling BN27 1RY**
email: accom@wartlingplace.prestel.co.uk **web:** www.wartlingplace.co.uk
dir: 2.5m SE of Herstmonceux. Exit A271 to Wartling. Wartling Place opposite village church

Located in a sleepy village, this beautiful Grade II listed country home is set in two acres of well-tended gardens. The individually decorated bedrooms, two featuring four-poster beds, are luxurious and have a host of thoughtful extras. Award-winning breakfasts are served at the communal table in the elegant dining room. Guests can also enjoy free WiFi access and relaxing walks in the garden.

Rooms 4 en suite (1 fmly) **Facilities** tea/coffee Dinner available WiFi **Conf** Max 12 **Parking** 10 **Notes** ⊗

See Brighton & Hove

Premier Collection

Broadacres

★★★★★ ⬠ ⬡ BED AND BREAKFAST

tel: 07568 083616 **Lewes Rd, Whitesmith BN8 6JG**
email: joannawild@hotmail.co.uk **web:** www.broadacres-bandb.co.uk
dir: A22 towards Eastbourne, right onto B2124 just before Golden Cross. 1m on left behind black metal gates

This beautiful property, located very near to Lewes, has a single, spacious, self-contained suite for guest use. The richly decorated rooms are all well-equipped and the bedroom features a large flat-screen TV, super king-size sleigh bed, and its own sitting area. There is also generous storage space. The well-equipped and luxurious bathroom has a rolltop bath and separate shower. Breakfast is a real treat and is served in the suite's own dining room. Dinner is also available on request. You can also expect WiFi, parking, all in extensive well-kept grounds. AA Friendliest B&B of the Year Award Finalist 2016-2017.

Rooms 1 en suite (1 GF) **Facilities** FTV tea/coffee Dinner available WiFi Riding 🔒
Extras Speciality toiletries, home-made biscuits **Parking** 4 **Notes** LB ⊗
No Children 12yrs Closed 24-28 Dec ⊜

Premier Collection

Knelle Dower B&B

★★★★★ ⬠ GUEST ACCOMMODATION

tel: 01797 253163 **Rye Rd TN31 6NJ**
email: knelledower@btconnect.com **web:** www.knelledower.co.uk
dir: A21 to Flimwell onto A268, then A28. In Northiam onto B2088 opposite primary school, on left between Talisman & Boundary House

Located in a rural location close to both Rye and the village of Northiam, this converted barn hosts a prime location with uninterrupted countryside views. The accommodation is spacious with high-quality decor and furnishings, and there is a private terrace leading off the main living area for guests to enjoy during summer months. Breakfast can be served here or in the main house. AA Friendliest B&B of the Year Award Finalist 2016-2017.

Rooms 1 annexe en suite (1 GF) **Facilities** FTV DVD iPod docking station tea/coffee WiFi ⬒ ♿ 18 🔒 **Parking** 2 **Notes** ⊗ No Children 3yrs Closed 21-28 Dec

See also Hastings & St Leonards

Premier Collection

Jeake's House

★★★★★ ⬠ GUEST ACCOMMODATION

tel: 01797 222828 **Mermaid St TN31 7ET**
email: stay@jeakeshouse.com **web:** www.jeakeshouse.com
dir: Approach from High St or The Strand

Previously a 16th-century wool store and then a 19th-century Baptist school, this delightful house stands on a cobbled street in one of the most beautiful parts of this small, bustling town. The individually decorated bedrooms combine elegance and comfort with modern facilities. Breakfast is served at separate tables in the galleried dining room, and there is an oak-beamed lounge as well as a stylish, book-lined bar complete with old pews.

Rooms 11 rms (10 en suite) (1 pri facs) (2 fmly) S £70-£85; D £95-£150*
Facilities FTV iPod docking station Lounge tea/coffee Licensed WiFi 🔒
Parking 20 **Notes** LB No Children 5yrs

See advert on opposite page

Premier Collection

Manor Farm Oast

★★★★★ 🏆 BED AND BREAKFAST

tel: 01424 813787 & 07866 818952 **Windmill Ln TN36 4WL**
email: manor.farm.oast@lineone.net **web:** www.manorfarmoast.co.uk
dir: *4m SW of Rye. A259 W past Icklesham church, left at x-rds into Windmill Ln, after sharp left bend, left (follow sign) into farmland*

Manor Farm Oast is a charming 19th-century environmentally-friendly oast house peacefully located amid orchards in open countryside. Spacious bedrooms are individually styled and include numerous thoughtful extras including free WiFi. A choice of lounges is available, one heated by a roaring log fire during the winter.

Rooms 3 rms (2 en suite) (1 pri facs) (1 fmly) S £80-£105; D £105 **Facilities** FTV Lounge tea/coffee Licensed WiFi 🔒 **Extras** Speciality toiletries, fruit, chocolates **Conf** Max 20 Thtr 20 Board 12 **Parking** 8 **Notes** LB ⊗ No Children 11yrs Closed 31 Dec

Premier Collection

Willow Tree House

★★★★★ GUEST ACCOMMODATION

tel: 01797 227820 & 07715 991325 **Winchelsea Rd TN31 7EL**
email: info@willow-tree-house.com **web:** www.willow-tree-house.com
dir: *On A259, 500mtrs from town centre*

Willow Tree House is an early 17th-century farmhouse which has been sympathetically refurbished to retain many of its charming original features. There are six individually furnished bedrooms, all appointed to a high standard – four doubles, one four-poster bedroom and a king size/twin; each has an en suite shower room. There is also ample free parking in the secure on-site car park. Willow Tree House is only ten minutes' walk away from Rye town centre with its antique shops restaurants, pubs, and cobbled streets.

Rooms 6 en suite S £90-£105; D £90-£140* **Facilities** FTV DVD iPod docking station Lounge tea/coffee WiFi ⚓ 18 🔒 **Extras** Speciality toiletries **Parking** 6 **Notes** LB ⊗ No Children 14yrs

---

Jeake's House

Mermaid Street, Rye, East Sussex TN31 7ET
Tel: 01797 222828 · Email: stay@jeakeshouse.com
Website: www.jeakeshouse.com

Jeake's House provides outstanding accommodation in Rye. The 16th Century house plays host to the discerning guest who wants to recapture the feel of history while at the same time enjoying a high standard of modern comfort and relaxed hospitality. Rye accommodation is very special and Jeake's House certainly lives up to this reputation. Guests will be invariably welcomed by our flirtatious Tonkinese, Freddie and Monte, cordially complemented by the friendly service of the proprietors, Jenny Hadfield and Richard Martin. Breakfast is served in our galleried dining room and there is a booklined honesty bar to relax in.

Staying at Jeake's House also provides access to the surrounding countryside. There are many historical and beautiful villages and towns nearby. Jenny and Richard are always happy to advise on leisurely trips to historic castles, beautiful gardens and picturesque villages; and can recommend the best local restaurants and friendly inns.

Parking in this small town is notoriously difficult to find and we are happy to be some of the only accommodation in Rye to guarantee guests a space in our private car park. There is a small charge. Our car park is a three minute walk from Jeake's House and we advise that you park on Mermaid Street so that we can assist you with your luggage and provide you with a parking permit.

RYE *continued*

Strand House

★★★★ ⑧ ☕ GUEST ACCOMMODATION

tel: 01797 226276 **Tanyards Ln, Winchelsea TN36 4JT**
email: info@thestrandhouse.co.uk **web:** www.thestrandhouse.co.uk
dir: *M20 junct 10, A2070 to Lydd. A259 through Rye to Winchelsea, house in 2m*

This charming 15th-century house is just a few miles from Rye. Traditional
character is maintained in comfortably appointed rooms and the public areas,
while the annexe rooms offer a more contemporary style. Both the main house and
the annexe rooms are available for exclusive use. The dining room is also open to
the public on certain days of the week, where local produce is a feature of the well
balanced menu. Homemade jams and marmalade, together with honey from the
garden and other local produce are offered at breakfast. Secure parking available.

Rooms 10 rms (9 en suite) (1 pri facs) 3 annexe en suite (4 fmly) (3 GF) S £60-£85;
D £75-£200* **Facilities** FTV DVD iPod docking station Lounge tea/coffee Dinner
available Licensed WiFi 🛀 **Extras** Mini-fridge in annexe rooms **Parking** 15 **Notes** LB
No Children 5yrs RS wknds (high season) 2 night bookings only Civ Wed 30

The Windmill Guest House

★★★★ GUEST ACCOMMODATION

tel: 01797 224027 **Ferry Rd TN31 7DW**
email: info@ryewindmill.co.uk **web:** www.ryewindmill.co.uk

This white smock windmill has been a Rye landmark since 1820 and was more
recently a bakery. Bedrooms located in the purpose-built extension have good beds
and en suite facilities and are generously proportioned. Breakfast, taken in the old
granary, is a freshly-cooked affair using well-sourced local ingredients including
butchers' sausages and some good fruit juices.

Rooms 10 en suite (4 GF) S £60-£75; D £80-£170* **Facilities** FTV Lounge TVL tea/
coffee Licensed WiFi 🛀 **Extras** Mineral water - complimentary **Conf** Max 30 Thtr 25
Class 30 Board 12 **Parking** 12 **Notes** No Children 12yrs Closed 24-26 Dec

The Kings Head Inn

★★★★ ☕ INN

tel: 01797 225962 & 07762 404958 **Rye Hill TN31 7HN**
email: info@kingsheadrye.co.uk **web:** www.kingsheadrye.co.uk

This inn is located just a couple of miles from the centre of Rye. Bedrooms are
stylish and contemporary in style and very comfortable and are split between the
main pub and converted annexe rooms with private parking. The pub and
restaurant is an ideal place to relax and enjoy a traditional pub lunch or dinner.
Breakfast is served in this area daily.

Rooms 5 en suite 6 annexe en suite (4 fmly) (5 GF) S £65-£100; D £120
Facilities FTV TV9B tea/coffee Dinner available WiFi **Parking** 40 **Notes** No coaches

The AA on Social Media - follow us:

twitter: @TheAA_Lifestyle
facebook: www.facebook.com/TheAAUK

Find us on **Facebook**

Little Saltcote

★★★★ GUEST ACCOMMODATION

tel: 01797 223210 & 07940 742646 **22 Military Rd TN31 7NY**
email: info@littlesaltcote.co.uk **web:** www.littlesaltcote.co.uk
dir: 0.5m N of town centre. Exit A268 into Military Rd signed Appledore, house 300yds on left

This delightful family-run establishment stands in quiet surroundings within walking distance of Rye town centre. The bright and airy en suite bedrooms are equipped with modern facilities including WiFi, and guests can enjoy afternoon tea in the garden conservatory. A hearty breakfast is served at individual tables in the dining room.

Rooms 4 en suite (2 fmly) (1 GF) **Facilities** FTV DVD Lounge tea/coffee WiFi 🔒
Parking 5 **Notes** Closed 25-26 Dec

ST LEONARDS

See Hastings & St Leonards

SEAFORD   Map 6 TV49

Ab Fab Rooms

★★★★ 🏠 BED AND BREAKFAST

tel: 01323 895001 & 07713 197915 **11 Station Rd, Bishopstone BN25 2RB**
email: stay@abfabrooms.co.uk **web:** www.abfabrooms.co.uk

Just a short walk from Bishopstone station and sandy beaches, this is a perfect base for visiting local sights and attractions. The three bedrooms are styled in a contemporary fashion and offer superior comfort and amenities – freshly-baked flapjacks are only one of the many baked goods offered. Breakfast, served in the garden conservatory, includes home-made jams and local Sussex produce. There is parking and a rear garden to enjoy during the warmer months.

Rooms 3 en suite S £55-£65; D £75-£85 **Facilities** STV DVD iPod docking station tea/coffee WiFi **Parking** 2 **Notes** ⊗ ⊜

The Avondale

★★★ GUEST ACCOMMODATION

tel: 01323 890008 **Avondale Rd BN25 1RJ**
email: info@theavondale.co.uk **web:** www.theavondale.co.uk
dir: In town centre, off A259 behind war memorial

A warm welcome is offered by the caring owners at this friendly, family-run guest accommodation which is ideally placed for the Newhaven to Dieppe ferry service. The bedrooms are pleasantly furnished and thoughtfully equipped. Breakfast is served in the attractive dining room and guests also have the use of a cosy lounge.

Rooms 14 rms (8 en suite) (4 fmly) **Facilities** FTV DVD TVL tea/coffee Lift Licensed WiFi **Conf** Max 15 Class 15 Board 15 **Notes** ⊗

WADHURST   Map 6 TQ63

Little Tidebrook Farm (TQ621304)

★★★★ FARMHOUSE

tel: 01892 782688 & 07970 159988 **Riseden TN5 6NY**
email: info@littletidebrook.co.uk **web:** www.littletidebrook.co.uk
dir: A267 from Tunbridge Wells to Mark Cross, left onto B2100, 2m, right at Best Beech Inn, left after 1m into Riseden Rd, farm on left

This traditional farmhouse has cosy log fires in winter and wonderful garden dining in warmer months. The imaginative decor sits well with modern amenities, such as WiFi, to provide both leisure and business guests with excellent accommodation. It is close to Bewl Water and Royal Tunbridge Wells.

Rooms 3 rms (2 en suite) (1 pri facs) S £60-£90; D £70-£90* **Facilities** FTV DVD TVL tea/coffee WiFi 🔒 **Parking** 8 **Notes** ⊗ No Children 12yrs ⊜ 50 acres horses

| **WILMINGTON** | Map 6 TQ50 |

Crossways

★★★★ ◎◎ RESTAURANT WITH ROOMS

tel: 01323 482455 **Lewes Rd BN26 5SG**
email: stay@crosswayshotel.co.uk **web:** www.crosswayshotel.co.uk
dir: On A27 between Lewes & Polegate, 2m E of Alfriston rdbt

Proprietors David Stott and Clive James have been welcoming guests to this elegant restaurant with rooms for over 25 years. Crossways sits amid stunning gardens and attractively tended grounds. The well-presented bedrooms are tastefully decorated and provide an abundance of thoughtful amenities including free WiFi. Guest comfort is paramount and the warm hospitality ensures guests often return.

Rooms 7 en suite S £79-£85; D £145-£165* **Facilities** FTV tea/coffee Dinner available Direct Dial WiFi 🔒 **Extras** Speciality toiletries, mini-bar, fresh milk **Parking** 30 **Notes** LB ⊗ No Children 12yrs Closed 24 Dec-23 Jan No coaches

WEST SUSSEX

| **AMBERLEY** | Map 6 TQ01 |

Woody Banks Cottage

★★★★ BED AND BREAKFAST

tel: 01798 831295 & 07719 916703 **Crossgates BN18 9NR**
email: enquiries@woodybanks.co.uk **web:** www.woodybanks.co.uk
dir: Off B2139 into village, right at Black Horse pub, Woody Banks 0.5m on left past Sportsman pub

Located close to Arundel in an elevated position with stunning views over the Wildbrooks, this immaculately maintained house and gardens is very popular with walkers. It provides two comfortable, homely bedrooms filled with thoughtful extras. Imaginative breakfasts are served in the spacious lounge-dining room.

Rooms 2 rms (1 pri facs) (1 fmly) S £40-£50; D £70-£85* **Facilities** FTV DVD TVL tea/coffee WiFi 🔒 **Extras** Fruit teas **Parking** 2 **Notes** LB ⊗ No Children 6yrs Closed 24-27 Dec 🐾

| **ANGMERING** | Map 6 TQ00 |

Angmering Manor

★★★★ 🛏 GUEST ACCOMMODATION

tel: 01903 859849 **High St BN16 4AG**
email: angmeringmanor@thechapmansgroup.co.uk **web:** www.relaxinnz.co.uk
dir: Follow A27 towards Portsmouth, exit A280, follow signs for Angmering

This former manor house in the heart of the village has been stylishly appointed. It offers good food, a bar, an indoor pool, and good parking. Staff are friendly and helpful and rooms are very comfortable.

Rooms 17 en suite (3 fmly) (4 GF) **Facilities** FTV TVL tea/coffee Dinner available Direct Dial Licensed WiFi 🕹 Sauna Gym Beauty salon **Parking** 25 **Notes** LB ⊗ Civ Wed 50

| **ARUNDEL** | Map 6 TQ00 |

See also Amberley

Hanger Down House B&B

★★★★ BED AND BREAKFAST

tel: 01903 882904 & 07753 595191 **Priory Ln, Tortington BN18 0BG**
email: hangerdownhouse@btinternet.com **web:** www.hangerdownhouse.co.uk
dir: A27 to Arundel, take road signed Ford/Climping at Arundel rdbt. Priory Ln 0.5m on right

Set in picturesque Sussex countryside, Hanger Down House is conveniently and quietly located one mile from the historic town of Arundel. All three bedrooms are stylishly decorated and provide comfortable accommodation for guests. Bedrooms include king-size beds, a leather sofa, fridge, digital LCD TVs and free WiFi. There are great views of the local countryside and a walled garden which guests are free to use. A cooked or continental breakfast can be enjoyed in the dining room.

Rooms 3 en suite (2 fmly) (1 GF) S £65-£95; D £95-£130 **Facilities** Lounge tea/coffee WiFi 🎾 ⛳ 🔒 Trampoline Football pitch Outdoor table tennis **Extras** Speciality toiletries - complimentary; fridges **Parking** 5 **Notes** LB ⊗ 🐾

The Town House

★★★★ ◎◎ RESTAURANT WITH ROOMS

tel: 01903 883847 **65 High St BN18 9AJ**
email: enquiries@thetownhouse.co.uk **web:** www.thetownhouse.co.uk
dir: A27 to Arundel, into High Street, establishment on left at top of hill

This is an elegant, Grade II listed Regency building overlooking Arundel Castle, just a short walk from the shops and centre of the town. Bedrooms and public areas retain the building's unspoilt character. The ceiling in the dining room is particularly spectacular and originated in Florence in the 16th century. The excellent food has been awarded two AA Rosettes.

Rooms 5 en suite (1 fmly) S £75-£110; D £110-£150* **Facilities** FTV iPod docking station Dinner available WiFi 🔒 **Extras** Speciality toiletries **Notes** ⊗ Closed 2wks Etr & 2wks Oct RS Sun-Mon Restaurant closed No coaches

White Swan

★★★★ INN

tel: 01903 882677 **16 Chichester Rd BN18 0AD**
email: thewhiteswan.arundel@pebblehotels.com **web:** www.pebblehotels.com
dir: From Arundel follow A27 towards Chichester, premises on right hand side at top of hill

The White Swan offers very comfortable and stylish accommodation. There is a character bar, a lounge and a restaurant, and informal service is provided by the friendly team. Substantial snacks and meals can be ordered throughout the day and evening. Complimentary WiFi is available in the public areas.

Rooms 20 en suite (6 GF) **Facilities** FTV TVL tea/coffee Dinner available Direct Dial WiFi **Extras** Speciality toiletries **Conf** Max 100 Thtr 100 **Parking** 100 **Notes** Civ Wed 70

BOGNOR REGIS
Map 6 SZ99

The Old Priory
★★★★ ⚱ GUEST HOUSE

tel: 01243 863580 & 07947 877733 **80 North Bersted St PO22 9AQ**
email: bookings@old-priory.com **web:** www.old-priory.com
dir: *1.6m NW of Bognor. Off A259 (Chichester road) to North Bersted. Old Priory sign on left. Or A29 to rdbt (McDonalds). Turn right into Rowan Way, follow signs*

Located in the mainly residential area of North Bersted, this 400-year-old property retains many original features. Bedrooms, which are all individual in style, are homely, with a couple featuring four-poster beds and sunken jacuzzi baths. All have en suites or a private bathroom. Delicious breakfasts, featuring home-made jams and cake, as well as excellent cooked dishes, are served at an impressive communal table in the grand dining room. There is also an outdoor pool, hot tub and delightful grounds for guests to enjoy.

Rooms 3 rms (2 en suite) (1 pri facs) 3 annexe en suite (3 GF) S £45-£52; D £72-£112* **Facilities** STV tea/coffee WiFi ⚲ 🔒 Hot tub **Parking** 6

BOLNEY
Map 6 TQ22

8 Bells Bed & Breakfast
★★★★ ⚬ INN

tel: 01444 881396 **The Long House, The Street RH17 5QP**
email: stay@8bellsbandb.com **web:** www.8bellsbandb.com
dir: *A23/A272 junct. Village situated between Ansty & Cowfold on A272*

This Tudor property is situated in a peaceful village, close to both Gatwick and Brighton. Many original features, including exposed beams, remain, along with high-quality, modern and comfortable accommodation. Guests check in at the pub located directly opposite and it is here that breakfast, lunch and dinner can be enjoyed.

Rooms 3 en suite (1 fmly) (1 GF) **Facilities** FTV DVD Lounge tea/coffee Dinner available WiFi Pool table **Extras** Bottled water - complimentary **Parking** 15 **Notes** LB ⊗

CHARLTON — Map 6 SU81

Charlton Twenty Eight

★★★★ ☀ BED AND BREAKFAST

tel: 01243 811756 **28 Charlton PO18 0HU**
email: info@charlton-28.co.uk **web:** www.charlton-28.co.uk
dir: *A286 in Singleton follow signs for Charlton. In village turn opposite The Fox Goes Free pub, continue straight, immediately after right hand bend*

Charlton Twenty Eight is an attractive Grade II listed 18th-century cottage which lies at the foot of the South Downs and close to the Goodwood Estate. Julie and Trevor offer a warm welcome, as well as delicious refreshments on arrival. Bedrooms are light, spacious, attractively presented and comfortably furnished, all with en suite facilities. Breakfast is a delight, while dinner can be taken at one of many local pubs and restaurants in the area.

Rooms 2 en suite **Facilities** FTV DVD tea/coffee WiFi 🔒 **Extras** Bottled mineral water, robes, slippers **Parking** 4 **Notes** ⊗ No Children 12yrs Closed 23-27 Dec, Feb-2 Mar

The Fox Goes Free

★★★★ INN

tel: 01243 811461 **PO18 0HU**
email: enquiries@thefoxgoesfree.com **web:** www.thefoxgoesfree.com
dir: *In village centre*

This former hunting lodge has retained much original character and is located in lovely countryside at the foot of the South Downs National Park. The bedrooms are well appointed and the pub boasts low ceilings, brick floors and three inglenook fireplaces. The inn serves its own ale and has an inviting, daily-changing menu. During the summer months, guests can take advantage of the rear garden.

Rooms 3 en suite 2 annexe en suite (3 fmly) (2 GF) S £70-£180; D £95-£180* **Facilities** FTV tea/coffee Dinner available WiFi 🔒 **Parking** 50

CHICHESTER — Map 5 SU80

See also West Marden

Premier Collection

Rooks Hill

★★★★★ ☀ GUEST HOUSE

tel: 01243 528400 & 07802 415639 **Lavant Rd, Lavant PO18 0BQ**
email: info@rookshill.co.uk **web:** www.rookshill.co.uk

This beautiful Grade II listed country house is at the foot of the South Downs yet is only a few minutes from Chichester. Goodwood is also close by and a 15 minute drive will take guests to the coast. The house is lovingly maintained with attractive rooms, all of which are presented in a way that balances the period features with contemporary style. All of them also feature modern en suites. The oak-beamed breakfast room and lounge is delightful and looks out to the wisteria-clad courtyard. Breakfasts are memorable for their quality, choice and the emphasis on local produce. Hospitality is also a highlight here.

Rooms 4 en suite (1 GF) D £110-£175* **Facilities** FTV Lounge tea/coffee WiFi 🔒 **Parking** 4 **Notes** ⊗ No Children 14yrs

To help you navigate safely and easily, use the AA Big Road Atlas Britain 2017. Available from: shop.theAA.com

BEST SELLING ROAD ATLASES OF BRITAIN

AA 2017
BIG ROAD ATLAS
BRITAIN

BRITAIN'S CLEAREST MAPPING

Safety cameras with speed limits
Clear, route planner map
Top 300 AA-inspected Caravan and Camping sites
Scenic routes
Large 3 miles to 1 inch scale

Premier Collection

The Royal Oak Inn

★★★★★ ◉◉ ⚲ INN

tel: 01243 527434 **Pook Ln, East Lavant PO18 0AX**
email: info@royaloakeastlavant.co.uk **web:** www.royaloakeastlavant.co.uk
dir: *2m N of Chichester. Exit A286 to East Lavant centre*

Located close to the Goodwood estate and Rolls-Royce HQ this delightful inn is full of character with beamed ceilings, timber floors and open fires in the public areas. Bedrooms are finished to a very high standard with comfortable beds and state-of-the-art electronic equipment. The food in the popular restaurant has been awarded two AA Rosettes.

Rooms 3 en suite 5 annexe en suite (1 fmly) (2 GF) S £95-£145; D £125-£295* **Facilities** FTV DVD iPod docking station tea/coffee Dinner available Direct Dial WiFi ⚡ 27 Riding **Extras** Speciality toiletries, chocolate, fresh milk - free **Parking** 25 **Notes** ⊗ No coaches

Musgrove House

★★★★ ⚲ BED AND BREAKFAST

tel: 01243 790179 & 07885 586344 **63 Oving Rd PO19 7EN**
email: enquiries@musgrovehouse.co.uk **web:** www.musgrovehouse.co.uk
dir: *From A27 onto B2144 towards city centre, at corner of Oving Rd & St James Rd*

Located just outside Chichester city centre, this establishment offers three stylish bedrooms with light, airy decor and modern fixtures and fittings, including free WiFi and digital TVs. Expect a friendly welcome on arrival and a choice of both cooked and continental dishes at breakfast, which makes good use of high-quality and locally sourced produce.

Rooms 3 en suite S £70-£90; D £75-£95* **Facilities** FTV DVD iPod docking station tea/coffee WiFi ⚲ **Extras** Speciality toiletries **Parking** 3 **Notes** ⊗ No Children 12yrs

---

The Bulls Head Inn

The Bulls Head is a 17th Century converted farmhouse situated in the picturesque village of Fishbourne West Sussex. *The Bulls Head* Fishbourne is an ideal location for business or pleasure close to many top local attractions and a short distance to Portsmouth, Southampton and Brighton.

A relaxing comfortable beamed pub that is famous for its good promptly served wholesome food (all freshly prepared and home cooked with children's and smaller portions available) excellent real ales and quality wines. A warm and intimate atmosphere awaits you in this typical English Village Pub. Fishbourne is an ideal location to be based whether for business or pleasure five minutes by car to the centre of Chichester and thirty minutes to Portsmouth with its Historic Dockyard and great waterfront shopping.

The Bulls Head is also close to many other popular attractions including Fontwell, Fishbourne Roman Villa and Goodwood famous for its Racecourse, the Goodwood Festival of Speed and the Goodwood Revival.

The Bulls Head serves the best in cask conditioned real ales with five to choose from including London Pride, Seafarers H.S.B and E.S.B along with other popular bottled and draught lagers with something for every taste bud.

99 Fishbourne Road, Fishbourne, Chichester, West Sussex PO19 3JP
Tel: 01243 839895 · **Website:** www.bullsheadfishbourne.net · **Email:** enquiries@bullsheadfishbourne.net

CHICHESTER *continued*

The Bulls Head
★★★★ INN

tel: 01243 839895 **99 Fishbourne Road West PO19 3JP**
email: enquiries@bullsheadfishbourne.net **web:** www.bullsheadfishbourne.net
dir: *A27 onto A259, 0.5m on left*

Located in Fishbourne, yet just a short drive from the centre of Chichester, and within easy access of Portsmouth, The Bulls Head offers comfortably appointed bedrooms in a former coach house. The bedrooms are light and airy with modern decor and furnishings. The pub is traditional in style and offers a wide selection of home-cooked pub classics as well as a good range of cask ales. Breakfast is served in the restaurant.

Rooms 4 annexe en suite (1 fmly) (4 GF) S fr £67; D fr £99* **Facilities** FTV DVD tea/coffee Dinner available WiFi ☕ **Parking** 35

See advert on page 309

82 Fishbourne
★★★★ 🍽 BED AND BREAKFAST

tel: 07854 051013 **82 Fishbourne Road West PO19 3JL**
email: nik@nikwestacott.plus.com **web:** www.82fishbourne.co.uk
dir: *A27 at Chichester rdbt, towards Fishbourne & Bosham on A259. 0.5m on right diagonally opposite Woolpack pub*

Warm and friendly hospitality abounds at 82 Fishbourne, which is just a short drive from historic Chichester. Accommodation is spacious and well equipped. Breakfast provides a substantial start to the day and includes delicious fresh eggs from the free-range hens that live in the back garden. Scheduled activities include 'mushroom hunts', and wine tastings are held throughout the year.

Rooms 3 en suite (1 fmly) (1 GF) **Facilities** FTV tea/coffee Dinner available Licensed WiFi ☕ Cookery lessons, fly fishing trips **Parking** 3 **Notes** LB

The George & Dragon
★★★ 🍽 INN

tel: 01243 785660 **51 North St PO19 1NQ**
email: info@georgeanddragoninn.co.uk **web:** www.georgeanddragoninn.co.uk
dir: *At top of North St, off A286, near Chichester Festival Theatre*

This inn, located at one end of Chichester's high street boasts attractively styled rooms and a friendly atmosphere. Rooms are comfortable with all the amenities needed for a pleasant night's stay. There is a light and airy dining room set apart from the popular central bar area where dinner and breakfast is served. Regional ales are available.

Rooms 10 annexe en suite (5 GF) **Facilities** FTV tea/coffee Dinner available WiFi **Notes** RS 25-26 Dec No bkfst service & pub closed No coaches

The Vestry
★★★ INN

tel: 01243 773358 **23 Southgate PO19 1ES**
email: info@the-vestry.co.uk **web:** www. the-vestry.co.uk

The Vestry is conveniently located in the town centre. Bedrooms are spacious and well equipped, including beverage making facilities and WiFi. The bar and restaurant are spacious with comfortable seating areas; during the winter months guests can keep cosy in front of the log fires, and live music features frequently. A wide choice of food is served during the day and a good range of continental and cooked breakfasts are available.

Rooms 11 en suite (2 fmly) **Facilities** FTV tea/coffee Dinner available WiFi **Notes** Closed 24-26 Dec & 31 Dec-1 Jan

CHILGROVE	Map 5 SU81

Premier Collection

The White Horse
★★★★★ ⓐ RESTAURANT WITH ROOMS

tel: 01243 519444 **High St PO18 9HX**
email: info@thewhitehorse.co.uk **web:** www.thewhitehorse.co.uk
dir: *From Chichester take A286 N, turn left onto B2141 to village*

Part of The Epicurean Collection, this spacious property offers stylish and relaxed surroundings on the edge of the South Downs. The bar and dining areas have an opulent feel, with lots of quirky touches and interesting features. Guests are welcome to enjoy a pint and relax, or dine from the appealing and wide-ranging menus. The emphasis is on local produce and food is a highlight. Bedrooms offer an attractive blend of traditional and contemporary features, with wooden beams, sheepskin rugs and king-size beds. Most open out onto the private courtyard and feature either copper baths or large rain showers, with a couple even having hot tubs. AA Funkiest B&B of the Year Award Runner-Up 2016-2017.

Rooms 15 en suite **Facilities** FTV Lounge tea/coffee Dinner available Direct Dial WiFi Fishing **Conf** Max 20 **Parking** **Notes** LB

COMPTON
Map 5 SU71

Apiary Cottage
★★★★ BED AND BREAKFAST

tel: 023 9263 1306 **PO18 9EX**
email: janesmckellar1@hotmail.co.uk **web:** www.apiarycottagebandb.co.uk
dir: A3 at Horndean into Rowlands Castle road. Left into Finchdean road, left onto B1246 to West Marden, then Compton

This beautiful cottage near Chichester has two highly individual bedrooms with their own private bathrooms. The richly decorated rooms are well equipped and are ideal for business or leisure use. Public areas include a comfortable lounge and the dining area is a sociable setting for breakfast, which overlooks the gardens. There is also parking available.

Rooms 2 rms (2 pri facs) S £60-£70; D £70-£85* **Facilities** FTV TVL tea/coffee WiFi 🔒 **Extras** Sweets, chocolate **Parking** 6 **Notes** ⊗ 🐾

CRAWLEY
For accommodation details see Gatwick Airport (London)

GATWICK AIRPORT (LONDON)
Map 6 TQ24

Old House Inn
★★★★ 😊 INN

tel: 01342 718529 **Effingham Rd RH10 3JB**
email: info@theoldhouseinn.co.uk **web:** www.theoldhouseinn.co.uk
dir: On B2037

Part of The Epicurean Collection, and conveniently located just ten minutes from Gatwick, this stylish inn offers a modern restaurant and bar, and has retained many original features. All of the bedrooms are en suite with stylish decor and very comfortable furnishings. There is plenty of parking on site and a large beer garden for guests to enjoy. Both cooked and continental breakfasts are served daily in the main restaurant.

Rooms 6 annexe en suite (1 fmly) (4 GF) **Facilities** FTV Lounge tea/coffee Dinner available Direct Dial WiFi 🛎🏌 🔒 **Parking** 50

Vulcan Lodge Guest House
★★★★ BED AND BREAKFAST

tel: 01293 771522 & 07980 576012 **27 Massetts Rd RH6 7DQ**
email: reservations@vulcan-lodge.com **web:** www.vulcan-lodge.com
dir: M23 junct 9, A23 into Horley, off A23 Brighton Rd

A particularly warm and friendly welcome is offered by the hosts of Vulcan Lodge, a charming period house, which sits back from the main road and is convenient for Gatwick Airport. Bedrooms are well equipped and feature many thoughtful extras. A choice of breakfast is offered, including vegetarian, and is served in a delightful dining room.

Rooms 4 rms (3 en suite) (1 pri facs) (1 fmly) S £49-£56; D £70 **Facilities** FTV TVL tea/coffee WiFi **Extras** Bottled water **Parking** 13 **Notes** Closed 23-27 Dec & 31 Dec-2 Jan

Gainsborough Lodge
★★★ GUEST ACCOMMODATION

tel: 01293 783982 **39 Massetts Rd RH6 7DT**
email: enquiries@gainsborough-lodge.co.uk **web:** www.gainsborough-lodge.co.uk
dir: 2m NE of airport off A23 Brighton Rd

Close to Gatwick, this fine Edwardian house offers a courtesy service to and from the airport. The bright bedrooms are comfortably appointed, and a varied breakfast, including a vegetarian option is served in the cheerful conservatory-dining room. There is also an attractive lounge.

Rooms 15 rms (14 en suite) (1 pri facs) 7 annexe en suite (5 fmly) (12 GF) S £37-£42; D £47-£52* **Facilities** FTV TVL tea/coffee Licensed WiFi **Parking** 20 **Notes** ⊗

Gatwick White House
★★ GUEST ACCOMMODATION

tel: 01293 402777 & 0800 612 3605 **50-52 Church Rd RH6 7EX**
email: hotel@gwhh.com **web:** www.gwhh.com
dir: In Horley centre off A23 Brighton Rd

Convenient for the airport and major routes, this establishment offers efficient and functional accommodation. There is a bar and a restaurant that serves good curries as well as traditional dishes. The house has ample parking, and a 24-hour transfer service to Gatwick is available on request.

Rooms 27 en suite (2 fmly) (10 GF) S £35-£45; D £45-£55 **Facilities** FTV TVL tea/coffee Dinner available Direct Dial Licensed WiFi 🔒 **Parking** 30 **Notes** ⊗

HORSHAM
Map 6 TQ13

Springfields
★★★★ GUEST ACCOMMODATION

tel: 01403 246770 **Springfield Park Rd RH12 2PW**
email: enquiries@springfieldshotel.co.uk **web:** www.springfieldshotel.co.uk

This purpose-built guest accommodation is located in the very heart of Horsham, bedrooms are modern in style, spacious and come well equipped with stylish furnishings, free WiFi, digital TV and well stocked beverage trays. Breakfast is served in the main dining room on the ground floor and ample parking is available on site. There are a number of restaurants within walking distance including a good selection of traditional meals at the neighbouring pub.

Rooms 11 en suite **Facilities** WiFi

LITTLEHAMPTON
Map 6 TQ00

Premier Collection

Glendales
★★★★★ 😊 BED AND BREAKFAST

tel: 01903 775383 & 07970 845689 **Pigeonhouse Ln, Rustington BN16 2AZ**
email: jenny@glendales.co.uk **web:** www.glendales.co.uk

Glendales is located in a quiet setting and is only a 10-minute walk away from the beach. The luxurious en suite accommodation is attractively presented and well-equipped. Guests have the use of the conservatory and attractive garden, and there is also off-street parking. Breakfast is also noteworthy and not to be missed.

Rooms 1 en suite (1 GF) S £75-£100; D £90-£140* **Facilities** FTV DVD tea/coffee WiFi **Extras** Speciality toiletries, fruit, snacks - free **Parking** 2 **Notes** ⊗ No Children 🐾

LITTLEHAMPTON *continued*

Premier Collection

Berry House

★★★★★ ☺ GUEST ACCOMMODATION

tel: 01903 726260 & 07799 425136 **Berry Ln BN17 5HD**
email: info@berryhouse.biz **web:** www.berryhouse.biz

Berry House is located in the heart of Littlehampton and has spacious, modern and comfortably appointed accommodation. The house was built in 2012, so all rooms have modern facilities including complimentary WiFi and digital TV. Breakfast is served in the main dining room and there is a wide selection of both cooked and continental dishes. Secure off-road parking is provided, and there are gardens for guests to enjoy during the summer months.

Rooms 4 en suite (1 fmly) (2 GF) **Facilities** STV FTV tea/coffee WiFi ⬇ 18 🔒
Extras Bottled water - complimentary; fruit, chocolates **Parking** 7 **Notes** ⊗
No Children 16yrs

East Beach Guest House

★★★★ GUEST HOUSE

tel: 01903 714270 **71 South Ter BN17 5LQ**
email: admin@eastbeachguesthouse.co.uk **web:** www.eastbeachguesthouse.co.uk
dir: *On South Terrace, opposite beach, 200mtrs from junct with Pier Rd*

This guest house offers individually styled and comfortable accommodation; all rooms are equipped with a good range of amenities including flat-screen TVs and WiFi; some bedrooms have sea views. A freshly cooked breakfast, using local produce, is served in the first-floor breakfast room that overlooks the sea.

Rooms 9 en suite (2 fmly) (2 GF) **Facilities** FTV DVD TVL tea/coffee WiFi 🔒
Extras Speciality toiletries - complimentary **Notes** LB ⊗ No Children 3yrs

Leeside

★★★★ GUEST ACCOMMODATION

tel: 01903 723666 & 07791 797131 **Rope Walk BN17 5DE**
email: leeside1@tiscali.co.uk **web:** www.leesidebandb.com
dir: *From A259 into Ferry Rd signed Rope Walk & West Beach. 1m, turn right into Rope Walk, Leeside on right*

Leeside is a bright bungalow, close to local sailing clubs, the River Arun and the beach. Visitors will enjoy a warm welcome, and comfortable modern bedrooms have flat-screen TVs and free WiFi. The hearty breakfasts make a good start to the day.

Rooms 4 en suite (3 GF) **Facilities** FTV TVL tea/coffee WiFi 🔒 **Parking** 4 **Notes** ⊗
No Children 14yrs

Who are the AA's award-winning B&Bs? For details see pages 12-15

Premier Collection

The Halfway Bridge Inn

★★★★★ ⍟ ☺ INN

tel: 01798 861281 & 07971 872655 **Halfway Bridge GU28 9BP**
email: enquiries@halfwaybridge.co.uk **web:** www.halfwaybridge.co.uk
dir: *From Petworth on A272 towards Midhurst, 3m on right*

This inn, located between Petworth and Midhurst, has attractively styled rooms in a converted barn setting; the spacious rooms, each with their own contemporary country-style decor, have many thoughtful extras. The popular inn offers warming fires, and intimate dining areas where guests can enjoy award-winning cuisine. The central bar is popular and guest ales feature strongly. The friendly team are key to the business here, making for a memorable stay.

Rooms 7 en suite (1 fmly) (7 GF) **Facilities** FTV DVD iPod docking station tea/coffee Dinner available WiFi **Extras** Speciality toiletries, fresh milk - complimentary **Parking** 30 **Notes** No coaches

Loves Farm *(SU912235)*

★★★★ FARMHOUSE

tel: 01730 813212 & 07789 228400 **Easebourne St GU29 0BG**
email: lovesl@btinternet.com **web:** www.lovesfarm.com
dir: *2m NE of town centre. Exit A272 at Easebourne church into Easebourne St, follow signs for Loves Farm*

This 17th-century farmhouse is set on a 300-acre farm with wonderful views of the South Downs from the windows. The comfortable rooms have their own entrance and benefit from king-size beds and en suite or private facilities. This is a great location for access to Midhurst, Cowdray Park and Goodwood.

Rooms 3 rms (2 en suite) (1 pri facs) (2 fmly) (1 GF) **Facilities** FTV tea/coffee WiFi **Parking** 3 **Notes** ⊗ ⊕ 300 acres arable/horses

The Old Railway Station

★★★★ GUEST ACCOMMODATION

tel: 01798 342346 **Station Rd GU28 0JF**
email: info@old-station.co.uk **web:** www.old-station.co.uk
dir: *1.6m S of Petworth on A285*

This building, once the railway station for Petworth, retains much of its railway history and atmosphere. Guest rooms are available in both the Station House and the fully restored Edwardian Pullman railway carriages. The original ticket windows can still be seen in the reception area. Breakfast is served in the 'waiting room' which has a six-metre high vaulted ceiling; weather permitting, breakfast can be taken outside on the platform. Both WiFi and parking are available.

Rooms 2 en suite 8 annexe en suite (1 GF) S £75-£120; D £100-£198* **Facilities** FTV Lounge tea/coffee Licensed WiFi 🔒 **Extras** Speciality toiletries **Parking** 11 **Notes** LB ⊗ No Children 10yrs Closed 23-26 Dec

Willow Barns

★★★★ BED AND BREAKFAST

tel: 01798 867493 & 07747 634011 **Graffham GU28 0NU**
email: infowillowbarns@aol.com **web:** www.willowbarns.co.uk

This bed and breakfast comprises five en suite bedrooms set in modern converted barns overlooking an RHS Silver Gilt awarded, professionally designed courtyard. This makes a fabulous choice for those walking the South Downs Way. Cyclists and horse riders are also welcomed, with stabling and turn-out facilities available by prior arrangement. Breakfast, lunch and dinner are served in the nearby inn, The White Horse.

Rooms 5 en suite (2 fmly) (5 GF) S fr £110; D fr £110* **Facilities** FTV DVD Lounge tea/coffee Dinner available Licensed WiFi **Parking** 8 **Notes** ⊗ No Children 12yrs Closed 2wks Xmas

The Angel Inn

★★★★ 🛏 INN

tel: 01798 344445 & 342153 **Angel St GU28 0BG**
email: reception@angelinnpetworth.co.uk **web:** www.angelinnpetworth.co.uk
dir: Leave one-way system onto A283 E, 100yds on left

Located in the heart of the historic town of Petworth, The Angel Inn has stylish yet traditionally decorated bedrooms and bathrooms. Guests can enjoy breakfast, lunch or dinner in the bar and restaurant area, and there is a large walled garden for alfresco dining during the warmer months. There is parking on site and the inn is just a two-minute walk from the town centre.

Rooms 6 en suite D £100-£160* **Facilities** FTV tea/coffee Dinner available WiFi **Parking** 15 **Notes** No coaches

RUSTINGTON — Map 6 TQ00

Kenmore Guest House

★★★★ GUEST ACCOMMODATION

tel: 01903 784634 **Claigmar Rd BN16 2NL**
email: enquiries@kenmoreguesthouse.co.uk **web:** www.kenmoreguesthouse.com
dir: A259 follow signs for Rustington, turn for Claigmar Rd by war memorial. Kenmore on right as Claigmar Rd bends

A warm welcome is assured at this Edwardian house, located close to the sea and convenient for touring West Sussex. Spacious bedrooms, all individually decorated, are provided with many useful extras. There is a comfortable lounge in which to relax and a bright dining room where a good choice of breakfast is served.

Rooms 8 rms (7 en suite) (1 pri facs) (1 fmly) (2 GF) S £45-£55; D £80-£85* **Facilities** FTV Lounge tea/coffee WiFi 🔒 **Parking** 9 **Notes** ⊗ No Children 6yrs

Rustington Manor

★★★★ 🛏 GUEST ACCOMMODATION

tel: 01903 788782 **12 Broadmark Ln BN16 2HH**
email: enquiries@rustingtonmanor.com **web:** www.rustingtonmanor.co.uk

A warm welcome is assured at family-run Rustington Manor where guests are made to feel at home. Attentive service and excellent food make for a wonderful dining experience. Six comfortable, en suite rooms offer all the amenities that the modern guest requires. The property is just a short walk from the beach.

Rooms 6 en suite S £70-£100; D £90-£170* **Facilities** FTV DVD TVL tea/coffee Dinner available Direct Dial Licensed WiFi ⚓ 18 **Conf** Max 40 Thtr 40 Class 40 Board 40 **Parking** 14 **Notes** ⊗ No Children 10yrs

SIDLESHAM — Map 5 SZ89

Premier Collection

The Crab & Lobster

★★★★★ ◉◉ 🍴 RESTAURANT WITH ROOMS

tel: 01243 641233 **Mill Ln PO20 7NB**
email: enquiries@crab-lobster.co.uk **web:** www.crab-lobster.co.uk
dir: A27 onto B2145 signed Selsey. 1st left after garage at Sidlesham into Rookery Ln to Crab & Lobster

Hidden away on the south coast near Pagham Harbour and only a short drive from Chichester is the stylish Crab & Lobster. Bedrooms are superbly appointed, and bathrooms are a feature with luxury toiletries and powerful 'raindrop' showers. Guests can enjoy lunch or dinner in the smart restaurant where the menu offers a range of locally caught fresh fish together with other regionally-sourced, seasonal produce.

Rooms 4 en suite S £90; D £165-£195* **Facilities** FTV DVD iPod docking station tea/coffee Dinner available WiFi **Extras** Speciality toiletries, fresh milk **Parking** 12 **Notes** ⊗ No coaches

STEYNING — Map 6 TQ11

The Castle Inn

★★★ INN

tel: 01903 816629 **The Street, Bramber BN44 3WE**
email: steve@castleinnhotel.co.uk **web:** www.castleinnhotel.co.uk
dir: A283 at rdbt take exit signed Bramber

A family-run independent inn located in the quaint village of Bramber, just a stone's throw from the ruined medieval Bramber Castle. The inn has retained many of its original character, yet all rooms and public areas have been refurbished to meet the needs of modern guests. There is a range of well-appointed rooms to meet all budgets, as well as fine ales and an appealing menu with daily-changing dishes. There is a relaxing beer garden and a convenient car park to the rear of the property.

Rooms 16 rms (15 en suite) (1 pri facs) (5 fmly) (1 GF) S £50-£90; D £70-£110* **Facilities** STV tea/coffee Dinner available WiFi 🔒 **Extras** Chocolates **Conf** Max 40 Thtr 40 Class 30 Board 22 **Parking** 16

TILLINGTON — Map 6 SU92

The Horse Guards Inn

★★★★ ◉ 🍴 INN

tel: 01798 342332 **Upperton Rd GU28 9AF**
email: info@thehorseguardsinn.co.uk **web:** www.thehorseguardsinn.co.uk
dir: Off A272 to Tillington, up hill opposite All Hallows church

This inn is conveniently located close to Petworth and Midhurst in a quiet village setting opposite the quaint church, and is perfect for exploring the beautiful surrounding countryside. The comfortable bedrooms are simply decorated, and delicious breakfasts are prepared to order using the finest local ingredients. The same principles apply to the substantial and flavoursome meals served in the cosy restaurant-bar dining areas.

Rooms 2 en suite 1 annexe en suite (1 fmly) S £80-£130; D £100-£150* **Facilities** FTV DVD tea/coffee Dinner available WiFi 🔒 **Extras** Speciality toiletries - complimentary **Notes** Closed 25-26 Dec

WEST CHILTINGTON
Map 6 TQ01

The Roundabout

★★★★ GUEST ACCOMMODATION

tel: 01798 817336 **Monkmead Ln RH20 2PF**
email: roundabout@relax.co.uk **web:** www.theroundabouthotel.webs.com

The Roundabout was originally designed by Reginald Wells in 1925, and many of the original features have been retained and sympathetically blended with contemporary touches to create accommodation that is suitable for the modern traveller. There is a choice of room types, comfortable public areas, a restaurant, and meeting rooms. The rear garden offers peace and tranquillity.

Rooms 26 en suite

WEST DEAN
Map 5 SU81

The Dean Ale & Cider House

★★★★ INN

tel: 01243 811465 **Main Rd PO18 0QX**
email: thebar@thedeaninn.co.uk **web:** www.thedeaninn.co.uk
dir: On A286, opposite West Dean primary school

The Dean Ale & Cider House, formerly The Selsey Arms, is located in the heart of West Dean village and has been the local village watering hole for the past 200 years. Set in the valley of the River Lavant in the South Downs, The Dean is five miles north of Chichester and five miles south of Midhurst. The inn boasts a restaurant extension and large courtyard with decked garden. The barns at the rear of the pub have been sympathetically renovated and now house comfortable bed and breakfast accommodation. A robust breakfast is part of the offering with plenty of on site parking available.

Rooms 6 annexe en suite (3 GF) **Facilities** FTV tea/coffee Dinner available WiFi **Parking** 30 **Notes** No coaches

WEST MARDEN
Map 5 SU71

Grandwood House

★★★★ GUEST ACCOMMODATION

tel: 07971 845153 & 023 9263 1436 **Watergate PO18 9EG**
email: info@grandwoodhouse.co.uk **web:** www.grandwoodhouse.co.uk

Set in the South Downs and built in 1907, Grandwood House was originally a lodge belonging to Watergate House, which was accidentally burnt down by troops during WWII. All rooms are en suite and enjoy views of the garden, open farmland or both. Large security gates leading onto the driveway ensure secure parking at all times. Only a short walk away, in nearby Walderton, is the local pub which serves lunches and evening meals.

Rooms 4 annexe en suite (4 GF) **Facilities** FTV DVD tea/coffee WiFi Riding 🐴 **Parking** 8 **Notes** LB

WORTHING
Map 6 TQ10

The Beacons

★★★★ GUEST ACCOMMODATION

tel: 01903 230948 **18 Shelley Rd BN11 1TU**
email: thebeacons@btconnect.com **web:** www.beaconsworthing.com
dir: 0.5m W of town centre. Exit A259 Richmond Rd into Crescent Rd, 3rd left

This splendid Edwardian property is ideally situated close to the shopping centre, marine garden and pier. Bedrooms are bright, spacious and attractively furnished with many thoughtful amenities, including free WiFi. Guests can enjoy the comfortable lounge with honesty bar, and breakfast is served in the sunny dining room.

Rooms 8 en suite (1 fmly) (3 GF) S £55-£60; D £82-£90* **Facilities** FTV Lounge tea/coffee Licensed WiFi **Parking** 8 **Notes** ⊗

The Burlington

★★★★ GUEST ACCOMMODATION

tel: 01903 211222 **Marine Pde BN11 3QL**
email: info@theburlington.net **web:** www.theburlington.net
dir: On seafront 0.5m W of Worthing Pier, Wordsworth Rd junct opposite Heene Terrace

This imposing seafront building has a modern contemporary look that appeals to a mainly youthful clientele. The light bar and terrace extends to a night club open at the weekends. Bedrooms are spacious and thoughtfully furnished, with some modern touches. The staff are friendly.

Rooms 26 en suite (6 fmly) **Facilities** FTV Lounge tea/coffee Dinner available Direct Dial Licensed WiFi **Conf** Max 100 Thtr 50 Class 35 Board 40 **Notes** ⊗

The Conifers

★★★★ 🛏 GUEST ACCOMMODATION

tel: 01903 265066 & 07947 321096 **43 Parkfield Rd BN13 1EP**
email: conifers@hews.org.uk **web:** www.theconifers.org.uk
dir: A24 or A27 onto A2031 at Offington rdbt, over lights, Parkfield Rd 5th right

The Conifers is located in a quiet residential area of west Worthing close to the town centre and seafront. Bedrooms are traditionally decorated and offer guests comfortable accommodation. There are a number of thoughtful extras such as chocolates, fluffy white robes, water and magazines, which make this a true home-from-home experience. Guests can enjoy a selection of both cooked and continental dishes for breakfast which has achieved an AA Breakfast Award. There is a well-kept, award-winning garden for guests to enjoy during the summer months. The Conifers was an AA Friendliest B&B of the Year Finalist in 2013-2014.

Rooms 2 rms (1 pri facs) (2 fmly) S £60-£65; D £82-£85* **Facilities** FTV tea/coffee WiFi **Extras** Chocolates, water, magazines - free; robes **Notes** LB ⊗ No Children 12yrs Closed 24-27 Dec

Merton House

★★★★ GUEST ACCOMMODATION

tel: 01903 238222 & 07767 163059 **96 Broadwater Rd BN14 8AW**
email: stay@mertonhouse.co.uk **web:** www.mertonhouse.co.uk
dir: A24 into Worthing, on left past Manor Green

This family run establishment is located on the A24 leading into Worthing, just a couple of minutes from the town centre and seafront. There are seven en suite bedrooms, all of a very traditional style yet providing up-to-date facilities including free WiFi and digital TV. A cooked and continental breakfast is served daily in the dining room. Parking available on site.

Rooms 7 en suite (2 GF) S £50-£70; D £75-£110 **Facilities** FTV Lounge tea/coffee WiFi 🐴 **Extras** Chocolates - complimentary **Parking** 5 **Notes** ⊗ No Children 12yrs

Moorings

★★★★ GUEST ACCOMMODATION

tel: 01903 208882 **4 Selden Rd BN11 2LL**
email: themooringsworthing@hotmail.co.uk **web:** www.mooringsworthing.co.uk
dir: *0.5m E of pier off A259 towards Brighton*

Moorings is a well-presented Victorian house, located in a quiet residential street just a short walk from the seafront and town centre. Bedrooms are attractively co-ordinated with plenty of extras such as WiFi and Freeview TV. Breakfast is served in a homely, traditional dining room and there is a very useful kitchenette with a microwave, fridge and crockery available. The friendly owners also offer secure parking for bicycles and motorcycles.

Rooms 6 en suite (1 fmly) S £60-£80; D £85-£100 **Facilities** FTV DVD Lounge tea/coffee WiFi ⚓ **Notes** LB ⊗ No Children 3yrs

High Beach Guest House

★★★ GUEST ACCOMMODATION

tel: 01903 236389 **201 Brighton Rd BN11 2EX**
email: info@highbeachworthing.com **web:** www.highbeachworthing.com
dir: *On A259, 200yds past Splashpoint swimming pool*

High Beach Guest House is situated within a short walk of Worthing town centre, and its seafront location offers uninterrupted sea views from front-facing rooms and the breakfast room. Bedrooms are traditionally decorated and come well equipped. A conservatory with comfortable seating leads onto the front garden where guests can sit during summer months.

Rooms 7 rms (3 en suite) (1 GF) S £33-£40; D £75-£85 **Facilities** FTV Lounge TVL tea/coffee WiFi ⚓ **Parking** 3 **Notes** ⊗ No Children 8yrs

Marina Guest House

★★★ GUEST ACCOMMODATION

tel: 01903 207844 **191 Brighton Rd BN11 2EX**
email: marinaworthing@ntlworld.com **web:** www.marina-guesthouse.co.uk
dir: *M27 onto A259 to Worthing; or M23 onto A24 to Worthing*

This Victorian establishment is in a great location with uninterrupted sea views, and is a short distance from the town centre. The property is well maintained with comfortable accommodation. A cooked breakfast can be enjoyed in the family-style breakfast room that looks out over the sea.

Rooms 5 rms (2 en suite) (2 fmly) **Facilities** tea/coffee Direct Dial WiFi **Notes** ⊗

TYNE & WEAR

| BIRTLEY | Map 19 NZ25 |

Bowes Incline

★★★★ ⇔ INN

tel: 0191 410 2233 **Northside DH3 1RF**
email: info@thebowesinclinehotel.co.uk **web:** www.thebowesinclinehotel.co.uk
dir: *From rdbt on A1231 NE of Washington follow Wreckenton sign. Pass lakes on left, approx 0.5m 1st left (signed). Approx 0.5m*

Located just one mile from the A1 but surrounded by open countryside, close to the protective arms of *The Angel of the North*. The family-run inn takes its name from the Bowes Incline Railway & Museum located close by. Bedrooms are of a good size and very well appointed with modern en suites. The large bar and restaurant offers good food chosen from the large blackboards. The hands on team are friendly and welcoming making this inn a perfect base to tour the North East.

Rooms 18 en suite (2 fmly) (18 GF) S £55-£80; D £65-£90* **Facilities** FTV tea/coffee Dinner available Direct Dial WiFi **Parking** 40 **Notes** ⊗ Closed 24 Dec-2 Jan No coaches

| SOUTH SHIELDS | Map 21 NZ36 |

Forest Guest House

★★★★ ⌂ GUEST HOUSE

tel: 0191 454 8160 & 07834 690989 **117 Ocean Rd NE33 2JL**
email: enquiries@forestguesthouse.com **web:** www.forestguesthouse.com

Forest Guest House is centrally located, close to both beach and town centre. It offers comfortable and modern bedrooms and many thoughtful extras provided as standard. The hospitable owners are always on hand to offer help and recommendations. A well-cooked breakfast is served on individual tables giving a great start to the day.

Rooms 6 en suite (2 fmly) S £35-£40; D £60-£74* **Facilities** STV FTV DVD tea/coffee WiFi ⚓ **Extras** Speciality toiletries - complimentary **Notes** ⊗

The Sir William Fox

★★★ GUEST ACCOMMODATION

tel: 0191 456 4554 **5 Westoe Village NE33 3DZ**
email: enquiries@sirwilliamfoxhotel.com **web:** www.sirwilliamfoxhotel.com
dir: *A194 into John Reid Rd, then King George Rd into Sunderland Rd. Over rdbt, turn right & right again*

Located in the picturesque village of Westoe in the heart of South Shields, The Sir William Fox offers value-for-money accommodation. It benefits from some off-road parking and is within easy walking distance of the Metro, and South Tyneside College. Dinner is available and the property is fully licensed.

Rooms 15 en suite (4 fmly) (2 GF) **Facilities** FTV DVD TVL tea/coffee Dinner available Direct Dial Licensed WiFi ⚓ **Parking** 10

WHITLEY BAY   Map 21 NZ37

Park Lodge

★★★★ GUEST HOUSE

tel: 0191 253 0288 **158-160 Park Av NE26 1AU**
email: parklodgehotel@hotmail.com **web:** www.parklodgewhitleybay.com
dir: *From S A19 through Tyne Tunnel, right onto A1058 to seafront. Left, after 2m left at lights onto A191. On left*

Set on a leafy avenue, overlooking the park and just minutes from the town centre and coastline, you can expect a friendly atmosphere at this Victorian house. Bedrooms are very comfortable, stylishly furnished and feature homely extras. A hearty breakfast is served and free WiFi is available. AA Friendliest B&B of the Year Award Finalist 2016-2017.

Rooms 5 en suite (1 fmly) (2 GF) **Facilities** FTV DVD iPod docking station TVL tea/coffee WiFi 🔒 **Parking** 2

WARWICKSHIRE

ALDERMINSTER   Map 10 SP24

The Bell at Alderminster

★★★★ ⊛ INN

tel: 01789 450414 **Shipston Rd CV37 8NY**
email: info@thebellald.co.uk **web:** www.thebellald.co.uk

This former 18th-century coaching inn is situated in Alderminster just a few miles away from Stratford-upon-Avon. It's a warm and friendly place where guests can enjoy a range of AA Rosette-worthy, home-cooked dishes and a range of ales and fine wines. The accommodation is smart, stylish and contemporary in design and bedrooms offer a high level of comfort with many thoughtful extras.

Rooms 4 en suite 5 annexe en suite (2 fmly) (3 GF) S £70-£80; D £95-£165*
Facilities FTV iPod docking station tea/coffee Dinner available Direct Dial WiFi
Extras Speciality toiletries, home-made biscuits, milk **Conf** Max 12 Thtr 12 Class 12 Board 12 **Parking** 50

ARMSCOTE   Map 10 SP24

The Fuzzy Duck

★★★★ ⊛ INN

tel: 01608 682635 **Ilmington Rd CV37 8DD**
email: info@fuzzyduckarmscote.com **web:** www.fuzzyduckarmscote.com

The Fuzzy Duck is an English country pub offering boutique bed and breakfast accommodation. The bedrooms are sumptuous, providing guests with lovely accessories such as luxury robes, and fluffy socks and slippers. Dinner can be enjoyed in the sophisticated restaurant where the chef uses only the finest quality and fresh ingredients.

Rooms 4 en suite (2 fmly) **Facilities** FTV iPod docking station Lounge Dinner available Direct Dial WiFi **Extras** Sherry, robes, fruit, snacks, slippers **Conf** Max 20 **Parking** 15

BAGINTON   Map 11 SP37

The Oak

★★★ INN

tel: 024 7651 8855 **Coventry Rd CV8 3AU**
email: thebagintonoak@aol.com **web:** www.thebagintonoak.co.uk

Located close to major road links and Coventry Airport, this popular inn serves a wide range of food throughout the open-plan public areas. Families are especially welcome. Modern, well-equipped bedrooms are situated in a separate building.

Rooms 13 annexe en suite (2 fmly) (6 GF) S £45-£65; D £45-£65 (room only)*
Facilities FTV tea/coffee Dinner available WiFi **Conf** Max 40 Thtr 40 Class 40 Board 25 **Parking** 110

COLESHILL   Map 10 SP28

Innkeeper's Lodge Birmingham (NEC) Coleshill

★★★ INN

tel: 08451 551551 *(Calls cost 2p per minute plus your phone company's access charge)* **High St B46 3BL**
email: info@innkeeperslodge.com **web:** www.innkeeperslodge.com

At Innkeeper's Lodge you'll find accommodation with comfort and character in equal measure, and everything needed for a relaxing stay, from easy check-in and free parking to complimentary breakfast and a cosy pub serving great value food and drink on the doorstep. Each Lodge has quality rooms, and there are Lodges in a variety of locations from towns and cities to countryside settings across the UK.

Rooms 33 en suite (7 fmly) (1 GF) **Facilities** FTV tea/coffee Dinner available Direct Dial WiFi **Parking** 44 **Notes** ⊗

EDGEHILL
Map 11 SP34

Castle at Edgehill
★★★★ ◉◉ ⚑ RESTAURANT WITH ROOMS

tel: 01295 670255 **Main St OX15 6DJ**
email: enquiries@castleatedgehill.co.uk **web:** www.castleatedgehill.co.uk

Built in 1742 to mark the centenary of the battle of Edgehill, where Charles I raised his standard at the start of the Civil War, the building has a unique history. Sympathetically refurbished in recent years, many of the original features have been restored and the exposed stone walls, along with the wood-panelled restaurant, really add to the character of the building. The Tower bedrooms boast panoramic views from their elevated position and bedrooms are all well-appointed. Dinner is not to be missed in the two AA Rosette award-winning restaurant and breakfast features the best in local produce.

Rooms 2 en suite 2 annexe en suite (1 fmly) (1 GF) **Facilities** FTV tea/coffee Dinner available WiFi **Parking** 22

FILLONGLEY
Map 10 SP28

Heart of England Conference & Events Centre
★★★★ GUEST ACCOMMODATION

tel: 01676 540333 **Meriden Rd CV7 8DX**
email: pa@heartofengland.co.uk **web:** www.heartofengland.co.uk

The Heart of England Conference & Events Centre is a charming stone-built house that offers attractively presented, well-equipped bedrooms and sleek modern bathrooms. This fine old house has bags of character and the spacious, comfortable lounge has a wood-burning stove, which proves a real bonus on cooler evenings. Delicious hot breakfasts are served at individual tables in the well-appointed breakfast room. The nearby Quicken Tree restaurant serves an extensive choice of imaginative dishes and makes a good choice for evening meals. As the name implies, first-rate conference and business facilities are available on site.

Rooms 7 en suite 1 annexe en suite (1 GF) S £85-£130; D £95-£140* **Facilities** FTV TVL tea/coffee Dinner available Direct Dial Licensed WiFi Fishing **Conf** Max 600 Thtr 600 Class 200 Board 50 **Parking** 36 **Notes** LB ⊗ Civ Wed 300

HENLEY-IN-ARDEN
Map 10 SP16

Bridge House
★★★ GUEST ACCOMMODATION

tel: 01564 794469 & 07481 885554 **289 High St B95 5DH**
email: hnly922@aol.com **web:** www.bridge-househotel.co.uk
dir: At junct of A4189 & A3400 in Henley-in-Arden

Located at the end of Henley-in-Arden's historic high street, Bridge House is within easy walking distance of shops, restaurants and central attractions. A warm welcome is assured at this former coaching inn that provides a range of thoughtfully furnished bedrooms. Breakfast is served in an attractive dining room. A guest lounge, free WiFi and on-site parking are also available.

Rooms 7 en suite (1 fmly) S £70-£75; D £85-£90* **Facilities** FTV Lounge tea/coffee WiFi 🍴 **Parking** 7 **Notes** ⊗

ILMINGTON
Map 10 SP24

The Howard Arms
★★★★★ ◉ INN

tel: 01608 682226 **Lower Green CV36 4LT**
email: info@howardarms.com **web:** www.howardarms.com

This 400-year-old Cotswold stone former coaching inn has been totally refurbished and the new bedrooms are all beautifully presented. The Howard Arms enjoys a prominent position in the heart of the pretty village of Ilmington. The bar/restaurant has been sympathetically restored and many original features have been retained. Real fires burn bright, and there is a great range of local ales along with an award-winning restaurant.

Rooms 8 en suite (2 fmly) (1 GF) S £72-£95; D £90-£130* **Facilities** FTV DVD iPod docking station tea/coffee Dinner available Direct Dial WiFi **Extras** Speciality toiletries **Parking** 18

KENILWORTH
Map 10 SP27

Ferndale House
★★★★ GUEST HOUSE

tel: 01926 853214 **45 Priory Rd CV8 1LL**
email: info@kenilworth-guesthouse-accommodation.com
web: www.kenilworth-guesthouse-accommodation.com
dir: From M40 junct 15 onto A46 towards Coventry, then onto A452, Priory Rd on right

Ferndale House is situated five minutes' walk from Kenilworth, and is on the local bus route close to the university. Each of the bedrooms is attractively designed and modern, and the beds provide a very good night's sleep. Both parking and WiFi are free of charge.

Rooms 7 en suite (1 GF) S £39; D £60-£65 **Facilities** FTV TVL tea/coffee WiFi **Parking** 4 **Notes** ⊗

Milsoms Kenilworth
★★★★ ⊖ INN

tel: 01926 515450 **Clarendon House Hotel, High St CV8 1LZ**
email: kenilworth@milsomshotel.co.uk **web:** www.milsomshotel.co.uk
dir: A452 signs to town centre, at small rdbt with clock tower, 2nd exit Abbey Hill. At lights, Milsoms immediately on left

Milsoms enjoys a prominent position in the heart of Kenilworth and benefits from secure parking for guests. The bedrooms are beautifully appointed and very well equipped; complimentary WiFi is available. Dinner in the Loch Fyne Restaurant should not be missed as guests are assured of great food along with attentive and friendly service. There is also a charming bar and a comfortable lounge. The NEC and Birmingham Airport are a short drive away.

Rooms 28 en suite 3 annexe en suite (1 fmly) (5 GF) **Facilities** FTV Lounge tea/coffee Dinner available WiFi 🍴 **Extras** Bottled water - complimentary **Conf** Max 25 Thtr 16 Class 18 **Parking** 19 **Notes** ⊗ No coaches

KENILWORTH *continued*

Stoneleigh Park Lodge

★★★★ GUEST HOUSE

tel: 024 7669 0123 **Stoneleigh Park CV8 2LZ**
email: info@stoneleighparklodge.com **web:** www.stoneleighparklodge.com
dir: *2m E of Kenilworth in Stoneleigh Park*

This house lies within the grounds of the National Agricultural Centre and provides modern, well-equipped accommodation. Meals, using local produce, are served in the Park View Restaurant overlooking the showground. Various conference and meeting facilities are available.

Rooms 58 en suite (4 fmly) (26 GF) S £60-£100; D £80-£120* **Facilities** FTV TVL tea/coffee Dinner available Direct Dial Licensed WiFi Fishing **Conf** Max 10 **Parking** 60 **Notes** Closed Xmas

| LONG COMPTON | Map 10 SP23 |

The Red Lion

★★★★★ ⑮ INN

tel: 01608 684221 **Main St CV36 5JS**
email: info@redlion-longcompton.co.uk **web:** www.redlion-longcompton.co.uk
dir: *5m S of Shipston on Stour on A3400*

Located in the pretty rural village of Long Compton, this mid 18th-century posting house retains many original features which are complemented by rustic furniture in the public areas. A good range of ales is offered, and interesting menus capitalise on quality local produce. The bedrooms are well appointed, and have a good range of facilities.

Rooms 5 en suite (1 fmly) S £60-£65; D £95-£150* **Facilities** tea/coffee Dinner available WiFi Pool table Children's play area **Extras** Speciality toiletries, home-made biscuits **Parking** 60 **Notes** No coaches

| RUGBY | Map 11 SP57 |

Innkeeper's Lodge Rugby, Dunchurch

★★★ INN

tel: 08451 551551 *(Calls cost 2p per minute plus your phone company's access charge)*
The Green, Dunchurch CV22 6NJ
email: info@innkeeperslodge.com **web:** www.innkeeperslodge.com

At Innkeeper's Lodge you'll find accommodation with comfort and character in equal measure, and everything needed for a relaxing stay, from easy check-in and free parking to complimentary breakfast and a cosy pub serving great value food and drink on the doorstep. Each Lodge has quality rooms, and there are Lodges in a variety of locations from towns and cities to countryside settings across the UK.

Rooms 16 en suite (2 fmly) (6 GF) **Facilities** FTV tea/coffee Dinner available WiFi **Parking Notes** ⊗

| SHIPSTON ON STOUR | Map 10 SP24 |

Holly End Bed & Breakfast

★★★★ ⑮ GUEST ACCOMMODATION

tel: 01608 664064 **London Rd CV36 4EP**
email: hollyend.hunt@btinternet.com **web:** www.holly-end.co.uk
dir: *0.5m S of Shipston on Stour on A3400, just beyond Old Rd*

Located between Oxford and Stratford-upon-Avon and a short walk from the town centre, this immaculate detached house offers bedrooms with lots of thoughtful extras. Accommodation is all you would expect from a four-star establishment yet still manages to maintain a home-from-home atmosphere. Comprehensive breakfasts use the best of local produce and comprise an award-winning range of options, one of which is full English.

Rooms 3 rms (2 en suite) (1 pri facs) (1 GF) **Facilities** FTV iPod docking station tea/coffee WiFi ⌁ 18 ♨ **Extras** Speciality toiletries, bottled water - free **Parking** 6 **Notes** LB ⊗ No Children 11yrs ⊜

The White Bear

★★★ INN

tel: 01608 664199 **High St CV36 4AJ**
email: thewhitebear@donnington-brewery.com **web:** www.whitebearinn.com

Overlooking the market square this 18th-century coaching inn is a popular meeting place for the local community thanks to its welcoming atmosphere. There's a friendly locals bar with log-burning stove, offering a selection of cask ales, and a lounge bar with dining room where good home cooked meals are served. Bedrooms are comfortable. Free WiFi and parking available.

Rooms 10 en suite **Facilities** Dinner available WiFi **Parking**

| STRATFORD-UPON-AVON | Map 10 SP25 |

Premier Collection

Cherry Trees

★★★★★ ⑮ GUEST ACCOMMODATION

tel: 01789 292989 **Swans Nest Ln CV37 7LS**
email: cherrytreesstratforduponavon@gmail.com
web: www.cherrytrees-stratford.co.uk
dir: *M40 junct 15 to A439, one-way system (A3400) over bridge, pass Cherry Trees, continue on to rdbt & double back. Then take 1st left into Swans Nest Ln*

Near to the theatre and the centre of Stratford, Cherry Trees offers three spacious, luxurious and well-appointed suites. The Garden Suite and Terrace Suite each have a conservatory and outdoor seating, while the Tiffany Suite has its own private TV room. Each room is decorated in calming tones, has a king-sized bed and benefits from many extra touches, such as Roberts radios and fridges. A warm welcome is assured, with home-made cake served on arrival. Breakfast is also a highlight and includes Drambuie porridge and marmalade omelette, alongside the more traditional offerings.

Rooms 3 en suite (3 GF) D £115-£135 **Facilities** FTV tea/coffee WiFi ♨ **Extras** Home-made biscuits & cake - complimentary **Parking** 4 **Notes** LB ⊗ No Children 12yrs Closed 4 Dec-2 Mar

Adelphi Guest House

★★★★ ⑮ GUEST ACCOMMODATION

tel: 01789 204469 **39 Grove Rd CV37 6PB**
email: info@adelphi-guesthouse.com **web:** www.adelphi-guesthouse.com
dir: *M40 junct 15 onto A46 towards Stratford, then A3400. Straight over at 2 rdbts, at lights right into Arden St (A4390). This becomes Grove Rd, on right opposite park*

Based in the centre of Stratford-upon-Avon, the Adelphi is ideally located for those visiting the Royal Shakespeare, Swan or Courtyard Theatres. The bedrooms offer comfort throughout and are all tastefully decorated in period design with many thoughtful extras. All guests will receive a warm and friendly welcome, and breakfast is not to be missed with a wide selection of high-quality dishes offered. Free parking and WiFi are also available.

Rooms 6 rms (5 en suite) (1 pri facs) (1 fmly) (1 GF) **Facilities** FTV DVD iPod docking station tea/coffee WiFi ♨ **Parking** 5 **Notes** LB ⊗ No Children 10yrs

Ambleside Guest House

★★★★ GUEST HOUSE

tel: 01789 297239 **41 Grove Rd CV37 6PB**
email: peter@amblesideguesthouse.com **web:** www.amblesideguesthouse.com
dir: *250mtrs from town centre on A4390 opposite Firs Gdns*

Ambleside, situated less than five minutes' walk from the town centre, is very popular with theatre goers and tourists. It is tastefully decorated in a contemporary style and offers a choice of breakfasts in the bright and airy dining room which overlooks the small park opposite. Free on-site parking and WiFi are provided.

Rooms 6 rms (5 en suite) (1 pri facs) (2 fmly) S £38-£45; D £60-£85* **Facilities** FTV tea/coffee WiFi 🐾 **Parking** 9 **Notes** ⊗ No Children 7yrs

Twelfth Night

★★★★ GUEST ACCOMMODATION

tel: 01789 414595 **13 Evesham Place CV37 6HT**
email: twelfthnight@fsmail.net **web:** www.twelfthnight.co.uk
dir: *In town centre off A4390 Grove Rd*

This delightful Victorian villa is within easy walking distance of the town centre. Quality decor and furnishings enhance the charming original features, and the elegant dining room is the setting for imaginative English breakfasts.

Rooms 7 rms (6 en suite) (1 pri facs) **Facilities** tea/coffee **Parking** 6 **Notes** ⊗ Closed 11-25 Feb

Arden Way Guest House

★★★★ GUEST ACCOMMODATION

tel: 01789 205646 **22 Shipston Rd CV37 7LP**
email: info@ardenwayguesthouse.co.uk **web:** www.ardenwayguesthouse.co.uk
dir: *On A3400, S of River Avon, 100mtrs on left*

A warm welcome is assured at this non-smoking house, located within easy walking distance of the Butterfly Farm and cricket ground. The homely bedrooms are filled with lots of thoughtful extras and an attractive dining room, overlooking the pretty rear garden, is the setting for comprehensive breakfasts.

Rooms 6 en suite (1 fmly) (2 GF) S £45-£60; D £64-£80* **Facilities** FTV DVD tea/coffee WiFi 🐾 **Parking** 6 **Notes** LB ⊗

Moonraker House

★★★★ GUEST ACCOMMODATION

tel: 01789 268774 **40 Alcester Rd CV37 9DB**
email: info@moonrakerhouse.com **web:** www.moonrakerhouse.com
dir: *200yds from rail station on A422 (Alcester Rd)*

Just a short walk from the railway station and the central attractions, this establishment provides a range of comfortable bedrooms. Freshly cooked breakfasts are served in the sitting area. The attractive exterior is enhanced by a magnificent floral display during the warmer months.

Rooms 7 en suite (1 fmly) (2 GF) **Facilities** FTV tea/coffee WiFi **Parking** 7 **Notes** LB ⊗ No Children 6yrs

Barbette Guest House

★★★ BED AND BREAKFAST

tel: 01789 297822 **165 Evesham Rd CV37 9BP**
email: barbette@sitgetan.demon.co.uk **web:** www.barbette.co.uk
dir: *B439 S, 0.5m from town centre*

Expect a friendly welcome at this B&B, a compact but comfortable establishment close to the main road, with parking and a landscaped rear garden. Bedrooms are comfortable and well equipped, and guests have use of a TV lounge.

Rooms 4 rms (2 en suite) **Facilities** FTV TVL tea/coffee WiFi **Parking** 5 **Notes** ⊗ ⊜

STRATFORD-UPON-AVON *continued*

Stretton House

★★★ GUEST ACCOMMODATION

tel: 01789 268647 **38 Grove Rd CV37 6PB**
email: shortpbshort@aol.com **web:** www.strettonhouse.co.uk
dir: *On A439 in town centre road behind police station*

This attractive, Edwardian terrace house is within easy walking distance of the railway station and Shakespeare's Birthplace. Bedrooms are carefully decorated, well equipped, and many have modern shower rooms en suite. The pretty front garden is a welcoming feature.

Rooms 6 rms (5 en suite) (1 pri facs) (4 fmly) (1 GF) **Facilities** FTV tea/coffee WiFi
🔒 **Parking** 6 **Notes** ⊗

Salamander Guest House

★★★ Ⓐ GUEST HOUSE

tel: 01789 205728 **40 Grove Rd CV37 6PB**
email: p.delin@btinternet.com **web:** www.salamanderguesthouse.co.uk
dir: *250yds W of town centre on A439 ring road, opposite Firs Garden*

Ideally located within easy walking distance of central attractions, this well-maintained Edwardian house provides a range of thoughtfully furnished bedrooms most with the benefit of modern and efficient en suite shower rooms. Breakfast is served in an attractive dining room overlooking a pretty park, and private parking is also available.

Rooms 7 rms (6 en suite) (1 pri facs) (5 fmly) (1 GF) **Facilities** FTV tea/coffee Dinner available WiFi **Parking** 12 **Notes** ⊗

TEMPLE GRAFTON   Map 10 SP15

The Blue Boar

★★★ INN

tel: 01789 750010 **B49 6NR**
email: info@theblueboar.co.uk **web:** www.theblueboar.co.uk
dir: *From A46 (Stratford-upon-Avon - Alcester), turn left, Blue Boar at 1st x-rds*

A warm welcome is guaranteed at this country inn. The bedrooms are comfortable and homely, and the dining room and bar menus offer extensive choice, plus additional specials. There is also a beer garden to sit in when the weather allows.

Rooms 14 en suite (5 fmly) (1 GF) **Facilities** FTV Dinner available WiFi **Conf** Max 30 Thtr 30 Class 30 Board 30 **Parking** 35

WELLESBOURNE   Map 10 SP25

Innkeeper's Lodge Stratford-upon-Avon

★★★ INN

tel: 08451 551551 *(Calls cost 2p per minute plus your phone company's access charge)* **Warwick Rd CV35 9LX**
email: info@innkeeperslodge.com **web:** www.innkeeperslodge.com

At Innkeeper's Lodge you'll find accommodation with comfort and character in equal measure, and everything needed for a relaxing stay, from easy check-in and free parking to complimentary breakfast and a cosy pub serving great value food and drink on the doorstep. Each Lodge has quality rooms, and there are Lodges in a variety of locations from towns and cities to countryside settings across the UK.

Rooms 9 en suite (2 fmly) **Facilities** FTV tea/coffee Dinner available WiFi **Parking** 35 **Notes** ⊗

WEST MIDLANDS

BIRMINGHAM   Map 10 SP08

Tri-Star

★★★ GUEST ACCOMMODATION

tel: 0121 782 1010 & 782 6131 **Coventry Rd, Elmdon B26 3QR**
email: info@tristarhotel.co.uk **web:** www.tristarhotel.co.uk
dir: *On A45*

Just a short drive from the airport, Birmingham International station and the NEC, this owner-managed property provides a range of thoughtfully furnished bedrooms with modern bathrooms. The open-plan ground-floor area includes a bright, attractive dining room and a comfortable lounge and bar. A separate room is available for conferences or functions.

Rooms 15 en suite (3 fmly) (6 GF) **Facilities** FTV TVL tea/coffee Dinner available Licensed WiFi Pool table Games room **Conf** Max 20 Thtr 20 Class 10 Board 20 **Parking** 25 **Notes** ⊗

Innkeeper's Lodge Birmingham West (Quinton)

★★★ INN

tel: 08451 551551 *(Calls cost 2p per minute plus your phone company's access charge)* **563 Hagley Road West, Quinton B32 1HP**
email: info@innkeeperslodge.com **web:** www.innkeeperslodge.com

At Innkeeper's Lodge you'll find accommodation with comfort and character in equal measure, and everything needed for a relaxing stay, from easy check-in and free parking to complimentary breakfast and a cosy pub serving great value food and drink on the doorstep. Each Lodge has quality rooms, and there are Lodges in a variety of locations from towns and cities to countryside settings across the UK.

Rooms 24 en suite (8 fmly) (8 GF) **Facilities** FTV tea/coffee Dinner available Direct Dial WiFi **Parking** **Notes** ⊗

BIRMINGHAM (NATIONAL EXHIBITION CENTRE)

See Solihull

COVENTRY   Map 10 SP37

Innkeeper's Lodge Birmingham (NEC) Meriden

★★★★ 🍴 INN

tel: 08451 551551 *(Calls cost 2p per minute plus your phone company's access charge)* **Main Rd, Meriden CV7 7NN**
email: info@innkeeperslodge.com **web:** www.innkeeperslodge.com

At Innkeeper's Lodge you'll find accommodation with comfort and character in equal measure, and everything needed for a relaxing stay, from easy check-in and free parking to complimentary breakfast and a cosy pub serving great value food and drink on the doorstep. Each Lodge has quality rooms, and there are Lodges in a variety of locations from towns and cities to countryside settings across the UK.

Rooms 13 en suite (3 fmly) (4 GF) **Facilities** FTV tea/coffee Dinner available Direct Dial WiFi **Parking** **Notes** ⊗

SOLIHULL
Map 10 SP17

Premier Collection

Hampton Manor

★★★★★ ◉◉◉◉ 🍴 RESTAURANT WITH ROOMS

tel: 01675 446080 **Shadowbrook Ln, Hampton-in-Arden B92 0EN**
email: info@hamptonmanor.com **web:** www.hamptonmanor.com
dir: M42 junct 6 follow signs for A45 (Birmingham). At 1st rdbt, 1st exit onto B4438 (Catherine de Barnes Ln). Left into Shadowbrook Ln

Hampton Manor is set in 45 acres of mature woodland, only minutes from Birmingham's major air, rail and road links and the NEC. The manor offers luxurious accommodation with a contemporary and sophisticated style while still maintaining many of its original features and heritage. The bedrooms are all beautifully and uniquely designed and boast sumptuous beds. Fine dining can be enjoyed at Peel's restaurant, which is a fabulous venue for innovative cooking, and will prove the highlight of any stay.

Rooms 15 en suite (3 fmly) (1 GF) S £160-£350; D £160-£350 (room only) **Facilities** FTV DVD iPod docking station Lounge tea/coffee Dinner available Direct Dial WiFi ⤓ 18 Beauty treatments **Extras** Bottled water, home-made cookies, fresh fruit **Conf** Max 120 Thtr 120 Class 60 Board 35 **Parking** 30 **Notes** LB ⊗ Civ Wed 120

Innkeeper's Lodge Solihull, Knowle

★★★ INN

tel: 08451 551551 *(Calls cost 2p per minute plus your phone company's access charge)* **Warwick Rd, Knowle B93 0EE**
email: info@innkeeperslodge.com **web:** www.innkeeperslodge.com

At Innkeeper's Lodge you'll find accommodation with comfort and character in equal measure, and everything needed for a relaxing stay, from easy check-in and free parking to complimentary breakfast and a cosy pub serving great value food and drink on the doorstep. Each Lodge has quality rooms, and there are Lodges in a variety of locations from towns and cities to countryside settings across the UK.

Rooms 11 en suite (1 fmly) **Facilities** FTV tea/coffee Dinner available WiFi **Parking** **Notes** ⊗

WILTSHIRE

AMESBURY
Map 5 SU14

Park House Motel

★★★★ GUEST ACCOMMODATION

tel: 01980 629256 **SP4 0EG**
email: info@parkhousemotel.com **web:** www.parkhousemotel.co.uk
dir: 5m E of Amesbury. Junct A303 & A338

Park House Motel is a family-run establishment that offers a warm welcome and is extremely convenient for the A303. Bedrooms are practically equipped with modern facilities and come in a variety of sizes. There is a large dining room where dinner is served during the week, and a cosy bar in which to relax.

Rooms 30 rms (27 en suite) (1 pri facs) (9 fmly) (25 GF) **Facilities** STV FTV TVL tea/coffee Dinner available Licensed WiFi **Parking** 40

BOWERCHALKE
Map 5 SU02

Greenbank Bed & Breakfast

★★★★ BED AND BREAKFAST

tel: 01722 780350 & 07812 486045 **Church St SP5 5BE**
email: enquiries@greenbank101.com **web:** www.greenbank101.com
dir: A354 from Salisbury to Coombe Bissett. Right at 1st junct, follow signs for Broad Chalke. Left by public house & follow signs for Bowerchalke

Located in the scenic Chalke Valley, a short drive out from Salisbury, Greenbank offers contemporary en suite accommodation. There is ample off-road parking and a warm welcome from your hosts Sue and Paul, who will ensure that your stay is a relaxing and pleasurable experience. Accommodation consists of two non-smoking, en suite double rooms. Guests also have use of a fridge and their own conservatory-lounge where there is access to all indoor and outdoor areas, games, magazines and items of local interest.

Rooms 2 en suite (2 GF) S £50-£60; D £80-£90 **Facilities** FTV Lounge tea/coffee WiFi **Extras** Fruit, snacks - complimentary **Parking** 4 **Notes** ⊗ No Children 12yrs

BOX
Map 4 ST86

Premier Collection

The Northey Arms

★★★★★ ◉ INN

tel: 01225 742333 **Bath Rd SN13 8AE**
email: thenorthey@ohhcompany.co.uk **web:** www.ohhcompany.co.uk

This stylish inn combines modern facilities and quality with relaxed and welcoming hospitality. The bedrooms and bathrooms are especially comfortable and well equipped, with large walk-in showers, luxurious towels and toiletries. Food is served throughout the day and utilises high quality produce on a menu which has something for everyone.

Rooms 5 en suite S £75-£130; D £99-£150* **Facilities** STV tea/coffee Dinner available Direct Dial WiFi **Parking** 30 **Notes** No coaches

BRADFORD-ON-AVON
Map 4 ST86

The Muddy Duck

★★★★★ ◉ INN

tel: 01225 858705 **Monkton Farleigh BA15 2QH**
email: dishitup@themuddyduckbath.co.uk **web:** www.themuddyduckbath.co.uk
dir: A363 from Bath towards Bradford-on-Avon. Left towards Monkton Farleigh, then left into village

The Muddy Duck is full of character and is quietly located in a pleasant village almost mid-way between Bath and Bradford-on-Avon. Bedrooms and bathrooms vary in terms of space but all are very well furnished and equipped. One bedroom in particular is very large. A menu offering carefully prepared dishes to suit all tastes is available at both lunch and dinner. Breakfast offers a range of high quality produce and a generous choice of hot dishes. Outdoor seating is available to both the front and rear of the inn.

Rooms 3 en suite 2 annexe en suite (2 GF) S £100-£250; D £120-£250 **Facilities** FTV DVD iPod docking station TVL tea/coffee Dinner available Direct Dial WiFi ⚭ **Parking** 20 **Notes** No coaches

BRADFORD-ON-AVON *continued*

The Beeches Farmhouse

★★★★ BED AND BREAKFAST

tel: 01225 865170 **Holt Rd BA15 1TS**
email: stay@beeches-farmhouse.co.uk **web:** www.beeches-farmhouse.co.uk
dir: *1m E of Bradford-on-Avon on B3107, on left just past garden centre*

Peacefully located and surrounded by delightful countryside, this relaxed and welcoming accommodation offers guest bedrooms in well furnished, converted barns and stables adjacent to the main building. There are various leisure facilities in the grounds including a games room. Breakfast is served in the conservatory of the main farmhouse.

Rooms 1 en suite 4 annexe en suite (1 fmly) (4 GF) **Facilities** FTV DVD Lounge tea/coffee WiFi ⅃ 18 Pool table ♨ **Extras** Mineral water, fruit, local biscuits & fudge **Conf** Max 8 Board 8 **Parking** 11 **Notes** RS Xmas & New Year room only (no breakfast)

The Tollgate Inn

★★★★ ⇔ INN

tel: 01225 782326 **Ham Green, Holt BA14 6PX**
email: laura@tollgateinn.co.uk **web:** www.tollgateholt.co.uk
dir: *A363 Bradford-on-Avon turn left onto B3105, left onto B3107, 100yds on right at W end of Holt*

The Tollgate Inn combines the comforts of a traditional hostelry with excellent food, served in delightful surroundings. It stands near the village green in Holt, only a short drive from Bath. The bedrooms, varying in size, are comfortable and thoughtfully equipped with welcome extras. An on-site café, deli and farm shop provide lunches and interesting picnic items.

Rooms 4 en suite 1 annexe en suite (1 GF) **Facilities** FTV DVD tea/coffee Dinner available Direct Dial WiFi Boules pitch **Extras** Fresh fruit, still & sparkling mineral water **Parking** 30 **Notes** ⊗

BROAD HINTON · Map 5 SU17

The Crown at Broad Hinton

★★★★ INN

tel: 01793 731302 **SN4 9PA**
email: enquiries@thecrownatbroadhinton.co.uk **web:** www.thecrownatbroadhinton.co.uk
dir: *M4 junct 16 follow signs for Wroughton, then Salthrop. A4361 right towards Devizes, next right to Broad Hinton. Left at T-junct, on right*

A warm welcome is guaranteed at this owner-run inn; traditional in style with a great range of ales on tap. Home-cooked pub fare is served, with specials changing daily. Located just moments from the M4 in a peaceful village, with good transport links, it's great for exploring the local area, including Avebury Stone Circles, Swindon and Devizes. Rooms are well designed and spacious with luxurious finishing touches; en suites are modern and finished to a high standard. Dylan and Flo (the pub dogs) are sure to greet all guests with a friendly wag of their tails.

Rooms 2 en suite (1 fmly) **Facilities** FTV iPod docking station Lounge tea/coffee Dinner available WiFi ♨ ⅃ 27 ♨ **Conf** Max 20 Board 12 **Parking** 90 **Notes** Closed 25 Dec

BURCOMBE · Map 5 SU03

Burcombe Manor B&B

★★★★ BED AND BREAKFAST

tel: 01722 744288 & 07967 594449 **Burcombe Ln SP2 0EJ**
email: enquiries@burcombemanor.co.uk **web:** www.burcombemanor.co.uk
dir: *A30 from Wilton, after 0.75m turn left over bridge. At T-junct turn right, 100mtrs on left*

Located in the village of Burcombe, only five miles west of Salisbury, this family home is set at the edge of a 1300-acre farm with views out over the water meadows. Bedrooms, including two en suite rooms, offer comfortable accommodation. Breakfast is served in one of the drawing rooms and there is a spacious lounge for guests to relax in.

Rooms 3 rms (2 en suite) (1 pri facs) S £60; D £85* **Facilities** FTV Lounge tea/coffee WiFi **Parking** 6 **Notes** ⊗

BURTON · Map 4 ST87

Premier Collection

The Old House at Home

★★★★★ ⇔ INN

tel: 01454 218227 **SN14 7LT**
email: office@ohhcompany.co.uk **web:** www.ohhcompany.co.uk
dir: *M4 junct 18, A46, B4040 to Acton Turvill, right onto B4039. 1.5m to Burton*

In a pleasant setting, just a couple of miles from the delightful village of Castle Combe, this well-established country inn is run personally by the resident proprietors and family. Six purpose-built, high-quality bedrooms and bathrooms provide plenty of welcome extras, and are located in a stylish block adjacent to the main building. Dinner here should not be missed, with a varied selection of carefully prepared ingredients used in the dishes, including the daily specials.

Rooms 6 annexe en suite (6 GF) S £75-£130; D £89-£150* **Facilities** FTV tea/coffee Dinner available Direct Dial WiFi **Parking** 20 **Notes** LB Closed 25 Dec

CALNE · Map 4 ST97

The White Horse

★★★★ ⊛ ⇕ INN

tel: 01249 813118 **Compton Bassett SN11 8RG**
email: info@whitehorse-comptonbassett.co.uk
web: www.whitehorse-comptonbassett.co.uk
dir: *M4 junct 16 onto A3102, after Hilmarton village turn left to Compton Bassett*

Nestled in the Wiltshire countryside, this free house offers a warm welcome and remains part of the local community. Inside the pub there is a modern, comfortable restaurant where high-quality food is served at breakfast, lunch and dinner. The bedrooms, located separately from the bar and restaurant areas, are individually styled.

Rooms 8 annexe en suite (3 fmly) (6 GF) **Facilities** FTV DVD tea/coffee Dinner available WiFi Boules **Extras** Home-made cookies, crisps, bottled water - free **Parking** 40 **Notes** Closed 25 Dec

The Lansdowne

★★★ INN

tel: 01249 812488 **The Strand SN11 0EH**
email: lansdowne@arkells.com **web:** www.lansdownestrand.co.uk

Situated in a picturesque market town, The Lansdowne was built in the 16th century as a coaching inn, and it still retains much of the charm and character of that era. Bedrooms are spacious and furnished in a traditional style. Guests can enjoy dinner in the pleasant bistro, in either of the bar areas, or choose from a varied room-service menu. An outdoor courtyard seating area is also available.

Rooms 21 en suite 4 annexe en suite (2 fmly) S £40-£60; D £70-£75* **Facilities** FTV tea/coffee Dinner available WiFi 🔒 **Conf** Max 50 Thtr 45 Class 45 Board 50 **Parking** 7 **Notes** ✕

CASTLE COMBE
Map 4 ST87

Fosse Farmhouse Chambre d'Hote

★★★★ 🍽 BED AND BREAKFAST

tel: 01249 782286 **Nettleton Shrub SN14 7NJ**
email: caroncooper@fossefarmhouse.com **web:** www.fossefarmhouse.com
dir: 1.5m N from Castle Combe on B4039, left at Gib, 1m on right

Set in quiet countryside not far from Castle Combe, this bed and breakfast has well-equipped bedrooms decorated in keeping with its 18th-century origins. Excellent dinners are served in the farmhouse, and cream teas can be enjoyed in the old stables or the delightful garden.

Rooms 2 en suite (1 fmly) S £99-£125; D £125-£160 **Facilities** FTV DVD Lounge tea/coffee Dinner available Licensed WiFi 🏊 18 🔒 **Extras** Speciality toiletries, bottled water, flowers **Conf** Max 15 Thtr 10 Class 10 Board 10 **Parking** 12 **Notes** LB

CHIPPENHAM
Map 4 ST97

Diana Lodge Bed & Breakfast

★★★ BED AND BREAKFAST

tel: 01249 650306 **Grathie Cottage, 72 Marshfield Rd SN15 1JR**
email: diana.lodge@talktalk.net **web:** www.dianalodgebedandbreakfast.co.uk
dir: 500yds NW of town centre on A420, into West End Club car park

A cheerful welcome awaits at Diana Lodge Bed & Breakfast, a late 19th-century cottage within walking distance of the town centre and the railway station. The comfortable bedrooms are well appointed, and there is a small, adjacent car park.

Rooms 5 rms (3 en suite) (2 pri facs) (1 fmly) (2 GF) **Facilities** FTV tea/coffee WiFi **Parking** 1 **Notes** ✕

Follow us on Facebook
www.facebook.com/TheAAUK

Find us on
f Facebook

COLLINGBOURNE KINGSTON
Map 5 SU25

Manor Farm B&B *(SU238556)*

★★★★ FARMHOUSE

tel: 01264 850859 **SN8 3SD**
email: stay@manorfm.com **web:** www.manorfm.com
dir: *Opposite church in centre of village*

An attractive, Grade II-listed farmhouse with comfortable and spacious rooms on a working family farm, this is the ideal base from which to explore the surrounding countryside, whether walking or cycling, directly from the farm. All rooms have been individually appointed and offer a range of practical amenities. Sumptuous traditional, vegetarian and special diet breakfasts are served at the communal table in the dining room.

Rooms 3 rms (2 en suite) (1 pri facs) (2 fmly) S £60-£70; D £70-£85 **Facilities** FTV tea/coffee WiFi 🔒 **Extras** Speciality toiletries, bottled water - free **Parking** 6 **Notes** LB ✕ No Children 8yrs 550 acres arable

CORSHAM
Map 4 ST87

Premier Collection

The Methuen Arms

★★★★★ ◉◎ INN

tel: 01249 717060 **2 High St SN13 0HB**
email: info@themethuenarms.com **web:** www.themethuenarms.com
dir: *M4 junct 17, A350 towards Chippenham, at rdbt take A4 towards Bath. 1m after lights, at next rdbt sharp left into Pickwick Rd, establishment 0.5m on left*

This well-established inn, in the centre of the thriving town of Corsham, provides very high levels of quality and comfort. The bedrooms are modern and stylish with large comfortable beds and spacious, well-equipped bathrooms. Guests can enjoy a drink in the relaxing bar, a light snack in the day or evening, and should not miss the carefully prepared, award-winning dishes at dinner.

Rooms 14 en suite (3 fmly) S £120-£155; D £140-£175* **Facilities** FTV tea/coffee Dinner available WiFi 🏊 18 🔒 **Extras** Speciality toiletries, digital radios **Conf** Max 60 Thtr 50 Board 14 **Parking** 40 **Notes** Closed 25-26 Dec

CORSHAM *continued*

Church Farm B+B

★★★★ BED AND BREAKFAST

tel: 01249 715180 & 07977 910775 **Hartham Ln, Hartham SN13 0PU**
email: churchfarmbandb@hotmail.com **web:** www.churchfarmbandb.com
dir: *M4 junct 17 onto A350 signed Poole & Chippenham. Onto A4 signed Bath &*
Corsham, pass Cross Keys Pub, right into Hartham Ln. Church Farm 500yds on left
just before church

This rural property is close to Bath, Lacock and Castle Combe and has easy access
to the M4. Here there is an emphasis on peace, tranquillity and lovely countryside
views. Bedrooms are located in a barn conversion next to the farmhouse, with two
of them on the ground floor. All are spacious and well equipped, with a double and
a single bed in each, and children over 12 are welcome. Guests also have the
benefit of outside seating areas and parking nearby. Breakfast is served
farmhouse-style in the main house dining room where guests can enjoy the view
across fields of dairy cows out to a Grade II listed mansion.

Rooms 3 annexe en suite (2 fmly) (2 GF) S £60-£65; D £80-£90* **Facilities** tea/
coffee WiFi ⌁ 18 ⚓ **Extras** Bath robes **Parking** 6 **Notes** LB ⊗ No Children 12yrs
Closed Xmas-Jan ⊜

Pickwick Lodge Farm B&B *(ST857708)*

★★★★ ⌂ FARMHOUSE

tel: 01249 712207 **Guyers Ln SN13 0PS**
email: bandb@pickwickfarm.co.uk **web:** www.pickwickfarm.co.uk
dir: *Exit A4, Bath side of Corsham, into Guyers Ln, farmhouse at end on right*

This Grade II listed, 17th-century farmhouse is peacefully located on a 300-acre
beef and arable farm, within easy reach of Bath. The spacious bedrooms are well
equipped with modern facilities and many thoughtful extras. A hearty breakfast,
using the best local produce, is served at a communal table in the dining room.

Rooms 3 rms (2 en suite) (1 pri facs) **Facilities** FTV TVL tea/coffee WiFi Fishing ⚓
Extras Speciality toiletries, fruit, home-made cake **Parking** 6 **Notes** ⊗
No Children 12yrs 300 acres arable/beef

CRICKLADE Map 5 SU09

The Red Lion Inn

★★★★ ⊛ ⌂ INN

tel: 01793 750776 **74 High St SN6 6DD**
email: info@theredlioncricklade.co.uk **web:** www.theredlioncricklade.co.uk
dir: *Off A419*

This historic pub is proud to feature real ales from its very own microbrewery on site
along with ciders and other guest ales. A range of menu options are available from
pub classics to modern British dishes. There are five spacious en suite bedrooms,
all designed individually and providing a high level of quality and comfort. Dogs are
welcome in some of the accommodation.

Rooms 5 annexe en suite (2 GF) **Facilities** FTV DVD iPod docking tea/coffee
Dinner available WiFi ⚓ **Notes** No coaches

DEVIZES Map 4 SU06

Premier Collection

Blounts Court Farm

★★★★★ ⌂ BED AND BREAKFAST

tel: 01380 727180 **Coxhill Ln, Potterne SN10 5PH**
email: carys@blountscourtfarm.co.uk **web:** www.blountscourtfarm.co.uk
dir: *A360 to Potterne, into Coxhill Ln opposite George & Dragon, at fork turn left, follow*
drive uphill to farmhouse

A warm welcome is assured at this peacefully located, delightful arable farm,
overlooking the village cricket field. The character barn has been converted to
provide three attractive bedrooms on the ground floor – one has a four-poster
bed. The elegant decor is in keeping with the character of the house. Breakfast,
which features home-made and local produce, is served in the farmhouse
dining room.

Rooms 3 en suite (3 GF) S £55-£60; D £85-£96* **Facilities** FTV DVD iPod docking
station TVL tea/coffee WiFi ⚓ **Extras** Speciality toiletries, home-made biscuits -
free **Parking** 5 **Notes** ⊗ No Children 8yrs

Premier Collection

The Peppermill

★★★★★ ⊛⊛ RESTAURANT WITH ROOMS

tel: 01380 710407 **40 Saint John's St SN10 1BL**
email: philip@peppermilldevizes.co.uk **web:** www.peppermilldevizes.co.uk
dir: *Situated in the market place*

Situated in the heart of Devizes, The Peppermill offers seven bedrooms located
above the restaurant, in one of the oldest buildings in the town. The en suite
bath/shower rooms have underfloor heating, limestone floors and heated mirrors.
Hypnos Royal Lansdowne beds, three of which split into twins if needed, have
goose-down bedding and Egyptian cotton bed linen to ensure a good night's
sleep. The restaurant serves breakfast, lunch and dinner, all offered daily.

Rooms 7 en suite D £115-£175* **Facilities** FTV iPod docking station TVL tea/
coffee Dinner available WiFi ⌁ 18 ⚓ **Extras** Robes **Notes** LB

Avalon Lodge

★★★★ BED AND BREAKFAST

tel: 01380 728189 **Devizes Rd, Rowde SN10 2LU**
email: stay@avalonlodge.co.uk **web:** www.avalonlodge.co.uk
dir: *1m from Devizes on A342. On left*

Avalon Lodge, located on the outskirts of Devizes, offers a great base for visiting a
host of local historical sites. Expect a very warm welcome from owners Nick and
Jenny. Rooms are individually decorated, offering very good levels of comfort, with
lots of thoughtful extras provided.

Rooms 4 rms (3 en suite) (1 pri facs) S £60-£70; D £80-£95* **Facilities** FTV DVD
iPod docking station Lounge tea/coffee Dinner available Licensed WiFi ⚓
Extras Fresh milk - complimentary; snacks - chargeable **Parking** 6 **Notes** LB ⊗
No Children 12yrs

Magnolia Tree Bed and Breakfast

★★★★ BED AND BREAKFAST

tel: 01380 738459 **27 Roundway Park SN10 2ED**
email: info@magnoliatreebedandbreakfast.co.uk
web: www.magnoliatreebedandbreakfast.co.uk
dir: *In centre of Devizes onto A361 (signed Swindon), pass Wiltshire Police Headquarters on left. Turn left into Roundway Park*

Located a short walk from the centre of the market town of Devizes, the Magnolia Tree is within easy reach of the Wessex Ridgeway and the Kennet and Avon Canal's Caen Hill flight of 29 locks. Salisbury, Stonehenge and Bath are also in close proximity. A warm welcome is guaranteed from Candy, Lloyd, and Daisy the dog. Bedrooms are comfortably furnished, serviced to a high standard, and come equipped with a range of accessories. Breakfast is served in the light and airy dining room. Free WiFi is accessible throughout.

Rooms 3 en suite S £45; D £75* **Facilities** FTV DVD tea/coffee WiFi 🔒 **Extras** Home-made biscuits, bottled water **Parking** 6 **Notes** ⊗

Vine Cottage Bed & Breakfast

★★★★ 🛏 BED AND BREAKFAST

tel: 01380 728360 & 07501 504948 **26 Bunnies Ln, Rowde SN10 2QB**
email: vinecottagebb@btinternet.com **web:** www.vinecottagebb.co.uk
dir: *2m from Devizes town centre on A342, signed Chippenham. In Rowde at George & Dragon pub take 2nd left into Bunnies Ln*

Vine Cottage is located in the quiet village of Rowde and is a good base for exploring the Wiltshire countryside. All rooms offer comfortable accommodation and are well equipped. The award-winning breakfast is served at the communal table in the cosy breakfast room. Parking available.

Rooms 3 en suite (1 fmly) (1 GF) S £65-£85; D £80-£110 **Facilities** FTV DVD Lounge tea/coffee WiFi Sauna 🔒 **Extras** Speciality toiletries, robes, bottled water, fruit **Parking** 4 **Notes** ⊗

EDINGTON — Map 4 ST95

Premier Collection

The Three Daggers

★★★★★ ⊜ INN

tel: 01380 830940 **Westbury Rd BA13 4PG**
email: hello@threedaggers.co.uk **web:** www.threedaggers.co.uk
dir: *A36 towards Warminster, A350 to Westbury, B3098 to Edington*

Stylishly refurbished to offer luxurious standards of quality and comfort throughout, The Three Daggers combines traditional hospitality with contemporary furnishings and decor. Bedrooms and bathrooms come in a range of shapes and sizes but all are appointed with high quality Egyptian cotton bedding, large shower heads and a generous range of welcome extras. The bar and dining area menus offer high quality, carefully prepared ingredients at both dinner and breakfast. A large lounge with a real fire and comfortable seating is also available to guests. Adjoining is a newly opened farm shop and brewery.

Rooms 3 rms (2 en suite) (1 pri facs) (1 fmly) S £85-£110; D £100-£165* **Facilities** FTV DVD iPod docking station TVL tea/coffee Dinner available WiFi Riding 🔒 **Extras** Fruit, speciality toiletries, fresh flowers **Conf** Max 14 **Parking** 45 **Notes** LB

FONTHILL BISHOP — Map 4 ST93

The Riverbarn

★★★★ ⊛ GUEST HOUSE

tel: 01747 820232 **SP3 5SF**
web: www.theriverbarn.org.uk
dir: *From Wincanton towards Amesbury on A303 take B3089, through Hindon to Fonthill Bishop. Property on right. Or from Amesbury on A303 left onto unclassified road after Wylye signed Fonthill Bishop. Property on left*

Surrounded by lawns stretching down to the river, The Riverbarn is the central hub of the village of Fonthill Bishop. Parts of the barn are 600 years old and it has been operated as a business for the last 100 years. The annexe bedrooms are spacious and well appointed. The café-bar offers sumptuous cakes and cream teas, light lunches and evening meals.

Rooms 3 annexe en suite (3 GF) S £65-£70; D £80-£90* **Facilities** FTV DVD tea/coffee Dinner available Licensed WiFi 🔒 **Parking** 20 **Notes** LB ⊗ No Children 14yrs

FOXHAM — Map 4 ST97

The Foxham Inn

★★★★ ⊛ INN

tel: 01249 740665 **SN15 4NQ**
email: info@thefoxhaminn.co.uk **web:** www.thefoxhaminn.co.uk
dir: *Off B4069 between Sutton Benger & Lyneham*

The Foxham Inn is an unpretentious family-run country inn, which serves award-winning food, real ale and fine wines. The two rooms are well configured and have been completed to a very good standard, and both offer a range of amenities including free WiFi. The main restaurant is a versatile venue suitable for a range of different occasions.

Rooms 2 en suite S £75; D £90 **Facilities** FTV Lounge tea/coffee Dinner available WiFi Fishing Riding 🔒 **Conf** Max 40 Thtr 40 Class 40 Board 20 **Parking** 20 **Notes** Closed 2-14 Jan RS Mon No coaches

HEYTESBURY — Map 4 ST94

The Resting Post

★★★★ BED AND BREAKFAST

tel: 01985 840204 & 07519 059910 **67 High St BA12 0ED**
email: enquiries@therestingpost.co.uk **web:** www.therestingpost.co.uk
dir: *From A36 Warminster bypass rdbt into Heytesbury. Pass Red Lion & church on right, 200yds past church on right*

This Grade II-listed building is located in the main High Street and was formerly the village post office. Bedrooms and bathrooms are all comfortably furnished and include some welcome extras. Parking is available on the main road outside, although one private parking space is also available to the rear of the property. Two pubs are within a short stroll. Breakfast is served in the cosy dining room.

Rooms 3 en suite (1 fmly) S £55-£75; D £75-£85 **Facilities** FTV tea/coffee WiFi 🔒 **Notes** ⊗

HORNINGSHAM

Map 4 ST84

The Bath Arms at Longleat

★★★★ ⊛ INN

tel: 01985 844308 **Longleat Estate BA12 7LY**
email: enquiries@batharms.co.uk **web:** www.batharms.co.uk
dir: *In village, on Longleat Estate*

Peacefully located at the edges of the Longleat Estate, this delightful inn is perhaps best described as offering 'quirky luxury'. Bedrooms come in a variety of shapes and sizes; each individually decorated in a range of styles and designs. High-quality produce is used to prepare delicious, AA Rosette award-winning dinners which are served in the relaxed main restaurant.

Rooms 9 en suite 8 annexe en suite (8 fmly) (8 GF) **Facilities** FTV DVD tea/coffee Dinner available Direct Dial WiFi ♨ 18 **Extras** Flavoured vodka - complimentary **Parking** 6

LOWER CHICKSGROVE

Map 4 ST92

Compasses Inn

★★★★ ⊛ INN

tel: 01722 714318 **SP3 6NB**
email: thecompasses@aol.com **web:** www.thecompassesinn.com
dir: *Exit A30 signed Lower Chicksgrove, 1st left into Lagpond Ln, single-track lane to village*

This charming 17th-century inn, within easy reach of Bath, Salisbury, Glastonbury and the Dorset coast, offers comfortable accommodation in a peaceful setting. Carefully prepared dinners, awarded an AA Rosette, are enjoyed in the warm atmosphere of the bar-restaurant, while breakfast is served in a separate dining room.

Rooms 5 en suite (2 fmly) S £65-£95; D £85-£95 **Facilities** FTV iPod docking station tea/coffee Dinner available WiFi ♨ **Extras** Speciality toiletries, bottled water, chocolate **Conf** Max 16 Thtr 16 Class 16 Board 14 **Parking** 40 **Notes** LB Closed 25-26 Dec RS Mon lunch winter closed

LUDWELL

Map 4 ST92

The Grove Arms

★★★★ INN

tel: 01747 828811 **SP7 9ND**
email: ninabartlett123@gmail.com **web:** www.grovearms-ludwell.co.uk
dir: *2m E of Shaftesbury on A30*

This 16th-century, Grade II listed building is located between Salisbury and Shaftesbury, and provides a great base for exploring the Wiltshire and Dorset countryside. The six en suite bedrooms are comfortable and well equipped. Lunch and dinner menus offer a great choice, enhanced with daily specials; traditional ales are also available.

Rooms 6 en suite (1 fmly) S £55-£75; D £75-£100* **Facilities** FTV DVD Lounge tea/coffee Dinner available WiFi Pool table ♨ **Parking** 35 **Notes** LB

MALMESBURY

Map 4 ST98

Kings Arms

★★★ INN

tel: 01666 823383 **29 High St SN16 9AA**

Located on Malmesbury High Street, a stone's throw from the Abbey, this traditional coaching inn is split between either side of the original delivery passage. One side features a cosy bar, the ideal place to enjoy a pint of Arkell's ale; while the more contemporary restaurant is located opposite and is perfect for dining and breakfast. Bedrooms are en suite and located above the main pub building or in the former coach house and stables at the rear. Owned by the Arkell's family brewers, a great range of traditionally brewed beers are available.

Rooms 12 en suite

PEWSEY

Map 5 SU15

Premier Collection

Red Lion Freehouse

★★★★★ ⊛⊛⊛ ⌂ INN

tel: 01980 671124 **East Chisenbury SN9 6AQ**
email: enquiries@redlionfreehouse.com **web:** www.redlionfreehouse.com
dir: *A345 to Upavon, left at T-junct, right signed East Chisenbury*

The Red Lion Freehouse at East Chisenbury offers an interesting blend of sumptuous accommodation and food, yet it retains the informality and laidback atmosphere of a traditional pub. Each of the five rooms have been individually appointed and offer plenty of in-room amenities coupled with beautiful views of the surrounding countryside. The cooking is confident and a particular flair is brought to the dishes based on seasonal, local ingredients. The pub rears its own pigs and keeps rescue hens. Tucked behind the Red Lion is a tranquil tree-shaded beer garden.

Rooms 5 en suite (1 fmly) (5 GF) S £135-£290; D £135-£290 (incl.dinner) **Facilities** FTV tea/coffee Dinner available WiFi ♨ 18 Fishing **Extras** Speciality toiletries, snacks, robes **Conf** Max 16 **Parking** 5 **Notes** LB No coaches

---

The Bell at Ramsbury

★★★★★ ◉◉ INN

tel: 01672 520230 **The Square SN8 2PE**
email: thebell@thebellramsbury.com **web:** www.thebellramsbury.com
dir: From Hungerford on B4192 towards Swindon. After 3.5m, left into Newton Rd. 1m on right

Owned by the local Ramsbury Brewery, this inn offers excellent en suite accommodation. Various dining options are available; traditional pub classics served in the bar or garden for a relaxed experience, the more formal dining options in the two AA-Rosette restaurant where the head chef demonstrates a modern and inventive approach to British food, and also the Shaker-influenced Café Bella (open daily) offering delicious cakes and much more.

Rooms 6 en suite 3 annexe en suite **Facilities** FTV tea/coffee Dinner available WiFi ⚓ 18 🔒 **Conf** Max 8 Board 8 **Parking** 20 **Notes** Closed 25 Dec

---

The George & Dragon

★★★★ ◉◉ RESTAURANT WITH ROOMS

tel: 01380 723053 **High St SN10 2PN**
email: thegandd@tiscali.co.uk **web:** www.thegeorgeanddragonrowde.co.uk
dir: 1.5m from Devizes on A350 towards Chippenham

The George & Dragon dates back to the 14th century when it was a meeting house. Exposed beams, wooden floors, antique rugs and open fires create a warm atmosphere in the bar and restaurant. Bedrooms and bathrooms are very well decorated and equipped with some welcome extras. Dining in the bar or restaurant should not be missed, as local produce and fresh fish deliveries from Cornwall are offered on the daily-changing blackboard menu.

Rooms 3 rms (2 en suite) (1 pri facs) (1 fmly) S £75-£95; D £75-£125*
Facilities FTV DVD iPod docking station Lounge TVL tea/coffee Dinner available WiFi ch fac 🔒 **Extras** Mini-bar, snacks - free **Parking** 15 **Notes** No coaches

---

See also Amesbury

Websters

★★★★ GUEST HOUSE

tel: 01722 339779 **11 Hartington Rd SP2 7LG**
email: enquiries@websters-bed-breakfast.com **web:** www.websters-bed-breakfast.com
dir: From city centre onto A360 (Devizes Rd), 1st turn on left

A warm welcome is assured at Websters, a delightful property, located in a quiet cul-de-sac close to the city centre. The charming, well-presented bedrooms are equipped with numerous extras including broadband. There is one ground-floor room with easier access.

Rooms 5 en suite (1 GF) **Facilities** FTV TVL tea/coffee WiFi **Parking** 5 **Notes** ⊗ No Children 12yrs Closed 31 Dec & 1 Jan RS Xmas & New Year continental breakfast only at Xmas

---

Cricket Field House

★★★★ GUEST ACCOMMODATION

tel: 01722 322595 **Skew Bridge, Wilton Rd SP2 9NS**
email: cricketfieldcottage@btinternet.com **web:** www.cricketfieldhouse.co.uk
dir: A36, 1m W of Salisbury, towards Wilton & Warminster

Cricket Field House is a 19th-century gamekeeper's cottage set in award-winning gardens overlooking the South Wiltshire Cricket Ground. It is within walking distance of the city centre and railway station, and provides high levels of accommodation, hospitality and customer care.

Rooms 8 annexe en suite (4 GF) D £75-£140* **Facilities** FTV tea/coffee Licensed WiFi 🔒 **Parking** 25 **Notes** ⊗ No Children 14yrs Closed 21 Dec-4 Jan

---

Spread Eagle Inn

★★★★ ⬤ INN

tel: 01747 840587 **Church Lawn BA12 6QE**
email: enquiries@spreadeagleinn.com **web:** www.spreadeagleinn.com
dir: 0.5m W off B3092 at entrance to Stourhead Gardens

Set in the beautiful grounds of Stourhead House with its Palladian temples, lakes and inspiring vistas, the Spread Eagle Inn is an impressive red-brick building with a good reputation for simple, honest and locally-sourced food. In the bedrooms, National Trust antiques sit side by side with modern comforts. The large Georgian windows, low ceilings and uneven floors add to the authentic atmosphere of this delightful country house.

Rooms 5 en suite **Facilities** tea/coffee Dinner available Direct Dial WiFi **Conf** Max 30 Thtr 30 Board 20 **Notes** ⊗

Sun Inn

★★★★ INN

tel: 01793 523292 **Coate SN3 6AA**
email: sun-inn@arkells.com **web:** www.suninn-swindon.co.uk
dir: M4 junct 15 onto A419, take 1st exit signed Swindon & hospital. 1st exit at rdbt, 1m on left

Located on the outskirts of Swindon, adjacent to the popular Coate Water Country Park, the inn features a large garden and children's play area with a thatched summer house. Accommodation is suitable for both business and leisure guests, offering free WiFi throughout. A regularly-changing blackboard menu offers well-prepared dishes, available throughout the day and evening. The popular Sunday lunch should not be missed. Owned by the Arkell's family brewers, a great range of traditionally brewed beers are available.

Rooms 10 en suite **Facilities** FTV DVD tea/coffee Dinner available WiFi **Parking** 80 **Notes** No coaches

SWINDON *continued*

The Angel

★★★★ ⊛ INN

tel: 01793 851161 **47 High St, Royal Wootton Bassett SN4 7AQ**
email: theangel.wbassett@arkells.com **web:** www.theangelhotelwoottonbassett.co.uk

Located directly on the high street of historic Royal Wootton Bassett, The Angel offers everything from morning coffee in the lounge, to a drink at the bar or a meal in the popular restaurant. Public areas are intimate and comfortably furnished. Accommodation is located at the rear of the property in a purpose-built wing overlooking the courtyard. Its location makes it ideal for corporate guests and those exploring the local area. The property also includes a boardroom and larger function room.

Rooms 3 en suite 14 annexe en suite S £60-£89; D £60-£110* **Facilities** FTV Lounge tea/coffee Dinner available WiFi **Conf** Max 100 Thtr 100 Class 36 Board 14 **Notes** ⊗ Closed 26 Dec & 1 Jan RS 25 Dec

Ardecca

★★★★ GUEST ACCOMMODATION

tel: 01793 721238 & 07791 120826 **Fieldrise Farm, Kingsdown Ln, Blunsdon SN25 5DL**
email: chris-graham.ardecca@fsmail.net **web:** www.ardecca-bedandbreakfast.co.uk
dir: *A419 onto B4019 to Blunsdon/Highworth, then into Turnpike Rd at Cold Harbour pub, left into Kingsdown Ln*

Ardecca is quietly located in sixteen acres of pastureland with easy access to Swindon and the Cotswolds. All bedrooms are on the ground floor and are well furnished and equipped. An especially friendly welcome is provided and arts and crafts workshops are available on site.

Rooms 4 rms (4 pri facs) (1 fmly) (4 GF) **Facilities** FTV tea/coffee WiFi Art & Crafts workshops **Extras** Bottled water, sweets **Conf** Class 16 **Parking** 5 **Notes** ⊗ No Children 6yrs ⊚

The Old Post Office Guest House

★★★★ GUEST HOUSE

tel: 01793 823114 **Thornhill Rd, South Marston SN3 4RY**
email: theoldpostofficeguesthouse@yahoo.co.uk
web: www.theoldpostofficeguesthouse.co.uk
dir: *M4 junct 15, A419 signed Cirencester/Swindon (East), approx 3m, left onto A420 towards Oxford, at next rdbt 2nd exit into Merlin Way, 0.3m, at White Hart rdbt 3rd exit onto A420. At Gablecross rdbt follow South Marston signs*

This attractive property is about two miles from Swindon. Guests are welcomed by the enthusiastic owner, a professional opera singer with a wonderful sense of humour. The comfortable bedrooms vary in size, and all are equipped with numerous facilities. An extensive choice is offered at breakfast, which is freshly cooked and uses the best local produce. AA Friendliest B&B of the Year Award Finalist 2016-2017.

Rooms 5 en suite (1 fmly) **Facilities** STV tea/coffee WiFi ⚓ Use of nearby country club **Extras** Snacks, chocolate **Parking** 6 **Notes** ⊗

Tawny Owl

★★★★ INN

tel: 01793 706770 **Queen Elizabeth Dr, Taw Hill SN25 1WR**
email: thetawnyowl.swindon@arkells.com **web:** www.arkells.com
dir: *2.5m NW of town centre, signed from A419*

Expect a genuinely friendly welcome from the staff at this modern inn on the north-west outskirts of Swindon. It has comfortable, well-equipped bedrooms and bathrooms. A varied selection of enjoyable home-cooked meals is on offer at both lunch and dinner, together with a range of Arkell's ales and wines. A private function room is available.

Rooms 5 en suite (2 fmly) **Facilities** TVL tea/coffee Dinner available Direct Dial WiFi Stairlift **Conf** Max 55 Thtr 55 Class 55 Board 55 **Parking** 75 **Notes** RS Xmas/New Year Civ Wed 50

The White Hart

★★★★ INN

tel: 01793 822272 & 07789 717368 **Oxford Rd, Stratton St Margaret SN3 4JD**
email: info@whitehartstratton.co.uk **web:** www.whitehartstratton.co.uk
dir: *On White Hart rdbt, at intersection of A420 & A419*

Located on the outskirts of Swindon, with good access to the M4 just a five-minute drive from junction 15, with its close links to Cirencester and the M5. Accommodation has been purpose built, offering comfortable and spacious rooms, suitable for both business and leisure guests. Free WiFi is available throughout, with ample free parking. A classic pub menu offers well-prepared dishes, available throughout the day and evening, and a popular carvery is available on Sundays. Function rooms are available. Owned by the Arkell's family brewers, a great range of traditionally brewed beers are available.

Rooms 24 en suite (6 fmly) (12 GF) **Facilities** FTV Lounge TVL tea/coffee Dinner available WiFi Pool table ⚓ **Extras** Speciality toiletries **Conf** Max 42 Thtr 42 Class 30 Board 20 **Parking** 60 **Notes** ⊗

Heart in Hand

★★★ INN

tel: 01793 721314 **43 High St, Blunsdon SN26 7AG**
email: leppardsteve@aol.com **web:** www.heartinhand.co.uk
dir: *Exit A419 into High St, 200yds on right*

Right in the village centre, this family-run inn offers a friendly welcome together with a wide selection of home-cooked food. Bedrooms are spacious, well equipped and offer a number of useful extras. A pleasant patio and rear garden with seating is also available.

Rooms 4 en suite (1 fmly) **Facilities** tea/coffee Dinner available **Parking** 17 **Notes** ⊗

Internos B&B

★★★ BED AND BREAKFAST

tel: 01793 721496 **3 Turnpike Rd, Blunsdon SN26 7EA**
web: www.internos-bedandbreakfast.co.uk
dir: *4m N of Swindon. Alongside A419 access from Cold Harbour End*

Situated just off the A419, Internos B&B offers comfortable accommodation in a relaxed and informal atmosphere. The gardens open onto a field, which is a haven for wildlife. Guests can enjoy the freshly-cooked breakfasts, served in the dining room, and a cosy lounge is also available.

Rooms 3 rms (1 fmly) **Facilities** FTV TVL tea/coffee WiFi **Parking** 6 **Notes** ⊗ ⊚

Saracens Head

★★ INN

tel: 01793 762284 **High St, Highworth SN6 7AG**
email: saracenshead@arkells.com **web:** www.arkells.com
dir: *5m NE of Swindon*

The Saracens Head stands on the main street of a pleasant market town, close to Swindon. It has lots of character, including a popular bar dating from 1828. The fine selection of real ales, and some excellent home-cooked food are highlights. Bedrooms, which vary in size, are generally compact. A rear car park and a patio area are available.

Rooms 12 en suite (1 fmly) **Facilities** tea/coffee Dinner available WiFi **Conf** Max 10 Thtr 10 Class 10 Board 10 **Parking** 30

■ TISBURY · Map 4 ST92

Hare Lodge Bed and Breakfast

★★★★ BED AND BREAKFAST

tel: 01747 870582 & 07754 044815 **Monmouth Rd, Tuckingmill SP3 6NR**
email: harelodge@btinternet.com **web:** www.hare-lodge.co.uk
dir: *In Tisbury, at The Square, exit signed Semley/Newtown. Pass church on left, over mini rdbt & continue on road. Into Tuckingmill, 3rd house on left*

Located on the edge of the village within an Area of Outstanding Natural Beauty, this Scandinavian-style house is a perfect base for exploring the area. A warm welcome is assured with every effort made to ensure a relaxing and rewarding stay. Bedrooms provide generous levels of space and comfort, one room having the benefit of a balcony, the other a suite with separate lounge area. Tasty breakfasts are served around the dining table, or outside in the summer if preferred. This is a popular area for walkers, and helpful advice is always on offer to help plans routes.

Rooms 2 en suite (1 fmly) S £80-£90; D £90* **Facilities** FTV DVD tea/coffee WiFi 🛁
Extras Speciality toiletries, fresh milk **Parking** 3 **Notes** ⊗ Closed 23 Dec-3 Jan ⊛

■ TOLLARD ROYAL · Map 4 ST91

King John Inn

★★★★★ ⊛⊛ RESTAURANT WITH ROOMS

tel: 01725 516207 **SP5 5PS**
email: info@kingjohninn.co.uk **web:** www.kingjohninn.co.uk
dir: *From A354 or A350 onto B3081*

Part of The Epicurean Collection, the King John Inn is a traditional style country inn located in a country village. It has a Victorian-style garden pavilion serving seasonal classics such as chargrilled lobster and pigeon salad. The recently added Dove Cottage offers three more en suite bedrooms to go with the five rooms at the inn. All have feature bathrooms. Food and wine is a real feature here with local ingredients much in evidence, alongside excellent levels of hospitality and customer care. Ample parking for residents.

Rooms 5 en suite 3 annexe en suite (2 GF) **Facilities** FTV Lounge tea/coffee Dinner available Direct Dial WiFi ⅃ **Parking Notes** RS 25 & 31 Dec restaurant closed for dinner

■ UPTON LOVELL · Map 4 ST94

Prince Leopold

★★★ ⊜ INN

tel: 01985 850460 **54 Upton Lovell BA12 0JP**
email: info@princeleopold.co.uk **web:** www.princeleopold.co.uk

Located on the banks of the River Wylye, this delightful inn enjoys views across the meadows from the dining room and outdoor seating in the riverside garden. An excellent range of good quality home-cooked dishes is available for lunch and dinner. Bedrooms and bathrooms vary in size and are all located on the first floor above the inn. Local ales are provided in the comfortable bar.

Rooms 6 rms **Facilities** Dinner available

■ WANBOROUGH · Map 5 SU28

The Harrow Inn

★★★ ⊜ INN

tel: 01793 791792 **SN4 0AE**
email: info@theharrowwanborough.co.uk **web:** www.theharrowwanborough.co.uk

Steeped in history and with many original features retained this cosy inn provides a warm welcome. The three en suite bedrooms are set in the 'old forge' opposite the main pub and all have their own external entrance. Hearty meals using much locally sourced produce are available daily.

Rooms 3 annexe en suite (3 GF) S £95; D £95* **Facilities** FTV DVD tea/coffee Dinner available WiFi 🛁 **Parking** 50

■ WESTBURY · Map 4 ST85

The Hollies Inn

★★★★ INN

tel: 01373 864493 **55 Westbury Leigh BA13 3SF**
email: info@theholliesinn.com **web:** www.theholliesinn.com

This traditional style inn provides plenty of quality and comfort in both bedrooms and bathrooms, and throughout the public areas. The inn is open during the day when lighter meals are offered, and there is a full menu in the evening along with a good range of ales. Quiz nights and live music are regular features. A car park is available, together with outdoor seating for the warmer months.

Rooms 3 en suite **Facilities** Dinner available **Parking**

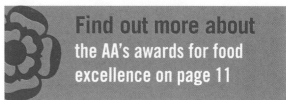

Find out more about the AA's awards for food excellence on page 11

WEST GRAFTON
Map 5 SU26

Mayfield Bed & Breakfast
★★★★ ⏣ BED AND BREAKFAST

tel: 01672 810339 & 07771 996811 **SN8 3BY**
email: angela.orssich@gmail.com **web:** www.mayfieldbandb.com
dir: *M4 junct 14 onto A338, through Hungerford. Turn left to West Grafton, 300mtrs on right*

Dating from the 15th century, this cosy bed and breakfast is located in a quiet hamlet just seven miles from the famous market town of Marlborough. Bedrooms are comfortable with many thoughtful extras. Hearty breakfasts feature as much home-made produce as possible, and are served around a family-style table.

Rooms 4 rms (2 en suite) (2 fmly) S £70-£90; D £90-£110 **Facilities** STV FTV TVL tea/coffee WiFi ⚲ ⚘ 🔒 **Extras** Fruit, snacks - complimentary **Parking** 8 **Notes** ⊗ Closed Xmas

ZEALS
Map 4 ST73

Cornerways Cottage
★★★★ BED AND BREAKFAST

tel: 01747 840477 **Longcross BA12 6LL**
email: cornerways.cottage@btinternet.com **web:** www.cornerwayscottage.co.uk
dir: *A303 onto B3092 signed Stourhead. At bottom of slip road, right under bridge, follow signs for Zeals. On left by 40mph sign*

A warm friendly welcome, comfortable rooms and hearty breakfasts await in Cornerways Cottage, a charming 250-year-old stone building. Situated right on the borders of Somerset, Dorset and Wiltshire it is ideal for visiting Longleat and Stourhead house and gardens. Horseriding, fishing, the Wiltshire Cycleway and plenty of great walks are all on the doorstep.

Rooms 3 rms (2 en suite) (1 pri facs) S fr £60; D £65-£75* **Facilities** FTV Lounge TVL tea/coffee WiFi ⚲ 9 🔒 **Extras** Speciality toiletries, bottled water - free **Parking** 10 **Notes** ⊗ Closed Xmas & New Year

WORCESTERSHIRE

ABBERLEY
Map 10 SO76

Premier Collection

The Manor Arms
★★★★★ ◉ INN

tel: 01299 890300 & 890453 **The Village WR6 6BN**
email: enquiries@themanorarms.co.uk **web:** www.themanorarms.co.uk
dir: *N of Worcester on A443, follow brown tourist signs for The Manor Arms*

This charming inn was totally refurbished in 2015 and offers guests a range of high quality, stylish bedrooms. The inn enjoys a prominent position in the heart of the pretty village of Abberley and many of the bedrooms have views overlooking the rolling countryside. The award-winning restaurant is very popular and the bar has been sympathetically restored, and many of the original features retained. The Manor Arms is an ideal base from which to explore the historic towns of Worcester and Malvern both of which are a short drive away.

Rooms 6 en suite **Facilities** FTV tea/coffee Dinner available WiFi **Extras** Speciality toiletries, bottled water - free **Parking** 40 **Notes** Civ Wed 70

ALVECHURCH
Map 10 SP07

Alcott Farm
Ⓤ

tel: 01564 824051 & 07736 445188 **Icknield St, Weatheroak B48 7EH**
email: alcottfarm@btinternet.com **web:** www.alcottfarm.co.uk
dir: *2m NE of Alvechurch. M42 junct 3, A435 for Birmingham, left signed Weatheroak, left at x-rds down steep hill, left opposite pub, farm 0.5m on right up long driveway*

Currently the rating for this establishment is not confirmed. This may be due to a change of ownership or because it has only recently joined the AA rating scheme.

Rooms 4 en suite 2 annexe en suite (1 GF) S £50; D £70* **Facilities** FTV TVL tea/coffee WiFi Fishing **Extras** Snacks **Parking** 20 **Notes** No Children 10yrs

ASTWOOD BANK
Map 10 SP06

Corner Cottage
★★★ BED AND BREAKFAST

tel: 01527 459122 & 07917 582884 **1194 Evesham Rd B96 6AA**
email: marilyn_alan1194@hotmail.co.uk **web:** www.corner-cottagebb.co.uk
dir: *A441 through Astwood Bank, Corner Cottage at lights*

A warm welcome awaits you at Corner Cottage, a beautiful Victorian cottage set in a delightful village location within walking distance of pubs, shops and restaurants. Convenient for Stratford-upon-Avon, Evesham, Warwick, Birmingham and Worcester.

Rooms 4 rms (3 en suite) (1 pri facs) S £40; D £65* **Facilities** FTV TVL tea/coffee WiFi 🔒 **Notes** LB ⊗ ⊗ ⊜

BEWDLEY
Map 10 SO77

AA GUEST ACCOMMODATION OF THE YEAR
FOR ENGLAND 2016-2017

Premier Collection

Kateshill House

★★★★★ 🍴 GUEST ACCOMMODATION

tel: 01299 401563 **Red Hill DY12 2DR**
email: info@kateshillhouse.co.uk **web:** www.kateshillhouse.co.uk
dir: *A456 onto B4195 signed Bewdley. Bear left over bridge, 1st left into Severnside South. Right into Lax Ln, at T-junct turn left, up hill on right*

A very warm welcome awaits at Kateshill House, a Georgian manor house overlooking Bewdley. Two acres of landscaped gardens provide a dramatic backdrop to the house, as well as fruit for breakfasts and home-made jams. The elegant bedrooms are individually styled, sumptuously decorated with rich fabrics and period furniture, and equipped with a wealth of amenities for guests' use. Small private functions are also catered for.

Rooms 7 en suite S £75-£80; D £90-£110 **Facilities** FTV Lounge TVL tea/coffee WiFi 🛁 **Parking** 10 **Notes** LB ⊗

The Mug House Inn

★★★★ 🍴 INN

tel: 01299 402543 **12 Severnside North DY12 2EE**
email: drew@mughousebewdley.co.uk **web:** www.mughousebewdley.co.uk
dir: *In town centre on riverfront*

Located on the opposite side of the River Severn to Bewdley Rowing Club, this 18th-century inn combines high standards of comfort and facilities with many original features. Bedrooms are thoughtfully furnished, there is a separate breakfast room, and imaginative dinners are served in the restaurant.

Rooms 4 en suite 3 annexe en suite (1 GF) S £70-£100; D £80-£100* **Facilities** FTV tea/coffee Dinner available WiFi **Notes** No Children 10yrs No coaches

Royal Forester Country Inn

★★★★ 🍴 INN

tel: 01299 266286 **Callow Hill DY14 9XW**
email: royalforesterinn@btinternet.com **web:** www.royalforesterinn.co.uk

Located opposite the Wyre Forest on the town's outskirts, this inn dates back to 1411 and has been sympathetically restored to provide high standards of comfort.

Stylish modern bedrooms are complemented by smart bathrooms, and equipped with many thoughtful extras. Decor styles throughout the public areas highlight the many period features, and the restaurant serves imaginative food featuring locally sourced produce.

Rooms 7 en suite (2 fmly) S £69-£75; D £79-£99* **Facilities** STV FTV TVL tea/coffee Dinner available WiFi **Parking** 40 **Notes** LB No coaches

Welchgate Guest House

★★★★ GUEST HOUSE

tel: 01299 402655 **1 Welch Gate DY12 2AT**
email: info@welchgate-guesthouse.co.uk **web:** www.welchgate-guesthouse.co.uk

Welchgate Guest House is a 400-year-old former inn providing modern comfort and good facilities. Bedrooms are equipped with fine furnishings and thoughtful extras, and have smart, modern en suite shower rooms. Hearty breakfasts are taken in a rustic-look café, which is also open to the public during the day.

Rooms 4 en suite **Facilities** tea/coffee Licensed WiFi 🛁 **Notes** LB ⊗ No Children

Bank House

★★★ BED AND BREAKFAST

tel: 01299 402652 **14 Lower Park DY12 2DP**
email: fleur.nightingale@virgin.net **web:** www.bewdley-accommodation.co.uk
dir: *In town centre. From junct High St & Lax Ln, Bank House after junct on left*

Once a private bank, this Victorian house retains many original features and offers comfortable accommodation. The cosy dining room is the setting for tasty English breakfasts served at one family table. Owner Mrs Nightingale has a comprehensive knowledge of the town and its history.

Rooms 4 rms (1 fmly) S £37-£40; D £62-£65* **Facilities** FTV tea/coffee WiFi 🛁 **Parking** 2 **Notes** ⊗ Closed 24-26 Dec 📧

BROADWAY
Map 10 SP03

Premier Collection

Abbots Grange

★★★★★ 🍴 GUEST HOUSE

tel: 020 8133 8698 **Church St WR12 7AE**
email: rooms@abbotsgrange.com **web:** www.abbotsgrange.com
dir: *M5 junct 9 follow signs to Evesham & Broadway*

A warm welcome awaits at Abbots Grange, a 14th-century monastic manor house believed to be the oldest dwelling in Broadway. A Grade II listed building, it stands proudly in eight acres of grounds. The bedrooms are luxurious and comprise twin and four-poster suites. Among the thoughtful extras in the rooms are fruit bowls and a selection of alcoholic drinks. The stunning medieval Great Hall is the guests' lounge and makes a romantic setting with its log fire and candles. Tea and cake is offered on arrival, and quality breakfasts are served at the large communal table in the wood-panelled dining room. Abbots Grange has a tennis court and croquet lawn along with a helicopter landing pad.

Rooms 4 rms (3 en suite) (1 pri facs) **Facilities** STV FTV DVD iPod docking station Lounge tea/coffee WiFi 🌸 🍷 🛁 **Extras** Port, whisky, sherry, soft drinks, mineral water **Conf** Board 10 **Parking** 8 **Notes** ⊗ No Children 6yrs

BROADWAY *continued*

Premier Collection

Mill Hay House

★★★★★ ⚲ GUEST ACCOMMODATION

tel: 01386 852498 **Snowshill Rd WR12 7JS**
email: info@millhay.co.uk **web:** www.millhay.co.uk
dir: *0.7m S of Broadway towards Snowshill, house on right*

Set in three acres of immaculate grounds beside a medieval watermill, this impressive early 18th-century stone house has many original features complemented by quality decor, period furniture and works of art. The spacious bedrooms are filled with thoughtful extras and one has a balcony. Imaginative breakfasts are served in the elegant dining room, and there is a spacious drawing room.

Rooms 3 en suite D £185-£245* **Facilities** FTV TVL tea/coffee Direct Dial WiFi 🔒 **Extras** Mineral water - complimentary **Parking** 15 **Notes** LB ⊗ No Children 12yrs

Premier Collection

Russell's

★★★★★ ⚙⚙ ⚲ RESTAURANT WITH ROOMS

tel: 01386 853555 **20 High St WR12 7DT**
email: info@russellsofbroadway.co.uk **web:** www.russellsofbroadway.co.uk
dir: *Opposite village green*

Situated in the centre of picturesque Broadway, this restaurant with rooms makes a great base for exploring local attractions. The superbly appointed bedrooms, each with its own character, have air conditioning and a wide range of extras. The cuisine is a real draw here with skilful use made of freshly-prepared, local produce.

Rooms 4 en suite 3 annexe en suite (4 fmly) (2 GF) S £98-£300; D £120-£300* **Facilities** FTV DVD tea/coffee Dinner available Direct Dial WiFi **Extras** Honesty bar **Conf** Max 12 Board 12 **Parking** 16 **Notes** No coaches

Cowley House

★★★★ GUEST ACCOMMODATION

tel: 01386 858148 **Church St WR12 7AE**
email: joan.peter@cowleyhouse-broadway.co.uk **web:** www.cowleyhouse-broadway.co.uk
dir: *Follow signs for Broadway. Church St adjacent to village green, 3rd on left*

A warm welcome is assured at this 18th-century Cotswold-stone house, just a stroll from the village green. Fine period furniture enhances the interior, and the elegant hall has a polished flagstone floor. Tastefully equipped bedrooms include thoughtful extras and smart shower rooms. Comprehensive breakfasts feature local produce.

Rooms 8 rms (7 en suite) (1 pri facs) (2 fmly) (2 GF) **Facilities** FTV TVL TV7B tea/coffee WiFi 🔒 **Parking** 8

The Vernon

★★★★ ⊚ INN

tel: 01527 821236 **Droitwich Rd, Hanbury B60 4DB**
email: info@thevernonhanbury.co.uk **web:** www.thevernonhanbury.co.uk
dir: *M5 junct 5, A38 to Droitwich. Turn left into Bromsgrove Rd (B4065). Left into Hanbury Rd (B4090), opposite junction*

Situated in the rural parish of Hanbury close to Bromsgrove and Droitwich, this 18th-century inn is sometimes known as the 'Birthplace of *The Archers*', because Godfrey Baseley, the original creator of the famous soap, was a regular. The inn boasts modern and comfortable accommodation, and fine dining can be enjoyed in the attractive restaurant.

Rooms 5 en suite S fr £65; D fr £105* **Facilities** STV FTV Lounge TVL tea/coffee Dinner available Direct Dial WiFi **Parking** 74 **Notes** ⊗

South House Bed & Breakfast

★★★★ BED AND BREAKFAST

tel: 01386 830848 & 07956 254990 **South House, Main St, South Littleton WR11 8TJ**
email: amanda@southhouse.co.uk **web:** www.southhouse.co.uk
dir: *From Evesham take B4035 signed Badsey. In Badsey left onto B4085 signed Bidford. In South Littleton, house on right*

South House is a stunning Grade II listed property, located in a quiet Worcestershire village within easy reach of the Cotswolds and historic Stratford. Both spacious en suite rooms are located in the eves of the former coach house. Guests are welcome to relax in the elegant drawing room in the main house. Aga-cooked breakfasts are washed down with home-pressed apple juice. A warm welcome is assured from the owners and friendly alpacas. Alpaca trekking is available by prior arrangement.

Rooms 2 annexe en suite **Facilities** FTV TVL tea/coffee Dinner available WiFi 🦜 ⚲ Gym 🔒 Alpaca trekking/feeding **Extras** Speciality toiletries, home-made biscuits **Conf** Max 14 Board 14 **Parking** 6 **Notes** No Children 14yrs

---

The Boot Inn

★★★★ ⌂ INN

tel: 01386 462658 **Radford Rd WR7 4BS**
email: enquiries@thebootinn.com **web:** www.thebootinn.com
dir: *In village centre, signed from A422*

An inn has occupied this site since the 13th century, though The Boot itself dates from the Georgian period. Much historic charm remains in the pub, while the bedrooms, furnished in antique pine, are equipped with practical extras and have modern bathrooms. A range of ales, wines and imaginative food is offered in the cosy public areas, which include an attractive conservatory and patio.

The Boot Inn

Rooms 5 annexe en suite (2 GF) **Facilities** FTV DVD iPod docking station Lounge tea/coffee Dinner available WiFi ⚓ 27 Pool table **Parking** 30 **Notes** LB

HIMBLETON
Map 10 SO95

Phepson Farm *(SO941598)*

★★★★ ☺ FARMHOUSE

tel: 01905 391205 **WR9 7JZ**
email: info@phepsonfarm.co.uk **web:** www.phepsonfarm.co.uk
dir: M5 junct 5 onto A38 (Droitwich). Left at 1st lights, left at next lights onto B4090. After 2m right to Himbleton. Phepson Farm 2m on right

Set in 50 acres of peaceful Worcestershire countryside, Phepson Farm has a one and a half acre coarse fishing lake. The farm is run in an eco-friendly manner and guests are welcome to walk the wildlife route. There are four individually-styled bedrooms; two large rooms are in the main farmhouse and two are in the converted stables, with their own entrances. Award-winning breakfasts include asparagus in season, damsons and plums from the farm, and locally sourced sausages and bacon. There is also a guest lounge.

Rooms 2 en suite 2 annexe en suite (2 GF) S £55-£60; D £80* **Facilities** FTV TVL tea/coffee WiFi Fishing **Extras** Bottled water **Parking** 4 **Notes** LB Closed Xmas & New Year 50 acres sheep/beef

---

KEMPSEY
Map 10 SO84

Walter de Cantelupe Inn

★★★ INN

tel: 01905 820572 **Main Rd WR5 3NA**
email: info@walterdecantelupe.co.uk **web:** www.walterdecantelupe.co.uk
dir: On A38 in village centre

This inn provides cosy bedrooms with smart bathrooms, and is convenient for the M5 and Worcester. The intimate, open-plan public areas are the setting for a range of real ales, and imaginative food featuring local produce and a fine selection of British cheeses.

Rooms 3 en suite (1 fmly) S £65-£85; D £80-£125* **Facilities** FTV DVD iPod docking station Lounge tea/coffee Dinner available WiFi **Parking** 24 **Notes** LB No coaches

---

MALVERN
Map 10 SO74

Ashbury Bed & Breakfast

★★★★ BED AND BREAKFAST

tel: 01684 574225 **Ashbury, Old Hollow WR14 4NP**
email: ashburybandb@btinternet.com **web:** www.ashburybedandbreakfast.co.uk
dir: A449 onto B4053, 2nd left into Hornyold Rd. Right at T-junct into Cowleigh Rd, 250yds on left

A warm and friendly welcome awaits you from Karen and Graham at Ashbury Bed & Breakfast. This beautiful and grand Victorian property offers modern, comfortable and stylish bedrooms; the many period features that have been retained add to the overall charm of the house. An enjoyable breakfast made with all fresh ingredients can be enjoyed with some views across the Malvern countryside. This is a good location for those wishing to go walking in the Malvern area. Free WiFi is available.

Rooms 3 en suite (2 GF) S £55-£105; D £75-£125* **Facilities** FTV TVL tea/coffee WiFi ⚓ **Extras** Home-made biscuits - complimentary **Conf** Max 10 Board 10 **Parking** 4 **Notes** LB ⊗ No Children 12yrs

---

Cowleigh Park Farm

★★★★ ☺ BED AND BREAKFAST

tel: 01684 566750 & 07954 121570 **Cowleigh Rd WR13 5HJ**
email: info@cowleighparkfarm.co.uk **web:** www.cowleighparkfarm.co.uk
dir: From A449 onto B4219 signed Bromyard. Take 1st right to stay on B4219 (Cowleigh Rd), driveway 0.5m on right

A warm welcome is assured at this 400 year old timber-framed former farmhouse peacefully set in attractive and deceptively large gardens below The Malvern Hills. Carefully modernised over hundreds of years this property blends modern day comforts with period features in abundance. Comfortably furnished en suites are complemented by a large sitting room with wood-burning stove. Home-cooked breakfasts are served in the attractive dining room and make for an excellent start to the day ahead.

Rooms 3 en suite S £55-£75; D £80-£95 **Facilities** FTV DVD Lounge tea/coffee WiFi ⚓ **Parking** 8

The Dell House

★★★★ BED AND BREAKFAST

tel: 01684 564448 **2 Green Ln WR14 4HU**
email: stay@thedellhouse.co.uk **web:** www.thedellhouse.co.uk

This former rectory dates back to the 1820s and is quietly located in its own large garden. Retaining many original features, rooms are thoughtfully furnished and provide good levels of comfort with suitable extras, and each bedroom benefits from countryside views. The breakfast menu features a number of vegetarian options. This is a good location for those wishing to go walking in the Malverns, or to attend events at the Three Counties Showground.

Rooms 4 en suite S £60-£75; D £85-£115* **Facilities** FTV Lounge TVL tea/coffee WiFi ⚓ **Conf** Max 10 Thtr 10 Class 8 Board 8 **Parking** 4 **Notes** LB ⊗

MALVERN continued

Wyche Inn

★★★★ INN

tel: 01684 575396 **74 Wyche Rd WR14 4EQ**
email: thewycheinn@googlemail.com **web:** www.thewycheinn.co.uk
dir: 1.5m S of Malvern. On B4218 towards Malvern & Colwall. Off A449 (Worcester to Ross/Ledbury road)

Located in an elevated position on the outskirts of Malvern, this inn is popular with locals and visiting walkers. The thoughtfully furnished bedrooms provide good levels of comfort with suitable guest extras; all bathrooms have a bath and shower. Each bedroom benefits from stunning countryside views. The menus feature home-cooked dishes, including good-value options, and a comprehensive range of real ales is available from the bar.

Rooms 4 en suite 2 annexe rms (2 pri facs) (1 GF) **Facilities** FTV DVD tea/coffee Dinner available WiFi Pool table **Extras** Speciality toiletries, bottled mineral water **Parking** 6 **Notes** LB No coaches

Sidney House

★★★ BED AND BREAKFAST

tel: 01684 574994 **40 Worcester Rd WR14 4AA**
email: info@sidneyhouse.co.uk **web:** www.sidneyhouse.co.uk
dir: On A449, 200yds N from town centre

Believed to have been purpose-built as a guest house in 1823, this Grade II listed property has a long history of welcoming visitors to Great Malvern. This tradition is continued today by Alexandra and Anthony, whose warm welcome is assured. Situated within easy walking distance of local attractions and restaurants, and within easy reach of the Malvern Hills, the property boasts enviable views across the Severn Vale and beyond. En suite rooms are comfortably furnished with a guest lounge, on-site parking and complimentary WiFi all provided.

Rooms 6 en suite S £55-£65; D £67-£90 **Facilities** FTV TVL tea/coffee Licensed WiFi Discounts at local beauty salon **Extras** Speciality toiletries **Parking** 8 **Notes** LB ⊗ No Children 12yrs

The Pembridge

★★★ GUEST ACCOMMODATION

tel: 01684 574813 **114 Graham Rd WR14 2HX**
email: info@thepembridge.co.uk **web:** www.thepembridge.co.uk
dir: From A449 into Church St, 1st left

Located on a leafy residential road close to the town centre, this large Victorian house retains many original features, including a superb staircase. Bedrooms are well equipped. Other areas include a comfortable sitting room and an elegant dining room.

Rooms 7 en suite (1 fmly) S £45-£53; D £64-£69 **Facilities** FTV TVL tea/coffee Direct Dial WiFi **Parking** 9 **Notes** LB ⊗ No Children 7yrs RS 25-26 Dec No cooked English breakfast

Portocks End House

★★★ BED AND BREAKFAST

tel: 01684 310276 **Little Clevelode WR13 6PE**
email: email@portocksendbandb.co.uk **web:** www.portocksendbandb.co.uk
dir: On B4424, 4m N of Upton upon Severn, opposite Riverside Caravan Park

Peacefully located, yet convenient for the showground and major road links, this period house retains many original features; the traditional furnishings and decor

highlight its intrinsic charm. The bedrooms are equipped with lots of thoughtful extras, and breakfasts are taken in a cosy dining room overlooking the garden.

Rooms 3 rms (1 en suite) (2 pri facs) (1 fmly) S £35; D £60-£65* **Facilities** Lounge tea/coffee WiFi **Extras** Speciality toiletries - complimentary **Parking** 4 **Notes** Closed Dec-Feb ⊗

PERSHORE   Map 10 SO94

Evesham Lodge Bed & Breakfast

★★★★ ☕ BED AND BREAKFAST

tel: 01386 710285 & 07816 203960 **Evesham Lodge, Bricklehampton WR10 3HQ**
email: kerry@eveshamlodge.co.uk **web:** www.eveshamlodge.co.uk
dir: B4084 Pershore to Evesham road, exit signed Bricklehampton. At T-junct turn right, through village, road bears right, 2nd on right

Located in the Vale of Evesham and within easy reach of The Cotswolds, the historic city of Worcester and the Malvern Hills, this former gate house offers the best of both worlds; easily accessible from the motorway, yet peacefully nestled on the edge of the 30 acre Bricklehampton Hall estate. Both en suite rooms are very well appointed, one features a Juliet balcony with views across the garden and parkland beyond. A freshly cooked breakfast using free-range eggs and local produce is served in the dining room overlooking the garden.

Rooms 2 en suite S £60-£70; D £75-£85* **Facilities** FTV DVD Lounge tea/coffee WiFi **Extras** Speciality toiletries, fridge, home-made biscuits **Parking** 2 **Notes** LB ⊗ ⊗

UPTON UPON SEVERN   Map 10 SO84

The Swan

★★★★ INN

tel: 01684 594948 & 07501 223754 **Waterside WR8 0JD**
email: info@theswanhotelupton.co.uk **web:** www.theswanhotelupton.co.uk

Set in the historic riverside town of Upton upon Severn this 400-year-old inn offers plenty of charm and quirkiness. The bedrooms provide good comfort and practicality and are modern in design, with some having views of the river. Enjoy good quality bar meals and cask conditioned ales in the waterside bar. A separate restaurant is also available for functions.

Rooms 6 en suite S £57.50-£97.50; D £75-£115* **Facilities** FTV tea/coffee Dinner available Direct Dial WiFi **Extras** Slippers **Notes** No coaches

The Star Inn

★★★ INN

tel: 01684 593432 & 07721 594001 **3 High St WR8 0HQ**
email: info@richmondhillbreweries.co.uk **web:** www.thestarinnupton.co.uk
dir: M5 junct 8 onto M50. Exit after 1m at junct 1, signed Malvern (A38). Continue on A38, after 6m left signed Upton & follow signs to town centre

This charming property is located opposite one of the town's most famous landmarks known locally as 'The Pepperpot'; a copper-clad coppola which is a remnant of a former church that stands on the historic battle site. Run by a husband and wife team, The Star sits back from the riverbank and offers a range of comfortably furnished en suite rooms. There is a large sun terrace to the rear which overlooks the River Severn. Evening meals are served in the traditional dining room to the rear of the property.

Rooms 17 en suite (3 fmly) **Facilities** FTV DVD TVL tea/coffee Dinner available WiFi

WICHENFORD
Map 10 SO76

Premier Collection

Laughern Hill Estate

★★★★★ GUEST ACCOMMODATION

tel: 01886 888065 **Laughern Hill WR6 6YB**
email: enquiries@laughernhill.co.uk **web:** www.laughernhill.co.uk
dir: *From A443 onto B4204 (Martley Rd). Located at Willow Rd junct, with white gates*

This charming and attractive Grade II listed manor house, nestled in the Worcestershire countryside, offers a quiet and relaxing stay. A wonderful location for civil ceremonies and private parties. The bedrooms have been elegantly furnished with some thoughtful extras, and breakfast can be enjoyed in the grand dining room.

Rooms 5 en suite (4 fmly) **Facilities** FTV DVD iPod docking station Lounge TV4B tea/coffee WiFi 🎣 Riding 🛇 **Extras** Robes **Parking** 8 **Notes** ⊗
Closed 24-26 Dec Civ Wed 100

WORCESTER
Map 10 SO85

Church House Bed & Breakfast *(SO849587)*

★★★★ FARMHOUSE

tel: 01905 452366 & 07909 968938 **Church House, Claines WR3 7RL**
email: wr37rl@btinternet.com **web:** www.churchhousebandb.co.uk
dir: *M5 junct 6 onto A449, after 3m at rdbt take 1st exit. 1st drive on right before Claines church*

Church House Bed & Breakfast is situated on a working farm in a peaceful area of Worcestershire, within easy reach of the motorway network. This Grade II listed Georgian building offers relaxing and comfortable accommodation. Each bedroom is en suite, with WiFi and large screen TVs. The comfortable beds offer a good night's sleep, and the enjoyable breakfast, with home-made produce from the farm, will provide a good start for the day.

Rooms 3 en suite S £50-£65; D £70-£85* **Facilities** FTV tea/coffee WiFi 🎣 Fishing 🛇 **Extras** Home-made biscuits - complimentary **Parking** 10 **Notes** No Children 12yrs ⊜ 600 acres mixed

Wyatt Guest House

★★★★ GUEST HOUSE

tel: 01905 26311 **40 Barbourne Rd WR1 1HU**
email: info@wyattguest.co.uk **web:** www.wyattguest.co.uk
dir: *On A38 0.5m N from city centre*

Located within easy walking distance of shops, restaurants and central attractions, this lovely Victorian house provides a range of thoughtfully furnished bedrooms. Breakfast is served in an attractive dining room, a warm welcome is assured, and the attractive frontage is a regular winner in Worcester's 'Britain in Bloom' competition.

Rooms 8 rms (7 en suite) (1 fmly) (1 GF) S £40-£50; D £70* **Facilities** FTV DVD Lounge tea/coffee WiFi

EAST RIDING OF YORKSHIRE

BEVERLEY
Map 17 TA03

Premier Collection

Newbegin House

★★★★★ 🌿 BED AND BREAKFAST

tel: 01482 888880 **10 Newbegin HU17 8EG**
email: wsweeney@wsweeney.karoo.co.uk **web:** www.newbeginhousebbbeverley.co.uk
dir: *At end of M62 onto B1230 signed North Cave. Through North Cave & Walkington. Left at mini rdbt, 1st left at at next mini rdbt into Admiral Walker Rd. 5th right into Newbegin. House on left*

Newbegin House is a delightful Georgian manor house located on a quiet one way street in the centre of this historic market town. It is an impressive family home, very spacious and with many original period features and a homely, inviting feel. Excellent breakfasts are served in the grand dining room. The walled garden is also available for guests to enjoy and private parking is provided.

Rooms 3 en suite (1 fmly) S £50-£60; D £65-£85* **Facilities** FTV DVD iPod docking station TVL tea/coffee WiFi 🛇 **Conf** Max 30 Thtr 30 Class 20 Board 12 **Parking** 3 **Notes** LB RS Closed owners annual holiday ⊜

Trinity Guest House

★★★★ GUEST HOUSE

tel: 01482 869537 **Trinity Ln, Station Square HU17 0AR**
email: trinity_house@hotmail.com **web:** www.trinityguesthouse.com
dir: *Opposite railway station*

This well presented Victorian town house is located next to the train station in the historic town centre. Guests simply need to cross the quiet street if they arrive by train. There is a convenient public car park opposite the house or permits are available for on-street parking. The house combines traditional and modern decor with a comfortable lounge also provided. WiFi access is also available. A secluded, walled garden provides additional space for guests to relax in warmer weather.

Rooms 6 en suite (2 fmly) **Facilities** FTV DVD TVL tea/coffee WiFi 🛇 **Notes** ⊗

BRIDLINGTON
Map 17 TA16

Premier Collection

Marton Grange

★★★★★ GUEST ACCOMMODATION

tel: 01262 602034 & 07708 211071 **Flamborough Rd, Marton cum Sewerby YO15 1DU**
email: info@marton-grange.co.uk **web:** www.martongrange.co.uk
dir: *2m NE of Bridlington. On B1255, 600yds W of Links golf club*

This Grade II listed former farmhouse is set in well-maintained gardens and offers high levels of comfort, service and hospitality. Bedrooms are well appointed with quality fixtures and fittings and public areas offer wonderful views of the gardens. Thoughtful extras, provided as standard, help create a delightful guest experience.

Rooms 11 en suite (3 GF) **Facilities** FTV DVD iPod docking station Lounge tea/coffee Lift Licensed WiFi ♿ 18 🛇 **Extras** Home-made shortbread, speciality toiletries - free **Parking** 11 **Notes** LB RS Jan-Feb restricted opening for refurbishments

BRIDLINGTON *continued*

The Royal Bridlington

★★★★ GUEST ACCOMMODATION

tel: 01262 672433 **1** Shaftesbury Rd YO15 3NP
email: info@royalhotelbrid.co.uk **web:** www.royalhotelbrid.co.uk
dir: *A615 N to Bridlington (Kingsgate), right into Shaftesbury Rd*

Just off the promenade, this immaculate property has a range of thoughtfully furnished bedrooms with smart modern bathrooms. The spacious public areas include a large dining room, conservatory-sitting room, and a cosy TV lounge. Freshly-cooked dinners are a feature and a warm welcome is assured.

Rooms 14 rms (13 en suite) (1 pri facs) 4 annexe en suite (7 fmly) (4 GF) S £42-£52; D £74-£84* **Facilities** FTV DVD Lounge TVL tea/coffee Dinner available Licensed WiFi 🛴 18 🔒 **Conf** Max 85 Thtr 85 Class 20 Board 40 **Parking** 7 **Notes** LB ⊗ No Children 12yrs

The Brockton

★★★★ GUEST ACCOMMODATION

tel: 01262 673967 & 401771 **4** Shaftesbury Rd YO15 3NP
email: brocktonhotel@yahoo.co.uk **web:** www.brockton-bridlington.co.uk
dir: *Off A167 coast road, right at golf course, through lights, 2nd on left*

Located close to the seafront, this family-run property offers comfortable bedrooms, some with sea views, and all with en suite shower rooms. A lounge and bar area is available, and dinner and breakfast are served in the dining room.

Rooms 10 en suite (2 fmly) (2 GF) S £40; D £70* **Facilities** FTV DVD Lounge TVL tea/coffee Dinner available Licensed WiFi 🛴 18 🔒 **Conf** Max 20 **Parking** 10 **Notes** LB ⊗

Rosebery House

★★★★ GUEST HOUSE

tel: 01262 670336 **1** Belle Vue YO15 2ET
email: info@rosebery-house.com **web:** www.rosebery-house.com
dir: *From B1254 (Promenade) into Tennyson Ave, Belle Vue on left*

This beautiful, quietly positioned Grade II listed Georgian house is only 100 metres from the seafront and promenade. The harbour is only a few minutes' walk and within five to ten minutes guests can walk to a wide choice of shops, restaurants and cafés or explore the historic Old Town. Private parking, parking permits and secure cycle storage are all provided as well as free WiFi access. Bedrooms are comfortable and the front rooms have views of the garden, public gardens and the sea beyond.

Rooms 7 en suite (1 fmly) D £60-£80 **Facilities** FTV TVL tea/coffee WiFi 🔒 **Parking** 6 **Notes** ⊗ No Children 3yrs Closed Nov-Feb

HUGGATE
Map 19 SE85

The Wolds Inn

★★★ ⌂ INN

tel: 01377 288217 Driffield Rd YO42 1YH
email: woldsinn@gmail.com **web:** www.woldsinn.co.uk
dir: *Huggate signed off A166 & brown signs to Wolds Inn*

At the end of the highest village in the Yorkshire Wolds, midway between York and the coast, this ancient inn is a rural haven beside the Wolds Way walk. Substantial meals are served in the dining room and a good range of well-kept beers is available in the bar. Bedrooms, varying in size, are well equipped and comfortable.

Rooms 3 en suite S £45-£53; D £60-£76* **Facilities** FTV tea/coffee Dinner available WiFi 🔒 **Extras** Bottled water - complimentary **Parking** 30 **Notes** ⊗

MARKET WEIGHTON
Map 17 SE84

Robeanne House

★★★ GUEST ACCOMMODATION

tel: 01430 873312 & 07720 468811 Towthorpe Ln, Shiptonthorpe YO43 3PW
email: enquiries@robeannehouse.co.uk **web:** www.robeannehouse.co.uk
dir: *1.5m NW on A614*

Set back off the A614 in a quiet location, this delightful, modern family home was built as a farmhouse. York, the coast, and the Yorkshire Moors and Dales are within easy driving distance. All bedrooms have country views and include a large family room. A charming wooden chalet is available in the garden.

Rooms 2 en suite 6 annexe en suite (3 fmly) (3 GF) **Facilities** FTV TVL tea/coffee Dinner available WiFi 🔒 **Extras** Guest kitchen, robes - complimentary **Conf** Max 8 Board 8 **Parking** 10

NORTH NEWBALD
Map 17 SE93

Premier Collection

Boxtree House Boutique B&B

★★★★★ ⌂ BED AND BREAKFAST

tel: 01430 801092 & 07805 875533 22 Monckton Rise YO43 4RX
email: enquiries@boxtreehouse.co.uk **web:** www.boxtreehouse.co.uk
dir: *M62 junct 39 (South Cave) onto A1034 towards Market Weighton. After 3.5m right into South Newbald Rd, then right into Monckton Rise. House on right*

Nestled among of a small collection of residential properties is this owner-run bed and breakfast. A warm welcome is offered alongside a hot drink and home-made scones on arrival. The property as a whole has a modern appeal, and bedrooms offer high levels of comfort in stylish surroundings. Many thoughtful extras such as fresh flowers are provided alongside modern technology; flat-screen TVs, music systems and complimentary WiFi. Breakfasts are a treat with home-made and local produce on offer. Dogs are welcome.

Rooms 2 rms (1 en suite) (1 pri facs) **Facilities** FTV DVD iPod docking station Lounge tea/coffee WiFi 🔒 **Extras** Fresh fruit & milk, flowers **Parking** 3 **Notes** No Children

SOUTH DALTON
Map 17 SE94

Premier Collection

The Pipe and Glass Inn

★★★★★ ⌂⌂ INN

tel: 01430 810246 West End HU17 7PN
email: email@pipeandglass.co.uk **web:** www.pipeandglass.co.uk

The former coaching inn stands on the site of the original gatehouse to Dalton Park on the beautiful Dalton Estate, with parts of the current building dating back to the 17th century. After an initial major refurbishment in 2006, James and Kate have updated the premises regularly, including an exclusive private dining suite. Most recently, three new accommodation rooms and a kitchen garden were added as part of an ambitious garden redesign. The restaurant is more contemporary in style and the conservatory looks out over the garden. James sources top-notch local and seasonal produce for a range of modern British menus.

Rooms 5 annexe en suite (5 GF) S £145; D £225* **Facilities** FTV DVD iPod docking station Lounge tea/coffee Dinner available Direct Dial WiFi **Parking** 60 **Notes** ⊗ Closed 2wks Jan RS Mon closed (ex BHs) No coaches

WILLERBY
Map 17 TA03

Innkeeper's Lodge Hull, Willerby
★★★ INN

tel: 08451 551551 *(Calls cost 2p per minute plus your phone company's access charge)* **Beverley Rd HU10 6NT**
email: info@innkeeperslodge.com **web:** www.innkeeperslodge.com

Conveniently located for the city centre which is just five minutes away and also close to the M62 and the Humber Bridge. Bedrooms are modern and offer good space and comfort. There is a Toby Carvery pub on site where guests can enjoy a wide range of drinks and food, including fresh roast dinners. Complimentary WiFi is provided and there is also on-site parking.

Rooms 32 en suite (12 fmly) (8 GF) **Facilities** FTV tea/coffee Dinner available WiFi **Parking** 70 **Notes** ⊗

NORTH YORKSHIRE

ALLERSTON
Map 19 SE88

Rains Farm Holidays *(SE879808)*
★★★★ FARMHOUSE

tel: 01723 859333 **YO18 7PQ**
email: rainsholidays@btconnect.com **web:** www.rains-farm-holidays.co.uk
dir: 1.5m S of A170 Pickering to Scarborough road, through village, 1m on right between Allerston & Yedingham

A warm welcome awaits you at Rains Farm Holidays situated a short drive from the popular town of Pickering. Bedrooms and bathrooms are comfortably appointed. A lounge area is available as well as a modern kitchen for guest use. Delicious hearty cooked breakfasts are served at a communal dining table. Gardens are an attractive feature with outdoor seating available in the summer months. Car parking is generous.

Rooms 3 en suite (1 GF) S £60-£90; D £90-£120* **Facilities** FTV TVL tea/coffee WiFi **Extras** Use of kitchen **Parking** 6 **Notes** LB ⊗ No Children 12yrs Closed Xmas & New Year 7 acres non-working

AMPLEFORTH
Map 19 SE57

Premier Collection

Shallowdale House
★★★★★ 🍴 ⚘ GUEST ACCOMMODATION

tel: 01439 788325 **West End YO62 4DY**
email: stay@shallowdalehouse.co.uk **web:** www.shallowdalehouse.co.uk
dir: Off A170 at W end of village, on turn to Hambleton

An outstanding example of an architect-designed 1960s house, Shallowdale lies in two acres of hillside gardens. There are stunning views from every room, and the elegant public rooms include a choice of lounges. Spacious bedrooms blend traditional and 1960s style with many home comforts. Expect excellent service and genuine hospitality from Anton and Phillip. The very imaginative, freshly cooked dinners are not to be missed.

Rooms 3 rms (2 en suite) (1 pri facs) S £100-£115; D £120-£145* **Facilities** FTV Lounge tea/coffee Dinner available Licensed WiFi 🛝 **Extras** Speciality toiletries - complimentary **Parking** 3 **Notes** ⊗ No Children 12yrs Closed Xmas & New Year

ARKENGARTHDALE
Map 18 NY90

Charles Bathurst Inn
★★★★ ⊛ 🍴 INN

tel: 01748 884567 **DL11 6EN**
email: info@cbinn.co.uk **web:** www.cbinn.co.uk
dir: B6270 to Reeth, at Buck Hotel turn N to Langthwaite, pass church on right, inn 0.5m on right

The CB Inn, as it is known to locals, is surrounded by magnificent scenery high in the Dales. Food is the focus of the pub, where a choice of rustic eating areas makes for atmospheric dining. The well-equipped bedrooms blend contemporary and traditional styles, and cosy lounge areas are available. A function suite is also available.

Rooms 19 en suite (3 fmly) (5 GF) **Facilities** Lounge tea/coffee Dinner available Direct Dial WiFi Fishing Riding Pool table 🛝 **Extras** Speciality toiletries, home-made shortbread **Conf** Max 70 Thtr 70 Class 30 Board 30 **Parking** 35 **Notes** LB Closed 25 Dec Civ Wed 70

ASENBY
Map 19 SE37

Premier Collection

Crab Manor
★★★★★ ⊛⊛ RESTAURANT WITH ROOMS

tel: 01845 577286 **Dishforth Rd YO7 3QL**
web: www.crabandlobster.co.uk
dir: A1(M) junct 49, on outskirts of village

This stunning, 18th-century Grade II listed Georgian manor is located in the heart of the North Yorkshire Dales. Each bedroom is themed around the world's most famous hotels and has high-quality furnishings, beautiful wallpaper, and thoughtful extras. Scandinavian log cabins are also available in the grounds, which have their own terrace with hot tubs. There is a comfortable lounge bar where guests can relax in the Manor before enjoying dinner next door in the Crab & Lobster Restaurant, which specialises in fresh local seafood. The attractive gardens offer a lovely backdrop.

Rooms 8 en suite 9 annexe en suite (3 fmly) D £165-£265* **Facilities** FTV iPod docking station Lounge tea/coffee Dinner available Direct Dial WiFi Sauna 🛝 **Conf** Max 16 Board 16 **Parking** 90 **Notes** ⊗ No coaches Civ Wed 105

AUSTWICK — Map 18 SD76

Premier Collection

The Traddock

★★★★★ ◉◉ 🍴 RESTAURANT WITH ROOMS

tel: 015242 51224 **Settle LA2 8BY**
email: info@thetraddock.co.uk **web:** www.thetraddock.co.uk
dir: *From Skipton take A65 towards Kendal, 3m after Settle turn right signed Austwick, cross hump back bridge, 100yds on left*

Situated within the Yorkshire Dales National Park and a peaceful village environment, this fine Georgian country house with well-tended gardens offers a haven of calm and good hospitality. There are two comfortable lounges with real fires and fine furnishings, as well as a cosy bar and an elegant dining room serving fine cuisine. Bedrooms are individually styled with many homely touches.

Rooms 12 en suite (2 fmly) (1 GF) D £95-£250* **Facilities** FTV DVD Lounge tea/coffee Dinner available Direct Dial WiFi ch fac ⏚ ⚓ 18 🐾 **Extras** Speciality toiletries, fruit, bottled water - free **Conf** Max 24 Thtr 24 Class 16 Board 16 **Parking** 20 **Notes** LB No coaches

AYSGARTH — Map 19 SE08

The Aysgarth Falls

★★★★★ ◉ INN

tel: 01969 663775 **DL8 3SR**
email: info@aysgarthfallshotel.com **web:** www.aysgarthfallshotel.com
dir: *On A684 between Leyburn & Hawes*

A friendly, high-quality inn, perfect for exploring the Yorkshire Dales, and the grounds lead down to Aysgarth Falls. Excellent meals are served throughout the bar and dining areas, and also on the outdoor terraces in warmer weather. Bedrooms are contemporary, featuring comfortable beds, flat-screen TVs and luxurious en suites. Residents also have use of a drying room for waterproofs and boots.

Rooms 11 en suite 2 annexe en suite (2 fmly) (2 GF) **Facilities** FTV DVD tea/coffee Dinner available WiFi 🐾 **Parking** 30 **Notes** No coaches

BAINBRIDGE — Map 18 SD99

Premier Collection

Yorebridge House

★★★★★ ◉◉◉ 🍴 RESTAURANT WITH ROOMS

tel: 01969 652060 **DL8 3EE**
email: enquiries@yorebridgehouse.co.uk **web:** www.yorebridgehouse.co.uk
dir: *A648 to Bainbridge. Yorebridge House N of centre on right before river*

Yorebridge House is situated by the river on the edge of Bainbridge, in the heart of the North Yorkshire Dales. In the Victorian era this was a schoolmaster's house and school, the building now offers luxury boutique-style accommodation. Each bedroom is individually designed with high-quality furnishings and thoughtful extras. All rooms have stunning views of the Dales and some have their own terrace with hot tub. There is a comfortable lounge bar where guests can relax before enjoying an excellent, three AA Rosette award-winning dinner in the attractive and elegant dining room.

Rooms 7 en suite 4 annexe en suite (11 fmly) (5 GF) **Facilities** STV FTV DVD iPod docking station Lounge tea/coffee Dinner available Direct Dial WiFi 🐾 Fishing **Extras** Speciality toiletries **Conf** Max 70 Thtr 70 Class 60 Board 30 **Parking** 30 **Notes** No coaches Civ Wed 100

BIRSTWITH — Map 19 SE25

The Station Hotel

★★★★ ⚑ INN

tel: 01423 770254 **Station Rd HG3 3AG**
email: admin@station-hotel.net **web:** www.station-hotel.net
dir: *A59 Harrogate to Skipton road, turn into Chain Bar Ln, signed Hampsthwaite. At T-junct left into Hollins Ln, in 1m at next T-junct right into Hampsthwaite High St. 1.6m to Birstwith, right into Wreaks Rd. 0.5m on left*

The Station Hotel is a family-owned country inn in the village of Birstwith, on the edge of Nidderdale, which means stunning scenery and great walks right on the doorstep. The restaurant serves food daily and vegetarians are well catered for. There are four bedrooms on the first floor of the main pub building and there is also a ground floor room in a separate annexe. All rooms are furnished with traditional oak furniture and comfortable beds. There are also useful facilities such as tea- and coffee-making facilities, alarm clocks, free internet access and flat-screen Freesat TVs. On-site parking and a hearty Yorkshire breakfast are included in the price.

Rooms 4 en suite 1 annexe en suite (1 fmly) (1 GF) S £80; D £100-£120* **Facilities** STV FTV iPod docking station tea/coffee Dinner available WiFi 🐾 **Parking** 25

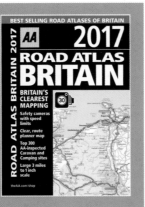

To help you navigate safely and easily, use the AA Road Atlas Britain 2017. Available from: shop.theAA.com

BEST SELLING ROAD ATLASES OF BRITAIN
AA 2017
ROAD ATLAS BRITAIN
BRITAIN'S CLEAREST MAPPING
Safety cameras with speed limits
Clear, route planner map
Top 300 AA-inspected Caravan and Camping sites
Large 3 miles to 1 inch scale
theAA.com/shop

BOLTON ABBEY   Map 19 SE05

Howgill Lodge

★★★★ GUEST ACCOMMODATION

tel: 01756 720655 **Barden BD23 6DJ**
email: info@howgill-lodge.co.uk **web:** www.howgill-lodge.co.uk
dir: B6160 from Bolton Abbey signed Burnsall, 3m right at Barden Tower signed
Appletreewick, Howgill Lodge 1.25m on right at phone box

In an idyllic position high above the valley, this converted stone granary provides a
quality get-away. The stylish bedrooms provide a host of thoughtful touches and are
designed to feature original stone walls, flagstone floors and timber beams. All of
the rooms boast spectacular, memorable views. Breakfasts make excellent use of
fresh local ingredients.

Rooms 4 en suite (1 fmly) (4 GF) S £65-£82; D £82* **Facilities** FTV tea/coffee
Extras Fridge **Parking** 6 **Notes** LB ⊗ Closed 24-26 Dec

BOROUGHBRIDGE   Map 19 SE36

The Crown Inn

★★★★ ⓐⓐ ⓨ RESTAURANT WITH ROOMS

tel: 01423 322300 **Roecliffe YO51 9LY**
email: info@crowninnroecliffe.co.uk **web:** www.crowninnroecliffe.co.uk
dir: A1(M) junct 48, follow signs for Boroughbridge. At rdbt exit towards Roecliffe & brown
tourist signs

The Crown is a 16th-century coaching inn providing an excellent combination of
traditional charm and modern comforts. Service is friendly and professional and
food is a highlight of any stay. The kitchen team use the finest of Yorkshire produce
from the best local suppliers to create a weekly-changing seasonal menu.
Bedrooms are attractively furnished with stylish en suite bathrooms.

Rooms 4 en suite (1 fmly) S £80-£90; D £90-£120 **Facilities** FTV DVD tea/coffee
Dinner available WiFi ch fac ⓐ **Extras** Sherry, espresso coffee machine, chocolate
Conf Max 100 Thtr 100 Class 60 Board 30 **Parking** 40 **Notes** No coaches Civ Wed 120

BURNSALL   Map 19 SE06

The Devonshire Fell

★★★★ ⓐ RESTAURANT WITH ROOMS

tel: 01756 729000 & 718111 **BD23 6BT**
email: manager@devonshirefell.co.uk **web:** www.devonshirefell.co.uk
dir: On B6160, 6m from Bolton Abbey rdbt, A59 junct

Located on the edge of the attractive village of Burnsall, The Devonshire Fell is
colourful, contemporary and quirky. Originally a gentleman's club it enjoys what
may be one of the finest locations in the country. Overlooking the village of Burnsall
in the heart of the Dales, the views are quite wonderful. A brasserie-style menu is
served in the light and airy conservatory restaurant, with views of the Fells and
Dales on the outside and original modern art work within. Intimate and friendly, The
Devonshire Fell is a superb choice for those looking to escape from it all. Expect
quality surroundings, home comforts and a friendly, warm welcome.

Rooms 16 en suite (2 fmly) **Facilities** STV FTV DVD tea/coffee Dinner available Direct
Dial WiFi ⓐ Fishing ⓐ Free use of spa facilities at sister hotel **Conf** Max 50 Thtr 50
Class 30 Board 24 **Parking** 40 **Notes** Civ Wed 80

CLAPHAM   Map 18 SD76

Premier Collection

The New Inn

★★★★★ ⓨ ⓤ INN

tel: 015242 51203 **The Green LA2 8HH**
email: info@newinn-clapham.co.uk **web:** www.newinn-clapham.co.uk
dir: From Skipton take A65 towards Kendal. Follow Clapham signs

The New Inn has been in operation since 1745 and is ideally located in the heart
of the conservation village of Clapham, beside Clapham Beck in the Yorkshire
Dales National Park. The whole property has been refurbished to a very high
standard that is sympathetic to the character of the building and to the
environment. Fully en suite, bedrooms cater well for visitors to this lovely and
peaceful village. There is a small but comfortable lounge on the first floor and
the bars are full of charm and character enhanced with a log-burning stove. The
restaurant and menus show imagination and flair, and an extensive and hearty
breakfast is served. AA Friendliest B&B of the Year Award Finalist 2016-2017.

Rooms 15 en suite 5 annexe en suite (3 fmly) (2 GF) S £95-£115; D £110-£145*
Facilities FTV DVD Lounge TVL TV19B tea/coffee Dinner available WiFi ⓐ 18 ⓐ
Seasonal game shooting **Extras** Speciality toiletries, bottled water **Conf** Max 30
Thtr 30 Class 25 Board 25 **Parking** 40 **Notes** LB

Brookhouse Guest House

★★★★ ⓤ GUEST HOUSE

tel: 015242 51580 **Station Rd LA2 8ER**
email: admin@brookhouseclapham.co.uk **web:** www.brookhouse-clapham.co.uk
dir: Off A65 into village

Beside the river, in the pretty conservation village of Clapham, this personally run
guest house provides comfortable accommodation and warm hospitality.
Brookhouse also provides an evening bistro, popular with locals, which offers an
interesting selection of home-made meals. Secure storage for cycles is also
available.

Rooms 3 rms (2 en suite) (1 pri facs) (1 fmly) **Facilities** FTV tea/coffee Dinner
available Licensed WiFi ⓐ ⓐ 18 **Notes** ⊗ ⓐ

CONEYSTHORPE   Map 19 SE77

Lime Kiln House

★★★★★ ⓐ BED AND BREAKFAST

tel: 01653 648213 **YO60 7DD**
email: gillianharris_slt@yahoo.co.uk **web:** www.limekiln-coneysthorpe.com
dir: From York on A64, turn left at sign for Castle Howard. 0.5m after Castle Howard
entrance, turn right then 1st left

With tasteful and spacious rooms, Lime Kiln House is a sympathetically modernised
traditional Yorkshire stone property. Breakfast produce is locally sourced and served
in the guest sitting room, which boasts features such as an open fireplace, an
antique leather rocking chair and views across the village green to Castle Howard.
Coneysthorpe is convenient for A64, the charming market town of Malton, York and
the Yorkshire coast. This is an ideal area for foodies and nature lovers.

Rooms 2 en suite (1 fmly) S £75; D £90-£100* **Facilities** FTV DVD TVL tea/coffee
WiFi ⓐ **Extras** Speciality toiletries, home-made biscuits - free **Parking** 4 **Notes** LB

CRAYKE
Map 19 SE57

Premier Collection

The Durham Ox
★★★★★ △ RESTAURANT WITH ROOMS

tel: 01347 821506 **Westway YO61 4TE**
email: enquiries@thedurhamox.com **web:** www.thedurhamox.com
dir: *A19 to Easingwold. Through market place to Crayke, 1st left up hill*

The Durham Ox is some 300 years old. The owners pride themselves on offering a friendly and efficient service, plus traditional pub food using only the best local ingredients. The pub has breathtaking views over the Vale of York on three sides, and a charming view up the hill to the medieval church on the other. Accommodation is mainly in four converted farm cottages. Crayke is in the heart of 'Herriot Country' and less than 20 minutes from York city centre.

Rooms 1 en suite 5 annexe en suite (1 fmly) (3 GF) S £80-£120; D £90-£150*
Facilities FTV DVD iPod docking station tea/coffee Dinner available WiFi ⌔ 18 🔒 Shooting, fishing, riding by arrangement **Extras** Speciality toiletries, honesty bar **Conf** Max 80 Thtr 80 Class 60 Board 30 **Parking** 35 **Notes** LB

DANBY
Map 19 NZ70

Church House Farm *(SE707088)*
★★★★ FARMHOUSE

tel: 01287 669303 & 07866 743331 **Danby Head YO21 2NH**
email: andrewdmorris@yahoo.co.uk **web:** www.churchhousefarmyorkshire.co.uk

Church House Farm is set in the beautiful Danby Dale on a working farm. The en suite accommodation is comfortable and homely with modern accessories such as flat-screen TVs and complimentary WiFi. Freshly cooked breakfasts are served in the spacious ground floor dining room at a communal dining table, which makes for a truly engaging breakfast experience.

Rooms 2 en suite S £52.50-£60; D £70-£80* **Facilities** FTV DVD TVL tea/coffee WiFi 🔒 **Extras** Fruit **Parking** 2 **Notes** LB ⊗ No Children 85 acres mixed

EASINGWOLD
Map 19 SE56

George at Easingwold
★★★★ ⇔ INN

tel: 01347 821698 **Market Place YO61 3AD**
email: info@the-george-hotel.co.uk **web:** www.the-george-hotel.co.uk
dir: *From A19 follow signs for Easingwold. Into Market Place, on right*

The George has a prominent position in the centre of the village and is only a 30 minute ride into York. The inn is very well managed and run by the owners Kay and Michael. Accommodation is comfortable, with modern en suite bathrooms, and public areas are quite spacious. Food is a must here; local produce, good sized portions and all freshly cooked. Hand-pulled beers and a good choice of wines are also available. There is some limited parking.

Rooms 15 en suite (2 fmly) (6 GF) S £75-£100; D £85-£120* **Facilities** FTV DVD Lounge tea/coffee Dinner available Direct Dial WiFi 🔒 Complimentary use of adjacent gymnasium **Parking** 8 **Notes** LB ⊗ Closed 24-25 Dec

ELLERBY
Map 19 NZ71

Ellerby Residential Country Inn
★★★★ INN

tel: 01947 840342 **12-14 Ryeland Ln TS13 5LP**
email: relax@ellerbyhotel.co.uk **web:** www.ellerbyhotel.co.uk
dir: *From A171 onto B1266, follow signs for Ellerby. Or from A174 (Whitby) follow signs for Ellerby*

This friendly, family-run inn is in a quiet country setting just eight miles from Whitby and a short drive from the North York Moors National Park. There is a traditional bar with open fire and real ales as well as a spacious restaurant. There is also a beautiful secluded garden and a residents' conservatory lounge. A range of bedrooms is available including ground-floor rooms, family rooms and a disabled accessible room. Complimentary WiFi is also provided and there is secure bicycle storage.

Rooms 10 en suite (4 fmly) (4 GF) S £65-£100; D £95-£130* **Facilities** STV FTV Lounge tea/coffee Dinner available Direct Dial WiFi 🔒 **Extras** Fresh milk, fridge, robes **Parking** 30 **Notes** LB

FILEY
Map 17 TA18

Premier Collection

All Seasons Guesthouse
★★★★★ 🛏 GUEST HOUSE

tel: 01723 515321 & 07870 267945 **11 Rutland St YO14 9JA**
email: lesley@allseasonsfiley.co.uk **web:** www.allseasonsfiley.co.uk
dir: *From A165 at rdbt follow signs for Filey. Continue to town centre, right into West Ave, 2nd left into Rutland St*

This immaculately presented, contemporary guest house is a short stroll from the seafront and is also close to the Crescent Gardens and town centre. There is a friendly, welcoming atmosphere and a lovely lounge for guests to relax in. Bedrooms and bathrooms are stylish and very comfortable. They include a luxury suite, a king-size room, family and twin rooms. Breakfast is a highlight of any stay with all produce either locally sourced or home-made. Complimentary WiFi is also provided.

Rooms 6 en suite (2 fmly) **Facilities** FTV DVD TVL tea/coffee WiFi 🛏⌔ 19 🔒 **Extras** Dressing gowns, slippers - complimentary **Notes** LB ⊗ No Children 10yrs

FLIXTON
Map 17 TA07

Orchard Lodge

★★★★ 🛏 GUEST ACCOMMODATION

tel: 01723 890202 & 07789 228682 **North St YO11 3UA**
email: orchardlodgescarborough@gmail.com **web:** www.orchard-lodge.com
dir: Off A1039 in village centre

A warm welcome is guaranteed at this owner-run property situated in the small village of Flixton near the popular seaside resort of Scarborough. Bedrooms are comfortably appointed with modern accessories such as complimentary WiFi. Award-winning breakfasts are served in the spacious dining room which is also open as a tearoom throughout the afternoon. A focus on local and home-made produce means eggs are sourced from the resident hens and the fruit used for jams and juices is picked from the on-site orchard. Free parking is also available.

Rooms 6 en suite (1 fmly) S £70; D £80* **Facilities** FTV TVL tea/coffee WiFi 🔔 **Extras** Fridge **Conf** Max 12 **Parking** 6 **Notes** LB No Children 12yrs

FYLINGTHORPE
Map 19 NZ90

Flask Inn

★★★★ 🍺 INN

tel: 01947 880305 & 880592 **YO22 4QH**
email: info@flaskinn.com **web:** www.theflaskinn.co.uk
dir: On A171 from Whitby, on left

This traditional inn offers spacious bar and dining areas along with smart, contemporary bedrooms. The rooms are very well equipped and feature modern en suites. There is a friendly atmosphere and food is a highlight of any stay with a high standard of cooking and a wide choice on the appealing menus. The inn has a very convenient location, close to the main road offering a scenic drive between Whitby and Scarborough and set in the beautiful North Yorkshire countryside.

Rooms 9 en suite (2 fmly) (3 GF) S fr £70; D fr £80* **Facilities** FTV tea/coffee Dinner available WiFi Pool table 🔔 **Extras** Bottled water **Parking** 25 **Notes** LB Closed 2 Jan-7 Feb No coaches

GILLING EAST
Map 19 SE67

The Fairfax Arms

★★★★ 🍴 INN

tel: 01439 788212 & 788819 **Main St YO62 4JH**
email: info@thefairfaxarms.co.uk **web:** www.thefairfaxarms.co.uk
dir: From A170 turn right onto B1257, right again onto B1363 to Gilling East, pub on right

This independently owned inn is situated in the quiet village of Gilling East within easy driving distance of Helmsley. A perfect balance between the appeal of up-to-date facilities and original features such as wooden beams and open fires has been struck by the owners. Bedrooms are well appointed with comfortable beds guaranteed to provide a good night's sleep; a range of thoughtful accessories are provided such as iPod docking stations, flat-screen TVs and luxurious toiletries. PlayStation consoles are also available on request. Award-winning dinners that focus on excellent quality local produce can be enjoyed both in the bar and restaurant areas. On-site parking is available.

Rooms 8 en suite 4 annexe en suite (2 fmly) (3 GF) S £75-£130; D £100-£170* **Facilities** FTV DVD iPod docking station Dinner available Direct Dial WiFi ⚓ 10 🔔 **Extras** Speciality toiletries **Parking** 14 **Notes** LB

GOLDSBOROUGH
Map 19 SE35

Premier Collection

Goldsborough Hall

★★★★★ ◎ 🛏 GUEST ACCOMMODATION

tel: 01423 867321 **Church St HG5 8NR**
email: info@goldsboroughhall.com **web:** www.goldsboroughhall.com
dir: A1(M) junct 47, A59 to Knaresborough. 2nd left into Station Rd, at T-junct left into Church St

It's not every day that you get the chance to stay in the former residence of a Royal Princess, in this case HRH Princess Mary (1897-1965), who was one of the Queen's aunts. Hospitality at Goldsborough Hall is second to none. The luxury bedrooms are appointed to the highest standards, and the bathrooms have a real 'wow' factor. Some of the main house bedrooms feature hand-made mahogany four-poster beds, chesterfields and 60" TVs. The popular seasonal afternoon tea is served either in front of the roaring fire in the Jacobean Library or in the Dining Room. Reservations for dinner from non-residents are welcomed.

Rooms 6 en suite 6 annexe en suite (4 fmly) S £125-£515; D £125-£515* **Facilities** FTV DVD iPod docking station Lounge tea/coffee Dinner available Direct Dial Lift Licensed WiFi 👶 ⚓ 18 🔔 Outdoor hot tub **Extras** Speciality toiletries; mini-bar - chargeable **Conf** Max 150 Thtr 150 Class 50 Board 30 **Parking** 50 **Notes** LB ⊗ Closed 24-26 Dec Civ Wed 150

GRASSINGTON
Map 19 SE06

Premier Collection

Grassington House

★★★★★ ◎◎ 🛏 RESTAURANT WITH ROOMS

tel: 01756 752406 **5 The Square BD23 5AQ**
email: bookings@grassingtonhouse.co.uk **web:** www.grassingtonhouse.co.uk
dir: A59 into Grassington, in town square opposite post office

Located in the square of the popular village of Grassington, this beautifully converted Georgian house is personally run by owners John and Sue. Delicious food, individually designed bedrooms and warm hospitality ensure an enjoyable stay. There is a stylish lounge bar looking out to the square and the restaurant is split between two rooms; here guests will find the emphasis is on fresh, local ingredients and attentive, friendly service.

Rooms 9 en suite (2 fmly) S £105; D £120-£140* **Facilities** STV FTV tea/coffee Dinner available Direct Dial WiFi 🔔 **Conf** Thtr 26 Class 20 Board 20 **Parking** 25 **Notes** LB ⊗ Civ Wed 44

GRASSINGTON *continued*

Premier Collection

Ashfield House

★★★★★ GUEST ACCOMMODATION

tel: 01756 752584 **Summers Fold BD23 5AE**
email: sales@ashfieldhouse.co.uk **web:** www.ashfieldhouse.co.uk
dir: *B6265 to village centre, from main street left into Summers Fold*

Guests are greeted like old friends at this beautifully maintained 17th-century house, peacefully tucked away a few yards from the village square. The smart lounges offer a high level of comfort and an honesty bar. The attractive bedrooms are well furnished and thoughtfully equipped.

Rooms 7 rms (6 en suite) (1 pri facs) 1 annexe en suite S £65-£90; D £88-£210* **Facilities** FTV Lounge tea/coffee Licensed WiFi **Extras** Home-baked cookies, speciality toiletries **Conf** Max 8 Board 8 **Parking** 8 **Notes** LB ⊗ No Children 5yrs

HARROGATE — Map 19 SE35

Premier Collection

The Grafton Boutique B&B

★★★★★ GUEST ACCOMMODATION

tel: 01423 508491 **1-3 Franklin Mount HG1 5EJ**
email: enquiries@graftonhotel.co.uk **web:** www.graftonhotel.co.uk
dir: *Follow signs to International Centre, into Kings Rd (with Centre on left), Franklin Mount 450yds on right*

The Grafton is a stylish townhouse, in a quiet location, just a short walk from the conference centre and town. It is a period property but with contemporary interior design throughout and a luxurious feel. There is a beautifully appointed lounge looking out to the garden, and breakfast is served in a spacious and striking dining room. Complimentary WiFi is provided.

Rooms 13 en suite (1 GF) D £100-£150 **Facilities** FTV Lounge tea/coffee Direct Dial Licensed WiFi ↕ 18 ♣ **Parking** 1 **Notes** LB ⊗ Closed 15 Dec-6 Jan

Shelbourne House

★★★★ GUEST ACCOMMODATION

tel: 01423 504390 **78 Kings Rd HG1 5JX**
email: sue@shelbournehouse.co.uk **web:** www.shelbournehouse.co.uk
dir: *Follow signs to International Centre, over lights by Holiday Inn, premises on right*

Situated opposite the conference centre and close to the town centre, this elegant Victorian house features attractive well-equipped bedrooms. There is a beautifully presented guest lounge and smart dining room. The friendly owners provide attentive service and offer a wide choice at breakfast, with emphasis on local ingredients. Complimentary WiFi access is provided.

Rooms 8 en suite (2 fmly) **Facilities** FTV DVD iPod docking station TVL tea/coffee WiFi **Conf** Board 16 **Parking** 1 **Notes** ⊗

Innkeeper's Lodge Harrogate (West)

★★★★ INN

tel: 08451 551551 *(Calls cost 2p per minute plus your phone company's access charge)* **Beckwith Knowle, Otley Rd HG3 1UE**
email: info@innkeeperslodge.com **web:** www.innkeeperslodge.com

Located close to town in Beckwith Knowle, this period property is ideal for exploring historic and vibrant Harrogate and the Yorkshire Dales National Park. The spacious public areas are stylish and full of character. Seasonally-changing menus feature traditional favourites as well as Mediterranean influences and the chef's daily specials. Bedrooms are modern, spacious and well furnished. Complimentary WiFi is provided.

Rooms 12 en suite (4 fmly) **Facilities** FTV tea/coffee Dinner available WiFi **Parking** 60 **Notes** ⊗

Harrogate Brasserie with Rooms

★★★★ GUEST ACCOMMODATION

tel: 01423 505041 **28-30 Cheltenham Pde HG1 1DB**
email: info@harrogatebrasserie.co.uk **web:** www.harrogatebrasserie.co.uk
dir: *On A61 town centre behind theatre*

This town centre establishment is distinctly continental in style. The brasserie covers three cosy dining areas, richly decorated and adorned with artefacts. Live jazz is featured every night except Saturdays. The individual bedrooms feature period collectibles; many rooms have DVD players and all have plentiful amounts of reading material.

Rooms 13 en suite 3 annexe en suite (3 fmly) (1 GF) **Facilities** FTV tea/coffee Dinner available Direct Dial Licensed WiFi ♣ **Parking** 12 **Notes** LB

HAWNBY — Map 19 SE58

The Inn at Hawnby

★★★★ INN

tel: 01439 798202 **YO62 5QS**
email: info@innathawnby.co.uk **web:** www.innathawnby.co.uk
dir: *Exit B1257 between Stokesley & Helmsley*

This charming 19th-century inn is located in a peaceful village. Service is attentive and friendly, with guests able to relax and browse menus in the cosy bar where there is a good wine list and range of ales. Delicious, home-cooked meals are served in the restaurant, overlooking the gardens and surrounding countryside. Bedrooms are well equipped, with some in the converted stables.

Rooms 6 en suite 3 annexe en suite (1 fmly) (3 GF) **Facilities** FTV DVD tea/coffee Dinner available Direct Dial WiFi Fishing Riding **Extras** Speciality toiletries, sherry - complimentary **Conf** Max 20 Thtr 12 Class 20 **Parking** 9 **Notes** Closed 25 Dec RS Feb & Mar Restricted lunch service Mon & Tue

HELMSLEY — Map 19 SE68

See also Hawnby

Premier Collection

Shallowdale House

★★★★★ GUEST ACCOMMODATION

tel: 01439 788325 **West End YO62 4DY**
email: stay@shallowdalehouse.co.uk **web:** www.shallowdalehouse.co.uk

(For full entry see Ampleforth)

Plumpton Court

★★★★ GUEST ACCOMMODATION

tel: 01439 771223 **High St, Nawton YO62 7TT**
email: mail@plumptoncourt.com **web:** www.plumptoncourt.com
dir: 2.5m E of Helmsley. Exit A170 in Nawton, signed

Situated in the small village of Nawton between Helmsley and Kirkbymoorside, Plumpton Court has six modern and individually decorated bedrooms. Guests can relax in front of a real fire in the homely lounge with a bottle of wine from the well-stocked bar and enjoy a leisurely breakfast with locally sourced ingredients. Chris is a convivial host and takes delight in helping guests make the most of their visit to North Yorkshire. To the rear of the house is a private, secure car park and a secluded garden.

Rooms 6 en suite (1 GF) S £60-£65; D £74-£84* **Facilities** FTV DVD Lounge tea/coffee Licensed WiFi ⛷ 18 ⚓ **Parking** 8 **Notes** ⊗ No Children 12yrs Closed 22-29 Dec & 4-31 Jan

The Feathers

★★★★ ⇔ INN

tel: 01439 770275 **Market Place YO62 5BH**
email: feathers@innmail.co.uk **web:** www.feathershotelhelmsley.co.uk
dir: A1(M) junct 49 onto A168 signed Thirsk. Bear left, then take 2nd exit at rdbt onto A170 to Helmsley. In Market Place

This fine old property enjoys a prominent position overlooking the busy town square in pretty Helmsley. The bar and lounge areas are full of character and real fires glow on the cooler evenings. There is an extensive dinner menu along with a nightly specials board, which uses the best in local, seasonal produce. Bedrooms have been decorated to a high standard and are most comfortable. Some secure parking is available for guests at the rear of the inn. The Feathers is an ideal base from which to explore the North York Moors National Park, and Helmsley is situated on the Cleveland Way walk.

Rooms 21 en suite 4 annexe en suite (2 fmly) (2 GF) S £59-£99; D £69-£129* **Facilities** FTV tea/coffee Dinner available WiFi ⛷ 18 ⚓ **Conf** Max 100 Thtr 100 Class 70 Board 40 **Parking** 15 **Notes** LB

HETTON
Map 18 SD95

Premier Collection

The Angel Inn

★★★★★ ⚜⚜ ⚑ RESTAURANT WITH ROOMS

tel: 01756 730263 **BD23 6LT**
email: info@angelhetton.co.uk **web:** www.angelhetton.co.uk
dir: B6265 from Skipton towards Grassington. At Rylstone turn left by pond, follow signs to Hetton

This roadside inn is steeped in history; parts of the building go back more than 500 years. The restaurant and bar are in the main building, which has ivy and green canopies at the front. Food is a highlight of any stay, offering excellent ingredients, skilfully prepared and carefully presented. The large, stylish bedrooms are across the road in a converted barn which has great views of the Dales, private parking and its own wine cave.

Rooms 9 en suite (3 GF) **Facilities** FTV tea/coffee Dinner available Direct Dial WiFi ⚓ Wine tasting cave **Conf** Max 16 Board 14 **Parking** 40 **Notes** Closed 25 Dec & 1wk Jan No coaches Civ Wed 40

HUNTON
Map 19 SE19

The Countryman's Inn

★★★ ⇔ INN

tel: 01677 450554 & 07734 556845 **South View DL8 1PY**
email: tony@countrymansinn.co.uk **web:** www.countrymansinn.co.uk
dir: Exit A1(M) at Leeming Bar onto A684 towards Bedale/Leyburn. Through Patrick Brompton, right at x-rds. After 1.25m turn left signed Hunton

This traditional country pub offers a friendly atmosphere, cask ales and great food. The bar features a real fire and beamed ceiling and there is a beer garden for warmer weather. A wide choice of freshly prepared meals are served and there is a smartly presented dining room. Bedrooms and bathrooms are more contemporary with a fresh, bright style with good provision made for families and a designated 'pet friendly' room. Other facilities include complimentary WiFi and private parking.

Rooms 4 en suite (2 fmly) S £55-£70; D £60-£110* **Facilities** FTV DVD iPod docking station TVL tea/coffee Dinner available WiFi ⛷ Riding ⚓ **Extras** Still & sparkling water **Parking** 8 **Notes** LB

KETTLEWELL
Map 18 SD97

Belk's Bed & Breakfast

★★★ ⚑ BED AND BREAKFAST

tel: 01756 761188 & 07979 149019 **Middle Ln BD23 5QX**
email: davidbelk23@gmail.com **web:** www.zarinaskettlewell.co.uk
dir: Into Kettlewell on B6160, turn opposite Racehorses Hotel, 200mtrs on right

Belk's Bed & Breakfast is located in the picturesque village of Kettlewell, and is popular with cyclists and walkers. The house provides guests with a warm and friendly welcome. Bedrooms are comfortable and well equipped with many thoughtful extras. Memorable breakfasts served in the pleasantly appointed tea room feature eggs from the Belk's own chickens, as well as home-made preserves. Outside garden seating area is available in warmer weather.

Rooms 3 en suite S £49; D £79-£89* **Facilities** FTV DVD tea/coffee Licensed WiFi ⚓ **Extras** Mini-bar **Parking** 2 **Notes** LB ⊗ No Children 18yrs Closed Jan-Feb

KEXBY
Map 17 SE65

Premier Collection

Kexby House

★★★★★ ⓘ GUEST ACCOMMODATION

tel: 01759 380254 **Kexby YO41 5LE**
email: info@bradfordowen.com **web:** www.kexbyhouse.co.uk
dir: On A1079, E of York

This beautifully presented 18th-century farmhouse is just a few miles outside of York, yet enjoys an idyllic setting in 13 acres of grounds, with 400 yards of private fishing. The marble-floored hall leads to an impressive and elegant dining room and the three bedrooms in the main house are individually furnished with bathrooms featuring cast iron roll top baths. The Cottage Room is located within the grounds and gives guests the added benefits of a kitchenette, living room and private patio. Delicious breakfasts feature free-range eggs from the owners' own hens.

Rooms 3 en suite 1 annexe en suite (1 fmly) (1 GF) **Facilities** DVD tea/coffee WiFi Fishing **Parking** 8 **Notes** ⊗ No Children 11yrs Closed 30 Nov-15 Jan

KIRKBY FLEETHAM
Map 19 SE29

Premier Collection

Black Horse Inn

★★★★★ ⓘ INN

tel: 01609 749010 & 749011 **7 Lumley Ln DL7 0SH**
email: reservations@blackhorseinnkirkbyfleetham.com
web: www.blackhorseinnkirkbyfleetham.com
dir: A1 onto A648 towards Northallerton. Left into Ham Hall Ln, through Scruton. At T-junct left into Fleetham Ln. Through Great Fencote to Kirkby Fleetham, into Lumley Ln, inn on left past post office

The Black Horse Inn is set in the heart of Kirkby Fleetham, in North Yorkshire countryside. It offers free parking, free WiFi in public areas, a bar, a garden and a restaurant. Each of the seven bedrooms have been decorated in neutral colours and boast antique furniture, breakfast hamper, flat-screen TV and mini refrigerator with fresh orange juice, milk and water. The en suite bathrooms feature bath and/or power shower with complimentary toiletries. Some bedrooms benefit from an in-room roll-top bath. Guests can relax in the bar or in the garden, and the restaurant serves traditional British dishes, all prepared using local produce. The Black Horse Inn is just ten minutes' drive from Catterick Racecourse and 40 from Yorkshire Dales National Park.

Rooms 7 en suite (1 fmly) (2 GF) D £59-£239* **Facilities** FTV tea/coffee Dinner available WiFi ⅃ 18 Fishing Quoits pitch **Extras** Fridge, fresh milk, orange juice - free **Conf** Max 40 Thtr 40 Class 30 Board 24 **Parking** 90 **Notes** LB

Find out more about this county with *The AA Guide to Yorkshire* – see shop.theAA.com

KIRKBY MALZEARD
Map 19 SE27

The Moorhouse

★★★★ ⓘ BED AND BREAKFAST

tel: 01765 658371 **HG4 3RH**
email: enquiries@moorhousebnb.co.uk **web:** www.moorhousebnb.co.uk
dir: From Ripon on B6265 to Pateley Bridge, turn right to Grantley. Left after pub to T-junct, turn right. On left after 1.5m

A warm welcome is guaranteed along with afternoon tea, served by the open fire in the guest lounge, on colder days. This friendly B&B is situated in the countryside, with popular destinations such as Ripon and Harrogate easily reachable by car. Bedrooms are well appointed and comfortable. Thoughtful extras such as bathrobes, luxurious toiletries and well-stocked hospitality trays are provided. Hearty Yorkshire breakfasts are served in the dining room alongside more healthy options such as fresh fruit smoothies. Plenty of parking is provided.

Rooms 5 en suite (2 GF) S £55-£60; D £80-£90* **Facilities** FTV TVL tea/coffee Licensed WiFi **Parking** 5 **Notes** ⊗ No Children 12yrs Closed Aug-Mar

KNARESBOROUGH
Map 19 SE35

Premier Collection

General Tarleton Inn

★★★★★ ⓘⓘ RESTAURANT WITH ROOMS

tel: 01423 340284 **Boroughbridge Rd, Ferrensby HG5 0PZ**
email: gti@generaltarleton.co.uk **web:** www.generaltarleton.co.uk
dir: A1(M) junct 48 at Boroughbridge, take A6055 to Knaresborough. 4m on right

This 18th-century coaching inn is both beautiful and stylish. Though the physical aspects are impressive, the emphasis here is on food with high-quality, skilfully prepared dishes served in the smart bar-brasserie and in the Orangery. There is also a richly furnished cocktail lounge with a galleried private dining room above it. Bedrooms are very comfortable and business guests are also well catered for.

Rooms 13 en suite (7 GF) S £75-£95; D £129-£150* **Facilities** FTV Lounge tea/coffee Dinner available Direct Dial WiFi 🔒 **Extras** Speciality toiletries, home-made biscuits **Conf** Max 40 Thtr 40 Class 35 Board 20 **Parking** 40 **Notes** LB ⊗ Closed 24-26 Dec, 1 Jan No coaches

Newton House

★★★★ ⓘ GUEST ACCOMMODATION

tel: 01423 863539 **5-7 York Place HG5 0AD**
email: info@newtonhouseyorkshire.com **web:** www.newtonhouseyorkshire.com
dir: A1(M) junct 47 onto A59 towards Knaresborough. Right at 1st rdbt, continue to town centre, on right before lights, entrance through archway

This elegant Georgian guest accommodation is only a short walk from the river, castle and market square; the property is entered by an archway into the courtyard. Attractive, very well-equipped bedrooms include some four-poster beds and also king-sized double rooms. There is a comfortable lounge with honesty bar and memorable breakfasts are served in the attractive dining rooms.

Rooms 9 rms (8 en suite) (1 pri facs) 3 annexe en suite (2 fmly) (4 GF) S £55-£60; D £95-£125* **Facilities** FTV DVD Lounge tea/coffee Licensed WiFi ⅃ 18 🔒 Special arrangement for guests to use nearby spa **Extras** Speciality toiletries, mini-bar in most rooms **Conf** Max 20 Thtr 20 Board 12 **Parking** 9 **Notes** LB

Innkeeper's Lodge Harrogate (East)

★★★ INN

tel: 08451 551551 *(Calls cost 2p per minute plus your phone company's access charge)* **Wetherby Rd, Plompton HG5 8LY**
email: info@innkeeperslodge.com **web:** www.innkeeperslodge.com

This country pub and lodge is convenient for Harrogate, with its tourist attractions, shops and tearooms as well as the Conference Centre. It is also well located for visiting picturesque Knaresborough, Ripon and the Yorkshire Dales. Hearty, seasonal food and cask ales are noteworthy, along with real fires and a range of areas in which to relax. There is a lovely beer garden when the weather's warmer. Bedrooms are comfortable. Complimentary WiFi and on-site parking are also provided.

Rooms 10 en suite (2 fmly) **Facilities** FTV tea/coffee Dinner available Direct Dial WiFi **Parking Notes** ⊗

LEEMING BAR　　　　　　　　　　　**Map 19 SE28**

Premier Collection

Little Holtby

★★★★★ ⬚ BED AND BREAKFAST

tel: 01609 748762 **DL7 9LH**
email: littleholtby@yahoo.co.uk **web:** www.littleholtby.co.uk
dir: *0.5m N of A684 (junct with A1)*

Little Holtby is a charming farmhouse on land which used to form part of an estate that is mentioned in the Domesday Book, although the current house dates back to the late 17th century. Ideally located close to the A1 and convenient for Leeming Bar and Bedale, this is a great location for touring this part of North Yorkshire. A warm welcome awaits along with cakes and a drink. Bedrooms are generous in size with all necessary facilities including a well-stocked hospitality tray. The gardens and surrounding countryside add to the experience as do the open log fires which keep away the chill of outside. An award-winning breakfast will be sure to get your day off to the right start.

Rooms 3 en suite S £50; D £85-£90* **Facilities** FTV DVD TVL tea/coffee WiFi ⌁ 18 🔒 **Extras** Speciality toiletries, fruit, snacks - free **Parking** 7 **Notes** LB ⊗ No Children 12yrs ✉

LEVISHAM　　　　　　　　　　　　**Map 19 SE89**

Premier Collection

Moorlands Country House

★★★★★ ⬚ ⬚ GUEST HOUSE

tel: 01751 460229 & 07733 980392 **YO18 7NL**
email: info@moorlandslevisham.co.uk **web:** www.moorlandslevisham.co.uk
dir: *A169 from Pickering or Whitby, take turn signed Lockton/Levisham. Through Lockton to Levisham*

An elegant and luxuriously appointed house located in the peaceful village of Levisham in the heart of the North York Moors National Park. The gardens are beautiful and the view over the valleys beyond is stunning. The lounge, dining room and bedrooms are richly furnished and there is a wealth of personal touches and thoughtful accessories. Food is also a highlight, with delicious evening meals and impressive breakfasts offered.

Rooms 4 en suite **Facilities** FTV DVD iPod docking station Lounge tea/coffee Dinner available Licensed WiFi ⌁ 18 Riding 🔒 **Extras** Snacks **Parking** 9 **Notes** ⊗ No Children Closed Nov-May

---

The Horseshoe Inn

★★★★ ⬚ INN

tel: 01751 460240 **Main St YO18 7NL**
email: info@horseshoelevisham.co.uk **web:** www.horseshoelevisham.co.uk
dir: *From Pickering on A169, after 4m past Fox & Rabbit Inn on right. 0.5m left to Lockton, then steep winding road to village*

The Horseshoe Inn is a charming 19th-century inn with a peaceful location in Levisham village. The spacious bar and dining area are traditionally furnished and food is a highlight with a wide choice and generous portions. The attractive bedrooms include seven garden rooms, and most rooms in the main house have lovely views of the village.

Rooms 13 rms (11 en suite) (7 GF) S £40-£50; D £80-£120* **Facilities** FTV Lounge tea/coffee Dinner available WiFi **Parking** 30 **Notes** LB No coaches

---

LEYBURN　　　　　　　　　　　　**Map 19 SE19**

Premier Collection

Braithwaite Hall

★★★★★ ⬚ BED AND BREAKFAST

tel: 01969 640287 **East Witton DL8 4SY**
email: info@braithwaitehall.co.uk **web:** www.braithwaitehall.co.uk
dir: *1.5m from East Witton on single track road*

This impressive 17th-century building is set in open farmland in Coverdale with views over the Pennines bordering Wensleydale. Inside are many period features including antique furnishings and a stunning oak staircase. The drawing room comes complete with oak panelling from the 1660s. Bedrooms are spacious and very comfortable. Delicious breakfasts are served in the elegant dining room and there is a friendly, welcoming atmosphere.

Rooms 3 rms (2 en suite) (1 pri facs) **Facilities** FTV DVD tea/coffee WiFi ⬛ Fishing **Extras** Speciality toiletries, fruit, port **Parking** 7 **Notes** ⊗ No Children 12yrs Closed Nov-Feb ✉

Premier Collection

Capple Bank Farm

★★★★★ ⬚ BED AND BREAKFAST

tel: 01969 625825 & 07836 645238 **West Witton DL8 4ND**
email: julian.smithers@btinternet.com **web:** www.capplebankfarm.co.uk
dir: *A1 to Bedale, onto A684 to Leyburn, turn left to Hawes, through Wensley, 1st left in West Witton. Up hill, left bend, gates straight ahead*

Ideal for walking and touring in the Yorkshire Dales National Park, Capple Bank Farm is a spacious house. Guests have use of a lovely lounge with a real fire lit on cooler days, and breakfast is served at a beautiful table in the open-plan kitchen and dining room. All bedrooms are en suite with bath and a shower.

Rooms 2 en suite 1 annexe en suite **Facilities** STV FTV Lounge tea/coffee WiFi 🔒 **Extras** Toiletries, hairdryers **Parking** 6 **Notes** ⊗ No Children 10yrs Closed Xmas

LEYBURN *continued*

Premier Collection

Low Mill Guest House

★★★★★ 🍽 ➘ GUEST HOUSE

tel: 01969 650553 **Bainbridge DL8 3EF**
email: lowmillguesthouse@gmail.com **web:** www.lowmillguesthouse.co.uk
dir: *A1 junct 51 onto A684 towards Hawes. In Bainbridge turn right by junct on village green*

A truly unique, luxurious retreat tucked away in the beautiful Dales village of Bainbridge. Grade II listed, Low Mill Guest House has been refurbished to an impressive standard with the original mill works and waterwheel restored. Bedrooms are spacious with original features blended with stylish design. There is a stunning lounge with working range, and an attractive dining room where breakfast and candlelit evening meals are served.

Rooms 3 en suite S £82-£135; D £110-£180* **Facilities** FTV DVD iPod docking station TVL tea/coffee Dinner available Direct Dial Licensed WiFi Fishing 🎣 **Extras** Speciality toiletries, home-made biscuits **Parking** 3 **Notes** LB No Children 10yrs

The Queens Head

★★★★ ➘ INN

tel: 01677 450259 **Westmoor Ln, Finghall DL8 5ND**
email: enquiries@queensfinghall.co.uk **web:** www.queensfinghall.co.uk
dir: *From Bedale follow A684 W towards Leyburn, just after pub & caravan park turn left signed to Finghall. Follow road, on left*

Located in the quiet village of Finghall, this country inn dates back to the 18th century and has original oak beams. A wide choice of freshly prepared meals are served in either the bar or more contemporary restaurant, which has lovely views of the surrounding countryside. Bedrooms are spacious and located in an adjacent annexe.

Rooms 3 annexe en suite (1 fmly) (3 GF) **Facilities** FTV DVD tea/coffee Dinner available WiFi 🎣 **Parking** 40

LOW ROW Map 18 SD99

The Punch Bowl Inn

★★★★ 🍽 ➘ INN

tel: 03337 000779 **DL11 6PF**
email: info@pbinn.co.uk **web:** www.pbinn.co.uk
dir: *From Scotch Corner take A6108 to Richmond then B6270 to Low Row*

This friendly inn is appointed in a contemporary style. Real ales and freshly-cooked meals are served in either the spacious bar or dining room. The modern bedrooms are stylish yet simply furnished, with well-equipped bathrooms. Guests also have use of a lounge which has stunning views of the Dales.

Rooms 9 en suite 2 annexe en suite (1 fmly) (1 GF) **Facilities** FTV Lounge tea/coffee Dinner available Direct Dial WiFi Fishing 🎣 **Extras** Speciality toiletries, home-made shortbread **Parking** 20 **Notes** LB Closed 25 Dec

MALHAM Map 18 SD96

The Lister Arms

★★★★ INN

tel: 01729 830330 **BD23 4DB**
email: relax@listerarms.co.uk **web:** www.listerarms.co.uk
dir: *From A59 into Malham, right in centre of village*

Located in Malham in the Yorkshire Dales National Park, The Lister Arms is a traditional country inn with wood beams and open fires. It is close to the village green and a babbling stream. The accommodation is comfortable and well equipped, and a wide selection of imaginative dishes, together with real ales and fine wines, are served in the busy bar and restaurant, where the atmosphere is relaxed and comfortable.

Rooms 15 en suite (3 fmly) **Facilities** FTV tea/coffee Dinner available WiFi **Parking** 20 **Notes** No coaches

River House

★★★★ 🍽 GUEST HOUSE

tel: 01729 830315 **BD23 4DA**
email: info@riverhousehotel.co.uk **web:** www.riverhousemalham.co.uk
dir: *Off A65, N to Malham*

Expect a warm welcome at River House, which dates from 1664. The house is nestled right in the centre of this scenic Malhamdale village and is perfect for walking and cycling routes. Bedrooms are bright and comfortable, with one on the ground floor. Public areas include an inviting lounge and a large, well-appointed dining room. The establishment is also licensed and offers excellent evening meals for groups of six or more. Breakfast is another highlight with delicious Dales cooked breakfasts featuring eggs from the owners' own hens. Other facilities also include free WiFi and secure storage for bikes.

Rooms 8 en suite (1 GF) S £65-£90; D £70-£100* **Facilities** FTV Lounge tea/coffee Dinner available Licensed WiFi Fishing 🎣 Drying room **Extras** Wine, flowers, fruit - chargeable **Parking** 5 **Notes** LB ⊗ No Children 12yrs Closed 21-26 Dec

The Buck Inn at Malham

★★★ INN

tel: 01729 830317 **Cove Rd BD23 4DA**
email: buck-inn@btconnect.com **web:** www.thebuckinnmalham.co.uk
dir: *From Skipton on A65 towards Kendal, after 2.5m turn right to Malham. Follow road to village*

The friendly owners and staff ensure guests are well looked after when they arrive at this traditional 19th-century coaching inn in the centre of Malham. Cask beers and a wide choice of hearty meals are served at lunchtimes and throughout evenings, with a log fire adding to the cosy atmosphere in the lounge bar. The colourful Hikers Bar features a Yorkshire flagstone floor, and dogs, families and muddy boots are all welcome. Free WiFi is available and there is also a heated patio, very popular during the busy summer months.

Rooms 12 en suite (1 fmly) S £45-£70; D £70-£90* **Facilities** tea/coffee Dinner available WiFi 🎣 **Conf** Max 40 Thtr 40 Class 20 Board 20 **Parking** 20

The Coach House at Middleton Lodge

Kneeton Lane, Middleton Tyas, Richmond, North Yorkshire DL10 6NJ
Tel: 01325 377 977
Email: info@middletonlodge.co.uk   **Web:** www.middletonlodge.co.uk

Located in the heart of rural North Yorkshire, *The Coach House at Middleton Lodge* is an award-winning restaurant with rooms, which takes a fresh approach to a country retreat.

Full of original character, *The Coach House* has nine characterful and sophisticated bedrooms, all personalised and designed to reflect the heritage of the retreat. There's an additional five bedrooms in the restored Farmhouse, alongside a private living and chill out area, all sat in its own tranquil wild garden.

Once you have settled into your bedroom, take a walk along the woodland trial or pop on one of the coach house's vintage bicycles, and explore the 200-acre grounds of the Georgian country estate. For those looking for some pampering, visit The Treatment Rooms, with a organic and holistic menu of soothing massages, body wraps, and facials from VOYA and REN.

In the evening, enjoy a meal at *The Coach House* restaurant, with a modern British menu, all created by Gareth Rayner, and inspired by the Yorkshire countryside. Remember to stop by the cocktail bar complete with a top flight team of mixologists, cool sounds and a laid back, brick-walled, atmosphere. It's the coolest way to end the night.

MIDDLETON TYAS
Map 19 NZ20

Premier Collection

The Coach House

★★★★★ ◎◎ RESTAURANT WITH ROOMS

tel: 01325 377977 **Middleton Lodge DL10 6NJ**
email: info@middletonlodge.co.uk **web:** www.middletonlodge.co.uk

Nestled within a 200-acre estate, surrounded by tall trees and winding footpaths, this picturesque setting really sets the tone for your stay. Bedrooms are annexed in a courtyard style setting and are furnished to a luxurious standard. Traditional features such as exposed beams and high ceilings are coupled with a wide range of modern accessories such as flat-screen TV, Nespresso machines and complimentary WiFi. The kitchen takes a modern approach, using calender-correct regional produce for an interesting range of meals that are served in the modern restaurant; a selection of cocktails is also offered. Beauty treatments are also available. Weddings and private functions can also be booked in the main house, Middleton Lodge.

Rooms 9 en suite (6 GF) **Facilities** STV FTV DVD Lounge tea/coffee Dinner available Direct Dial WiFi ॐ ॐ ॑ 18 ♨ **Extras** Snacks, juice - complimentary **Conf** Thtr 180 Class 100 Board 60 **Parking** 70 **Notes** LB Civ Wed 100

See advert on page 347

NEWTON UNDER ROSEBERRY
Map 19 NZ51

The Kings Head Inn

★★★ INN

tel: 01642 722318 **The Green TS9 6QR**
email: info@kingsheadinn.co.uk **web:** www.kingsheadinn.co.uk
dir: *A171 towards Guisborough, at rdbt onto A173 to Newton under Roseberry, under Roseberry Topping landmark*

The Kings Head Inn enjoys a wonderful location with the Roseberry Topping providing an iconic back drop, and is located at the edge of the North York Moors within easy striking distance of Whitby, York and Newcastle. Newly created, comfortable bedrooms are located in the adjacent 17th-century cottages. The pub serves good, home-cooked food and the staff are friendly and welcoming.

Rooms 12 annexe en suite (1 fmly) (6 GF) **Facilities** tea/coffee Dinner available WiFi **Parking** 50

OLDSTEAD
Map 19 SE57

Premier Collection

The Black Swan at Oldstead

★★★★★ ◎◎◎◎ ♟ RESTAURANT WITH ROOMS

tel: 01347 868387 **YO61 4BL**
email: enquiries@blackswanoldstead.co.uk **web:** www.blackswanoldstead.co.uk
dir: *Exit A19, 3m S Thirsk for Coxwold, left in Coxwold, left at Byland Abbey for Oldstead*

The Black Swan is set amidst the stunning scenery of the North York Moors National Park, and parts of the building date back to the 16th century. Well appointed, very comfortable bedrooms provide the perfect get-away; some are on the ground floor overlooking the newly created kitchen garden, others are in the Georgian House and feature both baths and wet-room showers. These bedrooms, together with welcoming open fires, a traditional bar and an award-winning restaurant that has become a destination in its own right, all combine to make this a 'little gem' of a property.

Rooms 4 en suite 5 annexe en suite (6 GF) D £200-£450* (incl.dinner) **Facilities** FTV tea/coffee Dinner available WiFi **Extras** Home-made biscuits, speciality toiletries **Parking** 20 **Notes** ⊗ No Children 18yrs No coaches

OSMOTHERLEY
Map 19 SE49

Premier Collection

The Cleveland Tontine

★★★★★ ◎◎ ♟ RESTAURANT WITH ROOMS

tel: 01609 882671 **Staddlebridge DL6 3JB**
email: bookings@theclevelandtontine.co.uk **web:** www.theclevelandtontine.co.uk
dir: *Just off A172 junct on A19 Nbound*

This iconic destination restaurant with rooms is a stunning place. Contemporary public areas sit alongside a traditional restaurant with open fires, tiled flooring and great food. Afternoon tea can be taken in the conservatory overlooking the gardens. Bedrooms are individually designed, with modern furniture and feature bathrooms. The service is friendly and relaxed, there is ample parking and major road links are close by.

Rooms 7 en suite (4 fmly) **Facilities** FTV Lounge tea/coffee Dinner available Direct Dial WiFi **Extras** Speciality toiletries **Conf** Max 70 Thtr 56 Class 28 Board 38 **Parking** 60 **Notes** ⊗ Civ Wed 56

PATELEY BRIDGE | Map 19 SE16

Roslyn House

★★★★ GUEST ACCOMMODATION

tel: 01423 711374 **9 King St HG3 5AT**
email: enquiries@roslynhouse.co.uk **web:** www.roslynhouse.co.uk
dir: B6165 into Pateley Bridge, right at end of High St at newsagents into King St, house 200yds on left

You are assured of a warm welcome at well-maintained Roslyn House in the centre of the village. Bedrooms are attractively furnished, with homely touches and contemporary en suites. A comfortable lounge is provided and hearty breakfasts will ensure you are set up for the day. Complimentary WiFi is also available. Cyclists and walkers on the famous Nidderdale Way are well catered for.

Rooms 7 en suite **Facilities** FTV TVL tea/coffee WiFi **Extras** Chocolates, water, sweets - complimentary **Conf** Max 8 Board 8 **Parking** 6 **Notes** ⊗ No Children 3yrs

PICKERING | Map 19 SE78

Premier Collection

17 Burgate

★★★★★ GUEST ACCOMMODATION

tel: 01751 473463 **17 Burgate YO18 7AU**
email: info@17burgate.co.uk **web:** www.17burgate.co.uk
dir: From A170 follow sign to Castle. 17 Burgate on right

An elegant house close to the centre of Pickering and the castle, 17 Burgate offers comfortable, individually designed bedrooms with all modern facilities, including free broadband, iPod docks, DVD/CD player and comfy sofas. Public areas include a restful lounge bar, and breakfast features a wide choice of local, healthy foods. The proprietors here make every effort to maintain green and sustainable credentials.

Rooms 3 en suite S £90-£95; D £90-£110 **Facilities** FTV DVD iPod docking station Lounge tea/coffee Licensed WiFi **Extras** Chocolate, snacks - chargeable **Conf** Max 12 Thtr 12 Class 12 Board 12 **Parking** 7 **Notes** LB No Children 10yrs Closed 24 Oct-10 Apr RS 15-29 Dec

Fox & Hounds Country Inn

★★★★ INN

tel: 01751 431577 **Main St, Sinnington YO62 6SQ**
email: fox.houndsinn@btconnect.com **web:** www.thefoxandhoundsinn.co.uk
dir: 3m W of Pickering. Off A170 between Pickering & Helmsley

An attractive village inn offering smart, well-equipped bedrooms. The public areas include a bar, a cosy lounge and a restaurant which offers an impressive range of well presented and well cooked dishes. Food here has been awarded an AA Rosette.

Rooms 10 en suite (4 GF) S £59-£84; D £70-£170* **Facilities** FTV Lounge tea/coffee Dinner available Direct Dial WiFi **Parking** 40 **Notes** LB Closed 25-27 Dec Civ Wed

Grindale House

★★★★ GUEST ACCOMMODATION

tel: 01751 476636 **123 Eastgate YO18 7DW**
email: info@grindalehouse.com **web:** www.grindalehouse.com

Close to the North York Moors National Park and North Riding Forest Park, Grindale House is a charming stone building with self-catering cottages to the side and behind. The guest accommodation is comfortable and attractive and breakfasts are memorable. Much of the produce that goes into it has come from local farms and suppliers. There is also on-site parking, WiFi, and secure bike lock-up.

Rooms 6 rms (5 en suite) (1 pri facs) 3 annexe en suite (2 fmly) (3 GF) **Facilities** FTV TVL tea/coffee WiFi **Parking** 8 **Notes** ⊗ Closed mid Dec-Mar

REDCAR | Map 19 NZ62

Springdale House

★★★★ BED AND BREAKFAST

tel: 01642 297169 & 07834 615147 **3 Nelson Ter TS10 1RX**
email: reservations@springdalehouse.co.uk **web:** www.springdalehouse.co.uk
dir: From A1 take A19 towards Teesside. Then take A174 to Redcar

Springdale House is a Victorian town house situated on a quiet terraced row and has delightful and friendly accommodation with a focus on quality furnishings and comfort. Each room is individually decorated and has flat-screen TV with Freeview. It is situated only five minutes' walk from the town's bars and restaurants, and near to the promenade.

Rooms 5 rms (4 en suite) (1 pri facs) S £45; D £80* **Facilities** FTV tea/coffee WiFi **Extras** Robes **Notes** ⊗ No Children 16yrs

Edwardian House B&B

AA Advertised

tel: 01642 506228 & 07901 746710 **45 High Street West TS10 1SF**
email: edwardianhouse@gmail.com **web:** www.edwardianhouseredcar.co.uk

Edwardian House enjoys far reaching sea views over Coatham Bay to the rear, and the town centre and other amenities are within walking distance. All rooms come with flatscreen Freeview TV and free WiFi, as well as tea and coffee making facilities and complimentary toiletries. Breakfast is served in the dining room.

Rooms 3 rms (2 en suite) (1 pri facs) 1 annexe en suite S £40; D £70* **Facilities** FTV tea/coffee WiFi **Notes** ⊗ No Children 14yrs

REETH
Map 19 SE09

Arkleside Guesthouse Bed and Breakfast

★★★ GUEST HOUSE

tel: 01748 884200 **DL11 6SG**
email: enquiries@arklesidereeth.co.uk **web:** www.arklesidereeth.co.uk
dir: *From Richmond on A6108, right onto B6270 signed Reeth. In village bear right at village green*

Arkleside is located in a quiet courtyard in the peaceful village of Reeth, with stunning views of Swaledale and Fremington Edge. Bedrooms are well appointed and presented, and the high quality breakfast uses produce from local butchers and farmers, giving a great start to the day. Reeth is an ideal base for touring the Dales, for walking, or for cyclists to replicate the 2014 Tour de France stage.

Rooms 4 en suite S £45-£65; D £55-£85 **Facilities** FTV tea/coffee Licensed WiFi 🔒 **Parking** 4

RICCALL
Map 16 SE63

White Rose Villa

★★★★ 🅰 BED AND BREAKFAST

tel: 01757 248115 **33 York Rd YO19 6QG**
email: whiterosevilla@btinternet.com **web:** www.whiterosevilla.info
dir: *S of York, from A19, signed Riccall, 50mtrs on right*

Expect a warm and friendly welcome from Viv and Steve when visiting White Rose Villa. Conveniently located in the heart of the Yorkshire countryside, the popular village of Riccall is close to both York and Selby. All bedrooms are en suite and well equipped. There is a TV lounge to relax in, complete with a selection of DVDs, CDs, books and board games. Breakfast is served in the sunny dining room, and special diets are catered for by prior arrangement.

Rooms 3 en suite (2 fmly) S £35-£40; D £65-£75* **Facilities** FTV DVD TVL tea/coffee WiFi **Extras** Speciality toiletries **Parking** 4 **Notes** LB ⊗ Closed 24-26 & 31 Dec

Per Bacco at The Park View

★★★ RESTAURANT WITH ROOMS

tel: 01757 249146 **20 Main St YO19 6PX**
email: gianlucasechi@hotmail.co.uk **web:** www.per-bacco.co.uk
dir: *A19 from Selby, left for Riccall by water tower, house 100yds on right*

This spacious detached property is located in a quiet residential area and is convenient for York. The ground floor has been converted into an authentic Italian restaurant and there is a wide choice of fresh, home-made dishes, all in a friendly atmosphere. The restaurant is the main part of the business but there is also a range of comfortable en suite bedrooms. Ample parking is available.

Rooms 4 en suite (2 fmly) **Facilities** STV FTV iPod docking station Lounge TVL tea/coffee Dinner available WiFi ♿ 🔒 **Parking** 30 **Notes** LB No coaches

RICHMOND
Map 19 NZ10

Rosedale Guest House

★★★★ GUEST HOUSE

tel: 01748 824465 & 07894 726132 **2 Pottergate DL10 4AB**
email: rosedalerichmond@hotmail.com **web:** www.richmondbedandbreakfast.co.uk
dir: *A1(M), A6108 to Richmond. Pottergate 0.5m before town centre*

A short stroll away from the centre of the small town of Richmond, Rosedale Guest House is an attractive Grade II listed building which has been tastefully decorated throughout. Walks can be taken near the beautiful River Swale which is nearby. The hosts offer warm hospitality alongside stylishly furnished and comfortably equipped bedrooms. The public rooms include a dining area and a private lounge with free WiFi.

Rooms 4 en suite 2 annexe en suite (1 fmly) (1 GF) **Facilities** FTV Lounge tea/coffee WiFi 🔒 **Notes** ⊗ No Children 16yrs

Whashton Springs Farm (NZ149046)

★★★★ FARMHOUSE

tel: 01748 822884 **DL11 7JS**
email: whashtonsprings@btconnect.com **web:** www.whashtonsprings.co.uk
dir: *In Richmond N at lights towards Ravensworth, 3m down steep hill, farm at bottom on left*

A friendly welcome awaits at Whashton Springs Farm, situated in the heart of the countryside yet convenient for major routes. Bedrooms are split between the courtyard rooms and the main farmhouse. Traditional hearty breakfasts are served with free range eggs from the farms own hens as well as ample amounts of home-made and local produce. The spacious dining room overlooks the beautiful gardens.

Rooms 3 en suite 5 annexe en suite (2 fmly) (5 GF) **Facilities** FTV tea/coffee WiFi **Conf** Max 16 Board 16 **Parking** 10 **Notes** ⊗ No Children 3yrs Closed late Dec-Jan 🌾 600 acres arable/beef/mixed/sheep

The Frenchgate Guest House

★★★★ GUEST HOUSE

tel: 07889 768696 **66 Frenchgate DL10 7AG**
email: frenchgate66@icloud.com **web:** www.66frenchgate.co.uk
dir: *From Scotch Corner, enter Richmond, straight over rdbt & lights. Left at 1st rdbt, turn sharp left after 100mtrs, drive to top of Frenchgate*

Tucked away on a charming cobbled street in an historic market town, this attractively presented Victorian town house has an elevated position with stunning views. Bedrooms are comfortable and well equipped with complimentary WiFi access provided. The spacious conservatory-lounge and breakfast room has panoramic south-facing views of the Swale Valley and Easby Abbey.

Rooms 8 rms (7 en suite) (1 pri facs) (3 fmly) (2 GF) S £40-£80; D £80-£96* **Facilities** FTV Lounge tea/coffee WiFi ♿ 18 🔒 **Extras** Fridges, bottled water, fruit, chocolates **Conf** Max 20 Thtr 15 Class 15 Board 15 **Notes** LB ⊗ No Children 5yrs

Black Lion

★★★ INN

tel: 01748 826217 **12 Finkle St DL10 4QB**
email: info@blacklionhotelrichmond.co.uk web: www.blacklionhotelrichmond.co.uk
dir: *A1M take A1/A66. At rdbt take A6108 to Richmond*

Nestled in the historic market town of Richmond, the Black Lion is a traditional family run inn which dates back to 1697. Bedrooms are well appointed and comfortable. Public areas are full of original character and charm and offer a range of seating areas including the snug. Menus offer a good selection of pub classics. Breakfasts are served in the Shiraz restaurant which is also available to hire as a function room. On-site car parking is available to the rear.

Rooms 14 rms (13 en suite) (1 pri facs) (2 fmly) **Facilities** FTV TVL tea/coffee Dinner available WiFi ⚓ 18 🔒 **Conf** Max 30 Class 30 Board 30 **Parking** 10 **Notes** No coaches

Farmers Arms

★★★ 🍴 INN

tel: 01748 818062 & 07966 984272 **Gatherley Rd, Brompton on Swale DL10 7HZ**
email: info@farmersarmsyorkshire.com web: www.farmersarmsyorkshire.com
dir: *From A1 junct 51 take A6136*

This cosy inn is situated in the small village of Brompton-on-Swale, near Richmond with easy access to the A1. A warm welcome awaits at the Farmers Arms; a family-run inn full of original character and charm, dating back to 1700. Bedrooms are comfortable and well equipped with modern amenities such as large flat-screen TVs and complimentary WiFi. Evening and lunch menus offer an interesting selection of modern dishes, coupled with traditional home-cooked classics. An ample amount of on-site parking is available.

Rooms 4 en suite (1 fmly) **Facilities** FTV tea/coffee Dinner available WiFi ⚓ 18 Pool table 🔒 **Parking** 40

RIPON   Map 19 SE37

Premier Collection

Mallard Grange *(SE270704)*

★★★★★ 🍴 FARMHOUSE

tel: 01765 620242 & 07720 295918 **Aldfield HG4 3BE**
email: maggie@mallardgrange.co.uk web: www.mallardgrange.co.uk
dir: *B6265 W fom Ripon, Mallard Grange 2.5m on right*

Located near Fountains Abbey, a genuine welcome is always guaranteed at Mallard Grange. The original features of this early 16th-century, Grade II listed farmhouse are highlighted by quality furnishings and decor. Bedrooms, two of

which are in a converted smithy, are filled with a wealth of thoughtful extras, and comprehensive breakfasts feature home-reared and local produce.

Rooms 2 en suite 2 annexe en suite (2 GF) D £85-£105* **Facilities** FTV iPod docking station Lounge tea/coffee WiFi **Extras** Speciality toiletries, home-made biscuits **Parking** 6 **Notes** LB ⊗ No Children 12yrs Closed Xmas & New Year 500 acres mixed/beef/sheep/arable

The Old Coach House

★★★★★ 🅰 GUEST ACCOMMODATION

tel: 01765 634900 & 07912 632296 **2 Stable Cottages, North Stainley HG4 3HT**
email: enquiries@oldcoachhouse.info web: www.oldcoachhouse.info
dir: *From Ripon take A6108 to Masham. Once in North Stainley, on left opposite Staveley Arms*

The Old Coach House has been part of the local community for over twenty years, so if you need information on the local area, don't hesitate to ask. This 18th-century building stands in the grounds of North Stainley Hall. All bedrooms are designed to a high specification and are individually decorated. Each room is named after a famous Yorkshire landmark or place and each offers a range of facilities. All rooms are en suite and some have wet rooms.

Rooms 8 en suite (4 GF) S £70-£100; D £80-£110* **Facilities** FTV iPod docking station Lounge tea/coffee Direct Dial WiFi ⚓ 18 🔒 **Extras** Speciality toiletries - complimentary **Parking** 8 **Notes** ⊗ No Children 14yrs

Bay Tree Farm *(SE263685)*

★★★★ 🍴 FARMHOUSE

tel: 01765 620394 **Aldfield HG4 3BE**
email: val@baytreefarm.co.uk web: www.baytreefarm.co.uk
dir: *4m W of Ripon. S off B6265 in village of Aldfield*

A warm welcome awaits at Bay Tree Farm, a well presented farmhouse set in the countryside close to Fountains Abbey and Studley Park. Bedrooms are comfortable, with flat-screen TVs, WiFi and luxury toiletries. There is a cosy lounge with a log-burning stove in winter and plenty of outside space for the summer months. Food is a highlight of any stay with delicious breakfasts served at the large farmhouse table. Memorable home cooked dinners are also available by prior arrangement.

Rooms 4 en suite 2 annexe en suite (1 fmly) (3 GF) S £45-£65; D £90-£110 **Facilities** FTV Lounge tea/coffee Dinner available WiFi **Parking** 10 **Notes** LB 400 acres beef/arable

St George's Court *(SE237697)*

★★★★ 🍴 FARMHOUSE

tel: 01765 620618 **Old Home Farm, Grantley HG4 3PJ**
email: info@stgeorgescourt.co.uk web: www.stgeorgescourt.co.uk
dir: *B6265 W from Ripon, up hill 1m past Risplith sign & next right, 1m on right*

This renovated farmhouse is in a great location, in the delightful countryside close to Fountains Abbey. The attractive, well-equipped, ground-floor bedrooms are located around a central courtyard and provide modern accessories such as in-room fridges and flat-screen TVs. Imaginative breakfasts are served in the breakfast room, and a guest lounge is available, both with views of the surrounding countryside.

Rooms 4 en suite (1 fmly) (4 GF) **Facilities** Lounge tea/coffee WiFi Fishing 🔒 **Conf** Max 12 **Parking** 12 **Notes** 20 acres beef/sheep/pigs

RUNSWICK
Map 19 NZ81

The Firs

★★★★ GUEST HOUSE

tel: 01947 840433 **26 Hinderwell Ln TS13 5HR**
email: info@the-firs.co.uk **web:** www.the-firs.co.uk
dir: *From Whitby on A174, turn right signed Runswick. At T-junct turn left, 150yds on right*

The Firs is a spacious, family-run property located in the picturesque village of Runswick on the stunning North Yorkshire coast. The house is just eight miles north of Whitby and is on the edge of the North York Moors National Park. Free private parking, complimentary WiFi and comfortable bedrooms are offered along with a friendly welcome. The ground floor rooms are wheelchair accessible and have en suite wet rooms. (Please note credit cards may only be used for online transactions.)

Rooms 9 en suite (3 fmly) (6 GF) **Facilities** FTV DVD iPod docking station Lounge tea/coffee Direct Dial WiFi ♨ **Extras** Sweets, mineral water, home-made cake - free **Parking** 14 **Notes** LB No Children 2yrs Closed Nov-Mar

SCARBOROUGH
Map 17 TA08

Downe Arms Country Inn

★★★★ INN

tel: 01723 862471 **Main Rd, Wykeham YO13 9QB**
email: info@downearmshotel.co.uk **web:** www.downearmshotel.co.uk
dir: *On A170 Pickering to Scarborough road in Wykeham*

Downe Arms Country Inn is a family-orientated inn on the doorstep of the North York Moors National Park and close to the coast and tourist areas in and around York. Part of the Dawnay estate, this 17th-century former farmhouse has been tastefully modernised. Expect comfortable public areas supported by good cooking, and well-appointed bedrooms with a contemporary feel. The property also caters well for functions and is a popular wedding venue. Ample car parking is available.

Rooms 10 en suite (2 fmly) **Facilities** FTV Lounge tea/coffee Dinner available WiFi Fishing ♨ Pheasant & grouse shooting **Conf** Max 150 Thtr 150 Class 90 Board 50 **Parking** 85 **Notes** Civ Wed 120

The Grainary *(SE965959)*

★★★★ FARMHOUSE

tel: 01723 870026 **Keesbeck Hill Farm, Harwood Dale YO13 0DT**
email: info@grainary.co.uk **web:** www.grainary.co.uk
dir: *From N - exit A171 signed Harwood Dale. From S - exit A171 in Burniston, into Stone Quarry Rd*

The Grainary is a delightful property set in acres of its own land with animal enclosures and duck ponds – very appealing for children and families. The tea room has stunning views over the countryside and is a real delight, with home-baked produce being a feature. Evening meals are also served and the Grainary is licensed. The accommodation is comfortable and very well presented. Public areas are a real feature. True Yorkshire hospitality guarantees a warm welcome and attentive service.

Rooms 14 en suite (5 fmly) (4 GF) S £45-£50; D £77-£87 **Facilities** FTV Lounge TVL tea/coffee Dinner available Licensed WiFi Fishing Pool table ♨ Geocache **Parking** 40 **Notes** LB Closed Dec-Jan Civ Wed 120 200 acres mixed

Olivers

★★★★ GUEST ACCOMMODATION

tel: 01723 368717 **34 West St YO11 2QP**
email: info@olivershotelscarborough.co.uk **web:** www.olivershotelscarborough.co.uk
dir: *Take A64 to B1427 (Margarets Rd). Right onto A165 (Filey Rd). 2nd left into Granville Rd*

Well-equipped, spacious bedrooms are a feature of this Victorian gentleman's residence; one bedroom was originally the nursery. Close to the cliff lift which takes you down to the spa, beaches and gardens, and centrally located on the South Cliff.

Rooms 6 en suite (2 fmly) (1 GF) D £68-£80* **Facilities** FTV DVD tea/coffee WiFi **Notes** LB ⊗ Closed 20-28 Dec

Paragon

★★★★ GUEST ACCOMMODATION

tel: 01723 372676 **123 Queens Pde YO12 7HU**
web: www.paragonhotel.com
dir: *On A64, follow signs for North Bay. Establishment on clifftop*

This welcoming Victorian terraced house has been carefully renovated to provide stylish, thoughtfully equipped, non-smoking accommodation. Hearty English breakfasts are served in the attractive dining room and there is also a lounge bar with a fabulous sea view.

Rooms 14 en suite (1 fmly) **Facilities** Lounge tea/coffee Direct Dial Licensed WiFi **Parking** 6 **Notes** Closed 20 Nov-24 Jan

The Whiteley

★★★★ GUEST ACCOMMODATION

tel: 01723 373514 **99-101 Queens Pde YO12 7HY**
email: thewhiteley@gmail.com **web:** www.yorkshirecoast.co.uk/whiteley
dir: *A64, A165 to North Bay & Peasholm Park, right into Peasholm Rd, 1st left*

The Whiteley is an immaculately run, sea-facing home-from-home. Bedrooms, though compact, are carefully decorated and have many thoughtful extras. There's a small garden at the rear, a choice of lounges and a bar. The establishment has superb views, and the owners provide personal attention and a substantial breakfast.

Rooms 10 en suite (3 fmly) (1 GF) S £36.50-£38; D £61-£72* **Facilities** Lounge TVL tea/coffee Licensed WiFi **Parking** 8 **Notes** LB ⊗ No Children 3yrs Closed 30 Nov-Jan

The Barrington Guest House

★★★ GUEST HOUSE

tel: 01723 379494 **3 Palace Hill, Eastborough YO11 1NL**
email: valeriehotchin@talktalk.net **web:** www.barringtonguesthouse.co.uk
dir: *From A64 follow signs for South Bay, left into Eastborough, on right*

This charming house is in an elevated position just a short walk from the sandy beaches of South Bay and all the amenities of the town. Bedrooms are ranged over three floors and all are tastefully decorated in a contemporary style; they include family rooms.

Rooms 5 en suite (2 fmly) **Facilities** FTV tea/coffee WiFi **Notes** LB Closed 24 Dec-2 Jan

The Albert

★★★ GUEST ACCOMMODATION

tel: 01723 447260 & 07792 902745 **58 North Marine Rd YO12 7PE**
email: alberthotel@btinternet.com **web:** www.thealbert-scarborough.co.uk
dir: *From rail station turn left onto Northway. Turn right at lights then straight on. At rdbt turn left, The Albert 100yds on left*

Located within a few minutes' walk of Scarborough's North Bay and the town centre, this refurbished traditional seaside pub offers a range of locally sourced dishes as well as a wide selection of real ales. The en suite accommodation is comfortable and offers a range of modern accessories such as flat-screen TVs and complimentary WiFi.

Rooms 3 en suite (2 fmly) **Facilities** FTV tea/coffee Dinner available Licensed WiFi Pool table 🔒 **Parking** 6

North End Farm Country Guesthouse

★★★ GUEST ACCOMMODATION

tel: 01723 862965 **88 Main St, Seamer YO12 4RF**
email: northendfarm@tiscali.co.uk **web:** www.northendfarmseamer.co.uk
dir: *A64 N onto B1261 through Seamer, next to rdbt*

Located in Seamer, a village inland from Scarborough, this 18th-century guest accommodation contains comfortable, well-equipped en suite bedrooms. Breakfast is served at individual tables in the smart dining room, and the cosy lounge has a large-screen TV.

Rooms 3 en suite (1 fmly) S £40-£50; D £70-£80* **Facilities** FTV TVL tea/coffee WiFi
🔒 **Parking** 6 **Notes** ⊗

Peasholm Park

★★★ GUEST ACCOMMODATION

tel: 01723 500954 **21-23 Victoria Park YO12 7TS**
email: peasholmparkhotel@btconnect.com **web:** www.peasholmpark.co.uk
dir: *Opposite entrance to Peasholm Park, off Columbus Ravine*

A warm welcome awaits you at Peasholm Park, a family-run guest accommodation, which is within easy walking distance of the beach or the town centre. Bedrooms are comfortable, and feature homely extras. Breakfast is served at individual tables in the dining room, which looks over Peasholm Park itself. Free WiFi is also available.

Rooms 12 en suite (3 fmly) S £42-£50; D £66-£90 **Facilities** FTV TVL tea/coffee Licensed WiFi **Notes** LB ⊗ No Children 6yrs Closed Dec-Feb

The Phoenix Guest House

★★★ GUEST HOUSE

tel: 01723 368319 & 07847 102337 **157 Columbus Ravine YO12 7QZ**
email: jnnlms@aol.co.uk **web:** www.phoenixscarborough.wordpress.com
dir: *From railway station at junct of A64 & A165, take A165 signed North Bay. On right, 100mtrs from Peasholm Park*

Located close to Peasholm Park and just a few minutes' walk from the North Bay, this friendly guest house offers clean, comfortable bedrooms. There is a cosy lounge where guests can relax, exchange books or play games at the card table. Complimentary WiFi is provided and packed lunches can also be purchased.

Rooms 6 en suite (2 fmly) S £30-£35; D £40-£45 (room only)* **Facilities** FTV DVD TVL tea/coffee WiFi **Notes** LB ⊗ ✉

The Sheridan

★★★ 🅰 GUEST ACCOMMODATION

tel: 01723 372094 **108 Columbus Ravine YO12 7QZ**
email: kim@thesheridan.co.uk **web:** www.thesheridan.co.uk
dir: *From railway station left into Northway, over 2 mini rdbts, establishment 300yds on left*

Set on an attractive, tree-lined road close to all North Bay attractions, and only five minutes' walk away from the beach, The Sheridan is a welcoming place to stay. At breakfast, try a full English – special diets are catered for. Traditional Yorkshire cuisine is available in the evening.

Rooms 8 en suite (2 fmly) (1 GF) **Facilities** FTV tea/coffee Dinner available WiFi **Parking** 5 **Notes** ⊗ No Children 5yrs Closed Xmas & New Year

| SCOTCH CORNER | Map 19 NZ20 |

The Vintage

★★ 🅰 INN

tel: 01748 824424 **DL10 6NP**
email: thevintagescotchcorner@btinternet.com **web:** www.thevintagehotel.co.uk
dir: *Exit A1 at Scotch Corner onto A66 towards Penrith, premises 200yds on left*

A warm welcome and attentive service awaits you at The Vintage, a family-run establishment. Bedrooms come in a variety of styles and sizes and all are well equipped. You can choose either a continental or a cooked breakfast, and a tempting selection of evening meals is available either in the bar or restaurant.

Rooms 8 rms (5 en suite) S £25-£40; D £45-£60 (room only)* **Facilities** FTV TVL tea/coffee Dinner available WiFi **Extras** Snacks - complimentary **Conf** Max 40 Thtr 40 Class 24 Board 20 **Parking** 40 **Notes** LB Closed Xmas & New Year No coaches

| SEAMER | Map 17 TA08 |

The Mayfield

★★★ GUEST ACCOMMODATION

tel: 01723 863160 **YO12 4RF**
email: info@themayfieldseamer.co.uk **web:** www.themayfieldseamer.co.uk
dir: *From Thirsk follow A170 to Seamer village. From York follow A64 to Staxton rdbt, turn left. At next rdbt turn left into Seamer village*

The Mayfield is set in the quiet village of Seamer near the popular seaside resort of Scarborough. The stylish accommodation boasts many modern extras such as complimentary WiFi, wine fridges and iPod docking stations. The bar is child friendly with family room and large soft play area. Menus offer a wide selection of home-made 'pub classics' as well as a full carvery offering.

Rooms 9 en suite (1 fmly) S £55-£90; D £60-£100 (room only)* **Facilities** STV FTV DVD iPod docking station tea/coffee Dinner available Direct Dial Licensed WiFi **Extras** Fridge, safe **Conf** Max 70 Thtr 70 Class 48 Board 30 **Parking** 22

SETTLE
Map 18 SD86

See also Clapham

The Lion at Settle

★★★★ INN

tel: 01729 822203 **Duke St BD24 9DU**
email: relax@thelionsettle.co.uk **web:** www.thelionsettle.co.uk
dir: *In town centre opposite Barclays Bank*

Located in the heart of the market town of Settle, this is a traditional coaching inn with an inglenook fireplace. The accommodation is comfortable and well equipped. A wide selection of imaginative dishes, together with real ales and fine wines, is served in the busy bar, and also the restaurant where the atmosphere is relaxed and comfortable; alfresco dining is possible in the courtyard.

Rooms 14 en suite (3 fmly) **Facilities** FTV tea/coffee Dinner available WiFi 🔒

SKIPTON
Map 18 SD95

The Woolly Sheep

★★★★ 🛏 INN

tel: 01756 700966 **38 Sheep St BD23 1HY**
email: woolly.sheep@btconnect.com **web:** www.woollysheepinn.co.uk
dir: *At bottom of High St*

Situated right in the centre of Skipton's vibrant market town, close to the medieval castle and railway station, this popular inn offers good quality and comfortable accommodation. All bedrooms are en suite and well equipped with traditional pine furniture, colour TV and tea/coffee making facilities. Good home-cooked food is served alongside a range of Timothy Taylor real ales. There is an attractive courtyard seating area and free secure parking to the rear.

Rooms 9 en suite (3 fmly) **Facilities** FTV tea/coffee Dinner available WiFi **Parking** 14 **Notes** ⊗ No coaches

TADCASTER
Map 16 SE44

The Old Presbytery Guest House

★★★ BED AND BREAKFAST

tel: 01937 557708 **London Rd, Saxton LS24 9PU**
email: guest@presbytery.plus.com **web:** www.presbyteryguesthouse.co.uk
dir: *4m S of Tadcaster on A162. 100yds N of Barkston Ash on E side of road*

Dating from the 18th century, this former dower house has been modernised to provide comfortable accommodation, while retaining many original features. The hall lounge features a wood-burning stove, and delicious breakfasts are served at an old oak dining table in a cosy breakfast room. The beautiful gardens are a feature in their own right, with an attractive wooden bower providing sheltered outdoor seating space. Secure parking and complimentary WiFi are provided.

Rooms 4 rms (3 en suite) (1 pri facs) (1 fmly) **Facilities** FTV TVL tea/coffee WiFi ⅄ 18 🔒 **Parking** 6 **Notes** ⊗ Closed 21 Dec-6 Jan

THIRSK
Map 19 SE48

Meadowcroft Bed & Breakfast

★★★★ BED AND BREAKFAST

tel: 01845 527497 & 07798 768129 **86 Topcliffe Rd YO7 1RY**
email: sue@meadowcroft-thirsk.co.uk **web:** www.meadowcroft-thirsk.co.uk
dir: *A1(M) junct 49 onto A168. After 5m onto B1448, B&B on left just past school in 1.5m*

This attractive detached family home was built in 1937 and has many original art deco features. The house is very spacious and is set in attractive, mature gardens in a peaceful location just a short stroll from the town centre. Guests can expect warm hospitality, and breakfasts feature local and home-made produce including eggs from the friendly owner's own hens. The two bedrooms are very well equipped with thoughtful accessories, comfortable beds and flat-screen TVs.

Rooms 2 en suite S £65-£75; D £75-£95* **Facilities** FTV DVD tea/coffee WiFi 🔒 **Extras** Mineral water - complimentary **Parking** 4 **Notes** LB ⊗ No Children 11yrs

Newsham Grange Farm Bed and Breakfast

★★★★ BED AND BREAKFAST

tel: 01845 588047 & 07808 903044 **Newsham Grange Farm YO7 4DF**
email: sue@newshamgrangefarm.co.uk **web:** www.newshamgrangefarm.co.uk
dir: *A1(M) junct with A61, follow signs to Thirsk for 4m. Left at rdbt onto A167, 3m on left*

This impressive Georgian farmhouse is set in extensive grounds on the outskirts of Thirsk. It's family run and the friendly owners have refurbished the property to a high standard. The four spacious bedrooms feature luxurious touches, such as under-floor heating, and can also be reconfigured to provide family rooms. The grounds are stunning with a decked terrace, outdoor swimming pool and hot tub adding to the idyllic setting overlooking the orchard. Secure parking with CCTV and lockable storage for bicycles add to the range of facilities. Complimentary WiFi is also available.

Rooms 2 en suite 2 annexe rms (2 pri facs) (2 fmly) (4 GF) **Facilities** FTV tea/coffee Licensed WiFi ⅄ ⅄ 18 Riding 🔒 Hot tub **Parking** 4 **Notes** LB ⊗ No Children 7yrs

WESTOW
Map 19 SE76

Woodhouse Farm *(SE749637)*

★★★★ 🏠 FARMHOUSE

tel: 01653 618378 & 07904 293422 **YO60 7LL**
email: stay@wood-house-farm.co.uk **web:** www.wood-house-farm.co.uk
dir: *Exit A64 to Kirkham Priory & Westow. Right at T-junct, farm drive 0.5m out of village on right*

The owners of this house are a young farming family who offer caring hospitality in their rural home. Bedrooms are spacious and there is a comfortable lounge also available for guests. Complimentary WiFi is provided. Home-made bread, preserves and farm produce turn breakfast into a feast, and the views from the house across open fields are splendid.

Rooms 2 en suite (1 fmly) S £40-£50; D £70-£80* **Facilities** FTV DVD iPod docking station TVL tea/coffee WiFi Fishing 🔒 **Extras** Robes **Parking** 12 **Notes** LB ⊗ Closed Xmas, New Year & mid Mar-mid Apr 🖙 500 acres arable/sheep/beef

WEST WITTON
Map 19 SE08

Premier Collection

The Wensleydale Heifer
★★★★★ ◉ ⬤ RESTAURANT WITH ROOMS

tel: 01969 622322 **Main St DL8 4LS**
email: info@wensleydaleheifer.co.uk **web:** www.wensleydaleheifer.co.uk
dir: A1 to Leeming Bar junct, A684 towards Bedale for approx 10m to Leyburn, then towards Hawes 3.5m to West Witton

Describing itself as 'boutique style', this 17th-century former coaching inn is very much of the 21st century. The bedrooms, with Egyptian cotton linen and Molton Brown toiletries as standard, are each designed with an interesting theme – for example, Black Sheep, Night at the Movies, True Romantics and Shooters, and for chocolate lovers, there's a bedroom where you can eat as much chocolate as you like! The food is very much the focus here in both the informal fish bar and the contemporary style restaurant. The kitchen prides itself on sourcing the freshest fish and locally reared meats.

Rooms 9 en suite 4 annexe en suite (2 fmly) (2 GF) S £80–£100; D £120–£140
Facilities FTV DVD Lounge tea/coffee Dinner available Direct Dial WiFi
Extras Speciality toiletries, fruit, snacks **Parking** 30 **Notes** LB

WHITBY
Map 19 NZ81

Abbotsleigh of Whitby
★★★★ ⬤ GUEST HOUSE

tel: 01947 606615 & 07866 880707 **5 Argyle Rd YO21 3HS**
email: enquiries@abbotsleighofwhitby.co.uk **web:** www.abbotsleighofwhitby.co.uk
dir: From train station onto Bagdale. At mini rdbt turn right onto Chubb Hill. At next rdbt take 2nd exit & right at next rdbt. Right into Argyle Rd

Guests can be sure of friendly service at this immaculately presented Victorian house where tea and home-made cake are offered on arrival. The attractively furnished bedrooms, and stylish en suite wet rooms have a luxurious feel. Thoughtful accessories such as coffee machines, iPod docking stations and DVD players are provided. Complimentary WiFi is also available.

Rooms 5 en suite (1 GF) D £100 **Facilities** STV DVD iPod docking station tea/coffee WiFi **Extras** Speciality toiletries, home-made biscuits, milk **Parking** 3 **Notes** LB ⊗ No Children 12yrs ⊗

Estbek House
★★★★ ◉◉ ⬤ RESTAURANT WITH ROOMS

tel: 01947 893424 **East Row, Sandsend YO21 3SU**
email: info@estbekhouse.co.uk **web:** www.estbekhouse.co.uk
dir: From Whitby take A174. In Sandsend, left into East Row

The speciality seafood restaurant on the first floor is the focus of this listed building in a small coastal village north west of Whitby. The seasonal menu is based on fresh, local ingredients, and is overseen by Tim the chef, who has guided his team to two AA Rosettes. There is also a small bar and breakfast room, and four individually appointed bedrooms offering high levels of comfort.

Rooms 4 rms (3 en suite) (1 pri facs) **Facilities** tea/coffee Dinner available WiFi **Conf** Board 20 **Parking** 6 **Notes** ⊗ No Children 14yrs No coaches

Netherby House
★★★★ ⬤ ⬤ GUEST ACCOMMODATION

tel: 01947 810211 **90 Coach Rd, Sleights YO22 5EQ**
email: info@netherby-house.co.uk **web:** www.netherby-house.co.uk
dir: In village of Sleights, off A169 (Whitby-Pickering road)

This fine Victorian house offers thoughtfully furnished, individually styled bedrooms together with delightful day rooms. There is a fine conservatory and the grounds are extensive, with exceptional views from the summer house at the bottom of the garden. Imaginative dinners feature produce from the extensive kitchen garden.

Rooms 6 en suite 5 annexe en suite (1 fmly) (5 GF) S £42.50–£52.50; D £85–£105*
Facilities FTV Lounge TVL tea/coffee Dinner available Licensed WiFi ⬤ ⬤
Parking 17 **Notes** LB ⊗ No Children 2yrs Closed 25-26 Dec

Overdale Guest House
★★★★ GUEST HOUSE

tel: 01947 605612 **39 Prospect Hill YO21 1QE**
email: jayneoates@hotmail.co.uk **web:** www.overdaleguesthouse.co.uk
dir: A171 to Whitby, onto A174 signed Town Centre. Guest house on right

This fine Victorian terraced house has been sympathetically refurbished and offers guests four charming, very well appointed bedrooms. Built originally for a local sea captain, the house is a short walk from the town centre and Whitby's lovely beaches. Free WiFi is available throughout the house and parking is available. A warm welcome is guaranteed and breakfast is served at individual tables in the light-filled breakfast room.

Rooms 4 en suite (2 fmly) S fr £65; D £85–£110* **Facilities** FTV Lounge tea/coffee WiFi ⬤ **Parking** 6 **Notes** ⊗

WHITBY *continued*

Whitehaven Guest House

★★★★ GUEST ACCOMMODATION

tel: 01947 601569 & 07748 374683 **29 Crescent Av YO21 3EW**
email: simon@whitehavenguesthouse.co.uk **web:** www.whitehavenguesthouse.co.uk
dir: *Follow signs to West Cliff, A174 into Crescent Av*

Occupying a corner position close to the sports complex and indoor swimming pool, this house provides colourful bedrooms in contrasting styles. All rooms have mini-fridges and most have DVD players. Vegetarian options are available at breakfast, which is served in the attractive dining room. Complimentary WiFi access is also available.

Rooms 4 rms (3 en suite) (1 pri facs) (1 fmly) D £75-£85* **Facilities** STV FTV DVD tea/coffee WiFi 🔒 **Extras** Speciality toiletries **Notes** LB ⊗ Closed 23-26 Dec ⊜

Argyle House

★★★★ GUEST ACCOMMODATION

tel: 01947 821877 **18 Hudson St YO21 3EP**
email: argyle-house@fsmail.net **web:** www.argyle-house.co.uk
dir: *Follow signs for West Cliff & Whitby Pavilion, with the sea on left, turn into Royal Crescent & exit through the rear of crescent. Hudson St is also known as Abbey Terrace*

Built originally in the 1850s and enjoying a prominent position in a conservation area, Argyle House is a short walk from Whitby's town centre, harbour and beaches. Recently restored, there are a range of comfortable, well-appointed bedrooms. Guests are guaranteed a warm welcome from the friendly owners and delicious breakfast is served at individual tables in the light-filled breakfast room. Free WiFi is available throughout.

Rooms 7 en suite (2 fmly) D £60-£86* **Facilities** STV FTV DVD iPod docking station tea/coffee WiFi **Extras** Fruit **Notes** LB ⊗ No Children 5yrs

Boulmer Guest House

★★★★ GUEST HOUSE

tel: 01947 604284 **23 Crescent Av YO21 3ED**
email: info@boulmerguesthouse.co.uk **web:** www.boulmerguesthouse.co.uk
dir: *Follow signs for West Cliff, from Royal Crescent into Crescent Av, pass church on right. Road bears to right, 3rd house on left before sorting office*

This friendly guest house is just a short walk from the beautiful beach and Whitby Pavilion on the picturesque West Cliff, and is also convenient for shops, cafés and restaurants. The range of attractively presented bedrooms include family rooms, a twin, a single, and with prior arrangement, dog-friendly bedrooms. Modern facilities are provided including complimentary WiFi. Free on-street parking is available.

Rooms 7 rms (5 en suite) (2 fmly) (1 GF) S £37.50; D £80* **Facilities** FTV DVD TVL tea/coffee WiFi 🔒 **Notes** LB ⊜

Kimberley House

★★★★ GUEST ACCOMMODATION

tel: 01947 604125 **7 Havelock Place YO21 3ER**
email: enquiries@kimberleyhouse.com **web:** www.kimberleyhouse.com
dir: *Follow signs for West Cliff, close to Whalebone Arch and Captain Cook Monument, behind Royal Crescent at corner of Hudson St*

Warm and genuine hospitality is offered at this attractive house in the centre of Whitby, just a short stroll away from the local attractions. Bedrooms are pleasantly co-ordinated and comfortably furnished, with an attic family suite available. Freshly prepared breakfasts are served in the attractive ground floor dining room which has a cosy sitting area, where guests can enjoy complimentary teas and coffees.

Rooms 8 rms (7 en suite) (1 pri facs) (1 fmly) (1 GF) S £40; D £60-£75* **Facilities** FTV DVD TVL tea/coffee WiFi 🔒 **Extras** Speciality toiletries, guest fridge **Notes** LB ⊗ Closed 15-27 Dec

| WOMBLETON | Map 19 SE68 |

New Buckland

★★★★ BED AND BREAKFAST

tel: 01751 433369 & 07850 738001 **Flatts Ln YO62 7RU**
email: nbabandb@gmail.com **web:** www.new-buckland-apartment.co.uk
dir: *From A170 turn right 3m from Helmsley, left at Plough Inn follow round, last property on right*

New Buckland offers two attractive bedrooms and excellent bathrooms in a well-presented countryside property. Whether one or both rooms are booked, guests have exclusive use of the spacious, contemporary lounge and a very well-equipped small kitchen. Complimentary WiFi access is available. Guests also have use of an area of the attractive garden with summer house and garden furniture.

Rooms 2 rms (2 pri facs) **Facilities** FTV DVD TVL tea/coffee WiFi 🔒 **Parking** 2 **Notes** LB ⊗

| YORK | Map 16 SE65 |

Premier Collection

The Judge's Lodging

★★★★★ ⍟ INN

tel: 01904 638733 **9 Lendal YO1 8AQ**
email: relax@judgeslodgingyork.co.uk **web:** www.judgeslodgingyork.co.uk

The Judge's Lodgings is a Grade I listed Georgian townhouse situated in the heart of the city centre, just a stone's throw from the Minster. The building has a wealth of charm and character throughout the public areas and in the well-equipped bedrooms. The public rooms include a cellar bar with original vaulted ceilings and cosy dining/drinking areas; a Cask Bar and a superb glass box, where you can dine inside yet still feel like you're outside. The property also has a choice of sun terraces for alfresco dining.

Rooms 23 rms S £115-£190; D £120-£200* **Facilities** FTV DVD iPod docking station tea/coffee Dinner available WiFi **Extras** Fresh milk **Conf** Max 8 Board 8 **Notes** ⊗ No coaches

Ascot House

★★★★ GUEST ACCOMMODATION

tel: 01904 426826 **80 East Pde YO31 7YH**
email: admin@ascothouseyork.com **web:** www.ascothouseyork.com
dir: 0.5m NE of city centre. Exit A1036 (Heworth Green) into Mill Ln, 2nd left

Ascot House is a 15-minute walk from York Minster. All bedrooms are en suite and the first-floor rooms all have four-poster or antique canopy beds and attractive period furniture, while those on the second floor have a more contemporary style. All rooms are well equipped with TV and free WiFi. The dining room offers a range of breakfast options including traditional English, vegetarian and continental. The comfortable residents' lounge is the ideal place to enjoy tea or coffee, or something stronger from the Butler's Pantry.

Rooms 12 en suite (3 fmly) (2 GF) S £90-£100; D £99-£115 **Facilities** FTV TVL tea/coffee Licensed WiFi 🔒 **Extras** Bottled water - complimentary **Parking** 13 **Notes** LB Closed 21-28 Dec

Burswood Guest House

★★★★ 🛏 GUEST HOUSE

tel: 01904 702582 **68 Tadcaster Rd, Dringhouses YO24 1LR**
email: info@burswoodguesthouse.co.uk **web:** www.burswoodguesthouse.co.uk
dir: On A1036 Tadcaster Rd

Located on the main Tadcaster Road just opposite York race course, this well presented accommodation offers very well equipped bedrooms and bathrooms including some on the ground floor. Breakfast is taken in the comfortable dining room and is freshly cooked to order using good quality ingredients. Off-street car parking is a welcome feature and a number of pubs and hotels are within easy walking distance for dinner.

Rooms 6 en suite (1 fmly) (3 GF) **Facilities** FTV Lounge tea/coffee WiFi 🔒 **Extras** Fresh milk, robes, slippers **Parking** 6 **Notes** LB ⊗

Guy Fawkes Inn

★★★★ 🌑 INN

tel: 01904 623716 **25 High Petergate YO1 7HP**
email: reservations@guyfawkesinnyork.com **web:** www.guyfawkesinnyork.com
dir: A64 onto A1036 signed York & inner ring road. Over bridge into Duncombe Place, right into High Petergate

The Guy Fawkes Inn stands next to York Minster and was the birthplace of the notorious Gunpowder Plotter. The inn offers rooms with free WiFi and flat-screen TVs, furnished with antiques and Italian fabrics. Many rooms have views of the city or the courtyard, and bathrooms have luxury toiletries from Aromatherapy Associates. Old or original features include the timber staircase, gas lighting and real log fires. The world-famous Guy Fawkes Ghost Walk leaves every night just around the corner. Dine by candlelight in the restaurant, which serves traditional food from locally-sourced ingredients. The bar stocks a wide range of real ales and a selection of fruit wines.

Rooms 13 en suite (1 fmly) (2 GF) **Facilities** FTV tea/coffee Dinner available Direct Dial WiFi

Symbols and abbreviations are explained on page 7

YORK *continued*

The Heathers Guest House

★★★★ GUEST ACCOMMODATION

tel: 01904 640989 **54 Shipton Rd, Clifton-Without YO30 5RQ**
email: aabbg@heathers-guest-house.co.uk **web:** www.heathers-guest-house.co.uk
dir: *N of York on A19, halfway between A1237 ring road & York city centre*

This spacious detached house offers off-street parking and a peaceful setting, only a short drive or walk from the city centre. Each room is individually designed, using quality fabrics. The light, airy breakfast room looks out onto the beautiful large rear garden, which is visited daily by local wildlife. Complimentary WiFi access is provided.

Rooms 5 en suite D £78-£120 **Facilities** FTV Lounge tea/coffee WiFi 🔒 **Parking** 9 **Notes** ⊗ No Children 12yrs Closed Xmas & Jan

Lamb & Lion Inn

★★★★ ◉◉ INN

tel: 01904 612078 & 654112 **2-4 High Petergate YO1 7EH**
email: reservations@lambandlioninnyork.com **web:** www.lambandlioninnyork.com
dir: *A64 onto A1036. 3.5m, at rdbt 3rd exit, continue on A1036. 2m, right into High Petergate*

In the heart of York, just beyond the entrance of Bootham Bar, the Lamb & Lion Inn offers hearty food, real ales, and luxurious bedrooms, some with spa baths. The bedrooms are beautifully decorated in earthy colours and all have en suite bathrooms. Guests can also enjoy free WiFi, a flat-screen TV and tea and coffee making facilities. The restaurant serves authentic, rustic dishes, including a cooked Yorkshire breakfast. A wide range of real ales and lagers is available at the bar. York Minster is just close by, while the National Railway Museum is a 15-minute walk, and Harrogate is a 40-minute drive.

Rooms 12 en suite **Facilities** FTV tea/coffee Dinner available WiFi **Conf** Max 20 Thtr 20 Class 20 Board 20

Holmwood House

★★★★ GUEST ACCOMMODATION

tel: 01904 626183 **112/114 Holgate Rd YO24 4BB**
email: info@holmwoodhousehotel.co.uk **web:** www.holmwoodhousehotel.co.uk

A 15-minute walk from Holmwood House takes you into the centre of York. The individually styled bedrooms are richly decorated and smartly furnished with many antiques. There is a comfortable lounge and a substantial breakfast is served in the pleasant basement dining room. Some private parking and complimentary WiFi are also available.

Rooms 14 en suite (1 fmly) (3 GF) **Facilities** FTV Lounge tea/coffee Licensed WiFi 🔒 **Parking** 8 **Notes** ⊗ Closed 24-27 Dec

Ashley Guest House

★★★★ 🛎 GUEST HOUSE

tel: 01904 647520 & 07955 250271 **76 Scott St YO23 1NS**
email: stay@ashleyguesthouse.co.uk **web:** www.ashleyguesthouse.co.uk
dir: *From A64 take York West exit onto A1036 (Tadcaster Rd) follow city centre signs. After racecourse (on right) at 2nd lights right into Scarcroft Rd. Scott St 2nd last street before lights*

Ashley Guest House is a Victorian end-terrace that has been given modern treatment resulting in stylish interiors and a distinctive character. Attractively furnished bedrooms and caring hospitality are hallmarks of this well-located city centre establishment.

Rooms 6 rms (5 en suite) (1 pri facs) (1 fmly) S £45-£75; D £60-£90 **Facilities** FTV Lounge tea/coffee WiFi 🔒 **Notes** ⊗ No Children 5yrs

City Guest House

★★★★ GUEST ACCOMMODATION

tel: 01904 622483 **68 Monkgate YO31 7PF**
email: info@cityguesthouse.co.uk **web:** www.cityguesthouse.co.uk
dir: *NE of city centre on B1036*

Just a five-minute walk from York Minster and close to the city wall and other sights, this charming Victorian town house is well located for business, shopping and sightseeing. Carefully furnished bedrooms are attractively presented and offer a range of thoughtful touches. The traditional and beautifully presented dining room provides a pleasant venue for the hearty breakfast.

Rooms 7 rms (6 en suite) (1 pri facs) (1 fmly) (1 GF) **Facilities** FTV iPod docking station Lounge tea/coffee WiFi ⚡ 9 🔒 **Parking** 6 **Notes** ⊗ No Children 8yrs Closed Xmas & 1st 2wks Jan

Fifth Milestone Cottage

★★★★ GUEST HOUSE

tel: 01904 489361 & 07885 502420 **Hull Rd YO19 5LR**
email: mrsmartyn@hotmail.com **web:** www.milestonecottage.co.uk
dir: *From A64 onto A1079 towards Hull. On left after Philip Welch Garage*

As the name suggests, this spacious cottage is just five miles from York centre. The property is set in large, well-kept grounds with private parking. Guests can relax in the pretty garden where there is also a large decked area. There is a wide range of bedrooms available from doubles, including a four-poster room, to twins and family rooms. Some also have their own terrace and several offer very good disabled facilities and good access for wheelchair users.

Rooms 3 en suite 3 annexe en suite (1 fmly) (4 GF) S £65; D £80-£85* **Facilities** FTV DVD iPod docking station tea/coffee WiFi 🔒 Animal farm **Parking** 12 **Notes** ⊗ RS 25-26 Dec room only

Greenside

★★★ GUEST HOUSE

tel: 01904 623631 **124 Clifton YO30 6BQ**
email: greenside@onebillnet.co.uk **web:** www.greensideguesthouse.co.uk
dir: A19 N towards city centre, over lights for Greenside, on left opposite Clifton Green

Overlooking Clifton Green, this charming detached conservation house is within walking distance of the city centre. Accommodation consists of comfortably furnished bedrooms and the traditional full English breakfast is served in the dining room. Secure parking and WiFi are additional bonuses.

Rooms 8 rms (3 en suite) (2 fmly) (3 GF) S £32-£35; D £60-£70* **Facilities** FTV tea/coffee WiFi **Parking** 6 **Notes** LB Closed Xmas & New Year ⊛

The Willows Bed & Breakfast

★★★ BED AND BREAKFAST

tel: 01904 738206 **Willow Close, Hessay YO26 8JU**
email: willowsinfo@aol.com **web:** www.thewillowsbb.co.uk

Located on the A59 near to York, this welcoming property is ideal for business travellers and tourists visiting the North Yorkshire countryside. Set in 7.5 acres of mature grounds featuring two fishing lakes and landscaped gardens, the house offers two well presented en suite bedrooms. Off-road parking and hearty breakfasts are an added bonus along with friendly hospitality. There is a no-shoe policy for guests staying here.

Rooms 2 en suite **Facilities** FTV DVD tea/coffee WiFi Fishing ▲ **Parking** 20 **Notes** ⊛ No Children

SOUTH YORKSHIRE

DONCASTER	Map 16 SE50

Innkeeper's Lodge Doncaster, Bessacarr

★★★ INN

tel: 08451 551551 *(Calls cost 2p per minute plus your phone company's access charge)* **Bawtry Rd, Bessacarr DN4 7BS**
email: info@innkeeperslodge.com **web:** www.innkeeperslodge.com

Comfortable, modern accommodation ideal for Doncaster racecourse and also convenient for Doncaster airport. There is a Toby Carvery offering a friendly pub atmosphere and roast dinners every day. There is also a pub menu, free WiFi throughout and Sky Sports is shown in the bar. Ample on-site parking is also available.

Rooms 25 en suite (3 fmly) (6 GF) **Facilities** FTV tea/coffee Dinner available Direct Dial WiFi **Parking Notes** ⊛

SHEFFIELD	Map 16 SK38

Cross Scythes

★★★★ INN

tel: 0114 236 0204 **Baslow Rd, Totley S17 4AE**
email: enquiries@cross-scythes.com **web:** www.cross-scythes.com

Located approximately five miles south of Sheffield city centre and just ten minutes' drive from Chatsworth House, this 18th-century building has been sympathetically renovated. There are four tastefully decorated double rooms and all are en suite. Food is served all day throughout the spacious public areas.

Rooms 4 en suite D £64 (room only)* **Facilities** FTV tea/coffee Dinner available WiFi ♿ 18 **Parking** 51 **Notes** ⊛

Dog & Partridge

★★★★ INN

tel: 01226 763173 **Bord Hill, Flouch S36 4HH**
email: info@dogandpartridgeinn.co.uk **web:** www.dogandpartridgeinn.co.uk
dir: M1 junct 37 onto A628. At Flouch rdbt, straight over follow signs for Manchester. 1m on left

This comfortable family-run inn is located within the Peak District National Park. Bedrooms are situated in the 18th-century barn adjoining the inn, all rooms are comfortably furnished and some superior rooms are available. The beer garden has stunning views of the surrounding moorland and a selection of real ales and imaginative food is served in the public areas.

Rooms 10 en suite (2 fmly) (7 GF) **Facilities** FTV tea/coffee Dinner available Direct Dial WiFi ▲ **Conf** Max 50 Thtr 50 Class 36 Board 20 **Parking** 70 **Notes** ⊛ Closed 25-27 Dec Civ Wed 80

Innkeeper's Lodge Hathersage, Peak District

★★★ INN

tel: 08451 551551 *(Calls cost 2p per minute plus your phone company's access charge)* **Hathersage Rd, Longshaw S11 7TY**
email: info@innkeeperslodge.com **web:** www.innkeeperslodge.com

At Innkeeper's Lodge you'll find accommodation with comfort and character in equal measure, and everything needed for a relaxing stay, from easy check-in and free parking to complimentary breakfast and a cosy pub serving great value food and drink on the doorstep. Each Lodge has quality rooms, and there are Lodges in a variety of locations from towns and cities to countryside settings across the UK.

Rooms 9 en suite (6 fmly) (4 GF) **Facilities** FTV tea/coffee Dinner available WiFi **Parking Notes** ⊛

WEST YORKSHIRE

ADDINGHAM	Map 16 SE04

Craven Heifer

★★★★ ⊛⊛ RESTAURANT WITH ROOMS

tel: 01943 830106 **Main St LS29 0PL**
email: info@wellfedpubs.co.uk **web:** www.thecravenheifer.com
dir: A65 Skipton to Otley road, at rdbt onto B6160 signed Addingham. Craven Heifer at next junct.

The Craven Heifer is located close to the town of Skipton and boasts themed rooms based on Yorkshire celebrities (e.g. Dame Judi Dench, David Hockney and Henry Moore). The bar is a traditional 'Dalesway' inn with stone and oak floors, open fires, leather seating, real ale and outstanding food. The two AA Rosette cuisine is beautifully complemented by a carefully chosen wine list. A warm and very friendly welcome from the well-informed staff is guaranteed.

Rooms 7 en suite **Facilities** FTV iPod docking station Lounge TVL tea/coffee Dinner available WiFi ▲ **Extras** Speciality toiletries, bottled water **Conf** Max 20 **Parking** 10 **Notes** Closed 2 Jan RS Mon restaurant closed

CASTLEFORD   Map 16 SE42

The Wheldale

★★ INN

tel: 01977 553403 **Wheldon Rd WF10 2SD**
email: wheldalecas@hotmail.co.uk **web:** www.wheldalehotel.co.uk
dir: *Opposite Castleford Tigers rugby stadium*

This inn is well established locally, and public areas are modern and provide spacious areas for families. The bar is very much a local's bar and has good real ales on offer. The Wheldale is situated opposite the Castleford Tigers Rugby ground so match days can be busy. Good parking is available and there is a very spacious beer garden where events are often held. Bedrooms are comfortable and offer both en suite and standard rooms.

Rooms 10 rms (5 en suite) (1 fmly) S £20-£29; D £39-£55* **Facilities** STV FTV Lounge TVL tea/coffee WiFi ♨ 18 Pool table 🔒 **Parking** 10 **Notes** ⊗ No Children 12yrs

HALIFAX   Map 19 SE02

Premier Collection

Shibden Mill Inn

★★★★★ ◎◎ 🍴 INN

tel: 01422 365840 **Shibden Mill Fold, Shibden HX3 7UL**
email: enquiries@shibdenmillinn.com **web:** www.shibdenmillinn.com
dir: *3m NE of Halifax off A58*

Nestling in a fold of Shibden Dale, this 17th-century inn features exposed beams and open fires. Guests can relax with a choice of lounge areas, and meals can be taken in the award-winning restaurant, the new Grill Room (Thursday- Saturday) or outside in summer. The stylish bedrooms are all individually designed and come in a variety of sizes, all thoughtfully equipped, with access to a free video library. Service is friendly and obliging.

Rooms 11 en suite (1 GF) S £90-£165; D £95-£195* **Facilities** FTV DVD tea/ coffee Dinner available Direct Dial WiFi ♨ 18 Free use of local fitness centre **Conf** Max 12 Board 12 **Parking** 100 **Notes** Closed 25-26 Dec & 1 Jan

HAWORTH   Map 19 SE03

Premier Collection

Ashmount Country House

★★★★★ 🥂 🍴 GUEST HOUSE

tel: 01535 645726 & 643822 **Mytholmes Ln BD22 8EZ**
email: info@ashmounthaworth.co.uk **web:** www.ashmounthaworth.co.uk
dir: *M65 junct 13A Laneshaw Bridge, turn right over moors to Haworth. Turn left after car park on right, 100yds on right*

Ashmount Country House is a stunning property in the heart of Brontë Country, just a short stroll from the centre of Haworth. It is an ideal location for those seeking a relaxing retreat with luxury touches. Each bedroom is designed with high-quality furnishings, attractive decor and many thoughtful extras; some have their own terrace with hot tub or sauna. There is also a comfortable lounge bar and an elegant dining room. The restaurant is open the both residents and non-residents, seven days a week and offers British food with a modern twist. The landscaped gardens provide a lovely backdrop and a pleasant location to relax or enjoy afternoon tea on the lawn.

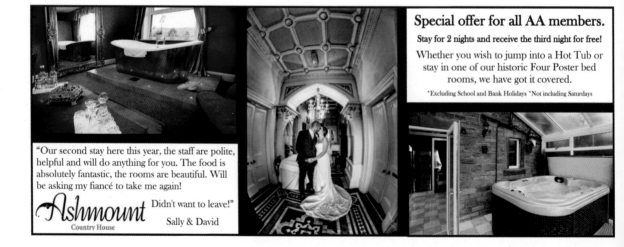

"Our second stay here this year, the staff are polite, helpful and will do anything for you. The food is absolutely fantastic, the rooms are beautiful. Will be asking my fiancé to take me again!
Didn't want to leave!"
Sally & David

Ashmount
Country House

Special offer for all AA members.
Stay for 2 nights and receive the third night for free!
Whether you wish to jump into a Hot Tub or stay in one of our historic Four Poster bed rooms, we have got it covered.
*Excluding School and Bank Holidays *Not including Saturdays

Ashmount Country House

Rooms 8 en suite 4 annexe en suite (5 GF) S £70–£150; D £95–£275*
Facilities FTV iPod docking station Lounge tea/coffee Dinner available Licensed
WiFi 🍴 🔒 **Extras** Fruit, home-made biscuits, sherry - complimentary **Conf** Max
25 Class 25 Board 15 **Parking** 12 **Notes** ⊗ No Children 10yrs Civ Wed 40

See advert on opposite page

HOLMFIRTH
Map 16 SE10

Rooms at the Nook

★★★★ GUEST ACCOMMODATION

tel: 01484 682373 & 07841 646308 **Victoria Square HD9 2DN**
email: office@thenookbrewhouse.co.uk **web:** www.roomsatthenook.co.uk
dir: From A6024 in Holmfirth. On A635 (Victoria St), at bottom of Victoria St

A warm welcome is assured at this centrally-located former 18th-century inn, which
offers eight stylish bedrooms. The Nook pub retains many original features and
benefits from an on-site microbrewery serving award-winning ales and a good wine
selection. An adjacent bar and restaurant, known as The Tap House, specialises in
tapas with a Yorkshire twist.

Rooms 8 en suite (3 fmly) S £70–£95; D £70–£95* **Facilities** FTV DVD TVL tea/coffee
Dinner available Licensed WiFi 🚲 18 Pool table 🔒 **Notes** ⊗

Old Bridge Inn & Coffee House

★★★ INN

tel: 01484 681212 **Market Walk HD9 7DA**
web: www.oldbridgeholmfirth.co.uk

The Old Bridge Inn & Coffee House is a modern inn in the centre of the popular town
of Holmfirth. Bedrooms are more traditional and offer good levels of comfort.
Cocktails and drinks can be enjoyed in the stylish bar before dinner in the cosy
restaurant with open fire. Menus offer an interesting choice. Home-made cakes can
also been enjoyed throughout the day in the coffee shop bar area with a choice of
comfortable sofas available. A large car park is available to all residents which is
an asset.

Rooms 21 en suite **Facilities** tea/coffee Dinner available WiFi **Parking**

HUDDERSFIELD
Map 16 SE11

Premier Collection

315 Bar and Restaurant

★★★★★ ◉◉ RESTAURANT WITH ROOMS

tel: 01484 602613 **315 Wakefield Rd, Lepton HD8 0LX**
email: info@315barandrestaurant.co.uk **web:** www.315barandrestaurant.co.uk
dir: M1 junct 38, A637 towards Huddersfield. At rdbt take A642 towards Huddersfield.
Establishment on right in Lepton

In a wonderful setting, 315 Bar and Restaurant is very well presented and
benefits from countryside views from the well-appointed dining room and
conservatory areas. The interior is modern with open fires that add character
and ambiance, while the chef's table gives a real insight into the working of the
two AA Rosette award-winning kitchen. Bedrooms are well appointed and
modern, and most have feature bathrooms. Staff are friendly and attentive, and
there are excellent parking facilities.

Rooms 10 en suite (2 fmly) S fr £80; D fr £90* **Facilities** FTV DVD tea/coffee
Dinner available Lift WiFi **Conf** Max 150 Thtr 100 Class 75 Board 60 **Parking** 97
Notes ⊗ Civ Wed 120

Woodman Inn

★★★★ 🍴 INN

tel: 01484 605778 **Thunder Bridge Ln HD8 0PX**
email: info@woodman-inn.com **web:** www.woodman-inn.com

(For full entry see Kirkburton)

Innkeeper's Lodge Huddersfield, Kirkburton

★★★ INN

tel: 08451 551551 *(Calls cost 2p per minute plus your phone company's access charge)*
36a Penistone Rd, Kirkburton HD8 0PQ
email: info@innkeeperslodge.com **web:** www.innkeeperslodge.com

Situated on the Penistone Road, with easy reach of the National Coal Mining
Museum and Huddersfield town centre. The lodge provides modern bedrooms and is
attached to the Foxglove Vintage Inn; an attractive 19th-century building with real
fires and spacious dining areas. A continental buffet breakfast is complimentary
for all guests – a cooked option available at a supplement. Free WiFi is available
throughout plus ample parking space.

Rooms 23 en suite (3 fmly) (13 GF) **Facilities** FTV tea/coffee Dinner available WiFi
Parking Notes ⊗

ILKLEY
Map 19 SE14

Innkeeper's Lodge Ilkley

★★★ INN

tel: 08451 551551 *(Calls cost 2p per minute plus your phone company's access
charge)* **Hangingstone Rd LS29 8BT**
email: info@innkeeperslodge.com **web:** www.innkeeperslodge.com

This Innkeeper's Lodge is a 19th-century Victorian property idyllically located in the
Yorkshire Dales, with stunning views over Wharfedale. Perfect for walkers, browsing
the spa town of Ilkley, close to Ben Rhydding golf course and only a short drive from
Leeds and Bradford. There is lots of period charm in the inviting public areas,
where hearty food and cask ales are served. The bedrooms are modern and
comfortable. Complimentary WiFi is provided.

Rooms 14 en suite (2 fmly) **Facilities** FTV TV13B tea/coffee Dinner available WiFi
Parking Notes ⊗

KIRKBURTON
Map 16 SE11

Woodman Inn

★★★★ ⇌ INN

tel: 01484 605778 **Thunder Bridge Ln HD8 0PX**
email: info@woodman-inn.com **web:** www.woodman-inn.com
dir: *1m SW of Kirkburton. Off A629 in Thunder Bridge*

The Woodman Inn is extremely popular with locals. The popular bar offers a wide selection of real ales, lagers and draught ciders. Bedrooms are comfortable and comprehensively furnished, making this an ideal base for walking, visiting the National Mining Museum, or simply escaping to the country. Weddings and small functions are also well catered for.

Rooms 13 en suite (3 fmly) (3 GF) **Facilities** FTV Lounge tea/coffee Dinner available Direct Dial WiFi ⚓ 18 **Extras** Speciality toiletries **Conf** Max 60 Thtr 50 Class 60 Board 30 **Parking** 60 **Notes** Civ Wed 80

LEEDS
Map 19 SE23

Innkeeper's Lodge Leeds Calverley

★★★ INN

tel: 08451 551551 *(Calls cost 2p per minute plus your phone company's access charge)* **Calverley Ln, Pudsey LS28 5QQ**
email: info@innkeeperslodge.com **web:** www.innkeeperslodge.com

A striking 19th-century Victorian lodge peacefully located in the picturesque village of Calverley, yet very convenient for Bradford and Leeds and only six miles from Leeds Bradford International Airport. The spacious bar and dining areas are comfortable, with cask ales and a wide choice of food offered. Bedrooms are spacious and suitably equipped, and there is a large garden with outside seating. Complimentary WiFi is also provided.

Rooms 14 en suite (5 fmly) **Facilities** FTV tea/coffee Dinner available WiFi **Parking Notes** ⊗

Hinsley Hall

★★★ GUEST ACCOMMODATION

tel: 0113 261 8000 **62 Headingley Ln LS6 2BX**
email: info@hinsley-hall.co.uk **web:** www.hinsley-hall.co.uk
dir: *On A660 Leeds to Skipton road, past university & Hyde Park lights. Turn right into Oakfield*

Set in extensive landscaped gardens, Hinsley Hall enjoys a peaceful setting just a short drive from Leeds city centre and the nearby university. Bedrooms are all comfortable, well equipped and well appointed. A lounge is available for guests along with a small bar area. There are large conferencing facilities on site along with a number of meeting rooms. Headingley Stadium is a 10 minute walk away.

Rooms 50 rms (47 en suite) (3 pri facs) (1 fmly) (4 GF) S fr £52.50; D fr £69.95 **Facilities** FTV Lounge TVL TV9B tea/coffee Dinner available Lift Licensed WiFi ⚓ **Conf** Max 90 Thtr 90 Class 50 Board 36 **Parking** 100 **Notes** ⊗ Closed 24 Dec-2 Jan

LINTON
Map 16 SE34

The Windmill Inn

★★★★ ⇌ INN

tel: 01937 582209 **Main St LS22 4HT**
email: enquiries@thewindmillinnlinton.co.uk **web:** www.thewindmillinnlinton.co.uk
dir: *A1(M) junct 45, then 2nd exit at Moore Grange rdbt. Left on A58, right onto A659. Right into Linton Ln, follow road into Main St*

The Windmill is a beautiful, traditional country inn tucked away in a charming village. Food is locally sourced and the two rooms are converted outbuildings that are just across the car park. They are spacious suites with lounge areas, WiFi, flat-screen TVs and modern bathrooms. There is ample car parking and an award-winning beer garden. Families are very welcome in the pub.

Rooms 2 annexe en suite (1 GF) D £95* **Facilities** FTV DVD Lounge TVL tea/coffee Dinner available WiFi ⚓ 18 Access to Wood Hall Spa & Swimming Pool **Parking** 48 **Notes** No Children Closed 1 Jan No coaches Civ Wed 80

MIRFIELD
Map 16 SE21

Mirfield Monastery B&B

★★ GUEST ACCOMMODATION

tel: 01924 483346 & 494318 **Stocks Bank Rd WF14 0BN**
email: enquiries@mirfield.org.uk **web:** www.monastery-stay.co.uk
dir: *M62 junct 25 towards Mirfield. At rdbt, fork left onto A62 (Leeds). 1st right at lights, 0.5m*

This is a quiet haven; set within the walls of Mirfield Monastery, in beautiful gardens tended by the resident monks. Rooms are modestly appointed and decorated in calming neutral tones. WiFi is available. A continental breakfast is provided on a self-service basis. The emphasis is on peace and quiet, with guests welcome to attend services if they wish.

Rooms 8 en suite **Facilities** FTV Lounge tea/coffee Licensed WiFi **Conf** Max 70 Thtr 70 Class 40 Board 25 **Parking** 10 **Notes** ⊗ No Children 5yrs

NORMANTON
Map 16 SE32

The Grange

★★★★ BED AND BREAKFAST

tel: 01924 892203 & 07970 505157 **2 Snydale Rd WF6 1NT**
email: enquiries@thegrangenormanton.co.uk **web:** www.thegrangenormanton.co.uk

The house has been in Sarah's family for over 100 years, and is a well maintained property with gardens that were designed by 2002 Chelsea Flower Show winner, Peter Garnett-Orme. The individually styled bedrooms are well appointed and have many thoughtful extras. Guests have use of the lounge with large screen TV. Full English breakfast is served in the dining room.

Rooms 3 rms (2 en suite) (1 pri facs) (1 fmly) S £45-£55; D £70-£90* **Facilities** FTV TVL tea/coffee Dinner available WiFi 🔒 **Extras** Fruit juice, bottled water **Parking** 4 **Notes** LB ⊗ No Children 18mths Closed 24-29 Dec

SILSDEN
Map 19 SE04

Pickersgill Manor Farm Bed and Breakfast

★★★★ 🍴 BED AND BREAKFAST

tel: 01535 655228 **Low Ln BD20 9JH**
email: lisa.preston@btconnect.com **web:** www.pickersgillmanorfarm.co.uk
dir: *N of Silsden on A6034, left into Cringles Ln. After 1.5m turn left into Low Ln. 0.5m turn left at B&B sign, at end of lane into Pickersgill Manor Farm*

A warm welcome awaits you at this family built and run farmhouse. Set on a rural working farm on Silsden Moors this property boasts breathtaking views of the surrounding countryside. Bolton Abbey is just a short drive from the property. Bedrooms are comfortable and provide modern amenities such as complimentary WiFi, flat-screen TVs and iPod docking station. An excellent breakfast can be enjoyed around the communal dining table.

Rooms 1 en suite 1 annexe en suite (1 fmly) (1 GF) **Facilities** FTV iPod docking station tea/coffee WiFi 🔒 **Extras** Speciality toiletries, fridge **Parking** 4 **Notes** ⊗

CHANNEL ISLANDS
JERSEY

ST AUBIN
Map 24

Premier Collection

The Panorama

★★★★★ 🍴 GUEST ACCOMMODATION

tel: 01534 742429 & 07797 742429 **La Rue du Crocquet JE3 8BZ**
email: info@panoramajersey.com **web:** www.panoramajersey.com
dir: *In village centre*

Enjoying spectacular views across St Aubin's Bay, The Panorama is a long-established favourite with visitors. The welcome is genuine and many of the well-equipped bedrooms have wonderful views; the bathrooms are finished to a high standard. Public areas also look seaward and have attractive antique fireplaces. Breakfast is excellent and served in two dining areas.

Rooms 14 en suite (3 GF) **Facilities** STV Lounge tea/coffee WiFi 🔒 **Extras** Robes, slippers, fridge **Notes** ⊗ No Children 18yrs Closed mid Oct-mid Apr

Harbour View

★★★★ GUEST HOUSE

tel: 01534 741585 **Le Boulevard JE3 8AB**
email: harbourview@localdial.com **web:** www.harbourviewjersey.com

Harbour View is situated in a beautiful location overlooking St Aubin harbour. The guest house has been lovingly restored and it retains many original features. Bedrooms are all smartly presented and come with a host of facilities. Food can be taken at 'Danny's at the Harbour View' and parking is an added bonus. A substantial continental breakfast, along with cooked options, is available in the well-appointed breakfast room.

Rooms 16 en suite (4 fmly) (2 GF) **Facilities** STV TVL tea/coffee Licensed WiFi 🚶 18 **Parking** 8 **Notes** Closed Dec-Feb

ST HELIER
Map 24

Bay View Guest House

★★★★ GUEST ACCOMMODATION

tel: 01534 720950 & 07700 720100 **12 Havre des Pas JE2 4UQ**
email: enquiries@bayviewjersey.com **web:** www.bayviewjersey.com
dir: *Through tunnel, right at rdbt, down Green St & left, 100yds on left*

The Bay View is just across the road from the Havre des Pas Lido and beach, and a ten-minute walk from the centre of St Helier. The bedrooms are well equipped, and extra facilities include a bar and a TV lounge both with Sky TV. Free WiFi is available throughout the property. There is a small patio garden to the front of the establishment, and at the rear, another secluded terrace and a hot tub.

Rooms 12 rms (12 pri facs) (3 fmly) S £38-£54; D £76-£108 **Facilities** FTV DVD iPod docking station TVL tea/coffee Licensed WiFi 🔒 Hot tub **Extras** Speciality toiletries, robes, fridge **Notes** LB ⊗

ISLE OF MAN

PORT ST MARY
Map 24 SC26

Premier Collection

Aaron House

★★★★★ 🍴 GUEST HOUSE

tel: 01624 835702 **The Promenade IM9 5DE**
web: www.aaronhouse.co.uk
dir: *Follow signs for South & Port St Mary, left at Post Office. House in centre of Promenade*

Aaron House is truly individual. From the parlour down to the cast-iron baths, the house overlooking the harbour has maintained its Victorian origins. The family work hard to offer the best quality, whether it's providing luxury and comfort in the bedrooms, or offering home-made cakes, or perhaps a full afternoon tea on arrival. Breakfast is worth the trip alone and features super home baking alongside the obligatory full English.

Rooms 4 rms (3 en suite) (1 pri facs) **Facilities** TVL TV1B tea/coffee **Notes** ⊗ No Children 12yrs Closed 21 Dec-3 Jan 🍴

Scotland

ABERDEENSHIRE

ABOYNE
Map 23 NO59

The Lodge on the Loch of Aboyne
★★★★ ◛ GUEST ACCOMMODATION

tel: 013398 86444 **Aboyne Loch Golf Centre AB34 5BR**
email: info@thelodgeontheloch.com **web:** www.thelodgeontheloch.com
dir: 1m E of Aboyne on A93

The beautiful location of this lochside property ensures stunning views and a peaceful stay. The wide range of facilities include a nine-hole golf centre with driving range, osprey viewing deck, fitness centre and a wide range of treatments offered in the Reflect Spa. Dining options include the restaurant and the bistro bar, with very good function and wedding facilities also available.

Rooms 14 en suite (2 fmly) (7 GF) S £100-£150; D £115-£205* **Facilities** FTV tea/coffee Dinner available Direct Dial Licensed WiFi ᐃ 9 Sauna ⛱ Hot tub Holistic spa treatments **Conf** Max 80 Thtr 80 Class 40 Board 25 **Parking** 30 **Notes** LB Civ Wed 120

BALLATER
Map 23 NO39

The Auld Kirk
★★★★ ◒ GUEST HOUSE

tel: 01339 755762 & 07918 698000 **Braemar Rd AB35 5RQ**
email: info@theauldkirk.com **web:** www.theauldkirk.com
dir: From Aboyne on A93 into Ballater, through village, past The Old Railway Station, 250yds on left

This Victorian Scottish Free Church building has been carefully converted to make an unusual guest house. Many original features of the kirk have been restored and incorporated in the design, and all seven rooms are purpose-built and situated on the first floor, accessed by a wide staircase from the large entrance hallway. Breakfasts using the finest local produce are served in the Spirit restaurant, where private dining is available by appointment. Packed lunches can also be provided.

Rooms 7 en suite (1 fmly) S £75-£95; D £115-£145* **Facilities** FTV Lounge tea/coffee Licensed WiFi ᐃ 18 ⛱ **Extras** Mineral water **Parking** 6 **Notes** Closed 24-25 Dec & Jan

The Deeside
★★★★ INN

tel: 01339 755413 **45 Braemar Rd AB35 5RQ**
email: deeside@crerarhotels.com **web:** www.crerarhotels.com/the-deeside-inn
dir: On A93 (Braemar Rd)

Located in the Royal Deeside village of Ballater, in the heart of the Grampian Highlands, The Deeside is a great base from which to explore the area. Relax in the stylish bar or public lounge with its large open fires. Comfortable accommodation is provided in the spacious bedrooms.

Rooms 25 en suite (2 fmly) **Facilities** STV FTV tea/coffee Direct Dial WiFi

ELLON
Map 23 NJ93

Premier Collection

Aikenshill House (NJ968218)
★★★★★ FARMHOUSE

tel: 01358 742990 **Aikenshill, Foveran AB41 6AT**
email: enquiries@aikenshill.co.uk **web:** www.aikenshill.co.uk
dir: From Aberdeen N on A90, pass Cock & Bull restaurant & Trump International Golf Links. Turn left signed Aikenshill, 500mtrs at end of road

This farmhouse enjoys spectacular views from its elevated position overlooking Donald Trump's golf course and the Aberdeenshire coastline beyond. Located close to Aberdeen, the house is well situated for either a peaceful getaway or a city break. Decorated and furnished to an impressive standard, the modern feel of the property is complemented by friendly hospitality from the whole family. Memorable breakfasts include the best ingredients, and dinners by request are also available.

Rooms 4 en suite **Facilities** FTV TVL Dinner available WiFi ᔒ ⛱ **Notes** 300 acres arable

KILDRUMMY
Map 23 NJ41

Kildrummy Inn
★★★★ ◉◉ ◒ INN

tel: 01975 571227 **AB33 8QS**
email: enquiries@kildrummyinn.co.uk **web:** www.kildrummyinn.co.uk
dir: On A97, 2m from junct with A944 at Mossat in direction of Strathdon & Cairngorms National Park

Located in the heart of rural Aberdeenshire, this popular inn is the perfect base for touring the Grampian Mountains and beyond. Personally run and with a unique history, Kildrummy Inn provides four comfortable bedrooms, all en suite and featuring TV, DVD player and free WiFi. The lounge bar with roaring fire and a good selection of beers and whiskies is a great place in which to while away the time. No visit would be complete without sampling the food on offer with skilfully created dishes highlighting the best in local produce.

Rooms 4 en suite D £65-£85* **Facilities** FTV DVD Lounge tea/coffee Dinner available WiFi Fishing ⛱ **Extras** Speciality toiletries **Conf** Max 12 Board 12 **Parking** 20 **Notes** ⊗ Closed Jan Civ Wed 70

STONEHAVEN
Map 23 NO88

The Ship Inn
★★★ INN

tel: 01569 762617 **5 Shorehead AB39 2JY**
email: enquiries@shipinnstonehaven.com **web:** www.shipinnstonehaven.com
dir: From A90 follow signs to Stonehaven, then signs to harbour

This popular inn overlooks the harbour in Stonehaven, and has been a fixture since 1771. Bedrooms and bathrooms offer good levels of comfort; many with views of the harbour. The Lounge Bar serves a host of whiskies and real ales, while the Captain's Table restaurant specialises in fresh local fish and some spectacular meats. Close to Aberdeen and the A90, the property is in an excellent location for those looking for some peace and tranquillity.

Rooms 11 en suite (2 fmly) S £80-£105; D £110-£140* **Facilities** FTV tea/coffee Dinner available WiFi **Notes** No coaches

TARLAND
Map 23 NJ40

The Commercial
★★★★ INN

tel: 01339 881922 **The Square AB34 4TX**
email: info@thecommerical-hotel.co.uk **web:** www.thecommerical-hotel.co.uk
dir: *From Aboyne on A93 follow signs for Tarland. In village turn left into The Square, on right by monument*

This property benefits from a stunning location in the heart of Royal Deeside in the 'Howe O' Cromar'. Near to Aberdeen, the Grampian Mountains and the Cairngorm National Park, The Commercial is ideally located, family-run and offers comfortable accommodation and a range of dining options, including the cosy lounge bar or the more formal Cromar restaurant.

Rooms 9 en suite S £59-£65; D £89-£99* **Facilities** FTV DVD iPod docking station Lounge tea/coffee Dinner available WiFi Pool table **Extras** Bottled water - complimentary **Parking** 17 **Notes** No coaches

ANGUS

ARBROATH
Map 21 NO64

Hayswell Guest House
★★★ BED AND BREAKFAST

tel: 01241 430385 **29 Hayswell Rd DD11 1TU**
email: info@hayswellguesthouse.co.uk **web:** www.hayswellguesthouse.co.uk

This small Victorian property is situated close to the centre of Arbroath and the historic Abbey where the 'Declaration of Arbroath', intended to confirm Scotland's right to independence, was signed in 1320. The two bedrooms are presented to a good standard with fridges and flat-screen TVs as standard. Warm hospitality is provided throughout any stay here, whether relaxing in the attractive lounge or enjoying one of the signature breakfasts in the dining room. Parking is easy to find next to the house.

Rooms 2 rms (1 en suite) (1 pri facs) (1 GF) S £40-£45; D £65-£75* **Facilities** FTV Lounge tea/coffee WiFi 18 **Notes**

INVERKEILOR
Map 23 NO64

Premier Collection

Gordon's
★★★★★ RESTAURANT WITH ROOMS

tel: 01241 830364 **Main St DD11 5RN**
email: gordonsrest@aol.com **web:** www.gordonsrestaurant.co.uk
dir: *Exit A92 between Arbroath & Montrose into Inverkeilor*

It's worth a detour off the main road to this family-run restaurant with rooms set in the centre of the village. The food in the restaurant has been awarded three AA Rosettes, and the excellent breakfasts are equally memorable. A huge fire dominates the restaurant on cooler evenings. Individually designed rooms all come with contemporary wenge furniture, oversized headboards, chandeliers, high decorative cornice and designer wallpaper. The showcase 'Thistle Suite' is in purple, stone and lavender and has an en suite bathroom with roll-top bath and monsoon shower.

Rooms 4 en suite 1 annexe en suite (1 GF) S £110; D £130-£160* **Facilities** FTV tea/coffee Dinner available WiFi **Extras** Speciality toiletries - complimentary **Parking** 6 **Notes** No Children 12yrs Closed 3wks Jan No coaches

MONTROSE
Map 23 NO75

Oaklands Guest House
★★★ GUEST HOUSE

tel: 01674 672018 **10 Rossie Island Rd DD10 9NN**
email: oaklands1@btopenworld.com **web:** www.oaklands.sm4.biz
dir: *On A92 at S end of town*

A genuine welcome and attentive service are assured at Oaklands Guest House, a smart, detached house situated on the south side of the town. Bedrooms come in a variety of sizes and are neatly presented. There is a lounge on the ground floor next to the attractive dining room, where hearty breakfasts are served. Motorcycle guided tours can be arranged for those travelling with their own motorbikes.

Rooms 7 en suite (1 fmly) (1 GF) S £35-£45; D £60-£70* **Facilities** FTV TVL tea/coffee WiFi **Extras** Mints - complimentary **Parking** 8 **Notes**

ARGYLL & BUTE

APPIN
Map 20 NM94

Pineapple House
★★★★ GUEST HOUSE

tel: 01631 740350 **Duror PA38 4BP**
email: info@pineapplehouse.co.uk **web:** www.pineapplehouse.co.uk
dir: *In Duror, off A828. 5m S of A82*

Situated in the pretty village of Duror on the Argyll Coastal Route, Pineapple House is within easy reach of both Fort William and Oban. The property is in an excellent location for tourists, walkers and cyclists who wish to explore the Highlands. Appointed to a very high standard, the guest house is family run and all bedrooms have en suite facilities. Bike storage and drying facilities are also available. The hearty breakfasts and warm hospitality make for a memorable stay.

Rooms 6 en suite (1 fmly) **Facilities** FTV TVL tea/coffee WiFi **Extras** Sweets, bottled water, speciality toiletries **Parking** 8 **Notes** No Children 7yrs Closed mid Nov-mid Mar

BARCALDINE
Map 20 NM94

Premier Collection

Ardtorna
★★★★★ BED AND BREAKFAST

tel: 01631 720125 & 07867 785524 **Mill Farm PA37 1SE**
email: info@ardtorna.co.uk **web:** www.ardtorna.co.uk
dir: *N from Connel on A828, 0.5m from Scottish Sea Life Sanctuary*

Purpose-built as a luxury bed and breakfast, Ardtorna enjoys a commanding position overlooking the Firth of Lorn near Oban. Warm hospitality can always be found here. Floor-to-ceiling windows in the bedrooms let you watch the glorious sunsets in comfort, and the excellent king-size beds will provide a great night's sleep. Bathrooms have luxury toiletries and huge towels. Breakfast will leave you spoilt for choice. 'Butler' and 'romantic' packages are also available for those wishing to be pampered further.

Rooms 4 en suite (4 GF) **Facilities** FTV DVD iPod docking station tea/coffee WiFi 9 Leisure facilities available at nearby hotel **Extras** Fresh fruit, flowers, malt whisky, Baileys **Parking** 10 **Notes** LB No Children 12yrs

CAIRNDOW
Map 20 NN11

Cairndow Stagecoach Inn

★★★ INN

tel: 01499 600286 & 600252 **PA26 8BN**
email: enq@cairndowinn.com **web:** www.cairndowinn.com
dir: *From N, take either A82 to Tarbet, A83 to Cairndow, or A85 to Dalmally, A819 to Inveraray & A83 to Cairndow*

A relaxed, friendly atmosphere prevails at the 18th-century Cairndow Stagecoach Inn, overlooking the beautiful Loch Fyne. Bedrooms offer individual decor and thoughtful extras. Traditional public areas include a comfortable beamed lounge, a well-stocked bar where food is served all day, and a spacious restaurant with conservatory extension. Deluxe bedrooms offer more space and luxury.

Rooms 13 en suite 5 annexe en suite (2 fmly) (5 GF) **Facilities** STV FTV Lounge tea/coffee Dinner available Direct Dial WiFi ☇ 9 Sauna Pool table ♨ **Conf** Max 30 Thtr 30 Class 30 Board 30 **Parking** 30 **Notes** LB

LUSS
Map 20 NS39

The Inn on Loch Lomond

★★★★ ⬭ INN

tel: 01436 860678 **Inverbeg G83 8PD**
email: res@innonlochlomond.co.uk **web:** www.innonlochlomond.co.uk
dir: *A82 N of Balloch*

Dating back to the 18th century, this inn offers very stylish, comfortable bedrooms (many with stunning views), bathrooms, and equally attractive public areas that boast open fires and cow-hide sofas. Food is as much of a feature as the property itself, with a varied menu offered. The inn has its own chip shop fryer which proves most popular. The Beach House accommodation, just a short walk from the inn, is a real treat for those looking for a little more privacy.

Rooms 25 en suite 8 annexe en suite (1 fmly) (5 GF) **Facilities** TVL tea/coffee Dinner available WiFi ♨ **Parking** 60 **Notes** LB Civ Wed 60

OBAN
Map 20 NM82

Premier Collection

Blarcreen House

★★★★★ GUEST HOUSE

tel: 01631 750272 & 07557 977225 **Ardchattan, Connel PA37 1RG**
email: info@blarcreenhouse.com **web:** www.blarcreenhouse.com
dir: *N over Connel Bridge, turn right signed Bonawe, 6.7m to Blarcreen*

This elegant Victorian mansion house on the side of Loch Etive is the ideal base for exploring the Highlands. Warm hospitality and log fires await guests arriving at this property, where they can relax and enjoy comfortable bedrooms and fantastic views. Evening meals are also available by prior arrangement.

Rooms 3 en suite S £90-£110; D £110-£130* **Facilities** FTV DVD iPod docking station TVL tea/coffee Dinner available Licensed WiFi ♨ **Extras** Speciality toiletries, chocolates - complimentary **Parking** 5 **Notes** No Children 16yrs Closed Dec-Jan

MacKay's Guest House

★★★★ ⬭ GUEST HOUSE

tel: 01631 563121 & 566356 **Corran Esplanade PA34 5AQ**
email: info@mackaysguesthouse.co.uk **web:** www.mackaysguesthouse.co.uk
dir: *A85 into town, at rdbt 2nd exit to seafront (Corran Esplanade). Pass Cathedral, 300yds on right*

Boasting fantastic views across Oban Bay, this property offers comfort and quality as well as warm traditional hospitality. All front-facing bedrooms are spacious and very well appointed. Award winning breakfast is served in the bright conservatory and breakfast room. Dedicated off-road parking and outdoor seating overlooking the bay add to this wonderful guest experience.

Rooms 8 en suite (2 GF) **Facilities** FTV DVD iPod docking station tea/coffee WiFi **Extras** Robes, snacks, water, sherry - complimentary **Parking** 10 **Notes** ⊗ No Children 15yrs Closed 13 Nov-21 Mar

The Barriemore Guest House

★★★★ GUEST HOUSE

tel: 01631 566356 & 571084 **Corran Esplanade PA34 5AQ**
email: info@barriemore.co.uk **web:** www.barriemore.co.uk
dir: *A85 into Oban, 1st rdbt exit towards sea. Right at 2nd rdbt, continue with sea on left, last guest house on right*

This splendid three-storey Victorian town house is in a fantastic location on Oban's seafront and enjoys great views over Oban Bay. Friendly service and spacious rooms with modern decor can be found at this family-run property. A hearty Scottish breakfast will set guests up for the day ahead.

Rooms 15 en suite (2 fmly) (2 GF) S £65-£90; D £105-£165* **Facilities** FTV DVD iPod docking station Lounge tea/coffee WiFi **Extras** Fruit, bottled water, sherry, robes, slippers **Parking** 14 **Notes** ⊗ Closed Nov-Apr

The Glenrigh Guest House

★★★★ GUEST HOUSE

tel: 01631 562991 **Corran Esplanade PA34 5AQ**
email: info@glenrigh.co.uk **web:** www.glenrigh.co.uk
dir: *Down hill into Oban, turn right (with sea on left), along esplanade*

This former Victorian mansion has fantastic views of Oban Bay and the far away islands, and has the added bonus of on-site parking. Close to the heart of Oban town centre, it is also within walking distance of local amenities. Glenrigh offers comfortable bedrooms, impressive bathrooms and a hearty breakfast. A friendly team are waiting to make your stay memorable.

Rooms 15 en suite (1 fmly) (5 GF) S £60-£65; D £90-£120* **Facilities** FTV DVD iPod docking station TVL tea/coffee WiFi 🛋 **Extras** Snacks, drinks **Parking** 20 **Notes** ⊗ Closed Nov-Mar

---

TAYNUILT   Map 20 NN03

The Taynuilt

★★★ ⊛⊛ ⊖ INN

tel: 01866 822437 **PA35 1JN**
email: enquiries@taynuilthotel.co.uk **web:** www.taynuilthotel.co.uk
dir: *In Taynuilt, on A85*

This small inn enjoys a great location in the heart of stunning Highand countryside, not far from Oban. Accommodation has been offered on this site for centuries, and it continues to provide comfortable bedrooms, and cosy public areas including the main restaurant, snug restaurant and lounge bar. A stay here would not be complete without sampling the quality cuisine on offer; Scottish produce treated with respect. Craft ales and a great selection of whiskies are also features of the inn.

Rooms 9 en suite (1 fmly) S £80-£100; D £115-£199* (incl.dinner) **Facilities** FTV DVD iPod docking station tea/coffee Dinner available WiFi ⌕ 9 🛋 **Conf** Max 50 Thtr 50 Class 30 Board 28 **Parking** 15

NORTH AYRSHIRE

WEST KILBRIDE   Map 20 NS24

Carlton Seamill B&B

AA Advertised

---

tel: 01294 822075 & 07887 611738 **53 Ardrossan Rd, Seamill KA23 9NE**
email: stay@carlton-seamill.co.uk **web:** www.carlton-seamill.co.uk
dir: *On A78 coastal road*

Carlton Seamill is an impressive, stone-built Victorian house, set in an ideal location at Seamill, on the Ayrshire coast. It enjoys commanding views to the Firth of Clyde and the Isle of Arran. The Rennie family have been at Carlton for over 60 years, and provide a relaxing atmosphere. On the ground floor, the handsome reception room has magnificent views over the Rose Garden and Croquet Lawn; and the elegant Victorian staircase leads up to the comfortable, first-floor accommodation. Carlton's garden gate leads to the sandy beach, so guests can enjoy a walk before heading to a local hostelry for dinner.

Rooms 3 rms S £40-£75; D £70-£75* **Facilities** FTV DVD tea/coffee WiFi 🛋 **Parking** 6 **Notes** ⊛

DUMFRIES & GALLOWAY

CASTLE DOUGLAS   Map 21 NX76

Craigadam

★★★★ ⊖ ⌂ GUEST HOUSE

tel: 01556 650233 & 650100 **Craigadam DG7 3HU**
email: inquiry@craigadam.com **web:** www.craigadam.com
dir: *From Castle Douglas E on A75 to Crocketford. In Crocketford turn left on A712 for 2m. House on hill*

Set on a farm, this elegant country house offers gracious living in a relaxed environment. The large bedrooms, most set around a courtyard, are strikingly individual in style. Public areas include a billiard room, and the panelled dining room which features a magnificent 15-seater table, the setting for Celia Pickup's delightful meals.

Rooms 10 en suite (2 fmly) (7 GF) S £65; D £94* **Facilities** FTV DVD Lounge TVL tea/coffee Dinner available Licensed WiFi ch fac ⌕ Fishing Snooker 🛋 Shooting **Extras** Speciality toiletries **Conf** Max 22 **Parking** 12 **Notes** LB Closed Xmas & New Year Civ Wed 150

Wallamhill House

★★★★ BED AND BREAKFAST

tel: 01387 248249 **Kirkton DG1 1SL**
email: wallamhill@aol.com **web:** www.wallamhill.co.uk
dir: *3m N of Dumfries. Off A701 signed Kirkton, 1.5m on right*

Wallamhill House is set in well-tended gardens, in a delightful rural area three miles from Dumfries. Bedrooms are spacious and extremely well equipped. Beds feature luxurious Egyptian linens while bathrooms have underfloor heating. There is a peaceful drawing room, and a mini health club with sauna, steam shower and gym equipment.

Rooms 3 en suite (1 fmly) (3 GF) **Facilities** FTV TVL tea/coffee WiFi ⤳ Sauna Gym ⚖ Steam room Hot tub **Extras** Fridge **Parking** 6 **Notes** ⊗

Rivendell

★★★★ GUEST HOUSE

tel: 01387 252251 **105 Edinburgh Rd DG1 1JX**
email: info@rivendellbnb.co.uk **web:** www.rivendellbnb.co.uk
dir: *On A701 Edinburgh Rd, 400yds S of A75 junct*

Situated just north of the town and close to the bypass, this lovely Charles Rennie Mackintosh inspired 1920s house, standing in extensive landscaped gardens, has been restored to reflect the period style of the property. Bedrooms are thoughtfully equipped, many are spacious and all offer modern facilities. Traditional breakfasts are served in the elegant dining room.

Rooms 7 rms (6 en suite) (1 pri facs) 3 annexe en suite (2 fmly) (5 GF) **Facilities** FTV iPod docking station tea/coffee WiFi **Parking** 12 **Notes** ⊗

Southpark House

★★★★ GUEST ACCOMMODATION

tel: 01387 711188 & 0800 970 1588 **Quarry Rd, Locharbriggs DG1 1FA**
email: info@southparkhouse.co.uk **web:** www.southparkhouse.co.uk
dir: *3.5m NE of Dumfries. Exit A701 in Locharbriggs into Quarry Rd, last house on left*

With a peaceful location commanding stunning views, this well-maintained property offers comfortable, attractive and well-equipped bedrooms. The peaceful lounge has a log fire on colder evenings, and e-mail facilities are available. Friendly proprietor Ewan Maxwell personally oversees the hearty Scottish breakfasts served in the conservatory breakfast room.

Rooms 4 en suite (1 fmly) **Facilities** STV FTV Lounge TVL tea/coffee WiFi 2 acres of garden **Parking** 13 **Notes** ⊗

Surrone House

★★★★ GUEST ACCOMMODATION

tel: 01461 338341 **Annan Rd DG16 5DL**
email: enquiries@surronehouse.co.uk **web:** www.surronehouse.co.uk
dir: *In town centre on B721*

Guests are assured of a warm welcome at this well-maintained property in attractive gardens set back from the road. Bedrooms are sensibly furnished and include a delightful honeymoon suite. The property is located only 500 yards from the centre of Gretna. Complimentary parking is available on site.

Rooms 6 en suite (3 fmly) (1 GF) S £50; D £70-£75* **Facilities** FTV TVL tea/coffee WiFi ⚖ **Extras** Speciality toiletries - complimentary **Parking** 10 **Notes** ⊗

Bridge House

★★★★ ⬮ GUEST HOUSE

tel: 01683 220558 **Well Rd DG10 9JT**
email: info@bridgehousemoffat.co.uk **web:** www.bridgehousemoffat.co.uk
dir: *Exit A708 (The Holm) into Burnside, bear right into Well Rd, house 0.5m on left*

A fine Victorian property, Bridge House stands in attractive gardens in a quiet residential area on the outskirts of the town. The atmosphere is very friendly and relaxed. The chef-proprietor provides interesting dinners (by prior arrangement) featuring local produce. There is a cosy guest lounge, and free WiFi is available.

Rooms 7 en suite (1 fmly) **Facilities** FTV Lounge tea/coffee Dinner available WiFi ⚖ **Parking** 7 **Notes** LB ⊗ No Children 2yrs Closed Xmas & New Year

Blackaddie House

★★★ ⦿⦿ RESTAURANT WITH ROOMS

tel: 01659 50270 **Blackaddie Rd DG4 6JJ**
email: ian@blackaddiehotel.co.uk **web:** www.blackaddiehotel.co.uk
dir: *300 yds from A76 on N side of Sanquhar*

Overlooking the River Nith, in two acres of secluded gardens, this family-run country house offers friendly and attentive hands-on service. The bedrooms and suites, including family accommodation, are all well-presented and comfortable, with many useful extras provided as standard. The award-winning food, served in the restaurant, with its lovely garden views, is based on prime Scottish ingredients.

Rooms 6 en suite 1 annexe en suite (1 fmly) S £85-£190; D £95-£210* **Facilities** FTV DVD Lounge tea/coffee Dinner available Direct Dial WiFi ⚲ 9 ⚖ **Extras** Speciality toiletries, mineral water **Conf** Max 16 Thtr 16 Class 16 Board 12 **Parking** 20 **Notes** LB No Children Civ Wed 24

WEST DUNBARTONSHIRE

The Waterhouse Inn

★★★★ INN

tel: 01389 752120 **34 Balloch Rd G83 8LE**
email: info@waterhouseinn.co.uk **web:** www.waterhouseinn.co.uk
dir: *M8 junct 30 onto M898. Over Erskine bridge, take exit for Crianlarich onto A82 head towards Loch Lomond. Right at rdbt onto A811*

The Waterhouse Inn is located on the high street of Balloch, close to the park and the mouth of Loch Lomond. Bedrooms are well equipped and spacious, with modern bright bathrooms. The inn is welcoming and friendly, with a café that serves home-cooked food throughout the day, and is a perfect base for touring Loch Lomond and the Trossachs National Park.

Rooms 7 en suite (2 fmly) **Facilities** STV FTV Lounge TVL tea/coffee Dinner available WiFi 🔒 **Notes** ⊗

Innkeeper's Lodge Loch Lomond

★★★ INN

tel: 08451 551551 *(Calls cost 2p per minute plus your phone company's access charge)*
Balloch Rd G83 8LQ
email: info@innkeeperslodge.com **web:** www.innkeeperslodge.com

This property enjoys an excellent location, a stone's throw from Loch Lomond and the nearby Balloch Castle Country Park. The historic lodge provides modern, spacious accommodation. The cosy and welcoming lounge bar is a popular place to dine below the exposed wooden beams. Enjoy a cask ale by the open fire or a dish from their wide and varying menu. Parking available on site.

Rooms 11 en suite (3 fmly) **Facilities** FTV tea/coffee Dinner available WiFi
Parking 52 **Notes** ⊗

CITY OF EDINBURGH

EDINBURGH	Map 21 NT27

See also Livingston (West Lothian)

Premier Collection

Kew House

★★★★★ 🗟 GUEST ACCOMMODATION

tel: 0131 313 0700 **1 Kew Ter, Murrayfield EH12 5JE**
email: info@kewhouse.com **web:** www.kewhouse.com
dir: *1m W of Princes St*

Forming part of a listed Victorian terrace, Kew House lies within walking distance of the city centre, and is convenient for Murrayfield Stadium and tourist attractions. Meticulously maintained in contemporary style throughout, it offers attractive bedrooms in a variety of sizes, all thoughtfully equipped to suit business and leisure guests. There is a comfortable lounge. Both parking and WiFi are complimentary.

Kew House

Rooms 6 en suite (1 fmly) (2 GF) D £99-£190* **Facilities** FTV Lounge tea/coffee Direct Dial WiFi 🔒 **Extras** Speciality toiletries, sherry, chocolates, fridge **Parking** 6 **Notes** LB ⊗ Closed approx 5-31 Jan

Premier Collection

Six Brunton Place

★★★★★ 🗟 GUEST HOUSE

tel: 0131 622 0042 & 07748 858892 **6 Brunton Place EH7 5EG**
email: contact@sixbruntonplace.com **web:** www.sixbruntonplace.com
dir: *On London Road (B1350), opposite London Road Gardens*

This award-winning Georgian town house is located within easy walking distance of the centre of Edinburgh. The building and its lovingly restored features cannot help but impress, and the warmth and hospitality make this a 'little gem'. Bedrooms are extremely well equipped with quality and comfort a given. Guests can also relax in either the walled garden or attractive lounge area.

Rooms 4 en suite (1 fmly) (1 GF) S £89-£159; D £109-£199 **Facilities** STV FTV DVD iPod docking station Lounge tea/coffee WiFi ⌁ 18 🔒 **Extras** Speciality toiletries, home-baked goods - free **Notes** ⊗ No Children 10yrs

Premier Collection

21212

★★★★★ ⊚⊚⊚⊚ RESTAURANT WITH ROOMS

tel: 0131 523 1030 **3 Royal Ter EH7 5AB**
email: reservations@21212restaurant.co.uk **web:** www.21212restaurant.co.uk
dir: *Calton Hill, city centre*

A real jewel in Edinburgh's crown, this establishment takes its name from the number of choices at each course on the five-course dinner menu. Located on the prestigious Royal Terrace this light and airy, renovated Georgian town house stretches over four floors. The four individually-designed bedrooms epitomise luxury living and the bathrooms certainly have the wow factor. At the heart of this restaurant with rooms is the creative and impressive four AA Rosette award-winning cooking of Paul Kitching. Service throughout is friendly and very attentive.

Rooms 4 en suite D £95-£295* **Facilities** STV FTV iPod docking station Lounge Dinner available WiFi **Extras** Speciality toiletries, mineral water, sloe gin **Notes** ⊗ No Children 5yrs Closed 1wk Jan & 1wk Autumn RS Sun & Mon restaurant closed No coaches

EDINBURGH *continued*

Premier Collection

The Witchery by the Castle

★★★★★ ◉ ≘ RESTAURANT WITH ROOMS

tel: 0131 225 5613 **Castlehill, The Royal Mile EH1 2NF**
email: mail@thewitchery.com **web:** www.thewitchery.com
dir: *Top of Royal Mile at gates of Edinburgh Castle*

Originally built in 1595, The Witchery by the Castle is situated in a historic building at the gates of Edinburgh Castle. The two luxurious and theatrically decorated suites, known as the Inner Sanctum and the Old Rectory, are located above the restaurant and are reached via a winding stone staircase. Filled with antiques, opulently draped beds, large roll-top baths and a plethora of memorabilia, this ancient and exciting establishment is often described as one of the country's most romantic destinations.

Rooms 4 en suite 5 annexe en suite (1 GF) **Facilities** STV FTV DVD tea/coffee Dinner available Direct Dial WiFi **Extras** Bottled water - complimentary **Notes** ⊗ No Children 12yrs Closed 25-26 Dec No coaches

Bonnington Guest House

★★★★ GUEST HOUSE

tel: 0131 554 7610 & 07880 312820 **202 Ferry Rd EH6 4NW**
email: booking@thebonningtonguesthouse.com **web:** www.thebonningtonguesthouse.com
dir: *On A902, near corner of Ferry Rd & Newhaven Rd*

This delightful Georgian house offers individually furnished bedrooms on two floors that retain many of their original features. A family room is also available. A substantial freshly prepared breakfast is served in the dining room. Off-street parking is an added bonus.

Rooms 6 rms (4 en suite) (2 pri facs) (1 fmly) S £65-£85; D £75-£140*
Facilities FTV tea/coffee WiFi **Extras** Speciality toiletries, sherry - free; robes **Parking** 9 **Notes** ⊗ Closed Nov-Mar RS 27 Dec-2 Jan Open for New Year & some wknds Nov-Mar

Fraoch House

★★★★ GUEST ACCOMMODATION

tel: 0131 554 1353 **66 Pilrig St EH6 5AS**
email: info@fraochhouse.com **web:** www.fraochhouse.com
dir: *1m from Princes St*

Situated within walking distance of the city centre and convenient for many attractions, Fraoch House, which dates from the 1900s, has been appointed to offer well-equipped and thoughtfully furnished bedrooms. Delicious, freshly cooked breakfasts are served in the charming dining room on the ground floor.

Rooms 9 rms (7 en suite) (2 pri facs) (1 fmly) (1 GF) **Facilities** FTV tea/coffee WiFi Free use of DVDs and CDs & internet access **Notes** ⊗

Kingsway Guest House

★★★★ ≘ GUEST HOUSE

tel: 0131 667 5029 **5 East Mayfield EH9 1SD**
email: booking@kingswayguesthouse.com **web:** www.edinburgh-guesthouse.com
dir: *A701 to city centre, after 4m road name changes to Mayfield Gdns. Right at lights into East Mayfield*

Well situated for the city centre and with off-road parking, this well-presented Victorian building maintains a number of original features, and genuine and warm hospitality is assured. All the bedrooms are comfortable, and the quality Scottish breakfasts make an excellent start to the day. AA Friendliest B&B of the Year Award Finalist 2016-2017.

Rooms 7 rms (6 en suite) (1 pri facs) (2 fmly) **Facilities** FTV DVD iPod docking station Lounge tea/coffee WiFi ⅃ 18 🔒 **Extras** Speciality toiletries **Parking** 4 **Notes** ⊗

Southside Guest House

★★★★ ≘ GUEST HOUSE

tel: 0131 668 4422 **8 Newington Rd EH9 1QS**
email: info@southsideguesthouse.co.uk **web:** www.southsideguesthouse.co.uk
dir: *E end of Princes St into North Bridge to Royal Mile, continue S, 0.5m, house on right*

Situated within easy reach of the city centre and convenient for the major attractions, Southside Guest House is an elegant sandstone building. Bedrooms are individually styled, comfortable and thoughtfully equipped. Traditional, freshly cooked Scottish breakfasts are served at individual tables in the smart, ground-floor dining room.

Rooms 8 en suite (2 fmly) (1 GF) **Facilities** FTV DVD tea/coffee Direct Dial Licensed WiFi **Extras** Speciality toiletries **Notes** LB ⊗ No Children 10yrs

Ashlyn Guest House

★★★★ GUEST HOUSE

tel: 0131 552 2954 **42 Inverleith Row EH3 5PY**
email: info@ashlynguesthouse.com **web:** www.ashlynguesthouse.com
dir: *Adjacent to Edinburgh Botanic Gardens. Follow signs for North Edinburgh & Botanics*

The Ashlyn Guest House is a warm and friendly Georgian home, ideally located to take advantage of Edinburgh's attractions. The city centre is within walking distance and the Royal Botanical Gardens are minutes away. Bedrooms are all individually decorated and furnished to a high standard. A generous and hearty breakfast gives a great start to the day.

Ashlyn Guest House

Rooms 5 rms (3 en suite) (2 pri facs) D £75-£100* **Facilities** FTV Lounge tea/coffee WiFi ⚲ **Extras** Mineral water **Notes** ⊗ No Children 10yrs Closed 23-28 Dec

Sherwood Guest House

★★★★ GUEST HOUSE

tel: 0131 667 1200 **42 Minto St EH9 2BR**
email: vivienne@sherwood-edinburgh.com **web:** www.sherwood-edinburgh.com
dir: On A701, S of city centre

The Sherwood Guest House is located on the south side of the city, and is well served by buses. Bedrooms vary in size, and the smaller ones are thoughtfully appointed to make the best use of space. Many thoughtful extras are provided and a continental breakfast is served in the bright and welcoming dining room. The property has limited parking space on a "first come first served" basis.

Rooms 6 rms (5 en suite) (1 pri facs) (2 fmly) (1 GF) S £50-£90; D £60-£120* **Facilities** FTV iPod docking station tea/coffee WiFi **Extras** Fridge **Parking** 3 **Notes** ⊗ Closed Jan

Ravensdown Guest House

★★★★ 🅰 GUEST HOUSE

tel: 0131 552 5438 **248 Ferry Rd EH5 3AN**
email: david@ravensdownhouse.com **web:** www.ravensdownhouse.com
dir: N of city centre, close to Royal Botanic Gardens, A902 Goldenacre

This substantial end-of-terrace house enjoys wonderful views of the city skyline. It offers comfortable, individually styled bedrooms with smart bathrooms. Guests are

made to feel welcome with good hospitality and customer care. Freshly prepared breakfasts are served at individual tables in the dining room.

Rooms 7 en suite (3 fmly) (1 GF) **Facilities** FTV iPod docking station tea/coffee WiFi ⚲ **Parking** 2 **Notes** ⊗

Arden Guest House

★★★ GUEST HOUSE

tel: 0131 664 3985 **126 Old Dalkeith Rd EH16 4SD**
email: ardenguesthouse@btinternet.com **web:** www.ardenedinburgh.co.uk
dir: 2m SE of city centre near Craigmillar Castle. On A7, 200yds W of hospital

Arden Guest House is well situated on the south-east side of the city, close to the hospital, and benefits from off-road parking. Many thoughtful extras are provided as standard, including WiFi. Attentive and friendly service enhances the guest experience.

Rooms 8 en suite (2 fmly) (3 GF) S £45-£90; D £65-£90* **Facilities** FTV DVD tea/coffee WiFi ⚡ 18 **Parking** 8 **Notes** Closed 22-27 Dec

Elder York Guest House

★★★ GUEST HOUSE

tel: 0131 556 1926 **38 Elder St EH1 3DX**
email: reception@elderyork.co.uk **web:** www.elderyork.co.uk
dir: Close to Princes St, next to bus station

Elder York Guest House is centrally located just minutes from the bus station, Harvey Nichols and the St James Shopping Centre. Accommodation is situated up flights of stairs and all bedrooms are well appointed with many thoughtful extras including WiFi. Quality breakfast is served on individual tables overlooking Queen Street.

Rooms 12 rms (11 en suite) (1 pri facs) (1 fmly) **Facilities** FTV tea/coffee WiFi **Notes** ⊗

Averon Guest House

★★★ GUEST HOUSE

tel: 0131 229 9932 **44 Gilmore Place EH3 9NQ**
email: info@averon.co.uk **web:** www.averon.co.uk
dir: From W end of Princes St onto A702, right at Kings Theatre

Situated within walking distance of the west end of the city and close to the Kings Theatre, Averon Guest House offers comfortable, good-value accommodation, with a secure car park to the rear.

Rooms 10 rms (6 en suite) (1 pri facs) (3 fmly) (5 GF) S £32-£60; D £64-£130 **Facilities** tea/coffee **Parking** 19 **Notes** ⊗

Innkeeper's Lodge Edinburgh, Corstorphine

★★★ INN

tel: 08451 551551 *(Calls cost 2p per minute plus your phone company's access charge)*
St Johns Rd, Corstorphine EH12 8AX
email: info@innkeeperslodge.com **web:** www.innkeeperslodge.com

At Innkeeper's Lodge you'll find accommodation with comfort and character in equal measure, and everything needed for a relaxing stay, from easy check-in and free parking to complimentary breakfast and a cosy pub serving great value food and drink on the doorstep. Each Lodge has quality rooms, and there are Lodges in a variety of locations from towns and cities to countryside settings across the UK.

Rooms 28 en suite (4 fmly) (6 GF) **Facilities** FTV tea/coffee Dinner available Direct Dial WiFi **Parking** 46 **Notes** ⊗

EDINBURGH *continued*

Halcyon House

★★ GUEST HOUSE

tel: 0131 556 1033 & 556 1032 **8 Royal Ter EH7 5AB**
email: patricia@halcyon-hotel.com **web:** www.halcyon-hotel.com

Halcyon House benefits from a fantastic location, and has retained many of its original Georgian features. It is within easy walking distance of the theatre and the centre of Edinburgh. Rooms are split over three floors, come in a variety of sizes, and are decorated in a basic but comfortable fashion. Front or back rooms offer wonderful views of the gardens or views across to the Forth.

Rooms 14 rms (11 en suite) (1 pri facs) (7 fmly) (2 GF) **Facilities** TVL tea/coffee WiFi **Notes** ⊗

RATHO   Map 21 NT17

The Bridge Inn at Ratho

★★★★ ⊛ ⊜ INN

tel: 0131 333 1320 **27 Baird Rd EH28 8RA**
email: info@bridgeinn.com **web:** www.bridgeinn.com

Located beside the Union Canal and in use as a hostelry since the 19th century, this inn offers modern, spacious and well-furnished bedrooms with views of the canal. The busy bistro's kitchen uses home-grown produce to create award-winning food. Outdoor seating is an added bonus as are the two restaurant barges that serve lunch, afternoon tea and dinner.

Rooms 4 en suite **Facilities** FTV tea/coffee Dinner available WiFi ⌚ **Extras** Speciality toiletries - complimentary **Parking** 40 **Notes** Closed 25 Dec Civ Wed 80

SOUTH QUEENSFERRY   Map 21 NT17

Innkeeper's Lodge Edinburgh South Queensferry

★★★ INN

tel: 08451 551551 *(Calls cost 2p per minute plus your phone company's access charge)* **7 Newhalls Rd EH30 9TA**
email: info@innkeeperslodge.com **web:** www.innkeeperslodge.com

At Innkeeper's Lodge you'll find accommodation with comfort and character in equal measure, and everything needed for a relaxing stay, from easy check-in and free parking to complimentary breakfast and a cosy pub serving great value food and drink on the doorstep. Each Lodge has quality rooms, and there are Lodges in a variety of locations from towns and cities to countryside settings across the UK.

Rooms 14 en suite (5 fmly) (3 GF) **Facilities** FTV tea/coffee Dinner available Direct Dial WiFi **Parking** 40 **Notes** ⊗

FIFE

ANSTRUTHER   Map 21 NO50

The Spindrift

★★★★ ⊜ ⊜ GUEST HOUSE

tel: 01333 310573 & 07713 597996 **Pittenweem Rd KY10 3DT**
email: info@thespindrift.co.uk **web:** www.thespindrift.co.uk
dir: *Enter town from W on A917, 1st building on left*

This immaculate Victorian villa stands on the western edge of the village. The attractive bedrooms offer a wide range of extra touches; the Captain's Room, a replica of a wood-panelled cabin, is a particular feature. The inviting lounge has an honesty bar, while imaginative breakfasts, and enjoyable home-cooked meals by arrangement, are served in the cheerful dining room. Free WiFi is available.

Rooms 8 rms (7 en suite) (1 pri facs) (2 fmly) S £45-£65; D £66-£100 **Facilities** FTV DVD iPod docking station TVL tea/coffee Dinner available Direct Dial Licensed WiFi ⌚ 18 ⌚ **Extras** Speciality toiletries, shortbread, chocolates - free **Parking** 9 **Notes** LB No Children 10yrs Closed Xmas-late Jan

The Bank

★★★★ INN

tel: 01333 310189 **23-25 High Street East KY10 3DQ**
email: enquiries@thebank-anstruther.co.uk **web:** www.thebank-anstruther.co.uk
dir: *From St Andrews, in Anstruther turn right towards Pittenweem. 50mtrs on left*

Located in the heart of Anstruther where the Dreel Burn meets the Forth, this friendly inn serves real ales and great pub food; there is a separate building next door for the accommodation. Modern, high quality, en suite bedrooms cater well for guests' needs and some offer great views. The beer garden is a real suntrap and has a children's play area.

Rooms 8 en suite (1 fmly) (1 GF) S £30-£60; D £45-£140* **Facilities** STV FTV iPod docking station tea/coffee Dinner available Direct Dial WiFi ⌁ 18 Pool table ▟ **Extras** Bottled water - complimentary; fridge, safe **Parking** 3 **Notes** LB ⊗

The Waterfront

★★★★ 🍴 RESTAURANT WITH ROOMS

tel: 01333 312200 **18-20 Shore St KY10 3EA**
email: info@anstruther-waterfront.co.uk **web:** www.anstruther-waterfront.co.uk
dir: *Off A917 opposite marina*

Situated overlooking the harbour, The Waterfront offers spacious, stylish, contemporary accommodation, with bedrooms located in lovingly restored buildings in a courtyard behind the restaurant. There is a comfortable lounge with a smartly fitted kitchen and dining room, and laundry facilities are available in the granary. Dinner and breakfast are served in the attractive restaurant that offers a comprehensive menu featuring the best of local produce.

Rooms 10 en suite (3 fmly) (2 GF) S £25-£60; D £50-£140* **Facilities** FTV DVD Lounge tea/coffee Dinner available WiFi ⌁ Pool table ▟ **Extras** Mineral water **Notes** LB ⊗

ELIE
Map 21 NO40

The Ship Inn

★★★★ 🍴 INN

tel: 01333 330246 **The Toft KY9 1DT**
email: info@shipinn.scot **web:** www. shipinn.scot

You'd have to travel along way to find views better than the ones from this recently refurbished inn. Overlooking the harbour in Elie, the Ship Inn has a beer garden and views over the sea and beach. They even organise cricket matches on the beach when the weather and tides allow. A comfortable lounge bar and expansive dining space enjoy beautiful views and sunsets when weather permits. Bedrooms and bathrooms continue the quality theme with Egyptian linens, coffee machines and beautiful toiletries a feature. No visit would be complete without sampling the food or trying one of the cask ales. The Ship Inn is the AA Pub of the Year for Scotland 2016-2017.

Rooms 6 en suite (1 GF) **Facilities** FTV iPod docking station tea/coffee Dinner available WiFi ⌁ 18 ▟

INVERKEITHING
Map 21 NT18

The Roods

★★★★ BED AND BREAKFAST

tel: 01383 415049 **16 Bannerman Av KY11 1NG**
email: isobelmarley@hotmail.com **web:** www.the-roods.co.uk
dir: *N of town centre off B981(Church St/Chapel Place)*

This charming house stands in secluded, well-tended gardens close to the train station. Bedrooms are individually styled and have state-of-the-art bathrooms. There is an inviting lounge, and breakfast is served at a large shared table in an attractive conservatory.

Rooms 3 en suite (2 GF) **Facilities** FTV DVD iPod docking station TVL tea/coffee Direct Dial WiFi ▟ **Parking** 4 **Notes** ⊗

Premier Collection

The Peat Inn

★★★★★ ◉◉◉ RESTAURANT WITH ROOMS

tel: 01334 840206 **KY15 5LH**
email: stay@thepeatinn.co.uk **web:** www.thepeatinn.co.uk
dir: *At junct of B940 & B941, 5m SW of St Andrews*

This 300-year-old former coaching inn enjoys a rural location is close to St Andrews. The Peat Inn is spacious, very well appointed, and offers rooms that all have lounge areas. The inn is steeped in history and for years has proved a real haven for food lovers. The three dining areas create a romantic setting, and chef/owner Geoffrey Smeddle produces excellent, award-winning dishes. Expect welcoming open fires and a relaxed ambiance. An extensive continental breakfast selection is served to guests in their bedrooms each morning.

Rooms 8 annexe en suite (3 fmly) (8 GF) **Facilities** FTV Lounge tea/coffee Dinner available Direct Dial WiFi 🌡 **Extras** Speciality toiletries, fruit, sherry - free **Parking** 24 **Notes** ⊗ Closed 25-26 Dec, 2wks Jan, 1wk Nov RS Sun-Mon closed No coaches

Lorimer House

★★★★ 🅰 GUEST HOUSE

tel: 01334 476599 **19 Murray Park KY16 9AW**
email: info@lorimerhouse.com **web:** www.lorimerhouse.com
dir: *A91 to St Andrews, left into Golf Place, right into The Scores, right into Murray Park*

A warm and friendly welcome is assured at Lorimer House, set in a delightful Victorian terrace, situated within easy reach of the famous Old Course, the seafront and town centre. Bedrooms are attractive, comfortably furnished and well equipped. Freshly prepared Scottish breakfasts are served in the stylish dining room, which also has a lounge area and offers free broadband internet access.

Rooms 5 en suite (1 GF) D £80-£140* **Facilities** STV FTV TVL tea/coffee WiFi ⌁ 🌡 **Extras** Chilled water, use of fridge **Notes** ⊗ No Children 12yrs

CITY OF GLASGOW

ABode Glasgow

★★★★ GUEST ACCOMMODATION

tel: 0141 221 6789 **129 Bath St G2 2SZ**
email: reservationsglasgow@abodehotels.co.uk **web:** www.abodehotels.co.uk

Located a moment's walk from Glasgow's shopping centres and central transport links, this impressive building provides comfortable luxury accommodation with a boutique feel. Bedrooms are all recently refurbished and tastefully appointed; many with high ceilings that allude to the fantastic history of the property. Bedrooms feature air conditioning and 32 inch TVs as standard. The modern restaurant offers an interesting range of dishes, and a hearty traditional Scottish breakfast sets you up for the day ahead.

Rooms 59 en suite

Georgian House

★★ GUEST HOUSE

tel: 0141 339 0008 & 07973 971563 **29 Buckingham Ter, Great Western Rd G12 8ED**
email: thegeorgianhouse@yahoo.com **web:** www.thegeorgianhousehotel.com
dir: *M8 junct 17 towards Dumbarton, through 4 sets of lights & right into Queen Margaret Dr, then right into Buckingham Ter*

Georgian House offers good-value accommodation and is situated at the west end of the city in a peaceful tree-lined Victorian terrace near the Botanic Gardens. Bedrooms vary in size and are furnished in a modern style. A continental style breakfast is served in the first-floor lounge-dining room.

Rooms 11 rms (10 en suite) (1 pri facs) (4 fmly) (3 GF) **Facilities** FTV tea/coffee WiFi **Parking** 6

HIGHLAND

AVIEMORE
Map 23 NH81

Eriskay Bed & Breakfast
★★★ BED AND BREAKFAST

tel: 01479 810717 & 07702 009614 **Craig Na Gower Av PH22 1RW**
email: enquiries@eriskay-aviemore.co.uk **web:** www.eriskay-aviemore.co.uk
dir: *From S turn left into Craig Na Gower Av, follow signs to Aviemore dental practice. At end of lane next to dentist*

This family-run B&B enjoys a quiet location close to the centre of Aviemore and is a great base for exploring the Cairngorms National Park and further afield. All bedrooms have en suite facilities and provide comfortable accommodation. A spacious guest lounge is also provided. Warm hospitality and a memorable breakfast are major aspects of any stay here. Newly built, self-contained ecopods in the grounds of the property are an alternative to the main accommodation.

Rooms 3 en suite (1 fmly) (3 GF) S £45-£80; D £60-£80 (room only)* **Facilities** FTV TVL tea/coffee WiFi **Parking** 3 **Notes** LB ⊗

BOAT OF GARTEN
Map 23 NH91

Moorfield House
★★★★ ⚑ GUEST HOUSE

tel: 01479 831646 **Deshar Rd PH24 3BN**
email: enquiries@moorfieldhouse.com **web:** www.moorfieldhouse.com
dir: *Off A9 at Carrbridge junct. Follow signs for Boat of Garten, in centre next to church*

Moorfield House is a charming family-run Victorian guest house, close to the Cairngorms. Bedrooms, named after tartans, are en suite and have flat-screen satellite TV and a variety of useful amenities. Breakfast offers a wide choice and the owners are happy to advise on local walks and attractions. The premises are licensed.

Rooms 6 en suite (1 GF) **Facilities** STV Lounge tea/coffee Licensed WiFi ⚓ 18 🔒
Extras Sweets, bottled water - complimentary **Parking** 6 **Notes** ⊗ No Children 12yrs Closed 31 Oct-26 Dec

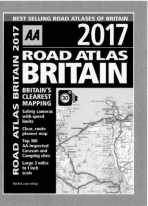

To help you navigate safely and easily, use the AA Road Atlas Britain 2017. Available from: shop.theAA.com

BRACHLA
Map 23 NH53

Premier Collection

Loch Ness Lodge
★★★★★ ⚏ GUEST ACCOMMODATION

tel: 01456 459469 **Loch Ness-Side IV3 8LA**
email: escape@loch-ness-lodge.com **web:** www.loch-ness-lodge.com
dir: *A9 from Inverness onto A82 signed Fort William, 9m, at 30mph sign. Lodge on right immediately after Clansman Hotel*

This house enjoys a prominent position overlooking Loch Ness, and each of the individually designed bedrooms enjoys views of the loch. The bedrooms are of the highest standard, and are beautifully presented with a mix of traditional luxury and up-to-date technology, including WiFi. There is a spa with a hot tub, sauna and a therapy room offering a variety of treatments. Guests have a choice of attractive lounges which feature real fires in the colder months and where decadent afternoon teas are served.

Rooms 7 en suite (1 GF) S £105-£260; D £175-£330 **Facilities** FTV DVD Lounge Direct Dial Licensed WiFi ⚓ 18 Fishing Sauna Hot tub Therapy room
Extras Speciality toiletries **Conf** Max 14 Thtr 14 Class 10 Board 14 **Parking** 10
Notes LB ⊗ No Children 10yrs Closed 2 Nov-27 Mar (dates may vary)
Civ Wed 14

CARRBRIDGE
Map 23 NH92

Cairn
★★★ INN

tel: 01479 841212 **Main Rd PH23 3AS**
email: info@cairnhotel.co.uk **web:** www.cairnhotel.co.uk

Conveniently located in the centre of the Cairngorms National Park, this property is the hub of the local community. The traditional bar and restaurant are complemented by a range of cosy bedrooms featuring modern touches. Guests can relax in front of the log fire with a cask ale or local malt whisky. The inn is an ideal base from which to participate in a number of outdoor activities with activity breaks and packages available to book.

Rooms 7 rms

CROMARTY
Map 23 NH76

Premier Collection

The Factor's House

★★★★★ ◉ ⬡ GUEST ACCOMMODATION

tel: 01381 600394 & 07917 799143 **Denny Rd IV11 8YT**
email: info@thefactorshouse.com **web:** www.thefactorshouse.com
dir: *Situated on A832 as you approach Cromarty on left from Fortrose*

Situated overlooking the historic town of Cromarty and only a short drive from Inverness, this refurbished house provides luxury accommodation in a secluded and peaceful setting. Spacious bedrooms feature Egyptian linens, a host of thoughtful touches and even home-made soaps to complement an impressive range of toiletries. Award-winning dinners and breakfasts are available; both making good use of the best of local produce, including fruit from the garden and eggs from the resident hens. Dinner must be booked 24 hours in advance. AA Friendliest B&B of the Year Award Finalist 2016-2017.

Rooms 3 en suite (1 GF) S £107-£117; D £127-£140 **Facilities** FTV DVD iPod docking station Lounge tea/coffee Dinner available WiFi 🔒 **Parking** 3 **Notes** LB ⊗ No Children 5yrs

DORNOCH
Map 23 NH78

Premier Collection

Links House at Royal Dornoch

★★★★★ ◉◉ ⬡ GUEST ACCOMMODATION

tel: 01862 810279 **Links House, Golf Rd IV25 3LW**
email: info@linkshousedornoch.com **web:** www.linkshousedornoch.com
dir: *From A9 onto A949 into Dornoch. From Castle St, right into Church Street then left into Golf Rd. House at junct of Golf Rd & Kennedy Ave*

This beautifully restored former manse house enjoys a stunning setting overlooking the famous Royal Dornoch Golf Course. The property provides an exceptional level of accommodation with stunning bedrooms and bathrooms, as well as delightful public areas including a wood-panelled library and a drawing room both with open fires; also an outside patio with a fire. The small dining room has a peat fire and provides the backdrop for memorable service, whether enjoying an elaborate evening meal or a sumptuous breakfast. Afternoon teas are also available by prior booking. The property is not just a great base for golf but also for shooting, fishing, stalking and a host of other activities in this beautiful part of the Highlands.

Rooms 5 en suite 3 annexe en suite (2 GF) D £270-£360* **Facilities** STV Lounge TVL Dinner available Licensed WiFi 🔒 18 🔒 Leisure activities can be booked in advance **Extras** Speciality toiletries, fruit - complimentary **Conf** Max 12 Thtr 12 Class 12 Board 12 **Parking** 3 **Notes** ⊗ Closed 25-27 Dec & 4 Jan-18 Mar

Premier Collection

2 Quail

★★★★★ ⬡ ⬡ GUEST ACCOMMODATION

tel: 01862 811811 **Castle St IV25 3SN**
email: theaa@2quail.com **web:** www.2quail.com
dir: *On main street, 200yds from cathedral*

The saying 'small is beautiful' applies to this property set in the main street. The cosy public rooms are ideal for conversation, but there are masses of books for those just wishing to relax. The stylish, individual bedrooms match the character of the house and are thoughtfully equipped with a number of thoughtful touches. Dinner and breakfast are both worth sampling at the property.

Rooms 3 en suite S £70-£120; D £80-£120* **Facilities** FTV DVD Lounge tea/coffee Dinner available Direct Dial Licensed WiFi 🔒 **Extras** Speciality toiletries **Notes** ⊗ No Children 8yrs Closed Xmas & 2wks Feb/Mar RS Nov-Mar winter hours - check when booking

DRUMNADROCHIT
Map 23 NH53

Highland Bear Lodge

★★★★ ⬡ GUEST HOUSE

tel: 01456 476213 **IV63 6TN**
email: mark@beyondextreme.co.uk **web:** www.highlandbearlodge.co.uk

Highland Bear Lodge offers a unique experience in the heart of the Highlands. Set amidst breathtaking scenery, near to Loch Ness, the house is lovingly run by an adventurous family who also run a paragliding and activities business. The baronial style house features spacious public areas with roaring fires and guests are invited to sit together for breakfast. Bedrooms are comfortable and luxurious. Walks can be taken around the 14 acres of peaceful grounds. This is the place to come if you want to feel like a Highland Laird for a night.

Rooms 3 rms (2 en suite) (1 pri facs) (1 GF) S £70-£130; D £90-£150* **Facilities** FTV Lounge WiFi 🔒 **Parking** 3 **Notes** LB ⊗ No Children 10yrs

EVANTON
Map 23 NH66

Balconie Inn

★★★ INN

tel: 01349 832908 **10 Balconie St IV16 9UN**
email: viewfirth_hotels@btconnect.com **web:** www.balconieinn.com
dir: *From A9 onto B817 signed Evanton. 1m on left*

The small village of Evanton lies in Easter Ross, only a short drive from Inverness. This family-run inn is the hub of the community, and is popular for both food and drinks, with monthly quiz nights and weekly Sunday music sessions a highlight. Decorated and furnished to a good standard, bedrooms and public areas are comfortable and inviting. Parking is available on site.

Rooms 5 rms (2 en suite) (3 pri facs) (3 fmly) **Facilities** FTV DVD tea/coffee Dinner available WiFi Pool table 🔒 **Extras** Speciality toiletries - complimentary **Parking** 14 **Notes** ⊗ No coaches

FORT WILLIAM
Map 22 NN17

See also Spean Bridge

Mansefield Guest House
★★★★ GUEST HOUSE

tel: 01397 772262 **Corpach PH33 7LT**
email: mansefield@btinternet.com **web:** www.fortwilliamaccommodation.com
dir: *2m N of Fort William. A82 onto A830, house 2m on A830 in Corpach*

Peacefully set in its own well-tended garden, this friendly, family-run guest house provides comfortable, attractively decorated and well-equipped accommodation. There is a cosy lounge, where a roaring coal fire burns on cold evenings, and an attractive dining room where delicious, home-cooked evening meals and breakfasts are served at individual tables.

Rooms 6 en suite (1 GF) **Facilities** FTV DVD TVL tea/coffee Dinner available WiFi
⌀ 18 🔒 **Parking** 7 **Notes** LB ⊗ No Children 12yrs

FOYERS
Map 23 NH42

The Craigdarroch Inn
★★★★ INN

tel: 01456 486400 **IV2 6XU**
email: info@hotel-loch-ness.co.uk **web:** www.thecraigdarrochinn.co.uk
dir: *Take B862 from either end of loch, then B852 signed Foyers*

Craigdarroch Inn is located in an elevated position, high above Loch Ness on the south side. Bedrooms vary in style and size but all are comfortable and well equipped; those that are front-facing have wonderful views. This friendly inn offers relaxed dining, many tables have loch views, and the staff are friendly and welcoming.

Rooms 8 en suite (1 fmly) S £60-£85; D £70-£140 **Facilities** FTV Lounge TVL tea/coffee Dinner available WiFi 🔒 **Conf** Max 30 Thtr 30 Class 30 Board 30 **Parking** 24 **Notes** No coaches

Foyers Bay Country House
★★★ GUEST HOUSE

tel: 01456 486624 **Lochness IV2 6YB**
email: info@foyersbay.co.uk **web:** www.foyersbay.co.uk
dir: *Off B852 into Lower Foyers*

Situated in sloping grounds with pines and abundant colourful rhododendrons, this delightful Victorian villa has stunning views of Loch Ness. The attractive bedrooms vary in size and are well equipped. There is a comfortable lounge next to the plant-filled conservatory-café, where delicious evening meals and traditional breakfasts are served.

Rooms 7 en suite (1 GF) **Facilities** FTV TVL tea/coffee Dinner available Licensed WiFi
🔒 **Parking** 7 **Notes** ⊗ No Children 16yrs

GRANTOWN-ON-SPEY
Map 23 NJ02

AA GUEST ACCOMMODATION OF THE YEAR FOR SCOTLAND 2016-2017

Premier Collection

The Dulaig
★★★★★ ⌀ BED AND BREAKFAST

tel: 01479 872065 **Seafield Av, Aviemore PH26 3JF**
email: enquiries@thedulaig.com **web:** www.thedulaig.com
dir: *A9 onto A95 to B9102. Into High St, left into Seafield Av for 200mtrs, past Rhuarden Court, The Dulaig on left*

Presented to an exceptional standard, this bed and breakfast benefits from a tranquil setting in 1.5 acres of stunning gardens. Featuring a summer house, duck pond and plenty of wildlife, the grounds provide a relaxing backdrop to the house. Located only a short walk from the centre of the town, features include luxurious, spacious bedrooms with Arts and Crafts antique furniture, and immaculately presented bathrooms with luxury toiletries. A welcoming drawing room is available and memorable breakfasts are served around a large shared table, making use of the best local produce and including eggs from the collection of hens. Carol and Gordon provide memorable hospitality which is appreciated by their many regular guests.

Rooms 3 en suite S £120-£140; D £160-£180* **Facilities** STV DVD Lounge tea/coffee WiFi 🔒 **Extras** Speciality toiletries, fruit, chocolates - free **Parking** 6 **Notes** LB ⊗ No Children 12yrs Closed 15 Dec-8 Jan

Trafford Bank

Premier Collection

Daviot Lodge

★★★★★ 🅰 GUEST ACCOMMODATION

tel: 01463 772215 **Daviot Mains IV2 5ER**
email: margaret.hutcheson@btopenworld.com **web:** www.daviotlodge.co.uk
dir: *Exit A9 5m S of Inverness onto B851 signed Croy. 1m on left*

Standing in 80 acres of peaceful pasture land, this impressive establishment offers attractive, well-appointed and well-equipped bedrooms. The master bedroom is furnished with a four-poster bed. There is a tranquil lounge with deep sofas and a real fire, and a peaceful dining room where hearty breakfasts featuring the best of local produce are served. Full disabled access for wheelchairs is provided.

Rooms 5 en suite (1 GF) S £68-£75; D £95-£130* **Facilities** FTV DVD Lounge TVL tea/coffee Licensed WiFi **Extras** Speciality toiletries, snacks **Parking** 10 **Notes** LB No Children 10yrs Closed 23 Dec-2 Jan

Premier Collection

Trafford Bank

★★★★★ 🅰 GUEST HOUSE

tel: 01463 241414 **96 Fairfield Rd IV3 5LL**
email: info@traffordbankhotel.co.uk **web:** www.traffordbankhotel.co.uk
dir: *Exit A82 at Kenneth St, 2nd left into Fairfield Rd, 600yds on right*

This impressive Victorian house lies in a residential area close to the canal. Lorraine Pun has made great use of her interior design skills to blend the best in contemporary styles with the house's period character and the results are simply stunning. Delightful public areas offer a choice of lounges, while breakfast is taken in a beautiful conservatory featuring eye-catching wrought-iron chairs. Each bedroom is unique in design and has TV, DVD and CDs, sherry, silent mini-fridges and much more.

Rooms 5 en suite (2 fmly) **Facilities** STV FTV TVL tea/coffee WiFi **Parking** 10 **Notes** ⊗

See advert on opposite page

Avalon Guest House

★★★★ GUEST HOUSE

tel: 01463 239075 & 07936 226241 **79 Glenurquhart Rd IV3 5PB**
email: avalon@inverness-loch-ness.co.uk **web:** www.inverness-loch-ness.co.uk

Avalon Guest House is just a short walk from the city centre, and five minutes' drive from Loch Ness. Breakfast can be taken in the well-appointed dining room where fresh local produce is the highlight of the menu. Bedrooms are spacious with a host of thoughtful extras including WiFi, fridges, fluffy towels and complimentary toiletries. A guest lounge is also provided.

Rooms 6 rms (5 en suite) (1 pri facs) (4 GF) **Facilities** FTV DVD iPod docking station TVL tea/coffee WiFi **Extras** Fridge, chocolates, flowers **Parking** 10 **Notes** ⊗ No Children 10yrs

Ballifeary Guest House

★★★★ 🅰 GUEST HOUSE

tel: 01463 235572 **10 Ballifeary Rd IV3 5PJ**
email: info@ballifearyguesthouse.co.uk **web:** www.ballifearyguesthouse.co.uk
dir: *Exit A82, 0.5m from town centre, left into Bishops Rd, sharp right into Ballifeary Rd*

This charming detached house has a peaceful residential location within easy walking distance of the town centre and Eden Court Theatre. The attractive bedrooms are carefully appointed and well equipped. There is an elegant ground-floor drawing room and a comfortable dining room, where delicious breakfasts, featuring the best of local produce, are served at individual tables.

Rooms 7 en suite (1 GF) S £50-£70; D £70-£85 **Facilities** FTV DVD Lounge tea/coffee WiFi 🅰 **Extras** Mineral water - complimentary **Parking** 6 **Notes** LB ⊗ No Children 15yrs Closed 24-28 Dec

Trafford Bank
Guest House

Koshal and Lorraine Pun purchased Trafford Bank in 2002 with the vision to make it into one of the top boutique guest houses in Scotland.

From the paintings on our walls to the cushions on our beds, these are all from local highland businesses. Our breakfast menu is all locally sourced, we have a variety of options which caters for all guests.

This former Bishop's home has been refurbished from top to bottom and mixes antique and contemporary furniture, some of which has been designed by Lorraine herself – an accomplished interior designer.

The guest house is non-smoking throughout, and is surrounded by mature gardens that the guests can enjoy and has ample parking.

AA
Breakfast
Award

AA ★★★★★

Trafford Bank Guest House
96 Fairfield Road, Inverness, Highland IV3 5LL
Tel: 01463 241414
E-Mail: info@traffordbankhotel.co.uk

www.traffordbankhotel.co.uk

INVERNESS *continued*

Moyness House

★★★★ GUEST HOUSE

tel: 01463 233836 **6 Bruce Gardens IV3 5EN**
email: info@moyness.co.uk **web:** www.moyness.co.uk
dir: *Off A82 (Fort William road), almost opposite Highland Regional Council headquarters*

Situated in a quiet residential area just a short distance from the city centre, this elegant Victorian villa dates from 1880 and offers beautifully decorated, comfortable bedrooms and well-appointed bathrooms. There is an attractive sitting room and an inviting dining room, where traditional Scottish breakfasts are served. Guests are welcome to use the secluded and well-maintained back garden.

Rooms 6 en suite (1 fmly) (2 GF) **Facilities** FTV Lounge tea/coffee WiFi
Extras Speciality toiletries, robes **Parking** 10 **Notes** ⊗

Dunhallin Guest House

★★★★ GUEST HOUSE

tel: 01463 220824 **164 Culduthel Rd IV2 4BH**
email: relax@dunhallin.co.uk **web:** www.dunhallin.co.uk
dir: *From city centre follow Castle St then Culduthel Rd for 1m. At mini rdbt take 1st exit, right at lights. 100mtrs on right*

Located in the Highland capital, this comfortable guest house offers a relaxing home-from-home. Margaret and Sandy love what they do and this shows in the friendly hospitality and helpful service they provide to all guests. Breakfasts are a feature of any stay here with a wide range of dishes offering something for everybody. Bedrooms are spaciously appointed with a great range of modern accessories including flat-screen TVs, DVD players and iPod docks. Complimentary parking on site.

Rooms 5 en suite S £48-£118; D £58-£128* **Facilities** FTV DVD iPod docking station Lounge tea/coffee WiFi 🔒 **Extras** Fridges in rooms **Parking** 5 **Notes** LB ⊗ No Children 12yrs

Heathcote B&B

★★★★ BED AND BREAKFAST

tel: 01463 236596 & 07833 730849 **59 Glenurquhart Rd IV3 5PB**
email: info@heathcotebandb.co.uk **web:** www.heathcotebandb.co.uk
dir: *On A82, 1m from city centre*

Only a few minutes' walk from the Eden Court Theatre and the centre of Inverness, this Victorian townhouse is ideally situated for touring the city and beyond, whether you are searching for the Loch Ness Monster or just castle-hunting. Modern bedrooms and bathrooms offer spacious and comfortable accommodation. Friendly hospitality and memorable breakfasts are also features here. Ample off street-private parking is provided.

Rooms 3 en suite S £45-£70; D £50-£90* **Facilities** FTV tea/coffee WiFi 🔒
Extras Bottled water **Parking** 6 **Notes** ⊗

Lyndon Guest House

★★★★ GUEST HOUSE

tel: 01463 232551 **50 Telford St IV3 5LE**
email: lyndon@invernessbedandbreakfast.com **web:** www.invernessbedandbreakfast.com
dir: *A9 onto A82, over Friars Bridge, right at rdbt into Telford St. House on right*

A warm Highland welcome awaits at Lyndon Guest House, family-run accommodation close to the centre of Inverness. All bedrooms are en suite and are equipped with plenty of useful facilities including full internet access. Gaelic is spoken here.

Rooms 6 en suite (4 fmly) (2 GF) S £35-£50; D £60-£90 **Facilities** FTV TVL tea/coffee WiFi 🔒 **Parking** 7 **Notes** ⊗ Closed 20 Dec-5 Jan

Sunnyholm

★★★ GUEST ACCOMMODATION

tel: 01463 231336 **12 Mayfield Rd IV2 4AE**
email: sunnyholm@invernessguesthouse.com **web:** www.invernessguesthouse.com
dir: *500yds SE of town centre. Exit B861 (Culduthel Rd) into Mayfield Rd*

Situated in a peaceful residential area within easy walking distance of the city centre, Sunnyholm offers comfortably proportioned and well-equipped bedrooms. A spacious conservatory-lounge overlooks the beautiful rear gardens, and there is another lounge next to the bright, airy dining room. Off-street parking is available to all guests.

Rooms 4 en suite (4 GF) S £40-£48; D £70-£75* **Facilities** FTV DVD Lounge tea/coffee WiFi 🔒 **Extras** Snacks - complimentary **Parking** 6 **Notes** ⊗ No Children 3yrs 🐾

Fraser House

★★★ GUEST ACCOMMODATION

tel: 01463 716488 & 07502 980034 **49 Huntly St IV3 5HS**
email: fraserlea@btopenworld.com **web:** www.fraserhouse.co.uk
dir: A82 W over bridge, left into Wells St leading into Huntly St, house in 100yds

Situated on the west bank of the River Ness, Fraser House has a commanding position overlooking the city, and is within easy walking distance of the central amenities. Bedrooms, all en suite, vary in size and are comfortably furnished and well equipped. The ground-floor dining room is the setting for freshly cooked Scottish breakfasts.

Rooms 5 en suite (2 fmly) **Facilities** FTV DVD iPod docking station tea/coffee WiFi ✿ **Notes** ⊗ Closed Feb-Mar ⊜

KINGUSSIE	Map 23 NH70

The Cross

★★★★★ ⊛⊛⊛ ☺ RESTAURANT WITH ROOMS

tel: 01540 661166 **Tweed Mill Brae, Ardbroilach Rd PH21 1LB**
email: relax@thecross.co.uk **web:** www.thecross.co.uk
dir: From lights in Kingussie centre take Ardbroilach Rd, 300yds left into Tweed Mill Brae

Built as a water-powered tweed mill in the late 19th century, The Cross is situated in the picturesque Cairngorms National Park and surrounded by four acres of riverside grounds that teem with an abundance of wildlife, including red squirrels. Comfortable lounges and a selection of well-appointed bedrooms are offered, and award-winning dinners are served by an open fire in the stone-walled and wood-beamed restaurant.

Rooms 8 en suite (1 fmly) S £60-£150; D £100-£180* **Facilities** FTV DVD Lounge tea/coffee Dinner available Direct Dial WiFi Riding ✿ **Extras** Bottled water, speciality toiletries **Conf** Max 20 Thtr 20 Class 20 Board 20 **Parking** 20 **Notes** LB Closed Jan No coaches

---

MEY	Map 23 ND27

Mey House Luxury Rooms and Breakfast

★★★★★ ⒜ BED AND BREAKFAST

tel: 01847 851852 **East Mey KW14 8XL**
email: info@meyhouse.co.uk **web:** www.meyhouse.co.uk
dir: From John O'Groats on A836, W towards Thurso. Continue to East Mey, right at brown tourist sign

Mey House is perfectly located for those visiting Orkney and The Castle of Mey. The generously proportioned suites all have panoramic ocean views, feature super king-sized beds, separate dressing areas and large bathrooms (with separate walk-in high pressure showers and feature baths). Mey House is licensed, so you can enjoy a wee dram and then take advantage of the free Mey House 'Restaurant Express' service which takes you to and from local restaurants. WiFi is available throughout the house, and there is ample off-street parking

Rooms 2 en suite D £115-£130* **Facilities** FTV iPod docking station Lounge tea/coffee Licensed WiFi ✿ **Extras** Speciality toiletries, home-made biscuits **Parking** 8 **Notes** ⊗ No Children 11yrs Closed Nov-Feb

---

NAIRN	Map 23 NH85

Premier Collection

Boath House

★★★★★ ⊛⊛⊛⊛ ☺ RESTAURANT WITH ROOMS

tel: 01667 454896 **Auldearn IV12 5TE**
email: info@boath-house.com **web:** www.boath-house.com
dir: 2m past Nairn on A96, E towards Forres, signed on main road

Standing in its own 20-acre grounds, with an ornamental lake, walled garden and secluded seating areas, this splendid Georgian mansion was built in 1825 for the Dunbar family, but there has been occupation on the site since the 16th century. Hospitality here is first class; the owners are passionate about what they do, and have a real ability to establish a special relationship with their guests. The food is memorable; head chef Charlie Lockley is a devotee of slow and organic cooking which also includes using foraged produce. The five-course dinners are a culinary adventure, matched only by the excellence of breakfasts. The house itself is delightful, with inviting lounges and a dining room overlooking a trout loch. The bedrooms, with lake and woodland views, are striking and very comfortable; Orangerie Rooms have their own conservatory.

Rooms 8 en suite S £190-£260; D £295-£365 **Facilities** FTV DVD tea/coffee Dinner available Direct Dial WiFi ⤙ Fishing **Parking** 20 **Notes** Civ Wed 32

POOLEWE	Map 22 NG88

Premier Collection

Pool House

★★★★★ ☺ ⊜ GUEST HOUSE

tel: 01445 781272 **IV22 2LD**
email: stay@pool-house.co.uk **web:** www.pool-house.co.uk
dir: 6m N of Gairloch on A832 in the centre of village by bridge

Set on the shores of Loch Ewe where the river meets the bay, the understated roadside façade gives little hint of its splendid interior, nor of the views facing the bay. Memorable features include delightful public rooms and stunningly romantic suites, each individually designed and with feature bathrooms. Pool House is run very much as a country house — the hospitality and guest care by the Harrison family are second to none.

Rooms 4 en suite D £250-£325* **Facilities** FTV DVD iPod docking station Lounge tea/coffee Dinner available Direct Dial Licensed WiFi Snooker **Extras** Sherry, speciality toiletries - complimentary **Parking** 10 **Notes** LB No Children 12yrs Closed Nov-mid Mar

---

ROY BRIDGE	Map 22 NN28

Homagen

★★★★ BED AND BREAKFAST

tel: 01397 712411 **PH31 4AN**
email: stay@homagen.co.uk **web:** www.homagen.co.uk
dir: On A86, opposite Roy Bridge Hotel

Homagen is a family-run property in a great location for touring the Highlands, with links to Fort William, Aviemore and beyond. Bedrooms feature modern decor and comfortable beds. Hearty breakfasts are served in the dining room at a communal table. Free WiFi is provided. Packed lunches are available for making day trips.

Rooms 4 rms (3 en suite) (1 pri facs) (4 GF) S £38-£45; D £65-£75* **Facilities** FTV Lounge tea/coffee WiFi Fishing ✿ **Parking** 6 **Notes** LB Closed 23 Dec-3 Jan

SPEAN BRIDGE   Map 22 NN28

Smiddy House

★★★★★ ◎◎ 🍴 RESTAURANT WITH ROOMS

tel: 01397 712335 **Roy Bridge Rd PH34 4EU**
email: enquiry@smiddyhouse.com **web:** www.smiddyhouse.com
dir: In village centre, A82 onto A86

Set in the Great Glen which stretches from Fort William to Inverness, this was once the village smithy, and is now a very friendly restaurant with rooms. The attractive bedrooms, named after places in Scotland, are comfortably furnished and well equipped. A relaxing garden room is available for guest use. Delicious evening meals are served in Russell's restaurant.

Rooms 4 en suite (1 fmly) **Facilities** FTV Lounge tea/coffee Dinner available WiFi **Extras** Speciality toiletries, mineral water - free **Parking** 15 **Notes** ⊗ No coaches

Distant Hills Guest House

★★★★ 🍴 GUEST HOUSE

tel: 01397 712452 **Roy Bridge Rd PH34 4EU**
email: enquiry@distanthills.com **web:** www.distanthillsspeanbridge.co.uk
dir: From A82 onto A86 signed Newtonmore. 0.5m on right

Distant Hills Guest House in the heart of the Highlands offers stylish bedrooms, award-winning breakfasts and friendly hospitality. Set amongst wonderful scenery, the house enjoys a quiet setting in its own impressive grounds. An ideal base for touring Fort William, Oban, Inverness and the Highlands whether walking, climbing or driving. Off-road parking and free WiFi are some of the numerous features of the house.

Rooms 7 en suite (7 GF) S £70-£85; D £85-£100 **Facilities** FTV DVD iPod docking station TVL tea/coffee WiFi ⌀ 9 ⌀ **Extras** Speciality toiletries **Parking** 10 **Notes** ⊗ No Children 12yrs Closed 15 Nov-1 Mar

STRATHPEFFER   Map 23 NH45

Inver Lodge

★★★ GUEST HOUSE

tel: 01997 421392 **IV14 9DL**
email: derbyshire@inverlg.fsnet.co.uk **web:** www.inverlodgestrathpeffer.com
dir: A834 through Strathpeffer centre, turn beside Spa Pavilion signed Bowling Green, Inver Lodge on right

You are assured of a warm welcome at this Victorian lodge, secluded in its own tree-studded gardens yet within easy walking distance of the town centre. Bedrooms are comfortable and well equipped, and the cosy lounge is ideal for relaxation. Breakfasts, and evening meals (by arrangement), are served at a communal table.

Rooms 2 rms (1 fmly) S £35-£37; D £52* **Facilities** FTV Lounge tea/coffee Dinner available WiFi ⌀ 18 ⌀ **Parking** 2 **Notes** LB ⊗ Closed Xmas & New Year ⊛

TORRIDON   Map 22 NG95

The Torridon Inn

★★★★ 🍺 INN

tel: 01445 791242 **IV22 2EY**
email: inn@thetorridon.com **web:** www.thetorridon.com/inn

The Torridon Inn enjoys an idyllic location and is set in 58 acres of parkland, overlooking Loch Torridon and surrounded by steep mountains on all sides. Bedrooms are lodge style with adjacent parking and are smartly appointed with comfy beds and modern facilities. Freshly prepared food is served in the adjacent inn, where over 80 whiskies, and several real ales, including a local Torridon Ale, are firm favourites.

Rooms 12 en suite (3 fmly) (5 GF) **Facilities** STV tea/coffee Dinner available WiFi ⌀ Fishing Pool table ⌀ Outdoor adventure activities available **Parking** 12 **Notes** LB Closed Jan Civ Wed 55

ULLAPOOL   Map 22 NH19

The Arch Inn

★★★ 🍺 INN

tel: 01854 612454 **10-11 West Shore St IV26 2UR**
email: info@thearchinn.co.uk **web:** www.thearchinn.co.uk
dir: Into Ullapool, continue along Shore St. Pass pier, inn on right

The Arch Inn is situated on Ullapool waterfront on the shores of Loch Broom, only a two-minute walk from the Outer Hebrides ferry terminal. The accommodation provided is comfortable, and most rooms have stunning views over the loch to the mountains in the distance. The relaxed bar and grill offers a selection of fresh local produce including seafood.

Rooms 10 en suite (1 fmly) (2 GF) S £45-£75; D £75-£85* **Facilities** STV FTV tea/coffee Dinner available WiFi Pool table **Extras** Sweets **Conf** Max 60 Thtr 40 Class 30 Board 35 **Parking** 5 **Notes** ⊗

INVERCLYDE

INVERKIP
Map 20 NS27

The Inverkip

★★★ ☕ INN

tel: 01475 521478 **Main St PA16 0AS**
email: enquiries@inverkip.co.uk **web:** www.inverkip.co.uk
dir: Just off A78, near Inverkip Marina

This family-run property enjoys a great location at the centre of the historic village of Inverkip and is only a short stroll from the popular Inverkip Marina. This is a great place for those with an interest in great pub food and a passion for cask ales, whiskies (over 200) and gin. A small public bar and a larger restaurant are most atmospheric, and a friendly face is always present with staff eager to please. Bedrooms and bathrooms are modern and well presented. Ample parking on site.

Rooms 5 en suite (2 fmly) S £59-£69; D £84-£94* **Facilities** STV FTV Lounge tea/coffee Dinner available WiFi ⬇ 18 ♨ **Parking** 33 **Notes** Closed 24-25 & 31 Dec-1 Jan (accommodation) RS 1 Jan closed for accommodation & food No coaches

NORTH LANARKSHIRE

MOTHERWELL
Map 20 NS75

Innkeeper's Lodge Glasgow

★★★ INN

tel: 08451 551551 *(Calls cost 2p per minute plus your phone company's access charge)*
1 Hamilton Rd ML1 3RB
email: info@innkeeperslodge.com **web:** www.innkeeperslodge.com

This property enjoys an excellent location for those travelling to and from Scotland, or as a base for visiting anywhere in the central belt. The inn is located just off the M74 with links to nearby Glasgow and Edinburgh. Modern, spacious bedrooms occupy an attractive building, where friendly service, wide-ranging breakfasts, free WiFi and complimentary parking are also available. Next door is the ever-popular Toby Carvery where food and real ales are available all day.

Rooms 28 en suite (13 fmly) (14 GF) **Facilities** FTV tea/coffee Dinner available WiFi **Conf** Max 35 **Parking** 150 **Notes** ⊗

SOUTH LANARKSHIRE

STRATHAVEN
Map 20 NS74

Rissons at Springvale

★★★ ◉ RESTAURANT WITH ROOMS

tel: 01357 521131 & 520234 **18 Lethame Rd ML10 6AD**
email: info@rissons.co.uk **web:** www.rissonsrestaurant.co.uk
dir: A71 into Strathaven, W of town centre off Townhead St

Guests are assured of a warm welcome at this charming establishment close to the town centre. The bedrooms and bathrooms are stylish and well equipped. The main attraction here is the food – a range of interesting, well-prepared dishes served in Rissons Restaurant.

Rooms 9 en suite (1 fmly) (1 GF) S £47.50; D £85* **Facilities** FTV Lounge TVL tea/coffee Dinner available WiFi ⬇⬇ 18 Fishing ♨ **Parking** 10 **Notes** ⊗ Closed 1st wk Jan No coaches

EAST LOTHIAN

ABERLADY
Map 21 NT47

Ducks Inn

★★★★ ◉◉ ⬤ RESTAURANT WITH ROOMS

tel: 01875 870682 **Main St EH32 0RE**
email: kilspindie@ducks.co.uk **web:** www.ducks.co.uk
dir: A1 (Bankton junct) take 1st exit to North Berwick. At next rdbt 3rd exit onto A198 signed Longniddry, left towards Aberlady. At T-junct, facing river, right to Aberlady

The name of this restaurant with rooms is referenced around the building – Ducks Restaurant for award-winning cuisine; Donald's Bistro and the Ducklings informal coffee shop. The warm and welcoming public areas include a great bar offering real ales and various *objets d'art*. The bedrooms are comfortable and well-appointed with stylish en suites. The team are informal and friendly, taking the time to chat to their guests.

Rooms 23 en suite (1 fmly) (6 GF) S £60-£95; D £80-£130* **Facilities** STV FTV Lounge TVL tea/coffee Dinner available Direct Dial WiFi ⬇ 18 ♨ **Conf** Max 100 Thtr 100 Class 60 Board 30 **Parking** 15

WEST LOTHIAN

EAST CALDER
Map 21 NT06

Ashcroft Farmhouse

★★★★ ⬤ GUEST HOUSE

tel: 01506 881810 & 07788 926239 **EH53 0ET**
email: ashcroftinfo@aol.com **web:** www.ashcroftfarmhouse.com

(For full entry see Livingston)

Whitecroft Bed & Breakfast

★★★★ BED AND BREAKFAST

tel: 01506 882494 **7 Raw Holdings EH53 0ET**
email: lornascot@aol.com **web:** www.whitecroftbandb.co.uk

(For full entry see Livingston)

LINLITHGOW
Map 21 NS97

Premier Collection

Arden Country House

★★★★★ ⬤ GUEST ACCOMMODATION

tel: 01506 670172 **Belsyde EH49 6QE**
email: info@ardencountryhouse.com **web:** www.ardencountryhouse.com
dir: 1.3m SW of Linlithgow. A706 over Union Canal, entrance 200yds on left at Lodge Cottage

Situated in the picturesque grounds of the Belsyde country estate and close to the Royal Burgh of Linlithgow, Arden Country House offers immaculate, stylishly furnished and spacious bedrooms. There is a cosy ground-floor lounge and a charming dining room where delicious breakfasts feature the best of local produce.

Rooms 3 en suite (1 GF) **Facilities** FTV DVD iPod docking station Lounge tea/coffee WiFi **Extras** Savoury snacks, chocolates **Parking** 4 **Notes** ⊗ No Children 12yrs Closed 25-26 Dec

LINLITHGOW *continued*

Belsyde House

★★★★ ⌂ GUEST ACCOMMODATION

tel: 01506 842098 **Lanark Rd EH49 6QE**
email: info@belsydehouse.com **web:** www.belsyde.com
dir: *1.5m SW on A706, 1st left over Union Canal*

Reached by a tree-lined driveway, this welcoming farmhouse is peacefully situated in attractive grounds close to the Union Canal. There are well-proportioned bedrooms including a family room; all are nicely furnished and well equipped. Breakfast, including a vegetarian menu, is served at good-sized tables in the dining room, next to the lounge. AA Friendliest B&B of the Year Award Finalist 2016-2017.

Rooms 3 en suite (1 fmly) **Facilities** FTV TVL tea/coffee WiFi 🔒 **Extras** Speciality toiletries, robes, mints **Parking** 10 **Notes** ⊗ No Children 12yrs Closed Xmas

Bomains Farm Guest House

★★★★ GUEST HOUSE

tel: 01506 822188 & 07974 736480 **Bo'ness EH49 7RQ**
email: bunty.kirk@onetel.net **web:** www.bomains.co.uk
dir: *A706, 1.5m N towards Bo'ness, left at golf course x-rds, 1st farm on right*

From its elevated location this friendly farmhouse has stunning views of the Firth of Forth. The bedrooms, which vary in size, are beautifully decorated and well-equipped with many thoughtful extra touches. Delicious home-cooked fare, featuring the best local produce, is served in a stylish lounge-dining room.

Rooms 6 rms (4 en suite) (1 pri facs) (1 fmly) (2 GF) **Facilities** STV FTV DVD Lounge TVL tea/coffee WiFi ⌕ 18 Fishing 🔒 **Extras** Sweets **Parking** 12

The AA on Social Media - follow us:

twitter: @TheAA_Lifestyle
facebook: www.facebook.com/TheAAUK

Find us on Facebook

Kirkland House

★★★★ BED AND BREAKFAST

tel: 01506 822188 & 07974 736480 **Bomains Farm EH49 7RQ**
email: bunty.kirk@onetel.net **web:** www.bomains.co.uk
dir: *A706, 1.5m N towards Bo'ness, left at golf course x-rds, 1st farm on right*

Kirkland House is a new purpose-built property adjacent to the family-run Bomains Farm Guest House, where a number of guest services are provided. Large bedrooms come with high quality fixtures and fittings, and patio doors that lead onto the garden which has a children's play area and views onto the River Forth. A peaceful location within striking distance of Linlithgow, Edinburgh and the Central Belt.

Rooms 3 en suite (1 fmly) (3 GF) **Facilities** FTV TVL tea/coffee WiFi ⚓ 18 Fishing
Parking 6 **Notes** ⊗ ⊜

LIVINGSTON   Map 21 NT06

Ashcroft Farmhouse

★★★★ ⌂ GUEST HOUSE

tel: 01506 881810 & 07788 926239 **East Calder EH53 0ET**
email: ashcroftinfo@aol.com **web:** www.ashcroftfarmhouse.com
dir: *On B7015, off A71, 0.5m E of East Calder, near Almondell Country Park*

With over 40 years' experience in caring for guests, Derek and Elizabeth Scott ensure a stay at Ashcroft will be memorable. Their modern home sits in lovely, award-winning landscaped gardens and provides attractive and well-equipped ground-floor bedrooms. The comfortable lounge includes a video and DVD library. Breakfast, featuring home-made sausages and the best of local produce, is served at individual tables in the stylish dining room. Free WiFi is available, and a Park and Ride facility is nearby.

Rooms 6 en suite (2 fmly) (6 GF) S£50-£60; D£80-£90* **Facilities** FTV TVL tea/coffee
WiFi ⛐ **Parking** 8 **Notes** ⊗ No Children 12yrs

Whitecroft Bed & Breakfast

★★★★ BED AND BREAKFAST

tel: 01506 882494 **7 Raw Holdings, East Calder EH53 0ET**
email: lornascot@aol.com **web:** www.whitecroftbandb.co.uk
dir: *A71 onto B7015, establishment on right*

A relaxed and friendly atmosphere prevails at Whitecroft, a charming, modern bed and breakfast. The bedrooms, all of which are on the ground floor, are attractively colour co-ordinated, well-equipped and contain many thoughtful extra touches. Breakfast is served at individual tables in the smart dining room.

Rooms 3 en suite (3 GF) **Facilities** FTV DVD tea/coffee WiFi **Parking** 5
Notes No Children 12yrs

Visit shop.theAA.com

for a wide variety of AA publications, including Walking books, Lifestyle Guides, Atlases, and International Travel Guides

MIDLOTHIAN

DALKEITH Map 21 NT36

The Sun Inn

★★★★ INN

tel: 0131 663 2456 **Lothian Bridge EH22 4TR**
email: thesuninn@live.co.uk **web:** www.thesuninnedinburgh.co.uk
dir: *On A7 towards Galashiels, opposite Newbattle Viaduct*

The Sun Inn dates back to 1697 and is situated within easy striking distance of Edinburgh. It has boutique-style bedrooms (one featuring a copper bath) and modern bathrooms. High quality, award-winning food is served in stylish surroundings; drinks can be enjoyed in the terraced garden area.

Rooms 5 en suite S £75; D £95* **Facilities** STV FTV tea/coffee Dinner available WiFi ⛳ 18 Fishing **Parking** 100 **Notes** LB ⊗

ROSLIN Map 21 NT26

The Original Rosslyn Inn

★★★★ INN

tel: 0131 440 2384 **4 Main St EH25 9LE**
email: enquiries@theoriginalhotel.co.uk **web:** www.theoriginalhotel.co.uk
dir: *From A701 at rdbt take B7003 signed Roslin & Rosewell, into Roslin. At T-junct, inn opposite. Or from mini rdbt on A701 at Bilston take B7006 to Roslin. Inn on left*

Whether on *The Da Vinci Code* trail or in the area on business, this property is ideally placed for a visit to the famous Rosslyn Chapel, which is just a short walk away. It is a delightful village inn that offers well-equipped bedrooms with en suites; four of the bedrooms have four-poster beds. The Grail Restaurant, the lounge and conservatory offer a comprehensive selection of dining options.

Rooms 7 en suite (2 fmly) **Facilities** FTV DVD Lounge tea/coffee Dinner available WiFi 🔒 **Conf** Max 130 Thtr 130 Class 80 Board 60 **Parking** 8 **Notes** Civ Wed 180

MORAY

FORRES Map 23 NJ05

Cluny Bank

★★★★ RESTAURANT WITH ROOMS

tel: 01309 674304 **69 St Leonards Rd IV36 1DW**
email: info@clunybankhotel.co.uk **web:** www.clunybankhotel.co.uk

Historic, listed Cluny Bank occupies a quiet location within walking distance of the centre of Forres, and is an ideal base for exploring the North East of Scotland. Family-run, the building retains many original architectural features. Public areas include the 'Altyre Bar' with a wide range of whiskies, and 'Franklin's Restaurant' where a real taste of Moray can be experienced. Room service, complimentary WiFi and memorable breakfasts are also provided for guests. AA Friendliest B&B of the Year Award Finalist 2016-2017.

Rooms 6 en suite 1 annexe en suite (2 GF) S £80-£85; D £125-£165* **Facilities** FTV iPod docking station Lounge tea/coffee Dinner available Direct Dial WiFi **Parking** 7 **Notes** LB ⊗ No coaches

PERTH & KINROSS

ABERFELDY Map 23 NN84

Errichel House

★★★★ GUEST ACCOMMODATION

tel: 01887 829562 & 07921 507458 **Errichel, Crieff Rd PH15 2EL**
email: paulnewman@errichel.co.uk **web:** www.errichel.co.uk
dir: *2m from Aberfeldy on Crieff road (A826)*

The guest accommodation on this family-run working farm occupies a stunning location in an elevated location above Aberfeldy, with breathtaking views of the Perthshire hills. Beautiful grounds feature a duck pond, and are home to an array of wildlife. Bedrooms and public areas are luxuriously presented and deeply comfortable. A stay here is not complete without sampling the food on offer at the restaurant 'Thyme at Errichel', or taking home some of the many home-made delicacies from their 'Thyme to Eat' shop. In fact all of the lamb, beef and pork sold here comes from the farm itself.

Rooms 4 en suite (1 fmly) S £70-£110; D £90-£150 **Facilities** FTV iPod docking station Lounge tea/coffee Dinner available Licensed WiFi 🔒 **Conf** Max 40 Thtr 40 Class 16 Board 20 **Parking** 12 **Notes** LB ⊗ Closed 3-12 Jan RS 12 Jan-1 Mar rest open Thu-Fri & Sat eve Civ Wed 120

ALYTH
Map 23 NO24

Premier Collection

Tigh Na Leigh Guesthouse

★★★★★ ⬛ ⬛ GUEST ACCOMMODATION

tel: 01828 632372 **22-24 Airlie St PH11 8AJ**
email: book@tighnaleigh.com web: www.tighnaleigh.co.uk
dir: *In town centre on B952*

Situated in the heart of this charming country town, Tigh Na Leigh (Gaelic for 'The House of the Doctor') is an equally charming property. It has an imposing, yet welcoming appearance, and inside has been completely restored to blend its Victorian architecture with contemporary interior design. Bedrooms, including a superb suite, have state-of-the-art bathrooms and spa baths. There are three lounges, and delicious meals are served in the conservatory/dining room overlooking a spectacular landscaped garden. Free WiFi is provided.

Rooms 5 en suite (1 GF) **Facilities** FTV DVD iPod docking station Lounge TVL tea/coffee Dinner available Licensed WiFi ⬛ 18 ⬛ **Extras** Fruit, mineral water **Parking** 5 **Notes** No Children 12yrs Closed Dec-Feb

BLAIR ATHOLL
Map 23 NN86

The Firs

★★★★ GUEST HOUSE

tel: 01796 481256 **PH18 5TA**
email: kirstie@firs-blairatholl.co.uk web: www.firs-blairatholl.co.uk
dir: *A9 follow signs to Blair Atholl, 1st left after Blair Atholl garage*

The Firs is located in the peaceful village of Blair Atholl, home of Europe's only legal private army, the Atholl Highlanders. This is a well-presented property with lovely gardens. Bedrooms are comfortable and have quality decor. Public areas are warm and welcoming, and are enhanced by a log fire, while breakfast is served in the conservatory at individual tables.

Rooms 6 en suite (3 fmly) (2 GF) S £45-£60; D £70-£105* **Facilities** FTV DVD Lounge tea/coffee WiFi ⬛ **Extras** Speciality toiletries **Parking** 7 **Notes** LB Closed Nov-Feb

CALVINE
Map 23 NN86

The Struan Inn

★★★★ GUEST ACCOMMODATION

tel: 01796 483714 **PH18 5UB**
email: thestruan.calvine@btinternet.com web: www.thestruan-inn.co.uk
dir: *From N - A9 turn right onto B847, turn right for Kinloch Rannoch. Under bridge, 1st right. From S - A9 turn left onto B847, turn right for Kinloch Rannoch, then as for From N*

Located on the edge of the Cairngorms National Park in a peaceful location yet just two minutes from the A9, this historic inn is comfortable and welcoming. Inside there is a residents' bar with a log fire, comfortable lounge, and a restaurant serving hearty dinners. Bedrooms are well appointed with modern features. Hospitality is warm and friendly.

Rooms 5 en suite (2 fmly) (1 GF) S £55-£70; D £70-£105 **Facilities** STV DVD iPod docking station TVL tea/coffee Dinner available Licensed WiFi ⬛ **Parking** 8 **Notes** ⊗ Closed 18 Dec-13 Jan

MEIKLEOUR
Map 21 NO13

Meikleour Arms

★★★★ INN

tel: 01250 883206 & 883406 **PH2 6EB**
email: contact@meikleourarms.co.uk web: www.meikleourarms.co.uk
dir: *N of Perth on A93*

This family-run country inn has been a popular venue for almost 200 years. It was first established as a coach and posting house. Today it welcomes both locals and visitors who come to the area for fishing and shooting. Bedrooms are spacious and comfortable with impressive bathrooms. An attractive restaurant serves high quality local produce, and the lounge bar is a cosy area where beer connoisseurs can sample the property's own real ale. The Meikleour Arms is currently undergoing a major refurbishment process which should be completed by the end of 2016.

Rooms 5 en suite 4 annexe en suite (2 fmly) (7 GF) **Facilities** FTV Lounge tea/coffee Dinner available WiFi ⬛ 45 Fishing Snooker ⬛ **Extras** Speciality toiletries, bottled water, sherry - free **Parking** 25

PERTH
Map 21 N012

Premier Collection

The Townhouse
★★★★★ GUEST HOUSE

tel: 01738 446179 **17 Marshall Place PH2 8AG**
email: info@thetownhouseperth.co.uk **web:** www.thetownhouseperth.co.uk
dir: *M90 junct 10 towards Perth. Into centre of town, left into Marshall Place*

This traditional, Georgian terraced property enjoys a great location in the heart of Perth city centre, and several of the large beautifully appointed rooms benefit from great views over picturesque South Inch Park. Luxurious beds and antique furniture sit alongside contemporary design. Breakfasts feature local and home-made produce. Complimentary parking and WiFi are provided.

Rooms 5 en suite (1 fmly) (1 GF) S £70-£80; D £110-£145 **Facilities** STV FTV DVD iPod docking station tea/coffee Direct Dial WiFi ⊕ **Parking** 5

Ballabeg Guest House
★★★ BED AND BREAKFAST

tel: 01738 620434 **14 Keir St PH2 7HJ**
email: ballabeg@btopenworld.com **web:** www.ballabegguesthouse.co.uk
dir: *NE of city centre, Keir St accessed from A93 (E of river) or from A94 (Strathmore St)*

Well situated for the town centre and benefiting from off-road parking, this property offers modern, comfortable bedrooms of a good overall size with a number of extras provided as standard. Well-cooked breakfasts together with warm and genuine hospitality ensure a pleasant stay. All major credit cards are accepted.

Rooms 4 rms (3 en suite) (1 pri facs) S £42-£48; D £63-£66 **Facilities** FTV DVD tea/coffee WiFi ⊕ **Parking** 4 **Notes** ⊗ No Children 16yrs Closed Dec-Jan

More than 2,000 professionally inspected restaurants, from village inns to smart city eateries. Authoritative and reliable - Over 50 years of experience.

AA

THE RESTAURANT GUIDE 2017

INSPECTING RESTAURANTS FOR OVER 50 YEARS

shop.theAA.com

SCOTTISH BORDERS

BONCHESTER BRIDGE
Map 21 NT51

The Horse and Hound Country Inn
★★★ INN

tel: 01450 860645 **TD9 8JN**
email: kathrynlawley@fsmail.net **web:** www.horseandhoundcountryinn.co.uk
dir: *On A6088*

The Horse and Hound is a traditional coaching inn, parts of which date back to 1701. This is an ideal base for touring the Scottish Borders. Hawick and Jedburgh are just a short drive away as is the magnificent Kielder Water and Observatory. The property offers value-for-money accommodation, with the pub offering quality home-cooked food and real ales. An open log fire during the winter months adds to the charm and character.

Rooms 9 en suite S £49-£77; D £60-£99* **Facilities** TVL tea/coffee Dinner available WiFi Pool table ⊕ **Extras** Speciality toiletries - complimentary **Conf** Max 40 Class 30 Board 20 **Parking** 24 **Notes** LB

See advert on opposite page

BROUGHTON
Map 21 NT13

The Glenholm Centre

★★★ ≜ ⬤ GUEST ACCOMMODATION

tel: 01899 830408 **ML12 6JF**
email: info@glenholm.co.uk **web:** www.glenholm.co.uk
dir: *1m S of Broughton. Off A701 to Glenholm*

Surrounded by peaceful farmland, this former schoolhouse has a distinct African theme. The home-cooked meals and baking have received much praise and are served in the spacious lounge-dining room. The bright airy bedrooms are thoughtfully equipped, and the service is friendly and attentive.

Rooms 3 en suite 1 annexe en suite (1 fmly) (2 GF) **Facilities** FTV DVD TVL tea/coffee Dinner available Licensed WiFi ⬤ **Parking** 10 **Notes** Closed 20 Dec-1 Feb

EDDLESTON
Map 21 NT24

The Horseshoe Restaurant with Rooms

★★★★ ≜ RESTAURANT WITH ROOMS

tel: 01721 730225 **Edinburgh Rd EH45 8QP**
email: reservations@horseshoeinn.co.uk **web:** www.horseshoeinn.co.uk
dir: *A703, 5m N of Peebles*

The Horseshoe is five miles north of Peebles and only 18 miles south of Edinburgh. Originally a blacksmith's shop, it has a very good reputation for its delightful atmosphere and excellent cuisine. There are eight luxuriously appointed and individually designed bedrooms. Please note: children are welcome, but dinner is not served to under fives except in the private dining room.

Rooms 8 en suite (1 fmly) (6 GF) **Facilities** FTV Lounge tea/coffee Dinner available Direct Dial WiFi **Extras** Speciality toiletries, fruit, mineral water - free **Parking** 20 **Notes** Closed 25 Dec, 1st 2wks Jan & 2wks Jul RS Mon & Tue closed

INNERLEITHEN
Map 21 NT33

Caddon View

★★★★ ≜ ⬤ GUEST ACCOMMODATION

tel: 01896 830208 **14 Pirn Rd EH44 6HH**
email: stay@caddonview.co.uk **web:** www.caddonview.co.uk
dir: *Signed from A72 in Innerleithen*

Set in its own well maintained gardens this well-presented Victorian house was originally built in the 1850s. Caddon View offers high standards of accommodation along with wonderful hospitality and customer care awareness. Located in the beautiful Tweed Valley, it's ideally located for all the border areas as well as Edinburgh. The property is licensed and serves quality evening meals (by prior arrangement), in a bright, welcoming and well-appointed dining room.

Rooms 8 rms (7 en suite) (1 pri facs) (2 fmly) (2 GF) S £53-£55; D £80-£110* **Facilities** FTV DVD Lounge tea/coffee Dinner available Licensed WiFi ⬤ **Parking** 7 **Notes** Closed 25-26 Dec RS Sun & Mon no dinner available

JEDBURGH
Map 21 NT62

Ferniehirst Mill Lodge

★★ GUEST HOUSE

tel: 01835 863279 **TD8 6PQ**
email: ferniehirstmill@aol.com **web:** www.ferniehirstmill.co.uk
dir: *2.5m S of Jedburgh on A68, onto private track to end*

Reached by a narrow farm track and a rustic wooden bridge, this chalet-style house has a secluded setting by the River Jed. Bedrooms are small and functional, and there is a comfortable lounge in which to relax. Home-cooked and hearty breakfasts are served in the cosy dining room.

Rooms 7 en suite (1 GF) S £30; D £60* **Facilities** TVL tea/coffee WiFi Fishing Riding ⬤ **Parking** 10

The Horse and Hound Country Inn
☎ 441450860645 ✉ kathrynlawley@fsmail.net 🌐 horseandhoundcountryinn.co.uk/
📍 Bonchester Bridge, Hawick, Sark, TD9 8JN, United Kingdom

The Horse and Hound is a traditional inn dating from 1701, situated in Bonchester Bridge, a quiet hamlet 7 miles from the famous knitwear town of Hawick, offering a friendly atmosphere within its lounge and bar. A restaurant is also available serving a variety of fresh, home cooked meals, with a varied wine list to complement your meal.

There are a variety of beers, lagers and ciders as well as cask ales, spirits and malt whiskies on offer in the bar and lounge areas.

Outside patio areas are sun traps in the summer, with a roaring log fire in the bar for those cooler evenings.

MELROSE
Map 21 NT53

Premier Collection

Fauhope Country House

★★★★★ 👜 GUEST HOUSE

tel: 01896 823184 & 07816 346768 **Gattonside TD6 9LU**
email: info@fauhopehouse.com **web:** www.fauhopehouse.com
dir: *0.7m N of Melrose over River Tweed. N off B6360 at Gattonside 30mph sign (E) up long driveway*

It's hard to imagine a more complete experience than a stay at Fauhope Country House, set high on a hillside on the north-east edge of the village. Hospitality is first class, breakfasts are excellent, and the delightful country house has a splendid interior. Bedrooms are luxurious, each individual and superbly equipped. Public areas are elegantly decorated and furnished, and enhanced by beautiful floral arrangements; the dining room is particularly stunning. AA Friendliest B&B of the Year Award Finalist 2016-2017.

Rooms 3 en suite S £80-£100; D £130-£145* **Facilities** FTV DVD Lounge tea/coffee Dinner available WiFi 🦆 🏇 Riding Treatment room **Extras** Speciality toiletries, fruit, sherry - free **Parking** 10 **Notes** LB

NEWCASTLETON
Map 21 NY48

Liddesdale

★★★★ INN

tel: 01387 375255 **Douglas Sq TD9 0QD**
email: reception@theliddesdalehotel.co.uk **web:** www.theliddesdalehotel.co.uk

Liddesdale is located in the peaceful 17th-century village of Newcastleton, overlooking the village square. There are well-appointed bedrooms and bathrooms, and the public areas offer various locations in which to dine. The welcoming public bar is well used by locals and residents alike, and there is also a beer garden. Relaxed and informal menus use the best local produce available.

Rooms 6 en suite (2 fmly) **Facilities** STV FTV Lounge TVL tea/coffee Dinner available Direct Dial WiFi 🎣 🏇 9 Fishing ⛳ **Conf** Max 60 Thtr 40 Class 40 Board 40 **Notes** LB

PEEBLES
Map 21 NT24

Premier Collection

Kingsmuir House

★★★★★ 👜 🛏 BED AND BREAKFAST

tel: 01721 724413 & 07776 405842 **Springhill Rd EH45 9EP**
email: malcolm@kingsmuirhouse.co.uk **web:** www.kingsmuirhouse.co.uk
dir: *From High St, over bridge then 2nd right into Springhill Rd. 0.25m opposite tennis court*

Kingsmuir House was built in 1855 and is set in a slightly elevated position to the south west of Peebles, just a few minutes' walk from the high street. This period building still boasts many original features, and the decor and furnishings are in keeping with its character. Hospitality is warm and genuine; and the bedroom suites are generous in size and beautifully presented with many thoughtful extras provided as standard. The en suites are also a feature, with walk-in showers and free-standing roll-top baths available. Dinner can be requested in advance and is well worth the 'night in'. If you want to bring your own wine this will be happily prepared and served on your behalf. Gardens are pleasing to the eye, and include a delightful summer house. Kingsmuir House was the AA Guest Accommodation of the Year for Scotland 2015-2016.

Rooms 2 en suite S £90; D £140 **Facilities** FTV DVD iPod docking station tea/coffee Dinner available WiFi 🏇 18 ⛳ **Extras** Home-made shortbread & truffles, fruit **Parking** 5 **Notes** ⊗

See advert on opposite page

STIRLING

CALLANDER   Map 20 NN60

Lubnaig House

★★★★ Ⓐ GUEST HOUSE

tel: 01877 330376 **Leny Feus FK17 8AS**
email: info@lubnaighouse.co.uk **web:** www.lubnaighouse.co.uk
dir: *From town centre take A84 W, 1st street on right after Poppies Hotel*

Lubnaig House is set in a delightful tree-lined secluded garden, just a five-minute walk from the town centre. The house, built in 1864, has comfortable, well-appointed bedrooms. There are two cosy lounges, and an impressive dining room where hearty traditional breakfasts are served at individual tables.

Rooms 6 en suite 2 annexe en suite (4 GF) **Facilities** FTV iPod docking station Lounge tea/coffee WiFi ⓐ **Parking** 10 **Notes** ⊗ No Children 7yrs Closed Nov-1 Apr

STIRLING   Map 21 NS79

Victoria Square Guest House

★★★★★ Ⓐ GUEST HOUSE

tel: 01786 473920 **12 Victoria Square FK8 2QZ**
email: info@vsgh.co.uk **web:** www.victoriasquareguesthouse.com
dir: *M9 junct 10 into Stirling, at Smith Museum 1st right into Victoria Place. 1st left into Victoria Square*

This classic Victorian building is situated in the peaceful and prestigious Kings Park area of Stirling, just a short walk away from Stirling Castle, Stirling Golf Club, the Smith Museum & Art Gallery and other attractions. Bedrooms are spacious and well-appointed and offer the space and comfort to ensure a peaceful and relaxing stay. Combining contemporary elegance with a strong sense of history, each room's decor and facilities enhance Victoria Square Guest House's welcome.

Rooms 7 en suite (1 GF) S £68-£85; D £83-£135* **Facilities** FTV iPod docking station Lounge tea/coffee WiFi ⓛ 18 **Extras** Speciality toiletries, mini-fridge, robes **Parking** 5 **Notes** ⊗ No Children 12yrs Closed 23-29 Dec

STRATHYRE   Map 20 NN51

Premier Collection

Creagan House

★★★★★ ◉◉ ⓢ RESTAURANT WITH ROOMS

tel: 01877 384638 **FK18 8ND**
email: eatandstay@creaganhouse.co.uk **web:** www.creaganhouse.co.uk
dir: *0.25m N of Strathyre on A84*

Originally a farmhouse dating from the 17th century, Creagan House has operated as a restaurant with rooms for many years. The baronial-style dining room provides a wonderful setting for the award-winning cuisine which is classic French with some Scottish influences. The warm hospitality and attentive service are noteworthy.

Rooms 5 en suite (1 fmly) (1 GF) S £90-£110; D £135-£155 **Facilities** FTV Lounge tea/coffee Dinner available WiFi ⓐ **Extras** Speciality toiletries **Conf** Max 35 Thtr 35 Class 12 Board 35 **Parking** 16 **Notes** LB Closed 26 Oct-6 Apr RS Wed & Thu closed

SCOTTISH ISLANDS

ISLE OF ARRAN

BRODICK   Map 20 NS03

Dunvegan House

★★★★ GUEST HOUSE

tel: 01770 302811 **Dunvegan Shore Rd KA27 8AJ**
email: dunveganhouse1@hotmail.com **web:** www.dunveganhouse-arran.co.uk
dir: *Turn right from ferry terminal, 500yds along Shore Rd*

Situated close to the shore and enjoying spectacular views of the bay, this establishment is a popular choice for visitors to the island. The property benefits from having a hands-on approach from the friendly owner while public areas and bedrooms have great views.

Rooms 9 en suite (3 GF) S £60; D £85* **Facilities** FTV Lounge tea/coffee Dinner available Licensed WiFi ⓐ **Parking** 8 **Notes** ⊗ Closed 23 Dec-3 Jan ⓔ

KINGSMUIR HOUSE – Peebles

Kingsmuir House, Springhill Road, Peebles, Scottish Borders, EH45 9EP
Tel: 01721 724413   Email: malcolm@kingsmuirhouse.co.uk
All the warmth of a B&B with the comfort and luxury of a small hotel.

"Luxury as standard"

Kingsmuir House in Peebles is a comfortable luxurious Award winning Victorian home, situated a short walk from the River Tweed and Peebles High Street. The two guest rooms are in the form of luxurious bedroom suites, each suite consisting of a separate sitting room, bedroom with super king size bed and a luxury bathroom with roll top bath and separate shower. The interior takes inspiration from its Victorian features yet with a modern twist, entering the hallway to a sweeping staircase and Scottish tartan carpets.

The overall ambiance of the house is relaxed and informal providing a great escape.

ISLE OF ISLAY

GLENEGEDALE
Map 20 NR35

Premier Collection

Glenegedale House
★★★★★ ⬥ GUEST HOUSE

tel: 01496 300400 & 07554 669664 **PA42 7AS**
email: info@glenegedalehouse.co.uk **web:** www.glenegedalehouse.co.uk

Situated midway between Bowmore and Port Ellen, this luxury guest house enjoys some of the best views on the island with the Mull of Oa and the glory of the Atlantic Ocean in full view. Modern accommodation is complemented by a range of comfortable lounges. The strength here lies with the hosts who go out of their way to ensure guests enjoy both the house and all the island has to offer. Memorable breakfasts served in the stunning dining room are not to be missed. AA Friendliest B&B of the Year Award Finalist 2016-2017.

Rooms 4 en suite (1 GF) S £90-£110; D £125-£145 **Facilities** FTV Lounge tea/coffee WiFi ⬥ 18 Fishing ⬥ **Parking** 8 **Notes** LB ⊗ No Children 12yrs Closed Dec

LISMORE

BACHUIL
Map 20 NM84

Bachuil Country House
★★★★ GUEST ACCOMMODATION

tel: 01631 760256 **PA34 5UL**
email: anita@clanlivingstone.com **web:** www.bachuilcountryhouse.co.uk
dir: On Isle of Lismore - 45 minute car ferry from Oban or 10 minute passenger ferry from Port Appin. There is no fuel available on Lismore

Situated on the Isle of Lismore, the most easterly of the southern Hebrides, Bachuil Country House provides a great place to enjoy the tranquillity of this historic and picturesque island. Hearty breakfasts and enjoyable dinners are provided daily. Guests can relax in the drawing room and enjoy open log fires.

Rooms 3 en suite **Facilities** iPod docking station TVL tea/coffee Dinner available WiFi ⬥ Fishing ⬥ **Extras** Fruit, snacks - complimentary **Parking** 4 **Notes** No Children 8yrs Closed Nov-Mar

SHETLAND

LERWICK
Map 24 HU44

Glen Orchy House
★★★★ ⬥ GUEST HOUSE

tel: 01595 692031 **20 Knab Rd ZE1 0AX**
email: glenorchy.house@virgin.net **web:** www.guesthouselerwick.com
dir: Next to coastguard station

This welcoming and well-presented house lies above the town with views over the Knab, and is within easy walking distance of the town centre. Bedrooms are modern in design and there is a choice of lounges with books and board games, one with an honesty bar. Substantial breakfasts are served, and the restaurant offers a delicious Thai menu.

Rooms 24 en suite (4 fmly) (4 GF) **Facilities** STV FTV DVD Lounge TVL tea/coffee Dinner available Licensed WiFi **Extras** Locally-made fudge **Parking** 10

ISLE OF SKYE

EDINBANE
Map 22 NG35

Shorefield House
★★★★ GUEST HOUSE

tel: 01470 582444 **Edinbane IV51 9PW**
email: stay@shorefield-house.com **web:** www.shorefieldhouse.com
dir: 12m from Portree & 8m from Dunvegan, off A850 into Edinbane, 1st on right

Shorefield House stands in the village of Edinbane and looks out to Loch Greshornish. Bedrooms range from single to family options, and one of the ground-floor rooms has easy access. All rooms are thoughtfully equipped and have WiFi, fridges, safes, DVD and CD players. The choices at breakfast are impressive, and the house has a child-friendly garden.

Rooms 3 en suite (1 fmly) (2 GF) S £55-£70; D £100-£140 **Facilities** STV FTV DVD tea/coffee WiFi ⬥ **Extras** Robes, mini-fridge **Parking** 10 **Notes** LB ⊗ Closed Oct-Apr

STRUAN
Map 22 NG33

Premier Collection

Ullinish Country Lodge
★★★★★ ⬤⬤⬤ ⬥ RESTAURANT WITH ROOMS

tel: 01470 572214 **IV56 8FD**
email: ullinish@theisleofskye.co.uk **web:** www.theisleofskye.co.uk
dir: Take A863 N. Lodge signed on left

Set in some of Scotland's most dramatic landscape, with views of the Black Cuillin and MacLeod's Tables, this lodge has lochs on three sides. Samuel Johnson and James Boswell stayed here in 1773 and were impressed with the hospitality even then. Hosts Brian and Pam hope to extend the same welcome to their guests today. As you would expect, all bedrooms have amazing views, and come with half-tester beds. The restaurant team combine the best in local produce with foraged items like seaweed, clams and herbs to create some truly impressive cooking.

Rooms 6 en suite S £115-£155; D £170-£250* (incl.dinner) **Facilities** FTV Lounge tea/coffee Dinner available WiFi **Extras** Sherry, sweets, mineral water - complimentary **Parking** 8 **Notes** LB ⊗ No Children 16yrs Closed 24 Dec-Jan No coaches

UIG
Map 22 NG36

Woodbine House
★★★★ GUEST ACCOMMODATION

tel: 01470 542243 & 07904 267561 **IV51 9XP**
email: contact@woodbineskye.co.uk **web:** www.woodbineskye.co.uk
dir: From Portree into Uig Bay, pass Ferry Inn, right onto A855 (Staffin road), house 300yds on right

Built in the late 19th century, Woodbine House occupies an elevated position overlooking Uig Bay and the surrounding countryside, and is well suited for walking and bird-watching enthusiasts. The ground-floor dining room has lovely sea views, as do the front-facing bedrooms.

Rooms 5 en suite (1 fmly) (1 GF) S £50-£65; D £69-£85* **Facilities** FTV Lounge tea/coffee WiFi ⬥ Mountain Bike/Sea kayak hire Boat trips **Parking** 5 **Notes** LB ⊗ RS Nov-Feb long stays or group bookings only

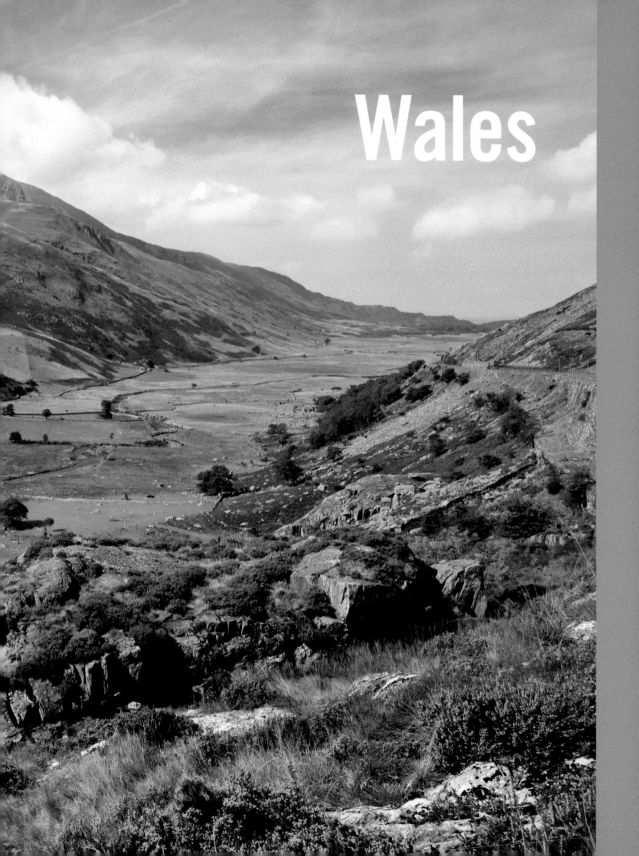

Wales

ISLE OF ANGLESEY

BEAUMARIS   Map 14 SH67

Premier Collection

The Bull - Beaumaris

★★★★★ ⑳⑳⑳ INN

tel: 01248 810329 **Castle St LL58 8AP**
email: info@bullsheadinn.co.uk **web:** www.bullsheadinn.co.uk
dir: *Located on Main St in town centre*

Both Charles Dickens and Samuel Johnson visited this inn, and the interior still features exposed beams and antique weaponry. Bedrooms are richly decorated and traditional, while The Townhouse, just across a side street, offers additional boutique bedrooms, each with vibrant decor. The food continues to attract high praise in both the Loft Restaurant and the less formal Brasserie, and cask-conditioned ales are served in the traditional bar. Meeting and functions can be catered for.

Rooms 25 en suite (2 fmly) (5 GF) S £95-£157.50; D £110-£170* **Facilities** FTV Lounge tea/coffee Dinner available Direct Dial Lift WiFi ⚡ 18 **Extras** Speciality toiletries **Parking** 10 **Notes** LB Closed 24-26 Dec No coaches

HOLYHEAD   Map 14 SH28

Blackthorn Farm

★★★★ ☒ GUEST ACCOMMODATION

tel: 01407 765262 **Penrhosfeilw, Trearddur Bay LL65 2LT**
email: enquiries@blackthornfarm.co.uk **web:** www.blackthornleisure.co.uk
dir: *A55 to Holyhead, take 1st exit at rdbt, turn immediately right between two pubs. At end of road, turn right, 0.5m on left*

Blackthorn Farm is a family-run establishment that is also a camping and touring site. Set in 18 peaceful acres on Holy Island, the farm enjoys outstanding panoramic views of the Irish Sea, Snowdonia, and coastal views of Anglesey. There is a beach, and coastal trails, within easy reach. A full Welsh breakfast is served. Please note pets are welcome.

Rooms 8 rms (6 en suite) (3 fmly) (1 GF) S £67-£80; D £80-£104* **Facilities** FTV DVD tea/coffee Licensed WiFi ⚓ **Conf** Thtr 25 Class 25 Board 20 **Parking** 10 **Notes** LB Closed 22-31 Dec

LLANFACHRAETH   Map 14 SH38

Black Lion Inn

★★★★ ⑳ INN

tel: 01407 730718 **Llanfaethlu LL65 4NL**
email: info@blacklionanglesey.co.uk **web:** www.blacklionanglesey.com
dir: *A55 junct 3, A5025 (follow Wylfa Power Station signs). Right at lights. 6m to inn*

After being derelict for many years, this inn has been lovingly brought back to life. The smartly whitewashed rural property stands on the main road between Valley and Cemaes Bay. Two spacious, modern bedrooms offer enhanced comfort for guests and are complemented by bathrooms complete with oversized rain showers. The busy and vibrant restaurant focuses on local produce, with the meat coming directly from the family farm. The bar also concentrates on local ales.

Rooms 2 en suite (1 fmly) S fr £90; D fr £115* **Facilities** DVD tea/coffee Dinner available WiFi **Extras** Speciality toiletries, home-made biscuits **Parking** 38 **Notes** Closed 5-15 Jan RS Out of season closed Sun-Tue

MENAI BRIDGE   Map 14 SH57

Bulkeley Arms

★★★ INN

tel: 01248 712715 **Uxbridge Square LL59 5DF**
email: tafarnwr@gmail.com **web:** www.bulkeleyarms.com

This family-run, friendly pub is easy to locate with its whitewashed walls standing prominently amongst the high street shops. A smart bar on the ground floor offers good quality dining and there is a separate area with pool tables and large screen TVs. Bedrooms are spacious and well equipped, all with en suite shower rooms. The small car park is a welcome addition.

Rooms 3 en suite (1 fmly) S £55; D £65* **Facilities** FTV tea/coffee Dinner available WiFi Pool table ⚓ **Parking** 6 **Notes** LB No coaches

RHOSNEIGR   Map 14 SH37

Cefn Dref

★★★★ ☒ BED AND BREAKFAST

tel: 01407 810714 **LL64 5JH**
email: bookings@cefndref.co.uk **web:** www.cefndref.co.uk
dir: *A55 junct 5 (signed Rhosneigr), onto A4080 to Llanfaelog. Turn right signed Rhosneigr, 1st house on right after 30mph sign*

Enjoying stunning coastal views, this welcoming Edwardian shooting lodge has been transformed into a very comfortable and inviting bed and breakfast. Bedrooms, complemented by smart, stylish bathrooms, are very well equipped with extras including WiFi and luxury toiletries. Breakfast is a memorable experience, with home-made or locally sourced produce from an extensive and imaginative menu. The town centre, with many dining options, is a short walk away, as is the sea.

Rooms 3 en suite (1 fmly) D £80-£125* **Facilities** FTV DVD tea/coffee WiFi ⚡ 18 ⚓ **Extras** Speciality toiletries, fridges in rooms **Parking** 10 **Notes** ⊗ Closed Nov-Etr

BRIDGEND

BRIDGEND   Map 9 SS97

Hazelwood Guest House

★★★★ GUEST HOUSE

tel: 01656 647780 **Tondu Rd CF31 4LJ**
email: info@hazelwood-house.co.uk **web:** www.hazelwood-house.co.uk

Located just outside Bridgend, this popular guest house offers a range of well-equipped bedrooms and bathrooms including some on the ground floor. Breakfast is taken in the comfortable conservatory and a large car park is also provided. There are a range of options for dinner, all within a short walk of the accommodation, including a pleasant inn.

Rooms 8 en suite (3 GF) S £45-£60; D £60-£70 (room only)* **Facilities** FTV TVL tea/coffee WiFi ⚓ **Parking** 14 **Notes** LB ⊗ Closed 24-27 Dec

CARDIFF

CARDIFF
Map 9 ST17

Innkeeper's Lodge Cardiff
★★★★ INN

tel: 08451 551551 *(Calls cost 2p per minute plus your phone company's access charge)*
The Beverley Hotel, 75-77 Cathedral Rd CF11 9PG
email: info@innkeeperslodge.com **web:** www.innkeeperslodge.com
dir: *M4 junct 29 (from E) onto A48. Left onto A4119, 0.5m left again (Cathedral Rd). Lodge on right*

Located in the Pontcanna district of Cardiff, this former Victorian villa has been tastefully restored as an inn. The modern bedrooms are equipped to a good standard, offering a range of extras for both the business and leisure traveller. The popular bar and restaurant offers home-cooked classics, with a number of real ales on tap. Just a short walk away are the Swalec Stadium, Cardiff University and the Millennium Centre.

Rooms 17 en suite (9 fmly) **Facilities** FTV tea/coffee Dinner available WiFi **Notes** ⊗

CARMARTHENSHIRE

CARMARTHEN
Map 8 SN42

Sarnau Mansion
★★★★ GUEST ACCOMMODATION

tel: 01267 211404 **Llysonnen Rd SA33 5DZ**
email: d.fernihough@btinternet.com **web:** www.sarnaumansion.co.uk
dir: *5m W of Carmarthen. Exit A40 onto B4298, becomes Bancyfelin road (signed Bancyfelin), Sarnau Mansion on right*

Located west of Carmarthen in 16 acres of grounds and gardens, including a tennis court, this large Grade II listed, late Georgian house retains much original character and is stylishly decorated. There is a lounge with a log fire, an elegant dining room, and spacious bedrooms with stunning rural views.

Rooms 4 rms (3 en suite) (1 pri facs) S £45-£60; D £85-£95* **Facilities** DVD TVL tea/coffee WiFi ⚓ 18 🔒 **Parking** 10 **Notes** ⊗ No Children 5yrs

Silver Stars

The AA Silver Star rating denotes a B&B that we highly recommend. They have a superior level of quality within their star rating, high standards of hospitality, service and cleanliness.

FELINGWM UCHAF
Map 8 SN52

Allt Y Golau Farmhouse *(SN510261)*
★★★★ 🏡 FARMHOUSE

tel: 01267 290455 **Allt Y Golau Uchaf SA32 7BB**
email: alltygolau@btinternet.com **web:** www.alltygolau.com
dir: *A40 onto B4310, N for 2m. 1st on left after Felingwm Uchaf*

This delightful Georgian farmhouse has been furnished and decorated to a high standard by the present owners, and enjoys panoramic views over the Tywi Valley to the Black Mountains beyond. Guests are welcome to take a relaxing walk through the two acres of mature garden. Many thoughtful extras are provided in the comfortable bedrooms, and there is a separate lounge. Breakfast is provided in the cosy dining room and served around a communal table.

Rooms 3 rms (2 en suite) (1 pri facs) (2 GF) S £45; D £70 **Facilities** TVL tea/coffee WiFi 🔒 **Extras** Speciality toiletries, snacks - complimentary **Parking** 3 **Notes** ⊗ No Children 12yrs Closed 20 Dec-2 Jan ⊜ 2 acres small holding

LAUGHARNE
Map 8 SN31

Broadway Country House
★★★★ ⊜ GUEST ACCOMMODATION

tel: 01994 427969 **Broadway SA33 4NU**
email: enquiries@broadwaycountryhouse.co.uk **web:** www.broadwaycountryhouse.co.uk
dir: *From A40 at St Clears onto A4066 to Laugharne. 0.75m past Laugharne on right*

This family-run business offers a relaxed and peaceful retreat. Set in seven acres of grounds and gardens it has delightful views over Carmarthen Bay and the Gower Peninsula. Bedrooms and bathrooms are well decorated and furnished and include some welcome extras. Both dinner and breakfast offer a range of carefully prepared quality ingredients and are a highlight of any visit.

Rooms 9 en suite (1 fmly) (6 GF) **Facilities** FTV TVL tea/coffee Dinner available Direct Dial Licensed WiFi **Conf** Max 150 Thtr 150 Class 20 Board 40 **Parking** 50 **Notes** Civ Wed 104

LLANARTHNE
Map 8 SN51

Premier Collection

Llwyn Helyg Country House

★★★★★ 🎧 BED AND BREAKFAST

tel: 01558 668778 & 07464 106085 **SA32 8HJ**
email: enquiries@llwynhelygcountryhouse.co.uk
web: www.llwynhelygcountryhouse.co.uk
dir: *A48 onto B4310, at rdbt at entrance of National Botanic Gardens of Wales take 1st exit (B4310). After 0.3m turn right at farm along lane then sharp left, 1m on left*

The owners of Llwyn Helyg, a newly-built 'country house', have used the finest quality materials to create this luxury bed and breakfast accommodation. Situated in three acres of landscaped gardens and surrounded by countryside, it's on the outskirts of Llanarthne, midway between Carmarthen and Llandeilo. All the individually designed, en suite bedrooms have 6-foot wide beds and luxurious Vi-Spring mattresses. Private parking is available. AA Friendliest B&B of the Year Award Finalist 2016-2017.

Rooms 3 en suite D £135-£155 **Facilities** FTV DVD iPod docking station Lounge TVL tea/coffee WiFi ⚓ 18 ⚓ Therapy/Holistic treatment room **Extras** Speciality toiletries, fruit, snacks - free **Conf** Max 6 Board 6 **Parking** 10 **Notes** LB ⊗ No Children 16yrs Closed Xmas & New Year

LLANDOVERY
Map 9 SN73

Llanerchindda Farm

★★★ 🏠 GUEST HOUSE

tel: 01550 750274 **Cynghordy SA20 0NB**
email: info@cambrianway.com **web:** www.cambrianway.com
dir: *A483 Llandovery to Builth Wells road, after 40mph sign turn left at brown tourist sign (Llanerchindda), 2.75m to farm*

Set in 50 acres of Welsh countryside with spectacular views over the Black Mountains and the Brecon Beacons, this farmhouse-style accommodation is the ideal base for various activities including walking, fishing, quad-bike riding and bird watching. Bedrooms and bathrooms are comfortable and guests also have use of the lounge. In addition to a substantial breakfast, dinner is available by prior arrangement and features delicious home cooking.

Llanerchindda Farm

Rooms 9 en suite (1 fmly) (2 GF) S £40-£44; D £80-£88* **Facilities** FTV Lounge TVL tea/coffee Dinner available Licensed WiFi ⚓ 18 Fishing ⚓ Clay pigeon shooting 4x4 driving experience **Parking** 31 **Notes** LB Closed 2-16 Jan

See advert on opposite page

LLANSTEFFAN
Map 8 SN31

Mansion House Llansteffan

★★★★ ◉◉ RESTAURANT WITH ROOMS

tel: 01267 241515 & 07768 194539 **Pantyrathro SA33 5AJ**
email: info@mansionhousellansteffan.co.uk **web:** www.mansionhousellansteffan.co.uk
dir: *From Carmarthen on B4312 towards Llansteffan, follow brown signs*

Mansion House has been lovingly restored by the current owners, and is set in five acres of grounds with enviable views over the Towy Estuary and Carmarthen Bay. While bedrooms differ in size and style all are well-equipped and complemented by smart bathrooms. With a wealth of quality produce right on the doorstep it's not surprising that the head chef focuses on using seasonal, local, and home-grown produce on the constantly changing, interesting menu. Pre-dinner drinks can be taken in the bar, where there is an excellent range of gins.

Rooms 9 en suite (1 fmly) S £99-£170; D £119-£200* **Facilities** FTV DVD iPod docking station Lounge tea/coffee Dinner available Direct Dial WiFi ⚓ 18 ⚓ **Extras** Speciality toiletries, robes, home-made cookies **Conf** Max 200 Thtr 150 Class 80 Board 40 **Parking** 50 **Notes** LB ⊗ Civ Wed 120

LLANYBYDDER
Map 8 SN54

Glasfryn Guest House

★★★★ GUEST HOUSE

tel: 01570 481400 & 07980 576491 **Glasfryn SA40 9TY**
email: ron@glasfrynguesthouse.co.uk **web:** www.glasfrynguesthouse.co.uk
dir: *On A485. On entering Llanybydder located on right*

Glasfryn is a spacious, double-fronted Victorian villa standing in the centre of market town of Llanybydder. Renowned for its livestock markets and monthly pony sales, the location is ideal for exploring the nearby Cardigan Bay, the Brecon Beacons, and shopping centres of Carmarthen and Aberystwyth. The friendly owners welcome you into their home, and bedrooms are of a good size. Most have en suite facilities. A wealth of original features have been retained, with high ceilings and original woodwork and architrave. Dinners can be provided on request, or there are a number of good quality eating places within a short drive.

Rooms 4 rms (3 en suite) (1 pri facs) (1 fmly) S £50-£100; D £68-£120*
Facilities FTV DVD tea/coffee Dinner available WiFi Fishing ⊕ **Parking** 6

ST CLEARS
Map 8 SN21

Premier Collection

Coedllys Country House

★★★★★ ⬤ BED AND BREAKFAST

tel: 01994 231455 **Coedllys Uchaf, Llangynin SA33 4JY**
email: coedllys@btinternet.com **web:** www.coedllyscountryhouse.co.uk
dir: *A40 St Clears rdbt, take 3rd exit, at lights turn left. After 100yds turn right, 3m to Llangynin, pass village sign. 30mph sign on left, turn immediately down track (private drive)*

Set in a peaceful valley, Coedllys is the home of the Harbers, who make visitors feel like honoured guests. Bedrooms are lavishly furnished, and the thoughtful and useful extras make a stay most memorable. There is a cosy, well-furnished lounge, and an extensive breakfast choice is served in the pleasant dining room. A further cottage-style annexe, suitable as a self-catering let, is also available. For the energetic there is a fitness suite, but guests can also relax in small indoor pool.

Rooms 2 en suite (1 GF) **Facilities** FTV DVD iPod docking station Lounge tea/coffee WiFi ⊙ Gym ⊕ **Extras** Speciality toiletries, home-made biscuits - free **Parking** 6 **Notes** No Children 12yrs Closed 22-28 Dec

CEREDIGION

ABERAERON
Map 8 SN46

Premier Collection

Feathers Royal

★★★★★ ⬤ INN

tel: 01545 571750 **Alban Square SA46 0AQ**
email: enquiries@feathersroyal.co.uk **web:** www.feathersroyal.co.uk
dir: *A482, Lampeter Road, Feathers Royal opposite recreation grounds*

This is a family-run inn, ideally located in the picturesque Georgian town of Aberaeron. It is a charming Grade II listed property, built in 1815 as a traditional coaching house, and later transformed to coincide with the town's bicentenary celebrations. Accommodation is very comfortable with modern fittings and accessories provided, and the public areas are well appointed. There is a large suite available for private or business functions.

Rooms 13 en suite (2 fmly) S £79; D £130* **Facilities** FTV Lounge tea/coffee Dinner available Direct Dial WiFi ⊕ **Conf** Max 200 Thtr 200 Class 100 Board 50 **Parking** 20 **Notes** LB ⊗ Civ Wed 200

The Castle

★★★★ ⬤ INN

tel: 01545 570205 **Market St SA46 0AU**
email: castle_hotel@btconnect.com **web:** www.the-castlehotel.co.uk
dir: *On A487, in centre of town*

The Castle is a Grade II listed building right in the centre of the pretty harbour town of Aberaeron. Pastel coloured houses are a feature of this Georgian town, ideally situated for many walks, including the Llanerchaeron Trail and Wales Coastal Path. A smart café bar serves very good quality home cooked dishes throughout the day. The modern bedrooms have flat-screen TVs, WiFi, Egyptian linen and duck-down duvets.

Rooms 8 en suite (1 fmly) **Facilities** FTV tea/coffee Dinner available WiFi ⊕ **Conf** Max 45 Thtr 30 Class 40 Board 20 **Notes** LB

LLANERCHINDDA FARM

Family run 3 star guest house situated in a rural location with spectacular views of the Cynghordy Viaduct, Black Mountain & Brecon Beacons. Ideally situated for exploring Mid & South Wales with great walking, mountain biking, bird watching and fantastic scenery all on our doorstep. The 9 rooms in the guest house are en-suite with a comfortable lounge bar, open log fire and a restaurant on site offering breakfast and evening meals using local fresh produce where possible. There are also 2 self catering cottages one sleeping 6 and one sleeping 10 people available.

Llanerchindda Farm, Cynghordy, Llandovery, Carmarthenshire SA20 0NB • Tel: 01550 750274 • Fax: 01550 750300
Email: info@cambrianway.com • Website: www.cambrianway.com

ABERAERON *continued*

Aromatherapy Reflexology Centre

★★★ BED AND BREAKFAST

tel: 01974 202581 **The Barn House, Pennant Rd SY23 5LZ**
email: aromareflex@googlemail.com **web:** www.aromatherapy-breaks-wales.co.uk
dir: *S of Aberystwyth to Llanon, leave village, turn left at 40mph sign. 2nd left to Barn House*

Expect a warm welcome from this family-run bed and breakfast where Welsh is spoken. Set in its own grounds in a tranquil position with lovely views of Cardigan Bay. Bedrooms are comfortable and smartly presented, and there is a choice of traditional, vegetarian or vegan breakfasts. Aromatherapy and reflexology are available at the centre.

Rooms 3 rms (2 en suite) (1 pri facs) **Facilities** FTV DVD tea/coffee WiFi 🛁 Massage/Reflexology by appointment **Parking** 7 **Notes** LB ☺

ABERYSTWYTH	Map 8 SN58

Premier Collection

Awel-Deg

★★★★★ BED AND BREAKFAST

tel: 01970 880681 **Capel Bangor SY23 3LR**
email: awel-deg@tiscali.co.uk **web:** www.awel-deg.co.uk
dir: *5m E of Aberystwyth. On A44 in Capel Bangor*

Located five miles from the historic university town of Aberystwyth, this attractive bungalow, set in pretty gardens, provides high standards of hospitality, comfort and facilities. Immaculately maintained throughout, spacious bedrooms are equipped with a wealth of thoughtful extras and smart, modern en suite shower rooms. Comprehensive breakfasts are served at one table in the elegant dining room and a choice of lounges is available.

Rooms 2 en suite (2 GF) S £50; D £59* **Facilities** FTV TVL tea/coffee WiFi **Parking** 8 **Notes** LB ☺ No Children 11yrs Closed 20-30 Dec ☺

Bodalwyn Guest House

★★★★ GUEST HOUSE

tel: 01970 612578 **Queen's Av SY23 2EG**
email: enquiries@bodalwyn.co.uk **web:** www.bodalwyn.co.uk
dir: *500yds N of town centre. Exit A487 (Northgate St) into North Rd to end*

Located a short walk from the promenade, this imposing Edwardian house, built for a college professor, has been appointed to provide high standards of comfort and good facilities. Smart modern bathrooms complement the spacious bedrooms, which are equipped with a wealth of thoughtful extras; family rooms are available. Welsh breakfasts are served in the elegant conservatory-dining room.

Rooms 7 en suite (2 fmly) S £45-£55; D £73-£80* **Facilities** FTV DVD tea/coffee WiFi **Notes** ☺ Closed 22 Dec-2 Jan ☺

Glyn-Garth

★★★★ GUEST HOUSE

tel: 01970 615050 & 07890 401498 **South Rd SY23 1JS**
email: glyngarth@aol.com **web:** www.glyngarth.pages.qpg.com
dir: *In town centre. Off A487 into South Rd, off South Promenade*

Privately owned and personally run by the same family for over 50 years, this immaculately maintained guest house provides a range of thoughtfully furnished bedrooms with smart modern bathrooms. Breakfast is served in the attractive dining room and a lounge is also available.

Rooms 10 rms (6 en suite) (2 fmly) (1 GF) S £33-£65; D £66-£88 **Facilities** STV FTV TVL tea/coffee WiFi ⌖ 18 🔒 **Parking** 2 **Notes** ☺ ☺

Yr Hafod

★★★★ GUEST HOUSE

tel: 01970 617579 **1 South Marine Ter SY23 1JX**
email: johnyrhafod@aol.com **web:** www.yrhafod.co.uk
dir: *On south promenade between harbour & castle*

Yr Hafod is an immaculately maintained end of terrace Victorian house with a commanding location overlooking South Bay. The spacious bedrooms are comfortable, some with delightful sea views and many have particularly well-appointed bathrooms. Breakfast is served in the front-facing dining room.

Rooms 6 rms (3 en suite) S £36-£38; D £72-£96 **Facilities** STV FTV TVL tea/coffee WiFi 🛁 **Extras** Chocolates, mineral water - complimentary **Parking** 1 **Notes** ☺ Closed Xmas & Jan ☺

Find out more about the **AA Friendliest B&B of the Year** on page 17

Y Gelli

★★★ GUEST HOUSE

tel: 01970 617834 **Dolau, Lovesgrove SY23 3HP**
email: pat@plasdolau.co.uk **web:** www.plasdolau.co.uk
dir: Off A44 2.75m E of town centre

Set in spacious grounds on the town's outskirts, this modern detached house contains a range of practical furnished bedrooms, with three further rooms available in an adjacent Victorian property. Comprehensive breakfasts are served in the attractive dining room with evening meals available on request. A comfortable lounge is also available for guests' use.

Rooms 6 rms (3 en suite) 3 annexe rms 1 annexe en suite (3 fmly) (1 GF) **Facilities** TVL TV8B tea/coffee Dinner available Snooker Pool table Table tennis Stabling can be provided **Conf** Thtr 30 Class 30 Board 20 **Parking** 20 **Notes** ⊗

CARDIGAN
Map 8 SN14

AA GUEST ACCOMMODATION OF THE YEAR FOR WALES 2016-2017

Premier Collection

Caemorgan Mansion

★★★★★ ♀ ☞ GUEST HOUSE

tel: 01239 613297 **Caemorgan Rd SA43 1QU**
email: guest@caemorgan.com **web:** www.caemorgan.com
dir: N of Cardigan on A487 towards Aberporth. Left into Caemorgan Rd, entrance in 200mtrs

Caemorgan Mansion stands in its own peaceful grounds, a haven for local wildlife, on the fringes of Cardigan, and is ideally located for visiting the glorious local beaches. Bought in a derelict state, the owners have breathed new life into the property, now fully refurbished. Bedrooms are spacious, with high quality bathrooms; several have feature showers and baths. The smart dining room overlooking the gardens is the ideal place to sample the innovative cuisine made from locally sourced produce at breakfast and dinner. The friendly hosts are on hand to offer suggestions for places to visit during your stay.

Rooms 5 en suite D £110-£130* **Facilities** FTV DVD iPod docking station Lounge tea/coffee Dinner available Licensed WiFi ❀ Massage/beauty therapy **Extras** Robes, slippers, speciality toiletries, safe **Conf** Max 20 Thtr 20 Class 10 Board 10 **Parking** 10 **Notes** ⊗ No Children 15yrs

NEW QUAY
Map 8 SN35

The Swallows Bed and Breakfast

★★★★ BED AND BREAKFAST

tel: 07516 905548 **Blaenwaun Fawr SA44 6JD**
email: theswallowsbandb@gmail.com **web:** www.the-swallows-bed-and-breakfast.com
dir: S of New Quay on A487. Through Synod Inn hamlet turn opposite parking sign for layby

The Swallows Bed and Breakfast is set just off the main coast road with stunning views over the countryside of Cardigan Bay, and a short distance from the coast. This relaxed and friendly property offers three spacious bedrooms located apart from the main house, offering guests total privacy and their own front door. Each room has a conservatory which acts as a dining room for breakfast and dinner. Hearty homemade dinners after a day exploring the nearby Coastal Path, or spotting dolphins, are delivered to your door to enjoy at your leisure. Large modern walk-in wet rooms complement these three ground floor rooms for easy access and use.

Rooms 3 annexe en suite (3 fmly) (3 GF) **Facilities** FTV DVD tea/coffee Dinner available WiFi ❀ ♨ **Extras** Fresh milk, fruit - complimentary **Parking** 3

Cambrian Inn & Restaurant

★★★ INN

tel: 01545 560295 **New Rd SA45 9SE**
email: cambrianhotel@gmail.com **web:** www.cambrianhotel-newquay.co.uk
dir: From A487 at Llanarth onto B4342 for 2m

Situated in a quiet location on the outskirts of popular New Quay, this family-run inn offers a good selection of dishes at both lunch and dinner. Bedrooms include a range of sizes and are all located on the first floor. Breakfast is served in the conservatory restaurant, and a garden with outdoor seating is also available.

Rooms 4 en suite S £50-£60; D £60-£85* **Facilities** FTV TVL tea/coffee Dinner available WiFi ♨ **Extras** Trouser press **Parking** 9 **Notes** LB RS Dec-Mar bar & restaurant closed

TREGARON
Map 9 SN65

Y Talbot

★★★★★ ◉ INN

tel: 01974 298208 **The Square SY25 6JL**
email: info@ytalbot.com **web:** www.ytalbot.com
dir: From Lampeter or Aberystwyth on A485, in Tregaron turn opposite NatWest, 100yds in Square

Located in the heart of this quiet town, Y Talbot has been appointed to provide a range of very high-quality bedrooms and bathrooms with luxury showers. Some smaller standard rooms are also available. There is a traditional bar serving real ales and a contemporary-style main restaurant and lounge. Dinner offers a very good selection of dishes using quality produce.

Rooms 11 en suite 2 annexe en suite (3 fmly) (1 GF) S £60-£110; D £85-£140* **Facilities** FTV iPod docking station Lounge tea/coffee Dinner available WiFi ♨ ♨ Drying room **Extras** Speciality toiletries, mineral water **Conf** Max 120 Thtr 80 Class 120 Board 40 **Parking** 7 **Notes** LB Civ Wed 140

CONWY

ABERGELE	Map 14 SH97

Premier Collection

The Kinmel Arms

★★★★★ ⦿⦿ RESTAURANT WITH ROOMS

tel: 01745 832207 **The Village, St George LL22 9BP**
email: info@thekinmelarms.co.uk **web:** www.thekinmelarms.co.uk
dir: *From A55 junct 24a to St George. E on A55, junct 24. 1st left to Rhuddlan, 1st right into St George. 2nd right*

This converted 17th-century coaching inn stands close to the church in the village of St George. The restaurant specialises in skilfully prepared produce from Wales and north-west England. Friendly, helpful staff will ensure you have a relaxing stay, in one of four attractive suites. All are kitted out with small kitchenettes where continental breakfasts are placed each day to enjoy at your leisure. Each suite is individually designed in a clean, natural style with luxurious bathrooms to match.

Rooms 4 en suite (2 GF) S £115-£135; D £115-£175* **Facilities** STV DVD Lounge tea/coffee Dinner available ⚓ 18 🛇 **Extras** Speciality toiletries, fruit, snacks - free **Parking** 50 **Notes** LB No Children 16yrs Closed 25 Dec & 1 Jan RS Sun & Mon closed (ex BHs) No coaches

The Black Lion

★★★★ ⊖ INN

tel: 01745 720205 **Swan Square, Llanfair Talhaiarn LL22 8RY**
web: www.theblacklionnorthwales.co.uk

This Welsh inn provides a warm and friendly welcome in the picturesque village of Llanfair Talhaiarn. Meals are available throughout the week with the focus on local produce and hearty, honest cooking but a modern twist here and there ensures everyone is catered for. Relax beside the fire to enjoy real ales on tap. Five stylish bedrooms are comfortable and offer all the mod cons.

Rooms 5 en suite (2 fmly) **Facilities** FTV tea/coffee Dinner available WiFi Pool table **Parking** 15 **Notes** ⊗

BETWS-Y-COED	Map 14 SH75

Premier Collection

Penmachno Hall

★★★★★ ⊖ GUEST ACCOMMODATION

tel: 01690 760410 **Penmachno LL24 0PU**
email: stay@penmachnohall.co.uk **web:** www.penmachnohall.co.uk
dir: *4m S of Betws-y-Coed. A5 onto B4406 to Penmachno, over bridge, right at Eagles pub signed Ty Mawr. 500yds at stone bridge*

Set in more than two acres of mature grounds including a mountain stream and woodland, this impressive Victorian rectory provides high standards of comfort and good facilities. Stylish decor and quality furnishings highlight the many original features throughout the ground-floor areas, and the bedrooms have a wealth of thoughtful extras. Alongside the main building is a superb two-bedroom, self-catering unit in a former coach house. Pre-booked set menu, party-style evening meals are served on Saturday nights, while buffet-style meals are served Tuesday through Friday.

Rooms 3 en suite D £90-£100* **Facilities** STV DVD Lounge tea/coffee Dinner available Licensed WiFi 🛇 **Extras** Fruit - complimentary; robes **Parking** 5 **Notes** LB ⊗ Closed Xmas & New Year RS Sun-Mon no evening meals

Afon View Guest House

★★★★ GUEST HOUSE

tel: 01690 710726 **Holyhead Rd LL24 0AN**
email: welcome@afon-view.co.uk **web:** www.afon-view.co.uk
dir: *On A5, 150yds E of HSBC bank*

A warm welcome is assured at this elegant Victorian house, located between Waterloo Bridge and the village centre. Bedrooms are equipped with lots of thoughtful extras, and day rooms include an attractive dining room and comfortable guest lounge.

Rooms 7 en suite (1 fmly) **Facilities** FTV Lounge tea/coffee WiFi 🛇 **Parking** 7 **Notes** ⊗ No Children 5yrs Closed 23-26 Dec

Bryn Bella Guest House

★★★★ GUEST HOUSE

tel: 01690 710627 **Lon Muriau, Llanrwst Rd LL24 0HD**
email: welcome@bryn-bella.co.uk **web:** www.bryn-bella.co.uk
dir: *A5 onto A470, 0.5m right onto driveway signed Bryn Bella*

Located in an elevated position on the outskirts of the village, with stunning views of the surrounding countryside, this elegant Victorian house provides a range of thoughtfully equipped bedrooms and smart, modern bathrooms. An eco-friendly approach is to be commended and this ethos runs through the whole operation from local sourcing to reduce food-miles to water reclamation. A warm welcome is assured and guest services include a daily weather forecast.

Rooms 5 en suite (1 GF) **Facilities** FTV DVD TVL tea/coffee WiFi 🛇 **Extras** Robes, microwave **Parking** 6 **Notes** ⊗ No Children 16yrs

Cwmanog Isaf Farm *(SH799546)*

★★★★ FARMHOUSE

tel: 01690 710225 & 07808 421634 **Fairy Glen LL24 0SL**
email: h.hughes165@btinternet.com **web:** www.cwmanogisaffarmholidays.co.uk
dir: *1m S of Betws-y-Coed off A470 before stone bridge, 500yds on farm lane*

Peacefully located in 30 acres of undulating land, where the Fairy Glen (a well known beauty spot on the River Conwy) can be found, this 200-year-old house on a working livestock farm has been restored to provide comfortable, thoughtfully furnished bedrooms. Breakfasts use home-reared or organic produce. The property's elevated position provides stunning views of the surrounding countryside.

Rooms 3 en suite (1 GF) S £45-£65; D £65-£75* **Facilities** STV Lounge tea/coffee 🛇 **Parking** 4 **Notes** ⊗ No Children 15yrs Closed Nov-15 Mar ⊛ 30 acres sheep

Park Hill

★★★★ GUEST HOUSE

tel: 01690 710540 **Llanrwst Rd LL24 0HD**
email: welcome@park-hill.co.uk **web:** www.park-hill.co.uk
dir: *0.5m N of Betws-y-Coed on A470 (Llanrwst road)*

A warm welcome is assured at this guest house, which benefits from a peaceful location overlooking the village of Betws-y-Coed and valley beyond. Well-equipped bedrooms, including one with a four-poster, offer comfortable beds and modern extras. There is a sun lounge to the front, a heated swimming pool, sauna and whirlpool bath for guests' use. Ample parking onsite.

Rooms 8 en suite S £72-£99; D £72-£99 **Facilities** FTV DVD Lounge tea/coffee WiFi 🏊 ⚓ 9 Sauna 🛇 **Parking** 11 **Notes** LB ⊗ No Children 8yrs

Ty Gwyn Inn

★★★ ⊜ INN

tel: 01690 710383 **LL24 0SG**
email: mratcl1050@aol.com **web:** www.tygwynhotel.co.uk
dir: Junct of A5 & A470, by Waterloo Bridge

Situated on the edge of the village, close to the Waterloo Bridge, this historic coaching inn retains many original features. Quality furnishings and memorabilia enhance its intrinsic charm. Bedrooms, some with antique beds, are equipped with thoughtful extras. Imaginative food is provided in the cosy bars and the restaurant.

Rooms 13 rms (10 en suite) (3 fmly) (1 GF) **Facilities** TVL tea/coffee Dinner available WiFi **Parking** 14 **Notes** Closed Mon-Wed in Jan

CAPEL CURIG   Map 14 SH75

Bryn Tyrch Inn

★★★★ ❀ INN

tel: 01690 720223 & 07855 762791 **LL24 0EL**
email: info@bryntyrchinn.co.uk **web:** www.bryntyrchinn.co.uk
dir: On A5 at top end of village

Dating from the 19th century, this former posting house has been sympathetically refurbished to provide public areas of real character and stylish modern bedrooms with smart en suite bathrooms. Hog and lamb roasts are a feature on certain days throughout the year and the award-winning restaurant also impresses. The enthusiastic proprietors, assisted by a friendly team are constantly making improvements to ensure a visit to Bryn Tyrch is worth the trip.

Rooms 11 en suite **Facilities** FTV Lounge tea/coffee Dinner available WiFi ⚓ 9 Drying facilities **Extras** Home-made biscuits **Parking** 30 **Notes** Closed 15-27 Dec & 3-20 Jan RS Feb-Mar open wknds only & school hols No coaches Civ Wed 75

COLWYN BAY   Map 14 SH87

The Northwood

★★★★ GUEST HOUSE

tel: 01492 549931 **47 Rhos Rd, Rhos-on-Sea LL28 4RS**
email: welcome@thenorthwood.co.uk **web:** www.thenorthwood.co.uk
dir: Exit at A55 junct 22 (Old Colwyn). At T-junct right, to next T-junct (facing sea). Left, pass pier, opposite harbour left into Rhos Rd. On left adjacent to church

A short walk from the seafront and shops, this constantly improving guest house has a warm and friendly atmosphere and welcomes back many regular guests. The bedrooms are en suite, comfortable and well equipped for the modern traveller.

Rooms 9 en suite (3 fmly) (2 GF) S £27-£37; D £54-£74 **Facilities** FTV DVD TVL tea/coffee Licensed WiFi ⚓ **Conf** Max 20 Class 20 Board 20 **Parking** 12 **Notes** LB

CONWY   Map 14 SH77

Premier Collection

The Groes Inn

★★★★★ ⊜ INN

tel: 01492 650545 **Tyn-y-Groes LL32 8TN**
email: enquiries@thegroes.com **web:** www.groesinn.com
dir: A55, over Old Conwy Bridge, 1st left through Castle Walls on B5106 (Trefriw Road), 2m on right

Located in the picturesque Conwy Valley, this historic inn dates from 1573 and was the first licensed house in Wales. The exterior and gardens have an abundance of shrubs and seasonal flowers that create an impressive welcome, which is matched by the friendly and professional staff. Public areas are decorated and furnished with flair to highlight the many period features. The spacious bedrooms, in renovated outbuildings, are equipped with a wealth of thoughtful extras; many have balconies overlooking the countryside.

Rooms 14 en suite (1 fmly) (6 GF) **Facilities** FTV tea/coffee Dinner available Direct Dial WiFi ⚓ 18 Petanque **Conf** Max 20 Thtr 20 Class 20 Board 20 **Parking** 100 **Notes** LB Civ Wed 100

Premier Collection

Sychnant Pass Country House

★★★★★ ⊜ GUEST ACCOMMODATION

tel: 01492 596868 **Sychnant Pass Rd LL32 8BJ**
email: office@sychnantpasscountryhouse.co.uk
web: www.sychnant-pass-house.co.uk

A warm welcome is assured from the friendly team at Sychnant Pass Country House. Located just on the northern edge of the Snowdonia National Park and within minutes of Conwy and Llandudno, it enjoys a secluded position in this Area of Outstanding Natural Beauty, and is ideally located for visiting the many attractions in North Wales. There is a relaxing comfortable lounge, or for the more energetic there is an indoor swimming pool, sauna and gym. Guests can enjoy dinner served in the smart dining room overlooking the gardens, feasting on the finest local seasonal produce. A range of bedrooms styles are offered, including one room with its own private hot tub.

Rooms 12 en suite (4 fmly) (2 GF) S £85-£135; D £105-£195* **Facilities** FTV Lounge tea/coffee Dinner available Licensed WiFi ☜ Sauna Gym ♨ Outside heated hot tub **Parking** 20 **Notes** Civ Wed 45

DWYGYFYLCHI   Map 14 SH77

The Gladstone

★★★★ INN

tel: 01492 623231 **Ygborwen Rd LL34 6PS**
email: thegladstonepub@hotmail.co.uk **web:** www.thegladstone.co.uk
dir: A55 junct 16 turn left, then left again towards Dwygyfylchi, 0.25m on right

The Gladstone is first and foremost a great pub enjoying a superb sea-facing outlook with views of Puffin Island and Great Orme. Guests can sit inside or out to take in the sunset with drinks and an extensive menu served in a friendly, informal style. Comfortable, stylish bedrooms are individually designed, equipped with plenty of modern extras and luxurious bathrooms. Off-road parking is available.

Rooms 6 en suite S £65-£95; D £75-£140* **Facilities** FTV Lounge TVL tea/coffee Dinner available WiFi ♨ **Conf** Max 20 Board 20 **Parking** 25 **Notes** LB Civ Wed 40

LLANDUDNO
Map 14 SH78

Premier Collection

Bryn Derwen

★★★★★ BED AND BREAKFAST

tel: 01492 876804 **34 Abbey Rd LL30 2EE**
email: brynderwen34@btinternet.com **web:** www.bryn-derwen.co.uk
dir: *A470 into Llandudno, left at The Parade promenade to cenotaph, left, over rdbt, 4th right into York Rd, Bryn Derwen at top*

A warm welcome is assured at this impressive Victorian house, which retains many original features such as tiled floors and fine stained-glass windows. Decor and furnishings highlight the historic charm of the property, which is most apparent in the sumptuous lounges and attractive dining room, the setting for generous, locally sourced breakfasts. A choice of individually styled bedrooms is available and these are equipped with many thoughtful extras.

Rooms 9 en suite (1 fmly) S £56-£62; D £82-£106 **Facilities** FTV DVD iPod docking station Lounge TVL tea/coffee Licensed WiFi ⅃ 18 🏌 **Extras** Speciality toiletries, water, chocolates - free **Parking** 9 **Notes** LB ⊗ No Children 12yrs Closed Dec-Jan

Brigstock House

★★★★ GUEST HOUSE

tel: 01492 876416 **1 St David's Place LL30 2UG**
email: brigstockguesthouse@gmail.com **web:** www.brigstockhouse.co.uk
dir: *A470 into Llandudno, left into The Parade promenade, left into Lloyd St, left into St David's Rd & left into St David's Place*

This impressive Edwardian property in a quiet residential corner of the town is within easy walking distance of the seafront and central shopping area. The atmosphere is relaxed and refined. Attractive, modern bedrooms are tastefully decorated with suites available for those who like to spread out. A comfortable lounge is also available with honesty bar. Substantial breakfasts are served in the elegant dining room.

Rooms 8 en suite **Facilities** FTV DVD TVL tea/coffee Licensed WiFi 🏌 **Parking** 6 **Notes** LB ⊗ No Children 12yrs Closed Dec-Jan

The Cliffbury

★★★★ GUEST ACCOMMODATION

tel: 01492 877224 **34 St David's Rd LL30 2UH**
email: info@thecliffbury.co.uk **web:** www.thecliffbury.co.uk

Located on a leafy avenue within easy walking distance of the town centre, this elegant Edwardian house sets high standards. Bedrooms, furnished in a bright, modern style, provide a range of practical and thoughtful extras. Two popular suites are available. A warm welcome is assured for all with comfort at the heart of everything the hosts provide. Off-street parking available.

Rooms 6 en suite S £45-£60; D £70-£82* **Facilities** FTV DVD tea/coffee WiFi **Parking** 6 **Notes** LB ⊗ No Children 14yrs Closed Jan

St Hilary Guest House

★★★★ GUEST ACCOMMODATION

tel: 01492 875551 **16 Craig-y-Don Pde, The Promenade LL30 1BG**
email: info@sthilaryguesthouse.co.uk **web:** www.sthilaryguesthouse.co.uk
dir: *0.5m E of town centre. On B5115 seafront road near Venue Cymru*

Anne-Marie and Howard offer a warm and personal welcome in their guest house sitting at the more peaceful Craig-y-Don end of The Promenade. Many of the elegant bedrooms have sea views and are all equipped with modern facilities such as WiFi and large TVs. The attractive front-facing dining room is the scene for hearty breakfasts. A bright and comfortable guest lounge is also now available with an honesty bar, should refreshment be needed.

Rooms 9 en suite (1 GF) S £49-£80; D £70-£90* **Facilities** FTV DVD iPod docking station Lounge tea/coffee Licensed WiFi **Notes** LB ⊗ No Children 8yrs Closed mid Dec-mid Jan

Stratford House

★★★★ GUEST ACCOMMODATION

tel: 01492 877962 **8 Craig-y-Don Pde, The Promenade LL30 1BG**
email: stratfordhtl@aol.com **web:** www.thestratfordbandb.com
dir: *A470 at rdbt take 4th exit, on Queens Rd to promenade, on right*

This immaculately presented spacious house is located on the seafront with spectacular views. Bedrooms are attractively decorated, some with four-poster beds, and all have an excellent range of accessories, such as flat-screen TVs. The traditionally decorated dining room is also beautifully presented. The friendly owners are very welcoming.

Rooms 9 en suite (1 fmly) (1 GF) S £50-£75; D £65-£80 **Facilities** FTV tea/coffee WiFi **Extras** Chocolates - complimentary **Notes** LB ⊗ No Children 10yrs Closed Jan-Feb RS Dec & Mar

Britannia Guest House

★★★★ GUEST HOUSE

tel: 01492 877185 & 07890 765071 **15 Craig-y-Don Pde, The Promenade LL30 1BG**
email: info@thebritanniaguesthouse.co.uk **web:** www.thebritanniaguesthouse.co.uk
dir: *A55 onto A470 to Llandudno, at rdbt take 4th exit signed Craig-y-Don, right at promenade*

This family-run Victorian guest house offers a warm welcome and friendly service. The bedrooms are very comfortable and well equipped, and many have fantastic views of Llandudno's bay. Ground-floor rooms are available, and hearty breakfasts are served in the dining room that has sea views.

Rooms 10 en suite (2 GF) D £72-£92* **Facilities** FTV tea/coffee WiFi **Extras** Speciality toiletries **Notes** LB ⊗ No Children 10yrs Closed 28 Nov-1 Mar

Can-Y-Bae

★★★★ GUEST ACCOMMODATION

tel: 01492 874188 **10 Mostyn Crescent, Central Promenade LL30 1AR**
email: canybae@btconnect.com **web:** www.can-y-baehotel.com
dir: A55 junct 19, A470, signed Llandudno/Promenade. Can-Y-Bae on seafront promenade between Venue Cymru Theatre & band stand

A warm welcome is assured at this tastefully renovated house, centrally located on the Promenade. Bedrooms are equipped with both practical and homely extras and upper floors are serviced by a modern lift. Public rooms include a panoramic lounge, cosy bar with souvenirs of famous guests and an attractive ground floor dining room. AA Friendliest B&B of the Year Award Runner-Up 2016-2017.

Rooms 16 en suite (2 GF) S £40-£50; D £80-£90* **Facilities** FTV Lounge tea/coffee Dinner available Direct Dial Lift Licensed WiFi **Extras** Speciality toiletries, mineral water - free **Notes** LB No Children 12yrs

Epperstone

★★★★ GUEST ACCOMMODATION

tel: 01492 878746 & 07749 304394 **15 Abbey Rd LL30 2EE**
email: epperstonehotel@btconnect.com **web:** www.theepperstone.co.uk
dir: A550, A470 to Mostyn St. Left at rdbt, 4th right into York Rd. Epperstone at junct of York Rd & Abbey Rd

This delightful property is located in wonderful gardens in a residential part of town, within easy walking distance of the seafront and shopping area. Bedrooms are attractively decorated and thoughtfully equipped. Two lounges and a Victorian-style conservatory are available.

Rooms 8 en suite (5 fmly) (1 GF) **Facilities** FTV Lounge tea/coffee Dinner available Direct Dial Licensed WiFi **⚓ Parking** 8 **Notes** LB No Children 6yrs

Glenavon Guest House

★★★★ GUEST HOUSE

tel: 01492 877687 **27 St Mary's Rd LL30 2UB**
email: postmaster@glenavon.plus.com **web:** www.glenavon-llandudno.co.uk
dir: From A470 signed Llandudno, left at lights into Trinity Av. 3rd right into St Mary's Rd. Glenavon on right

Supporters of Liverpool Football Club are especially welcome here and they can admire the extensive range of memorabilia throughout the comfortable day rooms. Bedrooms are equipped with thoughtful extras and Welsh breakfasts provide a good start to the day.

Rooms 7 en suite (1 fmly) S £50-£55; D £75-£80 **Facilities** FTV TVL tea/coffee WiFi **⚓ Parking** 4 **Notes** LB ⊗

The Lilly Restaurant with Rooms

★★★★ ⧆ ⧠ RESTAURANT WITH ROOMS

tel: 01492 876513 **West Pde, West Shore LL30 2BD**
email: thelilly@live.co.uk **web:** www.thelilly.co.uk
dir: Phone for detailed directions

Located on the seafront on the West Shore with views over the Great Orme, this establishment has bedrooms that offer high standards of comfort, and good facilities. Children are very welcome here, and a relaxed atmosphere is found in Madhatter's Brasserie, which takes its name from Lewis Carroll's *Alice's Adventures in Wonderland*, some of which may have been written while the author was staying on the West Shore. A fine dining restaurant is also available.

Rooms 5 en suite **Facilities** FTV iPod docking station Lounge tea/coffee Dinner available Direct Dial WiFi **Extras** Speciality toiletries **Conf** Max 35 Thtr 25 Board 20 **Notes** ⊗ No coaches

No. 9 Guest House

★★★ BED AND BREAKFAST

tel: 01492 877251 & 07950 445524 **9 Chapel St LL30 2SY**
web: www.no9llandudno.co.uk
dir: See website for detailed directions

No. 9 Guest House is centrally located in Llandudno with the promenade, shopping areas and restaurants all within a few minutes' walk. This Victorian building is traditionally styled, with a warm welcome assured from the friendly owner. Bedrooms vary in size and offer comfortable facilities for guests. A hearty breakfast is provided including homemade jams and seasonal special dishes in addition to the traditional breakfast.

Rooms 8 en suite (2 fmly) S £30-£32; D £64-£68* **Facilities** FTV DVD TVL WiFi **⚓**

LLANDUDNO *continued*

The Trevone

★★★ GUEST ACCOMMODATION

----

tel: 01492 876314 **10 St Georges Crescent LL30 2LF**
email: info@trevone.net **web:** www.trevone.net
dir: *A55 follow signs for Llandudno & central promenade*

The Trevone is in a splendid location at the heart of the Llandudno seafront and a friendly welcome and service is assured. Bedrooms and bathrooms come in a range of shapes and sizes; some have excellent sea views. Guests can relax in a choice of lounges and a well-stocked bar is provided.

Rooms 24 en suite (5 fmly) (1 GF) S £40-£44; D £80-£88* **Facilities** FTV Lounge TVL tea/coffee Lift Licensed WiFi 🔒 **Notes** LB ⊗ Closed Dec-Feb

LLANDUDNO JUNCTION	Map 14 SH77

Premier Collection

Queens Head

★★★★★ 🍴 INN

----

tel: 01492 546570 **Glanwydden LL31 9JP**
email: enquiries@queensheadglanwydden.co.uk
web: www.queensheadglanwydden.co.uk
dir: *A55 onto A470 towards Llandudno. At 3rd rdbt right towards Penrhyn Bay, 2nd right into Glanwydden, on left*

The Queens Head is an attractive stone inn located in a small village just a couple of miles from both Llandudno and Colwyn Bay. The friendly team ensure all guests are well cared for during their stay. Storehouse Cottage stands just a few steps away from the inn and offers quaint, cosy accommodation. With a smart fully equipped kitchen, lounge, bedroom and dressing room, there is plenty of space to relax and unwind after a busy day. There is a small sun-trap garden with seating area. A substantial continental breakfast is provided for guests in the cottage. Other meals are available in the inn or can be delivered to the cottage on request. There is a minimum two night stay for bed and breakfast.

Rooms 1 annexe en suite **Facilities** DVD Dinner available WiFi 🔒 **Extras** Sherry, fruit - complimentary **Parking** 40 **Notes** LB ⊗ Closed 25 Dec No coaches

Find out more about the AA B&B of the Year for Wales on page 14

RHOS-ON-SEA	Map 14 SH88

See also Colwyn Bay

Premier Collection

Plas Rhos

★★★★★ 🍴 GUEST ACCOMMODATION

tel: 01492 543698 **Cayley Promenade LL28 4EP**
email: info@plasrhos.co.uk **web:** www.plasrhos.co.uk
dir: *A55 junct 20 onto B5115 for Rhos-on-Sea, right at rdbt into Whitehall Rd to promenade*

Stunning sea views are a feature of this lovely Victorian house, which provides high standards of comfort and hospitality. Cosy bedrooms are filled with a wealth of thoughtful extras, and public areas include a choice of sumptuous lounges featuring smart decor, quality soft furnishings and memorabilia. Breakfast is served in the attractive dining room, overlooking the patio garden.

Rooms 5 en suite S £65-£85; D £85-£110* **Facilities** FTV Lounge TVL tea/coffee Licensed WiFi 🔒 **Parking** 4 **Notes** LB ⊗ No Children 12yrs Closed Nov-Feb

Whitehall Guest House

★★★★ GUEST HOUSE

----

tel: 01492 547296 **51 Cayley Promenade LL28 4EP**
email: mossd.cymru@virgin.net **web:** www.whitehall-hotel.co.uk
dir: *A55 onto B5115 (Brompton Av), right at rdbt into Whitehall Rd to seafront*

Overlooking the Rhos-on-Sea promenade, this popular, family-run establishment is convenient for the shops and local amenities. Attractively appointed bedrooms include family rooms and a room on the ground floor; all benefit from an excellent range of facilities such as video and CD players as well as air-conditioning. Facilities include a bar and a foyer lounge.

Rooms 12 en suite (4 fmly) (1 GF) S £32-£36; D £67-£72* **Facilities** FTV DVD Lounge TVL tea/coffee Direct Dial Licensed WiFi 🔒 **Parking** 5 **Notes** LB

TAL-Y-CAFN
Map 14 SH77

Premier Collection

Bodnant Welsh Food Centre
★★★★★ ⬤ RESTAURANT WITH ROOMS

tel: 01492 651100 & 651102 **Furnace Farm LL28 5RP**
email: reception@bodnant-welshfood.co.uk **web:** www.bodnant-welshfood.co.uk
dir: Off A470, 4m from A55 junct 19, follow signs for A470

Overlooking the River Conwy and neighbouring Bodnant Gardens, this 18th-century farm has been fully restored and is now the home to Bodnant Welsh Food Centre. It is ideally placed to explore the North Wales coastline, Snowdonia, and the nearby surf park. The buildings have been transformed into a tea room, farm shop and wine merchants with a focus on Welsh products. The Hayloft Restaurant serves interesting lunches and dinners, including a 7-course taster menu. A range of room types and sizes can be found in the comfortable accommodation, with a guest lounge and kitchen also available. There is a cookery school on-site, and small conferences and weddings can be accommodated here.

Rooms 6 en suite (1 GF) **Facilities** FTV Lounge TVL tea/coffee Dinner available Lift WiFi **Parking** 80 **Notes** LB ⊗ Closed 25-26 Dec Civ Wed 80

TREFRIW
Map 14 SH76

Premier Collection

Yr Hafod Country House
★★★★★ ⬤ BED AND BREAKFAST

tel: 01492 642444 **LL27 0RQ**
email: enquiries@hafod-house.co.uk **web:** www.hafod-house.co.uk
dir: From N - A470 onto B5279, after 1m left onto B5106. 5.5m to Trefriw, over bridge 200mtrs on left. From S - A470 into Llanrwst, left over bridge onto B5106. 1.5m on right

Situated in tranquil countryside and ideally located for the Conwy Valley and Snowdonia National Park, this cosy, family-run guest house offers four smartly turned-out bedrooms, which are tastefully designed and comfortable, each with separate access and its own balcony. Breakfast is served in the traditional dining room; dishes are freshly prepared using as much home-grown and local produce as possible. A well-stocked bar and lounge are also part of the package.

Rooms 4 en suite S £72.50-£75; D £85-£100* **Facilities** FTV DVD TVL tea/coffee Licensed WiFi ⬤ **Extras** Speciality toiletries, sweets, bottled water **Parking** 4 **Notes** ⊗ Closed Dec-13 Feb

Ty Newydd B&B
★★★ GUEST ACCOMMODATION

tel: 01492 641210 **Conwy Rd LL27 0JH**
email: tynewyddtrefriw@aol.com **web:** www.tynewyddtrefriw.co.uk
dir: In village centre, near post office

Nestled in a small village in the unspoilt Conwy Valley, Ty Newydd is just a short drive from Llandudno. The hosts of this large Victorian house offer a genuine warm Welsh welcome on arrival. Comfortable rooms are well equipped, and the property is within easy walking distance of a number of pubs and restaurants.

Rooms 4 rms (2 en suite) (2 pri facs) (1 fmly) S £35; D £70 **Facilities** STV FTV TVL tea/coffee WiFi ⤢ 9 ⬤

DENBIGHSHIRE

CORWEN
Map 15 SJ04

Bron-y-Graig
★★★★ GUEST HOUSE

tel: 01490 413007 **LL21 0DR**
email: info@north-wales-hotel.co.uk **web:** www.north-wales-hotel.co.uk
dir: On A5 on E edge of Corwen

A short walk from the town centre, Bron-y-Graig is an impressive Victorian house that has retained many original features including fireplaces, stained glass, and a tiled floor in the entrance hall. Bedrooms, complemented by luxurious bathrooms, are thoughtfully furnished; two are to be found in a coach house. Ground-floor areas include a traditionally furnished dining room and a comfortable lounge. A warm welcome and attentive service are assured.

Rooms 7 en suite 2 annexe en suite (4 fmly) S £39-£59; D £59-£68 **Facilities** STV FTV DVD Lounge tea/coffee Direct Dial Licensed WiFi ⬤ **Conf** Max 20 Class 20 Board 15 **Parking** 15 **Notes** LB

CORWEN *continued*

Plas Derwen Country House

★★★★ GUEST ACCOMMODATION

tel: 01490 412742 & 07773 965874 **London Rd LL21 0DR**
email: bandb@plasderwen.supanet.com **web:** www.plasderwen.co.uk
dir: *On A5 0.5m E of Corwen*

Set in an elevated position within four acres of mature gardens and natural meadow, this elegant late 18th-century house has been restored to provide top-notch levels of comfort and facilities. Quality furnishings and stylish decor highlight the many original features, and a warm and personal welcome is assured. An extensive continental or locally sourced full Welsh breakfast is served.

Rooms 2 en suite (2 fmly) **Facilities** FTV TVL tea/coffee WiFi 🛝 **Parking** 6 **Notes** ⊗ Closed Dec-Jan

DENBIGH
Map 15 SJ06

Guildhall Tavern

★★★★ INN

tel: 01745 816533 **Hall Square LL16 3NU**
email: info@guildhalltavernhotel.co.uk **web:** www.guildhalltavernhotel.co.uk

Standing in the centre of this historic medieval town, this 16th-century inn has had a number of different uses including a stint as a military HQ in 1646, when it was taken over by Generals Mytton and Myddleton. A wealth of historic features are still evident throughout, including the ornate carved staircases. Rooms are individually decorated and complemented by good quality bathrooms, many with feature baths or showers. There is a friendly bar area frequented by guests and locals, serving a range of local ales and ciders, alongside home-cooked dishes.

Rooms 10 rms

Food Allergies

A recent EU regulation makes it easier for those with food allergies to choose safer foods when eating out. 14 allergens are listed in the regulation, and pubs and restaurants must now list any of these used in the dishes they offer.

LLANDYRNOG
Map 15 SJ16

Premier Collection

Pentre Mawr Country House

★★★★★ 🍽 GUEST ACCOMMODATION

tel: 01824 790732 **LL16 4LA**
email: info@pentremawrcountryhouse.co.uk
web: www.pentremawrcountryhouse.co.uk
dir: *From Denbigh follow Bodfari/Llandyrnog signs. Left at rdbt to Bodfari, 50yds, left into country lane, Pentre Mawr on left*

Expect a warm welcome from Graham and Bre at this superb family country house, set in nearly 200 acres of meadows, park and woodland. The property has been in Graham's family for over 400 years. Bedrooms are individually decorated, very spacious, and each is thoughtfully equipped. Breakfast and dinner are served in the conservatory-restaurant overlooking the salt water swimming pool on the terrace. A formal dining room is available for larger parties. There are also six luxury Safari lodges and two suites, all with private hot tubs.

Rooms 3 en suite 8 annexe en suite (7 GF) **Facilities** FTV DVD iPod docking station Lounge tea/coffee Dinner available Licensed WiFi ↘ 🏊 ⛳ Fishing 🛝 **Extras** Robes **Conf** Max 20 Class 20 Board 20 **Parking** 14 **Notes** No Children 13yrs

LLANGOLLEN
Map 15 SJ24

See also Corwen

Tyn Celyn Farmhouse

★★★★ BED AND BREAKFAST

tel: 01978 861117 **Tyndwr LL20 8AR**
email: j.m.bather-tyncelyn@talk21.com **web:** www.tyncelyn-bnb-llangollen.co.uk
dir: *A5 to Llangollen, pass golf club on right, next left signed Tyndwr outdoor centre, 0.5m sharp left into Tyndwr Rd, past Tyndwr Hall on left. Tyn Celyn 0.5m on left*

This 300-year-old timber-framed farmhouse has stunning views over the Vale of Llangollen. Bedrooms, one of which is located on the ground floor, provide a range of thoughtful extras in addition to fine period furniture. Breakfast is served at a magnificent carved table in a spacious sitting-dining room.

Rooms 3 en suite (1 fmly) (1 GF) D £65-£70* **Facilities** DVD TVL tea/coffee WiFi 🛝 **Parking** 5 **Notes** LB ⊗ 🍽

RUTHIN	Map 15 SJ15

Premier Collection

Firgrove Country House B&B

★★★★★ ☺ ☕ BED AND BREAKFAST

tel: 01824 702677 & 07710 251606 **Firgrove, Llanfwrog LL15 2LL**
email: meadway@firgrovecountryhouse.co.uk **web:** www.firgrovecountryhouse.co.uk
dir: *0.5m SW of Ruthin. A494 onto B5105, 0.25m past Llanfwrog church on right*

Standing in immaculate mature gardens in a peaceful rural location, this well-proportioned house retains many original features, highlighted by the quality decor and furnishings throughout. Bedrooms, complemented by smart modern bathrooms, are equipped with a wealth of thoughtful extras. Memorable breakfasts, using home-made or local produce, are served in an elegant dining room. Imaginative dinners are also available by prior arrangement and a warm welcome is assured.

Rooms 2 en suite 1 annexe en suite (1 GF) S £65-£80; D £80-£110*
Facilities FTV Lounge tea/coffee Dinner available WiFi 🛁 **Extras** Mineral water, fresh milk - complimentary; fridge **Parking** 4 **Notes** ⊗ No Children Closed Dec-Feb

ST ASAPH	Map 15 SJ07

Premier Collection

Tan-Yr-Onnen Guest House

★★★★★ ☺ GUEST HOUSE

tel: 01745 583821 **Waen LL17 ODU**
email: tanyronnenvisit@aol.com **web:** www.northwalesbreaks.co.uk
dir: *W on A55 junct 28, turn left in 300yds*

A warm welcome is assured at Tan-Yr-Onnen Guest House, which is quietly located in six acres of gardens, conveniently close to the A55. The very well-equipped accommodation includes four ground-floor rooms with French windows that open onto the terrace. Upstairs, there are two luxury suites with lounge areas. Hearty breakfasts are served in the dining room overlooking the gardens, and a conservatory-lounge and WiFi access are also available.

Rooms 6 en suite (1 fmly) (4 GF) **Facilities** FTV Lounge tea/coffee Licensed WiFi 🛁 **Parking** 8 **Notes** ⊗

GWYNEDD

ABERDYFI
Map 14 SN69

Premier Collection

Penhelig Arms
★★★★★ ⊛ INN

tel: 01654 767215 **Terrace Rd LL35 0LT**
web: www.penheligarms.com

Originally a collection of fishermen's cottages, the charming Penhelig Arms overlooks the picturesque Dyfi Estuary within the Snowdonia National Park. Bedrooms in the main house are charming, with many taking in the impressive views. Award-winning cuisine is a real feature at the inn; local produce is a key factor in the popular dining room and bar, where bookings are essential to avoid disappointment. Penhelig Arms is the AA Pub of the Year for Wales 2016-2017.

Rooms 15 en suite **Facilities** Dinner available WiFi

BANGOR
Map 14 SH57

Gors-Yr-Eira Guest House B&B
★★★★ BED AND BREAKFAST

tel: 01248 601353 & 07887 394511 **Mynyddllandega LL57 4DZ**
email: einir@gorsyreira.co.uk **web:** www.gorsyreira.co.uk
dir: A55 onto A5, follow Betws-y-Coed road to Bethesda. Right onto B4409, after 1m turn left, up steep hill, B&B on brow of hill

A warm welcome is assured at this detached extended property with lovely country views, located between Bangor and Bethesda and also convenient for Llanberis and Mount Snowdon. Bedrooms and bathrooms vary in size and all are equipped with good furnishings, homely and practical extras including free WiFi. Hearty breakfasts are taken in a conservatory dining room overlooking the rear garden which is home to chickens, ducks and goats.

Rooms 3 en suite **Facilities** FTV DVD TVL tea/coffee WiFi 🔒 **Parking** 3

Tregarth Homestay B&B
★★★ BED AND BREAKFAST

tel: 01248 600532 & 07711 710364 **Llain-Y-Grug, Dob, Tregarth LL57 4PW**
email: tregarth.homestay@btinternet.com **web:** www.tregarth-homestay.com
dir: From A55 junct 11 onto A5 (Betwys), then 1st right onto A4244. Left onto B4409 signed Tregarth. Take 3rd right after chapel

Ideally located for both Bangor and Llanberis, this modern split-level house has cosy bedrooms at the lower level, with fine views over the pretty rear garden, surrounding coast and mountains. A comfortable lounge and small kitchen area are on hand. Hearty breakfasts utilise quality local produce and there is a choice of good eating pubs within reach.

Rooms 3 rms (1 en suite) (2 pri facs) S £45; D £70-£75* **Facilities** FTV TVL tea/coffee WiFi 🔒 **Parking** 3 **Notes** LB ⊗

BARMOUTH
Map 14 SH61

See also Dyffryn Ardudwy

Morwendon House
★★★★ ⊜ ⊜ GUEST ACCOMMODATION

tel: 01341 280566 **Llanaber LL42 1RR**
email: info@morwendon-house.co.uk **web:** www.morwendon-house.co.uk
dir: A496 at Llanaber N of Barmouth. On seaward side 250yds past Llanaber Church

Sitting in an impressive high location overlooking Cardigan Bay, Morwendon House is an ideal base for exploring the surrounding area and its many attractions. The bedrooms are comfortable and brightly decorated; many with sea views. Dinner is available by arrangement and worth a try with fresh cookery a highlight of any stay. Meals are taken in the attractive dining room and there is also a relaxing lounge both facing stunning sunsets in the summer months.

Rooms 5 en suite 1 annexe en suite (1 GF) D £70-£112* **Facilities** FTV DVD Lounge tea/coffee Dinner available Licensed WiFi ⅃ 18 🔒 **Extras** Bottled water **Parking** 6 **Notes** LB ⊗ No Children 12yrs Closed 24-27 Dec

Llwyndu Farmhouse
★★★★ ⊜ GUEST ACCOMMODATION

tel: 01341 280144 **Llanaber LL42 1RR**
email: intouch@llwyndu-farmhouse.co.uk **web:** www.llwyndu-farmhouse.co.uk
dir: A496 towards Harlech where street lights end, on outskirts of Barmouth, next right

This converted 16th-century farmhouse offers warm hospitality and traditional guest accommodation. Many original features have been retained, including inglenook fireplaces, exposed beams and timbers. There is a cosy lounge and meals can be enjoyed in the licensed restaurant. Bedrooms are and well equipped; some have four-poster beds and extraordinary views over Cardigan Bay. Four bedrooms are in the old dairy building.

Rooms 3 en suite 4 annexe en suite (2 fmly) S £60-£124; D £98-£124* **Facilities** FTV TVL tea/coffee Dinner available Licensed WiFi 🔒 **Extras** Speciality toiletries, fruit, snacks - free **Conf** Max 10 **Parking** 10 **Notes** LB ⊗ Closed 25-26 Dec RS Sun no dinner

BEDDGELERT
Map 14 SH54

Tanronnen Inn
★★★★ INN

tel: 01766 890347 **LL55 4YB**
email: tanbedd@12freeukisp.co.uk **web:** www.tanronnen.co.uk
dir: In village centre opposite river bridge

This delightful village inn offers comfortable, modern and attractively appointed accommodation, including rooms suitable for families. There is a selection of pleasant and relaxing public areas. The wide range of bar food is popular with tourists and locals alike. More formal meals are served in the restaurant. Real ales are another draw here with a good selection available.

Rooms 7 en suite (3 fmly) S £60-£65; D £100-£110* **Facilities** FTV tea/coffee Dinner available Direct Dial 🔒 **Parking** 9 **Notes** LB ⊗ No coaches

CAERNARFON   Map 14 SH46

Premier Collection

Plas Dinas Country House

★★★★★ 🍴 ☕ GUEST ACCOMMODATION

tel: 01286 830214 **Bontnewydd LL54 7YF**
email: info@plasdinas.co.uk **web:** www.plasdinas.co.uk
dir: *3m S of Caernarfon, off A487, 0.5m down private drive*

Situated in 15 acres of beautiful grounds in Snowdonia, this delightful Grade II listed building dates back to the mid-17th century, but has many Victorian additions. It was once the home of the Armstrong-Jones family, so there are many family portraits, memorabilia and original pieces of furniture on view. The bedrooms are individually decorated and include four-poster beds along with modern facilities. There is a stylish drawing room where a fire burns in the winter, and fresh local produce features on the dinner menu.

Rooms 10 en suite (2 fmly) (1 GF) **Facilities** FTV Lounge tea/coffee Dinner available Licensed WiFi **Extras** Speciality toiletries, mini-bar **Conf** Max 14 Board 14 **Parking** 16 **Notes** No Children 12yrs Civ Wed 32

Black Boy Inn

★★★★ INN

tel: 01286 673604 **LL55 1RW**
email: office@black-boy-inn.com **web:** www.black-boy-inn.com
dir: *A55 junct 9, A487, follow signs for Caernarfon. Inn within town walls between castle & Victoria Dock*

Located within Caernarfon's historic town walls, this fine 16th-century inn has low ceilings, narrow staircases and thick wooden beams originally from old ships. It is one of the oldest inns in north Wales, and has a wealth of charm and character. The bedrooms provide modern accommodation, and hearty meals are available in both the restaurant and bar area. On-site parking is available.

Rooms 16 en suite 10 annexe en suite (5 fmly) (3 GF) S £50-£70; D £70-£140 (room only) **Facilities** FTV tea/coffee Dinner available Direct Dial WiFi ⅃ 18 🍷 **Conf** Max 40 Thtr 40 Class 20 Board 30 **Parking** 26 **Notes** LB ⊗

CRICCIETH   Map 14 SH43

Bron Rhiw

★★★★ 🍴 GUEST ACCOMMODATION

tel: 01766 522257 **Caernarfon Rd LL52 0AP**
email: clairecriccieth@yahoo.co.uk **web:** www.bronrhiwhotel.co.uk
dir: *From High St onto B4411 & Bron Rhiw is 300yds on right*

A warm welcome, and high standards of comfort and facilities are assured at Bron Rhiw, a constantly improving Victorian property, just a short walk from the seafront. Bedrooms are equipped with lots of thoughtful extras and ground-floor areas include a sumptuous lounge, a cosy bar, and an elegant dining room, the setting for imaginative breakfasts. AA Friendliest B&B of the Year Award Finalist 2016-2017.

Rooms 9 en suite S £50; D £79-£81* **Facilities** FTV Lounge tea/coffee Licensed WiFi 🍷 **Parking** 3 **Notes** LB ⊗ No Children 10yrs Closed Nov-Feb

Min Y Gaer

★★★★ GUEST HOUSE

tel: 01766 522151 **Porthmadog Rd LL52 0HP**
email: info@minygaer.co.uk **web:** www.minygaer.co.uk
dir: *On A497 200yds E of junct with B4411*

Min Y Gaer is Welsh for 'near the fort', and so some of the fine views are of Criccieth Castle from this friendly guest house. The smart, modern bedrooms are furnished in pine, and the welcoming proprietors also a traditionally furnished lounge. Pets are welcome and parking is available.

Rooms 10 en suite S £46-£48; D £76-£84 **Facilities** FTV DVD Lounge tea/coffee WiFi 🍷 **Parking** 12 **Notes** Closed 18 Oct-mid Mar

DOLGELLAU   Map 14 SH71

Premier Collection

Tyddynmawr Farmhouse (SH704159)
★★★★★ FARMHOUSE

tel: 01341 422331 **Cader Rd, Islawrdref LL40 1TL**
email: olwynevans@btconnect.com **web:** www.wales-guesthouse.co.uk
dir: *From town centre left at top of square, left at garage into Cader Rd for 3m. 1st farm on left after Gwernan Lake*

A warm welcome is assured at this 18th-century farmhouse which lies at the foot of Cader Idris amid breathtaking scenery. The bedrooms are spacious and have Welsh oak furniture; the upper room has a balcony and the ground-floor room has a patio area. The bathrooms are large and luxurious. Breakfast offers an excellent choice of home-made items including bread, preserves, muesli or smoked fish. Self-catering cottages are also available.

Rooms 2 en suite (1 GF) S £68; D £88 **Facilities** Lounge TVL tea/coffee WiFi 🌢 **Parking** 8 **Notes** ⊗ No Children Closed Dec-Jan 🌑 800 acres beef/sheep

Dolgun Uchaf Guesthouse
★★★★ GUEST HOUSE

tel: 01341 422269 **Dolgun Uchaf LL40 2AB**
email: dolgunuchaf@aol.com **web:** www.guesthousessnowdonia.com
dir: *Exit A470 at Little Chef just S of Dolgellau. Dolgun Uchaf 1st property on right*

Located in a peaceful area with stunning views of the surrounding countryside this 500-year-old was a rich history as a Quaker meeting place. The house retains many original features including exposed beams and open fireplaces. The bedrooms, some in the house and others with external access are well-equipped. Ample parking onsite, a lounge for guests and a spacious breakfast room complete the facilities.

Rooms 3 en suite 1 annexe en suite (1 GF) **Facilities** TVL tea/coffee Dinner available WiFi 🌢 **Parking** 6 **Notes** No Children 5yrs

DYFFRYN ARDUDWY

Map 14 SH52

Cadwgan Inn

★★★★ INN

tel: 01341 247240 **LL44 2HA**
email: cadwgan.hotel@virgin.net **web:** www.cadwganhotel.co.uk
dir: *In Dyffryn Ardudwy into Station Rd, over railway crossing*

Privately-owned Cadwgan Inn stands in its own grounds, a stone's throw from Dyffryn Ardudwy station, between Barmouth and Harlech. With the beach just a short walk away, this well-equipped and modern accommodation includes family rooms and a luxury four-poster bedroom. Public areas include an attractive dining room and popular bar, serving honest pub food. Families are ably catered for.

Rooms 6 en suite (3 fmly) **Facilities** TVL tea/coffee Dinner available Sauna Gym Pool table **Notes** ⊗ No coaches Civ Wed 60

LLANBEDR

Map 14 SH52

Victoria Inn

★★★★ INN

tel: 01341 241213 **LL45 2LD**
email: junevicinn@aol.com **web:** www.vic-inn.co.uk
dir: *In village centre*

A former coaching inn, the Victoria Inn lies beside the River Artro in a very pretty village. Many original features remain, including the Settle bar with its flagstone floor, black polished fireplace and unusual circular wooden settle. The menu is extensive and is supplemented by blackboard specials. Bedrooms are spacious and thoughtfully furnished.

Rooms 5 en suite (1 fmly) **Facilities** FTV tea/coffee Dinner available 🔒 **Conf** Max 40 **Parking** 75

PORTHMADOG

Map 14 SH53

Tudor Lodge

★★★★ GUEST ACCOMMODATION

tel: 01766 515530 **Tan-Yr-Onnen, Penamser Rd LL49 9NY**
email: res@tudorlodge.co.uk **web:** www.tudorlodge.co.uk
dir: *From main Porthmadog rdbt into Criccieth Rd, house 40mtrs on left*

Tudor Lodge is a large property conveniently situated within a short walk of the town centre. It has good quality, modern accommodation, including family rooms. Separate tables are provided in the breakfast room, where a substantial self-service continental breakfast buffet is provided. There is also a pleasant garden for guests to use.

Rooms 13 en suite (3 fmly) (6 GF) **Facilities** STV tea/coffee WiFi ⅃ 18 🔒 **Parking** 25 **Notes** LB ⊗

PWLLHELI

Map 14 SH33

Premier Collection

The Old Rectory

★★★★★ BED AND BREAKFAST

tel: 01758 721519 **Boduan LL53 6DT**
email: theashcrofts@theoldrectory.net **web:** www.theoldrectory.net
dir: *From Pwllheli take A497 signed Nefyn. Continue 3m, after villlage sign for Boduan turn left. 1st house on right*

The Old Rectory is a lovely Georgian property set in delightful grounds. Ideally located for the marina in Abersoch, it is centrally placed for walkers on the Welsh Coast Path. The proprietors take great pride in their home and provide very well appointed bedrooms, spacious public areas and super gardens. Breakfast is also a delight, featuring local produce and taken at a large communal table in the dining room.

Rooms 4 en suite (1 fmly) S £80-£95; D £95-£115* **Facilities** FTV TVL tea/coffee WiFi ⅃ 18 🔒 **Extras** Chocolates, sherry **Conf** Max 8 Board 8 **Parking** 6 **Notes** LB ⊗ Closed 24-27 Dec

MERTHYR TYDFIL

MERTHYR TYDFIL

Map 9 SO00

The Mount Pleasant Inn

★★★★ GUEST HOUSE

tel: 01443 693555 & 07918 763640 **Mount Pleasant CF48 4TD**
email: jwacmorgan@aol.com **web:** www.themountpleasantinn.co.uk
dir: *A470 at Abercynnon rdbt onto A4054 towards Aberfan. 2.5m to Mount Pleasant*

With pleasant views across the valley, this friendly and welcoming guest house provides a relaxed and homely ambience. Bedrooms offer a range of shapes and sizes and are well equipped. Mount Pleasant is fully licensed, and dinner is available to residents; good quality, home-cooked dishes are on offer. Guests may enjoy a drink on the outdoor seating terrace to the rear of the property or laze in the outdoor spa pool.

Rooms 5 en suite (1 fmly) S fr £50; D fr £80* **Facilities** STV FTV DVD Lounge TVL tea/coffee Dinner available Licensed WiFi 🔒 Heated spa pool **Extras** Speciality toiletries - complimentary **Notes** ⊗ Closed 23 Dec-2 Jan

PONTSTICILL
Map 9 SO01

Penrhadw Farm

★★★★ GUEST HOUSE

tel: 01685 723481 & 722461 **CF48 2TU**
email: treghotel@aol.com **web:** www.penrhadwfarm.co.uk
dir: *5m N of Merthyr Tydfil*

Expect a warm welcome at this 19th-century former farmhouse in the glorious Brecon Beacons National Park. The house is appointed to provide quality modern accommodation. The well-equipped, spacious bedrooms include two large suites in cottages adjacent to the main building. There is also a comfortable lounge. Separate tables are provided in the cosy breakfast room.

Rooms 5 en suite 5 annexe en suite (5 fmly) (1 GF) S fr £50; D fr £75* **Facilities** FTV TVL tea/coffee Dinner available WiFi ⅃ 18 ⚓ **Conf** Max 10 Thtr 10 Class 10 **Parking** 22 **Notes** LB ⊗

MONMOUTHSHIRE

LLANDOGO
Map 4 SO50

The Sloop Inn

★★★★ INN

tel: 01594 530291 **NP25 4TW**
email: thesloopinn@btinternet.com **web:** www.thesloopinn.co.uk
dir: *On A466 in village centre*

This welcoming inn is centrally located in the village of Llandogo, close to the River Wye in an outstandingly beautiful valley. The Sloop Inn offers a selection of traditional food, as well as friendly hospitality. The dining room has delightful views over the valley, and the spacious bedrooms and bathrooms are equipped for both business and leisure guests.

Rooms 4 en suite (1 fmly) **Facilities** tea/coffee Dinner available Pool table **Parking** 50 **Notes** LB RS Mon-Fri closed between 3-6

MONMOUTH
Map 10 SO51

#7 Church Street

★★★★ ◉◉ RESTAURANT WITH ROOMS

tel: 01600 712600 **7 Church St NP25 3BX**
email: enquiries@numbersevenchurchstreet.co.uk
dir: *Travelling N A40 at lights left turn, T-junct left turn, 2nd right, at rear of car park*

Located in the centre of Monmouth #7 Church Street is open for light lunches and dinner and is popular with both guests and locals. Award-winning food is prepared with care and an emphasis on local sourcing and seasonality. Rooms are located above the restaurant and vary in size and shape, a comfortable private guest lounge is also available.

Rooms 8 en suite (2 fmly) S £50-£65; D £70-£85* **Facilities** FTV DVD TVL tea/coffee Dinner available WiFi ⚓ **Notes** ⊗ Closed 25-26 Dec

Church Farm Guest House

★★★ GUEST HOUSE

tel: 01600 712176 **Mitchel Troy NP25 4HZ**
email: info@churchfarmguesthouse.eclipse.co.uk **web:** www.churchfarmmitcheltroy.co.uk
dir: *From A40 S, left onto B4293 for Trelleck before tunnel, 150yds turn left and follow signs to Mitchel Troy. Guest House on main road on left, 200yds beyond campsite*

Located in the village of Mitchel Troy, this 16th-century former farmhouse retains many original features including exposed beams and open fireplaces. There is a range of bedrooms and a spacious lounge, and breakfast is served in the traditionally furnished dining room. Dinner is available by prior arrangement.

Rooms 8 rms (6 en suite) (2 pri facs) (3 fmly) S £37-£38; D £74-£76 **Facilities** FTV Lounge TVL tea/coffee Dinner available WiFi ⚓ **Parking** 12 **Notes** LB Closed Xmas

ROCKFIELD
Map 9 SO41

The Stonemill & Steppes Farm Cottages

★★★★ ◉◉ RESTAURANT WITH ROOMS

tel: 01600 775424 **NP25 5SW**
email: bookings@thestonemill.co.uk **web:** www.steppesfarmcottages.co.uk
dir: *A48 to Monmouth, take B4233 to Rockfield. 2.6m*

Located in a small hamlet just west of Monmouth, close to the Forest of Dean and the Wye Valley, this operation offers accommodation comprising six very well-appointed cottages. The comfortable rooms (available for self-catering or on a B&B basis) have been lovingly restored to retain many original features. In a separate, converted 16th-century barn is Stonemill Restaurant with oak beams, vaulted ceilings and an old cider press. Breakfast is served in the cottages on request. This establishment's location proves handy for golfers, with a choice of many courses in the area.

Rooms 6 en suite (6 fmly) (6 GF) S £65-£120; D £85-£145 (room only)* **Facilities** FTV DVD TVL tea/coffee Dinner available WiFi ⅃ 18 ⚓ Free golf **Conf** Max 60 Thtr 60 Class 56 Board 40 **Parking** 53 **Notes** LB ⊗ No coaches Civ Wed 120

TINTERN PARVA
Map 4 SO50

Parva Farmhouse Riverside Guest House & Restaurant

★★★★ ⌑ GUEST HOUSE

tel: 01291 689411 **Monmouth Rd NP16 6SQ**
email: parvahoteltintern@hotmail.co.uk **web:** www.parvafarmhouse.co.uk
dir: *On A466 at N edge of Tintern. Next to St Michael's Church on the riverside*

Parva Farmhouse is a relaxed and friendly family-run guest house, situated on a sweep of the River Wye with far-reaching views of the valley. Dating from the 17th century, this establishment has many excellent features, providing character and comfort in an informal atmosphere. The cosy Inglenook Restaurant is the place for quality ingredients at breakfast and dinner. The individually designed bedrooms are tastefully decorated and enjoy pleasant views; one has a four-poster.

Rooms 8 en suite (2 fmly) S £65-£78; D £80-£92* **Facilities** FTV Lounge tea/coffee Dinner available Licensed WiFi ⚓ **Parking** 8 **Notes** No Children 12yrs

USK
Map 9 SO30

Newbridge on Usk
★★★★ ⊛ ⬤ RESTAURANT WITH ROOMS

tel: 01633 451000 & 410262 **Tredunnock NP15 1LY**
email: newbridgeonusk@celtic-manor.com **web:** www.celtic-manor.com
dir: *M4 junct 24, signed Newport, onto B4236. At Ship Inn turn right, over mini rdbt onto Llangybi/Usk road. Turn right opposite Cwrt Bleddyn Hotel, signed Tredunnock, through village & down hill*

This cosy gastropub is tucked away in a beautiful village setting with the River Usk nearby. The well-equipped bedrooms, in a separate building, provide comfort and a good range of extras. Guests can eat at rustic tables around the bar or in the upstairs dining room where award-winning, seasonal food is served; there is also a small private dining room. Breakfast is one of the highlights of a stay with quality local ingredients offered in abundance.

Rooms 6 en suite (2 fmly) (4 GF) **Facilities** STV FTV DVD tea/coffee Dinner available Direct Dial WiFi ⏰ ⬤ ♨ 18 Fishing Sauna Gym Facilities available at Celtic Manor Resort **Extras** Speciality toiletries - complimentary **Conf** Max 14 Thtr 14 Class 14 Board 14 **Parking** 60 **Notes** ⊗ Civ Wed 80

WHITEBROOK
Map 4 SO50

Premier Collection

The Whitebrook
★★★★★ ⊛⊛⊛⊛ ⬤ RESTAURANT WITH ROOMS

tel: 01600 860254 **NP25 4TX**
email: info@thewhitebrook.co.uk **web:** www.thewhitebrook.co.uk
dir: *4m from Monmouth on B4293, left at sign to Whitebrook, 2m on unclassified road, on right*

Peacefully located and surrounded by woods and rivers, this delightful restaurant with rooms offers a peaceful escape. All the bedrooms are located above the main restaurant and come in a range of shapes and sizes. All are very comfortably decorated and furnished. The AA Rosette award-winning food makes great use of the finest local produce and the relaxing surroundings and friendly service provide a memorable dining experience. The Whitebrook is the winner of the Notable Wine Award for Wales 2016-2017.

Rooms 8 en suite S £159-£232; D £214-£324* (incl.dinner) **Facilities** FTV Lounge tea/coffee Dinner available Direct Dial WiFi **Extras** Speciality toiletries, Welsh cakes **Parking** 20 **Notes** ⊗ No Children 12yrs Closed 2-15 Jan No coaches

NEATH PORT TALBOT

NEATH
Map 9 SS79

Cwmbach Cottages Guest House
★★★★ GUEST HOUSE

tel: 01639 639825 **Cwmbach Rd, Cadoxton SA10 8AH**
email: l.morgan5@btinternet.com **web:** www.cwmbachguesthouse.co.uk
dir: *1.5m NE of Neath. A465 onto A474 & A4230 towards Aberdulais, left opposite Cadoxton church, guest house signed*

This terrace of former miners' cottages has been restored to provide a range of thoughtfully furnished bedrooms, with one on the ground floor for easier access. Spacious public areas include a comfortable lounge and a pleasant breakfast room with separate tables. A superb decked patio overlooks a wooded hillside rich with wildlife.

Rooms 5 en suite (2 fmly) (1 GF) S £44-£55; D £62-£80* **Facilities** FTV DVD iPod docking station Lounge TVL tea/coffee WiFi ♨ 18 ⚓ **Parking** 13 **Notes** LB ⊗

PEMBROKESHIRE

EGLWYSWRW
Map 8 SN13

Premier Collection

Ael y Bryn
★★★★★ ⬤ ⬤ BED AND BREAKFAST

tel: 01239 891411 **SA41 3UL**
email: stay@aelybrynpembrokeshire.co.uk **web:** www.aelybrynpembrokeshire.co.uk
dir: *In Eglwyswrw at junct of B4332 & A487 turn right signed Cardigan. Left after car park, 0.5 on left*

Set in beautiful countryside between Cardigan and Fishguard, a mere four miles from the coastal path, Ael y Bryn is a long, single-storey building that offers impressive levels of accommodation. Obviously, all rooms are on the ground floor, which means access is easy for all. Alongside the four luxurious bedrooms, guests have use of a conservatory, a lounge/music room, a library, an inner courtyard and a delightful garden. Breakfast and evening meals – available with prior notice – are served in the attractive dining room. Cyclists and walkers are welcome and safe storage and drying space is provided.

Rooms 4 en suite (4 GF) D £100-£130* **Facilities** FTV DVD Lounge tea/coffee Dinner available WiFi ⚓ **Extras** Fresh milk, mini-fridge - complimentary **Parking** 4 **Notes** ⊗ No Children 14yrs Closed mid Dec-mid Jan

FISHGUARD
Map 8 SM93

Premier Collection

Erw-Lon Farm (SN028325)
★★★★★ FARMHOUSE

tel: 01348 881297 **Pontfaen SA65 9TS**
email: lilwenmcallister@btinternet.com web: www.erwlonfarm.co.uk
dir: *5.5m SE of Fishguard on B4313*

Located in the Pembrokeshire Coast National Park, with stunning views of the Gwaun Valley, this attractive farmhouse has been converted to provide modern well-equipped bedrooms with a wealth of homely extras. The McAllisters give the warmest of welcomes, and their memorable dinners feature the finest local produce.

Rooms 3 en suite S £50-£60; D £70-£80* **Facilities** FTV TVL tea/coffee Dinner available WiFi Parking 5 **Notes** LB ⊗ No Children 10yrs Closed Dec-Mar 128 acres beef/sheep

Cefn-y-Dre
★★★★ BED AND BREAKFAST

tel: 01348 875663 **Cefn-y-Dre House SA65 9QS**
email: welcome@cefnydre.co.uk web: www.cefnydre.co.uk
dir: *On A40 in Scleddau turn opposite Gate Inn. Pass garden centre on left, 200yds turn right into No Through Rd*

Perched in delightful countryside along the end of a winding lane, this peaceful accommodation is located approximately a mile above the town and harbour of Fishguard. Bedrooms and bathrooms are very well decorated and furnished and include some welcome extras. Breakfast makes use of high quality ingredients and offers a number of daily specials. The owners offer a very friendly and relaxed style of accommodation with tea and cake offered on arrival. Guests are welcome to use the lounge and play the piano if the mood takes them.

Rooms 3 rms (2 en suite) (1 pri facs) **Facilities** FTV Lounge tea/coffee Dinner available Licensed WiFi Parking 8 **Notes** LB ⊗

HAVERFORDWEST
Map 8 SM91

See also Narberth

Premier Collection

Slebech Park Estate
★★★★★ ◉◉ GUEST ACCOMMODATION

tel: 01437 752000 & 752002 **SA62 4AX**
email: enquiries@slebech.co.uk web: www.slebech.co.uk
dir: *E of Haverfordwest on A40, take exit signed Picton Castle*

A delightful and peaceful retreat located on the shores of Dau Cleddau River – one of Europe's largest natural harbours. The estate covers 650 acres, with an array of walks from the door through meadows, woodlands and the riverside. Guests are ensured a warm welcome and excellent service throughout their stay. Bedrooms offer a range of shapes and sizes – all full of quality. Both the award-winning dinner and breakfast are served in the separate restaurant, and offer a range of carefully prepared dishes making use of top quality local produce. Lunch and afternoon tea are also available.

Rooms 15 en suite (5 fmly) (3 GF) S fr £95* **Facilities** STV FTV Lounge TVL tea/coffee Dinner available Direct Dial Licensed WiFi 18 Fishing Shooting **Extras** Speciality toiletries, home-made cakes **Conf** Max 200 Thtr 200 Class 180 Board 160 **Parking** 60 **Notes** LB Civ Wed 90

See advert on opposite page

Premier Collection

The Paddock

★★★★★ GUEST HOUSE

tel: 01437 731531 & 07973 636510 **Lower Haythog, Bethlehem SA62 5QL**
email: joss@thepaddockwales.co.uk **web:** www.thepaddockwales.co.uk
dir: *From Haverfordwest on A40 towards Fishguard. At next rdbt, 3rd exit onto B4329, 4.5m to Bethlehem, on right*

Peacefully located and surrounded by pleasant countryside, this modern, detached accommodation stands alongside the traditional farmhouse building and provides high levels of quality and comfort. Spacious bedrooms and bathrooms are all on the ground floor and include some welcome extras. Both breakfast and dinner (available by prior arrangement) make good use of a range of high quality produce.

Rooms 3 en suite (3 GF) **Facilities** FTV DVD Lounge tea/coffee Dinner available WiFi **Extras** Speciality toiletries, fridge, water **Parking** 4 **Notes** ⊗ No Children 12yrs

College Guest House

★★★★ GUEST HOUSE

tel: 01437 763710 **93 Hill St, St Thomas Green SA61 1QL**
email: colinlarby@aol.com **web:** www.collegeguesthouse.com
dir: *In town centre, along High St, pass church, keep in left lane. 1st exit by Stonemason Arms pub, follow signs for St Thomas Green/Leisure Centre/Police Station. 300mtrs on left by No Entry sign*

Situated in a mainly residential area within easy walking distance of Haverdfordwest's attractions, this impressive Georgian house offers good levels of comfort and facilities. There is a range of practically equipped bedrooms, along with public areas that include a spacious lounge (with internet access) and an attractive pine-furnished dining room – the setting for comprehensive breakfasts.

Rooms 8 en suite (4 fmly) **Facilities** FTV DVD TVL tea/coffee WiFi **Extras** Bottled water

Slebech Park, Haverfordwest, SA62 4AX
Tel: 01437 752000
Fax: 01437 752000
Email: enquiries@slebech.co.uk
Web: Slebech.co.uk

The *Slebech Park Estate* is set in 650 acres in the stunning Pembrokeshire National Park in West Wales. The facilities at the Estate revolve around the 18th century Grade II listed coach house, once the centre of the traditional agricultural Estate. A haven away from the rigours of the modern world.

The Coach house and its 15 bespoke bedrooms command a stunning position on the shores of the Dau Cleddau River Estuary. We have a host of walks along the shore, through fallow fields and mature woodlands.

Our 2 Rosette restaurant is open all year and prides itself with old fashioned hospitality and showcasing the finest of Welsh and locally sourced ingredients supplemented from our vintage kitchen gardens.

We are perfectly placed to explore beautiful Pembrokeshire with the stunning coastline of the county only 10 to 20 minutes away.

KILGETTY
Map 8 SN10

The Begelly Arms
★★★ INN

tel: 01834 812601 **New Rd SA68 0YF**
email: info@begellyarms.co.uk **web:** www.begellyarms.co.uk
dir: *On A40 at St Clears rdbt onto A477, signed Tenby/Pembroke Dock. At next rdbt take 3rd exit signed Kilgetty, into village, on left*

Being located very close to Oakwood Theme Park, this is a popular inn with families. Rooms are located in two areas – some above the main inn and others in an adjacent block. Food is served throughout the day and children are well catered for in terms of menus and the garden to the rear of the building. Function rooms are also available and a large car park is provided.

Rooms 7 en suite 9 annexe en suite (3 fmly) (4 GF) (2 smoking) **Facilities** STV FTV DVD tea/coffee Dinner available WiFi ⅃ 18 Pool table 🅿 **Parking** 60 **Notes** ⊗

MANORBIER
Map 8 SS09

Castlemead
★★★★ ☕ RESTAURANT WITH ROOMS

tel: 01834 871358 **SA70 7TA**
email: castlemeadhotel@aol.com **web:** www.castlemeadhotel.com
dir: *A4139 towards Pembroke, B4585 into village, follow signs to beach & castle, establishment on left*

Benefiting from a superb location with spectacular views of the bay, the Norman church and Manorbier Castle, this family-run business is friendly and welcoming. Bedrooms, which include some in a converted former coach house at ground floor level, are generally quite spacious and have modern facilities. Public areas include a sea-view residents' lounge and a restaurant accessed by stairs, which is open to non-residents, along with a cosy bar. There are extensive gardens to the rear of the property.

Rooms 5 en suite 3 annexe en suite (2 fmly) (3 GF) **Facilities** FTV Lounge tea/coffee Dinner available Direct Dial WiFi 🅿 **Parking** 20 **Notes** Closed Jan-Feb RS Nov maybe B&B only No coaches

NARBERTH
Map 8 SN11

Canaston Oaks
★★★★★ 🅰 BED AND BREAKFAST

tel: 01437 541254 **Canaston Bridge SA67 8DE**
email: enquiries@canastonoaks.co.uk **web:** www.canastonoaks.co.uk
dir: *Turn left off A40 at Canaston Bridge onto A4075. 600yds on left*

Canaston Oaks is a skilful blend of converted traditional farm stables with modern additions, all designed and built by Pembrokeshire craftsmen. The decor blends classic and contemporary elements to produce high levels of comfort in a peaceful setting.

Rooms 2 en suite 8 annexe en suite (2 fmly) (7 GF) D £98-£150* **Facilities** FTV DVD iPod docking station tea/coffee WiFi 🅿 **Extras** Bottled water, chocolates - complimentary **Parking** 10 **Notes** LB ⊗

NEWPORT
Map 8 SN03

Llys Meddyg
★★★★ ⚜⚜ RESTAURANT WITH ROOMS

tel: 01239 820008 **East St SA42 0SY**
email: info@llysmeddyg.com **web:** www.llysmeddyg.com
dir: *On A487 in centre of town*

Llys Meddyg is a Georgian town house offering a blend of old and new, with elegant furnishings, deep sofas and a welcoming fire. The owners of the property employed local craftsmen to create a lovely interior that has an eclectic style. The focus of the quality restaurant menu is on fresh, seasonal, locally sourced ingredients. The spacious bedrooms are comfortable and contemporary in design; bathrooms vary in style.

Rooms 5 en suite 3 annexe en suite (3 fmly) (1 GF) **Facilities** FTV DVD iPod docking station Lounge tea/coffee Dinner available WiFi ⅃ 18 Riding 🅿 **Extras** Speciality toiletries, mini-bar **Conf** Max 20 Class 20 Board 20 **Parking** 8 **Notes** No coaches Civ Wed 90

Salutation Inn
★★★ 🅰 INN

tel: 01239 820564 & 07793 488262 **Filindre Farchog SA41 3UY**
email: johndenley@aol.com **web:** www.salutationcountryhotel.co.uk
dir: *On A487 between Cardigan & Fishguard. 3m N of Newport*

John and Gwawr Denley offer a warm welcome at this 16th-century coaching inn in the heart of the Pembrokeshire Coast National Park. The old part of the inn blends well with the modern and well equipped bedrooms. The two bars have oak beams and an old country atmosphere. The inn overlooks lawned gardens that lead down to the river. All bedrooms are on the ground floor, en suite, and equipped with flat-screen TV.

Rooms 8 en suite (2 fmly) (8 GF) **Facilities** FTV tea/coffee Dinner available Direct Dial WiFi ⅃ 18 Pool table **Conf** Max 25 Thtr 25 Class 12 Board 12 **Parking** 60

Over 2,100 places, from country inns and historic taverns to town hostelries and gastro-pubs. Now in its 20th year.

THE PUB GUIDE 2017

BRITAIN'S BEST PUBS FOR BEER AND FOOD

shop.theAA.com

ST DAVIDS
See also Solva

Map 8 SM72

Ramsey House
★★★★★ GUEST HOUSE

tel: 01437 720321 & 07795 575005 **Lower Moor SA62 6RP**
email: info@ramseyhouse.co.uk **web:** www.ramseyhouse.co.uk
dir: *From Cross Sq in St Davids towards Porthclais, house 0.25m on left*

This pleasant guest house, under the ownership of Suzanne and Shaun Ellison, offers the ideal combination of professional management and the warmth of a family-run guest house. The property is quietly located on the outskirts of St Davids and is surrounded by unspoilt countryside. It provides modern, well-equipped bedrooms, most with en suite bathrooms, along with a good range of welcome extras. Breakfast provides a choice of home-made items, including breads and preserves.

Rooms 6 rms (5 en suite) (1 pri facs) (3 GF) S £70-£120; D £90-£120*
Facilities FTV Lounge tea/coffee Licensed WiFi 🔒 **Extras** Speciality toiletries - complimentary **Parking** 10 **Notes** LB ⊗ No Children 16yrs Closed Nov-13 Feb

The Waterings
★★★★ BED AND BREAKFAST

tel: 01437 720876 **Anchor Dr, High St SA62 6QH**
email: enquiries@waterings.co.uk **web:** www.waterings.co.uk
dir: *On A487 on E edge of St Davids*

Situated a short walk from the centre of St Davids, The Waterings offers spacious bedrooms that are accessed from a courtyard garden; most bedrooms have their own separate seating area. Breakfast, made from a good selection of local produce, is served in a smart dining room in the main house.

Rooms 2 en suite 5 annexe en suite (4 fmly) (5 GF) S £55-£80; D £75-£100
Facilities FTV tea/coffee Licensed WiFi 🦢 ⅃ 9 **Conf** Max 15 Board 15 **Parking** 20
Notes No Children 5yrs

ST DAVIDS continued

The City Inn

★★★ INN

tel: 0845 347 3102 *(Calls cost 7p per minute plus your phone company's access charge)*
& 01437 720829 **New St SA62 6SU**
email: info@cityinnstdavids.co.uk **web:** www.cityinnstdavids.co.uk

Located just ten minutes' walk from St Davids Cathedral and even closer to the main town, this well-furnished accommodation provides a relaxed and informal atmosphere. Guests can choose from a range of bar and restaurant menus at both dinner and lunch. Meals are served in the spacious lounge or the main dining room. The car park is a welcome feature.

Rooms 9 en suite (5 fmly) S £52.50; D £77.50-£78* **Facilities** FTV Dinner available WiFi ⚓ 9 Pool table ⚓ **Parking** 12 **Notes** Closed 23-26 Dec

| SOLVA | Map 8 SM82 |

Premier Collection

Crug Glâs Country House

★★★★★ ⚙ 🍴 RESTAURANT WITH ROOMS

tel: 01348 831302 **Abereiddy SA62 6XX**
email: janet@crug-glas.co.uk **web:** www.crug-glas.co.uk
dir: *From Solva to St Davids on A487. From St Davids take A487 towards Fishguard. 1st left after Carnhedryn, house signed*

This house, on a dairy, beef and cereal farm of approximately 600 acres, is situated about a mile from the coast on the St Davids Peninsula. Comfort, relaxation and flawless attention to detail are provided by the charming host, Janet Evans. Each spacious bedroom has the hallmark of assured design plus a luxury bathroom with both bath and shower; one suite on the top floor has great views. In addition there are two suites in separate buildings.

Rooms 7 en suite (1 fmly) (2 GF) S £110; D £150-£190* **Facilities** FTV Lounge tea/coffee Dinner available WiFi ⚓ **Extras** Speciality toiletries **Conf** Max 200 Thtr 200 Class 200 Board 200 **Parking** 10 **Notes** No Children 12yrs Closed 22-29 Dec Civ Wed 220

| TENBY | Map 8 SN10 |

Premier Collection

Trefloyne Manor

★★★★★ GUEST ACCOMMODATION

tel: 01834 842165 & 844429 **Trefloyne Ln, Penally SA70 7RG**
email: tom@trefloyne.com **web:** www.trefloyne.com
dir: *A478 to Tenby onto A4139 signed Penally. Turn right opposite Kiln Park Garage, then 1st right to Trefloyne, 150 mtrs along Trefloyne Ln turn left into Trefloyne Manor*

Delightfully located in a peaceful valley, surrounded by an 18-hole golf course, this relaxing accommodation offers an excellent range of high quality bedrooms and bathrooms. Some rooms are in the main house while others are in an adjacent coach house – decorated to very high standards including a number of suites. Both dinner and breakfast use local produce and are served in the light and airy conservatory overlooking the golf course.

Rooms 5 en suite 7 annexe en suite (4 fmly) (3 GF) S £75-£185; D £90-£200*
Facilities FTV iPod docking station Lounge TVL tea/coffee Dinner available Licensed WiFi ⚓ 18 ⚓ **Extras** Speciality toiletries, home-made biscuits **Parking** 150 **Notes** LB Closed 25 Dec Civ Wed 110

Esplanade

★★★★ GUEST ACCOMMODATION

tel: 01834 842760 & 843333 **1 The Esplanade SA70 7DU**
email: esplanadetenby@googlemail.com **web:** www.esplanadetenby.co.uk
dir: *Follow signs to South Beach, exit South Parade into St Florence Parade. Premises on seafront adjacent to town walls*

Located beside the historic town walls of Tenby, with stunning views over the sea to Caldey Island, the Esplanade provides a range of standard and luxury bedrooms, some ideal for families. Breakfast is offered in the elegant front-facing dining room, which contains a comfortable lounge-bar area.

Rooms 14 en suite (4 fmly) (1 GF) S £55-£120; D £75-£130 **Facilities** FTV DVD Lounge tea/coffee Direct Dial Licensed WiFi ⚓ **Extras** Mineral water - complimentary **Notes** LB Closed 15 Dec-6 Jan

| POWYS |

| BRECON | Map 9 SO02 |

Premier Collection

Peterstone Court

★★★★★ ⚙ RESTAURANT WITH ROOMS

tel: 01874 665387 **Llanhamlach LD3 7YB**
email: info@peterstone-court.com **web:** www.peterstone-court.com
dir: *3m from Brecon on A40 towards Abergavenny*

Situated on the edge of the Brecon Beacons, this establishment affords stunning views overlooking the River Usk. The atmosphere is friendly and informal, with no unnecessary fuss. No two bedrooms are alike, but all share comparable levels of comfort, quality and elegance. Public areas reflect similar standards, eclectically styled with a blend of the contemporary and the traditional. Quality produce is cooked with care in a range of enjoyable dishes.

Rooms 8 en suite 4 annexe en suite (2 fmly) S £125-£185; D £125-£275*
Facilities FTV DVD iPod docking station Lounge tea/coffee Dinner available Direct Dial WiFi ⚓ Fishing Riding Sauna Gym ⚓ Pool open mid Apr-1 Oct Spa facilities **Conf** Max 100 Thtr 100 Class 100 Board 60 **Parking** 60 **Notes** LB Civ Wed

Llanddetty Hall Farm *(SO124205)*

★★★★ FARMHOUSE

tel: 01874 676415 **Talybont-on-Usk LD3 7YR**
dir: *SE of Brecon. Off B4558*

This impressive Grade II listed, 17th-century farmhouse in the beautiful Usk Valley is full of character, and the friendly proprietors ensure a comfortable stay. Bedrooms are very pleasant and feature traditional furnishings, exposed timbers and polished floorboards. Welcoming log fires are lit during cold weather in the comfortable lounge, and guests dine around one table in the dining room.

Rooms 3 rms (2 en suite) (1 pri facs) 1 annexe en suite (1 GF) S £50-£75; D £70-£80* **Facilities** TVL TV1B tea/coffee **Parking** 6 **Notes** ⊗ No Children 12yrs Closed 15 Dec-15 Jan ⊜ 15 acres non-working

The Beacons Guest House

★★★ GUEST HOUSE

tel: 01874 623339 **16 Bridge St LD3 8AH**
email: guesthouse@thebreconbeacons.co.uk **web:** www.thebreconbeacons.co.uk
dir: On B4601 opposite Christ College

Located west of the historic town centre over the bridge, this 17th-century former farmhouse by the river has a range of homely bedrooms, some in converted barns and outbuildings. There is a guests' lounge and a cosy bar. This is a non-smoking establishment.

Rooms 11 rms (9 en suite) (2 pri facs) 3 annexe en suite (4 fmly) (3 GF)
Facilities FTV Lounge TVL tea/coffee Licensed WiFi 🔒 **Conf** Max 30 Thtr 30 Class 25 Board 20 **Parking** 20 **Notes** LB ⊗

Borderers Guesthouse

★★★ GUEST ACCOMMODATION

tel: 01874 623559 **47 The Watton LD3 7EG**
email: info@borderers.com **web:** www.borderers.com
dir: 200yds SE of town centre on B4601, opposite church

A warm welcome awaits at Borderers Guesthouse, originally a 17th-century drovers' inn. On offer are comfortable, attractively decorated bedrooms, some in the main building; annexe bedrooms are centred around a courtyard that provides secure car and bike parking. A private chalet is also available. Hearty breakfasts are served in the original part of the inn.

Rooms 4 rms (3 en suite) (1 pri facs) 5 annexe en suite (2 fmly) (4 GF) S £45-£50; D £65-£90* **Facilities** FTV tea/coffee WiFi **Parking** 6

BUILTH WELLS   Map 9 SO05

Rhedyn Guest House

★★★★ 🛏 🍴 GUEST HOUSE

tel: 01982 551944 & 07703 209721 **Rhedyn, Cilmery LD2 3LH**
email: info@rhedynguesthouse.co.uk **web:** www.rhedynguesthouse.co.uk
dir: From Builth Wells on A483 towards Garth. Rhedyn Guest House on right, through farm gate, closing all gates once through

This detached property stands just off the main road outside Cilmery, which is a short drive from Builth Wells. Three comfortable bedrooms provide all the modern facilities including WiFi and a range of guest extras. Two bedrooms are on the ground floor with their own entrances. Dinner, bookable at the time of reservation, offers imaginative menus. A hearty breakfast, including a selection of home-made preserves, is served in the delightful dining room around a communal table. Access to the guest house is via two gates through a field.

Rooms 1 en suite 2 annexe en suite (2 GF) S £85; D £95* **Facilities** STV FTV DVD Lounge tea/coffee Dinner available WiFi 🔒 **Extras** Sherry/Welsh cakes - complimentary **Parking** 3 **Notes** 🍽

CEMMAES   Map 14 SH80

The Penrhos Arms

★★★★ INN

tel: 01650 511243 & 07808 589349 **SY20 9PR**
email: dawndavies8@hotmail.com **web:** www.penrhosarms.com

The Penrhos Arms provides a warm welcome to new and returning guests alike, an historic inn with a charming and comfortable interior. Bedrooms are smartly appointed and have very comfortable beds. A hearty range of menu choices are offered, using local produce where possible.

Rooms 5 en suite 2 annexe en suite (1 fmly) **Facilities** FTV DVD TVL tea/coffee Dinner available WiFi ch fac ⚓ Pool table 🔒 **Conf** Max 40 **Notes** Civ Wed 50

CRICKHOWELL   Map 9 SO21

The Bear

★★★★★ 🌐 INN

tel: 01873 810408 **High St NP8 1BW**
email: info@bearhotel.co.uk **web:** www.bearhotel.co.uk
dir: Town centre, off A40 (Brecon road). 6m from Abergavenny

The Bear is a favourite with locals as well as visitors; the character and friendliness of this 15th-century coaching inn are renowned. The bedrooms come in a variety of sizes and include some with four-posters. The bar and restaurant are furnished in keeping with the style of the building, and provide comfortable areas in which to enjoy some of the very popular dishes that use the finest locally-sourced ingredients, served from a menu to suit all tastes.

Rooms 34 en suite (4 fmly) (6 GF) S £84-£141; D £104-£177* **Facilities** FTV Lounge tea/coffee Dinner available Direct Dial WiFi Fishing 🔒 **Parking** 40

CRIGGION   Map 15 SJ21

Brimford House (SJ310150)

★★★★ FARMHOUSE

tel: 01938 570235 **SY5 9AU**
email: info@brimford.co.uk **web:** www.brimford.co.uk
dir: Exit B4393 after Crew Green left for Criggion, Brimford 1st on left after pub

This elegant Georgian house stands in lovely open countryside and is a good base for touring central Wales and the Marches. The bedrooms are spacious, and thoughtful extras enhance guest comfort. A cheery log fire burns in the lounge during colder weather; the hospitality is equally warm and creates a relaxing atmosphere throughout.

Rooms 3 en suite S £50-£60; D £75-£85* **Facilities** FTV TVL tea/coffee WiFi Fishing **Parking** 4 **Notes** LB 250 acres arable/beef/sheep

ERWOOD
Map 9 SO04

Hafod-y-Garreg

★★★★ ⌂ BED AND BREAKFAST

tel: 01982 560400 **LD2 3TQ**
email: john-annie@hafod-y.wanadoo.co.uk **web:** www.hafodygarreg.co.uk
dir: *1m S of Erwood. Off A470 at Trericket Mill, sharp right, up track past cream farmhouse towards pine forest, through gate*

This remote Grade II listed farmhouse dates in part from 1401 and has been confirmed, by dendrochronology, as the 'oldest dwelling in Wales'. As you would expect, the house has tremendous character, and is decorated and furnished to befit its age; even so, the bedrooms have all the modern facilities. There is an impressive dining room and a lounge with an open fireplace. Warm hospitality from John and Annie here is a major strength here.

Rooms 2 en suite **Facilities** STV iPod docking station tea/coffee Dinner available WiFi 🔒 **Extras** Speciality toiletries, sherry, mags/books - free **Parking** 6 **Notes** No Children Closed Xmas ⊛

HAY-ON-WYE
Map 9 SO24

See also Erwood

Old Black Lion Inn

★★★★ ⊛ INN

tel: 01497 820841 **26 Lion St HR3 5AD**
email: info@oldblacklion.co.uk **web:** www.oldblacklion.co.uk
dir: *From B4348 in Hay-on-Wye into Lion St. Inn on right*

This fine old coaching inn, with a history stretching back several centuries, has a wealth of charm and character. It was occupied by Oliver Cromwell during the siege of Hay Castle. Privately owned and personally-run, it provides cosy and well-equipped bedrooms, some located in an adjacent building. A wide range of well-prepared food is provided, and the service is relaxed and friendly.

Rooms 6 rms (5 en suite) (1 pri facs) 4 annexe en suite (2 GF) S £50-£55; D £89-£125* **Facilities** FTV Lounge tea/coffee Dinner available Direct Dial WiFi 🔒 **Parking** 12 **Notes** Closed 24-26 Dec RS 3-12 Jan Limited services

LLANDRINDOD WELLS
Map 9 SO06

Holly Farm *(SO045593)*

★★★★ FARMHOUSE

tel: 01597 822402 **Holly Ln, Howey LD1 5PP**
web: www.hollyfarmbandb.co.uk
dir: *2m S on A483 of Llandrindod Wells near Howey*

This working farm dates from Tudor times, and is situated with easy access to the larger towns of Builth Wells and Llandrindod Wells. The bedrooms are homely and full of character. A comfortable lounge has a warming log fire in cooler months and pleasant gardens offer a peaceful area to sit in the warmer summer months. A hearty farmhouse breakfast can be enjoyed in the quaint dining room.

Rooms 3 en suite (1 fmly) S £42-£45; D £70-£76* **Facilities** FTV DVD TVL tea/coffee WiFi 🔒 **Parking** 4 **Notes** LB 70 acres beef/sheep

LLANGAMMARCH WELLS
Map 9 SN94

The Cammarch

★★★★ GUEST ACCOMMODATION

tel: 01591 620545 **LD4 4BY**
email: mail@cammarch.com **web:** www.cammarch.com
dir: *Exit A483 at Garth, signed Llangammarch Wells, opposite T-junct*

This property dates from the 1850s and was built as a railway hotel. Owner Kathryn Dangerfield offers a warm welcome to all guests and the establishment provides modern, well-equipped bedrooms that are tastefully decorated. There is a comfortable spacious bar and lounge, with a log-burning fire, ideal for colder evenings. The conservatory dining room, overlooking the attractive gardens and pond, offers fresh local produce on the dinner menu and the hearty Welsh breakfast makes a good start to the day. Parking is provided at the side of the property.

Rooms 12 en suite (3 fmly) S £69; D £95* **Facilities** FTV DVD Lounge TVL tea/coffee Dinner available Licensed WiFi ⤴ Fishing 🔒 **Extras** Speciality toiletries **Conf** Max 20 Thtr 20 Class 15 Board 15 **Parking** 16 **Notes** LB RS Xmas-New Year

LLANGEDWYN
Map 15 SJ12

Plas Uchaf Country House

★★★★ ⌂ GUEST HOUSE

tel: 01691 780588 & 07817 419747 **SY10 9LD**
email: info@plasuchaf.com **web:** www.plasuchaf.com
dir: *Mile End services Oswestry A483/Welshpool. After 2m right at White Lion public house, 4.5m Llangedwyn. 150yds after school on right*

Located in an elevated position in extensive mature parkland, this elegant Queen Anne house provides high standards of comfort and facilities. The interior flooring was created from recycled ship timbers taken from the Armada fleet of 1588, and furnishing styles highlight the many period features. Imaginative dinners are available, and a warm welcome is assured.

Rooms 6 en suite (1 fmly) (1 GF) S £67.50; D £95-£110* **Facilities** FTV DVD iPod docking station Lounge tea/coffee Dinner available Licensed WiFi ⊛ ⤴ 🔒 **Extras** Speciality toiletries - complimentary **Conf** Max 15 Thtr 15 Class 15 Board 15 **Parking** 30 **Notes** LB

Find out more about
the AA's awards for food
excellence on page 11

LLANGURIG
Map 9 SN97

The Old Vicarage
★★★★ GUEST HOUSE

tel: 01686 440280 **SY18 6RN**
email: info@theoldvicaragellangurig.co.uk **web:** www.theoldvicaragellangurig.co.uk
dir: A470 onto A44, signed

Located in pretty, mature grounds, which feature a magnificent holly tree, this elegant Victorian house provides a range of thoughtfully furnished bedrooms, some with fine period objects. Breakfast is served in a spacious dining room, and a comfortable guest lounge is also available.

Rooms 4 en suite (1 fmly) S £42; D £70* **Facilities** DVD TVL tea/coffee Licensed WiFi
🔒 **Parking** 6 **Notes** LB No Children 6yrs ☺

LLANWRTYD WELLS
Map 9 SN84

Lasswade Country House
★★★★ ◉◉ RESTAURANT WITH ROOMS

tel: 01591 610515 **Station Rd LD5 4RW**
email: info@lasswadehotel.co.uk **web:** www.lasswadehotel.co.uk
dir: Exit A483 into Irfon Terrace, right into Station Rd, 350yds on right

This friendly establishment on the edge of the town has impressive views over the countryside. Bedrooms are comfortably furnished and well equipped, while the public areas consist of a tastefully decorated lounge, an elegant restaurant with a bar, and an airy conservatory which looks towards the neighbouring hills. The kitchen makes good use of fresh, local produce to provide an enjoyable, award-winning dining experience.

Rooms 8 en suite (1 fmly) **Facilities** FTV Lounge TVL tea/coffee Dinner available WiFi
🔒 Riding 🔒 **Conf** Max 20 Thtr 20 Class 20 Board 20 **Parking** 6 **Notes** LB No coaches

MONTGOMERY
Map 15 SO29

The Nags Head Inn
🔟

tel: 01686 640600 **Garthmyl SY15 6RS**
email: reservations@nagsheadgarthmyl.co.uk **web:** www.nagsheadgarthmyl.co.uk
dir: On A483 between Welshpool & Newtown

Currently the rating for this establishment is not confirmed. This may be due to a change of ownership or because it has only recently joined the AA rating scheme.

Rooms 4 en suite D £65-£120* **Facilities** FTV Lounge TVL tea/coffee Dinner available Licensed WiFi 🔒 9 **Conf** Max 16 **Parking** 40

WELSHPOOL
Map 15 SJ20

See also Criggion

Heath Cottage *(SJ239023)*
★★★ 🏠 FARMHOUSE

tel: 01938 580453 **Kingswood, Forden SY21 8LX**
email: heathcottagewales@tiscali.co.uk
dir: 4m S of Welshpool. Off A490 behind Forden Old Post Office, opposite Parrys Garage

The furnishings and decor at Heath Cottage highlight the original features of this early 18th-century farmhouse. Bedrooms have stunning country views, and a choice of lounges, one with a log fire. Memorable breakfasts feature free-range eggs and home-made preserves.

Rooms 3 en suite (1 fmly) S £35; D £70* **Facilities** TVL tea/coffee WiFi 🔒 **Parking** 4 **Notes** ⊗ Closed Oct-Etr 🚜 6 acres poultry/sheep

SWANSEA

LLANGENNITH
Map 8 SS49

Kings Head
★★★★ INN

tel: 01792 386212 **Town House SA3 1HX**
email: info@kingsheadgower.co.uk **web:** www.kingsheadgower.co.uk
dir: M4 junct 47 follow signs for Gower A483. At next rdbt, 2nd left follow signs to Gowerton. At lights right onto B495, through old walls, keep left at fork. Kings Head on right

The Kings Head is made up of three 17th-century buildings set behind a splendid rough stone wall; it stands opposite the church in this coastal village. The well-equipped bedrooms, including some on the ground floor, are in two of the buildings. This is an ideal base for exploring the Gower Peninsula, whether for walking, cycling or surfing. Evening meals and breakfasts can be taken in the inn.

Rooms 27 en suite (3 fmly) (14 GF) **Facilities** FTV tea/coffee Dinner available Direct Dial WiFi Pool table 🔒 **Parking** 35 **Notes** LB Closed 25 Dec RS 24 Dec closed for check-in

PARKMILL (NEAR SWANSEA)
Map 8 SS58

Parc-le-Breos House (SS529896)

★★★★ FARMHOUSE

tel: 01792 371636 **SA3 2HA**
email: info@parclebreos.co.uk **web:** www.parc-le-breos.co.uk
dir: *On A4118, right 300yds after Shepherds shop, next left, signed*

This imposing, early 19th-century house is at the end of a forest drive and set in over 60 acres of delightful grounds. Many charming original features have been retained in the public rooms, which include a lounge and a games room. The bedrooms have comfortable furnishings, and many are suitable for families.

Rooms 10 en suite (7 fmly) (1 GF) **Facilities** FTV Lounge TVL tea/coffee Dinner available Licensed WiFi Fishing Riding Pool table **Conf** Max 30 Thtr 30 **Parking** 12 **Notes** LB ⊗ Closed 25-26 Dec 65 acres arable/horses/pigs/chickens

REYNOLDSTON
Map 8 SS48

Premier Collection

Fairyhill

★★★★★ ◉◉ ⌁ RESTAURANT WITH ROOMS

tel: 01792 390139 **SA3 1BS**
email: postbox@fairyhill.net **web:** www.fairyhill.net
dir: *M4 junct 47, A483, at next rdbt right onto A484. At Gowerton take B4295 for 10m*

Peace and tranquillity are never far away at this charming Georgian mansion set in the heart of the beautiful Gower Peninsula. Bedrooms are furnished with care and are filled with many thoughtful extras. There is also a range of comfortable seating areas, with crackling log fires, to choose from. The smart restaurant offers menus based on local produce that are complemented by an excellent wine list.

Rooms 8 en suite S £180-£310; D £200-£330 **Facilities** FTV DVD iPod docking station Lounge TVL tea/coffee Dinner available Direct Dial WiFi ᕫ Holistic treatments **Extras** Speciality toiletries, home-made Welsh cakes **Conf** Max 32 Thtr 32 Board 16 **Parking** 50 **Notes** LB No Children 8yrs Closed 24-26 Dec & 5-30 Jan RS Nov-Mar Closed Mon-Tue No coaches Civ Wed 40

SWANSEA
Map 9 SS69

Hurst Dene Guest House

★★★ GUEST HOUSE

tel: 01792 280920 **10 Sketty Rd, Uplands SA2 0LJ**
email: hurstdenehotel@yahoo.co.uk **web:** www. hurstdene.co.uk
dir: *1m W of city centre. A4118 through Uplands shopping area into Sketty Rd, Hurst Dene on right*

This friendly guest house has a private car park and provides soundly maintained bedrooms with modern furnishings and equipment. Facilities include an attractive breakfast room with separate tables and a small comfortable lounge.

Rooms 10 rms (8 en suite) (3 fmly) (1 GF) **Facilities** FTV TVL tea/coffee WiFi **Parking** 7 **Notes** ⊗ Closed 22 Dec-1 Jan

TORFAEN

PONTYPOOL
Map 9 SO20

The Lion

★★★★ ⚫ INN

tel: 01495 792516 **41 Broad St, Blaenavon NP4 9NH**
email: info@thelionhotelblaenavon.co.uk **web:** www.thelionhotelblaenavon.co.uk
dir: N of Pontypool, in centre of Blaenavon

The Lion is set in the beautiful village of Blaenavon, part of a UNESCO World Heritage Site, ideally located for walking and mountain biking in the Brecon Beacons. The restaurant offers a full service from breakfast to dinner, and prides itself on using the best of Welsh produce in its cooking. Rooms at The Lion fuse contemporary chic with classic luxury. Bedrooms all feature en suite bathroom or shower and a wide range of amenities including Freeview flat-screen TV/DVD, hair dryer, alarm clock, tea and coffee making facilities, free WiFi and a choice of pillows.

Rooms 12 en suite (2 fmly) **Facilities** FTV DVD TVL tea/coffee Dinner available Direct Dial WiFi Sauna steam room **Notes** ⊗

VALE OF GLAMORGAN

HENSOL
Map 9 ST07

Premier Collection

Llanerch Vineyard

★★★★★ ⚫ ☖ GUEST ACCOMMODATION

tel: 01443 222716 **CF72 8GG**
email: info@llanerch-vineyard.co.uk **web:** www.llanerch-vineyard.co.uk
dir: M4 junct 34, follow brown tourist signs

Llanerch Vineyard is delightfully set on a working Welsh vineyard with views over the vines to the countryside beyond. Bedrooms and bathrooms come in a range of shapes and sizes including sumptuously appointed suites in the main building. The Cariad Restaurant & Bistro is open for lunch, afternoon tea and dinner, with outdoor seating on the terrace in the warmer months. The vineyard's own wines are available to purchase in the small shop area, and are also on the wine list at dinner.

Rooms 3 en suite 8 annexe en suite (4 fmly) (7 GF) D £95-£125* **Facilities** FTV TVL tea/coffee Dinner available Direct Dial Licensed WiFi ⌁ 18 Wine tasting & vineyard tour **Extras** Bottled water - complimentary **Conf** Max 150 Thtr 150 Class 80 Board 40 **Parking** 100 **Notes** LB Civ Wed 150

LLANCARFAN
Map 9 ST07

Fox and Hounds

★★★★ ⚫ INN

tel: 01446 781287 **CF62 3AD**
email: foxandhoundsllancarfan@gmail.com **web:** www.foxandhoundsllancarfan.co.uk
dir: M4 junct 33, at rdbt 4th exit onto A48. Left onto A4226, turn right signed Fox and Hounds

Located in a peaceful village, this country-style inn offers a relaxed ambience combined with an excellent choice of dishes with good quality ingredients utilised at both dinner and breakfast. Bedrooms and bathrooms are all located on the first floor of the inn and come in a range of shapes and sizes. Outdoor seating is also available.

Rooms 8 en suite (1 fmly) **Facilities** FTV tea/coffee Dinner available Direct Dial WiFi ⌁ 18 **Parking** 18 **Notes** ⊗ Closed 25-27 Dec No coaches

PENARTH
Map 9 ST17

Premier Collection

Restaurant James Sommerin

★★★★★ ⓦⓦⓦ RESTAURANT WITH ROOMS

tel: 029 2070 6559 **The Esplanade CF64 3AU**
email: info@jamessommerinrestaurant.co.uk
web: www.jamessommerinrestaurant.co.uk

Restaurant James Sommerin stands proudly by the pier in Penarth with unrivalled views across the bay, just a short distance from Cardiff centre. Cuisine is accomplished and exciting with three different tasting menus offered in addition to the à la carte, showcasing the passion for food from this innovative chef and his team. The latest addition is the accommodation, which offers comfortable, quality facilities for guests wanting to take full advantage of the interesting and extensive wine list. This is truly a family business; the friendly front of house team are under the watchful eye of Louise Sommerin and often their oldest daughter can be seen assisting in the kitchen. Restaurant James Sommerin is the AA Restaurant of the Year for Wales 2016-2017.

Rooms 9 en suite S £150-£190; D £150-£190* **Facilities** FTV tea/coffee Dinner available Direct Dial Lift WiFi **Conf** Max 60 **Notes** LB RS Mon closed

See advert on page 428

Restaurant James Sommerin with Rooms

The restaurant opened in May 2014 with its 9 bedrooms only opening in February 2016.

The family run Restaurant with Rooms is situated on the Esplanade in Penarth with panoramic views over the Severn Estuary. James and eldest daughter, Georgia, can be found cooking up a storm in the kitchen and Louise, front of house.

There are 9 en-suite bedrooms, elegantly decorated with 5 benefiting from unobstructed sea views and 4 with views over the courtyard. All rooms benefit from flat screen Freeview TVs, hot drinks tray, complimentary water and toiletries. All rooms are accessible via a lift, one room has complete disabled access and facilities, and another is dog friendly (there is an additional £25 charge per dog staying in the room).

The restaurant offers A la Carte and Tasting Menus, all dietary requirements are catered for.

Free wifi access available.

The Esplanade, Penarth CF64 3AU   Tel: 029 20706559
jamessommerinrestaurant.co.uk   info@jamessommerinrestaurant.co.uk

WREXHAM

LLANARMON DYFFRYN CEIRIOG
Map 15 SJ13

The Hand at Llanarmon

★★★★ ◉ INN

tel: 01691 600666 **Ceiriog Valley LL20 7LD**
email: reception@thehandhotel.co.uk **web:** www.thehandhotel.co.uk
dir: Exit A5 at Chirk onto B4500 signed Ceiriog Valley, 11m to village

Appointed to a high standard, this inn provides a range of thoughtfully furnished bedrooms, with smart modern bathrooms. Public areas retain many original features including exposed beams and open fires. Imaginative food makes great use of the finest local produce. A warm welcome and attentive service ensure a memorable guest experience.

Rooms 13 en suite (4 GF) S £55-£90; D £90-£135* **Facilities** FTV Lounge tea/coffee Dinner available Direct Dial WiFi Pool table **Conf** Max 15 Thtr 10 Class 10 Board 15 **Parking** 19 **Notes** LB

WREXHAM
Map 15 SJ35

The Lemon Tree

★★★ ⬭ RESTAURANT WITH ROOMS

tel: 01978 261211 **29 Rhosddu Rd LL11 2LP**
email: info@thelemontree.org.uk **web:** www.thelemontree.org.uk
dir: A483 junct 5 follow signs for town centre, pass university & football stadium. Keep left, left at 1st rdbt

A modern and stylish restaurant setting awaits within this unassuming Gothic, Grade II listed building in the heart of Wrexham. The owners have a relaxed approach and offer locally sourced, modern British cuisine in the evenings. Straightforward and good value bedrooms are smartly appointed and comfortable; available in a range of sizes.

Rooms 12 en suite S £55-£70; D £60-£85* **Facilities** FTV TVL tea/coffee Dinner available WiFi **Conf** Max 40 Thtr 40 Class 20 Board 20 **Parking** 15 **Notes** LB ⊗ No coaches

Buck House

★★★ INN

tel: 01978 780336 **High St, Bangor-on-Dee LL13 0BU**
email: enquiries@thebuckhousebangorondee.co.uk **web:** www.thebuckhousebangorondee.co.uk

Located in the centre of the historic village, Buck House offers a warm welcome to all including many race goers from the nearby Bangor-on-Dee race course. Bedrooms vary in size and shape across the property with each comfortably appointed. Following a recent refurbishment the property can now provide a large function space alongside the cosy bar dining room which is very popular with locals and has a good selection of ales on tap.

Rooms 7 en suite (1 fmly) S £40-£60; D £45-£70 (room only)* **Facilities** FTV Lounge TVL tea/coffee Dinner available Direct Dial WiFi Pool table ⬭ **Conf** Max 60 Thtr 35 Class 45 Board 40 **Parking** 18 **Notes** LB

Ireland

NORTHERN IRELAND

COUNTY ANTRIM

BUSHMILLS
Map 1 C6

Premier Collection

Causeway Lodge
★★★★★ ⬤ GUEST HOUSE

tel: 028 2073 0333 **52 Moycraig Rd, Dunseverick BT57 8TB**
email: stay@causewaylodge.com **web:** www.causewaylodge.com

Causeway Lodge offers high-quality, contemporary accommodation in an idyllic setting on the north Antrim coast. Each of the individually designed bedrooms is thoughtfully presented and the Causeway Suite is very stylish. The house is close to the Giant's Causeway, Carrick-A-Rede rope bridge and the famous Bushmills Distillery. WiFi is available and a warm welcome is assured from the friendly owners.

Rooms 4 en suite 1 annexe en suite (2 fmly) (1 GF) S £90-£120; D £100-£140*
Facilities STV FTV iPod docking station TVL tea/coffee WiFi Sauna Gym ⬤ Hot tub **Extras** Speciality toiletries, fridge, bottled water, milk **Parking** 6 **Notes** ⊗

Premier Collection

Whitepark House
★★★★★ ⬤ GUEST ACCOMMODATION

tel: 028 2073 1482 **150 Whitepark Rd, Ballintoy BT54 6NH**
email: bob@whiteparkhouse.com **web:** www.whiteparkhouse.com
dir: On A2 at Whitepark Bay, 6m E of Bushmills

Whitepark House nestles above a sandy beach and has super views of the ocean and Scotland's Western Isles. The house features *objets d'art* gathered from Far Eastern travels, while the traditional bedrooms are homely. Breakfasts are served around a central table in the open-plan hallway, and hospitality is warm and memorable.

Rooms 3 en suite S £80; D £120* **Facilities** Lounge tea/coffee WiFi **Extras** Bottled water, robes **Parking** 6 **Notes** ⊗ No Children 10yrs

BELFAST

BELFAST
Map 1 D5

Tara Lodge
★★★★ GUEST ACCOMMODATION

tel: 028 9059 0900 **36 Cromwell Rd BT7 1JW**
email: pauline@taralodge.com **web:** www.taralodge.com
dir: M1 onto A55, left onto A1, right into Fitzwilliam St, left into University Rd, proceed to Botanic Av

Friendly staff and comfortable bedrooms make Tara Lodge popular for leisure or business guests. The stylish dining room is the scene of memorable breakfasts, while secure off-road parking is a bonus so close to the city centre. Tara Lodge was the AA Guest Accommodation of the Year for Northern Ireland 2015-2016.

Rooms 19 en suite 15 annexe en suite (3 GF) S £78-£93; D £83-£103* **Facilities** STV FTV DVD TVL tea/coffee Direct Dial Lift WiFi **Parking** 19 **Notes** LB ⊗ Closed 24-28 Dec

Springfield B&B
★★★ BED AND BREAKFAST

tel: 07711 971188 **16 Springfield Rd BT12 7AG**
email: k.obrien@live.co.uk **web:** www.bnbbelfast.com

Located just 10-15 minutes' walk from the city centre, Springfield B&B offers budget accommodation and genuine hospitality. Bedrooms and en suites are generally compact but cater well for the guest. Complimentary super-fast WiFi and good-sized TVs feature throughout. Breakfast offers a great start to the day with the traditional Ulster Fry — not for the faint-hearted, but not to be missed.

Rooms 5 en suite **Facilities** WiFi

COUNTY DOWN

COMBER
Map 1 D5

The Old Schoolhouse Inn
★★★★ ⬤⬤ ⬤ RESTAURANT WITH ROOMS

tel: 028 9754 1182 **100 Ballydrain Rd BT23 6EA**
email: info@theoldschoolhouseinn.com **web:** www.theoldschoolhouseinn.com
dir: A22 to Comber, right at end of road. 0.5m past Castle Espie to property

Located close to the shore of Strangford Lough, The Old Schoolhouse Inn enjoys a peaceful rural location, and is just a short drive from Comber and 20 minutes from Belfast. This family-run operation is in the capable hands of Will Brown who has learnt his trade in some of London's best kitchens and in establishments closer to home. Bedrooms are spacious and well appointed, while service is warm and genuine. The refurbished restaurant has been awarded two AA Rosettes and serves local produce with flair and imagination.

Rooms 12 en suite (12 GF) **Facilities** TVL tea/coffee Dinner available Direct Dial **Conf** Max 60 Thtr 60 Class 30 Board 30 **Parking** 100

DONAGHADEE
Map 1 D5

Pier 36
★★★★ ⬤ GUEST HOUSE

tel: 028 9188 4466 **36 The Parade BT21 0HE**
email: info@pier36.co.uk **web:** www.pier36.co.uk
dir: A2 left onto flyover before Bangor, follow signs for Donaghadee (right across bridge). In 3m take 3rd exit at rdbt towards harbour. Pier 36 on right

Pier 36 is right on the quayside of Donaghadee Harbour. The en suite bedrooms are well furnished, and both superior and standard rooms are available, all with fabulous views over the harbour and Copeland Islands. The breakfast menu is extensive, and there's is also a restaurant where guests can enjoy anything from sirloin and fillet steaks to a wide range of seafood, or a home-made scone beside the fire. Entertainment is offered most weekends.

Rooms 6 en suite (2 fmly) S £50-£75; D £79-£99* **Facilities** STV FTV TVL tea/coffee Dinner available Licensed WiFi ♿ 18 ⬤ **Extras** Bottled water **Conf** Max 36 Thtr 28 Class 20 Board 16 **Notes** LB

COUNTY FERMANAGH

ENNISKILLEN
Map 1 C5

Belmore Court & Motel

★★★★ GUEST ACCOMMODATION

tel: 028 6632 6633 **Tempo Rd BT74 6HX**
email: info@motel.co.uk **web:** www.motel.co.uk
dir: On A4, opposite Tesco on corner of Tempo Rd (B80)

Situated in the centre of Enniskillen, the Belmore Court offers an ideal location for visiting the north west and Fermanagh lakes. The accommodation offered has a range of styles from rooms with small kitchen areas to executive suites. All are stylish and have flat-screen TVs and free WiFi. Some also come with coffee makers. The public areas are also modern, and the breakfast room catches all the morning sun. Parking available.

Rooms 30 en suite 30 annexe en suite (17 fmly) (12 GF) **Facilities** FTV DVD iPod docking station TVL tea/coffee Direct Dial Lift WiFi ⅃ 18 🔒 **Extras** Speciality toiletries **Conf** Max 45 Thtr 45 Class 25 Board 16 **Parking** 60 **Notes** LB ⊗ Closed 24-28 Dec

COUNTY LONDONDERRY

COLERAINE
Map 1 C6

Greenhill House (C849210)

★★★★ 🏠 FARMHOUSE

tel: 028 7086 8241 & 07719 884103 **24 Greenhill Rd, Aghadowey BT51 4EU**
email: greenhill.house@btinternet.com **web:** www.greenhill-house.co.uk
dir: A29 from Coleraine, S for 7m, left onto B66 (Greenhill Rd) for 300yds. House on right (AA sign at front gate)

Set in the tranquil Bann Valley, overlooking the Antrim Hills, this delightful Georgian house nestles in well-tended gardens with views to open rolling countryside. Public rooms are traditionally styled and include a comfortable lounge and an elegant dining room. The pleasant bedrooms vary in size and style and have a host of thoughtful extras.

Rooms 4 en suite (1 fmly) **Facilities** FTV TVL tea/coffee Direct Dial WiFi 🔒 **Extras** Snacks, bottled water, fruit **Parking** 10 **Notes** ⊗ Closed Nov-Feb RS Mar-Oct 150 acres beef

MAGHERA
Map 1 C5

AA GUEST ACCOMMODATION OF THE YEAR FOR NORTHERN IRELAND 2016-2017

Ardtara Country House

★★★★ ⭐⭐ RESTAURANT WITH ROOMS

tel: 028 7964 4490 **8 Gorteade Rd BT46 5SA**
email: info@ardtara.com **web:** www.ardtara.com

Set in its own extensive gardens Ardtara Country House enjoys a secluded location just a short drive from the beautiful North Antrim Coast and the famous Giant's Causeway. This fine 19th-century house offers guests spacious bedrooms with views over the landscaped gardens. There is a comfortable lounge, a cosy bar and many of the original features have been sympathetically restored. The award-winning restaurant offers the best in fresh seasonal produce and the hearty breakfasts served in the conservatory are not to be missed. The city is of Derry is a short drive away as is the challenging Royal Portrush golf course.

Rooms 9 en suite (1 GF) **Facilities** Lounge tea/coffee Dinner available Direct Dial WiFi ⅃ 18 Fishing Riding **Conf** Max 50 **Parking** 100 **Notes** LB ⊗ Civ Wed 65

REPUBLIC OF IRELAND

COUNTY CARLOW

CARLOW
Map 1 C3

Avlon House Bed & Breakfast

★★★★ BED AND BREAKFAST

tel: 059 9174222 **Green Ln, Dublin Rd**
email: avlonhouse@eircom.net **web:** www.carlowbedandbreakfast.com
dir: N of town centre

Avlon House is a property built with visiting guests in mind. Located on the main approach from Dublin, there is secure parking and an attractively landscaped garden terrace. All of the bedrooms are well appointed, and guests have the choice of two comfortable lounge areas. While it is a non-smoking house, there is a dedicated smoking lodge in the garden.

Rooms 5 en suite (1 fmly) **Facilities** STV FTV TVL tea/coffee Dinner available Direct Dial WiFi **Parking** 7 **Notes** ⊗

Barrowville Town House

★★★★ GUEST HOUSE

tel: 059 9143324 & 086 2520013 **Kilkenny Rd**
email: barrowvilletownhouse@eircom.net **web:** www.barrowville.com
dir: Carlow Town, N9 Kilkenny Rd near Institute of Technology

The Smyths are the friendly owners of this carefully maintained 18th-century town house. Many of the very comfortable bedrooms are spacious, and the public rooms are elegant and relaxing. The conservatory, with its fruiting vine, is where breakfasts are served, overlooking well tended gardens. Ample parking is available.

Rooms 7 en suite (3 fmly) **Facilities** STV TVL tea/coffee Direct Dial WiFi **Parking** 11 **Notes** ⊗ Closed 24-26 Dec

To help you navigate safely and easily, use the AA Big Road Atlas Britain 2017. Available from: shop.theAA.com

BEST SELLING ROAD ATLASES OF BRITAIN
AA 2017 BIG ROAD ATLAS BRITAIN
BRITAIN'S CLEAREST MAPPING
Safety cameras with speed limits
Clear, route planner map
Top 300 AA-inspected Caravan and Camping sites
Scenic routes
Large 3 miles to 1 inch scale
BIG ROAD ATLAS BRITAIN 2017
theAA.com/shop

COUNTY CLARE

BALLYVAUGHAN
Map 1 B3

Ballyvaughan Lodge

★★★ 🛏 GUEST HOUSE

tel: 065 7077292 & 086 2511512
email: ballyvaughanlodge@yahoo.ie **web:** www.ballyvaughanlodge.com
dir: *From Galway take N6. Exit at junct 19 onto N18 (Oranmore). In Kilcolgan right onto N69 signed Ennistimon. Lodge on right on entering Ballyvaughan*

The warm and welcoming home of the O'Sullivans is the ideal base for touring the wonderful Burren region and Galway Bay. The village has a number of craft shops and atmospheric pubs, most of which serve evening meals. Bedrooms are comfortably appointed and the relaxing lounges include a sun room, with reading material, guides and some interesting pieces of original art. Breakfast is a delight; an array of fresh and poached fruits and local farmhouse cheeses followed by a selection of options cooked to order by Pauline.

Rooms 11 en suite (1 fmly) (5 GF) S €50-€60; D €80-€100* **Facilities** FTV Lounge TVL tea/coffee Direct Dial WiFi 🔒 **Extras** Bottled water, snacks, chocolates **Parking** 11 **Notes** Closed 23-28 Dec

DOOLIN
Map 1 B3

Cullinan's Seafood Restaurant & Guest House

★★★ ❀❀ 🛏 GUEST HOUSE

tel: 065 7074183
email: info@cullinansdoolin.com **web:** www.cullinansdoolin.com
dir: *In town centre at x-rds between McGanns Pub & O'Connors Pub*

A charming guest house and restaurant, where award-winning food is served in the conservatory dining room (in season; closed Wed and Sun) overlooking the River Aille. Chef-patron James Cullinan features locally caught fresh fish on the dinner menu, which also includes steaks, lamb and vegetarian dishes, and there is a popular Early Bird menu. Bedrooms are attractively decorated in a traditional style. There is a cosy guest lounge and ample off-street parking.

Rooms 8 en suite 2 annexe en suite (3 fmly) (3 GF) **Facilities** STV FTV Lounge TVL tea/coffee Dinner available Direct Dial WiFi **Parking** 15 **Notes** ⊗ No Children 4yrs Closed mid Dec-mid Feb

LAHINCH
Map 1 B3

Premier Collection

Moy House

★★★★★ ❀❀ 🛏 GUEST HOUSE

tel: 065 7082800
email: moyhouse@eircom.net **web:** www.moyhouse.com
dir: *1km from Lahinch on Miltown Malbay Rd, signed from Lahinch N67*

Moy House, an 18th-century former hunting lodge, overlooks Lahinch Bay, the world-famous surfing beach and championship golf links. Individually designed bedrooms and suites are decorated with luxurious fabrics and fine antique furniture. The elegant drawing room has an open turf fire and guests can enjoy breathtaking views of the ocean while enjoying a pre-dinner drink from the honesty bar. The Conservatory Restaurant adjoins the elegant dining room and features award-winning cookery. The menu is based on local seafood and seasonal produce from small independent farmers. A gourmet tasting menu is served on selected nights. Dinner must be pre-booked. Breakfast is also a treat, with a number of healthy options on offer together with the traditional Irish selection.

Rooms 9 en suite (2 fmly) (4 GF) S €145-€240; D €165-€380 **Facilities** STV FTV DVD Lounge Dinner available Direct Dial Licensed WiFi 🔒 🔒 Private access to beach **Extras** Speciality toiletries **Conf** Max 16 Board 16 **Parking** 30 **Notes** LB ⊗ Closed Nov-Feb Civ Wed 35

LISCANNOR
Map 1 B3

Moher Lodge (R043917)

★★★★ FARMHOUSE

tel: 065 7081269 **Cliffs of Moher**
email: moherlodge@gmail.com **web:** www.cliffsofmoher-ireland.com
dir: *1m from Cliffs of Moher on R478*

This very comfortable farmhouse is within walking distance of the world famous Cliffs of Moher. Three of the well appointed bedrooms are on the ground floor. There is a cosy sitting room with a turf fire and guests are greeted with tea and Mary's Guinness cake on arrival; there is a selection of dishes and freshly baked scones for breakfast. The locality offers restaurants, pubs with Irish music, ferries to the Aran Islands and the links golf course at Lahinch.

Rooms 4 en suite (1 fmly) (3 GF) **Facilities** FTV TVL tea/coffee WiFi **Parking** 4 **Notes** ⊗ Closed Nov-Mar 🐄 300 acres dairy/beef

Follow us on twitter
@TheAA_Lifestyle

LISDOONVARNA
Map 1 B3

Wild Honey Inn

★★★★ ◎◎ RESTAURANT WITH ROOMS

tel: 065 7074300 **Kincora**
email: info@wildhoneyinn.com **web:** www.wildhoneyinn.com
dir: *N18 from Ennis to Ennistymon. Continue through Ennistymon towards Lisdoonvarna, located on the right at edge of town*

Set in a former hotel dating from the 1860s, when the town prospered as a spa, the Wild Honey Inn has created a solid reputation for its two AA Rosette award-winning cuisine. 'Modern bistro style' is Aidan McGrath's description of the food on offer, served in the comfortable atmospheric bar at both lunch and dinner. Great attention is paid to the provenance of the ingredients, most of which are organic and sourced as close to County Clare as possible. Reservations are not taken. Bedrooms come in a number of styles, and the garden rooms have private patios. Residents have the use of a relaxing lounge, filled with reading material, not surprisingly featuring food and cookery. Breakfast is also a highlight of any visit, with a range of interesting options.

Rooms 14 en suite (3 GF) S €65; D €100–€130 **Facilities** STV Lounge Dinner available Direct Dial WiFi 🛁 **Extras** Bottled water, speciality toiletries **Notes** LB ⊗ No Children 12yrs Closed Nov-Feb RS Mar-Apr Open Thu-Sun No coaches

TUAMGRANEY
Map 1 B3

Clareville House

★★★★ ⚲ BED AND BREAKFAST

tel: 061 922925
email: info@clarevillehouse.net **web:** www.clarevillehouse.net
dir: *On R352 in village adjacent to Scarriff*

Clareville House is situated in the pretty lakeside village of Tuamgraney. Bedrooms are attractively decorated and furnished to a high standard, and there is a cosy guest sitting room. Teresa's breakfast is a special treat. Walking tours are organised by Derek, who knows all about fishing and golf in the area, and also offers a taxi service and airport collection.

Rooms 4 en suite (4 fmly) **Facilities** FTV TVL tea/coffee WiFi 🛁 18 Riding 🛁 Fishing tackle storage & bait bridge **Extras** Bottled water, magazines **Parking** 8 **Notes** ⊗

COUNTY CORK

BALTIMORE
Map 1 B1

Rolfs Country House

★★★ ◎ RESTAURANT WITH ROOMS

tel: 028 20289 **Baltimore Hill**
email: info@rolfscountryhouse.com **web:** www.rolfscountryhouse.com
dir: *Before village turn sharp left up hill. House signed*

Situated on a hill above the fishing village of Baltimore, these 400-year-old stone buildings have been successfully converted by the Haffner family. There are ten traditionally furnished en suite bedrooms in an annexe, a cosy bar with an open fire, and a rustic restaurant on two levels. Dinner is served nightly during the high season and at weekends in the winter; the menu features quality meats, artisan cheeses and fish landed at the busy pier. This is a lovely place to stay and the hosts are very friendly.

Rooms 10 annexe en suite S €60–€80; D €80–€120 **Facilities** FTV Lounge tea/coffee Dinner available WiFi **Parking** 60 **Notes** LB ⊗ Closed 20-26 Dec No coaches

CLONAKILTY
Map 1 B2

Duvane House (W349405)

★★★★ ⚲ FARMHOUSE

tel: 023 8833129 **Ballyduvane**
email: duvanefarm@eircom.net **web:** www.duvanehouse.com
dir: *1km SW from Clonakilty on N71*

This Georgian farmhouse is on the N71 Skibbereen road. Bedrooms are comfortable and include four-poster and brass beds. There is a lovely sitting room and dining room, and a wide choice is available at breakfast (dinner is available by arrangement). Local amenities include Blue Flag beaches, riding and golf.

Rooms 4 en suite (1 fmly) **Facilities** TVL tea/coffee Dinner available WiFi 🛁 9 Fishing Pool table 🛁 **Parking** 20 **Notes** ⊗ Closed Nov-Mar ⊜ 100 acres beef/dairy/mixed/sheep/horses

DURRUS
Map 1 B2

Blairscove House & Restaurant

★★★★ ◎◎ RESTAURANT WITH ROOMS

tel: 027 61127
email: mail@blairscove.ie **web:** www.blairscove.ie
dir: *From Durrus on R591 towards Crookhaven, 2.4km, blue gate on right*

Blairscove comprises four elegant suites located in the courtyard of a Georgian country house outside the pretty village of Durrus near Bantry; each room is individually decorated in a contemporary style and has stunning views over Dunmanus Bay and the mountains. The restaurant is renowned for its wide range of *hors d'oeuvres* and its open wood-fire grill. The piano-playing and candlelight add to a unique dining experience.

Rooms 4 annexe en suite (1 fmly) S €105–€160; D €150–€260* **Facilities** STV DVD tea/coffee Dinner available Direct Dial WiFi 🛁 **Extras** Sherry - complimentary; wine - chargeable **Parking** 30 **Notes** ⊗ Closed Nov-mid Mar No coaches Civ Wed 30

GOLEEN   Map 1 A1

The Heron's Cove
★★★★ ◉ 🎗 BED AND BREAKFAST

tel: 028 35225 & 0868 073072 **The Harbour**
email: suehill@eircom.net **web:** www.heronscove.com
dir: By harbour in Goleen

There are charming views of the harbour, fast-flowing stream and inland hills from The Heron's Cove, at Ireland's most south-westerly point, near Mizen Head. Bedrooms are comfortably furnished, some with balconies. The restaurant and wine bar is run by chef-patron Sue Hill, where the freshest fish and local produce feature and guests can choose their own wines from the cocktail bar shelves. Breakfast is a special treat and the best of West Cork ingredients can be enjoyed while watching the famous herons.

Rooms 5 en suite (2 fmly) S €50-€60; D €80-€90 **Facilities** STV tea/coffee Dinner available Direct Dial Licensed WiFi 🔒 **Extras** Bottled water **Parking** 10 **Notes** LB ⊗ Closed Xmas & New Year RS Oct-Mar bookings essential

KINSALE   Map 1 B2

Friar's Lodge
★★★★★ GUEST HOUSE

tel: 086 2895075 & 021 4777384 **5 Friars St**
email: mtierney@indigo.ie **web:** www.friars-lodge.com
dir: In town centre next to parish church

This family-run and owned lodge was purpose-built and is near the Friary, on a quiet street just a short walk from Kinsale, renowned for its restaurants and bars. Bedrooms and suites are particularly spacious and furnished with comfort in mind. Being close to The Old Head Golf Club, and many others, there is storage for clubs and a drying room available, with secure parking to the rear. There is a cosy lounge where a wine and snack menu is available. The elegant dining room is the setting for imaginative Irish breakfasts.

Rooms 18 en suite (2 fmly) (4 GF) **Facilities** STV tea/coffee Direct Dial Lift WiFi **Parking** 20 **Notes** Closed Xmas ◉

Long Quay House
★★★★ GUEST ACCOMMODATION

tel: 021 470 9833 **Long Quay**
email: info@longquayhousekinsale.com **web:** www.longquayhousekinsale.com
dir: Follow R600 from Cork to Kinsale, on entering the town house on right

Located at the entrance to the picturesque coastal town of Kinsale, Long Quay House is a Georgian residence and the home of Rasa and Peter Deasy. Many of the comfortable rooms retain the original proportions of the building, but don't miss out on today's creature comforts. Breakfast is a particular feature; beautiful presentation of interesting options. Kinsale is renowned for its restaurants, and is also an ideal base for touring West Cork

Rooms 8 en suite (2 fmly) (1 GF) S €80-€160; D €90-€200 **Facilities** FTV TVL Direct Dial WiFi 🛝 🔒 **Notes** ⊗ Closed 15 Nov-27 Dec

The White House
★★★★ ◉ RESTAURANT WITH ROOMS

tel: 021 4772125 **Pearse St, The Glen**
email: info@whitehouse-kinsale.ie **web:** www.whitehouse-kinsale.ie
dir: In town centre

Centrally located among the narrow, twisting streets of the charming maritime town of Kinsale, this restaurant with rooms dates from 1850. It is a welcoming hostelry with smart, comfortably appointed contemporary bedrooms. The atmospheric bar and bistro are open for lunch and dinner, with Restaurant d'Antibes also open during the evenings. The varied menu features local fish and beef. The courtyard at the rear makes a perfect setting in summer and there is regular entertainment in the bar.

Rooms 10 en suite (2 fmly) S €65-€100; D €100-€160* **Facilities** STV tea/coffee Dinner available Direct Dial WiFi **Notes** LB ⊗ Closed 24-25 Dec

The Old Bank House
Ⓤ

tel: 021 4772206 **10/11 Pearse St**
email: info@oldbankhousekinsale.com **web:** www.oldbankhousekinsale.com
dir: On main road into Kinsale from Cork Airport (R600). House on right at start of Kinsale, next to Post Office

Currently the rating for this establishment is not confirmed. This may be due to a change of ownership or because it has only recently joined the AA rating scheme.

Rooms 17 en suite (3 fmly) **Facilities** FTV TVL tea/coffee Direct Dial Lift WiFi 🔒 **Conf** Max 15 Thtr 15 Class 10 Board 12 **Notes** LB ⊗ Closed 25 Dec

SHANAGARRY
Map 1 C2

Premier Collection

Ballymaloe House

★★★★★ ⊚⊚ 🍴 GUEST HOUSE

---

tel: 021 4652531
email: res@ballymaloe.ie **web:** www.ballymaloe.ie
dir: *N25 onto R630 at Midleton rdbt. After 0.5m, left onto R631 to Cloyne. 2m after Cloyne on Ballycotton road*

This charming country house is on a 400-acre farm, part of the Geraldine estate in east Cork. Bedrooms upstairs in the main house retain many original features, and the ground floor and courtyard rooms have garden patios. The relaxing drawing room and dining rooms have enchanting old-world charm. Ballymaloe House is renowned for excellent meals, many of which are created using ingredients produced on the farm. There is a craft shop, café, tennis and small golf course on the estate.

Rooms 20 en suite 9 annexe en suite (2 fmly) (3 GF) S €150–€220; D €210–€310 **Facilities** Lounge TVL Dinner available Direct Dial Licensed WiFi ch fac ₹ 🐴 ⚜ ⚓ 9 🐴 Children's sand pit/slide **Conf** Max 200 Thtr 200 Class 50 Board 50 **Parking** 50 **Notes** LB Closed 23-26 Dec, 8-28 Jan RS Jan-Feb Closed Sun-Tue rooms & dinner Civ Wed 170

COUNTY DONEGAL

CARRIGANS
Map 1 C5

Mount Royd Country Home

★★★★ 🍴 BED AND BREAKFAST

---

tel: 074 914 0163
email: jmartin@mountroyd.com **web:** www.mountroyd.com
dir: *From Letterkenny on N14. At Dry Arch rdbt 2nd exit onto N13. At next rdbt 2nd exit onto N14 towards Lifford. Left at R236 to Carrigans. Or from Derry take A40 to Carrigans*

Mount Royd is a creeper-clad house with beautifully maintained gardens in the pretty village of Carrigans, a short distance from Derry City. The friendly Martins have brought hospitality to new heights – nothing is too much trouble for them. It is no wonder so many of their visitors are return guests. Breakfast is a feast of choices including home-baking and eggs from their own hens. Each of the individually designed bedrooms are very comfortable, with lots of personal touches.

Rooms 4 en suite (1 fmly) (1 GF) S €40–€45; D €70–€75* **Facilities** FTV TVL tea/coffee WiFi **Parking** 7 **Notes** LB ⊗ No Children 12yrs RS Nov-Feb ⊛

DONEGAL
Map 1 B5

The Red Door Country House

★★★★ ⊚ RESTAURANT WITH ROOMS

---

tel: 074 9360289 **Fahan, Inishowen**
email: info@thereddoor.ie **web:** www.thereddoor.ie
dir: *In Fahan village, church on right, The Red Door signed on left*

Nestled among mature trees and landscaped gardens, this warm and welcoming restaurant with rooms stands proudly on the shore of Lough Swilly, in the historic village of Fahan, just south of Buncrana. Dating from 1789, the original features of the house are cleverly combined with contemporary styling. Bedrooms are cosy and comfortable, each individually decorated and all en suite. The house has a fine reputation in the region for the quality of its restaurant for evening dining, and alfresco lunches. Breakfast is also a highlight and is designed to be lingered over.

The Red Door Country House was the AA Guest Accommodation of the Year for the Republic of Ireland 2015-2016.

Rooms 4 en suite D €120–€140* **Facilities** FTV Lounge tea/coffee Dinner available WiFi ⚓ 18 **Conf** Max 100 Thtr 100 Board 100 **Parking** 40 **Notes** RS Mon & Tue closed Civ Wed 160

DUBLIN

DUBLIN
Map 1 D4

Premier Collection

Glenogra Town House

★★★★★ GUEST HOUSE

---

tel: 01 6683661 **64 Merrion Rd, Ballsbridge**
email: info@glenogra.com **web:** www.glenogra.com
dir: *Opposite Royal Dublin Showgrounds & Intercontinental Hotel*

This fine 19th-century red brick house is situated across from the RDS and close to the Aviva Stadium. The bedrooms are comfortably appointed and include many thoughtful extras; three bedrooms are on the ground floor. There is an elegant drawing room and dining room, and the interesting breakfast menu offers a range of dishes. Secure parking is available, and The Aircoach and city-centre buses stop in Merrion Road; the DART rail is around the corner.

Rooms 13 en suite (1 fmly) (3 GF) S €59–€129; D €79–€249* **Facilities** STV TVL tea/coffee Direct Dial WiFi ⚓ **Parking** 10 **Notes** LB ⊗ Closed 23-28 Dec

Premier Collection

Harrington Hall

★★★★★ GUEST HOUSE

---

tel: 01 4753497 **69-70 Harcourt St**
email: harringtonhall@eircom.net **web:** www.harringtonhall.com
dir: *St Stephen's Green via O'Connell St, in Earlsfort Ter pass National Concert Hall & right into Hatch St, right into Harcourt St*

Harrington Hall is a Georgian house on a one-way street, just off St Stephen's Green in the centre of the city. The spacious bedrooms are well appointed and include comfortable suites. A lovely plasterwork ceiling adorns the relaxing drawing room, and an extensive breakfast menu is served in the basement dining room. A lift, porter service and limited off-street parking are available.

Rooms 28 en suite (3 fmly) (3 GF) **Facilities** STV FTV tea/coffee Direct Dial Lift Licensed WiFi ⚓ **Parking** 14 **Notes** ⊗ Closed 24-26 Dec

Charleville Lodge Guest House

★★★★ GUEST HOUSE

---

tel: 01 8386633 **268/272 North Circular Rd, Phibsborough**
email: info@charlevillelodge.ie **web:** www.charlevillelodge.ie
dir: *N from O'Connell St to Phibsborough, left fork at St Peter's Church, house 250mtrs on left*

Situated close to the city centre near Phoenix Park, this elegant terrace of Victorian houses provides accommodation of a high standard. The two interconnecting lounges are welcoming, and the smart dining room offers a choice of breakfasts. Bedrooms are very comfortable with pleasant decor, and there is a secure car park.

Rooms 30 en suite (2 fmly) (4 GF) **Facilities** STV FTV Lounge TVL Direct Dial Licensed WiFi ⚓ 18 **Conf** Max 10 Thtr 10 Class 10 Board 10 **Parking** 18 **Notes** LB ⊗

DUBLIN *continued*

Ardagh House

★★★ GUEST HOUSE

tel: 01 4977068 **1 Highfield Rd, Rathgar**
email: enquiries@ardahouse.com **web:** www.ardahouse.com
dir: *S of city centre through Rathmines*

Ardagh House is an early 19th-century house with modern additions, and stands in a premier residential area on the outskirts of the city, close to local restaurants and pubs. It retains many original features and has a relaxing lounge that overlooks a delightful garden. There is an attractive dining room where hearty breakfasts are served at individual tables. The comfortable bedrooms vary in size. Ample off-street parking is available.

Rooms 19 en suite (4 fmly) (1 GF) S €65-€110; D €80-€160 **Facilities** FTV TVL tea/coffee Direct Dial WiFi **Parking** 20 **Notes** ⊗ Closed 22 Dec-3 Jan

Leeson Bridge Guest House

★★★ GUEST HOUSE

tel: 01 6681000 & 6682255 **1 Upper Leeson St**
email: info@leesonbridgehouse.ie **web:** www.leesonbridgehouse.ie
dir: *At junct of N11 & N7, Leeson St*

This guest house is located right by Leeson Street Bridge, close to the city centre and is easily accessible from the ferry ports. Centred around a Georgian house, many of its original architectural features are retained. It offers a range of en suite bedroom styles, some with spa baths, sauna or galley kitchenette. Residents have access to ample parking at the rear. A take-away breakfast is offered to guests departing early in the morning.

Rooms 20 en suite (1 fmly) (2 GF) (10 smoking) **Facilities** STV FTV TVL tea/coffee Direct Dial Lift WiFi Fishing **Parking** 18 **Notes** LB ⊗

COUNTY GALWAY

CLIFDEN	Map 1 A4

Ardmore House (L589523)

★★★★ FARMHOUSE

tel: 095 21221 & 076 6030227 **Sky Rd**
email: info@ardmore-house.com **web:** www.ardmore-house.com
dir: *N59 from Galway to Clifden. Just N of Clifden centre follow signs on left for 'Sky Road', 5km, house on left*

Ardmore House is set among the wild scenery of Connemara, between hills and the sea on the Sky Road. Bedrooms are attractively decorated and the house is very comfortable throughout. A path leads from the house to the coast. A good hearty breakfast is provided featuring home baking.

Rooms 6 en suite (3 fmly) (6 GF) S €45-€55; D €70-€90* **Facilities** STV FTV TVL tea/coffee WiFi **Parking** 8 **Notes** LB ⊗ Closed Oct-Mar ⊜ 25 acres non-working

Faul House (L650475)

★★★★ FARMHOUSE

tel: 095 21239 **Ballyconneely Rd**
email: info@ireland.com **web:** www.faulhouse.com
dir: *1.5km from town right at rugby pitch signed Rockglen Hotel*

Faul House, a fine modern farmhouse, stands on a quiet and secluded road overlooking Clifden Bay. It is smart and comfortable with large bedrooms, all well furnished and with good views. Kathleen offers a hearty breakfast with home baking. There are Connemara ponies available for trekking.

Rooms 6 en suite (3 fmly) (3 GF) **Facilities** FTV TVL tea/coffee WiFi **Parking** 10 **Notes** Closed Nov-26 Mar ⊜ 35 acres sheep/ponies/hens/ducks

Mallmore House

★★★★ BED AND BREAKFAST

tel: 095 21460 **Ballyconneely Rd**
email: info@mallmore.com **web:** www.mallmorecountryhouse.com
dir: *1.5km from Clifden towards Ballyconneely take 1st right*

Mallmore House is a charming and lovingly maintained 17th-century house. It is situated close to the town and has a beautiful garden and mature woodland, and overlooks Clifden Bay. Bedrooms are spacious and very well appointed with antique furniture. The drawing room is delightfully relaxing with a turf fire. There is a wide choice available at breakfast including home baking and locally smoked fish. Mallmore is a lovely place to stay and enjoy the peace and quiet of Connemara.

Rooms 6 en suite (1 fmly) (6 GF) D €80-€90* **Facilities** FTV DVD Lounge tea/coffee WiFi 🔒 **Parking** 15 **Notes** ⊗ Closed Oct-1 Apr ⊜

Ben View House

★★★ GUEST HOUSE

tel: 095 21256 **Bridge St**
email: benviewhouse@ireland.com **web:** www.benviewhouse.com
dir: *Enter town on N59, opposite Esso fuel station*

This house is well located in the centre of the town with ample on-street parking. Dating from 1824, it offers good quality accommodation at a moderate cost. The breakfast room and lounge feature an old world atmosphere, with antique furniture and sparkling silverware in everyday use.

Rooms 10 rms (9 en suite) (3 fmly) **Facilities** TVL TV9B tea/coffee **Notes** ⊗

GALWAY	Map 1 B3

Marian Lodge Guest House

★★★★ GUEST HOUSE

tel: 091 521678 **Knocknacarra Rd, Salthill Upper**
email: celine@iol.ie **web:** www.marian-lodge.com
dir: *From Galway to Salthill on R336, through Salthill, 1st right after Spinnaker Hotel into Knocknacarra Rd*

This large modern house just 50 metres from the seafront, is an ideal base for both Galway City and the wilderness of Connemara. The comfortable bedrooms have orthopaedic beds and en suite facilities. There is also a cosy lounge and separate breakfast room where your welcoming host Celine is on hand to make recommendations for what to do with your day. There's plenty of parking available.

Rooms 6 en suite (4 fmly) **Facilities** STV TVL tea/coffee Direct Dial **Parking** 10 **Notes** ⊗ No Children 3yrs Closed 23-28 Dec

COUNTY KERRY

DINGLE (AN DAINGEAN)
Map 1 A2

Premier Collection

Castlewood House
★★★★★ ⌕ GUEST HOUSE

tel: 066 9152788 **The Wood**
web: www.castlewooddingle.com
dir: *R559 from Dingle, 0.5km from Aquarium*

Less than a ten minute stroll from the bustling centre of Dingle, Castlewood House is the perfect place to park the car and take in all the delights the town has to offer. Quality standards exceed the expectations of many a hotel, but it is the personal attention that proprietors Helen and Brian give their guests that really impresses here. Wonderfully spacious bedrooms are well-appointed and accessed by lift. Breakfast is a real highlight; so many options are available that choosing is difficult. The drawing room is a great place to relax after a day's walking and plan the next day's activities.

Rooms 12 en suite (3 fmly) (4 GF) S €70-€120; D €99-€210 **Facilities** STV tea/coffee Direct Dial Lift **Parking** 15 **Notes** LB ⊗ Closed 4-27 Dec & 4 Jan-4 Feb Civ Wed 20

Premier Collection

Gormans Clifftop House & Restaurant
★★★★★ ⊛ GUEST HOUSE

tel: 066 9155162 & 083 0033133 **Glaise Bheag, Ballydavid**
email: info@gormans-clifftophouse.com **web:** www.gormans-clifftophouse.com
dir: *R559 to An Mhuirioch, turn right at T-junct, N for 3km*

Sile and Vincent Gorman's guest house and restaurant is perched over the cliffs on the western tip of the Slea Head Peninsula near Ballydavid village. The beauty of the rugged coastline, rhythm of the sea and the sun going down on Smerwick Harbour can be enjoyed over a delicious dinner in the smart dining room. The menu includes produce from the garden, local seafood and lamb. Bedrooms are comfortably proportioned and thoughtfully equipped and have breathtaking views of the ocean or mountains, the ground-floor rooms are adapted for the less mobile. Bracing cliff walks can be accessed across from the house.

Rooms 8 en suite (2 fmly) (4 GF) D €110-€175* **Facilities** tea/coffee Dinner available Direct Dial Licensed WiFi Bicycles for hire **Parking** 15 **Notes** LB ⊗ Closed 24-26 Dec RS Oct-Mar reservation only Civ Wed 25

KENMARE
Map 1 B2

Muxnaw Lodge
★★★★ BED AND BREAKFAST

tel: 064 6641252 **Casletownbere Rd**
email: muxnaw@eircom.net **web:** www.muxnawlodge.ie

Located on the Castletownbere Road, within easy walking distance of Kenmare town, this warm and friendly house is a former hunting lodge dating from the early 19th century. It is set on an elevated site in mature gardens. Bedrooms and en suites are individually decorated, with some enjoying views of the Kenmare River. The lounge retains much of its original character, in addition to the bright and airy sun room. Ample parking is available to the rear.

Rooms 5 en suite (2 fmly) D €90* **Facilities** STV DVD TVL tea/coffee WiFi ⌕ 🔒 **Parking** 5 **Notes** ⊗ Closed 24-25 Dec ⊜

Sea Shore Farm Guest House
★★★★ GUEST HOUSE

tel: 064 6641270 & 6641675 **Tubrid**
email: seashore@eircom.net **web:** www.seashorekenmare.com
dir: *1.6km from Kenmare off N70 Ring of Kerry /Sneem road. Signed at junct N70 & N71*

Overlooking Kenmare Bay on the Ring of Kerry road, this modern farm guest house is close to town and has spacious bedrooms. Ground-floor rooms open onto the patio and have easier access. Guests are welcome to enjoy the farm walks through the fields to the shore, and nearby salmon and trout fishing on the Roughty River. There is a comfortable sitting room and dining room and a delightful garden.

Rooms 6 en suite (2 fmly) (2 GF) **Facilities** FTV Lounge tea/coffee Direct Dial WiFi ⌕ 18 🔒 **Extras** Speciality toiletries, snacks - complimentary **Parking** 10 **Notes** ⊗ No Children 5yrs Closed Nov-19 Mar

KILLARNEY
Map 1 B2

Premier Collection

Fairview Guest House
★★★★★ ⌕ GUEST HOUSE

tel: 064 6634164 **College St**
email: info@fairviewkillarney.com **web:** www.killarneyfairview.com
dir: *In town centre off College St*

Great attention to detail is demonstrated in the design of this smart guest house, handily located in the town centre close to the bus/railway station. Bedrooms include some with air conditioning and jacuzzi baths, and all are comfortable, with quality furnishings and fittings. There is a lift to all floors, and the impressive penthouse suite enjoys views over the town towards the Kerry mountains. There is a relaxing sitting area and the breakfast menu offers a selection of dishes cooked to order. Local activities and excursions include lake cruises, championship golf courses and the Killarney National Park.

Rooms 29 en suite (2 fmly) (1 GF) (2 smoking) **Facilities** STV DVD TVL tea/coffee Dinner available Direct Dial Lift Licensed WiFi ⌕ 18 Jacuzzi suites available **Parking** 11

KILLARNEY *continued*

Premier Collection

Foleys Town House

★★★★★ 🏠 GUEST HOUSE

tel: 064 6631217 **22/23 High St**
email: info@foleystownhouse.com **web:** www.foleystownhouse.com
dir: *In town centre*

Charming, individually-designed bedrooms are a feature of this well-established town house right in the centre of the town. Bedrooms are all well appointed and decorated with elegance. A warm welcome is assured at this property, which is family-owned and run by Carol Hartnett. Carol is also the chef in the adjoining popular bar and restaurant that specialises in seafood. There is a relaxing first-floor lounge reserved for guests, together with secure off-street parking to the rear.

Rooms 28 en suite S €60-€90; D €100-€150 **Facilities** STV Lounge TVL tea/coffee Dinner available Direct Dial Lift Licensed WiFi 🔒 **Parking** 60 **Notes** LB ⊗ Closed 6 Nov-16 Mar

Ashville House

★★★★ GUEST HOUSE

tel: 064 6636405 & 6636778 **Rock Rd**
email: info@ashvillekillarney.com **web:** www.ashvillekillarney.com
dir: *In town centre. Exit at N end of High St into Rock Rd*

This inviting house is just a stroll from the town centre and near the N22 (Tralee road). Bedrooms are comfortably furnished, and there is a pleasant sitting room and dining room. There is a private car park, and tours can be arranged.

Rooms 12 en suite (4 GF) S €50-€110; D €70-€150* **Facilities** STV FTV TVL tea/coffee Direct Dial WiFi ⚓ 18 🔒 **Parking** 13 **Notes** LB ⊗ Closed Nov-1 Mar

Kingfisher Lodge

★★★★ GUEST HOUSE

tel: 064 6637131 & 086 3741379 **Lewis Rd**
email: info@kingfisherlodgekillarney.com **web:** www.kingfisherlodgekillarney.com
dir: *Dublin link straight through 1st rdbt. Right at next rdbt towards town centre, Lodge on left*

This welcoming, modern guest house is home to the Carroll family. It is situated within walking distance of the town centre, and has comfortable and well-appointed bedrooms, all of which are en suite. Breakfast is served in the attractively decorated dining room and there is also a relaxing lounge and conservatory with WiFi. A drying room is available for fishing and wet gear. Golf, walking and fishing trips can be arranged. There is ample parking, and complimentary pick-up from the bus and train station are offered.

Rooms 10 en suite (1 fmly) (2 GF) **Facilities** STV FTV Lounge TVL tea/coffee Direct Dial WiFi ⚓ 18 🔒 Walking Fishing Horseriding Golf can be booked **Parking** 12 **Notes** LB Closed 29 Nov-13 Feb

Premier Collection

Carrig House Country House & Restaurant

★★★★★ ◎ 🍴 GUEST HOUSE

tel: 066 9769100 **Caragh Lake**
email: info@carrighouse.com **web:** www.carrighouse.com
dir: *N70 to Killorglin*

Located on the shores of Lake Caragh a short drive from Killorglin, amid natural green woodlands, this family-run house is the perfect retreat for a relaxing break. There is a range of room styles on offer, with some having lake views. Each is decorated to a high standard, with guest comfort in mind. Public rooms include elegant drawing rooms and cosy nooks. There is a true passion for food in evidence at dinner, where local seafood and seasonal produce is cooked and presented with care in the Lakeshore Restaurant. With over fifteen golf courses and a range of other outdoor pursuits available, there is something to suit all tastes.

Rooms 16 en suite **Facilities** Lounge TVL Dinner available Direct Dial Licensed WiFi ⚓ 18 Fishing **Extras** Bottled water **Parking** 20 **Notes** ⊗ No Children 8yrs Closed Oct-Feb Civ Wed 63

COUNTY KILKENNY

Butler House

★★★★ GUEST HOUSE

tel: 056 7765707 & 7722828 **Patrick St**
email: res@butler.ie **web:** www.butler.ie
dir: *In centre near Kilkenny Castle*

Once the dower house of Kilkenny Castle, this fine Georgian building fronts onto the main street, with secluded gardens at the rear, through which you stroll to have a full Irish breakfast in the Kilkenny Design Centre. A continental breakfast is served in the bedrooms, which all feature contemporary decor. There is a comfortable foyer lounge and conference/banqueting suites.

Rooms 13 en suite (4 fmly) **Facilities** STV FTV Lounge tea/coffee Direct Dial WiFi 🔒 **Extras** Bottled water - complimentary; safe in all rooms **Conf** Max 120 Thtr 120 Class 40 Board 40 **Parking** 24 **Notes** ⊗ Closed 24-29 Dec Civ Wed 80

CO LAOIS

Mahers B&B

★★★★ BED AND BREAKFAST

tel: 087 212 9236 **Beech Av, Rathleague**
email: mahersbandb@rathleague.com **web:** www.mahers-bnb.com

This Georgian home has been creatively renovated with attention to every detail, keeping original features where possible together with every modern facility. Built in the late 1700s, it has been in the Maher family for over 100 years. Outbuildings include storage for bikes, fishing tackle and hiking gear, and there is even an ornamental plant nursery on the site. Above all, it is the natural warm welcome from the family that endears visitors to this fine family home.

Rooms 4 rms (2 en suite) (2 pri facs) (3 fmly) **Facilities** STV FTV TVL tea/coffee WiFi ch fac ⚓ 18 🔒 **Conf** Max 20 Thtr 20 Class 16 Board 20 **Parking** 10

COUNTY LOUTH

CARLINGFORD
Map 1 D4

Ghan House

★★★★ ◉◉ 🍴 GUEST ACCOMMODATION

tel: 042 9373682
email: info@ghanhouse.com **web:** www.ghanhouse.com
dir: M1 junct 18 signed Carlingford, 5mtrs on left after 50kph speed sign

Dating from 1727, Ghan House oozes charm and comfort. Set in two acres of walled gardens, the house is within 50 metres of the centre of the medieval village of Carlingford, making it an ideal base for walking and touring the Cooley peninsula. Bedrooms are warm and well appointed, either in the house itself or in a converted barn in the grounds. Comfortable public rooms feature log fires and relaxing armchairs. Food is an important element of the business, and a successful cookery school has operated here for many years. Dinner has an emphasis on artisan produce and the renowned Cooley lamb. Breakfast is a treat, with a choice of fruit compôtes and preserves.

Rooms 4 en suite 8 annexe en suite (3 fmly) (4 GF) S €75-€95; D €150-€250*
Facilities FTV iPod docking station Lounge tea/coffee Dinner available Licensed WiFi ⅃ 18 Riding 🔔 **Extras** Home-made biscuits **Conf** Max 50 Thtr 50 Class 26 Board 32 **Parking** 35 **Notes** LB ⊗ Civ Wed 50

COUNTY MAYO

CASTLEBAR
Map 1 B4

Lough Lannagh Lodge

★★★ GUEST ACCOMMODATION

tel: 094 9027111 **Old Westport Rd**
email: info@loughlannagh.ie **web:** www.loughlannagh.ie
dir: N5/N60/N84 to Castlebar. At ring road follow signs for N5 Westport, signed Lough Lannagh village approaching Westport rdbt

Lough Lannagh Lodge is in a delightful wooded area within walking distance of Castlebar. There is a conference centre, fitness centre, tennis, table tennis, laundry and drying facilities, a private kitchen, and many activities for children. Bedrooms are well appointed and breakfast is served in the café. Dinner is available by appointment for groups.

Rooms 24 en suite (24 fmly) (12 GF) S €69; D €89* **Facilities** FTV Lounge TVL Dinner available Direct Dial WiFi ⅃ 18 🔔 **Conf** Max 100 Thtr 100 Class 54 Board 34 **Parking** 24 **Notes** LB ⊗ Closed mid Dec-mid Jan RS Sun no arrivals Civ Wed 100

WESTPORT
Map 1 B4

Bertra House *(L903823)*

★★★ FARMHOUSE

tel: 098 64833 & 086 0667233 **Thornhill, Murrisk**
email: bertrahse@eircom.net **web:** www.bertrahouse.com
dir: W of Westport off R335, near Croagh Patrick on L1833

This attractive bungalow overlooks the Bertra beach of Clew Bay, at the foot of Croagh Patrick, locally known as "The Reek". Located about a 10 minute drive from Westport, it is an ideal location for browsing the shops and touring the North of Mayo. Four bedrooms are en suite with the fifth having a dedicated bathroom. Breakfast is generous and features Margaret Gill's home baking, some of which might just be available with a cup of tea on your arrival in the cosy lounge!

Rooms 5 rms (4 en suite) (1 pri facs) (1 fmly) (5 GF) S €40-€50; D €60-€70
Facilities FTV Lounge TVL tea/coffee WiFi **Parking** 7 **Notes** LB ⊗ No Children 6yrs Closed 15 Nov-15 Mar 🐑 40 acres beef/sheep

COUNTY MEATH

SLANE
Map 1 D4

Premier Collection

Tankardstown

★★★★★ ◉◉ 🍴 GUEST ACCOMMODATION

tel: 041 9824621
email: info@tankardstown.ie **web:** www.tankardstown.ie
dir: N51 (Navan-Slane road), take turn directly opposite main entrance to Slane Castle, signed Kells. Continue for 5km

Tankardstown is a magical place. Set in 80 acres of parkland, it has many strings to its bow. The main house is host to elegant rooms, with others in cottages in the converted stableyard. Each is individually decorated to a very high standard. The cottages have the benefit of spacious kitchens and living areas, ideal for longer stays. The property is also host to the award-winning Brabazon, a fine dining restaurant, and there's a bistro for more casual fare. Excellent breakfasts are served in the main house, with the option of having it delivered to the cottages. This fine property is ideal for family gatherings and intimate wedding celebrations.

Rooms 7 en suite 15 annexe en suite (6 fmly) (2 GF) S €100-€250; D €200-€350
Facilities STV FTV DVD Lounge TVL tea/coffee Dinner available Direct Dial Licensed WiFi ⅃ 36 Fishing 🔔 Hot tub **Extras** Still water - free; mini-bar - chargeable **Conf** Max 150 Thtr 150 Class 80 Board 50 **Parking** 200 **Notes** Civ Wed 200

COUNTY MONAGHAN

GLASLOUGH
Map 1 C5

Premier Collection

The Castle at Castle Leslie Estate

★★★★★ GUEST HOUSE

tel: 047 88100
email: info@castleleslie.com **web:** www.castleleslie.com
dir: M1 junct 14, N2 to Monaghan then N12 onto R185 for Glaslough

Set in 1000 acres of rolling countryside, The Castle is the centre of the Leslie Estate which has been in the family since the 1660s. Bedrooms are all decorated in keeping with the age and style of the period, and are ideal for relaxing breaks where guests enjoy the peace and tranquillity of the property without any interference from televisions or other distractions. With a successful equestrian centre and a private fishing lake, this is an ideal location for those who enjoy country pursuits.

Rooms 20 rms (19 en suite) (1 pri facs) **Facilities** Lounge TVL Direct Dial Lift Licensed WiFi ⌂ ⌂ 18 Fishing Riding Snooker Spa treatment rooms Private cinema Falconry **Extras** Speciality toiletries **Conf** Max 280 Thtr 260 Class 150 Board 65 **Parking** 100 **Notes** LB ⊗ Closed 22-27 Dec Civ Wed 90

COUNTY SLIGO

BALLYSADARE
Map 1 B5

Seashore House

★★★ BED AND BREAKFAST

tel: 071 9167827 **Lisduff**
email: info@seashoreguests.com **web:** www.seashoreguests.com
dir: N4 onto N59 W at Ballisadore, in 4km Seashore signed on right. Turn down road, 600mtrs on right

Seashore House is an attractive dormer bungalow in a quiet seashore location. A comfortable lounge with open turf fire and sunny conservatory-dining room look out over attractive landscaped gardens and further sea and mountain views. Bedrooms are attractively appointed and comfortable, and there is also a tennis court and bicycle storage. Credit cards only accepted during high season.

Rooms 4 en suite (2 fmly) (2 GF) S €45-€55; D €80 **Facilities** STV FTV TVL WiFi ⌂ ⌂ 18 ⚓ **Parking** 6 **Notes** LB ⊗ No Children ⊛

ENNISCRONE (INISHCRONE)
Map 1 B5

Waterfront House

★★★★ ⊛ ⌂ RESTAURANT WITH ROOMS

tel: 096 37120 **Sea Front, Cliff Rd**
email: relax@waterfronthouse.ie **web:** www.waterfronthouse.ie

Located less than a five minute stroll from the town, Waterfront House has great views of the beach and Killalla Bay. This is a warm and friendly place, with proprietor Martina and her loyal team going to great lengths to ensure guests enjoy their stay. Bedrooms are spacious and very comfortably appointed. The award-winning restaurant has a well-deserved reputation, where the menu features fresh seafood, but there are plenty of other options available. Breakfast is a particular highlight in terms of range and food quality. This is an ideal location for the golf and surfing facilities in the area, or the famed Warm Seaweed Baths!

Rooms 11 en suite **Facilities** STV tea/coffee Dinner available Lift WiFi ⌂ 18 **Parking** 16 **Notes** ⊗

STRANDHILL
Map 1 B5

Strandhill Lodge and Suites

★★★★ GUEST HOUSE

tel: 071 9122122 **Top Rd**
email: info@strandhilllodgeandsuites.com **web:** http://strandhilllodgeandsuites.com
dir: From Sligo onto R292 for Strandhill

Located in the centre of Strandhill village, just five kilometres from Sligo, this property offers particularly spacious accommodation, finished to a very high standard. Many of the rooms have stunning views of the bay. Public areas are open plan in design, with a bright and airy breakfast room where continental breakfast is served. This is an ideal property for those playing golf or participating in the many other pursuits available in the region. There is a meeting room on the first floor, and ample parking to the rear. A number of cosy pubs and quality restaurants are located in the village.

Rooms 21 en suite 1 annexe en suite (7 fmly) (8 GF) S €59-€119; D €79-€169* **Facilities** STV FTV DVD iPod docking station Lounge TVL tea/coffee Direct Dial Lift WiFi ⌂ ⌂ 18 Fishing Riding ⚓ **Extras** Bottled water **Conf** Max 20 Thtr 20 Class 10 Board 8 **Parking** 22 **Notes** LB ⊗ Closed Jan-5 Feb

COUNTY TIPPERARY

CASHEL
Map 1 C3

Ashmore House

★★★ BED AND BREAKFAST

tel: 062 61286 & 0861 037010 **John St**
email: info@ashmorehouse.com **web:** www.ashmorehouse.com
dir: M8 exit 8 to town centre, into John St opposite Cashel Palace Hotel, house 100mtrs on right

Ashmore House is a Georgian building set in a colourfully planted walled garden, right in the centre of the town, within walking distance of the Rock of Cashel. There is secure parking at the rear. Guests have use of a large sitting and dining room, and bedrooms come in a variety of sizes from big family rooms to a more compact double. Children are welcome and guests have WiFi access.

Rooms 5 en suite (2 fmly) S €45-€55; D €70-€80 **Facilities** FTV TVL tea/coffee Dinner available WiFi **Parking** 10 **Notes** ⊗

THURLES
Map 1 C3

Premier Collection

The Castle

★★★★★ BED AND BREAKFAST

tel: 0504 44324 **Twomileborris**
email: bandb@thecastletmb.com **web:** www.thecastletmb.com
dir: 7km E of Thurles. On N75 200mtrs W of Twomileborris at Castle

Pierce and Joan are very welcoming hosts. Their fascinating house, sheltered by a 16th-century tower house, has been in the Duggan family for 200 years. Bedrooms are comfortable and spacious, there is a relaxing lounge, and the dining room overlooks the delightful garden. Golf, fishing, hill walking, and traditional pubs and restaurants are all nearby. Dinner is available by arrangement.

Rooms 4 en suite (3 fmly) **Facilities** STV FTV TVL tea/coffee Dinner available WiFi ⌂ ⌂ ⌂ 18 Fishing Pool table ⚓ **Conf** Max 40 Board 20 **Parking** 30 **Notes** ⊗

Inch House Country House & Restaurant

★★★★★ ◉ ♟ GUEST HOUSE

tel: 0504 51348 & 51261
email: mairin@inchhouse.ie **web:** www.inchhouse.ie
dir: 6.5km NE of Thurles on R498

This lovely Georgian house, at the heart of a working farm, was built in 1720 and is lovingly maintained by the Egan family. The elegant drawing room ceiling is particularly outstanding among the grand public rooms, and the five spacious bedrooms are delightfully appointed. Reservations are essential in the fine restaurant, where an imaginative choice of freshly prepared dishes is on offer, with an emphasis on local produce. Some of the produce from the kitchen is available in a number of specialist outlets throughout the country.

Rooms 5 en suite (1 fmly) **Facilities** TVL tea/coffee Dinner available Direct Dial Licensed WiFi **Parking** 40 **Notes** ⊗ Closed 2wks Xmas RS Sun & Mon Restaurant closed during day Civ Wed 50

TIPPERARY
Map 1 C3

Aisling

★★★ BED AND BREAKFAST

tel: 087 227 8230 **Glen of Aherlow**
email: ladygreg@oceanfree.net **web:** www.aislingbedandbreakfast.com
dir: From town centre R664 for 2.4km, past golf club

Aisling is close to Tipperary on the R664, Glen of Aherlow road. The bedrooms are well furnished and attractively decorated. There is a comfortable guest sitting room and a delightful garden with patio seating. Marian and Bob are helpful hosts, happy to arrange day trips, and provide maps and information on the locality.

Rooms 5 rms (3 en suite) (2 pri facs) (2 fmly) (5 GF) S €40; D €80* **Facilities** STV FTV DVD Lounge TVL WiFi ♿ 🔒 **Extras** Snack on arrival - complimentary **Parking** 5 **Notes** LB ⊛

COUNTY WATERFORD

TRAMORE
Map 1 C2

Seacourt

★★★★ BED AND BREAKFAST

tel: 051 386244 **Tivoli Rd**
email: seacourthouse@gmail.com **web:** www.seacourt.ie
dir: Leave Waterford City on R675 to Tramore. Over 2 rdbts, at 3rd rdbt (boat in middle) straight over, 1st B&B on left

Seacourt is a very comfortable house situated in the seaside town close to Splashworld, the beach and Tramore Race Course, with many other tourist attractions available locally. Bedrooms are comfortably furnished with a spacious family room on the ground floor. There is a cosy guest sitting room, a wide choice of cooked breakfast served in the dining room, and ample off-street parking is available.

Rooms 5 rms (5 pri facs) (1 fmly) (1 GF) **Facilities** STV TVL tea/coffee WiFi ♿ 18 🔒 **Parking** 10 **Notes** No Children 6yrs Closed Oct-2 Apr

WATERFORD
Map 1 C2

Belmont House

★★★ BED AND BREAKFAST

tel: 051 832174 **Belmont Rd, Rosslare Rd, Ferrybank**
email: belmonthouse@eircom.net
dir: Exit N25 at Luffany rdbt onto N29. At Slieverue rdbt follow R711 (Waterford N). Belmont House 4km from junct, 2nd B&B on left after service station

This comfortable bed and breakfast is within walking distance of the city centre. A hospitality tray is available in the relaxing guest sitting room and a hearty breakfast is served in the dining room at separate tables. Bedrooms are well appointed and offer good quality and space.

Rooms 6 rms (4 en suite) (3 fmly) **Facilities** TVL WiFi **Parking** 6 **Notes** ⊗ No Children 7yrs Closed Nov-Apr ⊛

COUNTY WEXFORD

CAMPILE
Map 1 C2

Kilmokea Country Manor & Gardens

★★★★★ ♟ GUEST ACCOMMODATION

tel: 051 388109 & 086 6641946 **Great Island**
email: stay@kilmokea.com **web:** www.kilmokea.com
dir: R733 from New Ross to Campile, right before village for Great Island & Kilmokea Gardens

This fine property is an 18th-century former rectory, lovingly restored and maintained by the hospitable Emma Hewlett and her husband Mark. The house is located in wooded and beautifully landscaped gardens that are in themselves a popular visitor attraction. In the grounds there is a spa with an indoor heated swimming pool, and aromatherapy treatments are available. The bedrooms are richly furnished in a mix of styles, but all have particularly comfortable beds. The drawing and reading rooms reflect 18th-century style and proportions, and there is an honesty bar. Dinner is available by prior arrangement, in what was the original dining room of the house, or in the conservatory in summer.

Rooms 4 en suite 2 annexe en suite (1 fmly) (2 GF) S €75-€90; D €150-€200 **Facilities** STV Lounge TVL TV2B tea/coffee Dinner available Direct Dial Licensed WiFi ch fac 🔒 ♿ ♿ ♿ 18 Fishing Riding Sauna Gym Pool table 🔒 Aromatherapy treatments Meditation room Jacuzzi **Conf** Max 75 Thtr 40 Class 30 Board 25 **Parking** 23 **Notes** LB RS Nov-end Jan Civ Wed 60

Premier Collection

Clonganny House

★★★★★ ◎◎ GUEST ACCOMMODATION

tel: 053 948 2111 **Ballygarrett**
email: info@clonganny.com **web:** www.clonganny.com
dir: *Just off R742 between Ballygarrett & Kilmuckridge*

Located 3km south of Ballygarrett village, Clonganny House is a recent addition to the area. Brona and Phillipe Brillant, who ran a similar property in England for a number of years, have painstakingly restored this 1825 house to its former glory. The breakfast room and lounge retain many of the original architectural features, and are beautifully presented with guest comfort and relaxation in mind. The accommodation features four individually decorated double rooms all at ground floor level, some with French windows overlooking the walled garden. There are walks set among the ten acres of woodland grounds. Breakfast is served in the charming dining room, which is also the venue for some outstanding cooking at dinner, overseen by Phillippe. Please note: The restaurant is only open to non-residents on Friday and Saturday. Booking is essential.

Rooms 4 annexe en suite (4 GF) D €160–€180 **Facilities** FTV iPod docking station Lounge tea/coffee Dinner available Licensed WiFi ⅃ 18 🛎 **Parking** 13 **Notes** ⊗ No Children 16yrs

Premier Collection

Killiane Castle Country House & Farm *(T058168)*

★★★★★ 🍃 FARMHOUSE

tel: 053 9158885 **Drinagh**
email: info@killianecastle.com **web:** www.killianecastle.com
dir: *Off N25 between Wexford and Rosslare*

This 17th-century house is run by the Mernagh family on a working dairy farm at Drinagh south of Wexford town. The house is part of a 13th-century Norman castle. The comfortable reception rooms and bedrooms are beautifully furnished. Many have been recently refurbished to a very high standard, in classic decor schemes. Breakfast is a real treat and includes farm produce and feature homemade baking and preserves.

Rooms 9 en suite (2 fmly) (2 GF) S €75–€85; D €110–€130 **Facilities** STV FTV DVD iPod docking station Lounge TVL Dinner available Licensed WiFi 🌊 ⅃ 18 🛎 Driving range 18 hole pitch & putt **Parking** 10 **Notes** ⊗ Closed Dec-Feb 230 acres dairy/sheep

Aldridge Lodge Restaurant and Guesthouse

★★★★ ◎◎ RESTAURANT WITH ROOMS

tel: 051 389116 **Duncannon**
email: info@aldridgelodge.com **web:** www.aldridgelodge.com

Just a 45-minute drive from the ferryport at Rosslare, Aldridge Lodge is an ideal first night stop-off following an afternoon sailing from the UK, and it's tempting to return for the final night of a visit to Ireland given the warm welcome. It makes a great base for exploring the many attractions and activities of The Hook Peninsula. Hosts Joanne and Billy, who is also the chef, take a keen interest in their guests – it's no wonder so many of them return, making advance weekend reservations essential. While each of the three guest rooms is warm and cosy, what brings most visitors here is the food. Billy has a strong reputation for his use of local ingredients and seasonality is also very much to the fore. The breakfast experience is also a feature – quality ingredients cooked with skill and care in a relaxed environment.

Rooms 3 en suite S fr €85; D €160–€170* (incl.dinner) **Facilities** FTV tea/coffee Dinner available WiFi **Notes** ⊗ Closed 6 Jan-1 Feb RS Mon-Tue closed

Tynte House *(N870015)*

★★★★ FARMHOUSE

tel: 045 401561
email: info@tyntehouse.com **web:** www.tyntehouse.com
dir: *N81 at Hollywood Cross, right at Dunlavin, follow finger signs for Tynte House, past market house in town centre*

This 19th-century farmhouse stands in the square of the quiet country village of Dunlavin, in the west of County Wicklow. The friendly hosts have carried out a lot of restoration resulting in cosy bedrooms and a relaxing guest sitting room. Breakfast, featuring Caroline's home baking, is a highlight of a visit to this house. An all-weather tennis court is located in the grounds, together with an indoor games room. This house is an ideal base for touring the Wicklow and Kildare areas with their many sporting attractions.

Rooms 7 en suite (2 fmly) **Facilities** Lounge TVL tea/coffee Direct Dial WiFi ch fac 🎾 ⅃ 18 Playground Games room **Parking** 16 **Notes** Closed 16 Dec-9 Jan 200 acres beef/tillage

COUNTY MAPS

England

1 Bedfordshire
2 Berkshire
3 Bristol
4 Buckinghamshire
5 Cambridgeshire
6 Greater Manchester
7 Herefordshire
8 Hertfordshire
9 Leicestershire
10 Northamptonshire
11 Nottinghamshire
12 Rutland
13 Staffordshire
14 Warwickshire
15 West Midlands
16 Worcestershire

Scotland

17 City of Glasgow
18 Clackmannanshire
19 East Ayrshire
20 East Dunbartonshire
21 East Renfrewshire
22 Perth & Kinross
23 Renfrewshire
24 South Lanarkshire
25 West Dunbartonshire

Wales

26 Blaenau Gwent
27 Bridgend
28 Caerphilly
29 Denbighshire
30 Flintshire
31 Merthyr Tydfil
32 Monmouthshire
33 Neath Port Talbot
34 Newport
35 Rhondda Cynon Taff
36 Torfaen
37 Vale of Glamorgan
38 Wrexham

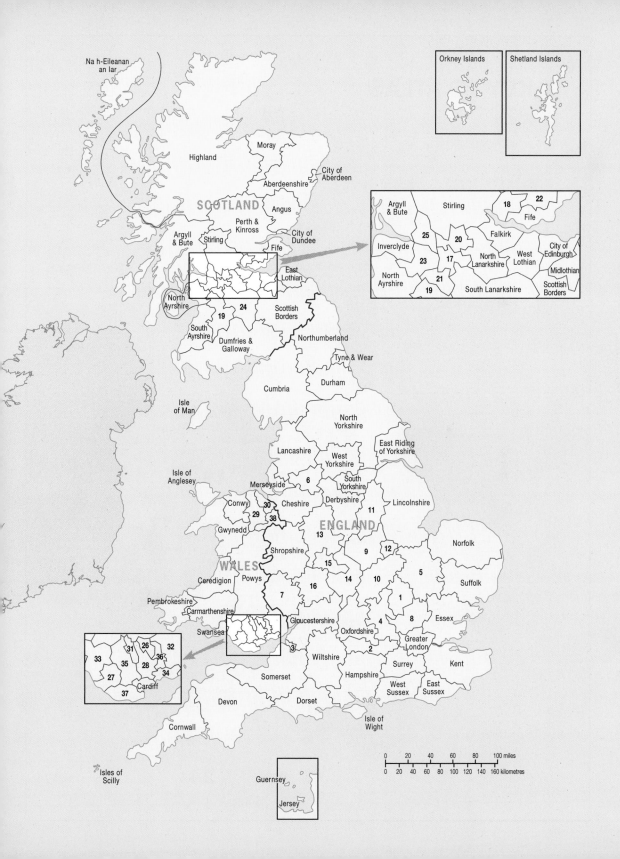

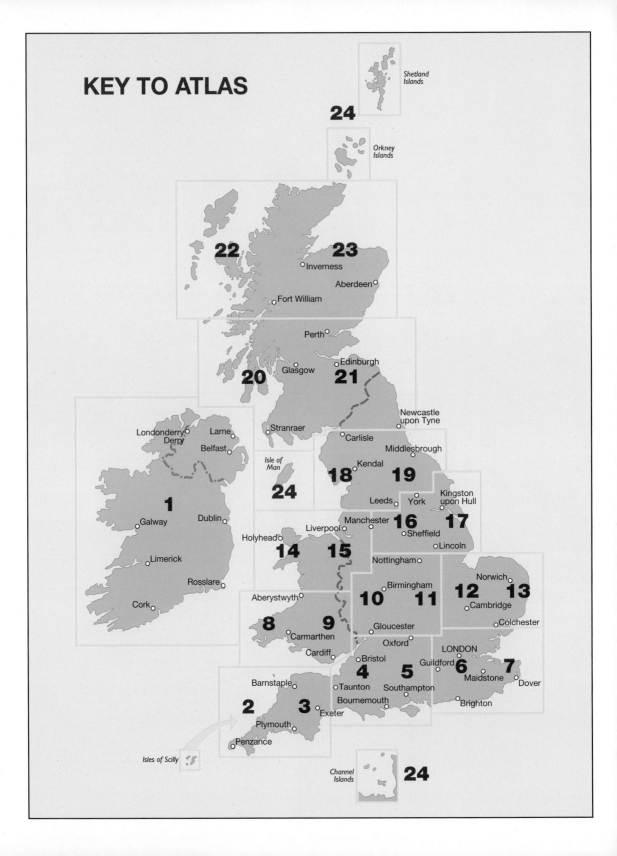

KEY TO ATLAS

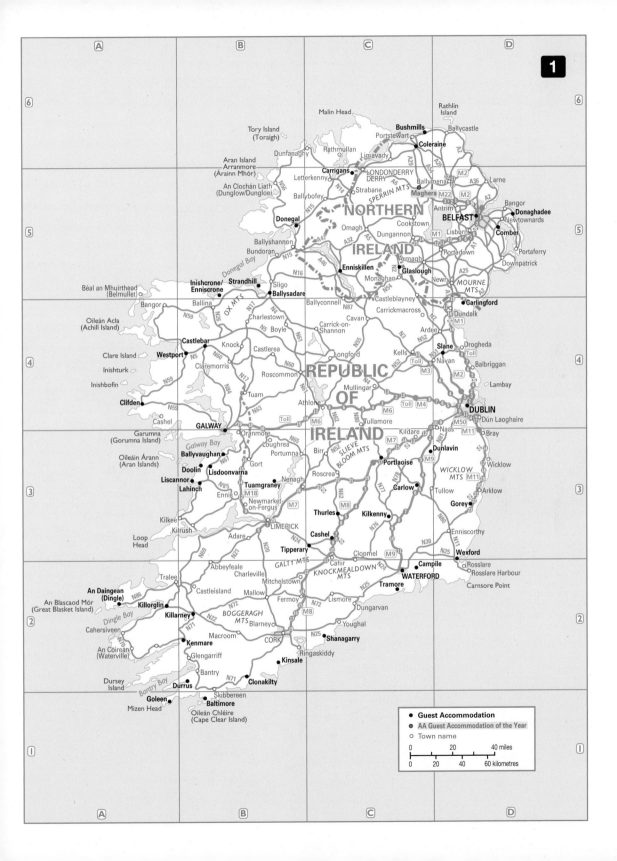

Legend

M6	Motorway/toll motorway
	Motorway junction full/restricted. Service area
A33	Primary route single/dual carriageway
A34	Other A road single/dual carriageway
B3409	B road
	Unclassified road
V	Vehicle ferry
C	Fast vehicle ferry or catamaran
● Stamford	Guest Accommodation
● Brighton	AA Guest Accommodation Award Winners
○ King's Cliffe	Town/Village name
	National boundary
ESSEX	English county name & boundary
CONWY	Welsh county name & boundary
MORAY	Scottish county name & boundary
	National Park

ISLES OF SCILLY
Bryher Tresco St Martin's
New Grimsby Higher Town
Hugh Town St Mary's
Middle Town Old Town
St Agnes
ISLES OF SCILLY TO SV
SV

SW

Lundy

Hartland Point
Hartland

Medd
Morwenstow

Kilkhampton

Bude Bay
Bude Str

Widemouth Bay

Crackington Haven Week
St Mary

Boscastle
Tintagel A39

Delabole
Port Gaverne Camelford Laneast
Port Isaac Pendoggett Bolventor
Polzeath St Tudy BODMIN MOOR
Rock St Kew A39 Blisland A30
Harlyn Padstow A389 Wadebridge Bolventor
Porthcothan CORNWALL St Cleer
Mawgan Porth St Mawgan Bodmin Dobwalls
St Columb Major Lanivet A38
Newquay Liskeard
West Pentire St Keyne
Roche Bugle Lostwithiel
Perranporth Summercourt Luxulyan Pelynt
Mitchell St Blazey Par
Ladock St Austell Bodinnick
St Agnes Marazanvose St Stephen Fowey Polperro
Porthtowan Grampound Polruan
Portreath Pentewan
St Day Truro Tregony Mevagissey
St Ives Gwithian Carnon Downs Gorran Haven
St Ives Bay Redruth Ruan High Lanes
Zennor Lelant Camborne St Just-in-Roseland Portloe
Hayle A393 Veryan
Marazion Penryn Portscatho
Leedstown Falmouth St Mawes
St Just Penzance Helston Constantine Mawnan Smith
Newlyn Perranuthnoe Gweek Manaccan
Land's End St Buryan Praa Sands Porthleven
Sennen Mousehole St Keverne
Porthcurno Treen Mount's Bay Mullion Coverack
Lizard Cadgwith
Lizard Point

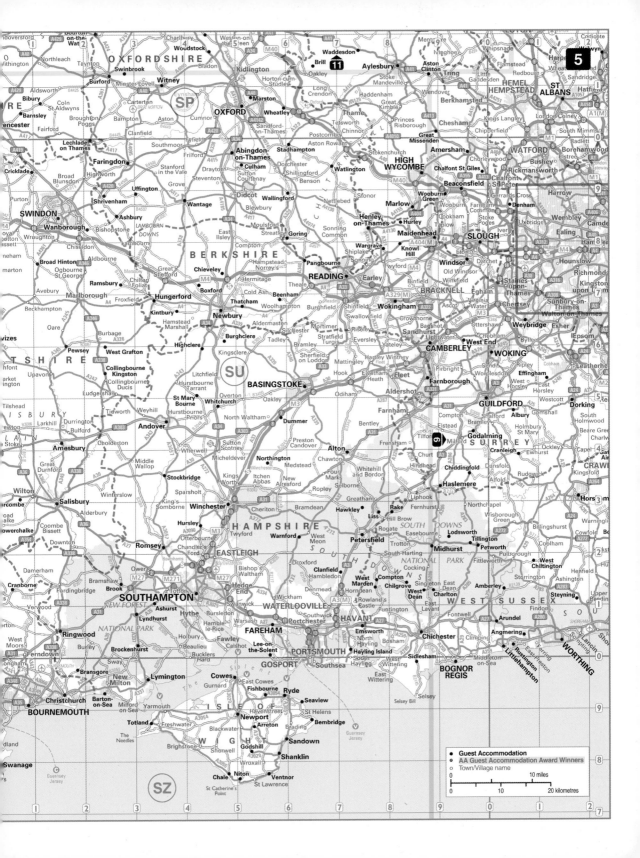

8

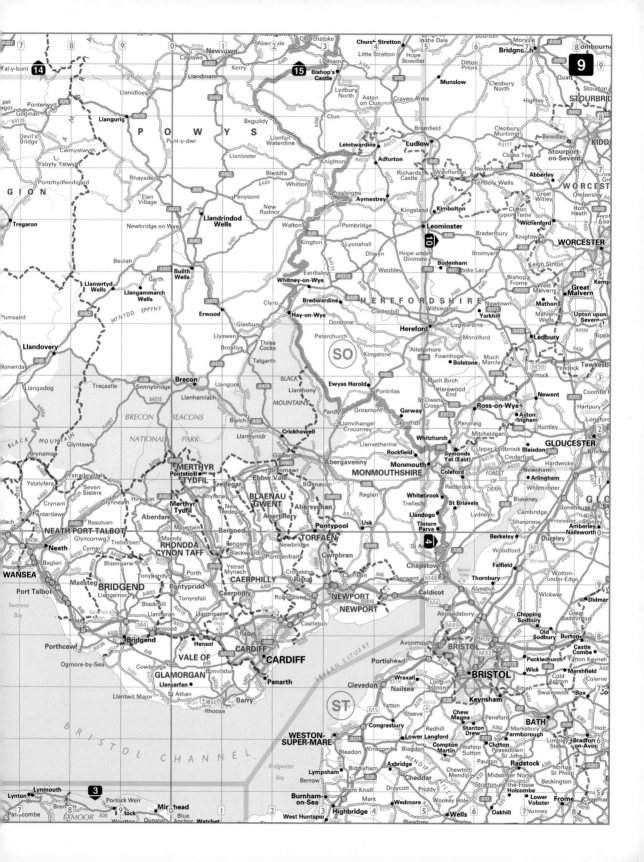

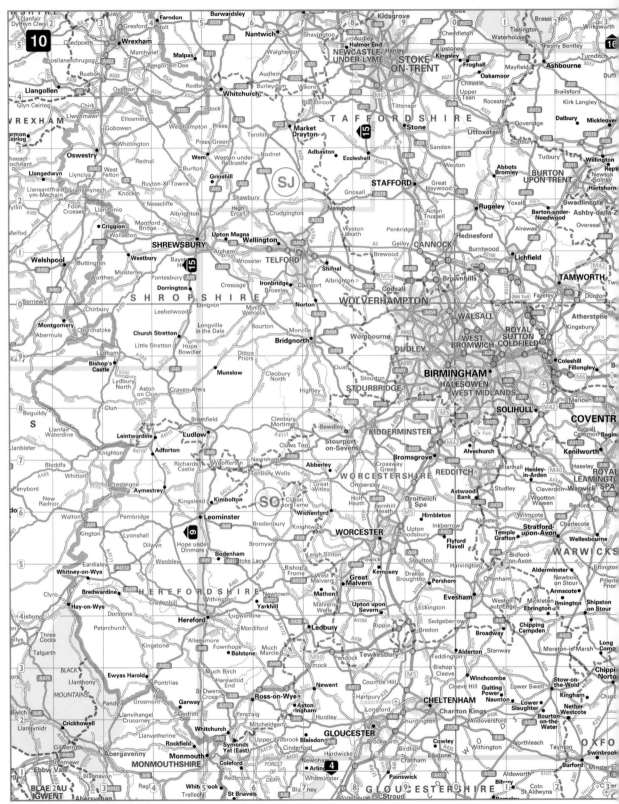

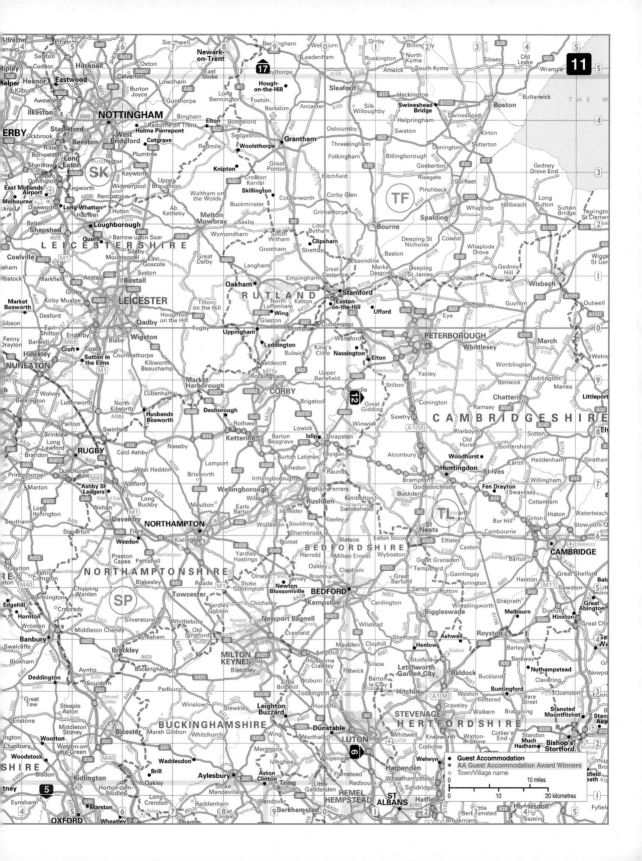

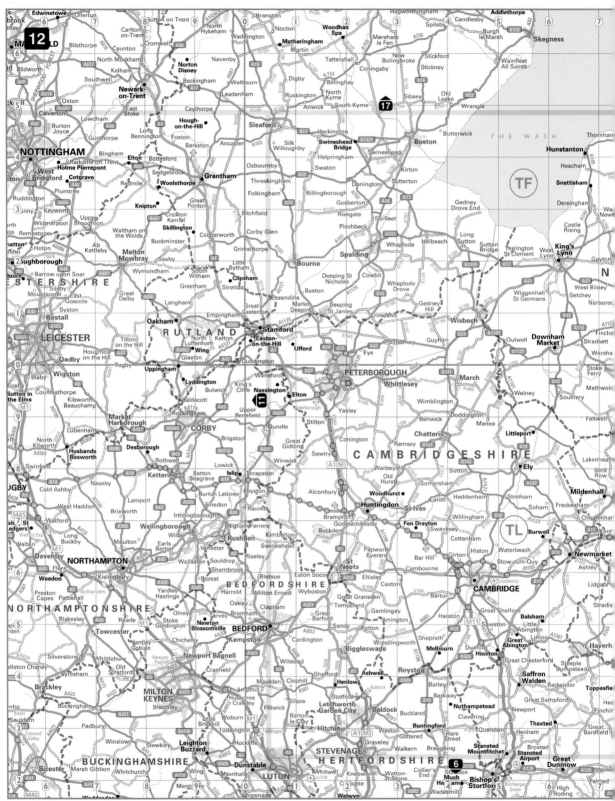

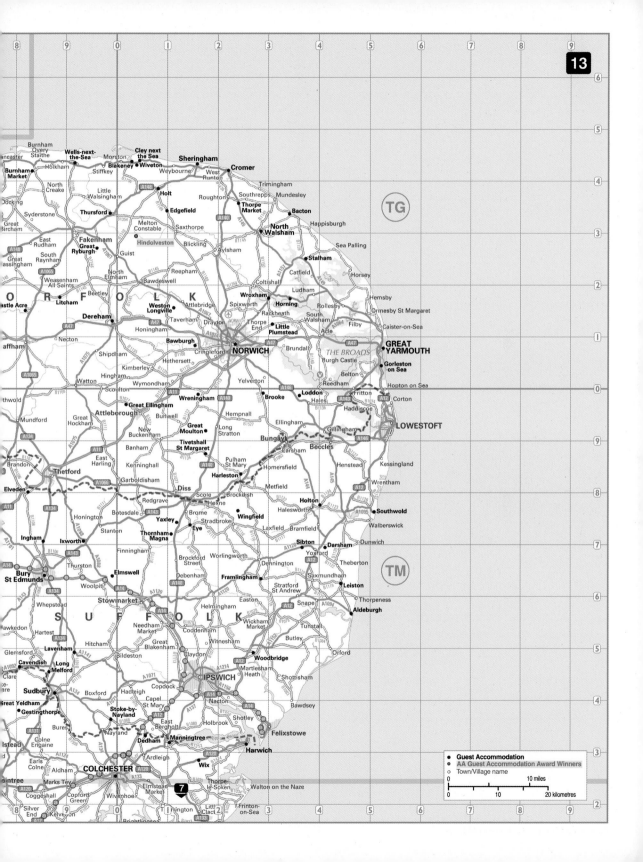

14

For continuation pages refer to numbered arrows

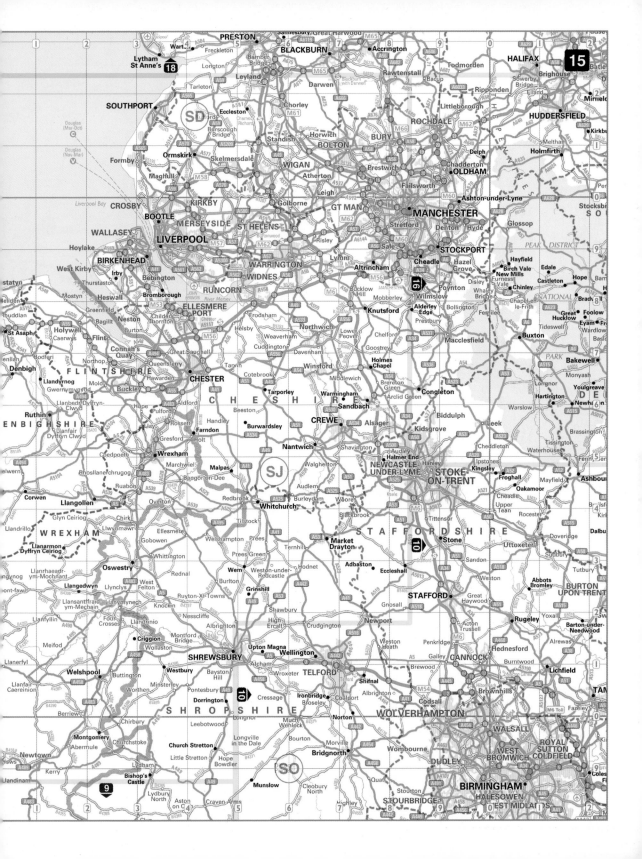

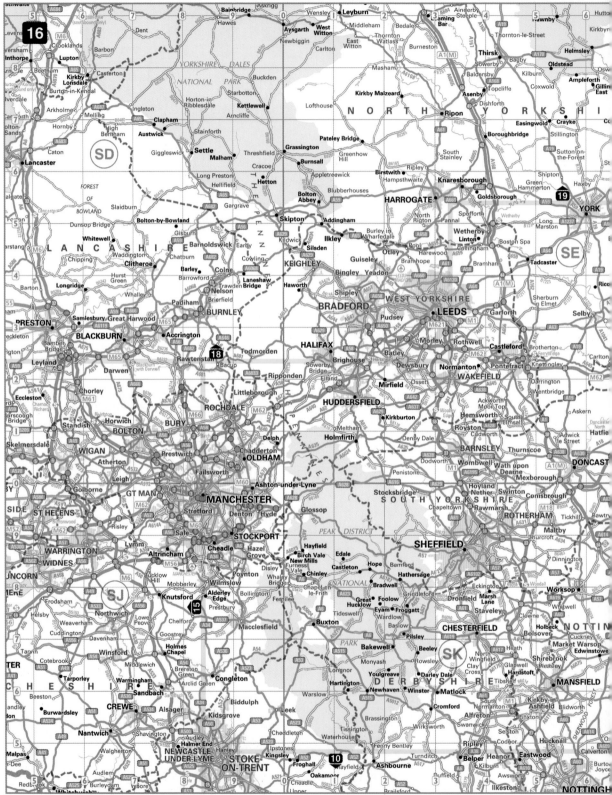

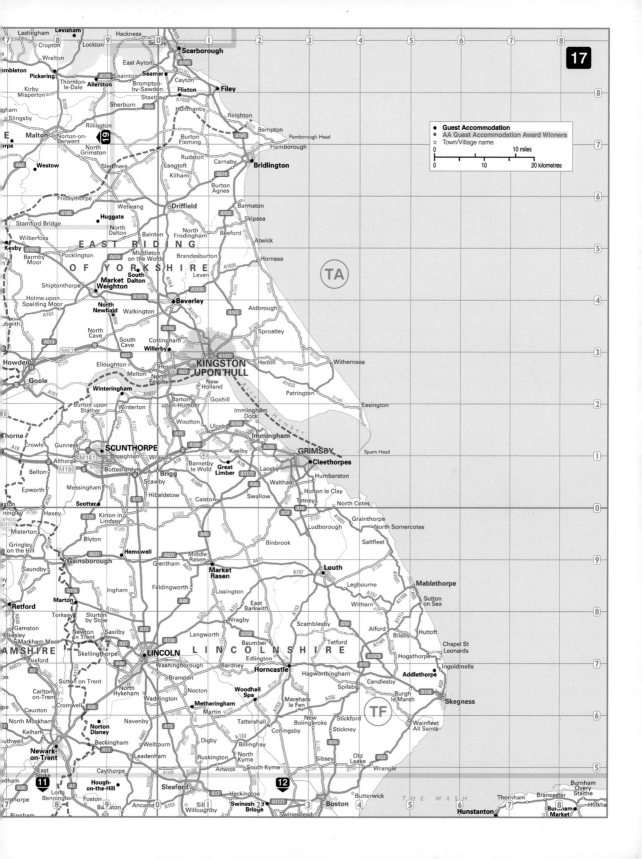

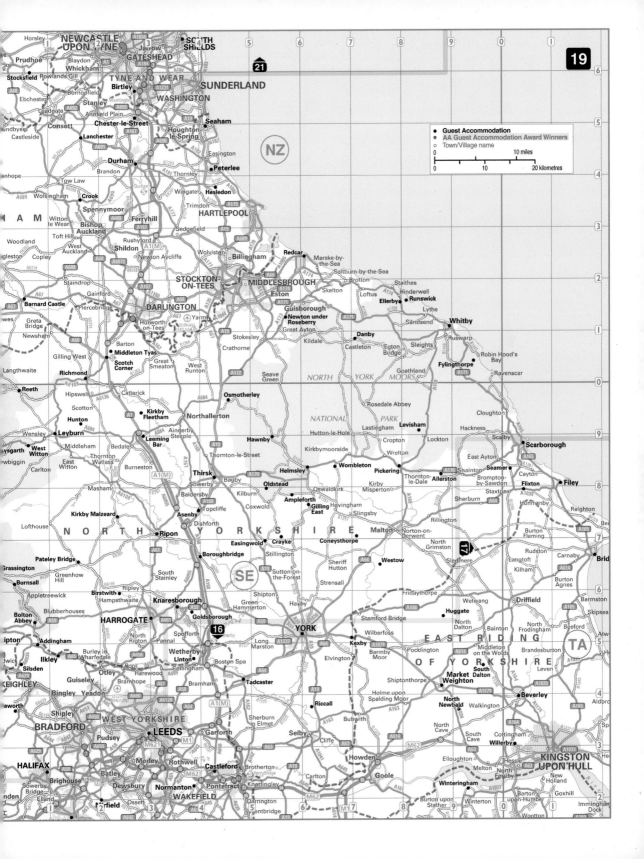

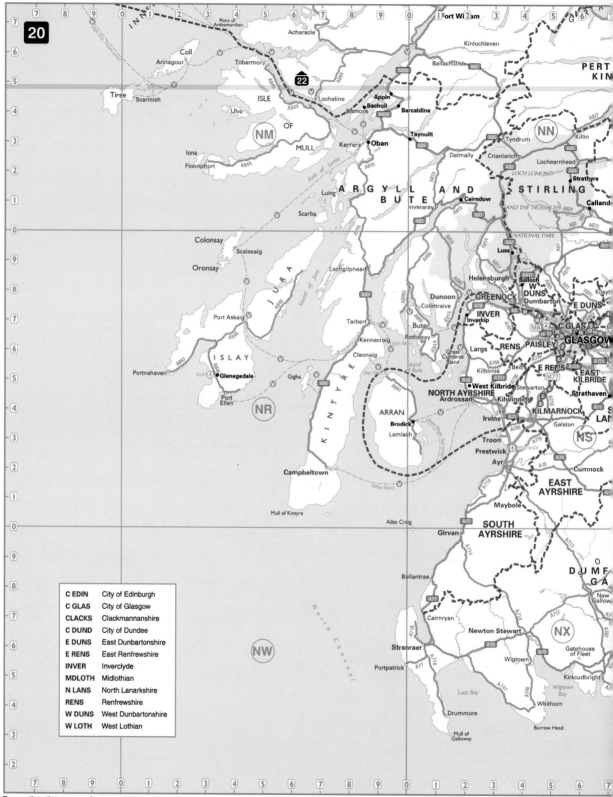

20

C EDIN	City of Edinburgh
C GLAS	City of Glasgow
CLACKS	Clackmannanshire
C DUND	City of Dundee
E DUNS	East Dunbartonshire
E RENS	East Renfrewshire
INVER	Inverclyde
MDLOTH	Midlothian
N LANS	North Lanarkshire
RENS	Renfrewshire
W DUNS	West Dunbartonshire
W LOTH	West Lothian

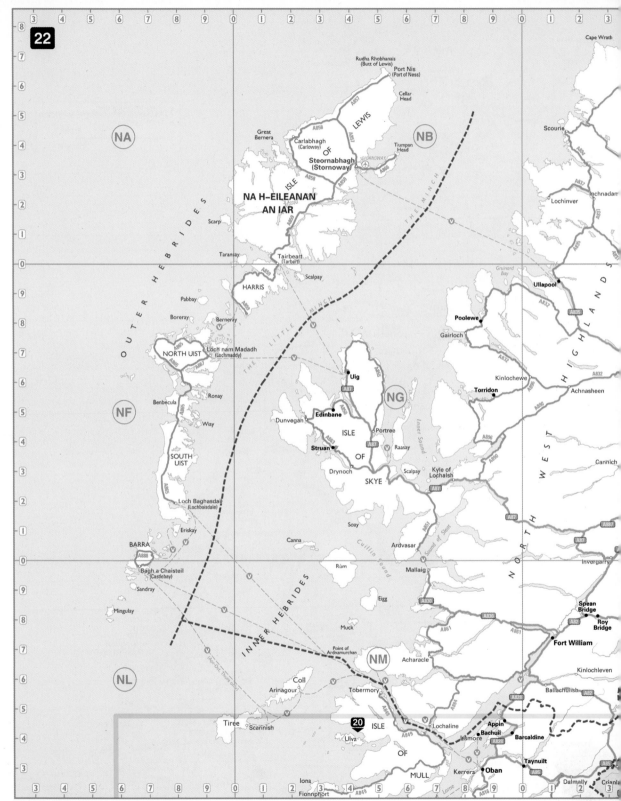

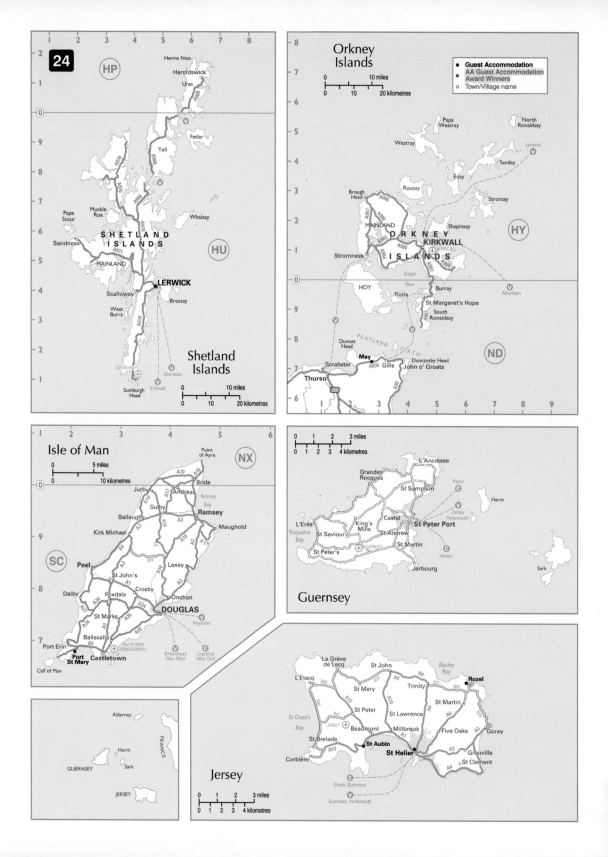

Central London

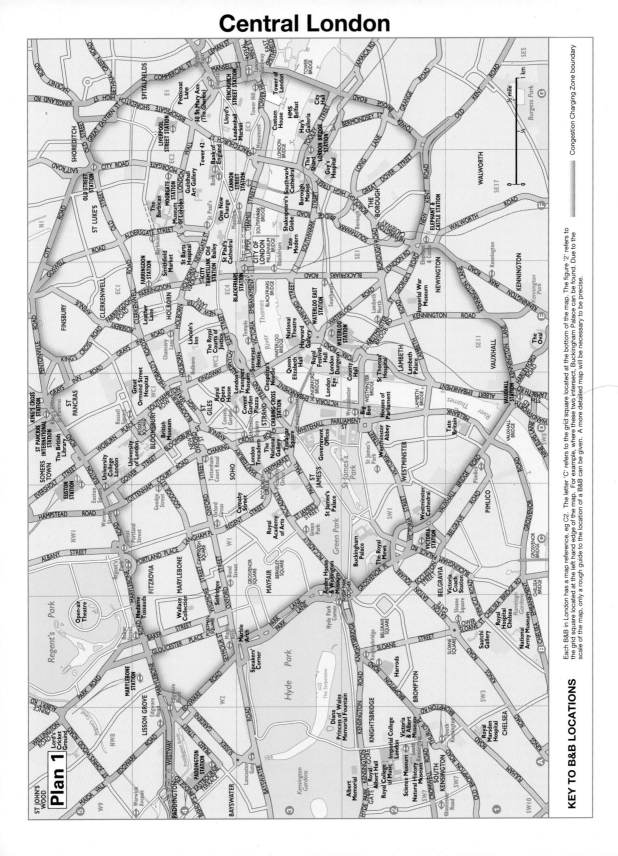

Plan 1

KEY TO B&B LOCATIONS

Each B&B in London has a map reference, eg C2. The letter 'C' refers to the grid square located at the bottom of the map. The figure '2' refers to the grid square located at the left hand edge of the map. For example, where these two intersect, Buckingham Palace can be found. Due to the scale of the map, only a rough guide to the location of a B&B can be given. A more detailed map will be necessary to be precise.

Congestion Charging Zone boundary

Index of Bed & Breakfasts

Acknowledgements

The Automobile Association wishes to thank the following photographers and organisations for their assistance in the preparation of this book.

Abbreviations for the picture credits are as follows – (t) top; (b) bottom; (l) left; (r) right; (c) centre; (AA) AA World Travel Library

3 Courtesy of Errichel House, Perth & Kinross; 4 Courtesy of Old Downton Lodge, Shropshire; 6 Courtesy of Benson House, Cambridgeshire; 9 Courtesy of The Downs, Devon; 10 Courtesy of The Rosemary, Cornwall; 12 Courtesy of Kit Fanner - On Location Events; 13l Courtesy of Snooze, Brighton; 13r Courtesy of Kateshill House; 12-13bg AA/Photodisc; 14l Courtesy of The Dulaig, Highland; 14r Courtesy of Caemorgan Mansion, Ceredigion; 15 Courtesy of Ardtara Country House, County Londonderry; 16-19 All images Courtesy The Old Bakery B&B, Hindolveston; 20 AA/S Lewis; 30-31 AA/A Burton; 364-365 AA/J Smith; 395 AA/S Whitehorne; 396-397 AA/M Bauer; 429 AA/AJ Hopkins; 430-431 AA/C Jones; 445 AA/S Day.

Every effort has been made to trace the copyright holders, and we apologise in advance for any unintentional omissions or errors. We would be pleased to apply any corrections in a following edition of this publication.

Readers' Report Form

Please send this form to:–
Editor, The B&B Guide,
Lifestyle Guides,
AA Media,
Fanum House,
Basingstoke RG21 4EA

e-mail: lifestyleguides@theAA.com

Please use this form to recommend any guest house, farmhouse or inn where you have stayed, that is not currently listed in the guide. If you have any comments about your stay at an establishment listed in the guide, please let us know, as feedback from readers helps to keep our Guide accurate and up to date. If you have a complaint during your stay, we recommend that you discuss the matter with the establishment.

Please note that the AA does not undertake to arbitrate between you and the establishment, or to obtain compensation or engage in protracted correspondence.

Date

Your name (BLOCK CAPITALS)

Your address (BLOCK CAPITALS)

Post code

E-mail address

Name of establishment

Location

Comments

(please attach a separate sheet if necessary)

Please tick here ☐ if you DO NOT wish to receive details of AA offers or products

PTO

Readers' Report Form *continued*

Have you bought this guide before? ☐ YES ☐ NO

Do you regularly use any other accommodation, restaurant, pub or food guides? ☐ YES ☐ NO
If YES, which ones?

_____

_____

Why did you buy this guide? (tick all that apply)

Holiday ☐   Short break ☐   Business travel ☐   Special occasion ☐
Overnight stop ☐   Find a venue for an event e.g. conference ☐
Other (please state)
_____

How often do you stay in B&Bs? (tick one choice)

More than once a month ☐   Once a month ☐   Once in 2-3 months ☐
Once in six months ☐   Once a year ☐   Less than once a year ☐
Other (please state)
_____

Please answer these questions to help us make improvements to the guide:

Which of these factors are the most important when choosing a B&B? (tick all that apply)

Price ☐   Location ☐   Awards/ratings ☐   Service ☐
Decor/surroundings ☐   Previous experience ☐   Recommendation ☐
Other (please state)
_____

Do you read the editorial features in the guide? ☐ YES ☐ NO

Do you use the location atlas?   ☐ YES ☐ NO

What elements of the guide do you find most useful when choosing somewhere to stay? (tick all that apply)

Description ☐   Photo ☐   Advertisement ☐   Star rating ☐

Is there any other information you would like to see added to this guide?

_____

_____

_____

_____